PRINCIPLES OF
PUBLIC INTERNATIONAL LAW

Seventh Edition

BY

IAN BROWNLIE, CBE, QC, FBA

Bencher of Gray's Inn
Chichele Professor of Public International
Law in the University of Oxford (Emeritus)
Distinguished Fellow of All Souls College, Oxford
Member of the Institute of International Law
Member and Former Chairman of the International Law Commission

OXFORD
UNIVERSITY PRESS

OXFORD
UNIVERSITY PRESS

Great Clarendon Street, Oxford OX2 6DP

Oxford University Press is a department of the University of Oxford.
It furthers the University's objective of excellence in research, scholarship,
and education by publishing worldwide in

Oxford New York

Auckland Cape Town Dar es Salaam Hong Kong Karachi
Kuala Lumpur Madrid Melbourne Mexico City Nairobi
New Delhi Shanghai Taipei Toronto

With offices in

Argentina Austria Brazil Chile Czech Republic France Greece
Guatemala Hungary Italy Japan Poland Portugal Singapore
South Korea Switzerland Thailand Turkey Ukraine Vietnam

Oxford is a registered trade mark of Oxford University Press
in the UK and in certain other countries

Published in the United States
by Oxford University Press Inc., New York

British Library Cataloguing in Publication Data

Data available

Library of Congress Cataloging in Publication Data

Data available

Typeset by Newgen Imaging Systems (P) Ltd, Chennai, India
Printed in Great Britain
on acid-free paper by
CPI Antony Rowe, Chippenham, Wiltshire

ISBN 978–0–19–921770–0 (Pbk)
ISBN 978–0–19–955683–0 (Hbk)

1 3 5 7 9 10 8 6 4 2

PREFACE TO THE SEVENTH EDITION

Changes have occurred in many areas of the law since the last edition of this book. Care has been taken to renovate the treatment of a number of topics, including jurisdictional immunities, the responsibility of states, indirect expropriation, international criminal justice and informal extradition.

At the same time, the procedure of renovation has been accompanied by certain inhibitions stemming from the inherent nature of a single volume treatment of the principles of public international law. The temptation to include a detailed treatment of recent complex events (the invasion and occupation of Iraq, for example) has been resisted. To deal adequately with such events would involve excursions well beyond the ambit of a legal handbook. If the situation of Iraq be taken as an example, the limitations can be seen immediately. In the first place, the determination of the material facts would involve considerable difficulty. Secondly, there is the central problem which is the tendency of the State actors to adopt convenient suppositions of fact, this tendency leading to the risk of positing a State practice based upon fiction.

The recent episodes of unilateralism have usually involved law-breaking rather than the development of the law, and it is inappropriate to appear to characterise law-breaking actions as 'precedents' or 'practice'. The book continues to present an analysis of the principles of public international law when the law is being applied in a framework of normality.

The new text reflects the substantial case law of the International Court of Justice and the recent work of the International Law Commission.

I would thank the Hague Academy of International Law and Mr Steven van Hoogstraten for his permission to make use of some passages of my General Course delivered in 1995 and published by the Academy under the title *The Rule of Law in International Affairs* (pp. 65–74) in 1998. I would also like to thank the staff of Oxford University Press, and in particular Rebecca Gleave and Rekha Summan, for their care and consideration. I am grateful for assistance received from Lavonne Pierre and Adam Sloane of Blackstone Chambers.

Finally, my thanks go to my wife for her assistance.

IAN BROWNLIE, Q.C.
Blackstone Chambers
Temple

TRANSLATIONS

Russian edition of the second edition,
by Professor G. I. Tunkin, Moscow, 1977

Japanese edition of the third edition,
by Seibundo Shinkosha Publishing Co. Ltd., 1989

Portuguese edition of the fourth edition,
by Fundaçao Calouste Gulbenkian, Lisbon, 1998

Simplified Chinese edition of the fifth edition
By Law Press, Beijing, 2001

Korean edition of the fifth edition,
By Hyon Am Publishing Co., Seoul, 2003

Complex Chinese edition of the sixth edition,
By Wu-Nan Book Company, Taiwan, 2007

OUTLINE CONTENTS

CONTENTS

PART I PRELIMINARY TOPICS

PART II PERSONALITY AND RECOGNITION

PART III TERRITORIAL SOVEREIGNTY

PART IV LAW OF THE SEA

PART VI STATE JURISDICTION

PART VII RULES OF ATTRIBUTION
(APART FROM TERRITORIAL SOVEREIGNTY
AND STATE JURISDICTION)

PART VIII THE LAW OF RESPONSIBILITY

PART XII INTERNATIONAL ORGANIZATIONS AND TRIBUNALS

PART XIII   THE USE OR THREAT OF FORCE BY STATES

TABLE OF CASES

ABBREVIATIONS

AJ	*American Journal of International Law*
Ann. Digest	*Annual Digest of Public International Law Cases*
Ann. de l'Inst.	*Annuaire de l'Institut de droit international*
Ann. français.	*Annuaire frunçais de droit international*
Austral. Yrbk.	*Australian Year Book of International Law*
Briggs	Briggs, *The Law of Nations* (2nd edn., 1952)
British Practice in IL	E. Lauterpacht (ed.), *British Practice in International Law* (1962–7)
Brownlie, *Documents*	Brownlie (ed.), *Basic Documents in International Law* (5th edn., 2002)
Brownlie and Goodwin-Gill, *Human Rights*	Brownlie and Goodwin-Gill (eds.), *Basic Documents on Human Rights* (5th edn., 2006)
BY	*British Year Book of International Law*
Canad. Yrbk.	*Canadian Yearbook of International Law*
Cmd., Cmnd.	United Kingdom, Command Papers
Daillier, and Pellet	*Droit International Public* (6th edn., 1999)
Europ. Journ.	*European Journal of International Law*
German Yrbk.	*German Yearbook of International Law*
Grot. Soc.	*Transactions of the Grotius Society*
Hague Court Reports	Scott (ed.), Hague Court Reports
Hague *Recueil*	*Recueil des cours de l'Académie de droit international*
Hudson, *Int. Legis.*	Hudson (ed.), *International Legislation* (9 vols., 1931–50)
ICJ Pleadings	International Court of Justice: Pleadings, Oral Arguments, Documents
ICJ Reports	Reports of Judgments, Advisory Opinions and Orders of the International Court of Justice
ICLQ	*International and Comparative Law Quarterly*
ILC	International Law Commission
ILQ	*International Law Quarterly*
Indian Journ.	*Indian Journal of International Law*
ILM	*International Legal Materials*

ILR	International Law Reports (continuation of the *Annual Digest*)
JDI	*Journal du droit international*
La Pradelle and Politis	*Recueil des arbitrages internationaux* (3 vols., 2nd edn., 1957)
LQR	*Law Quarterly Review*
McNair, *Opinions*	McNair, *International Law Opinions* (3 vols., 1956)
Neths. Int. L.R.	*Netherlands International Law Review (Nederlands tijdschrift voor internationaal recht)*
Neths. Yrbk.	*Netherlands Yearbook of International Law*
Oppenheim	Oppenheim, *International Law* (vol. i, 9th edn. (1992) by Sir Robert Jennings and Sir Arthur Watts)
PCIJ	Publications of the Permanent Court of International Justice
RDI (La Pradelle)	*Revue de droit international* (Paris, ed. by La Pradelle)
RDILC	*Revue de droit international et de législation comparée* (Brussels)
RGDIP	*Revue générale de droit international public* (Paris)
RIAA	United Nations, *Reports of International Arbitral Awards*
Rousseau, i, ii, iii, iv, v	*Droit international public* (5 vols., 1971, 1974, 1977, 1980, 1983)
Treaty Series	*United Kingdom Treaty Series*
UNTS	United Nations Treaty Series
US	United States; or United States Supreme Court Reports
Whiteman	Whiteman, *Digest of International Law* (1963–73)
Yrbk. ILC	United Nations, *Yearbook of the International Law Commission*

GLOSSARY

amicus curiae. A person permitted to present arguments bearing upon issues before a tribunal yet not representing the interests of any party to the proceedings.

animus. An intention, a state of mind.

animus manendi. An intention to remain.

animus revertendi. An intention to return.

ante litem motam. Prior to the existence of legal proceedings.

causa sine qua non. A necessary cause of the event.

compromis. A special agreement between states to submit a particular issue either to an arbitral tribunal or to the International Court.

conflict of laws. Or, private international law. A part of the municipal law of each state which provides rules for deciding cases involving foreign factual elements, for example, a contract made abroad.

cujus est solum est usque ad caelum et ad inferos. He who owns the surface has title both to the airspace above and the subsoil.

culpa. The civil law or Roman law term employed by lawyers from non-common law countries to refer to negligence, lack of reasonable care.

de lege ferenda. Relating to the law as it should be if the rules were changed to accord with good policy.

delicta juris gentium. Wrongs recognised by public international law.

détournement de pouvoir. A term of French administrative law originally, meaning abuse of administrative powers by public officials.

dicta. The lesser propositions of law stated by tribunals or by individual members of tribunals; propositions not directed to the principal matters in issue.

diligentia quam in suis. The standard of care normally exercised by a particular person in the conduct of his affairs.

dolus. The intention to inflict some harm, together with the foreseeable consequences of the intended harm.

dominium. Title or ownership.

equity infra legem. Equity defined by legal principles.

erga omnes. Opposable to, valid against, 'all the world', i.e. all other legal persons, irrespective of consent on the part of those thus affected.

ex aequo et bono. Equity in the most general sense.

ex gratia. As a matter of discretion.

ex injuria non oritur jus. The principle that no benefit can be received from an illegal act.

force majeure. Under the influence of duress.

imperium. Government, or a governmental interest.

in limine. At the outset.

in statu nascendi. In the process of formation.

in territorio alieno. In the territory of another.

inter se. Between the parties to a specific agreement or other transaction.

jura in re aliena. Rights in another property.

jus cogens. Peremptory norms of general international law.

lato sensu/stricto sensu. The broad sense/the narrow sense.

lex ferenda. See *de lege ferenda*.

locus delicti. The place or, more usually, the particular state or jurisdiction in which a wrong was committed.

locus standi. The power to apply to a tribunal for a particular remedy; more specifically, the existence of a sufficient legal interest in the matter in issue.

mala in se. Recognised as morally wrong.

ne bis in idem. No person should be proceeded against twice over the same matter.

obiter dicta. See *dicta*.

opinio juris et necessitatis. The element in the practice of States which denotes that the practice is required by contemporary international law.

pacta sunt servanda. Simply, the principle that agreements are binding and are to be implemented in good faith.

petitio principii. Begging the question.

prima facie. In principle; presumptively.

ratio; ratio decidendi. The principal proposition or propositions of law determining the outcome of a case; or, the only legal consideration necessary for the decision of a particular case.

ratione materiae. By reason of the subject-matter.

ratione personae. Determined by the status and dignity of the person or entity as such.

ratione temporis. Conditioned by reference to time.

rebus sic stantibus. The implication of a term that the obligations of an agreement come to an end with a change of circumstances.

res communis. Not subject to the sovereignty of a single state.

res inter alios acta. A matter affecting third parties and not opposable to the legal persons between whom there is an issue.

res judicata. The principle that an issue decided by a court should not be reopened.

res nullius. An asset susceptible of acquisition but presently under the ownership or sovereignty of no legal person.

stare decisis. The principle that a tribunal should follow its own previous decisions and those of other tribunals of equal or greater authority.

stipulation pour autrui. Contractual obligation in favour of a third party.

sui generis. Atypical, not falling within the normal legal categories.

travaux préparatoires. Preparatory work; preliminary drafts, minutes of conferences, and the like, relating to the conclusion of a treaty.

ultra vires. Unauthorised by legal authority.

PART I

PRELIMINARY TOPICS

1

SOURCES OF THE LAW[1]

1. INTRODUCTION

As objects of study, the sources of international law and the law of treaties (treated in Chapter 27) must be regarded as fundamental: between them they provide the basic particles of the legal regime.

It is common for writers to distinguish the formal sources and the material sources of law. The former are those legal procedures and methods for the creation of rules of general application which are legally binding on the addressees. The material sources provide evidence of the existence of rules which, when proved, have the status of legally binding rules of general application. In systems of municipal law the concept of formal source refers to the constitutional machinery of law-making and the status of the rule is established by constitutional law. In the context of international relations the use of the term 'formal source' is awkward and misleading since the reader is put in mind of the constitutional machinery of law-making which exists within states. No such machinery exists for the creation of rules of international law. Decisions of the International Court, unanimously supported resolutions of the General Assembly of the United Nations concerning matters of law, and important multilateral treaties concerned to codify or develop rules of international law, are all lacking the quality to bind states generally. In a sense 'formal sources' do not exist in international law. As a substitute, and perhaps an equivalent, there is the principle that the general consent of states creates rules of general application. The definition of custom in international law[2] is essentially a statement of this principle (and not a reference to ancient custom as in municipal law).

---

[1] See generally Sørensen, 101 Hague *Recueil* (1960, III), 16–108; Fitzmaurice, *Symbolae Verzijl* (1958), 153–76; Parry, *The Sources and Evidences of International Law* (1965); Lauterpacht, *International Law: Collected Papers*, i (1970), 58–135; Elias, in Friedmann, Henkin, and Lissitzyn (eds.), *Transnational Law in a Changing Society* (1972), 34–69; Schachter, in Macdonald and Johnston (eds.), *The Structure and Process of International Law* (1983), 745–99; *Études en l'honneur de Roberto Ago* (1987), i; Cassese and Weiler (eds.), *Change and Stability in International Law-Making* (1988); Thirlway, 61 *BY* (1990), 31–131 and 76 (2005), 77–119; Charney, 87 *AJ* (1993), 529–51; Tomuschat, 241 Hague *Recueil* (1993, IV), 195–374; Fidler, 39 *German Yrbk.* (1996), 198–248; Zemanek, 266 Hague *Recueil* (1997), 131–232; Degan, *Sources of International Law* (1997); Boyle and Chinkin, *The Making of International Law* (2007).

[2] *Infra*, pp. 6–12.

The consequence is that in international law the distinction between formal and material sources is difficult to maintain. The former in effect consist simply of a quasi-constitutional principle of inevitable but unhelpful generality. What matters then is the variety of material sources, the all-important *evidences* of the existence of consensus among states concerning particular rules or practices. Thus decisions of the International Court, resolutions of the General Assembly of the United Nations, and 'law-making' multilateral treaties are very material evidence of the attitude of states toward particular rules, and the presence or absence of consensus. Moreover, there is a process of interaction which gives these evidences a status somewhat higher than mere 'material sources'. Thus neither an unratified treaty nor a report of the International Law Commission to the General Assembly has any binding force either in the law of treaties or otherwise. However, such instruments stand as candidates for public reaction, approving or not, as the case may be: they may stand for a threshold of consensus and confront states in a significant way.

The law of treaties concerns the question of the content of obligations between individual states: the incidence of obligations resulting from express agreement. In principle, the incidence of particular obligations is a matter distinct from the sources. Terminology presents some confusion in this respect. Thus treaties binding a few states only are dubbed 'particular international law' as opposed to 'general international law' comprising multilateral 'law-making' treaties[3] to which a majority of states are parties. Yet in strictness there is no fundamental distinction here: both types of treaty only create particular obligations and treaties are *as such* a source of obligation and not a source of rules of general application. Treaties may form an important material source, however: see section 4 below.

It is perhaps useful to remark on two other usages of the term 'sources'. Thus the term may refer to the source of the binding quality of international law as such and also to the literary sources of the law as sources of information.

2. THE STATUTE OF THE INTERNATIONAL COURT OF JUSTICE

The pertinent provisions are as follows:

Article 38. 1. The Court, whose function is to decide in accordance with international law such disputes as are submitted to it, shall apply:

(a) international conventions, whether general or particular, establishing rules expressly recognized by the contesting States;

(b) international custom, as evidence of a general practice accepted as law;

(c) the general principles of law recognized by civilized nations;

---

[3] See *infra*, pp. 12–14.

(d) subject to the provisions of Article 59, judicial decisions and the teachings of the most highly qualified publicists of the various nations, as subsidiary means for the determination of rules of law.

2. This provision shall not prejudice the power of the Court to decide a case ex aequo et bono, if the parties agree thereto.

Article 59. The decision of the Court has no binding force except between the parties and in respect of that particular case.

These provisions are expressed in terms of the function of the Court, but they represent the previous practice of arbitral tribunals, and Article 38 is generally regarded as a complete statement of the sources of international law.[4] Yet the article itself does not refer to 'sources' and, if looked at closely, cannot be regarded as a straightforward enumeration of the sources. The first question which arises is whether paragraph 1 creates a hierarchy of sources. The provisions are not stated to represent a hierarchy, but the draftsmen intended to give an order and in one draft the word 'successively' appeared.[5] In practice the Court may be expected to observe the order in which they appear: (a) and (b) are obviously the important sources, and the priority of (a) is explicable by the fact that this refers to a source of mutual obligations of the parties. Source (a) is thus not primarily a source of rules of general application, although treaties may provide evidence of the formation of custom. Sources (b) and, perhaps, (c) are formal sources, at least for those who care for such classification. Source (d), with its reference 'as subsidiary means for the determination of rules of law', relates to material sources. Yet some jurists regard (d), as a reference to formal sources, and Fitzmaurice has criticized the classification of judicial decisions as 'subsidiary means'.[6]

In general Article 38 does not rest upon a distinction between formal and material sources, and a system of priority of application depends simply on the order (a) to (d), and the reference to subsidiary means. Moreover, it is probably unwise to think in terms of hierarchy dictated by the order (a) to (d) in all cases.[7] Source (a) relates to *obligations* in any case; and presumably a treaty contrary to a custom or to a general principle part of the *jus cogen*[8] would be void or voidable. Again, the interpretation of a treaty may involve resort to general principles of law or of international law.[9] A treaty may be displaced or amended by a subsequent custom, where such effects are recognized by the subsequent conduct of the parties.[10]

---

[4] See Hudson, *The Permanent Court of International Justice*, (1943), 601 ff. See also the Revised General Act for the Pacific Settlement of International Disputes, Art. 28; Model Rules on Arbitral Procedure adopted by the ILC, Art. 10, *Yrbk. ILC* (1958), ii. 83; Report of Scelle, ibid. 8. Art. 38 has often been incorporated textually or by reference in the *compromis* of other tribunals.

[5] Cf. *Castillo* v. *Zalles*, ILR 22 (1955), 540. See also Quadri, 113 Hague *Recueil*, 342–5; Judge Tanaka, Diss. Op., *South West Africa Cases* (Second Phase), ICJ Reports (1966), 300; Akehurst, 47 BY (1974–5), 273–85.

[6] *Symbolae Verzijl*, at p. 174.

[7] See Judge Moreno Quintana, *Right of Passage Case*, ICJ Reports (1960), 90.

[8] *Infra*, ch. 23, on *jus cogens* and its effects.

[9] See *infra*, pp. 16–19.

[10] *Air Transport Services Agreement Arbitration*, 1963, ILR 38, 182; *RIAA* xvi, 5; Award, Pt. IV, s. 5.

3. INTERNATIONAL CUSTOM[11]

DEFINITION

Article 38 refers to 'international custom, as evidence of a general practice accepted as law', and Brierly[12] remarks that 'what is sought for is a general recognition among States of a certain practice as obligatory'. Although occasionally the terms are used interchangeably, 'custom' and 'usage' are terms of art and have different meanings. A usage is a general practice which does not reflect a legal obligation,[13] and examples are ceremonial salutes at sea and the practice of exempting diplomatic vehicles from parking prohibitions.[14]

EVIDENCE

The material sources of custom are very numerous and include the following:[15] diplomatic correspondence, policy statements, press releases, the opinions of official legal advisers, official manuals on legal questions, e.g. manuals of military law, executive decisions and practices, orders to naval forces etc., comments by governments on drafts produced by the International Law Commission, state legislation,[16] international and national judicial decisions,[17] recitals in treaties and other international instruments, a pattern of treaties in the same form, the practice of international organs,[18]

---

[11] See *supra*, n. 1, and see further: Lauterpacht, *The Development of International Law by the International Court* (1958), 368–93; Guggenheim, in *Études en l'honneur de Georges Scelle* (1950), i. 275–84; id., *Traité* i. 93–113; Skubiszewski, 31 *Z.a.ö.R.u.V.* (1971), 810–54; Thirlway, *International Customary Law and Codification* (1972); Barberis, *Neths. Int. LR* (1967), 367–81; Manin, 80 *RGDIP* (1976), 7–54; Akehurst, 47 *BY* (1974–5), 1–53; Meijers, *Neths. Yrbk.* (1978), 3–26; Stern, *Mélanges Reuter* (1981), 479–99; Bos, *German Yrbk.*, 25 (1982), 9–53; Cheng, in Macdonald and Johnston (eds.) *The Structure and Process of International Law*, pp. 513–50; Virally, 183 Hague *Recueil*, (1983, V), 167–206; Jiménez de Aréchaga, in *Essays in Honour of Judge Manfred Lachs* (1984), 575–85; Abi-Saab, in *Études en l'honneur de Roberto Ago*, i. 53–65; Thirlway, 61 *BY* (1990), 31–110 and 76 *BY* (2005), 92–108; Wolfke, *Custom in Present International Law*, 2nd edn. (1993); id., 24 *Neths. Yrbk.* (1993), 1–16; Mendelson, 66 *BY* (1995), 177–208; Zemanek, *Recueil des Cours*, vol. 266 (1997), 149–67; I.L.A., *Report of the Sixty-Ninth Conference* (London), 2000, 712–90; Kammerhofer, *Europ. Journ.* 15 (2004), 523–53; Arangio-Ruiz, *Mélanges Salmon* (2007), 93–124.

[12] *Law of Nations*, 6th edn. (1963), 61. See also Judge Read in the *Fisheries* case, ICJ Reports (1951), 191: 'Customary international law is the generalization of the practice of States.'

[13] See further *infra*, pp. 8–10, on the *opinio juris*.

[14] See *Parking Privileges for Diplomats Case*, ILR 70, 396 (Fed. Admin. Ct., FRG).

[15] See in particular Parry, 44 *Grot. Soc.* (1958, 1959), 145–86; McNair, *Opinions*, i. Preface; Zemanek, *Festschrift für Rudolf Bernhardt* (1995), 289–306. Custom apart from the practice of *states* may be influential, e.g. in the general law of the sea; cf. the *Tolten* [1946] P. 135; *Ann. Digest* (1946), no. 42.

[16] Cf. the *Scotia* (1871) 14 Wallace 170.

[17] The latter provided a basis for the concept of the historic bay.

[18] In its Advisory Opinion in the *Genocide* case the ICJ refers to the practice of the Council of the League of Nations in the matter of reservations to multilateral conventions: ICJ Reports (1951), 25. See also the Joint Diss. Op., ibid. 34ff.

and resolutions relating to legal questions in the United Nations General Assembly. Obviously the value of these sources varies and much depends on the circumstances.

THE ELEMENTS OF CUSTOM

(a) Duration

Provided the consistency and generality of a practice are proved, no particular duration is required: the passage of time will of course be a part of the evidence of generality and consistency. A long (and, much less, an immemorial) practice is not necessary, and rules relating to airspace and the continental shelf have emerged from fairly quick maturing of practice. The International Court does not emphasize the time element as such in its practice.

(b) Uniformity, consistency of the practice

This is very much a matter of appreciation and a tribunal will have considerable freedom of determination in many cases. Complete uniformity is not required, but substantial uniformity is, and thus in the *Fisheries* case[19] the Court refused to accept the existence of a 10-mile rule for bays.[20]

The leading pronouncements by the Court appear in the Judgment in the *Asylum*[21] case:

The party which relies on a custom...must prove that this custom is established in such a manner that it has become binding on the other party...that the rule invoked...is in accordance with a constant and uniform usage practised by the States in question, and that this usage is the expression of a right appertaining to the State granting asylum and a duty incumbent on the territorial State. This follows from Article 38 of the Statute of the Court, which refers to international custom 'as evidence of a general practice accepted as law'.

The facts brought to the knowledge of the Court disclose so much uncertainty and contradiction, so much fluctuation and discrepancy in the exercise of diplomatic asylum[22] and in the official views expressed on different occasions; there has been so much inconsistency in the rapid succession of conventions on asylum, ratified by some States and rejected by others, and the practice has been so much influenced by considerations of political expediency in the various cases, that it is not possible to discern in all this any constant and uniform usage, accepted as law. ...

---

[19] ICJ Reports (1951), 116 at 131. See also the *Genocide* case, ibid. 25: 'In fact, the examples of objections made to reservations appear to be too rare in international practice to have given rise to such a rule.'

[20] See *infra*, pp. 176–8.

[21] ICJ Reports (1950), at 276–7. See also *U.S. Nationals in Morocco* case, ICJ Reports (1952), 200; *Nottebohm* case (Second Phase), ICJ Reports (1955), 30 per Judge Klaestad; *Right of Passage* case (*Merits*), ICJ Reports (1960), 40, 43; ibid. 62 per Judge Wellington Koo; p. 99 per Judge Spender, and ibid. 136 per Fernandes, judges *ad hoc*; *North Sea Continental Shelf Cases*, ICJ Reports (1969), 43; ibid. 86 per Judge Padilla Nervo; ibid. 229 per Judge Lachs; ibid. 246 per Judge Sørensen; *Nicaragua* v. *United States* (Merits), ICJ Reports (1986), p. 98, para. 186.

[22] The Court was concerned with the right to decide whether the offence was political and whether the case was one of urgency.

(c) Generality of the practice

This is an aspect which complements that of consistency. Certainly universality is not required, but the real problem is to determine the value of abstention from protest by a substantial number of states in face of a practice followed by some others. Silence may denote either tacit agreement or a simple lack of interest in the issue. It may be that the Court in the *Lotus* case[23] misjudged the consequences of absence of protest and also the significance of fairly general abstention from prosecutions by states other than the flag state.[24] In the *Fisheries Jurisdiction Case* (*United Kingdom* v. *Iceland*) the International Court referred to the extension of a fishery zone up to a 12-mile limit 'which appears now to be generally accepted' and to 'an increasing and widespread acceptance of the concept of preferential rights for coastal states' in a situation of special dependence on coastal fisheries.[25]

(d) *Opinio juris et necessitatis*[26]

The Statute of the International Court refers to 'a general practice *accepted as law*'.[27] Brierly[28] speaks of recognition by states of a certain practice 'as obligatory', and Hudson[29] requires a 'conception that the practice is required by, or consistent with, prevailing international law'. Some writers do not consider this psychological element to be a requirement for the formation of custom,[30] but it is in fact a necessary ingredient. The sense of legal obligation, as opposed to motives of courtesy, fairness, or morality, is real enough, and the practice of states recognizes a distinction between obligation and usage. The essential problem is surely one of proof, and especially the incidence of the burden of proof.

In terms of the practice of the International Court of Justice—which provides a general guide to the nature of the problem—there are two methods of approach. In many cases the Court is willing to assume the existence of an *opinio juris* on the bases of evidence of a general practice,[31] or a consensus in the literature, or the previous

---

[23] See *infra*, pp. 9–10.

[24] Lauterpacht, *Development*, pp. 384–6. See also the *Paquete Habana* (1900), 175 US 677.

[25] ICJ Reports (1974), 3 at 23–6. See also the *North Sea Continental Shelf Cases*, ICJ Reports (1969), 4 at 42. For reliance on the practice of a limited number of states see the *Wimbledon* (1923), PCIJ, Ser. A, no. 1. See also *Fernandez* v. *Wilkinson*, ILR, 87, 446, 455–8.

[26] See Chaumont, 129 Hague *Recueil* (1970, I), 434–45; Verzijl, *International Law in Historical Perspective*, i. 37–41; Barberis, 50 *Rivista di d.i.* (1967), 563–83; P. de Visscher, 136 Hague *Recueil* (1972, II), 70–5; Bos, *A Methodology of International Law* (1984), 236–44; Mendelson, 66 *BY* (1995), 177–208; Elias, 44 *ICLQ* (1995), 501–20; Schachter in, *Essays in Honour of Krzysztof Skubiszewski* (1996), 531–40; Sienho Yee. *German Yrbk.*, 43 (2000), 227–38.

[27] Italics supplied.

[28] p. 61.

[29] Quoted in Briggs, p. 25.

[30] See Guggenheim, *Études Scelle*, i. 275–80; Fischer Williams, *Some Aspects of Modern International Law* (1934), 44–6. See now Guggenheim, i. 103–5. For Kelsen the *opinio juris* is a fiction to disguise the creative powers of the judge: see *Revue internationale de la théorie du droit* (1939), 253–74; and cf. *Principles of International Law* (1952), 307; (2nd edn., 1967), 450–1.

[31] See Lauterpacht, *Development*, p. 380; id., *Coll. Papers*, i. 63; Baxter, 129 Hague *Recueil* (1970, I), 69; Guggenheim, i. 103–5. Cf. Sørensen, p. 134.

determinations of the Court or other international tribunals.[32] However, in a significant minority of cases the Court has adopted a more rigorous approach and has called for more positive evidence of the recognition of the validity of the rules in question in the practice of states. The choice of approach appears to depend upon the nature of the issues (that is, the state of the law may be a primary point in contention), and the discretion of the Court.

Three cases have involved the more exacting second method of approach, of which the first was the *Lotus*, in which the Permanent Court said:[33]

Even if the rarity of the judicial decisions to be found among the reported cases were sufficient to prove in point of fact the circumstances alleged by the Agent for the French Government, it would merely show that States had often, in practice, abstained from instituting criminal proceedings, and not that they recognized themselves as being obliged to do so; for only if such abstention were based on their being conscious of a duty to abstain would it be possible to speak of an international custom. The alleged fact does not allow one to infer that States have been conscious of having such a duty; on the other hand...there are other circumstances calculated to show that the contrary is true.

Presumably the same principles should apply to both positive conduct and abstention, yet in the *Lotus* the Court was not ready to accept continuous conduct as prima facie evidence of a legal duty and required a high standard of proof of the issue of *opinio juris*.[34]

In the *North Sea Continental Shelf Cases*[35] the International Court was also strict in requiring proof of the *opinio juris*. The Court did not presume the existence of *opinio juris* either in the context of the argument that the equidistance–special circumstances basis of delimiting the continental shelf had become a part of general or customary law at the date of the Geneva Convention of 1958, or in relation to the proposition that the *subsequent* practice of states based upon the Convention had produced a customary rule. However, it is incorrect to regard the precise findings as in all respects incompatible with the view that the existence of a general practice raises a presumption of *opinio juris*. In regard to the position *before* the Convention concerning the equidistance principle, there was little 'practice' apart from the records of the International Law Commission, which revealed the experimental aspect of the principle prior to 1958.[36] In considering the argument that practice *based upon* the Convention had produced a customary rule the Court made it clear that its unfavourable reception to the argument rested primarily upon two factors: (*a*) the peculiar form of the equidistance principle in Article 6 of the Convention was such that the rules were not of a norm-creating

---

[32] See the *Gulf of Maine* case, Judgment of the Chamber, ICJ Reports (1984), 293–4, paras. 91–3.

[33] Ser. A, no. 10, p. 28. See also the individual opinions of Nyholm and Altamira, ibid. 60, 97; the *European Commission of the Danube*, Ser. B, no. 14, p. 14 per Deputy-Judge Negulesco. Cf. the passage from the Judgment in the *Asylum* case quoted *supra*.

[34] See the criticisms of Lauterpacht, *Development*, p. 386. See, however, MacGibbon, 33 *BY* (1957), 131.

[35] ICJ Reports (1969), 3.

[36] Ibid. 28, 32–41.

character;[37] (*b*) the Convention had only been in force for less than three years when the proceedings were brought and consequently:[38]

Although the passage of only a short period of time is not necessarily, or of itself, a bar to the formation of a new rule of customary international law on the basis of what was originally a purely conventional rule, an indispensable requirement would be that within the period in question, short though it might be, State practice, including that of States whose interests are specially affected, should have been both extensive and virtually uniform in the sense of the provision invoked;—and should moreover have occurred in such a way as to show a general recognition that a rule of law or legal obligation is involved.

Nevertheless, the general tenor of the Judgment[39] is hostile to the presumption as to *opinio juris* and the Court quoted the passage from the *Lotus* case set out above.[40]

A broadly similar approach was adopted by the Judgment of the Court in the *Case of Nicaragua* v. *United States* (Merits),[41] and the Court expressly referred to the *North Sea Cases*:[42]

In considering the instances of the conduct above described, the Court has to emphasize that, as was observed in the *North Sea Continental Shelf* cases, for a new customary rule to be formed, not only must the acts concerned 'amount to a settled practice', but they must be accompanied by the *opinio juris sive necessitatis*. Either the States taking such action or other States in a position to react to it, must have behaved so that their conduct is 'evidence of a belief that this practice is rendered obligatory by the existence of a rule of law requiring it. The need for such a belief, i.e. the existence of a subjective element, is implicit in the very notion of the *opinio juris sive necessitatis*'. (*ICJ Reports* (1969), 44, para. 77.)

BILATERAL RELATIONS AND LOCAL CUSTOMS

In the case concerning *U.S. Nationals in Morocco*[43] the Court quoted the first of the passages from the *Asylum* case quoted earlier[44] and continued: 'In the present case there has not been sufficient evidence to enable the Court to reach a conclusion that a right to exercise consular jurisdiction founded upon custom or usage has been established *in such a manner that it has become binding on Morocco*'.[45]

In this case the Court may seem to have confused the question of law-making and the question of opposability, i.e. the specific relations of the United States and

---

[37] Ibid. 41–2.
[38] Ibid. 43.
[39] Ibid. 43–5, and see, in particular, p. 44, para. 77.
[40] For comment see Baxter, 129 Hague *Recueil* (1970, I), 67–9; D'Amato, 64 *AJ* (1970), 892–902; Marek, *Revue belge* (1970), 44–78. For the views of dissenting judges see ICJ Reports (1969), 156–8 (Koretsky), 175–9 (Tanaka), 197 (Morelli), 221–32 (Lachs), 241–2 (Sørensen). See also the Sep. Op. of Judge Petrén in the *Nuclear Tests Case*, ICJ Reports (1974), 253 at 305–6.
[41] ICJ Reports (1986), 14.
[42] Ibid. 108–9, para. 207. See also pp. 97–8, para. 184, pp. 97–103, paras. 184–93; pp. 106–8, paras. 202–6.
[43] ICJ Reports (1952), 199–200. See Lauterpacht, *Development*, pp. 388–92.
[44] *Supra*, p. 7.
[45] Italics supplied.

Morocco.[46] The fact is that general formulae concerning custom do not necessarily help in penetrating the complexities of the particular case. The case concerning a *Right of Passage over Indian Territory*[47] raised an issue of bilateral relations, the existence of a local custom in favour of Portugal in respect of territorial enclaves inland from the port of Daman (Damão). In this type of case the general law is to be varied and the proponent of the special right has to give affirmative proof of a sense of obligation on the part of the territorial sovereign: *opinio juris* is here not to be presumed on the basis of continuous practice and the notion of *opinio juris* merges into the principle of acquiescence.[48]

THE PERSISTENT OBJECTOR[49]

The way in which, as a matter of practice, custom resolves itself into a question of special relations is illustrated further by the rule that a state may contract out of a custom in the process of formation.[50] Evidence of objection must be clear and there is probably a presumption of acceptance which is to be rebutted. Whatever the theoretical underpinnings of the principle, it is well recognized by international tribunals,[51] and in the practice of states. Given the majoritarian tendency of international relations the principle is likely to have increased prominence.

THE SUBSEQUENT OBJECTOR

In the *Fisheries* case[52] part of the Norwegian argument was that certain rules were not rules of general international law, and, even if they were, they did not bind Norway, which had 'consistently and unequivocally manifested a refusal to accept them'. The United Kingdom admitted the general principle of the Norwegian argument here while denying that, as a matter of fact, Norway had consistently and unequivocally manifested a refusal to accept the rules. Thus the United Kingdom regarded the question as one of persistent objection. The Court did not deal with the issue in this way,

---

[46] See Fitzmaurice, 92 Hague *Recueil* (1957, II), 106. On opposability in general see *infra*, pp. 85–6. The *Asylum* case itself concerned a regional custom.

[47] ICJ Reports (1960), 6 at 39–43. Cf. Judges Wellington Koo at pp. 62–3; Armand-Ugon at pp. 82–4; and Spender at p. 110. See also Deputy-Judge Negulesco, *European Commission of the Danube*, PCIJ, Ser. B, no. 14, p. 114; and Judge Klaestad, *Nottebohm* (Second Phase), ICJ Reports (1955), 30.

[48] See generally MacGibbon, 33 *BY* (1957), 125–31; D'Amato, 63 *AJ* (1969), 211–23.

[49] See generally Akehurst, 47 *BY* (1974–5), 23–7; Bos, *German Yrbk*. 25 (1982), 43–53, id., *A Methodology of International Law* pp. 247–55; Stein, *Harvard Int. LJ*, 26 (1985), 457–82; Colson, *Washington LR*, 61 (1986), 957–69; Charney, 56 *BY* (1985), 1–24; id., 87 *AJ* (1993), 538–42; Thirlway, 61 *BY* (1990), 106–8.

[50] The principle was recognized by both parties in the *Anglo-Norwegian Fisheries* case; and also by authoritative opinion: see Fitzmaurice, 92 Hague *Recueil* (1957, II), 99–100; Waldock, 106 Hague *Recueil* (1962, II), 49–50; Sørensen, 101 Hague *Recueil* (1960, III), 43–4; Jiménez de Aréchaga, 159 Hague *Recueil* (1978, I), 30. See further Schachter, 178 Hague *Recueil* (1982, V), 36–8.

[51] See the *Anglo-Norwegian Fisheries* case ICJ Reports (1951), 131; *North Sea Continental Shelf* case, ibid. (1969), 26–7; Sep. Op. of Judge Ammoun, p. 131; Diss. Op. of Judge Lachs, pp. 235, 238; and Diss. Op. of Judge *ad hoc* Sørensen, p. 247. See also the *Asylum* case, ibid. (1950), 277–8.

[52] ICJ Reports (1951), 116. On which generally see *infra*, pp. 176ff.

however, and the *ratio* in this respect was that Norway had departed from the alleged rules, if they existed, *and other states had acquiesced* in this practice. But the Court is not too explicit about the role of acquiescence in validating a subsequent contracting out of rules.[53] Here one has to face the problem of change in a customary regime.[54] Presumably, if a substantial number of states assert a new rule, the momentum of increased defection, complemented by acquiescence, may result in a new rule,[55] as in the case of the law on the continental shelf. If the process is slow and neither the new rule nor the old have a majority of adherents then the consequence is a network of special relations based on opposability, acquiescence, and historic title.[56]

PROOF OF CUSTOM

In principle a court is presumed to know the law and may apply a custom even if it has not been expressly pleaded. In practice the proponent of a custom has a burden of proof the nature of which will vary according to the subject-matter and the form of the pleadings. Thus in the *Lotus* case[57] the Court spoke of the plaintiff's burden in respect of a general custom. Where a local or regional custom is alleged, the proponent 'must prove that this custom is established in such a manner that it has become binding on the other Party'.[58]

4. 'LAW-MAKING' TREATIES AND OTHER MATERIAL SOURCES

It may seem untidy to depart from discussion of the 'formal' sources, of which custom is the most important, and yet a realistic presentation of the sources involves giving prominence to certain forms of evidence of the attitude of states to customary rules and general principles of the law.[59] 'Law-making' treaties, the conclusions of international conferences, resolutions of the United Nations General Assembly, and drafts adopted by the International Law Commission have a direct influence on the content

---

[53] See Fitzmaurice, 30 *BY* (1953), 24–6; id., 92 Hague *Recueil* (1957, II), 99–101; Sørensen, 101 Hague *Recueil* (1960, III), 43–7. The dictum which requires explanation, at p. 131 of the Reports, is: 'In any event the ten-mile rule would appear to be inapplicable as against Norway inasmuch as she had always opposed any attempt to apply it to the Norwegian coast.'

[54] See *Lauritzen et al.* v. *Government of Chile*, ILR 23 (1956), 708 at 710–12.

[55] Since delict cannot be justified by an allegation of a desire to change the law, the question of *opinio juris* arises in a special form and in the early stages of change can amount to little more than a plea of good faith.

[56] Both forms of objection are restricted in any case by the norms of *jus cogens*: on which see *infra*, ch. 23, s. 5.

[57] PCIJ, Ser. A, no. 10, p. 18.

[58] *Asylum* case, ICJ Reports (1950), 276.

[59] See *infra*, pp. 16–19.

of the law, an influence the significance of which is not conveyed adequately by their designation as material sources.

'LAW-MAKING' TREATIES[60]

Such treaties create legal obligations the observance of which does not dissolve the treaty obligation. Thus a treaty for the joint carrying out of a single enterprise is not law-making, since fulfilment of its objects will terminate the obligation. Law-making treaties create *general* norms for the future conduct of the parties in terms of legal propositions, and the obligations are basically the same for all parties. The Declaration of Paris, 1856 (on neutrality in maritime warfare), the Hague Conventions of 1899 and 1907 (on the law of war and neutrality), the Geneva Protocol of 1925 (on prohibited weapons), the General Treaty for the Renunciation of War of 1928, and the Genocide Convention of 1948 are examples of this type. Moreover, those parts of the United Nations Charter which are not concerned with constitutional questions concerning competence of organs, and the like, have the same character.[61] Such treaties are in principle binding only on parties,[62] but the number of parties, the explicit acceptance of rules of law, and, in some cases, the declaratory nature of the provisions produce a strong law-creating effect at least as great as the general practice considered sufficient to support a customary rule.[63] By their conduct non-parties may accept the provisions of a multilateral convention as representing general international law:[64] this has been the case with Hague Convention IV[65] of 1907 and the rules annexed relating to land warfare. Even an unratified treaty may be regarded as evidence of generally accepted rules, at least in the short run.[66]

In the *North Sea Continental Shelf Cases*[67] the principal issue was to what extent, if at all, the German Federal Republic was bound by the provisions of the Continental Shelf Convention which it had signed but not ratified. The International Court concluded, by eleven votes to six, that only the first three articles of the Convention were emergent or

---

[60] See McNair, *Law of Treaties* (1961), 5, 124, 749–52; id., 11 *BY* (1930), 100–18 (repr. in *Law of Treaties*, p. 739); id., 19 *Iowa LR* (1934) (repr. in *Law of Treaties*, p. 729); Sørensen, 101 Hague *Recueil* (1958, III), 72–90; Baxter, 41 *BY* (1965–6), 275–300; id., 129 Hague *Recueil* (1970, I), 31–75; Shihata, 22 *Rev. égyptienne* (1966), 51–90; Manin, 80 *RGDIP* (1976), 7–54; Thirlway, 61 *BY* (1990), 87–102. See further ch. 27, s. 11.

[61] In particular the principles in Art. 2.

[62] But see ch. 27, s. 8.

[63] See McNair, *Law of Treaties*, pp. 216–18, for expression of a firm opinion on the effect of Art. 2, para. 3 and 4, of the Charter, which he describes as the 'nearest approach to legislation by the whole community of States that has yet been realised'.

[64] There must be evidence of consent to the extension of the rule, particularly if the rule is found in a regional convention: in the *Asylum* case the Court was unwilling to hold Peru bound by the rule contained in the Montevideo Conv. Cf. the *European Human Rights Convention Case*, ILR 22 (1955), 608 at 610.

[65] Scott, *The Hague Conventions and Declarations of 1899 and 1907* (3rd edn., 1915), 100. See the Nuremberg Judgment, *Ann. Digest*, 13 (1946), no. 92; and the declarations of both sides in the Korean war.

[66] See Baxter, 129 Hague *Recueil* (1970, I), 61; *Nottebohm* case (Second Phase), ICJ Reports (1955), 23; *Namibia* Opinion, ibid. (1971), 47. Cf. *North Sea Continental Shelf Cases*, ibid. (1969), 41–3.

[67] ICJ Reports (1969), 3.

pre-existing customary law.[68] The principles on which the Court discriminated between articles included reference to the faculty of making unilateral reservations which applied to some articles but not to those which, by inference, had a more fundamental status. With respect it may be doubted if the existence of reservations of itself destroys the probative value of treaty provisions.[69] The Court concluded, further, that the provision on delimitation of shelf areas in Article 6 of the Convention had not become a rule of customary law by virtue of the subsequent practice of states and, in particular, of non-parties.[70] The six dissenting judges regarded the Convention as having greater potency, more particularly in generating rules after its appearance.[71] Both in the *Gulf of Maine* case[72] and in the *Libya–Malta Continental Shelf* case,[73] the Chamber of the Court and the full Court, respectively, accorded evidential weight to certain aspects of the United Nations Convention on the Law of the Sea adopted in 1982 (but not then in force).

In any event, even if norms of treaty origin crystallize as new principles or rules of customary law, the customary norms retain a separate identity even if the two norms appear identical in content.[74]

OTHER TREATIES

Bilateral treaties may provide evidence of customary rules,[75] and indeed there is no clear and dogmatic distinction between 'law-making' treaties and others. If bilateral treaties, for example on extradition, are habitually framed in the same way, a court may regard the usual form as the law even in the absence of a treaty obligation.[76] However, considerable caution is necessary in evaluating treaties for this purpose.

THE CONCLUSIONS OF INTERNATIONAL CONFERENCES[77]

The 'Final Act' or other statement of conclusions of a conference of states may be a form of multilateral treaty, but, even if it be an instrument recording decisions not

---

[68] Ibid. 32–41. See also Padilla Nervo, Sep. Op., pp. 86–9; Ammoun, Sep. Op., pp. 102–6, 123–4.

[69] See Baxter, 129 Hague *Recueil* (1970, I), 47–51. See also Judges Tanaka, Diss. Op., ICJ Reports (1969), 182; Morelli, Diss. Op., p. 198; Lachs, Diss. Op., pp. 223–5; Sørensen, Diss. Op., p. 248.

[70] ICJ Reports (1969), pp. 41–5.

[71] Ibid. 56 (Bengzon); 156–8, 163, 169 (Koretsky); 172–80 (Tanaka); 197–200 (Morelli); 221–32 (Lachs); 241–7 (Sørensen).

[72] ICJ Reports (1982), 294–5, paras. 94–6.

[73] Ibid. (1985), 29–34, paras. 27–34.

[74] See the Judgment in the *Case of Nicaragua* v. *United States* (Merits), ibid. 92–6, paras. 174–9. See further on the same issue, ibid. 152–4 (Sep. Op., Nagendra Singh); 182–4 (Sep. Op., Ago); 204–8 (Sep. Op., Ni); 216–19 (Diss. Op., Oda); 302–6 (Diss. Op., Schwebel); 529–36 (Diss. Op., Jennings).

[75] See Baxter, 129 Hague *Recueil* (1970, I), 75–91; Sørensen, *Les Sources de droit international* (1946) 96–8. See also the *Wimbledon*, PCIJ Ser. A, no. 1, p. 25; *Panevezys–Saldutiskis Railway*, Ser. A/B, no. 76, pp. 51–2, per Judge Ehrlich; *Nottebohm*, ICJ Reports (1955), 22–3; see also *In re Lechin et al.*, Ann. Digest, 16 (1949), no. 1; *In re Dilasser et al.*, LR 18 (1951), no. 99; *The State (Duggan)* v. *Tapley*, ibid., no. 109; *Lagos* v. *Baggianini*, ibid. 22 (1955), 533; *Lauritzen* v. *Government of Chile*, ibid. 23 (1956), 708 at 715–16.

[76] Cf. *In re Muzza Aceituno*, ILR 18 (1951), no. 98; *Re Tribble*, ibid. 20 (1953), 366.

[77] See Johnson, 35 BY (1959), 1–33. See also *infra*, ch. 28, on international transactions.

adopted unanimously, the result may constitute cogent evidence of the state of the customary law on the subject concerned. Even before the necessary ratifications are received, a convention embodied in a Final Act and expressed as a codification of existing principles has obvious importance.[78]

RESOLUTIONS OF THE UNITED NATIONS GENERAL ASSEMBLY[79]

The law-making role of organizations is considered further in Chapter 31, section 10. In general these resolutions are not binding on member states, but, when they are concerned with general norms of international law, then acceptance by a majority vote constitutes *evidence* of the opinions of governments in the widest forum for the expression of such opinions.[80] Even when they are framed as general principles, resolutions of this kind provide a basis for the progressive development of the law and the speedy consolidation of customary rules. Examples of important 'law-making' resolutions are the Resolution[81] which affirmed 'the principles of international law recognized by the Charter of the Nuremberg Tribunal and the Judgment of the Tribunal'; the Resolution on Prohibition of the Use of Nuclear Weapons for War Purposes,[82] the Declaration on the Granting of Independence to Colonial Countries and Peoples;[83] the Declaration on Permanent Sovereignty over Natural Resources;[84] and the Declaration of Legal Principles Governing Activities of States in the Exploration and Use of Outer Space.[85] In some cases a resolution may have direct legal effect as an authoritative interpretation and application of the principles of the Charter.[86] In general each individual resolution must be assessed in the light of all the circumstances and also by reference to other evidence of the opinions of states on the point in issue.

[78] See *Re Cámpora et al.*, ILR 24 (1957); 518, *Namibia* Opinion, ICJ Reports (1971), 47.

[79] Generally see Cheng, 5 *Indian Journ.* (1965), 23–48; Castañeda, *Legal Effects of United Nations Resolutions* (1969); id., 129 Hague *Recueil* (1970, I), 211–331; Bastid, *Recueil d'études en hommage à Guggenheim* (1968), 132–45; Asamoah, *The Legal Significance of the Declarations of the General Assembly of the United Nations* (1966); Skubiszewski, 41 *BY* (1965–6), 198 at 242–8; Bishop, 115 Hague *Recueil* (1965, II), 241–5; Arangio-Ruiz, 137 Hague *Recueil* (1972, III), 431–628; P. de Visscher, 136 Hague *Recueil* (1972, II), 123–33; d., *Festschrift für Rudolf Bindschedler* (1980), 173–85; Schachter, 178 Hague *Recueil* (1982, V), III-23; Skubiszewski, *Annuaire de l'Inst.* 61 (1985), i. 29–358; id., *Études en l'honneur de Roberto Ago*, i. 503–19; Thierry, 167 Hague *Recueil* (1980, II), 432–44; Blaine Sloan, 58 *BY* (1987), 39–150. See further *South West Africa Cases* (Second Phase), ICJ Reports (1966), 171–2 (Sep. Op., van Wyk), 291–3 (Diss. Op., Tanaka), 432–41 (Diss. Op., Jessup), 455–7, 464–70 (Diss. Op., Padilla Nervo).

[80] See the Judgment in the *Case of Nicaragua v. United States* (Merits), ICJ Reports (1986), 98–104, paras. 187–95; pp. 107–8, paras. 203–5.

[81] Resol. no. 95; 11 Dec. 1946. Adopted unanimously.

[82] Resol. no. 1653 (XVI); 24 Nov. 1961. Adopted by 55 votes to 20; 26 abstentions.

[83] Resol. no. 1514 (XV), 14 Dec. 1960. Adopted by 89 votes to none; 9 abstentions.

[84] Resol. no. 1803 (XVII), 14 Dec. 1962; *UK Contemp. Practice* (1962), ii. 283. Adopted by 87 votes to 2; 12 abstentions.

[85] Resol. no. 1962 (XVIII), 13 Dec. 1963; 3 *ILM* (1964), 160; 58 *AJ* (1964), 477. Adopted unanimously.

[86] See e.g. the Decl. on the Elimination of All Forms of Racial Discrimination; adopted 20 Nov. 1963; Art. 1 (in Resol. 1904 (XVIII)); 3 *ILM* (1964), 164; Decl. on Principles of International Law Concerning Friendly Relations; adopted without vote, 24 Oct. 1970; Resol no. 2625; Brownlie, *Documents*, p. 27.

5. GENERAL PRINCIPLES OF LAW[87]

Article 38(1)(c) of the Statute of the International Court refers to 'the general principles of law recognized by civilized nations', a source which comes after those depending more immediately on the consent of states and yet escapes classification as a 'subsidiary means' in paragraph (d). The formulation appeared in the *compromis* of arbitral tribunals in the nineteenth century, and similar formulae appear in draft instruments concerned with the functioning of tribunals.[88] In the committee of jurists which prepared the Statute there was no very definite consensus on the precise significance of the phrase. The Belgian jurist, Baron Descamps, had natural law concepts in mind, and his draft referred to 'the rules of international law recognized by the legal conscience of civilized peoples'. Root considered that governments would mistrust a court which relied on the subjective concept of principles of justice. However, the committee realized that the Court must be given a certain power to develop and refine the principles of international jurisprudence. In the result a joint proposal by Root and Phillimore was accepted and this is the text we now have.[89]

Root and Phillimore regarded the principles in terms of rules accepted in the domestic law of all civilized states, and Guggenheim[90] holds the firm view that paragraph (c) must be applied in this light. However, the view expressed in Oppenheim[91] is to be preferred: 'The intention is to authorize the Court to apply the general principles of municipal jurisprudence, in particular of private law, in so far as they are applicable to relations of States'. The latter part of this statement is worthy of emphasis. It would be incorrect to assume that tribunals have in practice adopted a mechanical system of borrowing from domestic law after a census of domestic systems. What has happened is that international tribunals have employed elements of legal reasoning and private law analogies in order to make the law of nations a viable system for application in a judicial process. Thus, it is impossible, or at least difficult, for state practice to evolve the rules of

---

[87] Sørensen, 101 Hague *Recueil* (1960, III), 16–34, id., *Les Sources*, pp. 123–52; Guggenheim, *Traité*, i. 291–312; Verzijl, *International Law in Historical Perspective*, i. 47–74; Lauterpacht, *Private Law Sources and Analogies of International Law* (1927); id., *International Law: Collected Papers*, ii (1975), 173–212; id., *Development* pp. 158–72; Cheng, *General Principles of Law as Applied by International Courts and Tribunals* (1953), 163–80; McNair, 33 *BY* (1957), 1–19; Rousseau, *Droit international public*, i. 370–97; Jenks, *The Prospects of International Adjudication* (1964), 266–315; Parry, *The Sources and Evidences of International Law*, pp. 83–91; Verdross, *Recueil d'études en hommage* à *Guggenheim*, 521–30; Paul, 10 *Indian Journ.* (1970), 324–50; Akehurst, 25 *ICLQ* (1976), 813–25; Lammers, *Essays in Memory of H.F. van Panhuys* (1980), 53–75; Thirlway, 61 *BY* (1990), 110–27 and 76 *BY* (2005), 108–13; Shahabuddeen, *Essays in Honour of Sir Robert Jennings* (1996), 90–103. For the view that general principles of law provide a third system for disputes between corporations and governments see McNair, 33 *BY* (1957), 1–19, and the *Abu Dhabi* award (1951), 1 *ICLQ* (1952), 247.

[88] See the draft treaty for the establishment of an international prize court, 1907, Art. 7 (general principles of justice and equity). See also the European Conv. for the Protection of Human Rights and Fundamental Freedoms, Art. 7, para. 2.

[89] *Procés-verbaux* (1920), 316, 335, 344. Sørensen remarks that the compromise formula has an inherent ambiguity which is inimical to any rational interpretation of the provision: *Les Sources*, p. 125.

[90] 94 Hague *Recueil* (1958, II), 78.

[91] i. 29.

procedure and evidence which a court must employ. An international tribunal chooses, edits, and adapts elements from better developed systems: the result is a new element of international law the content of which is influenced historically and logically by domestic law.[92]

In practice tribunals show considerable discretion in the matter. The decisions on the acquisition of territory[93] tend not to reflect the domestic derivatives on the subject to be found in the textbooks, and there is room for the view that domestic law analogies have caused more harm than good in this sphere. The evolution of the rules on the effect of duress on treaties[94] has not depended on changes in domestic law. In the *North Atlantic Fisheries*[95] case the tribunal considered the concept of servitude and then refused to apply it. Moreover, in some cases, for example the law relating to expropriation of private rights, reference to domestic law might give uncertain results and the choice of models might reveal ideological predilections.

GENERAL PRINCIPLES OF LAW IN THE PRACTICE OF TRIBUNALS

(a) Arbitral tribunals[96]

Arbitral tribunals have frequently resorted to municipal analogies. In the *Fabiani*[97] case between France and Venezuela the arbitrator had recourse to municipal public law on the question of the responsibility of the state for the acts of its agents, including judicial officers, committed in the exercise of their functions. Reliance was also placed on general principles of law in the assessment of damages. The Permanent Court of Arbitration applied the principle of moratory interest on debts in the *Russian Indemnity* case.[98] Since the original Statute of the International Court came into force in 1920, tribunals not otherwise bound by it have treated Article 38(1)(c) as declaratory of the law applicable.[99]

(b) The International Court of Justice and its predecessor[100]

The Court has used this source sparingly, and it normally appears, without any formal reference or label, as a part of judicial reasoning. However, the Court has on occasion

---

[92] See Tunkin, 95 Hague *Recueil* (1958, III), 23–6; and de Visscher, *Theory and Reality in Public International Law* (1957), 356–8. Cf. McNair, ICJ Reports (1950), 148–50.

[93] See *infra*, ch. 7.

[94] See *infra*, ch. 27, s. 7. Nineteenth-century writers took the view that duress had no vitiating effect. Since 1920 the contrary view has been gaining ground.

[95] (1910) Hague Court Reports, i. 141.

[96] See Simpson and Fox, *International Arbitration*, pp. 132–7; Jenks, *Prospects of International Adjudication*, pp. 306–9; Lauterpacht, *Analogies*, pp. 60–7; id., *Function* pp. 115–18; Seidl-Hohenveldern, 53 *AJ* (1959), 853–72.

[97] (1896), La Fontaine, p. 344; *RIAA* x. 83. The claim was based on denial of justice by the Venezuelan courts.

[98] (1912), Hague Court Reports, p. 297. See also *Sarropoulos v. Bulgarian State* (1927), *Ann. Digest*, 4 (1927–8), no. 173 (extinctive prescription).

[99] Admin. Decision no. II (1923), Mixed Claims Commission, US–Germany; *Ann. Digest*, 2 (1923–4), no. 205; *Goldenberg & Sons v. Germany* (1928), ibid. 4 (1927–8), no. 369; *Lena Goldfields* arbitration (1930), ibid. 5 (1929–30), no. 1; 36 *Cornell LQ* 42.

[100] See Jenks, *Prospects of International Adjudication*, pp. 268–305; Lauterpacht, *Development*, pp. 158–72; Fitzmaurice, 35 *BY* (1959), 216–29; Waldock, 106 Hague *Recueil* (1962, II), 57–69; Beckett, *Corfu Channel* case, ICJ Pleadings; iii. 267ff.; Blondel, *Recueil d'études en hommage à Guggenheim*, 201–36.

referred to general notions of responsibility. In the *Chorzów Factory* case[101] the Court observed: '...one party cannot avail himself of the fact that the other has not fulfilled some obligation, or has not had recourse to some means of redress, if the former Party has, by some illegal act, prevented the latter from fulfilling the obligation in question, or from having recourse to the tribunal which would have been open to him'. In a later stage of the same case[102] the following statement was made: '...the Court observes that it is a principle of international law, and even a general conception of law, that any breach of an engagement involves an obligation to make reparation'. In a number of cases the principle of estoppel or acquiescence (*préclusion*) has been relied on by the Court,[103] and on occasion rather general references to abuse of rights and good faith may occur.[104] Perhaps the most frequent and successful use of domestic law analogies has been in the field of evidence, procedure, and jurisdictional questions. Thus there have been references to the rule that no one can be judge in his own suit,[105] litispendence,[106] *res judicata*,[107] various 'principles governing the judicial process',[108] and 'the principle universally accepted by international tribunals...to the effect that the parties to a case must abstain from any measure capable of exercising a prejudicial effect in regard to the execution of the decision to be given...'.[109] In the *Corfu Channel* case[110] the Court had recourse to circumstantial evidence and remarked that 'this indirect evidence is admitted in all systems of law, and its use is recognized by international decisions'. In his dissenting opinion in the *South West Africa* cases (Second Phase),[111] Judge Tanaka referred to Article 38(1)(c) of the Court's Statute as a basis for human rights concepts and pointed out that the provision contains natural law elements. The reasoning of the Court in the *Barcelona Traction* case (Second Phase)[112] related very closely to the general conception of the limited liability company to be found in systems of municipal law.

---

[101] *Chorzów Factory* (Indemnity; Jurisdiction), PCIJ, Ser. A, no. 9, p. 31.

[102] *Chorzów Factory* (Merits), PCIJ, Ser. A, no. 17, p. 29.

[103] See the *Eastern Greenland* case (1933), PCIJ, Ser. A/B, no. 53, pp. 52ff., 62, 69; *Arbitral Award of the King of Spain*, ICJ Reports (1960), 192 at 209, 213; the *Temple* case, ICJ Reports (1962), at 23, 31, 32 (see ch. 28, s. 4); ibid., individual op. of Judge Alfaro, pp. 39–51. See also ibid. 26, where the Court said: 'it is an established rule of law that a plea of error cannot be allowed as an element vitiating consent if the party advancing it contributed by its own conduct to the error'.

[104] e.g. the *Free Zones* case (1930), PCIJ, Ser. A, no. 24, p. 12; and (1932), Ser. A/B, no. 46, p. 167. For references to individual judges' use of analogies see Lauterpacht, *Development*, p. 167, n. 20, and see also ICJ Reports (1960), 66–7, 90, 107, 136.

[105] *Mosul Boundary* case (1925), PCIJ, Ser. B, no. 12, p. 32.

[106] *German Interests in Polish Upper Silesia* (1925), PCIJ, Ser. A, no. 6, p. 20.

[107] *Effect of Awards of the U.N. Administrative Tribunal*, ICJ Reports (1954), 53.

[108] Adv. Op. *Application for Review of Judgment No. 158*, ICJ Reports (1973), 166 at 177, 181, 210; Adv. Op. *Application for Review of Judgment No. 273*, ibid. (1982), 325 at 338–40, 345, 356.

[109] *Electricity Company of Sofia and Bulgaria* (1939), PCIJ, Ser. A/B, no. 79, p. 199.

[110] ICJ Reports (1949), 18. See also *Right of Passage over Indian Territory* (Prelim. Objection), ICJ Reports (1957), 141–2; *German Interests in Polish Upper Silesia*, PCIJ, Ser. A, no. 6 (1925), p. 19; and, on *forum prorogatum, infra*, ch. 32, s. 9.

[111] ICJ Reports (1966), 6 at 294–9.

[112] Ibid. (1970), at 33–5. See generally *infra*, ch. 22, s. 5.

6. GENERAL PRINCIPLES OF INTERNATIONAL LAW[113]

The rubric may refer to rules of customary law, to general principles of law as in Article 38(1)(c), or to logical propositions resulting from judicial reasoning on the basis of existing international law and municipal analogies. What is clear is the inappropriateness of rigid categorization of the sources. Examples of this type of general principle are the principles of consent, reciprocity, equality of states, finality of awards and settlements, the legal validity of agreements, good faith, domestic jurisdiction, and the freedom of the seas. In many cases these principles are to be traced to state practice. However, they are primarily abstractions from a mass of rules and have been so long and so generally accepted as to be no longer *directly* connected with state practice. In a few cases the principle concerned, though useful, is unlikely to appear in ordinary state practice. In general the subject-matter of 'general principles of law' overlaps that of the present section. However, certain fundamental principles have recently been set apart as overriding principles of *jus cogens* which may qualify the effect of more ordinary rules.[114]

7. JUDICIAL DECISIONS[115]

(a) Decisions of international tribunals

Judicial decisions are not strictly speaking a formal source, but in some instances at least they are regarded as authoritative evidence of the state of the law, and the practical significance of the label 'subsidiary means' in Article 38(1)(d) is not to be exaggerated.[116] A coherent body of jurisprudence will naturally have important consequences for the law.

ARBITRAL TRIBUNALS

The literature of the law contains frequent reference to decisions of arbitral tribunals. The quality of arbitral tribunals has varied considerably, but there have been a number

---

[113] See Rousseau, i. 389–95; Fitzmaurice, 92 Hague *Recueil* (1957, II), 57–8, Sørensen, *Les Sources*, pp. 112–22; Waldock, 106 Hague *Recueil* (1962, II), 62–4; Simpson and Fox, *International Arbitration*, p. 132. See also ICJ Reports (1958), 106–7 (Moreno Quintana); ibid. (1960), 136–7 (Fernandes); and ibid. (1962), 143 (Spender); Verdross, *Recueil d'études en hommage à Guggenheim*, pp. 521–30; Virally, ibid. 531–54. Cf. Fitzmaurice, 30 *BY* (1953), 2; 35 *BY* (1959), 185, rubric 'General Principles'; and id., *Symbolae Verzijl*, pp. 161–8.

[114] See ch. 23, s. 5.

[115] Lauterpacht, *Development*, pp. 8–22; Waldock, 106 Hague *Recueil* (1962, II), 88–95; Fitzmaurice, *Symbolae Verzijl*, pp. 168–73; Sørensen, *Les Sources*, pp. 153–76; Thirlway, 61 *BY* (1990), 127–33; and 76 *BY* (2005), 114–18.

[116] Fitzmaurice, *Symbolae Verzijl*, p. 174, criticizes the classification.

of awards which contain notable contributions to the development of the law by eminent jurists sitting as arbitrators, umpires, or commissioners.[117]

REFERENCE TO ARBITRAL AWARDS BY THE INTERNATIONAL COURT OF JUSTICE AND ITS PREDECESSOR

The Court has referred to particular decisions on only five occasions,[118] but on other occasions[119] has referred compendiously to the jurisprudence of international arbitration.

DECISIONS OF THE INTERNATIONAL COURT OF JUSTICE AND ITS PREDECESSOR

The Court applies the law and does not make it, and Article 59 of the Statute[120] in part reflects a feeling on the part of the founders that the Court was intended to settle disputes as they came to it rather than to shape the law. Yet it is obvious that a unanimous, or almost unanimous, decision has a role in the progressive development of the law. Since 1947 the decisions and advisory opinions in the *Reparation*,[121] *Genocide*,[122] *Fisheries*,[123] and *Nottebohm*[124] cases have had decisive influence on general international law. However, some discretion is needed in handling decisions. The *Lotus* decision, arising from the casting vote of the President, and much criticized, was rejected by the International Law Commission in its draft articles[125] on the law of the sea, and at its third session the Commission refused to accept the principles emerging from the *Genocide* case (a stand which was reversed at its fourteenth session).[126] Moreover, the

---

[117] See e.g. the *Alabama Claims* arbitration (1872), Moore, *Arbitrations*, i. 653; and the *Behring Sea Fisheries* arbitration (1893), Moore, *Arbitrations*, i. 755. See also *infra*, pp. 139–40 on the *Palmas Island* case, and pp. 403ff. on the *Canevaro* case, and, generally, the series of *Reports of International Arbitral Awards* published by the UN since 1948, and the foreword to vol. i.

[118] *Polish Postal Service in Danzig* (1925), PCIJ, Ser. B, no. 11, p. 30 (to the PCA in the case of the *Pious Funds of the Californias*, RIAA ix. 11); the *Lotus* (1927), PCIJ, Ser. A, no. 10, p. 26 (to the *Costa Rica Packet* case, Moore, *Arbitrations*, v. 4948); *Eastern Greenland* case (1933), PCIJ, Ser. A/B, no. 53, pp. 45–6; Hague Court Reports, iii, at p. 170 (to the *Island of Palmas* case, *infra*, pp. 141–2); *Nottebohm*, ICJ Reports (1953), 119 (to the *Alabama* arbitration, *infra*, p. 34); *Gulf of Maine* case, ibid., 1984, pp. 302–3, 324 (to the *Anglo–French Continental Shelf* arbitration, ILR 54, 6).

[119] *Chorzów Factory* (Jurisdiction) (1927), PCIJ, Ser. A, no. 9, p. 31; *Chorzów Factory* (Merits) (1928), PCIJ, Ser. A, no. 17, pp. 31, 47; *Fisheries* case, ICJ Reports (1951), 131. See also *Peter Pázmány University* (1933), PCIJ, Ser. A/B, no. 61, p. 243 (consistent practice of mixed arbitral tribunals); *Barcelona Traction* case (Second Phase), ICJ Reports (1970), at 40. The Court has also referred generally to decisions of other tribunals without specific reference to arbitral tribunals: *Eastern Greenland* case, *supra*, at p. 46; *Reparation for Injuries*, ICJ Reports (1949), 186.

[120] *Supra*, p. 4.

[121] *Infra*, ch. 31.

[122] *Infra*, ch. 27, s. 3.

[123] *Infra*, p. 176.

[124] *Infra*, ch. 19.

[125] See *infra*, pp. 239–40.

[126] See *infra*, ch. 27, s. 3.

view may be taken that it is incautious to extract general propositions from opinions and judgments devoted to a specific problem or settlement of disputes entangled with the special relations of two states.[127]

JUDICIAL PRECEDENT AND THE STATUTE OF THE COURT

It will be remembered that Article 38(1)(d) of the Statute starts with a proviso: 'Subject to the provisions of Article 59, judicial decisions...as subsidiary means for the determination of rules of law'. Article 59 provides: 'The decision of the Court has no binding force except as between the parties and in respect of that particular case'. Lauterpacht has argued[128] that Article 59 does not refer to the major question of judicial precedent but to the particular question of intervention. In Article 63 it is provided that, if a third state avails itself of the right of intervention, the construction given in the judgment shall be equally binding upon it. Lauterpacht concludes that 'Article 59 would thus seem to state directly what Article 63 expresses indirectly'. Beckett[129] took the view that Article 59 refers to the actual decision as opposed to the legal principles on which it is based. However, the debate in the committee of jurists responsible for the Statute indicates clearly that Article 59 was not intended merely to express the principle of *res judicata* but to rule out a system of binding precedent.[130] Thus in one judgment the Court said:[131] 'The object of [Article 59] is simply to prevent legal principles accepted by the Court in a particular case from being binding on other States or in other disputes'. In its practice, however, it has not treated earlier decisions in such a narrow spirit.

JUDICIAL PRECEDENT IN THE PRACTICE OF THE COURT[132]

Strictly speaking, the Court does not observe a doctrine of precedent,[133] but strives nevertheless to maintain judicial consistency. Thus, in the case on *Exchange of Greek and Turkish Populations*,[134] the Court referred to 'the precedent afforded by its Advisory

---

[127] On the *Genocide* case see McNair, *Law of Treaties*, pp. 167–8. On the *Nottebohm* case see the *Flegenheimer* case, ILR 25 (1958, I), 91 at 148–50.

[128] *Development*, p. 8. He relies on the final report of the committee of jurists in 1920.

[129] 39 Hague *Recueil* (1932, I), 141.

[130] See Descamps, *Procès-Verbaux*, pp. 332, 336, 584. See also Sørensen, *Les Sources*, p. 161; Hudson, *The Permanent Court of International Justice 1920–1942*, p. 207, and Waldock, 106 Hague *Recueil* (1962, II), 91. The latter observes: 'It would indeed have been somewhat surprising if States had been prepared in 1920 to give a wholly new and untried tribunal explicit authority to lay down law binding upon all States'.

[131] *German Interests in Polish Upper Silesia* (1926), PCIJ, Ser. A, no. 7, p. 19; World Court Reports, i. 510.

[132] See Thirlway, 61 *BY* (1990), 131–3; Lauterpacht, 12 *BY* (1931), 60; id., *Development*, pp. 9–20; Beckett, 39 Hague *Recueil* (1932, I), 138; Sørensen, *Les Sources*, pp. 166–76; *Case Concerning the Land, Island and Maritime Frontier Dispute*, ICJ Reports (1990), 52–3 (Diss. Op. of Judge Shahabuddeen), Shahabuddeen, *Precedent in the World Court* (1996).

[133] But precedent is firmly adhered to in matters of procedure.

[134] (1925), PCIJ, Ser. B, no. 10, p. 21. See also *Peace Treaties* case, ICJ Reports (1950), 89, 103, 106 (Winiarski, ZoriAib, and Krylov, dissenting); *South West Africa* cases, ICJ Reports (1962), 328, 345; *Cameroons* case, ibid. (1963), 27–8, 29–30, 37; *Aerial Incident* case, ibid. (1959), 192 (Joint Dissent); *South West Africa* cases

Opinion No. 3', i.e. the *Wimbledon* case, in respect of the view that the incurring of treaty obligations was not an abandonment of sovereignty. In the *Reparation*[135] case the Court relied on a pronouncement in a previous advisory opinion[136] for a statement of the principle of effectiveness in interpreting treaties. Such references are often a matter of 'evidence' of the law, but a fairly substantial consistency is aimed at and so the technique of distinguishing previous decisions may be employed. In the case on *Interpretation of Peace Treaties*[137] certain questions were submitted by the General Assembly to the Court for an advisory opinion. The questions concerned the interpretation of clauses in the peace treaties with Bulgaria, Hungary, and Romania, clauses relating to the settlement of disputes concerning the interpretation or execution of these treaties. In fact the request arose from allegations against these three states by other parties of breaches of the provisions of the treaties on the maintenance of human rights, a matter of substance. The Court rejected arguments to the effect that it lacked the power to answer the request for an opinion. The Court said:[138]

Article 65 of the Statute is permissive. It gives the Court the power to examine whether the circumstances of the case are of such a character as should lead it to decline to answer the Request. In the opinion of the Court, the circumstances of the present case are profoundly different from those which were before the Permanent Court of International Justice in the *Eastern Carelia* case[139] (Advisory Opinion No. 5), when that Court declined to give an Opinion because it found that the question put to it was directly related to the main point of a dispute actually pending between two States, so that answering the question would be substantially equivalent to deciding the dispute between the parties, and that at the same time it raised a question of fact which could not be elucidated without hearing both parties.

... the present Request for an Opinion is solely concerned with the applicability to certain disputes of the procedure for settlement instituted by the Peace Treaties, and it is justifiable to conclude that it in no way touches the merits of those disputes.

(Second Phase), ICJ Reports (1966), 240–1 (Koretsky, Diss. Op.); *North Sea Continental Shelf Cases*, ibid. (1969), 3 at 44, 47–9; ibid. 101–2, 121, 131, 138 (Ammoun, Sep. Op.); ibid. 210 (Morelli, Diss. Op.); ibid. 223, 225, 229, 231, 232–3, 236, 238 (Lachs, Diss. Op.); ibid. 243–4, 247 (Sørensen, Diss. Op.); *Namibia* Opinion ibid. (1971), 26ff., 53–4; *Case Concerning Kasikili/Sedudu Island*, ibid. (1999), 1073, 1076, 1097–1100; *Case Concerning the Land and Maritime Boundary Between Cameroon and Nigeria* (2002), paras. 68, 84, 223, 237–8, 286–90, 292–5, 301, 304, 321.

[135] ICJ Reports (1949), 182–3.

[136] *Competence of the I.L.O. to regulate, incidentally, the Personal Work of the Employer* (1926), PCIJ, Ser. B, no. 13, p. 18.

[137] ICJ Reports (1950), 65.

[138] ICJ Reports (1950), 72 (this is not the only significant passage). See Lauterpacht, *Development*, pp. 352–7, the criticism of the distinction between procedure and substance. See further Fitzmaurice, 29 *BY* (1952), 50–2 and the Diss. Ops. Cf. Joint Diss. Op. of Spender and Fitzmaurice, *South West Africa* cases, ICJ Reports (1962), 471–3; the *Cameroons* case, ibid. (1963), 35, 37–8, 62–4 (Wellington Koo, Sep. Op.), 68–73 (Sir Percy Spender, Sep. Op.); 108, 125–7 (Sir Gerald Fitzmaurice, Sep. Op.), 140–1 (Morelli, Sep. Op.), 150–1 (Badawi, Diss. Op.), 156–9, 170, 182 (Bustamante, Diss. Op.), 187–91, 194–6 (Beb a Don, Diss. Op.). The *Eastern Carelia* case was also distinguished in the *Namibia* Opinion, ICJ Reports (1971), 16 at 23.

[139] (1923), PCIJ, Ser. B, no. 5, at p. 27.

(b) Decisions of the Court of Justice of the European Communities[140]

Several decisions of this Court have involved issues of general importance.

(c) Decisions of national courts[141]

Article 38(1)(d) of the Statute of the International Court is not confined to international decisions and the decisions of national tribunals have evidential value. Some decisions provide indirect evidence of the practice of the state of the *forum* on the question involved;[142] others involve a free investigation of the point of law and consideration of available sources, and may result in a careful exposition of the law. Writers from common law jurisdictions make frequent reference to municipal decisions, and such use is universal in monographs from this source. French, German, and Italian jurists tend to use fewer case references, while Russian jurists are even more sparing. In the recent past there has been a great increase in the availability of decisions as evidence of the law.[143] Municipal decisions have been an important source for material on recognition of belligerency, of governments and of states, state succession, sovereign immunity, diplomatic immunity, extradition, war crimes, belligerent occupation, the concept of a 'state of war', and the law of prize.[144] However, the value of these decisions varies considerably, and many present a narrow national outlook or rest on a very inadequate use of the sources.

(d) *Ad hoc* international tribunals

Tribunals set up by agreement between a number of states, for some *ad hoc* purpose, may produce valuable pronouncements on delicate issues, much depending on the status of the tribunal and its members and the conditions under which it does its work. The Judgment of the International Military Tribunal for the Trial of German Major War Criminals,[145] the decisions of the Iran–United States Claims Tribunal, and the decisions of the International Criminal Court for the Former Yugoslavia contain a number of significant findings on issues of law.

(e) Municipal courts and disputes between parts of composite states[146]

The Supreme Court of the United States, the Swiss Federal Court, and the *Staatsgerichtshof* of the Weimar Republic have had occasion to decide disputes

---

[140] See Reuter, *Recueil d'études en hommage à Guggenheim*, p. 665 at pp. 673–85.

[141] See Lauterpacht, 10 *BY* (1929), 65–95 (also in Coll. Papers, ii. 238–68); Schwarzenberger, *International Law*, i (3rd edn., 1957), 32–4.

[142] Note the relation between English decisions and the Foreign Office Certificates: see Lyons, 23 *BY* (1946), 240–81. See also the *Lotus*, PCIJ, Ser. A, no. 10, pp. 23, 28–30; and the Diss. Ops. of Judges Finlay and Moore, pp. 54, 68–9 respectively; and the *Eichmann* case (1961), 56 *AJ* (1962), 805; ILR 36, 5.

[143] See the *Journal du droit international* (Clunet) and the *Annual Digest of Public International Law Cases*, now the International Law Reports.

[144] See also the *Scotia* (1871), 14 Wallace 170; the *Paquete Habana* (1900), 175 US 677; the *Zamora* [1916] 2 AC 77; *Gibbs* v. *Rodriguez* (1950), ILR 18 (1951), no. 204; *Lauritzen* v. *Government of Chile*, ILR 23 (1956), 708.

[145] Cmd. 6964; *Ann. Digest*, 13 (1946), no. 92.

[146] See 10 *BY* (1929), 74–5. See e.g. *New Jersey* v. *Delaware* (1934), 291 US 361; 29 *AJ* (1935), 309; *Labrador Boundary* case (1927), 43 TLR 289.

between members of the federal communities involved on the basis of doctrines of international law. The practice of the first of these is of importance in view of the fact that the United States has its origin in a union of independent states and this gives an international element to its internal relations.[147]

(f) Pleadings in cases before international tribunals

Pleadings before the International Court contain valuable collations of material and, at the least, have value as comprehensive statements of the opinions of particular states on legal questions.

8. THE WRITINGS OF PUBLICISTS[148]

The Statute of the International Court includes, among the 'subsidiary means for the determination of rules of law', 'the teachings of the most highly qualified[149] publicists of the various nations' or, in the French text, 'la doctrine'. Once again the source only constitutes evidence of the law, but in some subjects individual writers have had a formative influence. Thus Gidel has had some formative influence on the law of the sea.[150] It is, however, obvious that subjective factors enter into any assessment of juristic opinion, that individual writers reflect national and other prejudices, and, further, that some publicists see themselves to be propagating new and better views rather than providing a passive appraisal of the law.

Whatever the need for caution, the opinions of publicists are used widely. The law officers' opinions tendered confidentially to the executive in Great Britain contain references to the views of Vattel, Calvo, Hall, and others, and the opinions themselves represent the views of experts, including Harcourt, Phillimore, and Finlay.[151] Arbitral tribunals[152] and national courts[153] make use of the writings of jurists. National courts are unfamiliar with state practice and are ready to lean on secondary sources. Superficially the International Court might seem to make little use of doctrine,[154] and majority judgments contain few references: but this is because of the process of

---

[147] See also *infra*, pp. 58–9.

[148] See Lauterpacht, *Development*, pp. 23–5; Waldock, 106 Hague *Recueil* (1962, II), 95–6.

[149] This phrase is not given a restrictive effect by tribunals; but authority naturally affects the weight of the evidence.

[150] *Droit international public de la mer*, 3 vols. (1932–4). His work is associated with the concept of the contiguous zone. See also Colombos, *The International Law of the Sea* (6th edn., 1967), translated into French, Italian, Russian, Spanish, German, Portuguese, and Greek.

[151] See McNair, *Opinions*, i, Preface; iii. 402–6.

[152] Particularly in the period 1793 to 1914, using Grotius, Vattel, and Bynkershoek.

[153] See the judgments in the *Eichmann* case (1961), 56 *AJ* (1962), 805; ILR, 36, 5; *R. v. Keyn* (1876), 2 Ex. D. 63; *Public Prosecutor v. Oie Hee Koi* [1968] AC 829.

[154] But see the *Wimbledon* (1923), PCIJ, Ser. A, no. 1, p. 28 ('general opinion'); *German Settlers in Poland* (1923), PCIJ, Ser. B, no. 6, p. 36 ('almost universal opinion'); *Jaworzina* case (1923), PCIJ, Ser. B, no. 8, p. 37 (French text, 'une doctrine constante'); *German Interests in Polish Upper Silesia* (1925), PCIJ, Ser. A, no. 6, p. 20 ('the "teachings of legal authorities"' 'the jurisprudence of the principal countries'); the *Lotus* (1927),

collective drafting of judgments, and the need to avoid a somewhat invidious selection of citations. The fact that writers are used by the Court is evidenced by the dissenting and separate opinions[155] in which the 'workings' are set out in more detail and reflect the actual methods of approach of the Court as a whole. Many references to writers are to be found in the pleadings before the Court.

Sources analogous to the writings of publicists, and at least as authoritative, are the draft articles produced by the International Law Commission,[156] reports and secretariat memoranda prepared for the Commission,[157] Harvard Research drafts,[158] the bases of discussion of the Hague Codification Conference of 1930, and the reports and resolutions of the Institute of International Law and other expert bodies.[159]

9. EQUITY IN JUDGMENTS AND ADVISORY OPINIONS OF THE INTERNATIONAL COURT[160]

'Equity' is used here in the sense of considerations of fairness, reasonableness, and policy often necessary for the sensible application of the more settled rules of law. Strictly, it cannot be a source of law, and yet it may be an important factor in the process of decision. Equity may play a dramatic role in supplementing the law or appear unobtrusively as a part of judicial reasoning. In the case on *Diversion of Water from the River Meuse*[161] Judge Hudson applied the principle that equality is equity[162] and stated

PCIJ, Ser. A, no. 10, p. 26 ('teachings of publicists', 'all or nearly all writers'); *Nottebohm* (Second Phase), ICJ Reports (1955), 22 ('the writings of publicists').

[155] *Diversion of Water from the Meuse* (1937), PCIJ, Ser. A/B, no. 70, pp. 76–7 (Hudson); *South West Africa* case, ICJ Reports (1950), 146ff. (McNair); *Peace Treaties* case, ibid. 235 (Read); *Asylum* case, ibid. 335ff. (Azevedo); *Genocide* case, ICJ Reports (1951), 32ff. (Joint Dissent, Guerrero, McNair, Read, Hsu Mo); *Temple* case, ICJ Reports (1962), 39ff. (Alfaro); *Aerial Incident* case, ICJ Reports (1959), 174 (Joint Diss., Lauterpacht, Wellington Koo, Spender).

[156] See *LAFICO and the Republic of Burundi*, ILR 96, 279, 318–19; the Judgment of the International Court in the *Gabčikovo-Nagymaros Project* (Hungary/Slovakia), ICJ Reports (1997), 39–46, 55; and the *New Zealand* v. *France Arbitration*, Award of 30 April 1990, 20 *RIAA*, 215 at 252–5.

[157] See generally the *Yearbook of the International Law Commission*.

[158] See *AJ* 26 (1932), Suppl., p. 29 (1935), Suppl., p. 33 (1939), Suppl., and the *Genocide* case, ICJ Reports (1951), 32ff.

[159] See the decision of the New Zealand Court of Appeal in *KPMG Peat Marwick* v. *Davison*, ILR 104, 96 at p. 616.

[160] Jenks, *The Prospects of International Adjudication*, pp. 316–427; Lauterpacht, *Development*, pp. 213–17; *American and British Claims Arbitration*, *Report of Fred K. Nielsen* (1926), 51–72; Akehurst, 25 ICLQ (1976), 801–25; Schachter, 178 Hague *Recueil* (1982, V), 82–90; Thirlway, 60 *BY* (1989), 49–62; Lowe, 12 *Austral. Yrbk.*, 54–81; Higgins, *Peace and Process* (1994), 219–37; Miyoshi, *Considerations of Equity in the Settlement of Territorial and Boundary Disputes* (1993); Bernhardt, *Encyclopedia*, II (1995), 109–13.

[161] (1937), PCIJ, Ser. A/B, no. 70, p. 77. See also the *Wimbledon* (1923), PCIJ, Ser. A, no. 1, p. 32; World Court Reports, i. 163 (on the currency in which the damages were to be paid). Instances of equity in arbitral jurisprudence: *Orinoco Steamship Co.* case (1910); Hague Court Reports, i. 228; *RIAA* xi. 237; *Norwegian Shipowners' claims* (1922), Hague Court Reports, ii. 40; *RIAA* i. 309; *Eastern Extension, Australasia and China Telegraph Co., Ltd.* (1923), *RIAA* vi. 112; *Trail Smelter* arbitration (1938, 1941), *RIAA* iii. 1905.

[162] See also *supra*, p. 19, on 'general principles of international law'.

as a corollary that a state seeking the interpretation of a treaty must itself have completely fulfilled the obligations of that treaty. He observed that under 'Article 38 of the Statute, if not independently of that Article, the Court has some freedom to consider principles of equity as part of the international law which it must apply'.

In the *North Sea Continental Shelf Cases*[163] the Court had to resort to the formulation of equitable principles concerning the lateral delimitation of adjacent areas of continental shelf, as a consequence of its opinion that no rule of customary or treaty law bound the states parties to the dispute over the seabed of the North Sea. Considerations of equity advanced by Belgium in the *Barcelona Traction* case (Second Phase)[164] did not cause the Court to modify its views on the legal principles and considerations of policy. In the *Fisheries Jurisdiction* case (United Kingdom v. Iceland) the International Court outlined the elements of an 'equitable solution' of the differences over fishing rights and directed the parties to negotiate accordingly.[165] In the *Burkina Faso–Mali* case the Chamber of the Court applied 'equity *infra legem*' to the division of a frontier pool.[166]

Equity, in the present context, is encompassed by Article 38(1)(c) of the Statute, and not by Article 38(2),[167] which provides: 'This provision [para. I, *supra*, p. 3] shall not prejudice the power of the Court to decide a case *ex aequo et bono*, if the parties agree thereto'.

This power of decision *ex aequo et bono* involves elements of compromise and conciliation whereas equity in the English sense is applied as a part of the normal judicial function. In the *Free Zones* case[168] the Permanent Court, under a special agreement between France and Switzerland, was asked to settle the questions involved in the execution of the relevant provision in the Treaty of Versailles. While the Court was to declare on the future customs regime of the zones, the agreement contained no reference to decision *ex aequo et bono*. Switzerland argued that the Court should work on the basis of existing rights, and, by a technical majority including the vote of the President, the Court agreed with the argument. The Court said:[169]

...even assuming that it were not incompatible with the Court's Statute for the Parties to give the Court power to prescribe a settlement disregarding rights recognized by it and taking into account considerations of pure expediency only, such power, which would be of an absolutely exceptional character, could only be derived from a clear and explicit provision to the effect, which is not to be found in the Special Agreement. ...

---

[163] ICJ Reports (1969), 3 at 46–52. See also ibid. 131 ff. (Sep. Op., Ammoun), 165–8 (Diss. Op., Koretsky), 192–6 (Diss. Op., Tanaka), 207–9 (Diss. Op., Morelli), 257 (Diss. Op., Sørensen).

[164] Ibid. (1970), 3 at 48–50.

[165] ICJ Reports (1974), 3 at 30–5.

[166] Ibid. (1986), 554 at 631–3. See also Schwebel (Diss. Op.), Adv. Op. on *Application for Review* of *Judgment No. 273*, ibid. (1982), 325 at 536–7.

[167] Judge Kellogg in the *Free Zones* case (1930), PCIJ, Ser. A, no. 24, pp. 39–40, thought otherwise, but was in error. See the *North Sea Cases*, ICJ Reports (1969), 48.

[168] (1930), PCIJ, Ser. A, no. 24. See the earlier phase: (1929), Ser. A, no. 22; and Lauterpacht, *Development*, pp. 213–17; and *Function*, p. 318.

[169] Ser. A, no. 24, p. 10.

The majority of the Court expressed doubts as to the power of the Court to give deci-sions *ex aequo et bono*, but it would be unwise to draw general conclusions from such doubts since much depended on the nature of the special agreement. In any case the majority of the Court regarded the power to decide *ex aequo et bono* as distinct from the English notion of equity. However, the terminology of the subject is not well set-tled. The draftsmen of the General Act of Geneva, 1928,[170] seem to regard the power to decide *ex aequo et bono* and equity as synonymous. The converse, 'equity' to mean set-tlement *ex aequo et bono*, occurs in some arbitration agreements. On occasion equity is regarded as an equivalent of the general principles of law.[171]

10. CONSIDERATIONS OF HUMANITY

Considerations of humanity may depend on the subjective appreciation of the judge, but, more objectively, they may be related to human values already protected by posi-tive legal principles which, taken together, reveal certain criteria of public policy and invite the use of analogy. Such criteria have obvious connections with general prin-ciples of law and with equity, but they need no particular justification. References to principles or laws of humanity appear in preambles to conventions,[172] in resolutions of the United Nations General Assembly,[173] and also in diplomatic practice. The classical reference is the passage from the Judgment of the International Court in the *Corfu Channel* case,[174] in which the Court relied on certain 'general and well-recognized principles', including 'elementary considerations of humanity, even more exacting in peace than in war'. In recent years the provisions of the United Nations Charter concerning the protection of human rights and fundamental freedoms,[175] and refer-ences to the 'principles' of the Charter, have been used as a more concrete basis for considerations of humanity, for example in matters of racial discrimination and self-determination.[176]

---

[170] Art. 28. The provision was copied in other treaties.

[171] *Norwegian Shipowners' claim* (1922), Hague Court Reports, ii. 40; *RIAA* i. 309.

[172] Cf. Hague Conv. Concerning the Laws and Customs of War on Land, 1907, preamble, 'until a more complete code of the laws of war can be drawn up, the High Contracting Parties deem it expedient to declare that, in cases not covered by the rules adopted by them, the inhabitants and the belligerents remain under the protection and governance of the principles of the law of nations, derived from the usages established among civilized peoples, from the laws of humanity, and from the dictates of the public conscience'. This is known as the 'de Martens clause'. See also the draft provisions on war criminals debated at the Paris Peace Conference, 1919–20.

[173] See the Resol. on the Prohibition of the Use of Nuclear Weapons for War Purposes, 24 Nov. 1961.

[174] ICJ Reports (1949), 22. The statement was in respect of Albania's duty to warn of the presence of mines in her waters. See also the Judgment in the *Case of Nicaragua* v. *United States*, ibid. (1986), 112–14; and Thirlway, 61 *BY* (1990), 6–13.

[175] See generally ch. 25, s. 3.

[176] In approaching the issues of interpretation in the *South West Africa* cases (Second Phase), ICJ Reports (1966), 6 at 34, the International Court held that humanitarian considerations were not decisive. See also, in the same cases, Judge Tanaka, Diss. Op., pp. 252–3, 270, 294–9.

11. LEGITIMATE INTERESTS

In particular contexts rules of law may depend on criteria of good faith, reasonableness, and the like, and legitimate interests, including economic interests, may then be taken into account. However, legitimate interests may play a role in creating exceptions to existing rules and bringing about the progressive development of international law. Recognition of legitimate interest explains the extent of acquiescence in face of claims to the continental shelf[177] and fishing zones.[178] In this type of situation it is, of course, acquiescence and recognition which provide the formal bases for development of the new rules. In the *Fisheries* case[179] the International Court did not purport to do anything other than apply existing rules, but it had to justify the special application of the normal rules to the Norwegian coastline. In doing so the Court stated:[180] 'Finally, there is one consideration not to be overlooked...that of certain economic interests peculiar to a region, the reality and importance of which are clearly evidenced by a long usage'. Moreover, the Court referred to traditional fishing rights buttressed by 'the vital needs of the population' in determining particular baselines.[181]

Judge McNair, dissenting in the *Fisheries* case,[182] expressed disquiet:

In my opinion the manipulation of the limits of territorial waters for the purpose of protecting economic and other social interests has no justification in law; moreover, the approbation of such a practice would have a dangerous tendency in that it would encourage States to adopt a subjective appreciation of their rights instead of conforming to a common international standard.

This caution is no doubt justified, but the law is inevitably bound up with the accommodation of the different interests of states, and the rules often require an element of appreciation. Examples of such rules are those concerning the invalidity of treaties,[183] excuses for delictual conduct,[184] and the various compromises in conventions between the standard of civilization and the necessities of war.[185]

NOTE ON COMITY

International comity, *comitas gentium*, is a species of accommodation not unrelated to morality but to be distinguished from it nevertheless. Neighbourliness, mutual

---

[177] See *infra*, pp. 205ff.

[178] See *infra*, p. 198.

[179] See *infra*, pp. 176ff.

[180] ICJ Reports (1951), 133. See also at p. 128: 'In these barren regions the inhabitants of the coastal zone derive their livelihood essentially from fishing'. See also Fitzmaurice, 30 *BY* (1953), 69–70; id. 92 Hague *Recueil* (1957, II), 112–16; and Thirlway, 61 *BY* (1990), 13–20.

[181] ICJ Reports (1951), 142.

[182] p. 169.

[183] See ch. 27, s. 5.

[184] See ch. 21, s. 13.

[185] On the provisions in the Hague Regulations on Land Warfare and the Geneva Conventions of 1949 see Schwarzenberger, in *Mélanges Séfériadès* (1961), 13–21.

respect, and the friendly waiver of technicalities are involved, and the practice is exemplified by the exemption of diplomatic envoys from customs duties.[186] Oppenheim[187] writes of 'the rules of politeness, convenience and goodwill observed by States in their mutual intercourse without being legally bound by them'. Particular rules of comity, maintained over a long period, may develop into rules of customary law.

Apart from the meaning just explained, the term 'comity' is used in four other ways: (1) as a synonym for international law;[188] (2) as equivalent to private international law (conflict of laws);[189] (3) as a policy basis for, and source of, particular rules of conflict of laws;[190] and (4) as the reason for and source of a rule of international law.[191]

NOTE ON CODIFICATION

Narrowly defined, codification involves the setting down, in a comprehensive and ordered form, of rules of existing law and the approval of the resulting text by a law-determining agency. The process in international relations has been carried out by international conferences, such as the First and Second Hague Peace Conferences of 1899 and 1907, and by groups of experts whose drafts were the subjects of conferences sponsored by the League of Nations or the American states. However, the International Law Commission,[192] created as a subsidiary organ of the General Assembly of the United Nations, has had more success than the League bodies. Its membership combines technical qualities and experience of government work, so that its drafts are more likely to adopt solutions which are acceptable to governments. Moreover, its membership reflects a variety of political and regional standpoints and thus its agreed drafts provide a realistic basis for legal obligations. In practice the Commission has not maintained a strict separation of its tasks of codification and 'progressive development' of the law. Its work on various topics, including the law of the sea, has provided the basis for successful conferences of plenipotentiaries and the resulting multilateral conventions.

---

[186] Cf. now Art. 36 of the Vienna Conv. on Diplomatic Relations, 1961.

[187] i. 34, n. 1. French usage is 'convenance et courtoisie internationale'. See the *Alabama* arbitration, Moore, *Arbitrations*, i. 653; the *Paquete Habana* (1900), 175 US 677; and *Parking Privileges for Diplomats Case*, ILR 70, 396 (Fed. Admin. Ct., GFR).

[188] British and American courts often use the term thus, e.g. the *Parlement Belge* (1880), 5 PD 197, 214, 217, per Brett, LJ.

[189] See Phillimore, *Commentaries* (3rd edn., 1879), iv, para. 1.

[190] i.e. as an aspect of public policy. See *Hilton* v. *Guyot* (1895), 159 US 113; *Oetjen* v. *Central Leather Co.* (1918), 246 US 297, 303; *Foster* v. *Driscoll* [1929] 1 KB 470; and Briggs, pp. 407–8.

[191] *The Cristina* [1938] AC 485, 502, per Lord Wright; *Re A.B.* [1941] 1 KB 454, 457; *Krajina* v. *Tass Agency* [1949] 2 All ER 274, 280, per Cohen, LJ.

[192] See *International Law on the the Eve of the Twenty-first Century: Views from the International Law Commission* (1997), 1–18.

2

THE RELATION OF MUNICIPAL
AND INTERNATIONAL LAW

1. THEORETICAL PROBLEMS[1]

The present section has the modest object of presenting the various theories on the nature of the relation between municipal and international law in broad outline and in doing so to explore the nature of the problems. An extended theoretical exposition would be out of place in this book, and yet theoretical questions have had a certain, though not decisive, influence on writers dealing with substantive issues and also on courts. A simple example will indicate the type of situation to which the theoretical controversy relates. An alien vessel may be arrested and the alien crew tried before a municipal court of the arresting authority for ignoring customs laws. The municipal law prescribes a customs enforcement zone of x miles. The defendants argue that international law permits a customs zone of x–4 miles and that the vessel, when arrested, had not yet entered the zone in which enforcement was justified under international law.

The theoretical issue is normally presented as a clash between dualism (or pluralism) and monism. Both these schools of thought assume that there is a common field in which the international and municipal legal orders can operate simultaneously in regard to the same subject-matter, and the problem then is, which is to be master? It is at once obvious that when the issue is taken up in this form a limit has already been set to the controversy and certain solutions ruled out. Dualist doctrine[2] points to the essential difference of international law and municipal law, consisting primarily in the fact that the two systems regulate different subject-matter. International law is a law

---

[1] See Fitzmaurice, 92 Hague *Recueil* (1957, II), 68–94; Triepel, Hague *Recueil* (1923), 77–121; Kelsen, *Principles of International Law* (1952), 190–6, 401–50; ibid. (2nd edn., 1967), 290–4, 551–88; id., 84 Hague *Recueil* (1953, III), 182–200; Rousseau, 93 Hague *Recueil* (1958, I), 464–74; id., *Droit international public*, i. 37–48; Morgenstern, 27 *BY* (1950), 42–92; Ziccardi, 95 Hague *Recueil* (1958, III), 263–405; Verzijl, *International Law in Historical Perspective*, i (1968), 90–183; van Panhuys, 112 Hague *Recueil* (1964, II), 7–87; Quadri, 113 Hague *Recueil* (1964, III), 280–318; Lauterpacht, *International Law: Collected Papers*, i (1970), 151–77; Wengler, 72 *RGDIP* (1968), 921–90; Virally, *Mélanges offerts à Henri Rolin* (1964), 488–505; Wildhaber, 48 *Z.a.ö.R.u.V.* (1988), 163–207; Oppenheim, i. 52–4.

[2] Exponents: Triepel, *Völkerrecht und Landesrecht* (1899); id., 1 Hague *Recueil* (1923), 77–121; Oppenheim, i. (8th edn., 1955), 37 (not the view of the editor); Strupp, *Eléments* (2nd edn., 1930); id., 47 Hague *Recueil* (1934, I), 389–418.

between sovereign states: municipal law applies within a state and regulates the relations of its citizens with each other and with the executive. On this view neither legal order has the power to create or alter rules of the other. When municipal law provides that international law applies in whole or in part within the jurisdiction, this is merely an exercise of the authority of municipal law, an adoption or transformation of the rules of international law. In case of a conflict between international law and municipal law the dualist would assume that a municipal court would apply municipal law.

Monism is represented by a number of jurists whose theories diverge in significant respects. In the United Kingdom Hersch Lauterpacht[3] has been a forceful exponent of the doctrine. In his hands the theory has been no mere intellectual construction, and in his work monism takes the form of an assertion of the supremacy of international law even within the municipal sphere, coupled with well-developed views on the individual as a subject of international law. Such a doctrine is antipathetic to the legal corollaries of the existence of sovereign states, and reduces municipal law to the status of pensioner of international law. The state is disliked as an abstraction and distrusted as a vehicle for maintaining human rights: international law, like municipal law, is ultimately concerned with the conduct and welfare of individuals. International law is seen as the best available moderator of human affairs, and also as a logical condition of the *legal* existence of states and therefore of the municipal systems of law within the sphere of the legal competence of states.[4]

Kelsen[5] has developed monist principles on the basis of formal methods of analysis dependent on a theory of knowledge. According to the bases of Kelsen's thought, monism is scientifically established if international and municipal law are part of the same system of norms receiving their validity and contents by an intellectual operation from a basic norm. This basic norm he formulates as follows:[6] 'The states ought to behave as they have customarily behaved'. When the basic norm came to support a system of international law, the principle of effectiveness contained therein,[7] which allows revolution to be a law-creating fact, and accepts the first legislators of a state, provided the basic norm of national legal orders, i.e. the effectiveness of the new internal legal orders is established on the basis of acts which may be contrary to the previous constitution. Then, it follows: 'Since the basic norms of the national legal orders are determined by

---

[3] See Oppenheim, i. (8th edn., 1955), 38; 25 *Grot. Soc.* (1939), 62–7: 62 Hague *Recueil* (1937, IV), 129–48. See also the views of Scelle, *Précis de droit des gens* (1934), ii. 5; and Bourquin, 35 Hague *Recueil* (1931, I), 75–80. See also Lauterpacht, *International Law and Human Rights* (1950).

[4] See Oppenheim, i. 38: '...it is only by reference to a higher legal rule in relation to which they are all equal, that the equality and independence of a number of sovereign States can be conceived. Failing that superior legal order, the science of law would be confronted with the spectacle of some sixty sovereign States, each claiming to be the absolutely highest and underived authority'.

[5] *General Theory of Law and the State* (1945), 363–80; 43 *RGDIP* (1936), 5–49; *Principles of International Law* (1952), 401–47; ibid. (2nd edn.), 553–88. For views related to but not identical with those of Kelsen see the work of Verdross, 16 Hague *Recueil* (1927, I), 287–96; 30 Hague *Recueil* (1929, V), 290–3; Kunz, 10 *Grot. Soc.* (1924), 115–41; id., 6 *RDILC* (1925), 556–98; Guggenheim, i. 24–7; id. (2nd edn.), i. 58–61; Starke, 17 *BY* (1936), 66–81; id., *Studies*, pp. 1–19.

[6] *General Theory*, p. 369; *Principles of International Law*, pp. 417–18, ibid. (2nd edn.), 564.

[7] *General Theory*, p. 367.

a norm of international law, they are basic norms only in a relative sense. It is the basic norm of the international legal order which is the ultimate reason of validity of the national legal orders, too'.[8] While Kelsen establishes monism on the formal bases of his own theory, he does not support the 'primacy' of international law over municipal law: in his view the question of 'primacy' can only be decided on the basis of considerations which are not strictly legal. One may speculate whether Kelsen has avoided an element of assumption when he establishes that the basic norm of international law in some sense determines the validity of the national basic norm: the validity of each could rest on a relation of interdependence rather than a 'hierarchical' relation.

There is also a monist–naturalist theory, which, superficially at least, resembles Kelsen's provision of a universal basic norm. According to this theory the international and municipal legal orders are subordinate to a third legal order, usually postulated in terms of natural law or 'general principles of law', superior to both and capable of determining their respective spheres.[9]

2. THEORIES OF CO-ORDINATION

An increasing number of jurists wish to escape from the dichotomy of monism and dualism, holding that the logical consequences of both theories conflict with the way in which international and national organs and courts behave. Thus Sir Gerald Fitzmaurice[10] challenges the premiss adopted by monists and dualists that international and municipal law have a common field of operation. The two systems do not come into conflict as *systems* since they work in different spheres. Each is supreme in its own field. However, there may be a conflict of *obligations*, an inability of the state on the domestic plane to act in the manner required by international law: the consequence of this will not be the invalidity of the internal law but the responsibility of the state on the international plane.[11] Rousseau[12] has propounded similar views, characterizing international law as a law of co-ordination which does not provide for automatic abrogation of internal rules in conflict with obligations on the international

---

[8] *General Theory*, pp. 367–8; *Principles of International Law*, p. 415; ibid. (2nd edn.), 562; 84 Hague *Recueil* (1953, III), 196.

[9] See Lauterpacht, *Private Law Sources and Analogies of International Law* (1927), 58, for citations. Cf. the views of Scelle, *Précis*, ii. 5. See also Starke, in *Law, State and International Legal Order: Essays in Honor of Hans Kelsen* (1964), 308–16, referring to certain 'functional or constitutional norms' of international law.

[10] 92 Hague *Recueil* (1957, II), 68–94. In particular this writer criticizes monist doctrine on the role of the state. In his view the state cannot be regarded merely as an aggregation of individuals. At p. 77 he says that 'the concept of the State or nation as an indivisible entity possessing its own separate personality, is a necessary initial hypothesis, which has to be made before it is possible to speak significantly of international law at all...' See also Rousseau, i. 37–48.

[11] Ibid. 79–80. Anzilotti, *Cours de droit international*, i. (1929), 57, puts forward this view, but is often classified as a dualist.

[12] *Droit international public* (1953), 10–12; 93 Hague *Recueil* (1958, I), 473–4. Rousseau asserts the primacy of international law—but by this means primacy in its own field.

plane. These and other writers express a preference for practice over theory, and it is to the practice that attention will now be turned.

3. THE RELATION BETWEEN OBLIGATIONS OF STATES AND MUNICIPAL LAW[13]

The law in this respect is well settled. A state cannot plead provisions of its own law or deficiencies in that law in answer to a claim against it for an alleged breach of its obligations under international law.[14] The acts of the legislature and other sources of internal rules and decision-making are not to be regarded as acts of some third party for which the state is not responsible, and any other principle would facilitate evasion of obligations. In the *Alabama Claims* arbitration[15] the United States successfully claimed damages from Great Britain for breach of its obligations as a neutral during the American Civil War. The absence of legislation to prevent the fitting out of commerce raiders in British ports and their journey to join the Confederate forces was no defence. The Permanent Court of Arbitration,[16] the Permanent Court of International Justice,[17] and the International Court of Justice[18] have produced a consistent jurisprudence. In the *Free Zones* case[19] the Permanent Court observed '... it is certain that France cannot rely on her own legislation to limit the scope of her international obligations...'. And the Advisory Opinion in the *Greco-Bulgarian Communities* case[20] contains the statement: 'it is a generally accepted principle of international law that in the relations between Powers who are contracting Parties to a treaty, the provisions of municipal law cannot prevail over those of the treaty'. The same principle applies where the provisions of a constitution are relied upon; in the words of the Permanent Court:[21]

[13] See Marek, *Droit international et droit interne* (1961), 23 ff.; Lauterpacht, *The Development of International Law by the International Court* (1958), 262, 314–15, 332; Morgenstern, 27 BY (1950), 43–7; Fitzmaurice, 30 BY (1953), 26–7, 53–4, 35 BY (1959), 185–94, and 92 Hague *Recueil* (1957, II), 85–8; Oppenheim, i. 82–6. See also the *Wollemborg* claim, ILR 24 (1957), 654; *Ottoz* claim, ibid. 18 (1951), no. 136.

[14] See the Vienna Conv. on the Law of Treaties, 1969, Art. 27, referring to justification for failure to perform a treaty. See also *infra*, ch. 27, s. 5.

[15] (1872), Moore, *Arbitrations*, i. 653.

[16] References: Schwarzenberger, *International Law*, i (3rd edn., 1957) 68–9.

[17] See the *Wimbledon* (1923), PCIJ, Ser. A, no. 1, p. 29; *Mavrommatis*, Ser. A, no. 5; *German Interests in Polish Upper Silesia* (1926), Ser. A, no. 7, p. 19; *Chorzów Factory* (Merits) (1928), Ser. A, no. 17, pp. 33, 34; *Jurisdiction of the Courts of Danzig* (1928), Ser. B, no. 15, pp. 26, 27; *Free Zones Case* (1929), Ser. A, no. 24, p. 12. See also nn. 18, 19, 20 *infra*. Further references: Schwarzenberger, *International Law*, pp. 69–70.

[18] The leading cases are the *Fisheries* case, ICJ Reports (1951), 116 at 132; and the *Nottebohm* case, ibid. (1955), 4 at 20–1. See also *infra*, p. 292 on domestic jurisdiction. See further the *Guardianship* case, ICJ Reports (1958), 55 at 67. On the application of the Vienna Convention on Consular Relations with U.S. domestic law see the *La Grand Case*, I.C.J. Reports (2001), 466.

[19] (1932), PCIJ, Ser. A/B, no. 46, p. 167.

[20] (1930), PCIJ, Ser. B, no. 17, p. 32. See also the Adv. Op. on the *Applicability of the Obligation to arbitrate under the U.N. Headquarters Agreement* (*PLO Mission* case), ICJ Reports (1988), 12 at 31–2, para. 47.

[21] *Polish Nationals in Danzig* (1931), PCIJ, Ser. A/B, no. 44, p. 24. See also the *Pinson* claim (1928), *RIAA* v. 327; *Ann. Digest*, 4 (1927–8), no. 4.

It should...be observed that...a State cannot adduce as against another State its own Constitution with a view to evading obligations incumbent upon it under international law or treaties in force. Applying these principles to the present case, it results that the question of the treatment of Polish nationals or other persons of Polish origin or speech must be settled exclusively on the basis of the rules of international law and the treaty provisions in force between Poland and Danzig.

Arising from the nature of treaty obligations and from customary law, there is a general duty to bring internal law into conformity with obligations under international law.[22] However, in general a failure to bring about such conformity is not in itself a direct breach of international law, and a breach arises only when the state concerned fails to observe its obligations on a specific occasion.[23] In some circumstances legislation could of itself constitute a breach of a treaty provision and a tribunal might be requested to make a declaration to that effect. Another principle connected with these rules is to the effect that a change of government is not as such a ground for noncompliance with obligations.[24]

4. THE POSITION OF THE INDIVIDUAL

International law imposes duties of certain kinds on individuals as such, and thus national and international tribunals may try persons charged with crimes against international law, including war crimes and genocide.[25] The International Military Tribunal at Nuremberg and many national tribunals did not admit pleas by accused persons charged with war crimes that they had acted in accordance with their national law.[26] Conversely, in a great number of situations an individual or corporation may plead that a treaty has legal consequences affecting interests of the claimant which must be recognized by a municipal court.[27] And again, on a charge of crime, such as homicide, under municipal law, a plea of justification may be based on rules of international law, for example, that an act of killing was a lawful act of war.

---

[22] Fitzmaurice, 92 Hague *Recueil* (1957, II), 89; Oppenheim, i. 82–6; Guggenheim, i. 31–3; *Exchange of Greek and Turkish Populations* (1925), PCIJ, Ser. B, no. 10, p. 20. The principle applies to both unitary and federal states.

[23] McNair, *Law of Treaties* (1961), 100. Cf. Fitzmaurice, 92 Hague *Recueil* (1957, II), 89.

[24] On continuity of states: *infra*, pp. 80–2.

[25] See ch. 25, s. 2.

[26] See Morgenstern, 27 *BY* (1950), 47–8. For duties arising under a commercial treaty: *Institute National* v. *Mettes*, ILR 24 (1957), 584.

[27] See: *Restraint at Lobith* case, ILR 19 (1952), no. 34; *Pokorny* v. *Republic of Austria*, ibid., no. 98; *Soviet Re-quisition* case, ibid., no. 143; *People of the Philippines* v. *Acierto*, ibid. 20 (1953), 148; *Falcon Dam Constructors* v. *United States*, ibid. 23 (1956), 360; *Public Trustee* v. *Chartered Bank of India, Australia and China*, ibid. 687; *Revici* v. *Conference of Jewish Material Claims, Inc.*, ibid. 26 (1958, II), 362; *Indochina Railway* case, ibid. 28, p. 269; *Richuk* v. *State of Israel*, ibid. 442. See also *infra*, pp. 44ff. on incorporation.

5. ISSUES OF MUNICIPAL LAW BEFORE
INTERNATIONAL TRIBUNALS

(*a*) Cases in which a tribunal dealing with issues of international law has to examine the municipal law of one or more states are by no means exceptional.[28] As a matter of evidence, the spheres of competence *claimed* by states, represented by state territory and the territorial sea, jurisdiction, and nationality of individuals and legal persons, are delimited by means of legislation and judicial and administrative decisions.[29] The substantive law of nations brings the same matters in issue by setting limits of competence, represented especially by the concept of domestic jurisdiction[30] against which the municipal law on a given topic has to be measured. Thus a tribunal may have to examine municipal law relating to expropriation,[31] fishing limits,[32] nationality,[33] or the guardianship and welfare of infants[34] in order to decide whether particular acts are in breach of obligations under treaties or customary law. Issues relating to obligations to protect human rights,[35] the treatment of civilians during belligerent occupation, and the exhaustion of local remedies (as a question of the admissibility of claims)[36] concern internal law in nearly every case.

(*b*) A considerable number of treaties contain provisions referring directly to internal law or employing concepts which by implication are to be understood in the context of a particular national law. Many treaties refer to 'nationals' of the contracting parties, and the presumption is that the term connotes persons having that status under the internal law of one of the parties. Similarly, claims settlements involve references to legal interests of individuals and corporations existing within the cadre of a given national law.

(*c*) In the *Guardianship of Infants* case several of the individual judges rested their conclusions on the issues in the case on a principle of treaty law according to which the interpretation of treaties concerned with matters of private international law should take into account the nature of the subject-matter, in particular by the recognition of the principle of *ordre public* as applied locally.[37] In his separate opinion Judge Spender

---

[28] See generally Jenks, *The Prospects of International Adjudication* (1964), 547–603; Marek, *Droit international et droit interne*, pp. 267ff.; id., 66 *RGDIP* (1962), 260–98; Stoll, *L'application et l'interprétation du droit interne par les juridictions internationales* (1962); Strebel, 31 *Z.a.ö.R.u.V.* (1971), 855–84.

[29] See the United Nations Legis. Series. On municipal law as evidence of the intention of a government see the *Anglo-Iranian Oil Co.* case, ICJ Reports (1952), 93.

[30] *Infra*, pp. 290ff.

[31] *German Interests in Polish Upper Silesia* (1926), PCIJ, Ser. A, no. 7. See further ch. 24, s. 9.

[32] *Fisheries* case, ICJ Reports (1951), 116. See further *infra*, pp. 176ff.

[33] *Nottebohm* case, ICJ Reports (1955), 4. See further *infra*, ch. 19.

[34] *Guardianship of Infants* case, ICJ Reports (1958), 55.

[35] Ch. 25.

[36] Ch. 22, s. 6.

[37] ICJ Reports (1958), 72–3 (Spiropoulos); 74–8 (Badawi); 91ff. (Lauterpacht); 102–9 (Moreno Quintana). See Fitzmaurice, 35 *BY* (1959), 190–1. The Court, at p. 70, left the point open.

criticized this view of treaty interpretation, pointing to the variable content of *ordre public* and the importance of the principle *pacta sunt servanda*.[38]

(*d*) Treaties having as their object the creation and maintenance of certain standards of treatment of minority groups or resident aliens may refer to a national law as a method of describing the status to be created and protected. The protection of rights may be stipulated for 'without discrimination' or as 'national treatment' for the categories concerned.[39]

(*e*) On occasion an international tribunal may be faced with the task of deciding issues solely on the basis of the municipal law of a particular state. Such a case was the *Serbian Loans* case[40] before the Permanent Court. This arose from a dispute between the French bondholders of certain Serbian loans and the Serb-Croat-Slovene Government, the former demanding loan-service on a gold basis from 1924 or 1925 onwards, the latter holding that payment in French paper currency was in conformity with the terms of the contracts. This was not a dispute involving international law. The French Government, by virtue of the right of diplomatic protection,[41] took up the case of the French bondholders, and by a special agreement the dispute was submitted to the Permanent Court. The Court considered whether it had jurisdiction under its Statute in a case where the point at issue was a question which must be decided by application of a particular municipal law. The conclusion was that jurisdiction existed, the basis for this important finding being the wide terms of Article 36(1) of the Statute, which refers especially to cases brought by special agreement, and the duty of the Court to exercise jurisdiction when two states have agreed to have recourse to the Court, in the absence of a clause on the subject in the Statute. Applying itself to the issues arising from the loans the Court had to decide an issue of conflict of laws: did Serbian or French law govern the obligations at the time they were entered into? Public international law (as the law of the forum) provided no ready-made rules of conflict of laws, and the Court prescribed certain principles:[42]

The Court, which has before it a dispute involving the question as to the law which governs the contractual obligations at issue, can determine what this law is only by reference to the actual nature of these obligations and to the circumstances attendant upon their creation, though it may also take into account the expressed or presumed intentions of the Parties.

---

[38] pp. 120–31. See also Judge Córdova, Sep. Op., pp. 140–1, for a similar view.

[39] See *Memel Statute* case (1932) (PCJ) Ser. A/B, no. 49; *Jurisdiction of the Danzig Courts*, Ser. B, no. 15; *German Settlers in Poland* (1923), Ser. B, no. 6; *Minority Schools in Albania* (1935), Ser. A/B, no. 64. The Permanent Court did not regard a formal equality in law as the only criterion of equality. See further Fitzmaurice, 35 *BY* (1959), 191–2.

[40] (1929), PCIJ, Ser. A, no. 20. See also the *Brazilian Loans* case (1929), PCIJ, Ser. A, no. 21; Jenks, 19 *BY* (1938), 95–7; and Schwarzenberger, *International Law*, i (3rd edn.), 72–8. Cf. the *Norwegian Shipowners* claims (1922), *RIAA* i. 309; the *Diverted Cargoes* arbitration (1955), ILR 22 (1955), 820; and *Case No. 1*, Arbitration Tribunal for the Agreement on German External Debts, 34 *BY* (1958), 363.

[41] States may present, and negotiate concerning, claims which do not relate to international law. Sympathetic consideration may be given to such claims as a matter of general relations between the states concerned.

[42] PCIJ, Ser. A, no. 20, p. 41.

In the event the Court held that the substance of the debt and the validity of the clause defining the obligation of the debtor state was governed by Serbian law, but, with respect to the method of payment, the money of payment was the local currency of the place in which the debtor state was bound to discharge the debt. The money of payment was thus paper francs and the amount due in this currency was to be calculated, in accordance with the intention of the parties, by reference to gold francs, the money of account. The rate of conversion from the money of account to the money of payment was that prevailing at the time of the payment of the debt.

6. MUNICIPAL LAWS AS 'FACTS' BEFORE INTERNATIONAL TRIBUNALS

In the case of *Certain German Interests in Polish Upper Silesia*, the Permanent Court of International Justice observed:[43]

It might be asked whether a difficulty does not arise from the fact that the Court would have to deal with the Polish law of July 14th, 1920. This, however, does not appear to be the case. From the standpoint of International Law and of the Court which is its organ, municipal laws are merely facts which express the will and constitute the activities of States, in the same manner as do legal decisions or administrative measures. The Court is certainly not called upon to interpret the Polish law as such; but there is nothing to prevent the Court's giving judgment on the question whether or not, in applying that law, Poland is acting in conformity with its obligations towards Germany under the Geneva Convention.

This statement is to the effect that municipal law may be simply evidence of conduct attributable to the state concerned which creates international responsibility. Thus a decision of a court or a legislative measure may constitute evidence of a breach of a treaty or a rule of customary international law.[44] In its context the principle stated is clear. However, the general proposition that international tribunals take account of municipal laws only as facts 'is, at most, a debatable proposition the validity and wisdom of which are subject to, and call for, further discussion and review'.[45] In the practice of the International Court and other international tribunals the concept of 'municipal law as mere facts' has six distinct aspects, as follows.

(*a*) Municipal law may be evidence of conduct in violation of a rule of treaty or customary law, as stated already.

---

[43] PCIJ, Ser. A, no. 7, p. 19.

[44] See *Anglo-Iranian Oil Co.* case (Jurisdiction), ICJ Reports (1952), 106–7; Judge Badawi, Sep. Op., *Norwegian Loans* case, ibid. (1957), 31–2; Judge Lauterpacht, Sep. Op., ibid. 36–8, 40; Judge Morelli, *Barcelona Traction* case (Second Phase), ibid. (1970), 234; Judge Gros, Sep. Op., ibid. 272.

[45] Jenks, *Prospects of International Adjudication*, p. 552; and see, in that work, pp. 548–53, 569–70; and Jenks, 19 *BY* (1938), 89–92.

(*b*) Judicial notice does not apply to matters of municipal law. The tribunal will require proof of municipal law and will hear evidence of it, and, if necessary, may undertake its own researches.[46]

(*c*) Interpretation of their own laws by national courts is binding on an international tribunal.[47] This principle rests in part on the concept of the reserved domain of domestic jurisdiction[48] and in part on the practical need of avoiding contradictory versions of the law of a state from different sources.

(*d*) The *dicta* of international tribunals (already cited) rest to some extent on the assumption that, for any domestic issue of which a tribunal is seized, there must always be some applicable rule of municipal law, which will be ascertainable in the same way as other 'facts' in the case. This assumption is not uncommonly unsafe since municipal law may be far from clear.[49]

(*e*) International tribunals cannot declare the internal invalidity of rules of national law since the international legal order must respect the reserved domain of domestic jurisdiction.[50]

(*f*) Certain judges of the International Court have stated as a corollary of the proposition that 'municipal laws are merely facts' that an international tribunal 'does not interpret national law as such'.[51] This view is open to question. When it is appropriate to apply rules of municipal law, an international tribunal will apply domestic rules as such.[52] The special agreement may require the application of rules of municipal law to the subject matter of the dispute.[53] International law may designate a system of domestic law as the applicable law.[54] Moreover, in cases in which vital issues (whether classified as 'facts' or otherwise) turn on investigation of municipal law, the International Court has duly examined such matters, including the application of

[46] The *Mavrommatis Jerusalem Concessions* case, PCIJ, Ser. A. no. 5, pp. 29, 30; *Brazilian Loans,* ibid., nos. 20/1, p. 124; Judge Klaestad, Diss. Op., *Nottebohm* case (Second Phase), ICJ Reports (1955), 28–9; Judge Read, Diss. Op., ibid. 35–6; Judge Guggenheim, Diss. Op., ibid. 51–2; *Flegenheimer* claim, ILR 25 (1958, I), at 98. But see Judge Fitzmaurice, Diss. Op., Adv. Op., *Presence of South Africa in Namibia*, ICJ Reports (1971), 222.

[47] *Serbian Loans*, PCIJ, Ser. A. nos. 20–1, p. 46; *Brazilian Loans*, ibid. 124; Judge McNair, Sep. Op., *Fisheries* case, ICJ Reports (1951), 181; Judge Klaestad, Diss. Op., *Nottebohm* case (Second Phase), ibid. (1955), 28–9. See also the *Lighthouses* case, PCIJ, Ser. A/B, no. 62, p. 22; and the *Panevezys–Saldutiskis Railway* case, ibid., no. 76, p. 19.

[48] *Infra*, p. 291.

[49] See *R. v. Keyn*, *infra*, p. 42; *Burmah Oil* case [1965] AC 75.

[50] *Interpretation of the Statute of the Memel Territory*, PCIJ Ser. A/B, no. 49, p. 336; Judge Morelli, Sep. Op., *Barcelona Traction* case (Second Phase), ICJ Reports (1970), 234.

[51] See Judge Lauterpacht, *Guardianship* case, ICJ Reports (1958), Sep. Op., p. 91.

[52] The dictum of the PCIJ in the *Upper Silesia* case (quoted earlier) is not unequivocal in its remark that the Court was 'not called upon to interpret the Polish law as such'. See Judge Read, Diss. Op., *Nottebohm* case (Second Phase), ICJ Reports (1955), 36; Judge Guggenheim, ibid. 52. See also Judge Córdova, Diss. Op., *Administrative Tribunal of the I.L.O.*, ibid. (1956), 165; Judge Moreno Quintana, Sep. Op., *Guardianship* case, ibid. (1958), 108.

[53] *Lighthouses* case, PCIJ, Ser. A/B, no. 62, pp. 19–23. See also the *Lighthouses* Arbitration (1956), PCA, ILR, 23 (1956), 659.

[54] *Serbian and Brazilian Loans*, *supra*.

nationality laws,[55] the availability of local remedies,[56] and the law concerning guardianship of infants.[57] It is also necessary to make the point that in the particular state national courts may have a power to overrule local legislation on the ground that it is contrary to international law, for example, as laid down by the International Court.[58]

7. ISSUES OF INTERNATIONAL LAW BEFORE MUNICIPAL COURTS

IN GENERAL

English courts take judicial notice of international law: once a court has ascertained that there are no bars within the internal system of law to applying the rules of international law or provisions of a treaty,[59] the rules are accepted as rules of law and are not required to be established by formal proof, as in the case of matters of fact and foreign law. However, in the case of international law and treaties, the taking of judicial notice has a special character. In the first place, there is in fact a serious problem involved in finding reliable evidence on points of international law in the absence of formal proof and resort to the expert witness.[60] Secondly, issues of public policy and difficulties of obtaining evidence on the larger issues of state relations combine to produce the procedure whereby the executive is consulted on questions of mixed law and fact, for example, the existence of a state of war or the status of an entity claiming sovereign immunities.[61] The special considerations involved in this procedure do not affect the general character of rules of international law before the courts. Where, in a conflict of laws case, an expert gives evidence as to matters of foreign law, the method of ascertaining that law does not affect its character as law. However, in the absence of evidence offered by the parties, a court may presume that the foreign law is the same as the law of the forum in a conflict of laws case, but such a presumption cannot apply to matters of international law.

When a municipal court, in England or elsewhere, has decided, as a preliminary issue, that a rule of customary or treaty law is applicable to a case before it, the

---

[55] *Nottebohm* case (Second Phase), ICJ Reports (1955), 4. See also the *Flegenheimer* claim, ILR, 25 (1958, I), at 108–10.

[56] *Panevezys-Saldutiskis Railway* case, PCIJ, Ser. A/B, no. 76, pp. 18–22; *Case Concerning Elettronica Sicula S.p.A. (ELSI)*, ICJ Reports (1989), 44–8.

[57] *Guardianship* case, *supra*.

[58] See Judge Lauterpacht, Sep. Op., *Norwegian Loans* case, ICJ Reports (1957), 40–1.

[59] See *infra*, p. 41, on incorporation.

[60] See *infra*, pp. 42–3, on the decisions in *R. v. Keyn* and *West Rand Central Gold Mining Co. v. R.* See also *infra* on the sources employed by English courts.

[61] On the Foreign Office Certificate see *infra*, p. 49.

rule is applied as though it is a rule of the law of the forum.[62] For reasons set forth subsequently, the practice of municipal courts in this respect does not provide conclusive evidence for or against the dualist doctrine.[63] It is now necessary to examine the conditions in which rules of customary law and treaty provisions are given effect in the municipal sphere, a process variously described as 'incorporation', 'adoption', and 'transformation'. Whether the variant terminology reflects issues of substance is a question which must be reserved until later.[64]

8. THE DOCTRINE OF INCORPORATION IN BRITISH AND COMMONWEALTH COURTS[65]

(a) Customary international law

The dominant principle, normally characterized as the doctrine of incorporation, is that customary rules are to be considered part of the law of the land and enforced as such, with the qualification that they are incorporated only so far as is not inconsistent with Acts of Parliament or prior judicial decisions of final authority.[66] This principle is supported by a long line of authority[67] and represents a practical rather than theoretical policy in the courts. It would seem that the courts must first make a choice of law depending on the nature of the subject-matter. Where it is appropriate to apply international law, rather than the law of the forum or a foreign law, then the courts will take judicial notice of the applicable rules, whereas formal evidence is required of foreign (municipal) law. However, the courts still have to ascertain the existence of the rules

---

[62] See Seidl-Hohenveldern, 12 *ICLQ* (1963), 90–4; Fawcett, *The British Commonwealth in International Law* (1963), 16–74.

[63] Cf. Morgenstern, 27 *BY* (1950), 48–66.

[64] See *infra*, p. 53.

[65] See generally Lauterpacht, 25 *Grot. Soc.* (1939), 51–88 (also in *International Law: Collected Papers*, ii (1975), 537–69); Oppenheim, i. 56–63; Lauterpacht, *Coll. Papers*, i. 154–69, 218–22; Westlake, 22 LQR (1906), 14–26; and in Westlake, *Collected Papers* (1914), 498–518; Fawcett, *The British Commonwealth in International Law*, pp. 16–74; Castel, *International Law* (3rd edn., 1976), 28–40; Macdonald, Morris, and Johnston, *Canadian Perspectives on International Law and Organization* (1974), pp. 88–136; Collier, 38 *ICLQ* (1989), 924–35.

[66] Blackstone, *Commentaries*, iv., ch. 5; Brierly, pp. 86–8. Cf. Lord Finlay in the *Lotus* (1927), PCIJ, Ser. A, no. 10, p. 54; and the *Eichmann* case (1961), 56 *AJ* (1962), 805 at 806–7 (District Ct.) ILR 36, 18 at 24–5. (District Ct.); ibid. 277 at 280–1 (Israel, SC).

[67] *Barbuit's* case (1737), Cas. *temp.* Talbot. 281; *Triquet* v. *Bath* (1764), 3 Burr. 1478; *Heathfield* v. *Chilton* (1767), 4 Burr. 2015; *Dolder* v. *Lord Huntingfield* (1805), 11 Ves. 283; *Viveash* v. *Becker* (1814), 3 M. & S. 284, 292, 298; *Wolff* v. *Oxholm* (1817), 6 M. & S. 92, 100–6; *Novello* v. *Toogood* (1823), I B. & C. 554; *De Wütz* v. *Hendricks* (1824), 2 Bing. 314, 315; *Emperor of Austria* v. *Day* (1861), 30 LJ Ch. 690, 702 (reversed on appeal on another point); *Trendtex Trading Corporation* v. *Central Bank of Nigeria* [1977] 1 QB 529, CA. Cf. *R.* v. *Secretary of State, ex p. Thakrar* [1974] 1 QB 694, CA; *International Tin Council Appeals* [1988] 3 WLR 1033; ILR 80, 49, CA; [1989] 3 WLR 969; ILR 81, 670, HL; *Al-Adsani* v. *Government of Kuwait*, ILR 103, 420 at 428; ILR 107, 536 at 540–2.

of international law and their effect *within the municipal sphere*: the latter task is a
matter of some difficulty on which the rules of international law may provide no real
guidance. Lastly, the courts have to make sure that what they are doing is consonant
with the conditions of (internal) competence under which they must work. Thus the
rule of international law will not be applied if it is contrary to a statute,[68] and the courts
will observe the principle of *stare decisis*.[69] However, there is good reason to expect the
English courts to refuse to apply the rule of *stare decisis* if a previous decision rested
upon an obsolete rule of international law.[70]

However, the cases decided since 1876 are interpreted by some authorities[71] in such
a way as to displace the doctrine of incorporation by that of transformation, viz.: customary law is a part of the law of England *only in so far as* the rules have been clearly
adopted and made part of the law of England by legislation, judicial decision, or established usage.[72] The principal source of authority for this view is assumed by most writers to be the decision of the Court for Crown Cases Reserved in *Regina v. Keyn*.[73] In
that case the *Franconia*, a German ship, collided, as a result of the negligence of the
captain, with a British ship in British territorial waters. The British ship sank and a
passenger was drowned. The German captain was indicted for manslaughter at the
Central Criminal Court, and the question for the opinion of the Court for Crown
Cases Reserved was whether the Central Criminal Court, successor to the jurisdiction
of the Admiral, had jurisdiction. In a Court of thirteen it was decided by a majority
of one that there was no jurisdiction, the main ground for this opinion being that no
English statute conferred jurisdiction to try offences by foreigners on board foreign
ships, whether within or without the limit of territorial waters. The majority of the
judges were concerned primarily with heads of criminal jurisdiction in English law.[74]
Cockburn, CJ, whose long judgment is often a source for quotation, after considering
the English law, goes on to seek the relevant rule of international law.[75] He concludes
that the littoral sea beyond low water is not a part of British territory according to
English law,[76] and then, assuming that the law of nations says otherwise, he seeks

---

[68] See *Mortensen* v. *Peters* (1906) 8 F. (JC) 93 (Scotland: High Ct. of Justiciary); *Polites* v. *The Commonwealth*
(1945), 70 CLR 60 (High Ct. of Australia), *Ann. Digest*, 12 (1943–5), no. 61; *Roussety* v. *A.-G.*, ILR 44, 108.

[69] See *Chung Chi Cheung* v. *The King* [1939] AC 160, 169. For criticism of this application of *stare decisis* see Fawcett, *The British Commonwealth in International Law*, p. 39; Morgenstern, 27 *BY* (1950), 80–2;
Crawford, 48 *BY* (1976–7), 359; and *County of Saint John* v. *Fraser-Brace* (1958), 13 DLR (2d) 177; ILR 26
(1958, II), 165.

[70] See *Trendtex Trading Corporation* v. *Central Bank of Nigeria* [1977] 1 QB 529, at 554, 578–9, per Lord
Denning, MR, and Shaw, LJ, respectively; and *Iº Congreso del Partido* [1978] 1 QB 500 at 518 per Robert Goff
J. See also *Kaffraria Property Co.* v. *Government of Zambia*, ILR 64, 708 at 714. Cf. *Alcom Ltd.* v. *Republic of
Colombia* [1984] AC 580 at 597–600.

[71] Halsbury, *Laws of England* (3rd edn.), vii. 4, 264. The 4th edn. of *Halsbury* takes a different view of
Keyn: 4th edn., vol. XVIII, para. 1403, n. 1.

[72] Analytically the distinction between incorporation and transformation is probably only one of presumption for or against incorporation.

[73] (1876) 2 Ex D. 63, 202, 203. Cf. *Reg.* v. *Kent Justices, ex p. Lye* [1967] 2 QB 153, DC; 42 *BY* (1967), 293.

[74] Cf. Cockburn, CJ, pp. 161–73.

[75] pp. 173–93.

[76] pp. 193–202. See now the Territorial Waters Jurisdiction Act 1878, and *infra*, p. 192.

evidence of British assent to the rule of the law of nations, in the form of treaty or other express concurrence of a government, or by implication from established usage.[77] Further on[78] he introduces two special factors: the need for *evidence* of assent by the British Government and the constitutional consideration that the courts could not apply what would practically amount to a new law without usurping the province of the legislature. He is in general exercised by the vagueness and differing views of jurists on the precise point involved:[79] the exercise of criminal jurisdiction as a corollary of the territorial status of the littoral sea.

Holdsworth[80] considered that the court in *Keyn* displaced the doctrine of incorporation. On the other hand it is very doubtful if the majority of the judges directed themselves to the issue between incorporation and transformation.[81] The elements of 'transformation' in the judgment of Cockburn, CJ, are entirely compatible with the doctrine of incorporation if it is seen that he was concerned with the proof of the rules of international law: if the evidence is inconclusive and the issue affects the liberty of persons, then assent by the legislature of the forum is needed to supplement the evidence. Yet as a *general* condition he does not require express assent or a functional transformation by Act of Parliament.[82] In cases of first impression the courts are ready to apply international law without looking for evidence of 'assent'.[83]

In any case *Keyn* remains a somewhat ambiguous precedent for the present purpose, and the later cases must be considered. In *West Rand Central Gold Mining Co. v. R.*[84] a petition of right was denied on the basis that the conquering state (Great Britain) was not successor to the financial liabilities of the conquered state (the South African Republic) before the outbreak of war. The issue of incorporation was properly argued, and Lord Alverstone, CJ, dealt with the question at length. As the rules of international law did not favour the suppliants in any case his remarks are *obiter*. However, his words seem to rest on an assumption that the doctrine of incorporation holds good. At the same time he shares the concern of Cockburn, CJ, with questions of evidence of the rules of international law. He requires 'assent' in relation to rules based on the 'opinions of text-writers' as opposed to a subject-matter on which there is a 'particular and recognized rule of international law'.[85] Thus his Judgment *appears* to contain elements of the principle of transformation in the form of some 'assent' by Great Britain.

In *Mortensen* v. *Peters*[86] Lord Dunedin, the Lord Justice-General, regarded the question as to the extent of jurisdiction in the Moray Firth as one of construing the

---

[77] p. 202.

[78] p. 203.

[79] pp. 193, 203. The point was less obvious then than it would be now. See also the minority views of Brett, JA, and Grove, J.

[80] *Essays in Law and History* (1945), 263–6; and see Halsbury, *Laws of England*, vii. 4, 264.

[81] Sir Robert Phillimore, at p. 68, expressly reserves the question. See also Lauterpacht, *Coll. Papers*, i. 218–22.

[82] See Halsbury's *Laws of England*, 4th edn., xviii, para. 1403.

[83] See *In re Piracy Jure Gentium* [1934] AC 586; *Molvan* v. *A.-G. for Palestine* [1948] AC 351.

[84] [1905] 2 KB 391.

[85] pp. 407–8.

[86] *Supra*, n. 69.

relevant legislation. The *ratio* of the case was that the clear words of a statute bind the court even if the provisions are contrary to international law. The Judgment contains the following dictum which must be seen in the context of the *ratio*: 'It is a trite observation that there is no such thing as a standard of international law extraneous to the domestic law of a kingdom, to which appeal may be made. International law, so far as this Court is concerned, is the body of doctrine... which has been adopted and made a part of the law of Scotland'. This is equivocal but is commonly understood to be in favour of the transformation doctrine.

In *Commercial and Estates Co. of Egypt* v. *Board of Trade*, Atkin, LJ,[87] as he then was, uttered the following dictum which, not unambiguously, supports transformation: 'International Law as such can confer no rights cognisable in the municipal courts. It is only in so far as the rules of International Law are recognised as included in the rules of municipal law that they are allowed in municipal courts to give rise to rights and obligations'. Giving the opinion of the Privy Council in *Chung Chi Cheung* v. *The King*,[88] Lord Atkin stated that:

so far, at any rate, as the Courts of this country are concerned, international law has no validity save in so far as its principles are accepted and adopted by our own domestic law. There is no external power that imposes its rules upon our own code of substantive law or procedure. The Courts acknowledge the existence of a body of rules which nations accept amongst themselves. On any judicial issue they seek to ascertain what the relevant rule is, and, having found it, they will treat it as incorporated into the domestic law, so far as it is not inconsistent with rules enacted by statutes or finally declared by their tribunals.

This statement harks back to the problem of evidence of the relevant rules and is by no means incompatible with the principle of incorporation.[89] In the litigation concerning the debts of the International Tin Council the Courts have adopted the practical approach, which is to find the relevant rule on the basis of all the available evidence and not to be disconcerted by the general issue of 'incorporation': see, in this respect, the Court of Appeal decision in the *International Tin Council Appeals*.[90]

The authorities, taken as a whole, support the doctrine of incorporation, and the less favourable dicta are equivocal to say the least. Commonwealth decisions reflect the English accent on incorporation.[91]

---

[87] [1925] 1 KB 271, 295. A case of first impression on the right of a belligerent to seize neutral ships by way of necessity (the right of angary). See Morgenstern, 27 *BY* (1950), 51–2.

[88] [1939] AC 160, 167–8. Quoted: *Reference on Powers of City of Ottawa to Levy Rates on Foreign Legations* [1943] SCR 208; *Ann. Digest*, 10 (1941–2), no. 106; the *Rose Mary* [1953] 1 WLR 246; *Fraser-Brace* v. *Saint John County*, ILR 23 (1956), 217.

[89] Significantly, writers draw conflicting conclusions from the dictum. See Oppenheim, i. 39 n. 5; Brierly, p. 88. See further the dicta of Lords Macmillan and Wright in the *Cristina* [1938] AC 485 at 497 (quoting Lord Dunedin in *Mortensen* v. *Peters*) and 502 respectively, which also have these ambiguous aspects. But cf. *In re Ferdinand, Ex-Tsar of Bulgaria* [1921] 1 Ch. 107, especially the dictum of Warrington, LJ, at 137.

[90] [1988] 3 WLR 1033; ILR 80, 49.

[91] See *The Ship 'North'* v. *The King* [1906] 37 SCR 385 (Canada); *Wright* v. *Cantrell* [1943] 44 SR (NSW), 45; *Ann. Digest*, 12 (1943–5), no. 37; *Chow Hung Ching* v. *The King* (1948), 77 CLR 449 (Australia); *Virendra Singh* v. *State of Uttar Pradesh*, ILR 22 (1955), 131 (India); *Qureshi* v. *USSR*, ILR 64, 585 at 600 (Pakistan).

(b) Treaties[92]

In England, and also it seems in most Commonwealth countries, the conclusion and ratification of treaties are within the prerogative of the Crown (or its equivalent), and if a transformation doctrine were not applied, the Crown could legislate for the subject without parliamentary consent. As a consequence treaties are only part of English law if an enabling Act of Parliament has been passed. This rule applies to treaties which affect private rights or liabilities, result in a charge on public funds, or require modification of the common law or statute for their enforcement in the courts.[93] The rule does not apply to treaties relating to the conduct of war or treaties of cession. In any case, the words of a subsequent Act of Parliament will prevail over the provisions of a prior treaty in case of inconsistency between the two.[94]

9. TREATIES AND THE INTERPRETATION OF STATUTES IN THE UNITED KINGDOM[95]

The rule, stated in the previous section, is that in case of conflict statute prevails over treaty: this is a principle of constitutional law and not a rule of construction. There is, however, a well-established rule of construction which is normally stated thus: where domestic legislation is passed to give effect to an international convention, there is a presumption that Parliament intended to fulfil its international obligations.[96] The question then arises: what means should the courts use to discover the intention of Parliament in this connection?

Legislation to give effect in domestic law to the provisions may take various forms.[97] A statute may directly enact the provisions of the international instrument, which

---

[92] See McNair, *The Law of Treaties*, pp. 81–97; Mann, 44 *Grot. Soc.* (1958–9), 29–62; Doeker, *The Treaty-Making Power in the Commonwealth of Australia* (1966); Gotlieb, *Canadian Treaty-Making* (1968); Jacobs and Roberts (eds.), *The Effect of Treaties in Domestic Law* (1987).

[93] See *The Parlement Belge* [1880] 5 PD 197; *In re Californian Fig Syrup Co.* (1888), LR 40 Ch. D. 620 (Stirling, J., *obiter*); *Walker* v. *Baird* [1892] AC 491; *A.-G. for Canada* v. *A.-G. for Ontario* [1937] AC 326, 347, per Lord Atkin; *Theophile* v. *Solicitor-General* [1950] AC 186, 195–6; *Republic of Italy* v. *Hambro's Bank* [1950] 1 All ER 430; *Cheney* v. *Conn* [1968] 1 WLR 242; ILR 41, 421; *International Tin Council Appeals* [1988] 3 All ER 257, CA, at 291 per Kerr, LJ; at 335–6 per Nourse, LJ; at 349 per Ralph Gibson, LJ; [1989] 3 WLR 969, HL. See also *Ashby* v. *Minister of Immigration*, ILR. 85, 203 (New Zealand, CA).

[94] I.R.C. v. *Collco Dealings Ltd.* [1962] AC 1; ILR 33, 1 (see Bowett, 37 *BY* (1961), 548); *Woodend Rubber Company* v. *Commissioner of Inland Revenue* [1971] AC 321.

[95] See Sinclair, 12 *ICLQ* (1963), 508–51; Mann, *Foreign Affairs in English Courts* (1986), 97–112; annual notes on judicial decisions in *BY; Dicey and Morris on the Conflict of Laws* (14th edn., 2006), 12–18; Gardiner, *ICLQ* (1995), 620–8.

[96] *Salomon* v. *Commissioners of Customs and Excise* [1967], 2 QB 116, CA, at 141 (per Lord Denning, MR), 143 (per Diplock, LJ); ILR 41, 1; *Post Office* v. *Estuary Radio* [1967] 1 WLR 1396, CA, at 1404; [1968] 2 QB 740 at 757 (Diplock, LJ, delivering the judgment of the Court). *Corocraft Ltd.* v. *Pan American Airways Inc.* [1969] 1 QB 616; [1968] 3 WLR 1273, CA at 1281 per Lord Denning; ILR 41, 426.

[97] See Sinclair, 12 *ICLQ* (1963), 528–34; *British Practice* (1964), ii. 232–3.

will be set out as a schedule to the Act. Alternatively, the statute may employ its own substantive provisions to give effect to a treaty, the text of which is not directly enacted. In the latter situation, the international convention may be referred to in the long and short titles of the Act and also in the preamble and schedule. In *Ellerman Lines* v. *Murray*[98] their lordships adopted the view that if the relevant section of the Act had a 'natural meaning' it was improper to resort to the text of the Convention as an aid to interpretation. In recent cases, however, the Court of Appeal has held that the text of the relevant convention may be used as an aid to interpretation even if the statute does not in terms incorporate the convention nor even refer to it.[99] In the *Salomon* case Diplock, LJ,[100] stated two conditions for resort to the convention: (*a*) that the terms of the legislation are not clear but are reasonably capable of more than one meaning; (*b*) that there be cogent extrinsic evidence to the effect that the enactment was intended to fulfil obligations under a particular convention. These principles seem to represent the present law on the subject yet it is surely the case that Lord Diplock's second condition is the only necessary principle. The difficulty with the first condition is that it maintains the basic fault of the *dicta* in the *Ellerman Lines* decision, which is the question-begging involved. If the convention may be used on the correct principle that the statute is intended to implement the convention then, it follows, the latter becomes a proper aid to interpretation, and, more especially, may reveal a latent ambiguity in the text of the statute even if this was 'clear in itself'. Moreover, the principle or presumption that the Crown does not intend to break an international treaty must have the corollary that the text of the international instrument is a primary source of meaning or 'interpretation'. The courts have lately accepted the need to refer to the relevant treaty even in the absence of ambiguity in the legislative text when taken in isolation.[101] This approach is more readily adopted, as in the *Corocraft* case, when the statute expressly gives effect to the text of the convention as such and the text appears in a schedule as a translation into English of the only official text.[102] It is not clear, however, that the method chosen to give legislative effect to the treaty should determine whether reference should be made to the text of the convention, providing Lord Diplock's second condition (*supra*) is satisfied.

Since 1974 the English courts have with variable consistency been prepared to take the provisions of international conventions on human rights into account in the course of interpreting and applying statutes.[103]

---

[98] [1931] AC 126, at 147 per Lord Tomlin. See also *Barras* v. *Aberdeen Steam Trawling Co. Ltd.* [1933] AC 402; *Burns Philp & Co. Ltd.* v. *Nelson and Robertson Proprietaries Ltd.* (1957–8), 98 CLR 495, HC of A.

[99] *Salomon* v. *Commissioners of Customs and Excise, supra; Post Office* v. *Estuary Radio, supra.*

[100] [1967] 2 QB at 143, 144.

[101] See *Wilson, Smithett and Cope Ltd.* v. *Terruzzi* [1976] 2 WLR 418, CA; *The Jade, The Eischersheim* [1976] 1 WLR 430, HL; *Pan American World Airways Inc.* v. *Department of Trade* [1976] 1 Ll. LR 257, CA; *James Buchanan & Co. Ltd.* v. *Babco* [1978] AC 141, HL; *Fothergill* v. *Monarch Airlines Ltd.* [1980] 3 WLR 209, HL; *Garland* v. *British Rail Engineering Ltd.* [1983] 2 AC 751; *Goldman* v. *Thai Airways* [1983] 3 All ER 693, CA; *Gatoil* v. *Arkwright-Boston Manufacturers Mutual Insurance Co.* [1985] AC 255; *J.H. Rayner (Mincing Lane) Ltd.* v. *D.T.I.* (and other appeals), [1988] 3 All ER 257, CA; [1989] 3 WLR 969, HL.

[102] [1969] 1 QB 616; [1968] 3 WLR 1273.

[103] See e.g. *Waddington* v. *Miah* [1974] 1 WLR 692, HL; *Ahmad* v. *I.L.E.A.* [1978] 1 QB 36, CA; *R.* v. *Secretary of State, ex p. Brind* [1991] 1 AC 696, HL; *Derbyshire County Council* v. *Times Newspapers Ltd.* [1993]

British, American, and Commonwealth courts normally employ methods of interpretation similar in a general way to those of international tribunals and international law.[104]

10. TREATIES AND THE DETERMINATION OF COMMON LAW

Since 1979 the English courts have regularly taken into account treaty-based standards concerning human rights in order to resolve issues of common law, including the legality of telephone tapping,[105] the offence of criminal libel,[106] contempt of court,[107] and freedom of association.[108] This development is perfectly natural and should not be confined to 'human rights' issues. The decision in *Alcom* v. *Republic of Colombia*[109] involved reference to general international law for purposes of statutory interpretation in the context of state immunity, and this indicates the propriety of a wide range of reference in relation to both common law matters and interpretation of statutes.

11. THE RECEPTION OF INTERNATIONAL LAW IN OTHER STATES[110]

A very considerable number of states follow the principle of the incorporation, or adoption, of customary international law.[111] The principle may be applied in judicial practice or on the basis of constitutional provisions as interpreted by the courts. An

---

AC 534, HL; *Attorney-General* v. *Associated Newspapers Ltd.* [1994] 2 AC 238, HL. See further Staker, 64 *BY* (1993), 455–63; id., 15 *Austral. Yrbk.* (1993), 345–57; Cunningham, 43 *ICLQ* (1994), 537–67; and *Reference re Public Service Employee Relations Act*, ILR 94, 246 at 251–9 (Canada, S.C.).

[104] See *Fothergill* v. *Monarch Airlines Ltd.* [1980] 3 WLR 209, HL; *Commonwealth* v. *Tasmania* (1983) 46 ALR 625; ILR 68, 266, High Ct. of Australia.

[105] *Malone* v. *Metropolitan Police Commissioner (No. 2)* [1979] 1 Ch. 344, Megarry, VC. See further 50 *BY* (1979), 232–5 and notes on judicial decisions in current issues of *BY*.

[106] *Gleaves* v. *Deakin* [1980] AC 477, HL.

[107] *A.-G.* v. *B.B.C.* [1981] AC 303, HL.

[108] *Cheall* v. *Association of Professional, Executive, Clerical and Computer Staff* [1983] 2 AC 180, HL.

[109] [1984] AC 580, HL, at 597–600. Reference to general international law was made (in the cursory mode) by the courts involved in the ITC litigation.

[110] See generally Seidl-Hohenveldern, 12 *ICLQ* (1963), 88–124; Fawcett, *The British Commonwealth in International Law*, ch. 2; Mosler, 91 Hague *Recueil* (1957, I), 625–705; Lapidoth, *Les rapports entre le droit international public et le droit interne en Israël* (1959); Carsten Smith, 12 *Scandinavian Studies in Law* (1968), 153–201; *Norwegian Dentists Association* case, 96 *J.D.I.* (1969), 419, Supr. Ct., Norway; Benvenisti, 4 *Europ. Journ.* (1993), 159–83.

[111] Current evidence may be found in the International Law Reports. For use of English sources on the question: *Stampfer* v. *A.-G.*, ILR 23 (1956), 284 (Israel); *Re Lawless*, ILR 24 (1957) 420 (Eire). American authorities: *Hilton* v. *Guyot* (1895), 159 US 113; the *Paquete Habana* (1900), 175 US 677; *U.S.* v. *Melekh* (1960), 190 F. Supp. 67.

increasing number of states make appropriate provision in their constitutions, and thus Article 10 of the Italian constitution of 1947 provides that 'Italian law shall be in conformity with the generally recognized rules of international law'. In general it may be said that governments and lawyers are lately more conscious of the need to establish a constructive relationship between the municipal law and the system of international law. However, the subject-matter is complicated by issues of constitutional law peculiar to the given state and especially the distribution of power in a federal structure. Legal systems rarely adhere to any very pure form of incorporation. In Italy, to take an example already quoted, the courts have held that Article 10 of the constitution does not affect the validity of legislation passed before the constitution was brought into force. In the majority of states the rule obtains that international law must give way to national legislation. An important consideration is the fact that many rules of customary international law do not provide precise guidance for their application on the national plane. The principal task remains that of creating a sensible working relationship between the two systems within the jurisdiction of the particular state, an accommodation between them rather than the attainment of a formal 'harmony', or the 'primacy' of international law. The problems are obscured if they are placed in the context of the conflict between monists and dualists.[112]

These considerations apply with even greater force to the role of treaties in national courts. A number of countries adhere to the principle that treaties made in accordance with the constitution bind the courts without any specific act of incorporation. In fact in such states the principle is often applied with significant qualifications. Thus, in the United States, a later act of federal legislation overrides a treaty. Furthermore, a self-executing treaty may not be enforced internally until it has been published, and control over due publication introduces elements of formal constitutionality.[113] What is probably the more generally accepted principle requires specific legislative incorporation as a condition of internal force.

There also arises the category of 'self-executing' treaties. The term 'self-executing' may be used to state a principle of the particular system of national law that certain rules of international law do not need incorporation in order to have internal effect. However, the term is also used to describe the character of the rules themselves. Thus a national court may hold that, as a matter of interpretation, a treaty obligation could not be applicable internally without specific local legislation.[114] Both uses of the term appear in the decisions of American courts. The second of the uses described appears in *Fujii* v. *State of California*.[115] There the Supreme Court of California held that Articles

---

[112] *Supra*, pp. 31–3.

[113] See Seidl-Hohenveldern, 12 *ICLQ* (1963), 105–7.

[114] See Evans, 30 *BY* (1953), 178–205; Bishop, 115 Hague *Recueil* (1965, II) 202–9.

[115] (1952), 38 Cal. 2d. 718, 242 P. 2d. 617; ILR 19 (1952), no. 53; applied by the Supreme Court of Iowa in *Rice* v. *Sioux City Memorial Park Cemetery Inc.*, ILR 20 (1953), 244 and a District Court in *Comacho* v. *Rogers*, ILR 32, 368. See also Evans, 30 *BY* (1953), 178–205; Preuss, 51 *Michigan LR* (1953), 117; *A.J.K.* v. *Public Prosecutor*, ILR 28, 268; *Re Masini*, ILR 24 (1957), 11; *Rossier* v. *Court of Justice of Canton of Geneva*, ILR 32, 348. On the effect of the European Convention of Human Rights: *European Convention on Human Rights* case, ILR 40, p. 238, Austrian Const. Ct., 27 June 1960; *Ex parte Püschel*, ILR 38, p. 174, Austrian Const.

55 and 56 of the Charter of the United Nations, relating to human rights, were not self-executing and could not be applied in regard to individuals without the requisite legislation. The whole subject resists generalization, and the practice of states reflects the characteristics of the individual constitution. Treaties concluded by the European Community may be self-executing in the sense that they are binding within domestic legal systems without formal incorporation therein.[116]

12. RELATION OF EXECUTIVE AND JUDICIARY AND ISSUES OF NON-JUSTICIABILITY

To a great extent the problems of applying international law in the municipal sphere are related to the distribution of power within the state, and many of the principles noticed in the previous sections depend on a concern to maintain a proper relation between the courts and the legislature. Yet another field of problems arises when the relation of the executive and the courts is considered.[117] This relation has a number of facets. One of these is illustrated by the case of *Mortensen* v. *Peters*[118] in which the High Court of Justiciary of Scotland interpreted the Herring Fishery (Scotland) Act 1889 in such a way that it could apply in a manner contrary to international law—to prohibit fishing by aliens in areas outside the territorial sea. In fact the enforcement agencies have not applied the Act in this way.[119] In the realm of international relations the English courts seek the guidance of the appropriate department of government on the determination of a variety of issues, including the status of entities claiming to be independent states, the recognition of governments, the existence of a state of war, and the incidence of diplomatic immunity. This is formally a matter of evidence, a procedure for taking judicial notice of material facts, but the certificate of the Secretary of State is conclusive of the matter,[120] unless the certificate deliberately leaves the court free to construe a particular word or phrase, for example, 'war' in a time charter-party.[121] The

Ct., 14 Oct. 1961; *Deprivation of Liberty* case, ILR 40, 244, Austria, Admin. Ct., 15 Dec. 1961; *Kannas* v. *The Police*, ILR 41, 360. Cyprus, SC.

[116] See Mann, *Foreign Affairs in English Courts*, pp. 114–19.

[117] Of course, where the executive has the treaty-making power, a pure doctrine of incorporation applied by the courts would have the effect of bypassing the legislature: hence the English practice, *supra*, p. 45.

[118] (1906), 8 F. (JC), 93.

[119] *UK Contemp. Practice* (1962), i. 48. Similarly where an Act, without the interpretative intervention of the courts, could be applied in a particular way, the executive may enforce the law in such a way as to accord with international law as it is assumed to be by the executive: on the application of the Customs Consolidation Act 1876, so as to avoid a contiguous zone, see McNair, *Opinions*, i. 344, 345–6.

[120] See Lyons, 23 BY (1946), 240–81; 29 BY (1952), 227–64. But cf. *The Zamora* [1916] 2 AC 77 on the evidential effect of an Order in Council in respect of the effectiveness of a blockade. On American practice: Lyons, 24 BY (1947), 116–47. On continental and Latin American practice: id., 25 BY (1948), 180–210. See also *A.-G. of Israel* v. *Kamiar*, ILR 44, 197 at 250–2.

[121] See *Kawasaki Kisen Kabushiki Kaisha of Kobe* v. *Bantham Steamship Co. Ltd.* [1939] 2 KB 544; *Luigi Monta of Genoa* v. *Cechofracht Co. Ltd.* [1956] 2 QB 552; *In re Al-Fin Corporation's Patent* [1970] 1 Ch. 160; 44 BY (1970), 213; *Gur Corporation* v. *Trust Bank of Africa Ltd.* [1986] 3 WLR 583, CA (and see 57 BY (1986),

effect of this procedure is where necessary to subject the courts to the determination of important legal issues by the executive and so avoid the embarrassment of a conflict of opinion. Policy considerations of a similar kind have led courts to apply a form of the Act of State doctrine and, by holding a claim to be barred, because it concerned the acts of a foreign state, to leave the executive free in its conduct of foreign relations.

The act of State doctrine is referred to here more or less by way of a memorandum. It is a doctrine of English public law which, though long familiar in a general way, still has very uncertain operational limits. There is some evidence that the English courts are narrowing the scope of the doctrine on Rule of Law grounds. In principle, the doctrine prescribes that an issue which involves a court in determining the legal status of the relations of the British Government with foreign states (or international organizations) is non-justiciable. However, in *Nissan* v. *Attorney-General*[122] the House of Lords held that a British citizen whose house in Cyprus had been damaged by British troops, lawfully present in Cyprus as a consequence of an agreement with the Cyprus Government, was not prevented from pursuing remedies by the plea of act of State. The link with the Agreement with Cyprus was too tenuous. Similarly, in *Pinochet (No. 1)*[123] three of the Law Lords regarded the act of State doctrine as inapplicable. At the outset of the international law argument in *Pinochet (No. 3)*;[124] the presiding Law Lord, Lord Browne-Wilkinson, indicated to Counsel that there was no need to address the Act of State issue as extradition was an area already subject to a legal regime.

In any event, the act of State consists of several principles. Thus, whilst it is a principle of justiciability (or admissibility of claims *ab initio*), it is also an issue of substance (as a defence) once justiciability has been established (as in *Nissan* v. *Attorney-General*).[125] There is also the specialized principle that the validity of the transactions of foreign states cannot be the object of adjudication in the municipal courts of other States: this is known as '*Buttes* non-justiciability'.[126] However, whilst this principle applies to disputes concerning territorial sovereignty or maritime boundaries between States, it should not apply to protect acts in violation of international law from examination by an English court.[127] In any event it is clear that non-justiciability should not prevent the determination of private law rights.[128]

510–11). See also Merrills, 20 *ICLQ* (1971), 476–99. Edeson, 7 *Austral. Yrbk.* 1–26; Warbrick, 35 *ICLQ* (1986), 138–56; Wilmshurst, ibid. 157–69.

[122] [1970] AC 179; 43 *BY* (1968–69), 217–26.

[123] [1998] 3 WLR 1456; ILR 119, 50; Byers, 70 *BY* (1999), 277–95.

[124] [1999] 2 WLR 827; ILR 119, 135; Byers, op. cit.

[125] See above.

[126] See *Buttes Gas* v. *Hammer* [1982] AC 88 at 931–2, *per* Lord Wilberforce; Crawford, 53 *BY* (1982), 259–68. See also *Maclaine Watson* v. *Department of Trade and Industry* [1989] 3 WLR 969, 1001, ILR 81, 671, 700, *per* Lord Oliver.

[127] See Mance J. in *Kuwait Airways Corporation* v. *Iraqi Airways Company* [1999] CLC 31; ILR 116, 534; Byers, 69 *BY* (1998), 305–14; House of Lords, 16 May 2002, *per* Lord Nicholls, paras. 24–6.

[128] See *Republic of Ecuador* v. *Occidental Exploration and Production Co.* [2006] 2 WLR 70; 76 *BY* (2005), 585–9; and *AY Bank Ltd (in Liquidation)* v. *Bosnia and Herzegovina* [2006] 2 All ER (Comm), 463; 77 *BY* (2006), 489–99.

13. *RES JUDICATA* AND THE TWO SYSTEMS

There is no effect of *res judicata* from the decision of a municipal court so far as an international jurisdiction is concerned, since, although the subject-matter may be substantially the same, the parties will not be, and the issues will have a very different aspect. In the municipal court the legal person claiming is an individual or corporation: before an international tribunal the claimant will be a state exercising diplomatic protection with respect to its national.[129] Considerations of admissibility may have the effect of creating an exception to the general rule. Thus a respondent in an international claim may plead successfully that adequate remedies have been obtained before another tribunal, either national or international.[130] In the *Cysne*[131] an arbitral tribunal held that in matters of prize the judgments of national prize courts of final instance constituted international titles, which were generally recognized, and so had the force of *res judicata* as to the passing of property. The policy behind this ruling was based on considerations of security for third persons acquiring title in prize: however, the prize court's decision might create international responsibility for the state of the *forum* if it constituted a violation of international law. And of course an international tribunal may be bound by its constituent instrument, usually an agreement between two or more states, to accept certain categories of national decisions as conclusive of particular issues.[132]

In principle decisions by organs of international organizations are not binding on national courts without the co-operation of the internal legal system,[133] which may adopt a broad constitutional provision for 'automatic' incorporation of treaty norms or require specific acts of incorporation at least for certain categories of treaties.[134] It follows that a decision of the International Court, though it concerns substantially the same issues as those before a municipal court, does not of itself create a *res judicata* for the latter.[135] However, it does not follow that a municipal court could not, or should

---

[129] See *Certain German Interests in Polish Upper Silesia* (1925), PCIJ, Ser. A, no. 6, p. 20.

[130] See the *Ottoz* claim, ILR 18 (1951), no. 136 and the *Nartnick* and *Mayer* claims, ILR 21 (1954), 149, 150 respectively. It could be argued, however, that the commission deciding these claims (US International Claims Commission) was not strictly speaking an international tribunal.

[131] (1930), *RIAA*, ii. 1035. See also Oppenheim, ii. 475 n. 2.

[132] Cf. the *Pinson* claim (1928), *RIAA*, v. 327.

[133] See Sørensen, 101 Hague *Receuil* (1960, III), 120–5; Skubiszewski, 41 *BY* (1965–6), 198 at 267–71; id., 2 *Polish Yrbk.* (1968–9), 80–108; id., 46 *BY* (1972–3), 353–64; Schreuer, 27 *ICLQ* (1978), 1–17; *Diggs* v. *Richardson, Digest of US Practice* (1976), 50 (Security Council resol. held not to be self-executing); *Bradley* v. *Commonwealth of Australia* (1973), 1 ALR 241; 101 *JDI* (1974), 865.

[134] *Supra*, pp. 41–5.

[135] See *'Socobel'* v. *Greek State*, ILR 18 (1951), no. 2; 47 *AJ* (1953), 580; Rosenne, *The Law and Practice of the International Court 1920–1996* (1997), 221–6; and Jenks, *The Prospects of International Adjudication*, pp. 706–15. See also *Committee of United States Citizens Living in Nicaragua* v. *Reagan*, ILR 85, 248; and *Breard* v. *Greene*, U.S. Supreme Ct., 14 April 1998; ILR 118, 22.

not, recognize the validity of the judgment of an international tribunal of manifest competence and authority, at least for certain purposes.[136]

In a considerable number of countries municipal courts, in dealing with cases of war crimes and issues arising from belligerent occupation, for example the validity of acts of administration, of requisition, and of transactions conducted in occupation currency, have relied upon the findings of the International Military Tribunals at Nuremberg and Tokyo as evidence, even conclusive evidence, of the illegality of the war which resulted in the occupations.[137] In general the decisions of international tribunals provide evidence of the legally permitted extent of the jurisdiction and territorial sovereignty of the particular states involved.[138]

14. RELATION TO THE SOURCES OF INTERNATIONAL LAW

Judicial decisions in the municipal sphere and acts of legislation provide prima facie evidence of the attitudes of states on points of international law and very often constitute the only available evidence of the practice of states. Thus collections of municipal cases, such as the *Annual Digest of Public International Law Cases* (continued as the *International Law Reports*), and of legislation, which appears in the *United Nations Legislative Series*, are important in any assessment of the customary law.[139] In the pleadings before an international tribunal points of law will be dealt with at length by experts and the tribunal will in any case be qualified to handle the legal sources. The issues may be of great significance and the process of argument and decision will take some time. When points of international law arise in a municipal court, and resort to the executive for guidance does not occur, the court will commonly face very real difficulty in obtaining reliable evidence, in convenient form, of the state of the law,

---

[136] See *Messina* v. *Petrococchino* (1872) LR 4 PC 144; *Dallal* v. *Bank Mellat* [1986] 1 QB 441, Hobhouse, J., at 457–62. For comment see Fox, 37 *ICLQ* (1988), 24–38; Crawford, 57 *BY* (1986), 410–14. See further Schreuer, 24 *ICLQ* (1975), 153–83; Giardina, 165 Hague *Recueil* (1979, IV), 233–352; Schachter, 54 *AJ* (1960), 12–14; id., 178 Hague *Recueil* (1982, V), 226–8, 231–9. Cf. Mann, *Foreign Affairs in English Courts*, pp. 157–8 (para. 4).

[137] See Brownlie, *International Law and the Use of Force by States* (1963), 185–6, 407. See also *Hong Kong and Shanghai Banking Corporation* v. *Luis Perez-Samanillo Inc.*, *Ann. Digest*, 13 (1946), no. 157; *N.* v. *B.*, ILR 24 (1957), 941; *B.* v. *T.*, ibid. 962. On the special relationship between the Allied military tribunals in Germany under occupation and the IMT at Nuremberg see *Law Reports of Trials of War Criminals*, UNWCC xv. 17–20.

[138] See *Rex* v. *Cooper, Rex* v. *Martin*, ILR 20 (1953), 166, 167; *Administration des Habous* v. *Deal*, ibid. 19 (1952), no. 67; *Re Bendayan*, 49 *AJ* (1955), 267; *Mackay Radio Company* v. *El Khadar*, ILR 21 (1954), 136; 49 *AJ* (1955), 267, 413; *In re Krüger*, ILR 18 (1951), no. 68. See further *Anglo-Iranian Oil Co.* v. *Idemitsu Kosan Kabushiki Kaisha*, ILR 22 (1953), 305: *Anglo-Iranian Oil Co. Ltd.* v. *S.U.P.O.R.*, ILR 22 (1955), 23 at 41. Cf. *Steinberg* v. *Custodian of German Property*, ILR 24 (1957), 771; *Czechoslovak Agrarian Reform (Swiss Subjects)* case, *Ann. Digest*, 4 (1927–8), no. 94. See also Schreuer, 24 *ICLQ* (1975), 153–83.

[139] See further *infra*, pp. 297ff., 378ff.

and especially the customary law, on a particular point.[140] An *ad hoc*, yet extensive, research project is out of the question, and counsel cannot always fill the gap (unless a well prepared law officer of the Crown, or equivalent elsewhere, appears as an *amicus curiae*). In these circumstances it is hardly surprising that courts have leaned heavily on the opinions of writers.[141] It can and does happen that a municipal court makes for itself a very full investigation of all the legal sources,[142] including treaties and state practice—yet here also works of authority may be relied upon as repositories and assessors of state practice. And of course reference may be made to decisions and dicta of international tribunals[143] and the work of the International Law Commission.[144]

15. CONCLUSION

On the whole question of the relation between municipal and international law theoretical constructions have probably done much to obscure realities. If one has to choose between the theories considered earlier in this chapter,[145] then the views of Fitzmaurice and Rousseau might be preferred as coming closer to the facts. Each system is supreme *in its own field*, and neither has a hegemony over the other. And yet any generalities offered can only provide a background to the complex relations between the two systems. Three factors operate on the subject matter. The first is organizational: to what extent are the organs of states willing to apply rules of international law internally and externally?[146] This raises the problem of state responsibility, sanctions, and non-recognition of illegal acts. Exceptionally, as a result of international action followed by occupation, a state may suffer external direction in the application of international

---

[140] See *supra*, pp. 40ff.

[141] See *West Rand Central Gold Mining Co. v. R.* [1905] 2 KB 391 at 407–8. In some jurisdictions resort will be had to an expert witness.

[142] See *R. v. Keyn* (1876), 2 Ex. D. 63; *In re Piracy Jure Gentium* [1934] AC 586; *The State (Duggan) v. Tapley* [1952] IR 62; ILR 18 (1951), no. 109; *State of the Netherlands v. Federal Reserve Bank*, ibid. no. 174; *Aboitiz & Co. v. Price* (1951), 99 F. Supp. 602; ILR 18 (1951), no. 182; *Haw Pia v. China Banking Corp.*, ibid. no. 203; *Lauritzen v. Government of Chile*, ILR 23 (1956), 708; *Indonesian Tobacco Estates Case*, ILR 28, 16.

[143] See e.g. *Eichmann* (1961), 56 AJ (1962), 805; ILR 36, 5, 18, 277; *Murarka v. Bachrack Bros., Inc.*, ILR 20 (1953), 52; *Lauritzen v. Larsen*, ibid. 197; *The Rose Mary* [1953] 1 WLR 246; ILR 20 (1953), 316; *Heirs of Shababo v. Heilen (No. 2)*, ibid. 400; *Stampfer v. A.-G.*, ILR 23 (1956), 284; *Lauritzen v. Government of Chile*, ibid. 708 at 733, 738, 742, 750; *N.V. de Bataafsche Petroleum Maatschappij v. War Damage Commission*, ibid. 810 at 822, 832, 845; *Mobarik Ali Ahmed v. State of Bombay*, ILR 24 (1957), 156; *Re Application of Spanish-Swiss Conv. of Nov. 14, 1879*, ILR 28, 461.

[144] See *Cassirer and Geheeb v. Japan*, ILR 28, 396 at 407ff.

[145] *Supra*, pp. 31–4.

[146] Monists underestimate this aspect of the matter or gloss it over with conceptualism. The fact is that municipal law is more viable in terms of organization whereas international law is less of a system *in this sense*. From this point of view there is some substance in the view that international law derives from the activities of the constitutional organs of states. This view, characterized as monism in terms of internal law, was supported by Zorn, Kaufmann, Wenzel, and Decencière-Ferrandière (see the latter in 40 *RGDIP* (1933), 45–70). Critics have tended to caricature this view in order to criticize it: in fact it accords with widely held views that international law is *international* and not dependent on a supranational coercive order.

law both internally and externally. The second factor is the difficulty of proving the existence of particular rules of international law. In case of difficulty municipal courts may rely on advice from the executive or existing internal precedents, and the result may not accord with an objective appreciation of the law. Thirdly, courts, both municipal and international, will often be concerned with the more technical question as to which is the *appropriate* system to apply to particular issues arising. The question of appropriateness emphasizes the distinction between organization, i.e. the nature of the jurisdiction as 'national' or 'international', and the character of the rules of both systems as flexible instruments for dealing with disputes and regulating non-contentious matters. An international court may find it necessary to apply rules of municipal law,[147] while bodies, such as the United States Foreign Claims Settlement Commission, which are national in terms of organization and competence may find it appropriate, and be authorized, to apply rules of international law on a large scale. When a municipal court applies a rule of international law because it is appropriate, it is pointless to ask if the rule applied has been 'transformed', except in so far as 'transformation' describes a special process required by a particular municipal system before certain organs are permitted, or are willing, to apply rules of international law.[148]

---

[147] *Supra*, pp. 36–41.

[148] There are many areas of law in which the relation between the two systems has special features, for example the law of recognition, nationality of corporations, belligerent occupation, and the *res nullius*. Cf. Hackworth, i. 476 on the latter.

PART II

PERSONALITY AND RECOGNITION

3

SUBJECTS OF THE LAW[1]

1. INTRODUCTION

A subject of the law is an entity capable of possessing international rights and duties and having the capacity to maintain its rights by bringing international claims.[2] This definition, though conventional, is unfortunately circular since the *indicia* referred to depend on the existence of a legal person. All that can be said is that an entity of a type recognized by customary law as *capable* of possessing rights and duties and of bringing international claims, and having these capacities conferred upon it, is a legal person. If the first condition is not satisfied, the entity concerned may still have legal personality of a very restricted kind, dependent on the agreement or acquiescence of recognized legal persons and opposable on the international plane only to those agreeing or acquiescent. The principal formal contexts in which the question of personality has arisen have been: capacity to make claims in respect of breaches of international law, capacity to make treaties and agreements valid on the international plane, and the enjoyment of privileges and immunities from national jurisdictions. States have these capacities and immunities, and indeed the incidents of statehood as developed under the customary law have provided the *indicia* for, and instruments of personality in, other entities. Apart from states, organizations may have these capacities and immunities if certain conditions are satisfied.[3] The first of the capacities set out above, for organizations of a certain type, was established by the Advisory Opinion in the *Reparation for Injuries* case.[4] The first Waldock Report prepared for the International Law Commission on the law of treaties[5] recognized the capacity of

---

[1] See especially Lauterpacht, *International Law: Collected Papers*, ii. (1975), 487–533; Rousseau, ii; Broms in Macdonald and Johnston (eds.), *The Structure and Process of International Law* (1983), 383–423; Barberis, 179 Hague *Recueil* (1983, I), 145–304 (good biblio.); Cassese, *International Law in a Divided World* (1986), 74–104; Bedjaoui (ed.), *International Law: Achievements and Prospects* (1991), 23–132; Higgins, *Problems and Process* (1994), 39–55.

[2] *Reparation for Injuries* case, ICJ Reports (1949), 179.

[3] See *infra*, ch. 31, s. 8.

[4] See generally ch. 31. See also García Amador, *Yrbk. ILC* (1956), ii. 195, 198.

[5] See *Yrbk. ILC* (1962), ii. 31, 32, 35, 37. See also Brierly, ibid. (1950), ii. 230; Lauterpacht, ibid. (1953), ii. 96; Fitzmaurice, ibid. (1956), ii. 117–18; and (1958), ii. 24, 32: Waldock, ibid. (1962), ii. 31, 35–7. At a later stage the Commission decided to confine the specific provisions of the draft articles to the treaties of states: ibid. (1965), ii. 18; (1966), ii. 187, Art. 1, commentary.

international organizations to become parties to international agreements, and this recognition reflected the existing practice between organisations and also between states and organizations. Finally, while an organization probably cannot claim privileges and immunities like those of a sovereign state as of right, it can claim to be a suitable candidate for the conferment of like privileges and immunities.

It is states and organizations (if appropriate conditions exist) which represent the normal types of legal person on the international plane. However, as will become apparent in due course, the realities of international relations are not reducible to a simple formula and the picture is somewhat complex. The 'normal types' have congeners which create problems, and various entities, including non-self-governing peoples and the individual, have a certain personality. Moreover, abstraction of types of acceptable persons at law falls short of the truth, since recognition and acquiescence may sustain an entity which is anomalous, and yet has a web of legal relations on the international plane. But in spite of the complexities, it is as well to remember the primacy of states as subjects of the law. As Professor Friedmann observes:[6]

The basic reason for this position is, of course, that 'the world is to-day organized on the basis of the co-existence of States, and that fundamental changes will take place only through State action, whether affirmative or negative'.[7] The States are the repositories of legitimated authority over peoples and territories. It is only in terms of State powers, prerogatives, jurisdictional limits and law-making capabilities that territorial limits and jurisdiction, responsibility for official actions, and a host of other questions of co-existence between nations can be determined.... This basic primacy of the State as a subject of international relations and law would be substantially affected, and eventually superseded, only if national entities, as political and legal systems, were absorbed in a world state.

2. ESTABLISHED LEGAL PERSONS

(a) States

This category, the most important, has its own problems. The existence of 'dependent' states[8] with certain qualified and delegated legal capacities complicates the picture, but, providing the conditions for statehood exist,[9] the 'dependent' state retains its personality. The position of members of federal unions is interesting. In the constitutions of Switzerland and the German Federal Republic component states are permitted to exercise certain of the capacities of independent states, including the power to make treaties. In the normal case, such capacities are probably exercised as agents for

---

[6] *The Changing Structure of International Law* (1964), 213.
[7] Quoting Jessup, *A Modern Law of Nations* (1948), 17.
[8] See *infra*, pp. 72–4.
[9] See *infra*, pp. 70ff.

the union, even if the acts concerned are done in the name of the component state.[10] However, where the union originated as a union of independent states, the internal relations retain an international element, and the union may act as agent for the states.[11] The United States constitution enables the states of the Union to enter into agreements with other states of the Union or with foreign states with the consent of Congress.[12] In Canada the federal government has the exclusive power to make treaties with foreign states.[13]

(b) Political entities legally proximate to states

Political settlements both in multilateral and bilateral treaties have from time to time produced political entities, such as the former Free City of Danzig, which, possessing a certain autonomy, fixed territory and population, and some legal capacities on the international plane, are rather like states. 'Politically such entities are not sovereign states in the normal sense, yet legally the distinction is not very significant. The treaty origin of the entity and the existence of some form of protection by an international organization—the League of Nations in the case of Danzig—matter little if, in the result, the entity has autonomy and a nucleus of the more significant legal capacities, for example the power to make treaties, to maintain order and exercise jurisdiction within the territory, and to have an independent nationality law. The jurisprudence of the Permanent Court recognized that Danzig had international personality, except in so far as treaty obligations created special relations in regard to the League and to Poland.[14] The special relations of Danzig were based upon Articles 100–8 of the Versailles Treaty. The League of Nations had a supervisory function and Poland was placed in control of the foreign relations of Danzig. The result was very much a protectorate, the legal status and constitution of which were externally supervised. To describe legal entities like Danzig as 'internationalized territories'[15] is not very helpful since the phrase covers a number of distinct entities and situations and begs the question of legal personality. The Italian Peace Treaty of 1947 provided for the creation of

---

[10] See Brierly, *Yrbk. ILC* (1952), ii. 50; Lauterpacht, ibid. (1953), ii. 94–5, 137–9; Fitzmaurice, ibid. (1956), ii. 118; id., ibid. (1958), ii. 24, 32; Waldock, ibid. (1962), ii. 31, 36–7; Morin, 3 *Canad. Yrbk.* (1965), 127–86; Lissitzyn, 125 Hague *Recueil* (1968, III), 24–50; Rousseau, ii. 138–213, 264–8; Uibopuu, 24 *ICLQ* (1975), 811–45; Wildhaber, 12 *Canad. Yrbk.* (1974), 211–21; Ziegel, *Essays in Honour of Georg Schwarzenberger* (1988), 333–55; *Koowarta* v. *Bjelke-Petersen*, ILR 68, 181 (Australia); *Commonwealth of Australia* v. *State of Tasmania*, ibid. 266 (Australia); *Jenni* v. *Conseil d'État*, ILR 75, 99 (Switz.).

[11] This appears to be the position in Switzerland.

[12] See Whiteman, xiv. 15–17; Rodgers, 61 *AJ* (1967), 1021–8.

[13] See Gotlieb, *Canadian Treaty-Making* (1968), 27–32.

[14] See *Free City of Danzig and the ILO* (1930), PCIJ, Ser. B, no. 18; and *Polish Nationals in Danzig* (1932), Ser. A/B, no. 44, pp. 23–4. Germany occupied the Free City in 1939 and since 1945 the area has been part of Poland.

[15] See Rousseau, ii. 413, 423; Verzijl, *International Law in Historical Perspective*, ii. 500–2, 510–45; Crawford, *The Creation of States in International Law* (2nd edn., 2006), 233–44.

a Free Territory of Trieste with features broadly similar to those of the Free City of Danzig, but placed under the direct control of the United Nations Security Council.[16]

(c) Condominia

A *condominium*, as a joint exercise of state power within a particular territory by means of an autonomous local administration, may bear a resemblance to entities of the type considered latterly. However, the local administration can only act as an agency of the states participating in the *condominium*, and normally even its capacity as agent is limited.[17]

(d) Internationalized territories[18]

The label 'internationalized territory' has been applied by writers to a variety of legal regimes. It may be applied very loosely to cases like Danzig and Trieste where a special status was created by multilateral treaty and protected by an international organization.[19] In these instances the special status was attached to entities with sufficient independence and legal capacity to admit of legal personality. However, a special status of this kind may attach without the creation of a legal person. An area within a sovereign state may be given certain rights of autonomy under treaty without this leading to any degree of separate personality on the international plane: this was the case with the Memel Territory, which enjoyed a special status in the period 1924 to 1939, yet remained a part of Lithuania.[20] Another type of regime, more truly international, involves exclusive administration of a territory by an international organization or an organ thereof: this was the regime proposed for the city of Jerusalem by the Trusteeship Council in 1950 but never implemented.[21] In such a case no new legal person is established except in so far as an agency of an international organization may have a certain autonomy (*infra*).

---

[16] The Permanent Statute of Trieste was not implemented: the administration of the territory was divided by agreement in 1954; the partition was made definitive by the Treaty of Osimo, in force 3 Apr. 1977, *Rivista di d.i.* 60, 674. See Verzijl, *International Law in Historical Perspective*, 504–5; and, on the issue of sovereignty, *infra*, pp. 68–9. On the position of the Holy See and Taiwan see *infra*, pp. 67, 68.

[17] See 9 *ICLQ* (1960), 258. On the New Hebrides see O'Connell, 43 *BY* (1968–9), 71–145.

[18] See Rousseau, ii. 413–48; Crawford, *The Creation of States*, (2nd edn., 2006), 233–44; Yoshida, *Austrian Review*, Vol. 9 (2004), 63–118; Chesterman, *You, The People: The United Nations, Transitional Administration and State-Building* (2004).

[19] *Supra*, p. 59.

[20] *Interpretation of the Statute of the Memel Territory* (1932) PCIJ, Ser. A/B, no. 49, p. 313. See also the complex legal status of the International Zone of Tangier wound up in 1956; for which Rousseau, ii. 430–40; Ydit, *International Territories*, pp. 154–84; Whiteman, i. 595–8; Gutteridge, 33 *BY* (1957), 296–302.

[21] Ydit, *International Territories*, pp. 273–314; Whiteman, i. 593–5; Cassese, 3 *Palestine Yrbk.* (1986), 13–39; Hirsch, Housen-Couriel and Lapidoth, *Whither Jerusalem?*, 1995. Cf. Fitzmaurice, *Yrbk. ILC* (1958), ii. 24, 32 (para. 24). Cf. the Free City of Trieste, *supra*, p. 59.

(e) UN administration of territories immediately prior to independence

In relation to territories marked out by the United Nations as under a regime of illegal occupation and qualified for an expeditious transition to independence, an interim transitional regime may be installed under UN supervision. Thus the final phase of the attainment of Namibian independence involved the Security Council, the General Assembly, and the UN Transition Assistance Group, established by Security Council resolution 435 (1978) of 29 September 1978.[22]

In 1999 the long drawn out crisis concerning the illegal Indonesian occupation of East Timor was the subject of decisive action by the Security Council in Resolution 1272 (1999) of 25 October 1999.[23] This established the United Nations Transitional Administration in East Timor (UNTAET) with a mandate to prepare East Timor for independence. UNTAET had full legislative and executive powers and assumed its role independently of any competing authority. After elections, East Timor became independent in 2002.

(f) International organizations

The conditions under which an organization acquires legal personality on the international plane and not merely as a legal person within a particular system of national law are examined in Chapter 31. The most important person of this type is of course the United Nations.

(g) Agencies of states

Entities acting as the agents of states, with delegated powers, may have the appearance of enjoying a separate personality and considerable viability on the international plane. Thus components of federal states probably have treaty-making capacity, where this is provided for internally, as agents of the federal state.[24] By agreement states may create joint agencies with delegated powers of a supervisory, rule-making, and even judicial nature. Examples are the administration of a *condominium*,[25] an arbitral tribunal, the International Joint Commission set up under an agreement concerning boundary waters between Canada and the United States in 1909,[26] and the former European Commission of the Danube.[27] As the degree of independence and the legal powers of the particular agency increase it will approximate to an international organization.

---

[22] See 28 *ILM* (1989), 944–1017; Oppenheim, i. 300–7.

[23] See 39 *ILM* (2000), 240–2; 936–44. See further Chesterman, op. cit., *passim*; Drew, *Europ. Journ.*, 12 (2001), 651–84.

[24] See Fitzmaurice, *Yrbk. ILC* (1956), ii. 118 n.; and Morin, 3 *Canad. Yrbk.* (1965), 127–86. See further the draft articles on the law of treaties, ILC (1966), Art. 5 (2). On the role of the chartered companies such as the English East India Company and the Dutch East India Company, see Schwarzenberger, *International Law*, i. (3rd edn.), 80–1; McNair, *Opinions*, i. 41, 55; and the *Palmas* award, *RIAA*, ii at p. 858.

[25] *Supra*, p. 59; *infra*, pp. 113–14.

[26] See Baxter, *The Law of International Waterways* (1964), 107.

[27] Ibid. 103–6, 126–9.

3. SPECIAL TYPES OF PERSONALITY

(a) Non-self-governing peoples

Quite apart from the question of protected status,[28] and the legal effect of particular agreements under which territories have been placed under mandate or trusteeship, it is very probable that the populations of 'non-self-governing territories' within the meaning of Chapter XI of the United Nations Charter have legal personality, albeit of a special type. This proposition depends on the examination of the principle of self-determination to be found in Chapter 25, section 9.

(b) National liberation movements[29]

In the course of the anti-colonial actions conducted within the United Nations and within regional organizations, the practice of both the organs of the United Nations and the member States conferred legal status upon certain national liberation movements. Most, but by no means all, of the peoples represented by such movements have acquired statehood. In 1974 the General Assembly accorded recognition to the Angolan, Mozambican, Palestinian, and Rhodesian movements. These liberation movements were recognized as such by regional organizations. The political and legal roots of the concept of national liberation movements are to be found in the Declaration of Principles of International Law concerning Friendly Relations and Co-operation among States in accordance with the Charter of the United Nations (Resolution 2625 (XV), adopted without vote, 24 October 1970), and the principle of self-determination, of which the beneficiary is a 'people'.

National liberation movements may, and usually do, have other roles, as *de facto* governments and belligerent communities.

The political entities recognized as liberation movements have a number of legal rights and duties, the more significant of which are as follows:

(a) In practice liberation movements are accorded the capacity to conclude binding international agreements with other international legal persons.

(b) The rights and obligations set by the generally recognized principles of humanitarian law. The provisions of the Geneva Protocol I of 1977 apply to conflicts involving national liberation movements if certain conditions are fulfilled: see Articles 1(4) and 96(3) of the Protocol.

(c) The legal capacity of national liberation movements is reflected in the right to participate in the proceedings of the United Nations as observers, this right

---

[28] *Supra*, p. 61.

[29] See Lazarus, *Ann. Français*, 20 (1974), 173–200; Abi-Saab, Hague *Recueil*, 165 (1979–IV), 357–445; Barberis, Hague *Recueil* (1983, I), 239–68; Morgenstern, *Legal Problems of International Organisations*, 1986, 68–74; Wilson, *International Law and the Use of Force by National Liberation Movements*, 1988; Ranjeva, in Bedjaoui (ed.), *International Law: Achievements and Prospects*, 1991, 107–10; David, *Principes de Droit des Conflits Armés*, 2nd edn., 1999, 195–8; Cassese, *International Law*, 2001, 75–7.

being conferred expressly in various General Assembly resolutions. Thus the Palestine Liberation Organisation (PLO) was granted observer status in Resolution 3237 (XXIX), adopted on 22 November 1974.

In conclusion, it is necessary to recall the impact of the designation of a non-self-governing people engaged in a process of national liberation upon the colonial (or dominant) power. The colonial authorities do not, for example, have the legal capacity to make agreements affecting the boundaries or status of the territory to which the liberation process is applicable.[30]

(c) States in *statu nascendi*[31]

For certain legal purposes it is convenient to assume continuity in a political entity and thus to give effect, after statehood has been attained, to legal acts occurring before independence. Considerations relating to the principle of self-determination and the personality of non-self-governing peoples may of course reinforce a doctrine of continuity.

(d) Legal constructions

A state's legal order may be projected on the plane of time for certain purposes although politically it has ceased to exist.[32]

(e) Belligerent and insurgent communities

In practice, belligerent and insurgent bodies[33] within a state may enter into legal relations and conclude agreements valid on the international plane with states and other belligerents and insurgents. Sir Gerald Fitzmaurice[34] has attributed treaty-making capacity to 'para-Statal entities recognized as possessing a definite if limited form of international personality, for example, insurgent communities recognized as having belligerent status—*de facto* authorities in control of specific territory'. This statement is correct as a matter of principle,[35] although its application to particular facts will require caution. The status of the particular belligerent community may be affected by the considerations offered elsewhere as to the principle of self-determination and the personality of non-self-governing peoples.[36] A belligerent community often represents a political movement aiming at independence and secession.

---

[30] See the Award in the *Delimitation of the Maritime Boundary between Guinea-Bissau and Senegal* (1989): *RIAA*, Vol. XX, 138–9, paras. 49–52.

[31] *Infra*, p. 77.

[32] See further *infra*, pp. 78–9.

[33] See further Chen, *The International Law of Recognition* (1951), 303ff.; and *infra*, pp. 86–93.

[34] *Yrbk. ILC* (1958), ii. 24, 32; and see 92 Hague *Recueil* (1957, II), 10. The draft articles on the law of treaties adopted by the Commission referred to 'States or other subjects of international law': ibid. (1962), ii. 161. This phrase was intended to cover the case of insurgents. The 1966 draft articles related simply to treaties concluded between states.

[35] See Kelsen, *Principles of International Law* (2nd edn., 1967), 252; McNair, *Law of Treaties* (1961), 676.

[36] *Supra*, pp. 59–60.

(f) Entities *sui generis*

Whilst due regard must be had to legal principle, the lawyer cannot afford to ignore entities which maintain some sort of existence on the international legal plane in spite of their anomalous character. Indeed, the role played by politically active entities such as belligerent communities indicates that, in the sphere of personality, effectiveness is an influential principle. Furthermore, as elsewhere in the law, provided that no rule of *jus cogens* is broken, acquiescence, recognition, and the incidence of voluntary bilateral relations can do much to obviate the more negative consequences of anomaly. Some of the special cases may be considered very briefly. In a Treaty and Concordat in 1929, Italy recognized 'the Sovereignty of the Holy See in the international domain' and its exclusive sovereignty and jurisdiction over the City of the Vatican.[37] A number of states recognize the Holy See, and have diplomatic relations with it and the Holy See has been a party to multilateral conventions, including those on the law of the sea concluded in 1958. Functionally, and in terms of its territorial and administrative organization, the Vatican City is proximate to a state. However, it has certain peculiarities. It has no population, apart from the resident functionaries, and its sole purpose is to support the Holy See as a religious entity. Some jurists regard the Vatican City as a state, although its special functions make this doubtful. However, it is widely recognized as a legal person with treaty-making capacity.[38] Its personality seems to rest partly on its approximation to a state in function, in spite of peculiarities, including the patrimonial sovereignty of the Holy See, and partly on acquiescence and recognition by existing legal persons. More difficult to solve is the question of the personality of the Holy See as a religious organ apart from its territorial base in the Vatican City.[39] It would seem that the personality of political and religious institutions of this type can only be relative to those states prepared to enter into relationships with such institutions on the international plane. Even in the sphere of recognition and bilateral relations, the legal capacities of institutions like the Sovereign Order of Jerusalem and Malta[40] must be limited simply because they lack the territorial and demographic characteristics of states. In the law of war the status of the Order mentioned is merely that of a 'relief society' within the meaning of the Prisoner of War Convention, 1949, Article 125.

[37] See Whiteman, i. 587–93; Kunz, 46 *AJ* (1952), 308–14, Rousseau, ii. 353–77; de la Brière, 63 Hague *Recueil* (1938, I), 371–464; Ehler, 104 Hague *Recueil* (1961, III), 5–63; Verzijl, *International Law in Historical Perspective*, ii. 295–302, 308–38; Crawford, *The Creation of States*, (2nd edn., 2006), 221–33.

[38] See Fitzmaurice, *Yrbk. ILC* (1956), ii. 107, 118; *State of the Vatican City* v. *Pieciukiewicz*, ILR 78, 120; *Re Marcinkus, Mennini and De Strebel*, ibid., 87, 48; *Holy See* v. *Starbright Sales*, ibid., 102, 163.

[39] For acceptance of such personality see Kelsen, *Principles of International Law* (2nd edn.), 251; Oppenheim, i. 21; Ehler, 104 Hague *Recueil* (1961, III), 5–63; Kunz, 46 *AJ* (1952), 308–14; Guggenheim, i. 214–16. The problem of personality divorced from territorial base is difficult to isolate because of the interaction of the Vatican City, the Holy See, and the Roman Catholic Church. See also Waldock, *Yrbk. ILC* (1962), ii. 32, 36.

[40] See Farran, 3 *ICLQ* (1954), 217–34; id., 4 *ICLQ* (1955), 308–9; Whiteman, i. 584–7; Guggenheim, i. 216 n. 3, 489 n. 3; *Nanni* v. *Pace and the Sovereign Order of Malta*, *Ann. Digest*, 8 (1935–7), no. 2; *Scarfò* v. *Sovereign Order of Malta*, ILR 24 (1957), 1; *Sovereign Order of Malta* v. *Soc. An. Commerciale*, ibid. 22 (1955), 1; *Piccoli* v. *Italian Knights of the Sovereign Order of Malta*, ibid., 77, 613; O'Connell, 48 *BY* (1976–7), 433–4; *Répertoire suisse*, i. 498–9. See also *Bacchelli* v. *Comune di Bologna*, ILR 77, 621.

Two other political animals require classification. 'Exile governments' may be accorded considerable powers within the territory of most states and be active in various political spheres. Apart from voluntary concessions by states and the use of 'exile governments' as agencies for illegal activities against lawfully established governments and states, the legal status of an 'exile government' is consequential on the legal condition of the community it claims to represent, which may be a state, belligerent community, or non-self-governing people. Prima facie its legal status will be established the more readily when its exclusion from the community of which it is an agency results from acts contrary to the *jus cogens*,[41] for example, an unlawful resort to force.[42] Lastly, the case of territory the title to which is undetermined, and which is inhabited and has an independent administration, creates problems. On the analogy of belligerent communities and special regimes not dependent on the existence of the sovereignty of a particular state (for example, internationalized territories and trust territories), communities existing on territory with such a status may be treated as having a modified personality, approximating to that of a state. On one view of the facts, this is the situation of Taiwan (Formosa). Since 1972 the United Kingdom has recognized the Government of the People's Republic of China as the sole Government of China and acknowledges the position of the Chinese Government that Taiwan is a province of China.[43] The question will arise whether Taiwan is a 'country' within particular legal contexts.[44]

(g) Individuals

There is no general rule that the individual cannot be a 'subject of international law', and in particular contexts he appears as a legal person on the international plane. At the same time to classify the individual as a 'subject' of the law is unhelpful, since this may seem to imply the existence of capacities which do not exist and does not avoid the task of distinguishing between the individual and other types of subject. The position of the individual in international law is considered at large in Chapter 25.

4. CONTROVERSIAL CANDIDATURES

Reference to states and similar political entities, to organizations, to non-self-governing peoples, and to individuals, does not exhaust the tally of agencies active on the

---

[41] On this concept see *infra*, ch. 23, s. 5.

[42] See Talmon, *Essays in Honour of Ian Brownlie*, 1999, 499–537.

[43] See the official statements reported in 57 *BY* (1986), 509, 512; 62 *BY* (1991), 568; 66 *BY* (1995), 618, 620–1. See also Crawford, *The Creation of States*, (2nd edn., 2006) 197–221. Cf. the status of the Portuguese enclaves in Indian territory after 1954, when the Portuguese administration was expelled by the population; *Right of Passage Case* (Merits), ICJ Reports (1960), 6 at 53 (Judge Spiropoulos), 87 (Judge Armand-Ugon). On the status of Trieste: *Società Teatro Puccini* v. *Commissioner-General*, ILR 40, 43, Italy, Council of State: the issue of sovereignty was finally settled by the Treaty of Osimo, in force 3 Apr. 1977, *Rivista di d.i.* 60, 674.

[44] See *Rogers* v. *Cheng Fu Sheng*, ILR 31, 349; *Reel* v. *Holder* [1981] 1 WLR 1226; ILR 74, 105, CA.

international scene. Thus corporations of municipal law, whether private or public corporations, engage in economic activity in one or more states other than the state under the law of which they were 'incorporated' or in which they have their economic seat. The resources available to the individual corporation may be greater than those of the smaller states, and they may have powerful diplomatic backing from governments. Such corporations can and do make agreements, including concession agreements, with foreign governments, and in this connection in particular, jurists have argued that the relations of states and foreign corporations *as such* should be treated on the international plane and not as an aspect of the normal rules governing the position of aliens and their assets on the territory of a state. In principle, corporations of municipal law do not have international legal personality. Thus a concession or contract between a state and a foreign corporation is not governed by the law of treaties.[45] The question will be pursued further in Chapter 24. However, in the present connection it must be pointed out that it will not always be easy to distinguish corporations which are so closely controlled by governments as to be state agencies, with or without some degree of autonomy, and private corporations not sharing the international law capacity of a state. It will be clear that the conferment of separate personality by a particular national law is not necessarily conclusive of autonomy *vis-à-vis* the state for purposes of international law. Thus ownership of shares may give a state a controlling interest in a 'private law corporation'.[46]

Important functions are performed today by bodies which have been grouped under the labels 'intergovernmental corporations of private law' and 'établissements publics internationaux'.[47] The point is that states may by treaty create legal persons the status of which is regulated by the national law of one or more of the parties. However, the treaty may contain obligations to create a privileged status within the national law or laws to which the corporation is subjected. The parties by their agreement may accord certain immunities to the institution created and confer on it various powers. Where the independence from the national laws of the parties is marked, then the body concerned may simply be a joint agency of the states involved, with delegated powers effective on the international plane and with a privileged position *vis-à-vis* local law in respect of its activities.[48] Where there is, in addition to independence from national law, a considerable quantum of delegated powers and the existence of organs with autonomy in decision and rule-making, then the body concerned has the characteristics of an international organization. It is when the institution created by treaty has a viability and

---

[45] See Waldock, *Yrbk. ILC* (1962), ii. 32; and cf. the *Anglo-Iranian Oil Company* case, ICJ Reports (1952), 93 at 112.

[46] See McNair, *Opinions* ii. 39.

[47] See Adam, *Les Organismes internationaux spécialisés*, 4 vols. (1965–77); Sørensen, 101 Hague *Recueil* (1960, III), 139–41; Friedmann, *The Changing Structure*, pp. 181–4, 219–20; Sereni, 96 Hague *Recueil* (1959, I), 169ff., Goldman, 90 *JDI* (1963), 321–89; Angelo, 125 Hague *Recueil* (1968, III), 482ff. Salmon, *Dictionnaire* (2001), 453, 1029.

[48] For examples of such joint agencies see *supra*, p. 65. The treaty concerned may result in legal personality in terms of the national law of the parties: see *Vigoureux v. Comité des Obligataires Danube-Save-Adriatique*, ILR 18 (1951), 1.

special function which render the description 'joint agency' inappropriate, and yet has powers and privileges primarily within the *national* legal systems and jurisdictions of the various parties, that it calls for use of a special category. An example of intergovernmental enterprise of this kind is Eurofima, a company set up by a treaty involving fourteen states in 1955, with the object of improving the resources of railway rolling stock. The treaty[49] established Eurofima as a corporation under Swiss law with modifications in that law provided for in the treaty. The parties agreed that they would recognize this (Swiss) private law status, as modified by the treaty, within their own legal systems. The corporation is international in function and the fourteen participating railway administrations provide the capital. The corporation is also given privileges on the international plane, including exemption from taxation in Switzerland, the state of domicile. However, useful as the category 'établissements publics internationaux' may be, it is not an instrument of exact analysis, and does not represent a distinct species of legal person on the international plane. This type of arrangement is the product of a careful interlocking of the national and international legal orders on a treaty basis, and the nature of the product will vary considerably from case to case.

5. SOME CONSEQUENCES

The content of the previous sections must serve as a warning against facile generalizations on the subject of legal personality. In view of the complex nature of international relations and the absence of a centralized law of corporations, it would be strange if the legal situation had an extreme simplicity. The number of entities with personality *for particular purposes* is considerable. Moreover, the tally of autonomous bodies increases if agencies of states and organizations, with a quantum of delegated powers, are taken into account. The listing of candidates for personality, the characters the reader will encounter, has a certain value, and yet such a procedure has some pitfalls. In the first place, a great deal depends on the relation of the particular entity to the various aspects of the substantive law. Thus the individual is in certain contexts regarded as a legal person, and yet it is obvious that he cannot make treaties. The *context* of problems remains paramount. Further, subject to the operations of the *jus cogens*, comprising certain fundamental principles,[50] the institutions of acquiescence and recognition have been active in sustaining anomalous relations. And finally, the intrusion of agency and representation has created problems, both of application and of principle. Thus it is not always easy to distinguish a dependent state with its own personality from a subordinate entity with no independence, a joint agency of states from an organization, or a private or public corporation under some degree of state control from the state itself.

---

[49] Conv. signed 20 Oct. 1955; 378 UNTS 159.
[50] See *infra*, ch. 23, s. 5.

4

INCIDENCE AND CONTINUITY
OF STATEHOOD

1. INTRODUCTION

The state is a type of legal person recognized by international law. Yet, since there are other types of legal person so recognized—as emerges from the previous chapter—the possession of legal personality is not in itself a sufficient mark of statehood. Moreover, the exercise of legal capacities is a normal consequence, rather than conclusive evidence, of legal personality: a puppet state may have all the paraphernalia of separate personality and yet be little more than an agency for another power. It is sometimes said that statehood is a question of fact, meaning that it is not a question of law. However, as lawyers are usually asking if an entity is a state with a specific legal claim or function in view, it is pointless to confuse issues of law with the difficulties, which undoubtedly exist, of applying the legal principles to the facts and of discovering the important facts in the first place. The criteria of statehood are laid down by the law. If it were not so, then statehood would produce the same type of structural defect that has been detected in certain types of doctrine concerning nationality.[1] In other words, a state would be able by its own unfettered discretion to contract out of duties owed to another state simply by refusing to characterize the obligee as a state. Thus a readiness to ignore the law may be disguised by a plea of freedom in relation to a key concept, determinant of many particular rights and duties, like statehood or nationality. In starting from this position it will be apparent that the writer has in part anticipated the results of the examination of recognition in the next chapter. Nevertheless, as a matter of presentation the question whether recognition by other states is an additional determinant will be ignored in the present chapter.[2] The subject of state succession is also excluded from the discussion, and the subject-matter conventionally described by that label is considered in Chapter 29. However, when the continuity of states is considered some attempt will be made to distinguish this from state succession.[3]

---

[1] See *infra*, ch. 19.

[2] Certain special aspects of recognition and its congener, acquiescence, are noticed *infra*, (2nd edn., 2006).

[3] See *infra*, pp. 80ff.

In general the importance of the subject-matter is not reflected by the quantity of useful literature.[4] Three factors have contributed to the creation of this state of affairs. First, though the subject is important as a matter of principle, the issue of statehood does not often raise long-standing disputes. In practice disputes concern the facts rather than the applicable legal criteria. Moreover, many disputes do not concern statehood *simpliciter*, but specialized claims, for example, to membership of the United Nations.[5] Secondly, the literature is often devoted to the broad concepts of the sovereignty and equality of states[6] and so gives prominence to the incidents of statehood rather than its origins and continuity. Finally, the political and legal nature of many complete rifts in relations between particular states is represented by non-recognition of *governments* rather than of states.[7]

2. LEGAL CRITERIA OF STATEHOOD

Article I of the Montevideo Convention on Rights and Duties of States[8] provides: 'The State as a person of international law should possess the following qualifications: (a) a permanent population; (b) a defined territory; (c) government; and (d) capacity to enter into relations with the other States.' This brief enumeration of criteria is often adopted in substance by jurists,[9] but it is no more than a basis for further investigation. As will be seen, not all the conditions are peremptory, and in any case further criteria must be employed to produce a working legal definition of statehood. The four criteria enumerated above, and other conditions proposed from time to time, will now be considered.

(a) Population

The Montevideo Convention refers to 'a permanent population'. This criterion is intended to be used in association with that of territory, and connotes a stable

---

[4] Generally see Crawford, 48 *BY* (1976–7), 93–182; id., *The Creation of States in International Law* (2nd ed. 2006); Higgins, *The Development of International Law through the Political Organs of the United Nations* (1963), 11–57; Rousseau, ii. 13–93, Whiteman, i. 221–33, 283–476; Guggenheim, 80 Hague *Recueil* (1952, I), 80–96; Marek, *Identity and Continuity of States* in *Public International Law* (1954); Fawcett, *The British Commonwealth in International Law* (1963), 88–143; Lauterpacht, *International Law: Collected Papers*, iii (1977), 5–25; Mouskhély, 66 *RGDIP* (1962), 469–85; *Yrbk. ILC* (1949), 37–8, 62ff., 289; Verzijl, *International Law in Historical Perspective*, ii (1969), 62–294, 339–500; Lissitzyn, 125 Hague *Recueil* (1968, III), 5–87; Arangio-Ruiz, *L'État dans le sens du droit des gens et la notion du droit international* (1975).

[5] On the various specialized claims see *infra*, p. 77.

[6] See generally *infra*, ch. 14.

[7] See *infra*, ch. 5, s. 5.

[8] Signed 26 Dec. 1933; Hudson, *Int. Legis.*, vi. 620.

[9] See, e.g. Fitzmaurice, 92 Hague *Recueil*, 13; Higgins, *Development*, p. 13; Fawcett, *The British Commonwealth in International Law*, p. 92. See further Jessup, as US representative in the Security Council, 2 Dec. 1948, quoted in Whiteman, i. 230.

community. Evidentially it is important, since in the absence of the physical basis for an organized community, it will be difficult to establish the existence of a state.

(b) Defined territory

There must be a reasonably stable political community and this must be in control of a certain area. It is clear from past practice that the existence of fully defined frontiers is not required and that what matters is the effective establishment of a political community.[10] In 1913 Albania was recognized by a number of states in spite of a lack of settled frontiers, and Israel was admitted to the United Nations in spite of disputes over her borders.

(c) Government

The shortest definition of a state for present purposes is perhaps a stable political community, supporting a legal order, in a certain area. The existence of effective government, with centralized administrative and legislative organs,[11] is the best evidence of a stable political community. However, the existence of effective government is in certain cases either unnecessary or insufficient to support statehood. Some states have arisen before government was very well organized, as, for example, Poland in 1919[12] and Burundi and Rwanda, admitted to membership of the United Nations at the seventeenth session of the General Assembly.[13] The principle of self-determination[14] will today be set against the concept of effective government, more particularly when the latter is used in arguments for continuation of colonial rule. The relevant question may now be: in whose interest and for what legal purpose is government 'effective'? Once a state has been established, extensive civil strife or the breakdown of order through foreign invasion or natural disasters are not considered to affect personality. Nor is effective government sufficient, since this leaves open the questions of independence and representation by other states to be discussed below.

(d) Independence

In the enumeration contained in the Montevideo Convention, the concept of independence is represented by the requirement of capacity to enter into relations with other states.[15] Independence has been stressed by many jurists as the decisive criterion of statehood.[16] Guggenheim[17] distinguishes the state from other legal orders by means

---

[10] See Jessup, in Whiteman, i. 230; *Deutsche Continental Gas-Gesellschaft* v. *Polish State, Ann. Digest,* 5 (1929–30), no. 5, p. 15; *North Sea Continental Shelf Cases,* ICJ Reports (1969), 3 at 32; *In re Duchy of Sealand,* ILR 80, 683. See further Arbitration Commission, Conference on Yugoslavia, *Opinion No. 1,* ILR 92, 162; id., *Opinion No. 10,* ibid., 206.

[11] See Guggenheim, 80 Hague *Recueil* (1952, I), 83; Higgins, *Development,* pp. 20–5.

[12] Briggs, p. 104. See also ibid. 108–13, 117–19, on the position in Albania 1913–24.

[13] Higgins, *Development,* p. 22.

[14] See further ch. 25, s. 14.

[15] See Jessup, in Whiteman, i. 230.

[16] See, in particular, Rousseau, ii. 68ff.; Marek, *Identity,* pp. 161–90.

[17] 80 Hague *Recueil* (1952, I), 83, 96. Cf. Rousseau, ii. 68ff.; and Marek, *Identity,* p. 168.

of two tests which he regards as quantitative rather than qualitative. First, the state has a degree of centralization of its organs not found in the world community. Secondly, in a particular area the state is the sole executive and legislative authority. In other words the state must be independent of other state legal orders, and any interference by such legal orders, or by an international agency, must be based on a title of international law.[18] In the normal case independence as a criterion may create few problems. However, there are sources of confusion. In the first place, independence may be used in close association with a requirement of effective government,[19] leading to the issues considered earlier. Again, since a state is, in part, a legal order, there is a temptation to rely solely on formal criteria. Certainly, if an entity has its own executive and other organs, conducts its foreign relations through its own organs, has its own system of courts and legal system and, particularly important, a nationality law of its own, then there is prima facie evidence of statehood. However, there is no justification for ignoring evidence of foreign control which is exercised *in fact* through the ostensibly independent machinery of state. The question is that of foreign *control* overbearing the decision-making of the entity concerned on a wide range of matters of high policy and doing so systematically and on a permanent basis. The practice of states has been to ignore—so far as the issue of *statehood* is concerned—various forms of political and economic blackmail and interference directed against the weaker members of the community. Whilst it is a matter of appreciation, there is a distinction between agency and control, on the one hand, and *ad hoc* interference and 'advice', on the other.

DEPENDENT STATES

Foreign control of the affairs of a state may occur under a title of international law, for example as a consequence of a treaty of protection,[20] or some other form of consent to agency or representation in external relations, or of a lawful war of collective defence and sanction leading to an occupation of the aggressor and imposition of measures designed to remove the sources of aggression. Allied occupation of Germany under the Berlin Declaration of 5 June 1945 is an example of the latter: supreme authority was assumed in Germany by the Allies jointly.[21] Providing that the representation and agency exist in fact and in law, then there is no formal difficulty in saying that the criterion of independence is satisfied. Unfortunately writers have created confusion by rehearsing independence as an aspect of statehood and then referring to 'dependent

---

[18] Cf. ch. 16.

[19] In the *Aaland Islands* case (1920) the committee of jurists referred to the disorder existing in Finland and observed: 'It is therefore difficult to say at what exact date the Finnish Republic in the legal sense of the term actually became a definitely constituted sovereign State. This certainly did not take place until a stable political organization had been created, and until the public authorities had become strong enough to assert themselves throughout the territories of the State without the assistance of foreign troops'. (*LNOJ* (1920), Spec. Suppl. no. 3, p. 3.) This standard would have embarrassing consequences if widely applied.

[20] On the possible effect of the *jus cogens* on such treaties see ch. 23, s. 5.

[21] The occupation was not a belligerent occupation, nor was there a *debellatio* leading to extinction of Germany as a state: see Jennings, 23 *BY* (1946), 112–41.

states', which are presented as an anomalous category.[22] Here the incidents of personality are not sufficiently distinguished from its existence. The term 'dependent' is used to indicate the existence of one or more of the following distinct situations:

1. the absence of statehood, where the entity concerned is subordinated to a state so completely as to be within its control and the origin of the subordination does not establish agency or representation;

2. a state which has made concessions to another state in matters of jurisdiction and administration to such an extent that it has in some sense ceased to be sovereign;[23]

3. a state which has legally conferred wide powers of agency and representation in foreign affairs on another state;[24]

4. a state, which in fact suffers interference from another state and may be a 'client' state politically, but which quantitatively is not under the complete and permanent control of the 'patron';

5. a legal person of a special type, appearing on the international plane for certain purposes only, as in the case of mandated and trust territories and some protectorates;[25]

6. a state which fails to qualify as an 'independent' state for the purposes of a particular instrument.

The category of independence (or sovereignty used synonymously) can only be applied concretely in the light of the legal purpose with which the inquiry is made and the particular facts. In the *Austro-German Customs Union* case[26] the Permanent Court gave an advisory opinion on the question whether the proposed customs union was contrary to the obligations of Austria under a Protocol of 1922 'not to alienate its independence' and to 'abstain from any negotiations or from any economic and financial engagement calculated directly or indirectly to compromise this independence'. By a majority of eight to seven the Court held that the customs regime contemplated would be incompatible with these obligations. Here the term 'independence' referred to a specialized notion of economic relations in a treaty, and the obligations were not confined to abstention from actual and complete alienation of independence. In the case of the *Tunis and Morocco Nationality Decrees*[27] the Permanent Court emphasized that protectorates have 'individual legal characteristics resulting from the special conditions

[22] See Hall, *International Law* (8th edn., 1924), 18, 20, 33; Oppenheim, pp. 118–19 ('sovereignty' used as a synonym for 'independence').

[23] On the former legal position of Kuwait: Whiteman, i. 442–6.

[24] This may occur without subordination. Since 1919 by agreement the Swiss Federal Council has conducted the diplomatic relations of Liechtenstein.

[25] e.g. areas autonomous to some degree according to municipal law whose autonomy is placed under international guarantee.

[26] (1931), PCIJ, Ser. A/B, no. 41; World Court Reports, ii. 713.

[27] (1923), PCIJ, Ser. B, no. 4, p. 27; World Court Reports, i. 145.

under which they were created, and the stage of their development'. A protected state may provide an example of international representation which leaves the personality and statehood of the entity represented intact, though from the point of view of the *incidents* of personality the entity may be 'dependent' in one or more of the senses noted above. In the case of *U.S. Nationals in Morocco*[28] the International Court, referring to the Treaty of Fez in 1912, and the creation of a French protectorate, stated: 'Under this Treaty, Morocco remained a sovereign State but it made an arrangement of contractual character whereby France undertook to exercise certain sovereign powers in the name and on behalf of Morocco, and, in principle, all of the international relations of Morocco'. It should be pointed out that a common opinion is that the evidence supported the view that the relation was one of subordination and not agency.

It is sometimes said that international responsibility is a necessary correlative or criterion of independence.[29] Broadly this is true, but the principle must be qualified when a case of international representation arises and the 'protecting' state is the only available defendant.[30]

FEDERATIONS

The federal state as such has indisputable legal personality, and it is the status of the constituent states which creates problems. A federal constitution may confer treaty-making capacity and a power to enter into separate diplomatic relations on the constituent members. In the normal case, the constituent state is simply acting as a delegate or agent of the parent state.[31] However, by agreement or recognition, a federated state may assume a separate personality, as an analogue of statehood, on the international plane. Thus the Ukrainian SSR and Belorussian SSR, as members of the former Union of Soviet Socialist Republics, concluded treaties on their own behalf and were members of the United Nations.[32]

ASSOCIATIONS OF STATES

Independent states may enter into forms of co-operation by consent and on an equal basis. The basis for the co-operation may be the constitution of an international organization, such as the United Nations or the World Health Organization. However,

---

[28] ICJ Reports (1952), 176 at 188. See also Guggenheim, 80 Hague *Recueil* (1952, I), 96. Cf. the separate but dependent personality of India 1919–47; on which see McNair, *Law of Treaties* (1938), 76; Poulouse, 44 *BY* (1970), 201–12; and the opinion of Judge Moreno Quintana, ICJ Reports (1960), 95. Cf. also the position of Monaco in relation to France. On the status of Hungary after German occupation in 1944 see *Effects of Jews Deported from Hungary* case, ILR 44, 301 at 334–42 and on the status of the creation called Croatia in Yugoslavia during the German occupation see *Socony Vacuum Oil Company Claim*, ILR 21, 55 at 58–62.

[29] See Rousseau, 73 Hague *Recueil* (1948, II), 250; Marek, *Identity*, p. 189.

[30] On agency and joint tortfeasors see *infra*, pp. 456–8.

[31] See Fitzmaurice, *Yrbk. ILC* (1956), ii. 118; Reuter, *Mélanges offerts à Charles Rousseau* (1974), 199–218; Rousseau, ii. 138–213, 264–8; and *supra*, p. 64. Cf. Lauterpacht, *Yrbk. ILC* (1953), ii. 95, 137–9.

[32] See Dolan, 4 *ICLQ* (1955), 629–36; Rousseau, ii. 264–8.

by treaty or custom other structures for maintaining co-operation may be created. One such structure, the confederation, has in practice either disintegrated or been transformed into a federation. In recent times the British Commonwealth of Nations[33] and the French Community[34] have provided examples of associations of states of a special type. Membership of these two associations would not necessarily affect the primary legal capacities and personality of member states any more than membership of an organization and has less effect than membership of some organizations, for example, the European Union, which has a certain federal element, albeit on a treaty basis. However, the French Community accommodated a variety of relations, some more intimate than others.

(e) A degree of permanence[35]

If one relies principally on the concept of a stable political community, it might seem superfluous to stipulate for a degree of permanence. Time is an element of statehood, as is space. However, *permanence* is not necessary to the existence of a state as a legal order, and a state which has only a very brief life may nevertheless leave an agenda of consequential legal questions on its extinction.[36]

(f) Willingness to observe international law

In modern literature, this is not often mentioned as a criterion,[37] and it has been subjected to trenchant criticism.[38] The delictual and other responsibilities of states are consequences of statehood, and logically it is inexcusable to express as a criterion of statehood a condition which the entity has a capacity to accept only if it is a state.

(g) A certain degree of civilization

Hyde[39] states four qualifications for statehood (the first four above), but adds a fifth: 'the inhabitants must have attained a degree of civilization, such as to enable them to observe...those principles of law which are deemed to govern the members of the international society in their relations with each other'. This has a similarity to the last point considered, but is more fundamental. However, it is usually omitted from enumerations of criteria and is redolent of the period when non-European states were not accorded equal treatment by the European Concert and the United States. In modern law it is impossible to regard a tribal society which refuses to conduct diplomatic relations with other societies as a *res nullius*.

[33] See Fawcett, *The British Commonwealth in International Law*, esp. at pp. 144–94 (on the *Inter Se* Doctrine); Whiteman, i. 476–544; Rousseau, ii. 214–64.

[34] See Whiteman, i. 544–82.

[35] See Kelsen, *Principles of International Law* (2nd edn.), 381–3; Chen, *The International Law of Recognition*, pp. 59–60.

[36] Cf. the anti-Jewish legislation of the Italian Social Republic of Sálo: see the *Mosse* claim, ILR 20 (1953), 217; *Levi* claim, ibid. 24 (1957), 303; *Sonnino* claim, ibid. 647; *Wollemborg* claim, ibid. 654. British Somaliland became independent on 26 June 1960, but united with Somalia to form the Somali Republic on 1 July 1960.

[37] References: Chen, *The International Law of Recognition*, p. 61.

[38] See Chen, *The International Law of Recognition*, p. 61.

[39] i. 23 (and see Chen, *The International Law of Recognition*, pp. 127–9). See also Whiteman, i. 223.

(h) Sovereignty[40]

The term 'sovereignty' may be used as a synonym for independence, an important element in statehood considered already. However, a common source of confusion lies in the fact that 'sovereignty' may be used to describe the condition where a state has not exercised its own legal capacities in such a way as to create rights, powers, privileges, and immunities in respect of other states.[41] In this sense a state which has consented to another state managing its foreign relations, or which has granted extensive extra-territorial rights to another state, is not 'sovereign'. If this or a similar content is given to 'sovereignty' and the same ideogram is used as a criterion of statehood,[42] then the *incidents* of statehood and legal personality are once again confused with their existence. Thus the condition of Germany after 1945 involved considerable diminution of German sovereignty in this sense, and yet Germany continued to exist as a state.[43] Considerations of this sort have led some jurists to reject sovereignty as a criterion.[44] An alternative approach is that of the International Court in the case of *U.S. Nationals in Morocco*, where the Judgment described Morocco as a 'sovereign State', meaning that it had maintained its basic personality in spite of the French protectorate.[45] But it would be possible for a tribunal to hold that a state which had granted away piecemeal a high proportion of its legal powers had ceased to have a separate existence as a consequence. Obviously it may in law and fact be difficult to distinguish granting away of capacities and the existence of agency or representation.

(i) Function as a state

There remain some peripheral problems. Experience has shown that entities may exist which are difficult to regard as states in the political sense. The treaty of peace with Germany in 1919 created the Free City of Danzig, which had the legal marks of statehood in spite of the fact that it was placed under the guarantee of the League of Nations and Poland had the power to conduct its foreign relations.[46] The peace treaty with Italy in 1947 provided for the creation of the Free Territory of Trieste, which was to be placed under the protection of the Security Council.[47] The type of legal personality involved in these two cases is a congener of statehood, and it is the specialized political function of such entities, and their relation to an organization, which inhibits use of the category of statehood.[48]

---

[40] See generally *infra*, ch. 14.

[41] See *infra*, ch. 16.

[42] See Oppenheim, i. 118–19; Alfaro, 97 Hague *Recueil* (1959, II), 95–6.

[43] *Supra*, pp. 78–9.

[44] See Rousseau, 73 Hague *Recueil* (1948, II), 178ff. Cf. the dissenting judges in the *Austro-German Customs Union* case, PCIJ, Ser. A/B, no. 41 at p. 77; and Viscount Finlay in *Duff Development Co.* v. *Government of Kelantan* [1924] AC 747 at 814. See further Fawcett, *The British Commonwealth in International Law*, pp. 88–93; and the case concerning the *Lighthouses in Crete and Samos*, for which see *infra*, p. 115.

[45] *Supra*, pp. 73–4. See also Rolin, 77 Hague *Recueil* (1950, II), 326.

[46] *Supra*, p. 60. However, disputes between Danzig and Poland were referred to the Permanent Court of International Justice by means of its advisory jurisdiction in view of Art. 34 of the Statute of the Court, which gives *locus standi* in contentious cases only to states.

[47] *Supra*, p. 60.

[48] On the status of other entities *sui generis* see *supra*, pp. 64–5.

3. STATES *IN STATU NASCENDI*

A political community with considerable viability, controlling a certain area of territory and having statehood as its objective, may go through a period of travail before that objective has been achieved. In any case, since matters such as definition of frontiers and effective government are not looked at too strictly, the distinction between *status nascendi* and statehood cannot be very readily upheld.[49] States not infrequently first appear as independent belligerent entities under a political authority which may be called, and function effectively as, a provisional government. The influence of considerations of *jus cogens*, such as the principle of self-determination, on the status of belligerent entities is examined subsequently.[50] Apart from these considerations, once statehood is firmly established, it is justifiable, both legally and practically, to assume the retroactive validation of the legal order during a period prior to general recognition as a state, when some degree of effective government existed. Leaving questions of state succession on one side,[51] the principle of effectiveness dictates acceptance, for some legal purposes at least, of continuity before and after statehood is firmly established.[52] The legal consequences accorded by governments and foreign courts to the acts of governments recognized *de facto*[53] provide evidence for the views expressed above.

In exceptional circumstances, a people may be recognized by the international community, and by interested parties, as having an *entitlement* to statehood, and thus as being a state *in statu nascendi*. Normally, this transitional status leads, without too much delay, to independence under the auspices of the United Nations. However, in the case of the Palestinian people, there has been an eccentric bilateral process in which the question of statehood has been in issue between the Government of Israel and the PLO.[54] The agenda has, since 1993, included 'the permanent status negotiations', which were (it was assumed) to lead to an independent Palestinian State. Article I of the Washington Agreement of 1993[55] provides as follows:

The aim of the Israeli-Palestinian negotiations within the current Middle East peace process is, among other things, to establish a Palestinian Interim Self-Government Authority, the elected Council (the 'Council'), for the Palestinian people in the West Bank and the Gaza Strip, for a transitional period not exceeding five years, leading to a permanent settlement based on Security Council Resolutions 242 and 338.

---

[49] Cf. the cases of Albania in 1913; Poland and Czechoslovakia in 1917–18; Estonia, Latvia, and Lithuania, 1918–20. See Hackworth, i. 199–222. See also the case of Indonesia, 1946–9: Whiteman, ii. 165–7. Cf. the observations of Lord Finlay, *German Interests in Polish Upper Silesia* (Merits), PCIJ, Ser. A, no. 7 (1926), p. 84.

[50] *Infra*, pp. 510–12.

[51] See ch. 29.

[52] See *Ann. Digest*, 1 (1919–22), nos. 4–7, 24; ibid. 2 (1923–4), nos. 2, 122; ibid. 3 (1925–6), nos. 8, 9; ibid. 4 (1927–8), nos. 11, 94, 220: ibid. 5 (1929–30), no. 5.

[53] See *infra*, pp. 90–1. See, in particular, the *Gagara* [1919] p. 65.

[54] See Cassese, *Self-determination of peoples: A Legal Appraisal* (1995) 230–48; Shehadeh, *From Occupation to Interim Accords* (1997); Crawford, *Essays in Honour of Ian Brownlie* (1999), 95–124.

[55] *ILM* 32 (1993), 1525; Malanczuk, *Europ. Journ.*, 7 (1996), 485–500; Benvenisti, *Europ. Journ.*, 4 (1993), 542–54; Shehadeh, ibid., 555–63; Cassese, ibid., 564–71.

It is understood that the interim arrangements are an integral part of the whole peace process and that the negotiations on the permanent status will lead to the implementation of Security Council Resolutions 242 and 338.

Resolution 242 (1967) provides for the 'withdrawal of Israeli armed forces from territories occupied in the recent conflict' and Resolution 338 (1973) calls upon the parties concerned to begin the process of implementation of Resolution 242 (1967).

4. ILLEGAL OCCUPATION AND THE INFLUENCE OF *JUS COGENS*

Earlier it was stated that a state remains 'independent', in the sense of retaining separate personality, if a foreign legal order impinges on it, provided that the impingement occurs under a title of international law. It follows that illegal occupation cannot of itself terminate statehood.[56,57] Elsewhere[58] the general question of balancing effectiveness and the principle *ex injuria non oritur jus* is considered. Here it must suffice to point out that, when elements of certain strong norms (the *jus cogens*[59]) are involved, it is less likely that recognition and acquiescence will offset the original illegality. These issues will receive discussion when the identity and continuity of states are considered subsequently. One aspect of *jus cogens*, the principle of self-determination,[60] may justify the granting of a higher status to certain types of belligerent entities and exile governments than would otherwise be the case.[61]

5. NECESSARY LEGAL CONSTRUCTIONS

Political circumstances may lead to legal constructions which at first sight are excessively formalistic. A state's legal order may be projected on the plane of time for certain purposes although its physical and political existence has ceased. One view of the

---

[56] See Crawford, 48 *BY* (1976–7), 144–8, 173–6; Marek, *Identity*, pp. 553–87. Belligerent occupation clearly does not affect statehood: the occupant *ex hypothesi* does not displace the territorial sovereign though the *incidents* of statehood are affected. It is not correct to describe governments-in-exile as states without people or territory when the displacement is caused by a belligerent occupation (cf. Briggs, p. 66). Puppet states, such as Slovakia and Croatia, set up as a consequence of illegal threat or use of force in 1939 and 1941 respectively, received recognition from very few states. On the status of Burma in the Second World War see *Chettiar* v. *Chettiar, Ann. Digest*, 15 (1948), no. 178.

[57] On the Iraqi annexation of Kuwait in 1990 see *Kuwait Airways Corporation* v. *Iraqi Airways Company and the Republic of Iraq*, ILR 116, 535; *BYIL*, 71 (2000), 408 (CA).

[58] *Infra*, ch. 23.

[59] See *infra*, pp. 510–12.

[60] See ch. 25, s. 14.

[61] See Crawford 48 *BY* (1976–7), 144–73.

situation in Germany since 1945 is as follows. Subject to certain powers under the Berlin Declaration and the unconditional surrender, two German states existed. The German Federal Republic rested on a constitution of 1949 and certain agreements. The German Democratic Republic rested on a constitution of 1949 and an agreement with the USSR.[62] In the Moscow Treaty of 1990[63] it was provided that the newly united Germany (including the former German Democratic Republic and Berlin) was henceforth no longer subject to the quadripartite agreements of the former occupying powers. In this way the Germany which had surrendered in 1945 was finally wound up. In the *South-West Africa* cases[64] it was suggested by Judges Spender and Fitzmaurice in their joint dissenting opinion[65] that the principal Allied and associated powers of the First World War might retain a residual or reversionary interest in the ex-German territories placed under mandate. The five principal powers concerned were the United States,[66] the British Empire, France, Italy, and Japan, and, while they still exist as legal persons, their special capacity as principal Allied powers in 1919 may be projected on the plane of time.

6. MEMBERSHIP OF INTERNATIONAL ORGANIZATIONS AND AGENCIES

Membership in an international organization depends on the contractual terms arranged by the founding states. However, accession to membership may not be on the basis of right, by acceptance of a standing offer. Usually a leading organ of the institution will alone have competence to decide on qualifications for membership, and in practice political criteria may supplement the legal conditions laid down in a constituent instrument. These conditions will normally specify or assume the existence of statehood and may then refer to additional qualities.[67] Thus Article 4 of the United Nations Charter provides that membership of the organization 'is open to all peace-loving States which accept the obligations contained in the present Charter and, in the judgment of the Organization, are able and willing to carry out these obligations'. Admission to membership is to be by decision of the General Assembly upon the recommendation of the Security Council.[68]

---

[62] The situation was complicated by the fact that the German Federal Republic claims to be the successor to all German territory within the frontiers of 1937.

[63] 29 *ILM* (1990), p. 1186. See also Piotrowicz, 63 *BY* (1992), 367–414; *Re Treaty on the Basis of Relations*, ILR 78, 149; *Eastern Treaties Case*, ibid., 176.

[64] ICJ Reports (1962), 319.

[65] At pp. 482 (note), 486.

[66] The United States concluded a separate peace treaty in 1921: 16 *AJ* (1922), Suppl., p. 10.

[67] See Higgins, *Development*, pp. 11–57; and Fawcett, *The British Commonwealth in International Law*, pp. 223–39. On the concept of functional membership of organizations, see *infra*, ch. 31, s. 6.

[68] See the *Admission* case, ICJ Reports (1947–8), 63; Lauterpacht, *The Development of International Law by the International Court* (1958), 148–52; Rosenne, 39 *BY* (1963), 1 at 40–1.

7. IDENTITY AND CONTINUITY OF STATES[69]

The term 'continuity' of States is not employed with any precision, and may be used to preface a diversity of legal problems. Thus it may introduce the proposition that the legal rights and responsibility of states are not affected by changes in the head of state or the internal form of government.[70] This proposition can, of course, be maintained without reference to a concept of 'continuity' or 'succession', and it is in any case too general, since political changes may result in a change of circumstances sufficient to affect particular types of treaty relation.[71] More significantly, legal doctrine tends to distinguish between continuity (and identity) and state succession. The latter arises when one international personality takes the place of another, for example by union or lawful annexation. In general, it is assumed that cases of 'state succession'[72] are likely to involve important changes in the legal status and rights of the entities concerned, whereas if there is continuity, the legal personality and the particular rights and duties of the state remain unaltered.

Unfortunately the general categories of 'continuity' and 'state succession', and the assumption of a neat distinction between them, only make a difficult subject more confused by masking the variations of circumstance and the complexities of the legal problems which arise in practice. 'Succession' and 'continuity' are levels of abstraction unfitted to dealing with specific issues. Thus the view that Italy was formed not by union of other states with Sardinia, but by annexation to Sardinia, has the corollary that this was a case of continuity and not, with respect to Sardinia, a state succession.[73] Yet one may wonder if the difference in political procedure should make such a great legal difference. Further, political and legal experience provide several examples of situations in which there is 'continuity', but the precise circumstances, and the relevant principles of law and good policy, dictate solutions which are only partly conditioned by the element of 'continuity'. Legal techniques may well entail relying on continuity in one context, but denying its existence in another. Thus the political and legal transformation involved in destroying the Austro-Hungarian monarchy and establishing

---

[69] See, in particular, Whiteman, ii. 754–99; Kelsen, *Principles of International Law* (2nd edn.), 383–7; Marek, *Identity*; Clute, *The International Legal Status of Austria 1938–55* (1962); O'Connell, *State Succession in Municipal Law and International Law*, 2 vols. (1967) (particular states in Index); Kunz, 49 *AJ* (1955), 68–76; Crawford, *The Creation of States*, (2nd edn.,2006), 667–99; Rousseau, iii. 330–6; Green, in Keeton (ed.), *Law, Justice and Equity* (1967), 152–67, on dissolution of states and membership of the League of Nations and the United Nations.

[70] See McNair, *Opinions*, i. 3; Hackworth, i. 387–92; *Tinoco Concessions* arbitration (1923), *RIAA*, i. 369.

[71] See ch. 27, s. 6. A treaty of military and political co-operation may be invalidated if one party undergoes a change of regime inimical to the basis of the treaty.

[72] See *infra*, ch. 29. There is no single legal criterion for distinguishing partial and total succession of states (the latter involving change of personality).

[73] Marek, *Identity*, pp. 191–8. See also Guggenheim, i. 444–5; O'Connell, *State Succession*, i. 5; ii. 28–30, 365.

a new political settlement in central and south-east Europe produced Austria,[74] the Serb-Croat-Slovene state,[75] and Czechoslovakia,[76] which rested on new political and legal orders. Nevertheless for certain purposes principles of continuity with previous political entities were applied by state practice in these cases.

The functional approach has been prominent in a group of cases arising from the unlawful use of force. Ethiopia was conquered and annexed by Italy in 1936. Many states gave *de jure* or *de facto* recognition to Italian control, but Ethiopia remained formally a member of the League of Nations. After the outbreak of the Second World War the United Kingdom and other states treated Ethiopia, after liberation in 1941, as independent and cobelligerent.[77] Czechoslovakia was placed under German control in March 1939 as a result of the use and threat of force. *De jure* recognition was generally withheld in this case, and by 1941 an exile government was accepted by the Allies as a cobelligerent.[78] Albania was placed under Italian occupation in 1939 and was liberated in 1944.[79] Rather more difficult, since the community welcomed absorption, was the case of the Austrian Anschluss in 1938. Many states regarded this as illegal, and Austria was not regarded as responsible for her part in Axis aggression.[80] In all these cases foreign control can be ignored on the ground that its source was illegal: *ex injuria non oritur jus*. However, neither this principle nor that of continuity can provide an omnibus solution to the legal problems arising for solution after 1945. In all these cases, for slightly differing reasons, the occupation in fact and form went beyond belligerent occupation, since there was either absorption outright or the setting up of puppet regimes. Moreover, the control lasted for some time, and insistence on continuity is theoretical in these cases: what occurred on liberation was restoration, re-establishment of the former state. This is qualified continuity. Thus, in the case of Austria after 1945 state practice, including that of Austria, has supported the position that Austria is

[74] The Treaty of St Germain assumed continuity. State practice apart from this treaty favoured continuity in the matter of treaties. In respect of public debts and other matters, principles were applied indistinguishable from those related normally to 'state succession', i.e. continuity of obligation with modifications. See O'Connell, *State Succession*, index; Guggenheim, i. 444–5; Marek, *Identity*, pp. 199–236 (who uses the category of continuity too dogmatically); Kelsen, *Principles of International Law* (2nd edn.), 384.

[75] See O'Connell, *State Succession*, i. 5, 6; Marek, *Identity*, pp. 237–62; *Katz and Klump v. Yugoslavia*, Ann. *Digest*, 3 (1925–6), no. 24; *Ivanevic v. Artukovic*, ILR 21 (1954), 66.

[76] See O'Connell, *State Succession*, indices.

[77] See Marek, *Identity*, pp. 263–82; O'Connell, *State Succession*, index; *Azazh Kebbeda Tesema v. Italian Government*, Ann. *Digest*, 9 (1938–40), no. 36; UK-Ethiopia, Agreement of 31 Jan. 1942; Cmd. 6334; Peace Treaty with Italy, 1947, s. VII (cf. Fitzmaurice, 73 Hague *Recueil* (1948, II), 282).

[78] See Marek, *Identity*, pp. 283–330; *Hardtmuth v. Hardtmuth*, ILR 26 (1958, II), 40.

[79] See Marek, *Identity*, pp. 331–7; Peace Treaty with Italy, 1947, s. VI (cf. Fitzmaurice, 73 Hague *Recueil* (1948, II), 282).

[80] See Marek, *Identity*, pp. 338–68; Clute, *International Legal Status of Austria*; Guggenheim, ii. 470; *Security for Costs (Austria)* case, ILR 22 (1955), 58; *Republic of Austria v. City of Vienna*, ibid. 26 (1958, II), 77; *Schleiffer v. Directorate of Finance*, ibid. 609. The Austrian State Treaty of 1955 (text: 49 *AJ* (1955), Suppl., p. 162) is consonant with the view that Austria was re-established. See also n. 81 *infra*. Cf. *In re Mangold's Patent*, ILR 18 (1951), no. 59; 28 *BY* (1951), 406.

bound by pre-1938 treaties to which she was a party. Germany has been held respon-sible by the Allies for the payment of the bonded external debt of Austria for the period 1939–45: Austrian courts have not accepted succession in the public foreign debt from this period except where the principle of unjust enrichment required a different approach. Austria has accepted responsibility for the pre-Anschluss exter-nal debt. Nationality problems affecting Austria and Czechoslovakia show very clearly the need to approach issues free from the tyranny of concepts. After 1945 the government of these two states did not revoke the nationality law of the usurp-ing German administration retroactively. The law of the German Federal Republic allowed those who became German as a result of the Anschluss to maintain German nationality if since 1945 they had permanently resided on German territory (fron-tiers of 1937).[81]

The United Kingdom did not recognize the Iraqi occupation or control over the ter-ritory of Kuwait following the illegal Iraqi invasion in 1990. This policy was explicitly based upon the pertinent Security Council resolutions which called on all States not to recognize the regime set up by the occupying power.[82]

The political developments in Eastern Europe in the period 1990 to 1992 pro-duced some legal junctures involving the distinction between cases of secession, involving the 'core State' as a successor to the previous federal union, and cases of dissolution, involving no State succession on the part of the 'core State'. Thus British practice accepted that the Russian Federation was the successor to the former Soviet Union.[83] Paradoxically, perhaps, the surviving Federal Republic of Yugoslavia was not accepted as the continuation of the old Yugoslavia.[84] The treatment of the tran-sitions concerning Yugoslavia in the General Assembly resulted in marked differ-ences of opinion within the International Court in the *Case Concerning Legality of the Use of Force*.[85] In some instances, where the basis for continuity is tenuous, estoppel, special agreement, and principles of validation and effectiveness may provide elements of legal continuity. Lastly, the operation of the principle of self-determination as a part of the *jus cogens* may support a doctrine of reversion: for example, rights of way granted by a colonial power may not be opposable to the state which, in replacing the colonial power, is recovering an independence which it formerly had.[86]

---

[81] See Brownlie, 39 *BY* (1963), 326, 346; and the *Austrian Nationality* case, ILR 22 (1955), 430.

[82] See S.C. Resolution 662 (1990), adopted on 6 August 1990; see also the FCO letter to the Court in the *Kuwait Airways Corporation* case: *BYIL*, 68 (1997), 519. Cp. *Kuwait Airways Corporation* v. *Iraqi Airways Company and the Republic of Iraq*, ILR 116, 535 at 580–1.

[83] See 63 *BY* (1992), 639, 652, 653–5.

[84] See ibid., 636–7, 655–8. See also the Conference on Yugoslavia, Arbitration Commission, *Opinion No. 8*, ILR 92, 199; *Opinion No. 10*, ibid., 206.

[85] Judgment of 15 December 2004; ICJ Reports, 2004, 279 (Serbia and Montenegro v. Belgium).

[86] See the Diss. Op. of Judge Moreno Quintana in the *Right of Passage* case, ICJ Reports (1960), 95–6. The majority of the Court did not deal with this issue; on the evidence the passage had been maintained for some years after the British left India.

8. MICRO-STATES[87]

Membership of the United Nations is not expressed to be conditioned by the size[88] of the state concerned. However, Article 4 of the United Nations Charter makes an ability to carry out the obligations contained in the Charter a requirement of admission to membership and San Marino, Monaco, and Liechtenstein (among others) have not applied for membership. Nonetheless, however small geographically or modest in resources, an entity is a 'state' for general purposes of international law provided the criteria of statehood are satisfied. Thus the very small polities have become parties to the Statute of the International Court of Justice.

Since its early days quite small nations have been admitted to membership of the United Nations. Costa Rica, Luxembourg, and Iceland provide examples.[89] In recent years the increase in total membership and the modest size of some of the applicants for admission has caused United Nations organs to consider the possibility of establishing some form of associate membership of the United Nations. Such a regime might involve ineligibility for seats on the Security Council, the right to participate in General Assembly proceedings without a vote, favourable terms for contributions to expenses of the United Nations, and access to the resources of the specialized agencies, such as the World Health Organization. There are many problems to be faced, not least that of establishing criteria for ordinary membership.

[87] Other terms are 'diminutive' or 'mini-' states. See generally: UNITAR, *Status and Problems of Very Small States and Territories* (1969); Saint-Girons, 76 *RGDIP* (1972), 445–74; Rapoport, *ASIL Proceedings* (1968), 155–63; Fisher, ibid. 164–70; Harris, *Columbia Journ. Trans. Law* (1970), 23–53; Rousseau, ii. 329–47; Mendelson, 21 *ICLQ* (1972), 609–30; Schwebel, 67 *AJ* (1973), 108–16; Gunter, 71 *AJ* (1977), 110–24; Crawford, *The Creation of States*, (2nd edn., 2006), 182–6; Bernhardt, *Encyclopedia*, III (1997), 362–4.

On comparable issues within the British Commonwealth see Fawcett, Ann. Survey of Commonwealth Law (1967), 709–11; ibid. (1968), 785–8; ibid. (1969), 558–9; Broderick, 17 ICLQ (1968), 368–403.

[88] The most common indicator used is population, as opposed to geographical area, gross national product, etc.

[89] More recent examples: the Maldive Islands, Bhutan, Comoros, Cape Verde, Samoa, Grenada, and Sao Tomé and Principe. Western Samoa and Nauru have not applied to join the UN.

5

RECOGNITION OF STATES AND GOVERNMENTS[1]

1. RECOGNITION AS A GENERAL CATEGORY

Whenever a state acts in a way which may or does affect the legal rights or political interests of other states, the question arises of the legal significance of the reaction of other states to the event. In the *Eastern Greenland* case[2] it was held that Norway had, as a consequence of the declaration of her Foreign Minister, accepted Danish title to the disputed territory. There the acceptance by Norway of Denmark's claim was by informal agreement: in many instances formal treaty provisions will involve recognition of rights. However, apart from agreement, legally significant reaction may occur in the form of unilateral acts or conduct, involving estoppel, recognition, or acquiescence.[3] Frequently acts of states which are not within their legal competence will meet with protest from other states. Illegal acts are not in principle opposable to other states in any case, and protest is not a condition of the illegality. Conversely, a valid claim to territory is not conditioned as to its validity by the acceptance of the claim by the defending state. However, acts of protest and recognition play a subsidiary but, in practice, not insubstantial role in the resolution of disputes. Protest and recognition by other states may provide good evidence of the state of the law on the issues involved. Furthermore, there is a spectrum of issues involving areas of uncertainty in the law, novel and potentially law-changing claims (cf. the development of claims to resources

---

[1] State practice and other materials: Whiteman, ii. 1–746; Hackworth, i. 161–387; Moore, *Digest*, i. 67–248. Other literature: Chen, *The International Law of Recognition* (1951); Lauterpacht, *Recognition in International Law* (1947); id., *International Law: Collected Papers*, i (1970), 308–48; Brown, 44 *AJ* (1950), 617–40; Kelsen, *Principles of International Law* (2nd edn., 1967), 387–416; Fitzmaurice, 92 Hague *Recueil* (1957, II), 16–35; Jessup, *A Modern Law of Nations* (1948), 43–67; Jennings, 121 Hague *Recueil* (1967, II), 349–68; Mugerwa, in Sørensen, pp. 266–90; Verhoeven, *La Reconnaissance internationale dans la pratique contemporaine* (1975); Blix, 130 Hague *Recueil* (1970, II), 587–704; Crawford, 48 *BYIL* (1976–7), 93–107; Salmon, *La Reconnaissance d'état* (1971); Rousseau, iii. 513–611; Brownlie, 53 *BY* (1982), 197–211; Crawford, *The Creation of States in International Law* (2nd edn., 2006), 12–28, Oda, 28 *Japanese Annual* (1985), 29–46; Oppenheim, i. 126–203; Verhoeven, *Ann. Français*, 1993, 7–40; Talmon, *Recognition of Governments in International Law* (1998); Rich, *Europ. Journ.*, 4 (1993), 36–65; Hillgruber, *Europ. Journ.*, 9 (1998), 491–509; Murphy, *ICLQ*, 48 (1999), 545–81; Talmon, 75 *BY* (2004), 101–81.

[2] See *infra*, pp. 137ff. The better view is that the facts disclosed an agreement rather than an estoppel.

[3] On unilateral acts in general see ch. 28, s. 3.

of the continental shelf), and actually illegal activity (apart from issues involving fundamental principles, *jus cogens*),[4] within which issues are most sensibly settled on an *ad hoc* and bilateral basis: indeed, cases concerned with relatively well-settled areas of law are often decided on the basis of facts, including elements of acquiescence, establishing a special content of obligation between the parties, and this quite apart from treaty. Finally, it may be observed that protest and recognition may be pure acts of policy not purporting to be legal characterizations of acts of other states, and, whether having this purport or not, the protest or recognition, if unfounded in law and backed by state activity, may be simply a declaration of intent to commit a delict or, otherwise, to act *ultra vires*.

2. STATES AND GOVERNMENTS IN RELATION TO RECOGNITION

In international relations it is the recognition of states, governments, belligerency, and insurgency[5] which has been the most prominent aspect of the general category, and legal writing has adopted the emphasis and terminology of political relations. The dominance of the category 'recognition' has led to some perverse doctrine. When a state is in dispute over legal title to territory, for example, a legal forum will examine *all* the legally significant conduct and declarations of either party. A declaration by one party that it does not 'recognize' the title of the other will hardly determine the issue, and may be worth very little if it is simply a declaration of political interest and antagonism. Again, a statement registering the fact that at a certain date the opponent was in actual occupation will be a part of the evidence in the case, but only within the context of the particular case will the statement have a specific legal significance. Unfortunately, when the existence of states and governments is in issue, a proper legal perspective seems to be elusive.

Absurdly, the complexity one may expect of legal issues in state relations is compacted into a doctrinal dispute between the declaratory and constitutivist views on recognition of states and (in so far as the two matters are interdependent)[6] governments. According to the declaratory view,[7] the legal effects of recognition are limited,

---

4 See *infra*, pp. 510–12.

5 The recognition of '*de facto* governments' is related to belligerency and insurgency (see *infra*, pp. 96–7). On these topics see the general works cited *supra*, p. 89, and see further McNair, *Opinions*, ii. 325ff.; Lauterpacht, 3 *Mod. LR* (1939–40), 1–20; McNair, 53 *LQR* (1937), 471–500; Walker, 23 *Grot. Soc.* (1937), 177–210; and Wehberg, 63 Hague *Recueil* (1938, I), 7–126.

6 See *infra*, p. 90.

7 Modern adherents include Fischer Williams, *ubi supra*, n. 1; Chen, *The International Law of Recognition*; Brierly, p. 139; Rousseau, iii. 534–8; Waldock, 106 Hague *Recueil* (1962, II), 147–51; Rolin, 77 Hague *Recueil* (1950, II), 326–37; Kunz, 44 *AJ* (1950), 713; Kozhevnikov (ed.), *International Law* (n.d.), 117–18. Charpentier, *La Reconnaissance internationale*, in substance is a declaratist. See also the resolution of the Institute of International Law: *Annuaire* 39, ii. 175–255, 300–5.

since recognition is a mere declaration or acknowledgement of an existing state of law and fact, legal personality having been conferred previously by operation of law. As Hall says:[8] 'States being the persons governed by international law, communities are subjected to law... from the moment, and from the moment only, at which they acquire the marks of a State.' Thus, in a relatively objective forum, such as an international tribunal, it would be entirely proper to accept the existence of a state although the other party to the dispute, or third states, did not recognize it. The award in the *Tinoco Concessions* arbitration[9] adopted this approach. In that case Great Britain was allowed to bring a claim on the basis of concessions granted by the former revolutionary government of Costa Rica which had not been recognized by some other states, including Great Britain. The arbitrator, Taft, observed:

The non-recognition by other nations of a government claiming to be a national personality, is usually appropriate evidence that it has not attained the independence and control entitling it by international law to be classed as such. But when recognition *vel non* of a government is by such nations determined by inquiry, not into its *de facto* sovereignty and complete governmental control, but into its illegitimacy or irregularity or origin, their non-recognition loses something of evidential weight on the issue with which those applying the rules of international law are alone concerned. What is true of the non-recognition of the United States in its bearing upon the existence of a *de facto* government under Tinoco for thirty months is probably in a measure true of the non-recognition by her Allies in the European War. Such non-recognition for any reason, however, cannot outweigh the evidence disclosed by this record before me as to the *de facto* character of Tinoco's government, according to the standard set by international law.

The reasoning employed here applies also to recognition of states. In addition there is a substantial state practice behind the declaratory view. Unrecognized states are quite commonly the object of international claims, charges of aggression, and other breaches of the United Nations Charter, by the very states refusing recognition.[10]

The declaratory theory of recognition is opposed to the constitutive view. According to the latter, the political act of recognition is a precondition of the existence of legal rights: in its extreme form this is to say that the very personality of a state depends on

---

[8] *International Law* (8th edn., 1924), 19.

[9] (1923), *RIAA* i. 369. See also *Socony Vacuum Oil Company Claim*, ILR 21 (1954), 55, US Int. Claims Commission; *Standard Vacuum Oil Company Claim*, ILR 30, 168, US Foreign Claims Settlement Commission, 1959; *Clerget v. Représentation Commerciale de la République démocratique du Viet-Nam*, 96 JDI (1969), 894 at 898, Cour d'appel de Paris, 1969; *Wulfsohn v. R.S.F.S.R.* (1923), 234 NY 372; *Sokoloff v. National City Bank* (1924), 239 NY 158; *Salimoff v. Standard Oil Co.* (1933), 262 NY 220; *Deutsche Continental Gas-Gesellschaft v. Polish State, Ann. Digest*, 5 (1929–30), no. 5; Arbitration Commission, Conference on Yugoslavia, *Opinion No. 1*, ILR 92, 162; id., *Opinion No. 8*, ibid., 199; *Opinion No. 10*, ibid., 206. Cf. the *Reparation for Injuries* case, *infra*, ch. 31, in which the United Nations was held to have personality *vis-à-vis* Israel, a non-member.

[10] e.g. Arab charges against Israel; United States charges against North Vietnam, 1964–5. On the latter: Falk (ed.), *The Vietnam War and International Law*, i (1968), 583. See further *infra*, on implied recognition. See also the Montevideo Conv. on Rights and Duties of States, 1933, Art. 3; Hudson, *Int. Legis.*, vi. 620, Bogotá Charter, 1948, Art. 9; Briggs, p. 101.

the political decision of other states.[11] The result is as a matter of principle impossible to accept: it is clearly established that states cannot by their independent judgment establish any competence of other states which is established by international law and does not depend on agreement or concession.[12] Brierly comments:[13]

It is true that the present state of the law makes it possible that different states should act on different views of the application of the law to the same state of facts. This does not mean that their differing interpretations are all equally correct, but only that there exists at present no procedure for determining which are correct and which are not. The constitutive theory of recognition gains most of its plausibility from the lack of centralized institutions in the system, and it treats this lack not as an accident due to the stage of development which the law has so far reached, but as an essential feature of the system.

Constitutivist doctrine creates a great many difficulties. Its adherents may feel a need to rationalize the position of the unrecognized state and in doing so may adopt near-declaratory views.[14] Reference to recognition leads to various difficulties. How many states must recognize? Can existence be relative only to those states which do recognize? Is existence dependent on recognition only when this rests on an adequate knowledge of the facts? Cogent arguments of principle and the preponderance of state practice thus dictate a preference for declaratory doctrine, yet to reduce, or to seem to reduce, the issues to a choice between the two opposing theories is to greatly oversimplify the legal situation.

3. THE VARIED LEGAL CONSEQUENCES OF ACTS OF RECOGNITION AND POLICIES OF NON-RECOGNITION

There is no such thing as a uniform type of recognition or non-recognition. The terminology of official communications and declarations is not very consistent: there may be 'de jure recognition', 'de facto recognition', 'full diplomatic recognition', 'formal recognition', and so on. In any case 'recognition' is not a term of art. The term

---

[11] Constitutivist doctrine takes many forms, and in many cases the jurists concerned allow certain rights prior to recognition. Well-known adherents include Anzilotti, *Cours de droit international*, i (1929), 160; Oppenheim, i. 126; Kelsen, *ut supra*, n. 1 (earlier he was a declaratist: 4 *RDI* (1929), 617–18; and 42 Hague *Recueil* (1932, IV), 260–94); Lauterpacht, *ut supra*, n. 5. See further Chen, *The International Law of Recognition*, pp. 30ff. The *Polish Upper Silesia* case (1926), PCIJ, Ser. A, no. 7 at p. 28, does not unequivocally support the constitutive view, since the issue was the existence of a contractual nexus between Germany and Poland. The fact that Poland could not invoke a treaty against Germany did not connote the non-existence of the former. For the view that UN Secretariat practice has supported the constitutivist position see Schachter, 25 *BY* (1948), 109–15.

[12] See *infra*, pp. 292ff., 383ff.

[13] p. 139.

[14] Cf. the views of Rivier, Fauchille, and Hyde: *infra*, n. 16.

'recognition' may be absent, and thus recognition may take the form of an agreement, or declaration of intent, to establish diplomatic relations, or a congratulatory message on attainment of independence. The typical act of recognition has two legal functions. First, the determination of statehood, a question of law: such individual determination may have evidential[15] effect before a tribunal. Secondly, the act is a condition of the establishment of formal, optional, and bilateral relations, including diplomatic relations and the conclusion of treaties. It is this second function which has been described by some jurists as 'constitutivist', although here it is not a condition of statehood.[16] Since states cannot be required by the law (apart from treaty) actually to make a public declaration of recognition, and since they are obviously not required to undertake optional relations, the expression of state 'will' involved is political in the sense of being voluntary. But it may also be political in a more obvious sense. An absence of recognition may not rest on any legal basis at all, there being no attempt to pass on the legal question of statehood as such. Non-recognition may simply be part of a general policy of disapproval and boycott. Again, recognition may be part of a policy of aggression and the creation of puppet states: the legal consequences will here stem from the breaches of international law involved. The important point is that use of the term 'recognition' does not absolve the lawyer from inquiring into the intent of the government concerned and then placing this in the context of *all* the relevant facts and rules of law.

4. IS THERE A DUTY OF RECOGNITION?

Lauterpacht[17] and Guggenheim[18] adopt the view that recognition is constitutive, but that there is a legal duty to recognize. This standpoint has been vigorously criticized[19] as bearing no relation to state practice and for its inconsistency, since in an oblique way it comes close to the declaratory view. In principle the legal duty can only be valid if it is in respect of an entity already bearing the marks of statehood and (although Lauterpacht does not express it thus) it is owed to the entity concerned. The argument postulates personality on an objective basis. However, discussion of Lauterpacht's views often reveals a certain confusion among the critics. Recognition, *as a public*

---

[15] Recognition is rarely 'cognitive' in a simple sense: the issue is one of law as well as fact, and cognition, which may involve no outward sign, occurs before, often long before, public recognition. Cf. Whiteman, ii. 13 (Sec. of State, Dulles).

[16] Rivier, Fauchille, and Hyde draw the distinction between personality and the exercise of rights by a state.

Kelsen, Verdross, Kunz, and Guggenheim similarly regard recognition as declaratory of certain basic rights of existence but constitutive of more specific rights.

[17] *Recognition*; and in *Coll. Papers*, i. 312–14. See also UK comment on the draft Decl. of the Rights and Duties of States: Whiteman, ii. 15–17.

[18] i. 190–1.

[19] See Kunz, 44 *AJ* (1950), 713–19; Cohn, 64 *LQR* (1948), 404–8; Briggs, 43 *AJ* (1949), 113–21. See also Jessup, 65 *AJ* (1971), 214 at 217.

act of state, is an optional and political act and there is no legal duty in this regard. However, in a deeper sense, if any entity bears the marks of statehood,[20] other states put themselves at risk legally if they ignore the basic obligations of state relations. Few would take the view that the Arab neighbours of Israel can afford to treat her as a non-entity: the responsible United Nations organs and individual states[21] have taken the view that Israel is protected, and bound, by the principles of the United Nations Charter governing the use of force. In this context of state *conduct* there is a duty to accept and apply certain fundamental rules of international law: there is a legal duty to 'recognize' for certain purposes at least, but no duty to make an express, public, and political determination of the question or to declare readiness to enter into diplomatic relations by means of recognition. This latter type of recognition remains political and discretionary. Even recognition is not determinant of diplomatic relations, and absence of diplomatic relations is not in itself non-recognition of the state.

5. RECOGNITION OF GOVERNMENTS[22]

In principle most of the considerations set out previously apply equally to recognition of states and governments. It has been seen elsewhere[23] that the existence of an effective and independent government is the essence of statehood, and, significantly, recognition of states may take the form of recognition of a government. Thus in 1919 the British Foreign Office declared that the British Government recognized the Estonian National Council as a *de facto* independent body with the capacity to set up a prize court.[24] Everything depends on the intention of the recognizing government and the relevant circumstances. Although recognition of government and state may be closely related, they are not necessarily identical. Non-recognition of a particular regime is not necessarily a determination that the state represented by that regime does not qualify for statehood. Non-recognition of a government may have two legal facets: that it is not a government in terms of independence and effectiveness (a facet which does *necessarily* affect statehood),[25] or, that the non-recognizing state is unwilling to have normal relations with the state concerned.[26] Non-recognition of governments seems more 'political' than that of states because unwillingness to enter into normal relations is more often expressed by non-recognition of the organs of government. Recognition in the context of voluntary relations may be made conditional on the democratic character

---

[20] Strictly speaking it is superfluous to call in aid rights of independence, sovereignty, and self-determination.

[21] Arab representatives have frequently discussed relations with Israel in terms of inter-state obligation.

[22] See, in particular, Talmon, 63 *BY* (1992), 231–97, and *Recognition of Governments in International Law* (1998); and Ando, *Japanese Annual*, 28 (1985), 29–46.

[23] *Supra*, pp. 71ff.

[24] See the *Gagara* [1919] P. 95. See also Briggs, p. 105.

[25] *Supra*, pp. 71–2.

[26] See the *Tinoco Concessions* case, *supra*, p. 87.

of the regime, the acceptance of particular claims, or the giving of undertakings, for example on treatment of minorities.[27] The sphere of optional relations and voluntary obligations is one of discretion and bargain. In terms of bilateral voluntary relations, an unrecognized government is no better off than an unrecognized state.[28]

6. *DE JURE* AND *DE FACTO* RECOGNITION

General propositions about the distinction between *de jure* and *de facto* recognition are to be distrusted, since, as it was emphasized earlier, everything depends on the intention of the government concerned and the general context of fact and law.[29] At least it is unlikely that the epithets refer to internal constitutionality. On the international plane a statement that a government is recognized as the '*de facto* government' of a state may involve a purely political judgment, involving either a reluctant or cautious acceptance of an effective government, lawfully established in terms of international law and not imposed from without, or an unwarranted acceptance of an unqualified agency. On the other hand, the statement may be intended to be or to include a legal determination of the existence of an effective government, but with reservations as to its permanence and viability. It may of course happen that the legal and political bases for caution coincide. The distinction between '*de jure/de facto* recognition' and 'recognition as the *de jure/de facto* government' is insubstantial, more especially as the question is one of intention and the legal consequences thereof in the particular case.[30] If there is a distinction it does not seem to matter legally. Certainly the legal and political elements of caution in the epithet *de facto* in either context are rarely regarded as significant, and courts both national[31] and international[32] accord the same strength to *de facto* recognition as evidence of an effective government as they do to *de jure* recognition. The distinction occurs exclusively in the political context of recognition of governments. It is sometimes said that *de jure* recognition is irrevocable while *de facto* recognition can be withdrawn.[33] In the political sense recognition of either kind can always be withdrawn: in the legal sense it cannot be unless a change of circumstances warrants it. Of course, if a statement involving a legal determination of effectiveness is

[27] See Kelsen, *Principles of International Law* (2nd edn.), 403–4.

[28] There is a strong school of thought supporting the automatic recognition of *de facto* governments, exemplified by the 'Estrada doctrine' enunciated by the Mexican Secretary of Foreign Relations in 1930: Briggs, p. 123. As a means of reducing non-recognition as a source of interference in internal affairs this is laudable, but difficulties remain. Recognition cannot be automatic when competing governments appear or when there is an attempted secession and issues of government and statehood are linked.

[29] See, in particular, Talmon, *Recognition of Governments*, 44–111.

[30] For a different approach: Chen, *The International Law of Recognition*, pp. 273–300.

[31] See the *Gagara, supra,* n. 24; and *Luther v. Sagor, infra,* p. 96.

[32] See the *Tinoco Concessions* case, *supra,* p. 87.

[33] Writers usually conduct their investigations on the assumption that no illegality was involved in giving recognition. If the situation recognized is the product of illegality, it is the case that the recognition is invalid and revocation legally superfluous.

made, withdrawal as a political gesture is embarrassing, but no more so than the withholding of recognition on political grounds.

Situations do occur where there is a serious legal distinction between *de jure* and *de facto* recognition as those terms are employed in the particular context. Thus some governments accepted certain legal consequences of German control of Austria, 1938–45, and Czechoslovakia, 1939–45, for example in the fields of nationality law and consular agents. Yet these same governments did not accept the legality or the *origin* of the factual control of Germany.[34] In documents relating to these matters '*de facto* recognition' may be used to describe acceptance of facts with a dubious legal origin: *de jure* recognition would be inappropriate and legally unjustifiable.[35] In this context it is legally hazardous to accept the full legal competence of an administration accorded only '*de facto* recognition'. Thus, in *Bank of Ethiopia* v. *National Bank of Egypt and Liguori*,[36] the Court gave effect to an Italian decree in Abyssinia on the basis that the United Kingdom had recognized Italy as the *de facto* government. In fact Italy at the time was no more than a belligerent occupant. Furthermore, in situations where rival governments were accorded *de jure* and *de facto* recognition in respect of the same territory, problems arise if the same legal consequences are given to both types of recognition.[37]

7. RETROACTIVITY[38]

British and American courts have applied the principle of retroactivity in following or interpreting the views of the executive in matters of recognition,[39] but Oppenheim[40] describes the rule as 'one of convenience rather than of principle'. Once again one ought not to generalize except to say that on the international plane there is no rule of retroactivity.[41] When as state makes a late acceptance of the existence of a state then, in the field of the basic rights and duties of existence, this recognition *ex hypothesi* cannot be 'retroactive' because in a special sense it is superfluous. In the sphere of optional relations and voluntary obligation it may or may not be, since the area is one of discretion.[42]

[34] On the policies of the United Kingdom and United States see Brownlie, *International Law and the Use of Force by States* (1963), 414–16.

[35] British *de jure* recognition in 1938 of the Italian conquest of Ethiopia in 1936 was avoided subsequently: cf. *supra*, p. 81.

[36] [1937] Ch. 513.

[37] On the policy of the United Kingdom and the response of the courts in the cases of the Spanish Civil War and Italo-Ethiopian war see *infra*, pp. 102–5. See further *Carl Zeiss Stiftung* v. *Rayner and Keeler, Ltd. (No. 2)* [1966] 3 WLR 125 at 135–7 (Lord Reid) and 180–2 (Lord Wilberforce).

[38] See generally Whiteman, ii. 728–45; Fitzmaurice, 92 Hague *Recueil* (1957, II), 23n.; Hackworth, i. 381–5; Chen *The International Law of Recognition*, pp. 172–86.

[39] See Oppenheim, i. 161.

[40] i. 161.

[41] See Mervyn Jones, 16 *BY* (1935), 42–55; Kelsen, *Principles of International Law* (2nd edn.), 398; de Visscher, *Théories et réalités en droit international public* (4th edn., 1970), 262. *Contra*: Chen, *The International Law of Recognition*, pp. 177–8.

[42] Cf. the *Polish Upper Silesia* case, PCIJ, Ser. A, no. 7 (1926), 27–39 and 84 (Lord Finlay).

8. IMPLIED RECOGNITION[43]

Recognition is a matter of intention and may be express or implied. The implication of intention is a process aided by certain customary rules or, perhaps, presumptions. Thus Lauterpacht[44] concludes that, in the case of recognition of states, only the conclusion of a bilateral treaty which regulates comprehensively the relations between the two states, the formal initiation of diplomatic relations, and, probably, the issue of consular exequaturs, justify the implication. State practice shows that no recognition is implied from various forms of negotiation, the establishment of unofficial representation, the conclusion of a multilateral treaty to which the unrecognized entity is also a party, admission to an international organization (in respect to those opposing admission), or presence at an international conference in which the unrecognized entity participates. Confusion arises from two sources. First, the terminology of governmental statements may create confusion and lead tribunals to give high legal status to acts intended only to give a low level of recognition: for example, an authority with which only informal and limited contacts have been undertaken may be accorded sovereign immunity by national courts.[45] Secondly, different considerations ought to apply to different legal aspects of recognition, yet doctrine tends to generalize about the subject. Thus, in terms of evidence in an objective forum like an international tribunal, informal relations, without intent to recognize in the political sense, especially if these persist, have probative value on the issue of statehood.[46] However, as a matter of optional bilateral relations and readiness to undertake normal relations, recognition depends precisely on intention. The United Kingdom did not accord formal recognition of the statehood of Namibia, but it was implicit in the establishment of diplomatic relations in March 1990.

9. COLLECTIVE RECOGNITION: MEMBERSHIP OF ORGANIZATIONS[47]

Collective recognition may take the form of a joint declaration by a group of states, for example the Allied Supreme Council after the First World War, or of permitting a new state to become a party to a multilateral treaty of a political character, such as a

---

[43] See Lauterpacht, *Recognition*, pp. 369–408; id., 21 *BY* (1944), 123–50; Chen, *The International Law of Recognition*, pp. 201–16; Briggs, 34 *AJ* (1940), 47–57; Hackworth, i. 327–63; Whiteman, ii. 48–59, 524–604; Lachs, 35 *BY* (1959), 252–9.

[44] *Recognition*, p. 406. See also Oppenheim, i. 169–75.

[45] See the *Arantzazu Mendi*, considered *infra*, pp. 97–99.

[46] But not *incidental* relations like attendance at an international conference not primarily concerned with relations between the unrecognized state and non-recognizing state.

[47] See Briggs, *ASIL Proceedings* (1950), 169–81; Rosenne, 26 *BY* (1949), 437–47; Kelsen, *Principles of International Law* (2nd edn.), 398–9; Aufricht, 43 *AJ* (1949), 679–704; Schachter, 25 *BY* (1948), 109–15; Oppenheim, i. 147; Rousseau, iii. 548–51; Wright, 44 *AJ* (1950), 548–59; Higgins, *The Development of International Law through the Political Organs of the United Nations* (1963), 131–2, 140–4, 146–50; Jessup, *A Modern Law of Nations*, pp. 43–51; Lauterpacht, *Recognition*, pp. 400–3; Chen, *The International Law of Recognition*, pp. 211–16, 221–3; Jennings, 121 Hague *Recueil* (1967, II), 352–4; Dugard, *Recognition and the United Nations* (1987).

peace treaty. The functioning of international organizations of the type of the League of Nations and United Nations provides a variety of occasions for recognition, of one sort or another, of states. Recognition by individual members of other members, or of non-members, may occur in the course of voting on admission to membership[48] and consideration of complaints involving threats to or breaches of the peace. Indeed, it has been argued that admission to the League and the United Nations entailed recognition by operation of law by all other members, whether or not they voted against admission. The position, supported by principle and state practice, would seem to be as follows. Admission to membership is prima facie evidence of statehood, and non-recognizing members are at risk if they ignore the basic rights of existence of another state the object of their non-recognition. United Nations organs have consistently acted on the assumption that Israel is protected by the principles of the Charter on the use of force *vis-à-vis* her Arab neighbours. However, there is probably nothing in the Charter, or customary law apart from the Charter, which requires a non-recognizing state to give 'political' recognition and to enter into optional bilateral relations with a fellow member.[49] In any event the test of statehood in general international law is not necessarily applicable to the issue of membership in the specialized agencies of the United Nations.[50]

There are other elements in the situation in the case of organizations, adequate treatment of which cannot be given here. Can the Organization and its organs (including the Secretariat), *as such*, accord recognition? For the purposes of the Charter numerous determinations of statehood are called for: thus, for example, the UN Secretary-General acts as depositary for important treaties. Certainly such determinations are binding within the particular constitutional and functional context of the Charter. Whether, and to what extent, such determinations provide evidence of statehood for general purposes must depend on the relevance to general international law of the criteria employed in a given case.[51] Attitudes of non-recognition may depend on the political prejudices of individual members and the view that in any case the special qualifications for membership contained in Article 4 are not fulfilled: statehood may be necessary but is not sufficient. The approval of the credentials of state representatives by organs of the United Nations raises problems similar to, but not identical with, those concerning admission, since in practice the formal requirements for approving credentials have been linked with a challenge to the representation of a state by a particular government.[52]

---

[48] Cf. *Cameroons* case (Prelim. Objections), ICJ Reports (1963), 119–20, Sep. Op. of Judge Fitzmaurice.

[49] See Secretariat Memo., Doc. S/1466; Kelsen, *Law of the United Nations* (1951), 946 n.

[50] See Morgenstern, *Legal Problems of International Organizations* (1986), 46–68.

[51] United Nations organs have been involved in varying degrees in the process of political creation of some states, viz., Indonesia, Israel, Libya, Republic of Korea (South Korea), the Somali Republic and Namibia. On the UN role in such cases see ch. 8.

[52] See Higgins, *Development*, pp. 131–2, 140–4, 146–50; Kelsen; *Law of the United Nations*, p. 946 n.

10. NON-RECOGNITION AND SANCTIONS

One form of collective non-recognition commonly seen in practice is the resolution or decision of an organ of the League of Nations, and now the United Nations, based on a determination that an illegal act has occurred.[53] It is possible, though by no means necessary, to refer to such practice as collective non-recognition. There is no doubt a duty of states parties to a system of collective security or other multilateral conventions not to support or condone acts or situations contrary to the treaty concerned.[54] In some contexts such a duty will be carefully spelled out and a duty of non-recognition may be associated with measures recommended or commanded by an organ of the United Nations as a form of sanction or enforcement against a wrongdoer. The Security Council resolutions of 1965 and 1966 characterized the Smith regime in Rhodesia as unlawful in terms of the Charter of the United Nations[55] and called upon all states not to recognize the illegal regime.[56] Similar issues arise in relation to the situation in Namibia (formerly South West Africa) following the termination of the Mandate,[57] and in relation to the status of the Turkish-occupied area of Cyprus after the Turkish invasion of 1974.[58]

11. ISSUES OF RECOGNITION BEFORE NATIONAL COURTS[59]

Within the sphere of domestic law, recognition may have important practical consequences. Where the local courts are willing or are, as a matter of public law, obliged to follow the advice of the executive, the unrecognized state or government cannot claim

[53] See Lauterpacht, *Coll. Papers*, i. 321; C. de Visscher, *Théories et réalités en droit international public* (4th edn.), 266; Kelsen, *Principles of International Law* (2nd edn.), 415–16; Mugerwa, in Sørensen, pp. 278–9; Whiteman, v. 874–965; Radojković, *Mélanges Andrassy* (1968), 225–36; Dugard, *Recognition and the United Nations*, pp. 81–111; Crawford, *The Creation* of States (2nd edn., 2006), 157–73; Talmon, Tomuschat and Thouvenin (eds.), *Fundamental Rules of the International Legal Order* (2006), 99–125; Talmon, *La non-reconnaisance collective des Etats illégaux* (2007), Université Panthéon-Assas, *Cours et Travaux*.

[54] Cf. the Stimson Doctrine of 1932 on non-recognition of illegal changes brought about by the use of force contrary to the Kellogg–Briand Pact. See Lauterpacht, *Coll. Papers*, i. 337–48.

[55] See 60 *AJ* (1966), 921.

[56] On the UN resolutions concerning Rhodesia see Fawcett, 41 *BY* (1965–6), 103–21; McDougal and Reisman, 62 *AJ* (1968), 1–19; 71 *RGDIP* (1967), 442–504.

[57] See the *Namibia* Opinion, ICJ Reports (1971), 16, where the legal consequences of non-recognition are examined.

[58] See *R. v. Minister of Agriculture, Fisheries and Food, ex p. S.P. Anastasiou (Pissouri), Ltd.*; ILR 100, 257 (Ct. of J. of Europ. Comm.), *Loizidou v. Turkey* (Prelim. Objs.), ibid., 103, 622, and *Loizidou v. Turkey* (Merits), ibid., 108, 443 (Europ. Ct. of H.R.).

[59] See generally Merrills, 20 *ICLQ* (1971), 476–99; Nedjati, 30 *ICLQ* (1981), 388–415; Verhoeven, 192 Hague *Recueil* (1985, III), 13–232.

immunity from the jurisdiction, obtain recognition for purposes of conflict of laws of its legislative and judicial acts, or sue in the local courts as plaintiff. These are the normal consequences of non-recognition in British and American courts.[60] The attitude to questions of recognition adopted by municipal courts may thus reflect the policies of a particular state, and quite apart from this, the issue of recognition appears in relation to the special problems of private international law (conflict of laws). The manner in which municipal courts relate the generalities of pronouncements by the executive to specific cases is certainly a matter of interest, and it is proposed to examine some of the English cases on the subject. However, great caution is needed in using municipal cases to establish propositions about recognition in general international law. In particular, because of the constitutional position of the British and American courts in matters concerning foreign relations, it is unjustifiable to regard the cases as evidence supporting the constitutivist position.

LUTHER V. SAGOR[61]

The plaintiffs in this case were a company incorporated in the Russian Empire in 1898, and, it was held, retained Russian nationality at the time of the action. In pursuance of a decree of confiscation of June 1918 the Soviet authorities took possession of the plaintiff's factory and stock of manufactured wood. In August 1920 the defendants purchased a quantity of plywood boards from the Soviet authorities and imported them into England. The plaintiffs claimed a declaration that the goods were their property, an injunction restraining the defendants from dealing with them, and damages for conversion and detention of them. The defendants cotended, *inter alia*, that the seizure and sale of the goods were acts of a sovereign state and had validly transferred the property in the goods to them. After judgment against the defendants in the court below, letters from the Foreign Office of April 1921 stated that the British Government recognized the Soviet Government as the '*de facto* Government of Russia', and that the former Provisional Government, recognized by the British Government, had been dispersed on 13 December 1917. The Court of Appeal found for the defendants. On the issues concerning recognition the Court held that for the present purpose no distinction was to be drawn between *de facto* and *de jure* recognition. Bankes, LJ, said:[62] 'The Government of this country having…recognized the Soviet Government as the Government really in possession of the powers of sovereignty in Russia, the acts of that Government must be treated by the courts of this country with all the respect due to the acts of a duly recognized foreign sovereign State'. Bankes, LJ, did not discuss retroactivity of the recognition as such, but looked at the evidence, including the

---

[60] Exceptionally an unrecognized state has been accorded procedural competence: *Wulfsohn* v. *R.S.F.S.R.*, 234 NY 372 (1923); but the unrecognized government was not allowed to sue as plaintiff in *R.S.F.S.R.* v. *Cibrario*, 139 NE 259 (1923). See further *Restatement of the Law: The Foreign Relations Law of the United States* (1987), 91–3.

[61] [1921] 3 KB 532. See also the *Gagara* [1919] P. 95, as to the status of a *de facto* government.

[62] At p. 543.

information from the Foreign Office, and concluded that Soviet power dated from the end of 1917.[63] Warrington, LJ, observed:[64] 'Assuming that the acts in question are those of the government subsequently recognized I should have thought that in principle recognition would be retroactive at any rate to such date as our Government accept as that by which the government in question in fact established its authority'.

HAILE SELASSIE V. CABLE AND WIRELESS LTD. (NO. 2)[65]

On 9 May 1936 Italy proclaimed the annexation of Ethiopia following a war of conquest. Prior to this the plaintiff through an agent had made a contract with the defendants, and in 1937 he commenced proceedings to recover money due under the contract. Bennett, J., at first instance, held that the plaintiff, who was still recognized as *de jure* sovereign of Ethiopia by the United Kingdom, had not been divested of the right to sue for the debt in spite of the fact that the British Government recognized the Italian Government 'as the Government *de facto* of virtually the whole of Ethiopia'. The defendants had relied, *inter alia*, on *Luther* v. *Sagor* to establish the exclusive power to the *de facto* government. Bennett, J., distinguished that decision,[66] confining it to acts of the *de facto* government in relation to persons or property in the territory which it is recognized as governing in fact. The present case was not concerned with acts in relation to persons or property in Ethiopia but with a debt, a chose in action, recoverable in England. While an appeal by the defendants was pending, the British Government recognized the King of Italy as *de jure* Emperor of Ethiopia, and it was not disputed that this related back to the date when recognition of the King of Italy as *de facto* sovereign occurred in December 1936. Thus, when the action commenced, the debt, which was a part of the public property of the state of Abyssinia, vested in the King of Italy and the appeal was allowed.[67]

THE *ARANTZAZU MENDI*[68]

This case also concerned the comparative status of recognition *de facto* and *de jure*. The background was the civil war in Spain between rebel Nationalists under General Franco and the Republican Government which was finally overthrown in 1939. The

---

[63] At p. 544.

[64] At p. 549. See, to the same effect, Scrutton, LJ, at pp. 556–7. On retroactivity see also the *Jupiter (No. 3)* [1927] pp. 122, 250; *Princess Paley Olga* v. *Weisz* [1929] 1 KB 718; *Lazard Bros.* v. *Midland Bank, Ltd.* [1933] AC 298.

[65] [1939] Ch. 182. See also *Haile Selassie* v. *Cable and Wireless, Ltd. (No. 1)* [1938] Ch. 545, 839.

[66] See also, at pp. 190–2, his comments on *Bank of Ethiopia* v. *National Bank of Egypt and Liguori* [1937] Ch. 513, and *Banco de Bilbao* v. *Sancha* [1938] 2 KB 176, which contain strong dicta favouring prevalence of the acts of the *de facto* government. Cf. Lauterpacht, *Recognition*, pp. 284–8. The substantial distinction from *Luther* v. *Sagor* was the provenance of the *de facto* government in the present case, an unlawful foreign invasion.

[67] The principle of retroactivity operated in a particular context, that of state succession in the matter of public debts.

[68] [1939] AC 256; [1939] 1 All ER 719. In the Court of Appeal: [1939] P. 37; [1938] 4 All ER 267.

Arantzazu Mendi was a Spanish vessel registered at Bilbao and at the material time was requisitioned by the Nationalist authorities exercising power in northern Spain. Her master and the managing director of the owners agreed to hold the vessel, which was in the London docks under arrest by the Admiralty Marshal, at the disposal of the Nationalist authorities. At that stage the Republican Government issued the present writ, under which they claimed to have possession of the ship adjudged to them. The Nationalist authorities moved to set aside the writ on the ground that it impleaded a foreign sovereign state. The judge at first instance directed that inquiry be made of the Foreign Office as to the status of the Nationalist authorities. In reply[69] it was stated that the British Government recognized Spain as a foreign sovereign state and recognized the Government of the Spanish Republic as the only *de jure* Government of Spain or any part of it. It was also stated that:

5. His Majesty's Government recognises the Nationalist Government as a Government which at present exercises *de facto* administrative control over the larger portion of Spain.

6. His Majesty's Government recognizes that the Nationalist Government now exercises effective administrative control over all the Basque Provinces of Spain.

7. His Majesty's Government have not accorded any other recognition to the Nationalist Government.

8. The Nationalist Government is not a Government subordinate to any other Government in Spain.

9. The question whether the Nationalist Government is to be regarded as that of a foreign Sovereign State appears to be a question of law to be answered in the light of the preceding statements and having regard to the particular issue with respect to which the question is raised.

The House of Lords held that the Foreign Office letter established that at the date of the writ the Nationalist Government of Spain was a foreign sovereign state and could not be impleaded. Lord Atkin said:[70]

By 'exercising de facto administrative control' or 'exercising effective administrative control', I understand exercising all the functions of a sovereign government. ... There is ample authority for the proposition that there is no difference for the present purposes between a recognition of a State de facto as opposed to de jure. All the reasons for immunity which are the basis of the doctrine in international law as incorporated into our law exist.

This decision has some curious features.[71] Several sources of confusion existed. First, their Lordships[72] regarded the Foreign Office letter as conclusive as 'a statement of

---

[69] See [1938] P. 233, 242. See also the letter before the Court of Appeal in *Banco de Bilbao* v. *Sancha* [1938] 2 KB 176.

[70] At pp. 264–5.

[71] For comment see Lauterpacht, 3 *Mod. LR* (1939), 1–20; id., *Recognition*, pp. 288–94, 365–8; Briggs, 33 *AJ* (1939), 689–99.

[72] The other Lords substantially agreed with Lord Atkin.

fact'. Yet they interpreted and accepted it as conclusive on important issues of law. As a matter of interpretation, it was probably intended to be literally a statement of fact: its emphasis on 'administrative control' is significant. Moreover, at this time the Government had not 'recognized' the Franco authorities as *de facto* government of Spain.[73] Nor was the letter of the Foreign Office intended to be conclusive as its terms (para. 9) indicate. In previous cases like the *Gagara*,[74] *Luther* v. *Sagor*,[75] and *Haile Selassie* v. *Cable and Wireless Ltd. (No. 2)*[76] the recognition *de facto* had occurred as a public political act and in respect of a government of the state as a whole. As a matter of interpretation, and in view of the still effective competition of the *de jure* government within the state, the Foreign Office letter did not necessarily accord equality to the governments. To equate a government in partial control of a state territory with the state itself in these circumstances was an odd procedure.[77] However, two other aspects of Lord Atkin's speech may be noticed as providing a more pragmatic basis for the decision. First, he seems to say that the rationale of sovereign immunity was in any case applicable on the facts: a proposition controversial in terms of international law, but not absurd, since a belligerent entity may soon become a *de jure* government. Secondly, and this point is connected with the foregoing, Lord Atkin states a principle of inadmissibility which is attractive:[78] 'The non-belligerent state which recognizes two Governments, one *de jure* and one *de facto*, will not allow them to transfer their quarrels to the area of the jurisdiction of its municipal courts'. Such a principle would obviate the dubious acceptance of belligerent entities engaged in civil war as sovereign states for purposes of immunity from the jurisdiction.

CARL ZEISS STIFTUNG V. RAYNER AND KEELER, LTD. (NO. 2)[79]

This case raised, as in interlocutory question, the issue of the validity of title to property based upon legislative and administrative acts of the German Democratic Republic (East Germany). The Foreign Office certificate available stipulated that since the withdrawal of Allied forces from the zone allocated to the USSR in 1945 'Her Majesty's Government have recognized the State and government of the USSR as *de jure* entitled to exercise governing authority in respect of that zone... and... have not recognized either *de jure* or *de facto* any other authority purporting to exercise governing

---

73 See Briggs, 33 *AJ* (1939), 689–99; 34 *AJ* (1940), 47–57.

74 *Supra*, n. 24.

75 *Supra*, p. 96.

76 *Supra*, p. 97.

77 One might add that this approach involved an assumption that the executive intended to act in breach of international law by giving such a measure of recognition to belligerents or insurgents.

78 At p. 265.

79 [1967] 1 AC 853; [1966] 3 WLR 125; ILR, 43, 3. For comment see Jennings, 121 Hague *Recueil* (1967, II), 360–3; Greig, 83 *LQR* (1967), 96–145. Cf., *Salimoff* v. *Standard Oil Co.* (1933), 262 NY 220; *Upright* v. *Mercury Business Machines Company*, 213 NYS (2d) 417 (1961); ILR 32, 65. See also *In re Al-Fin Corporation's Patent* [1970] 1 Ch. 160; *Hesperides Hotels Ltd.* v. *Aegean Turkish Holidays Ltd.* [1978] 1 QB 205, CA; [1978] 3 WLR 378 at 386, per Lord Wilberforce; and *supra*, p. 52.

authority in or in respect of the zone'. In the face of this the Court of Appeal[80] held that no effect could be given to the acts of the East German legal system. The House of Lords allowed the appeal by the East German foundation. In their view the case should be approached in terms of the conflict of laws and East Germany was a law district with an established legal system, even though the sovereignty on which this was based must be placed in the USSR.[81] In an *obiter dictum* of great interest Lord Wilberforce stated that in his view it was 'an open question', in English law, whether the courts must accept the doctrine of the absolute invalidity of all acts flowing from unrecognized governments.

THE RHODESIAN CASES

Decisions of the Judicial Committee of the Privy Council concerning the validity of detentions in Rhodesia after the usurpation of power by the Smith regime in 1965,[82] and of the English courts as such concerning the recognition of Rhodesian divorce decrees,[83] raise substantially similar issues of policy to those presented by the *Carl Zeiss* proceedings. However, for English courts the major determinant was the constitutional illegality of the Smith regime.[84] Thus even divorce decrees emanating from the Rhodesian courts were refused recognition by the English courts.[85]

GUR CORPORATION V. TRUST BANK OF AFRICA LTD.[86]

In this litigation the 'Republic of Ciskei' counter-claimed for a declaration in relation to certain rights in a commercial case. Ciskei is a territory recognized by the United Kingdom Government, along with other governments, as subject to the sovereignty of South Africa. The Court of Appeal held that the 'Republic of Ciskei' had standing to sue and be sued in an English court on the basis of reasoning similar to that of the House of Lords in the *Carl Zeiss* case (*supra*). Thus the executive certificate produced, together with a process of judicial inference, was held to justify the view that the

---

[80] [1965] Ch. 596.

[81] This view has its difficulties since under the Allied arrangements of 1945 the four occupying Powers only had limited rights in their respective zones. United Kingdom declarations on the status of the East German Government were not intended to imply that the USSR had sovereignty over East Germany. See Mann, 16 *ICLQ* (1967), 760 esp. at 773 (n. 73), 776, 788.

[82] *Madzimbamuto* v. *Lardner-Burke* [1967] AC 645; ILR 39, 61 at 374. The latter volume contains the decisions of the High Court, General and Appellate Divisions of Rhodesia. For comment see Eekelaar, 32 *Mod. LR* (1969), 19–34.

[83] *Adams* v. *Adams* [1970] 3 All ER 572, Sir Jocelyn Simon, P.

[84] See the Southern Rhodesia Act 1965.

[85] See the Southern Rhodesia (Matrimonial Jurisdiction) Order 1970; SI 1970 no. 1540, which extends jurisdiction with respect to persons domiciled or resident in Southern Rhodesia.

[86] [1987] 1 QB 599; ILR 75, 675.

'Republic of Ciskei' was an emanation of the Republic of South Africa as a sovereign state, and was acting by virtue of a delegation of legislative power from South Africa.

12. BRITISH POLICY ON RECOGNITION OF GOVERNMENTS

In 1980 the British Government adopted a new practice concerning recognition of governments. The relevant statement was as follows:[87]

... we have decided that we shall no longer accord recognition to Governments. The British Government recognise States in accordance with common international doctrine.

Where an unconstitutional change of régime takes place in a recognised State, Governments of other States must necessarily consider what dealings, if any, they should have with the new régime, and whether and to what extent it qualifies to be treated as the Government of the State concerned. Many of our partners and allies take the position that they do not recognise Governments and that therefore no question of recognition arises in such cases. By contrast, the policy of successive British Governments has been that we should make and announce a decision formally 'recognising' the new Government.

This practice has sometimes been misunderstood, and, despite explanations to the contrary, our 'recognition' interpreted as implying approval. For example, in circumstances where there might be legitimate public concern about the violation of human rights by the new régime, or the manner in which it achieved power, it has not sufficed to say that an announcement of 'recognition' is simply a neutral formality.

We have therefore concluded that there are practical advantages in following the policy of many other countries in not according recognition to Governments. Like them, we shall continue to decide the nature of our dealings with régimes which come to power unconstitutionally in the light of our assessment of whether they are able of themselves to exercise effective control of the territory of the State concerned, and seem likely to continue to do so.

The practical result of this change has been unfortunate. Executive certificates, like the one supplied in the *Gur Corporation* case (*supra*) may be indecisive and reflect the premiss that the issues are unrelated to questions of general international law. Such a premiss is especially inappropriate in cases where the legitimacy of the régime in question raises the issue of validity in terms of general international law, for example, when the regime concerned is the product of a foreign intervention, or there are competing administrations and the internal validity thereof is linked to issues of international law. No doubt the facts are paramount in each case but the facts can only be assessed

---

[87] Written answer by the Secretary of State, H. of Lds., 28 Apr. 1980: see 51 *BY* (1980) 367–8. See Warbrick, 30 *ICLQ* (1981), 568–92.

within the appropriate legal framework.[88] The outcome is unhelpful for practitioners and for courts. In any event, when issues of international legality have been in question, the British Government has provided the necessary guidance, for example, in relation to the status of Kuwait under Iraqi occupation in 1990;[89] and the status of the 'Turkish Republic of Northern Cyprus'.[90]

---

[88] For criticism see Brownlie, 53 BY (1982), 209–11; Crawford, 57 BY (1986), 408–10; Talmon, *Recognition of Governments in International Law* (1998), 3–14. See also *Republic of Somalia* v. *Woodhouse Drake and Carey (Suisse) SA* [1993] QB 54; ILR 94, 620; and Kingsbury, *LQR*, 109 (1993), 377–82.

[89] See *Kuwait Airways Corporation* v. *Iraqi Airways Company and the Republic of Iraq*, ILR 116, 535 (at 580–1); Comm. Ct., Mance, J.

[90] See *Caglar* v. *Bellingham*, ILR 108, 510 (at 519); and *Veysi Dag* v. *Secretary of State*, ILR 122, 529 (at 536).

PART III

TERRITORIAL SOVEREIGNTY

6

TERRITORIAL SOVEREIGNTY

1. THE CONCEPT OF TERRITORY

In spatial terms the law knows four types of regime: territorial sovereignty, territory not subject to the sovereignty of any state or states and which possesses a status of its own (trust territories, for example), the *res nullius*,[1] and the *res communis*.[2] Territorial sovereignty extends principally over land territory, the territorial sea appurtenant to the land, and the seabed and subsoil of the territorial sea.[3] The concept of territory includes islands, islets, rocks, and reefs.[4] A *res nullius* consists of the same subject-matter legally susceptible to acquisition by states but not as yet placed under territorial sovereignty. The *res communis*, consisting of the high seas which for present purposes include exclusive economic zones and also outer space, is not capable of being placed under state sovereignty.[5] In accordance with customary international law and the dictates of convenience, the airspace above and subsoil beneath state territory, the *res nullius*, and the *res communis* are included in each category.

2. SOVEREIGNTY AND JURISDICTION

The state territory and its appurtenances (airspace and territorial sea), together with the government and population within its frontiers, comprise the physical and social manifestations of the primary type of international legal person, the state. The legal competence of states and the rules for their protection depend on and assume the existence of a stable, physically delimited, homeland.[6] The competence of states in respect of their territory is usually described in terms of sovereignty and jurisdiction

---

[1] See *infra*, p. 168.

[2] See *infra*, p. 169.

[3] See further *infra*, pp. 115–17 on the parts of the territory of a state.

[4] See 67 *AJ* (1973), 118–19; and the Award in the *Beagle Channel Arbitration*, 18 Apr. 1977, *Dispositif* of the Decision. See further the *Red Sea Islands* case, Phase One, Award of 9 October 1998; ILR 114, 2, *Dispositif*, at 138–9; and *Qatar* v. *Bahrain*, Judgment of 16 March 2001, paras. 200–9.

[5] On the legal regime of the *res communis* see *infra*, p. 169, on the high seas, *infra*, pp. 223ff.; on outer space, *infra*, pp. 254.

[6] On legal personality, see *supra*, ch. 3; on the criteria of statehood, *supra*, ch. 4.

and the student is faced with a terminology which is not employed very consistently in legal sources such as works of authority or the opinions of law officers, or by statesmen, who naturally place political meanings in the foreground. The terminology as used by lawyers is also unsatisfactory in that the complexity and diversity of the rights, duties, powers, liberties, and immunities of states are obscured by the liberal use of omnibus terms like 'sovereignty' and 'jurisdiction'. At the same time, a degree of uniformity of usage does exist and may be noticed. The normal complement of state rights, the typical case of legal competence, is described commonly as 'sovereignty': particular rights, or accumulations of rights quantitatively less than the norm, are referred to as 'jurisdiction'.[7] In brief, 'sovereignty' is legal shorthand for legal personality of a certain kind, that of statehood; 'jurisdiction' refers to particular aspects of the substance, especially rights (or claims), liberties, and powers. Immunities are described as such.[8] Of particular significance is the criterion of consent. State A may have considerable forces stationed within the frontiers of state B. State A may also have exclusive use of a certain area of state B, and exclusive jurisdiction over its own forces. If, however, these rights exist with the consent of the host state then state A has no sovereignty over any part of state B.[9] In such case there has been a derogation from the sovereignty of state B, but state A does not gain sovereignty as a consequence. It would be otherwise if state A had been able to claim that exclusive use of an area of state B was hers *as sovereign*, as of right by customary law and independently of the consent of any state.

3. SOVEREIGNTY AND OWNERSHIP

The analogy between sovereignty and ownership is evident and, with certain reservations, useful. For the moment it is sufficient to establish certain distinctions. The legal competence of a state includes considerable liberties in respect of internal organization and the disposal of territory. This general power of government, administration, and disposition is *imperium*, a capacity recognized and delineated by international law. *Imperium* is thus distinct from *dominium* either in the form of public ownership of property within the state[10] or in the form of private ownership recognized as such by the law.[11]

4. ADMINISTRATION AND SOVEREIGNTY

It may happen that the process of government over an area, with the concomitant privileges and duties, falls into the hands of another state. Thus after the defeat of Nazi Germany in the Second World War the four major Allied powers assumed

---

[7] See Verzijl, *International Law in Historical Perspective*, i. (1968), 256–92.
[8] See *infra*, ch. 16, on the jurisdictional immunities of states.
[9] See McNair, *Opinions*, i. 69–74.
[10] Or elsewhere: cf. the John F. Kennedy Memorial Act 1964, s. 1.
[11] Cf. Lauterpacht, *International Law: Collected Papers*, i (1970), 367–70.

supreme power in Germany.[12] The legal competence of the German state did not, however, disappear. What occurred is akin to legal representation or agency of necessity. The German state continued to exist, and, indeed, the legal basis of the occupation depended on its continued existence. The very considerable derogation of sovereignty involved in the assumption of powers of government by foreign states, without the consent of Germany, did not constitute a transfer of sovereignty. A similar case, recognized by the customary law for a very long time, is that of the belligerent occupation of enemy territory in time of war.[13] The important features of 'sovereignty' in such cases are the continued existence of a legal personality and the attribution of territory to that legal person and not to holders for the time being.

5. SOVEREIGNTY AND RESPONSIBILITY: THE OWNERSHIP OF RIGHTS

A possible source of confusion is the fact that sovereignty is not only used as a description of legal personality accompanied by independence[14] but also as a reference to various types of rights, indefeasible except by special grant, in the patrimony of a sovereign state, for example the 'sovereign rights' a coastal state has over the resources of the continental shelf,[15] or a prescriptive, or historic, right to fish in an area of territorial sea belonging to another state, or a prescriptive right of passage between the territorial homeland and an enclave. Exercise of rights which are 'owned' and, therefore, in this special sense, 'sovereign' is not to be confused with *territorial* sovereignty.

6. ADMINISTRATION DIVORCED FROM STATE SOVEREIGNTY

While the concept of territorial sovereignty normally applies in relation to states, there is the likelihood that international life will comprehend situations in which international organizations not only administer territory in the capacity of legal representatives[16] but also assume legal responsibility for territory in respect of which no state has

---

[12] For the purpose of argument it is assumed that the form which the occupation took was lawful. See Jennings, 23 *BY* (1946), 112–41.

[13] See *L. v. N., Ann. Digest*, 14 (1947), no. 110. Another instance is provided by the situation in which the ceding state still administers the ceded territory, by agreement with the state taking cession: *Gudder Singh and Another* v. *The State*, ILR 20 (1953), 145. Further examples of delegated powers: ILR 19 (1952), nos. 32 and 33 (Italian Ct. of Cassation *in re* Italian administration of Trieste and Libya).

[14] See *supra*, pp. 75–6.

[15] At least according to the Conv. on the Continental Shelf, see *infra*, p. 214.

[16] See ch. 28, s. 5.

territorial sovereignty.[17] Such a situation arose in 1966 when the General Assembly terminated the Mandate of South West Africa.[18] The nature of the legal relations of an organization to the territory would cause few difficulties of substance, but some difficulties of terminology can be foreseen solely because terms and concepts like 'sovereignty' and 'title' are historically associated with the patrimony of states with definable sovereigns.

7. TERRITORY THE SOVEREIGNTY OF WHICH IS INDETERMINATE[19]

It may happen, and recent history has provided some interesting examples, that a piece of territory not a *res nullius* has no determinate sovereign. The situation envisaged is not that in which two states have conflicting legal claims to territory. In such a case a settlement of the dispute does not, apart from special agreement, have retroactive effect. If a disputed parcel of territory previously in the possession of state A is declared to belong to state B, it does not follow that, prior to the execution of the settlement, the sovereignty in respect of the land was indeterminate. The parcel was, until the settlement, the subject-matter of a claim, but its sovereignty was not, as a consequence, 'indeterminate'. Sovereignty may also be indeterminate in so far as the process of secession[20] may not be seen to be complete at any precise point in time.

Existing cases spring chiefly from the renunciation of sovereignty by the former holder and the coming into being of an interregnum with disposition postponed until a certain condition is fulfilled or the states having power of disposition for various reasons omit to exercise a power or fail to exercise it validly. For example, in a peace treaty Japan renounced all right to Formosa. However, Formosa has not been the subject of any act of disposition; it has not been transferred to any state. In the former view of the British Government:[21] 'Formosa and the Pescadores are…territory the *de jure* sovereignty over which is uncertain or undetermined'. Since 1972 the British

---

[17] The problem of substance is whether organizations have the capacity to acquire territory: see *infra*, p. 167. In case of the mandate and trust territories international organizations have assumed a large measure of legal responsibility in relation to territory.

[18] See *infra*, ch. 8, s. 1.

[19] Pending final settlement territory the subject of dispute may be placed under a form of *condominium*: see the *Lighthouses* arbitration, ILR 23 (1956), 659 at 664–6, 668–9; Oppenheim, i. 566–7; Guggenheim, i. 436. It is not always obvious whether a particular disposition is final or not: see *Ditmar and Linde* v. *Ministry of Agriculture*, Ann. Digest, 8 (1935–7), no. 52.

[20] i.e. rebellion having as its object the formation of a new state or union with another state. Cf. Jennings, *The Acquisition of Territory in International Law* (1963), 7–8.

[21] Written answer by the Secretary of State, 4 Feb. 1955, in 5 *ICLQ* (1956), 413–14. Cf. ibid. 8 (1959), 166. See also Jain, 57 *AJ* (1963), 25–45. For further examples of a similar kind: 6 *ICLQ* (1957), 513–16; and *UK Contemp. Practice* (1962), i. 43. Cf. *De Wurts* v. *Wurts*, Ann. Digest, 6 (1931–2), no. 52; *Re An Inquiry by the Italian Ministry for Foreign Affairs*, ILR 26 (1958, II), 68, and *Weiss* v. *Inspector-General of the Police*, ibid. 210 (and see note at p. 221).

Government has acknowledged the position of the Chinese Government that Taiwan is a province of China.

8. TERMINABLE AND REVERSIONARY RIGHTS[22]

Territorial sovereignty may be defeasible in certain circumstances by operation of law, for example by fulfilment of a condition subsequent or the failure of the condition under which sovereignty was transferred where there is an express or implied condition that title should revert to the grantor. The first situation is exemplified by the status of Monaco,[23] the independence of which exists subject to there being no vacancy in the Crown of Monaco. Until such a condition operates the tenant has an interest equal in all respects to that of sovereignty.

The second type of case gives rise to many problems. On one view, the system of mandates created after the First World War provides a useful example. The mandatories, or administering states for the various ex-German territories, were nominated by the five principal Allied and associated powers, in whose favour Germany had renounced sovereignty over these territories in the Treaty of Versailles. By reason of the facts that the principal Allied powers had taken the cession from Germany, and that it was they who took the decision to place the territories under mandate, it has been concluded[24] that, in this capacity, 'the Principal Powers retained, and may still retain on a dormant basis, a residual or reversionary interest in the actual territories concerned except where these have attained self-government or independence'. The precise nature of such reversionary interests will depend on the facts of each case, but it seems clear that they do not necessarily amount to sovereignty but rather take the form of a power of disposition, or of intervention or veto in any process of disposition.

The concept of reversion is to be distinguished from that of 'residual sovereignty', considered subsequently, the principal point of difference consisting in the fact that reversion involves a change of sovereignty, whilst in the case of 'residual sovereignty', the territorial sovereign has not lost status as such.

9. RESIDUAL SOVEREIGNTY

Occupation of foreign territory in time of peace may occur on the basis of a treaty with the territorial sovereign. The grantee under the treaty may receive very considerable powers of administration amounting to a delegation of the exercise of many of

---

[22] No precise parallel with concepts of the English law of real property is intended.

[23] See Verzijl, *International Law in Historical Perspective*, ii. (1969), 459–61.

[24] See the Joint Diss. Op. of Judges Spender and Fitzmaurice in the *South West Africa* cases (Prelim. Objections), ICJ Reports (1962), 482 n.; and see ibid. 496.

the powers of the territorial sovereign to the possessor for a particular period. Thus, in Article 3 of the Treaty of Peace of 8 September 1951, Japan agreed that, pending any action to place the Ryukyu Islands under the trusteeship system of the United Nations, 'The United States will have the right to exercise all and any powers of administration, legislation and jurisdiction over the territory and inhabitants of these islands, including their territorial waters'. In 1951 the United States Secretary of State referred to the 'residual sovereignty' of Japan over the islands. United States courts, in holding that inhabitants of the Ryukyus were not nationals of the United States and that the islands were a 'foreign country' in connection with the application of various United States statutes, have referred to the '*de facto* sovereignty' of the United States and to the Japanese interest in terms of 'residual sovereignty' or '*de jure* sovereignty'.[25] Restoration of full Japanese sovereignty was the subject of bilateral agreements of 1968, 1969, and 1970.[26]

Referring to similar cases Oppenheim[27] describes the grantor's interest as 'nominal sovereignty', and points out that this type of interest may have practical consequences. For example, in the case concerning the *Lighthouses in Crete and Samos* (1937)[28] the Permanent Court of International Justice held that in 1913 the islands of Crete and Samos were under the sovereignty of Turkey, which therefore had the power to grant or renew concessions with regard to the islands. As regards Crete the Court said:

Notwithstanding its autonomy, Crete has not ceased to be a part of the Ottoman Empire. Even though the Sultan had been obliged to accept important restrictions on the exercise of his rights of sovereignty in Crete, that sovereignty had not ceased to belong to him, however it might be qualified from a juridical point of view.

Another practical consequence of the grantor's interest in such a case is the continuance of his right of disposition—a far from insignificant proprietary right. Thus in the *Lighthouses* case the Court pointed out that evidence for the existence of Turkish sovereignty consisted, in part, in the fact that Turkey was able, subsequently, to carry out an act of disposition in regard to the islands by ceding them to Greece.

10. INTERNATIONAL LEASES

The heading, it must be emphasized, is more a concession to usage than the product of legal analysis. The use of the term is excusable, but it cannot be regarded as more than a superficial guide to the nature of the interest concerned: each case depends on

---

[25] See *Brewer v. United States, Ann. Digest*, 15 (1948), no. 169; *Cobb v. United States*, ILR 18 (1951), no. 173; *United States v. Ushi Shiroma*, ILR 21 (1954), 82; *Burma v. United States*, ILR 24 (1957), 89; 70 *RGDIP* (1966), 160. See also Oda and Owada (eds.), *The Practice of Japan in International Law 1961–1970* (1982), 76–96.

[26] *ILM* vii (1968), 554; 74 *RGDIP* (1970), 717; 64 *AJ* (1970), 647.

[27] i. 567–8.

[28] PCIJ, Ser. A/B, no. 71; World Court Reports, iv. 241; *Ann. Digest*, 8 (1935–7), no. 49. See also Lauterpacht, *Coll. Papers*, i. 372–3; id., 62 Hague Recueil (1937, IV), 253–6; and the Sep. Op. of Judge Hudson in the case, PCIJ, Ser. A/B, no. 71, p. 117 at pp. 126–30.

its particular facts and especially on the precise terms of the grant. Certainly there is a presumption that the grantor retains residual sovereignty. By a Convention signed on 6 March 1898 China 'cedes to Germany on lease, provisionally for ninety-nine years, both sides of the entrance to the Bay of Kiao-Chau'. Article 3 of the convention provides that China 'will abstain from exercising rights of sovereignty in the ceded territory during the term of the lease...'. In this case China clearly retained residual sovereignty, and the grantee had, for example, no right to dispose of the territory to a third state.[29]

The difficulties concerning the nature of the grantor's interest in this type of case, new examples of which are unlikely to arise, are not present in the amenity providing 'lease' of railway station or a military, naval, or air base.[30] Here the rights conferred by a treaty, executive agreement, or other intergovernmental agreement are of a more limited nature: consequently the grantor has a right to revoke the 'contractual licence', and, after a reasonable time has elapsed, force may be employed to evict the trespasser.

11. USE AND POSSESSION GRANTED IN PERPETUITY

By a Convention of 18 November 1903 Panama granted to the United States 'in perpetuity the use, occupation and control of a zone of land and land under water for the construction...and protection' of the Panama Canal, 10 miles in width.[31] In such a case the residual sovereignty remains with the grantor. However, not only has the exercise of all rights of jurisdiction been delegated but the grantor might seem to have renounced even the right of disposition. A licence can be terminated; a grant in

---

[29] In 1919 the rights under the lease were assigned to Japan. The lease was terminated in 1922. See generally Basdevant, *Dictionnaire de la terminologie du droit international* (1960), S.V. 'Bail'; Lauterpacht, *Private Law Sources and Analogies of International Law* (1927), 183–90; Verzijl, *International Law in Historical Perspective*, iii (1970), 397–408; Brierly, pp. 189–90; Oppenheim, i. 568–71; Lauterpacht, *Coll. Papers*, i. 372; Guggenheim, i. 402. See further *State of Madras* v. *Cochin Coal Co.*, ILR 26 (1958, II), 116. The British lease of territory on the Chinese mainland north of Kowloon expired in 1997: see 56 *BY* (1985), 483–5; 57 *BY* (1986), 513–14, 529–34. Certain types of 'lease' were, in fact and law, cessions of territory: see *Cook* v. *Sprigg* [1899] AC 572; and *Secretary of State for India* v. *Sardar Rustam Khan, Ann. Digest*, 10 (1941–2), no. 21. See also *British and Foreign State Papers*, vol. 162, p. 92. On the dispute between the Philippines and Malaysia over Sabah (North Borneo) see 10 *Malaya LR* (1968), 306; 2 *Phil. Journ. of IL.* (1963), *passim*; Ortiz, *Legal Aspects of the North Borneo Question* (1964); Marston, *Austral. Yrbk* (1967), 103; Rousseau, 66 *RGDIP* (1962), 806. See also *Union of India* v. *Sukumar Sengupta*, ILR 92, 554, India, S.C.

[30] See e.g. the Agreement of 27 Mar. 1941 between the United States and the United Kingdom: 35 *AJ* (1941), Suppl., pp. 134–59.

[31] See Oppenheim, ii. 571; Lauterpacht, *Coll. Papers*, i. 372; *In re Cia. de Transportes de Gelabert, Ann. Digest*, 9 (1938–40), no. 45 (Panama, Supr. Ct.; held, that Panama retained 'its jurisdictional rights of sovereignty' in the airspace of the Canal Zone). Cf. *Stafford Allen & Sons, Ltd.* v. *Pacific Steam Navigation Co.* [1956] 1 WLR 629; [1956] 2 All ER 716; ILR 23 (1956), 116, CA. The Panama Canal Treaty signed on 7 Sept. 1977 supersedes the Conv. of 1903: see 16 *ILM* (1977), 1022.

perpetuity by definition cannot. However, the grantee's right rests on an agreement and would be defeated by a disposition of the residual sovereignty to a third state in regard to which the grant was *res inter alios acta*. In other words, the restriction on disposition consists in an inability to grant similar rights to another state: the residual sovereignty remains transferable and the grantee has no power of disposition.

12. DEMILITARIZED AND NEUTRALIZED TERRITORY

Restrictions on use of territory, accepted by treaty, do not affect territorial sovereignty as a title, even when the restriction concerns matters of national security and preparation for defence.[32]

13. THE CONCEPT OF TERRITORY: THE PRINCIPLE OF EFFECTIVE CONTROL APPLIED BY NATIONAL COURTS

National courts, though concerned indirectly with the large problems of residual sovereignty, territory the sovereignty of which is indeterminate, and the like, are usually presented with questions of narrow aspect which invite a pragmatic approach. Thus in a treaty or statute the term 'territory' may connote jurisdiction.[33] Moreover, courts are very ready to equate 'territory' with the actual and effective exercise of jurisdiction even when it is clear that the state exercising jurisdiction has not been the beneficiary of any lawful and definitive act of disposition. In the *Schtraks*[34] case the Israeli Government asked for the extradition of the appellant in pursuance of an agreement with the United Kingdom Government that the Extradition Act 1870, should apply subject to the terms of the Israel (Extradition) Order, 1960. The appellant, having been committed to prison to await extradition, applied for a writ of habeas corpus on the grounds, *inter alia*, that Jerusalem, where the offences charged were alleged to have been committed, was not 'territory' within the meaning of the agreement. The basis of the argument was the fact that the United Kingdom Government did not recognize the

---

[32] See *A.-G. of Israel* v. *El-Turani*, ILR 18 (1951), no. 39.

[33] *R.* v. *Governor of Brixton Prison, ex parte Minervini* [1959] 1 QB 155; [1958] 3 WLR 559, where the Div. Ct. held that 'territory' in a treaty of extradition meant jurisdiction and therefore included ships of the other party.

[34] [1964] AC 556; ILR 33, 319. But cf. *In Re Ning Yi-Ching and Others* (1939), 56 TLR 3; *Ann. Digest*, 9 (1938–40), no. 44.

de jure sovereignty of Israel in Jerusalem but only its *de facto* authority. On this point the House of Lords held that the instruments concerned were not concerned with sovereignty but with territory in which territorial jurisdiction is exercised.[35] Viscount Radcliffe[36] concluded that 'territory' in the present context included whatever is under the state's effective jurisdiction.

Such an approach avoids a legal vacuum in such territories and provides sensible solutions without the necessity for lengthy inquiry into roots of title, or the legal quality of a protectorate or trusteeship. Further, the equation of territory and jurisdiction is theoretically sound. Abstract discussion as to whether ships, aircraft, territorial sea, and embassies are 'territory' lacks reality, since in a legal context the word denotes a particular sphere of legal competence and not a geographical concept. Ultimately territory cannot be distinguished from jurisdiction for certain purposes. Both terms refer to legal powers, and, when a concentration of such powers occurs, the analogy with territorial sovereignty justifies the use of the term 'territory' as a form of shorthand.

14. *CONDOMINIA*

It may be asserted that sovereignty is divisible both as a matter of principle and as a matter of experience. International law recognizes the *condominium*, which 'exists when two or more states exercise sovereignty conjointly over a territory'.[37] Great Britain and Egypt had *condominium* over the Sudan between 1898 and 1955.[38] Worthy of comment is the fact that the theoretical consequences of this type of regime may be qualified by agreement.[39] Moreover, national legislation and jurisdiction will not automatically extend to territory under the special regime of *condominium*. On occasion it has been suggested that in certain cases, for example with reference to land-locked lakes and bays[40] bounded by the territory of two or more states,[41] the riparian states have *condominium* over the area by the operation of law. This is doubtful, but it is possible for the regime to arise by prescription.[42] In relation to the Gulf of Fonseca a Chamber of the

---

[35] Lord Reid at pp. 579, 1022, 532, respectively.

[36] Viscount Radcliffe at pp. 587, 1029, 537, respectively.

[37] Oppenheim, ii. 565–7. See also Verzijl, *International Law in Historical Perspective*, iii. 429–43; Lauterpacht, *Coll. Papers*, i. 370–2; O'Connell, 43 *BY* (1968–9), 71–145; and Bastid, 107 Hague *Recueil* (1962, III), 391–5; Rousseau, iii. 22–30.

[38] See Taha, 76 *BY* (2005), 337–82.

[39] Thus, in the case of the New Hebrides, the two sovereigns, Great Britain and France, exercised a separate jurisdiction over their own (metropolitan) subjects. The New Hebrides became independent (as Vanuatu) in 1980: 51 *BY* (1980), 395–8. The legal regime may be used to deal with problems of neighbourhood relating to frontier rivers and the like: *Dutch–Prussian Condominium* (1816) case, *Ann. Digest*, 6 (1931–2), no. 23. See also E. H. Brown, *The Saudi Arabia Kuwait Neutral Zone* (1963).

[40] See *Ann. Digest*, 7 (1933–4), no. 53, for decisions on the position of Lake Constance.

[41] See *infra*, p. 117.

[42] On which see *infra*, pp. 146ff.

International Court has held that its waters, other than the three-mile maritime belts, 'are historic waters and subject to a joint sovereignty of the three coastal states'.[43]

In any case, the particular regime will depend on the facts of each case, and it is unsafe to rely on any general theory of the community of property. This type of problem concerns a particular status *in rem*,[44] and the fact that one state cannot alienate the territory without the consent of the other or others[45] does not justify the application of the general category of joint tenancy, as opposed to tenancy in common.

15. VASSALAGE, SUZERAINTY, AND PROTECTION

Condominium is a case of sovereignty which is jointly exercised by two or more states on a basis of equality. Historically, other types of shared sovereignty have occurred in which the dominant partner, state A, has acquired a significant role in the government of state B, and particularly in the taking of executive decisions relating to the conduct of foreign affairs. The legal aspects of the relationship will vary with the circumstances of each case, and not too much can be deduced from the terminology of the relevant instruments.[46] It may be that the protected community or 'state' is a part of state A and, as a colonial protectorate, has no international legal personality, although for purposes of internal law it will have a special status.[47] The question of the status of colonial protectorates is complex and best approached on a case by case basis.[48] The protected state may retain a measure of externally effective legal personality, although the exercise of its legal capacities be delegated to state A. In this latter case treaties by state A will not necessarily apply to state B. However, for certain purposes, including the law of neutrality and war, state B may be regarded as an agent of state A. Thus if state A declares war the protected state may be treated as belligerent also, although much will depend on the precise nature of the relations between states A and B.[49] These

---

[43] *Case Concerning the Land, Island and Maritime Frontier Dispute*, ICJ Reports, 1992, p. 601, para. 404.

[44] Cf. *International Status of South-West Africa*, ICJ Reports (1950), 128.

[45] See *Costa Rica* v. *Nicaragua* (1916), and *El Salvador* v. *Nicaragua* (1917), decisions of the Central American Court of Justice, cited by Parry, *Nationality and Citizenship Laws*, p. 18, n. 13, reported in 11 *AJ* (1917), 181, 674, and discussed by Lauterpacht, *Analogies*, pp. 288–9.

[46] See Verzijl, *International Law in Historical Perspective*, ii. 339–454; Rousseau, ii. 276–300; Oppenheim, i. 266–74; and *supra*, pp. 72–4. On the unique co-seigneury of Andorra see *Cruzel* v. *Massip*, ILR 39, 412; *Re Boedecker and Ronski*, ibid. 44, 176; Verzijl, *International Law in Historical Perspective*, iii. 3, 325; Rousseau, ii. 342–7; Crawford, 55 *RDI* (Sottile), 258–72.

[47] See *Ex parte Mwenya* [1960] 1 QB 241; [1959] 3 WLR 509, CA (held, the sovereignty of the British Crown over the protectorate of Northern Rhodesia appeared to be indistinguishable in legal effect from that of a British colony or country acquired by conquest). See, however, ch. 25, s. 9, on self-determination.

[48] See *Agarwala and the Union of India*, ILR 118, 421; *Case Concerning the Land and Maritime Boundary between Cameroon and Nigeria*, Judgment of 10 October 2002, paras. 201–9; and the *Written Pleadings* of Nigeria in the same case.

[49] Cf. *Nationality Decrees in Tunis and Morocco* (1923), *supra*, p. 78. On other examples see Whiteman, i. 431–53.

questions, though important for the determination of the legal status of territory, pertain closely to the question of the independence of states, considered previously.[50]

16. PARTS OF STATE TERRITORY

Apart from land permanently above low-water mark, territorial sovereignty may be exercised over various geographical features associated with or analogous to land territory. By reason of their practical importance certain forms of the subject-matter of sovereignty will be treated separately and in a more appropriate context. Thus discussion of the territorial sea occurs in Chapter 9. The consideration of specialized rights over the high seas in Chapters 9 and 10 involves reference to legally protected interests, particularly in regard to the continental shelf,[51] proximate in varying degrees to the concept of territorial sovereignty. Other questions, for example international rivers, canals, and straits, commonly discussed in the present context, are reserved for Chapter 12 on common amenities and co-operation in the use of resources. The topics which remain, though somewhat disparate, may be considered conveniently together.

TERRITORIAL SUBSOIL

The rule universally accepted is that the subsoil belongs to the state which has sovereignty over the surface.[52]

AIRSPACE[53]

The airspace superjacent to land territory, internal waters, and the territorial sea is in law a part of state territory, and as a consequence other states may only use such airspace for navigation or other purposes with the agreement of the territorial sovereign. With the development of aviation in the early years of the present century, and the impact of the First World War, the customary law emerged in a relatively short period.[54] Its content, the application of the maxim of private law *cujus est solum est usque ad caelum et ad inferos,* was dictated primarily by the concern of states for

---

[50] *Supra*, pp. 71ff.

[51] *Infra*, pp. 205–14.

[52] See Verzijl, *International Law in Historical Perspective*, iii. 47–51.

[53] On jurisdiction over aircraft see *infra*, pp. 320–21. On the nationality of aircraft see *infra*, pp. 425–26. Much of the 'law of the air' is devoted to the problems of private law, and chiefly conflict of laws, relating to international air traffic. On the public international law aspects see Oppenheim, ii. 650–61; Jennings, 22 *BY* (1945), 191–209; id., 75 Hague *Recueil* (1949, II), 513–96; Goedhuis, 81 Hague *Recueil* (1952, II), 204–305; Johnson, *Rights in Air Space* (1965); *Grand-Duchy of Luxembourg* v. *Compagnie Luxembourgeoise de Télédiffiusion*, ILR 91, 281 (Lux., Superior Ct. of Justice).

[54] For treaties embodying the rule, *infra*, p. 174 n. 3.

national security and the integrity of neutral states in time of armed conflict. To this factor may be added the desire to prevent aerial reconnaissance by potential enemies, a fear of surprise attack, and the economic value of granting the right to fly to foreign commercial agencies. Consequently, the law does not permit a right of innocent passage, even through airspace over the territorial sea.[55] Aerial trespass may be met with appropriate measures of prevention, but does not normally justify instant attack with the object of destroying the trespasser.[56]

Two other issues must be noticed. First, the beginning of space exploration by satellites has led to discussion of the question of determining the outer limit of state sovereignty.[57] Secondly, airspace is generally assumed to be appurtenant to land territory and territorial waters.[58] It follows that a disposition of territory includes the superjacent airspace. However, the principle of appurtenance will not necessarily apply where the grantee is not to receive sovereignty but the possession and use of territory acknowledged to remain under the sovereignty of the grantor.[59]

INTERNAL WATERS[60]

Lakes and rivers included in the land territory of a state, as well as waters on the landward side of baselines from which the breadth of the territorial sea is calculated, comprise internal waters subject to state sovereignty. Large bodies of water such as land-locked seas[61] and historic bays[62] come within this category. The legal regime is that of territorial sovereignty, but in the case of ports, rivers, and canals, special questions arise relating to the sharing of amenities: these will be considered in Chapter 12. In this connection it is convenient to refer to the Convention on the Territorial Sea and Contiguous Zone of 1958,[63] which provides in Article 5:

1. Waters on the landward side of the baseline of the territorial sea form part of the internal waters of the State.

2. Where the establishment of a straight baseline in accordance with Article 4[64] has the effect of enclosing as internal waters areas which previously had been considered as part of the territorial sea or of the high seas, a right of innocent passage, as provided in Articles 14 to 23, shall exist in those waters.

---

[55] On the position concerning international straits, see p. 267.
[56] See Lissitzyn, 47 *AJ* (1953), 559–89; Anon., 61 *Columbia LR* (1961), 1074–102.
[57] See further *infra*, pp. 255–9.
[58] On the principle of appurtenance, *infra*, p. 117.
[59] Cf. *In re Cia. de Transportes de Gelabert, Ann. Digest*, 9 (1938–40), no. 45.
[60] Otherwise described as national or interior waters. Generally see McDougal and Burke, *The Public Order of the Oceans* (1962), pp. 89–173. A sea is not 'land-locked' in this sense if it is surrounded by the territory of two or more international persons: see *A.M.S.S.V.M. & Co.* v. *The State of Madras*, ILR 20 (1953), 167 and the note at 169. See also *Re Ownership of the Strait of Georgia*, ILR 73, 186 (Br. Columbia CA).
[61] *Infra*, p. 118.
[62] *Infra*, pp. 158–9.
[63] See *infra*, p. 173.
[64] See *infra*, p. 176.

It is to be emphasized that for purposes of international law the distinction between internal waters and territorial sea is important, in spite of the fact that the legal interest of the coastal state amounts to sovereignty in either case. Thus no right of innocent passage for foreign vessels exists in the case of internal waters (apart from the treaty provision quoted above).[65] Again, the rules relating to jurisdiction over foreign vessels differ.[66]

In the case of lakes and inland seas bounded by the territory of two or more states the legal position in practice depends either on the creation of prescriptive rights or on a treaty regime.[67] Thus the water boundary through the Great Lakes of Ontario, Erie, Huron, and Superior rests on a Convention of 1909 between Canada and the United States.[68] No doubt in the absence of agreement there is a presumption in favour of the middle line where only two states are involved.[69]

17. RESTRICTIONS ON DISPOSITION OF TERRITORY

TREATY PROVISIONS

States may by treaty agree not to alienate certain parcels of territory in any circumstances, or they may contract not to transfer to a particular state or states.[70] Moreover, a state may agree not to unite with another state: in the State Treaty of 1955[71] Austria was placed under an obligation not to enter into political or economic union with Germany. Previously, in the Treaty of St Germain of 1919, the obligation was expressed differently: the independence of Austria, it was provided,[72] 'is inalienable otherwise than with the consent of the Council of the League of Nations'. An obligation not to acquire territory may also be undertaken. In case of a breach of a treaty obligation not to alienate, or acquire, territory, it is doubtful if the title of the grantee is affected. The grantee may regard the treaty as *res inter alios acta*, and it is doubtful if the existence of a claim by a third state for breach of a treaty can result in the nullity of the transfer.

---

[65] On an alleged customary right of access to ports by foreign merchant vessels, see Guggenheim, i. 419.

[66] On jurisdiction over vessels in the territorial sea, *infra*, pp. 190–1; on jurisdiction over vessels in internal waters, *infra*, pp. 315–17.

[67] See *Ann. Digest*, 7 (1933–4), no. 53; Hackworth, i. 615; Oppenheim, ii. 589–91; Verzijl, *International Law in Historical Perspective*, iii. 18–20, 95–103; Hyde, i. 483; Riva, 24 *Ann. suisse* (1967), 43–66; and Pondaven, *Les Lacs-frontiére* (1972). Cf. the case of bays, *infra*, p. 181. See also *infra*, pp. 223–4 on closed seas.

[68] Cohen, 146 Hague *Recueil* (1975, III), 219–340.

[69] Cf. Oppenheim, ii. 666–7; Rousseau, iii. 263–5; Colombos (6th edn.), 165; Verzijl, *International Law in Historical Perspective*, iii. 576–90; *Frontier Dispute case (Burkina Faso/Republic of Mali)*, ICJ Reports (1986), 631–3, 640–1.

[70] Oppenheim, ii. 679 n.; Rousseau, iii. 197–8; Verzijl, *International Law in Historical Perspective*, ii. 477–8.

[71] Art. 4. Text: 49 *AJ* (1955), Suppl., p. 162.

[72] Art. 88. Text: 14 *AJ* (1920), Suppl., at p. 30. On the *Austro-German Customs Union* case see *supra*, p. 73.

THE PRINCIPLE OF APPURTENANCE

The territory of a state by definition and legal implication includes a territorial sea and the airspace above land territory and the territorial sea. Thus if state A merges into state B the present extent of the latter includes by implication the territorial sea and the airspace of state A.[73] This simple proposition is sometimes described as the principle of appurtenance,[74] and high authority supports the view that as a corollary, the territorial sea cannot be alienated without the coast itself[75] (and no doubt similarly in the case of airspace). With respect, the logical, and therefore the legal, basis for the corollary is not compelling. Another form of the doctrine of appurtenance appears in the Judgment of Judge McNair in the *Fisheries* case.[76] In his words: 'International law imposes upon a maritime State certain obligations and confers upon it certain rights arising out of the sovereignty which it exercises over its maritime territory. The possession of this territory is not optional, not dependent upon the will of the State, but compulsory'. Attractive though this view may seem at first sight, it raises many difficulties. How many of the various territorial extensions are possessed by compulsion of law?[77] The desire to invest the coastal state with responsibility for the maintenance of order and navigational facilities evinced by one authority[78] is not a sufficient basis for the rule supported by Judge McNair, and, indeed, this kind of logic would equally support a doctrine of closed seas. States are permitted to abandon territory, leaving it a *res nullius*, whereas the presumable consequence of disclaiming the territorial sea is simply to extend a *res communis*, the high seas.

18. CAPACITY TO TRANSFER OR ACQUIRE TERRITORY[79]

The last section relates to restrictions of a kind which may apply to transfer or acquisition by states with normal powers. However, the more basic questions of capacity may arise when a dependent state purports to acquire or transfer title.[80] When the principal

---

[73] Claims to territory and treaties of transfer usually refer to territory as specified, or islands, without referring to territorial waters: see e.g. the Italian peace treaty, 1947, Arts. 11 and 14; treaty between US and Cuba relating to the Isle of Pines, 19 *AJ* (1925), 95; and correspondence between Canada and Norway, 27 *AJ* (1933), 93.

[74] See the PCA in the *Grisbadarna* case, Hague Court Reports, pp. 122, 487. Cf. *Procurator General v. D., Ann. Digest*, 15 (1948), no. 26, and, on the power of the mandatory to legislate for the territorial waters of the mandated territory, see *Molvan v. A.-G. for Palestine* [1948] AC 351.

[75] Oppenheim, i. (8th edn.), 463, 488 n. 2. What is the legal consequence of ignoring the supposed rule?

[76] ICJ Reports (1951), 160. See also Fitzmaurice, 31 *BY* (1954), 372–3 and id., 92 Hague *Recueil* (1957, II), 137–8. See also 8 *ICLQ* (1959), 171.

[77] The Continental Shelf Conv. of 1958 adopts the principle of appurtenance: see *North Sea Continental Shelf Cases*, ICJ Reports (1969), 3 at 22, and *infra*, pp. 205–9.

[78] Fitzmaurice, 31 *BY* (1954), 372–3; id., 92 Hague *Recueil* (1957, II), 137–8.

[79] On the capacity of the UN to administer and to make dispositions of territory, see *infra*, p. 167.

[80] On the criteria of statehood, *supra*, pp. 70–6; on vassalage, suzerainty, and protection, *supra*, p. 114.

or dominant state opposes the transaction entered into by the dependency, the effect of the transfer will depend on the operation of the law relating to prescription, acquiescence, and recognition.[81] In other cases the principal will tacitly or expressly ratify the transfer. Here the situation is cognate with the existence of agency, a delegation of power, and the question of capacity cannot arise as such.[82] Related issues, for example the powers of a mandatory in relation to the mandated territory, are better considered in relation to the principle *nemo dat quod non habet*.[83]

19. THE CONCEPT OF TITLE[84]

The content of sovereignty has been examined from various points of view elsewhere.[85] By and large the term denotes the legal competence which a state enjoys in respect of its territory. This competence is a consequence of title and by no means conterminous with it. Thus an important aspect of state competence, the power of disposition, may be limited by treaty,[86] but the restriction, provided it is not total, leaves the title unaffected.[87] However, the materials of international law employ the term sovereignty to describe both the concept of title and the legal competence which flows from it. In the former sense the term 'sovereignty' explains (1) why the competence exists and what its fullest possible extent may be; (2) whether claims may be enforced in respect of interference with the territorial aspects of that competence against a particular state.

The second aspect mentioned is the essence of title: the validity of claims to territorial sovereignty against other states. The equivalent concept in French, 'titre', has been defined as follows: 'Terme qui, pris dans le sens de titre juridique, désigne tout fait, acte ou situation qui est la cause et le fondement d'un droit'.[88] In principle the concept of ownership, opposable to all other states and unititular,[89] can and does exist in international law. Thus the first and undisputed occupation of land which is *res nullius*,[90] and of immemorial and unchallenged attribution (as in the case of England and Wales), may give rise to title which is equivalent to the *dominium* of Roman law. However, in practice the concept of title employed to solve disputes approximates to

---

[81] *Infra*, pp. 146ff.

[82] See *T.P. Sankara Rao v. Municipal Council of Masulipatam*, ILR 26 (1958, II), 104; Hyde, i. 379.

[83] *Infra*, pp. 120–1.

[84] The student will find the following works helpful, since the problems in the sphere of international law are basically the same: Buckland and McNair, *Roman Law and Common Law* (2nd edn., 1965), 71–88 (Excursus by Lawson); Honoré, in Guest (ed.), *Oxford Essays in Jurisprudence* (1961), 107–47 and especially at pp. 134–41. See also ch. 7.

[85] *Supra*, pp. 109–11; *infra*, ch. 14.

[86] *Supra*, pp. 117–18.

[87] So also belligerent occupation and other forms of foreign control will not affect title.

[88] Basdevant, *Dictionnaire, s.v.*

[89] See Honoré, *Oxford Essays*, p. 137, for a definition of a unititular system: 'Under it, if the title to a thing is in A, no title to it can be acquired (independently) by B, except by a process which divests A. There is only one 'root of title' for each thing, and the present title can ultimately be traced back to that root.'

[90] See *infra*, p. 133.

the notion of the better right to possess familiar in the common law.[91] The operation of the doctrines of prescription, acquiescence, and recognition[92] makes this type of approach inevit-able, but in any case tribunals will surely favour an approach which reckons with the limitations inherent in a procedure dominated by the presentation of evidence by two claimants, the result of which is not automatically opposable to third states.[93]

20. THE DETERMINATION OF FRONTIERS

In a broad sense many questions of title arise in the context of 'frontier disputes', but as a matter of principle the determination of the location in detail of the frontier line is distinct from the issue of title. Considerable dispositions of territory may take place in which the grantee enjoys the benefit of a title derived from the grant although no determination of the precise frontier line is made.[94] On the other hand precise determination of the frontier may be made a suspensive condition in a treaty of cession. The process of determination is carried out in accordance with a special body of rules, the best known being the *thalweg* principle. According to the doctrine of the *thalweg* in the case of a navigable river, the middle of the principal channel of navigation is accepted as the boundary.[95] In the case of non-navigable watercourses the boundary is constituted by the median line between the two banks. Judicial practice follows these principles.[96]

The practical aspects of frontiers must be emphasized. Agreement as to the precise details of a frontier, enshrined in a written instrument, is often followed by the separate procedure of demarcation, that is, the marking, literally, of the frontier on the ground by means of posts, stone pillars, and the like. A frontier may be legally definitive, for some purposes, and yet remain undemarcated. Frontiers which are '*de facto*', either because of the absence of demarcation or because of the presence of an unsettled

---

[91] Jennings, *Acquisition of Territory*, pp. 5–6. The common law is 'multititular' (see Honoré, *Oxford Essays*, p. 139). See also the *Eastern Greenland* case, PCIJ, Ser. A/B, no. 53 at p. 46; World Court Reports, iii at p. 171; the *Palmas* award, *RIAA* ii at p. 480; and *infra*, pp. 160–1.

[92] *Infra*, pp. 151ff.

[93] See, in particular, the Statute of the International Court of Justice, Art. 59.

[94] See on the effect of treaties of cession or renunciation relating to territories the frontiers of which are undetermined: the *Mosul* case, PCIJ, Ser. B, no. 12 (1925), at 21 (and see Jennings, *Acquisition of Territory*, p. 14). Cf. Decl. of Potsdam, 2 Aug. 1945; on which *infra*, p. 138. On occasion the distinction between cession and the fixing of a boundary involves considerations of convenience rather than logic: see the cases in *Ann. Digest*, 6 (1931–2), no. 55.

[95] See Oppenheim, ii. 664–5; E. Lauterpacht, 9 *ICLQ* (1960), 208–36.

[96] *Case Concerning Kasikili/Sedudu Island* (Botswana/Namibia) I.C.J. Reports, 1999, p. 1062. para. 24; *Case Concerning the Frontier Dispute* (Benin/Niger), ibid., 2005, pp. 149–50, paras. 143–5. Generally see de Lapradelle, *La Frontière* (1928); Verzijl, *International Law in Historical Perspective*, iii. 513–621; Cukwurah, *The Settlement of Boundary Disputes in International Law* (1967); de Visscher, *Problèmes de confins en droit international public* (1969); Rousseau, iii. 231–72; Brownlie, *African Boundaries* (1979); Shaw, *Title to Territory in Africa* (1986), 221–63.

territorial dispute, may nevertheless be accepted as the legal limit of sovereignty for some purposes, for example those of civil or criminal jurisdiction, nationality law, and the prohibition of unpermitted intrusion with or without the use of arms.

21. *NEMO DAT QUOD NON HABET*[97]

This maxim, together with some exceptions, is a familiar feature of English commercial law, and the principle which the maxim represents is undoubtedly a part of international law. In the *Palmas* case, Huber, arbitrator, stated:[98]

The title alleged by the United States of America as constituting the immediate foundation of its claim is that of cession, brought about by the Treaty of Paris, which cession transferred all rights of sovereignty which Spain may have possessed in the region. ... It is evident that Spain could not transfer more rights than she herself possessed.

The effect of the principle is in practice very much reduced by the operation of the doctrines of prescription, acquiescence, and recognition.[99]

Certain connected principles require consideration. Except when there are only two possible claimants, the adjudication by a tribunal of a piece of territory as between states A and B is not opposable to state C. The tribunal, in so far as adjudication of itself gives title,[100] only has jurisdiction to decide as between the parties before it.[101] The fact that state C claims a particular parcel of territory does not deprive the tribunal of power to adjudicate and does not prevent states A and B from defining their rights in relation to the parcel mutually.[102] In certain cases, the principle operates through particular rules governing special problems. Thus an aggressor, having seized territory by force and committed a delict, may purport to transfer the territory to a third state. The validity of the cession will depend on the effect of specific rules relating to the use of force by states.[103] Again, a state may transfer territory which it lacks the capacity to

---

[97] Or, *nemo plus juris transferre potest quam ipse habet*: no man can give another any better title than he himself has. See the *Case Concerning the Land and Maritime Boundary between Cameroon and Nigeria*, Judgment of 10 October 2002, paras. 194–209.

[98] *RIAA* ii. 829 at 842. See also McNair, *The Law of Treaties* (1961), 656, 665; Hyde, i. 360; Fitzmaurice, 32 *BY* (1955–6), 22; and O'Connell, *The Law of State Succession* (1st edn., 1956), 50.

[99] See *infra*, pp. 145ff. Indeed, if one accepts extreme forms of the doctrine of effective control as the basis of sovereignty, the principle can have no relevance except in relation to the actual construction of treaties of cession: cf. Guggenheim, i. 443.

[100] See *infra*, p. 132.

[101] *Brazil–British Guiana Boundary* arbitration (1904), *RIAA* xi. 21 at 22.

[102] See the Boundary Agreement between China and Pakistan, 2 Mar. 1963, which is expressed as fixing 'the alignment of the boundary between China's Sinkiang and the contiguous areas the defence of which is under the actual control of Pakistan'. Thus India's rights in respect of Kashmir are not foreclosed (see Art. 6 of the Agreement).

[103] See *infra*, pp. 510–12, on *jus cogens*.

transfer. In this type of situation much turns on the extent to which such defects of title may be cured by prescription, acquiescence, and recognition.[104]

Under certain conditions it is possible that the law accepts the existence of encumbrances passing with territory ceded. Lord McNair[105] refers to 'treaties creating purely local obligations' and gives as examples territory over which the ceding state has granted to another state a right of transit or a right of navigation on a river, or a right of fishery in territorial or internal waters.[106] These matters are considered further in Chapter 29.

[104] See *infra*, pp. 146ff.

[105] *The Law of Treaties*, p. 656. Others speak of 'international servitudes'. See generally *infra*, pp. 366–8, where McNair's views are questioned. Cf. *supra*, pp. 110–11, on international leases and licences.

[106] On the Ethiopia–Somaliland frontier dispute and the question of the permanence of grazing rights of Somali tribes over Ethiopian territory: Brown, 10 *ICLQ* (1961), 167–78. See also the *Right of Passage over Indian Territory* case, ICJ Reports (1960), 6.

7

THE CREATION AND TRANSFER OF TERRITORIAL SOVEREIGNTY[1]

1. INTRODUCTION

Disputes concerning title to territory, including islands, and the precise determination of boundaries are frequent, and are regularly the subject of proceedings before the International Court, or courts of arbitration, or of procedures of negotiation and mediation. On occasion, recourse to arbitration forms a part of an overall peace settlement, as in the case of the Eritrea–Ethiopia Boundary Commission.[2] Many disputes are dormant, and it is only when a dispute flares up, creating a threat to the peace or other political crisis, that it receives publicity. Even in the case of the acquisition of territory belonging to no state (*terra nullius*), while this may not occur currently, the relevance and existence of such occupation in the past are often issues in existing disputes. Legally relevant events may have occurred centuries ago.[3] The pressures of national sentiment, new forms of exploitation of barren and inaccessible areas, the strategic significance of areas previously neglected, and the pressure of population on resources, give good cause for a belief that territorial disputes will increase in significance. This is specially so in Africa and Asia, where the removal of foreign political domination has left the successor states with a long agenda of unsettled problems, legal and political. Moreover, the body of rules relating to title to land territory provides a

---

[1] Jennings, *The Acquisition of Territory in International Law* (1963); Bastid, 107 Hague *Recueil* (1962, III), 435–95; Fitzmaurice, 32 *BY* (1955–6), 20–76; Hackworth, i. 393–476; Waldock, 25 *BY* (1948), 311–53; Verzijl, *International Law in Historical Perspective*, iii (1970), 297–386; de Visscher, *Les Effectivités du droit international public* (1967), 101–17; Blum, *Historic Titles in International Law* (1965); McEwen, *International Boundaries of East Africa* (1971); Munkman, 46 *BY* (1972–3), 1–116; Rousseau, iii. 145–230; Bardonnet, Hague *Recueil* (1976, V), 17–166; Kaikobad, 54 *BY* (1983), 119–41; Shaw, *Title to Territory in Africa* (1986); Thirlway, 66 *BY* (1995), 10–38; Kohen, *Possession contestée et souveraineté territoriale* (1997); Sharma, *Territorial Acquisition, Disputes and International Law* (1997).

[2] Decision of 13 April 2002; *ILM* 41, 1057.

[3] In the *Minquiers and Ecrehos* case, ICJ Reports (1953), 47, the parties and, to a lesser extent, the Court considered it necessary to investigate legal transactions of the medieval period.

basic apparatus applicable, within certain limits, in the sphere of maritime territory and the seabed.[4] Finally, the principles developed in relation to territorial areas provide useful resources for those engaged in building a legal regime for outer space.[5]

2. HISTORICAL CHANGES IN CONCEPTS OF LAW

In one sense at least law is history, and the lawyer's appreciation of the meaning of rules relating to acquisition of territory, and of the manner of their application in particular cases, will be rendered more keen by a knowledge of the historical development of the law. In the Middle Ages the ideas of state and kingship prevalent in Europe tended to place the ruler in the position of a private owner, since feudal law, as the applicable 'public law', conferred ultimate title on the ruler, and the legal doctrine of the day employed analogies of Roman private law in the sphere of property to describe the sovereign's power. The growth of absolutism in the sixteenth and seventeenth centuries confirmed the trend. A treaty ceding territory had the appearance of a sale of land by a private owner, and sales of territory did in fact occur. In the eighteenth and nineteenth centuries the significance of private law notions declined. In the field of theory sovereignty was recognized as an abstraction and thus the ruler was a bearer and agent of a legal capacity which belonged to the state. The nineteenth century witnessed some important and to some extent contradictory developments. In Europe and Latin America the principle of nationalities appeared, which, as 'the principle of self-determination', has become increasingly important. At the same time the European powers made use of the concept of the *res nullius*, which was legal in form but often political in application, since it involved the occupation of areas in Asia and Africa which were in fact the seat of organized communities.[6] More recently the rule has become established that the use or threat of force by states to settle disputes or otherwise to effect a territorial gain is illegal. This principle, like that of self-determination, requires harmonization with the pre-existing law on acquisition of territory.

3. THE DOCTRINE OF INTER-TEMPORAL LAW[7]

The fact is that in many instances the rights of parties to a dispute derive from legally significant acts, or a treaty concluded, very long ago. Sir Gerald Fitzmaurice states the rule applicable in these cases:[8] 'It can now be regarded as an established principle of international law

---

4 *Infra*, p. 158.

5 See *infra*, pp. 255–9.

6 See Crawford, *The Creation of States in International Law* (2nd edn., 2006), 257–81.

7 Jennings, *Acquisition of Territory*, pp. 28–31; Fitzmaurice, 30 *BY* (1953), 5–8; *Annuaire de l'Inst.* (1973), i; (1975), 537; Rousseau, iii. 149–50; Elias, 74 *AJ* (1980), 285–307 (also in *The International Court of Justice and Some Contemporary Problems* (1983), 119–47); Thirlway, 66 *BY* (1995), 128–43; Higgins, in *Essays in Honour of Krzysztof Skubiszewski* (1996), 173–81.

8 30 *BY* (1953), 5. See also Hyde, i. 320 n. 5, 329 n. 27; Hackworth, i. 393–5.

that in such cases the situation in question must be appraised, and the treaty interpreted, in the light of the rules of international law as they existed at the time, and not as they exist today'. In the *Island of Palmas* case Judge Huber stated the principle[9] and continued: 'The effect of discovery by Spain is therefore to be determined by the rules of international law in force in the first half of the 16th century—or (to take the earliest date) in the first quarter of it ...'. The rule has also been applied in the interpretation of treaties.[10]

In the *Island of Palmas* case Judge Huber had to consider whether Spanish sovereignty over the island subsisted at the critical date[11] in 1898. In doing so he gave a new dimension to the rule under discussion. He said:

As regards the question which of different legal systems prevailing at successive periods is to be applied in a particular case (the so-called intertemporal law), a distinction must be made between the creation of rights and the existence of rights. The same principle which subjects the act creative of a right to the law in force at the time the right arises, demands that the existence of the right, in other words its continued manifestation, shall follow the conditions required by the evolution of law.

This extension[12] of the doctrine has been criticized on the grounds that logically the notion that title has to be maintained at every moment of time would threaten many titles and lead to instability.[13] It would seem that the principle represented by extension of the doctrine is logically inevitable, but that the criticism is in point in so far as it emphasizes the need for care in applying the rule.[14] In any case the principle cannot operate in a vacuum: its theoretical extent will in practice be reduced by the effect of recognition, acquiescence, estoppel, prescription, the rule that abandonment is not to be presumed, and the general condition of the pleadings and evidence.[15]

4. CRITICAL DATES[16]

In any dispute a certain date, or several dates, will assume prominence in the process of evaluating the facts. The choice of such a date, or dates, is within the province of the tribunal seized of the dispute and will depend in some circumstances on the inevitable

[9] Hague Court Reports, ii. 83 at 100. See also the award in the *Grisbadarna* case (1909), 4 *AJ* (1910), 226, 231, 232; Hackworth, i. 395; *RIAA* xi. 155 at 159, 160.

[10] See *U.S. Nationals in Morocco*, ICJ Reports (1952), 176 at 189; *Right of Passage over Indian Territory*, ICJ Reports (1960), 6 at 37; and see also the *Namibia* Advisory Opinion, ICJ Reports (1971), 16 at 31; and the *Aegean Sea* case, ICJ Reports (1978), 3 at 32.

[11] See *infra*.

[12] Lauterpacht, *Function*, pp. 283–5.

[13] See Jessup, 22 *AJ* (1928), 735 at 739–40; Jennings, *Acquisition of Territory*, pp. 28–31, and 121 Hague *Recueil* (1967, II), 422.

[14] This form of the doctrine was applied sensibly in the *Minquiers and Ecrehos* case, ICJ Reports (1953), 47 at 56; and see also *Western Sahara* case, ICJ Reports (1975), 12 at 38–9; and 168–71 (Sep. Op. of Judge de Castro).

[15] The doctrine had no very substantial effect in the *Minquiers and Ecrehos* case: see last note and Bastid, 107 Hague *Recueil* (1962, III), 448–50.

[16] Fitzmaurice, 32 *BY* (1955–6), 20–44; Blum, *Historic Titles in International Law* pp. 208–22; Thirlway, 66 *BY* (1995), 31–8. See also the Chamber of the International Court in the *Case Concerning the Land, Island and Maritime Frontier Dispute*, ICJ Reports, 1992, p. 401, para. 67. For the problems arising in the context

logic of the law applicable to the particular facts and, in other cases, on the practical necessity of confining the process of decision to relevant and cogent facts and thus to acts prior to the existence of a dispute.[17] In the latter context the tribunal is simply employing judicial technique in the use of evidence and more especially the exclusion of evidence consisting of self-serving acts of parties at a stage when it was evident that a dispute existed. Of course, evidence of acts and statements occurring after the critical date may be admissible if not self-serving, as in the case of admissions against interest. There are several types of critical date, and it is difficult and probably misleading to formulate general definitions:[18] the facts of the case are dominant (including, for this purpose, the terms of the special agreement empowering the tribunal to hear the case) and there is no necessity for a tribunal to choose any date whatsoever. In many cases there will be several dates of varying significance.

The dispute between Norway and Denmark which led to the *Eastern Greenland* case arose from a Norwegian proclamation on 10 July 1931 announcing occupation of the area. The Court in that case said:[19] 'It must be borne in mind, however, that as the critical date is July 10th, 1931 ... it is sufficient [for Denmark] to establish a valid title in the period immediately preceding the occupation.' In the *Palmas Island*[20] case the United States claimed as successor to Spain under a treaty of cession dated 10 December 1898, and everything turned on the nature of Spanish rights at that time. The Court did not specifically choose a critical date in the *Minquiers and Ecrehos* case.[21] In the *Argentine–Chile Frontier*[22] case the Tribunal reported that it 'had considered the notion of the critical date to be of little value in the present litigation and has examined all the evidence submitted to it, irrespective of the date of the acts to which such evidence relates'.

---

of treaties of cession and the rights of successor states see the *Lighthouses* arbitration (France/Greece), PCA (1956), ILR 23 (1956), 659 at 668.

[17] Cf, the exceptions to the hearsay rule in the law of evidence based on statements *ante litem motam*, and the rules of English equity evolved to regulate the evidence admissible to rebut a presumption of advancement.

[18] See Jennings, *Acquisition of Territory*, pp. 31–5; id., 121 Hague *Recueil* (1967, II), 423–6.

[19] PCIJ, Ser. A/B, no. 53, p. 45.

[20] See *infra*, p. 136.

[21] ICJ Reports (1953), 47. The French argument rested on the date of the Conv. of 2 Aug. 1839; that of the United Kingdom on the date of the *compromis* (29 Dec. 1950). See Johnson, 3 *ICLQ* (1954), 189 at 207–11. Critical dates *eo nomine* did not feature in the Judgment in the case of the *Temple of Preah Vihear*, ICJ Reports (1962), 6. However, the Court treated two dates as material: 1904, the date of a frontier treaty between France and Thailand, and 1954, when Thailand sent military or police forces to occupy the area. See also the *Rann of Kutch* case; Award, 1968; *ILM* vii. 633 at 666: ILR 50, 2 at 470; RIAA xvii at pp. 527–8.

[22] Award, 1966; ILR 38, 10 at 79–80; *RIAA* xvi. 109 at 166–7; 61 *AJ* (1967), 1071. See also the *Red Sea Islands* case (Phase One), ILR 114, 2 at 32; *Case Concerning Sovereignty over Pulao Ligitan and Pulao Sipidan*, I.C.J. Reports (2002), 682; and *Case Concerning Territorial and Maritime Dispute between Nicaragua and Honduras in the Caribbean Sea*, I.C.J. Reports (2007), paras. 117–31.

5. THE MODES OF ACQUISITION

Many of the standard textbooks,[23] and particularly those in English, classify the modes of acquisition in a stereotyped way which reflects the preoccupation of writers in the period before the First World War. According to this analysis (if the term is deserved) there are five modes of acquisition—occupation, accretion, cession, conquest,[24] and prescription. Apart from issues arising from the division and choice of the modes, the whole concept of modes of acquisition is unsound in principle and makes the task of understanding the true position much more difficult.[25] Labels are never a substitute for analysis. The inadequacies of the orthodox approach will perhaps be more apparent when the relevant questions have been examined in the sections which follow, but a few things may be usefully said here. A tribunal will concern itself with proof of the exercise of sovereignty at the critical date or dates, and in doing so will not apply the orthodox analysis to describe its process of decision.[26] The issue of territorial sovereignty, or title, is often complex, and involves the application of various principles of the law to the material facts. The result of this process cannot always be ascribed to any single dominant rule or 'mode of acquisition'. The orthodox analysis does not prepare the student for the interaction of principles of acquiescence and recognition with the other rules. Furthermore, a category like 'cession' or 'prescription' may bring quite distinct situations into unhappy fellowship.[27] Lastly, the importance of showing a better right to possess in contentious cases, i.e. of relative title,[28] is obscured if too much credit is given to the five 'models'. The headings employed in the sections of this chapter which follow represent categories of convenience and are not intended to prejudge any issues of principle.

6. ORIGINAL AND DERIVATIVE TITLE

It is common to classify the five orthodox modes of acquisition as 'original' or 'derivative'. Occupation and accretion are usually described as 'original' methods, cession as 'derivative'. Significantly, there are differences of opinion in regard to conquest

[23] See Brierly, pp. 163–73, and Akehurst, *A Modern Introduction to International Law* (6th edn., 1987), 143–50.

[24] This appears as 'subjugation' in Oppenheim, ii. 698.

[25] For critical comment see Johnson, *Camb. LJ* (1955), 215–17; Jennings, *Acquisition of Territory*, pp. 6–7. See also Rousseau, 93 Hague *Recueil* (1958, I), 415–16; Schwarzenberger, *International Law*, i (3rd edn.) 292–309. See also *infra*, pp. 156–8, on historical consolidation of title.

[26] Note the difficulty encountered in classifying the *Island of Palmas, Eastern Greenland,* and *Minquiers and Ecrehos* cases: *infra*, p. 142. And cf. *Case Concerning Sovereignty over Certain Frontier Land*, ICJ Reports (1959), 209.

[27] It may be noted that 'annexation' is not a term of art. The term commonly describes an official state act signifying an extension of sovereignty. It is not a root of title. See McNair, *Opinions*, i. 285 n. 1, 289; Hyde, i. 391; Hackworth, i. 446–9; and *infra*, p. 141, on symbolic annexation.

[28] See *infra*, pp. 154–6.

and prescription, and the classification has no practical value.[29] In one sense all titles are original, since much depends on the acts of the grantee in the case of a cession.[30] In any case the dual classification oversimplifies the situation, and the modes described as 'derivative' are so in rather different ways. Moreover the usual analyses do not explain how title is acquired when a new state comes into existence.[31] Here title is created as a consequence of legal procedure relating to the establishment and recognition of new legal persons.[32] The events leading to independence of the new state are matters within the domestic jurisdiction of another legal person, and yet they are legally relevant to territorial disputes involving the new state.[33] In this type of case there is no 'root of title' *as such*: title is a by-product of the revolution, secession, or other events leading to the creation of a state as a new source of territorial sovereignty.

7. ROOTS OF TITLE[34]

(a) A treaty of cession[35]

A right to possess certain territory as sovereign may be conferred by agreement between intending grantor and grantee, and, if the grantee takes possession in accordance with the treaty,[36] the treaty provides the legal basis of sovereignty.[37] An actual transfer is not of course possible or required if the grantee is already in occupation.[38] The date on which title changes may be determined by the treaty of cession. It will normally be the date on which the treaty comes into force.[39] Furthermore, the treaty itself

---

[29] See Johnson, *Camb. LJ* (1955), 217. Thus an 'original' mode does not necessarily give a title free of incumbrances: see ICJ Reports (1960), 6.

[30] Guggenheim, i. 438, 443; and see *infra*.

[31] See Jennings, *Acquisition of Territory*, pp. 7–11. See also Hyde, i. 390; Hackworth, i. 444–5.

[32] *Supra*, pp. 85ff.

[33] For example, disputes between India and Pakistan involve examination of many constitutional issues and acts of state by the United Kingdom before independence.

[34] This is a general description of content and not strictly a term of art.

[35] The term 'cession' is used to cover a variety of types of transaction, and it is important to seek the legal realities behind the term in each case. Cf. *Différends Sociétés Dufay et Gigandet*, *RIAA* xvi. 197 at 208–12. On the effect of cessions accompanied by the use or threat of force see *infra*, p. 167. See also p. 168, 486–90 on the relevance of the principle of self-determination and other rules.

[36] See Oppenheim, ii. 682; Rousseau, iii. 173; Schwarzenberger, *International Law*, i (3rd edn.), 302–4; *Franco-Ethiopian Railway Co.* claim, ILR 24 (1957), at 616, 623. See also *San Lorenzo Title and Improvement Co.* v. *City Mortgage Co. Ann. Digest*, 6 (1931–2), no. 55 at p. 116. Cf. *German Interests in Polish Upper Silesia* (1926), PCIJ, Ser. A, no. 7, p. 30; *Lighthouses in Crete and Samos* (1937), Ser. A/B, no. 71, p. 103.

[37] See the United States argument in the *Island of Palmas* case.

[38] This situation is more properly classified as renunciation: *Sorkis* v. *Amed*, ILR 17 (1950), no. 24 at p. 103, and see *infra*, p. 139. However, the term cession is sometimes used thus: see the *German Reparations* case (1924), *RIAA* i. 429 at 443; *Banin* v. *Laviani and Ellena, Ann. Digest*, 16 (1949), no. 27; *Différends Sociétés Dufay et Gigandet*, *RIAA* xvi. 197 at 208–12.

[39] *Versailles Treaty* case, ILR 32, 339; *N. Masthan Sahib* v. *Chief Commissioner*, ILR 49, 484; and see Treaty of Cession relating to the Kuria Muria Islands, *Treaty Series* no. 8 (1968), Cmnd. 3505.

gives the intending grantee an assignable interest, and the grantee can pass his interest to a third state. Presumably, for the third state to get title, transfer is still required, and, if the sovereign refuses to give possession, the assignee can be subrogated to the treaty right of the assignor.

(b) Other dispositions by treaty

Apart from cession and transfer in accordance with a treaty, title may exist on the basis of a treaty alone, the treaty marking a reciprocal recognition of sovereignty in solemn form and with attention to detail.[40] In the case of a disputed frontier line the boundary treaty which closes the dispute will *create* title, because previously the question of title was unsettled: in contrast a treaty of cession transfers a definitive title.[41]

(c) Consent in other forms

The existence of consent of the transfer of territory may be evidenced without the conclusion of any formal agreement.[42] For example, a treaty of cession may be invalid, in the absence of appropriate legislation by one of the parties, in the courts of that state, yet if an actual transfer has taken place and a change of sovereignty is accepted by the interested parties, the validity or otherwise of the treaty is irrelevant.[43] Informal expression of consent is not far removed from consent implied from conduct and a unilateral rather than consensual recognition of sovereignty. This field of problems relates to acquiescence, estoppel, and recognition, and these topics will be considered later on.[44]

(d) Uti possidetis (juris)[45]

In the region of Latin America consent as a means of disposition of territory has assumed an indirect form. By their practice the successor states of Spain agreed to apply, as between themselves, and later in their disputes with Brazil, a principle for the settlement of frontier disputes in an area in which *terra nullius* (territory belonging

---

[40] Consequently disputes as to title may involve the interpretation of the given treaty exclusively: see the *Beagle Channel Arbitration*, Award of 18 Apr. 1977; HMSO 1977; Bilingual edn., Rep. of Chile, 1977; 17 *ILM* (1978), 632; ILR 52, 93.

[41] See McNair, *Law of Treaties* (1961), 656–7; id., *Opinions*, i. 287; *Case Concerning Sovereignty over Certain Frontier Land*, ICJ Reports (1959), 209 at 226, 231, 256; *Case of Temple of Preah Vihear*, ICJ Reports (1962), 6 at 16, 52, 67, 73–4, 102–3; *Ditmar and Linde* v. *Ministry of Agriculture*, Ann. Digest, 8 (1935–7), no. 52; *Willis* v. *First Real Estate and Investment Co.*, Ann. Digest, 11 (1919–42), no. 52.

[42] Schwarzenberger, *International Law*, i (3rd edn.), 302, *Frontier Land* case, ICJ Reports (1959), 238–48, 251; *Temple* case, ibid. (1962), 133–42.

[43] *Union of India* v. *Jain and Others*, ILR 21 (1954), 256 at 257.

[44] *Infra*, pp. 151ff.

[45] For a full account: Hyde, i. 498–510. See also Alvarez, *Le Droit international américain* (1910), 65; the *Colombia–Venezuela Boundary* arbitration (1922), *RIAA* i. 223; *Ann. Digest*, I (1919–22), no. 54; *Beagle Channel Arbitration*, Award of 18 Apr. 1977, *supra*, n. 41, Decision, paras. 9–12; Hackworth, i. 732–7; Rousseau, iii. 238–40; Thirlway, 66 *BY* (1995), 15–17; Shaw, 67 *BY* (1996), 75–154; Antonopoulos, *Rev. hellénique*, 49 (1996), 29–88; Abi-Saab, *Liber Amicorum Lucius Caflisch*, 657–71. See also the use of the *uti possidetis* as a general principle of law by two Latin American judges in the *Case Concerning Sovereignty over Certain Frontier Land*, ICJ Reports (1959), 209 at 240, 255.

to no state) by political definition, did not exist—the independent republics regarded their titles as coextensive with that of the former Spanish empire. The principle has been expressed as follows:[46]

When the common sovereign power was withdrawn, it became indispensably necessary to agree on a general principle of demarcation, since there was a universal desire to avoid resort to force, and the principle adopted was a colonial *uti possidetis*; that is, the principle involving the preservation of the demarcations under the colonial regimes corresponding to each of the colonial entities that was constituted as a State.

The principle involves implied agreement to base territorial settlement on a rule of presumed possession by the previous Spanish administrative unit in 1821, in Central America, or in 1810, in South America.

The operation of such a principle does not give very satisfactory solutions, since much depends on the concept of possession to be employed, and, furthermore, the old Spanish administrative boundaries are frequently ill-defined or difficult of proof.[47] It must be emphasized that the principle is by no means mandatory and the states concerned are free to adopt other principles as the basis of a settlement.[48] However, the general principle, that pre-independence boundaries of former administrative divisions all subject to the same sovereign remain in being, is in accordance with good policy and has been adopted by governments and tribunals concerned with boundaries in Asia[49] and Africa.[50] The principle has also been applied in relation to the appearance of new States on the territory of the former Yugoslavia.[51]

(e) Disposition by joint decision of the principal powers

After the defeat of the Central Powers in the First World War, and the Axis Powers in the Second World War, the leading victor states assumed a power of disposition, to be exercised jointly, over the territory of the defeated states. In the years 1919 and 1920 decisions were taken by the Supreme Council of the Allied and Associated

[46] See Hyde, i. 499 n. 3. See also Judge Urrutia Holguin, ICJ Reports (1960), 226.

[47] See the *Guatemala–Honduras Boundary* arbitration (1933), *RIAA* ii. 1322; *Ann. Digest*, 7 (1933–4), no. 46. For comment see 27 *AJ* (1933), 403–27. Cf. Waldock, 25 *BY* (1948), at 325. See also *Land, Island and Maritime Frontier Dispute*, ICJ Reports, 1992, p. 351, and, in particular, pp. 386–95 (paras. 40–56); *Case Concerning the Frontier Dispute* (Benin/Niger), ibid. (2005), pp. 108–10, 133–49; *Case Concerning Territorial and Maritime Dispute between Nicaragua and Honduras in the Caribbean Sea*, ibid. (2007), paras. 229–36.

[48] See generally Hyde, i. 499 n. 3; Hackworth, i. 726–55.

[49] See the *Temple* case, ICJ Reports (1962), 6; *Rann of Kutch* case; Award, 1968; *ILM* vii. 633; ILR 50, 2. Cp. The Award in the *Red Sea Islands* case (Phase One), ILR 114, 2 at 32–4.

[50] OAU Resol. on Border Disputes, 21 July 1964; Touval, 21 *Int. Organization* (1967), 102–27; Judgment of the Chamber of the ICJ, *Frontier Dispute Case (Burkina Faso–Republic of Mali)*, ICJ Reports (1986), 554 at 565–7, paras. 20–6; p. 568, para. 30; pp. 586–7, para. 63; Award of the Tribunal in the *Guinea-Guinea (Bissau) Maritime Delimitation Case* (1985), ILR 77, 636 at 657 (para. 40); Award of the Tribunal in *Guinea (Bissau)-Senegal Delimitation Case* (1989), ILR 83, 1, 22 and Bedjaoui, Diss. Op., 56–85. See also the Separate Opinion of Judge Ad Hoc Ajibola in *Libya/Chad*, ICJ Reports, 1994, 6 at 83–92.

[51] See Opinions No. 2 and No. 3, Conference on Yugoslavia, Arbitration Commission, ILR 92, 167 and 170 respectively; and Craven, 66 *BY* (1995), 385–90.

States; in 1943 and 1945 by meetings of leaders at Tehran, Yalta, and Potsdam,[52] and subsequently by meetings of Foreign Ministers. States losing territory as a consequence of dispositions in this wise might, and often did, renounce title[53] by the provisions of a peace treaty to the areas concerned, but the dispositions were assumed to be valid irrespective of such renunciation and the recipients were usually in possession prior to the coming into force of a peace treaty.[54] The existence of this power of disposition or assignment is recognized by jurists,[55] but they find it difficult to suggest, or to agree upon, a satisfactory legal basis for it. Some translate political realities into legal forms by supposing that the community of states has delegated such a power to the 'principal' or 'great' powers.[56] Others, at least in relation to the Second World War, postulate a right to impose measures of security, which may include frontier changes, on an aggressor consequent on his defeat in a war of collective defence and sanction.[57]

Much turns on the extent to which recognition and acquiescence[58] may counteract any elements of illegality[59] which may infect such procedures in some cases. Dispositions of this kind normally are recognized by multilateral peace treaty or otherwise.[60] In some cases, for example, the Geneva Conference of 1954,[61] in regard to Indo-China, the express delegation of power prior to agreed disposition of territory ensures that a certain number of states are bound to accept the results of the procedure.

(f) Renunciation or relinquishment[62]

It is not uncommon for states to renounce title over territory in circumstances in which the subject-matter does not thereby become *terra nullius* (territory belonging to no state). This distinguishes renunciation from abandonment.[63] Furthermore, there is no element of reciprocity, and no contract to transfer, as in the case of a treaty of

---

[52] Text of declarations: 38 *AJ* (1944), Suppl., p. 9; 39 *AJ* (1945), Suppl. pp. 103, 245. See also Goodrich and Carroll (eds.), *Documents on American Foreign Relations* (1947), vii and viii.

[53] See *infra*, on renunciation.

[54] See Hyde, i. 360–3. Much depends on the particular facts of each case and especially the intentions of the parties involved. In this type of case the use of the term 'cession' does not aid legal analysis. The dismemberment of Austria-Hungary and its division among seven states was effected prior to the Treaties of St Germain-en-Laye and Trianon. See also the *German Reparations* case (1924), *RIAA* i. 429 at 442.

[55] Verzijl, *International Law in Historical Perspective*, i. (1968), 305–7; *Jaworzina Boundary*, PCIJ, Ser. B, no. 8 (1923); *Monastery of Saint-Naoum*, ibid., no. 9; Joint Diss. Op. of Judges Spender and Fitzmaurice, ICJ Reports (1962), 482; PCA in the *Lighthouses* arbitration (France-Greece), 1956; ILR 23 (1956), 659 at 663–9. See also *L. and J.J. v. Polish State Railways*, ILR 24 (1957), 77.

[56] Cf. *infra*, p. 163.

[57] See Brownlie, *International Law and the Use of Force by States* (1963), 408–9.

[58] On which *infra*, p. 151.

[59] e.g. operation of the principle of self-determination (see *infra*, pp. 161–2) and the prohibition of the threat or use of force to acquire territory or settle disputes (see *infra*, p. 160, and also Brownlie, *International Law and the Use of Force by States*, pp. 74ff., 251ff.).

[60] See generally Crawford, *The Creation of States in International Law* (2nd edn., 2006), 503–64.

[61] *Documents on International Affairs* (1954), 138; Cmd. 9186.

[62] See Hyde, i. 385–6, 392 n. 2; Whiteman, ii. 1229–32. For two recent examples: *Digest of US Practice* (1979), 781–4.

[63] *Infra*, p. 139.

cession. Renunciation may be a recognition that another state now has title[64] or a recognition of, or agreement to confer, a power of disposition to be exercised by another state or a group of states.[65]

A series of unilateral acts may constitute evidence of an implicit voluntary relinquishment of rights.[66] Renunciation is to be distinguished from reversion, i.e. recognition by an aggressor that territory seized is rightfully under the sovereignty of the victim. Here, there is no title to renounce.[67] Since the procedure of renunciation involves title alone, it may happen that the state losing title retains powers of administration by delegation.[68]

(g) Adjudication

While the subject is generally neglected, some jurists accept adjudication by a judicial organ[69] as a mode of acquisition.[70] The award of a tribunal is certainly a valuable root of title, but the award is not of itself dispositive. There is some analogy here with the effect of a treaty of cession, and in general sovereignty changes only when there is an occupation in pursuance of the award. The award then gives the value of sovereignty to the possession.[71] However, in certain cases the award has a dispositive effect: (1) when the nature of the territory is such that no physical acts are necessary to its effective appropriation;[72] (2) where the two disputants are both exercising acts of administration in respect of the territory concerned, and the award merely declares which of the two 'possessors' is a lawful holder;[73] (3) where the loser is to continue in

---

[64] For examples see the Treaty of St Germain-en-Laye of 10 Sept. 1919; 14 AJ (1920), Suppl., p. 1, Arts. 36, 43, 46, 47, 53, 54, 59. See also the German Reparations case (1924), RIAA i. 429 at 442.

[65] See the Treaty of St Germain, Arts. 89–91; and the Lighthouses arbitration (1956), ILR 23 (1956), 659 at 663–6 (as to the Treaty of London, 30 May 1913). On Italian renunciation of all right and title to Italian territories in Africa see the Treaty of Peace with Italy, 1947, Art. 23; Banin v. Laviani and Ellena, Ann. Digest, 16 (1949), no. 27; Sorkis v. Amed. ILR 17 (1950), no. 24 at p. 103; Farrugia v. Nuova Comp. Gen. Autolinee, ILR 18 (1951), no. 32; Cernograz and Zudich v. INPS, ILR 77, 627. See also Différends Sociétés Dufay et Gigandet, RIAA xvi. 197 at 208–12; and Art. 2 of the Japanese Peace Treaty of 8 Sept. 1951; 46 AJ (1952), Suppl., p. 71.

[66] See the Rann of Kutch case; Award, 1968; ILM vii. 633 at 667–73, 685–8; ILR 50, 2 at 474–500, 516–18; RIAA xvii. at pp. 531–53, 567–70.

[67] See infra, p. 154, and a decision of the Franco-Italian Conciliation Commission in ILR 24 (1957), 602 at 605.

[68] See supra, p. 107 n. 13 and cf. the constitutum possessorium, so-called, in Roman law.

[69] i.e. the International Court of Justice (and its predecessor), the Permanent Court of Arbitration, ad hoc arbitral tribunals, conciliation commissions, and other bodies acting judicially in respect of the issue of title, including, for example, the Council of the League of Nations. If a political organ like the Security Council does not decide the issue judicially and in accordance with the law, it is simply exercising a power of disposition which may be derived from the Charter (this is a difficult question) or from a treaty specially conferring such power.

[70] Rousseau, iii. 186; Guggenheim, i. 442 n. 2; Verzijl, International Law in Historical Perspective, 378–81. See also Strupp, Éléments (2nd edn., 1930), 155; Minquiers and Ecrehos case, ICJ Reports (1953), 56; Brazil-British Guiana Boundary arbitration (1905), RIAA xi. 21 at 22; Basdevant (ed.), Dictionnaire de la terminologie du droit international (1960), s.v.

[71] Thus, before execution of the award the successful claimant cannot seize the territory. See also the UN Charter, Art. 94, para. 2, and Brownlie, International Law and the Use of Force by States, p. 382.

[72] See infra, pp. 135ff., on the Island of Palmas, Clipperton Island, and Eastern Greenland cases.

[73] See infra, p. 134.

possession with delegated powers of administration and jurisdiction; (4) when the successful claimant is already in possession[74] (5) where the award relates only to the detailed fixing of a frontier line.[75] In principle the International Court might be asked to declare the status of territory and subsequently find that at the critical date the territory belonged to no state.[76]

(h) Agreements concluded with local rulers

In the Advisory Opinion concerning *Western Sahara*[77] the International Court stated that in the period beginning in 1884:

the State practice of the relevant period indicates that territories inhabited by tribes or peoples having a social and political organization were not regarded as *terrae nullius*. It shows that in the case of such territories the acquisition of sovereignty was not generally considered as effected unilaterally through 'occupation' of *terra nullius* by original title but through agreements concluded with local rulers... such agreements... were regarded as derivative roots of title, and not original titles obtained by occupation of *terrae nullius*.

8. EFFECTIVE OCCUPATION[78]

The concept of effective occupation in international law represents the type of legal relation which in private law would be described as possession. In the absence of a formal basis for title in a treaty or judgment, and in a system without registration of title, possession plays a significant role. Naturally, as in private law, the concept is complex, and many difficulties arise in applying principles to facts. It must be borne in mind that 'legal possession' involves a search for an interest worth protection by the law. Legal policy may lead a court to regard as sufficient a tenuous connection between claimant and territory in certain conditions. Moreover, what is important is *state activity*, and especially acts of administration. 'Occupation' here derives from *occupatio* in Roman law and does not necessarily signify occupation in the sense of actual settlement and a physical holding.

Effective occupation is commonly related to extension of sovereignty to *terra nullius*, i.e. new land, for example a volcanic island, territory abandoned by the former sovereign, or territory not possessed by a community having a social and political

---

[74] See the *Eastern Greenland* case, *infra*, p. 137.

[75] Rousseau, iii. 186. There are some objections to his view: (1) to distinguish disputes about frontier lines from other disputes is difficult; and (2) an award of this kind of its very nature demands careful execution, a process of demarcation, before the line is final (see ICJ Reports (1962), 69.

[76] Cf. PCIJ, Ser. A/B, no. 53, pp. 41–2; World Court Reports, iii. 167 (Norwegian suggestion).

[77] ICJ Report (1975), 12 at 39. See also ibid. 123–4, Sep. Op. of Judge Dillard.

[78] See Waldock, 25 *BY* (1948), 311–53; von der Heydte, 29 *AJ* (1935), 448–71; Genet, 15 *RDILC* (1934), 285–324, 416–50; Fitzmaurice, 32 *BY* (1955–6), at 49–71; Whiteman, ii. 1030–62.

organization.[79] The connection with the *terra nullius* is pointed to as an important point of distinction between effective occupation and acquisitive prescription.[80] In the latter case land *previously* under the unchallenged sovereignty of one state is subjected to acts of sovereignty by a competitor. Where the conditions for acquisitive prescription are satisfied it is clear that a paradigm of effective occupation is an important element in the process of establishing sovereignty. In practice it is not easy to distinguish effective occupation and prescription, and in the *Island of Palmas* and *Eastern Greenland* cases the award and judgment, respectively, do not employ the categories. Beckett[81] has classified the former as a case of prescription, the latter as resting on occupation.[82] However, it is submitted that in the *Palmas* case, as in the *Minquiers and Ecrehos* case in 1953, the issue was simply that of which of two competing sovereignties had the better right. Prescription classically involves usurpation, a sequence of peaceful possession and competition. Yet the two last-mentioned cases, as will appear subsequently, involve, for all practical purposes, contemporaneously competing acts of state sovereignty. In the *Minquiers and Ecrehos* case the Court stated the issue as one of possession,[83] which in the context was equated with sovereignty.[84] Its task, in part, was 'to appraise the relative strength of the opposing claims to sovereignty over the Ecrehos'.[85]

As a consequence must of the material to be considered under the heading 'effective occupation' has a relevance far beyond the acquisition of *terra nullius*. Its elements involve simply proof of possession by states, of manifestations of sovereignty legally more potent than those of the other claimant or claimants, or, in brief, proof of the better right. The intensity of state activity required will obviously be less in the case of *terra nullius* than in the case where a competing claimant takes an interest in territory.

Proof of animus occupandi. In the *Eastern Greenland* case the Permanent Court said:[86] '...a claim to sovereignty based not upon some particular act or title such as a treaty of cession but merely upon continued display of authority, involves two elements each of which must be shown to exist: the intention and will to act as sovereign, and some actual exercise or display of such authority'.[87]

---

[79] See the Adv. Op. concerning *Western Sahara*, quoted in the text above. On the principle of self-determination see *infra*, p. 167. On the regime of the *res nullius* see *infra*, p. 168.

[80] See *infra*, pp. 146ff., on the nature of acquisitive prescription.

[81] 50 Hague *Recueil* (1934, IV), 218–55 at 220.

[82] The *Eastern Greenland* case, PCIJ, Ser. A/B, no. 53; World Court Reports, iii. 151; is commonly assumed to have been decided on the basis that the area concerned was *terra nullius* at the critical date: but see de Visscher, *Les Effectivités du droit international public*, p. 105, citing the Judgment at p. 45. See also on the *Clipperton Island* arbitration, *infra*, p. 140.

[83] ICJ Reports (1953), 57. See also ibid. 55, 56.

[84] pp. 58–9.

[85] p. 67. Cf. the *Eastern Greenland* case, Ser. A/B, no. 53, at p. 46.

[86] Ser. A/B, no. 53, at pp. 45–6. See also ibid., p. 63; *Frontier Land* case, ICJ Reports (1959), 250 (Diss. Op. of Judge Armand-Ugon); Adv. Op. concerning *Western Sahara*, ICJ Reports (1975), 12 at 42–3.

[87] These criteria were applied by the International Court in the *Case Concerning Territorial and Maritime Dispute between Nicaragua and Honduras in the Caribbean Sea*, ibid. (2007), paras. 168–208.

The requirement of an intention to act as sovereign, otherwise referred to as *animus occupandi*[88] or *animus possidendi*,[89] is generally insisted upon in the literature. However, it is notorious that the notion of *animus possidendi* may create more problems than it solves, and Ross has described that subjective requirement of the 'will to act as sovereign' as 'an empty phantom'.[90] In truth the subjective criterion involves the imputation of a state of mind, involving a *legal* assessment and 'judgment', to those ordering various state activities. This approach expects too much and is unrealistic in seeking a particular and coherent intention in an activity involving numerous individuals. Furthermore, the criterion begs the question in many cases where there are competing acts of sovereignty. Significantly the award in the *Island of Palmas* case and the Judgment in the *Minquiers and Ecrehos* case place emphasis on the objective facts of state activity, on manifestations of sovereignty.

In three contexts, however, the *animus occupandi*, or rules akin to the notion, have a necessary function. First, the activity must be *à titre de souverain* in the sense that the agency must be that of the state and not of unauthorized natural or legal persons.[91] Secondly, the concept has a negative role: if the activity is by the consent of another state or that other is otherwise recognized as the rightful sovereign[92] then no amount of state activity is capable of maturing into sovereignty.[93] Thirdly, the dominant nature of the activity taken as a whole must be explicable only on the basis that the existence of sovereignty is assumed.[94] Thus in the *Minquiers and Ecrehos* case the fact that both parties had conducted official hydrographic surveys of the area could not be regarded as necessarily referable to an assertion of sovereignty. But certain forms of activity, whilst not exclusively and necessarily connected with territorial sovereignty, have some probative value, for example the exercise of criminal jurisdiction in respect of territory.

EFFECTIVE AND CONTINUOUS DISPLAY OF STATE AUTHORITY

Concrete acts of appropriation, or a display of state activity consonant with sovereignty, are the vital constituents of title. The older works on international law give the nineteenth-century view of occupation in terms of settlement and close physical possession.[95] In fact the law has been decisively changed as a consequence of three decisions.

---

[88] Cf. Fitzmaurice, 32 *BY* (1955–6), at 55–8; award in the *Clipperton Island* arbitration, *RIAA* ii. 1105 at 1110.

[89] See Judge Anzilotti, Diss. Op. *Eastern Greenland* case, Ser. A/B, no. 53, p. 83. See also *Frontier Land* case ICJ Reports (1959), 255 (Diss. Op. of Judge Moreno Quintana, referring to *animus domini*).

[90] *International Law* (1947), 147; quoted with approval in Brierly, *Law of Nations* (5th edn.), 152 n.; 6th edn. by Waldock, p. 163 n. 2.

[91] See *infra*, p. 138.

[92] See *supra*, pp. 106–7, 131.

[93] This is subject to the possibilities of prescription, *infra*, pp. 146ff.

[94] Fitzmaurice, 32 *BY* (1955–6), 56–8.

[95] See Hall, *International Law* (8th edn., 1924), 125. See also McNair, *Opinions*, i. 291, 315–16; and Hyde, i. 342.

In the *Island of Palmas* arbitration (1928)[96] the Netherlands and the United States agreed to submit to the Permanent Court of Arbitration a dispute concerning sovereignty over the Island of Palmas (or Miangas) lying about halfway between the Philippine Islands (then under United States sovereignty) and the Netherlands East Indies (as they then were). The United States founded its title upon the Treaty of Paris, under which all rights which Spain possessed in the region were transferred by cession to the United States. Everything turned on the nature of Spain's rights at the date when the treaty of cession came into force in 1898. Huber, arbitrator, stated that 'the continuous and peaceful display of territorial sovereignty (peaceful in relation to other states) is as good as a title'. And further:

Manifestations of territorial sovereignty assume, it is true, different forms, according to conditions of time and place. Although continuous in principle, sovereignty cannot be exercised in fact at every moment on every point of a territory. The intermittence and discontinuity compatible with the maintenance of the right necessarily differ according as inhabited or uninhabited regions are involved, or regions enclosed within territories in which sovereignty is incontestably displayed or again regions accessible from, for instance, the high seas.[97]

He then reiterated the view that 'the actual continuous and peaceful display of State functions is in case of dispute the sound and natural criterion of territorial sovereignty....'[98] Having disposed of United States arguments based upon discovery,[99] recognition by treaty,[100] and contiguity,[101] and having decided that there was insufficient evidence of Spanish activities in relation to the Island of Palmas, the arbitrator then examined the Netherlands' arguments based upon peaceful and continuous display of state authority over the island. In his opinion the people of the island were connected with the East India Company, and thereby the Netherlands, by contracts of suzerainty[102] from 1677 onwards, and, allowing for the isolated position of the island and the relation of a colonial power and a vassal state[103] (which in turn controlled the island), there was

---

[96] *RIAA* ii. 829; Hague Court Reports, ii. 83; 22 *AJ* (1928), 867. See also discussion by Jessup, 22 *AJ* 735–52; and F. de Visscher, 10 *RDILC* (1929), 735–62. See further the *Alp Craivarola* arbitration (1874), Moore, *Arbitrations*, ii. 2027; *Jones* v. *United States* (1890), 136 US 202; *Brazil–British Guiana Boundary* arbitration (1904), *RIAA* xi. 21; Hackworth, i. 404; *Grisbadarna* arbitration (1909), 4 *AJ* (1910), 226, 233; *RIAA* xi. 155 at 161–2; Hague Court Reports, i. 122, 130; Hackworth, i. 405. See further the *Rann of Kutch* case; Award, 1968; *ILM* vii, 633 at 673–90; ILR 50, 2 at 500–19; *RIAA* xvii at pp. 553–70, on which see Rousseau, 72 *RGDIP* (1968), 1100–21; Salmon, 14 *Ann. français* (1968), 217–36; Untawale, 23 *ICLQ* (1974), 818–39; Anand, *Studies in International Adjudication* (1969) 218–49.

[97] See further on the degree of effectiveness required the *Clipperton Island* arbitration, *infra*, the *Eastern Greenland* case, *infra*, p. 153; Lauterpacht, *The Development of International Law by the International Court* (1958), 240–2; id., 27 *BY* (1950), 415–19. Cf. *Frontier Land* case ICJ Reports (1959), 228.

[98] See also *RIAA* ii. 867; Hague Court Reports ii. 126, and quotation thereof by the Permanent Court in the *Eastern Greenland* case, PCIJ Ser. A/B, no. 53, p. 45; World Court Reports iii. at p. 170.

[99] *Infra*, p. 139.

[100] *Supra*, pp. 128–9.

[101] *Infra*, pp. 142–4.

[102] See *supra*, p. 114.

[103] See *supra*, pp. 72–3.

evidence 'which tends to show that there were unchallenged acts of peaceful display of Netherlands sovereignty in the period from 1700 to 1906,[104] and which…may be regarded as sufficiently proving the existence of Netherlands sovereignty'.

In 1931 an award was made in the *Clipperton Island* arbitration[105] which resolved a dispute between France and Mexico, arising in 1898, on the subject of the sovereignty over an uninhabited[106] island in the Pacific Ocean. The reasoning of the award related very closely to the particular facts, and caution is needed in deducing principles from it.[107] However, the arbitrator stated unequivocally that 'the actual, and not the nominal, taking of possession is a necessary condition of occupation', and the taking of possession consisted of an exercise of state authority sufficient in the circumstances of the territory concerned.

The Permanent Court in the *Eastern Greenland* case[108] considered the status of the disputed area at the critical date, 10 July 1931, when Norway had proclaimed its occupation. Norway maintained that the area was then *terra nullius*. Denmark, in part,[109] argued that valid title in her favour had existed for a long time on the basis of the actual display of state authority over the whole of Greenland.[110] In deciding in favour of the Danish contention, the Permanent Court had regard to a pattern of activity between 1921 and 1931, including the enforcement by legislation of a state trade monopoly, the granting of trading, mining, and other concessions, the exercise of governmental functions and administration, and the making of numerous treaties in the terms of which Danish rights over Greenland were explicit. The Norwegian occupation was illegal and invalid, since Denmark, at the very least in the 10 years previous to the Norwegian occupation, had 'displayed and exercised her sovereign rights to an extent sufficient to constitute a valid title to sovereignty'.

The emphasis on the display of state activity, and the interpretation of the facts in the light of a legal policy which favours stability and allows for the special characteristics of uninhabited and remote territories, are evidence of a change in the law. The modern law concentrates on title, evidence of sovereignty, and the notion of occupation has been refined accordingly.[111] In deciding in favour of the United Kingdom in the *Minquiers and Ecrehos* case,[112] the International Court applied, in a practical way,

---

[104] At which date the dispute arose. The critical date was in 1898.

[105] Award of the King of Italy; *RIAA* ii. 1105; 26 *AJ* (1932), 390; Hackworth, i. 404. See also Marston, 57 *BY* (1986), 337–56.

[106] A low coral lagoon reef, 670 miles south-west of Mexico.

[107] For further discussion see *infra*, pp. 140–1.

[108] *Supra*, n. 82.

[109] See *infra*, pp. 140, 154.

[110] See *infra*, pp. 142–4, on the extent of sovereignty.

[111] See von der Heydte, 29 *AJ* (1935), 448 at 462ff.; Rousseau, iii. 169.

[112] ICJ Reports (1953), 47. See also Johnson, 3 *ICLQ* (1954), 189–216; Fitzmaurice, 32 *BY* (1955–6), 20–76. See further *United States* v. *Fullard-Leo* (1943), 331 US 256; *Case Concerning Sovereignty over Certain Frontier Land*, ICJ Reports (1959), 209 at 228–9, 231–2, 248–50, 251, 255; *Case Concerning the Temple of Preah Vihear*, ICJ Reports (1962), 6 at 12, 29–30, 59–60, 72, 91–6; and ICJ Pleadings, *Antarctica Cases (United Kingdom* v. *Argentina; United Kingdom* v. *Chile)*, 1956; *Case Concerning Sovereignty over Pulao Ligitan and Pulao Sipidan*, I.C.J. Reports, (2002), 678–86, paras. 126–49.

the modern law. Thus in relation to the Ecrehos group the Court was concerned with acts involving the exercise of jurisdiction, local administration, such as the holding of inquests in Jersey on corpses found on the Ecrehos,[113] and also an act of legislation, a British Treasury Warrant of 1875 constituting Jersey a Port of the Channel Islands. In the *Frontier Land*[114] and *Temple*[115] cases the Court was reluctant to place reliance on acts of local administration.

Rann of Kutch case, 1968. The Award in this case remarked that in an agricultural and traditional economy, the distinction between state and private interests was not to be established with the firmness to be expected in a modern industrial economy.[116] In an agricultural economy grazing and other economic activities by private landholders may provide evidence of title.

SOVEREIGNTY AND THE DUTY OF PROTECTION

In his award in the *Island of Palmas* case Huber states[117] that territorial sovereignty involves the right to exclude the activities of other states, and that, as a corollary of this, a duty exists 'to protect within the territory the rights of other States, in particular their right to integrity and inviolability in peace and in war, together with the rights which each State may claim for its nationals in foreign territory'. Maintenance of a reasonable standard of administration is thus strong evidence of sovereignty. However, it is doubtful if the fulfilment of the duty is an absolute condition for the existence of sovereignty, as some jurists assert.[118] It is generally admitted that slight activity will suffice in the case of uninhabited and remote regions, but, apart from the special circumstances of such territories, the view asserted will prejudice the rights of underdeveloped countries.[119] Failure to provide the minimum standard of protection to aliens will give rise to a claim for damages if injury ensues.[120]

ACTS OF APPROPRIATION BY PRIVATE PERSONS

Acts by private persons purporting to appropriate territory for the state of which they are nationals may be ratified by the state and will then constitute evidence of effective occupation in the ordinary way.[121] The former doctrine, based upon agency in private law, was that ratification could only be of the acts of officials.

---

[113] ICJ Reports (1953), 65–6. On acts relating to the Minquiers see pp. 67–70.

[114] ICJ Reports (1959), 209 at 228–9, 231–2, 248–50, 251, 255.

[115] ICJ Reports (1962), 6 at 29–30.

[116] *ILM* vii. 633 at 673–5; ILR 50, 2 at 500–1; *RIAA* xvii at pp. 553–4.

[117] *RIAA* ii. 839; Hague Court Reports, ii. 93. Cf. the *Clipperton Island* award, *infra*, pp. 138–9.

[118] See Waldock, 25 *BY* (1948), 317; Fitzmaurice, 32 *BY* (1955–6), 51.

[119] See also the criticism of Huber's extension to the doctrine of inter-temporal law, *supra*, pp. 131–3; and on the emphasis of the International Court on stability and effectiveness in acquisition of territory, Lauterpacht, *Development*, pp. 240–2.

[120] *Infra*, ch. 24.

[121] Oppenheim, i. 677–8, 686–7; McNair, *Opinions*, i. 295, 314, 316–19, 323–5. See also Orent and Reinsch, 35 *AJ* (1941), 450–4.

9. ABANDONMENT OR *DERELICTIO*[122]

In the face of competing activity and claims by another, a state may by conduct or by express admission acquiesce in the extension of its competitor's sovereignty. This process is more properly considered elsewhere.[123] In other cases, and more especially in the case where a claimant asserts that territory previously occupied by a rival claimant had been *res nullius* at a particular time and open to acquisition, 'abandonment' is simply the negative counterpart of effective occupation. Absence of a reasonable level of state activity may cause loss of title.[124] However, by reason of the need to maintain stability and to avoid temptations to 'squatting', abandonment is not to be presumed. Tribunals require little in the way of maintenance of sovereignty, particularly in regard to remote and uninhabited areas.[125] Thus in the *Clipperton Island* award[126] it is stated: 'There is no reason to suppose that France has subsequently lost her right by *derelictio*, since she never had the *animus* of abandoning the island, and the fact that she has not exercised her authority there in a positive manner does not imply the forfeiture of an acquisition already definitively protected'. In the *Eastern Greenland* case[127] Norway had argued that Greenland became *terra nullius* after the disappearance of the early settlements. The Court, rejecting the argument, observed: 'As regards voluntary abandonment, there is nothing to show any definite renunciation on the part of the Kings of Norway or Denmark'. In the *Cameroon–Nigeria* case the Court found that Cameroon had not abandoned its title to the Bakassi region.[128]

10. DISCOVERY[129]

This category, though much employed, is less than satisfactory for the purpose of legal analysis. In principle it is to be distinguished from acts of state activity initiating an occupation, and also from symbolic annexation (the doubts existing in regard to this

---

[122] Hyde, i. 392–4; McNair, *Opinions*, i. 299–305; Oppenheim, ii. 716–18; Moore, *Digest*, i. 300; Beckett, 50 Hague *Recueil* (1934, IV), 252–5; Hackworth, i. 442–3; Fitzmaurice, 32 *BY* (1955–6), 67. See *supra*, p. 131, on renunciation or relinquishment.

[123] *Infra*, pp. 151.

[124] In principle the term 'abandonment' could be reserved for the rare situation in which a state *intends* to abandon and expressly and formally renounces title (without this involving a procedure by which the territory falls under another sovereignty: see *supra*, p. 131).

[125] Thus Huber in speaking of the duty of protection in the *Island of Palmas* award was too dogmatic in the context of abandonment.

[126] See *infra*, pp. 141–2.

[127] *Supra*, n. 83. See also the *Frontier Land Case*, ICJ Reports (1959), 227–30; and the *Argentine-Chile Frontier Case* (1966), *RIAA* xvi. 109 at 173.

[128] *Case Concerning the Land and Maritime Boundary Between Cameroon and Nigeria*, Judgment of 10 October 2002, para. 223; see also Judgment in *Sovereignty over Pedra Branca*, 23 May 2008, paras. 120–22.

[129] See Hyde, i. 312–30; von der Heydte, 29 *AJ* (1935), 448–71; Goebel, *The Struggle for the Falkland Islands* (1927), 47–119; Keller, Lissitzyn, and Mann, *Creation of Rights of Sovereignty Through Symbolic Acts, 1400–1800* (1938); McDougal, Lasswell, Vlasic, and Smith, 111 *U. of Penn LR* (1963), 543–4, 558–60, 598–611; McDougal, Lasswell, and Vlasic, *Law and Public Order in Space*, pp. 829–44; Waldock, 25 *BY* (1948), 322–5; Rousseau, iii. 161–2, 220–1.

institution are considered subsequently). In practice discovery may be accompanied by symbolic acts, the planting of a flag and the like, and the distinction becomes blurred. At one time it was believed that in the fifteenth and sixteenth centuries discovery without more conferred a complete title.[130] Modern research has given cause to doubt that it gave more than an inchoate title in this period: an effective act of appropriation seems to have been necessary.[131] The view accepted by many jurists as to the modern law is that it gives an inchoate title, an option, as against other states, to consolidate the first steps by proceeding to effective occupation within a reasonable time.[132] In the *Island of Palmas* case[133] the United States argued that, as successor to Spain, title derived from Spanish discovery in the sixteenth century. While reserving his opinion on this point, Huber stated that, even if discovery without more gave title at that time, the continued existence of the right must be determined according to the law prevailing in 1898, at the critical date. In his opinion the modern law is that 'an inchoate title of discovery must be completed within a reasonable period by the effective occupation of the region claimed to be discovered'. Modern British[134] and Norwegian[135] practice supports this view. The official American view[136] is that mere discovery gives no title, inchoate or otherwise, and this view has much to commend it. The 'law of discovery' only makes sense if it is placed firmly in the context of effective occupation, and the modern law could avoid the category altogether.[137] Further, the notion of inchoate title is misleading. Title, which is in practice a question of the relative strength of state activity, is never 'inchoate', though it may be 'weak' in that it rests on a small amount of evidence of state activity.[138] The distinct though related question of symbolic annexation will be examined presently.

[130] See Hall *International Law*, p. 126.

[131] See Goebel, *The Struggle for the Falkland Islands*, pp. 58, 69–73, 89–117; von der Heydte, 29 *AJ* (1935), 452ff.; Hyde, i. 324, 326. In the sixteenth century the Roman law relating to acquisition by finding was applied, and this emphasized actual taking. Bartolus, Gryphiander, and Grotius give a similar emphasis, and contemporary state practice usually demanded a first taking followed by a public and continuous possession evidenced by state activity. See the instructions of Charles V of Spain to his ambassador of 18 Dec. 1523 respecting the Spanish claim to the Moluccas: Goebel, *The Struggle for the Falkland Islands*, pp. 96–7; Hyde, i. 324. Keller, Lissitzyn, and Mann, *Creation of Rights*, pp. 148–9 (and see Hackworth, i. 398) consider that whereas mere discovery, 'visual apprehension', could not give a valid title, symbolic acts of taking of possession did have this result.

[132] Hall, *International Law*, p. 127; Oppenheim, ii. 689–90; Guggenheim, i. 439; McNair, *Opinions*, i. 285.

[133] *Supra*, p. 136. See also the *Clipperton Island* case, *infra*, pp. 141–2, in which Mexico relied unsuccessfully on alleged discovery by Spain.

[134] McNair, *Opinions*, i. 285, 287, 320; Hackworth, i. 455.

[135] Hackworth, i. 400, 453, 469. See also ibid. 459 (French view on Adélie Land), and Orent and Reinsch, 35 *AJ* (1941), 443–61, and cf. Hyde, i. 325 (Portuguese view in 1782).

[136] Hackworth, i. 398–400, 457, 460.

[137] The logical difficulty is the apparent assumption in some statements that mere discovery, without any state activity, bars any competitor 'for a reasonable time'. This seems to be clearly incompatible with the law on effective occupation. Cf. von der Heydte, 29 *AJ* (1935), 461–2.

[138] See further *infra*, p. 154.

11. SYMBOLIC ANNEXATION[139]

Symbolic annexation may be defined as a declaration or other act of sovereignty or an act of private persons, duly authorized, or subsequently ratified by a state, intended to provide unequivocal evidence of the acquisition of sovereignty over a parcel of territory or an island. The subject must be seen as a part of the general question of effective occupation. There is no magic in the formal declaration of sovereignty by a government, whether or not this is preceded, accompanied, or followed by a formal ceremony in the vicinity concerned. In the case of uninhabited, inhospitable, and remote regions little is required in the nature of state activity,[140] and a first and decisive act of sovereignty will suffice to create a valid title. In principle the state activity must satisfy the normal requirements of 'effective occupation'. 'Symbolic annexation' does not give title except in special circumstances (as in the *Clipperton Island* case below). However, in the case of a *res nullius*, or a situation of competing state activity,[141] it is a part of the evidence of state activity. It has been stated[142] that 'a prior State act of formal annexation cannot after a long interval prevail against an actual and continuous display of sovereignty by another State'. With respect it is thought that formal annexation creates something more than an 'inchoate title' and that the competitor can only succeed, if at all, on the basis of prescription[143] or acquiescence.[144] To require too much in respect of the maintenance of rights may well involve a return to the nineteenth-century concept of effectiveness and encourage threats to the peace.[145] In the case of remote islands, it is unhelpful to require a determinate minimum of 'effectiveness'.

In the *Clipperton Island* case[146] a lieutenant in the French navy, duly authorized, proclaimed French sovereignty in 1858 when cruising near the island, and the event was notified to the Government of Hawaii by the French consulate. In 1897, after inactivity in the intervening years, a French vessel called at the island and found three Americans collecting guano for an American company. The United States stated that it had no intention of claiming sovereignty. In the same year the island received its first visit from a Mexican gunboat and a diplomatic controversy began. The Mexican case rested on an allegation of Spanish discovery, and the arbitrator stated that even if a historic right existed it was not supported by any manifestation of Mexican sovereignty. Assuming the island to be *terra nullius* in 1858, the question was whether

[139] von der Heydte, 29 *AJ* (1935), 452ff.; McDougal *et al.*, 111 *U. of Penn. LR* (1963), 543–4, 558–60, 598–611; id., *Law and Public Order in Space*, pp. 829–44; Hackworth, i. 398–9; Waldock, 25 *BY* (1948), 323–5; McNair, *Opinions*, i. 314ff.; Orent and Reinsch, 35 *AJ* (1941), 443–61; Marston, 57 *BY* (1986), 337–56.

[140] See the Judgment in the *Eastern Greenland* case.

[141] *Supra*, p. 133.

[142] See Waldock, 36 *Grot. Soc.* (1950), 325. Cf. Fitzmaurice, 32 *BY* (1955–6), 65.

[143] See *infra*, pp. 146ff.

[144] See *infra*, pp. 151ff.

[145] See *supra*, p. 137, on abandonment.

[146] References: *supra*, p. 137, n. 104. On the establishment of British sovereignty over Rockall in 1955: Verzijl, *International Law in Historical Perspective*, iii. 351.

France had proceeded to an effective occupation. If she had not, Mexico had a right to treat the island as open to occupation in 1897. The arbitrator stated that a condition of occupation was an actual taking of possession which consisted in an act or series of acts by which the territory is reduced to possession. The award continues:

Strictly speaking, and in ordinary cases, that only takes place when the State establishes in the territory itself an organization capable of making its laws respected. But this step is, properly speaking, but a means of proceeding to the taking of possession, and, therefore, is not identical with the latter. There may also be cases where it is unnecessary to have recourse to this method. Thus, if a territory, by virtue of the fact that it was completely uninhabited, is, from the first moment when the occupying State makes its appearance there, at the absolute and undisputed disposition of that State, from that moment the taking of possession must be considered as accomplished, and the occupation is thereby completed.

Thus France acquired the island when sovereignty was proclaimed on 17 November 1858 and the purported annexation, though symbolic in form, had legal effect.

12. ORIGINAL OR HISTORIC TITLE

It may happen that a contemporary dispute involves not only reliance upon the exercise of state authority but the invocation of an ancient, original, or historic title. The concept also informs the principle of 'immemorial possession' and reliance upon evidence of general repute or opinion as to matters of historical fact. Particularly in Asia traditional boundaries play a significant role.[147]

International tribunals have recognized the concept of ancient or original title,[148] but will require appropriate evidence thereof.

13. EXTENT OF SOVEREIGNTY: GEOGRAPHICAL DOCTRINES[149]

We are here concerned with certain logical and equitable principles which are not roots of title[150] but are of importance in determining the actual extent of sovereignty derived from some orthodox source of title such as a treaty of cession or effective

---

[147] See Kaikobad, 54 *BY* (1983), 130–4.

[148] See the *Minquiers and Ecrehos* case, ICJ Reports, 1953, 53–7; ibid., Sep. Op. of Judge Basdevant, 74–9; *Rann of Kutch Arbitration* (1968), *ILR* 50, 2 at p. 474; *Western Sahara* Advisory Opinion, ICJ Reports (1975), 42–3, paras. 90–3; *Case Concerning Land, Island and Maritime Frontier Dispute*, ICJ Reports (1992), 351 at pp. 564–5, paras. 343–5; *Red Sea Islands* case, ILR, 114, 2 at 37–45.

[149] Hyde, i. 331–6; Waldock, 25 *BY* (1948), 339ff.; von der Heydte, 29 *AJ* (1935), 463–71; Fitzmaurice, 32 *BY* (1955–6), 72–5; Kelsen, *Wehberg Festschrift* (1956), 200–11, Lauterpacht, 27 *BY* (1950), 423–31; McNair, *Opinions*, i. 287–8, 292; Rousseau, iii. 193–203.

[150] It would probably be truer to say that geographical doctrines are not independent roots of title: they are subsidiary to some other root of title, normally that of effective occupation.

occupation. Principles of continuity, contiguity, and geographical unity come to the fore when the disputed territory is uninhabited, barren, or uncharted. In relation to islands contiguity is the relevant concept. The principles are simply a part of judicial reasoning, but have significance in other respects. In the context of effective occupation, continuity and contiguity are a facet of the modern view of sovereignty according to which it does not depend on close settlement but on state activity. State activity as evidence of sovereignty need not press uniformly on every part of territory.[151] Associated with this is the presumption of peripheral possession based on state activity, for example, on the coast of a barren territory.[152] Lastly, in giving effect to principles of geographical unity in the *Eastern Greenland* case,[153] and thus concluding that somewhat localized Danish activity gave title over the whole of Greenland, the Permanent Court was not swayed by an intellectual significance of unity isolated from the context of effective occupation. In writing of the decision Lauterpacht[154] remarked on 'those principles of finality, stability and effectiveness[155] of international relations which have characterized the work of the Court'. Contiguity is in itself an earnest of effectiveness and has undoubtedly been an element in claims to the continental shelf.[156]

In conclusion it may be said that the 'principle of contiguity' is little more than a technique in the application of the normal principles of effective occupation.[157] In the case of islands in particular the notion of contiguity may be unhelpful. Huber in his award in the *Island of Palmas*[158] case said that 'the alleged principle itself is by its very nature so uncertain and contested that even governments of the same State have on different occasions maintained contradictory opinions as to its soundness...'

---

[151] Thus the ordinary concept of effective occupation is the rationale of the *Eastern Greenland* case. It must be noted that some Danish legislation applied to Greenland as a whole.

[152] *British Guiana Boundary* arbitration (1904), *RIAA* xi. 21. Cf. the old hinterland doctrine. See also the *Island of Palmas* case, *RIAA* ii. 855; ind. op. of Judge Levi Carneiro, *Minquiers and Ecrehos* case, ICJ Reports (1953), 99; Jennings, *The Acquisition of Territory*, pp. 74–6.

[153] PCIJ, Ser. A/B, no. 53, pp. 45–52; World Court Reports iii. 170–7; and see the Adv. Op. concerning *Western Sahara*, ICJ Reports (1975), 12 at 42–3.

[154] *Development*, p. 241.

[155] See also the Diss. Ops. of Judge Moreno Quintana, *Case Concerning Sovereignty over Certain Frontier Land*, ICJ Reports (1959), 257; and the *Temple* case, ibid. (1962), 71.

[156] Cf. *infra*, p. 184, on archipelagos.

[157] For a different opinion: Guggenheim, i. 440–1. See also Whiteman, ii. 1104–8.

[158] *RIAA* ii. 854; Hague Court Reports, ii. 111. Other disputes involving arguments based on contiguity: *Bulama Island* case (1870), Moore, *Arbitration*, ii. 1909; Lobos Islands (1852), Moore, *Digest*, i. 265–6, 575; Navassa Island (1872), Moore, *Digest*, i. 266–7; *Aves Island* case *(Netherlands-Venezuela)* (1865), Moore, *Arbitrations*, v. 5037 (Spanish Report); La Pradelle and Politis, ii. 404, 412; *Aves Island* *(US-Venezuela*; diplomatic controversy), Moore, *Digest*, i. 266–71. See further Hyde, i. 343–6; McNair, *Opinions*, i. 315.

14. ARCTIC AND ANTARCTIC SECTORS[159]

Particularly in the case of the Arctic, the question of rights over frozen sea of 'ice territory' arises,[160] but otherwise the principles relating to discovery, symbolic annexation, effective occupation, and contiguity apply to territory situated in polar regions. In the making of claims to ice deserts and remote groups of islands, it is hardly surprising that governments should seek to establish the limits of territorial sovereignty by means of straight lines, and similar systems of delimitation may be found in different types of region, for example in North America.[161] In polar regions use has been made of lines of longitude converging at the Poles to produce a sector of sovereignty. While the 'sector principle' does not give title which would not arise otherwise, if the necessary state activity occurs, it represents a reasonable application of the principles of effective occupation as they are now understood, and as they were applied in the *Eastern Greenland* case.[162] It remains a rough method of delimitation, and has not become a separate rule of law. Confusion of claims has arisen primarily from the indecisive nature of state activity in polar regions. However, three reservations may be made: the 'sector principle' has the defects of any doctrine based upon contiguity; its application is a little absurd in so far as there is claim to a narrow sliver of sovereignty stretching to the Pole; and, lastly, it cannot apply so as to include areas of the high seas.

The state practice is thought to support the propositions advanced. In the Arctic, Denmark, Finland, Norway, and the United States have refrained from sector claims linked to territories peripheral to the polar seas. On the other hand Canada[163] and the former USSR[164] have made use of the sector principle. It is very probable that it is recognition by treaty or otherwise which creates title[165] in the Arctic rather than the sector principle as such.[166] Sector claims in Antarctica have been made by the United

---

[159] See for the Antarctic: Hackworth, i. 399–400, 449–76; Waldock, 25 BY (1948), 311–53; US Naval War College, *Int. Law Docs.* (1948–9), 217–45; Castles, in O'Connell (ed.), *International Law in Australia* (1965), 341–67; Hayton, 50 AJ (1956), 583–610; Toma, ibid. 611–26; Auburn, 19 ICLQ (1970), 229–56. On the Arctic: Lakhtine, 24 AJ (1930), 703–17; Hyde, i. 349–50; Head, 9 McGill LJ (1963), 200–26; Pharand, 19 *Univ. of Toronto LJ* (1969), 210–33, Reid, 12 *Canad. Yrbk.* (1974), 111–36. See further Smedal, *Acquisition of Sovereignty over Polar Areas* (1931); Dollot, 75 Hague *Recueil* (1949, II), 121–9; Whiteman, ii. 1051–61; Hyde, 19 *Iowa LR* (1933–4), 286–94; Rousseau, iii. 203 30; Boyd, 22 *Canad. Yrbk* (1984), 98–152. See also Oude Elferink and Rothwell (eds.), *The Law of the Sea and Polar Maritime Delimitation and Jurisdiction* (2001), 121–3, 276–7. On the status of Antarctica under the Antarctic Treaty see *infra*, pp. 254–5.

[160] Some writers take the view that permanently frozen ice shelves are susceptible to effective occupation. See Waldock, 25 BY (1948), 317–18; Hackworth, i. 449–52; Fitzmaurice, 92 Hague *Recueil* (1957, II), 155; Whiteman, ii. 1266–7.

[161] See also, on the delimitation of the territorial sea, pp. 173ff.

[162] See Wall, 1 ILQ (1947), 54–8.

[163] No precise declaration has been made, but see Hackworth, i. 463; Whiteman, ii. 1267.

[164] Decree of 15 Apr. 1926; Hackworth, i. 461; Kozhevnikov (ed.), *International Law*, p. 191.

[165] See *infra*, p. 151.

[166] See Hackworth, i. 463–8. See also Whiteman, ii. 1268.

Kingdom,[167] New Zealand, Australia, France, Norway, Argentina, and Chile.[168] The state practice calls for brief comment. First, some claims are made which do not depend in the first place on contiguity but on discovery. Secondly, claimants are not confined to peripheral neighbours as in the Arctic. And thirdly, recognition[169] is obviously important in establishing title in an otherwise fluid situation created by overlapping claims, many of which in law may amount to little more than claims to first option or declarations of interest.

15. ACCRETION, EROSION, AND AVULSION[170]

The three terms in the title describe similar processes resulting in the increase of territory through new formations. Thus, in the simple case, deposits on a sea coast may result in an extension of sovereignty. As Hyde puts it: 'No formal acts of appropriation are required'. The doctrine does not make an express choice between accretion, as a doctrine of appurtenance, and effective occupation: in the latter case there is a presumption of occupation (Hyde's formulation is in this sense correct), but the presumption could be met by evidence of renunciation. The usual assumption in the books is that accretion is a distinct 'mode of acquiring territory'. However, the general observations to be found under the heading are to be treated with reserve. Whenever, as, for example, in the case of boundary rivers and delta systems, the presumption of unchallenged occupation does not arise on the facts, accretion ceases to be a root of title. Thus, in relation to the southern boundary of New Mexico, the solution of disputes between the United States and Mexico depended on principles of acquiescence and the interpretation of agreements as to the outcome of natural changes.[171] In this type of case, even in the absence of applicable agreements, sudden, forcible, and significant changes in river courses (avulsion) will not be considered to have changed the frontier line,[172] which is normally the centre line of the former main channel or *thalweg*.[173] Accretion, the gradual and imperceptible addition of substance, is only valid in so far as the process

[167] This claim, the first sector claim in the area, was Letters Patent in 1917 defining the Falkland Islands Dependencies.

[168] For the various claims see: *Int. Law Docs.* (1948–9), 217–45; Hackworth, i. 456ff.; Reeves, 33 *AJ* (1939), 519–21; 34 *AJ* (1940), Suppl., p. 83.

[169] Thus the Norwegian proclamation of 1939 was accompanied by a minute of the Ministry of Foreign Affairs which recognized the British, New Zealand, Australian, and French claims. Norway does not accept the sector principle as such. Japan renounced her claims by the peace treaty of 8 Sept. 1951.

[170] See Oppenheim, ii. 696–8; Schwarzenberger, *International Law* (3rd edn.), 294–6; Hackworth, i. 409–21; Hyde, i. 355; Huber, arbitrator, in the *Island of Palmas* award, *RIAA*, ii. 829 at 839; the *Anna* (1805), 5 C. Rob. 373; Kanska and Manko, *Polish Yrbk.*, Vol. 26 (2002–03), 135–55.

[171] See the *Chamizal* arbitration, 5 *AJ* (1911), 785; *RIAA*, xi. 316; Briggs, p. 258; Hackworth, i. 409ff.; and the *San Lorenzo* case, *Ann. Digest*, 6 (1931–2), no. 55. See also the Chamizal Conv. of 1963, 58 *AJ* (1964), 336.

[172] *Nebraska v. Iowa* (1892), 143 US 359; *Kansas v. Missouri* (1943), 322 US 213. Cf. the decision of the commission in the *Chamizal* case, *supra*, n. 170.

[173] See *infra*, p. 160, on the meaning of this term.

gives rise to an extension to areas already under effective occupation[174] on the basis of principles of contiguity and certainty. The gradual nature of the process leads to a presumption of occupation by the riparian state and one of acquiescence by other states.

16. ACQUISITIVE PRESCRIPTION[175]

The reader will be well advised to regard the heading and the category it represents as no more than a conventional introduction to certain types of subject-matter, since the use of the general and convenient classification is very far from being a substitute for careful analysis. As a further preliminary it is necessary to distinguish extinctive prescription or 'prescription libératoire'. In English terms this concerns the limitation of actions. The failure to bring a claim before an international tribunal due to the negligence or laches of the claimant party may cause an international tribunal eventually seized of the dispute to declare the claim to be inadmissible. In a territorial dispute (or indeed a dispute over any property rights) lapse of time may create equities in favour of the possessor in the form of expenditure on, or investments in, the territory possessed.[176]

As a 'mode of acquisition' of territory prescription is accepted by many jurists, although some eminent opinions[177] of the nineteenth century denied that it was an institution of international law. The essence of prescription is the removal of defects in a putative title arising from usurpation of another's sovereignty by the consent and acquiescence of the former sovereign. The standard apology for the principle rests on considerations of good faith, the presumed voluntary abandonment of rights by the party losing title, and the need to preserve international order and stability.

ANALYSIS OF THE CONCEPT

Since the concept, alleged to be a part of international law, depends on the views of writers, it is hardly surprising that in form it reflects the variety of view expressed as well as the internal inconsistencies of some expositions.[178] At least the doctrine[179] reveals clearly that the concept is regarded by jurists as having three forms:

1. Immemorial possession. This is understood to give title when a state of affairs exists the origin of which is uncertain and may have been legal or illegal but is presumed to be legal.

---

[174] See Huber, *RIAA* ii. 839.

[175] See generally Whiteman, ii. 1062–84; Johnson, 27 *BY* (1950), 332–54; Verykios, *La Prescription en droit international public* (1934); Jennings, *Acquisition of Territory*, pp. 20–3; Hackworth, i. 432–42; MacGibbon, 31 *BY* (1954), 143 at 152–68; Fitzmaurice, 30 *BY* (1953), 1 at 27–43; id., 32 *BY* (1955–6), 20 at 31–7; Pinto, 87 Hague *Recueil* (1955, I), 433–8; Sørensen, 3 *Acta Scandinavica* (1932), 145–60; Blum, *Historic Titles in International Law*, pp. 6–37; Oppenheim ii. 705–8; Thirlway, 66 *BY* (1995), 12–14.

[176] See King, 15 *BY* (1934), 82–97.

[177] Heffter, F. de Martens, and Rivier.

[178] See Johnson, 27 *BY* (1950), 334–40.

[179] Exclusive of writing since the Second World War.

2. Prescription under conditions similar to those required for *usucapio* in Roman law: uninterrupted possession, *justus titulus* even if it were defective, good faith, and the continuance of possession for a period defined by the law.

3. *Usucapio*, modified and applying under conditions of bad faith. Thus Hall, Oppenheim, and Fauchille do not require good faith in the context of international law.

This analysis is helpful in revealing some of the problems to be faced. The principle of immemorial possession is supported by many jurists as a source of title,[180] though some deny that it is a form of 'acquisitive prescription'.[181] Since the origin of the possession is unknown, it is illogical to classify the principle as a form of prescription. It is inelegant, moreover, to describe it as a mode of acquisition or source of title: the genuine source in this type of case is recognition of or acquiescence[182] in the consequences of unchallenged possession.[183] Apart from this there is the distinct issue of the procedural effect of the presumption of legality. The parts of the analysis which rest on *usucapio* reveal the malaise inherent in the general doctrine of prescription. The doctrine refers to concepts of municipal law, and it is sometimes said that the International Court would accept acquisitive prescription as a general principle of law.[184] However, there is a certain lack of congruity between the good faith of *usucapio* and the concept of acquiescence which English law, for example, equates with prescription. A taking in bad faith may meet with acquiescence whilst an honest possession may meet with challenge. What is the content of the general principle, if indeed there is one?

Leaving aside the category of 'immemorial possession', the term 'prescription' is often used by contemporary jurists to describe two distinct situations.

COMPETING ACTIVITIES IN THE SAME PARCEL OF TERRITORY

It has been remarked previously[185] that in particular cases the difference between prescription and effective occupation is not easy to establish. The points commonly made are, first, that prescription applies to land already appropriated and is a supplanting of title, whereas occupation is of a *res nullius*; and, secondly, the analytical and not very relevant fact that prescription alone applies to rights over the sea.[186] However, in the *Island of Palmas* case and others like it,[187] the territory is not a *res nullius*, as it belongs to one of the two claimants, and yet there is no usurpation. There is simply contemporaneously competing state activity, and in deciding the question of title

---

[180] Hall, *International Law*, p. 143; Johnson, 27 *BY* (1950), 334–40; de Louter, *Le Droit international public positif* (1920), i. 341; Verykios, *La Prescription*, p. 76.

[181] F. de Martens; Rivier. See also Fitzmaurice, 32 *BY* (1955–6), 31, 34.

[182] See *infra*, pp. 151–2; and see further Johnson, *Camb. LJ* (1955), 218–19; and Schwarzenberger, *International Law*, i (3rd edn.), 306, 332.

[183] The adjective 'immemorial' is superfluous and rather misleading.

[184] See Johnson, 27 *BY* (1959), 343. See also *supra*, p. 15.

[185] *Supra*, p. 133.

[186] *Infra*, p. 158.

[187] *Supra*, pp. 136 ff.

the tribunal concerned will apply the tests of effective control associated with 'effective occupation'. To speak of prescription here is unhelpful,[188] and significantly Huber in the *Palmas* arbitration avoided the terminology, apart from a passing reference to 'so-called prescription', by which he meant merely 'continuous and peaceful display of State sovereignty'.

ACQUIESCENCE BY THE DISPLACED COMPETITOR

The writer's submission is that, in the second class of situation referred to above, acquiescence and estoppel may establish rights, and consequently an independent doctrine of 'prescription' has no function to fulfil. Some jurists have lately asserted the dependence of acquisitive prescription on acquiescence and consent.[189] For acquiescence and consent to operate they must have reference to a possession of territory.

THE CONDITIONS FOR ACQUISITIVE PRESCRIPTION[190]

Assuming, without prejudice to later conclusions, that acquisitive prescription exists as a separate category, its content must be examined. The conditions usually specified are in fact interrelated and to some extent repetitive. They are also very similar to the criteria of effective occupation, with three differences. The first is that, in the case of competing state activities, the degree of possession must be greater, but this is hardly a vital difference and the case is not properly to be regarded as prescription. Secondly, unequivocal state acts will be required to provide a basis for conduct by the other party to a dispute which amounts to acquiescence in law. And, finally, there is the important difference—the criterion of acquiescence. The conditions as set forth by Fauchille and Johnson[191] may now be considered.

1. Possession must be exercised *à titre de souverain*. This states an important and familiar element of effective occupation. There must be a display of state authority and the absence of recognition of sovereignty in another state, for example under conditions of a protectorate leaving the protected state with a separate personality.

2. Possession must be peaceful and uninterrupted. Huber in the *Palmas* case refers to 'continuous and peaceful display of State authority'. Though quoted often, this

---

[188] Examples of references to the *Palmas* case as an instance of prescription: Oppenheim, ii. 707; Beckett, 50 Hague *Recueil* (1934, IV), 220, 230; Johnson, 27 *BY* (1950), 342, 348. Other cases misleadingly classified in this way: *British Guiana Boundary* arbitration, Great Britain and Brazil (1904), 99 BFSP, p. 930; *RIAA* xi. 21; *Grisbadarna* arbitration, Sweden and Norway (1909), 4 *AJ* (1910), 226; *RIAA* xi. 155; Hague Court Reports, i. 121; *Guatemala-Honduras Boundary* arbitration (1933), *Ann. Digest*, 7 (1933–4), no. 46; *RIAA*, ii. 1322.

[189] MacGibbon, 31 *BY* (1954), 143; Schwarzenberger, *International Law*, i (3rd edn.), 307. And see *infra*, pp. 151–2 on acquiescence and recognition. See also Anzilotti, Diss. Op. in the *Eastern Greenland* case, PCIJ, Ser. A/B, no. 53 at pp. 94–5.

[190] See Beckett, 50 Hague *Recueil* (1934, IV), 249.

[191] See Johnson, 27 *BY* (1950), 343–8, adopting the classification of Fauchille, *Traité*, i, pt. ii, (1925), 759; Fauchille and Audinet, 3 *RGDIP* (1896), 313–25, based their classifications on Art. 2229 of the French Civil Code.

formula must be construed with great care. In the context of the *Palmas* case itself, it can only represent a rule of thumb, a useful standard, since in a situation of competing acts of sovereignty, the condition cannot be mandatory. The question is, which claimant has done the most in the way of state activity?

Apart from the case of contemporaneously competitive acts of sovereignty, the principle would seem to be a statement to the effect that there must be acquiescence by the former sovereign. Two sources of difficulty exist. First, it would be better if the principle were expressed as one of acquiescence, since, if a piece of territory were occupied shortly before the pre-existing sovereign was forcibly occupied by an aggressor, the 'prescribing' state would have a peaceful and uninterrupted possession, but there would be no acquiescence.[192]

The second problem is to decide what suffices to prevent possession from being peaceful and uninterrupted. In principle the answer is clear: any conduct indicating a lack of acquiescence. Thus protests will be sufficient.[193] In the *Chamizal* arbitration[194] the United States claimed, as against Mexico, a tract of the Rio Grande on the basis of prescription, but the claim failed on the ground that the possession of the United States had not been without challenge. The United States was precluded from acquiring on a basis of prescription by the terms of a Convention of 1884. Furthermore, possession must be peaceable to provide a basis for prescription, and, in the opinion of the Commissioners, diplomatic protests by Mexico prevented title arising. A failure to take action which might lead to violence could not be held to jeopardize Mexican rights.[195]

Certain modern jurists regard the protest as effecting merely a postponement for a reasonable period of the process of prescription. Since 1920, it is argued, the protest must be followed by steps to use available machinery for the settlement of international disputes, at present primarily constituted by the United Nations and International Court.[196] This view lacks solid foundations. If acquiescence is the crux of the matter (and it is believed that it is) one cannot dictate what its content is to be, with the consequences that the rule that jurisdiction rests on consent may be ignored,[197] and failure to resort to certain organs is penalized by loss of territorial rights. In any case,

[192] Except if there were an exile government with competence in this respect. See *infra*, p. 151 on recognition by third states, as opposed to acquiescence by the loser.

[193] This is the opinion of Hyde, i. 387, 388; Oppenheim, ii. 706–7; Fauchille, *Traité*, ii. 760. See generally MacGibbon, 30 *BY* (1953), 306–17. But see *infra*, p. 150 on those supporting adverse prescription.

[194] 5 *AJ* (1911), 782; *RIAA*, xi. 316; Hackworth, i. 441. For the eventual resolution of the matter: 58 *AJ* (1964), 336; and see Jessup, 67 *AJ* (1973), 423–45. See also the *Walfisch Bay* arbitration (1911), Great Britain and Germany, Hertslet, *Treaties* (1913), xxvi. 187–250 at 249; 104 *BFSP* (1911), 50; *RIAA* xi. 267; *Georgia* v. *South Carolina*, ILR, 91, 439, US, SC.

[195] Today it is a principle of international law that force may not be used to settle international disputes: see Art. 2, paras. 3 and 4, of the United Nations Charter.

[196] See MacGibbon, 30 *BY* (1953), 312–17 (materials on the view of the Government of the United Kingdom). See also Johnson, 27 *BY* (1950), 346, 353–4; Fitzmaurice, 30 *BY* (1953), 28–9, 42–3; id., 32 *BY* (1955–6), 33.

[197] See *infra*, pp. 151–2; ch. 32, s. 8.

as MacGibbon has pointed out,[198] in a number of situations it is quite inappropriate to require resort to an international tribunal or political organ.

3. The possession must be public. Johnson has remarked:[199] 'Publicity is essential because acquiescence is essential'. In a complicated situation of competing state activity, as in the *Palmas* case, publicity will not play an important role because acquiescence may not be relevant except in minor respects.

4. Possession must persist. Obviously the legal power of state activity depends in part on its persistence. In the case of a very recent possession it is difficult to adduce evidence of tacit acquiescence, and in cases like that of the *Island of Palmas* the principle is simply an element in the process of weighing the activity of the competing states. A few writers have prescribed fixed periods of years.[200] The appearance of such opinions is due to a yearning after municipal models and also to the influence of the view that 'acquiescence' may be 'implied' in certain conditions.[201] It is significant that modern writers usually hold the view that the length of time required is a matter of fact depending on the particular case.[202]

ADVERSE HOLDING OR NEGATIVE PRESCRIPTION

Some writers[203] support, or seem to do so, the doctrine that prescriptive title arises even without acquiescence, simply by lapse of time and possession which is not disturbed by measures of forcible self-help. A similar result is reached by formulations which presume acquiescence under certain conditions. Such views are today exceptional and are not supported by state practice or jurisprudence. They commonly antedate the period when forcible self-help and conquest were prohibited.[204] It is probably the law that prescription cannot create rights out of situations brought about by illegal acts,[205] and it is unlikely that this form can be presented, with any plausibility, as a general principle of law, since it does not rest on good faith. Finally, it must be remembered that in the *Island of Palmas*[206] and *Minquiers and Ecrehos*[207] cases, and others like them, the possession ultimately upheld by the tribunal is adverse only in a special

---

[198] 30 *BY* (1953), 314–17. See also Lauterpacht, 27 *BY* (1950), 396–7.

[199] 27 *BY* (1950), 347.

[200] Field, *Outlines of an International Code* (1872), para. 52; fifty years. The fifty-year period specified in Art. IV(a) of the arbitration treaty relative to the British Guiana-Venezuela boundary dispute, of 1897, represents an *ad hoc* rule of thumb.

[201] See *infra*, on adverse prescription.

[202] Oppenheim, ii. 706–7; Fauchille, *Traité*, I. ii. 762; Johnson, 27 *BY* (1950), 347–8, 354; Hyde, i. 388–9.

[203] See Hall, *International Law*, pp. 143–4 (but he refers to the acquiescence of other states); Moore, *Digest*, i. 293–5 (ambiguous and diverse dicta of publicists collected); Hyde, i. 386 (but at p. 387 he stresses the element of acquiescence); Guggenheim, i. 442.

[204] See *infra*, pp. 161, 488.

[205] Lauterpacht, 27 *BY* (1950), 397–8. See also *infra*, pp. 161–2, on the question of alienability.

[206] *Supra*, p. 136.

[207] *Supra*, p. 137.

sense; in such cases there is no deliberate usurpation of sovereignty with a sequel of adverse holding, but a more or less contemporaneous competition.

ACQUISITIVE PRESCRIPTION: AN EPITAPH

In summary, the submission is that (if one excludes adverse holding or negative prescription) the situations described under the rubric of prescription by the writers, on analysis, fall into three categories: cases of immemorial possession; competing acts of sovereignty (*Island of Palmas* case); and cases of acquiescence. The first two categories are not really cases of prescription, but, as to the third, it may be said that acquiescence is a form of prescription and that the question ends as a matter of terminology. However, the doctrine is so tangled that it would be a help if the more candid and unambiguous label were used. And, of course, this would make clear the position of adverse holding in the law. However, it is important to notice that, whilst it is intended as an aid to understanding, the threefold analysis offered is not necessarily reflected neatly by life. In some cases it is not entirely clear whether there has been an occupation by one claimant of a *res nullius* followed later on by competing acts by another state, or whether there have been contemporaneously competing acts from the outset.[208] Again, in either case, a court will take acts of acquiescence into account:[209] in other words the second and third categories may overlap in practice.[210] In conclusion one may doubt whether there is any role in the law for a doctrine of prescription as such.[211] In the *Kasikili/Sedudu Island*[212] case the International Court rejected the Namibian argument, based explicitly upon acquisitive prescription, on the facts, and stated that it was not concerned to examine the status of acquisitive prescription in international law.

17. ACQUIESCENCE AND RECOGNITION[213]

The effect of consent on the transfer of territory has been considered previously with respect to cession, which is a procedure which includes agreement to transfer. However, in many cases recognition and acceptance of territorial sovereignty may

---

[208] It is possible to take such a view of the *Palmas* case, since Spain had some sort of title by discovery before Holland took possession: Beckett, 50 Hague *Recueil* (1934, IV), 230.

[209] That is, in the process of weighing the significance of the various acts of state authority.

[210] See the *Minquiers and Ecrehos* case, ICJ Reports (1953), 47; MacGibbon, 31 *BY* (1954), 156–66; Fitzmaurice, 32 *BY* (1955–6), 58-ff. In that case Counsel for the UK referred to omissions amounting to 'virtual acquiescence' in the British claims, but no argument was rested on prescription expressly.

[211] Many modern writers admit the relation between acquiescence and prescription: see Schwarzenberger, *International Law*, i (3rd edn.) 307; Rousseau, 93 Hague *Recueil* (1958, I) 422; Jennings, *Acquisition of Territory*, pp. 23, 39. See also *Case Concerning Sovereignty over Certain Frontier Land*, ICJ Reports (1959), 209 at 227–30.

[212] *Case Concerning Kasikili/Sedudu Island*, ICJ Reports (1999), 1045 at 1101–5.

[213] See generally MacGibbon, 31 *BY* (1954), 143–86; Blum, *Historic Titles in International Law*; Suy, *Les Actes juridiques unilatéraux en droit international public* (1962), 61–8; Fitzmaurice, 32 *BY* (1955–6), 58–63;

occur in contexts where there is no agreement to transfer, as the claimant is in possession already, the transaction may be unilateral, and the recognition is on the part of
third states and not necessarily the 'losing' state. Recognition may take the form of a
unilateral express declaration, or may occur in treaty provisions which make it clear
that there has been no cession in the sense of transfer by agreement.[214] In the *Eastern
Greenland* case[215] the Court referred to treaties between Denmark and states other
than Norway and observed: 'To the extent that these treaties constitute evidence of
recognition of her sovereignty over Greenland in general, Denmark is entitled to rely
upon them'. Acquiescence played a major role in the case of *Sovereignty over Pedra
Branca*, 23 May 2008.

Acquiescence has the same effect as recognition, but arises from conduct, the absence
of protest when this might reasonably be expected. In appropriate circumstances a tribunal will infer recognition of sovereignty in a competitor. In the case of land territory
the term acquiescence is applied to the attitude of the 'losing' state in a dispute, whereas
recognition refers to the attitude of third states.[216] Acquiescence and recognition are
not essential to title in the normal case, but they give significance to actual control of
territory and acts of state authority in circumstances when these do not of themselves
provide a complete foundation for title in the holder, for example where there are competing acts of possession.[217] Acquiescence and recognition may establish that at some
material date a rival claimant regarded an area as *res nullius*.[218] Of contemporary significance is the effect in establishing title of a series of resolutions of the General Assembly
of the United Nations: the strength of institutionalized and general recognition is obvious.[219] In any case the determination of the precise location of a 'recognized' boundary
may produce a dispute: see the *Taba Award* (1988) involving Egypt and Israel.[220]

Lauterpacht, *Recognition in International Law* (1947), 409–12; Jennings, *Acquisition of Territory*, pp. 36–40;
Schwarzenberger, 51 *AJ* (1957), 316–23; Kaikobad, 54 *BY* (1983), 119–41.

[214] See *supra*, p. 130, on disposition by joint decision of the principal powers, and p. 131 on renunciation.
See further *Ditmar and Linde* v. *Ministry of Agriculture, Ann. Digest*, 8 (1935–7), no. 52 at p. 162; *Franco-
Ethiopian Railway Co.* claim, ILR, 24 (1957), 602 at 605; UK recognition of Norwegian sovereignty over Jan
Mayen Island and Canadian recognition of Norwegian sovereignty over the Sverdrup Islands, 27 *AJ* (1933),
Suppl., pp. 92, 93; and McNair, *Opinions*, i. 287.

[215] (1933), PCIJ, Ser. A/B, no. 53, pp. 51–2; World Court Reports, iii. 175–6. See also the Adv. Op. concerning *Western Sahara*, ICJ Reports (1975), 12 at 49–57: the Moroccan argument from recognition failed on the
evidence. See also ibid. 87–92 (Judge Ammoun).

[216] See further *infra*, pp. 154–5, on questions of relative title; and pp. 158–9 on maritime claims.

[217] See the *Grisbadarna* arbitration (1909), 4 *AJ* (1910), 226 at 233, 234–5; *RIAA* xi. 155 at 161–2; *Island
of Palmas* case, *supra*, *RIAA*, ii at pp. 868, 869; *Case Concerning Sovereignty over Certain Frontier Land*,
ICJ Reports (1959), 209 at 227, 231, 248–50, 255. In the latter case the Court gave an appraisal of 'routine
administrative acts' which contrasts with the significance given to British acts in the *Minquiers* case. In
the *Frontier Land* case Belgium was held to be excusably ignorant of acts by the Netherlands and not to
have made implied admissions. See further MacGibbon, 31 *BY* (1954), 154ff. See also the *Frontier Dispute
Case (Burkina Faso-Mali)*, ICJ Reports (1986), 172–6, concerning alleged acquiescence in relation to
particular methods of appraising the evidence; and see also pp. 654–5 (Luchaire, Sep. Op.).

[218] *Minquiers and Ecrehos* case, ICJ Reports (1953), 47, at 67.

[219] Jennings, *Acquisition of Territory*, p. 85. See further the following chapter.

[220] See 26 *ILM* (1987), 1 (*Compromis*); 37 *ILM* (1988), 1421; *ILR* 80, 226 (Award).

18. ESTOPPEL[221]

The principle of estoppel undoubtedly has a place in international law (see *infra*, Chapter 28), and it has played a significant role in territorial disputes which have come before international tribunals. Recognition, acquiescence, admissions constituting a part of the evidence of sovereignty,[222] and estoppel form an interrelated subject-matter, and it is far from easy to establish the points of distinction. It is clear that in appropriate conditions acquiescence will have the effect of estoppel. In the *Temple* case[223] the Court held that by her conduct Thailand had recognized the frontier line contended for by Cambodia in the area of the temple, viz., that marked on the map drawn up by the Mixed Delimitation Commission set up by the treaty of 1904.

In many situations acquiescence and express admissions are but part of the evidence of sovereignty. Estoppel differs in that, if it exists, if suffices to settle the issue because of its unambiguous characterization of the situation. Resting on good faith and the principle of consistency in state relations, estoppel may involve holding a government to a declaration which in fact does not correspond to its real intention.[224] Such a principle must be used with caution, more particularly in dealing with territorial issues.[225] However, in instances like the *Temple* case, where much of the evidence is equivocal, acquiescence over a long period may be treated as decisive: here it is not in itself a root of title but an aid in the interpretation of the facts and legal instruments.[226] Acquiescence of the kind which closes the principal issue (which therefore has an effect equivalent to estoppel) must rest on very cogent evidence. Express recognition in the treaty of the existence of title in the *other party* to a dispute (as opposed to recognition by third states) creates an effect equivalent to that of estoppel.[227]

---

[221] See Bowett, 33 *BY* (1957), 175–202; MacGibbon, 7 *ICLQ* (1958), 468 at 506–9; Jennings, *Acquisition of Territory*, pp. 41–51; Martin, *L'Estoppel en droit international public* (1979); Thirlway, *BY* 60 (1989), 29–49.

[222] See Fitzmaurice, 32 *BY* (1955–6), 60–2; Bowett, 33 *BY* (1957), 196–7.

[223] ICJ Reports (1962), 6 at 32. See also ibid. 39–51 (Sep. Op. of Alfaro); 62–5 (Sep. Op. of Fitzmaurice); 96–7 (Diss. Op. of Wellington Koo); 129–31, 142–6 (Diss. Op. of Spender). For comment see Johnson, 11 *ICLQ* (1962), 1183–1204; Verzijl, 9 *Neths. Int. LR* (1962), 229–63. See also *Laguna del Desierto* arbitration, Award of 21 October 1994, ILR 113, 1 at 129–4 (Judge Galindo Pohl. Diss. Op.).

[224] See *infra*, p. 643.

[225] See Bowett, 33 *BY* (1957), 197–201, 202; and the Diss. Op. of Judge Spender in the *Temple* case, ICJ Reports (1962), 142–6 (in his view, on the facts, the elements of estoppel were not present in any case).

[226] Jennings, *Acquisition of Territory*, p. 51.

[227] See McNair, *Law of Treaties* (1961), 487, referring to the *Eastern Greenland* case, PCIJ, Ser. A/B, no. 53, at pp. 68–9; World Court Reports, iii. 190: 'In accepting these bilateral and multilateral agreements [containing provisions which recognized that Greenland was part of Denmark] as binding upon herself, Norway reaffirmed that she recognized the whole of Greenland as Danish; and thereby she has debarred herself from contesting Danish sovereignty over the whole of Greenland, and, in consequence, from proceeding to occupy any part of it'. McNair takes a less strict view of estoppel than e.g. Bowett, 33 *BY* (1957), 197–207, 202: see *infra*, pp. 643–5.

19. NOVATION

Verzijl[228] refers to 'novation' as a distinct mode of acquisition and defines the principle thus: 'It consists in the gradual transformation of a right *in territorio alieno*, for example a lease, or a pledge, or certain concessions of a territorial nature, into full sovereignty without any formal and unequivocal instrument to that effect intervening'. Several modern disputes relate to this type of problem. The dispute over the former British Honduras (Belize) is the example used by Verzijl. In his view 'it is beyond all doubt that the British claims in respect of Spanish, later Guatemalan, Belice were in origin nothing more than the right, guaranteed by Spain to Great Britain on behalf of her nationals by Article 17 of their Peace Treaty of Paris of 10 February 1763...not to be molested in their trade of cutting Campeachy wood in the Spanish territories bordering the Bay of Honduras'.[229] The article concerned makes no mention of territorial limits. Other modern disputes which have raised the same issue are as follows: the 'neutral ground' adjacent to the north face of the Rock of Gibraltar (United Kingdom and Spain);[230] the *Right of Passage* case (Merits) (Portugal and India);[231] and the issue of title to Sabah (North Borneo) (Philippines and Malaysia).[232]

Whilst it is useful to regard these disputes as a type, the issue of tacit novation is in no way unique and concerns the matters reviewed in earlier sections devoted to acquisitive prescription, acquiescence, recognition, and estoppel.

20. DOCTRINE OF REVERSION

When a transfer of sovereignty occurs, and the successor is generally recognized as recovering a previous state of independence, the question arises whether the successor is bound by territorial grants or recognition of territorial changes by the previous holder. The matter is considered in Chapter 29, section 8.

21. RELATIVE TITLE[233]

Title to territory may be relative in several quite different contexts.

---

[228] *International Law in Historical Perspective*, iii. 384–6.

[229] Ibid., 385. See further *British Digest*, iib. 621–58; Bloomfield, *The British Honduras–Guatemala Dispute* (1953); Clegern, 52 *AJ* (1958), 280–97.

[230] See Fawcett, 43 *International Affairs* (1967), 236 at 238–43; White Papers, Misc. No. 12 (1965), Cmnd. 2632; Misc. No. 13 (1966), Cmnd. 3131; *Documents on Gibraltar* (Madrid, 1956); 69 *RGDIP* (1965), 123–49; ibid., 70 (1966), 461–6; ibid. 71 (1967), 404–13; *British Digest*, iib. 748–9 (and see vol. iia).

[231] ICJ Reports (1960), 6. See Thirlway, 66 *BY* (1995), 12–14.

[232] Materials cited *supra*, p. 111.

[233] See Fitzmaurice, 32 *BY* (1955–6), 20 at 64–6; Schwarzenberger, 51 *AJ* (1957), 308 at 320–2.

1. The principle *nemo dat quod non habet* (no donor can give a greater interest than that which he himself has) places a restrictive effect on titles dependent on bilateral agreement.[234]

2. A judicial decision on issues of title cannot foreclose the rights of third parties.[235]

3. In a situation where physical holding is not conclusive of the question of right, recognition becomes important, and this may be forthcoming from some states and not others. An example of this situation is provided by the Romanian occupation of Bessarabia in 1918. A number of states accepted the change, but the RSFSR, and later the USSR, pursued a policy of non-recognition.

4. The *compromis* or special agreement, on the basis of which a dispute is submitted to the International Court, or other tribunal, may assume that title is to go to one of the two claimants. Thus the Court interpreted the *compromis* in the *Minquiers and Ecrehos* case as excluding the examination of the status of the islets as *res nullius* or subject to a *condominium*.[236] In such a case, in the absence of any other claimant, the result, it seems, is a title valid against all: but the parties have not had to come up to any minimum requirements of effective control.

5. Apart from the form of the *compromis*, in instances such as the *Island of Palmas* and *Minquiers and Ecrehos*,[237] the Court will assess the relative intensity of the competing acts of state authority. It is not a question here of, who possesses?[238] but, which has the better right?

6. In appropriate circumstances the Court will lean in favour of title in one claimant even though there are grounds for a finding that the territory is *terra nullius*. Thus in the *Eastern Greenland* case[239] Danish activity in the disputed area had hardly been intensive, but the Court refused to declare the area *terra nullius*. In Lauterpacht's view:[240] 'Any such decision would have been contrary to those principles of finality, stability, and effectiveness of international relations which have characterized the work of the Court'.

7. In some cases the sheer ambiguity of the facts will lead the Court to rely on matters which are less than fundamental,[241] and in this class of case there is a

[234] See *supra*, p. 119.
[235] Ibid.
[236] ICJ Reports (1953), 47 at 52. See also the special agreement in the *Island of Palmas* case, *RIAA* ii. 831, 869. For the doctrine of *uti possidetis*, see *supra*, p. 129.
[237] See also the *Temple* case, ICJ Reports (1962), 6 at 72 (Judge Moreno Quintana).
[238] In physical terms a test for possession may give no clear answer: both claimants are, as it were, squatting in the same field.
[239] *Supra*, p. 143, n. 152.
[240] *Development*, p. 241. See also the award in the *Clipperton Island* case, *supra*, p. 137; and *supra*, pp. 142–4, on the extent of sovereignty.
[241] See the *Temple* case, *supra*, p. 152, and the *Case Concerning Sovereignty over Certain Frontier Land*, ICJ Reports (1959), 209 at 231 (Judge Lauterpacht), 232 (Judge Spiropoulos), and 249–51 (Judge Armand-Ugon). In this latter case a title resting on an ambiguous treaty conflicted with various acts of administration.

tendency to seek evidence of acquiescence by one party.[242] Moreover, in this context it is academic to use the classification 'inchoate'. A title, though resting on very preliminary acts, is self-sufficient as against those without a better title.[243] In coming to a decision on the question of right, it may be necessary to measure 'titles', if this is the correct term, against each other. In the *Palmas* case Huber explained his approach clearly:[244]

...the exercise of some act of State authority and the existence of external signs of sovereignty...has been proved by the Netherlands...

These facts at least constitute a beginning of establishment of sovereignty by continuous and peaceful display of State authority, of a commencement of occupation of an island not yet forming a part of the territory of a State; and such a state of things would create in favour of the Netherlands an inchoate title for completing the conditions of sovereignty. Such inchoate title, based on display of State authority, would...prevail over an inchoate title derived from discovery, especially if this latter title has been left for a very long time without completion by effective occupation; and it would equally prevail over any claim which, in equity, might be deduced from the notion of contiguity.

22. HISTORICAL CONSOLIDATION OF TITLE

In the *Anglo-Norwegian Fisheries*[245] case the Court, having established that Norway had delimited her territorial sea by a system of straight baselines since 1869, had to decide whether, as against other states, she had title to waters so delimited. The Court said:[246]

...it is indeed this system itself [of straight baselines] which would reap the benefit of general toleration, the basis of an historical consolidation which would make it enforceable as against all States.

The general toleration of foreign States with regard to the Norwegian practice is an unchallenged fact....

The notoriety of the facts, the general toleration of the international community, Great Britain's position in the North Sea, her own interest in the question, and her prolonged abstention would in any case warrant Norway's enforcement of her system against the United Kingdom.

The attitude of other states was taken as evidence of the legality of the system, but there were certain special features. The extension of sovereignty claimed here was over a

---

[242] *Supra*, p. 151.

[243] Cf. French rights as against Mexico in the *Clipperton* case; Danish rights as against Norway in the *Eastern Greenland* case. See Beckett, 50 Hague *Recueil* (1934, IV), 230, 254, 255.

[244] *RIAA* ii. 831 at 870. See also ibid., 869: 'An inchoate title [i.e. discovery] however cannot prevail over a definite title founded on continuous and peaceful display of sovereignty.'

[245] See *infra*, pp. 176ff.

[246] ICJ Reports (1951), 116 at 138–9. The whole of this section of the judgment should be read with care. See also ibid. 130.

res communis[247] and therefore the toleration of foreign states in general was of significance. Moreover, the Court appears to regard British silence as an independent basis of legality as against the United Kingdom.

Charles de Visscher[248] has explained the decision on these lines,[249] and has proceeded to take the decision as an example of the 'fundamental interest of the stability of territorial situations from the point of view of order and peace', which 'explains the place that consolidation by historic titles holds in international law'.[250] He continues:

This consolidation, which may have practical importance for territories not yet finally organized under a State regime as well as for certain stretches of sea-like bays, is not subject to the conditions specifically required in other modes of acquiring territory. Proven long use, which is its foundation, merely represents a complex of interests and relations which in themselves have the effect of attaching a territory or an expanse of sea to a given State.

'Consolidation' differs from prescription, occupation, and recognition, in de Visscher's doctrine. It is certain that the elements which he calls 'consolidation' are influential. In the preceding section such elements were examined in relation to the problems of relative title[251] and the principle of effectiveness. The essence of the matter is peaceful holding and acquiescence or toleration by other states[252] (but de Visscher has his own notion of acquiescence). Moreover, special factors, including economic interests, may be entertained by a court faced with rather equivocal facts. However, it is probably confusing to overemphasize, and to lump together, this penumbra of equities by discovering the concept of consolidation.[253] Apart from the concept of consolidation, the role of social, economic and other 'non-legal' considerations in the application by tribunals of the more orthodox legal principles is not to be denied.[254]

It is not clear to what extent the concept of historical consolidation is much more than a sophisticated compendium of pre-existing modes of acquisition. Certainly, it has been developed or approved by some leading authorities, including Charles de Visscher, a Judge of the Permanent Court and also of the International Court, and Sir Robert Jennings, sometime President of the Court. Nonetheless, in the *Cameroon–Nigeria* case the Court stated that 'the theory of historical consolidation is highly controversial and cannot replace the established modes of acquisition of title under international law…'.[255] In the Award in Phase One of the *Red Sea Islands* case, a

---

[247] See *infra*, p. 169.

[248] *Theory and Reality in Public International Law* (1957), 199; (4th edn.) (in French, 1970), 226. See also de Visscher, *Les Effectivités du droit international public*, pp. 107–9; and Oppenheim, ii. 709–10.

[249] But he does not regard the case as one of 'acquiescence properly so called'.

[250] Works cited *supra* n. 247, see also Johnson, *Camb. LJ* (1955), 215–25.

[251] Cf. Johnson, *Camb. LJ* (1955), 215–25.

[252] See Schwarzenberger, 51 *AJ* (1957), 308 at 316–24.

[253] Jennings, *Acquisition of Territory*, pp. 23–8, is critical of the concept. He also reminds us that the concept 'is based upon the merest hint in the case reports'. The passage relied upon by de Visscher and Johnson is concerned with general acquiescence: see MacGibbon, 31 *BY* (1954), 160.

[254] See the careful study by Munkman, 46 *BY* (1972–3), 1–116.

[255] *Case Concerning the Land and Maritime Boundary Between Cameroon and Nigeria*, Judgment of 10 October 2002, para. 65.

distinguished Arbitration Tribunal referred to the concept of consolidation of title with approval.[256]

23. ACQUISITION OF MARITIME TERRITORY[257] AND OTHER TOPICS

Rules of general international law, reinforced by the doctrine of necessary appurtenance, attribute internal waters and a territorial sea to littoral states. The issue here is inherent right. In other cases extension of rights over the high seas has occurred on the basis of historic title and prescription.[258] Since the high seas are *res communis*[259] in principle there must be *general* acquiescence or recognition from other states, and, partly for this reason and partly because the extension may be by means of relatively unpublicized municipal decrees, there must be affirmative evidence of acquiescence. Where a special claim has existed for a very long time the parallel is with the 'immemorial' possession of land territory:[260] in so far as adverse prescription exists (but this is doubtful) it is inappropriate to speak of it here, as the possession may well have existed before the now generally accepted criteria developed. Acquiescence is the key notion in this field, and yet one may assume certain limits set by public policy.[261]

HISTORIC BAYS (INTERNAL OR NATIONAL WATERS)

By general acquiescence bays may become a part of internal waters although the closing line exceeds the limits permitted by the general law.[262] This proposition is supported, in a general way, by the Judgment of the Court in the *Fisheries* case.[263] The principle of

---

[256] Award of 9 October 1998; ILR 114, 2 at 117 (para. 450).

[257] See Secretariat Memo., 1957, *U.N. Conf. on the Law of the Sea, Off. Recs.*, i. 1–38; Gidel, iii. 621–63; Fitzmaurice, 30 *BY* (1953), 27–42; id., 31 *BY* (1954), 375–6, 381–2, 400; MacGibbon, ibid. 159ff.; Waldock, 28 *BY* (1951), 159–66; de Visscher, *Theory and Reality in Public International Law*, pp. 199–201; Bourquin, *Mélanges Georges Sauser-Hall* (1952); Bowett, 33 *BY* (1957), 199–201; Johnson, 1 *ICLQ* (1952), 163–6; *Law of the Sea, Juridical Regime of Historic Waters, including Historic Bays*, UN Secretariat, A/CN. 4/143, 9. Mar. 1962; *Yrbk. ILC* (1952), i. 155, paras. 18, 24; ibid. (1955), i. 178, para. 8; ibid. (1962), ii. 1, 86, para. 12(c), 190, para. 60; ibid. (1967) ii. 339, 340, 368; Whiteman, iv. 233–58; Bouchez, *The Regime of Bays in International Law* (1964), 199–302; Blum, *Historic Titles in International Law*, pp. 241–334; McDougal and Burke, *The Public Order of the Oceans* (1962), 357–68; Hackworth, i. 698–712; Hyde, i. 469–70.

[258] See the *North Atlantic Fisheries* arbitration (1910), *RIAA* xi. 173; Scott, Hague Court Reports, p. 141; *El Salvador v. Nicaragua* (1917), 11 *AJ* (1917), 693; *Case Concerning the Land, Island and Maritime Frontier Dispute*, ICJ Reports (1992) 351, at pp. 586–606.

[259] See *infra*, p. 169.

[260] *Supra*, p. 146. On the relation between acquiescence and historic title see MacGibbon, 31 *BY* (1954), 165.

[261] See *infra*, pp. 161–2.

[262] See the UK replies to the questionnaire of the Preparatory Committee of the League; McNair, *Opinions*, i. 378; and see further the UK arguments in the *Fisheries* case and the view expressed at the Geneva Conference in 1958; 7 *ICLQ* (1958), 545.

[263] *Infra*, pp. 176ff.

decision in the case was simply that the Norwegian system of baselines was in accordance with the general rules of international law. However, as a secondary basis for decision,[264] the Court relied upon general acquiescence or recognition: the terminology used by the Court itself is rather loose, but the purport is clear. Furthermore, the precise point was not acquiescence in the possession of specific waters but in the *general system* of baselines.[265] In seeking evidence of toleration of a system of this sort caution must be exercised.[266] Many states claim historic bays,[267] but it is to be noted that, in view of the fact that the closing line permitted by the Convention on the Territorial Sea (1958) is 24 miles, the significance of the doctrine is much reduced.[268]

HISTORIC WATERS (TERRITORIAL SEA)

The rule regarding historic bays is framed, naturally in view of the result of having a closing line, in terms of accessions to internal waters.[269] However, it is assumed that *ex hypothesi* this affects the outer limit of the territorial sea. Moreover, there is in principle no obstacle to recognition of a special breadth for the territorial sea, for example in respect of one coast of a state which elsewhere maintains an orthodox regime. In the *Fisheries* case both parties and the Court[270] considered that historic title applied to both the territorial sea and internal waters.

SEDENTARY FISHERIES[271]

Continuous occupation and acquiescence on the part of other states may create rights in sedentary fisheries outside the normal ambit of the territorial sea. Sedentary fisheries, such as pearl and chank, are capable of possession: but it is probable that the rights obtained are less than sovereignty.[272]

[264] See also the concurrence of Judge Hackworth based solely upon historic title, ICJ Reports (1951), 144.

[265] ICJ Reports (1951), 138–9; and see Fitzmaurice, 30 *BY* (1953), 27.

[266] Criticism of the decision rests in part on the weak evidence for British acceptance of a *general* system, which did not emerge as such until recent times: see Fitzmaurice, 30 *BY* (1953), 33–42; and Wilberforce, 38 *Grot. Soc.* (1952), 165–7. See also the Diss. Ops. of Judges McNair and Read: ICJ Reports (1951), 171ff., 199ff., respectively. On the nature of acquiescence in this context see Fitzmaurice, 30 *BY* (1953), 27–42.

[267] France: Bay of Cancale or Granville (17 miles wide); Sweden: Laholm Bay; the United States: Santa Monica (29), Chesapeake (12), and Delaware (10) Bays. Canada claims Hudson Bay (50); the US opposes this, see 15 *BY* (1934), 1. The former USSR claimed Peter the Great Bay (102) in the Far East: see 7 *ICLQ* (1958), 112. See further *U.S. v. Louisiana*, ILR 91, 411 (U.S., SC.); and *U.S. v. State of Maine*, ibid., 427 (U.S., SC.).

[268] See *infra*, p. 181.

[269] Gidel iii. 624.

[270] ICJ Reports (1951), 130, 138–9. The Court does not express any precise opinion on the point, however. See further the Diss. Op. of Judge McNair, at p. 183, citing Lord Stowell in the *Twee Gebroeders* (1801), 3 C. Rob. 336, 339; and that of Judge Read (at pp. 201ff.). Note also the concurrence of Judge Hackworth (p. 144), referring to 'the disputed areas of water'. Gidel, iii. 626, has a contrary view. See further *Civil Aeronautics Board v. Island Airlines*, 235 F. Supp. 990 (1964); ILR 35, 68.

[271] See also *A.M.S.S.V.M. v. State of Madras*, ILR 20 (1953), 167.

[272] Cf. *infra*, pp. 208–9, on the concept of 'sovereign rights' in the Continental Shelf Conv. of 1958 and the Law of the Sea Convention, 1982.

BOUNDARY BETWEEN ADJACENT TERRITORIAL SEAS AND CONTIGUOUS ZONES[273]

In the case of opposite and adjacent coasts there is, in the absence of a regime based upon acquiescence or express agreement, a rule that the line of division depends on the principle of equidistance, i.e. on a median line. The authority for the principle is primarily its basis in common sense: it is a general principle of law. Moreover, it has been adopted in Article 12 of the Convention on the Territorial Sea and Contiguous Zone of 1958 (Article 15 of the 1982 Law of the Sea Convention).[274] However, apart from cases where acquiescence or treaty provide a source of obligation, the precise legal effect of the principle of equidistance is not clear. It is probably not a rule of attribution as yet, but serves to support claims when they are made.

BOUNDARY RIVERS[275]

The principle of delimitation apparently established in the law is that of the *thalweg*, which may be presumed to mean the middle of the main navigable channel. However, the term may have another meaning in particular instruments and treaties, viz., the line of deepest soundings. The two definitions will no doubt often coincide. The conditions prevailing, even within the same river system, are very variable and the learning in the books tends to be unhelpful in practice. Judicial expertise is called for, particularly in relation to the determination of the main channel among several arms of a river.[276]

BOUNDARY LAKES[277]

The principle of the median line applies, but as usual express agreement or acquiescence may produce other modes of division. Moreover, a *condominium* might be adopted.

---

[273] Padwa, 9 *ICLQ* (1960), 628–53; Gidel, iii. 765–74. On bays shared by two or more states see *infra*, pp. 182–3.

[274] See also the dictum in the *Grisbadarna* arbitration, Hague Court Reports, i. 129; *RIAA* xi. 160; and *infra* for the regime of boundary lakes.

[275] McEwen, *International Boundaries of East Africa* (1971), 76–96; E.L., 9 *ICLQ* (1960), 208–36; Rousseau, iii. 252–63; Kaikobad, *The Shatt-al-arab Boundary Question: A Legal Reappraisal* (1988); Bardonnet, Hague *Recueil*, 153 (1976, V), 83–95; Schroeter, *Ann. français*, 1992, 948–82.

[276] See *Argentine–Chile Frontier Case*, ILR 38, 10 at 93; *Case Concerning Kasikili–Sedudu Island*, ICJ Reports (1999), 1045 at 1060–74; *Decision of the Eritrea–Ethiopia Boundary Commission*, 13 April 2002, ILM 41 (2002), 1057 at 1116, para. 7.2; *Case Concerning the Frontier Dispute* (Benin/Niger), ibid. (2005), 149–50.

[277] Hackworth, i. 615–16; Guggenheim, i. 384–6; McEwen, *International Boundaries*, pp. 97–100, 201–5; Pondaven, *Les Lacs-frontière* (1972); Rousseau, iii. 263–5. Examples: Swiss frontiers through Lac Leman (Lake of Geneva) and Bodensee (Lake Constance). See also the *Frontier Dispute Case (Burkina Faso/Mali)*, ICJ Reports (1986), 631–3, 640–1.

24. PROBLEMS OF ALIENABILITY

Certain restrictions on the transfer of territory have been noticed earlier,[278] and the present section is devoted to consideration of more fundamental issues arising from principles of general international law. The even more general, and very complex, question of the effect of illegality on various situations is considered later in Chapter 23.[279] The immediate concern is the effect of certain rules on the power of alienation. Two problems will be considered, viz., the effect of the prohibition of the use or threat of force as a means of acquiring territory and the consequences of the principle of self-determination.

TRANSFER BY AN AGGRESSOR

In the older customary international law, when conquest was regarded as a source of title, it was yet forbidden to annex territory during the currency of the war and in the absence of a peace treaty. The modern law prohibits conquest and regards a treaty of cession imposed by force as a nullity. Even if—and this is open to considerable doubt—the vice in title can be cured by recognition by third states, it is clear that the loser is not precluded thus from challenging any title based upon a transfer from the aggressor. It is the force of a powerful prohibition, the stamp of illegality, which operates here rather than the principle *nemo dat quod non habet*. Apparent exceptions, when the right of the loser is precluded, occur when there is a disposition of territory by the principal powers or some other international procedure valid as against states generally.[280] Such dispositions may result in an aggressor keeping territory he seized: but the title thenceforth is not based upon the illegal seizure.

Suppose that, objectively speaking, the result of the transfer were in accordance with the principle of self-determination: would this circumstance supersede the illegality of the seizure? It is probable that, at the very least, recognition of the title of the transference by third states would then be justifiable and would consolidate the rights of the holder.[281]

THE RIGHT OF SELF-DETERMINATION

Some other aspects of this question are dealt with elsewhere,[282] and the object here is to consider whether there is a rule of law inhibiting the transfer of territory if

---

[278] *Supra*, pp. 117–18.

[279] For the effect of the principle of self-determination on the 'static' rights of the territorial sovereign see pp. 553–5; for the limits of prescription, acquiescence, and recognition in respect of the consequences of illegal acts or omissions see pp. 513–17; on the concepts of *res nullius* and self-determination see *supra*, p. 131.

[280] See *supra*, pp. 130–1, and *infra*, p. 163.

[281] See further *infra*, pp. 579–82.

[282] *Infra*, pp. 579–82. The right of self-determination may be given a content which varies from one context to the next. For a treaty provision see the Treaty of Dorpat, 1920.

certain minimum conditions are not fulfilled. Of course, no problem exists if one denies the existence of the right of self-determination under customary international law. However, it is at least an optional principle which particular states may agree to observe in their relations between themselves. Dispositions by the principal powers, transfers under procedures prescribed by international organizations,[283] and bilateral cessions in the period since 1919 are not infrequently expressed to be in accordance with the principle of self-determination. The machinery of the plebiscite is sometimes applied to provide solutions.[284]

Some opinions[285] support the view that transfers must satisfy the principle. However, at present there is insufficient practice to warrant the view that a transfer is invalid simply because there is no sufficient provision for expression of opinion by the inhabitants. The position would change if more states refused to recognize cessions precisely because the principle had been ignored. At present most claims are made in terms which do not include a condition as to due consultation of the population concerned. Those jurists who insist on the principle refer to exceptions, the principal among them being the existence of a joint decision of states representing the international community to impose measures of security on an aggressor[286] and the principle of respect for pre-independence administrative divisions following attainment of independence by former colonies (*uti possidetis*).[287] In any event the application of the principle may be difficult in practice. In relation to the British–Argentine dispute over the Malvinas/Falklands the relevant UN resolutions call for transfer by virtue of a principle of statutory decolonization while the United Kingdom regards transfer as a breach of the principle of self-determination.[288]

---

[283] *Infra*, pp. 163–6.

[284] See Hyde, i. 364–5, 372; Whiteman, ii. 1168–72.

[285] Kozhevnikov (ed.), *International Law*, pp. 175–7; Oppenheim, ii. 712–15.

[286] Cf. the debate between West German and Polish jurists over the Oder-Neisse frontier established by the Potsdam Decl. in 1945. See Brownlie, *International Law and the Use of Force by States*, p. 409 n. 3, and, for the Potsdam Decl. 39 *AJ* (1945), Suppl., p. 245, chs. 6 and 9.

[287] See the Judgment of the Chamber in the *Frontier Dispute Case*, ICJ Reports (1986), 566–7, paras. 23–6; cf. also pp. 652–3 (Luchaire, Sep. Op.). On the principle of *uti possidetis* see *supra*, pp. 129–30.

[288] See 56 *BY* (1985), 402–6, 473–4. See also Crawford, *The Creation of States* (2nd edn., 2006), pp. 637–47.

8

STATUS OF TERRITORY: FURTHER PROBLEMS

1. INTERNATIONAL PROCEDURES RELATING TO TERRITORIAL DISPOSITIONS[1]

(a) Agreement between the states concerned

A cession of territory may depend on the political decision of the states concerned in a dispute and may be the result of either a political claim, on grounds of justice or security, or a legal claim. The conditions under which transfer occurs may be influenced by the recommendations of political organs of international organizations and by the principle of self-determination.[2] On a number of occasions plebiscites have been organized under the auspices of the United Nations.[3]

(b) Joint decision of the principal powers

It was pointed out in the previous chapter[4] that on a number of occasions a group of leading powers, perhaps in association with a large number of other states, have assumed a power of disposition although the legal bases of such a power were problematical. It is possible that, as in the case of the creation of a new constitution by rebellion, the political and legal bases are indivisible:[5] certainly the legal consequences of this power of disposition are commonly accepted. The mandates system rested in part at least on such a power of disposition, and the International Court has accepted its consequences in its advisory opinions on the status of South-West Africa and its decisions in the *South West Africa* cases.[6]

---

[1] See esp. Jennings, *The Acquisition of Territory in International Law* (1963), 69–87; and Crawford, *The Creation of States in International Law* (2nd edn., 2006), 501–647.

[2] This begs the question of the legal content of the principle, on which *infra*, pp. 579–82.

[3] See Merle, *Ann. français* (1961), 425–45; Whiteman, ii. 1168–72.

[4] pp. 138–9.

[5] Cf. the Adv. Op. in the *Reparation* case, quoted *infra*, ch. 31, s. 2.

[6] ICJ Reports (1962), 319; see also the Joint Diss. Op. of Judges Spender and Fitzmaurice, ibid. 482; ibid. (1966), 6.

(c) Action by United Nations organs

It is doubtful if the United Nations has a 'capacity to convey title', in part because the Organization cannot assume the role of territorial sovereign: in spite of the principle of implied powers[7] the Organization is not a state and the General Assembly only has a power of recommendation. Thus the resolution of 1947 containing a partition plan for Palestine was probably *ultra vires*, and, if it was not, was not binding on member states in any case.[8] However this may be, the fact is that states may agree to delegate a power of disposition to a political organ of the United Nations, at least where the previous sovereign has relinquished title and there is no transfer of sovereignty and no disposition of a title inhering in the Organization. The latter acts primarily as a referee. The General Assembly played this type of role in relation to the creation of the new states of Libya and Somalia and in the case of territory relinquished by Italy under the peace treaty of 1947.[9] On similar principles, the General Assembly probably has a power to terminate a trusteeship status.[10] The application of such principles to the termination of a mandate is a matter of some difficulty, partly because the power of disposition technically inhered in the principal Allied powers participating in the Treaty of Versailles.[11] It may be that, in the cases of mandate and trusteeship, and also of territories to which Chapter 11 of the Charter applies,[12] the United Nations does not 'confer sovereignty', but merely decides on the manner in which the principle of self-determination shall be implemented. Certainly resolutions of the General Assembly play an important element in the consolidation of title over territory already in possession, and this is especially the case with the resolutions based on Resolution 1514 containing a Declaration on the Granting of Independence to Colonial Countries and Peoples.[13]

The United Nations General Assembly assumed the power to terminate the Mandate for South West Africa in Resolution 2145 (XXI) adopted on 27 October 1966.[14] The operative paragraphs of the resolution are as follows:

1. *Reaffirms* that the provisions of General Assembly Resolution 1514 (XV)[15] are fully applicable to the people of the Mandated Territory of South West Africa and that, therefore, the people of South West Africa have the inalienable right to

---

[7] On which see *infra*, ch. 31, s. 4.

[8] See Kelsen, *The Law of the United Nations* (1951), 195–7 (n. 7).

[9] See Resol. 289 (IV)A of 21 Nov. 1949, 387 (V) of 17 Nov. 1950, and 1418 (XIV) of 5 Dec. 1959. See further Resol. 515 (VI) of 1 Feb. 1952 on the transfer of Eritrea to Ethiopia. For these and other materials see Whiteman, iii. 4–32.

[10] This may be inferred from Arts. 76 and 85 of the Charter: Jennings, *Acquisition of Territory*, p. 81. No express provision appears. See Marston, 18 *ICLQ* (1969), 1–40.

[11] See also the Sep. Op. of Judge McNair, *Status of South-West Africa*, ICJ Reports (1950), 128 at 150; Sep. Op. of Judge Read, ibid. 168, Diss. Op. of Judge Alvarez, ibid. 180–1; and E. Lauterpacht, 6 *ICLQ* (1957), 514–15.

[12] See *infra*, ch. 25, s. 3.

[13] See *infra*, pp. 553–5. See further Jennings, *Acquisition of Territory*, pp. 82–7.

[14] Text: 5 *ILM* (1966), 1190; Whiteman, xiii. 760. For comment see Dugard, 62 *AJ* (1968), 78–97; Marston, 18 *ICLQ* (1969), 28ff.; Rousseau, 71 *RGDIP* (1967), 382–4.

[15] On which see *infra*, pp. 579–82.

self-determination, freedom and independence in accordance with the Charter of the United Nations;

2. *Reaffirms further* that South West Africa is a territory having international status and that it shall maintain this status until it achieves independence;

3. *Declares* that South Africa has failed to fulfil its obligations in respect of the administration of the Mandated Territory and to ensure the moral and material well-being and security of the indigenous inhabitants of South West Africa, and has, in fact, disavowed the Mandate;

4. *Decides* that the Mandate conferred upon His Britannic Majesty to be exercised on his behalf by the Government of the Union of South Africa is therefore terminated, that South Africa has no other right to administer the Territory and that henceforth South West Africa comes under the direct responsibility of the United Nations;

5. *Resolves* that in these circumstances the United Nations must discharge those responsibilities with respect to South West Africa;

6. *Establishes* an *Ad Hoc* Committee for South West Africa—composed of fourteen Member States to be designated by the President of the General Assembly—to recommend practical means by which South West Africa should be administered, so as to enable the people of the Territory to exercise the right of self-determination and to achieve independence, and to report to the General Assembly at a special session as soon as possible and in any event not later than April 1967;

7. *Calls upon* the Government of South Africa forthwith to refrain and desist from any action, constitutional, administrative, political or otherwise, which will in any manner whatsoever alter or tend to alter the present international status of South West Africa;

8. *Calls the attention* of the Security Council to the present resolution;

9. *Requests* all States to extend their whole-hearted co-operation and to render assistance in the implementation of the present resolution;

10. *Requests* the Secretary-General to provide all assistance necessary to implement the present resolution and to enable the *Ad Hoc* Committee for South West Africa to perform its duties.

Subsequently the General Assembly established the United Nations Council for South West Africa, appointed a United Nations Commissioner to administer the territory and renamed the territory 'Namibia'. South Africa failed to respond to these developments and the Security Council adopted resolutions in 1969 and 1970 'recognizing' the decision of the General Assembly to terminate the Mandate and calling upon all states to take measures to implement the finding that South Africa's continued presence in Namibia was illegal. In a further resolution the International Court was requested to give an advisory opinion on the question, 'What are the legal consequences for States of the continued presence of South Africa in Namibia notwithstanding Security Council Resolution 276 (1970)'? The principal views of the Court are considered elsewhere,[16] but as a preliminary to giving its views on the substance of the question posed the

---

[16] See *infra*, pp. 513–14.

Court considered the validity of General Assembly Resolution 2145 (XXI) in terms of the Charter.[17] The Court held that the power of the League of Nations, and therefore of the United Nations also, to revoke the Mandate for reasons recognized by general international law (termination on the ground of material breach of a treaty) was to be implied.[18] The role adopted by the General Assembly, assisted if need be by the Security Council, appears to involve taking such action as is necessary to ensure the application of the provisions of Resolution 1514 (XV) to the people of Namibia.[19] In formal terms at least, this does not involve a power of disposition as such, but the application of the existing provisions of the Charter, as interpreted by the practice of the organs, relating to the principle of self-determination.[20] Namibia eventually achieved independence in 1990 after elections supervised by the UN Transition Assistance Group.

The role of the General Assembly in the decolonization of Western Sahara involved a complex of issues concerning the principle of self-determination and the legal interests of Morocco and Mauritania.[21]

In the aftermath of the illegal Iraqi occupation of Kuwait the Security Council adopted Resolution 687 (1991) on 3 April 1991. The resolution specified the measures to be taken, acting under Chapter VII of the Charter. In particular, the Security Council:

2. **Demands** that Iraq and Kuwait respect the inviolability of the international boundary and the allocation of islands set out in the 'Agreed Minutes Between the State of Kuwait and the Republic of Iraq Regarding the Restoration of Friendly Relations, Recognition and Related Matters', signed by them in the exercise of their sovereignty at Baghdad on 4 October 1963 and registered with the United Nations and published by the United Nations in document 7063, United Nations, **Treaty Series**, 1964;

3. **Calls upon** the Secretary-General to lend his assistance to make arrangements with Iraq and Kuwait, drawing on appropriate material, including the map transmitted by Security Council document S/22412 and to report back to the Security Council within one month;

4. **Decides** to guarantee the inviolability of the above-mentioned international boundary and to take as appropriate all necessary measures to that end in accordance with the Charter of the United Nations.

In due course the Demarcation Commission created under the auspices of the Security Council submitted a Final Report on the demarcation of the international boundary between Iraq and Kuwait on 20 May 1993. In Resolution 833 (1993) the Security Council

---

[17] ICJ Reports (1971), 16 at 45–50.

[18] pp. 47–9; and see Dugard, 62 AJ at pp. 84–8.

[19] See para. 1 of Resol. 2145 (XXI), *supra*.

[20] For criticism of the Op. on the basis (i) that neither the General Assembly nor the Security Council has the power to abrogate or alter territorial rights and (ii) that the resolutions concerned had this purpose, see Judge Fitzmaurice, Diss. Op., ICJ Reports (1971), 280–3, 294–5.

[21] See the Adv. Op. concerning the *Western Sahara*, ICJ Reports (1975), 12; and also the Decl. of Judge Gros at pp. 69–77; Sep. Op. of Judge Petrén at pp. 105–15; Sep. Op. of Judge Dillard at pp. 116–26; Sep. Op. of Judge de Castro at pp. 127–72. See also Crawford, *The Creation of States*, (2nd edn., 2006), 637–47; Shaw, 49 BY (1978), 118–54.

adopted the decisions of the Commission as 'final'. The exercise was in form merely the demarcation of an already agreed alignment and no 'relocation' was intended (see Resolution 833 (1993)). However, when the Final Report is examined it is difficult to escape the impression that elements of delimitation were involved, especially in relation to the maritime delimitation.[22] The outcome is controversial but it is important to bear in mind that the Security Council expressly disclaimed an intention to use the demarcation process for the purpose of 'reallocating territory between Kuwait and Iraq' (see the *consideranda* to Resolution 833).

2. CAPACITY OF THE UNITED NATIONS TO ADMINISTER TERRITORY[23]

The United Nations has supervisory functions specified in the Charter, and supported by practice, in relation to trusteeship and non-self-governing territories. Moreover, in the context of maintaining international peace and security United Nations organs have been prepared to assume administrative functions in relation to the City of Jerusalem,[24] the Free City of Trieste,[25] and in East Timor.[26] The existence of such administrative powers rests legitimately on the principle of necessary implication and is not incompatible with the view that the United Nations cannot have territorial sovereignty.[27] In Resolution 2145 (XXI) the General Assembly assumed a power of administration in respect of South West Africa (see the previous section).

3. LEGAL REGIMES APART FROM STATE SOVEREIGNTY

(a) Territory *sub judice*

The analogy here is perhaps with the right of possession which the *sequester* or stakeholder had in Roman law. The existing regime rests on acts in the law which in principle could not create sovereignty in the existing holder but which do not

---

[22] See *Demarcation of the International Boundary between the State of Kuwait and the Republic of Iraq by the United Nations* (Kuwait, n.d.); Mendelson and Hulton, *BY* 64 (1993), 135–95; id., *Ann. français* (1993), 178–231.

[23] See Crawford, *The Creation of States*, (2nd edn., 2006), 546–64.

[24] See *supra*, p. 60.

[25] See *supra*, p. 59, and Whiteman, iii. 68–109.

[26] On the United Nations Transitional Administration in East Timor established in 1999 see Crawford, *The Creation of States*, (2nd edn., 2006), 560–62; and Chesterman, *You, The People* (2004), 135–43.

[27] See E. Lauterpacht, 5 *ICLQ* (1956), 409–13; and Seyersted, 37 *BY* (1961), 351 at 451–3. Cf. Kelsen, *Law of the United Nations* (1950), 195–7, (n. 7) 684–7.

render the region *terra nullius*.[28] For practical purposes the present possessor may be regarded as exercising normal powers of jurisdiction and administration, subject only to external limitations arising from the legal instruments determining the status of the region. Thus the relevant agreement may contain provisions for demilitarization. Furthermore, there must be an implied obligation not to act in such a way as to render fulfilment of the ultimate objective of the arrangement impossible. Thus if the stated objective is to provide for an expression of opinion by certain minority groups it would be *ultra vires* to deport or to harass and blackmail the groups concerned.[29] The status of the inhabitants in terms of nationality and citizenship will depend on the circumstances of the particular case. If one accepts the obligations inherent in the doctrine of the ultimate objective then the conferment and deprivation of nationality would not be a matter of domestic jurisdiction for the administering state.

(b) *Terra nullius*[30]

For practical purposes the cases of the *terra nullius* and territory *sub judice* may be to a certain extent assimilated.[31] In both cases activity is limited by principles similar to those protecting a reversioner's interest in municipal law. However, in the case of the *terra nullius* the state which is in the course of consolidating title[32] is in principle entitled to carry out acts of sovereignty. The important difference is that whereas the *terra nullius* is open to acquisition by any state, the territory *sub judice* is not susceptible to occupation, since the express conditions for its attribution may have been laid down already, and in any case there is an existing possessor whose interim possession may have received some form of general recognition.[33]

The *terra nullius* is subject to certain rules of law which depend on the two assumptions that such zones are free for the use and exploitation of all and that persons are not deprived of the protection of the law merely because of the absence of state sovereignty—the law of the sea provides the analogy for this. States may exercise jurisdiction in respect of individuals and companies carrying on activities in a *terra nullius*. Article 101 of the United Nations Convention of the Law of the Sea[34] defines piracy to include acts directed 'against a ship, aircraft, persons or property in a place outside the jurisdiction of any State'. Acts in the nature of aggression or breaches of the peace,

---

[28] Examples: the City of Jerusalem, Trieste, the former Italian colonies after 1947, and perhaps Taiwan. For administration by the United Nations see *supra*, p. 163.

[29] Such activity might amount to a breach of the standards laid down by the Genocide Conv.

[30] See *Island of Palmas* case, Hague Court Reports, ii. 92; Fitzmaurice, 92 Hague *Recueil* (1957, II), 140–4; Guggenheim, i. 456–7; Hackworth, i. 427, 465–8, 471, 474–6. See further *supra*, pp. 141ff. Cf. McNair, *Opinions* i. 314–25; *Jacobsen v. Norwegian Government*, *Ann. Digest*, 7 (1933–4), no. 42.

[31] Cf. *UK Contemp. Practice* (1962), i. 43–5.

[32] Since states do not always advertise an animus possidendi this is probably to be presumed, except where representations from other states provoke a disclaimer.

[33] This apart from the case of competing acts of state authority in the same region.

[34] See further Arts. 100 and 105 of the Conv.; Arts. 14, 15, and 19 of the Conv. on the High Seas, 1958; *Yrbk.* ILC (1956), ii. 282–3 (Arts. 38, 39 and 43 and commentary thereon).

war crimes, or crimes against peace and humanity, will equally be so in *terra nullius*.[35] Unjustified interference from agencies of another state with lawful activity will create international responsibility in the ordinary way. It is doubtful whether private interests established prior to the reduction into sovereignty of a *terra nullius* must be respected by the new sovereign.[36] Several issues remain unsettled. Thus it is not clear that a *terra nullius* has a territorial sea, and if so, what is the breadth thereof: the logic, such as it is, of the doctrine of appurtenance[37] does not apply here, and it would be reasonable to regard the adjacent waters as high seas.[38]

(c) *Res communis*

The high seas are commonly described as *res communis omnium*,[39] and occasionally as *res extra commercium*.[40] The use of these terms is innocent enough providing not too much is read into them. They represent only a few basic rules and do not provide a viable regime of themselves. The *res communis* may not be subjected to the sovereignty of any state, general acquiescence apart,[41] and states are bound to refrain from any acts which might adversely affect the use of the high seas by other states or their nationals. It is now generally accepted that outer space and celestial bodies have the same general character.[42] Legal regimes similar in type may be applied by treaty to other resources, for example an oilfield underlying parts of two or more states.[43]

(d) Territorial entities (other than states) enjoying legal personality

In the Advisory Opinion concerning the *Western Sahara*[44] the International Court considered the legal status of the 'Mauritanian entity' at the time of colonization by Spain in the years 1884 onwards. It was accepted that the entity was not a State. The Court concluded that the emirates and tribes which existed in the region did not constitute a 'legal entity'. However, in coming to this conclusion the Court accepted as a principle that in certain conditions a legal entity, other than a state, 'enjoying some form of sovereignty', could exist distinct from the several emirates and tribes which

---

[35] Fitzmaurice, 92 Hague *Recueil* (1957, II), 142.

[36] Guggenheim, i. 456–7, says that they must.

[37] *Supra*, p. 117.

[38] Art. 1 of the Conv. on the Territorial Sea and Contiguous Zone, 1958, and Art. 2 of the UN Conv. on the Law of the Sea, 1982, speak of the extension of the sovereignty of a state. The provisions of both Conv. relating to the continental shelf refer constantly to the 'coastal state'.

[39] Fitzmaurice, 92 Hague *Recueil* (1957, II), 143, 150–1, 156–7, 160–2. In Roman law the concept did not acquire a very definite content and was confused at times with res publicae.

[40] Schwarzenberger, *International Law*, i (3rd edn., 1957), 309. Lindley (quoted in Hackworth, i. 397) uses the term *territorium nullius*.

[41] *Supra*, pp. 145ff., 162ff.

[42] See *infra*, pp. 255–9.

[43] See Agreement relating to the Exploitation of Single Geological Structures extending across the Dividing Line on the Continental Shelf under the North Sea, U.K. and Netherlands, *Treaty Series* no. 24 (1967), Cmnd. 3254. Cf. the Antarctic Treaty, *infra*, pp. 261–2.

[44] ICJ Reports (1975), 12 at 57–65, 67–8.

composed it. These conditions were not described with any precision by the Court but were related to the existence of 'common institutions or organs' and of an entity which was in 'such a position that it possesses, in regard to its Members, rights which it is entitled to ask them to respect'.[45] Presumably, but the matter is far from clear, such legal entities will have rights and duties similar to those of states.

[45] ICJ Reports (1975), 12 at 63, referring to the *Reparation for Injuries* case, ICJ Reports (1949), 178, and see *infra*, p. 678.

PART IV

LAW OF THE SEA

9

TERRITORIAL SEA, CONTIGUOUS ZONES, AND EXCLUSIVE ECONOMIC ZONES[1]

A. Territorial Sea

1. INTRODUCTION

At the present time all states claim to exercise sovereignty, subject to treaty obligations and rules on general international law, over a belt of sea adjacent to their coastlines. On its outer edge this belt is bounded by the high seas, and it is founded on a baseline, related to the low-water mark and, in certain conditions, to other phenomena, which serves to divide the territorial sea from the interior or national waters comprised in rivers, bays, gulfs, harbours, and other water lying on the landward side of the baseline. The term of art now generally accepted is 'territorial sea', and it is employed in the most recent Conventions. Other terms employed to denote the same concept include 'the maritime belt', 'marginal sea', and 'territorial waters'.[2] The language of the

---

[1] See generally El-Hakim, *The Middle Eastern States and the Law of the Sea* (1979); Oda, *International Law of the Resources of the Sea* (1979); Rousseau iv. 340–402, 455–61; Rembe, *Africa and the International Law of the Sea* (1980); O'Connell, *The International Law of the Sea* (ed. Shearer), 2 vols. (1982, 1984); Platzöder (ed.), *Third United Nations Conference on the Law of the Sea* (Documents), 17 vols. (1982–8); Anand, *Origin and Development of the Law of the Sea* (1983); Bardonnet and Virally (eds.), *Le Nouveau Droit international de la mer* (1983); Rozakis and Stephanou (eds.), *The New Law of the Sea* (1983); Nordquist (ed.), *United Nations Convention on the Law of the Sea 1982: A Commentary* (1985); Dupuy and Vignes, *Traité du nouveau droit de la mer* (1985); Prescott, *The Maritime Political Boundaries of the World* (1985); Kittichaisaree, *The Law of the Sea and Maritime Boundary Delimitation in South-East Asia* (1987); Churchill and Lowe, *The Law of the Sea* (3rd edn., 1999); UN Office for Ocean Affairs and the Law of the Sea, *Law of the Sea Bulletin*; Vasciannie, *Land-locked and Geographically Disadvantaged States in the International Law of the Sea* (1990); Lucchini and Voelckel, *Droit de la Mer*, Tôme I (1990); Tôme 2, vol. 1 (1996); Tôme 2, vol. 2 (1996); Dupuy and Vignes (eds.), *A Handbook on the New Law of the Sea*, 2 vols. (1991); *Mélanges offerts à Laurent Lucchini et Jean-Pierre Quéneudec* (2003); Roach and Smith, *United States Responses to Excessive Maritime Claims* (2nd edn., 1996); *Handbook on the Delimitation of Maritime Boundaries* (United Nations, 2000).

[2] The term 'territorial waters' is perhaps confusing as it is used on occasion in national legislation to describe internal waters, or internal waters and territorial sea combined. Cf. also the *Fisheries* case, ICJ Reports (1951), 116 at 125. Constitutions, legislation, and treaties often refer to the 'maritime frontier'.

Convention on the Territorial Sea and Contiguous Zone[3] seems to assume that every state necessarily has a territorial sea, and some jurists assert a doctrine of inseparable and natural appurtenance.[4]

The view generally accepted by writers,[5] and which has found expression in Article 1 of the Convention on the Territorial Sea of 1958, is that states have rights amounting to sovereignty over the territorial sea.[6] Article 2 of the Convention of 1958 states that the sovereignty is exercised 'subject to the provisions of these articles and to other rules of international law'. The first part of the proviso is obvious, and the second part was intended to make it clear that the limitations set out in the Convention are not exhaustive. The sovereignty of the coastal state extends also to the seabed and subsoil of the territorial sea and the airspace over it. The Law of the Sea Convention of 1982 contains essentially similar provisions (Art. 2).

An understanding of the modern law and of the problems which remain unsolved must depend to a considerable extent on obtaining an historical perspective. In the eighteenth century extravagant claims to sovereignty over the seas were obsolete in many cases and were nearly so in others.[7] Before the abandonment of such claims in the case of states which had not pursued extensive claims to the seas, and as a consequence of such abandonment in other cases, a test of appurtenance, a definition of the maritime marches of states, had to be sought. In a work published in 1702[8] the Dutch jurist Bynkershoek propounded the doctrine that the power of the territorial sovereign extended to vessels within the range of cannon mounted on the shore. At first this doctrine seems to have rested on the control of the actual guns of ports and fortresses over adjacent waters: it was not originally a concept of a maritime belt of uniform breadth.[9] However, in the latter half of the eighteenth century several states laid down

---

[3] *Infra.* This important multilateral convention entered into force on 10 Sept. 1964. Together with three other Conv., on the High Seas, on Fishing and Conservation of the Living Resources of the High Seas, and on the Continental Shelf, it was adopted at the First United Nations Conference on the Law of the Sea in 1958. Only the Conv. on the High Seas is 'generally declaratory of established principles of international law' but the Territorial Sea and Continental Shelf Conv. provide evidence of the generally accepted rules bearing on their subject-matter. On the status of the provisions of the latter as rules of general law see ch. 10. On the status of the Territorial Sea Conv. as general law see *Reference Re Ownership of Offshore Mineral Rights* (1968), 65 DLR (2d) 353, SC of Canada. Texts of the Conventions: Brownlie, *Documents*, p. 66; 52 *AJ* (1958), 830. The other three Conv. came into force as follows: Conv. on the High Seas, 30 Sept. 1962; Conv. on the Continental Shelf, 10 June 1964; Conv. on Fishing and Conservation, 20 Mar. 1966.

[4] See *supra*, p. 118.

[5] Oppenheim, ii. 600; Gidel, iii. 181; O'Connell, 45 *BY* (1971), 303–83; id., *The International Law of the Sea*, i. 59–123.

[6] See the Air Navigation Conv. 1919, Art. 1; International Civil Aviation Conv. 1944, Art. 2; Hague Conv. XIII on the Rights and Duties of Neutral Powers in Time of War, 1907, Art. 1; Treaty of Peace with Japan, 1951, Art. 1; the *David, Ann. Digest*, 7 (1933–4), no. 52; *Yrbk. ILC* (1956), ii. 265. See also *Bonser* v. *La Macchia*, ILR 51, 39; *N.S.W. and others* v. *Commonwealth of Australia*, ibid. 89.

[7] See further *infra*, pp. 224ff., on the freedom of the seas.

[8] *De Dominio Maris*, ch. 2.

[9] This is the view of Walker, 22 *BY* (1945), 210–31. The concept of actual control is probably referable to the diplomatic practice of Holland and France in the seventeenth and eighteenth centuries.

limits for belts for purposes of customs or fishery control in legislation and treaties and Danish practice—after 1745 based on a four-mile belt[10] as the extent of sovereignty—had some impact on European thinking on the matter.[11]

In the last quarter of the century two decisive developments occurred. Writers and statesmen began to conceive of a hypothetical cannon-shot rule, a *belt* over which cannon could range if they were placed along the whole seaboard. Further, as 'cannon-shot' was by no means a definite criterion, suggestions for setting up a convenient standard equivalent, or rather substitute, began to appear. In 1782 the Italian writer Galiani proposed three miles, or one marine league,[12] and the diplomatic birth of the three-mile limit appears to be the United States Note to Britain and France of 8 November 1793, in which the limit was employed for purposes of neutrality.[13] During and after the Napoleonic wars the British and American prize courts translated the cannon-shot rule into the three-mile rule.[14]

A significant aspect of the development of the law is the intimate relation between claims to jurisdiction for particular purposes over the high seas, and extension of sovereignty to a maritime belt. Some claims, such as those of Denmark and Sweden, though commencing as pronouncements for neutrality purposes, fairly soon developed into assertions of sovereignty,[15] especially when associated with exclusive fishery limits. In other cases it remained for long uncertain whether a claim was only to certain types of jurisdiction or was a general limit of sovereignty.[16] What is certain is that claims to jurisdiction have always tended to harden into claims to sovereignty. This process was, however, arrested to some extent by general recognition of the basic legal distinction between territorial sea as an extension of sovereignty and special jurisdictional zones, 'contiguous zones' as they were later to be called, *over the high seas*.[17]

[10] So also Sweden, at least after 1779. Vattel in his influential *Le Droit des gens* (1758) adopted a theory of a maritime belt.

[11] See Kent, 48 *AJ* (1954), 537–53; O'Connell, 45 *BY* (1971), 320–3.

[12] Similar views were expressed by Azuni in 1795. See also Kent, 48 *AJ* (1954), 548.

[13] Hyde, i. 455. See also US Proclamation of Neutrality, 22 Apr. 1793, which refers to the range of cannonball 'usually stated at one sea league'.

[14] The *Twee Gebroeders* (1800), 3 C. Rob. 162; (1801), 3 C. Rob. 336; the *Anna* (1805), 5 C. Rob. 373; the *Brig Ann* (1815), 1 Gallison 62. See also McNair, *Opinions*, i. 331.

[15] In the case of Denmark and Norway, probably in 1812. See also Fulton, *The Sovereignty of the Sea* (1911), 566ff.; Verzijl, *International Law in Historical Perspective*, iii. (1970), 60–5.

[16] Cf. the Portuguese 6-mile limit for customs and neutrality; on which see Jessup, *The Law of Territorial Waters and Maritime Jurisdiction* (1927), 41. The Spanish 6-mile limit for a territorial sea appears to originate in customs legislation. The 12-mile zone claimed by Imperial Russia related to customs and fisheries legislation.

[17] The 'general recognition' certainly existed by 1920 and perhaps as early as 1880. See generally Masterson, *Jurisdiction in Marginal Seas* (1929), 375ff. In 1914 Chile, which already had a territorial sea with a 3-mile limit, declared the same limit for purposes of neutrality. British sources often refer to 'territorial jurisdiction'.

2. BASELINE FOR MEASUREMENT
OF THE TERRITORIAL SEA

The normal baseline from which the breadth of the territorial sea is measured is the low-water line along the coast. This follows from the concepts of maritime belt and appurtenance, and corresponds with state practice.[18] There is no uniform standard by which states in practice determine this line, and Article 5 of the Law of the Sea Convention defines the line 'as marked on large scale charts officially recognised by coastal States'.[19] In the case of tideless seas the baseline may be placed at the average waterline on the coast in question. The regime of bays, islands in the vicinity of coasts, and archipelagos will be considered subsequently. For the present, attention must be turned to the *Anglo-Norwegian Fisheries* case, which has had a decisive effect on the baseline issue.

The *Fisheries* case.[20] British fishermen have fished off the Norwegian coast since about 1906, and at various times incidents led to diplomatic correspondence about Norway's fishery limits. The Norwegian limit of four miles for territorial waters had been established by royal decree in 1812 and was not in issue in the case. However, later decrees of 1869, 1881, and 1889, and official explanations thereof, continued the measure of 1812 in terms of a system of straight lines drawn from certain outermost points of the 'skjaergaard' or rampart of rocks and islands which fringes much of the Norwegian coast. By a decree of 12 July 1935 Norway applied the system in a more detailed way than before, and the validity of the new limits was challenged by the United Kingdom. After a series of incidents involving British vessels the United Kingdom took the case before the International Court by unilateral application, asking for the award of damages for interferences with British fishing vessels outside the permissible limits.[21] The Court took the view that the system of straight baselines following the general direction of the coast had been consistently applied by Norway and had encountered no opposition on the part of other states. The United Kingdom had not made a formal

[18] Conv. on the Territorial Sea and Contiguous Zone (1958), Art. 3; Law of the Sea Conv. (1982), Art. 5; *ILC Yrbk.* (1956), ii. 266; the *Fisheries* case, ICJ Reports (1951), 116 at 128; Sep. Op. of Judge Hsu Mo, 154; Diss. Op. of Judge McNair, 162. Note especially Waldock, 28 *BY* (1951) at 131–7; McDougal and Burke, *The Public Order of the Oceans*, pp. 305ff.; Gihl, *Scand. Studies in Law* (1967), 119–74.

[19] The article states this as a definition and not as presumptive evidence: the relevant subcommittee of the Hague Codification Conference entered a proviso 'provided the latter line does not appreciably depart from the line of mean low-water spring tides': see Hackworth, i. 643–4; and the critical comment in McDougal and Burke, *The Public Order of the Oceans*, pp. 322–6. See also *Lia Ching Hsing* v. *Rankin* (1978), 23 ALR 151; ILR, 73, 173.

[20] ICJ Reports (1951), 116; ILR 18 (1951), no. 36. Literature: Waldock, 28 *BY* (1951), 114–71; Fitzmaurice, 30 *BY* (1953), 8–54 and 31 *BY* (1954), 371–429; Lauterpacht, *The Development of International Law by the International Court* (1958), 190–9; Hudson, 46 *AJ* (1952), 23–30; Johnson, 1 *ICLQ* (1952), 145–80; Evensen, 46 *AJ* (1952), 609–30; Wilberforce, 38 *Grot. Soc.* (1952), 151–68; Auby, 80 *JDI* (1953), 24–55.

[21] The 1935 decree was not strictly enforced until 16 Sept. 1948 and the UK claim was for interference between that date and the date of the application, 24 Sept. 1949. 48 fixed points were employed: 18 of the lines exceeded 15 miles in length, one line was 44 miles in length. The decree refers to a fisheries zone, but both parties assumed in their arguments that it delimited the territorial sea: ICJ Reports (1951), 125.

and definite protest on the issue of the position of baselines until 1933.[22] There is little doubt that, as the later parts of the Judgment indicate, the validity of the decree of 1935 could have been upheld on the basis of acquiescence,[23] and, indeed, Judge Hackworth gave, as a separate reason for concurring in the Judgment of the Court, the existence of historic title to the areas in question on the part of Norway.[24] However, while it is true that the Court refers to the absence of protest from other states, and also to the consolidation of the method 'by a constant and sufficiently long practice', the Judgment as a whole makes abundantly clear the fact that the Court believed that the Norwegian system of baselines was, as a matter of principle, in accordance with international law.[25] The course of the Court's reasoning brings this out.

The Court commences with a description of the topography of the coast of the mainland:

Very broken along its whole length, it constantly opens out into indentations often penetrating for great distances inland. ... To the West, the land configuration stretches out into the sea: the large and small islands, mountainous in character, the islets, rocks and reefs,[26] some always above water, others emerging only at low tide, are in truth but an extension of the Norwegian mainland. ... The coast of the mainland does not constitute... a clear dividing line between land and sea. What matters, what really constitutes the Norwegian coast line, is the outer line of the 'skjaergaard'.[27]

The Court then states that the problem which arises concerns the baseline from which the breadth of the territorial sea is to be measured and that, while the parties agree that the criterion is the low-water mark, they differ as to its application. The Court decides that the relevant low-water mark is the outer line of the 'skjaergaard' and states that this solution 'is dictated by geographical realities'.[28] The question which now presented itself was how the baseline was to be drawn in the case of the Norwegian coast. The method of the *tracé parallèle*, that is, drawing a line which is an exact image of the coastline, assumed by the Court to be the normal method of applying the low-water mark rule,[29] did not apply to the type of coast in question, since in this case the baseline could only be determined by means of a geometric construction. In a crucial passage the Judgment elaborates this concept:[30]

The principle that the belt of territorial waters must follow the general direction of the coast makes it possible to fix certain criteria valid for any delimitation of the territorial sea;

---

[22] ICJ Reports (1951), 138. But see the Diss. Op. of Judge McNair, ibid. 171–80.

[23] See *supra*, p. 151.

[24] ICJ Reports (1951), 206. See also the *Anglo-French Continental Shelf Case*, ILR 54, 6 at 74–83 (paras. 121–44) on acceptance of a basepoint *by* conduct.

[25] The later references to the attitude of other governments appear to have been intended, in part at least, as evidence of legality: see ICJ Reports (1951), 139.

[26] The 'skjaergaard' or rock rampart, containing about 120,000 insular formations.

[27] ICL Reports (1951), 127.

[28] Ibid. 128.

[29] See Waldock, 28 *BY* (1951), 132–7.

[30] ICJ Reports (1951), 129–30.

these criteria will be elucidated later. The Court will confine itself at this stage to noting that, in order to apply this principle, several States have deemed it necessary to follow the straight baselines method[31] and that they have not encountered objections of principle by other States. This method consists of selecting appropriate points on the low-water mark and drawing straight lines between them. This has been done, not only in the case of well-defined bays, but also in cases of minor curvatures of the coastline where it was solely a question of giving a simpler form to the belt of territorial waters.

The Court proceeds to discount the British contention that straight lines could only be drawn across bays.[32] An argument that, in any case, the length of straight lines must not exceed 10 miles was criticized in these terms:[33]

In this connection, the practice of States does not justify the formulation of any general rule of law. ... Futhermore, apart from any question of limiting the lines to ten miles, it may be that several lines can be envisaged. In such cases the coastal State would seem to be in the best position to appraise the local conditions dictating the selection.

Consequently, the Court is unable to share the view of the United Kingdom Government, that 'Norway, in the matter of base-lines, now claims recognition of an exceptional system'...all that the Court can see therein is the application of general international law to a specific case.

In the opinion of the Court certain basic considerations as to the nature of the territorial sea provided criteria by which the validity of systems of delimitation could be determined.[34] First, because of the close dependence of the territorial sea upon the land domain, 'the drawing of baselines must not depart to any appreciable extent from the general direction of the coast'. Secondly, a close geographical relationship between sea areas and land formations is a 'fundamental consideration' in deciding 'whether certain sea areas lying within [the baselines] are sufficiently closely linked to the land domain to be subject to the regime of internal waters'. The Court states that the other consideration is 'that of certain economic interests peculiar to a region, the reality and importance of which are evidenced by long usage'.[35]

The Judgment is then devoted to an examination of the consistency of the application of the Norwegian system of baselines, and of the attitude of other states. The conclusion reached[36] is that the method of straight lines 'was imposed by the peculiar

[31] Annex 112 of the Norwegian Rejoinder. See Waldock, 28 BY (1951), 142–3; and the Diss. Op. of Judge McNair, ICJ Reports (1951), 162.

[32] See *infra*, p. 181, on the 10-mile closing line for bays.

[33] ICJ Reports (1951), 131.

[34] Ibid. 133.

[35] See also the reference (p. 128) to the fact that 'in these barren regions the inhabitants of the coastal zone derive their livelihood essentially from fishing'.

[36] Ibid. 139. In an individual op. Judge Alvarez expresses the view that each state may determine the extent of its territorial sea and the way in which it is reckoned if certain conditions are satisfied, *inter alia*, that the delimitation is carried out reasonably (p. 150). His criteria of reasonableness include geographic and economic considerations. Judge Hsu Mo agrees in his Sep. Op. with the findings of the Court on the legality of the method of straight lines, but does not consider that all the actual lines fixed by the decree of 1935 are in conformity with international law (p. 154). In a substantial Diss. Op. Judge McNair states that the system

geography of the Norwegian coast', and had been consolidated by 'a constant and sufficiently long practice'.

3. STRAIGHT BASELINES: RECENT DEVELOPMENTS

Even if one regards the Judgment in the *Fisheries* case as an instance of judicial legislation, and not an application of pre-existing principles to the special facts, its significance for the development of the law cannot be underestimated. The pronouncements on the straight lines method are intended to have general application to coasts of that type.

Article 4 of the Convention on the Territorial Sea[37] includes a provision (para. 4) the effect of which is that account may be taken of economic interests in determining individual baselines if the geographical criteria justifying straight lines are satisfied. Substantially the article confirms the place of the principles of the *Fisheries* case in the law. A good number of states employ straight baselines which apply the Norwegian system or are at least compatible with it,[38] leaving aside certain extensive closing lines for bays and lines enclosing archipelagos. The provisions of Article 7 of the Law of the Sea Convention of 1982 affirm the existing principles governing straight baselines and deal with the problem of deltas and other unstable coastlines (para. 2).

of straight lines is not in accordance with law, that it will create practical difficulties for mariners, and that the effect of the decree of 1935 will be to injure the principle of the freedom of the seas (pp. 158, 171, 185). Moreover, he considered reliance on 'economic and other social interests' as a basis for delimitation to be impermissible (pp. 161, 169, 171). See also pp. 171–80 on the issue of acquiescence on the part of the United Kingdom. The Diss. Op. of Judge Read presents similar conclusions (p. 186). See also Moore, *Digest*, i. 785–8.

[37] 'Article 4. 1. In localities where the coastline is deeply indented and cut into, or if there is a fringe of islands along the coast in its immediate vicinity, the method of straight baselines joining appropriate points may be employed in drawing the baselines from which the breadth of the territorial sea is measured.

2. The drawing of such baselines must not depart to any appreciable extent from the general direction of the coast, and the sea areas lying within the lines must be sufficiently closely linked to the land domain to be subject to the regime of internal waters.

3. Baselines shall not be drawn to and from low-tide elevations, unless lighthouses or similar installations which are permanently above sea level have been built on them.

4. Where the method of straight baselines is applicable under the provisions of paragraph 1, account may be taken, in determining particular baselines, of economic interests peculiar to the region concerned, the reality and importance of which are clearly evidenced by long usage.

5. The system of straight baselines may not be applied by a State in such a manner as to cut off from the high seas the territorial sea of another State.

6. The coastal State must clearly indicate straight baselines on charts, to which due publicity must be given.'

[38] Approximately 48 states employ such baselines: see US Dept. of State, The Geographer, *Limits in the Seas*, no. 36. For the UK system of straight baselines: Territorial Waters Order in Council, 1964; *British Practice in IL* (1964, I), 49; *Limits in the Seas*, no. 23; and Orders in Council made under the Territorial Sea Act 1987. See further Law of the Sea Inst. (Rhode Island), Occasional Paper no. 13 (1972); Hydrographic Society (London), Special Publication no. 2; Voelckel, 19 *Ann. français* (1973), 820–36; US Dept. of State, Office of Ocean Law and Policy, *Limits in the Seas*, no. 106. See also Reisman and Westerman, *Straight Baselines in International Boundary Delimitation* (1992); Roach and Smith, *United States Responses to Excessive Maritime Claims*, 2nd edn. (1996), pp. 57–146.

4. BREADTH OF TERRITORIAL SEA[39]

In the seventeenth century several forms of limit were known, including the range of vision on a fair day and the range of cannons on shore.[40] By the last quarter of the eighteenth century the cannon-shot rule obtained in western and southern Europe.[41] It was not dominant, however, and other claims rested simply on a belt with a stated breadth.[42] In 1793, as we have seen, the cannon-shot rule was first given a standard value of one marine league or three miles in diplomatic practice.[43] By 1862,[44] and probably earlier, the cannon-shot rule and the three-mile limit were generally regarded as synonymous in the practice of states supporting a three-mile rule. The cannon-shot rule in its original form had become obsolete.[45]

Until recent years (1987 and 1988 respectively) the United States and the United Kingdom supported the three-mile limit and protested in the face of claims to a wider territorial sea.[46] British adherence to the three-mile limit was reinforced in the late nineteenth century by the abandonment of a special customs and excise jurisdiction over zones beyond three miles and the embodiment of the limit in legislation, commencing with the Territorial Waters Jurisdiction Act 1878. The three-mile limit gained considerable currency in the course of the nineteenth century.[47] However, the practice was far from uniform,[48] and some states, including France, Belgium, Portugal, Germany, and Imperial Russia, did not differentiate clearly in their practice between territorial sea and jurisdictional zones, and claimed zones for particular purposes. Many states supporting a three-mile limit claimed contiguous zones extending beyond three miles.

It is not surprising to find that several eminent jurists doubted whether the three-mile limit had been unequivocally settled.[49] Indeed, it was not until 1920 that claims

---

[39] See Gidel, iii. 62ff.; McDougal and Burke, *The Public Order of the Oceans*, pp. 446–564; Fulton, *The Sovereignty of the Sea*, pp. 537ff.; US Dept. of State, The Geographer, *Limits in the Seas*, no. 36; UN Office for Ocean Affairs and the Law of the Sea, *Law of the Sea Bulletin*. Of particular importance are the materials to be found in the *Yearbook of the International Law Commission* (1952–6, inclusive).

[40] *Supra*, pp. 174–5.

[41] Fulton, *The Sovereignty of the Sea*, pp. 566ff.

[42] Denmark and Norway, 4 miles (1745); Sweden, 4 miles (1779); Spain, 6 miles (1760). On the relation to special zones of jurisdiction, *supra*, p. 179.

[43] *Supra*, p. 175. Units of measurements: the marine or nautical mile is equivalent to 1,852 metres.

[44] Cf. Moore, *Digest*, i. 706–7.

[45] An isolated case of reliance on the rule to justify a limit of 12 miles occurred in 1912, when Russia referred to the rule to justify extensions of jurisdiction for customs and fishery purposes: Hackworth, i. 635. See also *Costa Rica Packet*, La Fontaine, p. 510; Moore, *Arbitrations*, iv. 4948; the *Alleganean*, Moore, *Arbitrations*, iv. 4332–5; La Pradelle and Politis, ii. 257.

[46] See *supra*, n. 39. For the diplomatic practice on the three-mile limit: Hackworth, i. 630–41; Hyde, i. 455–9; McNair, *Opinions*, i. 331–8.

[47] Adherents prior to 1914 included Argentina (1871), Austria (1846), Belgium (1832–91—fishing zone), Brazil (1859), Chile (1855), Ecuador (1889), France (1862—fishing zone), Greece (1869—fishing zone), Japan (1870), Liberia, Mexico (1902), Netherlands (1889), Panama, United Kingdom, and the United States.

[48] Spain had long had a 6-mile limit; Norway, Denmark, and Sweden claimed 4 miles. See also 20 *AJ* (1926), Spec. Suppl., pp. 73–4, and Gidel, iii. 69ff., on treaty practice.

[49] Hall, *International Law*, pp. 191–2; Westlake, *International Law*, pt. i. (1904), 184–6. See also Fulton, *The Sovereignty of the Sea*, p. 664. Oppenheim, i. (8th edn., 1955) 490–2, is very cautious on the subject (and see the first edition (1905), 241–2).

to special jurisdictional zones were generally seen to be distinct from full claims to territorial sea. Thus the results of the Hague Codification Conference of 1930 provide a significant balance sheet in view of the stage of development reached and the obvious role of the Conference and its preliminaries in crystallizing governmental attitudes. The preparatory material and the proceedings showed that although a majority of states favoured a three-mile limit, some of these also claimed contiguous zones.[50] In its report to the Conference the second committee explained that, in view of differences of opinion, it had preferred not to express an opinion on what ought to be regarded as the existing law. During the fourth, seventh, and eighth sessions the International Law Commission indicated that a majority of members did not regard 'the three-mile rule' as a part of positive law. In 1970 the United States adopted an Oceans Policy one component of which was an effort to obtain international agreement on a maximum of 12 miles. Article 3 of the Law of the Sea Convention of 1982 provides that 'every state has the right to establish the breadth of its territorial sea up to a limit not exceeding 12 nautical miles'. The great preponderance of states have a 12-mile limit and this has been adopted by recent legislation in the United Kingdom (the Territorial Sea Act 1987) and the United States (1988).[51] Claims apparently in excess of 12 miles call for careful assessment. Certain of these are fishing conservation zones which have been wrongly characterized. Those which are not will be incompatible with the Convention of 1982 and with general international law.

5. BASELINES: FURTHER PROBLEMS[52]

BAYS[53]

It is necessary to determine the closing line which leaves internal waters on its landward side and provides a baseline for delimiting the territorial sea. The drawing of a closing line is possible only where the coast of the bay belongs to a single state. To justify assimilation to the land domain there must be a certain degree of penetration.

---

[50] For the views expressed in the second committee: 24 *AJ* (1930), Suppl., p. 253; Hackworth, i. 628. 17 states favoured 3 miles; 4 favoured 4 miles; 12 states favoured 6 miles. Of the 17 states favouring 3 miles, 5 desired a contiguous zone.

[51] Useful information on claims to territorial seas (and other zones) may be found in: UN Office of Legal Affairs, *Law of the Sea Bulletin*. The current situation is as follows: 3 states claim 3 miles: Jordan, Palau, Singapore. 1 state claims 4 miles: Norway, 2 states claim 6 miles: Dominican Republic, Greece. 140 states claim 12 miles.

Seven states claim 200 miles: Benin, Congo (Brazzaville), Ecuador, El Salvador, Liberia, Panama, Peru, Sierra Leone, Somalia.

[52] Minor points are dealt with in Arts. 8, 9 and 13 of the Convention on the Territorial Sea and Arts. 9, 11, and 12 of the Law of the Sea Convention of 1982.

[53] In particular see: Gidel, iii. 532ff.; Fitzmaurice, 8 *ICLQ* (1959), 79–85; McDougal and Burke, *The Public Order of the Oceans*, pp. 327–73; Waldock, 28 *BY* (1951), 137–42; Whiteman, iv. 207–33; *Fisheries* case, Pleadings, I; Gihl, *Scand. Studies in Law* (1967), 119–74; Bouchez, *The Regime of Bays in International Law* (1964); Blum, *Historic Titles in International Law* (1965), 261–81; Edeson, *Austral. Yrbk.* (1968–9), 5–54; O'Connell, *The International Law of the Sea*, i. 338–416; Westerman, *The Juridical Bay* (1987).

Article 7, paragraph 2, of the Territorial Sea Convention of 1958, and Article 10, paragraph 2, of the Law of the Sea Convention of 1982, provide a semicircle, or rigid geometrical, test of such assimilation.[54] However, there is substantial authority for the view that this criterion is a necessary but not sufficient condition for the existence of a bay in legal terms. There must be 'a well-marked indentation with identifiable headlands', but this 'geographical test' is itself question-begging.[55] Gulfs, fjords, and straits, or parts thereof, are not excluded from the legal concept of a bay. The straight closing line applicable to bays is quite distinct from the system of baselines applicable in special circumstances as established in the *Fisheries* case. The provisions concerning bays in the Convention on the Territorial Sea of 1958 and the Law of the Sea Convention of 1982 are not intended to introduce the system of straight lines to coasts whose configuration does not justify this. It was asserted formerly that the closing line was limited to 10 miles. Practice was, however, far from uniform,[56] and in the *Fisheries* case the International Court concluded that 'the ten-mile rule has not acquired the authority of a general rule of international law'.[57] Article 7, paragraph 4, of the Convention on the Territorial Sea of 1958, and Article 10, paragraph 4, of the Law of the Sea Convention of 1982 prescribe 24 miles. Coastal states may derive title to bays as a consequence of the system of straight lines approved in the *Fisheries* case [58] where this is applicable. A considerable number of large claims related to 'bays' are based on historic title, a mode of acquisition which has been examined already as a question of general principle.[59]

BAYS BOUNDED BY THE TERRITORY OF TWO OR MORE STATES

Although the issue has not been uncontroversial, Article 15 of the Convention on the Law of the Sea of 1982 (see also Art. 12, para. 1, of the Territorial Sea Convention of 1958) probably represents the law as it has been generally understood and provides:[60]

[54] See the Conv. of 1982, Art. 10, para. 2: 'For the purposes of this Convention, a bay is a well-marked indentation whose penetration is in such proportion to the width of its mouth as to contain landlocked waters and constitute more than a mere curvature of the coast. An indentation shall not, however, be regarded as a bay unless its area is as large as, or larger than, that of the semi-circle, whose diameter is a line drawn across the mouth of that indentation'. On the application of this provision see *Post Office* v. *Estuary Radio* [1967] 1 WLR 1396. And see para. 3. See also *U.S.* v. *California*, 381 US 139; ILR 42, 86; *U.S.* v. *Louisiana et al.*, 389 US 155 (1967); ILR 57, 90; *U.S.* v. *Louisiana et al.*, 394 US 11 (1969); ILR 53, 206; *U.S.* v. *California*, ILR 57 (1952), 54; *Texas* v. *Louisiana*, ILR 59 (1976), 194; *Raptis* v. *South Australia* (1977) 15 ALR 223; ILR 69, 32.

[55] *North Atlantic Fisheries Arbitration* (1910), RIAA xi. 167 at 199; *U.S.* v. *Louisiana* (1969), ILR 53, 206 at 239–46; O'Connell, *The International Law of the Sea*, p. 384; Westerman, *The Juridical Bay*, pp. 79–98. Cf. *Raptis* v. *South Australia*, previous note.

[56] In the nineteenth century the content of the concept of a bay was assumed and not precisely defined: see McNair, *Opinions*, i. 353–6, 360. The 10-mile limit finds support in the documents of the 1930 Codification Conference and the practice of Belgium, France, Germany, and Holland.

[57] ICJ Reports (1951), 131. See also Judge McNair, at pp. 163–4. However, Judge Read, p. 188, regards the rule as a part of the customary law.

[58] *Supra*, pp. 176ff.

[59] *Supra*, p. 157. For bays claimed as 'historic bays' (over 30 in all), see Colombos, pp. 180–8; Jessup, *Law of Territorial Waters*, pp. 383–439. See further McDougal and Burke, *The Public Order of the Oceans*, pp. 357–68 (discounting the basis in authority of some claims); Gidel, iii. 621–63; Goldie *et al.*, ii *Syracuse Journ. of IL and Commerce* (1984), 211–376.

[60] See Oppenheim, ii. 632; Colombos, p. 188; Hyde, i. 475; Gioia, 24 *Neths. Yrbk.* (1993), 139–81.

Where the coasts of two States are opposite or adjacent to each other, neither of the two States is entitled, failing agreement between them to the contrary, to extend its territorial sea beyond the median line every point of which is equidistant from the nearest points on the baselines from which the breadth of the territorial seas of each of the two States is measured. The above provision does not apply, however, where it is necessary by reason of historic title[61] or other special circumstances[62] to delimit the territorial seas of the two States in a way which is at variance therewith.

STRAITS[63]

See the provision quoted above.

OCCASIONAL ISLANDS[64]

Whatever the size or population a formation is an island in the legal sense if two conditions are satisfied: (1) the formation must be natural and not an artificial installation; (2) it must always be above sea level. Formations visible only at low tide ('low-tide elevations'), and permanently submerged banks and reefs, do not in general produce a territorial sea, as islands do. However, the Law of the Sea of Convention of 1982, Article 121, paragraph 3, provides as follows: 'Rocks which cannot sustain human habitation or economic life of their own shall have no exclusive economic zone or continental shelf'. This provision does not represent the customary law and has no retrospective effect.

LOW-TIDE ELEVATIONS[65]

In two cases these formations are permitted to produce an effect on the limit of the territorial sea. Article 4, paragraph 3, of the Convention on the Territorial Sea of 1958 and Article 7, paragraph 4, of the Convention of 1982 provide that straight baselines

---

[61] The Central American Court of Justice, in an opinion and decision of 9 Mar. 1917, declared that the Gulf of Fonseca was 'an historic bay possessed of the characteristics of a closed sea' and further that, without prejudice to the rights of Honduras, El Salvador and Nicaragua had a right of co-ownership in the extraterritorial waters of the Gulf. See the *Case Concerning the Land, Island and Maritime Frontier Dispute*, ICJ Reports (1992) 351 at pp. 588–604. On claims to treat the Straits of Tiran and the Gulf of Aqaba as a closed sea see Gross, 53 *AJ* (1959), 564 at 566–72; Selak, 52 *AJ* (1958), 660 at 689–98.

[62] This is unfortunately vague. Geographical peculiarities and the elimination of practical problems are probably catered for. See the declaration on Art. 12 by Venezuela: McDougal and Burke, *The Public Order of the Oceans*, p. 1184.

[63] See Gidel, iii. 728ff.; McDougal and Burke, *The Public Order of the Oceans*, pp. 432–7; Hyde, i. 489; Harv. Research, 23 *AJ* (1929), Spec. Suppl., pp. 280–7.

[64] See the Conv. on the Territorial Sea of 1958, Art. 10; the Law of the Sea Convention of 1982, Art. 121, para. 1; *Yrbk. ILC* (1956), ii. 270; Fitzmaurice, 8 *ICLQ* (1959), 85–8; Gidel, iii. 670ff.; McNair, *Opinions*, i. 363ff.; McDougal and Burke, *The Public Order of the Oceans*, pp. 373, 391–8. See also Jayewardene, *The Regime of Islands in International Law* (1990).

[65] See the Judgment in *Qatar v. Bahrain*, ICJ Reports, 2001, 40 at pp. 100–3, paras. 200–9; Whiteman, *Digest*, IV (1965), 304–7; Marston, 46 *BY* (1972–73), 405–23; Weil, *Liber Amicorum Judge Shigeru Oda*, Vol. 1 (2002), 307–21; Guillaume, *Mélanges offerts à Laurent Lucchini et Jean-Pierre Quéneudec* (2003), 287–302.

shall not be drawn to or from low-tide elevations unless lighthouses or similar instal-lations which are permanently above sea level have been built on them.[66] Secondly, and apart from the effect of these provisions, the low-water line on an elevation situated at a distance not exceeding the breadth of the territorial sea from the mainland or an island may be used as the baseline.[67] Elevations not within the territorial sea have no territorial sea of their own.

ISLAND FRINGES TREATED AS NATURAL APPENDAGES OF THE COAST[68]

Quite apart from coasts to which a *system* of straight lines may properly apply, there is, in the opinion of Sir Humphrey Waldock, a 'considerable body of State practice' supporting the principle that under certain conditions coastal islands may be treated as part of the mainland.[69] The principle rests on considerations of geographical asso-ciation and appurtenance, and some but by no means all claims are supported by his-toric title and acquiescence. A baseline—not necessarily a straight line—is drawn in such cases from the low-water line on the seaward shore of the island chain. Such an approach could be justified as an application of the principles expounded in the Judgment in the *Fisheries* case[70] (in which the Court regarded the outer line of the 'skjaergaard' as constituting 'a whole with the mainland').

GROUPS OF ISLANDS; ARCHIPELAGOS[71]

Claims to a baseline drawn along the outer fringe of groups of islands in close associa-tion with the mainland may be justified on grounds considered in the last paragraph.[72]

---

[66] See Marston, 46 *BY* (1972–3), 405–23, for detailed consideration. See also *Qatar* v. *Bahrain*, Judgment of 16 March 2001, paras. 200–9.

[67] Art. 11 of the Conv. of 1958 and Art. 13 of the Conv. of 1982. See also the *Fisheries* case, ICJ Reports (1951), 128, and cf. UN Legis. Series, *Regime of the Territorial Sea*, pp. 14, 48, 54, 194, 245, 293, 563, 564; *Regina* v. *Kent Justices, ex p. Lye* [1967] 2 QB 153; *U.S.* v. *Louisiana et al.*, 394 US 11 (1969), ILR 53, 206.

[68] See Gidel, iii. 711, 719, 722; Colombos, pp. 122–3; Waldock, 28 *BY* (1951), 142; Gihl, *Scand. Studies in Law* (1967), 129–35. See also the *Anna* (1805), 5 C. Rob. 373; *U.S.* v. *Louisiana et al.*, n. 68 *supra*; *Raptis* v. *South Australia*, ILR 69, 32 at 63–5 (Mason, J.), 72–3 (Murphy, J.).

[69] 28 *BY* (1951), 142.

[70] ICJ Reports, (1951), 128.

[71] Gidel, iii. 706–27; Evensen, UN Conf. on the Law of the Sea, Off. Recs. i. 289–302; Fitzmaurice, 8 *ICLQ* (1959), 88–90; Waldock, 28 *BY* (1951), 142–7; McDougal and Burke, *The Public Order of the Oceans*, pp. 373–87; Sørensen, *Varia Juris Gentium*, pp. 315–31; *Yrbk. ILC* (1953), ii. 69, 77; Whiteman, iv. 274–303; Pharand, 21 *Univ. of Toronto LJ* (1971), 1–14; O'Connell, 45 *BY* (1971), 1–77; Law of the Sea Inst. (Rhode Island), Occasional Paper no. 13 (1972); Amerasinghe, 23 *ICLQ* (1974), 539–75; Bowett, *The Legal Regime of Islands in International Law* (1979), 73–113; Symmons, *The Maritime Zones of Islands in International Law* (1979), 62–81; Anand, 19 *Indian Journ.* (1979), 228–56; Lattion, *L'Archipel en droit international* (1984); Herman, 23 *Canad. Yrbk* (1985), 172–200; Rajan, 29 *German Yrbk* (1986), 137–53; Churchill and Lowe, *The Law of the Sea* (3rd edn., 1999), 118–31; Jayewardene, op. cit., 103–72. See also *Civil Aeronautics Board* v. *Island Airlines*, 235 F. Supp. 990 (1964).

[72] See legislation of Cuba, Ecuador, Egypt, Ethiopia, Iran, Saudi Arabia, and Yugoslavia. See also *Fisheries* case, Pleadings, i. 79–83, 465–95.

The International Law Commission failed to produce a draft article on the question, although in a comment (annexed to draft Art. 10) it pointed out that the straight baselines system might be applicable. However, neither this system nor what has been said above provides a solution to the problem of baselines associated with large island systems unconnected with any mainland. Indonesia and the Philippines[73] employ straight baselines to enclose such island systems, and it may be that a polygonal system is the only feasible one in such special cases. It is arguable that this is only a further application, to special facts, of principles of unity and interdependence inherent in the *Fisheries case*. The difficulty is to allow for such special cases without giving a general prescription which, being unrelated to any clear concept of mainland, will permit of abuse.

At the Third United Nations Conference on the Law of the Sea the archipelagic states as a group[74] had some success in advancing the cause of straight archipelagic baselines. Consequently the Law of the Sea Convention of 1982 includes a set of articles concerning archipelagic states (Arts. 46–54). These are defined as 'a state constituted wholly by one or more archipelagos and may include other islands'. For no very sound reason this definition excludes states, such as Ecuador and Canada, which consist in part of one or more archipelagos. According to the Convention archipelagic straight baselines may be employed subject to certain conditions: for example, that such baselines 'shall not depart to any appreciable extent from the general configuration of the archipelago'. The archipelagic state has sovereignty over the waters enclosed by the baselines subject to certain limitations created by the provisions of this Part of the Convention. These limitations consist of the right of innocent passage (see below) for ships of all states, and, unless the archipelagic state designates sea lanes and air routes above, 'the right of archipelagic sea lanes passages...through the routes normally used for international navigation' (Art. 53, para. 12).

REEFS

In the case of reef-bound coastlines the baseline is the seaward low-water line of the reef. This flows from principle in any case but is affirmed by the Law of the Sea Convention of 1982 (Art. 6).

HIGHLY UNSTABLE COASTLINES

Article 7, paragraph 2, of the Convention of 1982 provides as follows: 'Where because of the presence of a delta and other natural conditions the coastline is highly unstable,

[73] Philippines claim: *Yrbk. ILC* (1956), ii. 69–70. For the Indonesian claim and the United Kingdom protest: 7 *ICLQ* (1958), 538.

[74] There are currently 14 such states: Bahamas, Cape Verde, Comoros, Fiji, Indonesia, Maldives, Mauritius, Papua-New Guinea, Philippines, São Tomé and Príncipe, Seychelles, Solomon Islands, Trinidad and Tobago, Vanuatu. In the Judgment in *Qatar v. Bahrain* the International Court refused to accept the relevance of the claim of Bahrain to have the status of an archipelagic state: see the Judgment of 16 March 2001, paras. 180–3.

the appropriate points may be selected along the furthest seaward extent of the low-water line and, notwithstanding subsequent regression of the low-water line, the straight baselines shall remain effective until changed by the coastal state in accordance with this Convention'.

6. LEGAL REGIME OF THE TERRITORIAL SEA

In practical terms, the coastal state has rights and duties inherent in sovereignty, although foreign vessels have privileges, associated particularly with the right of innocent passage, which have no counterparts in respect of the land domain apart from special agreement or local customary rights. The coastal state may reserve fisheries for its own nationals, and indeed the first exercise of this power has often been the first evidence of a claim to a maritime belt. It may also exclude foreign vessels from navigation and trade along the coast (*cabotage*). Obviously, there is a general power of police in matters of security, customs, fiscal regulation, and sanitary and health controls. Particular limitations on this sovereignty to be found in general international law will now be considered.

INNOCENT PASSAGE[75]

Customary law recognizes the right of peaceful or innocent passage through the territorial sea.[76] Historically the right is related to a state of affairs in which special zones of jurisdiction were not clearly distinguished from full-blooded claims and in principle the maritime belt was high seas but with restrictions in favour of the coastal state. As a question of policy innocent passage is a sensible form of accommodation between the necessities of sea communication and the interests of the coastal state. Definition of innocent passage is a matter of some difficulty, not only in respect of precision in stating the conditions of innocence, but also with regard to the question of a presumption in favour either of the visitor or of the coastal state in case of doubt. The starting point must be Article 14 of the Convention on the Territorial Sea:[77]

1. Subject to the provisions of these articles, ships of all States, whether coastal or not, shall enjoy the right of innocent passage through the territorial sea.

---

[75] Gidel, iii. 193–291; Whiteman, iv. 343–417; McDougal and Burke, *The Public Order of the Oceans*, pp. 174–269; Fitzmaurice, 8 *ICLQ* (1959), 90–108; François, Report, *Yrbk. ILC* (1952), ii. 38; O'Connell, *The International Law of the Sea*, i. 260–98; Lucchini and Voelckel, *Droit de la Mer*, Tôme 2, vol. 2 (1996), 202–303; *The Law of the Sea: National Legislation on the Territorial Sea, the Right of Innocent Passage and the Contiguous Zone* (United Nations, New York, 1995).

[76] Not through internal waters. For an exception resulting from the use of a straight baseline, see Art. 5, para. 2, of the Conv. on the Territorial Sea of 1958, and Art. 8, para. 2, of the Conv. of 1982.

[77] Arts. 14 to 17 inclusive appear under the rubric 'Rules applicable to All Ships'. Art. 14 bears a close relation to Arts. 3 and 4 of the draft produced by the Second Committee of the Hague Codification Conference in 1930.

2. Passage means navigation through the territorial sea for the purpose either of traversing that sea without entering internal waters, or of proceeding to internal waters, or of making for the high seas from internal waters.

3. Passage includes stopping and anchoring, but only in so far as the same are incidental to ordinary navigation or are rendered necessary by *force majeure* or by distress.

4. Passage is innocent so long as it is not prejudicial to the peace, good order or security of the coastal State. Such passage shall take place in conformity with these articles and with other rules of international law.

5. Passage of foreign fishing vessels shall not be considered innocent if they do not observe such laws and regulations as the coastal State may make and publish in order to prevent these vessels from fishing in the territorial sea.[78]

In substance this article corresponds to the customary law, but it is more specific in certain respects. Though to some degree the text speaks for itself some comment is necessary. Vessels engaged in coastal trade (*cabotage*) are excluded by the definition of passage. Fishing vessels are included, though by an ill-drafted provision which makes compliance with local laws and regulations relating to the prevention of fishing a criterion of innocence. This approach contradicts paragraph 4. Paragraph 4 states that passage is innocent if 'not prejudicial to the peace, good order or security of the coastal State', but does not make compliance with local laws and regulations a criterion of innocence.[79] Apparently the text was intended to place emphasis on the manner in which the passage was carried out[80] rather than on factors such as the object of the particular passage, the cargo carried, ultimate destination, and so on. However, several commentators understand the words to extend to the object of the journey.[81]

At the Third United Nations Conference on the Law of the Sea (1973–9) the right of innocent passage was a matter of particular interest. The maritime states, faced with expanding claims to territorial seas affecting many seaways, were concerned to provide firmer outlines for the right. Consequently, the Law of the Sea Convention of 1982 contains the following detailed definition of 'innocent passage' (Art. 19):

1. Passage is innocent so long as it is not prejudicial to the peace, good order or security of the coastal State. Such passage shall take place in conformity with this Convention and with other rules of international law.

2. Passage of a foreign ship shall be considered to be prejudicial to the peace, good order or security of the coastal State if in the territorial sea it engages in any of the following activities:

   (a) Any threat or use of force against the sovereignty, territorial integrity or political independence of the coastal State, or in any other manner in violation

---

[78] Para. 6 contains a simple condition of passage rather than a criterion of innocence: 'Submarines are required to navigate on the surface and to show their flag.'

[79] See Fitzmaurice, 8 *ICLQ* (1959), 95.

[80] Cf. the *Corfu Channel* case (Merits), ICJ Reports (1949), 30–2; and Fitzmaurice, 27 *BY* (1950), 28–31.

[81] Fitzmaurice, 8 *ICLQ*, pp. 95–6; Sørensen, 101 Hague *Recueil* (1960, III), 188; id. *Int. Conciliation*, no. 520 (1958), 334. *Contra*, Gross, 53 *AJ* (1959), 582. Example of non–innocent passage on this interpretation: carriage of weapons to a state helping guerrillas operating against the coastal state.

of the principles of international law embodied in the Charter of the United
Nations;

(b) Any exercise or practice with weapons of any kind;

(c) Any act aimed at collecting information to the prejudice of the defence or security
of the coastal State;

(d) Any act of propaganda aimed at affecting the defence or security of the coastal
State;

(e) The launching, landing or taking on board of any aircraft;

(f) The launching, landing or taking on board of any military device;

(g) The loading or unloading of any commodity, currency or person contrary to
the customs, fiscal, immigration or sanitary laws and regulations of the coastal
State;

(h) Any act of wilful and serious pollution, contrary to this Convention;

(i) Any fishing activities;

(j) The carrying out of research or survey activities;

(k) Any act aimed at interfering with any systems of communication or any other
facilities or installations of the coastal State;

(l) Any other activity not having a direct bearing on passage.

Article 20 of the Convention provides: 'In the territorial sea, submarines and other
underwater vehicles are required to navigate on the surface and to show their flag'.

PASSAGE OF WARSHIPS[82]

Several opinions of considerable authority deny the right of passage of warships in
peacetime;[83] others allow such a right 'when the territorial waters are so placed that
passage through them is necessary for international traffic'.[84] It is clear that a significant number, and perhaps a majority, of states require prior authorization for the passage of warships, and, as a consequence, dogmatic assertions of a right of passage have
an aspect of advocacy. A draft article formulated by the International Law Commission
at its eighth session gave the coastal state the right to make passage subject to prior

[82] See McDougal and Burke, *The Public Order of the Oceans*, pp. 192–4, 216–21; Colombos, p. 133; Gidel,
iii. 227–89; Jessup, 59 *Columbia LR* (1959), 247–9; Harv. Research, 23 *AJ* (1929), Spec. Suppl., pp. 295–6;
François, *Yrbk. ILC* (1952), ii. 42–3; UN Legis. Series, *The Territorial Sea*, pp. 361–420; Verzijl, *International
Law in Historical Perspective*, iii. 59–60; McNair, *Opinions*, ii. 191–2; de Vries Reilingh, 2 *Neths. Yrbk.* (1971),
29–67; Delupis, 78 *AJ* (1984), 53–75; Oxman, 24 *Virginia JIL* (1984), 809–63; Butler, 81 *AJ* (1987), 331–47;
O'Connell, *The International Law of the Sea*, i. 274–98; Oppenheim, ii. 618–20; Roach and Smith, *United
States Responses to Excessive Maritime Claims* (2nd edn., 1996), 251–78. On passage through territorial
waters forming part of an international strait, *infra*, ch. 12.

[83] Hall, *International Law* p. 198; Sørensen, 101 Hague *Recueil* (1960, III), 192. Is 'peacetime' a bilateral
relation, or is it applicable to a war situation proximate geographically?

[84] Colombos, loc. cit. Cf. Guggenheim i. 421–2; Hyde, i. 516–18. Gidel, iii. 280. Cf. *Corfu Channel* case
(Merits), ICJ Reports (1949), 28.

authorization or notification.[85] At the Geneva Conference of 1958 this formula did not get the necessary support. However, Professor Sørensen[86] is of the opinion that a majority of delegations did not intend warships to have a right of passage, but no article in the Convention on the Territorial Sea deals with this question directly. The draft article of the Commission bearing directly on the subject was omitted.[87]

Certain jurists have deduced from the text of the Convention the sense that it recognizes a right of passage. In support of this position Sir Gerald Fitzmaurice, as he then was, states that Articles 14–17 are titled 'Rules applicable to All Ships', and the provision relating to submarines (Art. 14, para. 6) makes it clear by implication that 'All Ships' includes warships.[88] The *travaux préparatoires* contradict this implication.[89] It has also been argued[90] that the right of passage arises by implication from Article 23, which is the sole article under the title 'Rule applicable to Warships'. This provides: 'If any warship does not comply with the regulations of the coastal State concerning passage through the territorial sea and disregards any request for compliance which is made to it, the coastal State may require the warship to leave the territorial sea'.

The object of this provision was to deal with the case where a warship, having commenced passage in accordance with international law, being subject to local laws and regulations, has refused to comply therewith.[91] The immunity from jurisdiction[92] which warships enjoy necessitated a special provision: the hypothesis on which the article rests does not preclude the issue as to a *right* of passage. Moreover, the textual arguments advanced involve the unwarranted assumption that a question with a background of controversy was ultimately settled by leaving the issue dependent on inference. The Law of the Sea Convention of 1982 contains the same unresolved obscurities as the provisions of 1958 (Arts. 17–32).

RIGHTS OF THE COASTAL STATE

The coastal state may take the necessary steps in its territorial sea to prevent passage which is not innocent (Convention on the Territorial Sea, Art. 16, para. 1; Law of the Sea Convention of 1982, Art. 25, para. 1). Vessels exercising the right of passage are subject to local laws and regulations, providing these conform with international law

[85]   *Yrbk. ILC* (1956), ii. 276–7. States requiring prior authorization or notification: (*inter alia*) Belgium, Bulgaria, Colombia, Egypt, France, Honduras, Italy, Norway, Poland, Romania, the former USSR, Yugoslavia. See also reservations to Art. 23 of the Conv. on the Territorial Sea by Bulgaria, Belorussia, Czechoslovakia, Hungary, Romania, and the Ukraine. Those permitting a right of passage: (*inter alia*) Denmark, Netherlands, United Kingdom (see 7 *ICLQ* (1958), 544), United States, German Federal Republic, Iran, Peru, Sweden. The materials of the Hague Codification Conference are inconclusive.

[86]   *Int. Conciliation*, no. 520 (1958), 235.

[87]   See UN Conf. on the Law of the Sea, Off. Recs., ii. 66–8.

[88]   8 *ICLQ* (1959), 98–9, 102–3. See also O'Connell, *The International Law of the Sea*, pp. 290–1.

[89]   Cf. *Yrbk. ILC* (1956), ii. 272 (comment on Art. 15).

[90]   Jessup, *Law of Territorial Waters*, p. 248.

[91]   See *Yrbk. ILC* (1956), ii. 276–7: in this draft Subsection D 'Warships', has two subheads, 'Passage' and 'Non-observance of the regulations'. Art. 23 repeats the article under the latter subhead.

[92]   See *infra*, pp. 322, 371.

and treaty obligations (Art. 16, para. 2; Art. 17; Law of the Sea Convention of 1982, Art. 21, Art. 22, Art. 25, para. 2). The substance of such laws and regulations and the mode of enforcing compliance should not be such as to render passage impossible or impracticable. Article 16, paragraph 3 of the 1958 Convention (Law of the Sea Convention of 1982, Art. 25, para. 3) confers on the coastal state a right to suspend innocent passage *temporarily* in specified areas of the territorial sea if such suspension 'is essential for the protection of its security'.[93] Article 18 (Law of the Sea Convention of 1982, Art. 26) provides that no charge may be levied on foreign vessels by reason only of their passage, but only for specific services rendered to the ship.

CRIMINAL JURISDICTION OVER SHIPS IN PASSAGE[94]

This question does not arise in the case of warships or non-commercial government vessels, which enjoy complete immunity from local jurisdiction. Article 19 of the Convention on the Territorial Sea of 1958 substantially reproduces rules assumed to represent international law:[95]

1. The criminal jurisdiction of the coastal State should not be exercised on board a foreign ship passing through the territorial sea to arrest any person or to conduct any investigation in connexion with any crime committed on board the ship during its passage, save only in the following cases:

    (a) If the consequences of the crime extend to the coastal State; or

    (b) If the crime is of a kind to disturb the peace of the country or the good order of the territorial sea; or

    (c) If the assistance of the local authorities has been requested by the captain of the ship or by the consul of the country whose flag the ship flies; or

    (d) If it is necessary for the suppression of illicit traffic in narcotic drugs.

Subsection (d) was an innovation, however. A matter of controversy concerned the legality of arrest or investigation in connection with any crime committed before a ship entered the territorial sea if the vessel was merely passing through the territorial sea without entering internal waters. Gidel was of the opinion that arrest was permitted.[96] Paragraph 5 of Article 19 expressly prohibits the exercise of jurisdiction in this way, although logically the prohibition is inherent in the first paragraph. Paragraph 2 of Article 19 reserves a right of arrest and investigation on board foreign vessels

---

[93] The provision of 1982 adds the words 'including weapons exercises'.

[94] See McDougal and Burke, *The Public Order of the Oceans*, pp. 294–301; Lee, 55 *AJ* (1961), 77 at 86–93; Fitzmaurice, 8 *ICLQ* (1959), 103–6; UN Legis. Series, *The Territorial Sea*, pp. 319ff.; Guggenheim, i. 423; Rousseau, iv. 371–3; Hyde, i. 749; Report of François, *Yrbk. ILC* (1952), ii. 40–1; *Yrbk. ILC* (1956), ii. 274–5 (draft article and comment); Francioni, 1 *Ital. Yrbk.* (1975), 27–41; O'Connell, *The International Law of the Sea*, ii. 936–66.

[95] Fitzmaurice, 8 *ICLQ* (1959), 104, is not prepared to regard the rules as strict law but rather as international practice. Cf. the view of Fitzmaurice as delegate to the Geneva Conference, 7 *ICLQ* (1958), 545.

[96] iii. 261. Contradicted by other writers. See also Hyde, i. 749–50.

passing through the territorial sea after leaving internal waters. The Law of the Sea Convention of 1982 (Art. 27) with minor changes affirms the provisions of 1958.

CIVIL JURISDICTION OVER SHIPS IN PASSAGE[97]

(a) Persons on board

It is impermissible to stop or divert a foreign ship passing through the territorial sea for the purpose of exercising civil jurisdiction in relation to a person on board. The good sense of the rule is obvious, and it appears in the Territorial Sea Convention of 1958 (Art. 20, para. 1) and the Law of the Sea Convention of 1982 (Art. 28, para. 1).[98]

(b) Process against the vessel

Paragraph 2 of Article 20 of the Convention on the Territorial Sea of 1958 and paragraph 2 of Article 28 of the Convention of 1982 provide that the coastal state may not levy execution against or arrest a foreign ship for the purpose of any civil proceedings 'save only in respect of obligations or liabilities assumed or incurred by the ship itself in the course or for the purpose of its voyage through the waters of the coastal State'.[99] Under this provision the rights of the coastal states are more restricted than they would be under the Brussels Convention for the Unification of Certain Rules Relating to the Arrest of Sea-going Ships, 1952.[100] If the latter does not apply to arrest during passage through the territorial sea, as opposed to internal waters, there is, of course, no conflict. In any case many states have not ratified the Brussels Convention.[101]

SHIPS AT ANCHOR IN THE TERRITORIAL SEA

The rules considered previously apply, since stopping and anchoring, if these acts are incidental to ordinary navigation, or are rendered necessary by *force majeure* or by distress, are a part of passage.[102] In other cases ships at anchor may be treated in the same way as ships in internal waters: in such cases vessels are not exercising the right of innocent passage.[103]

---

[97] See McDougal and Burke, *The Public Order of the Oceans*, pp. 273–82; Lee, 55 *AJ* (1961), 77 at 93–5; Fitzmaurice, 8 *ICLQ* (1959), 106–8; UN Legis. Series, *The Territorial Sea*, pp. 319ff.; Report of François, *Yrbk. ILC* (1952), ii. 41–2; ibid. (1956), ii. 275–6 (draft article and comment); Jessup, 27 *AJ* (1933), 747–50; O'Connell, *The International Law of the Sea*, ii. 867–918.

[98] Colombos, p. 318; Art. 9, draft of Hague Codification Conference, 1930, 24 *AJ* (1930), Suppl., p. 244.

[99] See Art. 9, Hague draft, last note; *The Ship 'D. C. Whitney'* v. *St. Clair Navigation Co.* (1907), 38 SCR 303, 311. For a contrary opinion: *The David* (1933), *RIAA* vi. 382, relied on by Hyde, i. 749. See further the proviso in Art. 20, para. 3, of the Territorial Sea Conv. of 1958 and Art. 28, para. 3, of the Conv. of 1982.

[100] 439 UNTS, no. 6330.

[101] For the position of parties to both, see the Conv. on the Territorial Sea, Art. 25: 'The provisions of this Convention shall not affect conventions or other international agreements already in force as between States Parties to them' and Art. 311 of the Conv. of 1982.

[102] *Supra*, p. 186.

[103] Hyde, ii. 750; Gidel, iii. 276.

FOREIGN VESSELS IN INTERNAL WATERS

See *infra*, pp. 318–20.

B. *Specialized Rights*

1. INTRODUCTION

The territorial sea is by no means the only form in which the power of the coastal state is manifested over sea areas. It is, however, the form which involves a concentration of legal rights justifying the term 'sovereignty',[104] and the limit of the territorial sea marks the seaward frontier of states. Beyond this line stretch the high seas and the exclusive economic zone. A general interest in maintaining the substance of the principle of freedom of the seas outside the territorial sea has been reconciled with the tendencies of coastal states to extend their power seawards, by the development of generally recognized specialized extensions of jurisdiction, and of rights analogous to legally protected possession of land areas.

2. THE CONCEPT OF THE CONTIGUOUS ZONE[105]

The historical development of the territorial sea, and the appearance of a clear distinction between the plenitude of legal rights over the territorial sea called sovereignty and specialized rights arising from particular types of jurisdiction and control in contiguous zones, are matters which have been considered previously.[106] The opinions of jurists and of governments give very wide recognition to the fact that contiguous zones give jurisdiction *over the high seas* (or, more recently, over areas which may be claimed as exclusive economic zone) for special purposes. In the Convention on the Territorial Sea of 1958 the sole article on the contiguous zone, Article 24, refers to control by the coastal state 'in a zone of the high seas contiguous to its territorial sea'. Similarly, Article 33 of the Law of the Sea Convention of 1982 recognizes the institution of the contiguous zone but describes it simply as a zone contiguous to the territorial sea of the coastal state. It is clear from the provisions of Article 55 of the Convention that the

---

[104] *Supra*, pp. 105–6.

[105] Gidel, iii. 361–492; id., 48 Hague *Recueil* (1934, II), 241–73; François, Second Report, *Yrbk. ILC* (1951), ii. 91–4; Fitzmaurice, 8 *ICLQ* (1959), 108–21; Jessup, *Law of Territorial Waters*, pp. 75–112, 241–352; Oda, 11 *ICLQ* (1962), 131–53; Fell, 62 *Michigan LR* (1964), 848–64; Rousseau, iv. 378–82; Lowe, 52 *BY* (1981), 109–69; Pazarci, 18 *Revue belge* (1984–5), 249–71; O'Connell, *The International Law of the Sea*, ii. 1034–61; Roach and Smith, *United States Responses to Excessive Maritime Claims* (2nd edn., 1996), 163–72.

[106] *Supra*, pp. 173–5.

contiguous zone, if it is claimed, will be superimposed upon the exclusive economic zone (if such a zone is claimed). In the absence of a claim to an exclusive economic zone, the areas concerned form part of the high seas (see Art. 86 of the Convention of 1982). It follows that the rights of the coastal state in such a zone do not amount to sovereignty,[107] and thus other states have rights exercisable over the high seas except as they are qualified by the existence of jurisdictional zones. Moreover, these zones are not appurtenant as in the case of the territorial sea—they must be claimed.[108] However, like the territorial sea, they are contiguous, and they share the latter's baseline.[109]

The most important question concerns the purposes for which special rights of jurisdiction and policy may be asserted. Difficulty arises from two sources. From the doctrinal point of view it is only in relatively recent times that a consistent general doctrine of contiguous zones has made an appearance,[110] and sytematic development had not proceeded very far when the International Law Commission took up these problems.

The Law of the Sea Convention of 1982 provides for the creation of contiguous zones for the same purposes and on the same basis as before (Art. 33), except that (1) the contiguous zone is no longer expressed to be 'a zone of the high seas'; and (2) the maximum limit is expressed to be 24 miles.

In 2002 some 71 states had a contiguous zone extending beyond the outer limit of a 12-mile territorial sea, of which 63 states had a 24 mile limit.

3. PERMISSIBLE TYPES OF ZONE

In considering the purposes for which zones may be maintained, Article 24 of the Convention on the Territorial Sea may be taken as a point of departure. The article refers to exercise of control necessary to prevent infringement of 'customs, fiscal, immigration or sanitary regulations within the territory or territorial sea of the coastal State'. Subsequently other claims, including fishery and security zones, will be considered.

CUSTOMS ZONES

The exercise of this type of jurisdiction is very frequent and no doubt rests on customary international law.[111] Article 24 of the Convention on the Territorial Sea of 1958 and

---

[107] See Fitzmaurice, 8 *ICLQ* (1959), 111–13; id., 92 Hague *Recueil* (1957, II), 157; Sørensen, 101 Hague *Recueil* (1960, III), 155–8. See also *Sorensen and Jensen*, ILR 89, 78, Chilean SC.

[108] *Supra*, pp. 180–4. Note the permissive language of Art. 24 of the Conv. on the Territorial Sea of 1958 and Art. 33 of the Conv. of 1982.

[109] *Supra*, pp. 176–8, 181–5.

[110] Gidel (vol. iii, published in 1934) may be given the credit for giving the concept authority, system, and coherence. Cf. the materials of the Hague Codification Conference; and Renault, 11 *Annuaire de l'Inst.* (1889–92), 150. Generally see Gidel, iii. 372ff. Colombos gives a rather idiosyncratic treatment and so do McDougal and Burke, *The Public Order of the Oceans*, pp. 565–630.

[111] See Whiteman, iv. 483–94; Gidel, iii. 379–454, 476–9; Jessup, *Law of Territorial Waters*, p. 95; Oppenheim, ii. 625; Hackworth, i. 663ff.

Article 33 of the Convention of 1982 refer compendiously to 'customs and fiscal' regulations, other sources refer to 'revenue laws'. Modern vessels would find smuggling only too easy if a narrow enforcement area were employed, and customs zones of six and 12 miles are common. The United States has exercised customs jurisdiction over foreign vessels bound for the United States within a four-league zone since 1790. The United Kingdom had similar 'hovering acts' operating against foreign vessels from 1736 until 1876.[112] The content of the claim to enforcement of national legislation in areas of the high seas is presumably limited by a requirement of reasonableness, and regulations designed for revenue enforcement cannot be employed in such a way as to accomplish another purpose, for example the exclusion of foreign vessels.[113] Treaty regimes may be created for the mutual recognition of zones and enforcement procedures, thus reducing the likelihood of incidents.[114]

IMMIGRATION ZONES

In practice customs and fiscal regulations might be applied to deal with the question, and this type of jurisdiction shares the same basis in policy as the customs zone. Immigration zones are given a significant measure of recognition by inclusion in the Convention on the Territorial Sea of 1958 (and subsequently the Convention of 1982).[115] The limitation to immigration is perhaps significant, although in the relevant draft of the International Law Commission the term was intended to include emigration.

ZONES FOR SANITARY PURPOSES

Such zones are included in Article 24 of the Convention on the Territorial Sea of 1958 (and also the Convention of 1982). The comment of the International Law Commission on the relevant draft article states:[116] 'Although the number of States which claim rights over the contiguous zone for the purpose of applying sanitary regulations is fairly small, the Commission considers that, in view of the connection between customs and sanitary regulations, such rights should also be recognized for sanitary regulations'. Doctrine supports the validity of this type of claim.[117]

---

[112] On the British and American legislation and the diplomatic repercussions see Masterson, *Jurisdiction*.

[113] See the opinion excerpted in Hackworth, i. 657–9.

[114] See the Helsingfors Conv. of 19 Aug. 1925; UN Legis. Series, *The Territorial Sea*, p. 709, signed and ratified by 11 European states; ibid., Second Part, ch. 2, for bilateral treaties. On the 'liquor treaties' concluded by the United States see Masterson, *Jurisdiction*, pp. 326ff.

[115] The type had appeared in the ILC draft articles in 1955, but was deleted from the draft of the eighth session in 1956. *Yrbk. ILC* (1956), ii. 295, comment (7). See Fitzmaurice, 8 *ICLQ* (1959), 117–18 (critical of inclusion); and Oda, 11 *ICLQ* (1962), 146.

[116] *Yrbk. ILC* (1956), ii. 294–5.

[117] See Gidel, iii. 455–7, 476, 486; Oppenheim, ii. 625–7; Fitzmaurice, 8 *ICLQ*, 117.

PREVENTION OF POLLUTION OF THE SEA

The zones considered in the previous paragraph might well be held to accommodate measures to prevent pollution, particularly by oil, but the position is by no means clear.[118] In recent years jurisdiction to police pollution has been advanced principally by extension of the territorial sea and the appearance of the exclusive economic zone (see *infra*), in which the coastal state has the right of *conserving* the natural resources.

SECURITY ZONES

The Convention on the Territorial Sea of 1958 and the Convention of 1982 do not recognize such zones, and it is submitted that they have not received general acceptance in the practice of states.[119] In a commentary on the relevant draft article the International Law Commission states:[120]

The Commission did not recognize special security rights in the contiguous zone. It considered that the extreme vagueness of the term 'security' would open the way for abuses and that the granting of such rights was not necessary. The enforcement of customs and sanitary regulations will be sufficient in most cases to safeguard the security of the State. In so far as measures of self-defence against an imminent and direct threat to the security of the State are concerned, the Commission refers to the general principles of international law and the Charter of the United Nations.

To this it may be added that recognition of such rights would go far toward equating rights over the contiguous zone and rights in the territorial sea.

4. DELIMITATION OF THE CONTIGUOUS ZONE

BASELINES

It has always been assumed that the baselines for the delimitation of both contiguous zones and the territorial sea are identical. State practice and the terms of Article 24 of the Convention on the Territorial Sea of 1958 and Article 33 of the Convention of 1982 confirm the assumption.

---

[118] See Briggs, pp. 376–7, and references therein.

[119] See Gidel, iii. 455, 458–62, 476, 486–7; Whiteman, iv. 495–8. Many standard works contain no reference to such zones. See also Secretariat Memo., 1950, paras. 81–107, and François, Second Report, *Yrbk. ILC* (1951), ii. 93, paras. 117–18. Eighteen states appear to have claimed security zones in the recent past, apart from security zones not greater in breadth than the territorial sea. See also Roach and Smith, op. cit., 166–72.

[120] *Yrbk. ILC* (1956), ii. 295. See also Oda, 11 *ICLQ* (1962), 147–8.

BREADTH

The question is dealt with by Article 24 of the Convention on the Territorial Sea, which established a 12-mile limit for all purposes.[121] The Convention of 1982 prescribes 24 miles (Art. 33).

5. PROBLEMS OF ENFORCEMENT

As a matter of general international law the coastal state may take any steps necessary to enforce compliance with its laws and regulations in the prescribed zone or zones. The power is one of police and control, and transgressors cannot be visited with consequences amounting to reprisal or summary punishment. Forcible measures of self-help may not be resorted to as readily as in the case of trespass over a state frontier.

In this respect the text adopted both by the International Law Commission and by the Conference on the Law of the Sea in 1958 may be more restrictive from the point of view of a coastal state than general international law.[122] Article 24, paragraph 1, of the Convention on the Territorial Sea of 1958 provides:

In a zone of the high seas contiguous to its territorial sea, the coastal State may exercise the control necessary to:

(a) Prevent infringement of its customs, fiscal, immigration or sanitary regulations within its territory or territorial sea;

(b) Punish infringement of the above regulations committed within its territory or territorial sea...

Sir Gerald Fitzmaurice was prominent in promoting this text, and the interpretation which he has placed upon it deserves attention. In his view:[123]

It...is control, not jurisdiction, that is exercised...Although the two ensuing subheads (a) and (b) of the paragraph envisage punishment as well as prevention, yet taken as a whole, the power is essentially supervisory and preventative. The basic object is anticipatory. No offence against the laws of the coastal State is actually being committed at the time. The intention is to avoid such an offence being committed *subsequently*, when, by entering the territorial sea, the vessel comes within the jurisdiction of the coastal State; or else to punish such an offence already committed when the vessel was within such jurisdiction...it would seem that the following distinction can be drawn between the powers the coastal States can

---

[121] Para. 3 of the article provides for the case where the coasts of two states are opposite or adjacent to each other. Cf. Art. 12 of the Conv. The provision in Art. 24 does not provide for exceptions 'by reason of historic title or other special circumstances', contrasting thus with the provision on the territorial sea.

[122] See the article by Oda, 11 *ICLQ* (1962), 131–53; and McDougal and Burke, *The Public Order of the Oceans*, pp. 621–30.

[123] 8 *ICLQ* (1959), 73 at 113. See also id., 31 *BY* (1954), 371 at 378–9; and O'Connell, *The International Law of the Sea*, ii. 1057–9.

exercise under heads (a) and (b) of this paragraph, respectively...it is...clear that just as head (b)—punishment—can only apply to outgoing ships, head (a)—prevention—can only apply to incoming ones. But what are the ('necessary') powers of control which the coastal State can exercise in the case of an incoming ship, or rather, do they, in particular, include arrest and conduct into port? So far as arrest, as such, is concerned, the answer must be in the negative. Whatever the eventual designs of the vessel, she cannot *ex hypothesi* at this stage have committed an offence 'within [the coastal State's] territory or territorial sea'. There is consequently nothing in respect of which an arrest, as such, can be effected. ...As regards ordering, or conducting, the vessel into port under escort, the case is less clear. Though formally distinct from arrest, enforced direction into port is, in the circumstances, almost tantamount to it, and should therefore in principle be excluded: any necessary inquiries, investigation, examination, search, etc., should take place at sea while the ship is still in the contiguous zone. ...In case this may seem to be unduly restrictive, it must be observed that only by insistence on such limitations is it possible to prevent coastal States from treating the contiguous zone as virtually equivalent to territorial sea.

While this interpretation is perfectly possible as a matter of textual exegesis, neverthe-less in case of controversy reference may be made to the *travaux préparatoires*. From these it is apparent that the majority of states at the Law of the Sea Conference did not intend to restrict rights in contiguous zones, as hitherto understood,[124] by establish-ing the distinction between 'control' and 'jurisdiction'. The provisions of Article 33 of the Convention of 1982 are essentially the same as those of 1958. It is true that the new text no longer describes the contiguous zone as a zone 'of the high seas' but this change should not be given too much significance in view of the preservation of sev-eral important high seas freedoms by Article 58 of the Convention of 1982.[125]

6. OTHER ZONES FOR SPECIAL PURPOSES

The twentieth century has produced a number of national claims to non-contiguous, but adjacent, zones for special purposes, which represent attempts to apply the logic of claims to contiguous zones in a manner calculated to protect national interests to the utmost. Thus defence zones[126] in polygonal or similar forms extending beyond the ter-ritorial sea, and zones for purposes of air identification[127] have made their appearance in the practice of states. In so far as those zones represent claims to extra-territorial

---

[124] See Oda, 11 *ICLQ* (1962), 131–53; O'Connell, ii. 643–4. Note Art. 23 of the Conv. on the High Seas, and Art. 111 of the Conv. of 1982, which permit hot pursuit to commence within the contiguous zone (*infra*, pp. 235–7), thus strengthening the powers of the coastal state.

[125] For a different view: Churchill and Lowe, *The Law of the Sea*, pp. 117–18.

[126] See US Naval War College, *Int. Law Documents* (1941), 83–90; ibid. (1943), 51–67; ibid. (1948–9), 157ff., 169ff.; MacChesney, US Naval War College, *Int. Law Situation and Documents* (1956), p. iii; legislation of Ethiopia and South Korea, UN Legis. Series, *Regime of Territorial Sea*, pp. 128, 175.

[127] Such zones have appeared in recent American and Canadian practice: MacChesney, *Int. Law Situation*, pp. 577ff.; Murchison, *The Contiguous Air Space Zone in International Law* (1956); Whiteman, iv. 495–8.

jurisdiction over nationals they are not necessarily in conflict with general international law, and, furthermore, groups of states may co-operate and be mutually obligated to respect such zones by convention. Again, such zones may take the form of a lawful aspect of belligerent rights in time of war. Beyond these limits such zones would be incompatible with the status of waters beyond the limit of the territorial sea, at least if they involved the application of powers of prevention or punishment in regard to foreign vessels or aircraft.

FISHERY CONSERVATION ZONES

For some time coastal states with particular interest in offshore fisheries have sought means of limiting major operations by extra-regional fishing fleets. Paradoxically it was the United States, historically an opponent of fishing zones, which sowed the seeds of change. In the first place the United States took an important initiative in claiming the mineral resources of the continental shelf in 1945,[128] on the basis of the generous concept of 'adjacency'. It would not be surprising if other states were ready to claim the biological resources of the adjacent waters or 'epicontinental sea' by a general parity of reasoning. Secondly, the United States produced a Fisheries Proclamation of 28 September 1945,[129] which empowered the Government to establish 'explicitly bounded' conservation zones in areas of the high seas 'contiguous to the United States'.

Beginning in 1946 a number of Latin American states made claims to the natural resources of the epicontinental sea, in effect a fishery conservation zone of 200 miles breadth.[130] Icelandic legislation on these lines began in 1948. For a long while the tendency was lacking in coherence. Adherents were scattered and the legal quality of some of the claims was uncertain and varied. Some, for example, the Peruvian claim, were, on one view an extended territorial sea with a concession of the rights of overflight and free navigation. In 1970 only nine out of 20 Latin American states subscribed to the Montevideo Declaration on the Law of the Sea.[131] In this instrument a 200-mile zone is asserted by the states concerned, involving 'sovereignty and jurisdiction to the extent necessary to conserve, develop and exploit the natural resources of the maritime area adjacent to their coasts, its soil and its subsoil', but without prejudice to freedom of navigation and overflight.

---

[128] See ch. 10.

[129] 40 *AJ* (1946), Supp., p. 45; Whiteman, iv, 954. The Proclamation has never been implemented by Executive Order.

[130] Argentina (1946), Panama (1946), Peru (1947), Chile (1947), Ecuador (1947), Honduras (1950), El Salvador (1950).

[131] Text: 64 *AJ* (1970), 1021. See further the Lima Decl. 8 Aug. 1970; 10 *ILM* (1971), 207 and the Decl. of Santo Domingo, 9 June 1972; 11 *ILM* (1972), 892.

By 2008 some 21 states had fishing zones of 200 miles.[132] The adherents to 200-zones included the United States,[133] Japan,[134] and the members of the EEC (including the United Kingdom). Clearly the fishery conservation zone, not greater than 200 miles from the usual baselines, has become established as a principle of customary international law. However, in the early phase of the formation of the new rule such limits were opposable to non-adherents only on the basis of express recognition. Thus in the *Fisheries Jurisdiction Case* (United Kingdom v. Iceland)[135] an Icelandic fishing zone 50 miles in breadth was held to be not valid as against the United Kingdom as a consequence of the terms of a bilateral agreement of 1961. The Court avoided taking a position on the validity of the Icelandic claim in general international law. In a joint separate opinion[136] five judges expressed the firm view that no rule of customary law concerning maximum fishery limits had yet emerged. In any event by 1989 the development of 200-mile fishery zones had been made to an extent redundant by the legality and preponderance of exclusive economic zones. However, a number of States prefer to maintain fishing zones rather than to claim an exclusive economic zone. The United Kingdom has a 200-mile fishing zone (Fishery Limits Act 1976),[137] together with an 150-mile fishery conservation zone in respect of the Falklands.[138] It is common for States to apply fishing zones to certain coasts if the geography makes an exclusive economic zone of 200 nautical miles inappropriate. The status of fishery zones in customary law was recognized by the International Court in the *Jan Mayen Case* (Denmark v. Norway).[139]

PREFERENTIAL RIGHTS FOR THE COASTAL STATE

In the *Fisheries Jurisdiction Case* (United Kingdom v. Iceland)[140] the International Court held that the concept of preferential rights had crystallized as customary law: that is to say, 'preferential rights of fishing in adjacent waters in favour of the coastal state in a situation of special dependence on its coastal fisheries, this preference operating in regard to other states concerned in the exploitation of the same fisheries'. This concept has survived in customary law in spite of the absence of any reference to it in the Law of the Sea Convention of 1982.[141]

---

[132] US Dept. of State, The Geographer, *Limits in the Seas*, No. 36 and revisions. See Oppenheim, ii. 782–8; Quéneudec, *German Yrbk.*, 32 (1989), 138–55.

[133] Fishery Conservation and Management Act of 1976; 15 *ILM* (1976), 635. This legislation has some controversial features: see the statement by the President, ibid. 634.

[134] In 1977 on the basis of reciprocity.

[135] ICJ Reports (1974), 3 at 24. See also *Fisheries Jurisdiction Case (Fed. Rep. of Germany v. Iceland)*, ibid. 175. For comment: Fitzmaurice, *The Times*, 13 Sept. 1974.

[136] ICJ Reports (1974), 45 at 46.

[137] Subject to obligations arising from membership of the European Community.

[138] See Symmons, 37 *ICLQ* (1988), 283–324.

[139] ICJ Reports, 1993, 38 at 59, 61–2.

[140] ICJ Reports (1974), 3 at 23, 24–31.

[141] See Oppenheim, ii. 788, para. 328. For a more sceptical view: Churchill and Lowe, *The Law of the Sea* (3rd edn., 1999), 285.

EXCLUSIVE ECONOMIC ZONES[142]

The increase in claims to exclusive rights in respect of the fisheries in an adjacent maritime zone, described above, led eventually to claims encompassing all natural resources in and of the seabed and superjacent waters in a zone 200 miles in breadth. By 1972 this development was presented, in more or less programmatic form, as a 'patrimonial sea',[143] or 'economic zone'.[144] In 1973 documents presented at the meetings of the United Nations Committee on the Peaceful Uses of the Seabed and Ocean Floor proclaimed the right to establish 'an exclusive economic zone' with limits not exceeding 200 miles.[145]

At the Third United Nations Conference on the Law of the Sea (1973–9) there was widespread support for the exclusive economic zone. Consequently the Law of the Sea Convention of 1982 provides a detailed structure (Arts. 55–75). The zone is to extend no further than 200 miles from the baselines of the territorial sea. In the text the zone is not defined as a part of the high seas (Art. 86) and is *sui generis*. Apart from the freedom of fishing, the freedoms of the high seas apply (see Article 87 and see generally *infra*, pp. 230–5. The rights of the coastal state are described as follows (Art. 56, para. 1):

In the exclusive economic zone, the coastal State has:

(a) sovereign rights for the purpose of exploring and exploiting, conserving and managing the natural resources, whether living or non-living, of the waters superjacent to the sea-bed and of the sea-bed its sub-soil, and with regard to other activities for the economic exploitation and exploration of the zone, such as the production of energy from the water, currents and winds;

(b) jurisdiction as provided for in the relevant provisions of the present Convention with regard to:

    (i) the establishment and use of artificial islands, installations and structures;

---

[142] Phillips, 26 *ICLQ* (1977), 585–618; Extavour, *The Exclusive Economic Zone* (1979); Krueger and Nordquist, 19 *Virginia JIL* (1979), 321–99; Moore, ibid. 400–9; Conforti, 5 *Ital. Yrbk.* (1980–1), 14–21; Oda, 77 *AJ* (1983), 739–55; Robertson, 24 Virginia JIL (1983–4), 865–915; Castañeda, *Essays in Honour of Manfred Lachs* (1984), 605–23; Orrego (ed.), *The Exclusive Economic Zone: A Latin American Perspective* (1984); Charney, 15 *Ocean Development and IL* (1985), 233–88; Orrego, 199 Hague *Recueil* (1986, IV), 11–170; Smith, *Exclusive Economic Zone Claims* (1986); Juda, 16 *Ocean Development and IL* (1986), 1–58; id., 18 *Ocean Development and IL* (1987), 305–31; Attard, *The Exclusive Economic Zone in International Law* (1987); McLean and Sucharitkul, 63 *Notre Dame LR* (1988), 492–534; Kwiatkowska, *The 200 Mile Exclusive Economic Zone in the New Law of the Sea* (1989); Orrego, *The Exclusive Economic Zone* (1989); Oda, Max Planck Institute, *Encyclopaedia of P I.L.*, vol. 11 (1989), 102–9; Roach and Smith, op. cit., 173–92.

[143] See the Decl. of Santo Domingo, 9 June 1972; 11 *ILM* (1972), 892; Castañeda, 12 *Indian Journ.* (1972), 535–42; Nelson, 22 *ICLQ* (1973), 668–86; Gastines, 79 *RGDIP* (1975), 447–57; cf. the Decl. of Lima, 8 Aug. 1970, 10 *ILM* (1971), 207.

[144] Yaoundé Seminar of African States, Recommendations, 30 June 1972; Lay, Churchill, and Nordquist, *New Directions in the Law of the Sea*, i. 250.

[145] 12 *ILM* (1973), 1200, 1235, 1246, 1249. Other proposals of similar content did not use the same label. For an early reference to the 'exclusive economic zone concept': ibid. 33 (proposal of Kenya, 1972).

    (ii)   marine scientific research;

    (iii) the protection and preservation of the marine environment;

(c) other rights and duties provided for in this Convention.

The basic elements are clear enough, but the place of the concept within the overall picture calls for careful appreciation, and there are some complexities. No less than 128 states have made claims to an exclusive economic zone and it forms part of customary law, independently of the version to be found in the provisions of the Law of the Sea Convention of 1982. This customary law status has been recognized by the International Court[146] and also by the United States.[147] The customary law version of the concept is closely related to the version which emerged within the Third United Nations Conference on the Law of the Sea and indeed is to an extent based upon the Convention model. However, the extent of the coincidence is problematical.

In any event, both under the Convention and in customary law the zone is optional and its existence depends upon an actual claim. Some states, including the majority of the Mediterranean states, have no obvious advantage in making claims, and certain states, such as Canada, the German Federal Republic, and Japan, are content to maintain 200-mile exclusive fishing zones.

When claimed, an exclusive zone coexists with the regime of the continental shelf which governs rights with respect to the seabed and the subsoil (Law of the Sea Convention, Art. 56, para. 3). It may also coexist with a contiguous zone.

The United States takes the view that 'highly migratory species', including the commercially important tuna, are excluded from the jurisdiction of the coastal state, and therefore available for foreign distant water fishing fleets.[148] This position is difficult to substantiate. It is contradicted, rather than supported, by the provisions of Article 64 of the Convention of 1982, and is not reflected in the practice of states.[149]

The legal regime of the exclusive economic zone has various facets. Article 60 of the Law of the Sea Convention of 1982 provides (in part) as follows:

    1. In the exclusive economic zone, the coastal State shall have the exclusive right to construct and to authorise and regulate the construction, operation and use of:

    (a) artificial islands;

---

[146] *Tunisia–Libya Continental Shelf* case, ICJ Reports, (1982), 18 at 38, 47–9, 79; *Gulf of Maine* case, *ibid.* (1984), 246 at 294–5 (paras. 94–6); *Libya–Malta Continental Shelf* case, *ibid.* (1985), 13 at 32–4 (paras. 31–4). See also *Rego Sanles* v. *Ministère Public*, ILR 74, 141.

[147] Presidential Proclamation of 10 Mar. 1983; 22 *ILM* (1983), 461.

[148] See the US Proclamation of 1983, *supra.*

[149] See Attard, *The Exclusive Economic Zone*, pp. 184–7; Burke, 14 *Ocean Development and IL* (1984–5), 273–314. Art. 64 provides as follows: '1. The coastal State and other States whose nationals fish in the region for the highly migratory species listed in Annex I shall co-operate directly or through appropriate international organisations with a view to ensuring conservation and promoting the objective of optimum utilisation of such species throughout the region, both within and beyond the exclusive economic zone. In regions for which no appropriate international organisation exists, the coastal State and other States whose nationals harvest these species in the region shall co-operate to establish such an organisation and participate in its work. 2. The provisions of paragraph 1 apply in addition to the other provisions of this Part.'

(b) installations and structures for the purposes provided for in Article 56 and other economic purposes;

(c) installations and structures which may interfere with the exercise of the rights of the coastal State in the zone.

2. The coastal State shall have exclusive jurisdiction over such artificial islands, installations and structures, including jurisdiction with regard to customs, fiscal, health, safety and immigration laws and regulations.

The same article confirms that artificial islands, installations, and structures have no territorial sea of their own and do not affect the delimitation of the territorial sea, the exclusive economic zone, or the continental shelf (para. 8).

Article 61 elaborates upon the responsibility of the coastal state in managing the living resources in the zone by stipulating its duty to 'ensure through proper conservation and management measures that the maintenance of the living resources in the exclusive economic zone is not endangered by over-exploitation'. In the same general context Article 62 requires the coastal state to promote the optimum utilization of the living resources in the zone. In particular it is provided that:

2. The coastal State shall determine its capacity to harvest the living resources of the exclusive economic zone. Where the coastal State does not have the capacity to harvest the entire allowable catch, it shall, through agreements or other arrangements and pursuant to the terms, conditions, laws and regulations referred to in paragraph 4, give other States access to the surplus of the allowable catch, having particular regard to the provisions of Articles 69 and 70,[150] especially in relation to the developing States mentioned therein.

3. In giving access to other States to its exclusive economic zone under this article, the coastal State shall take into account all relevant factors, including, *inter alia*, the significance of the living resources of the area to the economy of the coastal State concerned and its other national interests, the provisions of Articles 69 and 70, the requirements of developing States in the subregion or region in harvesting part of the surplus and the need to minimise economic dislocation in States whose nationals have habitually fished in the zone or which have made substantial efforts in research and identification of stocks.

4. Nationals of other States fishing in the exclusive economic zone shall comply with the conservation measures and with the other terms and conditions established in the law and regulations of the coastal State...

The allocation of the respective rights and duties of the coastal state and those of other states in the zone involves a delicate balancing process which is articulated in fairly general terms in the provisions of the Convention.[151] Article 58 provides as follows:

---

[150] *Infra*, p. 214.

[151] Attard is of the opinion that in view of the phrasing of Art. 56(1)(a) ('Sovereign rights...') in case of doubt there will be a presumption in favour of the coastal state (*The Exclusive Economic Zone*, p. 48). This may well be true of the modalities of the recognized rights of the coastal state, but may not be true when independently constituted rights (like those of land-locked and geographically disadvantaged states) are in question (Arts. 69, 70, and 71). The general formulations of Art. 59 (see *infra*) beg the present question (but

1.   In the exclusive economic zone, all States, whether coastal or land-locked, enjoy, subject to the relevant provisions of this Convention, the freedoms referred to in Article 87 of navigation and overflight and of the laying of submarine cables and pipelines, and other internationally lawful uses of the sea related to these freedoms, such as those associated with the operation of ships, aircraft and submarine cables and pipelines, and compatible with the other provisions of this Convention.

2.   Articles 88 to 115 and other pertinent rules of international law apply to the exclusive economic zone in so far as they are not incompatible with this Part.

3.   In exercising their rights and performing their duties under this Convention in the exclusive economic zone, States shall have due regard to the rights and duties of the coastal State and shall comply with the laws and regulations adopted by the coastal State in accordance with the provisions of this convention and other rules of international law in so far as they are not incompatible with this Part.[152]

Article 59 appears under the rubric 'basis for the resolution of conflicts regarding the attribution of rights and jurisdiction in the exclusive economic zone' and provides:

In cases where this Convention does not attribute rights or jurisdiction to the coastal State or to other States within the exclusive economic zone, and a conflict arises between the interests of the coastal State and any other State or States, the conflict should be resolved on the basis of equity and in the light of all the relevant circumstances, taking into account the respective importance of the interests involved to the parties as well as to the international community as a whole.

The coastal state has the power to take reasonable measures of enforcement of its rights and jurisdiction within the zone in accordance with both the standards of general international law and, where applicable, the provisions of the Convention of 1982 (Art. 73).

It will be convenient to treat the problems of delimitation of the zone between states with opposite or adjacent coasts in conjunction with the same topic in the context of the continental shelf and therefore the question is reserved for the following chapter.

Churchill and Lowe, *The Law of the Sea* (3rd edn., 1999), 175–6, hold that the article rules out any presumption). See further Orrego, 199 Hague *Recueil* (1986, IV), 41–4.

[152] On the interpretation of Art. 58 and various related issues see the *M/V Saiga (No. 2)*, Int. Trib. for the Law of the Sea, 1 July 1999, *ILR* 120, 145 at 188–92.

10

THE CONTINENTAL SHELF: DELIMITATION OF SHELF AREAS AND EXCLUSIVE ECONOMIC ZONES

1. INTRODUCTION

Submarine areas may be classified as follows: (*a*) the seabed of the internal waters and territorial seas of coastal states; (*b*) the continental shelf area; (*c*) the seabed of the exclusive economic zone;[1] (*d*) the seabed and ocean floor beyond the outer limits of the continental shelf and exclusive economic zone. The first case is under the legal regime of territorial sovereignty. The continental shelf has a specialized regime which is considered subsequently. The fourth category partakes of the legal regime of the high seas. The presumption is that each of the categories includes the marine subsoil to the extent that the rules of the particular legal regime are intended so to apply. The legal regime of the ocean floor and the relevance of the International Seabed Area to be established in accordance with the Law of the Sea Convention of 1982 are topics reserved for the chapters which follow. The focus of the present chapter is the regime of the continental shelf and the related issues of delimitation as between opposite or adjacent States.

2. CONTINENTAL SHELF: BACKGROUND[2]

Much of the seabed consists of the deep ocean floor (the abyssal plain), several thousand metres deep. In many parts of the world the deep ocean floor is separated from the coast of the land masses by a terrace or shelf, which in geological terms is a part of

---

[1] On the EEZ, in general see ch. 9.

[2] See generally: Whiteman, iv. 740–931; Lauterpacht, 27 *BY* (1950), 376–433; Gutteridge, 35 *BY* (1959), 102–23; Secretariat Memo., *Yrbk*. ILC (1950), ii. 87–113; François, Fourth Report, ibid. (1953) ii. 1–50; Jennings, 121 Hague *Recueil* (1967, II), 387–408; Oda, 127 Hague *Recueil* (1969, II), 433–57; O'Connell, *The International Law of the Sea*, i (1982), 467–509; Jewett, 22 *Canad. Yrbk*. (1984), 153–93; id., 23 *Canad. Yrbk*. (1985), 201–25; Oppenheim ii. 764–82; Cook and Carleton (eds.), *Continental Shelf Limits* (2000).

the continent itself, overlain by the relatively shallow waters of the continental margin. The width of the shelf varies from a mile or so to some hundreds of miles and the depth ranges from 50 to 550 metres. The configuration of the seabed has certain regularities. The increase in depth is gradual until the shelf edge or break is reached, when there is a steep descent to the ocean floor. The average depth of the edge is between 130 and 200 metres. The relatively steep incline of the continental slope gives way to the often large apron of sediments, which masks the boundary between the deep ocean floor and the pedestal of the continental mass, and is called the continental rise.

The shelf carries substantial oil and gas deposits in many areas and the seabed itself provides sedentary fishery resources. In 1944 an Argentine Decree created zones of mineral reserves in the epicontinental sea. However, the decisive event in state practice was a United States proclamation on 28 September 1945 relating to the natural resources of the subsoil and seabed of the continental shelf.[3] The shelf was regarded as a geological feature and a press release stated that the shelf was regarded as extending up to the 100 fathoms line.[4] The resources concerned were described as 'appertaining to the United States, subject to its jurisdiction and control'. Of particular importance were the limitations of the claim to the resources themselves and the declaration that 'the character as high seas of the waters of the continental shelf and the right to their free and unimpeded navigation are in no way thus affected'.

The lines of the Truman proclamation were in substance followed by Orders in Council of 1948 relating to the Bahamas and Jamaica, and by proclamations issued by Saudi Arabia, in 1948, and nine sheikhdoms in the Persian Gulf under United Kingdom protection, in 1949.[5] The practice showed certain variations, however. The Truman proclamation and an Australian proclamation of 10 September 1953 relate the claim to the purpose of *exploitation of the resources* of the seabed and subsoil of the continental shelf, and stipulate that the legal status of the superjacent waters as high seas shall not be affected. A number of states claimed sovereignty over the seabed and subsoil of the shelf as such but expressly reserving the question of the status of the waters above as high seas.[6] In this development principles of geological continuity, self-protection, and effective control played a part and the development parallels, in a new sphere, the concepts of the territorial sea and contiguous zone.

The thesis contained in the Truman proclamation proved attractive to a diversity of states. The new principle provided a stable basis for exploitation of petroleum and

---

[3] Text: 40 *AJ* (1946), Suppl., p. 45: Whiteman, iv. 756. For the background: Hollick, 17 *Virginia JIL* (1976), 23–55; id., *United States Foreign Policy and the Law of the Sea* (1981).

[4] Approximately 200 metres or 600 feet.

[5] Surveys of state practice: Whiteman, iv. 752–814; UN Legis. Series, *The Regime of the High Seas*, i (1951); ibid., Suppl. (1959); UN Secretariat, Survey of National Legislation Concerning the Seabed and the Ocean Floor, and the Subsoil thereof, underlying the High Seas beyond the Limits of Present National Jurisdiction, A/AC. 135/11, 4 June 1968; UN Legis. Series, *National Legislation and Treaties Relating to the Territorial Sea...*, ST/LEG/SER.B/15 (1970) 319–476; US Dept. of State, The Geographer, *Limits in the Seas*, no. 36, 8th Revision (2000).

[6] e.g. Bahamas (1948), Saudi Arabia (1949), Pakistan (1950), India (1955).

at the same time made a reasonable accommodation for freedom of fishing and navigation in the superjacent waters. However, the practice was far from uniform[7] and the discussions in the International Law Commission in the years 1951–6 indicated the immaturity of the legal regime. As a consequence the text of the Convention on the Continental Shelf[8] adopted at the Law of the Sea Conference of 1958 represented in part at least an essay in the progressive development of the law.[9] Nevertheless, the first three articles represented pre-existing or at least emergent rules of customary international law:[10]

Article 1

For the purpose of these Articles, the term 'continental shelf' is used as referring (a) to the seabed and subsoil of the submarine areas adjacent to the coast but outside the area of the territorial sea, to a depth of 200 metres or, beyond that limit, to where the depth of the super-jacent waters admits of the exploitation of the natural resources of the said areas; (b) to the seabed and subsoil of similar submarine areas adjacent to the coasts of islands.

Article 2

1. The coastal State exercises over the continental shelf sovereign rights for the purpose of exploring it and exploiting its natural resources.

2. The rights referred to in paragraph 1 of this Article are exclusive in the sense that if the coastal State does not explore the continental shelf or exploit its natural resources, no one may undertake these activities, or make a claim to the continental shelf, without the express consent of the coastal State.

3. The rights of the coastal State over the continental shelf do not depend on occupation, effective or notional, or on any express proclamation.

4. The natural resources referred to in these Articles consist of the mineral and other nonliving resources of the seabed and subsoil together with living organisms belonging to sedentary species, that is to say, organisms which, at the harvestable stage, either are immobile on or under the seabed or are unable to move except in constant physical contact with the seabed or the subsoil.

Article 3

The rights of the coastal State over the continental shelf do not affect the legal status of the superjacent waters as high seas, or that of the air space above those waters.

---

[7] See the award of Lord Asquith as umpire in the *Abu Dhabi* arbitration, ILR 18 (1951), no. 37; Whiteman, iv. 747.

[8] Text: 52 *AJ* (1958), 858; Brownlie, *Documents*, p. 88. Entered into force 10 June 1964. For discussion see Whiteman, 52 *AJ* (1958), 629–53; Young, 55 *AJ* (1961), 359–73; Gutteridge, 35 *BY* (1959), 102–23.

[9] The date at which the legal concept of the shelf matured as part of customary law may be relevant in intra-federal disputes: *Re a Reference Concerning Continental Shelf offshore Newfoundland*, ILR 86, 593 (Canada, SC).

[10] *North Sea Continental Shelf* cases, ICJ Reports (1969), 3 at 39; ILR 41, 29.

3. SOURCES OF THE LAW

The three articles quoted above provide the essence of the legal regime and Articles 2 and 3 are reproduced in the Law of the Sea Convention of 1982 (Art. 77 and Art. 78, para. 1). The Convention of 1958 has 51 parties, and on occasion it may be relevant by reason of the fact that both parties to a dispute are parties to it.[11] However, the present position in general international law depends upon a variety of sources, each of which must be given appropriate weight, as proof of customary international law. The Chamber of the International Court which decided the *Gulf of Maine* case recognized the relevance of codification conventions, such as the Convention on the Continental Shelf of 1958, the decisions of the Court and of other international tribunals, and the Law of the Sea Convention of 1982, in so far as the proceedings of the Third United Nations Conference on the Law of the Sea indicated that certain provisions reflected a consensus among the participants.[12] In its decision in the *Case Concerning the Continental Shelf* (Libya–Malta), the full bench of the International Court adopted a similar approach and took careful account of certain aspects of the Convention of 1982 as evidence of customary international law.[13] In the same decision the Court emphasized the significance of state practice.[14] With respect to delimitation of shelf areas between opposite or adjacent states the subject is essentially a matter of customary law and of the principles established by decisions of the International Court and other international tribunals in a progression of decisions which began with the *North Sea Continental Shelf* cases (1969).[15]

4. RIGHTS OF THE COASTAL STATE IN THE SHELF

According to the provisions of Article 2 of the Continental Shelf Convention of 1958 (which are repeated in Art. 77 of the Law of the Sea Convention of 1982), the coastal state exercises over the shelf 'sovereign rights for the purpose of exploring it and exploiting its natural resources'. The term 'sovereignty' was deliberately avoided in 1958, as it was feared that this term, redolent of territorial sovereignty (which operates in three dimensions), would prejudice the status as high seas of the waters over the shelf. While the area within a claimed 200-mile EEZ (see *supra*, pp. 199–203) is not designated as 'high seas' in the 1982 Convention (Arts. 55 and 86), Article 78 of the Convention provides that 'the rights of the coastal State over the continental shelf do not affect the legal status of the superjacent waters or of the airspace above those waters' (para. 1; and cf. Art. 3 of the 1958 Convention *supra*). In the absence of a claimed EEZ, and also when the shelf extends beyond 200 miles from the coast, the legal status

---

[11] *Anglo-French C.S.* case, ILR 54, 6; 18 *ILM* 397; *Gulf of Maine* case, ICJ Reports (1984), 246 at 291 (para. 84), 300–3 (paras. 115–25); *Jan Mayen* case, ibid. (1993), pp. 57–9, paras. 44–6.
[12] ICJ Reports (1984), 246 at 288–95 (paras. 79–96).
[13] Ibid. (1985), 13 at 29–34 (paras. 26–34).
[14] Ibid. (1985), 29–30 (para. 27), 33 (para. 34), 38 (para. 44), 45 (para. 58).
[15] Ibid. (1969), 3.

of the superjacent waters will be that of high seas. When an EEZ exists, the superjacent waters are still subject to a significant number of high seas freedoms in accordance both with general international law and with Article 58 of the Convention of 1982.

A number of provisions in both Conventions attend to the delicate problem of balancing the rights of the coastal state in exploiting shelf resources and the rights and freedoms of other states. Article 78, paragraph 2, of the Convention of 1982 provides that 'the exercise of the rights of the coastal State over the continental shelf must not infringe or result in any unjustifiable interference with navigation and other rights and freedoms of other States as provided for in this Convention' (see also Art. 5, para. 1, of the Convention of 1958). Article 79 of the Convention of 1982 provides that 'all States are entitled to lay submarine cables and pipelines on the continental shelf' subject to certain conditions (see also Art. 4 of the Convention of 1958). It is also provided that the coastal state 'shall have the exclusive right to authorise and regulate drilling on the continental shelf for all purposes' (Art. 81 of the Convention of 1982).

A major objective has been to provide a stable basis for operations on the seabed and to avoid squatting by offshore interests. Thus the 'sovereign rights' inhere in the coastal state by operation of law and are not conditioned by occupation or express claim. They are not defeasible except by express grant. While it is true that coastal states apply various parts of criminal and civil law to activities in the shelf area, it is by no means clear that states do this either on the basis that the shelf is territorial or even as an aspect of their international law rights in the shelf area as such. Legislation of the United Kingdom[16] and other states indicates that the shelf regime is not assimilated to state territory.[17]

5. NATURAL RESOURCES OF THE SHELF[18]

The Truman proclamation of 1945 was concerned with the mineral resources of the shelf. Subsequently Latin American states pressed for recognition of the interest of coastal states in the fisheries of the shelf. The International Law Commission had decided to include sedentary fisheries[19] and Article 2, paragraph 4, of the Convention of 1958 defines 'natural resources' so as to include 'living organisms belonging to the sedentary species, that is to say, organisms which, at the harvestable stage, either are immobile on or under the seabed or are unable to move except in constant physical contact with the seabed or the subsoil'. The application of this distinction has met difficulties in relation to king crabs[20] and particular species of lobster.[21] The definition

---

[16] Continental Shelf Act 1964, c. 29; *British Practice* (1964), 53–7.

[17] See *In re Ownership and Jurisdiction over Offshore Mineral Rights*, 65 DLR 2d (1967) 353; ILR 43, 93; SC of Canada; *Bonser* v. *La Macchia*, 43 ALJR 275 (1969); 64 *AJ* (1970), 435; ILR 51, 39; High Ct. of Australia; *Clark (Inspector of Taxes)* v. *Oceanic Contractors, Inc.* [1983] 2 AC 130, HL.

[18] See Whiteman, iv. 856–71; Gutteridge, 35 *BY* (1959), 116–19; Report on Law of the Sea Conf., 1958, Cmnd. 584, para. 31; O'Connell, *The International Law of the Sea*, i (1982), 498–503.

[19] *Yrbk ILC* (1956), ii. 297–8.

[20] Oda, 127 Hague *Recueil* (1969, II), 427–30.

[21] Azzam, 13 *ICLQ* (1964), 1453–9; 67 *RGDIP* (1965), 364. See also decl. with French ratif.: *British Practice* (1965), 141.

excludes in principle dermersal species, such as halibut and plaice, which swim close to the seabed. The provision of the 1958 Convention is reproduced in the Convention of 1982 (Art. 77, para. 4). When an EEZ has been claimed in the area, such issues will no longer arise, as rights in all the living resources inhere in the coastal state (Convention of 1982, Art. 56, para. 1).

6. ARTIFICIAL ISLANDS AND INSTALLATIONS ON THE SHELF[22]

Article 5, paragraph 2, of the Continental Shelf Convention provides (in part) that:

the coastal State is entitled to construct and maintain or operate on the continental shelf installations and other devices necessary for its exploration and the exploitation of its natural resources, and to establish safety zones around such installations and devices and to take in those zones measures necessary for their protection.

Such installations do not have a territorial sea of their own.

The Convention provides no basis for the construction of defence installations on the shelf: nor does it prohibit such installations, so that they may be lawful if some other legal justification exists.[23] To suggest that the coastal state may create defence installations and prohibit comparable activities by other states[24] is to run the risk of justifying a security zone over the whole shelf area. The well-known North Sea Installations Act (1964) of the Netherlands asserted certain rights of jurisdiction over fixed installations on the shelf as a means of control over 'pirate' broadcasting. However, this measure was not based upon the doctrine of the continental shelf.[25]

Article 80 of the Convention of 1982 simply provides that Article 60 (see *supra*, p. 208) 'applies *mutatis mutandis* to artificial islands, installations and structures on the continental shelf'. It is to be noted that Article 60, paragraph 7, provides:

Artificial islands, installations and structures and the safety zones around them may not be established where interference may be caused to the use of recognised sea lanes essential to international navigation.

(And see Art. 5, para. 6 of the 1958 Convention.[26])

---

[22] Whiteman, iv. 888–903.

[23] See Gutteridge, 35 *BY* (1959), 119–22; Jennings, 121 Hague *Recueil* (1967, II), 389.

[24] See O'Connell, i. 507.

[25] See van Panhuys and van Emde Boas, 60 *AJ* (1966), 303 at 326–36. See further François, Bos, and Woodliffe, 12 *Neths. Int. LR* (1965), 113, 337, 365, respectively; Verzijl, *International Law in Historical Perspective*, iv. (1971), 145–51.

[26] The Convention of 1982 has a provision on removal of abandoned installations (Art. 60, para. 3) which is less onerous than the corresponding provision in the 1958 Conv. (Art. 5, para. 5). See further the UK Petroleum Act 1987; and 58 *BY* (1987), 604–8.

7. REGIME OF THE SUBSOIL[27]

Article 85 of the Convention of 1982 provides that its Part VI 'does not prejudice the right of the coastal State to exploit the subsoil by means of tunnelling irrespective of the depth of water above the subsoil' (and see also Art. 7 of the Convention of 1958). In other words, such activity falls outside the scope of the Convention and is governed by customary international law.[28] There is a notable distinction inherent in this arrangement. If exploitation of the subsoil occurs from above the shelf, the continental shelf regime applies; whereas if exploitation is by tunnels from the mainland, then a different regime applies.

8. OUTER LIMIT OF THE SHELF

For legal purposes the inner limit is the outer edge of the territorial sea and its seabed. As to the outer limit, the solution proposed by the Law of the Sea Convention of 1982 is substantially different from the criteria indicated in Article 1 of the Continental Shelf Convention of 1958.

The correct interpretation of Article 1 of the Convention of 1958 would seem to be as follows.[29] The 200-metre depth criterion is subject to the exploitability criterion, but the latter is controlled by the general conception of the shelf as a geological feature, and by the principle of adjacency in Article 1. It is clear from the preparatory materials (the records of the International Law Commission) that the legal conception was based substantially upon the geological conception. It was not thought that the whole ocean floor could be divided up as continental shelf and be subject ultimately to a median line division in accordance with Article 6. It makes no material difference that the legal conception was not based *exclusively* upon the geological conception.[30] Thus the legal definition *includes* (a) the shelves of islands; (b) shallow basins such as the North Sea and the Persian Gulf; (c) steep buttresses like that adjacent to the coast of Chile which can be exploited by tunnels from the mainland; and *excludes* the seabed of the territor-ial sea. The assumption that, with exploitability at greater depths, the 200-metre criterion becomes otiose is unjustified. If exploitability be applied as a dominant test the result would be that state A would concede part of a broad shelf

---

[27] See Whiteman, iv. 918–20; Gutteridge, 35 *BY* (1959), 122. On the Channel tunnel project: van den Mensbrugghe, 71 *RGDIP* (1967), 325–41; Marston, 47 *BY* (1974–5), 290–300.

[28] Generally, on the seabed and subsoil, *infra* ch. 11.

[29] See further Jennings, 121 Hague *Recueil* (1967, II), 392–400; id., 18 *ICLQ* (1969), 819–32; O'Connell, i. 509–11; Goldie, 8 *Natural Resources Journal* (1968), 323–77; id., 1 *Journal of Maritime Law and Commerce* (1970), 461–72; Weissberg, 18 *ICLQ* (1969), 62–83; Henkin, 63 *AJ* (1969), 504–10; Finlay, 64 *AJ* (1970), 42–61; O'Connell, *The International Law of the Sea*, i. 488–95; Hutchinson, 56 *BY* (1985), 111–88; Vasciannie, 58 *BY* (1987), 271–302.

[30] *Yrbk. ILC* (1956), ii. 296–7 (commentary on draft Art. 67).

'opposite' to state B's narrow shelf [but separated from it by abyssal plain] since the median line would fall across the 200-metre zone adjacent to state A. The median line solution in Article 6 only applies when states share the same shelf in the geological context. In other terms the submarine area extending to the 200-metre contour is always 'adjacent'.[31] The outcome is that when exploitability extends to great depths the coastal state will have rights over the entire shelf as a geological feature, including the continental slope and the continental rise.

A part of current state practice, which is based upon claims and legislation dating from before the Law of the Sea Convention of 1982, employs a 200-metre depth limit together with an exploitability criterion (36 states). It may be presumed that the exploitability criterion is itself limited by the geological/geomorphological criterion which flows from the legal concept of the shelf.

The Law of the Sea Convention of 1982 contains a significantly different approach, recognizes a 200-mile *breadth* limit as an independently valid criterion, and provides guidelines for determining the location of the 'outer edge of the continental margin'. Article 76 provides as follows:

1. The continental shelf of a coastal State comprises the sea-bed and subsoil of the submarine areas that extend beyond its territorial sea throughout the natural prolongation of its land territory to the outer edge of the continental margin, or to a distance of 200 nautical miles from the baselines from which the breadth of the territorial sea is measured where the outer edge of the continental margin does not extend up to that distance.

2. The continental shelf of a coastal State shall not extend beyond the limits provided for in paragraphs 4 to 6.

3. The continental margin comprises the submerged prolongation of the land mass of the coastal State, and consists of the sea-bed and subsoil of the shelf, the slope and the rise. It does not include the deep ocean floor with its oceanic ridges or the subsoil thereof.

4. (a) For the purposes of this Convention, the coastal State shall establish the outer edge of the continental margin wherever the margin extends beyond 200 nautical miles from the baselines from which the breadth of the territorial sea is measured, by either:

   (i) a line delineated in accordance with paragraph 7 by reference to the outermost fixed points at each of which the thickness of sedimentary rocks is at least 1 per cent of the shortest distance from such point to the foot of the continental slope; or

   (ii) a line delineated in accordance with paragraph 7 by reference to fixed points not more than 60 nautical miles from the foot of the continental slope.

   (b) In the absence of evidence to the contrary, the foot of the continental slope shall be determined as the point of maximum change in the gradient at its base.

5. The fixed points comprising the line of the outer limits of the continental shelf on the sea-bed, drawn in accordance with paragraph 4(a)(i) and (ii), either shall not exceed 350

---

[31] See Jennings, 121 Hague *Recueil* (1967, II), 398; and also in 18 *ICLQ* (1969), 819–32.

nautical miles from the baselines from which the breadth of the territorial sea is measured or shall not exceed 100 nautical miles from the 2,500 metre isobath, which is a line connecting the depth of 2,500 metres.

6. Notwithstanding the provisions of paragraph 5, on submarine ridges, the outer limit of the continental shelf shall not exceed 350 nautical miles from the baselines from which the breadth of the territorial sea is measured. This paragraph does not apply to submarine elevations that are natural components of the continental margin, such as its plateaux, rises, caps, banks and spurs.

7. The coastal State shall delineate the outer limits of its continental shelf, where that shelf extends beyond 200 nautical miles from the baselines from which the breadth of the territorial sea is measured, by straight lines not exceeding 60 nautical miles in length, connecting fixed points, defined by co-ordinates of latitude and longitude.

8. Information on the limits of the continental shelf beyond 200 nautical miles from the baselines from which the breadth of the territorial sea is measured shall be submitted by the coastal State to the Commission on the Limits of the Continental Shelf set up under Annex II on the basis of equitable geographical representation. The Commission shall make recommendations to coastal States on matters related to the establishment of the outer limits of their continental shelf. The limits of the shelf established by a coastal State on the basis of these recommendations shall be final and binding.

9. The coastal State shall deposit with the Secretary-General of the United Nations charts and relevant information, including geodetic data, permanently describing the outer limits of its continental shelf. The Secretary-General shall give due publicity thereto.

10. The provisions of this article are without prejudice to the question of delimitation of the continental shelf between States with opposite or adjacent coasts.

The general *modus operandi* presented in this provision (200-mile breadth limit or continental margin, whichever is the greater) is generally recognized as representing the new standard of customary law. There is always the technical possibility that states opposing the 200-mile breadth criterion may adopt the role of persistent objectors,[32] but this stance is difficult for the many states apparently willing to become parties to the Convention of 1982. Approximately 35 states have adopted criteria closely related to the provisions of the Convention.[33] It is also evident that a number of states with geological shelves falling short of a 200-mile breadth criterion will simply rely upon a claim to the resources of the EEZ. Article 56, paragraph 3, of the Convention of 1982 expressly provides that the rights in respect of the sea-bed and subsoil of the EEZ 'shall be exercised in accordance with' the provisions governing the continental shelf (Part VI of the Convention).

[32] See *supra*, p. 11.
[33] A number of states continue to have legislation based upon the definition in the 1958 Convention.

9. THE CONTINENTAL SHELF AND THE EXCLUSIVE ECONOMIC ZONE COMPARED

It is instructive to compare the legal concepts of the continental shelf and EEZ. They coexist both in the sphere of customary law and in the regime set by the Law of the Sea Convention of 1982, and contain significant elements of similarity and interpenetration. Both concepts focus upon control of economic resources and are based, in varying degrees, upon adjacency and the distance principle.[34] The EEZ includes the continental shelf interest in the seabed of the 200-mile zone (Art. 56, para. 3, of the 1982 Convention).

However, there are significant points of distinction:

(i)   The EEZ is optional, whereas rights to explore and exploit the resources of the shelf inhere in the coastal state by operation of law. Thus several states of the Mediterranean have shelf rights unmatched by an EEZ (which is less relevant in semi-enclosed seas in any case).

(ii)   Shelf rights exist beyond the limit of 200 miles from the pertinent coasts when the continental shelf and margin extend beyond that limit.[35] Consequently, within the regime of the Law of the Sea Convention of 1982 the rights of the International Sea-bed Authority[36] must be reconciled with those of the coastal state (Art. 82).

(iii) The EEZ regime involves the water column and consequently its resources (apart from sedentary species of fish) are subject to the rules about sharing the surplus of the living resources of the EEZ with other states and, in particular, with land-locked and geographically disadvantaged states of the same region or subregion (Law of the Sea Convention of 1982, Arts. 62, 68, 69, 70, and 71).

(iv)   The EEZ regime confers upon coastal states a substantial jurisdiction over pollution by ships, and also greater control in respect of marine scientific research.[37]

10. SHELF DELIMITATION BETWEEN OPPOSITE OR ADJACENT STATES[38]

SOURCES

Article 6 of the Continental Shelf Convention of 1958 is concerned with the cases where the 'same continental shelf' extends between two opposite or two adjacent

---

[34] See the Judgment of the full bench of the International Court in the *Libya–Malta C.S.* case, ICJ Reports (1985), 33, para. 33.

[35] As in the case of Argentina and Australia.

[36] *Infra*, pp. 242–5.

[37] See Arts. 56 and 246 of the Conv. of 1982.

[38] See generally: Bowett, *The Legal Regime of Islands in International Law* (1978); id., 49 *BY* (1978), 1–29; Symmons, *The Maritime Zones of Islands in International Law* (1979); Bilge, *Festschrift für Rudolf*

states. In separate provisions for the two cases the Convention stipulates that the boundary shall be determined by agreement but 'in the absence of agreement, and unless another boundary line is justified by special circumstances', the boundary shall be determined by a median line, that is, the principle of equidistance from the nearest points of the baselines from which the breadth of the territorial sea of each state is measured.

This approach—the equidistance/special circumstances rule—was held not to represent general international law in the *North Sea Continental Shelf* cases (1969).[39] Since that decision, and on the basis of a consistent jurisprudence, the relevant rules of customary law have taken the form of 'equitable principles' as elaborated in the course of the decisions of the International Court and other tribunals.[40]

The classical statement of 'the principles and rules of international law' applicable (in the absence of a relevant treaty) is to be found in the Judgment given in the *North Sea* cases[41] and is as follows:

(A) the use of the equidistance method of delimitation not being obligatory as between the Parties; and

(B) there being no other single method of delimitation the use of which is in all circumstances obligatory;

(C) the principles and rules of international law applicable to the delimitation as between the Parties of the areas of the continental shelf in the North Sea which appertain to each of them beyond the partial boundary determined by the agreements of 1 December 1964 and 9 June 1965, respectively, are as follows:

   (1) delimitation is to be effected by agreement in accordance with equitable principles, and taking account of all the relevant circumstances, in such a way as to leave as much as possible to each Party all those parts of the continental shelf that constitute a natural prolongation of its land territory into and under the sea, without encroachment on the natural prolongation of the land territory of the other;

   (2) if, in the application of the preceding sub-paragraph, the delimitation leaves to the Parties areas that overlap, these are to be divided between them in agreed proportions or, failing agreement, equally, unless they decide on a régime of joint jurisdiction, user, or exploitation for the zones of overlap or any part of them;

Bindschedler (1980), 105–27; Pazarci, *La Délimitation du plateau continental et les îles* (1982); O'Connell, *The International Law of the Sea*, ii (1984), 684–732; Hutchinson, 55 *BY* (1984), 133–87; Jagota, *Maritime Boundary* (1985); 171 Hague *Recueil* (1981, II), 81–223; Bowett, *Essays in Honour of Roberto Ago*, ii (1987), 45–63; Colliard, ibid. 87–105; Degan, ibid. 107–37; Jiménez de Aréchaga, ibid. 229–39; Virally, ibid. 523–34; Kittichaisaree, *The Law of the Sea and Maritime Delimitation in South-East Asia* (1987), 57–119; Weil, *Perspectives du droit de la délimitation maritime* (1988); Johnston and Saunders (eds.), *Ocean Boundary Making: Regional Issues and Developments* (1988); Evans, *Relevant Circumstances and Maritime Delimitation* (1989); Jennings, *Festschrift für Karl Doehring* (1989), 397–408; Evans, 40 *ICLQ* (1991), 1–33. On the Rockall dispute see Symmons, 35 *ICLQ* (1986), 344–73.

[39] ICJ Reports (1969), 3; ILR 41, 29. See also the Court of Arbitration, *Anglo-French Continental Shelf* case (Decision of 30 June 1977); ILR 55, 6 at 54–8, paras. 66–75.

[40] *Libya–Malta* case, ICJ Reports (1985), 38–9, para. 45.

[41] ICJ Reports (1969), 53–4, para. 101.

(D) in the course of the negotiations, the factors to be taken into account are to include:

    (1)   the general configuration of the coasts of the Parties, as well as the presence of any special or unusual features;

    (2)   so far as known or readily ascertainable, the physical and geological structure, and natural resources, of the continental shelf areas involved;

    (3)   the element of a reasonable degree of proportionality, which a delimitation carried out in accordance with equitable principles ought to bring about between the extent of the continental shelf areas appertaining to the coastal State and the length of its coast measured in the general direction of the coastline, account being taken for this purpose of the effects, actual or prospective, of any other continental shelf delimitations between adjacent States in the same region.

These 'equitable principles' have a normative character as a part of general international law, and their application is to be distinguished from decision *ex aequo et bono*.[42]

The provisions of the Convention of 1982 leave the issue of delimitation to the rules of general or customary international law. Thus Article 83, paragraph 1, provides that:

The delimitation of the continental shelf between States with opposite or adjacent coasts shall be effected by agreement on the basis of international law, as referred to in Article 38 of the Statute of the International Court of Justice, in order to achieve an equitable solution.

THE EQUITABLE PRINCIPLES

The 'principles' recognized as such, are rather general in character, and those most often formulated are as follows:

    (i)   Delimitation shall be effected by agreement on the basis of international law.[43]

    (ii)   The principle of non-encroachment by one party on the natural prolongation of the other.[44]

    (iii) The principle of preventing, as far as possible, any cut-off of the seaward projection of the coast of either of the states concerned.[45]

---

[42] *North Sea* cases, ICJ Reports (1969), 46, para. 83; pp. 46–7, para. 85; *Libya–Tunisia* case, ibid. (1982), 60, para. 71; *Libya–Malta* case, ICJ Reports (1985), 38–9, para. 45. See also Jennings, 42 *Ann. suisse* (1986), 27–38.

[43] Conv. of 1982, Art. 83, para. 1; *North Sea* cases, ICJ Reports (1969), 46–8, paras. 85–7; p. 53, para. 101; *Gulf of Maine* case, ICJ Reports (1984) 292–3, para. 90; p. 299, para. 112; *Libya–Malta* case, ibid. (1985), 39, para. 46.

[44] *North Sea* cases, ICJ Reports (1969), 46–7, para. 85; p. 53, para. 101; *Gulf of Maine* case, ibid. (1984), 312–13, para. 157; *Libya–Malta* case, ibid. (1985), 39, para. 46; *Dubai-Sharjah* Award, ILR 91, 543 at 659.

[45] *North Sea* cases, ICJ Reports (1969), 17–18, para. 8; *Gulf of Maine* case, ibid. (1984), 298–9, para. 110; pp. 312–13, para. 157; p. 328, para. 196; p. 335, para. 219; *Guinea–Guinea (Bissau)* case, ILR 77, 635 at 681, para. 103.

(iv) Delimitation is to be effected by the application of equitable criteria and by the use of practical methods capable of ensuring, with regard to the geographical configuration of the area and other relevant circumstances, an equitable result.[46]

(v) There is a presumption that the equitable solution is an equal division of the areas of overlap of the continental shelves of the states in dispute.[47]

RELEVANT CIRCUMSTANCES

The precise application of the equitable principles involves reference to the 'relevant circumstances', or 'factors to be taken into account', or 'auxiliary criteria' (the terminology is somewhat variable). The relevant circumstances recognized by international tribunals are as follows:

(i) The general configuration of the coasts of the parties.[48]

(ii) Given a geographical situation of quasi-equality as between a number of states, it is necessary to abate the effects of an incidental special feature from which an unjustifiable difference of treatment would result.

This principle has been employed to avoid, or at least to diminish, the effects of a concave coast,[49] the location of islands of state A near the coast of state B[50] and the eccentric alignment of small islands lying off a peninsula.[51] On occasion, the effect of a group of islands has been reduced by half when the geography was not markedly eccentric.[52]

(iii) The geological structure of the sea-bed and its geomorphology (or surface features).[53]

(iv) The disparity of coastal lengths in the relevant area.[54]

(v) The general geographical framework or context.[55]

---

[46] Gulf of Maine case, ICJ Reports (1984), 299–300, para. 112; Libya–Malta case, ibid. (1985), 38–9, para. 45; p. 57, para. 79.

[47] North Sea cases, ICJ Reports (1969), 36, para. 57; p. 52, para. 99; p. 53, para. 101C2; Gulf of Maine case, ibid. (1984), 300–1, para. 115; pp. 312–13, para. 157; pp. 327–32, paras. 195–210; Libya–Malta case, ibid. (1985), 47, paras. 62–3.

[48] North Sea cases, ICJ Reports (1969), 49, para. 89; pp. 53–4, para. 101; Tunisia–Libya case, ibid. (1982), 61–3, paras. 73–8; Gulf of Maine case, ibid. (1984), 327–31, paras. 195–207; Libya–Malta case, ibid. (1985), 50, para. 68; p. 52, para. 73; Guinea-Guinea (Bissau) case, ILR 77, 635 at 676–9, paras. 92–8.

[49] North Sea cases, ICJ Reports (1969), 49–50, para. 91. See also ibid., 36, para. 57.

[50] Anglo-French Continental Shelf case, ILR 54, 6 at 100–2, paras. 196–201 (Channel Islands enclaved).

[51] Ibid., 123–4, paras. 248–51 (Scilly Isles given half-effect).

[52] Tunisia–Libya case, ibid. (1982), 88–9, paras. 127–9. For criticism of this approach: ibid. 149–56 (Diss. Op. of Gros). See also the Dubai-Sharjah Award, ILR 91, 543 at 673–7.

[53] North Sea cases, ibid. (1969), 53–4, para. 101 D(2); Tunisia–Libya case, ibid. (1982), 58, para. 68; p. 64, para. 80.

[54] Gulf of Maine case, ICJ Reports (1984), 323, para. 185; Libya–Malta case, ibid. (1985), 48–50, paras. 66–8; Jan Mayen case, ibid. (1993), 65–70, paras. 61–71.

[55] Anglo-French Continental Shelf case, ILR 54, 6 at 95–8, paras. 181–2, 187; Libya–Malta case, ICJ Reports (1985), 42, para. 53; p. 50, para. 69; pp. 51–3, paras. 72–3; Guinea-Guinea (Bissau) case, ILR 77, 635 at 683–5, paras. 108–11.

(vi)   The conduct of the parties, such as the *de facto* line produced by the pattern of grants of petroleum concessions in the disputed area.[56]

(vii)   The incidence of natural resources (usually oil and natural gas) in the disputed area.[57]

(viii) The principle of equitable access to the natural resources of the disputed area.[58]

(ix)   Defence and security interests of the states in dispute.[59]

(x)   Navigational interests of the states in dispute.[60]

(xi)   Consistency with the general direction of the land boundary.[61]

PROPORTIONALITY[62]

The Judgment of the Court in the *North Sea* cases states that one of the factors 'to be taken into account' in delimitation is 'the element of a reasonable degree of proportionality, which a delimitation in accordance with equitable principles ought to bring about between the extent of the continental shelf areas appertaining to the coastal State and the length of the coast measured in the general direction of the coastline, account being taken for this purpose of the effects, actual or prospective, of any other continental shelf delimitations between adjacent States in the same region'.[63] In the first place, proportionality is not an independent principle of delimitation (based on the ratio of the lengths of the respective coasts), but only a test of the equitableness *of a result arrived at by other means.*[64] This process of *ex post facto* verification of a line arrived at on the basis of other criteria may take two forms. Exceptionally, it may take the form of a ratio loosely based on the lengths of the respective coastlines.[65] More generally, it takes the form of vetting the delimitation for evident disproportionality resulting from particular geographical features.[66]

---

[56] *Tunisia–Libya* case, ICJ Reports (1982), 83–4, paras. 117–18; *Gulf of Maine* case, ibid. (1984), 310–11, paras. 149–52; *Jan Mayen* case, ibid. (1993), 75–7, paras. 82–6.

[57] *North Sea* cases, ICJ Reports (1969), 54, para. 101D(2); *Tunisia–Libya* case, ibid. 77–8, para. 107; *Libya–Malta* case, ibid. (1985), 41, para. 50.

[58] *Jan Mayen* case, ibid., 70–3, paras. 72–8.

[59] *Anglo-French Continental Shelf* case, ILR 54, 6 at 98, para. 188; *Libya–Malta* case, ICJ Reports (1985), 42, para. 51; *Guinea–Guinea (Bissau)* case, ILR 77, 635 at 689, para. 124; *Jan Mayen* case, ICJ Reports (1993), 74–5, para. 81.

[60] *Anglo-French Continental Shelf* case, ILR 54, 6 at 98, para. 188.

[61] *Tunisia–Libya* case, ICJ Reports (1982), 64–6, paras. 81–5; *Guinea–Guinea (Bissau)* case, ILR 77, 635 at 682–3, para. 106.

[62] See Jaenicke, *Essays in Honour of Willem Riphagen* (1986), 51–69.

[63] ICJ Reports (1969), 53–4, para. 101D(3); and see also ibid. 52, para. 98.

[64] *Libya–Malta* case, ibid. (1985), 45–6, para. 58.

[65] *Tunisia–Libya* case, ibid. (1982), 75–6, paras. 103–4; p. 78, para. 108; p. 91, paras. 130–1; p. 93, para. 133B(5).

[66] *Anglo-French Continental Shelf* case, ILR 54, 6 at 67–8, paras. 98–101; *Gulf of Maine* case, ibid. (1984), 323, para. 185; *Libya–Malta* case, ibid. (1985), 53–5, paras. 74–5.

MODE OF APPLICATION OF THE EQUITABLE PRINCIPLES

In its judgments the International Court has emphasized that there must be a process of balancing up all the pertinent considerations and that the relative weight to be given to the various principles and factors varies with the circumstances of the case.[67] Apart from the 'relevant circumstances' or 'factors' rehearsed above, other factors which may be given some weight include the maintenance of the unity of any deposits,[68] the factor of perpendicularity to the coast,[69] existing fishing patterns,[70] and the maintenance of optimum conservation and management of living resources.[71] Economic factors, including disparities of wealth, have been ruled out as extraneous and variable from time to time.[72] However, the key criterion of acceptability appears to be whether the particular consideration advanced is related to the legal concept of the continental shelf.[73]

The practical application of the equitable principles normally involves drawing a boundary line and the method chosen will be the method (or combination of methods) which will produce an equitable result. Methods available include a median line, a median line subject to a factor of equitable correction, a perpendicular to the general direction of the coast, using a bisector of the angle of the lines expressing the general direction of the relevant coasts[74] and the creation of a zone of joint development.[75]

THE CONCEPT OF NATURAL PROLONGATION[76]

The precise relevance of this concept is problematical. Its original significance, reflected in the Judgment in the *North Sea* cases, was the emphasis on the geological aspect of the shelf as appurtenant to the land territory and as a natural prolongation of land territory into and under the sea.[77] This encouraged the view that geological factors should enjoy a certain pre-eminence in the process of delimitation. In practice, these formulations constitute no more than a simple epitome of the shelf concept and

[67] *North Sea* cases, ICJ Reports (1969), 50–1, paras. 92–4; *Tunisia–Libya* case, ibid. (1982), 59–61, paras. 70–2; *Libya–Malta* case, ibid. (1985), 40, para. 48.

[68] *North Sea* cases, ICJ Reports (1969), 51–2, paras. 97, 99.

[69] *Tunisia–Libya* case, ICJ Reports (1982), 85, para. 120.

[70] *Gulf of Maine* case, ICJ Reports (1984), 298–9, para. 110.

[71] *Gulf of Maine* case, previous note.

[72] *Tunisia–Libya* case, ICJ Reports (1982), 77–8, paras. 106–7; *Libya–Malta* case, ibid. (1985), 41, para. 50; *Guinea–Guinea (Bissau)* case, ILR 77, 635 at 688–9, paras. 121–3.

[73] *Libya–Malta* case, ICJ Reports (1985), 40, para. 48; pp. 41–2, paras. 50–1.

[74] See the Judgment of the Chamber in the *Gulf of Maine* case, ICJ Reports (1984), 313–14, para. 159; and the Judgment of the Full Court in the *Case Concerning Territorial and Maritime Delimitation between Nicaragua and Honduras in the Caribbean Sea*, ibid. (2007), paras. 283–98, 320.

[75] *North Sea* cases, ICJ Reports (1969), 53, para. 101C(2); Conciliation Commission, *Jan Mayen Continental Shelf* (Iceland–Norway), ILR 62, 108.

[76] See Hutchinson, 55 BY (1984), 133–87.

[77] ICJ Reports (1969), 22, para. 19; p. 32, para. 45; p. 37, para. 58; pp. 46–7, para. 85; p. 51, paras. 95–6; p. 53, para. 101C(1); Conciliation Commission, *Jan Mayen Continental Shelf, supra*.

the roots of title of the coastal state. Indeed, the International Court has more recently pointed to the principle of distance as a basis of entitlement and concluded that, within the areas at a distance of under 200 miles from either of the coasts in question, there is no role for geological or geophysical factors either in terms of verifying title or as factors in delimitation.[78] It has also been established that natural prolongation is not *as such* a test of what is equitable.[79] Even when the seabed contains marked declivities, these will not play any, or any significant, role as a criterion of equity, unless they 'disrupt the essential unity of the continental shelf' (and in practice they rarely do),[80] and unless they occur *outside* areas within 200 miles or less of the coasts in question.[81]

11. EXCLUSIVE ECONOMIC ZONE DELIMITATION BETWEEN OPPOSITE OR ADJACENT STATES[82]

The provisions of Article 74 of the Law of the Sea Convention of 1982 concerning delimitation of the EEZ between states with opposite or adjacent coasts are identical with those of Article 83 relating to continental shelf delimitation. Moreover, the basis of entitlement of the coastal state to the EEZ is less differentiated from that of shelf areas since the International Court emphasized the distance principle of 200 miles in the *Libya–Malta* case.[83] In general, it may be assumed that the principles of delimitation are similar, especially when the coasts involved are less than 400 miles apart. However, there will be some differences in balancing up of equitable factors, more especially when the EEZ areas to be delimited are significant on account of fisheries rather than oil and gas.

In this context, the state practice and decisions of international tribunals relating to single maritime boundaries are significant.[84] Such a boundary divides areas of different status, for example, an EEZ and a fisheries zone of 200 miles, as in the *Gulf of Maine* case.[85] The Judgment of the Chamber in that case applied equitable criteria

---

[78] *Libya–Malta* case, ICJ Reports (1985) 32–7, paras. 31–41; and, in particular, p. 35, para. 39.

[79] *Tunisia–Libya* case, ICJ Reports (1982), 46–7, para. 44.

[80] *Anglo-French Continental Shelf* case, ILR 54, 6 at 68–70, paras. 104–8. See also the *North Sea* cases, ICJ Reports (1969), 32, para. 45; *Tunisia–Libya* case, ibid. (1982), 57–8, paras. 66–8; p. 64, para. 80.

[81] *Libya–Malta* case, ICJ Reports (1985), 35–6, paras. 39–40.

[82] See generally Evensen, in Rozakis and Stephanou (eds.), *The New Law of the Sea* (1983), 107–54; O'Connell, *The International Law of the Sea*, ii. 727–32; Attard, *The Exclusive Economic Zone in International Law* (1987), 221–76; Orrego, 199 Hague *Recueil* (1986, IV), 121–9; Weil, *Perspectives du droit de la délimitation maritime*; id. *The Law of Maritime Delimitation: Reflections* (1989); Evans, *Relevant Circumstances and Maritime Delimitation*, pp. 39–62.

[83] ICJ Reports (1985), 35, para. 39. Cf. *Tunisia–Libya* case, ibid. (1982), 48–9, paras. 47–8; and ibid. 114–15, paras. 51–3 (Jiménez de Aréchaga); p. 222, para. 107 (Oda).

[84] See Oda, *Essays in Honour of Roberto Ago* (1987), ii. 349–61; Evans, 64 BY (1993), 283–332.

[85] ICJ Reports (1984), 246. For comment: Oda, *Essays in Honour of Roberto Ago*; Rhee, 75 AJ (1981), 590–628; Legault and McRae, 22 *Canad. Yrbk.* (1984), 267–90; Legault and Hankey, 79 AJ (1985), 961–91; Schneider, 79 AJ (1985), 539–77.

essentially identical with those applicable to shelf delimitation, while emphasizing the need to use criteria suited to a multi-purpose delimitation involving both the shelf and the superjacent water column.[86]

12. THE REGIME OF ISLANDS[87]

Islands may constitute a relevant circumstance for the purpose of delimiting areas of continental shelf or exclusive economic zone between opposite or adjacent states and in this context they may be given full effect[88] or half-effect,[89] or they may be snubbed and enclaved.[90]

In truth much will depend on the particular geographical relationships of the island rather than its classification as such. Article 121 of the Law of the Sea Convention of 1982 provides that islands count as land territory (see also Art. 10 of the Territorial Sea Convention of 1958), but then formulates (para. 3) an exception: 'Rocks which cannot sustain human habitation or economic life of their own shall have no exclusive economic zone or continental shelf'. This is a new principle and raises considerable problems of definition and application.

[86] ICJ Reports (1984), 326–7, paras. 191–4. See also the Court of Arbitration decision in the *Guinea–Guinea (Bissau)* case, ILR 77, 635 at 658–9, paras. 42–3; pp. 685–7, paras. 113–17; *Dubai-Sharjah* Award, ILR 91, 543; *St. Pierre and Miquelon* Award, ILR 95, 645 at pp. 663–4; *Red Sea Islands Arbitration* (Phase Two), *ILR* 119, 417 at 457–8, para. 132; *Qatar* v. *Bahrain*, Judgment of 16 March 2001, paras. 168–73; *Cameroon* v. *Nigeria*, Judgment of 10 October 2002, paras. 285–9; *Case Concerning Territorial and Maritime Delimitation between Nicaragua and Honduras in the Caribbean Sea*, Judgment of 8 October 2007, paras. 261–65.

[87] See generally O'Connell, *The International Law of the Sea*, ii. 714–23, 731–2; Bowett, *The Legal Regime of Islands in International Law* (1979); Symmons, *The Maritime Zones of Islands in International Law* (1979); Dipla, *Le Régime juridique des îles dans le droit international de la mer* (1984); Symmons, 35 *ICLQ* (1986), 344–73. Jayewardene, *The Regime of Islands in International Law* (1990). On artificial islands: Johnson, 4 ILQ (1951), 203–15; Papadakis, *The International Legal Regime of Artificial Islands* (1977); O'Connell, *The International Law of the Sea*, i. 196–7.

[88] *Anglo-French Continental Shelf* case, ILR 54, 6 at 123, para. 248 (Island of Ushant).

[89] *Tunisia–Libya* case, ICJ Reports (1982), 18 at 88–9, paras. 128–9 (Kerkennah Islands); *Anglo-French* case, ILR 54, 6 at 121–4, paras. 243–51 (Scilly Isles); *Gulf of Maine* case, ICJ Reports (1984) 246 at 336–7, para. 222 (Seal Island).

[90] *Anglo-French Continental Shelf* case, ILR 54, 6 at 98–104, paras. 189–203 (Channel Islands).

11

THE REGIME OF THE HIGH SEAS[1]

1. INTRODUCTION

At the outset, it must be emphasized that 'the term "high seas" has traditionally encompassed all parts of the sea that are not included in the territorial sea or in the internal waters of a State',[2] and therefore comprehends contiguous zones and the waters over the continental shelf and outside the limit of the territorial sea. However, the Convention on the Law of the Sea of 1982 states that the provisions of Part VII (High Seas) 'apply to all parts of the sea that are not included in the exclusive economic zone, in the territorial sea or in the internal waters of a State, or in the archipelagic waters of an archipelagic State' (Art. 86). This prescription invites two observations. First, the exclusive economic zone is optional and by no means all coastal states claim such a zone. Secondly, a significant proportion of the freedoms of the high seas are, according to the Convention of 1982, applicable in the exclusive economic zone (Arts. 58 and 86), and this is also the position in customary international law.[3] The regime of the high seas does not apply to international lakes and land-locked seas, and these are not open to free navigation except by special agreement.[4] However, by acquiescence and custom, perhaps reinforced by conventions on particular questions, seas which are

[1] Of considerable value and authority is the Secretariat Memo. of 14 July 1950, A/CN. 4/32, *Yrbk. ILC* (1950), ii. 67–79 (believed to be the work of Gidel). See also McDougal and Burke, *The Public Order of the Oceans* (1962), 730ff.; Oppenheim, ii. 719–64; Churchill and Lowe, *The Law of the Sea*, (3rd edn.), 203–432; Burke, *The New International Law of Fisheries* (1994); Freestone, 5 *Canterbury LR* (1994), 341–62; François, Reports on the Regime of the High Seas, *Yrbk. ILC* (1950), ii. 36; ibid. (1951), ii. 75; ibid. (1952), ii. 44; ibid. (1954), ii. 7; Bos, 12 *Neths. Int. LR* (1965), 337–64; Whiteman, iv. 499–739; Rousseau, iv. 273–339; Bardonnet and Virally (eds.), *Le Nouveau Droit international de la mer* (1983); O'Connell, *The International Law of the Sea*, ii (1984), 792–830; Dupuy and Vignes (eds.), *Traité du nouveau droit de la mer* (1985), 337–74.

On the legal status of the *res communis*, supra, p. 169; on the regulation of the high seas as a shared resource infra, pp. 252–4.

[2] Conv. on the High Seas, 1958, Art. 1. This multilateral convention entered into force on 30 Sept. 1962. See Brownlie, *Documents*, p. 74. In the preamble its provisions are expressed to be 'generally declaratory of established principles of international law'.

[3] See the reference to freedom of navigation in the exclusive economic zone by the International Court in the case of *Nicaragua v. United States* (Merits), ICJ Reports (1986), 14 at 111–12, paras. 213–14.

[4] Oppenheim, ii. 589–91. Lakes and land-locked seas entirely enclosed by the land of a single state are part of the territory of that state.

virtually land-locked may acquire the status of high seas: this is the case of the Baltic and Black Seas. In such cases much turns on the maintenance of freedom of transit through the straits communicating with other large bodies of sea.[5] It is doubtful whether, apart from acquiescence and special agreements on access and other issues, the Baltic and Black Seas would have the status of open seas.

2. THE FREEDOM OF THE HIGH SEAS

The modern law governing the high seas has its foundation in the rule that the high seas are not open to acquisition by occupation on the part of states individually or collectively: it is *res extra commercium*.[6] Historically the emergence of the rule is associated with the rise to dominance of maritime powers and the decline of the influence of states which had favoured closed seas.[7] In the fifteenth century states were in favour of appropriation of or at least an exercise of exclusive rights over large expanses of sea, and Papal Bulls of 1493 and 1506 partitioned the oceans of the world between Spain and Portugal. The Spanish monopoly of commerce in the West Indies was challenged by Tudor policies, and Elizabeth I affirmed the freedom of the seas in answer to a Spanish protest arising from the expedition of Drake.[8] After 1609 Stuart policies extended the principle of closed seas from Scotland to England and Ireland, and the political concept of the 'British Seas' appeared. The areas claimed extended to the opposite shores of the continent.[9] The seventeenth century marked the heyday of the *mare clausum* (closed sea) with claims by England, Denmark, Spain, Portugal, Genoa, Tuscany, the Papacy, Turkey, and Venice.

In the eighteenth century the position changed completely. Dutch policies had favoured freedom of navigation and fishing in the previous century, and the great publicist Grotius had written against the Portuguese monopoly of navigation and commerce in the East Indies.[10] After the accession of William of Orange to the English throne in 1689 English disputes with Holland over fisheries ceased. By the late

---

[5] On access to the Black Sea and its status see the Montreux Conv., 1936, 31 AJ (1937), Suppl., p. 1. Does the Conv. recognize the status of the Black Sea as an open or a closed sea?

[6] But encroachment may occur as a result of acquisition by general acquiescence, see supra, p. 176 on the *Fisheries* case and historic waters.

[7] For the history see Fulton, *The Sovereignty of the Sea* (1911).

[8] However, in instructions to her ambassadors in 1602, while contesting a Danish claim to dominion over the seas between Norway, on the one hand, and Iceland and Greenland, on the other, the Queen recognized a right of 'oversight and jurisdiction'. Russia asserted the principle of the freedom of the seas in 1587.

[9] See Selden, *Mare Clausum* (1635). The King's Chambers were a different concept. In 1604 James I caused the limits of bays, from which hostile acts of belligerents were excluded, to be marked on charts (see the map in Fulton, *The Sovereignty of the Sea*, p. 123). No claim to sovereignty was intended. It seems that no special rights exist today in respect of the King's Chambers: see the *Fagernes* [1927] P. 311, CA.

[10] *Mare Liberum sive de jure quod Batavis competit ad Indicana commercia dissertatio* (1609), being a chapter of the work *De iure praedae*.

eighteenth century the British claim to sovereignty was obsolete and the requirement of the flag ceremony was ended in 1805. By the late eighteenth century the cannon-shot rule predominated, and claims to large areas of sea faded away.[11] In the nineteenth century naval power and commercial interests dictated British, French, and American support for the principle of freedom of the seas. However, whatever special interests the principle may have served historically, it has obviously commended itself to states generally, as representing a sensible and wholesome concept of shared use.

The principle of the freedom of the high seas has been described by Gidel[12] as 'multiforme et fugace', and in truth it is a 'general principle of international law', or a policy concept, from which particular rules must be deduced. Its application to specific problems often fails to give precise results. Weapon testing which involves the closure of large areas of ocean is regarded by some as a legitimate form of enjoying the freedom of the seas and by others as a serious denial of that freedom.[13] The problems of reasonableness and mutuality involved are reminiscent of the law of nuisance and the doctrine of abuse of rights.[14] Like guarantees of freedoms in written constitutions the only successful form of prescription is that of specifying exceptions. Gidel regards the concept as essentially negative. However, the substance of the principle and its character as a principle provide certain presumptions which may aid in the resolution of particular problems, and some consideration of its positive content is, therefore, useful. Grotius stated two principles: first, that the sea could not be the object of private or state appropriation; secondly, that the use of the high seas by one state would leave the medium available for use by another.[15]

Gidel has stated his views as follows:[16]

La liberté de la haute mer, essentiellement négative, ne peut pas cependant ne pas comporter des conséquences positives. Dirigée contre l'exclusivité d'usage elle se résout nécessairement en une idée d'égalité d'usage. ... Tous les pavillons maritimes ont un droit égal à tirer de la haute mer les diverses utilités qu'elle peut comporter. Mais l'idée d'égalité d'usage ne vient qu'en second lieu. L'idée essentielle contenue dans le principe de liberté de la haute mer est l'idée d'interdiction d'interférence de tout pavillon dans la navigation en temps de paix de tout autre pavillon.

---

[11] *Supra*, pp. 174–5. The extravagant Portuguese and Spanish pretensions had ended before this. Spain supported a 6-mile limit in 1760.

[12] *Yrbk. ILC* (1950), ii. 68.

[13] See Whiteman iv. 544V.; Gidel, in *Festschrift für Jean Spiropoulos* (1957), 173–205; *Yrbk. ILC* (1956), ii. 278 (Art. 27, Commentary, para. 3); Oda and Owada (eds.), *The Practice of Japan in International Law 1961–1970* (1982), 110–21; and the applications of Australia and New Zealand in the *Nuclear Tests Cases*, ICJ Reports (1974), 253 (*Australia v. France*); 457 (*New Zealand v. France*). The claims were found to be without object: see infra, p. 475. Useful material may be found in the *Pleadings*. Nuclear tests in the atmosphere are restricted by the Test Ban Treaty signed in 1963.

[14] See *infra*, pp. 443–5.

[15] *Mare Liberum*, cap. v.

[16] *Spiropoulos Festschrift*, p. 69. See also the *Lotus* (1927), PCIJ, Ser. A, no. 10, p. 25.

To these propositions it is necessary to add that the general principle applies in time of war or armed conflict as well as time of peace.[17] On two occasions in its jurisprudence the International Court has taken the opportunity to invoke 'the principle of the freedom of maritime communication'.[18] An attempt to describe, in part, the content of the freedom of the seas is to be found in Article 2 of the Convention on the High Seas of 1958, which provides:

The high seas being open to all nations, no State may validly purport to subject any part of them to its sovereignty. Freedom of the high seas is exercised under the conditions laid down by these articles and by the other rules of international law. It comprises, *inter alia*, both for coastal and non-coastal States:

(1) Freedom of navigation;

(2) Freedom of fishing;[19]

(3) Freedom to lay submarine cables and pipelines;

(4) Freedom to fly over the high seas.

These freedoms, and others which are recognized by the general principles of international law,[20] shall be exercised by all States with reasonable regard to the interests of other States in their exercise of the freedom of the high seas.

The four freedoms itemized, and particularly the first two, are supported by arbitral jurisprudence and are inherent in many particular rules of law. Freedom of fishing is an assumption at the base of the decision in the *Fisheries* case[21] and the awards in the *Behring Sea Fisheries* arbitrations in 1893[22] and 1902.[23] Both arbitrations arose from attempts to enforce conservation measures on the high seas.[24] In the former case the United States had arrested Canadian sealers, and in the latter Russian vessels had arrested American sealers, with the object of preventing the depletion of seal stocks. The awards in both arbitrations rejected claims to enforce conservation measures against foreign vessels on the high seas. In the absence of a treaty, a coastal state could

---

[17] This aspect of the matter is obscured by the treatment in some works: naturally the exceptions to the principle are diVerent if the status of belligerent is acquired, but the principle is not thereby obliterated.

[18] *Corfu Channel Case (Merits)*, ICJ Reports (1949), 4 at 22; and see also *Nicaragua v. United States (Merits)*, ibid. (1986). 14 at 111–12, paras. 213–14.

[19] See also Art. 1 of the Conv. on Fishing and Conservation of the Living Resources of the High Seas of 1958.

[20] The United Kingdom in its comment on the ILC draft articles advocated the addition of two others: '5. Freedom of research, experiment and exploration. 6. The right to regulate the operation of foreign vessels in the coastal trade in those cases where such ships are permitted to engage in that trade'.

[21] *Supra*, p. 176. Cf. Judge Read, Diss. Op., ICJ Reports (1951), 187–9.

[22] See Moore, *Digest*, i, para. 172; McNair, *Opinions*, i. 241.

[23] See Moore, *Digest*, i, para. 173; *RIAA* ix. 51. The seal fishery was later regulated by the Conv. of Washington, 1911, between Great Britain, the United States, Russia, and Japan. See further Johnston, *The International Law of Fisheries* (1965), 264–9.

[24] The arbitration between Great Britain and the United States involved the question of compensation for abstention from fishing by Great Britain during the pendency of the arbitration; the arbitration between United States and Russia concerned claims for indemnity arising from seizures by Russian cruisers.

only apply such measures to vessels flying its own flag.[25] Of the questions submitted for decision to the tribunal of 1892 the fifth concerned an issue of general law: '5. Has the United States any right, and if so, what right of protection or property in the furseals frequenting the islands of the United States in Behring Sea when such seals are found outside the ordinary three-mile limit?' The arbitrators found, by a majority, that 'the United States has not any right of protection or property in the fur-seals frequenting the islands of the United States in Behring Sea, when such seals are found outside the ordinary three-mile limit'.

In conclusion it is necessary to give some account of the changes resulting from the Third United Nations Conference on the Law of the Sea.[26] The major change is the legitimation of the exclusive economic zone (see *supra*, pp. 206–9) to a maximum of 200 miles in breadth. According to the Convention on the Law of the Sea of 1982 the zone does not form part of the high seas (see Arts. 55 and 86), although some significant aspects of the regime of the high seas apply to the zone. A further change is the creation of a special regime for the resources of the seabed and subsoil beyond the limits of national jurisdiction under the control and management of the International Sea-bed Authority. These changes are reflected in the chronicle of freedoms of the high seas included in the Convention. The four freedoms set forth in the Convention of 1958 are formulated but freedom of fishing is subject (principally) to the reduction of area consequent upon exclusive economic zones, as well as the activities involved in exploitation of the seabed and ocean floor and subsoil thereof, beyond the limits of national jurisdiction, under control of the International Sea-bed Authority. The Convention formulates additional freedoms (Art. 87, para. 1):

(d) Freedom to construct artificial islands and other installations permitted under international law, subject to Part VI;[27] ...

(f) freedom of scientific research, subject to Parts VI[27] and XIII.[28]

It is to be noted that the exclusive economic zone as described in the Convention would confer jurisdiction on coastal states in respect of marine scientific research (Art. 56, para. 1). Moreover, while freedom of fishing is preserved (Art. 87, para. 1 (e)) this is subject to certain conditions, including 'the duty to take, or to co-operate with other States in taking, such measures for their respective nationals as may be necessary for the conservation of the living resources of the high seas' (Arts. 116–20; and, in particular, Art. 117).[29]

---

[25] On fishery conservation zones see *supra*, p. 198.
[26] See Conforti, *Ital. Yrbk.* (1975), 3–15.
[27] Concerning the continental shelf.
[28] Concerning marine scientific research in general.
[29] See Oda, 77 *AJ* (1983), 739–55.

3. THE MAINTENANCE OF ORDER
ON THE HIGH SEAS

States may agree among themselves to accept special procedures for the repression of the slave-trade and other wrongdoing on the high seas. In some cases the Convention on the High Seas confers the power to stop and seize foreign vessels by way of enforcement. In others the parties are obliged only to incorporate the prohibition in their national legislation, and enforcement is by national courts in respect of vessels flying the flag of the forum and persons subject to the jurisdiction of the forum state. The system of enforcement, whether specified by treaty or custom, rests on the co-operation of international law and the national laws of states possessing a maritime flag. Every state is under a duty to fix the conditions for the grant of nationality to its ships, for the registration of ships in its territory, and for the right to fly its flag. Ships have the nationality of the state whose flag they are entitled to fly, and each state has an obligation to issue to ships to which it has granted the right to fly its flag documents to that effect.[30]

The essential elements are the nationality of the ship;[31] the exclusive jurisdiction of the flag state over the ship (apart from treaty provisions to the contrary); the right of approach to verify the right of a ship to fly its flag; and the imposition on the flag state of obligations in respect of the maintenance of good order and general security on the high seas by customary rules and by treaties. The right to enjoy the protection of the law balances the responsibility of the flag state for the behaviour of its ships. The ship without nationality[32] loses the protection of the law with respect to boarding and seizure on the high seas.[33] However, such ships are not outside the law altogether, and their occupants are protected by elementary considerations of humanity.[34] The seizure of ships by insurgents has created some difficult problems, and the issues have been obscured by a tendency for courts to describe ships under the control of insurgents as pirates.[35] Such ships, it seems, should not be interfered with provided they do not attempt to exercise belligerent rights against foreign vessels and the lives of any 'neutral' aliens on board are not threatened.

---

[30] See Oppenheim, ii. 727; Conv. on the High Seas, Art. 5; Conv. on the Law of the Sea, 1982, Art. 91; van der Mensbrugghe, 11 *Revue belge* (1975), 56–102.

[31] On the nationality of ships: *infra*, p. 422.

[32] To which will be assimilated a vessel flying a flag without authority of the flag state and a ship sailing under the flags of two or more states, using them according to convenience: see Oppenheim, ii. 595–6; Conv. on the High Seas, Art. 6, para. 2; Law of the Sea Conv., 1982, Art. 92, para. 2.

[33] See *Naim Molvan v. A.G. for Palestine* [1948] AC 351 at 369, PC; and Report of François, *Yrbk. ILC* (1950), ii. 36 at 38. On the status of derelict vessels see the *Costa Rica Packet* case, La Fontaine, p. 510.

[34] On pirate ships, *infra*.

[35] See Colombos, pp. 450ff.; and *infra*, p. 231. On the *Santa Maria* incident in 1961: Green, 37 *BY* (1961), 496–505; Goyard, 66 *RGDIP* (1962), 123–42.

4. EXCEPTIONS TO THE PRINCIPLE OF THE FREEDOM OF THE HIGH SEAS

(a) Rules of customary law

(i) *Piracy.*[36] The dissenting opinion of Judge Moore in the *Lotus* case provides a useful starting-point.[37] He said that:

in the case of what is known as piracy by law of nations, there has been conceded a universal jurisdiction, under which the person charged with the offence may be tried and punished by any nation into whose jurisdiction he may come. I say 'piracy by law of nations', because the municipal laws of many States denominate and punish as 'piracy' numerous acts which do not constitute piracy by law of nations, and which therefore are not of universal cognizance, so as to be punishable by all nations. Piracy by law of nations, in its jurisdictional aspects, is *sui generis.* Though statutes may provide for its punishment, it is an offence against the law of nations; and as the scene of the pirate's operations is the high seas, which it is not the right or duty of any nation to police, he is denied the protection of the flag which he may carry, and is treated as an outlaw, as the enemy of all mankind—*hostis humani generis*—whom any nation may in the interest of all capture and punish.

The definition of piracy has long been a source of controversy,[38] but it is thought that Article 15 of the Convention on the High Seas represents the existing customary law.[39] This provides:

Piracy consists of any of the following acts:

(1) Any illegal acts of violence, detention or any act of depredation, committed for private ends by the crew or the passengers of a private ship or a private aircraft, and directed:

(a) On the high seas, against another ship or aircraft, or against persons or property on board such ship or aircraft;

---

[36] Gidel, i. 303–55; Whiteman, iv. 648–67; Verzijl, *International Law in Historical Perspective*, iv. 248–61; Secretariat Memo., *Yrbk. ILC* (1950), ii at p. 70; Oppenheim, ii. 746–55; Johnson, 43 *Grot. Soc.* (1957), 63–85; Harv. Research, 26 *AJ* (1932), Suppl., pp. 739ff.; McNair, *Opinions*, i. 265–81; Shubber, 43 *BY* (1968–9), 193–204; Rousseau, iv. 330–6; O'Connell, *The International Law of the Sea*, ii. 967–83.

[37] PCIJ, Ser. A, no. 10 (1927), p. 70.

[38] By way of caution, it may be pointed out that definitions by municipal courts are often out of date, and may involve an amalgam of municipal rules and international law, or the narrow issue of the meaning of 'piracy' in an insurance policy. The treatment in Oppenheim, ii. 610–14, presents an unusually wide conception of piracy. For judicial essays in definition see *The Serhassan Pirates* (1845), 2 Wm. Rob. 354; *The Magellan Pirates* (1853), 1 Sp. Ecc. & Ad. 81; *Republic of Bolivia v. Indemnity Mutual Marine Assurance Co.* [1909] KB 785; *In re Piracy Jure Gentium* [1934] AC 586, PC; *Athens Maritime Enterprises Corporation v. Hellenic Mutual War Risks Association (Bermuda) Ltd.* [1983] QB 647; *Castle John and Nederlandse Stichting Sirius v. NV Mabeco and NV Parfin*, ILR 77, 537.

[39] See also the ILC draft and comment: *Yrbk. ILC* (1956), ii. 282. See also Art. 101 of the Law of the Sea Conv., 1982 (virtually the same).

(b) Against a ship, aircraft, persons, or property in a place outside the jurisdiction of any State;

(2) Any act of voluntary participation in the operation of a ship or of an aircraft with knowledge of facts making it a pirate ship or aircraft;

(3) Any act of inciting or of intentionally facilitating an act described in sub-paragraph (1) or sub-paragraph (2) of this article.

The only innovation in the provision just quoted is the reference to aircraft, a sensible application of analogy.[40] The essential feature of the definition is that the acts must be committed for private ends. It follows that piracy cannot be committed by warships or other government ships, or government aircraft, except where the crew 'has mutinied and taken control of the ship or aircraft' (Art. 16 of the Convention on the High Seas, 1958; Art. 102 of the Law of the Sea Convention, 1982). Acts committed on board a ship by the crew and directed against the ship itself, or against persons or property on the ship are not within the definition.[41]

The Convention confines piracy to acts on the high seas or 'in a place outside the territorial jurisdiction of any State'. The latter phrase refers primarily to an island constituting *terra nullius* or the shore of an unoccupied territory.[42]

Article 19 of the Convention on the High Seas of 1958 provides:

On the high seas, or in any other place outside the jurisdiction of any State, every State may seize a pirate ship or aircraft,[43] or a ship taken by piracy and under the control of pirates, and arrest the persons and seize the property on board. The courts of the State which carried out the seizure may decide upon the penalties to be imposed, and may also determine the action to be taken with regard to the ships, aircraft or property, subject to the rights of third parties acting in good faith.[44]

The second part of this provision preserves the effect of the maxim '*pirata non mutat dominium*': the rightful owner is not deprived of his title by virtue of acts of piracy relating to his goods.[45] Seizures on account of piracy may only be carried out by warships or military aircraft, or other government ships or aircraft authorized to that effect (Art. 21, Convention of 1958; Art. 107 of the Law of the Sea Convention of 1982). Capture may occur in other circumstances as a consequence of acts of self-defence by an intended victim of piratical action.

---

[40] The ILC draft did not refer to attacks by aircraft on aircraft. See further the UK Tokyo Conv. Act 1967, s. 4 and Sched.

[41] *Contra*, Oppenheim, ii. 751 n. 2; Hall, *International Law* (8th edn., 1924), 314. See further O'Connell, *The International Law of the Sea*, ii. 970–3.

[42] On the legal regime of the *res nullius*, see *supra*, p. 168.

[43] Defined in Art. 17: 'A ship or aircraft is considered a pirate ship or aircraft if it is intended by the persons in dominant control to be used for the purpose of committing one of the acts referred to in Article 15. The same applies if the ship or aircraft has been used to commit any such act, so long as it remains under the control of the persons guilty of that act'. (And see also the Law of the Sea Conv. 1982, Art. 103).

[44] And see also Art. 105 of the Conv. on the Law of the Sea, 1982.

[45] See Wortley, 24 *BY* (1947), 258–72; id., 33 *Grot. Soc.* (1948), 25–35.

(ii) *Other illegal acts committed by ships on the high seas.* The use of force by ships against foreign vessels on the high seas may be unlawful and yet may not fall within the definition of piracy. However, from time to time tribunals, governments, and writers have assimilated certain categories of acts to piracy. The tendency to enlarge the concept of piracy thus evident is explicable partly by the existence of doubts relating to the definition of piracy and partly by a desire to affirm the illegality of certain types of activity in the most unequivocal manner. The subject as a whole is dominated by the problem of keeping order outside the territorial jurisdiction of states[46] and, in particular, of maintaining legal controls in respect of those not identifiable with a state on which responsibility may be placed. Thus Hall[47] considered piracy to include acts done 'by persons not acting under the authority of any politically organized community, notwithstanding that the objects of the persons so acting may be professedly political'. The categories of act causing difficulties of classification will now be briefly reviewed.

INSURGENCY

Ships controlled by insurgents may not, without a recognition of belligerency by third states[48] exercise belligerent rights against the shipping of other states. Forcible interference of this kind is unauthorized by law and may be resisted by all available means. However, it is very doubtful if it is correct to characterize such acts as piracy,[49] and this proposition is reinforced by the terms of the Convention on the High Seas. However, it may be that it is lawful to punish acts constituting *mala prohibita*—murder, robbery, and so on—carried out *ultra vires* by insurgents.[50] Opinions which favour the treatment of insurgents as such as 'pirates' are surely incorrect.[51]

UNLAWFUL ACTS COMMITTED WITH THE AUTHORITY OF A LAWFUL GOVERNMENT

Illegal attacks on or seizures of innocent merchant ships by warships or government ships result in the delictual responsibility of the aggressor's flag state, but the offending ships do not become pirate ships.[52] Again, a privateer, authorized by a belligerent to act in her service, is not a pirate, even if acts of violence are committed against neutral ships. In the latter case the belligerent is responsible as principal.

---

[46] See generally *supra*, pp. 227–8.

[47] *International Law* (8th edn.) 314 (and see p. 311). See also Johnson, 43 *Grot. Soc.* (1957), 77n.

[48] *Supra*, ch. 5, n. 5.

[49] For the view doubted see: Hall, *International Law*, pp. 314, 318–19; Oppenheim, ii. 751–2; Law Officers of the Crown *in re the Huascar* incident in 1877 (McNair, *Opinions*, i. 274–80); Lauterpacht, 46 *RGDIP* (1939), 513–49; Secretariat Memo., *Yrbk. ILC* (1950), ii. 70. See further van Zwanenberg, 10 *ICLQ* (1961), 798–817; Green, 37 *BY* (1961), 496–505.

[50] See the Conv. on the Rights and Duties of States in the Event of Civil Strife, 1928; Hudson, *Int. Legis*, iv, no. 195.

[51] See an American court in the case of the *Ambrose Light* [1885] 25 Fed. Rep. 408.

[52] *Supra*, pp. 243–5; Oppenheim, ii. 747–8; McNair, *Opinions*, i. 267, 268.

POLITICALLY MOTIVATED OPERATIONS BY ORGANIZED GROUPS

Harassing operations by organized groups deploying forces on the high seas may have political objectives, and yet may be neither connected with insurgency against a particular government nor performed by agents of a lawful government. Ships threatened by such activities may be protected, and yet the aggressors may not be regarded as pirates.

UNRESTRICTED SUBMARINE WARFARE

The term 'piracy' is employed on occasion to describe acts by ships acting on the orders of a recognized government 'which are in gross breach of International Law and which show a criminal disregard of human life'.[53] Thus by the Nyon Agreement of 14 September 1937[54] eight states agreed on collective measures 'against piratical acts by submarines' with regard to attacks on merchant ships in the Mediterranean during the Spanish Civil War. The acts were stated to be 'acts contrary to the most elementary dictates of humanity which should be justly treated as acts of piracy'. In this case the condemnation rests on the convention, and the use of the term 'piracy' adds nothing to the legal result.

(iii) *The right of approach in time of peace.*[55] In order to make a success of the system for maintaining order on the high seas, reviewed earlier, it is necessary to provide for an approach by warships in order to verify the identity and nationality of ships. Such a right of approach (*droit d'approche; enquéte ou vérification du pavillon; reconnaissance*) is recognized by customary law. The right of approach exists in all circumstances, but does not involve the actual examination of papers or seizure of the vessel.[56]

(iv) *Visit, search, and capture in time of peace.*[57] There is no general power of police exercisable over foreign merchant ships, and the occasions on which ships can be visited and seized by warships in time of peace are limited. In a report of a Law Officer of

---

[53] See Oppenheim, ii. 750.

[54] Treaty Series, no. 38 (1973); 31 *AJ* (1937), Suppl., p. 179. See also the unratified Treaty of Washington, 1922, Art. 3; 16 *AJ* (1922), Suppl., p. 57 (attacks on merchant ships contrary to the laws of war); and Johnson, 43 *Grot. Soc.* (1957), 81–5.

[55] Oppenheim, ii. 736–7; Gidel, i. 299; Colombos, p. 311; Report by François, *Yrbk. ILC* (1950), ii. 41; Second Report by François, ibid. (1951), ii. 81; Rousseau, iv. 322–3; O'Connell, *The International Law of the Sea*, ii. 802–3; the *Marianna Flora* (1826), 11 Wheaton 1. See also *infra*, n. 61. See *United States v. Postal*, ILR 91, 509; *United States v. Monroy*, ibid., 539.

[56] The treatments in Oppenheim, Colombos, and other Anglo-American sources do not show clarity on this point. In the context of piracy the right of approach tends to merge with the right of visit and capture. See Gidel, i. 290–3; and the reports by François *supra*, n. 55.

[57] McNair, *Opinions*, i. 229–45; Colombos, pp. 310–14; Gidel, i. 288–300; McDougal and Burke, *The Public Order of the Oceans*, pp. 885–93; van Zwanenberg, 10 *ICLQ* (1961), 785–93; Rousseau, iv. 323–4; O'Connell, *The International Law of the Sea*, ii. 757, 801–8, 1114–15. See *United States v. Cadena*, ILR 91, 467.

the Crown of 25 October 1854 there appears the statement:[58] 'I have further to observe that all interference with British Vessels on the High Seas by the Mexican Authorities on any pretence beyond the limit of three miles from the shore is *prima facie* illegal. No general right of search of foreign ships can be claimed on the High Seas by any Nation not a belligerent'.

The jurists have generally agreed that a right to resort to a threat or use of force to effect visit, search, and, if justified, seizure of a ship[59] only existed in the case of a known pirate ship or a ship the behaviour of which gave reasonable grounds for suspecting her of piracy.[60] This proposition is a corollary of the principle of the freedom of the seas and also of the rule that in general a merchant ship can only be boarded by a warship flying the same flag and therefore having a right of jurisdiction.[61] British and American jurisprudence refused to admit a right of visit in the case of ships suspected of taking part in the slave-trade,[62] and, apart from piracy, the right could only exist on the basis of treaty or if a ship refused to show its flag.

The legal regime outlined here has met with three threats to its stability. The first, attempts to extend the concept of piracy, has been noticed already.[63] Claims to a right of self-defence on the high seas constitute another source of instability, and some writers, having presented a strict regime in the matter of visit, somewhat inconsistently refer later to a right of self-defence without defining its limits. The third source of confusion lies in the definition of the right of approach or verification of flag. Some English writers link this closely with the right of visit and lay down the conditions for visit in seemingly expansive terms requiring only 'suspicion' of piracy.[64] However, it was realized by governments in the last century that the right of visit could be abused and that there must be reasonable ground for suspicion, for example a refusal by a ship to hoist her flag.[65]

[58] McNair, *Opinions*, i. 233. Note 1 on p. 231 reads: 'It is believed that, apart from cases of suspected piracy... and cases permitted by treaty (e.g. slave traffic treaties), Great Britain has always resisted the visit and search of her merchant ships on the high seas in time of peace . . . .' See also the US Dept. of State memo. and diplomatic correspondence set out in Hackworth, ii. 659–65; and Moore, *Digest*, ii. 987–1001.

[59] As a matter of customary law visit, search, and capture are a legal unity. For an attempt to distinguish visit and search see Wilson, 44 *AJ* (1950), 505 at 516. The right to interfere may be delimited by treaty: see the International Conv. for the Protection of Submarine Telegraph Cables, 1884, Art. 10.

[60] Gidel, i. 301, 303, 355; Colombos, pp. 310–11; Brierly, pp. 306–7; Wheaton, *Elements* (1866), s. 106; Moore, *Digest*, ii. 886; Guggenheim, i. 449–50; Hyde, i. 764.

[61] In the Judgment in the *Lotus* case, PCIJ, Ser. A, no. 10, p. 25, the Permanent Court expressed the rule: 'Vessels on the high seas are subject to no authority except that of the State whose flag they fly. In virtue of the principle of the freedom of the seas, that is to say, the absence of any territorial sovereignty upon the high seas, no State may exercise any kind of jurisdiction over foreign vessels upon them'. Cf. the *Jessie*, etc. (1921), RIAA vi. 57; the *Wanderer* (1921), ibid. 68.

[62] See the decisions of Lord Stowell in *Le Louis* (1817), 2 Dods. 210; and of the US Supreme Court in the *Antelope* (1825), 10 Wheaton 66. See further Moore, *Digest*, ii. 914–18.

[63] *Supra*, pp. 228–9. Activities described there as illegal may give rise to rights of self-defence but not ipso facto to a right of visit, search, and capture (except perhaps when insurgent vessels have foreign nationals on board).

[64] See Oppenheim, ii. 736–7; Colombos, p. 311.

[65] See Gidel, i. 299; Colombos, pp. 312–13; McNair, *Opinions*, i. 233, 240 ('vehement suspicion of Piracy'); Hall, *International Law*, pp. 317–18 ('when weighty reasons exist for suspecting'); François, Second Report, *Yrbk. ILC* (1951), ii. 81–3.

The provisions of the Convention on the High Seas of 1958 in general confirm the validity of the strict regime in these matters and include slaving as a justification for visit:

Article 22. 1. Except where acts of interference derive from powers conferred by treaty, a warship which encounters a foreign merchant ship on the high seas is not justified in boarding her unless there is reasonable ground for suspecting:

    (a) That the ship is engaged in piracy; or

    (b) That the ship is engaged in the slave trade; or

    (c) That, though flying a foreign flag or refusing to show its flag, the ship is, in reality, of the same nationality as the warship.

2. In the cases provided for in sub-paragraphs (a), (b) and (c) above, the warship may proceed to verify the ship's right to fly its flag. To this end, it may send a boat under the command of an officer to the suspected ship. If suspicion remains after the documents have been checked, it may proceed to a further examination on board the ship, which must be carried out with all possible consideration.

3. If the suspicions prove to be unfounded, and provided that the ship boarded has not committed any act justifying them, it shall be compensated for any loss or damage that may have been sustained.

The Law of the Sea Convention of 1982 contains essentially similar provisions except that two additional justifications for boarding are included: engaging in unauthorized broadcasting (see Art. 109) and the case in which the ship is without nationality (Art. 110, para. 1(c) and (d)). It is also provided that the right of visit may be carried out by military aircraft (para. 4) and also by 'any other duly authorized ships or aircraft clearly marked and identifiable as being on government service' (para. 5). The act of boarding, even when 'reasonable ground' for boarding exists, is a privilege, and, if no act justifying the suspicions has been committed by the ship boarded, there is strict liability, and the flag state of the warship must compensate for 'any loss or damage'.[66] In its comment[67] the International Law Commission stated that the severe penalty 'seems justified in order to prevent the right of visit being abused'.

(v) *The right of self-defence.* The particular claim to visit and seize vessels on the high seas may take the form of a 'security zone', a 'defence zone', or a 'neutrality zone', and the legality of these zones has been considered briefly in Chapter 9. However, quite apart from claims to contiguous and other zones some states, and particularly the United Kingdom, have on occasion asserted a right to use force to detain vessels on the ground of security or self-defence, and many of the English authorities support

---

[66] In the comment on the ILC draft the Yugoslav Government thought that the search of merchant ships by warships should not be discouraged by too strict sanctions: 'It is necessary therefore to consider whether a provision should be inserted freeing the warship from *damnum emergens*, if *dolus* or *culpa lata* cannot be charged to the warship'. (*Yrbk. ILC* (1956), ii. 97.) Cf. the *Marianna Flora* (1826), 11 Wheaton 1; Moore, *Digest*, ii. 886.

[67] *Yrbk. ILC* (1956), ii. 284.

such a right.[68] Nevertheless it may be said here that the legal basis of such a right, in the absence of an attack on other shipping by the vessel sought to be detained, is lacking. In the present context it is significant that the International Law Commission, and the majority of states, do not accept the legality of security zones and therefore are unlikely to regard an ambulatory exercise of a right of (anticipatory) self-defence with any favour. In its comment on the draft article which later appeared as Article 22 of the Convention on the High Seas the Commission stated:[69]

The question arose whether the right to board a vessel should be recognized also in the event of a ship being suspected of committing acts hostile to the State to which the warship belongs, at a time of imminent danger to the security of that State. The Commission did not deem it advisable to include such a provision, mainly because of the vagueness of terms like 'imminent danger' and 'hostile acts', which leaves them open to abuse.

(vi) *Blockade and contraband.* In time of war the exercise of belligerent rights will be justified and may take the form of a blockade of the enemy's ports and coast. Enforcement of the blockade may take place on the high seas adjoining the coast, and neutral merchant ships may be confiscated if they attempt to break the blockade. The right of visit, search, and capture may be exercised against neutral ships carrying contraband or engaged in acts of unneutral service.[70]

(vii) *The right of hot pursuit; droit de poursuite.*[71] The law as understood in the nineteenth century, and its rationale, is expressed by Hall as follows.[72]

. . . when a vessel, or some one on board her, while within foreign territory commits an infraction of its laws she may be pursued into the open seas, and there arrested. It must be added that this can only be done when the pursuit is commenced while the vessel is still within the territorial waters or has only just escaped from them. The reason for the permission seems to be that pursuit under these circumstances is a continuation of an act of jurisdiction which has been begun, or which but for the accident of immediate escape would have been begun,

---

[68] See e.g. Colombos, pp. 314–15; Hall, *International Law*, p. 328. See also US. memo. in *Yrbk. ILC* (1950), ii. 61–2. Generally on the use of force under this title see Brownlie, *International Law and the Use of Force by States* (1963), 305–8.

[69] *Yrbk. ILC* (1956), ii. 284. See also the Secretariat Memo., *Yrbk. ILC* (1950), ii. 71; and the view of the Commission on security zones, *supra*, p. 194.

[70] For useful accounts see Colombos, chs. 17–20. See also 57 *BY* (1986), 583–4 (invoking Art. 51 of the UN Charter).

[71] Gidel, iii. 339–60; Colombos, pp. 168–75; McDougal and Burke, *The Public Order of the Oceans*, pp. 893–923; Glanville Williams, 20 *BY* (1939), 83–97; Beck, 9 *Can. BR* (1931), 176–202, 249–70, 341–65; Hackworth, ii. 700–9; Report by François, *Yrbk. ILC* (1950), ii. 43–5; Second Report by François, ibid. (1951), ii. 89–91; Bowett, *Self-Defence in International Law* (1958), 82–6; McNair, *Opinions*, i. 253–5; Whiteman, iv. 677–87 (1958); Rousseau, iv. 328–30; O'Connell, *The International Law of the Sea*, ii. 1075–93; Gilmore, 44 *ICLQ* (1995), 949–58. See also *United States v. Postal*, ILR 91, 509. While not the *ratio decidendi*, the question of hot pursuit was among the issues raised by the *I'm Alone* arbitration between the United States and Canada (1933–5); *RIAA* iii. 1609. For discussion of the case see Fitzmaurice, 17 *BY* (1936), 82–111.

[72] *International Law*, p. 309 (written in the first edn., 1880). The Canadian courts relied on Hall to a great extent in the *North* (1905), 11 Exch. Rep. 141; (1906), 37 SCR 385; 2 *AJ* (1908), 688.

within the territory itself, and that it is necessary to permit it in order to enable the territorial jurisdiction to be efficiently exercised.

The right of pursuit[73] is thus an act of necessity, institutionalized and delimited by state practice. In its present form it had appeared in Anglo-American practice in the first half of the nineteenth century, and it was not until the Hague Codification of 1930 that there was sufficient evidence of general recognition by states. Article 11 of the regulations adopted by the second committee of the Conference provided the basis for the draft article adopted by the International Law Commission,[74] which, with some amend-ment, became Article 23 of the Convention on the High Seas of 1958.

   Paragraph 1 of Article 23 provides:

The hot pursuit of a foreign ship may be undertaken when the competent authorities of the coastal State have good reason to believe that the ship has violated the laws and regulations of that State. Such pursuit must be commenced when the foreign ship or one of its boats[75] is within the internal waters or the territorial sea or the contiguous zone of the pursuing State,[76] and may only be continued outside the territorial sea or the contiguous zone if the pursuit has not been interrupted. It is not necessary that, at the time when the foreign ship within the territorial sea or the contiguous zone receives the order to stop, the ship giving the order should likewise be within the territorial sea or the contiguous zone.[77] If the foreign ship is within a contiguous zone, as defined in Article 24 of the Convention on the Territorial Sea and the Contiguous Zone[78] the pursuit may only be undertaken if there has been a violation of the rights for the protection of which the zone was established.[79]

The British position has been to oppose any right of pursuit commencing within a contiguous zone,[80] but some continental[81] and American[82] opinions have been otherwise. The draft articles produced by the International Law Commission[83] provided that, whilst pursuit may *commence* in the contiguous zone, acts committed in the contiguous zone cannot confer a right of pursuit. However, during the Conference on the Law of the Sea a proposal was accepted to insert the words 'or the contiguous zone' in

---

[73] For other legal contexts in which the right might appear see Glanville Williams, 20 *BY* (1939), 83–97.

[74] See *Yrbk. ILC* (1956), ii. 284–5.

[75] Note the restrictive effect of the words 'one of its boats' (see *Yrbk. ILC* (1956), ii. 285) and the different effect of para. 3. On the doctrine of 'constructive presence' see the *Araunah* (1888); Moore, *Arbitrations*, i. 824; McNair, *Opinions*, i. 245; the *Grace and Ruby* (1922), 283 Fed. 475; the *Henry L. Marshall* (1923), 292 Fed. 486; François, Second Report, *Yrbk. ILC* (1951), ii. 89; Masterson, *Jurisdiction in Marginal Seas* (1929), 308–21; McNair, *Opinions*, i. 245.

[76] Art. 111, para. 1, of the Law of the Sea Conv. of 1982 refers also to 'the archipelagic waters' of the pursuing state.

[77] Thus patrol vessels will often cruise just outside the territorial sea.

[78] See now Art. 33 of the Conv. of 1982.

[79] See also the Law of the Sea Conv. of 1982, Art. 111, para. 1.

[80] See Fitzmaurice, 8 *ICLQ* (1959), 115–17; *Yrbk. ILC* (1956), ii. 82.

[81] Gidel, iii. 348–9; François, Second Report, p. 90.

[82] Judicial interpretation of the Anglo-American Liquor Treaty, 1924, e.g. in the *Vinces* (1927), 20 Fed. (2d) 164, 174–5; US arguments in the *I'm Alone* case.

[83] *Yrbk. ILC* (1956), ii. 284–5.

four places in the draft article. Sir Gerald Fitzmaurice[84] has argued that the paragraph provides for pursuit from a contiguous zone only if there 'has been a violation', a phrase appearing in the final sentence; and thus the right of pursuit only applies in respect of outgoing ships as regards violations already committed by them in the coastal state's internal waters or territorial sea. With respect, this construction is at variance both with the text of the article as a whole and with the *travaux préparatoires*.[85] Pursuit and arrest may relate to acts committed within the contiguous zone.

Paragraph 2 of the article is uncontroversial: 'The right of hot pursuit ceases as soon as the ship pursued enters the territorial sea of its own country or of a third state'.[86] Paragraph 3 states the conditions on which pursuit may commence:[87]

Hot pursuit is not deemed to have begun unless the pursuing ship has satisfied itself by such practicable means as may be available that the ship pursued or one of its boats or other craft working as a team and using the ship pursued as a mother ship are within the limits of the territorial sea, or as the case may be within the contiguous zone. The pursuit may only be commenced after a visual or auditory signal to stop has been given at a distance which enables it to be seen or heard by the foreign ship.

Paragraph 4 stipulates that pursuit must be undertaken by warships, military aircraft,[88] 'or other ships or aircraft on government service specially authorized to that effect'.[89] (See also Art. 111, para. 5, of the Convention of 1982.)

Paragraph 7 provides for compensation for 'any loss or damage' consequent on unjustified exercise of the right of pursuit. The criterion here is presumably the existence of reasonable ground for suspicion, since paragraph 1 refers to 'good reason' for belief that a violation of the laws of the coastal state has occurred, and the text of paragraph 7 differs significantly from the form of Article 22, paragraph 3.[90] (See also Art. 111, para. 8, of the Convention of 1982.)

The Law of the Sea Convention of 1982 provides that the right of hot pursuit shall apply to violations of laws of the coastal state relating to and occurring in the exclusive economic zone and on the continental shelf (Art. 111, para. 2).

(viii) *Ships without a flag.* Ships flying no flag, and refusing to show a flag when called upon to do so in a proper manner, may be boarded by the ships of any state.

---

[84] 31 *BY* (1954), 380; and in 8 *ICLQ* (1959), 116.

[85] See McDougal and Burke, *The Public Order of the Oceans*, pp. 906–8, 910–13.

[86] See Colombos, p. 171; and the American–Chilean Claims Commission in the *Itata*, Moore, *Arbitrations*, iii. 3067. See also Art. 111, para. 3, of the Convention of 1982.

[87] Cf. Glanville Williams, 20 *BY* (1939), 96 n. 5; François, Second Report, *ubi supra*. See also Art. 111, para. 4. of the Conv. of 1982.

[88] In this respect the Conv. developed the law. See also para. 5 of Art. 23.

[89] The latter category comprehends customs and police vessels. The ship finally arresting need not necessarily be the same as the one which began the pursuit, but must not be a mere interceptor. Cf. the facts of the *I'm Alone* case. The validity of an arrest is not affected by the fact that the ship arrested was escorted across a portion of the high seas (para. 6).

[90] Cf. the provision on visit on the high seas, *supra*, p. 249; and see Glanville Williams, 20 *BY* (1939), 96 n. 2, and Colombos, p. 168. Para. 7 is, however, not unequivocal.

(b) Restrictions by treaty[91]

Treaties conferring powers of visit and capture above and beyond those permitted to states by the customary law relate to a variety of subject-matter. Great Britain was a party to numerous bilateral treaties after 1815 concerning repression of the slave-trade, and on 20 December 1841 the Treaty of London, to which five states became parties,[92] was concluded. This provided that warships with special warrants could search, detain, or send in for trial suspected merchant ships flying the flags of contracting states. The General Act for the Repression of the Slave Trade, signed at Brussels on 2 July 1890, provided for a limited right of search of suspected vessels in a defined zone.[93] The General Act was in major part abrogated as between parties to the Treaty of St Germain, and the Slavery Conventions of 1926 and 1956 do not provide for visit, search, and seizure: a right of visit is provided for, however, in Article 23 of the Convention on the High Seas of 1958 and Article 110 of the Convention of 1982. Mutual powers of visit and search are conferred by bilateral treaties the parties to which are concerned to conserve fish stocks, to control smuggling, or to repress certain aspects of the trade in arms. Modern fishery conservation agreements are exemplified by the United States–Canada Convention for the Preservation of the Halibut Fishery of the Northern Pacific Ocean and the Bering Sea (1953),[94] the Treaty Concerning Pacific Salmon (1986),[95] and the Convention on the Conduct of Fishing Operations in the North Atlantic (1967).[96] Of particular significance is the Straddling Stocks Agreement (1995), which has the purpose of creating a regime for the conservation and management of straddling fish stocks and highly migratory fish stocks.[97] In the case of stocks which are available both in the areas of coastal state jurisdiction and in the high seas, the regime of conservation is problematical and there are conflicts of interest between the coastal states and the distant water fishing nations.

The important multilateral Convention for the Protection of Submarine Cables of 1884, in Article 10, confers the right to stop and verify the nationality of merchant ships suspected of breaking the treaty on warships of the signatories.[98] The relevant provisions of the Convention on the High Seas of 1958 (Arts. 26 to 29) do not refer

---

[91] It will be noticed that questions to which the Conv. on the High Seas of 1958 or the Law of the Sea Conv. of 1982 relate have been considered already since for the most part the provisions are closely related to general international law.

[92] Austria, Great Britain, Prussia, and Russia. Belgium acceded. France signed but did not ratify.

[93] UN Legis. Series, *The High Seas*, i. 269.

[94] A Protocol of Amendment was signed on 29 Mar. 1979: *Digest of US Practice* (1979), 1034–9.

[95] *Digest of US Practice* (1981–88), 333, 1928.

[96] Text: 6 *ILM* 760.

[97] Text: 34 *ILM* 1542. See Burke, *The New International Law of Fisheries* (1994), 82–150; Davies and Redgwell, 67 *BY* (1996), 199–274; Anderson, 45 *ICLQ* (1996), 463–75.

[98] The parties numbered 26, including Great Britain. Text: UN Legis. Series, *The High Seas*, i. 251. See also McDougal and Burke, *The Public Order of the Oceans*, p. 843; Franklin, US Naval War College liii; *The Law of the Sea: Some Recent Developments*, pp. 157–78; Whiteman, iv. 727–39.

to such a right, but the Convention[99] is not intended to supersede the Convention of 1884 automatically (see, likewise, the Convention of 1982, Art. 311, para. 2). States have also been willing to provide for the mutual exercise of the right of hot pursuit in treaties.

5. JURISDICTION OVER SHIPS ON THE HIGH SEAS

The Convention on the High Seas of 1958 and the Law of the Sea Convention of 1982 affirm the general principle enunciated by the Permanent Court in the *Lotus* case:[100] 'Vessels on the high seas are subject to no authority except that of the State whose flag they fly. In virtue of the principle of the freedom of the seas, that is to say, the absence of any territorial sovereignty upon the high seas, no State may exercise any kind of jurisdiction over foreign vessels upon them'. Thus Article 6, paragraph 1, of the Convention of 1958 (and see also Art. 92, para. 1, of the Convention of 1982) provides that 'Ships shall sail under the flag of one State only and, save in exceptional cases expressly provided for in international treaties or in these articles, shall be subject to its exclusive jurisdiction on the high seas'. The exceptions in the Conventions, dealt with earlier, are piracy, the slave-trade, hot pursuit, and the right of approach by warships where reasonable grounds exist for suspecting that a ship is of the same nationality as the warship.[101]

Article 11, paragraph 1, of the Convention of 1958 (and see also Art. 97, para. 1, of the Convention of 1982) provides:[102] 'In the event of a collision or of any other incident of navigation[103] concerning a ship on the high seas, involving the penal or disciplinary responsibility of the master or of any other person in the service of the ship, no penal or disciplinary proceedings may be instituted against such persons except before the judicial or administrative authorities either of the flag State or[104] of the State of which such person is a national'. This provision negatives the decision of the Permanent Court in the *Lotus*[105] case and reflects the view of the International Law Commission.[106] In its

---

[99] Art. 30 provides: 'The provisions of this Convention shall not affect Conventions or other international agreements already in force, as between States Parties to them'.

[100] (1927), PCIJ, Ser. A, no. 10, p. 25.

[101] *Supra*, p. 228.

[102] See also para. 3: 'No arrest or detention of this ship, even as a measure of investigation, shall be ordered by any authorities other than those of the flag State' (and see also Art. 97, para. 3, of the Conv. of 1982).

[103] e.g. damage to a submarine telegraph, telephone, or high voltage cable or pipeline.

[104] Thus states issuing certificates of competence and the like may wish to consider the conduct of the holders serving on board foreign vessels: hence the reference also to 'disciplinary proceedings'.

[105] Considered also *infra*, p. 300.

[106] *Yrbk. ILC* (1956), ii. 281. See also François, ibid. (1950), ii. 38, 39–40; Secretariat Memo., ibid. 74–5; François, ibid. (1951), ii. 77–80; ibid. (1952), ii. 45–6; ibid. (1953), ii. 51–3; ibid. (1954), ii. 13; Gidel, i. 281; Whiteman, ix. 58–62; Brierly, 44 *LQR* (1928), 154–63; McNair, *Opinions*, ii. 180–85; Fischer Williams, *Chapters on Current International Law and the League of Nations* (1929), 209–31 (and in 35 *RGDIP* (1928), 361–76); Verzijl, 55 *RDILC* (1928), 1–32; Rousseau, iv. 325–7.

commentary on the relevant draft article, the Commission commented on the *Lotus* case as follows:

This judgement, which was carried by the President's casting vote after an equal vote of six to six, was very strongly criticized and caused serious disquiet in international maritime circles. A diplomatic conference held at Brussels in 1952 disagreed with the conclusions of the judgement. The Commission concurred with the decisions of the conference, which were embodied in the International Convention for the Unification of Certain Rules relating to Penal Jurisdiction in matters of Collisions and Other Incidents of Navigation... [107] It did so with the object of protecting ships and their crews from the risk of penal proceedings before foreign courts in the event of collision on the high seas, since such proceedings may constitute an intolerable interference with international navigation.

6. OIL POLLUTION CASUALTIES, 'PIRATE' RADIO AND TERRORISM

States may claim special zones of jurisdiction over areas of high seas adjacent to their coasts in order to regulate activities of various kinds: the contiguous zone and certain other types of jurisdiction have been examined elsewhere.[108] Recently, a number of incidents have raised new problems relating to control of sources of harm to the coastal states, and perhaps states generally, which are sited beyond the territorial sea or any existing contiguous zone. Major accidents involving large tankers may release huge quantities of oil. The *Torrey Canyon*, registered in Liberia, ran aground on a reef off the Cornish coast in 1967 and lost some 60,000 tons of oil. The British Government ordered that the wreck be bombed, after salvage attempts had failed, in order to reduce the pollution. Even so, British and French coasts received serious pollution. This type of incident raises a variety of interesting legal issues.[109] Remedial action may be justified on the ground of necessity (but not of self-defence). The optional regime of the exclusive economic zone has removed the need for anti-pollution zones as such.[110] Agreement on the use of remedial measures against ships of other nations on the high seas is obviously desirable and events led to the signing in Brussels in 1969 of an International Convention Relating to Intervention on the High Seas in Cases of Oil Pollution Casualties.[111] The use of protective measures is now recognized by Article 221, paragraph 1, of the Law of the Sea Convention of 1982, which reserves the right

---

[107] Signed at Brussels 10 May 1952; Cmd. 8954.

[108] *Supra*, pp. 192ff.

[109] See Brown, 21 *Curr. Leg. Problems* (1968), 113–36; Queneudec, *Ann. français* (1968), 701–18; Caflisch, 8 *Revue belge* (1972), 7–33; O'Connell, *The International Law of the Sea*, ii. 997–1012; Churchill and Lowe, *The Law of the Sea* (3rd edn., 1999), 328–96.

[110] *Supra*, p. 213.

[111] Text: 64 *AJ* (1970), 471; 9 *ILM* (1970), 25.

of states 'to take and enforce measures beyond the territorial sea proportionate to the actual or threatened damage to protect their coast line or related interests, including fishing, from pollution or threat of pollution following upon a maritime casualty[112] or acts relating to such a casualty, which may reasonably be expected to result in major harmful consequences'. The discharge of oil into the sea by ships is regulated by conventions and, in particular the Law of the Sea Convention of 1982 contains an elaboration of the duties of states in respect of the protection and conservation of the marine environment (Arts. 192–237).[113]

The use of ships, aircraft, or installations fixed on a continental shelf, outside the territorial sea of any state, for broadcasting unregulated by any national legal system, has increased of late. This is regarded as a threat to national interests by states at whose population the broadcasts are aimed and may cause interference with licensed broadcasts and frequencies used for distress calls. Moreover, international regulation of telecommunications and allocation of radio frequencies depends upon the capacity of states to regulate these matters through their legal systems.[114] The Netherlands has based certain claims to control pirate radio upon the protective principle of jurisdiction.[115] The United Kingdom has preferred to take measures carefully restricted to the exercise of territorial jurisdiction.[116] The Council of Europe sponsored the conclusion in 1965 of an Agreement for the Prevention of Broadcasts Transmitted from Stations outside National Territories.[117] This provides for the use, in effective co-ordination, of criminal sanctions in national legal systems, aimed both at nationals and aliens. The provisions of the Convention are concerned to punish acts supporting 'pirate' broadcasting which are committed *within* the national jurisdiction of the states which are parties and do not warrant external interference with foreign ships, aircraft, or nationals. The Law of the Sea Convention of 1982 provides for broad bases of jurisdiction and powers of arrest in respect of 'the transmission of sound radio or television broadcasts from a ship or installation on the high seas intended for reception by the general public contrary to international regulations, but excluding the transmission of distress calls' (Arts. 109 and 110).

---

[112] Para. 2 provides: 'For the purposes of this article "maritime casualty" means a collision of vessels, stranding or other incident of navigation, or other occurrence on board a vessel or external to it resulting in material damage or imminent threat of material damage to a vessel or cargo'.

[113] Int. Conv. for the Prevention of Pollution of the Sea by Oil, 1954; 327 *UNTS*, p. 3; amended, 1962, *Treaty Series* no. 59 (1967), Cmnd. 3354; Agreement for Co-operation in Dealing with Pollution of the North Sea by Oil, 1969; *Treaty Series* no. 78 (1969), Cmnd. 4205; Int. Conv. for the Prevention of Pollution from Ships, 1973, 12 *ILM* (1973), 1319.

[114] Generally on 'pirate' radio see: Evensen, 115 Hague *Recueil* (1965, II), 563–78; Bowett, *The Law of the Sea* (1967), 52–5; van Panhuys and van Emde Boas, 60 *AF* (1966), 303–41; Hunnings, 14 *ICLQ* (1965), 410–36; François, 12 *Neths. Int. LR* (1965), 113–23; Bos, ibid. 337–64; Woodliffe, ibid. 365–84; Sørensen, in *Festschrift Castberg* (1963), 319–31; Whiteman, ix. 789–809; O'Connell, *The International Law of the Sea*, ii. 814–19.

[115] See further *infra*, p. 302.

[116] See the Marine Broadcasting (Offences) Act 1967.

[117] 4 *ILM* (1965), 115.

The suppression of terrorist activities against ships and the persons on board is the object of the Convention for the Suppression of Unlawful Acts against the Safety of Maritime Navigation adopted on 10 March 1988 at a diplomatic conference convened by I.M.O.[118]

7. THE SEABED AND OCEAN FLOOR BEYOND THE LIMITS OF NATIONAL JURISDICTION

(a) The pre-existing seabed regime[119]

The legal status of the high seas beyond the outer limit of the territorial sea has been considered earlier in the present chapter. In principle the seabed of the high seas is not susceptible of appropriation by states, and the regime of the freedom of the high seas applies (see the High Seas Convention of 1958, Art. 2; and the Law of the Sea Convention, 1982, Art. 89). However, historic title and prescription may play a role, and title to certain seabed (sedentary) fisheries (for example, pearl, oyster, and sponge fisheries) has been obtained on the basis of prescription.[120] Title to sedentary fisheries probably involves the exclusive right to take the harvest rather than a right to the seabed as such.[121]

To a great extent the legal category of sedentary fisheries in its traditional form has been made redundant as a consequence of the doctrines of the continental shelf, the fishery conservation zone (up to a limit of 200 miles), and the exclusive economic zone. However, sedentary fisheries remain as a separate issue in two situations: (1) where certain historic rights are maintained in a shelf area appurtenant to another state; and (2) where historic rights to sedentary fisheries of a coastal state (on its own shelf) are greater in extent than the rights granted by the legal regime of the continental shelf.[122]

(b) The convention of 1982 and the international sea-bed authority[123]

During the 1960s it was asserted that exploitation of the mineral resources of the deep seabed and ocean floor was technically possible in areas not included in the regime of

---

[118] Text: 27 *ILM* (1988), 668. See Ronzitti (ed.), *Maritime Terrorism and International Law* (1990).

[119] See Gidel, i. 493–501; Hackworth, ii. 672–9; Verzijl, *International Law in Historical Perspective*, iv. 277–84; O'Connell, 49 *AJ* (1955), 185–209; id., *The International Law of the Sea*, i (1982), 449–57; François, *Yrbk. ILC* (1951), ii. 94–9.

[120] *Supra*, p. 146.

[121] See McNair, *Opinions*, i. 258–64.

[122] See Young, 55 *AJ* (1961), 359–73; Goldie, 63 *AJ* (1969), 86–97; Papandréou, 11 *Revue hellénique de droit international* (1958), 1–158; O'Connell, *The International Law of the Sea*, i. 450–6.

[123] Anand, *Legal Regime of the Seabed and the Developing Countries* (1976); Bennouna, 84 *RGDIP* (1980), 120–43; Kronmiller, *The Lawfulness of Deep Seabed Mining*, 3 vols. (1980–1); Paolillo, 188 Hague *Recueil* (1984, IV), 135–337; Dupuy and Vignes (eds.) *Traité du nouveau droit de la mer* (1985), 499–686; Brown, *Sea-Bed Energy and Mineral Resources and the Law of the Sea*, vols. ii and iii (1986); Joyner, 35 *ICLQ*

the continental shelf, and proposals were made which would have permitted either the partition of the ocean floor between coastal states or the development of mining operations by individual enterprises. The prize in view took the form of the vast deposits of polymetallic nodules, principally in the Pacific and Indian Oceans, containing manganese, nickel, copper, and cobalt. On 1 November 1967, Dr Arvid Pardo, the representative of Malta, presented a proposal to the First Committee of the UN General Assembly, to the effect that the seabed and its resources beyond the limits of national jurisdiction should be declared to be part of the 'common heritage of mankind'.

This proposal subsequently became a part of the agenda of the Third United Nations Conference on the Law of the Sea (1973–82). The Law of the Sea Convention, which entered into force on 16 November 1994 and has not less than one hundred and twenty-two parties, contains a radical regime of the internationalization of the mineral resources of the deep seabed. These 'resources' (Art. 133 of the Convention) and the 'Area' (defined in Art. 1 as 'the sea-bed and ocean floor and subsoil thereof, beyond the limits of national jurisdiction') are declared to be 'the common heritage of mankind' (Art. 136).

It must be emphasized that this regime applies to the areas beyond the 200-mile limit applicable to the exclusive economic zone, and overlaps those areas of continental shelf which extend beyond the 200-mile limit (see Arts. 82 and 134 of the Convention).[124] In general the treaty regime for the mineral resources of the Area co exists *mutatis mutandis* with the legal regime of the high seas reviewed earlier in the present chapter. Thus Article 135 provides that the treaty regime does not affect the legal status of the waters superjacent to the Area or that of the airspace above those waters.[125]

The institutional underpinning of the regime relating to the resources of the Area consists of the International Sea-Bed Authority, of which all states parties are *ipso facto* members (Art. 156), which is empowered to organize and control activities in the Area (Art. 157). The Authority has as its 'principal organs' an Assembly, a Council, and a Secretariat (Art. 158).

The regime for the development of the resources of the Area has six key elements:

1. No state shall claim sovereignty or sovereign rights over any part of the Area or its resources and no State or natural or juridical person shall appropriate any part thereof (Art. 137, para. 1).

2. Activities in the Area shall be organized and controlled exclusively by the International Sea-Bed Authority, and shall be carried out for the benefit of mankind as a whole (Arts. 137 (para. 2), 140, 150(i), 153 (para. 1), 156 and 157).[126]

(1986), 190–9; Churchill and Lowe, *The Law of the Sea* (3rd edn., 1999), 223–54; Kirsch and Fraser, 26 *Canad. Yrbk.* (1988), 119–53; Zegers, 31 *German Yrbk.* (1988), 107–19.

[124] See also Art. 142 of the Conv. (deposits which lie across limits of national jurisdiction).

[125] Several provisions of this Part of the Conv. are concerned with the protection of other activities in the marine environment: see Arts. 138, 142, 143, 145, and 147.

[126] See also Art. 149:
Archaeological and historical objects

3. The system of public order, based upon state responsibility, appears in Article 139, paragraph 1, which provides:

States Parties shall have the responsibility to ensure that activities in the Area, whether carried out by States Parties, or state enterprises or natural or juridical persons which possess the nationality of States Parties or are effectively controlled by them or their nationals, shall be carried out in conformity with this Part. The same responsibility applies to international organizations for activities in the Area carried out by such organizations.[127]

4. The system of exploration and exploitation involves parallel activities by the Enterprise (an organ of the Authority), and by operators, in accordance with Article 153, which provides (in material part):

2. Activities in the Area shall be carried out as prescribed in paragraph 3:
(a) by the Enterprise, and
(b) in association with the Authority by States Parties, or state enterprises or natural or juridical persons which possess the nationality of States Parties or are effectively controlled by them or their nationals, when sponsored by such States, or any group of the foregoing which meets the requirements provided in this Part and in Annex III.

3. Activities in the Area shall be carried out in accordance with a formal written plan of work drawn up in accordance with Annex III and approved by the Council after review by the Legal and Technical Commission. In the case of activities in the Area carried out as authorised by the Authority by the entities specified in paragraph 2(b), the plan of work shall, in accordance with Annex III, Article 3, be in the form of a contract. Such contracts may provide for joint arrangements in accordance with Annex III, Article 11.

5. The Authority shall provide for the equitable sharing of the economic benefits derived from the activities in the Area (Art. 140, para. 2; Art. 160, para. 2(f)(i)).

6. In the exercise of its powers and functions the Authority may show special consideration for the interests of developing states: see Articles 140 (para. 1), Article 144 (para. 1), 148, 150, 152 (para. 2), 160 (para. 2(f)(i)).[128]

In 1994 the United Nations General Assembly adopted the Agreement relating to the Implementation of Part XI of the United Nations Convention on the Law of the Sea of 1982.[129] The Agreement and the Convention are to be interpreted and applied together

---

'All objects of an archaeological and historical nature found in the Area shall be preserved or disposed of for the benefit of mankind as a whole, particular regard being paid to the preferential rights of the State or country of origin, or the State of cultural origin, or the State of historical and archaeological origin'.

[127] See also Art. 153, para. 4.

[128] Reference is also made to the 'special need' of the land-locked and geographically disadvantaged states among the developing states: see Arts. 148, 152 (para. 2), 160 (para. 2(k)).

[129] Text: 33 *ILM* 1309; UN Doc. A/RES/48/263, 17 August 1994.

'as a single instrument' (Article 2). The Agreement modifies certain aspects of Part XI in order to meet objections raised by the United States.[130]

(c) Is the regime of the international sea-bed authority binding upon non-parties?

The status of the Area (subject to the International Sea-Bed Authority within the provisions of the Law of the Sea Convention of 1982) as against states which do not intend to become parties to the Convention is a vexed question.[131] For states who have signed the Convention, the rule is that an obligation of good faith arises to refrain from acts calculated to frustrate the objects of the treaty.[132] The position for non-parties is controversial. The opinion of the United States and certain other developed states is, quite simply, that the ordinary regime of the freedom of the seas is applicable to the resources of the deep seabed.[133] This approach is opposed by the large majority of non-aligned states in the General Assembly represented by the Group of 77. This body of opinion takes the view that the seabed beyond the limits of national jurisdiction is a part of the common heritage of mankind and consequently not subject to unilateral exploitation.[134] The Group of 77 has stated that the Declaration of Principles adopted by the General Assembly in 1970,[135] and other evidence, justifies the view that their position represents the present state of customary international law. The text of the Declaration of Principles of 1970 has a somewhat programmatic character, and it is generally recognized that resolutions of the General Assembly do not as such create binding rules.[136] However, 'Western' writers tend to ignore the fact that such resolutions may provide vehicles for the generation of state practice and, in the present context, that is precisely what has happened.[137] However, the dissident states, such as the United States, might be said to have the status of persistent objectors, having opposed

---

[130] See Nash, 88 *AJ* (1994), 733–8. See also Oxman, ibid., 687–95, Sohn, ibid., 696–705, and Charney, ibid., 705–14.

[131] See Jiménez de Aréchaga, 159 Hague *Recueil* (1978, I), 222–30; Conforti, 4 *Ital. Yrbk.* (1978–9), 3–19; Bennouna, 84 *RGDIP* (1980), 120–43; also in Bardonnet and Virally (eds.), *Le Nouveau Droit international de la mer*, pp. 117–39; Brown, *Sea-Bed Energy and Mineral Resources and the Law of the Sea*, ii, 2; Kronmiller, *The Lawfulness of Deep Seabed Mining*, i. 207–521; Jennings, *Mélanges offerts à Paul Reuter* (1981), 347–55.

[132] Vienna Conv. on the Law of Treaties, Art. 18.

[133] *Digest of US Practice* (1973), 263–7; ibid. (1974), 339–43; ibid. (1978), 1017–27.

[134] See the letter dated 24 Apr. 1979 from the Chairman of the Group of 77; *UNCLOS III, Off. Recs.*, xi. 80; letter dated 29 Aug. 1980 from the Chairman, ibid. xiv. 111. See also the statement of Mr Nandan, 15 Sept. 1978; ibid. ix. 103–4.

[135] Resol. 2749 (XXV), 17 Dec. 1970; Brownlie, *Documents*, p. 92 (108 in favour; none against; 14 abstentions). See also the 'Moratorium' resolution, GA Resol. 2574 (XXIV), 15 Dec. 1969; Lay, Churchill, and Nordquist, *New Directions in the Law of the Sea*, 6 vols. (1973–81), ii. 737 (62 in favour; 28 against; 28 abstentions).

[136] See Skubiszewski, *Annales d'études internationales* (1973), 237–48; Jennings, 20 *ICLQ* (1971), 438–40; Monnier, in *Festschrift für Rudolf Bindschedler* (1980), 129–44; Churchill and Lowe, *The Law of the Sea*, pp. 178–81.

[137] See Jiménez de Aréchaga, 159 Hague *Recueil* (1978, I), 32–3, 229–30; Bennouna, 84 *RGDIP* (1980), 132–3; and also in Bardonnet and Virally, *Le Nouveau Droit international de la mer*, pp. 127–31; Churchill and Lowe, *The Law of the Sea* (3rd edn., 1999), 226–8.

the new customary rule while it was in the process of formation; but to claim this status would involve conceding the existence of the new rule.

(d) The practical accommodation of competing claims

The United States adopted legislation permitting and regulating seabed mining in 1980, and other states have done the same. Those states (France, the German Federal Republic, the United Kingdom, and the United States) which originally expected to stay outside the regime created by the Law of the Sea Convention created a 'Reciprocating States Regime' involving mutual recognition of authorizations granted for deep seabed operations.[138] Alongside these developments the Preparatory Commission (Prep. Com.) established by the Final Act of the Third United Nations Conference on the Law of the Sea (Resolution I) has undertaken the recognition of the so-called 'pioneer investors' and the processing and registration of applications by states as pioneer investors or on behalf of other pioneer investors (Resolution II).[139] Registrations have been effected of sites for India, France, Japan, and the former USSR.

The recent tendency has been to promote arrangements to prevent overlapping claims as between states within the Convention regime and others: see the Agreement on the Resolution of Practical Problems with Respect to Deep Seabed Mining Areas dated 14 August 1987.[140] This, with the related Exchanges of Notes, involved a group of states which form part of the Preparatory Commission of the 1982 Convention (Belgium, Canada, Italy, Netherlands, USSR) and a group of non-signatories (the German Federal Republic, the United Kingdom, and the United States). Such arrangements do not, however, preclude issues of principle, and the Preparatory Commission for the International Seabed Authority has declared that:

Any claim, agreement or action regarding the Area and its resources undertaken outside the Preparatory Commission which is incompatible with the United Nations Convention on the Law of the Sea and its related resolutions shall not be recognised.[141]

In 2000 the International Seabed Authority adopted the Regulation on Prospecting and Exploration for Polymetallic Nodules in the Area. This, known as the Mining Code, enabled the Authority in 2001 to enter into a series of 15 year contracts for the exploration of polymetallic nodules. In this way the regime of Resolution II (above) came to an end.[142]

---

[138] Agreement Concerning Interim Arrangements Relating to Polymetallic Nodules of the Deep Sea Bed, signed on 2 Sept. 1982; 21 *ILM* (1982), 950; and see also the Provisional Understanding Regarding Deep Seabed Matters, in force, 2 Sept. 1984; 23 *ILM* (1984), 1354.

[139] See the interpretative statements by the Commission on the resolution of competing claims among pioneer investors: 25 *ILM* (1986), 1329; 26 *ILM* (1987), 1725. See generally the *Law of the Sea Bulletin* (UN Office for Ocean Affairs and the Law of the Sea).

[140] Text: 26 *ILM* (1987), 1502; *Law of the Sea Bulletin*, no. 11 (July 1988), 28–45.

[141] Decl. adopted on 30 Aug. 1985; *Law of the Sea Bulletin*, no. 6 (Oct. 1985), 85.

[142] See Oude Elferink and Rothwell, *Oceans Management*, 2004, 341–5.

PART V

COMMON AMENITIES AND CO-OPERATION IN THE USE OF RESOURCES

12

COMMON AMENITIES AND CO-OPERATION IN THE USE OF RESOURCES

1. INTRODUCTION

International law has tended so far to ape the individualistic manners of municipal law. Apart from the concepts of *res communis*[1] as applied to the high seas and outer space, and 'the common heritage of mankind',[2] international law depends to a great extent on 'voluntarist' devices, in the form of concessions by private law methods, treaties, and various types of international agencies and organizations, in order to provide access to resources outside national territory. Indeed, the use of 'voluntarist' devices in the political conditions of the past has led to a situation where the law, as applied by some states, had prevented a weak or ex-colonial state from having a reasonable level of command over its own resources and general economy: however, issues concerning vested rights[3] and expropriation[4] are considered elsewhere. Apart from these questions of economic self-determination, the subject as a whole is concerned with machinery and organization and also the influence of technical considerations to a degree uncommon in other areas of the law. Co-operation may take the form of internationalization of a territory, a qualitative change in its status, but this type of regime is more often employed to provide a solution to territorial problems creating political disputes and to maintain local conditions conducive to the maintenance of peace and security. In the subjects now to be considered customary international law plays a role, and at times a dynamic role, but caution may be needed to avoid giving normative effect to rules which merely reflect local or temporary factors. It must also be observed that the agenda must tend to grow with changes in technology, and lawyers are already concerned with activities which radically affect the environment of the earth, such as weapon testing and experiments in weather control.[5]

---

[1] *Supra*, p. 169.
[2] On the International Sea-Bed Area, see *supra*, pp. 241–6.
[3] *Infra*, pp. 651–2.
[4] *Infra*, pp. 531ff.
[5] See the *Draft Rules Concerning Changes in the Environment of the Earth*, David Davies Memorial Institute of International Studies (London, 1964); Stockholm Conference, Decl. on the Human Environment, 16 June 1972; 11 *ILM* (1972), 1416.

2. ECONOMIC AID

Though some distance from a genuine sharing of world resources, both of material wealth and of skill and knowledge, the provision of economic aid and technical assistance to underdeveloped areas is an object of the first importance in creating conditions of justice and stable foundations for peace. The United Nations Charter, in Chapters 9 and 10, recognizes the urgent need to deal with economic and social problems, and certain of its provisions create obligations for governments to maintain human rights. There is probably also a collective duty of member states to take responsible action to create reasonable living standards both for their own peoples and for those of other states.[6] The means by which economic aid may be provided are varied and include loans by governments, construction or technical assistance projects with no provision for payment or collateral advantages, loans by specialized agencies of the United Nations, and loans from, and aid projects supported by, private corporations with or without government sponsorship and support, for example by the requirement of guarantees from the recipient state on the international plane. These various forms of aid give rise to issues of private and public international law, although governments and corporations adopt devices to prevent issues arising from loans and concessions going before the national jurisdiction of the recipient or 'host' state.[7]

The objectives of aid must be lawful, and aid agreements may be affected by the *jus cogens*[8] and thus, for example, should not be intended to further preparation for unlawful resort to force. Nor should aid be given under conditions which lead to infringement of the principles of the sovereign equality of states and of permanent sovereignty over natural resources.[9] In 1964 the United Nations Conference on Trade and Development recommended certain principles to be observed in the giving of aid.[10]

A high proportion of aid is given on the basis of bilateral agreements, and so it is subject to conditions imposed by the giving states, while its incidence is governed by political factors. Some technical assistance programmes are sponsored by the United Nations directly by means of the United Nations technical assistance programme. The Special United Nations Fund for Economic Development and the Expanded Programme of Technical Assistance were merged in 1965 as the United Nations Development Programme.[11] Matters of study, planning, and expert advice on co-ordination of policies of states are within the sphere of the four United Nations

---

[6] See Resol. 1316 (XIII) of the UN General Assembly, 12 Dec. 1958, which refers to Art. 56 of the Charter; and Resol. 2158 (XXI) on Permanent Sovereignty over Natural Resources, 25 Nov. 1966; 6 *ILM* (1967), 147; Charter of Economic Rights and Duties of States, Resol. 3281 (XXIX), 12 Dec. 1974; Brownlie, *Documents*, p. 180; Art. 17, UNGA, Decl. on the Right to Development, Resol. 41/128, 4 Dec. 1986, Arts. 3, 4, and 10.

[7] See Sereni, 96 Hague *Recueil* (1959, I), 133–237.

[8] See *infra*, pp. 510–12.

[9] *Infra*, pp. 289ff., 539.

[10] *UN Monthly Chronicle* (July 1964), 49.

[11] *Yrbk. of the UN* (1965), 283–300.

Economic Commissions for Europe, Asia and the Far East, Latin America, and Africa. Apart from these sources the International Bank for Reconstruction and Development and its affiliates[12] provide very large sums for development projects. The Bank has the primary purpose of assisting in the reconstruction and development of its member countries by facilitating the investment of capital for productive purposes. The Bank is a specialized agency of the United Nations, but has more autonomy than other such agencies. In its long-term loan operations, it is confined to promotion of private enterprise, and there is discrimination in favour of governments willing to pursue *laissez-faire* policies. Moreover, all members of the Bank must be members of the International Monetary Fund and comply with its policy.

In 1964 the United Nations Conference on Trade and Development (UNCTAD) was established as a subsidiary organ of the General Assembly of the United Nations. In 1966 the United Nations Capital Development Fund was brought into operation also as a subsidiary organ of the General Assembly.[13] A further, associated, step was the establishment in 1966 of the United Nations Industrial Development Organization (UNIDO).[14]

3. ACCESS TO RESOURCES: THE PEACEFUL USES OF ATOMIC ENERGY

By analogy with the legal duty which may exist to provide economic aid to underdeveloped countries, it is possible to suggest that there is a general duty to provide access to resources under reasonable conditions binding all states. However, it is not easy to describe the precise incidents of such a duty in respect of resources governed by a regime of territorial sovereignty, and the real issues relate to forms of organization between states rather than general legal principles. Because of its importance, the relation to questions of security and disarmament, and the immense cost of development, the utilization of atomic energy for peaceful purposes has been a fruitful field for co-operation between states and between organizations and states. The most important organization, the International Atomic Energy Agency, was established in 1957[15] and has a relationship agreement with the United Nations. The Agency provides assistance of various kinds for the development of atomic energy in particular states under a system of inspection and control to ensure, *inter alia*, that the aid is not used for military purposes. Other organizations and agencies existing include the European Atomic Energy Agency (Euratom),[16] the European Nuclear Agency of the Organization for

---

[12] The International Development Association and the International Finance Corporation. Regional institutions include the Inter-American, Asian, and African Development Banks.

[13] *Yrbk. of the UN* (1966), 285–91.

[14] *Yrbk. of the UN* (1965), 338–47; (1966), 297–301.

[15] Text of Statute: 51 *AJ* (1957), 466.

[16] In existence 1 Jan. 1958; text of treaty: UNTS, vols. 294–8; 51 *AJ* (1957), 955.

Economic Co-operation and Development (OECD)[17] and the European Organization for Nuclear Research.[18]

4. CONSERVATION OF THE LIVING RESOURCES OF THE HIGH SEAS

The high seas, having the character of *res communis*, are open to the use and enjoyment of all states on an equal basis.[19] This principle of freedom, applied to fishing, has threatened to cause depletion of certain fish stocks and so to destroy the content of the right to fish by unregulated exploitation. States, by means of extension of their territorial sea, the creation of contiguous zones for fisheries purposes, and the exercise of rights over the resources of the continental shelf, have been successful in extending their legal powers not only to fish but to regulate fishing in given areas. *Ad hoc*, somewhat anomalous, claims to fishery conservation zones as such on the high seas have been made, notably in a proclamation by the United States President in 1945.[20] Whatever the justification for extended claims to take fish exclusively, unilateral claims to take conservation measures involving abstention by other states have been resisted;[21] in other words, the reference to conservation as a reason for unilateral assertion of rights to control fish stocks makes no legal difference.

Clearly treaty arrangements may provide a reasonably stable conservation regime involving also a negotiated distribution of marine resources. The object of a treaty will often be the maintenance of the maximum sustainable yield of the fish stock combined with principles of equal access and equal limitations on fishing. Conservation thus appears in conjunction with allocation of resources. Another relevant factor is a dislike of the principle of 'free competition' by states unable to compete on the same basis and which, as underdeveloped countries, claim a priority of needs. Moreover, commercial fishing by non-regional interests generates regional maritime zones.[22]

In the last decade attempts have been made to provide a broad multilateral basis for conservation. The United States has urged acceptance of the principle of abstention,[23] which:

relates to situations where States have, through the expenditure of time, effort and money on research and management, and through restraints on their fishermen, increased and

---

[17] The OECD was formed in 1961 as a replacement for the Organization for European Economic Co-operation (OEEC).

[18] Or, CERN set up by a Conv. of 1 July 1953, under the auspices of UNESCO.

[19] *Supra*, pp. 223ff.

[20] 28 Sept. 1945; Whiteman, Vol. 4, 956; contemporaneous with a continental shelf proclamation.

[21] Cf. the *Behring Sea Fisheries* arbitrations of 1893 and 1902, *supra*, pp. 226–7.

[22] The famous 200-mile claims by Peru, Ecuador, and Chile in 1952 were based on conservation rather than a concept of territorial sea. See Garcia Amador, *The Exploitation and Conservation of the Resources of the Sea* (2nd edn., 1959), 73–9; *Yrbk. ILC* (1956), i. 169.

[23] See e.g. *Yrbk. ILC* (1956), ii. 91, 93. The principle first appeared in the North Pacific Fisheries Conv. of 1952. See Allen, 46 *AJ* (1952), 319–23; Bishop, 62 *Columbia LR* (1962), 1206–29; id., 115 Hague *Recueil* (1965, II), 315–17; Yamamoto, 43 *Washington LR* (1967–8), 45–61; Oda and Owada (eds.), *The Practice of Japan in International Law, 1961–1970* (1982), 126–36.

maintained the productivity of stocks of fish, which without such action would not exist or would exist at far below their most productive level. Under such conditions and when the stocks are being fully utilized, that is, under such exploitation that an increase in the amount of fishing would not be expected to result in any substantial increase in the sustainable yield, then States not participating, or which have not in recent years participated in exploitation of such stocks of fish, excepting the coastal state adjacent to the waters in which the stocks occur, should be required to abstain from participation.

This principle has been criticized as resting on a one-sided principle of allocation, akin to acquisitive prescription and contrary to the principle of the freedom of the high seas,[24] and it did not find a place in the Convention on Fishing and Conservation of the Living Resources of the High Seas opened for signature in 1958.[25] The Convention is concerned with creating powers to institute conservation measures, establishing priorities of interest, and providing machinery for the settlement of disputes arising from the implementation of its provisions on matters of substance. Article 6, paragraph 1, recognizes that 'a coastal State has a special interest in the maintenance of the productivity of the living resources in any area of the high seas adjacent to its territorial sea'. Article 7 gives content to the special interest as follows:

1. ... any coastal State may, with a view to the maintenance of the productivity of the living resources of the sea, adopt unilateral measures of conservation ... in any area of the high seas adjacent to its territorial sea, provided that negotiations to that effect with the other States concerned have not led to an agreement within six months.

2. The measures ... shall be valid as to other States only if the following requirements are fulfilled:
    (a) That there is a need for urgent application of conservation measures in the light of the existing knowledge of the fishery;
    (b) That the measures adopted are based on appropriate scientific findings;
    (c) That such measures do not discriminate in form or in fact against foreign fishermen.

Articles 6 and 7 may well be subjected to a restrictive interpretation in the interest of those favouring fisheries off foreign shores.[26] In the United Nations Convention on the Law of the Sea of 1982 the provisions concerning the exclusive economic zone[27] (Arts. 55–75) constitute a regime of conservation and management based upon the specified powers and duties of the coastal state. The Convention (Arts. 117–20) also prescribes certain duties for all states in respect of the management and conservation of the living resources of the high seas (fish stocks and marine mammals), such duties being

[24] See Oda, *International Law of the Resources of the Sea* (1979), 41–60; and Van der Molen, *Liber Amicorum presented to J.P.A. François* (1959), 203–12.

[25] Text: 52 *AJ* (1958), 851; Brownlie, *Documents*, p. 82; *Treaty Series* no. 39 (1966), Cmnd. 3028. In force 20 Mar. 1966. The Conv. was signed by only 37 states, although 86 states were represented at the Geneva Conference. See also Oda, *International Law of the Resources of the Sea*, pp. 60–7; Oppenheim ii. 755–60; Burke, *The New International Law of Fisheries* (1994), 82–150.

[26] Cf. Oda, *International Control of Sea Resources* (1963), 116–18; McDougal and Burke, *The Public Order of the Oceans* (1962), 981ff.; Gros, 97 Hague *Recueil* (1959, II), 42–54.

[27] On which: *supra*, pp. 200–203.

of a very general nature. It has been observed that the new Convention is not really an advance on the 1958 Convention in respect of the problems of allocation of fishery resources.[28] In any case, within the Exclusive Economic Zone, 200 miles in breadth, a different regime of fisheries management obtains. In response to recent developments the FAO introduced a voluntary Code of Conduct for Responsible Fisheries.

5. ANTARCTICA

The issues arising from territorial claims in polar regions have been noticed earlier,[29] and it is now proposed to give a short account of the regime of co-operation established by the Antarctic Treaty.[30] The object of the treaty is to ensure that Antarctica is used for peaceful purposes only, and that freedom of scientific investigation, and co-operation towards that end, as applied during the International Geophysical Year, shall continue. However, military personnel and equipment may be used in pursuing peaceful purposes. Nuclear explosions, for whatever purpose, are prohibited. Article VI provides for the application of the treaty to the area south of 60° south latitude, includes all the shelves, but reserves the rights of states (and not only contracting parties) with regard to the high seas in the area. Article IV reserves the rights and claims of contracting parties to territorial sovereignty in the area and provides as follows:

No acts or activities taking place while the present Treaty is in force shall constitute a basis for asserting, supporting or denying a claim to territorial sovereignty in Antarctica or create any rights of sovereignty in Antarctica. No new claim, or enlargement of an existing claim, to territorial sovereignty in Antarctica shall be asserted while the present Treaty is in force.

This last-quoted provision is not expressed to apply only to contracting parties, and this, and indeed the treaty as a whole, leads to the question of the obligation of non-parties.[31] In principle the treaty as such can only bind parties to it,[32] although Article IV(2) quoted above may constitute a joint establishment by the parties of a policy of

---

[28] See Oda, 77 *AJ* (1983), 739 at 749–55.

[29] *Supra*, pp. 144–5.

[30] Text: Cmnd. 913, Misc. no. 21 (1959); 54 *AJ* (1960), 476; 9 *ICLQ* (1960), 475; and Whiteman, ii. 1232. Signed 1 Dec. 1959 by Argentina, Australia, Belgium, Chile, France, Japan, New Zealand, Norway, South Africa, USSR, the United Kingdom, and the United States. See also 10 *ICLQ* (1961) 562. At least 43 states are parties. For the UK see now the Antarctica Treaty Act 1967, c. 65. See further US Dept. of State Memo.; 70 *AJ* (1976), 115; Orrego Vicuña (ed.), *Antarctic Resources Policy* (1983); Rousseau, iii. 217–19; Francioni and Scovazzi (eds.), *International Law for Antarctica*, 2nd edn. (1996); Oppenheim ii. 694–6; Francioni, 260 Hague *Recueil* (1996), 249–403.

[31] See generally *infra*, pp. 627–9.

[32] Nevertheless, the treaty bears some resemblance to treaties classified as 'constitutive or semi-legislative' by Lord McNair, *Law of Treaties* (1961), ch. 14. Cf. also Art. X of the Antarctic Treaty: 'Each of the Contracting Parties undertakes to exert appropriate efforts, consistent with the Charter of the United Nations, to the end that no one engages in any activity in Antarctica contrary to the principles or purposes of the present Treaty'. This provision could be read as a clear admission that non-parties are not bound by the treaty itself.

closed options, i.e. non-parties are not physically excluded, but they cannot by their activities create a basis for new territorial claims. Thus the states with outstanding claims are protected from new sources of competition. In addition, however, the parties may also intend to reserve previously unclaimed areas for disposal by agreement among themselves. The validity of such a policy of options *vis-à-vis* non-parties and joint reservation will depend on general international law and not on the fact that the policy is expressed in a treaty.

Two other matters may be mentioned. First, there is a liberal inspection system involving a right to designate observers unilaterally and provision for complete freedom of access for such observers at any time to any or all areas of Antarctica. Secondly, the jurisdiction cannot in the context rest on the principle of territoriality. From the jurisdictional point of view the area is treated as *res nullius* and the nationality principle presumably governs. However, general principles will have to be resorted to when a national of one party commits an offence or civil wrong against a national of another party or of a non-party.[33]

The recent past has seen the development of the Antarctic Treaty system in two directions. In the first place a Convention for the Conservation of Antarctic Marine Living Resources was concluded in 1980[34] and, secondly, against the contingency of a discovery of ways of exploiting minerals beneath the icesheet, in 1988 a Convention on the Regulation of Antarctic Mineral Resource Activities[35] was concluded. The Convention has provoked opposition, and there is a body of opinion which supports a moratorium on the negotiations to establish a regime for exploitation of minerals. Certain, as yet unresolved, issues have arisen concerning the relation between the Antarctic regime and the Law of the Sea Convention of 1982.[36]

6. OUTER SPACE

There is no reason for believing that international law is spatially restricted, although, obviously, new areas of human activity will create problems, as in the case of exploitation of the continental shelf. The General Assembly of the United Nations has in any case adopted the view that 'International law, including the Charter of the United Nations, applies to outer space and celestial bodies'.[37] The analogy most applicable is that of the high seas, a *res communis*, but such a category is not a source of many

---

[33] See *infra*, pp. 289ff. The nationality principle (see *infra*, p. 303) is applied to observers and scientific personnel exchanged under the treaty: Art. VIII (1).

[34] Text: 19 *ILM* (1980), 841. See also: *Digest of U.S. Practice* (1978), 1010–17, 1485–91; 52 *BY* (1981), 461–2.

[35] Text: 27 *ILM* (1988), 868. See also: 53 *BY* (1982), 458–66; 54 *BY* (1983), 488–95; Joyner and Lipperman, 27 *Virginia JIL* (1986–7), 1–38; Rich, 31 *ICLQ* (1982), 709–25.

[36] See Joyner, 21 *Virginia JIL* (1980–1), 691–725; Harry, ibid. 727–44; Orrego Vicuña (ed.) *Antarctic Resources Policy*, Pt. 4.

[37] Resol. 1721 (XVI), adopted 20 Dec. 1961; 56 *AJ* (1962), 946. See also Art. 3 of the Outer Space Treaty of 1967, *infra*.

precise rules. However, although much remains to be done, particularly in relation to controlling military uses of space, a solid area of agreement on some basic rules has been achieved since space exploration began in 1957. The basis for agreement has been an early acceptance of the principle that outer space and celestial bodies are not susceptible to appropriation by states.[38] Evidence of generally accepted principles is provided by the General Assembly Resolution of 13 December 1963,[39] adopted unanimously, which contains 'a declaration of legal principles' governing activities of states in the exploration and use of outer space.

In 1967 as a sequel to the resolution of 1963 there was signed the Treaty on Principles governing the Activities of States in the Exploration and Use of Outer Space, Including the Moon and Other Celestial Bodies.[40] This will be binding on the parties and, apart from that obvious feature, will replace the resolution as the best evidence of the applicable principles for non-parties. The regime created is similar to that of the Antarctica Treaty of 1959. Article I provides that exploration and use of outer space 'shall be carried out for the benefit and in the interests of all countries... and shall be the province of all mankind'; and further, outer space (including the moon and other celestial bodies) 'shall be free for exploration and use by all states without discrimination of any kind, on a basis of equality and in accordance with international law, and there shall be free access to all areas of celestial bodies'. Freedom of scientific investigation is established.[41] Article 2 provides that outer space 'is not subject to national appropriation by claim of sovereignty, by means of use or occupation, or any other means'. There is no provision on the precise boundary between outer space and airspace, or, more precisely, between the regime of *res communis*[42] and the sovereignty of states over national territory. Until there is agreement on the legality of certain types of activity on the fringes of national airspace, states will tend to reserve their positions on a boundary line beyond which the application of sanctions against unlawful activities may be problematical.[43] The lowest limit above the earth sufficient to permit free

---

[38] Although existing principles on acquisition of territory would have been applicable, as they are to uninhabited polar regions.

[39] Resol. 1962 (XVIII); 58 *AJ* (1964), 477; 3 *ILM*, 157; GA, Off. Recs., 18th Sess., Suppl. no. 15 (A/5515), p. 15. On the relations of the Outer Space Treaty of 1967 and the resolution see Fawcett, *International Law and the Uses of Outer Space* (1968), 4–14.

[40] *Treaty Series* no. 10 (1968), Cmnd. 3519; 61 *AJ* (1967), 644; 41 *BY* (1965–6), 426; Brownlie, *Documents*, p. 154. In force 10 Oct. 1967; approx. 91 parties. For comment see Jennings, 121 Hague *Recueil* (1967, II), 410–15; Darwin, 42 *BY* (1967), 278–89; Cheng, 95 *JDI* (1968), 532–45; McMahon, 41 *BY* (1965–6), 417–25. See further Lay and Taubenfeld, *The Law Relating to Activities of Man in Space* (1970); Lachs, *The Law of Outer Space* (1972); Marcoff, *Traité de droit international public de l'espace* (1973); Goedhuis, 27 *ICLQ* (1978), 576–95, id., 19 *Columbia Journ. Trans. Law* (1981), 213–33; Rousseau, iv. 631–43; Christol, *The Modern International Law of Outer Space* (1982); Fawcett, *Outer Space* (1984); Matte (ed.), *Space Activities and Emerging International Law* (1984); Young, *Law and Policy in the Space Stations Era* (1989); Oppenheim ii. 826–45; Böckstiegel and Benkö, *Space Law: Basic Legal Documents* (1990), 3 vols; Lachs, in Bedjaoui (ed.), *International Law: Achievements and Prospects* (1991), 959–74; Bernhardt (ed.), *Encyclopedia*, III (1997), 837–9.

[41] See Arts. 1, 10, 11, and 12.

[42] *Supra*, p. 169.

[43] See Fawcett, *International Law and the Uses of Outer Space*, pp. 23–4; Goedhuis, 174 Hague *Recueil* (1982, I), 367–408; 55 *BY* (1984), 564–6; Lachs, *The Law of Outer Space*, pp. 55–9; Rousseau, iv. 636–8.

orbit of spacecraft would make a sensible criterion: this limit would be of the order of 100 miles since this is the lowest technically desirable altitude of orbit. Fawcett[44] has, on this basis, suggested that it would be necessary to convert the criterion into the arbitrary but precise limit of 100 miles. There may be a customary rule that satellites in orbit cannot be interfered with unless interference is justified in terms of the law concerning individual or collective self-defence.

The general regime is, like that of the high seas, based upon free use and a prohibition of claims to sovereignty by individual states. However, when the moon and other bodies are the objects of regular human activity, bases will be set up which may create some sort of possessory title. At any rate the existing rules need development to cope with the practical problems of peaceful but competing uses and matters of jurisdiction. In Article 8 it is provided that 'a State Party to the Treaty on whose registry an object launched into outer space is carried shall retain jurisdiction and control over such object, and over any personnel thereof, while in outer space or on a celestial body'. The same article provides that the ownership of space objects is not affected by their presence in outer space or on a celestial body or by their return to earth. In 1974 the General Assembly adopted the Convention on Registration of Objects Launched into Outer Space.[45]

Article 6 provides that states parties to the Treaty shall bear responsibility for national activities in space, whether such activities are carried on by governmental agencies or by non-governmental entities. Article 7 is as follows:

Each State Party to the Treaty that launches or procures the launching of an object into outer space, including the Moon and other celestial bodies, and each State Party from whose territory or facility an object is launched, is internationally liable for damage to another State Party to the Treaty or to its natural or juridical persons by such object or its component parts on the Earth, in airspace or in outer space, including the Moon and other celestial bodies.

The Legal Sub-Committee of the Space Committee of the United Nations General Assembly has prepared a more comprehensive treaty on these matters.[46] In the context of responsibility Article 9 contains some important provisions creating standards of conduct for states engaged in exploration and use of outer space. Thus activities shall be conducted 'with due regard to the corresponding interests of all other States Parties to the Treaty' and study and exploration shall be carried out so as to avoid harmful contamination of outer space and celestial bodies and also 'adverse changes in the environment of the Earth resulting from the introduction of extraterrestrial matter'.

---

[44] *International Law and the Uses of Outer Space*, pp. 23–4. See also McMahon, 38 *BY* (1962), 340–57.

[45] Resol. 3235 (XXIX). The Conv. came into force on 15 Sept. 1976. For the text see 14 *ILM* (1975), 43; and see also *Digest of US Practice* (1974), 398–404. See also the UK Outer Space Act 1986.

[46] See now the Conv. on International Liability for Damage Caused by Space Objects, signed 29 Mar. 1972; 66 *AJ* (1972), 702. See further Hailbronner, 30 *Z.a.ö.R.u.V.* (1970), 125–41; Malik, 6 *Indian Journ.* (1966), 335–62; Fawcett, *International Law and the Uses of Outer Space*, pp. 57–60; Cheng, *Curr. Leg. Problems* (1970), 216–39; Foster, 10 *Canad. Yrbk.* (1972), 137–85.

Article 4 creates a regime of demilitarization:[47]

States Parties to the Treaty undertake not to place in orbit around the Earth any object carrying nuclear weapons or any other kind of weapons of mass destruction, install such weapons on celestial bodies, or station such weapons in outer space in any other manner.

The Moon and other celestial bodies shall be used by all States Parties to the Treaty exclusively for peaceful purposes. The establishment of military bases, installations and fortifications, the testing of any type of weapons and the conduct of military manoeuvres on celestial bodies shall be forbidden. The use of military personnel for scientific research or for any other peaceful purposes shall not be prohibited. The use of any equipment or facility necessary for peaceful exploration of the Moon and other celestial bodies shall also not be prohibited.

Assistance to astronauts in case of emergency is the subject of Article 5 of the Outer Space Treaty and also of the Agreement on the Rescue of Astronauts, the Return of Astronauts and the Return of Objects Launched into Outer Space, signed on 22 April 1968.[48]

On 5 December 1979 the UN General Assembly adopted the text of an Agreement Governing the Activities of States on the Moon and Other Celestial Bodies.[49] In effect the instrument is intended to subject the moon and other celestial bodies to a regime of internationalization. Thus Article 11(1) provides that 'the moon and its natural resources are the common heritage of mankind'. However, the provisions concerning the appropriation of resources of the moon have certain obscurities.

An important feature of the use of outer space, as opposed to its exploration, has been the employment of satellites in orbit to develop telecommunications and systems of broadcasting. The major developments so far have been based upon the co-operative management of such activities by means of international organizations.[50] The principal organization is INTELSAT, first established as a consortium of interests in 1964, but placed on a permanent basis in 1973. The definitive arrangements consist of an inter-state agreement and an Operating Agreement,[51] to which both governments and designated entities, public or private, may be parties. In 1971 a number of socialist countries concluded an agreement for the creation of a satellite communications system called INTERSPUTNIK.[52] In addition there are regional systems in existence,

---

[47] See also Art. 3. Earlier developments: the Nuclear Test Ban Treaty signed on 5 Aug. 1963; 57 *AJ* (1963), 1026; and GA Resol. 1884 (XVIII), adopted on 17 Nov. 1963, prohibiting the placing in orbit around the earth of objects carrying weapons of mass destruction, the installing of such weapons on celestial bodies, or stationing such weapons in outer space in any other manner. See also Brownlie, 40 *BY* (1964), 1–31; Fawcett, *International Law and the Uses of Outer Space*, pp. 29–42.

[48] Text: 63 *AJ* (1969), 382; *Treaty Series* no. 56 (1969), Cmnd. 3997. For comment see Hall, 63 *AJ* (1969), 197–210; Cheng, 23 *Yr. Bk. of World Affairs* (1969), 185–208.

[49] Text: 18 *ILM* (1979), 1434; *Digest of US Practice* (1979), 1178. For comment: Cheng, *Curr. Leg. Problems* (1980), 213–37; Fawcett, *Outer Space*, pp. 11–14; Matte (ed.), *Space Activities*, pp. 104–8.

[50] Generally on these developments see Fawcett, *Outer Space*, pp. 54–79; Matte, 166 Hague *Recueil* (1980, I), 119–249; id., *Aerospace Law: Telecommunications Satellites* (1982); id., in Bos and Brownlie (eds.), *Liber Amicorum for Lord Wilberforce* (1987), 61–75.

[51] Text: 10 *ILM* (1971), 909.

[52] Later: Agreement of 1976 (Intercosmos programme), 16 *ILM* (1977), 1.

including EUTELSAT[53] and ARABSAT;[54] and a global specialized network, namely, the International Maritime Satellite Organization (INMARSAT).[55] Problems created by these developments include the conservation of the radio frequency spectrum and the powers of the ITU and UNESCO to take action in the matter,[56] and also the legal responsibility of international organizations for space activities. Article 6 of the Outer Space Treaty of 1967 provides that 'responsibility for compliance with this Treaty shall be borne both by the international organization [which carries on activities in outer space] and by the States Parties to the Treaty participating in such organisation.'[57]

Activities in outer space necessarily involve the type of problem met with in the context of the enjoyment of the freedoms of the high seas. In other words, certain activities are considered in certain quarters either to infringe the principle of non-appropriation or to involve breaches of other principles of general international law. The first category is exemplified by the phenomenon of geostationary (or synchronous) satellites, which rotate with the earth (in a near-equatorial orbit) and thus remain at a fixed point above a given point on the earth's surface. Eight equatorial states have claimed that the individual segments of the unique (and therefore finite) geostationary orbit are subject to a regime of national sovereignty.[58] Such claims are difficult to reconcile with Articles I and II of the Outer Space Treaty of 1967.[59] In any case there is a fine line to be drawn between excessive use of the orbit and appropriation. Space satellites can also be used for the collection of all kinds of data relating to the earth's surface and also subsurface conditions, a procedure known as remote sensing. The legality of remote sensing is to some extent problematical, but much will turn on the facts in each case and generalization is to be avoided.[60]

[53] The Interim EUTELSAT Agreement was signed on 13 May 1977; the Agreement became definitive on 1 Sept. 1985.

[54] Concluded in 1976 by member states of the Arab League: text in Jasentuliyana and Lee (eds.), *Manual on Space Law* (1979), ii. 345.

[55] Conv. signed on 3 Sept. 1976. Text: 15 *ILM* (1976), 219, 1051; amendments: 27 *ILM* (1988), 691.

[56] See Leive, *International Telecommunications and International Law: The Regulation of the Radio Spectrum* (1970); and UNGA Resol. 37/92, 10 Dec. 1982; 22 *ILM* (1983), 451.

[57] See also Art. 13. For comment see Fawcett, *Outer Space*, pp. 44–6; Darwin, 42 *BY* (1967), 286–8. See also the UK Outer Space Act 1986.

[58] See the Bogotá Decl., 1976, Jasentuliyana and Lee (eds.), *Manual on Space Law*, ii. 383; and see also *Digest of US Practice* (1979), 1187–8.

[59] See generally Goedhuis, 27 *ICLQ* (1978), 588–92; Gorove, 73 *AJ* (1979), 444–61; Matte (ed.), *Space Activities*, pp. 282–4; Theis, 29 *German Yrbk.* (1986), 227–51; 55 *BY* (1984), 565–6; *Digest of US Practice* (1977), 658–64, 669–70; ibid. (1979), 1185–88.

[60] See the Draft Principles adopted by the Legal Sub-Committee of the UN Committee on the Peaceful Uses of Outer Space, 1986; 25 *ILM* (1986), 1334. See also Christol, ibid. 1331–3; *Digest of US Practice* (1975), 473–9; Matte and De Saussure (eds.), *Legal Implications of Remote Sensing from Outer Space* (1976); Matte (ed.), *Space Activities*, pp. 389–419; Szafarz, *Polish Yrbk.* (1985), 135–43.

7. INTERNATIONAL RIVERS[61]

The term 'international' with reference to rivers is merely a general indication of rivers which geographically and economically affect the territory and interests of two or more states. Associated with rivers will be lakes and canals and other artificial works forming part of the same drainage system. Conceivably a river could be 'internationalized', i.e. given a status entirely distinct from the territorial sovereignty and jurisdiction of any state, on the basis of treaty or custom, either general or regional. However, in practice rivers separating or traversing the territories of two or more states are subject to the territorial jurisdiction of riparian states up to the *medium filum aquae*, usually taken to be the deepest channel of navigable waters.[62] For the most part the legal regime of rivers, creating rights for other riparians and non-riparian states and limiting the exercise of territorial jurisdiction for individual riparians, depends on treaty. Particularization of the regimes for various river systems would seem to be inevitable, since each system has its own character and technical problems. Moreover, no longer may general principles be founded on the assumption that the primary use will be navigation. Irrigation, hydro-electricity generation, and industrial uses are more prominent in many regions than navigation, fishing, and floating of timber.

On some sets of facts unilateral action, creating conditions which may cause specific harm, and not just loss of amenity, to other riparian states, may create international responsibility on the principles laid down in the *Trail Smelter* arbitration[63] and the decision in the *Corfu Channel* case (Merits).[64] The arbitral award concerning the waters of *Lake Lanoux*[65] in 1957 was concerned with the interpretation of a treaty between France and Spain. However, the tribunal made observations on certain Spanish arguments based on customary law. On the one hand, the tribunal seemed to accept the principle that an upstream state is acting unlawfully if it changes the waters of a river

---

[61] See generally *British Digest*, iib. 55–190; Verzijl, *International Law in Historical Perspective*, iii (1970), 103–220; Rousseau, iv. 484–564; Vitányi, *The International Regime of River Navigation* (1979); Chauhan, *Settlement of International Water Law Disputes in International Drainage Basins* (1981); Zacklin and Caflisch (eds.), *The Legal Regime of International Rivers and Lakes* (1981); Lammers, *Pollution of International Watercourses* (1984); Caflisch, 219 Hague *Recueil* (1989–VII), 9–226; Oppenheim, ii. 574–89; Fuentes, 67 *BY* (1996), 337–412. id, 69 *BY* (1998), 119–200; McCaffrey, *The Law of International Watercourses: Non-Navigational Uses* (2001); Bernhardt (ed.), *Encyclopedia*, III (1995), 1364–68.

[62] On the problems of river boundaries see E. Lauterpacht, 9 *ICLQ* (1960), 208 at 216–26. As in the case of maritime indentations a river may be subjected to a *condominium*.

[63] Award II, 1941; *RIAA* iii. 1905 at 1965 (no right to permit use of territory in such a manner as to cause injury by fumes to the territory of another state).

[64] *Infra*, p. 442.

[65] 62 *RGDIP* (1958), 79; *RIAA* xii. 281; 53 *AJ* (1959), 156; *ILR* 24 (1957), 101. See also Duléry, 62 *RGDIP* (1958), 469–516; and Griffin, 53 *AJ* (1959), 50–80. The arbitration concerned the diversion of water by the upstream state, France, opposed by the lower state, Spain. For the Conv. made subsequently by the parties, see 4 *Ann. français* (1958), 708. See Berber, *Rivers in International Law*, p. 150, and Vitányi, 26 *German Yrbk.* (1983), 54–85, for a suggestion of local European customary rules; and Brownlie, 10 *ICLQ* (1960), 656. See further the Treaty Relating to Co-operative Development of the Water Resources of the Columbia River Basin, 1961; US and Canada, 59 *AJ* (1965), 989; and the Helsinki Convention on the Protection and Use of Transboundary Watercourses and International Lakes, 1992; *ILM*, 31 (1992), 1312 (35 States Parties).

in their natural condition to the serious injury of a downstream state. On the other, the tribunal stated that 'the rule according to which States may utilize the hydraulic force of international watercourses only on condition of a prior agreement between the interested States cannot be established as a custom, or even less as a general principle of law'. The issues of liability for changes in the flow of a river as between riparian States will often be determined within the framework of the law of treaties in combination with the principles of State responsibility, as in the Judgment of the International Court in the *Hungary/Slovakia* case[66] relating to the provisions of a bilateral treaty between the two States. At the same time the Court referred to the 'basic right' of Hungary 'to an equitable and reasonable sharing of the resources of an international watercourse'.[67]

In the case of navigable rivers[68] it is generally accepted that customary law does not recognize a right of free navigation.[69] Significantly, only a minority of states have accepted the Barcelona Convention on the Regime of Navigable Waterways of International Concern of 1921,[70] which provided for free navigation as between the parties on navigable waterways of international concern. Several treaty regimes for specific river systems provide for free navigation and equality of treatment for riparian states only.[71] However, this is not always the case, and the treaty regime for the Danube for long conferred rights of navigation and control on non-riparians. The Belgrade Convention of 1948 maintained free navigation for all states whilst retaining powers of control for riparian states.[72] Navigation by warships of non-riparian states is prohibited. In construing a treaty which creates machinery for supervision of an international regime of navigation, a tribunal may prefer not to employ a restrictive interpretation of the powers of the agency of control as against the territorial sovereigns.[73] In its Judgment in the case on the *Jurisdiction of the International Commission of the River Oder*, the Permanent Court stated its view as to the conception on which international river law, as developed in conventions since the Act of the Congress of Vienna in 1815, is based. This conception was 'a community of interest of riparian States' which in a navigable river 'becomes the basis of a common legal right, the essential features of which are the perfect equality of all riparian States in the use of the whole course of the river and the exclusion of any preferential privilege of any one riparian State in relation to the others'.[74]

[66] *Gabčíkovo-Nagymaros Project* (Hungary/Slovakia), ICJ Reports (1997), 7.

[67] Ibid., para. 78.

[68] See generally, ILA, *Report of the Fiftieth Conference* (Brussels, 1962), 453ff.; Baxter, *The Law of International Waterways* (1964), 149–59.

[69] Baxter, *The Law of International Waterways*, p. 155; Oppenheim, ii. 582. See also the *Faber* case, *RIAA* x. 441; *British Digest*, iib. 55–190; Rousseau, iv. 493–6.

[70] *Treaty Series* no. 28 (1923), Cmd. 1993; 7 LNTS, 51. Some 28 states have become parties.

[71] See e.g. the Boundary Waters Treaty of 1909 between the United States and Canada; in Baxter (ed.), *Documents on the St. Lawrence Seaway* (1960), 7.

[72] Text: 33 UNTS, 181. The United Kingdom, the United States, and France, *inter alia*, contend that the previous Danube Conv. of 1921 is still in force. See Kunz, 43 *AJ* (1949), 104–13; Sinclair, 25 *BY* (1948), 398–404; Bokor-Szegö, 8 *Ann. français* (1962), 192–205. For the regime of navigation on the Rhine see 51 *BY* (1980), 462.

[73] See the *International Commission of the River Oder*, PCIJ, Ser. A, no. 23, p. 29; *Jurisdiction of the European Commission of the Danube*, PCIJ, Ser. B, no. 14, pp. 61, 63–4.

[74] *Ut supra*, p. 27. Ibid. 28, the Court referred also to the interest of non-riparian states in navigation on the waterways in question.

In 1966 the International Law Association adopted the Helsinki Rules on the Uses of Waters of International Rivers as a statement of existing rules of international law.[75] In 1970 the United Nations General Assembly recommended that the International Law Commission should take up the study of the law of the non-navigational uses of international watercourses with a view to its progressive development and codification.[76] The work of the Commission culminated in the adoption by the General Assembly of the Convention on the Law of Non-navigational Uses of International Watercourses on 21 May 1997.[77] Part II of the Convention is set out below.

PART II. GENERAL PRINCIPLES

Article 5

Equitable and reasonable utilization and participation

1. Watercourse States shall in their respective territories utilize an international watercourse in an equitable and reasonable manner. In particular, an international watercourse shall be used and developed by watercourse States with a view to attaining optimal and sustainable utilization thereof and benefits therefrom, taking into account the interests of the watercourse States concerned, consistent with adequate protection of the watercourse.

2. Watercourse States shall participate in the use, development and protection of an international watercourse in an equitable and reasonable manner. Such participation includes both the right to utilize the watercourse and the duty to cooperate in the protection and development thereof, as provided in the present Convention.

Article 6

Factors relevant to equitable and reasonable utilization

1. Utilization of an international watercourse in an equitable and reasonable manner within the meaning of Article 5 requires taking into account all relevant factors and circumstances, including:

(a) Geographic, hydrographic, hydrological, climatic, ecological and other factors of a natural character;

---

[75] *Report of the Fifty-Second Conference*, pp. 477–533. On the status of the Rules: 17 *Ann. suisse* (1971), 179. Further work by the ILA: *Report of the Fifty-Sixth Conference*, pp. xiii, 102–54; *Report of the Fifty-Seventh Conference*, pp. xxxiv, 213–66; *Report of the Fifty-Eighth Conference*, pp. 219–47; *Report of the Fifty-Ninth Conference*, pp. 359–99; *Report of the Sixtieth Conference*, pp. 531–52. See also Manner and Metsälampi (eds.), *The Work of the International Law Association on the Law of International Water Resources* (1988).

[76] See further *Yrbk. ILC* (1971), ii. 207–8; ibid. (1973), ii. 95–6; ibid. (1974), ii (Pt. 1), 300–4; ibid. (1974), ii (Pt. 2), 33–366; ibid. (1976), ii (Pt. 1), 147–91; ibid. (1976), ii (Pt. 2), 153–62; ibid. (1978), ii (Pt. 1), 253–61; ibid. (1979), ii (Pt. 1), 143–81; ibid. (1979), ii (Pt. 2), 160–9; ibid. (1980), ii (Pt. 1), 153–98; ibid. (1980), ii (Pt. 2), 104–36; ibid. (1982), ii (Pt. 1), 65–197; ibid. (1983), ii (Pt. 1), 155–99; ibid. (1983), ii (Pt. 2), 62–78; ibid. (1984), ii (Pt. 1), 101–27; ibid. (1984), ii (Pt. 2), 82–98; ibid. (1985), ii (Pt. 1), 87–96; ibid. (1985), ii (Pt. 2), 68–71; ibid. (1986), ii (Pt. 1), 87–144; ibid. (1986), ii (Pt. 2), 60–3; ibid. (1987), ii (Pt. 1), 15–46; ibid. (1987), ii (Pt. 2), 18–38; ibid. (1988), ii (Pt. 1), 205–50; ibid. (1988), ii (Pt. 2), 22–54; ibid. (1989), ii (Pt. 1), 91–130; ibid. (1989), ii (Pt. 2), 122–30; ibid. (1990), ii (Pt. 1), 41–82; ibid. (1990), ii (Pt. 2), 46–67; ibid. (1991), ii (Pt. 1), 45–69; ibid. (1991), ii (Pt. 2), 63–78. See further Reports of the ILC: 1993, 216–41; and 1994, 195–326.

[77] Text: 36 *ILM* 700. Not yet in force.

(b) The social and economic needs of the watercourse States concerned;

(c) The population dependent on the watercourse in each watercourse State;

(d) The effects of the use or uses of the watercourses in one watercourse State on other watercourse States;

(e) Existing and potential uses of the watercourse;

(f) Conservation, protection, development and economy of use of the water resources of the watercourse and the costs of measures taken to that effect;

(g) The availability of alternatives, of comparable value, to a particular planned or existing use.

2. In the application of Article 5 or paragraph 1 of this article, watercourse States concerned shall, when the need arises, enter into consultations in a spirit of cooperation.

3. The weight to be given to each factor is to be determined by its importance in comparison with that of other relevant factors. In determining what is a reasonable and equitable use, all relevant factors are to be considered together and a conclusion reached on the basis of the whole.

Article 7

Obligation not to cause significant harm

1. Watercourse States shall, in utilizing an international watercourse in their territories, take all appropriate measures to prevent the causing of significant harm to other watercourse States.

2. Where significant harm nevertheless is caused to another watercourse State, the States whose use causes such harm shall, in the absence of agreement to such use, take all appropriate measures, having due regard for the provisions of articles 5 and 6, in consultation with the affected State, to eliminate or mitigate such harm and, where appropriate, to discuss the question of compensation.

Article 8

General obligation to cooperate

1. Watercourse States shall cooperate on the basis of sovereign equality, territorial integrity, mutual benefit and good faith in order to attain optimal utilization and adequate protection of an international watercourse.

2. In determining the manner of such cooperation, watercourse States may consider the establishment of joint mechanisms or commissions, as deemed necessary by them, to facilitate cooperation on relevant measures and procedures in the light of experience gained through cooperation in existing joint mechanisms and commissions in various regions.

Article 9

Regular exchange of data and information

1. Pursuant to Article 8, watercourse States shall on a regular basis exchange readily available data and information on the condition of the watercourse, in particular that of a hydrological, meteorological, hydrogeological and ecological nature and related to the water quality as well as related forecasts.

2. If a watercourse State is requested by another watercourse State to provide data or information that is not readily available, it shall employ its best efforts to comply with the request but may condition its compliance upon payment by the requesting State of the reasonable costs of collecting and, where appropriate, processing such data or information.

3. Watercourse States shall employ their best efforts to collect and, where appropriate, to process data and information in a manner which facilitates its utilization by the other watercourse States to which it is communicated.

Article 10

Relationship between different kinds of uses

1. In the absence of agreement or custom to the contrary, no use of an international watercourse enjoys inherent priority over other uses.

2. In the event of a conflict between uses of an international watercourse, it shall be resolved with reference to Articles 5 to 7, with special regard being given to the requirements of vital human needs.

8. CANALS[78]

Canals, like rivers, are in principle subject to the territorial sovereignty and jurisdiction of the state or states which they separate or traverse. Where the canal serves more than one state or otherwise affects the interests of more than one state a treaty regime may be created to regulate user and administration. The history of three canals of international concern, by reason of use by foreign vessels, has provided the basic materials for jurists seeking to establish general rules applicable to all such canals, and these must be examined.

The Suez Canal was built and opened in 1869 under a private law concession for ninety-nine years by the Egyptian Government to the Universal Suez Maritime Canal Company. For most of its history the latter was a joint Franco-Egyptian company with the various aspects of its existence and function subjected either to French or to Egyptian municipal law. However, the British Government was the largest shareholder.[79] Eventually the affairs of the Canal were regulated by the Convention of Constantinople in 1888,[80] signed by nine states and to receive six accessions. In Article I it was provided that the Canal 'shall always be free and open, in time of war as in time of peace, to every vessel of commerce or of war, without distinction of flag'. The parties agreed not to interfere with the free use of the Canal and not to subject it to

---

[78] See generally *British Digest*, iib. 193–338; Whiteman, iii. 1076–261; Baxter, *The Law of International Waterways*; Verzijl, *International Law in Historical Perspective*, iii. 221–38; Rousseau, iv. 565–89; Oppenheim ii. 591–99; Bernhardt, *Encyclopedia*, I (1992), 523–7.

[79] On the problems of nationality and diplomatic protection see *infra*, pp. 419ff.

[80] See *The Suez Canal, A Selection of Documents*...(London, Soc. of Comp. Legis. and Int. Law, 1956), 48; *British Digest*, iib. 193–281, 341–67.

the right of blockade. It was further provided that, even if the territorial sovereign was a belligerent, no act of war should be committed in the Canal or its ports, as well as within a radius of three miles from these ports (Art. IV). However, in Article X there is a stipulation that the restrictions in Article IV, and similar restrictions in other articles, should not interfere with the measures which the territorial sovereign 'might find it necessary to take for securing by [his] own forces the defence of Egypt and the maintenance of public order'. Legal issues of some complexity arise when the territorial sovereign is engaged in hostilities, or is otherwise in a 'state of war', and Egyptian measures against Israeli shipping in the Canal since the Rhodes Armistice of 1949 between Egypt and Israel have been the subject of acute controversy.[81]

In 1954 Britain and Egypt concluded an agreement[82] under which British forces withdrew from the Suez Canal base (with rights of use reserved under certain conditions), and the parties recognized 'that the Suez Maritime Canal, which is an integral part of Egypt, is a waterway economically, commercially and strategically of international importance', and expressed a determination to uphold the Convention of Constantinople. In 1956 the Egyptian Government nationalized the Canal Company, under a law making provision for compensation,[83] but made no claim to alter the status of the Canal itself. Britain, France, and other states argued for the illegality of this measure, linking the status of the Company and the concession from the Egyptian Government with the status of the Canal, and alleging that the nationalization was unlawful both in itself and as being incompatible with the 'international status' of the Canal. As a result of the Franco-British invasion later in the same year Egypt abrogated her agreement with Britain of 1954. On 24 April 1957 Egypt made a declaration[84] to the effect that she would respect the rights and obligations arising from the Convention of Constantinople and would 'afford and maintain free and uninterrupted navigation for all nations within the limits and in accordance with the provisions' of that Convention. Egypt registered the instrument with the UN Secretariat as an 'international agreement', but it would seem that it has legal force as a unilateral act.[85] The Canal is operated by the Suez Canal Authority, which is a legal person under Egyptian law, attached to the Ministry of Commerce.

Until 1978 the Panama Canal Zone was occupied and administered by the United States under a treaty with Panama under which the latter had a residual sovereignty.[86] The United States administered the Canal directly and independently of Panama under the bilateral Hay–Bunau–Varilla Treaty of 1903,[87] which, inter alia, provided that the Canal should be neutral in perpetuity and open to the vessels of all nations. Before the

---

[81] See Mensbrugghe, Les Garanties de la liberté de navigation dans le Canal de Suez (1964), 147ff.

[82] Treaty Series no. 67 (1955), Cmd. 9586; Documents, ut supra, p. 69.

[83] For the law: Documents, ut supra, p. 41. On nationalization see infra, pp. 531ff.

[84] Text: 51 AJ (1957), 673; E. Lauterpacht, The Suez Canal Settlement (1960), 35; Mensbrugghe, Les Garanties, p. 397.

[85] On such transactions see infra, p. 640.

[86] On the type of territorial status involved see supra, p. 111.

[87] See Hyde, i. 63. See also supra, p. 111.

construction of the Canal had been provided for in this latter treaty, the United States had already concluded the Hay–Pauncefote Treaty[88] with Great Britain, under which free navigation, even in time of war, was guaranteed in terms borrowed from the Convention of Constantinople. Under the terms of a treaty signed in 1977[89] Panama is recognized as 'territorial sovereign' with rights of management of the Canal granted to the United States for the duration of the Treaty. Associated agreements[90] deal with 'permanent neutrality' of the Canal and aspects of implementation of the Panama Canal Treaty. The Treaty was ratified in 1978 by both Panama and the United States on the basis of certain 'amendments, conditions, reservations and understandings'.[91]

The Kiel Canal, though important for international commerce, was controlled by Germany untrammelled by special obligations until, in the Treaty of Versailles, it was provided that, except when Germany was a belligerent, the Canal was to be open to vessels of commerce and of war of all nations on terms of equality (Art. 380). In 1936 the relevant provisions of the Treaty of Versailles were denounced by Germany. Apart from the specific question of the voidable character of the treaty by reason of duress applied to Germany, other states seem to have acquiesced in German avoidance of the Versailles provisions.[92]

It is very doubtful if the existing materials justify a general theory of international canals. However, there is some authority to the contrary in the majority Judgment of the Permanent Court in the case of the *Wimbledon*.[93] In 1921 a British vessel chartered by a French company, *en route* to Danzig with munitions for the Polish Government, was refused access to the Kiel Canal by the German Government. The issue before the Court was whether, on the assumption that Poland and Russia were at war, Germany was justified in taking the view that Article 380 of the Versailles Treaty did not preclude the observance of neutral duties on her part. The question was primarily one of treaty interpretation, but the majority Judgment, against Germany, referred[94] to the Suez and Panama Canals as 'precedents' which were

merely illustrations of the general opinion according to which when an artificial waterway connecting two open seas has been permanently dedicated to the use of the whole world, such waterway is assimilated to natural straits in the sense that even the passage of a belligerent man-of-war does not compromise the neutrality of the sovereign State under whose jurisdiction the waters in question lie.

---

[88]   Text: Moore, *Digest*, iii. 219. See further *British Digest*, iib. 281–338.

[89]   Text: 16 *ILM* (1977), 1022.

[90]   Texts: ibid. 1040–98. The Protocol to the Treaty Concerning the Permanent Neutrality and Operation of the Panama Canal (ibid. 1042) is open to accession by all states.

[91]   Text: 17 *ILM* (1977), 817. See further *Digest of US Practice* (1977), 575–96; ibid. (1978), 732–4, 1027–70; and Meron, 49 *BY* (1978), 182–99.

[92]   Some authors take another view: see Brierly, p. 236. See also the *Kiel Canal Collision* case, ILR 17 (1950), no. 34 and Barabolya (and Others), *Manual of International Maritime Law* (1966); US edition (1968), i. 162, 180–1.

[93]   PCIJ, Ser. A, no. 1; World Court Reports, i. 163. Judges Anzilotti, Huber, and Schücking dissented.

[94]   p. 28. For criticism see Schwarzenberger, *International Law*, i (3rd edn.), 223–6.

It will be noted that this proposition was ancillary to an exercise in treaty interpretation and that even the general proposition as such depends on the incidence of 'permanent dedication', a notion to be examined later on. Moreover, interested states are reluctant to generalize: in 1956 the United States regarded the Suez Canal as having an 'international status', while denying this in the case of the Panama Canal.

If the legal regime of a particular canal is not to rest on territorial sovereignty as qualified by treaty obligations, when these exist, one has to look for some special circumstance which renders interference with shipping unlawful in relation to states which are not parties to a treaty with the riparian sovereign. One approach, which does not constitute a principle specific to canals, is to see the particular treaty regime as 'constitutive or semi-legislative' and therefore creative of third-party rights.[95] The basis of this principle is examined more appropriately in Chapter 26. Another basis is the solemn unilateral act which may create rights independent of a treaty regime.[96] Baxter prefers a principle of permanent dedication, reminiscent of the *Wimbledon* decision but coupled with the requirement of reliance, of actual user.[97] Apparently reliance by the international shipping community suffices to support a complaint by any state, user or not. This principle Baxter regards as applicable to both the Panama and Suez Canals.[98] It has attractions, but also the weakness of novelty, since user as such can be legally ambiguous. Moreover, the notion of dedication only leads back to the problem of deciding when, if at all, treaties bind third states and create permanent regimes. Its legal core is the concept of historic rights, but it is not easy to apply this to the present subject-matter, partly because, where there has been for long a treaty obligation to allow free navigation, it is difficult to read a radical significance into the fulfilment of the treaty obligation by the territorial sovereign.[99] In conclusion, it can be pointed out that, assuming a canal has an international status on one basis or another, this is not necessarily incompatible with control by an administrative body which is merely a legal person under the law of the territorial sovereign.

9. STRAITS[100]

Narrow seas joining two large zones of the high seas do not create any real problems providing the territorial seas of the littoral states do not meet. When the territorial seas do meet then problems arise as to the drawing of the boundary between them, although

---

[95] See McNair, *Law of Treaties*, pp. 265–8.

[96] See *infra*, p. 640.

[97] *The Law of International Waterways*, pp. 182, 308, 343.

[98] For the view that the Panama Canal is within the exclusive jurisdiction of the US see Colombos, p. 213.

[99] In the case of the Panama Canal Zone has the United States the legal capacity to allow historic rights to accrue which affect territory in which Panama has at least a residual sovereignty?

[100] See generally Whiteman, iv. 417–80; Brüel, *International Straits* (1947), 2 vols.; Kennedy, UN Conf. on the Law of the Sea, 1958, Off. Recs. i. 114 (UN Doc. A/CONF. 13/38); *British Digest*, iib. 3–51; Verzijl, *International Law in Historical Perspective*, iv (1971), 115–42; Lapidoth, *Les Détroits en droit international*

the applicable principle is generally that of a median line.[101] In general there is a right of innocent passage for foreign ships through straits which are used for international navigation between one part of the high seas and another. This right is recognized by the customary law and is incorporated in the Convention on the Territorial Sea and Contiguous Zone of 1958 (Article 16(4)).[102] Before the particular incidents of this right are considered, certain special cases may be mentioned. Functions in some respects similar to those of straits are fulfilled by boundary rivers linking international lakes with the high seas. Where this occurs, as in the case of the St Lawrence Seaway and the Great Lakes in North America, the rights of the riparians are regulated by agreement between them and the analogy with straits is not accepted in general legal principle.[103] A process of unilateral dedication may create an estoppel in favour of one or a number of states or, perhaps, states generally. Assuming that it could be argued that the Baltic and Black Seas are not open seas,[104] then a process of acquiescence, together with agreement on particular issues, may create rights of access which would not otherwise exist. Thus Denmark has ceased to demand tolls for passage through the Great and Little Belts and the Sound, although treaties on the subject exist with only a restricted number of states.[105] In the case of the Black Sea, passage through the Dardanelles, the Sea of Marmara, and the Bosphorus is regulated by the Montreux Convention of 1936.[106] Powers which are non-littoral states of the Black Sea have only a limited access in respect of total tonnage of warships in time of peace, but otherwise there is freedom of transit and navigation for all vessels in peacetime. In time of war, but only when Turkey is not a belligerent, warships have freedom of transit and navigation; with the

---

(1972); Giuliano, *Italian Yrbk.* (1975) 16–26; Pharand, in *The Law of the Sea* (*Thesaurus Acroasium*, vii) (1977), 64–100; Rousseau, iv. 402–21; O'Connell, *The International Law of the Sea* (ed. Shearer), i (1982), 299–337; Treves, *Essays in Honour of Willem Riphagen* (1986), 247–58; Caminos, 205 Hague *Recueil* (1987, V), 13–245; Churchill and Lowe, *The Law of the Sea* (3rd edn., 1999), 102–17; Nandan and Anderson, 60 *BY* (1989), 159–204; De Yturriaga, *Straits Used for International Navigation* (1991); Oppenheim, ii. 633–43; Jia, *The Regime of Straits in International Law* (1998); Roach and Smith, *United States Responses to Excessive Maritime Claims* (2nd edn., 1996), 281–365; Bernhardt, *Encyclopedia*, IV (2000), 693–6. See also Butler, *Northeast Arctic Passage* (1978); Leifer, *Malacca, Singapore and Indonesia* (1978); Pharand, *Canada's Arctic Waters in International Law* (1988), 215–43; Alexandersson, *The Baltic Straits* (1982); Lapidoth, *The Red Sea and the Gulf of Aden* (1982); Pak, *The Korean Straits* (1988).

[101] *Supra*, p. 182.

[102] Generally on the territorial sea see *supra*, pp. 173ff. As 12 miles becomes a widely accepted breadth for the territorial sea, it is obvious that the law of straits will become much more prominent.

[103] On the rights, if any, of non-riparian states see Eek, *Scand. Studies in Law* (1965), 75–6. See also *British Digest*, iib. 132–52; and Baxter, *The Law of International Waterways*, pp. 46–7.

[104] See *supra*, p. 173; and *British Digest*, iib. 12–28. If the Baltic Sea is an open sea by general acquiescence (which it almost certainly is), does this leave Denmark subject to the ordinary regime of international straits as a consequence, without acquiescence by Denmark in relation to this status for the straits? See also the *Case Concerning Passage Through the Great Belt* (Finland v. Denmark), ICJ Reports (1991) 12. The dispute related to the effect on the right of passage of the building of a bridge by Denmark. The existence of the right of passage as such was not challenged: ibid., 17, para. 22.

[105] See Brüel, *International Straits*, i. 198–200, ii. 11–115.

[106] Cmd. 5249; 31 *AJ* (1937), Suppl., p. 1; Hudson, *Int. Legis.*, vii. 386. See Brüel, *International Straits*, ii. 252–426; de Visscher, 17 *RDILC* (1936), 699–718; Rozakis and Stagos, *The Turkish Straits* (1987).

proviso that belligerent vessels shall not pass except in pursuance of obligations arising out of the sanctions provisions of the Covenant of the League of Nations (see the
Montreux Convention, Art. 25) and in cases of assistance rendered to a state victim of
aggression in virtue of a treaty of mutual assistance binding Turkey, concluded within
the framework of the League Covenant (Art. 19). Obviously the Convention is in need
of revision, but it is doubtful if it is, as a whole, invalidated by change of circumstances,
and the parties have not used the power of denunciation after twenty years provided
for in Article 28. The analogue of the formation of a general right of access by estoppel,
acquiescence, and general user is the acquisition of historic rights converting a strait
broader than the sum of the normal territorial seas into a territorial strait.[107] Article
16(4) of the Convention on the Territorial Sea takes care of another special case, since
it refers to straits 'which are used for international navigation between one part of the
high seas and another part of the high seas *or the territorial sea of a foreign State*'.[108]

Before the decision in the *Corfu Channel* case (Merits)[109] a number of authorities[110]
considered that a strait was 'international' for legal purposes if it was *essential* to passage between two sections of the high seas and was used by considerable numbers of
foreign ships. However, in the *Corfu Channel* case, the International Court of Justice
stated that the test was not relative importance for navigation. Of the North Corfu
Channel between Greek and Albanian territory it observed:[111]

the decisive criterion is rather its geographical situation as connecting two parts of the high
seas and the fact of its being used for international navigation. Nor can it be decisive that
this strait is not a necessary route between two parts of the high seas, but only an alternative
passage between the Aegean and the Adriatic Seas. It has nevertheless been a useful route for
international maritime traffic.

In its final articles on the law of the sea the International Law Commission referred
to straits 'normally used' for international navigation.[112] The intention was to follow
the *Corfu Channel* Judgment, but some thought the formulation was more restrictive.
Article 16(4) of the Territorial Sea Convention refers broadly to 'straits which are used
for international navigation'.

---

[107] Cf. the Juan de Fuca Strait, 10 miles across at its narrowest, divided between Canada and the United
States. Presumably historic rights may form the basis for denial of a right of passage also.

[108] Italics supplied. On the Arab–Israeli dispute over the Straits of Tiran, see Gross, 53 *AJ* (1959), 564–94;
Hammad, 15 *Revue égyptienne* (1959), 118–51; Lapidoth, 40 *RGDIP* (1969), 30–51.

[109] ICJ Reports (1949), 4.

[110] See Hyde, i. 488; Fauchille, *Traité* (8th edn.) i, pt. ii (1925), 246–7; Brüel, *International Straits*,
i. 43–5 (and see next note). Essentiality is a relative conception, as Brüel's examples show. See also Gidel,
iii. 729–64.

[111] ICJ Reports (1949), 28–9. For criticism of the views of the Court on this point and its acceptance of the
information provided by the British Agent see Brüel, *Festschrift für Rudolf Laun* (1953), 259 at 273, 276. The
passage in the *Corfu Channel* Judgment is not easy to reconcile with the Judgment in the *Anglo-Norwegian
Fisheries* case, ICJ Reports (1951), 116 at 132, referring to the Indreleia (the name of a navigational route): see
Fitzmaurice, 31 *BY* (1954), 419.

[112] *Yrbk. ILC* (1956), ii. 273 (Art. 17).

The coastal state has less control over passage than in the case of innocent passage through the territorial sea.[113] The coastal state may not suspend passage, but it can take precautions to safeguard its security and make rules concerning safe navigation, lighting, and buoys. Where passage through a territorial sea not forming part of a strait is concerned, the right of passage may be suspended temporarily by the coastal state 'if such suspension is essential for its security' (Territorial Sea Convention, Art. 16(3)). Suspension of passage through a strait is not permitted (ibid., Art. 16(3) and (4)), but particular vessels may be objected to in respect of particular passages not considered innocent.[114] The provisions in Article 16 leave the question of the passage of warships shrouded in obscurity: this problem of interpretation has already been considered in connection with passage through the territorial sea in general.[115] However, the *Corfu Channel* case[116] and the International Law Commission support a right of innocent passage for warships without prior authorization, although the Commission did require previous authorization or notification when passage was not through a strait.[117] Nevertheless the controversy at the first Law of the Sea Conference as to the passage of warships was overall and extended to territorial seas both in straits and in ordinary circumstances.[118] Thus the interpretation of Article 16(4) of the Territorial Sea Convention turns on the main issue, viz., what types of vessel qualify for innocent passage *ab initio*?

At the Third United Nations Conference on the Law of the Sea (1973–82) the question of passage through straits was regarded as a matter of the first importance by the United States, together with other maritime powers. The Law of the Sea Convention of 1982 contains articles concerning straits which have radical features involving a severe limitation on the powers of some coastal states. The concept of strait is characterized loosely, as before, in terms of 'straits used for international navigation' (Art. 34). The radical element is 'transit passage', which is 'the exercise… of the freedom of navigation and overflight solely for the purpose of continuous and expeditious transit of the strait between one area of the high seas or an exclusive economic zone and another area of the high seas or an exclusive economic zone' (Art. 38, para. 2). While ships and aircraft exercising this right have specified duties the coastal state has no power either to hamper or suspend 'transit passage' (Art. 44). Moreover, the duties owed to the coastal

---

[113] *Supra*, p. 186.

[114] Art. 16(1) provides: 'The coastal State may take the necessary steps in its territorial sea to prevent passage which is not innocent'.

[115] *Supra*, p. 188.

[116] ICJ Reports (1949), 28.

[117] *Yrbk. ILC* (1956), ii. 276–7 (Art. 24).

[118] On the connections between the two parts of the subject-matter, and the authorities denying a right of passage for warships, see Judge Azevedo, Diss. Op., ICJ Reports (1949), at 97–106; and cf. Gidel, iii. 278–89 and esp. 283–4; and *British Digest*, iib. 3–11. At the Hague Codification Conference in 1930 the United States denied the existence of a right of passage for warships. Affirming passage for warships through straits are Fauchille, *Traité*, i. ii. 257; Oppenheim, ii. 635–6; Sibert, *Traité* (1951), i. 725; Colombos, pp. 133, 198; McDougal and Burke, *The Public Order of the Oceans*, pp. 199–208; Baxter, *The Law of International Waterways*, pp. 167–8; Fitzmaurice, 8 *ICLQ* (1959), 100–1; Brüel, *International Straits*, i. 54–69, 202; O'Connell, *The International Law of the Sea* (ed. Shearer), i. 299–327. See also *British Practice* (1964), ii. 178.

state by ships and aircraft transiting are not matched by powers of enforcement vested in the coastal state, except in the case of violations 'causing or threatening to cause major damage to the marine environment of the straits' (Art. 233). There is no condition of innocence as such attached to 'transit passage'. However, 'if the strait is formed by an island of a state bordering the strait and its mainland, transit passage shall not apply if there exists seaward of the island a route through the high seas or through an exclusive economic zone of similar convenience with respect to navigational and hydrographic characteristics' (Art. 38, para. 1). In the latter case and in straits 'between a part of the high seas or an exclusive economic zone and the territorial sea of a foreign state' the regime of non-suspendable innocent passage is applicable (Art. 45).[119]

The provisions of the 1982 Convention concerning transit passage involve a substantial departure from the position of customary international law,[120] and cannot be invoked by non-parties. In principle the regime could be confirmed as customary law by state practice independently of the Convention, and there is some evidence of a trend in this direction, supported by the practice of France, the United States and the United Kingdom.[121] No doubt state relations in this field may evolve to some extent on the basis of recognition of transit rights and reciprocity.

10. LAND-LOCKED STATES AND ENCLAVES

There are 41 land-locked states and principalities in existence and numerous enclaves detached from a parent entity (and lacking access to the sea).[122] Rights of transit, particularly for trade purposes, are normally arranged by treaty, but they may exist by revocable licence or local custom.[123] A right of transit may be posited as a general principle of law in itself[124] or on the basis of a principle of servitudes or other general principles of law.[125] However, a general right of transit is difficult to sustain, and the principle of servitudes, and the other possibly available instruments, are controversial and depend, in any case, on the existence of special circumstances.

Against this unpromising background must be considered the recent attempts to improve the legal position of land-locked states. At the first United Nations Conference

---

[119] See Burke, 52 *Wash. LR* (1976–7), 193–200; Robertson, 20 *Virginia JIL* (1979–80), 801–51; Reisman, 74 *AJ* (1980), 48–76; Moore, ibid. 77–121; de Vries Lentsch, 14 *Neths. Yrbk.* (1983), 165–225.

[120] See Stevenson and Oxman, 68 *AJ* (1974), 3; and in 69 *AJ* (1975), 14–15; Oxman, 24 *Virginia JIL* (1984), 809 at 851–8; Schachter, 178 Hague *Recueil* (1982, V), 281; Lee, 77 *AJ* (1983), 558–9; *Digest of US Practice* (1979), 1065–9. Cf. 58 *BY* (1987), 599–601; Jia, op. cit., 129–208.

[121] Schachter, 178 Hague *Recueil* (1982, V), 281.

[122] See generally *British Digest*, iib. 727–38, 745–7; Whiteman, ix. 1143–63; Palazzoli, 70 *RGDIP* (1966), 667–735; Ibler, *Annales d'études internationales* (Geneva, 1973), 55–65; Verzijl, *International Law in Historical Perspective*, iii. 443–54. Churchill and Lowe, *The Law of the Sea* (3rd edn., 1999), 433–46.

[123] See the *Right of Passage* case (Merits), ICJ Reports (1960), 6; and, in particular at 66 (Judge Wellington Koo), 79–80 (Judge Armand-Ugon).

[124] Farran, 4 *ICLQ* (1955), 294 at 304. See also *supra*, p. 15.

[125] See *infra*, p. 376. See also UN Conference on the Law of the Sea, Off. Recs. i. A/CONF. 13/29, paras. 41–4.

on the Law of the Sea the Fifth Committee considered the question of free access to the sea of land-locked states.[126] The result was Article 3 of the Convention on the High Seas, which provides as follows:

1. In order to enjoy the freedom of the seas on equal terms with coastal States, States having no sea-coast should have free access to the sea. To this end States situated between the sea and a State having no sea-coast shall by common agreement with the latter and in conformity with existing international conventions accord:

(a) To the State having no sea-coast, on a basis of reciprocity, free transit through their territory, and

(b) To ships flying the flag of that State treatment equal to that accorded to their own ships, or to the ships of any other States, as regards access to sea ports and the use of such ports.

2. States situated between the sea and a State having no sea-coast shall settle, by mutual agreement with the latter, and taking into account the rights of the coastal State or State of transit and the special conditions of the State having no sea-coast, all matters relating to freedom of transit and equal treatment in ports, in case such States are not already parties to existing international conventions.

Article 4 of the same Convention recognizes the right of every state, whether coastal or not, to sail ships under its flag on the high seas. The United Nations Convention on the Transit Trade of Landlocked Countries[127] adopts the principle of free access and sets out the conditions under which freedom of transit will be granted. The Convention provides a framework for the conclusion of bilateral treaties and is not directly dispositive with respect to rights of access.

Part X of the Convention on the Law of the Sea of 1982 is devoted to the 'right of access of land-locked states to and from the sea and freedom of transit' (Arts. 124–32). The key provision is Article 125 as follows:

1. Land-locked States shall have the right of access to and from the sea for the purpose of exercising the rights provided for in this Convention including those relating to the freedom of the high seas and the common heritage of mankind. To this end, land-locked States shall enjoy freedom of transit through the territory of transit States by all means of transport.

2. The terms and modalities for exercising freedom of transit shall be agreed between the land-locked States and transit States concerned through bilateral, subregional or regional agreements.

3. Transit States, in the exercise of their full sovereignty over their territory, shall have the right to take all measures necessary to ensure that the rights and facilities

---

[126] There was a Preliminary Conference of Landlocked States in Geneva, 10–14 Feb. 1958, at which a statement of principles was adopted. See Whiteman, ix. 1150; Cmnd. 584, Misc. no. 15 (1958), 12–13.

[127] In force 9 June 1967. Text: Whiteman, ix. 1156.

provided for in this Part for land-locked States shall in no way infringe their legitimate interests.

While this Article constitutes a clear recognition of the principle involved, the modalities called for in paragraphs (2) and (3) must involve substantial qualifications in practice.[128]

---

[128] For comment: Caflisch, 49 *BY* (1978), 71–100.

13

LEGAL ASPECTS OF THE PROTECTION OF THE ENVIRONMENT

1. INTRODUCTION: THE RELEVANT LEGAL CATEGORIES

The increased sophistication in appreciating the risks to the earth's environment, and the irreversible damage which may be caused by human activity, has resulted in a conscious effort, both by governments acting collectively and also by non-governmental organizations, to invoke legal protection of the environment.[1] The resulting agenda is very extensive, and includes the problem of transboundary air pollution, the risks created by reliance upon nuclear power, the protection of Antarctica, the protection of endangered species of flora and fauna, and the control of the disposal of industrial waste. The policy issues generated by such an agenda are difficult to resolve because inevitably the issues do not concern the 'environment' in isolation, but relate to human and social priorities, systems of loss distribution, and the right to development.

The fact is that environmental concerns have for long been reflected in general international law and the relevant legal categories include the law of the sea, state respons-ibility, space law, the legal regime of Antarctica, and the non-navigational

[1] See generally Brownlie, *Natural Resources Journal* 13 (1973) 179; Teclaff and Utton (eds.), *International Environmental Law* (1974); Bilder, 144 Hague *Recueil* (1975, I), 139–240; Dupuy, *La Responsabilité internationale des états pour les dommages d'origine technologique et industrielle* (1976); Schneider, *World Public Order of the Environment* (1979); Kirgis, *Prior Consultation in International Law* (1983); Nascimento e Silva, *Annuaire de l'Institut*, 62–I (1987), 159–294; Smith, *State Responsibility and the Marine Environment* (1988); Wolfrum, 33 *German Yrbk* (1990), 308–30; Kiss and Shelton, *International Environmental Law* (1991); Magraw (ed.), *International Law and Pollution* (1991); Hohmann (ed.), *Basic Documents of International Environmental Law* (3 vols., 1992); Birnie and Boyle, *International Law and the Environment* (2nd edn., 2002); E. Brown Weiss (ed.), *Environmental Change and International Law: New Challenges and Dimensions* (1992); Barboza, 247 Hague *Recueil* (1994, III), 291–406; Sands, *Principles of Environmental Law*, (2nd edn., 2003); Kummer, *International Management of Hazardous Wastes* (1995); Birnie and Boyle, *Basic Documents on International Law and the Environment* (1995); Okowa, 67 *BY* (1996), 275–336; Fitzmaurice, in *Essays in Honour of Krzysztof Skubiszewski* (1996), 909–25. Okowa, *State Responsibility for Transboundary Air Pollution* (2000); Stephens, *Austral. Yrbk.*, 25 (2006), 227–71; Boyle, *Int. Journ. of Marine and Coastal Law*, 22, 369–81.

uses of international watercourses. At the same time, it is evident that general international law does not provide the focused problem-solving which results from carefully prepared standard-setting treaties linked with domestic and international support systems and funding. It is also appropriate that effective action will be set in train in the context of regional organizations such as the European Union.

2. THE RELEVANCE OF EXISTING PRINCIPLES OF GENERAL INTERNATIONAL LAW

The legal underpinnings of the protection of the environment continue to be the institutions of general international law. This is immediately apparent from the content of the major works devoted to the legal protection of the environment, which invoke the principles of state responsibility relating to the liability of the territorial sovereign for sources of danger to other states which are created or tolerated within its territory, and cite the *Trail Smelter* arbitration[2] and the *Corfu Channel* case.[3] It comes as no surprise that recent cases concerning environmental issues have all involved specific areas of international law which are not concerned with the environment as such. Thus the *Nuclear Tests* cases (1973–4)[4] concerned issues of admissibility and remedial law. The *Case Concerning Phosphate Lands in Nauru* (1992)[5] related to issues of admissibility, the regime of a former United Nations Trusteeship, and state responsibility.

In practice, specific transboundary problems will tend to have a background in treaty relations and other dealings between neighbouring states. Consequently, the *Hungary/Slovakia* case,[6] relating to a conjoint project on the Danube, was in legal terms concerned with points of the law of treaties, together with related points of state responsibility (issues of justification for alleged breaches of treaty obligations).

3. DEFICIENCIES IN THE USE OF THE ADVERSARIAL SYSTEM OF STATE RESPONSIBILITY

A particular difficulty in the sphere of environmental hazards and damage is the selection and deployment of an appropriate cause of action or basis of claim. The process of contamination is often, in physical terms, incremental and may involve complex causal mechanisms. Apart from the finding of a cause of action, the requirement of damage

---

[2] *RIAA* iii, 1905.
[3] ICJ Reports (1949), 4.
[4] Ibid. (1974), 253 (*Australia v. France*); ibid. (1974), 457 (*New Zealand v. France*).
[5] Ibid. (1992), 240.
[6] Ibid. (1997), 7.

as a necessary condition of claim bears an uneasy relation to the scientific proof of a certain threshold of damage caused by an overall rise in radiation or other forms of pollution and problems of multiple causation then arise.

In the *Nuclear Tests* case brought by Australia against France, the Australian application employed the international law equivalent to trespass to deal with this problem. Thus the deposit of radioactive fall-out on the territory of Australia was classified as a violation of Australia's territorial sovereignty.[7] In the same context, the concept of 'decisional sovereignty' was used, referring to the right of Australia to determine what acts should take place within its territory.

A particular source of difficulty is the controversy on the question of whether remedies can be sought in anticipation of actual damage. In general it seems clear that the International Court can give injunctive relief by way of a declaratory judgment. This was the view of the four Judges of the Court in the Joint Dissenting Opinion in the *Nuclear Tests* cases.[8]

It has been observed that the decisions in the *Nuclear Tests* cases 'suggest that an international tribunal cannot grant injunctions or prohibitory orders restraining violations of international law'.[9] This view does not seem to be justified, and declarations are given by the Court which are injunctive in effect.

No doubt requests for interim measures of protection addressed to the International Court have a certain role. The request, if it is successful, has considerable effects in the political sphere, in part as a result of the media attention and the revelation of facts which the respondent state finds it difficult to deny. In environmental cases, such effects would have particular value, always provided that credible scientific evidence was available.

4. EMERGENT LEGAL PRINCIPLES: THE PRECAUTIONARY PRINCIPLE[10]

The practice of states and the literature provide support for a number of emergent, but still evolving, legal principles. Probably the best known of these is the precautionary principle. Sands observes that: 'There is no uniform understanding of the meaning of the precautionary principle among States and other members of the international

---

7 See ICJ Pleadings, *Nuclear Tests*, i. 479–90 (Argument of Mr Byers).

8 ICJ Reports (1974), 312–71 and 494–523 respectively.

9 Birnie and Boyle, *International Law and the Environment* (1992), 150–1.

10 See Birnie and Boyle, *International Law and the Environment* (2nd edn., 2002), 115–21; Sands, *Principles of International Environmental Law* (2nd edn., 2003), 266–79; Freestone and Hey (eds.), *The Precautionary Principle and International Law* (1996); Hickey and Walker, 14 *Virginia Environmental LJ* (1995), 423–54; Orrego Vicuña, *The Changing International Law of High Seas Fisheries* (1999), 156–64; Ellis, *Europ Journ.*, 17 (2006), 445–62.

community'.[11] However, it receives clear support in the 1992 Rio Declaration on Environment and Development:

Principle 15: In order to protect the environment, the precautionary approach shall be widely applied by States according to their capabilities. Where there are threats of serious or irreversible damage, lack of full scientific certainty shall not be used as a reason for postponing cost-effective measures to prevent environmental degradation.

The principle has received recognition in the Dissenting Opinion of Judge Weeramantry in the 1974 *Nuclear Tests* case.[12] The point which stands out is that at least some applications of the precautionary approach, which is based upon the principle of foreseeable risk to other States, are encompassed within existing concepts of State responsibility. The precautionary principle was discussed in certain individual opinions in the *Southern Bluefin Tuna Cases*.[13]

5. EMERGENT LEGAL PRINCIPLES: THE CONCEPT OF SUSTAINABLE DEVELOPMENT

Judge Cassese classifies sustainable development as a 'general guideline' laid down in 'soft law' documents and relies upon the definition in the Report of the Brundtland Commission thus:[14]

...in promoting development, States should always be guided by the notion of 'sustainable development', propounded in many treaties and declarations. This notion intends to cover 'development that meets the needs of the present without compromising the ability of future generations to meet their own needs' (this is the definition offered in the Report made in 1987 to the UN GA by the World Commission on Environment and Development (WCED)...).

Birnie and Boyle make the effort to present the separate elements which compose this protean concept. The elements identified include the following:

(a) *The integration of environmental protection and economic development*[15]

This element reflects Principle 4 of the Rio Declaration which provides that 'environmental protection shall constitute an integral part of the development process and cannot be considered in isolation from it'.

(b) *The right to development*

Principle 3 of the Rio Declaration provides as follows:

The right to development must be fulfilled so as to equitably meet developmental and environmental needs of present and future generations.

---

[11] Op. cit., 212.

[12] ICJ Reports, 1995, 342–4.

[13] International Tribunal for the Law of the Sea (Request for Provisional Measures), 27 August 1999; ILR 117, at 172–4 (Laing); 179–80 (Treves); 186–7 (Shearer). See also Marr, *Europ. Journ.* 11 (2000), 815–31.

[14] Cassese, *International Law* (2001), 384.

[15] Birnie and Boyle (2nd edn., 2002), 86–7.

Birnie and Boyle emphasize that 'the legal status of the right to development has been and remains doubtful,'[16] but nevertheless rank it as an element of sustainable development.

(c) *Sustainable utilization and conservation of natural resources*

This is ranked as an 'element' of sustainable development by Birnie and Boyle[17] although it is not directly reflected in the Rio Declaration. The concept provides available standards, which, when they appear in a precise treaty context, will have a concrete meaning and purpose.

(d) *Inter-generational equity*

This forms a policy datum which falls within the penumbra of sustainable development and underlies a number of global environmental treaties. However, at the end of the day, as Birnie and Boyle point out, it is question-begging.[18]

(e) *Inequity within the existing economic system*

This is now referred to, unhelpfully, as 'intra-generational equity'.[19] This element has no clear legal status and lies outside the sphere of environmental concerns as such.

6. EMERGENT LEGAL PRINCIPLES: THE POLLUTER-PAYS PRINCIPLE

Cassese[20] recognizes this is a 'general guideline' and refers to Article 16 of the Rio Declaration which provides as follows:

National authorities should endeavour to promote the internalisation of environmental costs and the use of economic instruments, taking into account the approach that the polluter should, in principle, bear the cost of pollution, with due regard to the public interest and without distorting international trade and investment.

Birnie and Boyle include this principle as an 'element' of sustainable development, but describe it as 'essentially an economic policy'.[21] It is clear from the language of Article 16 of the Rio Declaration that the principle is essentially programmatic and hortatory. Sands observes that 'it is doubtful whether it has achieved the status of a generally applicable rule of customary international law...'.[22] There is here a certain difficulty. The content of the Polluter-pays principle is vague, but appears to involve strict liability. Doubts are expressed by reputable authorities about its legal status and, in this context, and in

---

[16] Op. cit., 87.
[17] Op. cit., 88–9. See also Sands, op. cit., 252–6.
[18] Op. cit., 89–91. See also Sands, op. cit., 256–7.
[19] See Birnie and Boyle, op. cit., 91–2.
[20] *International Law* (2001), 384.
[21] Op. cit., 92–5.
[22] Op. cit., 280.

order to avoid confusion, it is necessary to recall that the ordinary principles of State responsibility are applicable if damage affects the legal interest of another State.

7. RISK MANAGEMENT: THE PREVENTION OF TRANSBOUNDARY HARM FROM HAZARDOUS ACTIVITIES

At its fifty-third session in 2001 the International Law Commission adopted the text of a preamble and nineteen draft articles on the Prevention of Transboundary Harm from Hazardous Activities, and decided to recommend to the General Assembly the elaboration of a convention by the Assembly on the basis of the draft articles.[23] The key provisions are as follows:

Article 1

Scope

The present articles apply to activities not prohibited by international law which involve a risk of causing significant transboundary harm through their physical consequences.

Article 2

Use of terms

For the purposes of the present articles:

(a) 'Risk of causing significant transboundary harm' includes risks taking the form of a high probability of causing significant transboundary harm and a low probability of causing disastrous transboundary harm;

(b) 'Harm' means harm caused to persons, property or the environment;

(c) 'Transboundary harm' means harm caused in the territory of or in other places under the jurisdiction or control of a State other than the State of origin, whether or not the States concerned share a common border;

(d) 'State of origin' means the State in the territory or otherwise under the jurisdiction or control of which the activities referred to in Article 1 are planned or are carried out;

(e) 'State likely to be affected' means the State or States in the territory of which there is the risk of significant transboundary harm or which have jurisdiction or control over any other place where there is such a risk;

(f) 'States concerned' means the State of origin and the State likely to be affected.

---

[23] See *Report of the International Law Commission, Fifty-third session*, 2001; G.A. Off. Recs., Fifty-sixth session, Suppl. No. 10 (A/56/10). The Special Rapporteur was Mr Pemmaraju Sreenivasa Rao. In 2006 the Commission adopted a set of eight draft principles on the allocation of loss in case of transboundary harm arising out of hazardous activities; see the *Report of the International Law Commission, Fifty-eighth session* (2006), G.A. Off. Recs., *Sixty-first session*, Suppl. No. 10 (A/61/10), 101–82. See further Boyle, *Journ. of Environmental Law*, Vol. 17 (2005), 3–26. Unlike the case of prevention of harm, the adoption of a convention is not envisaged in relation to the allocation of loss.

Article 3

Prevention

The State of origin shall take all appropriate measures to prevent significant transboundary harm or at any event to minimize the risk thereof.

Article 4

Co-operation

States concerned shall co-operate in good faith and, as necessary, seek the assistance of one or more competent international organizations in preventing significant transboundary harm or at any event in minimizing the risk thereof.

Article 5

Implementation

States concerned shall take the necessary legislative, administrative or other action including the establishment of suitable monitoring mechanisms to implement the provisions of the present articles.

Article 6

Authorization

1. The State of origin shall require its prior authorization for:

(a) Any activity within the scope of the present articles carried out in its territory or otherwise under its jurisdiction or control;

(b) Any major change in an activity referred to in subparagraph (a);

(c) Any plan to change an activity which may transform it into one falling within the scope of the present articles.

[...]

Article 7

Assessment of risk

Any decision in respect of the authorization of an activity within the scope of the present articles shall, in particular, be based on an assessment of the possible transboundary harm caused by that activity, including any environmental impact assessment.

Article 8

Notification and information

1. If the assessment referred to in Article 7 indicates a risk of causing significant transboundary harm, the State of origin shall provide the State likely to be affected with timely notification of the risk and the assessment and shall transmit to it the available technical and other relevant information on which the assessment is based.

2. The State of origin shall not take any decision on authorization of the activity pending the receipt, within a period not exceeding six months, of the response from the State likely to be affected.

Article 9

Consultations on preventive measures

1. The States concerned shall enter into consultations, at the request of any of them, with a view to achieving acceptable solutions regarding measures to be adopted in order to prevent significant transboundary harm or at any event to minimize the risk thereof. The States concerned shall agree, at the commencement of such consultations, on a reasonable time-frame for the consultations.

2. The States concerned shall seek solutions based on an equitable balance of interests in the light of Article 10.

3. If the consultations referred to in paragraph 1 fail to produce an agreed solution, the State of origin shall nevertheless take into account the interests of the State likely to be affected in case it decides to authorize the activity to be pursued, without prejudice to the rights of any State likely to be affected.

Article 10

Factors involved in an equitable balance of interests

In order to achieve an equitable balance of interests as referred to in paragraph 2 of Article 9, the States concerned shall take into account all relevant factors and circumstances, including:

(a) The degree of risk of significant transboundary harm and of the availability of means of preventing such harm, or minimizing the risk thereof or repairing the harm;

(b) The importance of the activity, taking into account its overall advantages of a social, economic and technical character for the State of origin in relation to the potential harm for the State like to be affected;

(c) The risk of significant harm to the environment and the availability of means of preventing such harm, or minimizing the risk thereof or restoring the environment;

(d) The degree to which the State of origin and, as appropriate, the State likely to be affected are prepared to contribute to the costs of prevention;

(e) The economic viability of the activity in relation to the costs of prevention and to the possibility of carrying out the activity elsewhere or by other means or replacing it with an alternative activity;

(f) The standards of prevention which the State likely to be affected applies to the same or comparable activities and the standards applied in comparable regional or international practice.

Article 11

Procedures in the absence of notification

1. If a State has reasonable grounds to believe that an activity planned or carried out in the State of origin may involve a risk of causing significant transboundary harm to it, it may request the State of origin to apply the provision of Article 8. The request shall be accompanied by a documented explanation setting forth its grounds.

2. In the event that the State of origin nevertheless finds that it is not under an obligation to provide a notification under Article 8, it shall so inform the requesting State within a reasonable time, providing a documented explanation setting forth the reasons for such finding. If this finding does not satisfy that State, at its request, the two States shall promptly enter into consultations in the manner indicated in Article 9.

3. During the course of the consultations, the State of origin shall, if so requested by the other State, arrange to introduce appropriate and feasible measures to minimize the risk and, where appropriate, to suspend the activity in question for a reasonable period.

Article 12

Exchange of information

While the activity is being carried out, the States concerned shall exchange in a timely manner all available information concerning that activity relevant to preventing significant transboundary harm or at any event minimizing the risk thereof. Such an exchange of information shall continue until such time as the States concerned consider it appropriate even after the activity is terminated.

These draft articles provide a creative and original regime for prevention of transboundary harm and the management of risk. They are concerned with prevention rather than with State responsibility for activities which have caused harm. The articles are without prejudice to obligations incurred by States under relevant treaties or rules of customary law. Further provisions deal with notification of emergencies by the State of origin and the settlement of disputes.

The regime of prevention is based upon territorial jurisdiction as the dominant criterion. The title over territory is conclusive evidence of jurisdiction. However, the obligations of prevention also apply to 'situations in which a State is exercising *de facto* jurisdiction, even though it lacks jurisdiction *de jure*, such as in cases of unlawful intervention, occupation and unlawful annexation'.[24] The substance of the draft articles is radical and the perspective is still dominated by the fact that there are no substantive limitations on the activities which States may undertake on their own territory.

8. THE IMPORTANCE AND ROLE OF MULTILATERAL STANDARD-SETTING CONVENTIONS

At the end of the day the working part of environmental law consists of the collection of important standard-setting conventions devoted to particular problems.[25] A number of such instruments relate to the conservation of nature and living resources. Apart from these conventions, other significant instruments include the following:

---

[24] *Report of the International Law Commission* (2001), 384, para. 12.
[25] See Birnie and Boyle (eds.), *Basic Documents on International Law and the Environment* (1995). See also Scovazzi and Treves, *World Treaties for the Protection of the Environment* (1992).

(1) Convention on Long-Range Transboundary Air Pollution, Geneva, 13 November 1979;[26]

(2) The Convention for the Protection of the Ozone Layer, Vienna, 22 March 1985;[27]

(3) Convention on Early Notification of a Nuclear Accident, Vienna, 28 September 1986;[28]

(4) The Protocol on Substances that Deplete the Ozone Layer, Montreal, 16 September 1987;[29]

(5) Convention on the Control of Transboundary Movements of Hazardous Wastes and their Disposal, Basel, 22 March 1989;[30]

(6) Convention on environmental impact assessment in a Transboundary context, Espoo, Finland, 25 February 1991;[31]

(7) Convention on the Protection and Use of Transboundary Watercourses and Lakes, Helsinki, 17 March 1992;[32]

(8) Convention on the Transboundary Effect of Industrial Accidents, Helsinki, 17 March 1992;[33]

(9) Framework Convention on Climate Change, New York, 9 May 1992;[34]

(10) Convention on Biological Diversity, Nairobi, 22 June 1992;[35]

(11) Protocol on Further Reduction of Sulphur Emissions, Oslo, 14 June 1994;[36]

(12) United Nations Convention to Combat Desertification in those Countries Experiencing Serious Drought and/or Desertification, Particularly in Africa, Paris, 14 October 1994;[37]

(13) Convention on the Law of the Non-navigational Uses of International Watercourses, New York, 21 May 1997;[38]

(14) Kyoto Protocol to the United Nations Framework Convention on Climate Change, Kyoto, 11 December 1997.[39]

---

[26] Birnie and Boyle (eds), *Basic Documents*, 277.
[27] Ibid., 211.
[28] Ibid., 300.
[29] Ibid., 224.
[30] Ibid., 322.
[31] Ibid., 31.
[32] Birnie and Boyle (eds.), *Basic Documents*, 345.
[33] Ibid., 50.
[34] Ibid., 252.
[35] Ibid., 390.
[36] Ibid., 285.
[37] Ibid., 511.
[38] G.A. Resol. 51/229, adopted 8 July 1997.
[39] *ILM* 37 (1998), 22.

Further multilateral conventions deal with the protection of the marine environment of the Baltic[40] and Mediterranean Seas.[41]

9. EVALUATION

In the context of environmental problems, the way forward lies in the deployment of effective enforcement systems fully integrated into the legal and administrative systems of individual states. Moreover, enforcement must be based upon scientific data, and suitable economic desiderata, rather than the importunities of special interests and single issue advocates. It must follow that the appropriate vehicle for action is the multi-lateral standard-setting convention with a focus upon a specific type of problem or a specific region. Bilateral agreements relating to boundaries and frontier relations also have a role to play.

The continuing relevance of the principles of state responsibility is not to be underestimated. The difficulty is that state responsibility, like duty situations in the law concerning civil responsibility in national systems, depends ultimately upon the emergence of social and moral criteria which are generally acceptable. Candidate principles of general international law which do not satisfy the grand jury of state practice are unlikely to prosper. In any event, the existing principles of state responsibility are more versatile than the specialist writers are prepared to recognize. The role played by international principles of environmental law in national courts remains minimal.[42]

In any event the general obligation of States to ensure that activities within their jurisdiction and control respect the environment of other States (and of areas beyond national control) was affirmed by the International Court in its Advisory Opinion on the *Legality of the Threat or Use of Nuclear Weapons* (1996).[43]

---

[40] Convention on the Marine Environment of the Baltic Sea Area, 1974; 13 *ILM* (1974), 546.

[41] Convention for the Protection of the Mediterranean Sea Against Pollution, 1976; 15 *ILM* (1976), 290.

[42] See Anderson and Galizzi (eds.), *International Environmental Law in National Courts* (2002).

[43] ICJ Reports, 1996, p. 226 at pp. 241–2, para. 29. See also the Rio Declaration (1992), 31 *ILM* 874, Principle 2; the Institute of International Law, Resol. on Responsibility and Liability under International Law for Environmental Damage, 4 Sept. 1997; *Annuaire*, vol. 67–II (1998), 487; and the Judgment of the International Court in the *Gabčikovo/Nagymaros Project*, ICJ Reports (1997), p. 41 (para. 53).

PART VI

STATE JURISDICTION

14

SOVEREIGNTY AND EQUALITY
OF STATES

1. GENERAL[1]

The sovereignty and equality of states represent the basic constitutional doctrine of the law of nations, which governs a community consisting primarily of states having a uniform legal personality. If international law exists, then the dynamics of state sovereignty can be expressed in terms of law, and, as states are equal and have legal personality, sovereignty is in a major aspect a relation to other states (and to organizations of states) defined by law. The principal corollaries of the sovereignty and equality of states are: (1) a jurisdiction, prima facie exclusive, over a territory and the permanent population living there; (2) a duty of non-intervention in the area of exclusive jurisdiction of other states; and (3) the dependence of obligations arising from customary law[2] and treaties on the consent of the obligor.[3] The last of these has certain special applications: thus the jurisdiction of international tribunals depends on the consent of the parties; membership of international organizations is not obligatory; and the powers of the organs of such organizations to determine their own competence, to take decisions by majority vote, and to enforce decisions, depend on the consent of member states.

The manner in which the law expresses the content of sovereignty varies, and indeed the whole of the law could be expressed in terms of the coexistence of sovereignties. The

---

[1] See Rousseau, 73 Hague *Recueil* (1948, II), 171–253; id., *Droit international public*, iv. 21–33; Chaumont, *Hommage d'une génération de juristes au Président Basdevant* (1960), 114–51; Waldock, 106 Hague *Recueil* (1962, II), 156–91; van Kleffens, 82 Hague *Recueil* (1953, I), 5–130; Lauterpacht, *The Development of International Law by the International Court* (1958), 297–400; Fitzmaurice, 92 Hague *Recueil* (1957), II), 48–59; Kelsen, *Principles of International Law* (1952), 108–10, 155–7, 216–17, 315–17, 438–44; ibid. (2nd edn., 1967), 190–4, 247–50, 446–8, 581–5; id., 53 *Yale LJ* (1944), 207–20; McNair, *Law of Treaties* (1961), 754–66; *Preparatory Study Concerning a Draft Declaration on the Rights and Duties of States*, A/CN.4/2, 1948, pp. 49–74; Verzijl, *International Law in Historical Perspective*, i. (1968), 256–92; Lachs, 169 Hague *Recueil* (1980, IV), 77–84; Virally, 183 Hague *Recueil* (1983, V), 76–88; Anand, 197 Hague *Recueil* (1986, II), 9–228; Oppenheim i. 339–79; Broms, Bedjaoui (ed.), *International Law: Achievements and Prospects* (1991), 59–62.

[2] See *supra*, pp. 6–10. But see pp. 510–512 on *jus cogens*. In any case the conditions for 'contracting out' of rules are not easy to fulfil.

[3] See, in particular the Decl. on Principles of International Law Concerning Friendly Relations and Cooperation Among States, UNGA, 1970, 65 *AJ* (1971), 243; Brownlie, *Documents*, p. 27. See further *British Practice* (1964), 124–6, 128–30; ibid. (1966), 41–9; ibid. (1967), 35–41, 192–6; 56 *BY* (1985), 385–6.

problems can be approached through the concept of the reserved domain of domestic jurisdiction (section 5, *infra*, p. 290). Yet another perspective is provided by the notion of sovereignty as discretionary power within areas delimited by the law. Thus states alone can confer nationality for purposes of municipal law, delimit the territorial sea, and decide on the necessity for action in self-defence. Yet in all these cases the exercise of the power is conditioned by the law.[4]

2. SOVEREIGNTY AND THE APPLICATION OF RULES[5]

(a) The validity of obligations arising from treaties

In the *Wimbledon* the Permanent Court firmly rejected the argument that a treaty provision could not deprive a state of the sovereign right to apply the law of neutrality to vessels passing through the Kiel Canal:[6] 'The Court declines to see, in the conclusion of any treaty by which a State undertakes to perform or refrain from performing a particular act, an abandonment of its sovereignty...the right of entering into international engagements is an attribute of State sovereignty'.

(b) Interpretation of treaties

The principles of treaty interpretation are considered in Chapter 26. On occasion the International Court has referred to sovereign rights as a basis for a restrictive interpreta-tion of treaty obligations,[7] but everything depends on the context, the intention of the parties, and the relevance of other, countervailing, principles such as that of effectiveness.

(c) Presumptions and burdens

Many areas of international law are uncertain or contain principles which do not admit of easy application to concrete issues. Thus much could turn on the answer to the question whether there is a presumption in favour of sovereignty. In another form the issue is whether, in case of doubt as to the mode of application of rules or in case of an absence of rules, the presumption is that states have legal competence or is one

---

[4] On nationality see *infra*, ch. 19. On the territorial sea see the *Fisheries* case, *supra*, pp. 176ff. On the right of self-defence see Brownlie, *International Law and the Use of Force by States* (1963), 235ff. Cf. the problem of the automatic reservation of the optional clause (*infra*, pp. 716ff.). and the regulation of rights (*infra*, p. 376).

[5] See Lauterpacht, *Development*, pp. 359–67; Waldock, 106 Hague *Recueil* (1962, II), 159–69; Fitzmaurice, 92 Hague *Recueil* (1957, II), 49–59 id., 30 *BY* (1953), 8–18; McNair, *Law of Treaties*, pp. 754–66.

[6] (1923), PCIJ, Ser. A, no. 1, p. 25. Cf. the view of the International Court on reservations by states seeking to become parties to multilateral treaties: *Reservations to the Genocide Convention*, ICJ Reports (1951), at 24; and the views of certain members of the Court on the automatic reservation in acceptances of the optional clause, *infra*, pp. 688ff.

[7] See the *Wimbledon, supra*, p. 21; and the *Free Zones* cases (1930), PCIJ, Ser. A, no. 24, p. 12; (1932), PCIJ, Ser. A/B, no. 46, p. 167.

of incompetence. In the *Lotus* case[8] the Court decided the issue of jurisdiction on the basis that 'restrictions upon the independence of States cannot be presumed'. However, there is no general rule, and in judicial practice issues are approached empirically. It is also the case that a general presumption of either kind would lead to inconvenience or abuse. The context of a problem will determine the incidence of particular burdens of proof, which may be described in terms of the duty to establish a restriction on sovereignty on the part of the proponent of the duty. The jurisdictional 'geography' of the problem may provide useful indications. Thus in the *Asylum* case the Court stressed the fact that diplomatic asylum involves a derogation from sovereignty as represented by the normally exclusive jurisdiction of the territorial state. On the other hand, in the *Fisheries* case,[9] the dominant factor from this point of view was the international impact of the delimitation of frontiers, in that case the maritime frontier.

3. SOVEREIGNTY AND COMPETENCE

Sovereignty is also used to describe the legal competence which states have in general, to refer to a particular function of this competence, or to provide a rationale for a particular aspect of the competence.[10] Thus jurisdiction, including legislative competence over national territory, may be referred to in the terms 'sovereignty' or 'sovereign rights'. Sovereignty may refer to the power to acquire title to territory and the rights accruing from exercise of the power. The correlative duty of respect for territorial sovereignty,[11] and the privileges in respect of territorial jurisdiction, referred to as sovereign or state immunities, are described after the same fashion. In general 'sovereignty' characterizes powers and privileges resting on customary law and independent of the particular consent of another state.

4. MEMBERSHIP OF ORGANIZATIONS[12]

The institutional aspects of organizations of states result in an actual, as opposed to a formal, qualification of the principle of sovereign equality.[13] Thus an organization may adopt majority voting and also have a system of weighted voting; and organs may

---

[8] See *infra*, p. 300. Cf. *Lake Lanoux* arbitration, *supra*, p. 260. See further *De Pascale Claim*, *RIAA* xvi. 227; ILR 40, 250 at 256; Sultan, *Mélanges offerts à Andrassy* (1968), 294–306.

[9] *Supra*, pp. 176ff.

[10] See further ch. 6.

[11] See the *Corfu Channel* case (Merits), ICJ Reports (1949), 4 at 35; and Art. 2, para. 4, of the United Nations Charter.

[12] See Bourquin, *L'Etat souverain et l'organisation internationale* (1959); Broms, *The Doctrine of Equality of States as Applied in International Organizations* (1959); Korowicz, *Organisations internationales et souveraineté des états membres* (1961); Waldock, 106 Hague *Recueil* (1962, II), 20–38, 171–2; van Kleffens, 82 Hague *Recueil* (1953, I), 107–26; Rousseau, iv. 27–33; Lachs, 169 Hague *Recueil* (1980, IV), 141–2; Morgenstern, *Legal Problems of International Organizations* (1986), 46–68; Sands and Klein (eds.) *Bowett's Law of International Institutions* (5th edn., 2001), 533–64.

[13] Compare Art. 2, para. 1, of the UN Charter with the provisions on the Security Council, chs. 5–8.

be permitted to take decisions, and even to make binding rules, without the express consent of all or any of the member states.[14] Of course it can be said that on joining the organization each member consented in advance to the institutional aspects, and thus in a formal way the principle that obligations can only arise from the consent of states and the principle of sovereign equality are satisfied. In their practice the European Communities, while permitting integration which radically affects domestic jurisdiction for special purposes, have been careful not to jar the delicate treaty structures by a too ready assumption of implied powers.[15] In the case of the United Nations the organs, with the approval of the Court, have interpreted the Charter in accordance with the principles of effectiveness and implied powers at the expense, it may seem, of Article 2, paragraphs 1 and 7.[16] If an organization encroaches on the domestic jurisdiction of members to a substantial degree the structure may approximate to a federation, and not only the area of competence of members but their very personality will be in issue. The line is not easy to draw, but the following criteria of extinction of personality have been suggested: the obligatory nature of membership; majority decision-making; the determination of jurisdiction by the organization itself; and the binding quality of decisions of the organization apart from consent of member states.[17]

5. THE RESERVED DOMAIN OF DOMESTIC JURISDICTION

The corollary of the independence and equality of states is the duty on the part of states to refrain from intervention in the internal or external affairs of other states.[18] The duty of non-intervention is a master principle which draws together many particular rules on the legal competence and responsibility of states. Matters within the competence of states under general international law are said to be within the reserved domain, the domestic jurisdiction, of states.[19] This is tautology, of course, and as a matter of

---

[14] See generally ch. 31.

[15] See Pescatore, 103 Hague *Recueil* (1961, II), 9–238; Hahn, 108 Hague *Recueil* (1963, I), 195–300.

[16] See *infra*, pp. 676ff., 697ff., on the *Reparation and Expenses* cases.

[17] See van Kleffens, 82 Hague *Recueil* (1953, I), 117–26; Verzijl, *International Law in Historical Perspective*, i. 283–92; Waldock, 106 Hague *Recueil* (1962, II), 171–2. See also *supra*, pp. 71–4, on independence as a criterion of statehood.

[18] See the draft Decl. on the Rights and Duties of States, *Yrbk. ILC* (1949), 287, Art. 3. The duty binds international organizations also. One aspect of the duty concerns the illegality of the use or threat of force: see Brownlie, *International Law and the Use of Force by States*, pp. 74, 96–101, 117, 224–5. Cf. the *Lotus* case *infra*, p. 301. The duty includes large areas of law: see Whiteman, v. 321–702.

[19] On domestic jurisdiction see generally *Annuaire de l'Inst.* 44 (1952), i. 137–80; and 45 (1954), ii. 108–99, 292, 299; Preuss, 74 Hague *Recueil* (1949, I), 553–652; Rajan, *United Nations and Domestic Jurisdiction* (2nd edn., 1961) (pp. 407–48, 509–25, for notes on literature and a very full biblio.); Berthoud, 4 *Ann. suisse de d.i.* (1947), 17–104; Jones, 46 *Illinois LR.* (1951), 219–72; Waldock, 106 Hague *Recueil* (1962, II), 173–91; Kelsen, *Principles of International Law*, pp. 62–4, 191–2, 196–201; ibid. (2nd edn), 290–1, 294–300; Briggs, 93 Hague *Recueil* (1958, I), 309–63; id., *Mélanges Rolin* (1964), 13–29; Fitzmaurice, 92 Hague *Recueil* (1957,

general principle the problem of domestic jurisdiction is not very fruitful. However, as a source of confusion, it deserves some consideration. The general position is that the 'reserved domain' is the domain of state activities where the jurisdiction of the state is not bound by international law: the extent of this domain depends on international law and varies according to its development.[20] It is widely accepted that no subject is irrevocably fixed within the reserved domain, but some jurists have assumed that a list of topics presently recognized as within the reserved domain can be drawn up, including categories such as nationality and immigration.[21] This approach is misleading, since everything depends on the precise facts and legal issues arising therefrom. When, by legislation or executive decree, a state delimits a fishing zone or the territorial sea, the manner and provenance of the exercise of state power is clearly a matter for the state. But when it is a matter of enforcing the limit *vis-à-vis* other states, the issue is placed on the international plane. Similarly, the conferment and withdrawal of nationality may lead to a collision of interest between states if two states are in dispute over the right of one of them to exercise diplomatic protection.[22] One might conclude that the criterion depends on a distinction between internal competence—no outside authority can annul or prevent the internally valid act of state power—and international responsibility for the consequences of the *ultra vires* exercise of the competence declared by the legislation to exist. This distinction certainly has wide application, but is not absolute in character. Thus, in particular contexts, international law may place restrictions on the 'internal' territorial competence of states as a consequence of treaty obligations, for example, forbidding legislation which discriminates against certain groups among the population, or as a consequence of territorial privileges and immunities created by custom. In the case of various territorial privileges, created either by general or local custom or by treaty, other states are permitted to exercise governmental functions, sovereign acts, within the territorial domain.[23]

The relativity of the concept of the reserved domain is illustrated by the rule that a state cannot plead provisions of its own law or deficiencies in that law in answer to a claim against it for an alleged breach of its obligations under international law,[24] and also by the fact that a particular international obligation may refer to national law as a means of describing a status to be created or protected.[25]

As a separate notion in general international law, the reserved domain is mysterious only because many have failed to see that it really stands for a tautology. However, if

---

II), 59–67; Verzijl, *International Law in Historical Perspective*, i. 272–83 (also in *Scritti Perassi* (1957), ii. 389–403); Rousseau, ii. 84–91; Conforti, Bedjaoui (ed.), *International Law: Achievements and Perspectives* (1991), 467–82; Bernhardt, *Encyclopedia*, Vol. I (1992), 1090–6; Arangio-Ruiz, *Essays in Honour of Sir Robert Jennings* (1996), 440–64.

[20] Resol. of the Institute of International Law, *Annuaire de l'Inst.* 45 (1954), ii. 292, 299; and see also *Nationality Decrees in Tunis and Morocco* (1923), PCIJ, Ser. B, no. 4, p. 24.

[21] Cf. Rousseau, 73 Hague *Recueil* (1948, II), 239–46.

[22] See generally *infra*, pp. 399ff.

[23] See *infra*, pp. 323ff., 369ff.

[24] *Supra*, p. 34.

[25] *Supra*, pp. 36, 38. And see also the *Serbian Loans* case, *supra*, p. 37.

a matter is prima facie within the reserved domain because of its nature and the issue presented in the normal case, then certain presumptions against any restriction on that domain may be created.[26] Thus the imposition of customs tariffs is prima facie unrestricted by international law, whilst the introduction of forces into another state is not prima facie an internal matter for the sending state.[27]

6. ARTICLE 2, PARAGRAPH 7, OF THE UNITED NATIONS CHARTER[28]

The advent of international organizations with powers to settle disputes on a *political* basis caused some states to favour express references to the reserved domain. Thus in the League of Nations Covenant, Article 15, paragraph 8, provided, in relation to disputes submitted to the Council *and not to arbitration or judicial settlement*: 'If the dispute between the parties is claimed by one of them, and is found by the Council, to arise out of a matter which by international law is solely within the domestic jurisdiction of that party, the Council shall so report, and shall make no recommendation as to its settlement.'

In making a political settlement the Council might well touch on the reserved domain, since this contains matters frequently the cause of disputes, and the need to write in the legal limit of action was apparent.[29] During the drafting of the United Nations Charter similar issues arose, and the result was the provision in Article 2, paragraph 7:[30]

Nothing contained in the present Charter shall authorize the United Nations to intervene in matters which are essentially within the domestic jurisdiction of any State or shall require the Members to submit such matters to settlement under the present Charter; but this principle shall not prejudice the application of enforcement measures under Chapter VII.

---

[26] Cf. the remarks on sovereignty, *supra*, pp. 290–1.

[27] See, however, Judge Lauterpacht, Sep. Op., *Norwegian Loans* case, ICJ Reports (1957), at 51–2.

[28] See also Kelsen, *The Law of the United Nations* (1951), 769–91; Fincham, *Domestic Jurisdiction* (1948); Verdross, 36 *RGDIP* (1965), 314–25; Gross, *Austral. Yrbk.* (1965), 137–58; Gilmour, ibid. (1967), 153–210; id., 16 *ICLQ* (1967), 330–51; Verdross, *Mélanges offerts à Charles Rousseau* (1974), 267–76. For accounts of the practice of United Nations organs see *Repertory of Practice of United Nations Organs*, i. 55–156; Rajan, *United Nations*; Higgins, *The Development of International Law through the Political Organs of the United Nations* (1963), 58–130; Ross, *Mélanges Rolin*, pp. 284–99; Köck, 22 *Öst. Z. für öff. R.* (1971–2), 327–61; Watson, 77 *AJ* (1977), 60–83; Trindade, 25 *ICLQ* (1976), 715–65. See further the *Peace Treaties* case, ICJ Reports (1950), 65 at 70–1, quoted *infra*, p. 297.

[29] But the limitation could not be relied upon too readily: see the *Nationality Decrees* case, PCIJ, Ser. B, no. 4 and Lauterpacht, *Development*, pp. 270–2. The limitation does not appear in Arts. 12 to 14, which are concerned with arbitration and judicial settlement.

[30] See also Art. 10 of the Charter, Art. 1(3) of the UNESCO Constitution, and Art. 3 D of the Statute of the International Atomic Energy Agency.

Certain contrasts with the provision of the Covenant quoted above will be apparent. There is no reference to international law, the reference is to matters 'essentially' within the domestic jurisdiction, and there is no designation of the authority which is to have the power to qualify particular matters. The provision in the Charter was intended to be flexible and non-technical. At the same time the restriction was meant to be thoroughgoing, hence the formula 'essentially within', because of the wide implications of the economic and social provisions of the Charter (Chapter IX). These intentions have in practice worked against each other. The flexibility of the provision, and the assumption in practice that it does not override other, potentially conflicting, provisions,[31] have resulted in the erosion of the reservation of domestic jurisdiction, although its draftsmen had intended its reinforcement. Moreover, the word 'intervene' has been approached empirically. Discussion, recommendations in general terms, and even resolutions addressed to particular states have not been inhibited by the form of paragraph 7. At the same time the term 'intervene' is not to be conceived of only as dictatorial intervention in this context. Member states have proceeded empirically with an eye to general opinion and a clear knowledge that precedents created in one connection may have a boomerang effect.

In practice United Nations organs, particularly on the basis of Chapters IX and XI of the Charter and the provisions on human rights in Articles 55 and 56, have taken action on a wide range of topics dealing with the relations of governments to their own people. Resolutions on breaches of human rights,[32] the right of self-determination[33] and colonialism, and non-self-governing territories (as qualified by the General Assembly) have been adopted regularly. If the organ concerned felt that the acts complained of were contrary to the purposes and principles of the Charter and also that the issue was 'endangering international peace and security',[34] then a resolution was passed. Certain issues, principally those concerning the right of self-determination and the principle of non-discrimination in racial matters, are regarded as of international concern by the General Assembly, apart from express reference to any threat to international peace and security.[35] The Security Council adopted a resolution concerning apartheid *only partly* on the basis that the situation 'constitutes a potential threat to international peace and security'.[36]

A question which lacks a clear answer is the relation of Article 2, paragraph 7, to general international law. On its face the provision is a matter of constitutional competence for organs of the United Nations, and, as we have seen, it lacks reference to

[31] In particular, the provisions of chs. 9 and 10. See Kelsen, 55 *Yale LJ* (1946), 1006–7; Guggenheim, 80 Hague *Recueil* (1952, I), 105; Verdross, 83 Hague *Recueil* (1953, II), 73.

[32] Generally on human rights: ch. 25.

[33] *Infra*, pp. 579–82.

[34] Exceptionally, as in the Spanish question, and the issue of *apartheid* in South Africa, the form of government in a state was regarded as a potential threat to international peace.

[35] On the concept of international concern see Howell, 48 ASIL *Proceedings* (1954), 90; and Higgins, *Development*, pp. 77–81.

[36] See Resol. 282 (1970), 23 July 1970. It is relevant to notice that this and other resolutions of the SC on the same subject were adopted under ch. 6 of the UN Charter.

international law. Moreover, in their practice the political organs have avoided express determination of technical points arising from the provision. Thus in principle it has no necessary and direct impact on general law.[37] However, in a general way in a political document like the Charter, the provision corresponds to the principles of non-intervention and the reserved domain. And, further, *in relation to other articles* and especially Articles 55, 56, and 73(e), the interpretation of the provision by organs of the United Nations has had important effects on the reserved domain: but here we must again escape from tautology. What has happened is simply that a new content has been given to the obligations and legal competence of states through the medium of the Charter.

7. INTERNATIONAL TRIBUNALS AND THE PLEA OF DOMESTIC JURISDICTION[38]

The chief characteristic of the concept of domestic jurisdiction in relation to the practice of tribunals has been its lack of specific relevance. In the case of *Nationality Decrees in Tunis and Morocco*[39] the concept played a prominent role simply by reason of the special circumstances in which the League Council had requested an advisory opinion. The dispute between Great Britain and France had been brought before the League Council by Britain, as France had rejected her request to accept a judicial settlement.[40] In the Council proceedings France pleaded Article 15, paragraph 8, of the League Covenant. Eventually the two governments agreed that the League Council should request the Permanent Court to give an advisory opinion on the nature of the dispute, in other words, on the issue whether the Council's jurisdiction was barred by Article 15, paragraph 8, of the Covenant. The Court stressed that it was not concerned with the actual legal rights of the parties as in contentious proceedings but with the general character of the legal issues for the purpose of establishing the competence of the Council. In this task the Court contented itself with reaching a 'provisional conclusion' on the international character of the issues in the case.[41] However, it is doubtful if this approach on the basis of a 'provisional conclusion' is justifiable in the case where there is a preliminary objection to jurisdiction in a contentious case,[42] where

---

[37] Cf. Hambro, *Annuaire de l'Inst.* 44 (1952), i. 167.

[38] See Briggs, 93 Hague *Recueil* (1958, I), 309–63; Waldock, 31 *BY* (1954), 96–142; Fitzmaurice, 35, *BY* (1959), 197–207; Trindade, 16 *Indian Journ*, (1976). 187–218.

[39] PCIJ, Ser. B, no. 4.

[40] At this time neither state had accepted jurisdiction in advance under the optional clause in the Statute of the Permanent Court of International Justice.

[41] pp. 24–6.

[42] This approach has its supporters: see Waldock, 31 *BY* (1954), 111–14. For critical comment see Lauterpacht, *Development*, pp. 270–1; Verzijl, *The Jurisprudence of the World Court*, i (1965), 45–50; and Fitzmaurice, 35 *BY* (1959), 200–7. See further the *South-West Africa* cases (Second Phase), 1966.

the question of domestic jurisdiction is raised in relation to the precise issues before the Court. In practice the International Court has joined a plea of domestic jurisdiction to the merits,[43] since, although the plea is in form a preliminary objection,[44] it has an intimate connection with the issues of substance.

A further question which arises is application of the reservation in Article 2, paragraph 7, of the Charter to the jurisdiction of the Court, the object of arguing for its application being to benefit from the extensive formula 'essentially within'.[45] Whether the reservation in the Charter applies to the contentious jurisdiction or not,[46] the plea of domestic jurisdiction is available by operation of law, its success depending on the particular legal relations of the parties concerned.[47] The case is rather different where the advisory jurisdiction is challenged on the basis that the political organ concerned was incompetent to request an opinion as a consequence of Article 2, paragraph 7. In this situation the relevance of the Charter reservation is indisputable. In the *Peace Treaties* case, the Court considered objections to its competence based (1) upon the incompetence of the requesting organ and (2) upon the application of Article 2, paragraph 7, to the Court itself. The objections involved the argument that a matter may be 'essentially' within the domestic jurisdiction of a state although it is governed by a treaty. As to the competence of the requesting organ of the United Nations, the Court observed:[48]

The Court is not called upon to deal with the charges brought before the General Assembly since the Questions put to the court relate neither to the alleged violations of the provisions of the Treaties concerning human rights and fundamental freedoms nor to the interpretation of the articles relating to these matters. The object of the request is much more limited. It is directed solely to obtaining from the Court certain clarifications of a legal nature regarding the applicability of the procedure for the settlement of disputes [in the peace treaties with Bulgaria, Hungary, and Romania]. The interpretation of the terms of a treaty for this purpose could not be considered as a question essentially within the domestic jurisdiction of a State. It is a question of international law which, by its very nature, lies within the competence of the Court.

The Court then stated that these considerations sufficed to dispose of the objection based on Article 2, paragraph 7, directed specifically against the competence of the Court. While this is not unequivocal evidence that Article 2, paragraph 7, applies to

---

[43] See the *Losinger* case, PCIJ, Ser. A/B, no. 67, pp. 23–5; *Right of Passage* case, ICJ Reports (1957), 125 at 149–50.

[44] But see *Electricity Company of Sofia and Bulgaria,* PCIJ, Ser. A/B, no. 77, pp. 78, 82–3.

[45] In the *Anglo-Iranian Oil Co.* case the Court did not find it necessary to examine an Iranian argument on these lines. See the views of Judge Lauterpacht on the breadth of the formula employed in the French Decl. of acceptance of jurisdiction, ICJ Reports (1957), at 51–2.

[46] For references to the different views: Shihata, *The Power of the International Court to Determine its own Jurisdiction* (1965), 229–33.

[47] See the *Interhandel* case (Prelim. Objections), ICJ Reports (1959), 24–5; *Right of Passage* case (Merits), ibid. (1960), 32–3.

[48] See the *Peace Treaties* case, ICJ Reports (1950), 65 at 70–1.

the advisory jurisdiction,[49] the incident indicates that the Court will not in any case give any specific, and from the point of view of its jurisdiction more restrictive, content to the 'essentially within' formula as compared with the normal version of the principle of domestic jurisdiction: a matter regulated by treaty does not remain 'essentially within' the domestic jurisdiction of a state.

[49] See Waldock, 31 *BY* (1954), 138.

15

JURISDICTIONAL COMPETENCE

1. GENERAL

Jurisdiction refers to particular aspects of the general legal competence of states often referred to as 'sovereignty'. Jurisdiction is an aspect of sovereignty and refers to judicial, legislative, and administrative competence.[1] Distinct from the power to make decisions or rules (the prescriptive or legislative jurisdiction) is the power to take executive action in pursuance of or consequent on the making of decisions or rules (the enforcement or prerogative jurisdiction). The starting-point in this part of the law is the proposition that, at least as a presumption, jurisdiction is territorial. However, the territorial theory has been refined in the light of experience, and the law, which is still rather unsettled, is developing in the light of two principles. First, that the territorial theory, while remaining the best foundation for the law, fails to provide ready-made solutions for some modern jurisdictional conflicts. Secondly, that a principle of substantial and genuine connection between the subject-matter of jurisdiction, and the territorial base and reasonable interests of the jurisdiction sought to be exercised, should be observed.[2] It should also be pointed out that the sufficiency of grounds for jurisdiction is an issue normally considered relative to the rights of other states and not as a question of basic competence.[3]

---

[1] See generally: Mann, 111 Hague *Recueil* (1964, I), 9–162; also in Mann, *Studies in International Law* (1973), 1–139; id., 186 Hague *Recueil* (1984, III), 11–115; Jennings, 33 *BY* (1957), 146–75; id., 32 *Nord Tids.* (1962), 209–29; id., 121 Hague *Recueil* (1967, II), 515–26; Whiteman v. 216–19; vi. 88–183; *Digest of US Practice* (1973) (Ann. vols., ch. 6 in each); Akehurst, 46 *BY* (1972–3), 145–257; Griffin, 18 *Stanford JIL* (1982), 279–309; Bowett, 53 *BY* (1982), 1–26; Rosenthal and Knighton, *National Laws and International Commerce: The problem of Extraterritoriality* (1982); Lowe, *Extraterritorial Jurisdiction* (1983); Meessen, 78 *AJ* (1984), 783–810; id., 50 *Law and Contemporary Problems* (1987), 47–69; Olmstead (ed.), *Extra-territorial Application of Laws and Responses Thereto* (1984); Schachter, 178 Hague *Recueil* (1982, V), 240–65; Castel, 79 Hague *Recueil* (1983, I), 9–144; Lange and Born (eds.), *The Extraterritorial Application of National Laws* (1987); Neale and Stephens, *International Business and National Jurisdiction* (1988); Stern, *Ann. français* (1986), 7–52; Stern, ibid. (1992), 239–313; Bridge, 4 *Legal Studies* (1984), 2–29; Gilbert, 63 *BY* (1992), 415–42; Meessen (ed.), *Extra-territorial Jurisdiction in Theory and Practice* (1996); Meessen (ed.), *International Law of Export Control: Jurisdictional Issues* (1992); Bernhardt, *Encyclopedia*, III (1997), 55–60.

[2] Cf. the doctrine stated in the *Nottebohm* case, *infra*, in the matter of conferment of nationality; *Kingdom of Greece* v. *Julius Bär and Co.*, ILR 23 (1956), 195; and the statements in the *Guardianship* case, ICJ Reports (1958), 109 (Judge Moreno Quintana), 135–6 (Judge Winiarski), 145 (Judge Córdova), and 155 (Judge *ad hoc* Offerhaus).

[3] The last question may arise in relation to stateless persons or jurisdiction over non-nationals by agreement with other states. Cf. the European Agreement for the Prevention of Broadcasts Transmitted from

2. CIVIL JURISDICTION

In order to satisfy international law standards in regard to the treatment of aliens[4] a state must in normal circumstances maintain a system of courts empowered to decide civil cases and, in doing so, prepared to apply private international law where appropriate in cases containing a foreign element.[5] Municipal courts are often reluctant to assume jurisdiction in cases concerning a foreign element and adhere to the territorial principle conditioned by the *situs* of the facts in issue, and supplemented by criteria relating to the concepts of allegiance or domicile and doctrines of prior express submission to the jurisdiction and of tacit submission, for example on the basis of the ownership of property in the state of the forum.[6] Excessive and abusive assertion of civil jurisdiction could lead to international responsibility or protests at *ultra vires* acts. Indeed, as civil jurisdiction is ultimately reinforced by procedures of enforcement involving criminal sanctions, there is in principle no great difference between the problems created by assertion of civil and criminal jurisdiction over aliens.[7] In either case the prescriptive jurisdiction is involved and, in any case, anti-trust legislation often involves a process which, though formally 'civil', is in substance coercive and penal.

3. CRIMINAL JURISDICTION[8]

The discussion which follows concerns the general principles on which municipal courts may exercise jurisdiction in respect of acts criminal under the law of the forum, but of course the issue on the international plane is only acute when aliens, or other

Stations outside National Territories, signed 22 Jan. 1965, Cmnd. 2616; and see *British Practice in IL* (1964), i. 39–44; 59 *AJ* (1965), 715; van Panhuys and van Emde de Boas, 60 *AJ* (1966), 303–41; Bos, 12 *Neths. Int. LR* (1965), 337–64; and Woodliffe, ibid. 365–84.

   [4] On which see *infra*, ch. 24.

   [5] On the relations of public and private international law see Mann, 111 Hague *Recueil* (1964, I), 10–22; 54–62; Akehurst, 46 *BY* (1972–3), 216–31.

   [6] See Beale, 36 *Harv. LR* (1922–3), 241–62; *Rainford, Boston and Graham* v. *Newell-Roberts*, ILR 30, 106; *Royal Exchange Assurance* v. *Compania Naviera Santi*, SA ILR 33, 173; *Colt Industries, Inc* v. *Sarlie* ILR 42 108; *Banque Centrale de Turquie* v *Weston*, ILR 65, 417; *Universal Oil Trade Inc* v. *Islamic Republic of Iran*, ibid. 436. For a different view see Akehurst, 46 *BY* (1972–3), 170–7; and see *Derby & Co. Ltd.* v. *Larsson* [1976] 1 WLR 202, HL; 48 *BY* (1976–7), 352 (note by Crawford). See also *Thai-Europe Tapioca Service* v. *Government of Pakistan* [1975] 1 WLR 1485 at 1491–2, per Lord Denning.

   [7] There are many specialized areas, for example those relating to conscription and taxation. On the former see Parry, 31 *BY* (1954), 437–52, and Whiteman, viii. 540–72; on the latter see Mann, 111 Hague *Recueil* (1964, I), 109–19; Whiteman, viii. 507–39; Albrecht, 29 *BY* (1952), 145–85. See also *Rex* v. *Secretary of State, ex. p. Greenberg* [1947] 2 All ER 550 (extra-territorial jurisdiction to render a deportation order effective); and on the protection of alien infants see the *Guardianship* case, ICJ Reports (1958), 55 at 71; and *Re P. (G.E.) (an infant)* [1965] Ch. 568; ILR 40, 239.

   [8] See Mann, 111 Hague *Recueil* (1964, I), pp. 82ff.; O'Connell, ii. 823–31; Sarkar, 11 *ICLQ* (1962), 446–70; Jennings, 33 *BY* (1957), 146–75; Fawcett, 38 *BY* (1962), 181–215; Harv. Research, 29 *AJ* (1935), Spec. Suppl., pp. 439–651. And see further: Beckett, 6 *BY* (1925), 44–60; id., 8 *BY* (1927), 108–28; Fitzmaurice, 92 Hague *Recueil* (1957, II), 212–17.

persons under the diplomatic protection of another state,[9] are involved. The question only achieved prominence after about 1870, and the appearance of clear principles has been retarded by the prominence in the sources of the subject of municipal decisions, which exhibit empiricism and adherence to national policies, and also by the variety of the subject-matter. Several distinct principles have nevertheless received varying degrees of support from practice and opinion, and these will be examined individually before their relations with each other are established.

(a) The territorial principle

The principle that the courts of the place where the crime is committed may exercise jurisdiction has received universal recognition, and is but a single application of the essential territoriality of the sovereignty, the sum of legal competences, which a state has. In the case of crime, the principle has a number of practical advantages, including the convenience of the forum and the presumed involvement of the interests of the state where the crime is committed. In English and American decisions statements occur which suggest that the territorial principle is exclusive. However, the practice of states has not adopted this view.[10] and the United Kingdom legislature has conferred jurisdiction over nationals, *inter alia*, in respect of treason, murder, bigamy, and breaches of the Official Secrets Acts, wherever committed.[11] Moreover, in so far as they and other states have adopted the territorial principle, this principle has sometimes been given extensive application. In the first place, there is the subjective application, which creates jurisdiction over crimes commenced within the state, but completed or consummated abroad.[12] Generally accepted and often applied is the objective territorial principle, according to which jurisdiction is founded when any essential constituent element of a crime is consummated on state territory. The classical illustration is the firing of a gun across a frontier causing a homicide on the territory of the forum, but the principle can be employed to found jurisdiction in cases of conspiracy,[13] violation of anti-trust[14] and immigration laws[15] by activity abroad, and in many other fields of policy.[16] The objective principle received general support, and a controversial

---

[9] On the relation between nationality and diplomatic protection see *infra*, pp. 402–3.

[10] See Harv. Research, 29 *AJ* (1935), Spec. Suppl., pp. 439–651.

[11] On American divergence from the strict principle: Preuss, 30 *Grot. Soc.* (1944), 184–208.

[12] See Harv. Research, 29 *AJ* (1935), Spec. Suppl., pp. 484–7; the *Tennyson*, 45 *JDI* (1918), 739; *Public Prosecutor* v. *D.S.*, ILR 26 (1958, II), 209.

[13] *Board of Trade* v. *Owen* [1957], AC 602 at 634; *R.* v. *Cox* [1968] 1 All ER 410 at 414, CA; *D.P.P.* v. *Doot* [1973] AC 807, HL (and see the speech of Lord Wilberforce, p. 817); *D.P.P.* v. *Stonehouse* [1977] 2 All ER 909 at 916 *per* Lord Diplock. See also *State of Arizona* v. *Willoughby*, ILR 114, 586; Arizona S.C.

[14] See *U.S.* v. *Aluminium Company of America*, 148F. 2d. 416 (1944). In American anti-trust cases wide extension of the territorial principle might be explained by, though it is not expressed in terms of, a principle of protection: see Jennings, 33 *BY* (1957), 155, 161ff.; Baxter *et al.*, *UBCLR* (1960), 333–72; Verzijl, 8 *Neths. Int. LR* (1961), 3–30; George, 64 *Michigan LR* (1966), 609–38.

[15] Cf. *Naim Molvan* v. *A.-G. for Palestine* [1948] AC 531.

[16] See *Mobarik Ali Ahmed* v. *State of Bombay*, ILR 24 (1957), 156; *Public Prosecutor* v. *Y.*, ibid. 264: the *Cutting* case (on which see also *infra*, p. 304; *Public Prosecutor* v. *Janos V*, ILR 71, 229; *Ministère Public* v. *Brabant*, ILR 73, 369.

application to collisions on the high seas, in the *Lotus* case[17] before the Permanent Court of International Justice.

The *Lotus* case[18] originated in a collision on the high seas between a French steamer and a Turkish collier in which the latter sank and Turkish crew members and passengers lost their lives. The French steamer having put into port in Turkey, the officers of the watch on board at the time of the collision were tried and convicted of involuntary manslaughter. The Permanent Court was asked to decide whether Turkey had acted in conflict with international law by instituting proceedings, i.e. by the fact of exercising criminal jurisdiction and, if so, what reparation was due. France contended that the flag state of the vessel alone had jurisdiction over acts performed on board on the high seas. Turkey argued in reply, in part, that vessels on the high seas form part of the territory of the nation whose flag they fly. By the casting vote of the President (the votes were equally divided, six on either side), the Court decided that Turkey had not acted in conflict with the principles of international law by exercising criminal jurisdiction. The majority of six judges avoided dealing with the precise question of the compatibility of the relevant article of the Turkish penal code with international law. This article provided for punishment of acts abroad by foreigners against Turkish nationals and involved the protective principle of jurisdiction.[19] Judge Moore, in a separate opinion, agreed with the majority as to the outcome but expressly rejected the protective principle.[20]

The basis of the majority view on the Court (with which Judge Moore concurred, aside from the question of the principle of protective jurisdiction) was the principle of objective territorial jurisdiction. This principle was familiar but to apply it the Court had to assimilate the Turkish vessel to Turkish national territory. On this view the collision had affected Turkish territory.[21] In most respects the Judgment of the Court is unhelpful in its approach to the principles of jurisdiction, and its pronouncements are characterized by vagueness and generality. Thus, on the specific question of criminal jurisdiction, the Court observes that:

Though it is true that in all systems of law the territorial character of criminal law is fundamental, it is equally true that all, or nearly all these systems extend their jurisdiction to offences committed outside the territory of the State which adopts them and they do

---

[17] (1927), PCIJ, Ser. A, no. 10, p. 23; on which also see *supra*, pp. 254–5. The dissenting judges considered an objective application to be improper if the effects in the other jurisdiction were unintended: on this distinction see Beckett, 8 *BY* (1927), 108–28, and *R.* v. *Keyn* (1876) 2 Ex. Div. 63.

[18] For comment see Verzijl, 8 *Neths. Int. LR* (1961), 7–8; id., *The Jurisprudence of the World Court*, i (1965), 73–98; Fischer Williams, *Chapters on Current International Law and the League of Nations* (1929), 209–31; Jennings, 121 Hague *Recueil* (1967, II), 516–20; Mann, 111 Hague *Recueil* (1964, I), 33–6, 39, 92–3; Brierly, 44 *LQR* (1928), 154–63; *Annuaire de l'Inst.* 43 (1950), i. 295–365. See also *Sellers* v. *Maritime Safety Inspector*, ILR 120, 585 at 591–3; New Zealand, C.A.

[19] Hersch Lauterpacht has stated that in the *Lotus* case the Court 'declared the exercise of such protective jurisdiction to be consistent with international law'; 9 *Camb. LJ* (1947), at 343. But see Verzijl, *The Jurisprudence of the World Court*, i. 78–80; and in 8 *Neths. Int. LR* (1961), 7–8.

[20] pp. 65, 89–94.

[21] p. 23.

so in ways which vary from State to State. The territoriality of criminal law, therefore, is not an absolute principle of international law and by no means coincides with territorial sovereignty.[22]

On the question of jurisdiction in general the Court expressed its view in a passage which reads in part:

Far from laying down a general prohibition to the effect that States may not extend the application of their laws and the jurisdiction of their courts to persons, property or acts outside their territory, it leaves them in this respect a wide measure of discretion which is only limited in certain cases by prohibitive rules; as regards other cases, every State remains free to adopt the principles which it regards as best and most suitable.[23]

The passage of which this forms a part has been criticized by a substantial number of authorities[24] and its emphasis on state discretion is contradicted by the views of the International Court in the *Fisheries*[25] and *Nottebohm*[26] cases, which concerned the comparable competences of states, respectively, to delimit the territorial sea and to confer nationality on individuals.

In the *Woodpulp Cases* the Report for the Hearing in the European Court of Justice stated that 'the only two legal bases of jurisdiction in international law are the principles of nationality and territoriality...'[27]

(b) The nationality principle

Nationality,[28] as a mark of allegiance and an aspect of sovereignty, is also generally recognized as a basis for jurisdiction over extra-territorial acts.[29] The application of the principle may be extended by reliance on residence and other connections as evidence of allegiance[30] owed by aliens and also by ignoring changes of nationality.[31]

---

[22] p. 20.

[23] pp. 18–19.

[24] See e.g. Brierly, 58 Hague *Recueil* (1936, IV), 146–8, 183–4; Basdevant, ibid. 594–7; Fitzmaurice, 92 Hague *Recueil* (1957, II), 56–7; Lauterpacht, *International Law: Collected Papers*, i (1970), 488–9. See further the Opinion of the Inter-American Juridical Committee dated 23 Aug. 1996; CJI/Res.II-14/96.

[25] 176, p. 180.

[26] *Infra*, p. 396.

[27] *ILR* 96, 148 at 169. See also the Judgment of the Court, ibid., 196–7, para. 18.

[28] On which see generally *infra*, ch. 19. On the difficult question of the nationality of juristic persons see Harv. Research, 29 *AJ* (1935), Spec. Suppl., pp. 535–9.

[29] Judge Moore, Sep. Op. in the *Lotus, ubi supra*, p. 92; Harv. Research, 29 *AJ* (1935), Spec. Suppl. pp. 519ff.; Jennings, 121 Hague *Recueil* (1967, II), 153; Sarkar, II *ICLQ* (1962), 456–61; Sørensen, pp. 356–62. See also *U.S.* v. *Baker*, ILR 22 (1955), 203; *Re Gutierrez*, ibid. 24 (1957), 265; *Weiss* v. *Inspector-General*, ibid. 26 (1958, III), 210; *Public Prosecutor* v. *Günther B. and Manfred E.*, ILR 71, 247. Se also *Passport Seizure* case, ILR 73, 372; *Greek National Military Service* case, ibid. 606; 57 *BY* (1986), 561. See also Ergec, *La Compétence extra-territoriale á la lumiére du contentieux sur le gazoduc Euro-Sibérien* (1984), 53–68.

[30] See *Public Prosecutor* v. *Drechsler*, Ann. *Digest*, 13 (1946), no. 29; *Re Penati*, ibid., no. 30; *In re Buttner*, ibid. 16 (1949), no. 33; and cf. *D.P.P.* v. *Joyce* [1946] AC 347, and *Re P. (G.E.) (an infant)* [1964] 3 All ER 977. See also Sørensen, p. 361.

[31] See *In re Mittermaier*, Ann Digest, 13 (1946), no. 28; ibid. 14 (1947), 200–1 (Dutch decisions); *Ram Narain* v. *Central Bank of India*, ILR 18 (1951), no. 49. This type of case may rest on the protective principle: see *infra*.

On the other hand, since the territorial and nationality principles and the incidence of dual nationality create parallel jurisdictions and possible double jeopardy, many states place limitations on the nationality principle[32] and it is often confined to serious offences. In any event nationality provides a necessary criterion in such cases as the commission of criminal acts in locations such as Antarctica, where the 'territorial' criterion is inappropriate.

(c) The passive nationality principle[33]

According to this principle aliens may be punished for acts abroad harmful to nationals of the forum. This is the least justifiable, as a general principle, of the various bases of jurisdiction, and in any case certain of its applications fall under the principles of protection and universality considered below. In the *Cutting* case[34] a Mexican court[35] exercised jurisdiction in respect of the publication of defamatory matter by an American in a Texas newspaper. The defamation was of a Mexican, and the court applied the passive nationality principle among others. This judgment led to diplomatic protests from the United States,[36] although the outcome of the dispute was inconclusive. In the *Flatow* case a United States court held that extraterritoral jurisdiction, in actions by victims of alleged foreign state-sponsored terrorism, was supported by the principles of passive personality, protection and universal jurisdiction.[37]

(d) The protective or security principle[38]

Nearly all states assume jurisdiction over aliens for acts done abroad which affect the security of the state, a concept which takes in a variety of political offences, but is not necessarily confined to political acts.[39] Currency, immigration, and economic offences are frequently punished. The United Kingdom and the United States allow significant exceptions to the doctrine of territoriality though without express reliance upon the protective principle. Thus, courts of the former have punished aliens for abetment by acts on the high seas of illegal immigration,[40] and perhaps considerations of security

---

[32] Harv. Research, 29 *AJ* (1935), Spec. Suppl., pp. 519ff.

[33] See Jennings, 121 Hague *Recueil* (1967, II), 154; Sarkar, 11 *ICLQ* (1962), 461; Harv. Research, 29 *AJ* (1935), Spec. Suppl. pp. 445, 579; Bishop, 115 Hague *Recueil* (1965, II), 324; Mann, 111 Hague *Recueil* (1964, I), 40–1; Akehurst, 46 *BY* (1972–3), pp. 162–6; Watson, 28 *Texas Int. LJ* (1993), 1–46. See also *United States* v. *Yunis (No. 2)*, ILR 82, 343 at 349–51.

[34] See Moore, *Digest*, ii. 228–42; US For. Rel. (1887), 751–867.

[35] Decision set out in Briggs, p. 571.

[36] See also Whiteman, vi. 103–5 and *Digest of US Practice* (1975), 339.

[37] *Flatow* v. *Islamic Republic of Iran*, ILR 121, 618 at 633–4.

[38] See Harv. Research, 29 *AJ* (1935), Spec. Suppl. pp. 543–63; *Annuaire de l'Inst.* (1931), 236; Sarkar, 11 *ILCQ* (1962), 462–6; Garcia Mora, 19 *U. Pitt. LR* (1957–9), 567–90; van Hecke, 106 Hague *Recueil* (1962, II), 317–18; Bourquin, 16 Hague *Recueil* (1927, I), 121–89.

[39] See *Nusselein* v. *Belgian State*, ILR 17 (1950), no. 35; *Public Prosecutor* v. *L.*, ibid. 18 (1951), no. 48; *Re van den Plas*, ibid. 22 (1955), 205; *Rocha et al.* v. *U.S.*, 228 F. 2d 545 (1961), ILR 32, 112; *Italian South Tyrol Terrorism* case, ILR 71, 242.

[40] *Naim Molvan* v. *A.G. for Palestine* [1948] AC 531, *Ann. Digest*, 15 (1948), 115. See also *Giles* v. *Tumminello*, ILR 38, 120.

helped the House of Lords in *Joyce* v. *D.P.P.*[41] to the view that an alien who left the country in possession of a British passport owed allegiance and was guilty of treason when he subsequently broadcast propaganda for an enemy in wartime. In so far as the protective principle rests on the protection of concrete interests, it is sensible enough: however, it is obvious that the interpretation of the concept of protection may vary widely.

(e) The universality principle[42]

A considerable number of states have adopted, usually with limitations, a principle allowing jurisdiction over acts of non-nationals where the circumstances, including the nature of the crime, justify the repression of some types of crime as a matter of international public policy. Instances are common crimes, such as murder, where the state in which the offence occurred has refused extradition and is unwilling to try the case itself, and also crimes by stateless persons in areas not subject to the jurisdiction of any state, i.e. a *res nullius* or *res communis*. Anglo-American opinion is hostile to the general principle involved. In 2001 the following view was expressed on behalf of the British Government in the context of the International Criminal Court Bill:[43]

Many respondents sought to have this legislation extend the jurisdiction of British courts not only to UK nationals but also to anyone suspected of an ICC crime committed anywhere in the world. We do not favour the taking of such wide jurisdiction, so-called 'universal jurisdiction', in this case. This is an issue that we have considered with great care. The primary responsibility for the investigation of crimes committed outside the United Kingdom lies with the state where the crime occurred, or whose nationals were responsible. If that state is not able or willing to investigate, the ICC will be there to step in.

The British criminal justice system is based on a territorial link to the United Kingdom and there are significant practical difficulties when our courts have to prosecute crimes that have taken place elsewhere in the world. Even in the furtherance of a cause as great as that of upholding the rule of international law we have to be practical and ensure that we can deliver what we can undertake. It is our policy to assume universal jurisdiction only where an international agreement expressly requires it. The Rome statute does not. Rather than taking jurisdiction that will be difficult to enforce, we believe that those countries in which the offences took place should be encouraged to prosecute.

---

[41] [1946] AC 347; *Ann Digest*, 15 (1948), 91. On which see Lauterpacht, 9 *Camb. LJ*, 330–48; also *International Law: Collected Papers*, iii (1977), 221–41. See also *Board of Trade* v. *Owen* [1957] AC 602, at 634 per Lord Tucker; the Exchange Control Act 1947; and the Strategic Goods (Control) Order 1959, 9 *ICLQ* (1960), 226. See further the US Anti-Smuggling Act of 1935, Preuss, 30 *Grot. Soc.* (1944), 184–208 and Sarkar, 11 *ICLQ* (1962), 453–6.

[42] See Harv. Research, 29 *AJ* (1935), Spec. Suppl. pp. 563–92; Jennings, 121 Hague *Recueil* (1967, II), 156; Bishop, 115 Hague *Recueil* (1965, II), 323–4; Bowett, 53 *BY* (1982), 11–14; Brown, *New England L.R.* 35 (2001), 383–97; Reydams, *Universal Jurisdiction: International and Municipal Legal Perspectives* (2003); *Universal Jurisdiction (Austria)* case, ILR 28, 341; *R.* v. *Martin* [1956] 2 QB 272; ILR 20 (1953), 167; *Board of Trade* v. *Owen, supra*, and *Cox* v. *Army Council* [1963] AC 48; ILR 33, 194.

[43] 72 *BY* (2001), 620–1.

However, we have made one change to the Bill which is relevant to that issue. Under UK extradition law, it is the normal rule that we are unable to send people to another country to stand trial or to serve a period of imprisonment unless we could try that person under similar circumstances in the United Kingdom. This is the so-called 'dual criminality rule'. But under this Bill we are going to disapply that rule in the case of ICC crimes. This means that even though a state that requests the extradition of an individual suspect takes a wider jurisdiction than we do ourselves, we shall now be able to extradite that person to stand trial in the usual way. So even in cases where suspects were not liable to prosecution in this country or before the ICC they would be liable to extradition. This will ensure that non-UK nationals who have committed crimes overseas will not be able to come to the United Kingdom thinking that they will be immune from the reach of the law. They will be vulnerable to prosecution before the ICC, and they will be vulnerable to extradition.

Hijacking (unlawful seizure of aircraft)[44] and offences related to traffic in narcotics[45] are probably subject to universal jurisdiction.

(f) Crimes under international law

It is now generally accepted that breaches of the laws of war, and especially of the Hague Convention of 1907 and the Geneva Conventions of 1949, may be punished by any state which obtains custody of persons suspected of responsibility. This is often expressed as an acceptance of the principle of universality,[46] but this is not strictly correct, since what is punished is the breach of international law; and the case is thus different from the punishment, under national law, of acts in respect of which international law gives a liberty to all states to punish, but does not itself declare criminal.[47] In so far as the invocation of the principle of universality in cases apart from war crimes and crimes against humanity creates misgivings, it may be important to maintain the distinction. Certainly universality in respect of war crimes finds expression in the Geneva Conventions of 1949.[48] Moreover, in the *Eichmann* case[49] the Israeli courts were concerned, *inter alia*, with charges of crimes against

---

[44]   See Akehurst 46 *BY* (1972–3), 161–2; and cf. *Annuaire de l'Inst.* 54 (1971), ii. 455. See also *United States* v. *Yunis (No. 2)*, *ILR* 82, 343, at 348–9.

[45]   See *Drug Offences* case, ILR 74, 166. (F.R.G., Fed. Supr. Ct.).

[46]   See Cowles, 33 *Calif. LR* (1945), 177–218; Brand, 26 *BY* (1949), 414–27; Baxter, 28 *BY* (1951), 382–93; *In re Gerbsch*, *Ann. Digest*, 16 (1949), no. 143; *In re Rohrig*, ILR 17 (1950), no. 125. Cf. Röling, 100 Hague *Recueil* (1960, II), 357–62. See also the recent decisions of municipal courts: *Re Sharon and Yaron*, ILR 127, 110, Belgian Ct. of Cassation; *Javor and Others*, ILR 127, 126, French Court of Cassation; *Munyeshyaka*, ILR 127, 134, ibid.

[47]   On piracy see *supra*, pp. 229–30.

[48]   But Art. VI of the Genocide Conv. gives jurisdiction to the *forum delicti commissi*. See generally Carnegie, 39 *BY* (1963), 402–24. Cf. *In re Koch*, ILR 30, 496.

[49]   ILR 36, 5, 18, 227, 342 (biblio.). See Fawcett, 38 *BY* (1962), 181 at 202–8; Green, ibid. 457–71; Lasok, 11 *ICLQ* (1962), 355–74; Silving, 55 *AJ* (1961), 307–58; Baade, *Duke LJ* (1961), 400–20. Another issue which arises is the application of municipal rules on limitation (*verjährung*) to charges of war crimes and other crimes under international law: see Weiss, 53 *BY* (1982), 163–95; Conv. on the Non-Applicability of Statutory Limitations to War Crimes and Crimes Against Humanity, adopted by the UNGA, 26 Nov. 1968; in force 11 Nov. 1970; 8 *ILM* (1969), 68.

humanity arising from events before Israel appeared as a state. Again, in the *Barbie* case the French Court of Cassation held that crimes against humanity were defined in French law by reference to international agreements and were not subject to statutory limitation.[50]

It is to be noted that in the *Pinochet* case in the House of Lords[51] the issues of jurisdiction were overlaid by the specialized requirements of the European Convention on Extradition (1957), the Extradition Act (1989), and the date (1988) at which the Torture Convention became a part of English law. However, Lord Millett, dissenting, analysed the jurisdictional and historical background, including the question of universal jurisdiction:

In my opinion, crimes prohibited by international law attract universal jurisdiction under customary international law if two criteria are satisfied. First, they must be contrary to a peremptory norm of international law so as to infringe a *jus cogens*. Secondly, they must be so serious and on such a scale that they can justly be regarded as an attack on the international legal order. Isolated offences, even if committed by public officials, would not satisfy these criteria...

Every state has jurisdiction under customary international law to exercise extraterritorial jurisdiction in respect of international crimes which satisfy the relevant criteria. Whether its courts have extraterritorial jurisdiction under its internal domestic law depends, of course, on its consitutional arrangements and the relationship between customary international law and the jurisdiction of its criminal courts. The jurisdiction of the English criminal courts is usually statutory, but it is supplemented by the common law. Customary international law is part of the common law, and accordingly I consider that the English courts have and always have had extraterritorial criminal jurisdiction in respect of crimes of universal jurisdiction under customary international law...

In my opinion, the systematic use of torture on a large scale and as an instrument of state policy had joined piracy, war crimes and crimes against peace as an international crime of universal jurisdiction well before 1984. I consider that it had done so by 1973. For my own part, therefore, I would hold that the courts of this country already possessed extraterritorial jurisdiction in respect of torture and conspiracy to torture on the scale of the charges in the present case and did not require the authority of statute to exercise it. I understand, however, that your Lordships take a different view, and consider that statutory authority is required before our courts can exercise extraterritorial criminal jurisdiction even in respect of crimes of universal jurisdiction. Such authority was conferred for the first time by section 134 of the Criminal Justice Act 1988, but the section was not retrospective. I shall accordingly proceed to consider the case on the footing that Senator Pinochet cannot be extradited for any acts of torture committed prior to the coming into force of the section.

---

[50] Decisions of 1983 and 1984: ILR 78, 125. However, a different view was taken of war crimes: see the decision of 20 Dec. 1985; ibid. 136. See also *Regina* v. *Finta*, ILR 82, 424 (Canada: High Ct.).

[51] [1999] 2 WLR. 825 at 911–12; ILR 119, 135 at 229–30.

4. THE RELATIONS OF THE SEPARATE PRINCIPLES

The status of crimes under international law involves special considerations and can be left on one side. The various principles held to justify jurisdiction over aliens are commonly listed as independent and cumulative, although writers may grade them with some subjectivity, by labelling one or more as 'subsidiary' to some other. However, it must be remembered that the 'principles' are in substance generalizations of a mass of national provisions which by and large do not directly reflect categories of jurisdiction in the same way that, for example, the more recent legislation on jurisdiction over the continental shelf involves reference to a definite quantity of interest recognized by international law. It may be that each individual principle is only evidence of the reasonableness of the exercise of jurisdiction. The various principles often interweave in practice. Thus, the objective applications of the territorial principle and also the passive personality principle have strong similarities to the protective or security principle. Nationality and security may go together, or, in the case of the alien, factors such as residence may support a rather *ad hoc* notion of allegiance. These features of the practice have led some jurists, with considerable justification, to formulate a broad principle resting on some genuine or effective link between the crime and the state of the forum.[52] The significance of connecting links is evidenced by the provisions of the European Convention on Jurisdiction and the Enforcement of Judgments in Civil and Commercial Matters (1968)[53] and the European Convention on State Immunity (1972).[54] Such an approach would not necessarily solve issues of concurrence of jurisdiction, for example of the state of the nationality of the accused and the *locus delicti*.[55] Moreover, the principle of universality may still require a separate regime, with qualifications on competence arising from general principles of law, including the rule *ne bis in idem*.[56] Where there are connections with several law districts the forum which is not the *locus delicti* may allow the accused to plead the *lex loci delicti*.[57]

[52] Mann, 111 Hague *Recueil* (1964, I), 43–51, 82–126; Sarkar, 11 *ICLQ* (1962), 466–70; Fawcett, 38 *BY* (1962), 188–90; Steinberger, in Olmstead (ed.) *Extra-territorial Application*, pp. 91–3. Cf. Fitzmaurice, 92 Hague *Recueil* (1957, II), 215–17. See also the proper law approach in *U.S.* v. *R.P. Oldham Co. et al.*, ILR 24 (1957), 673; and cf. Seyersted, 14 *ICLQ* (1965), 31 at 33–43 (on jurisdiction over state organs on foreign territory). On the latter see also *Weiss* v. *Inspector-General*, ILR 26 (1958, II), 210. On the effective link doctrine in the law of nationality see *infra*, pp. 393ff. Such a principle applied to criminal jurisdiction would place reins on the permissiveness of the security principle. On the problem of jurisdiction in respect to United Nations forces see Bowett, *United Nations Forces* (1964), 244–8. See also *Drug Offences Case*, ILR 74, 166.

[53] Text: Collins, *The Civil Jurisdiction and Judgments Act 1982* (1983), 183.

[54] Text: 11 *ILM* (1972), 470. See also the UK State Immunity Act 1978; and *Explanatory Reports on the European Convention on State Immunity and the Additional Protocol*, Council of Europe (1972).

[55] See ILR 28, 143–4 (amnesty by state of nationality).

[56] Where the doctrine of substantial connection (the equivalent of a proper law as in private international law) is not applied, as in the case of the universality principle, it is possible that a choice of law problem is left open and that there is a tendency to solve this instinctively by reference to general principles of international law. As Mann, 111 Hague *Recueil* (1964, I), 17–22, points out, the 'private international law approach' and the 'public international law approach' are or should in principle be integrated, both in civil and criminal jurisdiction. The tendency towards a proper law approach supports this opinion.

[57] e.g. to obtain benefit of a prescription period or to place a limit on the severity of the punishment.

5. EXTRA-TERRITORIAL ENFORCEMENT
MEASURES[58]

The governing principle is that a state cannot take measures on the territory of another state by way of enforcement of national laws without the consent of the latter. Persons may not be arrested, a summons may not be served, police or tax investigations may not be mounted, orders for production of documents may not be executed, on the territory of another state, except under the terms of a treaty or other consent given.[59] In the field of economic regulation, and especially anti-trust legislation, controversy has arisen. It is probable that states will acquiesce in the exercise of enforcement jurisdiction in matters governed by the objective territorial principle of jurisdiction. Courts in the United States, for example, in the *Alcoa*[60] and *Watchmakers of Switzerland*[61] cases, have taken the view that whenever activity abroad has consequences or effects within the United States which are contrary to local legislation then the American courts may make orders requiring the disposition of patent rights and other property of foreign corporations, the reorganization of industry in another country, the production of documents, and so on. The American doctrine appears to be restricted to agreements abroad intended to have effects within the United States and actually having such effects.[62] Such orders may be enforced by action within the United States against the individuals or property present within the territorial jurisdiction, and the policy adopted goes beyond the normal application of the objective territorial principle. More recently United States courts have adopted a principle of the balancing of the various national interests involved, which, though unhelpfully vague could result in some mitigation of the cruder aspects of the 'effects doctrine'.[63]

American policies have provoked a strong reaction from a large number of foreign governments. Protest was provoked in particular by the Bonner Amendment to the Shipping Act, under which the US Federal Maritime Commission was given regulatory powers concerning the terms upon which non-American shipowners carry goods to and from the United States. The United Kingdom[64] and other states enacted legislation

---

[58] See Mann, 111 Hague *Recueil* (1964, I), 126–58; id., 13 *ICLQ* (1964), 1460–5; Jennings, 33 *BY* (1957), 146–75; Whiteman, vi. 118–83; ILA, *Report of the Fifty-First Conference* (1964), 304–592; *Report of the Fifty-Second Conference* (1966), 26–142; *Report of the Fifty-Third Conference* (1968), 337–402; Verzijl, 8 *Neths. Int. LR* (1961) 3–30; van Hecke, 106 Hague *Recueil* (1962, II), 257–356; Haight, 63 *Yale LJ* (1953–4), 639–54; Whitney, ibid. 655–62; Henry, 8 *Canad. Yrbk.* (1970), 249–83; Akehurst, 46 *BY* (1972–3), 179–212.

[59] The *Lotus* case, PCIJ, Ser. A, no. 10 (1927), 18; *Service of Summons Case*, ILR 38, 133, Austria, SC; *Répertoire suisse*, ii. 986–1017.

[60] *U.S.* v. *Aluminium Co. of America*, 148 F. 2d 416 (1945); Whiteman, vi. 136.

[61] *U.S.* v. *Watchmakers of Switzerland Information Center Inc.*, 133 F. Supp. 40 (1955); 134 F. Supp. 710 (1955).

[62] See O'Connell, ii. 821–2. Intention was not a prominent requirement in *U.S.* v. *I.C.I.*, 100 F. Supp. 504 (1951); 105 F. Supp. 215 (1952); and in many circumstances it can be inferred.

[63] See *Timberlane Lumber Company* v. *Bank of America*, ILR 66, 270; *Mannington Mills Inc.* v. *Congoleum Corporation*, ibid., 487. The 'balancing' approach was critcized in *Laker Airways Ltd.* v. *Sabena*, 731 F. 2d. 909 (DC Cir. 1984); 78 *AJ* (1984), 666. See also Meessen, ibid. 783–810.

[64] Shipping Contracts and Commercial Documents Act 1964.

to provide defensive measures against American policy. Similar episodes have arisen as a result of the application of the United States Export Administration Act, and, in particular, in face of United States measures directed against non-American corporations involved in contracts relating to the construction of the West Siberian pipeline.[65] Both the European Community[66] and the United Kingdom Government[67] protested and asserted the illegality of the actions of United States authorities, which actions were intended to prevent the re-export of machinery of American origin and the supply of products derived from American data. It must be noted that anti-cartel legislation in several European States is based on principles similar to those adopted in the United States.[68] Moreover, the Court of Justice of the European Communities has applied a principle similar to the American 'effects doctrine' in respect of company subsidiaries[69] and the Advocate-General espoused this view in his Opinion in the *Woodpulp Cases*.[70] In any event the legislation of Congress has continued to provoke protests from the European Communities (now the EU) and from individual States.[71] This legislation includes the Cuban Democracy Act (1992) and the Helms-Burton Act (1996).

The American courts, the United States Government,[72] and foreign governments in reacting to American measures assume that there are *certain* limits to enforcement jurisdiction but there is no consensus on what those limits are.[73] The view of the United Kingdom appears to be that a state 'acts in excess of its own jurisdiction when its measures purport to regulate acts which are done outside its territorial jurisdiction by persons who are not its own nationals and which have no, or no substantial, effect within its territorial jurisdiction'.[74] Judge Jennings has stated[75] the principle 'that extra-territorial jurisdiction may not be exercised in such a way as to contradict the local law at the place where the alleged offence was committed'. In the case of corporations with complex structures and foreign-based subsidiaries, a principle of

---

[65] See Lowe, 27 *German Yrbk.* (1984), 54–71; Kuyper, ibid. 72–96; Meessen, ibid. 97–108.

[66] See the Note dated 12 Aug. 1982 and comments, Lowe, *Extraterritorial Jurisdiction* (1983), 197.

[67] Note dated 18 Oct. 1982, 53 *BY* (1982), 453; Lowe, *Extraterritorial Jurisdiction*, p. 212.

[68] On the German position see Gerber, 77 *AJ* (1983), 756–83; Steinberger, in Olmstead (ed.), *Extraterritorial Application* pp. 77–95.

[69] *I.C.I.* v. *E.E.C. Commission*, ILR 48, 106 at 121–3.

[70] Delivered at the sitting of the Court of Justice on 25 May 1988, ILR 96, 174. However, the Court based its decision on 'the territoriality principle as universally recognized in public international law': Judgment of 27 Sept. 1988 ibid., 196–7, para. 18. See further Waelbroeck, in Olmstead, *Extra-territorial Application*, pp. 74–6; Akehurst, 59 *BY* (1988), 415–19.

[71] See 63 *BY* (1992), 724–9; 64 *BY* (1993), 643–5; 66 *BY* (1995), 669–71; 67 *BY* (1996), 763–5; 69 *BY* (1998), 534; 72 *BY* (2001), 627, 631.

[72] See Whiteman, vi. 133, 159, 164: 8 *Canad. Yrbk.* (1970), 267–8.

[73] See Judge Fitzmaurice, Sep. Op., *Barcelona Traction* case (Second Phase), ICJ Reports (1970), 103–6; the Belgian Memorial, ICJ Pleadings, *Barcelona Traction*, p. 114; ICJ Pleadings, *Barcelona Traction (New Application: 1962)*, I. Belgian Memorial, p. 165 and, in particular, p. 167, para. 336.

[74] The Attorney-General, Sir John Hobson, 15 July 1964; *British Practice* (1964), 146 at 153.

[75] 33 *BY* (1957), 151. See also *British Nylon Spinners Ltd.* v. *I.C.I. Ltd.* [1952] 2 All ER 780 and [1954] 3 All ER 88; Kahn-Freund, 18 *MLR* (1955), 65.

substantial or effective connection could be applied as a basis for jurisdiction.[76] This approach would accord with the highly relevant notions of the conflict of laws and, in particular, the notion of the 'proper law' of a transaction. The present position is probably this: a state has enforcement jurisdiction abroad only to the extent necessary to enforce its legislative jurisdiction. This latter rests upon the existing principles of jurisdiction and these, it has been suggested already, are close to the principle of substantial connection.

6. A GENERAL VIEW OF THE LAW

There is some risk in presenting the law in a schematic form, yet the usual presentation of the different facets of jurisdiction in separate compartments can obscure certain essential and logical points.

(a) In the case of substantive or legislative jurisdiction (the power to make decisions or rules enforceable within state territory), there is no major distinction between the types of jurisdiction. The 'types' used by writers in presenting materials (principally the civil, criminal, fiscal, and monetary jurisdictions) are not the basis of significant distinctions in the principles limiting extra-territorial jurisdiction.[77] Thus the exercise of civil jurisdiction in respect of aliens presents essentially the same problems as the exercise of criminal jurisdiction over them.

(b) There is again no essential[78] distinction between the legal bases for and limits upon substantive (or legislative) jurisdiction, on the one hand, and, on the other, enforcement (or personal, or prerogative) jurisdiction. The one is a function of the other. If the substantive jurisdiction is beyond lawful limits, then any consequent enforcement jurisdiction is unlawful.

(c) The two generally recognized bases for jurisdiction of all types are the territorial and nationality principles, but the application of these principles is subject to the operation of other principles (para. (d));

(d) Extra-territorial acts can only lawfully be the object of jurisdiction if certain general principles are observed:

(i) that there should be a substantial and bona fide connection between the subject-matter and the source of the jurisdiction;[79]

---

[76] See *supra*, n. 74; and see also *Carron Iron Co.* v. *Maclaren* (1855), 5 HLC 416, 442 per Lord Cranworth; *The Tropaioforos* (1962), 1 Lloyd's List LR 410; Mann, 111 Hague *Recueil*, at pp. 149–50.

[77] But see Mann, 111 Hague *Recueil* (1964, I), e.g. at p. 96; and Jennings, 121 Hague *Recueil* (1967, II), 517–18. The latter relies on the Judgment in the *Lotus* case. It is doubtful if the Court was concerned to establish any significant distinction.

[78] But see Mann, 111 Hague *Recueil* (1964, I), 13–14, 128.

[79] The various principles of criminal jurisdiction overlap and could be synthesized in this way: *supra*. See further Mann, 111 Hague *Recueil* (1964, I) 44–51, 126; *Survey of International Law* (Working Paper

(ii) that the principle of non-intervention in the domestic or territorial jurisdiction of other states should be observed;[80]

(iii) that a principle based on elements of accommodation, mutuality, and proportionality should be applied. Thus nationals resident abroad should not be constrained to violate the law of the place of residence.[81]

(e) The customary law and general principles of law relating to jurisdiction are emanations of the concept of domestic jurisdiction[82] and its concomitant, the principle of non-intervention in the internal affairs of other states. These basis principles do not apply or do not apply very helpfully to (i) certain cases of concurrent jurisdiction[83] and (ii) crimes against international law.[84] In these areas special rules have evolved. Special regimes also apply to the high seas,[85] continental shelf,[86] the exclusive economic zone,[87] outer space,[88] and Antarctica.[89]

(f) The principle of territorial jurisdiction is to be placed in a proper relation to the other principles. Thus it is not completely exclusive in its application to aliens within national territory. This qualification has several ramifications. First, the jurisdiction of the alien's state of origin is not excluded.[90] Secondly, the territorial jurisdiction may be excluded if there is an absence of substantial links between the alien or foreign corporation and the state asserting jurisdiction.[91]

(g) Jurisdiction is not based upon a principle of exclusiveness: the same acts may be within the lawful ambit of one or more jurisdictions. However, an area of

---

Prepared by the Sec.-Gen.), UN Doc. A/CN. 4/245, 23 Apr. 1971, paras. 80–90; Judge Padilla Nervo, Sep. Op., *Barcelona Traction* case (Second Phase), ICJ Reports (1970), 248–50, 262–3. Cf. Judge Fitzmaurice, Sep. Op., ibid. 103–6.

[80] See *Buck* v. *Attorney-General* [1965] Ch. 745, CA, per Diplock, LJ at 770–2; *Lauritzen* v. *Larsen*, 345 US 571 (1953); ILR, 20, 197; *Romero* v. *International Terminal Operating Co.*, 358 US 554 (1959); ILR 28, 145; *Rio Tinto Zinc Corporation* v. *Westinghouse* [1978] 2 WLR 81, at 93 (Lord Wilberforce), 108 (Lord Dilhorne). See also the view of the Federal Cartel Office, German Federal Republic, and the Const. Ct. (Gelber, 77 *AJ* (1983), 776–7). See further 49 *BY* (1978), 388–90; 55 *BY* (1984), 540; 56 *BY* (1985), 385–6. Cf. US Supreme Court decision in the *Aérospatiale* case, 26 *ILM* (1987), 1021, and see the dissent, ibid. 1037–41.

[81] Oppenheim, i. 406.

[82] *Supra*, p. 292.

[83] *Infra*. On jurisdiction of the sending state in respect of diplomatic missions see the Vienna Conv. on Diplomatic Relations, Art. 31(4); Hardy, *Modern Diplomatic Law* (1968), 55.

[84] *Supra*, p. 306.

[85] ch. 11.

[86] ch. 10.

[87] *Supra*, pp. 200–203.

[88] *Supra*, p. 255.

[89] *Supra*, p. 254.

[90] See Whiteman, v. 216–19, at 219; *Yrbk. ILC* (1949), 99.

[91] See the Belgian case, ICJ Pleadings, *Barcelona Traction*, Belgian Memorial, p. 114, para. 225; ICJ Pleadings, *Barcelona Traction (New Application: 1962)*, Belgian Memorial p. 165; Mann, 111 Hague *Recueil*, p. 50. Cf. Judge Fitzmaurice, Sep. Op., ICJ Reports (1970), 103–6.

exclusiveness may be established by treaty,[92] as in the case of offences committed on board aircraft.[93]

Excursus: British Aide-Mémoire *to the Commission of the European Communities*[94]

AIDE-MÉMOIRE

The United Kingdom Government have noted, in the *Journal Officiel* of the European Communities dated 7 August 1969, the publication of a decision of the Commission of 24 July 1969 (No. IV/26267) concerning proceedings pursuant to Article 85 of the Treaty establishing the European Economic Community in the matter of dyestuffs. Article 1 of this decision declares that 'the concerted practices of fixing the rate of price increases and the conditions of application of these increases in the dyestuffs sector…constitute violations of the provisions of Article 85 of the EEC Treaty'. Article 2 of the decision inflicts or purports to inflict certain fines upon the commercial undertakings who are alleged to have participated in these concerted practices. Among the undertakings specified in Articles 1 and 2 of the decision are Imperial Chemical Industries Limited (hereinafter referred to as 'I.C.I.'), which is a company incorporated and carrying on business in the United Kingdom. Article 4 of the decision declares that 'the present decision is directed to the undertakings mentioned in Article 1'; it then goes on to state that as far as I.C.I. and certain Swiss undertakings are concerned, '[the decision] may likewise be notified to them at the seat of one of their subsidiaries established in the Common Market'.

The United Kingdom Government neither wish nor intend to take issue with the Commission about the merits of this particular case. They accept that it is for the undertakings to whom the decision is directed to pursue whatever remedies are available under the E.E.C. Treaty if they desire for their part to challenge the legality or correctness of this measure taken by the Commission. It is in any event their understanding that certain of the undertakings to whom the decision is directed have already indicated their intention to institute proceedings before the European Court of Justice challenging the decision on various grounds.

The concern of the United Kingdom Government in this matter is rather directed towards the more fundamental point concerning the reach and extent of the jurisdiction exercisable by the Commission *vis-à-vis* undertakings which are neither incorporated in the territory of a member-State of the European Economic Community, nor carrying on business nor resident therein.

The Commission will be aware that certain claims to exercise extra-territorial jurisdiction in anti-trust proceedings have given rise to serious and continuing disputes between Western European Governments (including the Governments of some E.E.C. member-States) and the United States Government, inasmuch as these claims have been based on grounds which the Western European Governments consider to be unsupported by public international law.

In particular, the United Kingdom Government have for their part consistently objected to the assumption of extra-territorial jurisdiction in anti-trust matters by the courts or

---

[92] There may exist a rule of exclusiveness based upon customary law in the case of international crimes.

[93] *Infra*, p. 320.

[94] 20 Oct. 1969. Text in *British Practice* (1967), 58.

authorities of a foreign state when that jurisdiction is based upon what is termed the 'effects doctrine'—that is to say, the doctrine that territorial jurisdiction over conduct which has occurred wholly outside the territory of that State claiming jurisdiction may be justified because of the resulting economic 'effects' of such conduct within the territory of that State. This doctrine becomes even more open to objection when, on the basis of the alleged 'effects' within the State claiming jurisdiction of the conduct of foreign corporations abroad (that is to say, conduct pursued outside the territory of the State), such corporations are actually made subject to penal sanctions.

The United Kingdom Government are of the view that certain of the 'considerations' advanced in the decision of the Commission of 24 July 1969 conflict with the principles of public international law concerning the basis upon which personal and substantive jurisdiction may be exercised over foreign corporations in anti-trust matters. A summary statement of these principles as seen by the United Kingdom Government, is annexed to this *aide-mémoire* for ease of reference.

In particular, it will be noted that the method by which the decision of the Commission was purportedly notified to I.C.I. (Article 4 of the decision) ignores the clear legal distinction between a parent company and its subsidiaries and the separate legal personalities of the latter. The United Kingdom Government consider that this attempted 'notification' of a parent company through its subsidiary is designed to support a doctrine of substantive jurisdiction which is itself open to objection as going beyond the limits imposed by the accepted principles of international law.

So far as substantive jurisdiction is concerned, the United Kingdom Government are of the view that the decision of the Commission incorporates an interpretation of the relevant provisions of the E.E.C. Treaty which is not justified by the accepted principles of international law governing the exercise of extra-territorial jurisdiction over foreigners in respect of acts committed abroad.

The United Kingdom Government deem it necessary to bring these considerations to the attention of the Commission lest there be any misunderstanding as to their position in the matter.

STATEMENT OF PRINCIPLES ACCORDING TO WHICH, IN THE VIEW OF THE UNITED KINGDOM GOVERNMENT, JURISDICTION MAY BE EXERCISED OVER FOREIGN CORPORATIONS IN ANTI-TRUST MATTERS

The basis on which personal jurisdiction may be exercised over foreign corporations

(1) Personal jurisdiction should be assumed only if the foreign company 'carries on business' or 'resides' within the territorial jurisdiction.

(2) A foreign company may be considered to 'carry on business' within the jurisdiction by an agent only if the agent has legal power to enter into contracts on behalf of the principal.

(3) A foreign parent company may not be considered to 'carry on business' within the jurisdiction by a subsidiary company, unless it can be shown that the subsidiary is the agent for the parent in the sense of carrying on the parent's business within the jurisdiction.

(4) The separate legal personalities of a parent company and its subsidiary should be respected. Such concepts as 'enterprise entity' and 'reciprocating partnership' when applied

for the purpose of asserting personal jurisdiction over a foreign parent company by reason of the presence within the jurisdiction of a subsidiary (and a foreign subsidiary by reason of its parent company) are contrary to sound legal principle in that they disregard the distinction of personality between parent and subsidiary.[95]

(5) The normal rules governing the exercise of personal jurisdiction should not be extended in such a manner as to extend beyond proper limits the exercise of substantive jurisdiction in respect of the activities of foreigners abroad. Nor can the assertion of extended personal jurisdiction be justified on the basis that it is necessary for the enforcement of legislation which in itself exceeds the proper limits of substantive jurisdiction.

(6) There is no justification for applying a looser test to methods of personal service in anti-trust matters than is permissible in relation to other matters.

The basis on which substantive jurisdiction may be exercised in anti-trust matters

(1) On general principles, substantive jurisdiction in anti-trust matters should only be taken on the basis of either

    (a) the territorial principle, or

    (b) the nationality principle.

There is nothing in the nature of anti-trust proceedings which justifies a wider application of these principles than is generally accepted in other matters; on the contrary there is much which calls for a narrower application.

(2) The territorial principle justifies proceedings against foreigners and foreign companies only in respect of conduct which consists in whole or in part of some activity by them in the territory of the State claiming jurisdiction. A State should not exercise jurisdiction against a foreigner who or a foreign company which has committed no act within its territory. In the case of conspiracies the assumption of jurisdiction is justified:

    (a) if the entire conspiracy takes place within the territory of the State claiming jurisdiction; or

    (b) if the formation of the conspiracy takes place within the territory of the State claiming jurisdiction even if things are done in pursuance of it outside its territory; or

    (c) if the formation of the conspiracy takes place outside the territory of the State claiming jurisdiction, but the person against whom the proceedings are brought has done things within its territory in pursuance of the conspiracy.

(3) The nationality principle justifies proceedings against nationals of the State claiming jurisdiction in respect of their activities abroad only provided that this does not involve interference with the legitimate affairs of other States or cause such nationals to act in a manner which is contrary to the laws of the State in which the activities in question are conducted.

---

[95] See also the issues involving the Canadian Government; 5 *Canad. Yrbk.* (1967), 308–10, 313–17 (note inserted by author).

7. COGNATE QUESTIONS, INCLUDING
EXTRADITION, INFORMAL RENDITION
AND EXTRAORDINARY RENDITION

Ancillary issues abound and are of some complexity: some at least of these must be mentioned. In the first place, what are the precise legal consequences of a wrongful exercise of jurisdiction? In principle excess of jurisdiction gives rise to state responsibility even in the absence of an intention to harm another state.[96] Moreover, the state of which the accused is a national has *locus standi* in respect of proceedings which by object or mode involve a breach of existing standards protecting human rights.[97] Secondly, a change of sovereignty does not have the effect of an amnesty for criminals: the rule is in part the result of a principle of substitution, but particular applications may depend on genuine connection or the principle of universality.[98]

Apart from trial *in absentia*, an unsatisfactory procedure, states have to depend on the co-operation of the other states in order to obtain surrender of suspected criminals or convicted criminals who are, or have fled, abroad. Where this co-operation rests on a procedure of request and consent, regulated by certain general principles, the form of international judicial assistance is called extradition.[99] However, executive discretion to expel aliens may be employed *ad hoc* for similar ends.[100] With the exception of alleged crimes under international law,[101] in the absence of treaty, surrender of an alleged criminal cannot be demanded as of right.[102]

In the last five years there has been an increase in the practice of informal extradition. If this takes place with the consent of the State from the territory of which the transfer of custody takes place, there is no transgression of international law standards. Informal extradition, in the absence of the application of a treaty regime, is not necessarily unlawful. Issues of legality may arise in two types of case. In the first type, informal extradition takes place in a situation in which there is knowledge of the likelihood of physical abuse or torture of the suspect in the receiving State. In the second

---

[96] See the Belgian final submissions in the *Barcelona Traction* case (Second Phase), ICJ Reports (1970), 4 at 17–18. *Ultra vires* acts may justify diplomatic protests, of course: cf. US reaction in the *Cutting* case, *supra*, p. 304. See also Beckett, 6 *BY* (1925), 59–60.

[97] *Infra*, pp. 519ff.

[98] See Rosenne, 27 *BY* (1950), 267 at 282–7; Fawcett, 38 *BY* (1962), 181–215.

[99] Extradition is not easy to classify: McNair and Oppenheim place it under 'Individuals'; Briggs links it with jurisdiction over aliens.

[100] Cf. *R. v. Brixton Prison (Governor), ex. p. Soblen* [1963] 2 QB 283; ILR 33, 255. And see Thornberry, 12 *ICLQ* (1963), 414–74; O'Higgins, 27 *Mod. LR* (1964), 521–39; Bowett, 28 *BY* (1962), 479–83; Crawford, 54 *BY* (1983), 295–7; 56 *BY* (1985), 331–3.

[101] i.e. war crimes, crimes against humanity, and crimes against peace. See Neumann, 45 *AJ* (1951), 495–508; Green, 11 *ICLQ* (1962), 329–54.

[102] See generally Shearer, *Extradition in International Law* (1971); Whiteman, vi, ch. 16; Verzijl, *International Law in Historical Perspective* (1972), 269–401; 53 *BY* (1982), 402–9; 56 *BY* (1985), 423–6; 57 *BY* (1986), 535–9; Doehring, *Annuaire de l'Inst.* 59 (1981), i. 79–200; ibid. 60 (1984), ii. 304 (Resol.). On reciprocity as a self-sufficient basis for extradition: Rezek, 52 *BY* (1981), 171–203.

type of case there is no extradition of any kind, but the suspect is seized by the agents of a State in the absence of any legal process or the consent of the State from whose territory the seizure is made. This practice, generally described as 'extraordinary rendition', is clearly unlawful.[103] Much of the material on extradition depends on questions of internal and particularly of constitutional law and the effect of treaties on municipal rules. Thus, in the *Pinochet* case, the Law Lords were prepared to set aside the immunity of a former Head of State, but the requirements of English law and the European Convention reduced the available charges to a substantial degree.[104] However, some courts, in giving extradition in the absence of a treaty, have abstracted from existing treaties and municipal provisions certain 'general principles of international law'.[105] The two leading principles are that of double criminality, that the act charged must be criminal under the laws of both the state of refuge and the requesting state, and that of specialty, according to which the person surrendered shall be tried and punished exclusively for offences for which extradition had been requested and granted. Extradition may also be refused if the requesting state is not expected to observe reasonable procedural standards and also if the offence alleged is political.[106] The granting of political asylum[107] is a power which is limited in law in respect of international crimes, including genocide,[108] in certain conventions for the suppression of terrorist acts,[109] and in practice

---

[103] Sands, *Mélanges Salmon* (2007), 1074–94.

[104] *Regina v. Bow Street Metropolitan Stipendiary Magistrate, ex. p. Pinochet Ugarte (No. 3)* [2000] 1 AC 147; ILR 119, 135.

[105] See *Re D'Emilia*, ILR 24 (1957), 499; *Re Campora et al.*, ibid. 518; *Re Bachofner*, ibid. 28. 322. Cf. *Re Hartmann and Pude*, ILR 71, 232; *E. v. Police Inspectorate of Basle*, ILR 75, 106; *The State v. J. Furlong*, ILR 53, 9.

[106] Courts in England approach the definition of 'political offence' empirically: see *In re Castioni* [1891] 1 QB 149; *In re Meunier* [1894] 2 QB 415; *R. v. Governor of Brixton Prison, ex. p. Kolczynski* [1955] 1 QB 540; *Schtraks v. Government of Israel* [1964] AC 556; ILR 33, 319; (and note the Div. Ct., [1963] 1 QB 55 at 86–9 per Lord Parker, CJ); *R. v. Governor of Brixton Prison, ex. p. Kotronis* [1969] 3 All ER 304 at 306–7, per Lord Parker, CJ (point not taken in H. of Lds.); *Re Gross and Others* [1968] 3 All ER 804 at 807–10, per Chapman, J.; *Cheng v. Governor of Pentonville Prison* [1973] AC 931, HL; *R. v. Governor of Brixton Prison, ex. p. Keane* [1971] 2 WLR 194, DC; [1971] 2 WLR 1243, HL; *R. v. Governor of Winson Green Prison, ex. p. Littlejohn* [1975] 1 WLR 893, DC. The last two decisions relate to the hybrid procedure under the Republic of Ireland (Backing of Warrants) Act 1965, on which see O'Higgins, 15 *ICLQ* (1966), 369–94. See also Gutteridge, 31 *BY* (1954), 430–6; Evans, 57 *AJ* (1963), 1–24; Wortley, 45 *BY* (1971), 219–53; *Hungarian Deserter* case, ILR 28, 343; *Algerian Irregular Army* case, ILR 32, 294; *Jimenez v. Aristeguieta*, 311 F. 2d 547 (1963); ILR 33, 353; *The State v. Schumann*, ILR 39, 433; *Public Prosecutor v. Zind*, ILR 40, 214; *Karadzole v. Artukovic*, 247 F. 2d 198; ILR 24 (1957), 510; 170 F. Supp. 383, ILR 28, 326; *In re Gonzalez*, 217 F. Supp. 717; ILR 34, 139; *Digest of US Practice* (1975) 168–75; *State of Japan v. Mitsuyo Kono*, ILR 59, 472; *Kroeger v. Swiss Federal Prosecutor's Office*, ILR 72, 606; *Watin v. Ministère Public Fédéral*, ibid. 614; *Della Savia v. Ministère Public*, ibid. 619; *T. v. Swiss Federal Prosecutor's Office*, ibid. 632; *In the Trial of F.E. Steiner*, ILR 74, 478; *Baader-Meinhof Group* case, ibid. 493; *Folkerts v. Public Prosecutor*, ibid. 498; *Croissant*, ibid. 505; *Yugoslav Terrorism* case, ibid. 509; ILR, Vol. 79, index; *Lujambio Galdeano*, ILR 111, 505. See also the European Extradition Conv., 359 UNTS 273, Art. 3; and *Annuaire de l'Inst.* 60 (1984), ii. 304 (Resol., Arts. II, IV, and V).

[107] In some influential instruments there is provision for a *right* to seek asylum from persecution: Universal Decl. of Human Rights, Art. 14; and see also the materials in Whiteman, viii. 660–84.

[108] Genocide Conv., Art. VII. For the former attitude of the UK: *UK Contemp. Practice* (1962, II), 223.

[109] e.g. European Conv. on the Suppression of Terrorism, 1977; 15 *ILM* (1976), 1272 (and see the UK Suppression of Terrorism Act 1978).

by security measures between members of political and military alliances.[110] In general, states refuse to extradite nationals, but in some cases to do so without assuming responsibility for trying the suspect is an obvious abuse of power.

While international responsibility may arise as a consequence of the illegal seizure of offenders, the violation of the law does not affect the validity of the subsequent exercise of jurisdiction over them.[111] The position is similar in respect of defective extradition procedures and mistaken surrender of fugitive criminals.[112]

8. SPECIAL CASES OF CONCURRENT JURISDICTION

Elsewhere the exercise of jurisdiction over ships on the high seas[113] or enjoying the right of innocent passage through the territorial sea has been considered.[114] The matter which falls to be dealt with here is the relation between the territorial sovereign and the flag state in the matter of jurisdiction[115] over private[116] vessels in ports or other internal waters.[117] The view that a ship is a floating part of state territory has long fallen into disrepute, but the special character of the internal economy of ships is still recognized, the rule being that the law of the flag depends on the nationality of the ship[118] and the flag state has responsibility for and jurisdiction over the ship. But, when a foreign ship enters a port, except perhaps as a consequence of distress,[119] a temporary allegiance is owed to the territorial sovereign and a case of concurrent jurisdiction arises, since both the flag state and the local sovereign may exercise jurisdiction in respect of activities associated with the ship for breaches of their respective laws.[120] In the case of criminal jurisdiction there is some debate on the limits of the local jurisdiction. In principle, there are no limits provided action is taken with regard only to breaches of local law and

---

[110] Cf. the process of rendition under the Fugitive Offenders Act 1881; see *British Digest*, vi. 767ff. See now, for UK, the Fugitive Offenders Act 1967, c. 68 and the Criminal Justice Act 1988, c. 33 (Pt. I).

[111] This is the view adopted by courts in many states and by some writers. Much depends on the existence of independently sustainable grounds for the actual exercise of jurisdiction or of a waiver of a claim to reconduction.

[112] The award in the *Savarkar* case (1911), Hague Court Reports, p. 275, supports this statement in the case of mistaken surrender, although in fact the French Government had agreed that the fugitive should remain in British custody while on French territory (cf. McNair, *Opinions*, ii. 64).

[113] *Supra*, pp. 228ff.

[114] *Supra*, pp. 186–91.

[115] See Gidel, ii. 39–252; Jessup, *The Law of Territorial Waters and Maritime Jurisdiction*, (1927), 144–208; Harv. Research, 23 *AJ* (1929), Spec. Suppl., pp. 307–28; and 29 *AJ* (1935), Suppl., pp. 508–15; McDougal and Burke, *The Public Order of the Oceans* (1962), 161–73; Colombos, pp. 318–30; Whiteman, ix. 62–7.

[116] On the immunities from jurisdiction of public vessels and foreign armed forces, see *infra*, pp. 371ff. Concurrence may arise in these cases also.

[117] On the nature of internal waters see *supra*, p. 116. For analogous cases of concurrence see Beale, 36 *Harv. LR* (1922–3), 247–51; Lauterpacht, 9 *ICLQ* (1960), 208 at 231–2.

[118] On which see *infra*, p. 422. See also *Lauritzen* v. *Larsen*, ILR 20 (1953), 197 at 205–7.

[119] See Oppenheim, i. 503–4; Schwarzenberger, *International Law*, i. 199.

[120] See *U.S.* v. *Flores* (1933), 289 US 137; *Re Bianchi*, ILR 24 (1957), 173.

not to breaches of rules set by the law of the flag state.[121] However, it has been custom-ary to contrast the Anglo-American position with the French jurisprudence (which has been followed by some other states). During the preparatory work of the Hague Codification Conference of 1930, the United Kingdom stated its opinion on the issues as follows:[122]

...the State is entitled to exercise jurisdiction over a foreign merchant vessel lying in its ports and over persons and goods on board.

In criminal matters it is not usual for the authorities to intervene and enforce the local jurisdiction, unless their assistance is invoked by, or on behalf of the local representative of the flag State, or those in control of the ship, or a person directly concerned, or unless the peace or good order of the port is likely to be affected. In every case it is for the authorities of the State to judge whether or not to intervene.

Thus in the view of the United Kingdom derogation from the exercise of local crim-inal jurisdiction is a matter of comity and discretion. In *Wildenhus'* case[123] the United States Supreme Court took the view that a murder by one crew member of another, both Belgian nationals, committed on board a Belgian steamship in dock in Jersey City, *ipso facto* disturbed the public peace on shore. These Anglo-American attitudes are sometimes supposed to contrast with French practice based upon the opinion of the *Conseil d'État* in the cases of the *Sally* and the *Newton* in 1806.[124] The *Conseil d'État* maintained the principle of local jurisdiction in matters affecting the interest of the state, in matters of police, and for offences by members of the crew against strangers even on board. The local jurisdiction was stated not to apply to matters of internal discipline or offences by members of the crew not affecting strangers,[125] except when the peace and good order of the port are affected or the local authorities are asked for assistance. The French practice is said to be more liberal *vis-à-vis* the flag state and to involve a more explicit renunciation of jurisdiction in some cases than the Anglo-American doctrine. However, the points of contrast are seen to be minimal on closer examination, and the actual practice on both sides is fairly uniform.[126] The French practice accepts the overriding nature of the local jurisdiction, and French jurispru-dence has adopted the view that homicide of a fellow crew-member compromises the peace of the port.[127] In general, the local jurisdiction does not apply to acts taking place on board a ship before the vessel entered internal waters.[128]

---

[121] Oppenheim, i. 503–4; Gidel, ii. 204, 246.

[122] McNair, *Opinions*, ii. 194. See also *Wildenhus'* case (1887), 120 US 1.

[123] See last note.

[124] See Charteris, 1 *BY* (1920–1), 50 (translation of the opinion); 23 *AJ* (1929), Spec. Suppl., p. 325. It received imperial approval and had the force of legislation. See also the *Albissola*, *Ann. Digest*, 5 (1929–30), no. 67; and *U.S. v. Reagan*, ILR 57, 160.

[125] The instant cases involved assaults by members of the crews of American vessels in French ports on other crew members.

[126] Many states follow slight variants of the 'English' or 'French' rules: but the 'French' rule may be that of the *Tempest* (next note), not that laid down in 1806.

[127] *Cour de Cassation*: the *Tempest*, 1859, Dalloz *Recueil hébdomadaire*, i. 88; quoted in *Wildenhus'* case, *supra*, p. 321, n. 118. In the facts of the *Tempest* it will be found that disorder on shore had been caused.

[128] Colombos, pp. 301–3; Fitzmaurice, 92 Hague *Recueil* (1957, II), 211.

A problem of some consequence arises from the view of the New York Court of Appeals in *Incres Steamship Co. Ltd.* v. *International Maritime Workers Union et al.*[129] that a federal statue, the National Labour Relations Act, applied to labour disputes between foreign nationals operating ships under foreign flags and therefore the National Labour Relations Board had jurisdiction in respect of disputes concerning Liberian-registered ships operating from New York. In seeking to make intervention as *amicus curiae* in the appeal to the Supreme Court, the United Kingdom Government stated in the brief that to hold that such jurisdiction existed if the foreign flag vessel called at a United States port with any degree of regularity opposed 'the traditional internal economy doctrine long applied by all nations to foreign flag vessels temporarily in their ports' and gave 'an unwarranted extraterritorial effect to domestic law'. In its argument the United Kingdom Government seems to regard the exception as to matters involving the tranquillity of the port as a matter of law and not a matter of comity.[130] The dispute is not directly an issue of criminal jurisdiction, but the national policy involved is an important one, and such legislation employs penal sanctions as a longstop. Certainly the law of the flag doctrine needs more integration with the regime of vessels in port, and it may be that a doctrine of effective connection[131] is usable in questions of both criminal and civil jurisdiction. In the *Incres* case[132] and also in *McCulloch* v. *Sociedad Nacional*[133] the Supreme Court held that the National Labour Relations Act had no application to the operations of foreign-flag ships employing alien crews. In *McCulloch* the Supreme Court relied principally on the construction of the Act but also referred to the 'well-established rule of international law that the law of the flag State ordinarily governs the internal affairs of a ship'.

Aircraft have not fitted very readily into the jurisdictional rules of either domestic or international law, and crimes on board civil aircraft over the high seas or in the air-space of foreign states or *terra nullius* have been the subject of considerable variations of opinion. In the United Kingdom the extra-territorial commission of common law offences such as murder and theft is punishable,[134] and many provisions, apart from aeronautical regulations made under the Civil Aviation Act 1949, have no applica-tion to crimes on aircraft abroad or over the high seas.[135] The practice of states on the relation between the national law of the aircraft[136] and the law of any foreign territory

---

[129] 10 NY 2d 218, 176 NE. 2d 719 and other appeals (1963), 372 US 10; 57 *AJ* (1963), 659. The Supreme Court reaffirmed the jurisdiction of the flag state.

[130] See UK *Contemp. Practice* (1962, I), 18.

[131] *Supra*, p. 308.

[132] 372, US 24 (1963); ILR 34, 66.

[133] 372 US 10 (1963); ILR 34, 51. See further May, 54 *Georgetown LJ* (1966), 794–856; *Lopes* v. *S.S. Ocean Daphne*, 337 F. 2d 777; ILR 35, 97.

[134] *R.* v. *Martin* [1956] 2 QB 272 at 285–6, Devlin, J., *obiter*; *R.* v. *Naylor* [1962] 2 QB 527; ILR 33, 202.

[135] In *R.* v. *Martin* it was decided that s. 62 (1) of the Civil Aviation Act has procedural effect and confers jurisdiction only if a substantive rule makes the act concerned criminal when committed on board a British aircraft. In that case the indictment was quashed, as the Dangerous Drugs Regulations, 1953, applied only to the United Kingdom. See generally Cheng, 12 *Curr. Leg. Problems* (1959), 177–207.

[136] On which see *infra*, p. 425.

overflown is not very coherent,[137] and no doubt the general practice on criminal jurisdiction, considered earlier, supplies some useful principles. However, work sponsored by the International Civil Aviation Organization has produced a Convention on Offences and Certain Other Acts Commited on Board Aircraft,[138] the jurisdictional provisions of which are as follows:

Art. 3

1. The State of registration of the aircraft is competent to exercise jurisdiction over offences and acts committed on board.

2. Each Contracting State shall take such measures as may be necessary to establish its jurisdiction as the state of registration over offences committed on board aircraft registered in such State.

3. This Convention does not exclude any criminal jurisdiction exercised in accordance with national law.

Art. 4

A Contracting State which is not the State of registration may not interfere with an aircraft in flight in order to exercise its criminal jurisdiction over an offence committed on board except in the following cases:

(a) the offence has effect on the territory of such state;

(b) the offence has been committed by or against a national or permanent resident of such state;[139]

(c) the offence is against the security of such state;

(d) the offence consists of a breach of any rules or regulations relating to the flight or manœuvre of aircraft in force in such state;

(e) the exercise of jurisdiction is necessary to ensure the observance of any obligation of such state under a multilateral international agreement.

The practice of hijacking aircraft has prompted the promotion of multilateral conventions creating duties for states to punish the seizure of aircraft in flight and to exercise jurisdiction in specified conditions, for example, when the offence is committed on board an aircraft registered in the contracting state.[140]

---

[137] See the survey in Cheng, 12 *Curr. Leg. Problems* (1959), 180–1, based upon the UN Legis. Series, *Laws and Regulations on the Regime of the High Seas*, ii (1952; Suppl., 1959). See generally Mankiewicz, *Ann. français* (1958), 112–43; Lemoine, *Traité de droit aérien* (1947), 795ff.; Treaty on International Penal Law, signed at Montevideo, 19 Mar. 1940, Hudson, *Int. Legis.*, viii, no. 582; Oppenheim, i. 479–84.

[138] Signed at Tokyo, 14 Sept. 1963; 58 *AJ* (1964), 566; Cmnd. 2261. See Mendelsohn, 53 *Virginia LR* (1967), 509–63; and, for the UK, the Tokyo Convention Act 1967, c. 52; comment by Samuels, 42 *BY* (1967), 271.

[139] Cf. the principle of passive personality, *supra*, p. 304.

[140] Conv. for the Suppression of Unlawful Seizure of Aircraft, in force; 10 *ILM* (1971), 133; 65 *AJ* (1971), 440; Conv. for the Suppression of Unlawful Acts Against Civil Aviation, in force 26 Jan. 1973; 10 *ILM* (1971), 1151; 66 *AJ* (1972), 455; see the UK Aviation Security Act 1982. See further McWhinney, *Ann. de l'Inst.*, 54 (1971), i. 520–92; McWhinney (ed.), *Aerial Piracy and International Law* (1971); Green, 10 *Alberta LR* (1972), 72–88; Glaser, 76 *RGDIP* (1972), 12–35; ILA, *Report of the Fifty-Fourth Conference* (1970) 336–404.

16

PRIVILEGES AND IMMUNITIES
OF FOREIGN STATES

1. INTRODUCTION

By licence[1] the agents of one state may enter the territory of another and there act in their official capacity. The acts may include the disposition and even the use in the field of military forces and the exercise of jurisdiction in the specific sense of setting up courts and using power to enforce the findings of such courts.[2] The privilege of the entrant in such cases stands against the exclusive power of the territorial sovereign to regulate, and to enforce decisions of its organs respecting, the territory and its population.[3] A concomitant of the privilege to enter and remain is normally the existence of an immunity from the jurisdiction of the local courts and the local agencies of law enforcement. However, as a general principle this immunity is delimited by a right on the part of the receiving state to use reasonable force to prevent or terminate activities which are in excess of the licence conferred or are otherwise in breach of international law.

The subject is related to two matters which must be given brief notice. First, it is a consequence of the equality and independence of states that municipal courts accept the validity of the acts of foreign states and their agents, including legislation.[4] This is a highly controversial subject, and in practice courts may refuse to recognize foreign acts considered to be contrary to international law[5] or the public policy of the forum.[6] A very common practice is for courts to refuse to exercise jurisdiction in cases involving foreign acts of state on the ground that to pass on the question would embarrass the executive in arriving at an appropriate diplomatic settlement.[7] This approach,

---

[1] Cf. the Vienna Conv. on Diplomatic Relations, 1961, Art. 2: 'The establishment of diplomatic relations between States, and of permanent diplomatic missions, takes place by mutual consent.'

[2] See *infra*, pp. 372ff.

[3] See *supra*, pp. 290–1, on the relation between jurisdiction and sovereignty.

[4] See Oppenheim, i. 267.

[5] See *infra*, pp. 531ff., on expropriation.

[6] There is also a rule, in effect an adjunct of the public policy proviso, that no effect will be given to foreign penal, fiscal, or political laws.

[7] See *Banco Nacional de Cuba* v. *Sabbatino*, 84 Sup. Ct. 923 (1964); and the comment by Henkin, 64 *Col. LR* (1964), 805–32.

whatever the motivation, is akin to the notion that admissibility of a claim is related to the appropriateness of the forum.[8] The second related matter is the privilege, which as a matter of comity is usually allowed, of foreign states to appear as plaintiffs in national courts. The generally recognized limits to the privilege are the non-enforcement of penal or revenue laws by this means and the refusal to admit disputes between the plaintiff state and the state of the forum (or a third state) to be presented as civil actions.[9] In the latter case there is no dogmatic objection to the exercise of jurisdiction and the issue becomes one of appropriate forum, either diplomatic negotiation, arbitration, or judicial settlement on the international plane. When a foreign state brings an action in the courts of another state there is a submission to the jurisdiction which extends to any counter-claim which is in the nature of a defence to the action rather than a cross-action.[10]

2. THE DISTINCTION BETWEEN NON-JUSTICIABILITY AND IMMUNITY AS A JURISDICTIONAL BAR

The concept of state immunity is treated very often in the context of statements in which the immunity features as a bar to a jurisdiction of the state of the forum which would exist *but for* the doctrine of immunity, and which can be waived by the beneficiary state. The facts of well-known cases involve ships or other property actually within the territorial jurisdiction, the latter being 'excluded' by the existence of state immunity. Thus in *The Schooner Exchange*[11] the principles appear as implied conditions of a licence to enter foreign territory. It is, however, important to bear in mind that state immunity may appear as a doctrine of inadmissibility or non-justiciability rather than an immunity in a strict sense. In other words the national court has no competence to assert jurisdiction: it is a matter of the essential competence of the local courts in relation to the subject-matter.[12] In *Buck* v. *A.-G.*[13] the Court of Appeal refused to make declarations on the validity or otherwise of the constitution of Sierra Leone as created

---

[8] See *infra*, pp. 492, 503.

[9] Cf. *Secretary of State for India* v. *Kamachee Boye Sahaba* (1859), 13 Moo. PC 22; *Salaman* v. *Secretary of State for India* [1906] 1 KB 613.

[10] See *High Commissioner for India* v. *Ghosh*, [1906] 1 QB 134; *National City Bank* v. *Republic of China*, 348 US 356 (1965); ILR (1955), 211; *Banco Nacional de Cuba* v. *First National City Bank*, 270 F. Supp. 1004 (1967); ILR 42, 45; and generally Simmonds, 9 *ICLQ* (1960), 334–43.

[11] See *infra*.

[12] The same point arises in relation to diplomatic immunity: *infra*, p. 361.

[13] [1965] Ch. 745; ILR, 42, 11; 41 *BY* (1965–6), 435; Mann, 14 *ICLQ* (1965), 985–7. See also *Zoernsch* v. *Waldock* [1964] 1 WLR 675, at 684, 688–9, 691–2; and the *International Tin Council Appeals* [1989] 3 WLR 969.

by Order in Council at independence. The Court held that it had no jurisdiction to make a declaration of the kind claimed. Diplock, LJ,[14] stated the principles as follows:

The only subject-matter of this appeal is an issue as to the validity of a law of a foreign independent sovereign State, in fact, the basic law containing its constitution...

As a member of the family of nations, the Government of the United Kingdom (of which this court forms part of the judicial branch) observes the rules of comity, *videlicet* the accepted rules of mutual conduct as between State and State which each State adopts in relation to other States and expects other States to adopt in relation to itself. One of those rules is that it does not purport to exercise jurisdiction over the internal affairs of any other independent State, or to apply measures of coercion to it or to its property, except in accordance with the rules of public international law. One of the commonest applications of this rule...is the well-known doctrine of sovereign immunity...the application of the doctrine of sovereign immunity does not depend upon the persons between whom the issue is joined, but upon the subject-matter of the issue. For the English Court to pronounce upon the validity of a law of a foreign sovereign State within its own territory, so that the validity of that law became the *res* of the *res judicata* in the suit, would be to assert jurisdiction over the internal affairs of that State. That would be a breach of the rules of comity. In my view, this court has no jurisdiction so to do.

It is helpful to distinguish two principles on which sovereign immunity rests. The one, expressed in the maxim *par in parem non habet jurisdictionem*, is concerned with the status of equality attaching to the independent sovereign: legal persons of equal standing cannot have their disputes settled in the courts of one of them. This principle is satisfied if a sovereign state waives its immunity: the consent given upholds the status of equality. If there is a subject-matter over which the national courts of the other state may properly exercise jurisdiction *in rem* or if there is a basis for acquiring jurisdiction *in personam*, then jurisdiction follows consent. The existence of a ship or a fund or other assets may provide a basis in such cases for the exercise of civil jurisdiction in accordance with the principles of jurisdiction considered in Chapter 15. The other principle on which immunity is based is that of non-intervention in the internal affairs of other states. This produces an area of issues which are in essence non-justiciable and are exemplified by *Buck* v. *A.-G.* (*supra*). It is difficult to catalogue such issues but the nature of the subject matter will lead a municipal court to accept that it is not an appropriate forum and can do nothing useful or effective.[15] A good example would be the immunity of arbitrations between states from the jurisdiction of the state in which the arbitration takes place.[16] This principle of non-justiciability overlaps with the cases in which courts refuse to exercise jurisdiction over transactions flowing from

---

[14] [1965] Ch. at pp. 770–1. See further *Duke of Brunswick* v. *King of Hanover* (1848), 2 HLC 1; *Johnstone* v. *Pedlar* [1921] 2 AC 262, 291; *Nissan* v. *A.-G.* [1970] AC 179, at 216–18 per Lord Morris; Mann, 59 *LQR* (1943), 42–57, 155–71.

[15] See *National Institute of Agrarian Reform* v. *Kane*, 153 So. 2d 40 (1963); ILR 34, 12. Cf. the *Sabbatino* case in which, however, the US Supreme Court applied the Act of State doctrine as a doctrine of municipal law, neither required nor prohibited by international law: ILR 35, 25.

[16] See Mann, 42 *BY* (1967), 1–2.

the execution of treaties the provisions of which do not provide for enforcement in the municipal courts of either party.[17]

3. THE RATIONALE OF JURISDICTIONAL IMMUNITY

The most commonly quoted statement of the principle is the judgment of the United States Supreme Court in *The Schooner Exchange* v. *McFaddon*,[18] delivered by Marshall, CJ, who referred to the jurisdiction of a state within its own territory as being 'necessarily exclusive and absolute'. In his words:

This full and absolute territorial jurisdiction being alike the attribute of every sovereign, and being incapable of conferring extra-territorial power, would not seem to contemplate foreign sovereigns nor their sovereign rights as its objects. One sovereign being in no respect amenable to another, and being bound by obligations of the highest character not to degrade the dignity of his nation, by placing himself or its sovereign rights within the jurisdiction of another, can be supposed to enter a foreign territory only under an express license, or in the confidence that the immunities belonging to his independent sovereign station, though not expressly stipulated, are reserved by implication, and will be extended to him.

This perfect equality and absolute independence of sovereigns, and this common interest compelling them to mutual intercourse, and an interchange of good offices with each other, have given rise to a class of cases in which every sovereign is understood to waive the exercise of a part of that complete exclusive territorial jurisdiction, which has been stated to be the attribute of every nation.

The instances which were then enumerated were the exemption of the person of the sovereign from arrest or detention within a foreign territory, the immunity of foreign ministers, and the passage of foreign troops under licence. In an earlier period the immunity would be seen to attach to the person of the visiting sovereign, but in the view of the Supreme Court the immunity clearly extends to the various organs of the visiting nation, and the sovereign himself is considered somewhat in a representative capacity. The immunity is primarily from the jurisdiction of the territorial courts, but it has other facets.[19] The rationale rests equally on the dignity of the foreign nation, its organs and representatives, and on the functional need to leave them unencumbered in the pursuit of their mission. Historically the immunity of diplomatic agents was established by a well-developed practice before that of sovereigns and states.[20] However, the two doctrines are closely linked as to their underlying

---

[17] *Secretary of State* v. *Kamachee Boye Sahaba* (1859), 13 Moo. PC 22; *Cook* v. *Sprigg* [1899] AC 572; *Salaman* v. *Secretary of State* [1906] 1 KB 613; *Kingdom of Greece* v. *Gamet*, ILR 28, 153.

[18] (1812), 7 Cranch 116.

[19] See *infra*, pp. 342–3.

[20] The immunity of sovereigns would not be in issue often and must have been presumed to exist. Sovereign immunity seems to have derived doctrinally from that of the ambassador.

principles. They both contain an extra-territorial and a ceremonial element,[21] though the diplomatic immunity is more obviously functional.[22] It must be emphasized that the terms 'immunity', and 'extra-territoriality', are no more than general guides to the legal regime involved in each case. The 'immunity' is not absolute, for it can be waived; and there are limits and exceptions varying with the nature of the occasion for the licence.[23] Moreover, it must be stressed that there is no immunity from international responsibility where this exists under general international law.

4. STATE IMMUNITY: CONTROVERSY OVER ITS EXTENT[24]

In the course of the nineteenth century states appeared as commercial entrepreneurs on a considerable scale, creating monopolies in particular trades, and operating railway, shipping, and postal services. The First World War increased such activities, and the appearance of socialist states has given greater prominence to the public sector in national economies. Moreover, countries such as India have found it necessary to have a public sector as a basis for a planned development of a modern economy. After earlier doctrinal developments Belgian and Italian courts responded to the extension

[21] See Hall, *International Law* (8th edn., 1924), 217ff. at 219; Fitzmaurice, 92 Hague *Recueil* (1957, II), 187–8; and Simmonds, 11 *ICLQ* (1962), 1204–10.

[22] Cf. Oppenheim, i. 264–7, 271–5, 788, 792–3. Courts seeking to develop a restrictive doctrine of sovereign immunity are tempted to emphasize the distinction between state immunity and the very protected position of diplomatic agents: see *Lagoso* v. *Baggianini*, ILR 22 (1955), 533; *Foreign Press Attaché* case, ILR 38, 160; Austrian SC; comment by Abel, 11 *ICLQ* (1962), 842–3; *Yuglosav Military Mission* case, ILR 38, 162; German Fed. Rep., Fed. Const. Ct. See also Lalive, 84 Hague *Recueil* (1953, III), 252–3; *S.* v. *British Treasury*, ILR 24 (1957), 223; *Reference on Powers of City of Ottawa to Levy Rates on Foreign Legations* [1943] SCR 208; *Ann. Digest*, 10 (1941–2), no. 106.

[23] It is now generally recognized that exterritoriality or 'extra-territoriality' of warships and diplomatic agents is a fiction, and an unhelpful fiction at that, since there is no necessary coincidence between territorial sovereignty and jurisdiction: see *Chung Chi Cheung* v. *The King* [1939] AC 160, PC, at 175, quoting Brierly, p. 223.

[24] See Whiteman, vi. 553–726; Lémonon *et al.*, *Annuaire de l'Inst.* 44 (1952), i. 5ff.; 44 (1952), ii. 424–6; 45 (1954), ii. 200–27; Lauterpacht, 28 *BY* (1951), 220–72; Fitzmaurice, 14 *BY* (1933), 101–24; O'Connell, ii. 841–79; Riad, 108 Hague *Recueil* (1963, I), 607–29; Sucharitkul, 149 Hague *Recueil* (1976, I), 87–216; Lalive, 84 Hague *Recueil* (1953, III), 205–389; Rousseau, iv. 8–19, 117–38; Sinclair, 167 Hague *Recueil* (1980, II), 113–284; Crawford, 75 *AJ* (1981), 820–69; id., 54 *BY* (1983), 75–118, id., 8 *Austral. Yrbk.* (1983), 71–107; Sornarajah, 31 *ICLQ* (1981), 661–85; UN Legis. Series, *Materials on Jurisdictional Immunities of States and Their Property*, ST/LEG/Ser. B/20 (1982); ILA, *Report of the Sixtieth Conference* (Montreal, 1982), 5–10, 325–48; Molot and Jewett, 20 *Canad. Yrbk.* (1982), 79–122; Higgins, 29 *Neths. Int. LR* (1982), 265–76; Emanuelli, 22 *Canad. Yrbk.* (1984), 26–97; Badr, *State Immunity* (1984); Fox, 34 *ICLQ* (1985), 115–41; Trooboff, 200 Hague *Recueil* (1986, V), 235–432; *Annuaire de l'Inst.* 62 (1987), i. 13–158; ibid. 62 (1987), ii. 241–73; ibid., 63 (1989), i; ibid., 64, i. 80–9; ibid., 64, ii. 214–78; Schreuer, *State Immunity: Some Recent Developments* (1988); *Yrbk. ILC* (1979), ii (Pt. 1), 227–44; (1980), ii (Pt. 1), 199–230; (1981), ii (Pt. 1) 125–50; (1982), ii (Pt. 1), 199–229; (1983), ii (Pt. 1), 25–56; (1984), ii (Pt. 1), 5–58; (1985), ii (Pt. 1), 21–47; (1986), ii (Pt. 1), 21–37; ibid. (Pt. 2), 7–22; (1991), ii (Pt. 2), 12–62; Fox, *The Law of State Immunity* (2002).

of state activity by developing a distinction between acts of government, *jure imperii*, and acts of a commercial nature, *jure gestionis*, denying immunity from jurisdiction in the latter case. This approach, often called the doctrine of restrictive or relative immunity, has been adopted by the courts of at least twenty countries.[25] Another eleven states support the restrictive approach in principle.[26] The doctrine is also reflected in recent legislation in Australia, Canada, Pakistan, Singapore, South Africa, the United Kingdom, and the United States.[27]

In 1952 the Department of State announced its intention to follow the restrictive principle of immunity,[28] and in *Alfred Dunhill of London, Inc.* v. *Republic of Cuba*[29] four of the Justices of the Supreme Court expressed support for the restrictive approach to sovereign immunity. The restrictive doctrine of immunity is now codified in the

[25] Austria: *Holoubek* v. *US*, ILR 40, 73 (SC, 1961); *X* v. *Fed. Rep. of Germany*, ILR 65, 10 (SC, 1963); *Steinmetz* v. *Hungarian P.R.*, ibid. 15 (SC, 1970). *Belgium*: Suy, 27 *Z.a.ö.R.u.V.* (1967), 660–92; *S.A. 'Dhlellemes et Masurel'* v. *Banque Centrale de la République de Turquie*, ILR 45, 85 (CA of Brussels, 1963). *Canada*: *Government of D.R. of the Congo* v. *Venne*, ILR 64, 24 (SC, 1971); *Zodiak International Products* v. *Polish P.R.*, ILR 64, 51 (CA of Quebec, 1977); *Re Royal Bank of Canada and Corriveau*, ILR 64, 69 (Ontario High Ct., 1980); *Cargo Ex The Ship 'Atra'* v. *Lorac Transport Ltd.* (1986) 28 DLR (4th) 309. *Denmark*: *Czechoslovak Embassy Case*, 111 *JDI* (1984), 639. *Egypt*: *Yrbk. ILC* (1982), ii (Pt. 1), 214–15. *France*: *Etat espagnol* v. *Société Anonyme de L'Hôtel George V*, ILR 65, 61 (*Cour de Cassation*, 1973); *Blagojevic* v. *Bank of Japan*, ibid. 63 (*Cour de Cassation*, 1976). *German Fed. Rep.*; *Hungarian Embassy Case*, ILR 65, 110 (SC 1969); *Arms Sales Commission Agreement Case*, ibid. 119 (*Oberlandesgericht*, Coblenz, 1972); *Central Bank of Nigeria Case*, ibid. 131 (*Landgericht*, Frankfurt, 1975/6); *Spanish State Tourist Office Case*, ibid. 140 (*Oberlandesgericht*, Frankfurt, 1977); *Philippine Embassy Bank Account Case*, ibid. 146 (Fed. Const. Ct., 1977); *NIOC Revenues from Oil Sales Case*, ibid. 215 (Fed. Const. Ct., 1983). *Greece*: UN Legis. Series, *Materials* (1982), 89; *Embassy Eviction Case*, ILR 65, 248; *Purchase of Embassy Staff Residence Case*, ibid. 255. *Ireland*: *Government of Canada* v. *Employment Appeals Tribunal*, ILR 95, 467 (Ireland, SC). *Italy*: *Hungarian Papal Institute* v. *Hungarian Institute in Rome*, ILR 40, 59 (Ct. of Cassation, 1960); *U.S. Government* v. *Irsa*, ILR 65, 262 (Ct. of Cassation, 1963); *De Ritis* v. *United States*, ibid. 283 (Ct. of Cassation, 1971); *Campione* v. *Hungarian Republic*, ibid. 287 (Ct. of Cassation, 1972); *Italian Knights of the Order of Malta*, ibid. 308 (Ct. of Cassation, 1974); *Luna* v. *S.R. of Romania*, ibid. 313 (Ct. of Cassation, 1974); *Danish Cultural Institute and Krogh* v. *Hansen*, ibid. 325 (Ct. of Cassation, 1979); *Velloso* v. *Borla*, ibid. 328 (Ct. of Cassation, 1979). *Lebanon*: UN Legis. Series, *Materials* (1982), 579. *Netherlands*: *N.V. Cabolent* v. *N.I.O.C.*, ILR 47, 138 (CA of The Hague, 1965); *N.V. Exploitatie Maatschappij Bengkalis* v. *Bank of Indonesia*, ILR 65, 348 (CA of Amsterdam, 1963); *S.E.E.E.* v. *Socialist Fed. Rep. of Yugoslavia*, ibid. 356 (SC, 1973). *New Zealand*: *Marine Steel Ltd.* v. *Government of the Marshall Islands*, ILR 64, 539 (High Ct., 1981); *Buckingham* v. *The Aircraft Hughes 500 D Helicopter*, ibid. 551 (High Ct., 1982). *Pakistan*: *Secretary of State of U.S.A.* v. *Gammon-Layton*, ibid. 567 (High Ct. of W. Pakistan); *Qureshi* v. *U.S.S.R.*, ibid. 585 (SC, 1981). *Senegal*: UN Legis. Series, *Materials* (1982), 596. *South Africa*: *Inter-Science Research and Development Services* v. *Rep. Popular de Mocambique*, ILR 64, 689 (SC, 1979); *Kaffraria Property Co.* v. *Government of Rep. of Zambia*, ibid. 708 (SC, 1980). *Spain*: UN Legis. Series, *Materials* (1982), 599 (some doubt). *Sweden*: ibid. 602. *Switzerland*: *U.A.R.* v. *Mrs. X*, ILR 65, 385 (Fed. Trib., 1960); *Italian Rep.* v. *Beta Holdings*, ibid. 394 (Fed. Trib., 1966); *Banque Commerciale Arabe S.A. Case*, ibid. 412 (Fed. Trib., 1977); *Banque Centrale de la Rép. de Turquie* v. *Weston*, ibid. 417 (Fed. Trib., 1978); *Arab Rep. of Egypt* v. *Cinetelevision*, ibid. 425 (Fed. Trib., 1979). *United Kingdom*: *Trendtex* v. *Central Bank of Nigeria* [1977] QB 529; ILR 64, 111; *1° Congreso del Partido* [1983] AC 244, per Lord Wilberforce (p. 260) and Lord Diplock (p. 272); ILR 64, 307 (at 311, 324, respectively). *United States*: *Alfred Dunhill of London, Inc.* v. *Republic of Cuba*, ILR 66, 212. See also *Reid* v. *Republic of Nauru* [1993] 1VR 251 (Victoria, SC).

[26] Barbados, Chile, Finland, Iceland, Madagascar, Mexico, Norway, Qatar, Suriname, Togo, Yugoslavia.

[27] UN Legis. Series, *Materials on Jurisdictional Immunities of Foreign States and Their Property* (1982).

[28] In the 'Tate Letter': Dept. of St. Bull. 26 (1952), 984, on which see Bishop, 47 *AJ* (1953), 93–106; Note, 1 *Georgia Journ. of Int. and Comp. Law* (1970), 133–78.

[29] 425 US 682 (1976); 15 *ILM* (1976), 735; 70 *AJ* (1976), 828.

United States as a result of the Foreign Sovereign Immunities Act of 1976.[30] There is certainly a trend toward a restrictive principle, but the picture contains contrary elements. A certain number of states[31] still accept the principle of absolute immunity, according to which immunity is granted except in cases in which the defendant state has consented to the exercise of jurisdiction.

Many states, including the United States and the former USSR, agree by treaty to waive immunity in respect of shipping and other commercial activities,[32] and it could be said either that such treaties assume a broad doctrine of immunity or that they are part of a contrary trend. Reference to treaty practice should include mention of the Brussels Convention of 1926,[33] which subjected vessels engaged in trade owned or operated by foreign states to the local jurisdiction as if they were private persons. This Convention received only 13 ratifications and cannot be regarded as of general significance.[34] However, the provisions of two important treaties, the Convention on the Territorial Sea and Contiguous Zone and the Convention on the High Seas, signed at Geneva in 1958,[35] tend to assimilate for the purposes of the Conventions the position of government ships operated for commercial purposes to that of non-government merchant ships. The former Convention, in dealing with the right of innocent passage through the territorial sea,[36] distinguishes the position of 'government ships operated for commercial purposes' from that of 'government ships operated for non-commercial purposes'.[37] Article 9 of the latter Convention provides:[38] 'Ships owned or operated by a State and used only on government non-commercial service shall, on the high seas, have complete immunity from the jurisdiction of any State other than the flag State.' These provisions are by no means conclusive of the general issue as to the extent of sovereign immunity, but they establish the position[39] in the very important sector of state-operated merchant shipping. The more recent United Nations Convention on the Law of the Sea (1982) contains similar provisions (Arts. 31, 32, 95, and 96).

[30] In force 19 Jan. 1977. For the text: 15 *ILM* (1976), 1388. For the Dept. of State circular to foreign embassies: 27 *ICLQ* (1978), 253; *Digest of US Practice* (1976), 327. For comment: Von Mehren, 17 *Columbia Journ. Trans. Law* (1978), 33–66; Delaume, 71 *AJ* (1977), 399–422; id., *Festschrift für F. A. Mann* (1977), 338–65; Brower, Bistline, Loomis, 73 *AJ* (1979), 200–14.

[31] Brazil, Bulgaria, China, Czechoslovakia, Ecuador, Hungary, Japan, Poland, Portugal, Sudan, Syria, Thailand, Trinidad and Tobago, the former USSR and Venezuela. The Polish courts emphasize the principle of reciprocity. There is a trend toward restrictive immunity in the Argentine cases: Sucharitkul, 4th Report, *Yrbk. ILC* (1982), ii (Pt. 1), 222. The position in respect of Burma, Philippines, Tunisia (amongst others) is obscure. The issue was left open in *Mizra Ali Akbar Kashani* v. *U.A.R.*, ILR 64, 489 (SC of India, 1965).

[32] See Sucharitkul, *State Immunities*, pp. 151–4, 196–7; Zourek, 86 *JDI* (1959), 660.

[33] Hudson, *Int. Legis.*, iii, no. 154, Art. II.

[34] But see *Yrbk. ILC* (1956), ii. 276, commentary to Art. 22.

[35] *Supra*, pp. 179ff. On government ships employed in commerce see generally Sucharitkul, *State Immunities*, pp. 15–103; and Thommen, *Legal Status of Government Merchant Ships in International Law* (1962).

[36] *Supra*, p. 186.

[37] See Arts. 20, 21, and 22; and *Yrbk. ILC* (1956), ii. 276, Art. 22 and commentary.

[38] Contrast the ILC draft, *Yrbk. ILC* (1956), ii. 280, Art. 33 and commentary.

[39] However, Art. 20 (or Art. 21) of the Territorial Sea Conv. drew reservations from seven Communist states; and Art. 9 of the High Seas Conv. drew reservations from eight Communist states. See McDougal and Burke, *The Public Order of the Ocean* (1962), 1180–9. The UK Government informed the Secretariat of its objection to these reservations. See *Treaty Series* no. 5 (1963), Cmnd. 1929.

5. THE CURRENT LEGAL POSITION

It is far from easy to state the current legal position in terms of customary or general international law. Recent writers emphasize that there is a *trend* in the practice of states towards the restrictive doctrine of immunity but avoid firm and precise prescriptions as to the present state of the law.[40] Moreover, the practice of states is far from consistent and, as the comments of governments relating to the draft articles produced by the International Law Commission[41] indicate, there is a persistent divergence between adherents of the principle of absolute immunity and that of restrictive immunity.[42] This divergence of views and the unresponsive attitude of the Sixth Committee of the General Assembly is usually ignored in the academic sources. The most recent development is the publication of the Draft Articles on jurisdictional immunities of States and their property prepared by the UN Ad Hoc Committee on this topic dated 27 February 2003,[43] and the convention opened for signature in 2005.

In any event the materials of the law call for careful managing and the problems encountered in practice are not avoided simply by hoisting the conceptual flag of restrictive immunity. It is one thing to say that the principle of absolute immunity is inadequate to policy needs, or no longer represents the law; it is quite another to demarcate the new boundaries of immunity. The various items said to embody the principle of restrictive immunity (for example: the European Convention of 1972, the United Kingdom State Immunity Act of 1978, the Australian Foreign States Immunities Act of 1985, and the Canadian State Immunity Act of 1982) do not provide uniform solutions. In any case there have always been certain generally recognized exceptions to the principle of absolute immunity.[44]

What emerges in reality is an agenda of problems which cannot be approached effectively in terms of a simple focus on the dichotomy between 'absolute' and 'restrictive' immunity. Thus even those states which have accepted the restrictive principle are in general unwilling to apply it at the level of actual enforcement by means of the seizure of assets of the debtor state. In other words, the adherents of the restrictive principle do not apply it at the more critical phase of the judicial process. The central

---

[40] See Sucharitkul, 149 Hague *Recueil* (1976, I), 87–216; and Sinclair, 167 Hague *Recueil* (1980, II), 113–284. See also Fitzmaurice, 92 Hague *Recueil* (1957, II), 187; O'Connell, ii. 844–6; Emanuelli, 22 *Canad. Yrbk.* (1984), 26 at 96–7; Report of the International Law Commission, *Yrbk. ILC* (1986), ii (Pt. 2), 6 (commentary on Art. 6).

[41] Report of the International Law Commission on the Work of its Fortieth Session, Gen. Ass., Off. Recs., 43rd sess., Suppl. no. 10 (A/43/10), pp. 258–9, paras. 398–503.

[42] The conclusion of Schreuer, *State Immunity*, 168, does not reflect the evidence. In his words: 'From a general perspective it can be said that the doctrine of restrictive immunity has been strengthened to a point where practically all countries from which any substantive material is available have embraced it.'

[43] U.N. Doc. A/AC.262/L.4/Add. 1.

[44] Viz. proceedings relating to immovable property owned by a foreign state and proceedings relating to acquisition by a foreign state by succession or gift of movable or immovable property.

fact is that adopting the principle of restrictive immunity does not avoid the determination of the precise boundaries of immunity. Thus the English courts continue to uphold immunity when, in all the circumstances, this is justifiable: see *Littrell* v. *United States (No. 2)*[45] (hospital treatment affecting a United States serviceman in a United States Air Force Hospital in the United Kingdom); *Kuwait Airways Corporation* v. *Iraqi Airways Company*[46] (taking and removal by Iraqi government entity of aircraft at Kuwait Airport belonging to K.A.C.); and *Holland* v. *Lampen-Wolfe*[47] (education and training of foreign military personnel).

A connected question of considerable significance is the distinction, already noted (*supra*, pp. 320–22), between immunity as a plea based upon the *status* of the defendant as a sovereign state (*ratione personae*), and immunity *ratione materiae*, which affects the essential competence of the local courts in relation to the particular subject-matter. The immunity *ratione personae* (procedural immunity) is a bar to the jurisdiction of the state of the forum which would exist (or be presumed to exist) but for the existence of a title of immunity. In fact the proponents of the principle of restrictive immunity, by reducing the role of status as a basis for conferring a title to immunity, have inevitably given greater prominence to the nature of the subject-matter and the issue of the essential competence of the judicial organs of the forum state.

The agenda of legal issues (before a national court) is as follows:

(*a*) The issue of ordinary subject-matter jurisdiction on the basis of territorial and other appropriate connecting factors with the forum state:[48] see Chapter 15 above.

(*b*) The existence of immunity *ratione personae*, which is *either* a privilege derogating from a subject-matter jurisdiction which would otherwise exist *or* a privilege to be recognized on a contingency basis *in case* subject-matter jurisdiction exists.

(*c*) Even if there is no basis of immunity *ratione personae*, and a basis for subject-matter jurisdiction exists, the question still remains whether the courts of the forum have an essential competence (in terms of general international law) in respect of the issue. The issue here is essentially that of propriety in terms of the rules of general international law.

(*d*) There may be a problem of the relation between the category of diplomatic immunity (which is substantially *ratione personae*) and the scope of the privilege of the foreign state in right of immunity *ratione materiae*.[49] In case of conflict, a pertinent statutory provision may provide that in such a case the title to diplomatic immunity should prevail. On occasion, as in the case of bank accounts of diplomatic missions, the existence of diplomatic immunity may be questionable (such accounts are not protected by the inviolability provisions of the Vienna Convention on Diplomatic

---

[45] ILR 100, 438, C.A.

[46] [1995] 1 WLR 1147; ILR, 103, 340.

[47] ILR 119, 368.

[48] The need to investigate jurisdiction as well as immunity is sometimes ignored: cf. *Alcom, Ltd*. v. *Rep. of Colombia*, ILR 74, 170.

[49] See generally Fox, 34 *ICLQ* (1985), 115 at 126–32.

Relations), and immunity will then turn on either the existence of a rule of customary international law apart from the Vienna Convention or the scope of state immunity as such in the circumstances.[50]

(e) The last question involves the characterization of the facts (which can be complex) in terms of which facts are critical in attracting the title to immunity. Thus in the case of *1° Congreso del Partido*[51] the House of Lords experienced difficulty in relation to the ship *Marble Islands*, one of two ships operated by a Cuban state agency and carrying sugar to Chile under a contract with Cubazucar, another Cuban agency. In reaction to the coup overthrowing the Allende government in Chile, the Cuban Government ordered the *Marble Islands* (which was still on the high seas) not to proceed with the contractual voyage. The Republic of Cuba was not contractually liable for the carriage of the sugar in the *Marble Islands*, and only became owner of the ship after the coup. The House of Lords held by a majority that the Republic of Cuba was not entitled to immunity since the subsequent disposal of the cargo in Vietnam by the master took place on the basis of private law and therefore did not attract immunity.[52] However, Lord Wilberforce (with Lord Edmund-Davies) dissented from this conclusion, holding that in respect of the *Marble Islands* the Republic of Cuba was not involved in any trading relationship and its acts 'were and remained in their nature purely governmental'.[53] The issue in this context can be characterized as a relative of causation and the nature of the link between the conduct of the state and the private law relationships which are affected by that conduct directly or indirectly.

6. THE MODALITIES OF RESTRICTIVE IMMUNITY

In any event the courts and governments of a number of states apply the principle of restrictive immunity and therefore it is necessary to examine the modalities of its application. The method most commonly referred to is the distinction between acts *jure imperii* (acts of sovereign authority) and acts *jure gestionis* (acts of a private law character), and the merits of this distinction must be examined. The basic criterion appears to be whether the key transaction was accomplished on the basis of a private law relationship, such as a contract. Another form of this approach is to state that the act is *jure gestionis*, and therefore not immune, if the transaction can be made by an individual.

Another approach is to inquire into the purpose of the act, and at first sight this appears to be a more appropriate criterion. However, this criterion involves either

---

[50] See the *Philippine Embassy Case*, ILR 65, 146 (German Fed. Rep., Fed. Const. Ct., 1977); *Alcom Ltd.* v. *Rep. of Colombia*, ILR 74, 170 (England, H. of Lds.).

[51] [1983] AC 244; ILR 64, 307. See also Crawford, 54 *BY* (1983), 75 at 94–102.

[52] [1983] AC 273–6; ILR 74, 324–7; *per* Lord Diplock.

[53] [1983] AC 271–2; ILR 64, 323; and see Lord Edmund-Davies, 276–7, and 327–8, respectively.

a restatement of the problem or an essentially political distinction between what is acceptable as a state purpose and what is not according to the concepts of public policy prevalent in the state concerned.[54] The difficulty with the criterion of purpose is that it involves a considerable curtailment of the operation of the criterion based upon acts *jure gestionis*. Thus the Italian Court of Cassation has held that the distinction between acts *jure gestionis* and acts *jure imperii* is not decisive in cases involving a contract of employment with an economic agency attached to a foreign embassy,[55] a contract of employment with a foreign public agency of Denmark (the Danish Cultural Institute),[56] and the contract of employment of an Italian subject employed in a managerial capacity by a foreign embassy.[57]

On any view a satisfactory mode of application of the principle of restrictive immunity has yet to be developed. National courts applying the principle manage to produce conflicting decisions on the classification of the purchase of military equipment, the operation of state railways, the promotional activities of state tourist offices, and so forth.[58] A good number of distinguished critics have concluded that the distinction is substantially flawed.[59]

A fairly standard approach, to be seen in the United Kingdom State Immunity Act (1978) and the Australian Foreign States Immunities Act (1985), is to employ these elements: a general principle of immunity (from jurisdiction), a catalogue of detailed exceptions, and a provision to the effect that the process of enforcement is possible in respect of property of a foreign state in use or intended for use for commercial purposes (including ships). In the *Victory Transport* case,[60] the United States District Court of Appeals listed as exclusively sovereign acts, internal administrative acts, such as expulsion of an alien, legislative acts, such as nationalization, acts concerning the armed forces, acts concerning diplomatic activity, and public loans.

Another approach would be to employ a combination of two sets of criteria which are countervailing and therefore have to be 'balanced up' in relation to the facts of the case, rather than applied as autonomous propositions. Thus in determining the question of the competence of the legal system of the forum state each case is to be characterized on its merits in the light of the relevant facts and the relevant criteria, both of competence and incompetence; no presumption is to be applied concerning the dominance or priority of either group of criteria. This method is in fact a rather structured

---

[54] Fitzmaurice, 14 *BY* (1933), 101 at 121, observes: 'The truth is that a sovereign State does not cease to be a sovereign State because it performs acts which a private citizen might perform.' See also O'Connell, ii. 845–6.

[55] *Luna* v. *S.R. of Romania*, ILR 65, 313.

[56] *Danish Cultural Institute* v. *Hansen*, ibid. 325.

[57] *Velloso* v. *Borla*, ibid. 328. See also *Special Representative* v. *Pieciukiewicz*, ILR 78, 120.

[58] See Lalive, 84 Hague *Recueil* (1953, III), 255–7; Schreuer, *State Immunity*, 24–9.

[59] See Hersch Lauterpacht, 28 *BY* (1951), 222–7; Lalive, 84 Hague *Recueil* (1953, III), 255–7; Brierly, p. 250; Sinclair, 167 Hague *Recueil* (1980, II), 210–13; Molot and Jewett, 20 *Canad. Yrbk.* (1982), 96–104.

[60] ILR 35, 110. This decision has been cited often by courts in other jurisdictions: see e.g. *Government of the D.R. of the Congo* v. *Venne*, ILR 64, 24 at 37, 43; *Inter-Science Services* v. *Rep. de Mocambique*, ibid. 689 at 703.

version of the actual method of decision-making used in practice by municipal courts for many years. The origins of the method are explained at length in the Definitive Report prepared by the writer as Rapporteur of the Fourteenth Commission of the Institute of International Law.[61]

The following criteria are indicative of the incompetence *ratione materiae* of the legal system of the forum state but are not conclusive of the question of competence either individually or collectively:

(a) The validity, meaning, and effect of the transactions of sovereign states in terms of public international law cannot be the object of adjudication in the municipal courts of other states.[62]

(b) The validity, meaning, and effect of the internal administrative and legislative acts of sovereign states in terms of international law cannot be the object of adjudication in the municipal courts of other states.[63]

(c) The legal system of the forum state should not assume competence in respect of issues the resolution of which has been allocated to a remedial context other than the legal system of the forum.[64]

(d) The content, conduct, and precise implementation of the foreign and defence policies of foreign states are matters outside the competence of the legal system of the forum state.[65]

(e) Arbitrations between states are outside the jurisdiction of the state in the territory of which the arbitral procedure is conducted.[66]

---

[61] See *Annuaire de l'Institut*, 62, i. 45 at 54–85. Lady Fox, rather oddly, states that national courts 'have made little use of Brownlie's approach': see *The Law of State Immunity*, 91. But this is to ignore the fact that the approach is based upon a *previous* long-established judicial practice. Lady Fox does not refer to the contents of the *Reports* on which the conclusions of the present author are based. The 'Brownlie approach', which is descriptive rather than prescriptive, has in fact appeared in several significant sources: see the Australian Law Reform Commission Report No. 24, *Foreign State Immunity* (1984); the ILC, Report of Working Group on Jurisdictional Immunities of States and Their Property, 6 July 1999; *KPMG Peat Marwick v. Davison*, ILR 104, 526, 584–6, 616–19, New Zealand C.A.

[62] See Lord Denning in *Rahimtoola v. Nizam of Hyderabad* [1958] AC 379 at 422–3; Lord Wilberforce in *Buttes Gas v. Hammer* [1982] AC 888 at 931–2; *Arab Republic of Syria v. Arab Republic of Egypt*, ILR 91, 288 (Brazil S.C.).

[63] See Hersch Lauterpacht, 28 BY (1951), 237–8; Lalive, 84 Hague *Recueil* (1953, III), 285; Sinclair, 167 Hague *Recueil* (1980, II), 216; *Arab Republic of Libya v. SpA Imprese Maritimme Frassinetti*, ILR 78, 90 (Italy: Ct. of Cassation); *S. v. Socialist Republic of Romania*, ILR 82, 45 (Swiss Fed. Trib.); *Société Internationale de Plantations d'Hévéas v. Lao Import Company*, ILR 80, 688 (France: Ct. of Cassation).

[64] Examples cited in *Annuaire de l'Inst.* 62, i. 62–4.

[65] The principle was applied by the H. of Lds. in *1° Congreso del Partido* [1983] AC 244; ILR 64, 307; and in *Kuwait Airways Corporation v. Iraqi Airways Co.* [1995] 1 WLR 1147 at 1164–68. See also *Luna v. S.R. of Romania*, ILR 65, 313; *Danish Cultural Institute v. Hansen*, ibid. 325; *Velloso v. Borla*, ibid. 328; *I.O.M. v. OPEC*, ILR 66, 413 at 420; *Buckingham v. The Aircraft Hughes 500 D Helicopter*, ILR 64, 551; *Amanat Khan v. Fredson Travel, Inc.*, ibid. 733; *In re Sedco*, 21 *ILM* (1982), 318; ILR 72, 110; *Commonwealth of Australia v. Midford (Malaysia) Sdn Bhd*, ILR 86, 640.

[66] See Mann, 42 BY (1967), 1 at 2. This view was assumed by the Arbitration Tribunal in *Saudi Arabia v. Arabian American Oil Co.*, ILR 27, 117 at 155. See also *Annuaire de l'Inst.* 62, i. 67.

(*f*) Transactions relating to the validity, meaning, and implementation of an inter-governmental agreement creating agencies, institutions, or funds subject to the rules of public international law are not within the competence of the legal system of the forum State.[67]

The following criteria are indicative of the competence *ratione materiae* of the legal system of the forum state, but are not conclusive of the question of competence either individually or collectively:

(*a*) In the absence of agreement to the contrary, the legal system of the forum state is competent in respect of proceedings relating to a commercial transaction to which a foreign state (or its agent) is a party.[68]

(*b*) The legal system of the forum state is competent in respect of proceedings con-cerning legal disputes arising from relationships of a private law character to which a foreign state (or its agent) is a party; the class of relationships referred to includes (but is not confined to) the following legal categories: commercial contracts; contracts for the supply of services; loans and financing arrangements; guarantees or indem-nities in respect of financial obligations; ownership, possession, and use of property; the protection of industrial and intellectual property; the legal incidents attaching to incorporated bodies, unincorporated bodies and associations, and partnerships; actions *in rem* against ships and cargoes; and bills of exchange.[69]

(*c*) The legal system of the forum state is competent in respect of proceedings con-cerning legal disputes arising from relationships which are not classified in the forum as having a 'private law character' but which nevertheless are based upon elements of good faith and reliance (legal security) within the context of the local law.[70] Thus in certain legal systems contracts of employment may fall within the sphere of adminis-trative law.

(*d*) The legal system of the forum state is competent in respect of proceedings con-cerning contracts of employment and contracts for professional services to which a foreign state (or its agent) is a party provided that the relationship concerned does not involve sovereign activities, such as the running of a naval base.[71]

---

[67] See *U.S.A. and Republic of France* v. *Dollfus Mieg* [1952] AC 582; and esp. per Lord Radcliffe, pp. 615, 618–19; and *Rahimtoola* v. *Nizam of Hyderabad* [1958] AC 379 per Lord Denning at 423. The House of Lords reaffirmed this principle in the *International Tin Council Appeals* [1989] 3 WLR 969 at 983–5 *per* Lord Templeman, and at 1001–3, 1020–3 *per* Lord Oliver of Aylmerton.

[68] See *Yrbk. ILC* (1982), ii (Pt. 1), 207–29 (Fourth Report of Professor Sucharitkul); Draft Articles of the Commission, *Yrbk. ILC* (1991), ii (Pt. 2), 33–40.

[69] See *Annuaire de l'Inst.* 62, i. 75–6, for reference to the more recent decisions. See also *Yrbk. ILC* (1982), ii (Pt. 1), 207–29; ibid. (1984), ii (Pt. 1), 16–21, 25–54.See also *Her Majesty the Queen in Right of Canada* v. *Edelson*, ILR 131, 279; Israel S.C.

[70] See *Annuaire de l'Inst.* 62, i. 76.

[71] See *Yrbk. ILC* (1983), ii (Pt. 1), 32–8 (Fifth Report of Professor Sucharitkul); *Annuaire de l'Inst.* 62, i. 76–9; Draft Articles, *Yrbk. ILC* (1991), ii (Pt. 2), 41–4; Fox, 66 BY (1995), 97–176. But see *Van der Hulst* v. *United States*, ILR 94, 373 (Netherlands S.C.); and *U.S.A.* v. *The Public Service Alliance of Canada*, ibid., 264 (Canada S.C.); *Libyan Arab Jamahiriya* v. *Trobbiani*, ILR 114, 520 (Italian Ct. of Cassation); *Seidenschmidt* v. *United States*, ILR 116, 530 (Austria, S.C.); *Brazilian Embassy Employee Case*, ILR 116, 625 (Portugal, S.C.).

(e) The legal system of the forum state is competent in respect of proceedings concerning the death of, or personal injury to, a person, or loss of or damage to tangible property, attributable to an act or omission of a foreign state or its agent.[72] In this context it makes no difference if the act involved is a deliberate act of policy such as an assassination. The difficult question is whether this exception is applicable to *lawful* acts of State.

(f) The legal system of the forum state is competent in respect of proceedings relating to any interest of a foreign state in movable or immovable property, being a right or interest arising by way of succession, gift, or *bona vacantia*; or a right or interest in the administration of property forming part of the estate of a deceased person or a person of unsound mind or a bankrupt; or a right or interest in the administration of property of a company in the event of its dissolution or winding up; or a right or interest in the administration of trust property or property otherwise held on a fiduciary basis.[73]

(g) The legal system of the forum state is competent in respect of proceedings relating to fiscal liabilities, income tax, customs duties, stamp duty, registration fees, and similar impositions, provided that such liabilities are the normal concomitant of commercial and other legal relationships in the context of the local legal system and *provided further* that the relevant legislation is applied without discrimination.[74]

7. THE EUROPEAN CONVENTION ON STATE IMMUNITY

The adoption in 1972 of the European Convention on State Immunity[75] is an important development and provides further evidence of the trend toward a restrictive approach to immunity. At the same time the provisions have a cadence and economy of their own, and the Convention represents a compromise between the doctrines of absolute and relative immunity. The principal provisions of interest are as follows:

Article 6

1. A Contracting State cannot claim immunity from the jurisdiction of a court of another Contracting State if it participates with one or more private persons in a company, association

---

[72] See *Yrbk. ILC* (1983), ii (Pt. 1), 38–46; *Annuaire de l'Inst.* 62, i. 79–81; Crawford, 8 *Austral. Yrbk.*, pp. 88–9; Draft Articles, *Yrbk. ILC* (1991), ii (Pt. 2), 44–6. See also *Al-Adsani* v. *Government of Kuwait*, ILR 100, 465; ILR 107, 536 (English C.A.) (allegations of torture by officials of Kuwait); *Nelson* v. *Saudi Arabia*, ILR 88, 189 (U.S. Ct. of Appeals, Eleventh Circuit). Cp. *Jaffe* v. *Miller*, ILR 87, 197 (Ontario High Ct.).

[73] See *Yrbk. ILC* (1983), ii (Pt. 1), 46–52; Draft Articles, *Yrbk. ILC* (1991), ii (Pt. 2), 46–7.

[74] See *Yrbk. ILC* (1984), ii (Pt. 1), 21–5 (Sixth Report of Professor Sucharitkul); *Annuaire de l'Inst.* 62, i. 83.

[75] Opened for signature on 16 May 1972. For the text: 11 *ILM* (1972), 470. For comment: Sinclair, 22 *ICLQ* (1973), 254–83; Krafft, 31 *Ann. suisse* (1975), 11–30; Knierim, 12 *Columbia Journ. Trans. Law* (1973), 130–54; Council of Europe, *Explanatory Reports on the European Convention on State Immunity and the Additional Protocol* (1972).

or other legal entity having its seat, registered office or principal place of business on the territory of the State of the forum, and the proceedings concern the relationship, in matters arising out of that participation, between the State on the one hand and the entity or any other participant on the other hand.

2. Paragraph 1 shall not apply if it is otherwise agreed in writing.

Article 7

1. A Contracting State cannot claim immunity from the jurisdiction of a court of another Contracting State if it has on the territory of the State of the forum an office, agency or other establishment through which it engages, in the same manner as a private person, in an industrial, commercial or financial activity, and the proceedings relate to that activity of the office, agency or establishment.

2. Paragraph 1 shall not apply if all the parties to the dispute are States, or if the parties have otherwise agreed in writing.

The Convention formulates these and other exceptions to the principle of immunity, which applies apart from the express provisions (Art. 15). There is no immunity from execution but foreign States are obliged to give effect to judgments rendered against them (Art. 20). It is to be noted that the provisions do not incorporate the restrictive principle of immunity in terms, but a major part of activities of a commercial character will fall within Articles 6 and 7. The specification of connecting links is a special feature deriving from the need to provide a basis for recognition and enforcement of any resulting judgment.

8. THE UNITED KINGDOM STATE IMMUNITY ACT[76]

After an earlier adherence to the 'absolute' principle of immunity (which in fact included certain exceptions), the English courts have recently held that the 'restrictive' principle applied at common law.[77] The position is now regulated by the State Immunity Act (1978) and this is regarded as embodying the 'restrictive' theory of state immunity.[78] However, it would be incautious to assume that the Act is evidence of customary international law.[79] In a general way the purpose of the Act is to implement the European Convention on State Immunity, together with the Brussels Convention

---

[76] Entered into force 22 Nov. 1978. Text: ILR 64, 718. For comment: Mann, 50 BY (1979), 43–62; Delaume, 73 AJ (1979), 185–99. The substantive provisions are not retrospective: *Planmount* v. *Rep. of Zaire* [1981] 1 All ER 1110; ILR 64, 268.

[77] *Trendtex Trading Corporation* v. *Central Bank of Nigeria* [1977] QB 529; ILR 64, 111 (CA); *Hispano Americana Mercantil* v. *Central Bank of Nigeria* [1979] 2 Lloyd's Rep. 277; ILR 64, 221 (CA); *1° Congreso del Partido* [1983] AC 244, per Lord Wilberforce at 260; ILR 64, 307 at 311; per Lord Diplock, at pp. 272, 324, respectively.

[78] *1° Congreso del Partido*, previous note.

[79] *1° Congreso del Partido*, supra, n. 73, per Lord Wilberforce. Cp. *S.* v. *India*, ILR 82, 14 (Swiss Fed. Trib.); *Libya* v. *Actimon S.A.*, ILR 82, 30 (Swiss Fed. Trib.).

of 1926 on Immunity of State-owned Ships (and the Protocol thereto of 1934). The provisions of the Act are to be interpreted against the background of the principles of general international law.[80]

The Act enacts a general principle of immunity from the jurisdiction of the courts of the United Kingdom (s. 1(1)), and then provides for a catalogue of substantial exceptions to the general principle (ss. 2–11). The most important of these exceptions is section 3, which provides as follows:

3. (1) A State is not immune as respects proceedings relating to—
  (a) a commercial transaction entered into by the State; or
  (b) an obligation of the State which by virtue of a contract (whether a commercial transaction or not) falls to be performed wholly or partly in the United Kingdom.

(2) This section does not apply if the parties to the dispute are States or have otherwise agreed in writing; and subsection (1)(b) above does not apply if the contract (not being a commercial transaction) was made in the territory of the State concerned and the obligation in question is governed by its administrative law.
  (3) In this section 'commercial transaction' means—
  (a) any contract for the supply of goods or services;
  (b) any loan or other transaction for the provision of finance and any guarantee or indemnity in respect of any such transaction or of any other financial obligation; and
  (c) any other transaction or activity (whether of a commercial, industrial, financial, professional or other similar character) into which a State enters or in which it engages otherwise than in the exercise of sovereign authority;

but neither paragraph of subsection (1) above applies to a contract of employment between a State and an individual.

This provision is broadly cast. Thus, subsection (1) not only applies to commercial transactions 'entered into by the State', but also to 'an obligation of the State which by virtue of a contract (whether a commercial transaction or not) falls to be performed…'.[81]

The Court of Appeal has held that, whenever the issue of immunity arises under the Act, this question must be decided as a preliminary issue in favour of the plaintiff before the substantive action can proceed.[82] The Act does not affect immunities under the Diplomatic Privileges Act (1964) or the Consular Relations Act (1968) (s. 16(1)).[83]

---

[80] *Alcom* v. *Rep. of Colombia* [1984] AC 580, *per* Lord Diplock at 597; ILR 74, 170 at 180. See also Mann, 50 *BY* (1979), 49–50.

[81] See *Alcom* v. *Rep of Colombia* [1984] AC 580; ILR 74, 170 (HL); and the *International Tin Council Appeals* (Direct actions), CA. On the relation of s. 3 and s. 6 see *Intpro Properties Ltd.* v. *Sauvel* [1983] 1 QB 1019 at 1030–1; ILR 64, 384 at 389 (CA).

[82] *International Tin Council Appeals* (Direct actions) [1988] 3 All ER 257.

[83] See *Sengupta* v. *Rep. of India*, ILR 64, 352 at 357; *Intpro Properties* v. *Sauvel* [1983] 1 QB 1019; *Alcom* v. *Rep. of Colombia* [1984] AC 580; ILR 74, 170 (HL).

A 'separate entity' is immune only if (*a*) the proceedings relate to anything done by it 'in the exercise of sovereign authority', and (*b*) the circumstances are such that a state would have been immune (s. 14(1)). A 'separate entity' is any entity 'which is distinct from the executive organs of the government of the State and capable of suing or being sued' (s. 14(2)).[84]

In practice the issue of immunity has very often arisen in the context of indirect impleading, that is to say, cases in which the foreign state is not a defendant but the proceedings are alleged to affect property in which the foreign state has a proprietary, possessory, or other legal interest.[85] While the Act does not address this question as such, the practical effect of the provisions is to maintain the prohibition on indirect impleading as it was before the Act, with the exception of actions in respect of ships used for commercial purposes (s. 10).[86]

The Act provides that no process of enforcement can be invoked against a foreign state and that 'the property of a State shall not be subject to any process for the enforcement of a judgment or arbitration award or, in an action *in rem*, for its arrest, detention or sale' (s. 13(2)). This immunity applies to a central bank or other monetary authority of a State even if it is a 'separate entity' (s. 14(4)). However, injunctive relief or the issue of any process for enforcement may be given with the written consent of the state concerned (which may be contained in a prior agreement) (s. 13(3)). For this purpose a provision merely submitting to the jurisdiction of the courts is not to be regarded as a consent to execution (ibid.).

Apart from the effect of consent, there is no immunity from execution 'in respect of property which is for the time being in use or intended for use for commercial purposes' (s. 13(4)).[87] According to section 17(1), 'commercial purposes' means 'purposes of such transactions or activities as are mentioned in section 3(3)'. In *Alcom* v. *Republic of Colombia*[88] the balance standing to the credit of a diplomatic mission's current bank account was held to fall outside the words in section 13(4) on the basis of a certificate furnished by the head of the mission, which certificate is 'sufficient evidence of the fact unless the contrary is proved' (s. 13(5)).

The Act is in principle concerned with immunity *ratione personae* of the foreign state and it is reasonable to assume that, if a defendant state were not accorded immunity by virtue of its provisions, a plea of immunity *ratione materiae* would still be available in accordance with general international law, except where the relevant exception to immunity clearly extends to matters of immunity *ratione materiae*.

---

[84] See *Kuwait Airways Corporation* v. *Iraqi Airways Co.* [1995] 1 WLR 1147, HL.

[85] See *The Cristina* [1938] AC 485; *U.S.A. and Republic of France* v. *Dollfus Mieg* [1952] AC 582; *Rahimtoola* v. *Nizam of Hyderabad* [1958] AC 379.

[86] See Dicey and Morris, *The Conflict of Laws* (14th edn., 2000, i. 279). The key provisions are ss. 2(4) and 6(4).

[87] This exception does not apply (apart from actions *in rem* by virtue of s. 10) to property of a state party to the European Conv. on State Immunity, unless certain conditions are fulfilled (essentially on a basis of reciprocity).

[88] [1984] AC 580 at 604; ILR 74, 170 at 187–8. See Fox, 34 *ICLQ* (1985), 115–41.

9. WAIVER OF IMMUNITY[89]

Immunity here is not mandatory: subject to the distinction drawn in section 2 above, no fundamental principle prohibits the exercise of jurisdiction, and the immunity can be waived by the state concerned either expressly or by conduct. Waiver may occur, *inter alia*, in a treaty, in a diplomatic communication, or by actual submission to the proceedings in the local court. Voluntary submission to jurisdiction does not extend to measures of execution.[90] Waiver is not to be implied, by law as it were, from the fact that a given activity is commercial.[91] The problems of waiver are of course related to the controversy over the extent of immunity, and some courts utilize a doctrine of 'implied waiver' to restrict immunity. English courts, on the other hand, required a genuine and unequivocal submission in the face of the court: waiver was not constituted either by a prior contract to submit to the jurisdiction[92] or by an arbitration clause in a contract, even when an award had been made and the foreign state was applying to have it set aside.[93] Under the State Immunity Act 1978 immunity is denied when there is a prior written agreement to submit to the jurisdiction and when there is a written agreement to submit to arbitration: see sections 2 and 9 of the Act.[94] In various jurisdictions there are decisions (which have not produced a consistent jurisprudence) on the question whether and in what circumstances an arbitration clause in a state contract involves a waiver of immunity by the state party.[95]

10. POLITICAL SUBDIVISIONS AND STATE AGENCIES

The extent to which member states of federations and provinces of other types of state can claim immunity is unsettled.[96] Three approaches are possible: (1) on the basis that political subdivisions are organs of a state and entitled to the same immunity; (2) on

---

[89] See Harv. Research, 26 *AJ* (1932), Spec. Suppl., pp. 540–723; Cohn, 34 *BY* (1958), 260–73; Whiteman, vi. 674–9; Rousseau, iv. 18–19; Molot and Jewett, 20 *Canad. Yrbk.* (1982), 104–7; Crawford, 8 *Austral. Yrbk.*, pp. 96–102; Third Report by Sucharitkul, *Yrbk. ILC* (1981), ii (Pt. 1), 125–50; ibid. (1982), ii (Pt. 2), 107–11, ibid. (1983), ii (Pt. 2), 22–5; Draft Articles, *Yrbk. ILC* (1991), ii (Pt. 2), 25–33; Fox, *The Law of State Immunity* (2002), 262–71.

[90] See Second Report by Sucharitkul, *Yrbk. ILC* (1980), ii (Pt. 1), 15; Crawford, 75 *AJ* (1981), 860–1.

[91] Such a doctrine of implied waiver has been employed by the Italian courts: *Storelli* v. *Governo della Repubblica francese, Ann. Digest* (1923–4), no. 66; *Hungarian P.R.* v. *Onori*, ILR 23 (1956), 203.

[92] See *Kahan* v. *Pakistan Federation* [1951] 2 KB 1003; ILR 18 (1951), no. 50; *Baccus S.R.L.* v. *Servicio Nacional del Trigo* [1957] 1 QB 438; ILR 23 (1956), 160.

[93] *Duff Development Co.* v. *Government of Kelantan* [1924] AC 797. Cf. *Myrtoon Steamship Co.* v. *Agent Judiciaire du Trésor*, ILR 24 (1957), 205.

[94] See Dicey and Morris, *The Conflict of Laws* (14th edn., 2006), 285–6.

[95] See *Annuaire de l'Inst.*, 62 (1987), 82; Schreuer, *State Immunity*, pp. 70–1; *Yrbk. ILC* (1984), ii (Pt. 1), 54–8 (Sixth Report by Sucharitkul); ibid. (1985), ii (Pt. 2), 63–4 (Report to GA); Crawford, 8 *Austral. Yrbk.*, pp. 96–102; Mann, *Further Studies in International Law* (1990), 319; Oppenheim, i. 351–2. See also *Westland Helicopters* v. *A.O.I.*, 23 *ILM* (1984), 1071 at 1089 (Interim Award, ICC Ct. of Arbitration). See also Draft Articles, *Yrbk. ILC* (1991), ii (Pt. 2), 54–5.

[96] See Sucharitkul, *State Immunities*, pp. 106–12; id., 149 Hague *Recueil* (1976, 1), 101–3; Sucharitkul, Second Report, *Yrbk. ILC* (1980), ii (Pt. 1), 208–9; *Yrbk. ILC* (1986), ii (Pt. 2), 13–14; Rousseau, iv. 12;

the basis that sovereignty for this purpose inheres only in the central organs of a state; and (3) on a functional basis using criteria of the type surveyed in section 6 above. The existing case law is confused and reveals no consistent principles.[97] Decisions allowing immunity on the ground that an entity is 'sovereign' under the law of the forum are not very much in point.[98] The relevant provisions of the European Convention on State Immunity of 1972 (Arts. 27 and 28) appear to adopt the functional test, since the constituent states of a federal state are 'entities' for the purpose of Article 27.

Municipal courts have been prepared, apart from the effect of the restrictive doctrine, to extend immunity to various state agencies, including the United States Shipping Board,[99] the Spanish Servicio Nacional Del Trigo,[100] the Soviet Trade Delegation,[101] the Tass Agency,[102] and the New Brunswick Development Corporation.[103] However, in this sphere also the principles on which courts act are still unsettled.[104] At least it is doubtful if separate incorporation as a legal person under municipal law of itself should preclude immunity.[105] The general test seems to be that of effective control, and thus immunity may extend to a private corporation in which a foreign government has a controlling interest.[106] However, in decisions concerning central banks the criteria

---

O'Connell, ii. 877–8; Whiteman, vi. 589–92; Molot and Jewett, 20 *Canad. Yrbk.* (1982), 110–13; Crawford, 8 *Austral. Yrbk.*, pp. 94–6; Draft Articles, *Yrbk. ILC* (1991) ii (Pt. 2), 14–17; Fox, *The Law of State Immunity* (2002), 323–67.

[97] See *Feldman v. State of Bahia* (1907), 26 *AJ* (1932), 484; *Molina v. Comisión Reguladora del Mercado de Henequen* (1918), Hackworth, ii. 402; *State of Céara v. Dorr* (1932), *Ann. Digest*, 4 (1927–8), no. 21; *Van Heyningen v. Netherlands Indies* (1948), *Ann. Digest*, 15 (1948), no. 43; *Montefiore v. Belgian Congo*, ILR 44, 72; *Mellenger v. New Brunswick Development Corporation* [1971] 1 WLR 603, CA; 45 *BY* (1971), 396. Some writers regard the jurisprudence as supporting a rule denying immunity: see de Visscher, 102 Hague *Recueil* (1961, I), 421.

[98] See *Mighell v. Sultan of Johore* [1894] 1 KB 149; *Duff Development Co. v. Government of Kelantan* [1924] AC 797; *Kahan v. Federation of Pakistan* [1951] 2 KB 1003; *Sayce v. Bahawalpur* [1952] 2 All ER 64.

[99] *Compania Mercantil Argentina v. United States Shipping Board* (1924), 131 LT 388; *Ann. Digest*, 2 (1923–4), no. 73.

[100] *Baccus S.R.L. v. Servicio Nacional del Trigo* [1957] 1 QB 438; ILR 23 (1956), 160.

[101] *Russian Trade Delegation in Sweden*, *Ann. Digest* (1946), no. 33; *Bank of Netherlands v. State Trust*, *Ann. Digest* (1943–5), no. 26. Cf. *Borga v. Russian Trade Delegation* (1953), ILR 22 (1955), 235, where the Italian Court of Cassation applied the restrictive doctrine of immunity to trading activity. See Fensterwald, 63 *Harv. LR* (1950), 614–42.

[102] *Krajina v. Tass Agency* [1949] 2 All ER 274; *Ann. Digest*, 16 (1949), no. 37.

[103] *Mellenger v. New Brunswick Development Corporation* [1971] 1 WLR 603, CA.

[104] See generally Sucharitkul, *State Immunities*, pp. 104–61; id., 149 Hague *Recueil* (1976, I), 100–1; Sucharitkul, Second Report, *Yrbk. ILC* (1980), ii (Pt. 1), 209–10; *Yrbk. ILC* (1986), ii (Pt. 2), 13–14; Lalive, 84 Hague *Recueil* (1953, III), 243–7; Rousseau iv. 12–14; O'Connell, ii. 872–6; Schreuer, *State Immunity*, pp. 92–124; Molot and Jewett, 20 *Canad. Yrbk.* (1982), 107–10; Crawford, 8 *Austral. Yrbk.*, pp. 94–6; Draft Articles, *Yrbk. ILC* (1991) ii (Pt. 2), 14, 17–18. See also *Hungarian Academy in Rome* case, ILR 40, 59.

[105] See *Krajina v. Tass Agency, Baccus S.R.L. v. Servicio Nacional del Trigo, Mellenger, supra;* and *Czarnikow (C) Ltd. v. Rolimpex* [1978] QB 176, CA. This is not the approach of French and other civil law courts: cf. *Passelaigues v. Mortgage Bank of Norway*, ILR 22 (1955), 227. See also de Visscher, 102 Hague *Recueil* (1961, I), 423–6.

[106] Cf. *Re Investigation of World Arrangements with Relation to Petroleum* (1952), 13 F. 280; ILR 19 (1952), no. 41; 47 *AJ* (1953), 502, where the test applied was that of the 'object and purpose' of the Anglo-Iranian Oil Co., which was held to have a public purpose by reason of its connection with the British Government. See also *U.S. v. Deutsches Kalisyndikat Gesellschaft*, 31 F. 2d 199 (1929), *Ann. Digest* (1929–31), no. 71; *Ulen v. Bank Gospodarstwa*, 24 NYS 2d 201 (1940); Sørensen, pp. 428–9; *In re Grand Jury Investigation of the Shipping*

have been applied with rather different results and reserve banks under substantial governmental control have been held not to be organs or agents of government.[107]

An attractive solution, which has some support in the case-law[108] is to apply the criteria which indicate the application of immunity *ratione materiae*, either in the simple version distinguishing 'commercial transactions',[109] or the more flexible version of countervailing criteria indicated above (section 6).[110] It is also important to note that a state agency, such as a central bank, may exercise a variety of functions concurrently, and thus commercial functions may coexist with official functions as a bank of issue and/or as an administrator of the foreign exchange reserves of the state.

11. ATTACHMENT AND SEIZURE IN EXECUTION[111]

The issue of immunity from jurisdiction (procedural immunity) is distinct from the question of immunity from measures of constraint consequent upon the exercise of jurisdiction. Such measures comprise all measures of constraint directed against property of the foreign state (including funds in bank accounts) either for the purpose of enforcing judgments (*exécution forcée*) or for the purpose of pre-judgment attachment (*saisie conservatoire*). The distinction between 'immunity from jurisdiction' and 'immunity from execution' reflects the particular sensitivities of states in face of measures of forcible execution directed against their assets, and measures of execution may lead to serious disputes at the diplomatic level.[112] At the same time, there are strong considerations of principle which militate in favour of the view that, if there is competence of the municipal legal system in order to exercise jurisdiction and to render a judgment, enforcement jurisdiction in respect of that judgment should also be exercisable.

Industry, 186 F. Supp. 298 (1960); ILR 31, 209; *Et Ve Balik Kurumu* v. *B.N.S.*, 204 NYS 2d 971; ILR 31, 247; *Royal Nepal Airline Corporation* v. *Meher Singh Legha*, ILR 64, 430.

[107] See *Swiss Israel Trade Bank* v. *Government of Malta* [1972], 1 Lloyd's Rep. 497; 46 *BY* (1972–3), 427; *Trendtex Trading Corporation* v. *Central Bank of Nigeria* [1977] 1 QB 529, CA; 48 *BY* (1976–7), 353 at 354–5 (further citations). See also the material in *Digest of US Practice* (1973), 227–30; and Delaume, 71 *AJ* (1977), 399 at 412–13.

[108] See *Blagojevic* v. *Bank of Japan*, ILR 65, 63; *N.V. Exploitatie-Maatschappij Bengkalis* v. *Bank Indonesia*, ibid. 348; *Arab Republic of Egypt* v. *Cinetelevision*, ibid. 425; *Société Sonatrach* v. *Migeon*, ILR 77, 525.

[109] See Schreuer, *State Immunity*, p. 95.

[110] See *Annuaire de l'Inst.* 62, i. 85–7.

[111] See generally Whiteman, vi. 709–26; Bouchez *et al.*, 10 *Neths. Yrbk.* (1979), 3–289; Rousseau, iv. 16–17; Sinclair, 167 Hague *Recueil* (1980, II), 218–42; Crawford, 75 *AJ* (1981), 820–69; Molot and Jewett, 20 *Canad. Yrbk.* (1982), 113–18; Badr, *State Immunity*, pp. 107–12, 129–32; Fox, 34 *ICLQ* (1985), 115–41; Sucharitkul (Seventh Report), *Yrbk. ILC* (1985), ii (Pt. 1), 21–44; *Annuaire de l'Inst.* 62, i. 87–93; Schreuer, *State Immunity*, pp. 125–67; Draft Articles, *Yrbk. ILC* (1991), ii (Pt. 2), 56–9; Fox, *The Law of State Immunity* (2002), 368–417; Reinisch, *Europ. Journ.* 17 (2006), 803–36.

[112] Sinclair, 167 Hague *Recueil* (1980, II), 218–20; Fox, 34 *ICLQ* (1985), 121.

The majority of states almost certainly still recognize immunity from execution,[113] but it is very probable that this position will change as the views of governments are influenced by the developments in the doctrine and in the case-law of municipal courts. It is generally assumed that the preponderance of modern writers favour the application of the restrictive principle and reliance upon the distinction between acts *jure gestionis* and acts *jure imperii*.[114] However, some of the authorities do not speak with a clear voice,[115] and some respectable opinions continue to support the principle of absolute immunity.[116] While the picture is not without obscurities, some leading elements in the recent case-law have taken the position that the criteria of competence (of a municipal law court) are in principle the same for enforcement as for jurisdiction.[117] This is essentially the position adopted by the International Law Commission, in its Report to the General Assembly.[118] On this view, property in use or intended for use by the state for commercial (or non-governmental) purposes will not be immune from measures of enforcement. In this context, a bank account of a diplomatic mission used for the purpose of running the embassy is immune from enforcement measures.[119]

In the case of waiver, the principle which is still generally recognized is that consent to the exercise of jurisdiction does not involve an implicit waiver of the separate immunity from measures of execution.[120]

---

[113] See the replies to the Questionnaire in UN Legis. Series, *Materials on Jurisdictional Immunities of States and Their Property* (1982), 557–645.

[114] See Lalive, 84 Hague *Recueil* (1953, III), 279; Bouchez, 10 *Neths. Yrbk.* (1979), 17–32; Crawford, 75 *AJ* (1981), 820–69; Diez de Velasco, *Instituciones* (8th edn., 1988), i. 242–3; Pastor Ridruejo, *Curso* (2nd edn., 1987), 497.

[115] See e.g. Sørensen, p. 441; O'Connell, ii. 864–5; Daillier, and Pellet, *Droit international public* (6th edn., 1999), 448–9. See also Sucharitkul, *Yrbk. ILC* (1985), ii (Pt. 1), 36–7.

[116] See Johnson, 6 *Austral. Yrbk.* pp. 2–3; Rousseau, iv. 16.

[117] The case-law is examined by Sinclair, 167 Hague *Recueil* (1980, II), 218–42. See, in particular, *In re The Charkow*, ILR 65, 100 (FRG, *Landgericht* of Bremen), at pp. 104–5; *Philippine Embassy Bank Account* case, ibid. 146 (FRG, Fed. Const. Ct.), at 164–6; *N.I.O.C. Revenues from Oil Sales* case, ibid. 215 (FRG Fed. Const. Ct.); *United Arab Republic* v. *Mrs. X*, ibid. 385 (Switzerland, Fed. Trib.), at 391; *Italian Republic* v. *Beta Holding S.A.*, ibid. 394 (Switzerland, Fed. Trib.); *Banque Commerciale Arabe S.A.* case, ibid. 412 (Switzerland, Fed. Trib.); *Arab Republic of Egypt* v. *Cinetelevision International Registered Trust*, ibid. 425 (Switzerland, Fed. Trib.); *Trendtex* v. *Central Bank of Nigeria*, ILR 64, 111 (England, CA); *Hispano Americana Mercantil S.A.* v. *Central Bank of Nigeria*, ibid. 221 (England, CA); *Islamic Republic of Iran* v. *Société Eurodif*, ILR 77, 513 (France, Ct. of Cassation); *Société Sonatrach* v. *Migeon*, ibid. 525 (the same); *Republic of 'A' Embassy Bank Account* case, ibid. 489 (Austria, Supr. Ct.). See further the United Kingdom State Immunity Act (1978), s. 13(4); the Pakistan State Immunity Ordinance (1981), s. 14; the Canadian State Immunity Act (1982), s. 11; and the Australian Foreign States Immunities Act (1985), ss. 30 and 32.

[118] Draft Articles 18 and 19, *Yrbk.*, ILC (1991), 56–9.

[119] See *Clerget* v. *Banque Commerciale*, ILR 65, 54; the *Philippine Embassy* case, ILR 65, 146; *Alcom* v. *Rep. of Colombia*, ILR 74, 170; *Republic of 'A' Embassy* case, ILR 77, 489; *MK* v. *State Secretary for Justice*, ILR 94, 357; *LETCO* v. *Liberia*, ILR 89, 360; *Banamar-Capizzi* v. *Embassy of Algeria*, ILR 87, 56; *Libya* v. *Actimon S.A.*, ILR 82, 30 (Swiss Fed. Trib.); *Abbott* v. *Republic of South Africa*, ILR 113, 411 (Spain Const. Ct.); *Leasing West* v. *People's Democratic Republic of Algeria*, ILR 116, 526 (Austria, S.C.). See also *Kingdom of Spain* v. *Company XS.A.*, ILR 82, 38 (Swiss Fed. Trib.).

[120] See *Yrbk. ILC* (1986), ii (Pt. 2), 18 (draft article 22); Draft Articles, Article 18(2), *Yrbk. ILC* (1991), 56.

12. THE UNITED NATIONS CONVENTION ON JURISDICTIONAL IMMUNITIES OF STATES AND THEIR PROPERTY[121]

This instrument constitutes a significant codification of the principles governing jurisdictional immunity. The Convention originates in the set of draft articles adopted by the International Law Commission in 1991.[122] The final text was prepared by an Ad Hoc Committee established by the General Assembly, the final report being adopted on 5 March 2004.[123]

The Convention was opened for signature on 17 January 2005 and is subject to ratification. Apart from the rate of adoption by states, it is clear that the English courts will regard the Convention as evidence of the state of international opinion on the subject.[124] The provisions of the Convention reflect the pre-existing consensus of opinion on the subject and it follows that the Convention leaves in place the central problem, which is not that of 'restrictive immunity', but the issue of the boundary between immunity and the assertion of jurisdiction. In any event, according to the pertinent General Assembly resolution, the Convention does not cover criminal proceedings.

The Convention proceeds in the normal mode by propounding the principle of immunity 'subject to the provisions of the present Convention' (Article 5). The restrictions on immunity appear in Articles 10 to 17. The provisions include the following:

Article 10

Commercial transactions

1. If a State engages in a commercial transaction with a foreign national or juridical person and, by virtue of the applicable rules of private international law, differences relating to the commercial transaction fall within the jurisdiction of a court of another State, the State cannot invoke immunity from that jurisdiction in a proceeding arising out of that commercial transaction.

2. Paragraph 1 does not apply:
   (a) in the case of a commercial transaction between States; or
   (b) if the parties to the commercial transaction have expressly agreed otherwise.

3. Where a State enterprise or other entity established by a State which has an independent legal personality and is capable of:
   (a) suing or being sued; and

---

[121] 44 ILM (2005), 801. See Denza, *ICLQ*, 55 (2006), 395–8; Fox, ibid., 399–406.

[122] *Yrbk ILC* (1991, II), 8.

[123] U.N. Doc. A/59/22.

[124] See *AIG Capital Partners, Inc. v. Republic of Kazakhstan*, [2006] 1 W.L.R. 1420; I.L.R. 129, 589; and *Jones v. Saudi Arabia*, [2007] 1 AC 270, 278 (Lord Bingham) and see at page 293 (Lord Hoffmann); ILR 129, 629.

(b) acquiring, owning or possessing and disposing of property, including property which that State has authorised it to operate or manage,

is involved in a proceeding which relates to a commercial transaction in which that entity is engaged, the immunity from jurisdiction enjoyed by that State shall not be affected.

Article 11

Contracts of employment

1. Unless otherwise agreed between the States concerned, a State cannot invoke immunity from jurisdiction before a court of another State which is otherwise competent in a proceeding which relates to a contract of employment between the State and an individual for work performed or to be performed, in whole or in part, in the territory of that other State.

2. Paragraph 1 does not apply if:
   (a) the employee has been recruited to perform particular functions in the exercise of governmental authority;
   (b) the employee is:
       (i)   a diplomatic agent, as defined in the Vienna Convention on Diplomatic Relations of 1961;
       (ii) a consular officer, as defined in the Vienna Convention on Consular Relations of 1963;
       (iii) a member of the diplomatic staff of a permanent mission to an international organisation or of a special mission, or is recruited to represent a State at an international conference; or
       (iv) any other person enjoying diplomatic immunity;
   (c) the subject-matter of the proceeding is the recruitment, renewal of employment or reinstatement of an individual;
   (d) the subject-matter of the proceeding is the dismissal or termination of employment of an individual and, as determined by the head of State, the head of Government or the Minister for Foreign Affairs of the employer State, such a proceeding would interfere with the security interests of that State;
   (e) the employee is a national of the employer State at the time when the proceeding is instituted, unless this person has the permanent residence in the State of the forum; or
   (f) the employer State and the employee have otherwise agreed in writing, subject to any considerations of public policy conferring on the courts of the State of the forum exclusive jurisdiction by reason of the subject-matter of the proceeding.

Article 12

Personal injuries and damage to property

Unless otherwise agreed between the States concerned, a State cannot invoke immunity from jurisdiction before a court of another State which is otherwise competent in a proceeding which relates to pecuniary compensation for death or injury to the person, or damage to or loss of tangible property, caused by an act or omission which is alleged to be attributable to the State, if the act or omission occurred in whole or in part in the territory of that other State and if the author of the act or omission was present in that territory at the time of the act or omission.

Article 13

Ownership, possession and use of property

Unless otherwise agreed between the States concerned, a State cannot invoke immunity from jurisdiction before a court of another State which is otherwise competent in a proceeding which relates to the determination of:

(a) any right or interest of the State in, or its possession or use of, or any obligation of the State arising out of its interest in, or its possession of, immovable property situated in the State of the forum;

(b) any right or interest of the State in movable or immovable property arising by way of succession, gift or *bona vacantia*; or

(c) any right or interest of the State in the administration of property, such as trust property, the estate of a bankrupt or the property of a company in the event of its winding up.

The United Nations Convention affirms the immunity of the property of States from attachment and seizure in execution (Articles 18 to 21).

Article 19 provides (in part) as follows:

No post-judgment measures of constraint, such as attachment, arrest or execution, against property of a State may be taken in connection with a proceeding before a court of another State unless and except to the extent that:

(c) it has been established that the property is specifically in use or intended for use by the State for other than government non-commercial purposes and is in the territory of the State of the forum, provided that post-judgment measures of constraint may only be taken against property that has a connection with the entity against which the proceeding was directed.

And in this context the provisions of Article 21, on 'specific categories of property', are very helpful:

1. The following categories, in particular, of property of a State shall not be considered as property specifically in use or intended for use by the State for other than government non-commercial purposes under Article 19, subparagraphs (c):

   (a) property, including any bank account, which is used or intended for use in the performance of the functions of the diplomatic mission of the State or its consular posts, special missions, missions to international organisations or delegations to organs of international organisation or to international conferences;

(b) property of a military character or used or intended for use in the performance of military functions;

(c) property of the central bank or other monetary authority of the State;

(d) property forming part of the cultural heritage of the State or part of its archives and not placed or intended to be placed on sale;

(e) property forming part of an exhibition of objects of scientific, cultural or historical interest and not placed or intended to be placed on sale.

13. STATE IMMUNITY AND HUMAN RIGHTS

There is a persistent tension in the case law between the profile of state immunity and the principles of human rights. In this context the European Court of Human Rights has determined that the principles of state immunity under international law are compatible with the right of access to court by virtue of Article 6(1) of the European Convention on Human Rights. The Court has adopted the position that the grant of state immunity in civil proceedings pursued the legitimate aim of complying with international law in order to promote comity and good relations between the states.[125]

The English courts have adopted the same approach, also in the context of civil claims. Thus, in *Jones* v. *Saudi Arabia* the House of Lords, in a case involving claims of torture by officials of the Kingdom of Saudi Arabia, relied upon various sources, including the *Al-Adsani* decision by the Grand Chamber of the European Court. With respect to the United Nations Convention, Lord Bingham observed:[126]

26. Thirdly, the UN Immunity Convention of 2004 provides no exception from immunity where civil claims are made based on acts of torture. The Working Group in its 1999 Report makes plain that such an exception was considered, but no such exception was agreed. Despite its embryonic status, this Convention is the most authoritative statement available on the current international understanding of the limits of state immunity in civil cases, and the absence of a torture or jus cogens exception is wholly inimical to the claimants' contention.

The House of Lords expressly distinguished the decision in the *Pinochet (No.3)* case. Again, in the words of Lord Bingham:[127]

I would not question the correctness of the decision reached by the majority in *Pinochet (No 3)*. But the case was categorically different from the present, since it concerned criminal proceedings falling squarely within the universal criminal jurisdiction mandated by the

---

[125] See the decisions of the Grand Chamber in; *Al-Adsani* v. *United Kingdom*, ILR 123, 24; *Fogarty* v. *United*, ibid 53 and *McElhinney* v. *Ireland*, ibid., 73. See Bianchi, *Europ. Journ.*, 10 (1999), 237–77; Dicey, Morris and Collins, *Conflict of Laws*, 14th ed. (2006), 1, 273–4; *Europ. Human Rights Law Review* (2006), 100ff.

[126] [2007] 1 AC 270 at p. 289, ILR 129, at p.727.

[127] [2007] 1 AC at p. 286, ILR 129, at pp. 723–4.

Torture Convention and did not fall within Part 1 of the 1978 Act. The essential ratio of the decision, as I understand it, was that international law could not without absurdity require criminal jurisdiction to be assumed and exercised where the Torture Convention conditions were satisfied and, at the same time, require immunity to be granted to those properly charged. The Torture Convention was the mainspring of the decision, and certain members of the House expressly accepted that the grant of immunity in civil proceedings was unaffected: see p. 264 (Lord Hutton), p. 278 (Lord Millett) and pp. 280, 281, 287 (Lord Phillips of Worth Matravers). It is, I think, difficult to accept that torture cannot be a governmental or official act, since under article 1 of the Torture Convention torture must, to qualify as such, be inflicted by or with the connivance of a public official or other person acting in an official capacity. The claimants' argument encounters the difficulty that it is founded on the Torture Convention; but to bring themselves within the Torture Convention they must show that the torture was (to paraphrase the definition) official; yet they argue that the conduct was not official in order to defeat the claim to immunity.

17
DIPLOMATIC AND CONSULAR RELATIONS

1. DIPLOMATIC RELATIONS:[1] INTRODUCTION

In its simplest sense diplomacy comprises any means by which states establish or maintain mutual relations, communicate with each other, or carry out political or legal transactions, in each case through their authorized agents. Diplomacy in this sense may exist between states in a state of war or armed conflict with each other, but the concept relates to communication, whether with friendly or hostile purpose, rather than the material forms of economic and military conflict.

Normally, diplomacy involves the exchange of permanent diplomatic missions, and similar permanent, or at least regular, representation is necessary for states to give substance to their membership of the United Nations and other major intergovernmental organizations.[2] Then there are the categories of special missions or *ad hoc* diplomacy, and the representation of states at *ad hoc* conferences.[3]

The rules of international law governing diplomatic relations were the product of long-established state practice reflected in the legislative provisions and judicial decisions of national law. The law has now been codified to a considerable extent in the Vienna Convention on Diplomatic Relations.[4] Parts of the Convention are based

---

[1] See Hardy, *Modern Diplomatic Law* (1968); Whiteman, vii. 1–504; Denza, *Diplomatic Law* (3rd edn., 2008); *Yrbk. ILC* (1956) ii. 129; ibid. (1957), i. 2; ibid. (1958), i. 84; (1958), ii. 16, 89; *British Digest*, vii, ch. 19; Kiss, *Répertoire français de droit international public* (1962), iii. 277–359; Havana Conv., 1928, Hudson, *Int. Legis.*, iv. 2385; Giuliano, 100 Hague *Recueil* (1960, II), 81–202; Lyons, 30 *BY* (1953), 116–51; 31 *BY* (1954), 299–370; 34 *BY* (1958), 368–74. See also Cahier, *Le Droit diplomatique contemporain* (1962); Sen, *A Diplomat's Handbook of International Law and Practice* (1965), 1–197; Young, 40 *BY* (1964), 141–82; *Répertoire suisse*, iii. 1431–547; *Digest of US Practice* (1973) (ann. vols., ch. 4 in each); Dufour, 11 *Canad. Yrbk.* (1973), 123–65, ibid. 12 (1974), 3–37; do Nascimento e Silva, *Diplomacy in International Law* (1972); 58 *BY* (1987), 549–68; *Digest of US Practice* (1979), 571–650, 1471–92; Rousseau, iv. 139–210; Brown, 37 *ICLQ* (1988), 53–88; Salmon and Sucharitkul, *Ann. français* (1987), 163–94; Oppenheim, ii. 1053–125; Gore-Booth, *Satow's Guide to Diplomatic Practice* (5th edn., 1979); Salmon, *Manuel de Droit diplomatique* (1994).

[2] *Infra*, p. 675.

[3] *Infra*, p. 357.

[4] In force 24 Apr. 1964. Text: 500 UNTS 95; Brownlie, *Documents*, p. 162; 10 *ICLQ* (1961), 600; 55 *AJ* (1961), 1062. See further the Optional Protocol concerning Acquisition of Nationality and the Optional Protocol concerning the Compulsory Settlement of disputes: 500 UNTS 223, 241; also in force 24 Apr. 1964.

on existing practice and other parts constitute a progressive development of the law. However, as ratifications mount up even the latter portions provide the best evidence of generally accepted rules.[5] The Convention presently has at least 180 parties. The importance of the principles of law embodied in the Vienna Convention was stressed by the International Court in the *Case Concerning United States Diplomatic and Consular Staff in Tehran* (Order of 15 December 1979[6] and Judgment of 24 May 1980).[7] In its Judgment on the Merits the Court observed that 'the obligations of the Iranian Government here in question are not merely contractual . . . but also obligations under general international law'.[8] In that case the Government of Iran was held responsible for failing to prevent and for subsequently approving the actions of militants in invading the United States mission in Tehran and holding the diplomatic and consular personnel as 'hostages'.

For English courts the Diplomatic Privileges Act of 1708 was declaratory of the common law. The Act of 1708 has been repealed and replaced by the Diplomatic Privileges Act of 1964[9] which sets out in a schedule those provisions of the Convention which are incorporated into the law of the United Kingdom. The same Act replaces section 1(1) of the Diplomatic Immunities (Commonwealth Countries and Republic of Ireland) Act of 1952, which provided for immunity from suit. The Vienna Convention does not affect rules of customary law governing 'questions not expressly regulated' by its provisions[10] and, of course, states are free to vary the position by treaty and tacit agreements based upon subsequent conduct.

2. GENERAL LEGAL ASPECTS OF DIPLOMATIC RELATIONS

(a) Incidence

Article 2 of the Vienna Convention provides that 'the establishment of diplomatic relations between States, and of permanent diplomatic missions, takes place by mutual consent'. There is no right of legation in general international law, though all independent states have the capacity to establish diplomatic relations. The mutual consent involved may be expressed quite informally.

---

[5] Various sources refer to the Conv. as representing generally accepted principles of international law: 7 *Canad. Yrbk.* (1969), 305–6; ibid. 8 (1970), 339–40; *Hellenic Lines Ltd.* v. *Moore*, 345 F. 2d 978; ILR 42, 239; *Digest of US Practice* (1974), 164; (1976), 189, 194, 198; 14 *Canad. Yrbk.* (1976), 326–7.

[6] ICJ Reports (1979), 19.

[7] Ibid. (1980), 30–43.

[8] Ibid. 31, para. 62. See also at p. 33, para. 69; and p. 41, para. 90.

[9] 1964, c. 81. See *Empson* v. *Smith* [1966] 1 QB 426; ILR 41, 407; *Shaw* v. *Shaw* [1979] 3 WLR 24; CA; Buckley, 41 *BY* (1965–6), 321–67.

[10] See the *Philippine Embassy Case*, ILR 65, 146 at 161–2, 186–7; the *Republic of 'A' Embassy Bank Account Case*, ILR 77, 489; and *Abbott* v. *Republic of South Africa*, ILR 113, 411.

(b) Relation to recognition

While recognition[11] is a condition for the establishment and maintenance of diplomatic relations, the latter are not necessary consequences of recognition. The non-establishment or withdrawal of diplomatic representation may be the result of purely practical considerations or a form of non-military sanction.[12]

(c) Rationale of privileges and immunities[13]

The essence of diplomatic relations is the exercise by the sending government of state functions on the territory of the receiving state by licence of the latter. Having agreed to the establishment of diplomatic relations, the receiving state must take steps to enable the sending state to benefit from the content of the licence. The process of giving 'full faith and credit' to the licence results in a body of 'privileges and immunities'. One explanation, now discredited, for this situation has been that the diplomatic agent and the mission premises were 'exterritorial', in other words for all purposes legally assimilated to the territorial jurisdiction of the sending state.[14] The consequences of this theory were never worked out and the existing rules of law simply do not rest on such a premiss. The existing legal position in truth rests on no particular theory or combination of theories, though in a very general way it is compatible with both the representative theory, which emphasizes the diplomat's role as agent of a sovereign state, and the functional theory, which rests on practical necessity.[15] The latter theory is fashionable but somewhat question-begging.

In the final analysis, the question must be related to the double aspect of diplomatic representation: the sovereign immunity (immunity *ratione materiae*) attaching to official acts of foreign states, and the wider and overlying, yet more conditional, elements of 'functional' privileges and immunities of the diplomatic staff and the premises.[16]

(d) Fulfilment of duties by the host state

The observance of legal duties by the host state requires the taking of a variety of steps, both legislative and administrative, in the municipal sphere. Appropriate care must be shown in providing police protection for personnel and premises[17] and the state

---

[11] Ch. 5.

[12] On several occasions the General Assembly has recommended severance of diplomatic reltions. For the powers of the Security Council see the UN Charter, Art. 41.

[13] Hardy, *Modern Diplomatic Law*, pp. 8–12; *Yrbk. ILC* (1956), ii. 157–61; Montell Ogdon, *Juridical Bases of Diplomatic Immunity* (1936); *British Digest*, vii. 693–99; Preuss, 10 *NYULQR* (1933), 170–87.

[14] See 8 *Canad. Yrbk.* (1970), 337; and cases cited below, s. 6.

[15] *Yrbk. ILC* (1958), ii. 94–5; *Tietz v. People's Republic of Bulgaria*, ILR 38, 369; *Yugoslav Military Mission* case, ILR 28, 162; *Smith v. Office National de l'Emploi*, ILR 69, 276; *Parking Privileges Case*, ILR 70, 396; *Private Servant Case*, ILR 71, 546; *Dorf Case*, ibid. 552. The preamble to the Vienna Conv. refers to both considerations.

[16] See further s. 7 below. Courts seeking to develop a restrictive doctrine of state immunity are tempted to emphasize the distinction between state immunity and the, in one sense, more extensive immunity of diplomatic agents: see *Foreign Press Attaché* case, ILR 38, 160 and *supra*, p. 329.

[17] See ss. 4(a) and 5 below.

may incur responsibility if the judiciary fails to maintain the requisite privileges and immunities.

(e) Functions of missions

Article 3 of the Vienna Convention provides:

1. The functions of a diplomatic mission consist *inter alia* in:

    (a) representing the sending State in the receiving State;

    (b) protecting in the receiving State the interests of the sending State and of its nationals, within the limits permitted by the international law;[18]

    (c) negotiating with the Government of the receiving State;

    (d) ascertaining by all lawful means[19] conditions and developments in the receiving State, and reporting thereon to the Government of the sending State;

    (e) promoting friendly relations between the sending State and the receiving State, and developing their economic, cultural and scientific relations.

2. Nothing in the present Convention shall be construed as preventing the performance of consular relations by a diplomatic mission.

3. STAFF, PREMISES, AND FACILITIES OF MISSIONS

(a) Classification of personnel

The Vienna Convention, in Article 1, divides the staff of the mission into the following categories:

1. The diplomatic staff, namely, members of the mission having diplomatic rank as counsellors, diplomatic secretaries, or attachés.

2. The administrative and technical staff, such as clerical assistants and archivists.

3. The service staff, who are the other employees of the mission itself, such as drivers and kitchen staff, referred to in the Convention as 'in the domestic service of the mission'.

Two other terms are of importance in the Convention. A 'diplomatic agent' is the head of the mission or a member of the diplomatic staff of the mission; and the 'head of the mission' is 'the person charged by the sending State with the duty of acting in that capacity'.

---

[18] See Art. 41 which provides, *inter alia*, that persons enjoying privileges and immunities have a duty not to interfere in the internal affairs of the receiving state.

[19] i.e. under local law.

(b) Heads of mission

(i) *Accreditation and* agrément. Article 4 of the Vienna Convention provides as follows:

1. The sending State must make certain that the *agrément*[20] of the receiving State has been given for the person it proposes to accredit as head of the mission to that State.

2. The receiving State is not obliged to give reasons to the sending State for a refusal of *agrément.*

In this and other respects the receiving state is given a power of refusal and control in keeping with its role as licensor of the mission. In case of the appointment of a chargé d'affaires *ad interim* as provisional head of the mission, owing to the vacancy of the post of head or his inability, no *agrément* is required.[21]

The actual taking up of functions is regulated by Article 13 of the Vienna Convention:

1. The head of the mission is considered as having taken up his functions in the receiving State either when he has presented his credentials or when he has notified his arrival and a true copy of his credentials has been presented to the Ministry for Foreign Affairs of the receiving State, or such other ministry as may be agreed, in accordance with the practice prevailing in the receiving State which shall be applied in a uniform manner.

2. The order of presentation of credentials or of a true copy thereof will be determined by the date and time of the arrival of the head of the mission.

(ii) *Classes and precedence.*[22] The principal provision is Article 14 of the Vienna Convention:

1. Heads of mission are divided into three classes, namely:

(a) that of ambassadors or nuncios[23] accredited to Heads of State, and other heads of mission of equivalent rank;

(b) that of envoys, ministers and internuncios, accredited to Heads of State;

(c) that of *chargé d'affaires* accredited to Ministers for Foreign Affairs.

2. Except as concerns precedence and etiquette, there shall be no differentiation between heads of mission by reason of their class.

Article 16, paragraph 1, provides:

Heads of mission shall take precedence in their respective classes in the order of the date and time of taking up their functions in accordance with Article 13.

---

[20] A term of art meaning consent.

[21] Art. 19(1).

[22] For the background see Hardy, *Modern Diplomatic Law*, pp. 21–4. The practice was regulated previously by the Congress of Vienna, 1815, and the Conference of Aix-la-Chapelle, 1818, which established four classes. See further *British Digest*, vii. 655–71.

[23] Representatives of the Holy See: on their precedence see Art. 16(3).

(c) Appointment of members other than the head of mission

Article 7 of the Vienna Convention provides as follows:

Subject to the provisions of Articles 5, 8, 9 and 11, the sending State may freely appoint the members of the staff of the mission. In the case of military, naval or air attachés, the receiving State may require their names to be submitted beforehand, for its approval.

In the International Law Commission there was considerable difference of opinion as to the extent to which the consent of the receiving state conditioned the appointment of members other than the head of mission. The text of Article 7 may seem sufficiently clear[24] but at the Vienna Conference several delegations adopted the position that the Article was to be interpreted in accordance with prevailing custom,[25] namely that the consent of the receiving state was required in all cases. It may be that, if Article 7 is not so interpreted by a majority of states, then the prevailing custom will have changed, and such a position can only be preserved by means of a reservation.[26] In a recent controversial English decision[27] it was held that Article 7 was qualified by Article 10 and that a failure to notify the receiving state destroyed the appointee's entitlement to immunity. In any case the receiving state has special powers of control in case of appointments to more than one state (Art. 5(1)), appointment of non-nationals (Art. 8), and excessive appointments (see *infra*).[28]

In recent years there has been some pressure for limitation on the size of missions. The consequence of this was the provision in Article 11 of the Vienna Convention:

1. In the absence of specific agreement as to the size of the mission, the receiving State may require that the size of a mission be kept within limits considered by it to be reasonable and normal, having regard to circumstances and conditions in the receiving State and to the needs of the particular mission.

The test is thus not an objective one but rests simply on the opinion of the receiving state.[29] However, a decision of the latter which was discriminatory or otherwise unrelated to the considerations of size as such would be in breach of the provision. Article 11, paragraph 2, provides that 'the receiving State may equally, within similar bounds and on a non-discriminatory basis, refuse to accept officials of a particular category'.

---

[24] See Rousseau, iv. 158–9; and Brown, 37 *ICLQ* (1988), 54–9.

[25] See Harvard Research Draft Conv., Art. 8. Comment: 26 *AJ* (1932), Suppl., p. 67.

[26] Nepal has made a reservation.

[27] *R. v. Lambeth Justices, ex. p. Yusufu* [1985] TLR 114, DC; 56 *BY* (1985), 328–31. See further ibid. 440–1.

[28] And see also on the *persona non grata* procedure, *infra*.

[29] Art. 11(1) has attracted reservations from certain states.

(d) Termination of functions of individual diplomatic staff[30]

The sending state may for its own reasons, practical or political, terminate the functions of individual staff members on notification of this to the receiving state.[31] The receiving state may act under Article 9[32] of the Vienna Convention:

1. The receiving State may at any time and without having to explain its decision, notify the sending State that the head of the mission or any member of the diplomatic staff of the mission is *persona non grata* or that any other member of the staff of the mission is not acceptable. In any such case, the sending State shall, as appropriate, either recall the person concerned or terminate his functions with the mission. A person may be declared *non grata* or not acceptable before arriving in the territory of the receiving State.

2. If the sending State refuses or fails within a reasonable period to carry out its obligations under paragraph 1 of this Article, the receiving State may refuse to recognize the person concerned as a member of the mission.

The term *persona non grata* is simply the formal equivalent of 'not acceptable' in the case of staff not having diplomatic rank.

(e) Premises and facilities

Article 25 of the Vienna Convention provides that the receiving state 'shall accord full facilities for the performance of the functions of the mission'. Other provisions refer to freedom of movement for members of the mission, subject to legal restrictions established for reasons of national security,[33] and 'free communication on the part of the mission for all official purposes'.[34] A particular problem is the acquisition of premises since in some states the legal system may exclude a market in land or place restrictions on acquisition of land by aliens or foreign states. The International Law Commission draft[35] had required the receiving state either to permit acquisition by the sending state or to 'ensure adequate accommodation in some other way'. The Vienna Convention contains less decisive provisions in Article 21,[36] as follows:

1. The receiving State shall either facilitate the acquisition on its territory, in accordance with its laws, by the sending State of premises necessary for its mission or assist the latter in obtaining accommodation in some other way.

2. It shall also, where necessary, assist missions in obtaining suitable accommodation for their members.

---

[30] Of course, diplomatic relations may be terminated by armed conflict, extinction of the sending or receiving state, and withdrawal of the mission at the will of either the sending or receiving state. See the Vienna Conv., Art. 44, 45(a). On the effect of death see Art. 39(3) and (4). See further Whiteman, vii. 83–108; Denza, *Diplomatic Law* (3rd edn., 2008), 449–50. See also *Gustavo JL and Another*, ILR 86, 517 (Spain, S.C.).

[31] Art. 43(a).

[32] See also Art. 43(b).

[33] Art. 26. See Denza, *Diplomatic Law* (3rd edn., 2008), 205–10.

[34] Art. 27(1). See Kerley, 56 AJ (1962), 110–18; and Denza, *Diplomatic Law* (3rd edn., 2008), 211–24.

[35] Art. 19. See further Hardy, *Modern Diplomatic Law*, pp. 33–4.

[36] Conditions governing the use of premises appear in Arts. 12 and 41(3).

4. INVIOLABILITY[37] OF MISSIONS

(a) Premises[38]

A necessary consequence of the establishment and functioning of a mission is the protection of the premises from external interference. The mission premises, including the surrounding land, are the headquarters of the mission and benefit from the immunity of the sending state itself. The Vienna Convention recapitulates the position in the customary law in Article 22 as follows:

1. The premises of the mission[39] shall be inviolable. The agents of the receiving State may not enter them, except with the consent of the head of mission.

2. The receiving State is under a special duty to take all appropriate steps to protect the premises of the mission against any intrusion or damage and to prevent any disturbance of the peace of the mission or impairment of its dignity.

3. The premises of the mission, their furnishings and other property thereon and the means of transport of the mission shall be immune from search, requisition, attachment or execution.

The provisions of paragraph 1 contain no proviso relating either to cases of emergency, for example, the situation in which the premises present a pressing danger to the surrounding district by reason of fire breaking out or use as a firing point, or to countermeasures in case of a use of the premises by the staff themselves for unlawful purposes. It is a nice question whether on general principles,[40] if remedial steps were taken by the host state, a defence of necessity or *force majeure* could be sustained.[41] Evidence of the practical complications and threats to the peace caused by the location of foreign embassies, the abandonment of embassy premises, and the use of embassies for illegal

---

[37] Parry, in *British Digest*, vii. 700, observes that the term, which appears often in the Vienna Conv. is 'not particularly precise', and remarks: 'But it no doubt implies immunity from all interference, whether under colour of law or right or otherwise, and connotes a special duty of protection, whether from such interferences or from mere insult, on the part of the receiving State'. See also Giuliano, 100 Hague *Recueil* (1960, II), 111ff., 181–2; Whiteman, vii. 353–5, 373–4; Harvard Research, 26 *AJ* (1932), Suppl., pp. 52, 90–7; Guggenheim, i. 502–4; *Yrbk. ILC* (1956), ii. 161, 170; 8 *Canad. Yrbk.* (1970), 355–6; *Répertoire suisse* iii. 1504–28; Mann, *Further Studies in I.L.* (1990), 326–38; Oppenheim, ii. 1072–89; Denza (2nd edn., 1998), 112–48.

[38] See *British Digest*, vii. 887–901; Giuliano, 100 Hague *Recueil* (1960, II), 181–93; Whiteman, vii. 353–403; Dehaussy, 83 *JDI* (1956), 596; *Digest of US Practice* (1976), 205; Rousseau, iv. 179–83; *Embassy Eviction Case*, ILR 65, 248.

[39] Art. 1(i) defines 'the premises of the mission' as 'the buildings…and the land ancillary thereto…used for the purposes of the mission'; thus premises not so 'used' are outside the terms of Art. 22: see *Westminster City Council* v. *Government of the Islamic Republic of Iran* [1986] 1 WLR 979; 57 *BY* (1986), 423–6.

[40] *Infra*, p. 465.

[41] See the case of Sun Yat Sen, detained in the Chinese Legation in London in 1896; McNair, *Opinions*, i. 85; and the shooting episode at the Libyan embassy in London in Apr. 1984; 55 *BY* (1984), 459–94, and, in particular, at 582–4, on self-defence. See also Giuliano, 100 Hague *Recueil* (1960, II), 192–3; Kerley, 56 *AJ* (1962), 102–3; Guggenheim, i. 504; *Fatemi et al.* v. *United States*, 192 A. 2d 525 (1963); ILR 34, 148; *The Queen* v. *Turnbull, ex p. Petroff* (1971), 17 FLR 438; ILR 52, 303.

activities prompted the adoption in the United Kingdom legislation of various powers of control (in the Diplomatic and Consular Premises Act 1987).[42] It follows from
Article 22 that writs may not be served, even by post, within the premises of a mission
but only through the local Ministry of Foreign Affairs.[43] Paragraph 2 of the Article
creates a special standard of care apart from the normal obligation to show due diligence in protecting aliens present within the state. The International Court found that
breaches of Article 22 of the Convention had occurred in the *Case Concerning Armed
Activities on the Territory of the Congo*.[44]

Embassy bank accounts are protected by Article 24 of the Vienna Convention, as
archives or documents of the mission, which were 'inviolable at any time and wherever
they may be'.[45]

(b) Diplomatic asylum[46]

The Vienna Convention contains no provision on diplomatic asylum, although in
Article 41 the reference to 'special agreements' makes room for bilateral recognition
of the right to give asylum to political refugees within the mission. The reason for the
omission is substantially that it was deliberately excluded from the agenda during the
preparatory work by the International Law Commission. It is very doubtful if a right
of asylum for either political or other offenders is recognized by general international
law.[47] There is a qualified right under the Havana Convention on Asylum of 1928[48] and
it may be that a Latin-American regional custom exists.[49]

(c) Archives, documents, and official correspondence[50]

The Vienna Convention establishes the inviolability of the archives and documents of the mission 'at any time and wherever they may be'[51] and also of the official

---

[42] See 58 *BY* (1987), 540–2.

[43] See *Hellenic Lines, Ltd.* v. *Moore*, 345 F. 2d 978; ILR 41, 239.

[44] Judgment of 19 December 2005, paras. 334–44 (in relation to Uganda's second counter-claim). See also
the *Kenyan Diplomatic Residence Case*, ILR 128, 632, German Fed. Supr. Ct.

[45] See *Iraq* v. *Vinci Constructions*, ILR 127, 101, Court of Appeal of Brussels.

[46] See Morgenstern, 25 *BY* (1948), 236–61; Hackworth, ii. 621–32; Whiteman, vi. 428–95; *British Digest*,
vii. 905–23; Ronning, *Diplomatic Asylum* (1965); Sørensen, pp. 409–12; 13 *Canad. Yrbk.* (1975), 338–9; ibid.
14 (1976), 335–6; *Digest of US Practice* (1974), 115–19; (1975), 158–9; ibid. (1979), 427; Rousseau, iv. 186–8.

[47] Whiteman, vi. 440, 458; McNair, *Opinions*, ii. 67, 76; Guggenheim, i. 505; Harvard Research Draft, 26
AJ (1932), Suppl., Art. 6 and Comment, pp. 62–6; Sørensen, p. 409; *obiter dicta* of the International Court,
Asylum case, ICJ Reports (1950), 266 at 282–6. But see Morgenstern, 25 *BY* (1948), 236–61, and id., 67 *LQR*
(1951), 362 at 381, for a different view.

[48] Hudson, *Int. Legis.*, iv. 2412; Art. 2(1). See also the Montevideo Conv. on Political Asylum, 1933;
Hudson, *Int. Legis.*, vi. 607.

[49] See the *Asylum* case, ICJ Reports (1950), 266; ibid. 395; ibid. (1951), 71. See now the Inter-American
Conv. on Diplomatic Asylum, 1954, Whiteman, vi. 436, for a new Latin American regime. See the decision of
the Human Rights Committee; *Almeida de Quinteros and Quinteros Almeida* v. *Uruguay*, ILR 79, 168.

[50] See Hardy, *Modern Diplomatic Law*, p. 49; Cohen, 25 *BY* (1948), 404; Whiteman, vii. 389–92. Cf. *In re
Estate of King Faisal II*, ILR 31, 395. See also *Fayed* v. *Al-Tajir* [1987] 3 WLR 102, CA; 58 *BY* (1986), 438–47;
ILR 86, 131.

[51] Art. 24.

correspondence.[52] It is also provided simply that 'the diplomatic bag shall not be opened or detained'.[53] The evidence of abuse of the diplomatic bag in the form of commerce in drugs or the transport of the equipment for terrorist attacks has led to a decision by the United Kingdom Government to resort to the scanning of bags on specific occasions where there are strong grounds of suspicion and a member of the relevant mission is invited to be present.[54] In 1989 the International Law Commission adopted a set of more precise rules concerning the diplomatic bags and diplomatic couriers.[55]

(d) Other property

See the terms of the Vienna Convention, Article 22, paragraph 3, set out above.

5. INVIOLABILITY[56] OF DIPLOMATIC AGENTS

Article 29 of the Vienna Convention provides: 'The person of a diplomatic agent shall be inviolable. He shall not be liable to any form of arrest or detention. The receiving state shall treat him with due respect and shall take all appropriate steps to prevent any attack on his person, freedom or dignity'. This inviolability is distinct from the immunity from criminal jurisdiction (see *infra*). As in the case of the inviolability of the mission premises, there is no express reservation for action in cases of emergency, for example, a drunken diplomat with a loaded gun in a public place.[57]

Article 30 of the Vienna Convention provides as follows:

1. The private residence of a diplomatic agent shall enjoy the same inviolability and protection as the premises of the mission.

2. His papers, correspondence, and, except as provided in paragraph 3 of Article 31,[58] his property,[59] shall likewise enjoy inviolability.

The principle in paragraph 1 applies even to the temporary residence of an agent. However, there is no jurisdictional immunity in case of a real action concerning immovable property and, whilst no measures of execution may be taken against his property, courts may be unwilling to support measures of self-help undertaken by the diplomatic agent to recover premises from a person in possession under a claim

---

[52] Art. 27(2). See Denza, *Diplomatic Law* (3rd edn., 2008), 189–99, 225–6. On the issue of waiver see (by way of analogy) *Shearson Lehman Bros.* v. *Maclaine Watson & Co. Ltd. (No. 2)* [1988] 1 WLR 16, H.L.

[53] Art. 27(3); and see also Art. 27(4). See Denza, op. cit., 227–48.

[54] See 56 *BY* (1985), 446–9, 459–62; 58 *BY* (1987), 548–9, 566, 570–1.

[55] *Yrbk. ILC* (1989), ii. (Pt. 2), 8–49.

[56] On this term see *supra*, n. 37.

[57] See *British Digest*, vii. 785; Giuliano, 100 Hague *Recueil* (1960, II), 120–2; Denza, *Diplomatic Law*, op. cit., 162–5; *Fatemi et al.* v. *United States*, 192 A. 2d 525 (1963); ILR 34, 148.

[58] See *infra*, p. 360.

[59] This includes goods in the agent's private residence, and also other property such as his motor car, his bank account and goods which are intended for his personal use or essential to his livelihood: *Yrbk. ILC* (1958), ii. 98.

of right made in good faith.[60] The International Court found that breaches of Article 29 of the Convention had occurred in the *Case Concerning Armed Activities on the Territory of the Congo*.[61]

6. PERSONAL IMMUNITIES FROM LOCAL JURISDICTION[62]

(a) General

Diplomatic agents enjoy an immunity from the jurisdiction of the local courts and not an exemption from the substantive law.[63] The immunity can be waived[64] and the local law will then apply. Moreover, the Vienna Convention, Article 41, paragraph 1, stipulates that 'it is the duty of all persons enjoying such privileges and immunities to respect the laws and regulations of the receiving State'.[65]

In each jurisdiction a standard procedure will exist by which the qualification for immunity is established in such a way as to be conclusive for the local court.[66] In the United Kingdom, the Diplomatic Privileges Act 1964, provides as follows in section 4:

If in any proceedings any question arises whether or not any person is entitled to any privilege or immunity under this Act a certificate issued by or under the authority of the Secretary of State stating any fact relating to that question shall be conclusive evidence of that fact.

A court may act on information received from the executive by the parties.[67]

(b) Immunity from criminal jurisdiction[68]

Article 31, paragraph 1, of the Vienna Convention provides in simple terms and without qualification that 'a diplomatic agent shall enjoy immunity from the criminal jurisdiction of the receiving State'. This has long been the position in the customary law. A diplomatic agent guilty of serious or persistent breaches may be declared *persona non grata*.

---

[60] *Agbor* v. *Metropolitan Police Commissioner* [1969] 2 All ER 707, CA; ILR 52, 382.

[61] Judgment of 19 December 2005, paras. 334–44 (in relation to Uganda's second counter-claim).

[62] The jurisdiction of the sending state applies in principle: see Hardy, *Modern Diplomatic Law*, p. 55; Vienna Conv., Art. 31(4).

[63] *Dickinson* v. *Del Solar* [1930] 1 KB 376; *Empson* v. *Smith* [1966] 1 QB 426, CA; *Fatemi* v. *U.S.*, 192 A. 2d 525 (1963); ILR 34, 148. Cf. *Regele* v. *Federal Ministry*, ILR 26 (1958, II), 544.

[64] See *infra*, p. 360.

[65] See 52 BY (1981), 431–4.

[66] For the position in the United States see *Trost* v. *Tompkins*, 44 A. 2d 226 (1945); *Carrera* v. *Carrera*, 174 F. 2d 496 (1949); Cardozo, 48 *Cornell LQ* (1963), 461; Whiteman, vii. 108–26; Lyons, 24 BY (1947), 116–47.

[67] See generally, Lyons, 23 BY (1946), 240–81; 26 BY (1949), 433–7; 33 BY (1957), 302–10; *British Digest*, vii. 186–216.

[68] See generally Hackworth, iv. 515–33; *British Digest*, vii. 756–97; Giuliano, 100 Hague *Recueil* (1960, II), 91–2; Rousseau, iv. 200–2.

(c) Immunity from civil and administrative jurisdiction[69]

Article 31, paragraph 1, also confers immunity on the diplomatic agent from the local civil and administrative jurisdiction, except in the case of:

(a) a real action relating to private immovable property situated in the territory of the receiving State, unless he holds it on behalf of the sending State for the purposes of the mission;[70]

(b) an action relating to succession in which the diplomatic agent is involved as executor, administrator, heir or legatee as a private person and not on behalf of the sending State;

(c) an action relating to any professional or commercial activity exercised by the diplomatic agent[71] in the receiving State outside his official functions.

The jurisdictions referred to 'comprise any special courts in the categories concerned, e.g. commercial courts, courts set up to apply social legislation, and all administrative authorities exercising judicial functions'.[72]

The exceptions to this form of immunity represent a modern development in the law and reflect the principle that the personal immunities of diplomatic agents should not be conferred without qualification.

The exception relating to immovable property applies to the situation in which the property is the residence of the diplomatic agent. However, in that case such measures of execution as affect the inviolability of his person or of his residence are ruled out, as they are in respect of all three exceptions.[73]

(d) Waiver

This subject is dealt with in Article 32 of the Vienna Convention. It has always been accepted that the immunity from jurisdiction may be waived by the sending state.[74] Previous practice had been to some extent tolerant of implied waiver based on conduct but Article 32, paragraph 2, states that 'waiver must always be express'.[75] It further provides:

---

[69] See generally Hardy, *Modern Diplomatic Law*, 58–63; Hackworth, iv. 533–51; Giuliano, 100 Hague *Recueil* (1960, II), 92–104; Rousseau, iv. 197–200, 206–9. On proceedings begun before immunity applied see *Ghosh* v. *D'Rozario* [1963] 1 QB 106; ILR 33, 361.

[70] See *Intpro Properties (U.K.) Ltd.* v. *Sauvel* [1983] QB 1019, CA; ILR 64, 384.

[71] Art. 42 provides that 'a diplomatic agent shall not in the receiving state practise for personal profit any professional or commercial activity'. The exception in Art. 31(1) applies (*a*) to cases in which the receiving state allows exceptions to the operation of Art. 42; (*b*) to activities of members of the staff not of diplomatic rank.

[72] *Yrbk. ILC* (1958), ii. 98. Cf. *British Digest*, vii. 798.

[73] Art. 31(3).

[74] The Vienna Conference adopted a Resol. II, on 'Consideration of Civil Claims', which recommended that the sending state should waive immunity 'in respect of civil claims of persons in the receiving State when this can be done without impeding the performance of the functions of the mission'. It recommended, further, 'that in the absence of waiver the sending state should use its best endeavours to bring about a just settlement of claims'.

[75] For the position in English law see *Engelke* v. *Musmann* [1928] AC 433; *Regina* v. *Madan* [1961] 2 QB 1; 33 ILR 368, CCA; Diplomatic Privileges Act 1964, s. 2(3); *British Digest*, vii. 867–75. See also

3. The initiation of proceedings...shall preclude [the person enjoying immunity] from invoking immunity from jurisdiction in respect of any counter-claim directly connected with the principal claim.[76]

The fourth paragraph provides that waiver of immunity from civil or administrative jurisdiction shall not be held to imply waiver in respect of the execution of the judgment, for which a separate waiver shall be necessary.

7. IMMUNITY FROM JURISDICTION FOR OFFICIAL ACTS *RATIONE MATERIAE*[77]

In the case of official acts the immunity is permanent, since it is that of the sending state.[78] In respect of private acts the immunity is contingent and supplementary and it ceases when the individual concerned leaves his post. Article 39, paragraph 2, of the Vienna Convention refers to the termination of diplomatic functions and the concomitant immunities, and provides: 'However, with respect to acts performed by such a person in the exercise of his functions as a member of the mission, immunity shall continue to subsist'.[79] The definition of official acts is by no means self-evident. The conception presumably extends to matters which are essentially 'in the course of' official duties and this might include a road accident involving a car on official business.[80]

8. IMMUNITIES FROM APPLICATION OF CERTAIN LOCAL LAWS

Certain immunities from the application of the local law are obviously ancillary to the main body of privileges and immunities. Perhaps the most decisive of the ancillary immunities is that from measures of execution.[81] There is exemption from all

---

Armon v. Katz, ILR 60, 374 (Ghana CA); Nzie v. Vessah, ILR 74, 519; Public Prosecutor v. Orhan Olmez, ILR 87, 212 (Malaysia S.C.).

[76] See *High Commissioner for India* v. *Ghosh* [1960] 1 QB 134; 28 ILR 150, CA.

[77] See Hardy, *Modern Diplomatic Law*, pp. 64–7; van Panhuys, 13 *ICLQ* (1964), 1193; Dinstein, 15 *ICLQ* (1966), 76; Harvard Research, 26 *AJ* (1932), Suppl., pp. 97–9, 104–6, 136–7; Niboyet, 39 *Revue Critique de d.i. privé* (1950), 139; Giuliano, 100 Hague *Recueil* (1960, II), 166–80; *Yrbk. ILC* (1956), ii. 145, para. 101; Parry, *Cambridge Essays* (1965), 122 at pp. 127–32; *Foreign Press Attaché* case, ILR 38, 160, Austrian SC.

[78] See *Zoernsch* v. *Waldock* [1964] 1 WLR 675 at 684, 688–9, 691–2, CA, *per* Willmer, Danckwerts, and Diplock, LJJ.

[79] See also Art. 37(2) and (3), set out *infra*, p. 354; and Art. 38(1).

[80] See Kerley, 56 *AJ* (1962), 120–1. Cf. *Re Cummings*, ILR 26 (1958, II), 549; *Caisse Industrielle d'Assurance Mutuelle* v. *Consul Général de la République Argentine*, ILR 45, 381.

[81] See *supra*, Arts. 31(3) and 32(4).

dues and taxes with a number of exceptions, one of which is indirect taxes (normally incorporated in the price of goods or services).[82] Further immunities concern customs duties,[83] personal services, public service (for example, jury service), military obligations,[84] social security provisions,[85] and the giving of evidence as a witness.[86] The exemption from customs duties of articles for the personal use of the diplomatic agent or members of his family belonging to the household is a rendering of a long current practice into a rule of law. The exemption from dues and taxes probably existed in the previous customary law, though the practice was not very consistent.

9. SOME OTHER ASPECTS OF IMMUNITY

(a) Beneficiaries of immunities[87]

Diplomatic agents, who are not nationals of or permanently resident in, the receiving state, are beneficiaries of the privileges and immunities set out in the Vienna Convention, Articles 29 to 36.[88] The extent to which administrative and technical staff (as non-diplomatic members of the staff) should have these privileges and immunities was a matter on which state practice had not been uniform[89] and on which there was considerable debate at the Vienna Conference. The position for this group and also for members of service staff[90] was regulated as follows in Article 37:[91]

2. Members of the administrative and technical staff of the mission, together with members of their families forming part of their respective households, shall, if they are not nationals of or permanently resident in the receiving State, enjoy the privileges and immunities specified in Articles 29 to 35, except that the immunity from civil and administrative jurisdiction of the receiving State specified in paragraph 1 of Article 31 shall not extend to acts performed outside the course of their duties. They shall also enjoy the privileges specified in Article 36, paragraph 1,[92] in respect of articles imported at the time of first installation.

3. Members of the service staff of the mission who are not nationals of or permanently resident in the receiving State shall enjoy immunity in respect of acts performed in the course

---

[82] Vienna Conv., Arts. 23 and 34. Cf. Art. 37 concerning the family of the agent and administrative, technical, and service staff.

[83] Art. 36. Cf. Art. 37.

[84] Art. 35. Cf. Art. 37.

[85] Art. 33. This deals with a matter previously obscure. Cf. Art. 37.

[86] Art. 31(2). Cf. Giuliano, 100 Hague *Recueil* (1960, II), 118–19. Cf. also Art. 37.

[87] See Hardy, *Modern Diplomatic Law*, pp. 74–80; Giuliano, 100 Hague *Recueil* (1960, II), 141–65; Whiteman, vii. 260–70; Wilson, 14 *ICLQ* (1965), 1265–95; Denza, *Diplomatic Law* (3rd edn., 2008), 390–425.

[88] Art. 37(1). There had been some inconsistent practice in relation to diplomatic agents apart from heads of mission; see Gutteridge, 24 *BY* (1947), 148–59; cf. Giuliano, 100 Hague *Recueil* (1960, II), 142.

[89] See Gutteridge, 24 *BY* (1947), 148–59; Giuliano, 100 Hague *Recueil* (1960, II), 153–8.

[90] On the previous position: Giuliano, 100 Hague *Recueil* (1960, II), 159–62.

[91] This article has provoked reservations from some states.

[92] Concerning customs duties.

of their duties, exemption from dues and taxes on the emoluments they receive by reason of their employment and the exemption[93] contained in Article 33.

In the case of diplomatic agents and the administrative and technical staff of the mission the respective immunities extend to 'members of the family' 'forming part of' their households. In view of variations in family law and social custom a precise definition was inappropriate.[94]

(b) Duration of privileges and immunities[95]

The termination of the functions of individual members of the diplomatic staff has been considered already.[96] Termination of the mission may occur, for example, through its recall, the outbreak of war between the states concerned, or the extinction of one of the states concerned. The duration of privileges is governed by Article 39 of the Vienna Convention, the principal provisions being these:

1. Every person entitled to privileges and immunities shall enjoy them from the moment he enters the territory of the receiving State on proceeding to take up his post or, if already in its territory, from the moment when his appointment is notified to the Ministry for Foreign Affairs or such other ministry as may be agreed.

2. When the functions of a person enjoying privileges and immunities have come to an end, such privileges and immunities shall normally cease at the moment when he leaves the country, or on expiry of a reasonable period in which to do so,[97] but shall subsist until that time, even in case of armed conflict. However, with respect to acts performed by such a person in the exercise of his functions as a member of the mission,[98] immunity shall continue to subsist.

The Supreme Restitution Court of Berlin has held that premises or sites formerly occupied by diplomatic missions but no longer used for diplomatic purposes had lost their immunity from the local jurisdiction.[99]

---

[93] Concerning social security provisions.

[94] See *In re C. (an infant)* [1959] Ch. 363; ILR 26 (1958, II), 539; *Dutch Diplomat Taxation Case*, ILR 87, 76; see generally O'Keefe, 25 *ICLQ* (1976), 329–50; 49 *BY* (1978), 368; 56 *BY* (1985), 441; Rousseau, iv. 196–7; Brown, 37 *ICLQ* (1988), 63–6; Oppenheim, i. 110–12.

[95] See generally Whiteman, vii. 436–45; Jones, 25 *BY* (1948), 262–79; Hardy, *Modern Diplomatic Law*, pp. 80–3; Lauterpacht, *International Law: Collected Papers*, iii. (1970), 433–57; Denza, *Diplomatic Law* (3rd edn., 2008), 426–50; Rousseau, iv. 202–3.

[96] *Supra*, p. 355.

[97] See *Magdalena Steam Navigation Co. v. Martin* (1859) 2 El. & El. 94; *Musurus Bey v. Gadban* [1894] 2 QB 352; *Re Suarez* [1918] 1 Ch. 176, CA; *Shaffer v. Singh*, 343 F. 2d 324 (1965); ILR 35, 219; *Propend Finance Pty. v. Sing*, ILR 111, 611.

[98] On immunity *ratione materiae*, see *supra*, s. 7.

[99] See *Tietz v. People's Republic of Bulgaria*, ILR 28, 369. The Court emphasized that the non-user was permanent. See further Romberg, 35 *BY* (1959), 235; and *Westminster City Council v. Government of the Islamic Republic of Iran* [1986] 1 WLR 979. Peter Gibson, J.

10. CONSULAR RELATIONS[100]

Consuls are in principle distinct in function and legal status from diplomatic agents. Though agents of the sending state for particular purposes, they are not accorded the type of immunity from the laws and enforcement jurisdiction of the receiving state enjoyed by diplomatic agents. Consular functions are very varied indeed and include the protection of the interests of the sending state and its nationals, the development of economic and cultural relations, the issuing of passports and visas, the administration of the property of nationals of the sending state, the registration of births, deaths, and marriages, and supervision of vessels and aircraft attributed to the sending state.

Since the eighteenth century the status of consuls has been based upon general usage rather than law, together with special treaty provisions. The customary law as it has evolved is as follows.[101] The consul must have the authority of the sending state (his commission) and the authorization of the receiving state (termed an exequatur). The receiving state must give consular officials and premises special protection, i.e. a higher standard of diligence than that appropriate to protection of aliens generally.[102] The consular premises are not inviolable from entry by agents of the receiving state.[103] The consular archives and documents are inviolable[104] and members of the consulate are immune from the jurisdiction of the judicial and administrative authorities of the receiving state in respect of acts performed in the exercise of consular functions.[105] This immunity in respect of official acts is generally regarded as an aspect of state immunity.[106] Articles intended for the use of the consulate are exempt from customs duties, and members of the consulate, other than the service staff, are exempt from all public services, including military obligations. The authorities reveal differences of opinion concerning the personal inviolability of consular officials and in principle they are liable to arrest or detention.[107] In addition they are amenable to criminal and civil jurisdiction in respect of non-official acts, to local taxation, and to customs

---

[100] *British Digest*, viii; Harvard Research, 26 *AJ* (1932), Suppl., pp. 189–449; Hackworth, iv. 655–949; Whiteman, vii. 505–870; Guggenheim, i. 512–15; *Yrbk. ILC* (1961), ii. 55, 89, 129; Zourek, 106 Hague *Recueil* (1962, II), 365–497; id., 90 *JDI* (1963), 4–67; Lee, *Consular Law and Practice* (2nd edn., 1991); *Répertoire suisse*, iii. 1552–93; *Digest of US Practice* (1979), 654–75; Rousseau, iv. 211–63; Oppenheim, ii. 1132–53.

[101] See *Yrbk. ILC* (1961), ii. 110ff. There are differing views on the ambit of the customary law: compare Zourek, 106 Hague *Recueil*, at p. 451; Beckett, 21 *BY* (1944), 34–50; Guggenheim; Lee, *Consular Law and Practice* (2nd edn., 1991); *British Digest*, viii. 146, 151, 158, 164.

[102] *Infra*, p. 525.

[103] See *British Digest*, viii. 125; O'Connell, ii. 920–1; Oppenheim, ii. 841–2; Beckett, 21 *BY* (1944), 34–50; *Yrbk. ILC* (1961), ii. 109. Cf. Whiteman, vii. 744.

[104] The authorities all agree on this.

[105] *Princess Zizianoff* v. *Kahn and Bigelow, Ann. Digest* (1927–8), no. 266; Oppenheim, ii. 841; *British Digest*, viii. 146; Beckett, 21 *BY* (1944), 34–50; Whiteman, vii. 770; *Yrbk. ILC* (1961), ii. 117, Art. 43, Commentary; Parry, *Cambridge Essays*, p. 122 at pp. 127–32, 154.

[106] *Supra*, p. 318. See *Hallberg* v. *Pombo Argaez*, ILR 44, 190.

[107] Compare *British Digest*, viii. 103–22, 214; Whiteman, vii. 739; *Yrbk. ILC* (1961), ii. 115, Art. 41, Commentary.

duties. In a general way it could be said that the jurisdiction of the local sovereign is presumed in the customary law.

The existence of fairly uniform *practices* (whatever the customary law might be), evidenced by a large number of bilateral treaties, encouraged the International Law Commission to produce draft articles on consular relations, and subsequently the Vienna Convention on Consular Relations was signed in 1963.[108] It is provided that the Convention 'shall not affect other international agreements in force as between parties to them'. The Convention has a strong element of development and reconstruction of the existing law and brings the status of career consuls, as opposed to honorary consuls, nearer to that of diplomatic agents. Career consuls are exempted from taxation and customs duties in the same way as diplomats. Consular premises are given a substantial degree of inviolability (Art. 31) and are exempted from taxation (Art. 32). Immunities and the duty of protection already recognized by customary law are maintained.[109] A significant extension of protection and immunity occurs as follows:

Article 41 (Personal inviolability of consular officers):

1. Consular officers shall not be liable to arrest or detention pending trial, except in the case of a grave crime and pursuant to a decision by the competent judicial authority.

2. Except in the case specified in paragraph 1 of this article, consular officers shall not be committed to prison or liable to any other form of restriction on their personal freedom save in execution of a judicial decision of final effect.

3. If criminal proceedings are instituted against a consular officer, he must appear before the competent authorities. Nevertheless, the proceedings shall be conducted with respect due to him by reason of his official position and, except in the case specified in paragraph 1 of this article, in a manner which will hamper the exercise of consular functions as little as possible. When, in the circumstances mentioned in paragraph 1 of this article, it has become necessary to detain a consular officer, the proceedings against him shall be instituted with the minimum delay.

Although the Vienna Convention has attracted no less than 165 ratifications it is unsafe to regard its provisions in general as conclusive evidence on the present state of general international law on the subject.[110] Nevertheless, states and municipal courts[111] may use its provisions as the best evidence of the present state of the law quite

---

[108] In force 19 Mar. 1967. Text: 596 UNTS 261; 57 *AJ* (1963), 993; 13 *ICLQ* (1964), 1230. For comment see Lee, *Vienna Convention on Consular Relations* (1966); do Nascimento e Silva, 13 *ICLQ* (1964), 1214–64; Torres Bernardez, *Ann. français* (1963), 78–118. Substantial parts of the Conv. are incorporated into the law of the United Kingdom: Consular Relations Act 1968, c. 18, s. 1. See *Regina (B and Others)* v. *Secretary of State* [2005] QB 643; ILR 131, 616.

[109] See esp. Art. 40 (Protection of consular officers); 33 (Inviolability of consular archives and documents); 43 (Immunity from jurisdiction in respect of acts performed in the exercise of consular functions); and 52 (Exemption from personal services and contributions). See also *L.* v. *The Crown*, ILR 68, 175; *United States* v. *Lo Gatto*, ILR 114, 555; *Canada* v. *Cargnello*, ibid., 559.

[110] On the *North Sea Continental Shelf Cases*, see *supra*, p. 9.

[111] Cf. *Republic of Argentina* v. *City of New York*, 25 NY 2d 252 (1969), NY Ct. of Appeals; ILR 53, 544; *Heaney* v. *Government of Spain*, ibid. 57, 153; Whiteman, vii. 825–8; *Digest of US Practice* (1974), 183; (1975), 249–50, 259–60. See also *Honorary Consul of X* v. *Austria*, ILR 86, 553 (Austria, S.C.).

apart from its effect for actual parties. In its Judgment in the *Case Concerning United States Diplomatic and Consular Staff in Tehran* the International Court emphasized that the obligations disregarded by Iran were part of general international law and not merely contractual obligations established by the Vienna Convention on Consular Relations.[112] Two regional multilateral conventions should also be noted, namely the Pan-American Convention of 1928[113] and the European Convention on Consular Functions of 1967.[114]

In a series of cases[115] involving foreign nationals sentenced to death in various component states of the United States, requests for provisional measures have been addressed to the International Court. The requests have been based upon allegations of breaches of the provisions of the Vienna Convention on Consular Relations and, in particular, the provision that arresting authorities have a duty to inform foreign nationals of their right to contact the appropriate consulate (Art. 36(1)(b)).

11. SPECIAL MISSIONS[116]

Beyond the sphere of permanent relations by means of diplomatic missions or consular posts, states make frequent use of *ad hoc* diplomacy or special missions. These vary considerably in functions: examples include a head of government attending a funeral abroad in his official capacity, a foreign minister visiting his opposite number in another state for negotiations, and the visit of a government trade delegation to conduct official business. These occasional missions have no *special* status in customary law but it should be remembered that, since they are agents of states and are received by the consent of the host state, they benefit from the ordinary principles based upon sovereign immunity and the express or implied conditions of the invitation or licence received by the sending state. The United Nations General Assembly has adopted and opened for signature the Convention on Special Missions, 1969.[117] This provides a fairly flexible code of conduct based on the Vienna Convention on Diplomatic Relations with appropriate divergences.

---

[112] ICJ Reports (1979), 31, para. 62. See also at p. 33, para. 69, and p. 41, para. 90.

[113] Hudson, *Int. Legis.*, iv. 2394.

[114] European Treaty Series, no. 61.

[115] The *Breard Case* (Paraguay v. U.S.), ILR 118, 1; *Le Grand Case* (Germany v. U.S.), ibid., 37; and *Avena and Others (United States of Mexico v. U.S.)*, Hearings of 22 January 2003.

[116] Whiteman, vii. 33–47; *Yrbk. ILC* (1964), ii. 67; (1965), ii. 109; (1966), ii. 125; (1967), ii. 1; Hardy, *Modern Diplomatic Law*, pp. 89–94; Bartos, 108 Hague *Recueil* (1963, I), 431–560; Waters, *The Ad Hoc Diplomat* (1963); Bernhardt (ed.) *Encyclopedia*, Vol.4 (2000), 574–7; Ryan, *Canad. Yrbk*, 16 (1978), 157–96. On the arrest of the French Property Commission in the UAR in 1961 see 12 *ICLQ* (1963), 1383; *Ann. français* (1962), 1064. See also *R. v. Governor of Pentonville Prison, ex p. Teja* [1971] 2 QB 274, DC; ILR 52, 368.

[117] Resol. 2530 (XXIV), 8 Dec. 1969, Annex: (a) Conv.; (b) Optional Protocol concerning the Compulsory Settlement of Disputes. See also Resol. 2531 (XXIV) on settlement of civil claims. See Donnarumma, 8 *Revue belge* (1972), 34–79.

12. THE PREVENTION AND PUNISHMENT OF CRIMES AGAINST INTERNATIONALLY PROTECTED PERSONS

As a consequence of the high incidence of political acts of violence directed against diplomats and other officials, the General Assembly of the United Nations adopted the Convention on the Prevention and Punishment of Crimes Against Internationally Protected Persons, including Diplomatic Agents, which was annexed to Resolution 3166 (XXVIII) of 14 December 1973.[118] The offences envisaged are primarily the 'murder, kidnapping or other attack upon the person or liberty of an internationally protected person', the latter category including heads of state, foreign ministers and the like. Contracting parties undertake to make these crimes punishable by 'appropriate penalties which shall take into account their grave nature', and either to extradite alleged offenders or to apply the domestic law.

---

[118] The Conv. came into force on 20 Feb. 1977. For the text see: 68 *AJ* (1974), 383; 13 *ILM* (1974), 41; see Rozakis, 23 *ICLQ* (1974), 32–72; and Wood, ibid. 791–817. See also the UK Internationally Protected Persons Act 1978 and *Duff* v. *R.* (1979) 28 ALR 663; ILR 73, 678. There is also an OAS Conv. adopted on 2 Feb. 1971; 10 *ILM* (1971), 255. The European Conv. on the Suppression of Terrorism, opened for signature on 27 Jan. 1977, is concerned to render extradition more effective: for the text see 14 *ILM* (1976), 1272.

18

RESERVATIONS FROM TERRITORIAL SOVEREIGNTY

1. TERRITORIAL PRIVILEGES BY CONCESSION

The previous section relates the cases in which there exists immunity from territorial jurisdiction, primarily, but by no means exclusively, an immunity from the jurisdiction of the local courts. There is no very neat way of separating these instances from the cases of 'privilege' now to be considered. Thus, in the case of the diplomatic agent, the legal regime is by no means confined to negative rules of jurisdictional immunity: after all, these rules are only one facet of a situation involving privileges to carry out various governmental commissions and in certain cases even to grant diplomatic asylum on the basis of treaty or regional custom.[1] Conversely, the stay of foreign armed forces in time of peace involves both privileges and immunities. However, in this latter case and in some others placed under the present heading the aspect of privilege involving extra-territorial exercise of sovereign capacities is particularly prominent. While the classification is to some extent empirical, it is believed that the special rights involved in the stationing of armed forces on foreign territory, and other instances of the exercise of governmental functions on the territory of another state, are relatively less normal and more prominently 'privileges' than the other cases of official intercourse including the sending and receiving of diplomatic agents. Technically these other cases are also privileges, but the cases now to be considered all display a number of idiosyncrasies and, in view of their character, may more readily lead to the application of a presumption in favour of the exclusive jurisdiction of the territorial sovereign[2] in case of doubt. However, the situations are rather disparate, and generalizations are unlikely to be very helpful. If it is not sufficiently obvious it should be pointed out that what follows is not exhaustive of all forms of privilege and licence granted by territorial sovereigns.[3] The group of cases depends on the existence of agreement or *ad hoc* consent on the part of the receiving state and not

---

[1] On extra-territorial asylum see *supra*, p. 357. On diplomatic agents see ch. 17.

[2] Cf. *supra*, p. 291.

[3] On the enforcement and recognition in England of foreign judgments and arbitration awards see Dicey, *Conflict of Laws* (14th edn., 2006), chs. 14, 15 and 16; UN Conv. on the Recognition and Enforcement of Foreign Arbitral Awards (in force, 7 June 1959), 7 *ILM* (1968), 1046; and the UK Arbitration Act 1975.

on the operation of law. However, once the *occasion* has arisen by concession, in the absence of variations by special agreement, the law regulates the nature and extent of the privilege.

(a) Refugee and exile governments[4]

Where there is no breach of legal duty[5] involved, a state may tolerate the establishment of a refugee or exile government of a foreign state on its territory. In this type of case a considerable quantum of sovereign powers may be exercised by the exile government over the nationals, armed forces, and both public and private vessels in the host state and on the high seas. During the Second World War the United Kingdom gave extensive privileges and immunities to exile governments and their representatives, and such governments were permitted to carry out legislative, administrative, and other functions in the United Kingdom. The basis for such competence can only be the invitation and consent of the territorial sovereign. Similar concessions may be made in favour of visiting sovereigns.

(b) International Control Commissions

The internal affairs of a state may give rise to issues of international concern, for example because the right of self-determination is denied, or there is foreign intervention in a civil war, or the state had recently been defeated by a group of lawful belligerents conducting a war of collective defence and sanction against a source of aggression.[6] In such a case, with or without the support of organs of the United Nations,[7] interested states may by agreement, or otherwise, bring about a political solution, the principles of which are to be applied under the supervision of an external agency. Thus, the Geneva Agreements of 1954[8] provided for an International Control Commission to supervise the application of a political settlement to the succession states of French Indo-China. The regime of supervision may involve a grant of privileges to agents of other states, and may constitute a serious derogation from sovereignty. The regime of compliance imposed on Iraq by virtue of Security Council Resolution 687 (1991)[9] includes the supervision of the destruction of chemical and biological weapons. Compliance in this and other respects is monitored by a Special Commission (UNSCOM).

---

[4] See Oppenheim, i. 146–7; Oppenheimer, 36 *AJ* (1942), 568–95; Stein, 46 *Michigan LR* (1948), 341–70; Whiteman, vi. 354–78; McNair, *The Legal Effects of War* (4th edn., 1966), 424–46; id., *Opinions*, i. 69–70, 72–4; Bernhardt, *Encyclopedia*, II (1995), 607–11; Talmon, *Recognition of Governments in International Law* (1998), 115–273; *In re Amand* [1941] 2 KB 239; *Lorentzen* v. *Lydden* [1942] 2 KB 202. On deposed, abdicated, refugee, and captured monarchs see McNair, *Opinions*, i. 104–10, 127.

[5] On recognition of governments see *supra*, p. 90.

[6] On the situation in Germany after 1945, see *supra*, pp. 78–9.

[7] For cases of UN administration, *supra*, p. 167.

[8] *Docs. on International Affairs* (1954), 138; Cmnd. 9239, Misc. no. 20 (1954); 23 *Rev. int. française du droit des gens* (1954), 172. See also the Protocol to the Declaration on the Neutrality of Laos, 23 July 1962, 456 UNTS, no. 6564, p. 301. And see 9 *ICLQ* (1960), 259.

[9] 30 ILM 847.

(c) Foreign public ships[10]

The controversy as to the jurisdictional immunity of government ships used in commerce has been treated as an aspect of the general question of state control of economic activity,[11] and for the present purpose that issue will be left on one side. In any case the extra-territorial exercise of sovereign powers is normally the business of naval vessels and auxiliaries. The main principles are for the most part well settled[12] and have had influence on the law relating to the status of foreign armed forces in general. Apart from lawful belligerency, foreign warships using a police power in the territory of a state are violating the latter's territorial sovereignty and create a legal responsibility.[13] However, foreign public vessels lawfully entering territorial sea or internal waters have extensive privileges and immunities. The law was stated by Hyde[14] as follows:

The ship cannot be lawfully subjected to a civil action arising, for example, from a claim for salvage, or to a criminal action arising from the violation of a local regulation. No occupant while remaining on board the vessel is subject to the local jurisdiction, notwithstanding his infraction of the local criminal code by an act committed on shore or taking effect there. . . . The vessel of war and its occupants owe, nevertheless, well-defined duties to the local sovereign. The former is obliged to respect, for example, local regulations pertaining to navigation and quarantine, and special obligations, when, in time of war, the vessel attached to a belligerent service enters a neutral port.

The foreign public vessel, in the classical case, a warship, attracts the character of sovereign immunity,[15] and the sources treat the subject as a facet of sovereign immunity. However, the armed public vessel, by its function and physical autonomy, has a special inviolability, and it was not absurd to regard such vessels as extra-territorial. However, this is not strictly the case. Thus in *Chung Chi Cheung* v. *The King*[16] the Privy Council held that a local court has jurisdiction if the immunity is waived and can punish a member of the crew for a breach of the local law, in this case a murder, on board a

---

[10] The position of warships and other government ships in innocent passage through the territorial sea is considered *supra*, pp. 188–9. On concurrence of criminal jurisdiction in the case of non-governmental ships: *supra*, pp. 318–21.

[11] *Supra*, pp. 327ff.

[12] See McNair, *Opinions*, i. 90ff.; Brierly, pp. 267–9; Oppenheim, ii. 1165–74; Gidel, ii. 253–315; Colombos, pp. 264–84; id., *Mélanges Gidel* (1961), 159–65; Baldoni, 65 Hague *Recueil* (1938, III), 189–302; UN Legis. Series, *Laws and Regulations on the Régime of the Territorial Sea* (1957), ch. 3; *Annuaire de l'Inst.* 34 (1928), 475ff.; Cheng, 11 *Curr. Leg. Problems* (1958), 225–57; Hackworth, ii. 408–65; Whiteman, ix. 74–83; Rousseau, iv. 288–9; Bernhardt, *Encyclopedia* IV, (2000), 1413–19.

[13] See McNair, *Opinions*, i. 74–83 and cf. the *Corfu Channel* case (Merits), ICJ Reports (1949), 33–5 (on a British mine-sweeping operation in Albanian waters); and *Japan* v. *Kulikov*, ILR 21 (1954), 105. See also Delupis, 78 *AJ* (1984), 53–73.

[14] ii. 826–7.

[15] See Marshall, CJ, in the *Schooner Exchange* v. *McFaddon* (1812), 7 Cranch 116; *supra*, pp. 325–6; *infra*, p. 368. The decision influenced courts elsewhere: see the *Constitution* (1879), 4 PD 39; the *Parlement Belge* (1880), 5 PD 197; *Chung Chi Cheung* v. *The King* [1939] AC 160; *Wright* v. *Cantrell* (1943), 44 SRNSW 45; *Ann. Digest* (1943–5), no. 37; *Municipality of Saint John* v. *Fraser-Brace Overseas Corp.* (1958), 13 DLR (2d), 177; ILR 26 (1958, II), 165.

[16] *Ubi supra*, n. 14.

foreign public ship in territorial waters. Yet the warship remains for many purposes an independent area of foreign competence: the sending state can exercise governmental powers and undertake judicial action on the vessel. Members of the crew committing crimes when ashore on leave and recovering the ship are safe from apprehension by the local authorities. Moreover, it seems that members of the crew committing breaches of the local law when ashore on duty or on official mission are immune from the local jurisdiction.[17] The internal independence of the warship has led to opinions that political asylum may be granted on board, but no power exists in positive law.[18] If, however, asylum is granted, local fugitives from justice are taken on board, infractions of local regulations occur, or acts of violence issue from the vessel, no local police power may be exercised within the warship itself. The remedy lies in diplomatic representations and, ultimately, in termination of the licence to remain and measures of compulsion to enforce the withdrawal of consent or to prevent further acts of violence.

(d) Foreign military and other public aircraft[19]

The legal position is similar to that which obtains in the case of foreign military and other public ships.

(e) Foreign armed forces (apart from public ships and aircraft)[20]

This subject has complexities to which justice cannot be done in the present treatment. Any statement of general principle must be provisional in view of the confused state of the sources, and states commonly rely on a treaty regime to govern the status of visiting forces. The problems are a little more tractable if some classification, based on the occasion for the presence of foreign forces, is attempted. Foreign public ships and aircraft have a special legal regime which justifies separate treatment (*supra*).

(i) *A military force exercising a right of passage.* We are here concerned with a concession relating to a specific force on a specific occasion.[21] The decision in the *Schooner Exchange* has been used to support a variety of propositions about the immunities of armed forces, and it is important to recall that in this connection Marshall, CJ, was concerned exclusively with the case of the grant of free passage and not the stationing

---

[17] See Oppenheim, ii. 1169–70; and *Ministère Public* v. *Triandafilou, Ann. Digest* (1919–42), no. 86; 39 *AJ* (1945), 345. Some would deny this immunity; see Hyde, ii. 830; Hall, *International Law*, p. 249. Cf. *Japan* v. *Smith and Stinner*, ILR 19 (1952), no. 47.

[18] Opinion of Lord Stowell, 18 Nov. 1820; Hyde, ii. 829; Gidel, ii. 273–88. See also Baldoni, 65 Hague *Recueil* (1938, III), 285–92; Morgenstern, 25 *BY* (1948), 253–5; McNair, *Opinions*, ii. 67–73 (Stowell's opinion at 70). Other views: Hall, *International Law*, p. 247; Colombos, p. 278. See also the Havana Conv. on Asylum, 1928, 22 *AJ* (1928), Suppl., p. 158.

[19] Oppenheim, ii. 1165 fn. 1; Cheng, 11 *Curr. Leg. Problems* (1958), 225–57; Brierly, p. 269; Whiteman, ix. 75. See further, on the *Sea Harrier* case: 56 *BY* (1985), 462–7.

[20] See generally Whiteman, vi. 379–427; Wijewardane, 41 *BY* (1967), 122–54; Barton, 26 *BY* (1949), 380–413; 27 *BY* (1950), 186–234; and 31 *BY* (1954), 341–70; King, 36 *AJ* (1942), 539–67; 40 *AJ* (1946), 257–79; van Praag, *Jurisdiction et droit international public* (1915), 492ff., Suppl. (1935), 265ff.; Whitton, 63 *RGDIP* (1959), 5–20; Rousseau, iii. 72–92; Oppenheim, ii. 1154–64; Bernhardt, *Encyclopedia*, III (1997), 381–90.

[21] The conditions in which the concession is made may create issues arising from the duties of neutrals in time of war.

or sojourn of troops.[22] There is, of course, an analogy with the visit of a warship by invitation, and there is an immunity from the supervisory and, though this is less certain, the criminal jurisdiction of the territorial sovereign.[23] Moreover, the sending state has wide powers of control and jurisdiction over the force.

(ii) *Forces stationed in defined camp or base areas.* If the rationale of the privilege given to forces in transit is based on their organized and hermetic nature and the warship analogy is drawn on, and if it is correct to say that forces in passage have extensive privileges, then it can obviously be argued that visiting forces in defined camp and base areas have similar characteristics and should have similar privileges. However, this is almost certainly not the modern law.[24]

(iii) *Visiting forces in general.* Some writers have applied the principles stated in the *Schooner Exchange*, which in regard to land forces were expressed in the context of a right of free passage, to visiting forces in general, and thus support a doctrine of 'absolute' immunity, which can nevertheless be waived.[25] Others have interpreted the materials differently and, influenced by the content of the NATO Status of Forces Agreement[26] and various recent bilateral agreements, have denied, as a general principle, the immunity of members of a visiting force from the criminal jurisdiction of the local courts.[27] A number of writers,[28] supported by some judicial practice,[29] support a qualified immunity, operating in certain situations: the rule is normally stated as an acceptance of immunity from criminal jurisdiction for offences committed within the quarters of the force and elsewhere when on duty. Yet another approach, which is the most satisfactory in principle and therefore, in a confused situation, has a good claim to be the law on the subject, involves a return to the rationale of the words of Marshall CJ, in the *Schooner Exchange*.[30] Although

---

[22] (1812), 7 Cranch 116 at 139–40; Westlake, *International Law* (1904), i. 255; and see also Barton, 26 *BY* (1949), 383–5; and 27 *BY* (1950), 217–19; *In re Gilbert, Ann. Digest*, 13 (1946), no. 37, per Nonato, J. (cf. Barton, 31 *BY* (1954), 345).

[23] See Brierly, p. 269 ('passing through ... another State's territory as organized units'); Hall, *International Law*, pp. 250–1.

[24] See Barton, 27 *BY* (1950), 227–9; id., 31 *BY* (1954), 342–50. For a statement supporting a wide immunity see Oppenheim, ii. 1156–7. Cf. Brierly, p. 270. On lease of territory for bases see *Hans* v. *The Queen* [1955] AC 378; ILR 22 (1955), 154.

[25] King, 36 *AJ* (1942), 539–67; van Panhuys, 2 *Neths. Int. LR* (1955), 255.

[26] See *infra*.

[27] See Barton, 31 *BY* (1954), 341–70; Draper, 44 *Grot. Soc.* (1958, 1959), 12ff.

[28] e.g. Oppenheim, ii. 1156–7; Guggenheim, i. 518–19; O'Connell, ii. 879–86 (limited to matters of 'internal disciplinary organization').

[29] See Barton, 27 *BY* (1950), 227–31; 31 *BY* (1954), 342–63. Cf. Oppenheim, ii. 1157–64; *Reference re Exemption of United States Forces from Canadian Criminal Law* (1943), 4 DLR 11; *Ann. Digest*, 12 (1943–5), no. 36, Duff, CJC and Hudson, J.

[30] The key passage is as follows: 'In such case, without any express declaration waiving jurisdiction over the army to which this right of passage has been granted, the sovereign who should attempt to exercise it would certainly be considered as violating his faith. By exercising it, the purpose for which the free passage was granted would be defeated, and a portion of the military force of a foreign independent nation would be diverted from those national objects and duties to which it was applicable and would be withdrawn from the control of the sovereign whose power and safety might greatly depend on retaining the exclusive command

he referred to the *passage* of a force, his rationale for the immunity was the implied waiver by the receiving state of the exercise of any powers which would seriously affect the integrity and efficiency of the force.[31] Thus, in principle the visiting force has exclusive jurisdiction over matters of discipline and internal organization over offences by its members committed when on duty. In some situations it will not be immediately clear that the rationale precludes local jurisdiction-for example, where within the quarters one member of the visiting force not on duty murders another or a local civilian commits a breach of local law within the base area. In such cases it is thought that the principle of immunity should be complemented by principles of interest[32] or substantial connection.[33] In the case of forces stationed on territory, and not merely passing through it, it may be that the presumption should be in favour of the local jurisdiction.[34] In cases of doubt there is no reason why the modalities of an immunity should not be governed by the general principles governing jurisdiction over aliens.[35] The rationale referred to above provides a reasonable outcome to the difficult issue of civil jurisdiction: in most cases there will be no reason to allow a member of a visiting force immunity from civil action for harm caused to a local citizen even by acts committed in the course of duty.[36] On the other hand there will be immunity from local direct taxation.[37]

As a matter of political and administrative convenience, and no doubt partly because of the uncertainty of the customary law, states frequently rely on special agreement. In one case, that of the NATO Status of Forces Agreement,[38] 1951, the matter is regulated by a multilateral convention. Its provisions have created some problems of application, but the general scheme is as follows. The military authorities of the sending state may exercise criminal jurisdiction within the receiving state over all persons subject to the military law of the sending state and committing offences against that law. The receiving state may punish any breach of its own law by members of the visiting force and their dependants: when the breach is not also a breach of the law of the sending state

and disposition of this force. The grant of a free passage therefore implies a waiver of all jurisdiction over the troops during their passage, and permits the foreign general to use that discipline and to inflict those punishments which the government of his army require'. But see *Wilson* v. *Girard*, 354 US 524 (1957).

[31] See *Wright* v. *Cantrell* (1943), 44 SRNSW 45; *Ann. Digest*, 12 (1943–5), no. 37, Supreme Ct. of New South Wales. See further *Chow Hung Ching* v. *The King* (1948), 77 CLR 449; *Ann. Digest*, 15 (1948), no. 47, High Ct. of Australia; and US view in 58 *AJ* (1964), 994.

[32] See Nonato, J. in *In re Gilbert, Ann. Digest*, 13 (1946), no. 37; 31 *BY* (1954), 345–6.

[33] Cf. *supra*, p. 309. See also bilateral treaties concluded by the former Soviet Union with Hungary, Poland, and the German Democratic Republic: 52 *AJ* (1958), 219–27. These provided for local jurisdiction, as a general principle, but crimes by Soviet forces or members of their families solely against the Soviet Union or other persons in the Soviet forces, and crimes committed by these forces while discharging their duties, were excluded. And cf. the Visiting Forces Act 1952, ss. 2 and 3.

[34] See *Wilson* v. *Girard*, 354 US 524 (1957); Whiteman, vi. 382, 384–6.

[35] *Supra*, ch. 15.

[36] See *Wright* v. *Cantrell, supra*, n. 31.

[37] See Fairman and King, 38 *AJ* (1944), 258–77, and cf. *Reference on Powers of City of Ottawa* (1943), SCR 208, *Ann. Digest*, 10 (1941–2), no. 106. See also NATO Status of Forces Agreement, Art. 10.

[38] 48 *AJ* (1954), Suppl., p. 83. See also the Visiting Forces Act 1952; the International Headquarters and Defence Organizations Act 1964; 54 *BY* (1983), 441, 477–81; 58 *BY* (1987), 542–6, 587, 588.

(as it applies to such forces) this jurisdiction is exclusive. However, there is a large area of concurrence, and this treaty provides rules to decide which state has the 'primary right' to exercise jurisdiction.[39] Thus the sending state has primary jurisdiction if the offence arises out of any act or omission 'done in the performance of official duty'. Professor Baxter has expressed the view that the NATO formula for allocation of jurisdiction may pass into customary law.[40]

(iv) *Co-belligerent forces conducting operations on national territory.*[41] It could be said that the rationale of the position of warships and, perhaps, of forces in passage applies equally to the lines of allied forces helping the territorial sovereign to expel hostile forces. However, the evidence suggests that, apart from defences to international claims and criminal charges offered by the contingencies of war operations, such forces have a status basically no different from that of visiting forces in other circumstances. It is, of course, difficult to distinguish between the case of co-belligerent forces stationed in a country not yet the field of land operations, co-belligerent forces in action on state territory, and allied forces given facilities for deployment in time of peace as part of preparation for effective action in case of attack. In all three cases the position will normally be regulated by treaty.[42] However, it is probable that a source of limitations on the belligerent powers of the allied forces in action on state territory lies in the ordinary rules on belligerent occupation,[43] although these are normally conceived to apply only to enemy occupants.

(f) The inviolability of certain weapons deployed by foreign forces

It is today not uncommon for states supplying weapons or components thereof in pursuance of a joint military programme to reserve full 'ownership, custody, and control' of certain components, for example nuclear warheads for missiles.[44] The reservation is presumably necessary because otherwise the supply of such components might be regarded as a transfer of rights of ownership and control.

---

[39] See generally Snee and Pye, *Status of Forces Agreements and Criminal Jurisdiction* (1957); Rouse and Baldwin, 51 *AJ* (1957), 29–62; Baxter, 7 *ICLQ* (1958), 72–81; Draper, 44 *Grot. Soc.* (1958, 1959), 9–28; id., *Civilians and the NATO Status of Forces Agreement* (1966); Lazareff, *Status of Military Forces under Current International Law* (1971); Whiteman, vi. 392–427; van Panhuys, 2 *Neths. Int. LR* (1955), 253–78. See also *Re Labelle*, ILR 24 (1957), 251; *Whitley v. Aitchison*, ibid. 26 (1958, II), 196. Cf. *U.S. v. Copeland*, ibid. 23 (1956), 241; *Wilson v. Girard*, ibid. 24, 248; 354 US 524 (1957); *Japan v. Girard*, ibid. 26 (1958, II), 203. For some other aspects: Meron, 6 *ICLQ* (1957), 689–94.

[40] Foreword to Lazareff, *Status of Military Forces.*

[41] See King, 36 *AJ* (1942), 539–67; 40 *AJ* (1946), 257–79; Barton, 26 *BY* (1949), 387ff.; 27 *BY* (1950), 187ff. See also *Société Anonyme v. Office d' Aide Mutuelle*, ILR 23 (1956), 205; *Office d' Aide Mutuelle v. Veuve Eugéne Elias*, ILR 32, 588.

[42] e.g. Agreement between UK and Belgium on civil administration and jurisdiction in liberated territory, 1944, 90 UNTS, p. 283; Agreement between US and the Netherlands, 1944, 132 UNTS, p. 355; US and France, 1944, 138 UNTS, p. 247.

[43] See *Jakub l. v. Teofil B.*, ILR 26 (1958, II), 730; and the *UK Manual of Military Law*, iii (1958), 140 no. 3.

[44] United Kingdom and United States, Exchange of Notes, 22 Feb. 1958, *Dept. of State Bull.* 38 (1958), 418–19.

(g) United Nations forces

United Nations forces engaged in peace-keeping operations, not constituting enforcement action within the meaning of the Charter of the United Nations,[45] can only be deployed with the agreement of the state concerned. In the relevant formal agreements, considerable powers and immunities may be conferred, involving the establishing of bases and freedom of movement.[46]

(h) Grants of interests in territory

A state may grant a right of exclusive use over a part of its territory to another state, retaining sovereignty, but conceding the enjoyment of the liberties of the territorial sovereign. Such a grant may be described as a 'lease'.[47] However, the nature of the interest involved here is such that it is inappropriate to classify such grants with the privileges considered in this section. Nevertheless, in strictness, these grants do constitute privileges, and in principle their incidence depends on the consent of the territorial sovereign. In most cases where military and naval bases have been established by agreement the result is more akin to a contractual licence than it is to an interest in land in the English sense.[48]

(i) Servitudes[49]

The title 'servitudes' denotes only an area of problems, and its use as a legal category is a matter of controversy.[50] By treaty or otherwise, a state may have accommodation rights over the territory of a neighbour in the form of a right of way, user of a railway station or port facilities, maintenance of wireless stations, customs houses, or military bases, and so on. Again, the rights may take the form of an obligation on the neighbour

---

[45] There is a large issue as to the constitutional status of such forces within the Charter: see the *Expenses* case, *infra*, pp. 697–8.

[46] See generally Wijewardane, 41 *BY* (1967), 154–97; Bowett, *United Nations Forces* (1964), 428–67; Higgins, *United Nations Peacekeeping*, 4 vols. (1969, 1970, 1980, 1981); Siekmann, *Basic Documents on United Nations and Related Peacekeeping Forces* (1985); Oppenheim, i. 1164–5. See further *Jennings* v. *Markley*, 186 F. Supp. 611; 290 F. 2d 892; ILR 32, p. 367; *Nissan* v. *A.-G.* [1970] AC 179; 43 *BY* (1968–9), 217. On the position of UN observer groups: Bowett, *United Nations Forces*, pp. 83–4.

[47] *Supra*, pp. 110–11.

[48] On areas 'retained under full British sovereignty' in Cyprus after independence see Cmnd. 679, Misc. no. 4 (1959). See also Whiteman, ii. 1215–24.

[49] See generally McNair, 6 *BY* (1925), 111–27; Crusen, 22 Hague *Recueil* (1928, II), 5–79; Schwarzenberger, *International Law* (3rd edn., 1957), 209–15; Lauterpacht, *Private Law Sources and Analogies of International Law* (1927), 119–24, 237–43; id., *International Law: Collected Papers*, i (1970), 374–5; Esgain, in O'Brien (ed.), *The New Nations in International Law and Diplomacy* (1965), 42–97; *British Digest*, iib, ch. 8; O'Connell, i. 544–52; Reid, *International Servitudes in Law and Practice* (1932); id., 45 Hague *Recueil* (1933, III), 5–68; Váli, *Servitudes of International Law* (2nd edn., 1958); Hyde, i. 510–15; Whiteman, ii. 1173–224; Rousseau, iii. 43–6; *Répertoire suisse*, ii. 1049–53; Dominicé, 19 *Ann. suisse* (1962), 71–102; Bernhardt, *Encyclopedia*, IV (2000), 387–90.

[50] The subject has been regarded with great caution by tribunals, although they have not rejected the concept in principle: see the *North Atlantic Coast Fisheries* arbitration (1910), *RIAA* xi. 167; Hague Court Reports, i. 141; *British Digest*, iib. 585 (and see the comment at 405–6); and the *Wimbledon* (1923), PCIJ, Ser. A, no. 1, p. 24. See also Judge Moreno Quintana, Diss. Op., *Right of Passage* case, ICJ Reports (1960), 90.

to abstain from building in a given zone or from militarization of a defined area. The similarity to servitudes in municipal law and the influence of civil law doctrines on the writers have led to the advocacy of a concept of servitudes in international law, *jura in re aliena*, involving a relation of territory to territory, unaffected by change of sovereignty in either state, and terminable only by mutual consent, by renunciation on the part of the dominant state, or by consolidation of the territories concerned.[51] However, the majority of modern writers consider the category to be useless and, indeed, misleading.[52] It is certainly true that treaties, and local custom, may create obligations of a local character which survive a change in the sovereignty of one or both of the parties, but such instances are explicable without any reference to a concept of servitudes. Moreover, if the concept is adopted it is very difficult to explain why certain similar restrictions on territory are not transmissible, and further, why certain restrictions, clearly not like servitudes, are transmissible.

The concept is useless but the subject-matter to which it has been applied by various writers does have some real problems, and some brief account of these is necessary. At the outset two matters must be set apart. First, customary international law creates analogous accommodation rights in the case of the right of innocent passage through the territorial sea[53] and certain rights and duties of neighbourhood.[54] Secondly, in certain conditions, a multilateral treaty may create permanent local restrictions as part of an 'objective regime' in order to pursue an end of international public policy, as for example the neutralization of a sensitive area. The nature and basis of such 'objective regimes' varies, and the proper context of the problems is the law of treaties.[55] In general it is dangerous to argue that, if transmissibility arises from the principles of state succession[56] and/or the law of treaties,[57] then this proves the existence of a legal category 'servitude'.

Two situations may arise. The original parties to a treaty may stipulate for the granting of rights 'for ever' or use other words suggesting irrevocability. There is no question of transmissibility here,[58] and everything turns on the interpretation of the provisions.

[51] See Reid, *International Servitudes*, p. 25. Other advocates: Váli, *Servitudes*; Verzijl, *International Law in Historical Perspective* iii (1970), 413–28; O'Connell; Lauterpacht, *Analogies* and *Coll. Papers*, i; and Oppenheim, (8th edn., 1955) i. 535–43 (view of author and editor); Oppenheim, 9th edn., ii (1992), 670–6 (much more sceptical); Schücking, Dissent, the *Wimbledon, supra*, pp. 43 ff. Hall, *International Law* (8th edn., 1924), 203–5, bases servitudes on agreement. See also Parry, *British Digest*, iib. 373–409.

[52] See McNair, 6 *BY* (1925), 111–27; id., *Law of Treaties* (1961), 656; Guggenheim, i. 394–7; Schwarzenberger, *International Law*; Hyde, i. 513; Brierly, pp. 190–4. See also the Commission of Jurists, Aaland Islands dispute, 1920, *British Digest*, iib. 771.

[53] *Supra*, p. 186.

[54] Sauser-Hall, 83 Hague *Recueil* (1953, II), 553–8.

[55] See *infra*, p. 627.

[56] See ch. 29.

[57] On the effect of treaties on third states see *infra*, pp. 598–600. See also the *Free Zones* case, Ser. A/B, no. 46, p. 145; and Armand-Ugon, Diss. Op., ICJ Reports (1960), 81.

[58] See the *North Atlantic Coast Fisheries* arbitration, *supra*, in which by treaty Great Britain had granted a liberty of fishing 'forever' to inhabitants of the United States. The real issue was the extent to which a grantor can regulate the rights granted: see *infra*, p. 376. See also Schwarzenberger, *International Law*, pp. 210–12.

Thus, such language may be intended to exclude termination by the outbreak of war[59] or the operation of the *clausula rebus sic stantibus*.[60] More interesting are the cases in which local obligations affecting user of territory are considered to survive changes of sovereignty. Four possibilities exist.

1. Rights of passage and the like may rest on a local custom acquiesced in by transferees of the territory.[61]

2. If a successor in title participates in the enjoyment of rights which have their sources in a composite arrangement involving reciprocal benefits and duties, then, by the operation of estoppel, obligations of a territorial nature may devolve.[62] The estoppel could also be regarded as a consequence of various equitable principles, and especially the rule that one cannot both approbate and reprobate. Thus, if a frontier regime is established by agreement between A and B and part of the consideration for the agreement of B is the granting of grazing rights across the frontier in B's favour, then C, territorial successor to B, must accept or reject the arrangement as a whole: it cannot reject the frontier regime, but accept and enjoy the grazing rights.[63]

3. Another application of principles of equity is involved in the principle that a state, by transferring territory to C, cannot derogate from a previous grant of territorial rights to B, such as a right of navigation: *nemo plus juris transferre quam ipse habet* (no one can give a greater interest than he himself has).[64]

4. The three principles already mentioned may be complemented by other applications of the principle that the grant of rights should be reasonably effective. For example, if state A, which is the riparian sovereign of a river giving access to the sea, is granted a right of navigation on the river, the waters of which are under the sovereignty of B, the grantor, then it is arguable that A may construct and use jetties which penetrate B's sovereignty in order to implement the right of navigation.[65]

Of these four principles, the third is perhaps the most controversial and difficult of application. If state A, on becoming independent, or receiving a parcel of territory from B, allows C to retain a military base on the territory concerned, the basis of the

[59] *Infra*, pp. 620–1.

[60] *Infra*, pp. 623–5.

[61] *Right of Passage* case, ICJ Reports (1960), 6 at 40, 43; Hall, *International Law*, p. 203. See also *Union of India* v. *Sukumar Sengupta*, ILR 92, 554 (India, S.C.).

[62] Cf. Judge Anzilotti, *Diversion of Water* case, PCIJ, Ser. A/B, no. 70 (1937), 50, on the principle *inadimplenti non est adimplendum* (a party which has failed to execute a treaty cannot rely on it). See also Váli, *Servitudes*, p. 321.

[63] Cf. the Ethiopian-Somali dispute over grazing rights in the Haud: on which see Latham Brown, 5 *ICLQ* (1956), 245–64; 10 *ICLQ* (1961), 167–78. See also Fitzmaurice, *Yrbk. ILC* (1960), ii. 99–100.

[64] McNair, *Law of Treaties*, pp. 656–9; O'Connell, 30 *Can. BR* (1952), 810–15; id., *Law of State Succession* (1st edn., 1956), 53–6. See also Fitzmaurice, *Yrbk. ILC* (1960), ii. 99–100.

[65] On the position of the Shatt-al-Arab see E. Lauterpacht, 9 *ICLQ* (1960), 208 at 226–32; Kaikobad, *The Shatt-al-Arab Boundary Question: A Legal Reappraisal* (1988), 68–99.

right is probably now the agreement or acquiescence of A. If B had not reserved such a right in its grant to A, then B will answer to C, but the right of C cannot be 'sanctioned' at the expense of A. Nor, in this case, can the difficulty be avoided by saying that the right involved is a 'local obligation' serving other territory held by C, and even if it were, to speak of a 'local obligation' may be to resurrect the concept of servitude.

2. OTHER RESTRICTIONS ON TERRITORIAL SUPREMACY

Restrictions on the liberty of states to regulate the affairs of their territories as they wish are legion, stemming from treaty, local custom, estoppel, and the rules of customary law. Some of these restrictions have been classified in the three previous sections, but more comprehensive classification could be attempted.[66] However, to list such restrictions is simply to collect a great number of widely diverse topics ranging over much of international law. The nature of the restrictions vary, as is apparent if one compares the right of innocent passage through the territorial sea,[67] the obligation to avoid conditions on state territory causing harm to other states or their nationals,[68] the right of individual or collective self-defence which permits the use of force against or within other states, and the great mass of treaty obligations relating to labour standards, international traffic, commerce, nationality, and many other fields. Important restrictions concern shared resources and amenities.[69]

3. EXTERNAL IMPOSITION OF GOVERNMENTAL FUNCTIONS WITHOUT THE CONSENT OF THE SOVEREIGN

Executive and administrative powers may be exercised by alien authorities under the rules of belligerent occupation[70] in time of war and by forces taking enforcement action under Chapter 7 of the United Nations Charter.[71]

---

[66] Cf. Schwarzenberger, *International Law*, i (3rd edn.), Pt. III; Fitzmaurice, 92 Hague *Recueil* (1957, II), 186–90; Sørensen, 101 Hague *Recueil* (1960, III), 182–98; Hyde, i. 510–639.

[67] *Supra*, p. 186.

[68] *Infra*, p. 440.

[69] *Supra*, ch. 12.

[70] The concept of belligerent occupation is not confined to enemy forces: *supra*, p. 371. See generally U.K. Ministry of Defence, *The Manual of the Law of Armed Conflict* (2004), paras. 11.1–11.91.

[71] On the relevance of consent to the presence of peace-keeping forces not acting under ch. 7, see the controversial opinion of Bowett, *United Nations Forces*, pp. 231–2, 412–27.

PART VII

RULES OF ATTRIBUTION
(apart from Territorial Sovereignty
and State Jurisdiction)

19

THE RELATIONS OF
NATIONALITY

1. THE DOCTRINE OF THE FREEDOM OF STATES
IN MATTERS OF NATIONALITY[1]

As special rapporteur of the International Law Commission,[2] Manley O. Hudson expressed the view: 'In principle, questions of nationality fall within the domestic jurisdiction of each state'. This proposition already had high authority behind it, and there is no doubt that it expresses the 'accepted view'. The impetus to a wide acceptance of the principle enunciated by Hudson was given by the dictum of the Permanent Court in the Advisory Opinion concerning the *Tunis and Morocco Nationality Decrees*:[3]

The question whether a certain matter is or is not solely within the jurisdiction of a State is an essentially relative question; it depends upon the development of international relations. Thus, in the present state of international law, questions of nationality are, in the opinion of this Court, in principle within this reserved domain.

Whatever the intrinsic meaning and value of the statement of the Permanent Court *as such*,[4] its influence must be examined in terms of the construction placed upon it by others, to the effect that states are exclusively in control of nationality matters. Numerous textbooks and standard works have repeated the statement in the *Nationality Decrees* case, or have stated in their own words propositions obviously inspired by it.[5]

    There are compelling objections of principle to the doctrine of the freedom of states in the present context. However, before these are considered it is necessary to recall the

---

[1] Generally on nationality see Whiteman, viii. 1–193; Weis, *Nationality and Statelessness in International Law* (1956; 2nd edn., 1979); Fitzmaurice, 92 Hague *Recueil* (1957, II), 191–207; van Panhuys, *The Role of Nationality in International Law* (1959); de Castro y Bravo, 102 Hague *Recueil* (1961, I), 521–634; Briggs, *Annuaire de l'Inst.* (1965), i. 126–77; Rousseau, v. 101–27; Donner, *The Regulation of Nationality in International Law* (1983); Panzera, *Limiti internazionali in materia di cittadinanza* (1984); Rezek, 198 Hague *Recueil* (1986, III), 333–400; Bernhardt (ed.), *Encyclopedia*, III (1997), 501–10; Bederman, 42 *ICLQ* (1993), 119–36. See also Brownlie, 39 *BY* (1963), 284–364; and *British Digest*, v.

[2] *Yrbk. ILC* (1952), ii. 3 at 7. See also Hudson, *Cases* (2nd edn., 1936), 201; (3rd edn., 1951), 138.

[3] PCIJ, Ser. B, no. 4 (1923), 24; Whiteman, viii. 37–42.

[4] See further Brownlie, 39 *BY* (1963), 286–8.

[5] See e.g. Ralston, *The Law and Procedure of International Tribunals* (1926), 160; ibid., Suppl., p. 76; Brierly, pp. 283, 357. See further Oppenheim, ii. 643. But see the first edition, i. 348–9, para. 293, where the original context reduces the significance of the statement.

high significance which the concept of nationality has in the law. Thus a state, a national of which has suffered a wrong at the hands of another state, has the right to exercise diplomatic protection. This, the principle of nationality of claims, is all-important, in spite of certain qualifications to it recognized lately.[6] In former times, and, in the opinion of some jurists, even in the period of the United Nations Charter, the law recognized a right of forcible intervention to protect the lives and property of nationals.[7] Numerous duties of states in relation to war and neutrality, resting for the most part on the customary law, are framed in terms of the acts or omissions by nationals which states should prevent and, in some cases, punish. Aliens on the territory of a state produce a complex of legal relations consequent on their status of non-nationals. Acts of sovereignty may give rise to questions of international responsibility when they affect aliens or their property; witness the problems considered under the titles 'denial of justice', 'expropriation', and the like. Aliens may be expelled for sufficient cause and their home state is bound to receive them. Nationals will not, while aliens may, be extradited. Nationality provides a normal (but not exclusive) basis for the exercise of civil and criminal jurisdiction and this even in respect of acts committed abroad.

At the outset one might predicate a presumption of effectiveness and regularity which would abruptly resolve the apparent conflict between the reliance of so many institutions of the law on the concept of nationality, so far as application and enforcement are concerned, and the alleged freedom of states in the conferment of nationality. Nationality is a problem, in part of attribution, and regarded in this way resembles the law relating to territorial sovereignty.[8] National law prescribes the extent of the territory of a state, but this prescription does not preclude a forum which is applying international law from deciding questions of title in its own way, using criteria of international law. Sovereignty which is in principle unlimited, even by the existence of other states, is ridiculous, whether dominion is sought to be exercised over territory, sea, airspace, or populations. In a related matter, the delimitation of the territorial sea, the Court in the *Fisheries* case allowed that in regard to rugged coasts the coastal state would seem to be in the best position to appraise the local conditions dictating the selection of baselines, but the tenor of the judgment was not in support of legal autonomy, and the Court stated:[9]

The delimitation of sea areas has always an international aspect; it cannot be dependent merely upon the will of the coastal State as expressed in its municipal law. Although it is true that the act of delimitation is necessarily a unilateral act, because only the coastal State

---

[6] See *infra*, p. 477.

[7] Generally see Brownlie, *International Law and the Use of Force by States* (1963), 289–301; Bowett, *Self-Defence in International Law* (1958), 87–105.

[8] Parry, *Nationality and Citizenship Laws of the Commonwealth and the Republic of Ireland* (1957), i. 17–19, regards the analogy of territory as 'very attractive', but he also remarks that it should not be pushed too far (see p. 21). However, for the purpose of comment on the possible *results* of a certain type of doctrine the analogy would seem to be perfectly valid.

[9] ICJ Reports (1951), 116 at 132. See also Judge McNair, 160–1; and Judge Read, 189–90; and further, Fitzmaurice, 30 *BY* (1953), 11. Cf. the *Asylum* case, ICJ Reports (1950), 266 at 273–5.

is competent to undertake it, the validity of the delimitation with regard to other States depends upon international law.

This passage is of considerable importance, since the origins of nationality as a status are very similar to the process of delimitation here dealt with.

It is important to avoid reliance on general statements purporting to establish the boundaries of the reserved domain in abstract form.[10] Everything depends on the way in which a particular issue arises. Nationality is not capable of performing a role confined to the reserved domain or the realm of state relations: in principle it has two aspects, either of which may be dominant, depending on the facts and type of dispute. The approach of the International Court in the *Nottebohm* case[11] would seem to be perfectly logical in this respect. The Court said:[12]

It is for Liechtenstein, as it is for every sovereign State, to settle by its own legislation the rules relating to the acquisition of its nationality, and to confer that nationality by naturalization granted by its own organs in accordance with that legislation.[13] It is not necessary to determine whether international law imposes any limitations on its freedom of decision in this domain[14]... Nationality serves above all to determine that the person upon whom it is conferred enjoys the rights and is bound by the obligations which the law of the State in question grants to or imposes on its nationals. This is implied in the wider concept that nationality is within the domestic jurisdiction of the State.

But the issue which the Court must decide is not one which pertains to the legal system of Liechtenstein. It does not depend on the law or on the decision of Liechtenstein whether that State is entitled to exercise its protection... To exercise protection, to apply to the Court, is to place oneself on the plane of international law. It is international law which determines whether a State is entitled to exercise protection and to seise the Court.[15]

2. OPINIONS OF GOVERNMENTS ON THE ISSUE OF AUTONOMY

The significance of the views of governments, expressed in replies to questions of the Preparatory Committee for the Hague Codification Conference, does not need emphasis. Incidentally but usefully, these replies provide a commentary on the

---

[10] See de Visscher, *Theory and Reality in Public International Law* (1957), 222–3; and *supra*, p. 292.
[11] ICJ Reports (1955), 4.
[12] ICJ Reports (1955), 20–1.
[13] Cf. *Yrbk. ILC* (1954), ii. 164 (Belgian comment), 173 (United States comment).
[14] See *infra*.
[15] See also the *Fisheries* case, ICJ Reports (1951), 116 at 132.

Advisory Opinion concerning the *Nationality Decrees in Tunis and Morocco*.[16] In its reply the German Government stated:[17]

The general principle that all questions relating to the acquisition or loss of a specific nationality shall be governed by the laws of the State whose nationality is claimed or contested should be admitted. The application of this principle, however, should not go beyond the limits at which the legislation of one State encroaches on the sovereignty of another. For example, a State has no power, by means of a law or administrative act, to confer its nationality on all the inhabitants of another State or on all foreigners entering its territory. Further, if the State confers its nationality on the subjects of other States without their request, when the persons concerned are not attached to it by any particular bond, as, for instance, origin, domicile or birth, the States concerned will not be bound to recognize such naturalization.

The British reply[18] states the principle of exclusive jurisdiction and continues:

The mere fact, however, that nationality falls in general within the domestic jurisdiction of a State does not exclude the possibility that the right of the State to use its discretion in legislating with regard to nationality may be restricted by duties which it owes to other States (see *Tunis and Morocco Case*...). Legislation which is inconsistent with such duties is not legislation which there is any obligation upon a State whose rights are ignored to recognize. It follows that the right of a State to legislate with regard to the acquisition and loss of its nationality and the duty of another State to recognize the effects of such legislation are not necessarily coincident.

Even if the discretion of the State in the former case may be unlimited, the duty of the State in the latter case is not unlimited. It may properly decline to recognize the effects of such legislation which is prejudicial to its own rights as a State.

It is only in exceptional cases that this divergence between the right of a State to legislate at its discretion with regard to the enjoyment or non-enjoyment of its nationality and the duty of other States to recognize such legislation would occur. The criterion is that the legislation must infringe the *rights* of the State as apart from its *interests*.

The last paragraph of this reply confines the area of divergence to 'exceptional cases'. However, if exceptional cases are admitted to exist the force of emphasis on discretion in legislation is much diminished. Obviously there are limits to the discretion, and these are not concealed by the device whereby the exercise of the discretion occurs but is not recognized by other states. In terms of international law this would then seem to be a discretion within the limits set by the divergence referred to in the British reply. In other words, the principle is admitted. Moreover, there is a general duty to bring national law into conformity with obligations under international law;[19] and in this connection the opinion has been expressed[20] that where a state adopts legislation on its face contrary to its obligations the legislation may itself constitute the breach of an

---

[16] *Supra*, p. 383.
[17] *League of Nations, Conference for the Codification of International Law, Bases of Discussion*, I, *Nationality* (1929), V. 1. 13.
[18] Ibid. 17, 169. The replies of the Dominions and India are identical or substantially similar.
[19] *Supra*, p. 34.
[20] Fitzmaurice, 92 Hague *Recueil* (1957, II), 89.

obligation. In such a case, however, potential plaintiff states must await the occurrence of actual damage before presenting a claim. The contradiction and misconception inherent in the theory of divergence are to be found in the replies of other governments. Thus the majority relate the duty to recognize foreign nationality legislation to fulfilment of international obligations, but do not always place this in direct relation to the right to determine nationality. In view of the element of contradiction and the rules noted above, the statements in the replies of governments to the effect that 'in principle' the question of nationality falls within the exclusive competence of states lose much of their effect.

3. THE CONVENTION CONCERNING CERTAIN QUESTIONS RELATING TO THE CONFLICT OF NATIONALITY LAWS[21]

At the Hague Codification Conference of 1930 the First Committee stated in its report[22] that although nationality 'is primarily a matter for the municipal law of each State, it is nevertheless governed to a large extent by principles of international law'. In spite of the fact that the committee could not agree on the principles to which they referred, the Conference did produce a Convention of some interest, though of limited importance. Article 1 thereof provides:[23] 'It is for each State to determine under its own law who are its nationals. This law shall be recognized by other States in so far as it is consistent with international conventions, international custom, and the principles of law generally recognized with regard to nationality'. It will be at once apparent that the antithesis between autonomy in legislation and the limited duty of recognition, which is evident in the replies of governments, recurs. The antithesis, taken together with the independent force of the second part of the article, deprives the principle of autonomy of its integrity. However, the antithesis might perhaps equally be said to make the provision a legal curiosity, of little strength, and not giving respectability to any proposition. Article 18, paragraph 2, provides in part that the inclusion of the principles and rules stated in the Convention 'shall in no way be deemed to prejudice the question whether they do or do not already form part of international law'. In relation to Article 1 this takes one neither forwards nor backwards. But, with its limitations, Article 1

---

[21] *League of Nations Treaty Series*, vol. 179, p. 89; *Laws Concerning Nationality*, UN Legis. Series, ST/LEG/SER.B/4, July 1954, p. 567. In force 1 July 1937. Twenty-seven states signed but did not ratify. Approximately 19 states have ratified or acceded to the Convention.

[22] *League of Nations, Conference for the Codification of International Law, Acts of the Conference*, II, *Report of the Ist Committee* (1930), V. 8. 2–3.

[23] This text was adopted by the First Committee by thirty-eight votes to two and by the Conference by forty votes to one: *Acts of the Conference*, II, *Minutes of the Ist Committee* (1930), V. 15. 19–36, 205–9; ibid. I, *Plenary Meetings* (1930), V. 14. 38–41. See also Sixth Session, Asian–African Legal Consultative Committee, 1964, Whiteman, viii. 82.

remains a useful authority for the view that international law sets limits to the power of a state to confer nationality.[24]

It is to be noted that in Article 3 of the European Convention on Nationality, concluded in 1997, it is provided that national legislation must be consistent with conventions, customary law, and 'principles of law generally recognised with regard to nationality.'[25]

4. NATIONALITY RULES COMMONLY ADOPTED BY STATES

Certain principles concerning conferment of nationality are adopted in the legislation of states often enough to acquire the status of 'general principles'. It is proposed to give a relatively short exposition[26] of these principles while postponing a general consideration of their precise legal status. Without prejudging too much the question of their legal status, account will be taken of the existence of a sufficiency of adherence to a principle to establish the principle as 'normal' though not necessarily adopted generally in the sense of either a simple or absolute majority.

The two main principles on which nationality is based are descent from a national (*jus sanguinis*) and the fact of birth within state territory (*jus soli*).

JUS SANGUINIS

Weis[27] remarks that *jus sanguinis* and *jus soli* are 'the predominant modes of acquisition of nationality'. In 1935 Sandifer[28] concluded that legislation in 48 states followed the *jus sanguinis* principally and referred to 'the widespread extent of the rule of *jus sanguinis*, and its paramount influence upon the law of nationality throughout the world'. There is no reason to think that this assessment is out of place today.[29] The Harvard Research survey polled 17 states with law based solely on *jus sanguinis*; two equally on *jus sanguinis* and *jus soli*; and 26 principally on *jus soli* and partly on *jus sanguinis*. Experts[30] commonly regard the two principles as permissible criteria, but

---

[24] Thus Córdova, *Yrbk. ILC* (1953), ii. 167, paras. 13–15.

[25] Council of Europe: *European Treaties*; ETS No. 166; Strasbourg, 6 Nov. 1997.

[26] For extended surveys see Córdova, Special Rapporteur, *Yrbk. ILC* (1953), ii. 167, 170ff. (Pt. I); *Survey of the problem of multiple nationality prepared by the Secretariat*, A/CN. 4/84, *Yrbk. ILC* (1954), ii. 52, 63ff. (ch. I); Harv. Research, 23 *AJ* (1929), Spec. Suppl., p. 24; Sandifer, 29 *AJ* (1935), 248.

[27] *Nationality*, p. 98. See also Hudson, *Yrbk. ILC* (1952), ii. 3 at 7.

[28] 29 *AJ* (1935), at 256, 278.

[29] See new legislation in Parry, *Nationality and Citizenship Laws*; and UN Leg. Series, *Supplement to the Volume on the Laws Concerning Nationality*, 1954 (1959), ST/LEG/SER.B/9.

[30] Preparatory Committee of the Hague Codification Conference, *Bases of Discussion*, p. 20 (excised in the Committee on Nationality of the Conference by 18 votes to 17; Mervyn Jones, *British Nationality Law and Practice* (1956), 10–11; Guggenheim, i. 315–16; Makarov, 74 Hague *Recueil* (1949, I), 364–5.

do not always indicate an opinion on their precise legal status. Van Panhuys[31] considers the two principles to be sanctioned by customary law.

In regard to the modalities of the *jus sanguinis*, Sandifer[32] calculated that 47 states had rules under which the status of the father governed (conditional in 14 cases); 35 had rules under which the status of either parent or both governed (conditional in 22 cases); and 29, including the United States, had rules under which the status of the unmarried mother governed.

JUS SOLI

The role of *jus soli* will be evident from what has gone before. However, it may be remarked that, as a principle, it has a relative simplicity of outline, with fairly clear exceptions, when compared with *jus sanguinis*. Indeed, in terms of adherence to a particular system, with a minor degree of dilution, *jus soli* seems to have predominance in the world.[33] Except in so far as there may exist a presumption against statelessness, it is probably incorrect to regard the two most important principles as mutually exclusive: in varying degrees the law of a very large number of states rests on both, and recent legislation gives no sign of any change in the situation. However, the Harvard draft provided in Article 3 that states must choose between the two principles.[34] Of particular interest are the special rules relating to the *jus soli*, appearing as exceptions to that principle, the effect of the exceptions being to remove the cases where its application is clearly unjustifiable. A rule which has very considerable authority stipulated that children born to persons having diplomatic immunity shall not be nationals by birth of the state to which the diplomatic agent concerned is accredited. Thirteen governments stated the exception in the preliminaries of the Hague Codification Conference. In a comment[35] on the relevant article of the Harvard draft on diplomatic privileges and immunities it is stated: 'This article is believed to be declaratory of an established rule of international law'. The rule receives ample support from the legislation of states[36] and expert opinion.[37] The Convention on Certain Questions relating to the Conflict of Nationality Laws of 1930 provides in Article 12: 'Rules of law which confer nationality by reason of birth on the territory of a State shall not apply automatically

---

[31] *The Role of Nationality*, pp. 160–1.

[32] 29 *AJ* (1935), 254, 255, 258.

[33] According to Sandifer, 29 *AJ* (1935), 256, 29 states followed *jus soli*; and the study by the International Union for Child Welfare (1950) concluded that, of 49 states, 35 relied principally on the *jus soli*. See also *Yrbk. ILC* (1953), ii. 170–1; ibid. (1954), ii. 63ff. On the UK Nationality Act of 1981 see: 52 *BY* (1981), 409; White and Hampson, 31 *ICLQ* (1982), 849–55.

[34] 23 *AJ* (1929), Spec. Suppl., p. 27. See further Weis, *Nationality*, pp. 97–8, where he states: 'In the absence of historical examples it is a matter of conjecture whether a nationality law based equally on *jus soli* and *jus sanguinis* would be regarded as inconsistent with international law or the general principles of law'.

[35] 26 *AJ* (1932), Suppl., p. 133. See also the Harvard draft on nationality, ibid. 23 (1929), Spec. Suppl., p. 13, Art. 5.

[36] See the UN Legis. Series, *Laws Concerning Nationality* (1954), Suppl. Vol. 1959.

[37] Córdova, *Yrbk. ILC* (1953), ii. 166 at 176 (Art. III); Guggenheim, i. 317.

to children born to persons enjoying diplomatic immunities in the country where the birth occurs.'

In 1961 the United Nations Conference on Diplomatic Intercourse and Immunities adopted an Optional Protocol concerning Acquisition of Nationality,[38] which provided in Article II: 'Members of the mission not being nationals of the receiving State, and members of their families forming part of their household, shall not, solely by the operation of the law of the receiving State, acquire the nationality of that State'. Some states extend the rule to the children of consuls,[39] and there is some support for this from expert opinion.[40] The United Nations Conference on Consular Relations adopted an Optional Protocol Concerning Acquisition of Nationality containing a provision similar to that concerning diplomats.[41] In a few instances legislation[42] and other prescriptions[43] exclude the *jus soli* in respect of the children of persons exercising official duties on behalf of a foreign government. Another exception quite commonly adopted concerns the children of enemy alien fathers born in territory under enemy occupation.

EXTENSIONS OF THE *JUS SOLI*

The Harvard Research draft[44] refers to 'territory or a place assimilated thereto', and states have generally applied the principle of the *jus soli* to birth on ships and aircraft registered under the flag. Legislation formerly in force in Argentina[45] referred to birth in a 'legation or warship of the Republic', and the later legislation extends to birth 'in an international zone under the Argentine flag'.[46] Where apparent conflict may arise, as in the case of birth on a foreign ship in territorial waters, it is tolerably clear that the child does not in principle acquire *ipso facto* the nationality of the littoral state.[47] This is an obvious case where the matter is not one of exclusive jurisdiction. Moreover, the analogy is with the concept of aliens in transit, which appears in some laws, the presence being somewhat incidental and brief. However, some states, including the United States, Italy, and Japan, do at least claim the faculty of treating birth within their waters as productive of nationality.[48] Yet it would be strange if birth on a ship exercising the right of innocent passage had this consequence. In an attempt

---

[38] 18 Apr. 1961; 500 UNTS, 223. See Johnson, 10 *ICLQ* (1961), 597. The Protocol, in Art.II, reproduces the text of Art. 35 of the draft articles of the ILC: *Yrbk. ILC* (1958), ii. 89 at 101.

[39] See *Laws Concerning Nationality* (1954), 1, 152, 248, 459; Suppl. (1959), 15.

[40] *Yrbk. ILC* (1953), ii. 176–7.

[41] 24 Apr. 1963; 596 UNTS 469. See also *Yrbk. ILC* (1961), ii. 122, Art. 52.

[42] e.g. the Canadian Citizenship Act 1946, as amended, s. 5(2); constitution of Bolivia, 23 Nov. 1946, as amended; constitution of Brazil, 18 Sept. 1946.

[43] Art. 2 of the draft convention prepared by the Committee of Experts of the League of Nations.

[44] 23 *AJ* (1929), Spec. Suppl. See generally Córdova, *Yrbk. ILC* (1953), ii. 177–9.

[45] *Laws Concerning Nationality* (1954), 11; cf. 595.

[46] Ibid. 595. The countries taking this view include the UK, Commonwealth states, Germany, Belgium, and Norway.

[47] See Parry, *Nationality and Citizenship Laws*, pp. 151–3, 230, 412, 426, 537, 950, 960.

[48] See *Yrbk. ILC* (1953), ii. 178; Hackworth, iii. 10.

to avoid statelessness, Córdova, as rapporteur of the International Law Commission, proposed an article which subjected those born on ships and aircraft to the law of the state in the territory (or waters) of which the ship or aircraft was situated at the time.[49]

INVOLUNTARY NATURALIZATION OF INDIVIDUALS

As Special Rapporteur for the International Law Commission, Hudson expressed the following opinion:[50]

Under the law of some States nationality is conferred automatically by operation of law, as the effect of certain changes in civil status: adoption, legitimation, recognition by affiliation, marriage.

Appointment as teacher at a university also involves conferment of nationality under some national laws.

While these reasons for the conferment of nationality have been recognized by the consistent practice of States and may, therefore, be considered as consistent with international law, others have not been so recognized.

Some of these categories may be considered briefly.

MARRIAGE

A survey carried out by the Secretary-General of the United Nations in 1953 showed that a wife automatically acquired the nationality of her husband in 22 states, that in 44 states acquisition was conditional, and that in four states there was no effect. The development of opinion has culminated in the Convention on the Nationality of Married Women opened for signature by the General Assembly of the United Nations on 29 January 1957.[51] The Hague Convention of 1930 merely provides that naturalization of the husband during marriage shall not involve a change in the nationality of the wife except with her consent. The Convention of 1957 favours the principle of equality (and hence independence) of the wife, but compromises to some extent. Thus each contracting state agrees that neither the celebration nor the dissolution of marriage between one of its nationals and an alien, nor change of nationality by the husband during marriage, shall affect the wife's nationality automatically. However, it is provided that the alien wife of a national of a contracting state may, at her request, acquire her husband's nationality by means of privileged naturalization procedures.

---

[49] *Yrbk. ILC* (1953), ii. 177. See now the United Nations Conv. on the Reduction of Statelessness, signed 30 Aug. 1961, Art. 3 (test of flag of registration).

[50] *Yrbk. ILC* (1952), ii. 8. The rubric employed is: 'Conferment of nationality by operation of law'.

[51] Resol. 1040 (XI). Text: *Laws Concerning Nationality*, Supplement (1959), 91. In force in 1958. See *Mejia* v. *Regierungsrat des Kantons Bern*, ILR 32, 192 and the British Nationality Act 1981, sect. 8.

The Convention on the Elimination of All Forms of Discrimination against Women, adopted by the UN General Assembly on 18 Dec. 1979,[52] contains the following provisions (Art. 9):

1. States Parties shall grant women equal rights with men to acquire, change or retain their nationality. They shall ensure in particular that neither marriage to an alien nor change of nationality by the husband during marriage shall automatically change the nationality of the wife, render her stateless or force upon her the nationality of the husband.

2. States Parties shall grant women equal rights with men with respect to the nationality of their children.

LEGAL RECOGNITION OR LEGITIMATION

It is widely accepted in legislation that the child follows the father's nationality.[53]

ADOPTION

That the minor acquires the nationality of the adoptive parent is also generally recognized in legislation, but there are considerable variations from the norm.

ACQUISITION OF DOMICILE OR ANALOGOUS LINKS

Hudson, rather curiously, refers[54] to appointment as a teacher at a university as a mode recognized by the law, but omits other important items to some extent, at least, similar. Among the omissions are residence, domicile, and immigration *animo manendi*, with an intent to remain permanently. Similarly, it is common to permit resumption of nationality, for example where a marriage which changed nationality is now dissolved, by a renewal of domicile in the state concerned. Also akin to domicile is the conferment of nationality on members of particular ethnic or other defined groups belonging to the population of a state. In many states nationals of certain categories, such as naturalized citizens, citizens by registration (in Commonwealth countries), and analogous instances, may by acquisition of domicile abroad lose their nationality.[55]

In certain cases states have protested against legislation permitting involuntary naturalization of foreigners resident for a certain period on national territory or acquiring real estate in the territory.[56] However, it is important to determine the exact bases of such protests. Thus the United States was concerned to a great extent with the principle of voluntary expatriation. Other states, without being very articulate as to

---

[52] See Brownlie, *Basic Documents on Human Rights* (5th edn., 2006), 388.
[53] Sandifer, 29 *AJ* (1935), 259; *Yrbk. ILC* (1953), ii. 180–1. But cf. Weis, *Nationality* (2nd edn.), 110–11.
[54] *Yrbk. ILC* (1952), ii. 8. Cf. Austria, Citizenship Act 1949, Art. 2(4), 6.
[55] Cf. the United Nations Conv. on the Reduction of Statelessness, Art. 7.
[56] Reliance is placed on the materials set out in Weis, *Nationality*, pp. 103ff.

the reasons justifying their protests, were in substance reserving their rights and at the same time intimating that these matters were not within the discretion of the territorial sovereign.[57] The British view seems to have been that conferment of nationality on the basis of a number of years' residence, provided that due notice is given and a declaration of a contrary intention may be made, was lawful.[58] The available evidence does not indicate that states are hostile to domicile as a basis for conferment of nationality (as opposed to a temporary residence without *animus manendi*).

'VOLUNTARY' NATURALIZATION

The position is stated as follows by Weis:[59]

Naturalization in the narrower sense may be defined as the grant of nationality to an alien by a formal act, on the application of the *de cujus*. It is generally recognized as a mode of acquiring nationality. The conditions to be complied with for the grant of naturalization vary from country to country, but residence for a certain period of time would seem to be a fairly universal requisite.

Hudson remarks:[60] 'Naturalization must be based on an explicit voluntary act of the individual or of a person acting on his behalf'. Some jurists have concluded that prolonged residence is a precondition for a naturalization which conforms with international law.[61] Such a conclusion is probably sound, but in regard to *voluntary*[62] naturalization two points must be borne in mind. First, the voluntary nature of the act supplements other social and residential links. Not only is the act voluntary but, in regard to obtaining nationality, it is specific: it has that very objective. The element of deliberate association of individual and state is surely important and should rank with birth and descent, not to mention marriage, legitimation, and adoption. Secondly, while it is true that a considerable number of states allow naturalization on easy terms, the form of the legislation quite often presents the relaxed conditions as available exceptionally.[63]

---

[57] See the Law Officer's opinion quoted by Weis, *Nationality*, p. 104.

[58] See Weis, *Nationality*, p. 104 and *British Digest*, v. 28, 250. However, the British view may well have been that in appropriate circumstances what occurred was a voluntary naturalization.

[59] *Nationality*, p. 101.

[60] *Yrbk. ILC* (1952), ii. 8. His rubric is: 'Naturalization in the narrower sense. Option'. In his terminology naturalization means every nationality acquired subsequent to birth.

[61] See *infra*, pp. 407ff.

[62] Voluntary *sub modo*, since the individual does not have any control over the conditions under which naturalization may occur or under which it may be revoked. There is no right to naturalization unless this is conferred by treaty.

[63] See e.g. the Dominican Republic, Naturalization Act no. 1683 of 16 Apr. 1948; *Laws Concerning Nationality* (1954), 126, Art. 18: 'The President of the Republic may, as a special privilege, grant Dominican nationality by decree to such aliens as he considers worthy of exemption from the usual Dominican naturalization formalities because of services rendered to the Republic'.

NATIONALITY *EX NECESSITATE JURIS*

The rubric is convenient, but not in all respects satisfactory, since acquisition by marriage, legitimation, and adoption might be so described. However, the cases to be mentioned are sufficiently clear to justify the somewhat question-begging heading. The first group of generally recognized rules consists in modalities of the *jus soli*. There is in the legislation of many countries a provision that a child of parents unknown is presumed to have the nationality of the state on the territory of which it is found until the contrary is proved. Also in a great many instances it is provided that the rule applies to children born of parents of unknown nationality or who are stateless. The principal rule as to foundlings appears in the Hague Convention on Certain Questions relating to the Conflict of Nationality Laws, which provides in Article 14: 'A foundling is, until the contrary is proved, presumed to have been born on the territory of the State in which it was found'.[64]

5. LEGAL STATUS OF THE 'GENERAL PRINCIPLES'

A proportion, if not perhaps all, of the principles considered above are generally recognized principles as far as municipal law of the various states is concerned. Weis is very cautious in assessing such material in terms of state practice. He says:[65]

Concordance of municipal law does not yet create customary international law; a universal consensus of opinion of States is equally necessary. It is erroneous to attempt to establish rules of international law by methods of comparative law, or even to declare that rules of municipal law of different States which show a certain degree of uniformity are rules of international law.

This statement of principle is unexceptionable in so far as the reversal of the statement would result in a proposition obviously much too dogmatic. However, in substance, Weis is thought to underestimate the significance of legislation as evidence of the opinion of states. In the case of the territorial sea, the evidence of state practice available to the International Law Commission was chiefly in the form of legislation, and the comments of governments received by the Commission concentrated to some extent on the nature of their own legislation.

It may be said that, particularly in the field of nationality, the necessary *opinio juris et necessitatis* is lacking; but insistence on clear evidence of this may well produce capricious results. The fact is that municipal law overwhelmingly rests on significant links between the individual and the state. Such lack of uniformity as there

---

[64] See also the United Nations Conv. on the Reduction of Statelessness, 1961, Art. 2.

[65] *Nationality*, p. 98; see also p. 101. Similar views in Makarov, 74 Hague *Recueil* (1949, I), 304. Cf. Oppenheim, ii. 651ff.

is in nationality laws is explicable not in terms of a lack of *opinio juris*, but by reference to the fact that inevitably municipal law makes the attribution in the first place, and also to the occurrence of numerous permutations and hence possible points of conflict in legislation on a subject-matter so mobile and complex. There is no evidence that there is an absence of *opinio juris*, and, on the contrary, in spheres where conflict on the international plane is easily foreseeable, the rules are there to meet the case; witness the rules relating to children of diplomats and birth on ships and aircraft.

In view of considerations of this sort, the conclusions of the Court in the *Nottebohm* case are not particularly novel.[66] After considering the evidence[67] for the doctrine of the real or effective link favoured by the Court, the Judgment proceeds:[68]

The character thus recognized on the international level as pertaining to nationality is in no way inconsistent with the fact that international law leaves it to each State to lay down the rules governing the grant of its own nationality. The reason for this is that the diversity of demographic conditions has thus far made it impossible for any general agreement to be reached on the rules relating to nationality, although the latter by its very nature affects international relations. It has been considered that the best way of making such rules accord with the varying demographic conditions in different countries is to leave the fixing of such rules to the competence of each State. On the other hand, a State cannot claim that the rules it has thus laid down are entitled to recognition by another State unless it has acted in conformity with this general aim of making the legal bond of nationality accord with the individual's genuine connection with the State which assumes the defence of its citizens by means of protection as against other States.

. . . According to the practice of States, to arbitral and judicial decisions and to the opinions of writers, nationality is a legal bond having as its basis a social fact of attachment, a genuine connection of existence, interests and sentiments, together with the existence of reciprocal rights and duties. It may be said to constitute the juridical expression of the fact that the individual upon whom it is conferred, either directly by the law or as the result of an act of the authorities, is in fact more closely connected with the population of the State conferring nationality than with that of any other State. Conferred by a State, it only entitles that State to exercise protection *vis-à-vis* another State, if it constitutes a translation into juridical terms of the individual's connection with the State which has made him its national.

This important statement of principle and policy was supported by eleven members of the Court, there being only three dissenting opinions.

---

[66] The more precise implications of the decision are examined *infra*, pp. 407–18.

[67] See *infra*, pp. 409–12. The Court says, ICJ Reports (1955), 22: 'National laws reflect this tendency when, *inter alia*, they make naturalization dependent on conditions indicating the existence of a link, which may vary in their purpose or in their nature but which are essentially concerned with this idea. The Liechtenstein Law of 4 January 1934 is a good example'. For the Liechtenstein Law see ibid. 13–14.

[68] ICJ Reports (1955), 23.

6. THE LOGICAL APPLICATION OF RULES OF INTERNATIONAL LAW

The manner in which rules of international law often make use of the terms 'national' or 'nationality' has been noticed previously.[69] If these rules are to work effectively, or at all, there must be important limitations on the powers of individual states in the matter of attribution of persons for purposes of international law. Some of these limitations must now be considered.

MANDATED AND TRUST TERRITORIES[70]

In principle the status of the inhabitants of mandated and trust territories cannot be a domestic question. The mandatory does not have sovereignty over the territory,[71] nor does the administering authority over a trust territory.[72] It would seem that in principle the inhabitants cannot be nationals of the administering power, and thus, *in one sense*, they have no nationality. Weis observed:[73] 'The position of these persons is somewhat anomalous since they have, in consequence, no nationality in the sense of international law'. With respect this seems to be a *petitio principii*, since the absence of nationality *qua* internal law of the administering power, and the absence of nationality conferred by some other source, does not render the inhabitants stateless. For various purposes of the law they are attributable to the territory itself. Judicial decisions, such as *R.* v. *Ketter*,[74] do not take the matter very far, since they merely establish that the *de cujus* is not a national of the administering power, without deciding what his status is otherwise. The decisions, and particularly those concerning the former Mandated Territory of South West Africa,[75] often turn on questions of state succession. The existence of some system of attribution is recognized by the admission that the administering power may exercise the right of diplomatic protection in respect to the population of the territories.

STATES WITHOUT NATIONALITY LEGISLATION

It may happen that a state has not adopted any nationality laws on the modern pattern. Such cases are increasingly rare.[76] Historically, before the existence of general

---

[69] *Supra*, p. 383.

[70] See, in particular, Weis, *Nationality*, pp. 20–5; van Panhuys, *The Role of Nationality*, pp. 65–8. On ch. 11 of the UN Charter see *infra*, p. 573.

[71] Judge McNair, ICJ Reports (1950), 128, at 150; Art. 22 of the League Covenant.

[72] UN Charter, ch. 12.

[73] *Nationality*, p. 27.

[74] [1940] 1 KB 787; *Ann. Digest*, 9 (1938–40), no. 21.

[75] *Rimpelt* v. *Clarkson, Ann. Digest*, 14 (1947), no. 21; *Westphal et Uxor* v. *Conducting Officer of Southern Rhodesia* (1948), 2 SALR 18; *Ann. Digest*, 15 (1948), no. 54. See also, on the 'C' class mandates, *Wong Man On* v. *The Commonwealth and Others* (1952), 86 CLR 125; ILR 19 (1952), no. 58, on which see O'Connell, 31 BY (1954), 458.

[76] Cf. Parry, *Nationality and Citizenship Laws*, pp. 355ff.

statutory definitions, nationality was related to domicile (to some extent it still is), and in fact the two concepts were not differentiated. Recurrent examples of the absence of nationality legislation arise from the creation of new states. Of necessity—if they are states—they must possess a population which is their own. In a decision on the status of former Palestine citizens[77] prior to the enactment of the Israeli Nationality Law of 1952, a judge of the District Court of Tel-Aviv observed:[78]

So long as no law has been enacted providing otherwise, my view is that every individual who, on the date of the establishment of the State of Israel was resident in the territory which to-day constitutes the State of Israel, is also a national of Israel. Any other view must lead to the absurd result of a State without nationals—a phenomenon the existence of which has not yet been observed.

If a new state, relying on the absence of a municipal law, tried to deport a part of its permanent population, it would be acting in clear breach of its legal duties and might even involve its government in acts punishable as genocide.

PERSONS OUTSIDE NATIONAL LEGISLATION

The legislation of a number of states has categorized the population concerned into those who had a higher status, usually designated 'citizens', and others. Thus, in the case of the United Kingdom, the position is that the inhabitants of dependencies, whatever their internal status under the British Nationality Act 1981, are considered to have the status of national for purposes of international law.[79] In the past Italian law knew a distinction between citizens and colonial subjects, and in substance the latter were regarded as nationals in the international sphere. American law has the category '"non-citizen" nationals'. The legal necessity for making attribution in the absence of any internal provisions governing the status of a group, and also in cases where a deliberate denial of citizenship occurs, is apparent from two international cases. In an arbitral award of 22 January 1926 the status of Cayuga Indians, who had migrated from the United States to Canada, was established on the basis of factual connection. They were held to have become British nationals, and the assumption was that, for purposes of international law, they had previously been attached to the United States.[80] In *Kahane (Successor)* v. *Parisi and Austrian State*[81] the tribunal in substance regarded Romanian Jews as Romanian nationals, since Romania, while withholding citizenship, did not consider them to be stateless. However, the main point of the decision was to establish the meaning of the term 'ressortissant' in the Treaty of St Germain.[82]

Cases of state succession: see Chapter 29, section 5(a).

---

[77] Palestine citizenship had ceased to exist: *Hussein* v. *Inspector of Prisons*, 6 Nov. 1952; see ILR 17 (1950), 112.

[78] *A.B.* v. *M.B.*, ILR 17 (1950), 110. However, the same court in another case assumed the absence of nationality until the Nationality Law: *Oseri* v. *Oseri*, ibid. 111 (and cf. the *Shifris* case, ibid.). See also Rosenne, 81 *JDI* (1954), 4, n. 3, and cf. 6. See further *Malapa* v. *Public Prosecutor*, ILR 28, 80.

[79] See 52 *BY* (1981), 408 at 412.

[80] Award: 20 *AJ* (1926), 574; *RIAA* vi. 173.

[81] *Ann. Digest*, 5 (1929–30), no. 131.

[82] Arts. 249, 256.

7. STATE RESPONSIBILITY AND THE DOCTRINE OF THE GENUINE LINK

States cannot plead provisions of internal law in justification of international wrongs, and they are responsible for conditions on their territory which lead to the infliction of harm on other states. Delictual responsibility for damage arising from activities of persons on state territory will exist whether the delinquents are nationals or not.[83] However, many important duties of a specific nature are prescribed by reference to nationals of a state. Thus Oppenheim[84] states the existence of a duty to admit nationals expelled from other states and, the corollary, the duty not to expel nationals. Yet obviously *ad hoc* denationalization would provide a ready means of evading these duties. In appropriate circumstances responsibility would be created for the breach of duty if it were shown that the withdrawal of nationality was itself a part of the delictual conduct, facilitating the result.[85] Again, states could avoid rules governing the treatment of aliens if they could at *their discretion* impose nationality on aliens resident in or passing through state territory, however brief the sojourn. Similar considerations apply to the law of belligerent occupation[86] and the law of neutrality.[87]

The principles needed to solve this type of problem are simple enough if, on the facts of the case, the manipulation of the law of nationality was part and parcel of the delictual conduct. However, it is possible to postulate a general principle of *genuine* link relating to the *causa* for conferment of nationality (and the converse for deprivation), a principle distinguishable from that of effective link. Significantly enough, authors,[88] with support from state practice and the jurisprudence of international tribunals,[89] have often stated the rule that a diplomatic claim cannot be validly presented if it is based on a nationality which has been fraudulently acquired. Admittedly the rule is

---

[83] Cf. *Corfu Channel* case (Merits), ICJ Reports (1949), 4. As to activities outside state territory see McNair, *Opinions*, ii. 288–9.

[84] ii. 646, 695. See also Weis, *Nationality*, pp. 45–59 (very helpful); Whiteman, viii. 99, 367–8, 620–1; *British Digest*, vi. 112; and *Co-operative Committee on Japanese Canadians* v. *A.-G. for Canada*, *Ann. Digest*, 13 (1946), at 26.

[85] See Weis, *Nationality*, pp. 57, 127; Fischer Williams, 8 *BY* (1927), 55–60; Guggenheim, i. 318; Jennings, 20 *BY* (1939), 98 at 112–13. Generally on denationalization see *infra*, pp. 409, 560.

[86] Thus the German ordinance of 1942, which authorized the grant of nationality to certain classes of the population in territories not subject to German sovereignty but occupied by Germany, was not bound to be recognized by third states, as it was contrary to international law: see Guggenheim, ICJ Reports (1955), 54.

[87] In the *Nottebohm* case the Guatemalan argument, *per* Rolin, was that, because the motive of Nottebohm, a German national, was to acquire neutral status by his naturalization, there was no genuine link. This point was taken by the Court at the end of its Judgment, ICJ Reports (1955), 26. See *infra*, p. 412, n. 89. The dissenting judges regarded the question as a part of the issues concerning abuse of rights and fraud: ICJ Reports (1955), 32 (Klaestad), 48–9 (Read), 64–5 (Guggenheim). However, there was little or no evidence that Liechtenstein was attempting to avoid her neutral duties or that damage had been caused to Guatemala as a result of the naturalization. Nottebohm's motives could not easily be imputed to Liechtenstein.

[88] See, *inter alia*, Weis, *Nationality*, pp. 218–20, 246; Makarov, 74 Hague *Recueil* (1949, I), 331–4.

[89] See, *inter alia*, the *Salem* case, *Ann. Digest*, 6 (1931–2), no. 98; *Flegenheimer* claim, ILR 25 (1958, I), 91 at 98–101.

often formulated with the acts of the individual in mind, but in principle it is applicable to fraud on the part of the administration of a state. In the *Nottebohm* case[90] Guatemala contended that Liechtenstein had acted fraudulently in granting nationality to Nottebohm, and further, that Nottebohm himself acted fraudulently in applying for and obtaining the certificate of naturalization. The Court did not concern itself with these arguments explicitly, but, in adverting to Nottebohm's motive of acquiring neutral status at the end of the judgment,[91] the Court accepted the substance of the argument: in this context the doctrine of genuine link, in the narrow sense, and the broad concept of effective link were brought into close relation.[92] In a Dissenting Opinion, Judge Klaestad considered that as regards fraud by Nottebohm the issue could not be decided apart from the merits.[93] Judge Read, also dissenting, considered that he could not, in dealing with a plea in bar, look at the evidence as to fraud, but he did not regard the motive of avoiding belligerent status (if this were the case) as amounting to fraud.[94] Guggenheim, Judge *ad hoc*, expresses views similar to those of Read.[95]

In applying the principle of genuine link, two considerations are relevant. In the first place, there is a presumption of the validity of an act of naturalization, since the acts of governments are presumed to be in good faith. Secondly, this is reinforced by the concept of nationality as a status, since an act of conferment being acted upon is not to be invalidated except in very clear cases.[96] However, it is not entirely clear that the rule as to inquiry into fraudulent naturalization can be used to support a general principle of genuine link. The Conciliation Commission in the *Flegenheimer* claim justified the rule in terms of procedure and judicial necessity.[97]

8. NATIONALITY OF CLAIMS

When a government or court is concerned with the principle of diplomatic protection,[98] which rests primarily on the existence of the nationality of the claimant state attaching to the individual or corporation concerned both at the time of the alleged breach

---

[90] ICJ Reports (1955), 4.

[91] p. 26; see *supra*, n. 86.

[92] See further *infra*, p. 417.

[93] ICJ Reports (1955), 31–3.

[94] Ibid. 48–9. Read points out that at the time of naturalization Guatemala was making every effort to maintain neutrality. At p. 26, the judgement of the Court refers to 'his status as a national of a belligerent State', and, earlier, at p. 25, states that, when he applied for naturalization, Nottebohm had been a German national from the time of his birth. It would seem that the Court indirectly admits the fact that Nottebohm felt bound by his German ties. Cf. Read at p. 47 (surely he is inconsistent: cf. his views at pp. 48–9); and Guggenheim, at pp. 64–5.

[95] Ibid. 64–5. However, he regards the German nationality as the basis for 'belligerent status'.

[96] See Jennings, 121 Hague *Recueil* (1967, II), 458–60.

[97] ILR 25 (1958, I), 91 at 98.

[98] See further *infra*, pp. 477ff.

of duty[99] and at the time when the claim is presented, the issue is clearly placed on the international plane.[100] Situations will arise in which reference to the relevant national rules cannot give a solution.

In many cases the individual has nationality in both the claimant and defendant states. The discussions of this problem are generally presented by assigning the available evidence to two propositions, which are assumed to be incompatible. The first rule[101] is to be found in Article 4 of the Hague Convention of 1930: 'A State may not afford diplomatic protection to one of its nationals against a State whose nationality such person also possesses'. British practice appears to reflect this principle.[102] The other rule is that the effective nationality governs the question,[103] and has been applied by the Permanent Court of Arbitration in the *Canevaro* case,[104] the Italian–United States Conciliation Commission in the *Mergé* claim[105] and the United Nations Compensation Commission.[106] In the *Nottebohm* case the International Court stated,[107] with reference to 'the real and effective nationality': 'International arbitrators have decided in the same way numerous cases of dual nationality, where the question arose with regard to the exercise of protection'. The US Department of State applies the rule of effective nationality.[108]

Two points may be made. First, the principle of effective link is not to be regarded as forcing a choice. If the facts are consistent with a substantial connection with both states,[109] then the individual cannot expect international law to give him a privileged position as against other nationals of the two states—as would happen if he has a remedy in the international forum against his own government. Where, however, a choice can be made, then the principle of equality is not necessarily infringed, although it might be if tenuous links acknowledged by a municipal law were allowed to render the claim inadmissible. As a matter of principle the two rules usually cited in opposition

[99] The right of protection may extend to instances in which harm is merely apprehended.

[100] *Nottebohm* case, ICJ Reports (1955), 4 at 20–1.

[101] Proponents: van Panhuys, *The Role of Nationality*, pp. 73–81; Guggenheim, i. 312; Kunz, 54 *AJ* (1960), 558; Fitzmaurice, 92 Hague *Recueil* (1957, II), 193; *Annuaire de l'Inst.* (1965), ii. 260, 262; Rousseau, v. 127.

[102] See 52 *BY* (1981), 499; 53 *BY* (1982), 492–3; 54 *BY* (1983), 520–1, 524; 58 *BY* (1987), 622.

[103] See Weis, *Nationality*, pp. 196–7; Rousseau, v. 125–6; Rezek, 198 Hague *Recueil* (1986, III), 357–69.

[104] Hague Court Reports, p. 284; *RIAA* xi. 405.

[105] *RIAA* xiv. 236 at 241–8; ILR 22 (1955), 443 at 449–57 (the international jurisprudence is collected here). See also the cases set out in ILR 24 (1957), 452ff.; *Flegenheimer* claim, ibid. 25 (1958, I), at 147–50; *RIAA* xiv. 327 at 374–8; *Turri* claim, ILR 30, 371; the *Mathison* case, *RIAA* ix. 485; the *Schmeichler-Pagh* case, 92 *JDI* (1965), 689 (Danish Supr. Ct.); and *Shareholders of the Z.A.G.* v. *A. Bank*, ILR 45, 436 at 443 (Kammergericht, Berlin); the decision of the Iran–US Claims Tribunal, Case no. 18, ILR 75, p. 176 at pp. 188–94 (the Iranian members wrote a Diss. Op. (pp. 204–68) upholding the principle contained in Art. 4 of the Hague Conv.); and decisions of Chamber Two of the same Tribunal in *Esphahanian* v. *Bank Tejarat*, ILR 72, 478; *Golpira* v. *Iran*, ibid. 493; and *Saghi* v. *Iran*, 14 Iran–US CTR 3. See also the *Costa Rican Naturalization Provisions* Advisory Opinion, ILR 79, 283 at pp. 295–6 (paras. 35–38), 303 (para. 63) (Inter-Am. Ct. of Human Rights).

[106] *Claims Against Iraq* (Category 'A' Claims), ILR 109, 1 at 106–7 (paras. 29–30).

[107] ICJ Reports (1955), 22. Cf. the *Reparation case*, ibid. (1949), 186.

[108] See *Digest of US Practice* (1979), 693–4.

[109] See 39 *BY* (1963), 360–1.

are not incompatible.[110] The second point is that latitude may be allowed in this and other situations where the question is that of admissibility and the outcome does not directly affect the status of the individual.[111]

A different case of dual nationality is presented when one of two states of a dual national claims against a third state and the latter pleads that the other nationality of the individual is the effective or dominant nationality. A substantial jurisprudence supports the principle of the inopposability of the nationality of a third state in an international claim. In the *Salem* case[112] the tribunal found that Salem was a Persian national at the time of his American naturalization, and held that it was not open to Egypt to invoke the Persian nationality against the claimant state, the United States: 'the rule of International Law being that in a case of dual nationality a third Power is not entitled to contest the claim of one of the two Powers whose national is interested in the case by referring to the nationality of the other Power'. The tribunal referred to *Mackenzie* v. *Germany*,[113] but that case depended on a strict application of American law relating to expatriation and is not entirely in point. The same rule has been affirmed by the Italian–United States Conciliation Commission in its decision in the *Flegenheimer* claim.[114] However, in the *Mergé* claim the same Commission made it clear that for the Commission it was a question of treaty interpretation, and the working rule laid down was:[115] '(8) United States nationals who did not possess Italian nationality but the nationality of a third State can be considered "United States nationals" under the Treaty, even if their prevalent nationality was the nationality of the third State'.

The rule of inopposability invites some comment. In the *Salem* case the tribunal disapproved of the principle of effectiveness, whereas in the *Mergé* claim the commission approved of the principle where the dual nationality was that of the two states in dispute. One may ask whether and on what basis the principle is to be confined to certain permutations only. The short answer probably is, as it was in *Nottebohm*, that the issue is that of opposability as between the two parties. However, in treating the issue thus it must surely be relevant, on some facts at least, to point to the dominant nationality of a third state. This precise issue was not before the Court in *Nottebohm*, but the general principles propounded there extend logically to the present problem. The formulations

---

[110] Cf. Hyde, ii. 1131; and Verzijl, in the *Georges Pinson* case, *Ann. Digest*, 4 (1927–8), nos. 194, 195, quoted ILR 22 (1955), at 451. See also the *Spaulding* claim, *RIAA* xiv. 292; ILR 24 (1957), at 454–5.

[111] See *Feldman* v. *Mexico*, ILR 126, 1 at pp.16–17, NAFTA Tribunal.

[112] *Ann. Digest*, 6 (1931–2), no. 98; *RIAA* ii. 1161 at 1188.

[113] German–US Mixed Claims Commission; *RIAA* vii. 288; 20 *AJ* (1926), 595. See Schwarzenberger, *International Law* (3rd edn.), 366. The Umpire declared that 'while the American Department of State *may in the exercise of its sound discretion* well decline to issue a passport to, or intervene on behalf of, or otherwise extend diplomatic protection to an American by birth of foreign parents so long as he resides in the country of the nationality of his parents, it is not believed that it has, by departmental rule or otherwise asserted the power to strip of American citizenship one so born': *RIAA* vii, at 290. My italics.

[114] ILR 25 (1958, I), at 149–50; *RIAA* xiv, at 377.

[115] ILR 22 (1955), at 456; *RIAA* xiv, at 247. See also the *Vereano* claim ILR 24 (1957), 464; *RIAA* xiv. 321, and *Flegenheimer* claim, ILR 25 (1958, I), at 150; *RIAA* xiv, at p. 377.

of the Court refer in general terms to 'the courts of third States'.[116] However, it must be emphasized that the existence of a 'third nationality' will not be an automatic bar.

The last situation to consider is one in which prima facie the individual has one nationality or none. This was the problem in *Nottebohm*,[117] and the Court, by a large majority, stated and applied the principle of the real or effective link. In the *Flegenheimer* claim the Italian–United States Conciliation Commission distinguished *Nottebohm* on the ground that the case concerned opposability for the purposes of admitting the claim against Guatemala, but in substance the Commission disapproved of the principle of effective nationality as it was formulated by the Court in *Nottebohm*.[118] Any conclusion on the question obviously depends on the view held about the principle of effective nationality.[119]

9. DIPLOMATIC PROTECTION

It is trite learning that, with some exceptions,[120] states may only exercise diplomatic protection in respect of their nationals. The issue here is on the international plane and cannot be resolved by simple reference to the internal law of the states involved. A number of the problems have been discussed in terms of the question of the nationality of claims and, subsequently,[121] some comment will be made on the consequences of *Nottebohm* from the point of view of the effectiveness and availability of diplomatic protection. The assumption or, more correctly, the effect of the way in which the law is generally expressed is that diplomatic protection depends on nationality, but in reality the relation of the two is more complex. In the absence of formal evidence of ties with a particular state, the interest of a government in an individual, and especially the exercise or attempt to exercise protection in respect of that individual, may provide cogent evidence of nationality.[122] Moreover, if a right of protection arises by virtue of lawful administration of territory, then it would seem that nationality may be said to arise from the fact of the right of protection.[123] This is, in part at least, the justification

---

[116] ICJ Reports (1955), 22. Cf. ibid. 21. However, on p. 22 there are two such references and the latter reference is: 'the courts of third States, when they have before them an individual whom two other States hold to be their national…'. But the passages on pp. 22 and 23, taken as a whole, are general in effect: see *infra*, pp. 414–15. See also the *Laurent* case, Anglo-American Claims Commission, 1853, Hornby's *Report*, p. 299, where Mexican domicile of British subjects was a bar to claims against the United States, a view repudiated by the Commission in 1871: see *British Digest*, v. 315–22.

[117] Nottebohm had lost his German nationality as a consequence of the acquisition of Liechtenstein nationality in 1939. See Loewenfeld, 42 *Grot. Soc.* (1956), 13; Guggenheim, ICJ Reports (1955), 55.

[118] On the general significance of *Nottebohm* see *infra*, pp. 411ff.

[119] See *infra*, p. 407.

[120] *Infra*, pp. 477ff.

[121] *Infra*, p. 477.

[122] See also *infra*, p. 403, on the question of estoppel.

[123] In the *Cayuga Indians* case, the tribunal said, with reference to the Cayuga Indians in Canada: 'These Indians are British Nationals. They have been settled in Canada, under the protection of Great Britain and,

for treating British protected persons and similar categories of persons[124] in other systems as nationals of the administering power on the international plane. Persons not enjoying the protection of the state of their nationality (by internal law) are known as '*de facto* stateless', and the International Law Commission has considered means of alleviating their position.[125] If the effective link test were applied, then it might be that a refusal to give diplomatic protection would be regarded *on the international plane* as a severing of the more important links with the given state.

Three further observations are called for. First, it is important to notice, though it may seem obvious, that there is an element of circularity in much that is said about this subject. In the absence of any internal law provisions[126] or evidence of facts giving nationality by birth and other titles under internal provisions, a state may still claim to protect its population by virtue of its international competence, its sovereignty, and its very statehood (these three quantities being identical for the present purpose). If one accepts the existence of rules of attribution set by international law, then it is inelegant and illogical to say that diplomatic protection depends on 'nationality', especially when from the context the writer appears to refer to internal law. Secondly, what has been said is subject to the possible existence of the rule that neither state of a dual national may exercise diplomatic protection against the other.[127] Thirdly, diplomatic protection does not depend on nationality in either the internal or international sense in certain cases, because the right to protect may arise from a process of delegation by one sovereign to another or in other cases of representation in international relations.[128]

10. NATIONALITY BY ESTOPPEL

For the purpose of the discussion it is assumed, and the assumption is surely correct, that estoppel or *préclusion* is a principle of international law.[129] It seems that the principle can be applied to cases involving sovereignty over territory, and there is no reason

subsequently, of the Dominion of Canada, since the end of the eighteenth or early years of the nineteenth century'. (*RIAA* vi. 175 at 177). See also *Rothmann* v. *Austria and Hungary*, ibid. 253; *Margulies* v. *Austria and Hungary*, ibid. 279. Both these cases turn on the interpretation of an American statute, however. See further the *Mathison* case, ibid. ix. 485 at 490, 491–2; *Valeriani* v. *Amuna Bekri Sichera*, *Ann. Digest*, 8 (1935–7), no. 120; *Logan* v. *Styres et al.*, 20 DLR (2d). (1959), 416, ILR 27, 239 (as to the Six Nations Indians of Ontario); *British Digest*, v. 388–91.

[124] See Parry, *Nationality and Citizenship Laws*, pp. 11–15.

[125] See e.g. *Yrbk. ILC* (1954), i. 18 (246th Meeting); ibid. (1954), ii. 38 (draft article).

[126] See *supra*, p. 385.

[127] *Supra*, pp. 399–402.

[128] Poland conducted the external relations of Danzig by virtue of the treaty of 9 Nov. 1920. The whole question of protected states and criteria of statehood comes up. So also the diplomatic protection of the inhabitants of mandates arises from a concept akin to representation: cf. *Malapa* v. *Public Prosecutor*, ILR 28, 80. See further the *Pugh* claim, *Ann. Digest*, 7 (1933–4), no. 97; Parry, *Nationality and Citizenship Laws*, pp. 122–3.

[129] See Bowett, 33 *BY* (1957), 176–202; MacGibbon, 7 *ICLQ* (1958), 468.

why it should not be applied to the status of individuals. Indeed, in many cases where the basic facts concerning the individual are ambiguous,[130] the conduct of governments will provide the answer. Express declarations and admissions by diplomatic represent-atives may create an estoppel in the view of a court.[131] However, acts of administration of an incidental or routine nature, and in the absence of any dispute or apprehension thereof, may not have this effect. Thus in the *Nottebohm* case[132] Liechtenstein argued that Guatemala had recognized the naturalization in Liechtenstein on the basis of the entry of a visa in the Liechtenstein passport and official acts relating to the control of aliens. The Court observed:[133]

All of these acts have reference to the control of aliens in Guatemala and not to the exercise of diplomatic protection. When Nottebohm thus presented himself before the Guatemalan authorities, the latter had before them a private individual: there did not thus come into being any relationship between governments. There was nothing in all this to show that Guatemala then recognized that the naturalization conferred upon Nottebohm gave Liechtenstein any title to the exercise of protection.

Admissions and absence of dispute by the parties in the face of a court will normally[134] be relied upon by a tribunal in matters of nationality.[135] In some cases the tribunal has been prepared to rely on the conduct of governments in the absence of any declar-ation directly alluding to the issue. In the *Hendry* claim[136] the Mexican–United States General Claims Commission held that Mexico, the respondent state, was estopped from denying the American nationality of the deceased, Hendry, by reason of it hav-ing discharged him from employment because he was an American. However, in the *Flegenheimer* claim[137] the Italian–United States Conciliation Commission rejected an Italian argument that the claim was inadmissible because at the date of the acts com-plained of Flegenheimer's apparent nationality (in their phrase) was German, because he had used a German passport in dealings with the Italian authorities. This argument failed on the facts, but the Commission noted 'that the doctrine of apparent national-ity cannot be considered as accepted by the Law of Nations'.

---

[130] Cf. in a different sphere the *Temple* case, ICJ Reports (1961), 17.

[131] *Société De Bienfaisance* v. *Siag, Ann. Digest*, 6 (1931–2), no. 122; *Taamy* v. *Taamy*, ibid. 8 (1935–7), no. 128. Cf. the *Nottebohm* case, ICJ Reports (1955), 4 at 17–20.

[132] ICJ Reports (1955), 4 at 17–19. For a different conclusion see Judge Read's Diss. Op. at 47–8, and cf. Guggenheim, judge *ad hoc*, ibid. 53.

[133] At p. 18.

[134] But see 39 *BY* pp. 344–7, on nationality as a status. Presumably the doctrine of effective link would justify a court in refusing to rely on admissions (if it were free to do so under the terms of the *compromis*).

[135] *Expropriated Religious Properties* case, *RIAA* i. 7 at 46.

[136] *RIAA* iv. 616. Cf. the *Kelley* claim, ibid. 608. See also *British Digest*, v. 89, 369–70, 374, 379–80, 461.

[137] ILR 25 (1958, I), 91 at 151. The Commission went on: 'In international jurisprudence one finds decisions based on the "non concedit venire contra factum proprium" principle which...allows a Respondent State to object to the admissibility of a legal action directed against it by the national State of the allegedly injured party, when the latter has neglected to indicate his true nationality, or has concealed it, or has invoked another nationality at the time the fact giving rise to the dispute occurred, or when the national State has made erro-neous communications to another State thus fixing the conduct to be followed by the latter'.

11. COMPULSORY CHANGE OF NATIONALITY

Existing practice and jurisprudence does not support a general rule that deprivation of nationality is illegal.[138] The analogue of deprivation of nationality is provided by the cases described as compulsory change of nationality and 'collective naturalization'. The whole pattern of rules and the practice of states is based on the assumption that in terms of administration states set the conditions under which nationality is acquired and lost. The law concerned may call for expressions of will on the part of individuals directly, or indirectly, by their establishing residence or service in the armed forces, but the conditions are set by the law. Nevertheless tribunals have occasionally stated in terms that international law does not permit compulsory change of nationality.[139] The United States, the United Kingdom, France, and other states have often protested against 'forced naturalization provisions', as they are sometimes called, in the laws of various Latin American states.[140] This practice is bound up with the rule that international law does not permit states to impose their nationality on aliens resident abroad.[141] It is to be doubted whether this rule is correctly stated thus. The present writer would submit that the rule, and the practice referred to above, represents yet another aspect of the principle of effective link,[142] and is not to be stated unconditionally. The objective principle to emerge from the practice concerned is simply that nationality is not to be conferred on those already having a nationality unless the new nationality is based upon adequate links. Similarly, an illegal deprivation of nationality (for example on a racial basis) may become irreversible if the individual voluntarily establishes himself elsewhere at a stage when 'resumption' of the original citizenship would have been possible.[143]

---

[138] See the conclusions of Hudson, *Yrbk. ILC* (1952), ii. 10, and Weis, *Nationality*, pp. 123–4, 242. Standard works on international law do not state such a rule, but this is in some cases a consequence of their general position on the freedom of states in matters of nationality. See Oppenheim, ii. 657–8, and Guggenheim, i. 318. See also *Lempert v. Bonfol, Ann. Digest*, 7 (1933–4), no. 115 at pp. 293–4; *U.S. ex rel. Steinvorth v. Watkins*, ibid. 14 (1947), no. 41. An important fact, generally ignored by writers on the subject, is that municipal laws providing for deprivation normally provide for this in cases where residence and acts of allegiance have occurred abroad. See also the United Nations Conv. on the Reduction of Statelessness, 1961, Art. 8; Weis, *Nationality*, pp. 122–31; and the Universal Decl. of Human Rights, Art. 15, para. 2.

[139] *In re Rau, Ann. Digest*, 6 (1931–2), no. 124; decisions referred to ibid. 251n. (*Occelli* and *Barcena*, decisions of the Italian–Mexican and Spanish-Mexican Claims Commissions); *Compulsory Acquisition of Nationality Case*, ILR 32, 166, referring to Art. 1 of the Conv. on Conflict of Nationality Laws, 1930.

[140] e.g. laws referring to the purchase of land. For references: Briggs, pp. 461–2; and cf. Hudson, *Yrbk. ILC* (1952), ii. 8.

[141] See Morgenstern, note in *Ann. Digest*, 15 (1948), 211; and *In re Krüger*, ILR 18 (1951), no. 68 at p. 259 (referring to Universal Decl. of Human Rights, Art. 15, para. 2).

[142] Cf. Guggenheim, i. 317; Makarov, 74 Hague *Recueil* (1949, I), 305.

[143] See *Oppenheimer v. Cattermole* [1973] Ch. 264; CA; [1975] 2 WLR 347; ILR 72, 446; HL; Mann, 89 *LQR* (1973), 194; id., 48 *BY* (1976–7), 43–5, 50–1. Cf. *Loss of Nationality (Germany) Case*, ILR 45, 353. See further Hersch Lauterpacht, *International Law: Collected Papers*, iii (1977), 383–404.

12. THE FUNCTIONAL APPROACH
TO NATIONALITY

In spite of the reiteration from time to time of the principle that nationality depends on municipal law, it is common for legislation and judicial decisions to create functional nationality[144] whereby parts of national law are applied on the basis of allegiance, residence, and other connections. There seems to be general acquiescence in this splitting up of the legal content of nationality for particular purposes. Thus legislation in many countries has defined the enemy alien in functional terms and without dependence on the 'technical' nationality of the country in question. The control test has been widely applied to corporations[145] and goods in determining enemy character. Moreover, the use of factual tests occurs equally widely when the issue is one of the law of war and neutrality, for example taking under the law of prize.[146] However, France,[147] Germany, Italy, and Japan, among others, refer to formal nationality of individuals and the flag of vessels. Moreover, in the context of treaties rules are often functional rather than declaratory as to general status. Thus in the *IMCO* case[148] the issue was the interpretation of the phrase 'the largest ship-owning nations' in Article 28 of the Convention for the Establishment of the Inter-Governmental Maritime Consultative Organization, and the Advisory Opinion delivered rested on an inquiry into the legislative history of the provision and usage in other maritime conventions. In construing the phrase 'nationals of the United Nations' in the peace treaties after the Second World War, a court is likely to adopt an approach which will give effect to the intentions of the parties.[149] In the Geneva Convention on the Status of Refugees of 1951, Article 16, paragraph 3, provides that a refugee must be treated, in states parties to the Convention in which he is not habitually resident, on the same footing as a national of the state in which he is resident for certain purposes including access to the courts.[150] The Vienna Convention

---

[144] A different type of functionalism may occur when a forum is prepared to disregard dual nationality where policy demands a choice. Examples have already occurred earlier (see *supra*, pp. 398–9). Note also the provision in the staff regulations and rules of the United Nations which makes it mandatory for the Secretary-General to select a single nationality for the purpose of the staff rules: see *Julhiard* v. *Secretary-General of the United Nations*, ILR 22 (1955), 809.

[145] *Daimler* v. *Continental Tyre Co.* [1916] 2 AC 307; *Contomichalos* v. *Drossos* (1937), *Gazette des Tribunaux Mixtes d'Egypte*, 28 (1937–8), 49. See further Watts, 33 *BY* (1957), 78–83.

[146] *The Arisa, Ann. Digest*, 16 (1949), no. 206; *The Nyugat*, ILR 24 (1957), 916; *The S.S. Lea Lott*, ibid. 28, 652; *The Inginer N. Vlassopol*, ibid. 18 (1951), no. 223; *The Nordmeer, Ann. Digest*, 13 (1946), no. 172; *The Athinai*, ibid. 12 (1943–5), no. 128. Cf. *The Unitas* [1950] AC 536 on the conclusiveness of a vessel's flag and limitations thereon.

[147] However, by legislation and administrative action France has modified her position and introduced residence as an additional test.

[148] *Constitution of the Maritime Safety Committee of the Inter-Governmental Maritime Consultative Organization*, ICJ Reports (1960), 23; and see Simmonds, 12 *ICLQ* (1963), 56.

[149] See the *Mergé* claim, ILR 22 (1955), 456.

[150] See *Grundel* v. *Bryner*, ILR 24 (1957), 483.

on Diplomatic Relations[151] restricts the conferment of privileges and immunities in the case of members of the mission if they are nationals of the receiving state or 'permanently resident' therein.

13. THE PRINCIPLE OF EFFECTIVE LINK AND THE JUDGMENT IN THE *NOTTEBOHM* CASE

PROLOGUE

The thesis of the present writer is that, seen in a proper perspective, the decision in the *Nottebohm* case is a natural reflection of a fundamental concept which has long been inherent in the materials concerning nationality on the international plane. The doctrine of the effective link has been recognized for some time in continental literature[152] and the decisions of some municipal courts.[153] The recognition is commonly in connection with dual nationality, but the particular context of origin does not obscure its role as a general principle with a variety of possible applications. Several members of the International Law Commission were proponents of the principle (out of the context of dual nationality) during the fifth session.[154]

The reply of the German Government of 1929[155] to the Preparatory Committee of the Hague Codification Conference declared that 'a State has no power ... to confer its nationality on all the inhabitants of another State or on all foreigners entering its territory ... if the State confers its nationality on the subjects of other States without their request, when the persons concerned are not attached to it by any particular bond, as, for instance, origin, domicile or birth, the States concerned will not be bound to recognize such naturalization'. The internal legislation of states makes general use of residence, domicile, immigration *animo manendi* (with an intent to remain permanently), and membership of ethnic groups associated with the state territory, as connecting factors.[156] International law has rested on the same principles in dealing with the situations where a state has no nationality legislation and when certain parts of the population are outside nationality legislation. There is interesting evidence of reliance on settlement together with the existence of the political and diplomatic protection of

---

[151] See *supra*, p. 362.

[152] See Weis, *Nationality*, pp. 196–7; ILR 22 (1955), 452–4. See also Lipstein [1977] *Camb. LJ* 55–6, referring to Basdevant, 5 *Rev. de droit int. privé* (1909), 41, 60.

[153] *Magalhais* v. *Fernandes*, *Ann. Digest*, 10 (1941–2), no. 83; *In re Heinz S*, ibid. 11 (1919–42), no. 98. See also the *Johann Christoph* (1854), 2 Sp. Ecc. and Ad. 2; and the German Federal Constitutional Court, ILR 19 (1952), no. 56, p. 320; and see *supra*, p. 399. For a pronouncement to the contrary see *The King* v. *Burgess, ex parte Henry*, *Ann. Digest*, 8 (1935–7), no. 19 at p. 67.

[154] *Yrbk. ILC* (1953), i. 180, para. 24, p. 186, paras. 5, 7; p. 239, paras. 45, 46 (Yepes); p. 181, paras. 32, 33, p. 218, para. 63 (Zourek); p. 184, para. 57, p. 237, para. 24 (François); p. 239, para. 50 (Amado).

[155] *Supra*, p. 387.

[156] On the recognition of foreign divorce decrees by the English courts see *Indyka* v. *Indyka* [1969] 1 AC 33.

a particular sovereign. The principle of effective link is considered to underlie much of the state practice on state succession and the continuity of states and to support the concept of *ressortissant* found frequently in treaties.[157]

THE ISSUES IN THE *NOTTEBOHM* CASE (SECOND PHASE)[158]

In this case Liechtenstein claimed damages in respect of the acts of the Government of Guatemala in arresting, detaining, expelling, and refusing to readmit Nottebohm and in seizing and retaining his property without compensation. In the counter-memorial Guatemala asked the Court to declare the claim of Liechtenstein inadmissible, in part 'because Liechtenstein had failed to prove that M. Nottebohm, for whose protection it was acting, properly acquired Liechtenstein nationality in accordance with the law of that Principality; because even if such proof were provided, the legal provisions which would have been applied cannot be regarded as in conformity with international law; and because M. Nottebohm appears in any event not to have lost, or not validly to have lost, his German nationality'. In the final submissions, the third point was developed and the inadmissibility was contended for 'on the ground that M. Nottebohm appears to have solicited Liechtenstein nationality fraudulently, that is to say, with the sole object of acquiring the status of a neutral national before returning to Guatemala, and without any genuine intention to establish a durable link, excluding German nationality, between the Principality and himself'.

In its Judgment the Court regarded the plea relating to Nottebohm's nationality as fundamental. The issue was one of admissibility, and the Court observed:[159]

In order to decide upon the admissibility of the Application, the Court must ascertain whether the nationality conferred on Nottebohm by Liechtenstein by means of a naturalization which took place in the circumstances which have been described, can be validly invoked as against Guatemala, whether it bestows upon Liechtenstein a sufficient title to the exercise of protection in respect of Nottebohm as against Guatemala...what is involved is not recognition [of acquisition of Liechtenstein nationality][160] for all purposes but merely for the purposes of the admissibility of the Application, and, secondly, that what is involved is not recognition by all States but only by Guatemala.

---

[157] See Weis, *Nationality*, pp. 7–9; and *Kahane (Successor)* v. *Parisi and Austrian State, supra*, p. 396.

[158] ICJ Reports (1955), 4. Literature: Kunz, 54 *AJ* (1960), 536–71; Mervyn Jones, 5 *ICLQ* (1956), 230–44; Loewenfeld, 42 *Grot. Soc.* (1956), 5–22; de Visscher, 60 *RGDIP* (1956), 238–66; Bastid, *Revue critique de droit international privé*, 45 (1956), 607–33; Maury, 23 *Zeit. für ausl. und. int. Privatrecht* (1958), 515–34; Perrin, *Recueil d'études en hommage à Paul Guggenheim* (1968), 853–87; Grossen, *Festgabe Gutzwiller* (1959), 489–502; Makarov, 16 *Z.a.ö.R.u.V.* (1955–6), 407–26; Lipstein and Loewenfeld, in *Gedächtnisschrift Ludwig Marxer* (1963), 275–325; Knapp, *Ann. suisse* (1960), 147–78; De Burlet, *Revue belge de d.i.* (1976), 75–89; Hersch Lauterpacht, *International Law: Collected Papers*, iv (1978), 5–20. The effect of the decision is underestimated in O'Connell, ii. 678–81, and the evidence for the effective link principle is not reported.

[159] ICJ Reports (1955), 16–17. See also pp. 20, 21.

[160] The writer's parenthesis.

In the event, having applied the doctrine of the effective link to the facts, the Court held the claim to be inadmissible. Critics of the decision[161] and the dissenting judges[162] have pointed out that Guatemala had not argued the case on the basis that there was no effective link, and also that the precise *ratio* of the decision was the question of opposability as against Guatemala. The truth of this is obvious, but the effect of such formal arguments in limiting the significance of the judgment is negligible. The tendency to look for very precise grounds for decision is a common characteristic of judicial technique, and few jurists seriously believe that, apart from cases of treaty interpretation, the pronouncements of the Court can be placed in quarantine by formal devices.[163] Furthermore, the Court develops its views on the social bases of and legal policy concerning nationality in a manner which indicates the importance of the pronouncements on the genuine or effective link.[164] In any case, the fact that admissibility was involved was only a detour in the argument. As the Court said:[165] 'To exercise protection, to apply to the Court, is to place oneself on the plane of international law. It is international law which determines whether a State is entitled to exercise protection and to seise the Court'. The Court did not base its decision on estoppels as against Liechtenstein, but rested on the existence or not of a right of protection, an issue the outcome of which would logically affect states in general and not just the parties.[166] In view of all this it is not surprising to find authoritative acknowledgements of the general significance of the decision in the work of the International Law Commission[167] and other bodies.[168]

EVIDENCE OF THE 'LINK' DOCTRINE RELIED ON BY THE COURT

Commentators who are unsympathetic to the conclusions of the Court on questions of principle commonly emphasize the generality of the passages dealing with the preceding practice on which the Court purported to rely.[169] The survey is, in the view of the present writer, unsatisfactory if it is regarded in isolation and weighed simply as a material assessment of practice and jurisprudence. Moreover, to those who regard the

---

[161] e.g. Mervyn Jones, 5 *ICLQ* (1956), 238–9; Kunz, 54 *AJ* (1960), 541, 552; Weis, *Nationality*, pp. 176–81.

[162] See Judge Klaestad, ICJ Reports (1955), 30; Judge Read, ibid. 35, 38, 39–40; Guggenheim, judge *ad hoc*, p. 53 (cf. p. 62). See further the decision of the Italian–United States Conciliation Commission in the *Flegenheimer* claim, ILR 25 (1958, I), 91 at 148–50.

[163] Cf. the effect of the *Fisheries* case, ICJ Reports (1951), 116.

[164] See *supra*.

[165] p. 20.

[166] Cf. Guggenheim at pp. 60, 63, and Kunz, 54 *AJ* (1960), 564.

[167] *Yrbk. ILC* (1956), ii. 278–9 (draft article on nationality of ships and comment); ibid. (1956), i. 36, 66–7, 70–2 (p. 72, the genuine link test adopted by 9 votes to 3, with 3 abstentions). *Nottebohm* is not referred to expressly in these materials, but the terminology used, and the existence of a general problem beyond that of dual nationality, make the connection clear. For the replies of governments on the nationality of ships, see *Yrbk. ILC* (1956), ii. 14–16.

[168] See 51 *Annuaire de l'Inst.* (1965), ii. 269, Resol. II, Art. 4; and *Foreign Relations Law of the U.S., Restatement, Second*; 1962; para. 26 (and Briggs 61 *AJ* (1967), 214 for criticism).

[169] pp. 21–3. However, the Court does not, as a general rule, seem ready to undertake an examination of the details of practice and jurisprudence in its judgments; see the *Fisheries* case.

approach of the Court as a novelty,[170] the inadequacy of exposition in this connection is a particular source of disquiet. Three points would seem to be worth consideration here. First, to those who felt that the 'link' theory was self-evident, and well supported in the legal materials, it would not be apparent that a very full *exposé* was necessary. Secondly, the somewhat varied collection of propositions and references to previous practice reads not as a survey but rather as an attempt at further and better particulars as to the logical necessity of the *general principle* for which the Court was contending. The relevant section of the judgment commences[171] well before the 'survey of materials', and the logical burden of the section as a whole is that, to settle issues on the plane of international law, principles have to be applied apart from the rules of national laws. The major point is made on the basis of a 'general principle of international law' and not on the basis of a rule which could be classified as a customary rule of the usual sort. Thirdly, the critics of the judgment are probably seeking materials which support the 'link' theory explicitly as a specific rule. Not all the materials support any rule in this way, but there is much material, surveyed earlier in this chapter, which supports the general principle. There was very little on the international plane which expressly *denied* the effective link doctrine, and the incidental rejection of it in the *Salem* case[172] was regarded by contemporaries as a novelty.[173]

At any rate, it is true that, taken individually, the pieces of evidence deployed by the Court are not completely cogent. Thus it is plausible for Judge Read[174] to say that the provision on dual nationality in the Statute of the Court[175] has nothing to do with diplomatic protection. The Court was obviously as aware of this as he was, but the majority judges were concerned with a general principle. Again, the references by the Court[176] to bilateral treaties concluded by the United States with other states since 1868, the so-called Bancroft Treaties, and to the Pan-American Convention of 13 August 1906, do not provide unequivocal evidence on the effective link as a part of general international law. As Judge Read points out,[177] the treaty restrictions on the power to protect naturalized persons who return to their country of origin may indicate a lack of reliance on a rule of positive law.

---

[170] See Mervyn Jones, 5 *ICLQ* (1956), 240–2; Kunz, 54 *AJ* (1960), 552, 555; Judge Read, ICJ Reports (1955), 39–40; Perrin, *Recueil*, p. 874.

[171] At p. 20.

[172] *Supra*, pp. 389–90.

[173] See *Ann. Digest*, 6 (1931–2), no. 98 at p. 192, note by Hersch Lauterpacht, and Mervyn Jones, 5 *ICLQ* (1956), 242, n. 14.

[174] Diss. op., ICJ Reports (1955), 40.

[175] Art. 3 provides: '1. The Court shall consist of fifteen members, no two of whom may be nationals of the same State. 2. A person who for the purposes of membership in the Court could be regarded as a national of more than one State shall be deemed to be a national of the one in which he ordinarily exercises civil and political rights'. See the judgment of the Ct. at p. 22.

[176] pp. 22–3.

[177] p. 41. He also says: 'even within that part of the Western hemisphere which is South of the 49th Parallel, the ratifications of the multilateral Convention were not sufficiently general to indicate consensus of the countries concerned'. See also Guggenheim, i (1953), 59–60; and Kunz, 54 *AJ* (1960), 557.

Judge Read[178] and others[179] have also contended that the Court[180] relied irrelevantly on the principles adopted by arbitral tribunals in dealing with cases of double nationality,[181] since in the *Nottebohm* case the facts did not present this problem. Nottebohm either had Liechtenstein nationality or none. However, in establishing logical positions it may be that the critics have the onus of proving why the doctrine of effectiveness only applies to certain permutations of fact. Commentators who regard the rejection of the doctrine of effective link in the *Salem* case as odd do not explain the oddity by saying that in that case Egypt was pleading the nationality of a third state.[182] The principle of effectiveness is thus not restricted to dual nationality of the two parties to the dispute. If the principle exists it applies to the *Nottebohm* permutation also.

Both the majority and the minority opinions of the Court almost completely neglect the state practice apart from conventions.[183] The Judgment of the Court merely states:[184]

The practice of certain States which refrain from exercising protection in favour of a naturalized person when the latter has in fact, by his prolonged absence, severed his links with what is no longer for him anything but his nominal country, manifests the view of these States that, in order to be capable of being invoked against another State, nationality must correspond with the factual situation.

This consideration is far from conclusive.[185] Both sides seem to ignore the cumulative effect of the evidence set out earlier.[186] However, Guggenheim, Judge *ad hoc*, reviews a number of issues, including the proposition that ownership of land is not by itself a sufficient legal title for the grant of nationality, and remarks,[187] 'all these situations are, however, somewhat exceptional'. One may doubt if they are exceptional, but the point is that the *principle* of inopposability is accepted by him in this passage.

Judge Read completes his review of the evidence relied on by the majority with the statement:[188] 'It is noteworthy that, apart from the cases of double nationality, no instance has been cited to the Court in which a State has successfully refused to recognize that nationality, lawfully conferred and maintained, did not give rise to a right of diplomatic protection'. Here the phrase 'lawfully conferred' takes much force

---

[178] At pp. 41–2.

[179] See Kunz, 54 *AJ* (1960), 556–9; Guggenheim, ICJ Reports (1955), 59.

[180] p. 22.

[181] See *supra*, p. 390, and the *Mergé* claim, ILR 22 (1955), 443 at 450–2; *RIAA* xiv. 236 at 246–8.

[182] See Mervyn Jones, 5 *ICLQ* (1956), 242 n. 14.

[183] There is a reference by the Court to national laws on naturalization: 'National laws reflect this tendency when, *inter alia*, they make naturalization dependent on conditions indicating the existence of a link...'. (p. 22). Kunz (54 *AJ* (1960), 553) and Mervyn Jones (5 *ICLQ* (1956), 236) are much too grudging in their assessment of national legislation; see *supra*, pp. 378ff.

[184] p. 22.

[185] See *supra*, p. 403.

[186] *Supra*, pp. 385ff.

[187] p. 54.

[188] p. 42.

away from the proposition: no doubt Judge Read would agree that the imposition of nationality on aliens in transit through national territory is unlawful or, at least, inopposable. Thus, the question is begged. The non-opposability of nationality in internal law is obscured in the law of war and neutrality by the use of other or of supplementary connecting factors, but the effect is the same.[189] Enemy control may displace the 'nationality' of a person or goods or vessels for purposes of international law. Moreover, state practice has for long recognized the converse of Read's statement: absence of internal conferment does not lead to absence of a power of diplomatic protection.[190]

THE PRINCIPLE APPLIED TO THE FACTS

Nottebohm was German by birth and was still a German national when he applied for naturalization in Liechtenstein in October 1939. He had left Germany in 1905, but maintained business connections with that country. As a consequence of naturalization in Liechtenstein he lost his German nationality.[191] The Court decided that the effective nationality was not that of Liechtenstein (but without characterizing the links with Guatemala in terms of effective nationality):[192]

He had been settled in Guatemala for 34 years. He had carried on his activities there. It was the main seat of his interests. He returned there shortly after his naturalization, and it remained the centre of his interests and of his business activities. He stayed there until his removal as a result of war measures in 1943. He subsequently attempted to return there, and he now complains of Guatemala's refusal to admit him...In contrast, his actual connections with Liechtenstein were extremely tenuous...If Nottebohm went to Liechtenstein in 1946, this was because of the refusal of Guatemala to admit him...These facts clearly establish, on the one hand, the absence of any bond of attachment between Nottebohm and Liechtenstein and, on the other hand, the existence of a long-standing and close connection between him and Guatemala, a link which his naturalization in no way weakened.

The Court went on to consider the motive for and circumstances of the naturalization.[193]

The application of the principle of the link or *rattachement* to the facts of this case has been criticized from two points of view. The first approach deals with the alleged subjectivity of the test and is bound up with consideration of its attributes from the point of view of policy. The second approach is to say that *at the material time* the effective nationality was that of Liechtenstein. The question whether an absence of connection

---

[189] It is significant that the Court states at the end of the judgment (p. 26): 'Naturalization was asked for not so much for the purpose of obtaining a legal recognition of Nottebohm's membership in fact in the population of Liechtenstein, as it was to enable him to substitute for his status as a national of the belligerent State that of a national of a neutral State, with the sole aim of thus coming within the protection of Liechtenstein. ...Guatemala is under no obligation to recognize a nationality granted in such circumstances'. See also Hudson, 50 *AJ* (1956), 1 at 5. For the seeker after the narrowest *ratio decidendi* this would seem to be the answer.

[190] *Supra*, p. 397.

[191] See Guggenheim, ICJ Reports (1955), 55.

[192] pp. 25–6.

[193] *Supra*, n. 188.

when the nationality was originally acquired can be cured by later events[194] was not considered by the Court. As a question of principle it is surely consonant with the doctrine of effective link to permit curing by subsequent changes. In its Judgment the Court approves the view 'that, in order to be capable of being invoked against another State, nationality must correspond with the factual situation'. The events which related to the merits of the dispute occurred between 1943 and 1951, and for nine years, between 1946 and the beginning of the case, Nottebohm had resided in Liechtenstein. His applications to return to Guatemala in 1946 could perhaps be explained by the necessity to protect his interests and property there.[195] However, while it might be argued that in 1955 his effective nationality was that of Liechtenstein, when the principal losses and acts complained of occurred it was not:[196] it is doubtful, to say the least, if after receiving a wrong a national can then take on another nationality and, after a lapse of time, *retroactively* acquire a champion in the form of a 'foreign' state against the state of his former nationality.

THE CRITERIA OF EFFECTIVENESS

The principle of real and effective nationality applied by the Court is one of relatively close, factual connection. The Court said:[197]

International arbitrators have decided in the same way numerous cases of dual nationality...They have given their preference to the real and effective nationality,[198] that which accorded with the facts, that based on stronger factual ties between the person concerned and one of the States whose nationality is involved. Different factors are taken into consideration, and their importance will vary from one case to the next: the habitual residence of the individual concerned is an important factor,[199] but there are other factors such as the centre of his interests, his family ties, his participation in public life, attachment shown by him for a given country and inculcated in his children, etc.

Further on,[200] the Court refers to the practice of certain states which 'manifests the view of these States that...nationality must correspond with the factual situation'. On the next page[201] of the Judgment, in the same general context, there are references to the individual's 'genuine connection' and 'genuine connections' with the state, to nationality as based upon 'a social fact of attachment,[202] a genuine connection of existence,

---

[194] Mervyn Jones, 5 *ICLQ* (1956), 241 n. 8, thinks not.

[195] See Judge Read, ICJ Reports (1955), 44.

[196] The latest decree relating to expropriation occurred in 1951. The application of the relevant decrees to Nottebohm's property occurred as early as 1944 at least. The series of decrees concerning the property of aliens started in 1941.

[197] ICJ Reports (1955), 22. See also Córdova, *Yrbk. ILC* (1954), ii. 42 at 50; the Secretariat survey, ibid. 52 at 108, paras. 365–6.

[198] The phrase recurs later on the same page of the judgment and twice on p. 24.

[199] See Córdova, *Yrbk. ILC* (1954), ii. 50, for the precedents.

[200] p. 22.

[201] p. 23.

[202] Cf. p. 26, reference to 'bond of attachment'.

interests and sentiments, together with the existence of reciprocal rights and duties',
and to nationality as 'the juridical expression of the fact that the individual…is in fact
more closely connected[203] with the population of the State conferring nationality than
with that of any other state'.

In discussion of the draft Convention on the Elimination, and the Reduction, of
Future Statelessness at its fifth session, the International Law Commission was concerned to discover the criteria which states would accept as creating a sufficient link
between individual and state. Criticism, in relation to the reduction of future statelessness, was directed at a draft article which in part provided that[204] 'if a person does
not acquire any nationality at birth, either *jure soli* or *jure sanguinis*, he shall subsequently acquire the nationality of the State in whose territory he is born'. As a result
of the criticism the final draft[205] contained the provision (in para. 2): 'The national
law of the Party may make preservation of such nationality dependent on the person
being normally resident in its territory until the age of eighteen, and provide that to
retain nationality he must comply with such other conditions as are required from
all persons born in the Party's territory'. While the provision is rather tangential, it
reflects the concern of the Commission to provide for the establishment of sufficiently
close links. Yepes pointed out in discussion that *jus soli* countries made acquisition
by birth conditional: the place of birth was a matter of chance, and nationality could
not be left to chance.[206] In his phrase,[207] 'there must be a genuine relation between
the individual and the nation', and he proposed habitual residence, the domicile of the
parents, and option as links.[208] Žourek spoke of the need to prove the 'solidity' of the
individual's link with the state, and suggested that this was not provided by 'a mere
formality—the place of birth and the fact of residence'.[209] François stated[210] that the
draft article[211] resting on an unconditional *jus soli* 'was contrary to a basic principle of
law to which the Netherlands attached great importance, namely, that there should be
a link between countries and the individuals to whom they granted their nationality'.
In general the discussion showed the difficulty of codifying the factual criteria. Thus
Córdova's draft on the reduction of future statelessness[212] set out the links sufficient to
support nationality of the country of birth, viz., residence until military age, option

[203] See also, on p. 24 of the judgment, the references to 'factual connections between Nottebohm and
Liechtenstein', and the 'social fact of a connection': pp. 22ff. contain several other references to 'connection'
and 'link'.

[204] See *Yrbk. ILC* (1953), ii. 187.

[205] Ibid. 228.

[206] Ibid. (1953), i. 180, para. 24.

[207] Ibid. 186, para. 7 (and para. 5).

[208] Ibid. 239, para. 45. See the draft proposals at pp. 215, 220.

[209] See *Yrbk. ILC* (1953), ii. 218, para. 63. Cf. ibid. 181, para. 32, 33. Cf. Amado, p. 239, para. 50, where he
speaks of 'a sufficient link'.

[210] Ibid. 184, para. 57.

[211] Ibid. (1953), ii. 170. See Córdova's justification for this form in the draft on elimination of future statelessness, ibid. 174–5.

[212] Ibid. 187 (and see the comment by the rapporteur at pp. 188–9).

for that nationality on reaching military age, and service in the armed forces of that state. These criteria received considerable criticism.[213]

The principle, as expounded by the Court in *Nottebohm*, rests on all relevant facts in the given case, although habitual residence is an important factor. Three questions as to its application require immediate notice. First, it is said by Judge Read[214] that the criteria on which it rests are vague and subjective, and he states: 'Nationality, and the relation between a citizen and the State to which he owes allegiance, are of such a character that they demand certainty... There must be objective tests, readily established, for the existence and recognition of the status'. The form which such comment takes has certain flaws. The object of the test—to discover the effective nationality—is neither vague nor subjective. The 'tests' referred to are merely the relevant facts, which are 'objective'. It is true that there is the element of appreciation, of assessing facts, and this may lead to subjectivity. Yet if the difficulties of applying rules to facts were a bar to useful application of rules many significant outcrops of jurisprudence would stand as monuments to futility. Moreover, Judge Read himself applies the tests[215] and reaches a conclusion which he clearly regards as logical and definite.[216] Ignoring the fundamental incongruity of the principle of autonomy on the international plane, one may question the assumption that reference to national laws gives certain and objective criteria. In the *Nottebohm* situation this was hardly the case; even after investigation of the facts on the issue of admissibility by the Court, not all was clear: the obvious point surely is that in regard to cosmopolitans like Nottebohm no test is going to lead to nice results. A second question arising from the decision is whether an effective nationality can exist in the absence of a formal status in the internal law of the state concerned.[217] The statements of principle in the Judgment and the finding[218] that Nottebohm's close connection was with Guatemala lead to the conclusion that it can so exist. Of course, in many of the cases which lead to disputes, the facts on which internal law depends for its determination may not be established, or it may not be possible to establish the fact of the act of government creating the formal link. In many cases it will not be clear whether loss of nationality occurred *ipso facto* or only from the date of the issue of a certificate or other declaration of status by the state concerned.[219] Thirdly, it may be asked whether naturalization has certain special features in the context of effective nationality: this leads on to the next rubric, and will be dealt with thereunder.

---

[213] Ibid. (1953), i. 213ff.

[214] ICJ Reports (1955), 46. See also Guggenheim, ibid. 55–7.

[215] However, he uses his own terminology, referring to 'the establishment of legal relationships', and 'a series of legal relationships, rights and duties'.

[216] ICJ Reports (1955), 46–8.

[217] Reuter, 103 Hague *Recueil* (1961, II), 612, thinks not.

[218] ICJ Reports (1955), 26.

[219] Cf. Guggenheim, ICJ Reports (1955), 55, on Nottebohm's loss of German nationality.

EFFECTIVE LINKS AND THE INTERESTS OF GOVERNMENTS

The Judgment in *Nottebohm* presents the principle of effective nationality in terms of the links between the life of the person concerned and the population or community of a state and of a 'social fact of attachment'.[220] However, members of the International Law Commission who espoused the same principle (admittedly in a different context) during its fifth session were prone to stress the duality of relevant links, and to show concern for the loyalty of the individual toward the state, which on the international plane had the responsibility for protection of the individual. Thus Yepes[221] referred to 'a genuine relationship between the individual and the nation'. In his dissenting opinion Judge Read in effect provided his own interpretation of the principle of effective link, although he opposed the principle as such. In his words,[222] 'the State is a concept broad enough to include not merely the territory and its inhabitants but also those of its citizens who are resident abroad but linked to it by allegiance. ... In the case of many countries such as China, France, the United Kingdom and the Netherlands, the non-resident citizens form an important part of the body politic, and are numbered in their hundreds of thousands or millions'. In his view Nottebohm by his own conduct and that of Liechtenstein became a member of that body politic, 'the country of his allegiance'. These considerations would seem to be perfectly valid, and the general formulations of the Court could accommodate the more 'political' factors.[223] Certainly the reference by the Court to interests and intentions of the individual could include questions of allegiance. In a case where a businessman has international connections and social mobility, residence and interests may provide no choice and political ties may then take on particular significance.

In connection with political ties it is perhaps justifiable to regard the voluntary creation of such ties between individual and state by naturalization as a link of special strength. This consideration appears to have weighed with Judge Read,[224] and the Judgment of the Court is not really inimical to such a view. On the facts *as the Court saw them* the naturalization was not a real attempt to join Liechtenstein as a community, and, by reason of the motive involved, 'it was lacking in the genuineness requisite to an act of such importance'.[225] The matter of political ties may also arise in a rather different light when acts of protection and 'holding out' as a national have occurred. Where the facts of the individual connections are ambiguous the conduct of

---

[220] See esp. p. 23; quoted *supra*, p. 413. But at p. 24 the Court uses the phrase 'bond of allegiance'.

[221] *Yrbk. ILC* (1953), i. 186, para. 7. And see *supra*, p. 409.

[222] ICJ Reports (1955), 44–5. Cf. p. 46 for a further reference to allegiance.

[223] The Court includes, in a list of relevant factors, 'attachment shown by him for a given country and inculcated in his children'; Judgment, at p. 22. See also the *Canevaro* case, *RIAA* xi. 405, in which exercise of political rights and request to hold public office were important factors. Cf. the form of certain provisions in the United Nations Conv. on Reduction of Statelessness, 1961, especially Art. 8.

[224] ICJ Reports (1955), 44. See also *supra*, p. 393, and cf. Córdova, *Yrbk. ILC* (1953), ii. 189, para. J.

[225] ICJ Reports (1955), 26.

a government may provide a determinant.[226] Here, however, we approach the realm of estoppel, and, in principle, estoppel properly so-called could produce a result incompatible with the principle of effective link.

THE RELATION OF GENUINE AND EFFECTIVE LINKS

There is general agreement that naturalization on the basis of fraud or duress is voidable, and this rule relates to the question of genuine link in a narrow context.[227] In the *Nottebohm* Judgment a broader doctrine of 'genuine connection'[228] appears in intimate relation with the, more frequent, references to 'real and effective nationality' and the like. It is probably correct to treat the two elements as aspects of the same thing, the references to genuineness being intended to emphasize that the quality and significance of factual relations with a given country are to be taken into account. Where the individual has material and family connections in several states, inquiry into motive and intentions may become important. In the *Nottebohm* decision itself the Court gives some prominence at the end of its Judgment to the purpose for which, in its view, Nottebohm sought naturalization in a neutral state.[229] As a general principle 'genuine connection' is valuable, but in relation to special problems the principle may beg too many questions, presenting issues rather than providing solutions.[230]

THE EFFECT OF *NOTTEBOHM* ON DIPLOMATIC PROTECTION

Of the implications of the *Nottebohm* Judgment in the realm of policy, critics have concentrated on what is, in their view, a very unfortunate severance of diplomatic protection and nationality.[231] The practical result of the decision is seen to be a narrowing of the ambit of diplomatic protection.[232] Paul de Visscher,[233] on the other hand, takes the view that the field of diplomatic protection seems to have been extended by the principle of effective nationality. Before commenting on these opinions it may be remarked that the consequences of an affirmation of the principle of effective nationality are unlikely to be radical, because in a vast number of cases the effective nationality matches the formal nationality. In difficult cases like that of *Nottebohm* it will be the case that the approach on the basis of national rules will produce results no more

---

[226] Cf. Judge Read, ibid. 44–5, referring *inter alia* to Nottebohm obtaining the diplomatic protection of Liechtenstein in Oct. 1943, and on commencement of the confiscation of his properties.

[227] *Supra*, p. 387.

[228] ICJ Reports (1955), 23 (phrase used twice).

[229] See *supra*, p. 411, n. 188.

[230] See the *I.M.C.O.* case, 1960: Pleadings, Oral Arguments and Documents, pp. 364–6 (Seyersted); 383 (Vallat). The whole question of registration of ships remains delicate, but see *infra*, p. 410, for the provision in Art. 5 of the Conv. on the High Seas.

[231] See Judge Read, ICJ Reports (1955), 46.

[232] See Mervyn Jones, 5 *ICLQ* (1956), 244; Eagleton, 50 *AJ* (1956), 919–20; *Annuaire de l'Inst.* (1965), i. 75–80, 167–8; Knapp, *Ann. suisse* (1960), 147–78.

[233] 60 *RGDIP* (1956), 263–4.

certain than the 'real link' method. In many of these cases the national law or laws do not stand in isolation, but are overlaid by many other equally relevant facts, presumptions, and evidence of official acts and declarations: in establishing a proper basis for protection the 'real link' method probably gives reasonably satisfactory answers. Futhermore, if the exercise of diplomatic protection ignores the requirement of genuine connection, the state which it sought to hold to account may refuse to recognize the right of protection. Long-resident refugees are an important source of problems, and it would seem likely that the link doctrine is potentially more helpful here than reference to national laws. The latter method leaves the refugee stateless or links him to a community which he has tried to quit permanently in many cases.

Fears that effective nationality produces a narrow regime will be the less justified if the doctrine is applied in a liberal way. There is probably nothing in *Nottebohm* or the other sources of principle to prevent an approach which is not too exacting in the matter of effectiveness. The application of the principle in *Nottebohm* appeared to be strict because of the factors involved: the individual concerned had a variety of links with two states, the issue was between the two best candidates, and on the Court's view of the facts the question of *genuine* attachment was prominent.[234] Professor Jennings[235] has remarked: 'If the law is to work in practice... the presumption created by a juridical fact such as voluntary naturalization must be regarded by any tribunal as a very strong presumption, not easily rebutted'.

On 30 August 1961 there was signed the United Nations Convention on the Reduction of Statelessness,[236] the detailed provisions of which rely on various criteria of factual connection and evidence of allegiance. The United Nations Conference which gave rise to the Convention also adopted a resolution[237] recommending 'that persons who are stateless *de facto* should as far as possible be treated as stateless *de jure* to enable them to acquire an effective nationality'. Dr Weis remarks[238] that the Convention and recommendation 'clearly reflect the importance which is attached to an increasing degree to effectiveness of nationality'.

---

[234] *Supra*, p. 417.
[235] 121 Hague *Recueil* (1967, II), 459.
[236] Text: 11 *ICLQ* (1962), 1090. In force 1975.
[237] Ibid. 1096.
[238] Ibid. 1073 at 1087. He points out that delegates at the Conference tended to speak in terms of effective links: references, ibid., n. 38.

20

SOME RULES OF ATTRIBUTION: CORPORATIONS AND SPECIFIC ASSETS

1. GENERAL ASPECTS

The assignment of persons and property to particular legal persons is normally approached through the concept of nationality and primarily the nationality of individuals and corporations for purposes of diplomatic protection. Yet it is clear that the problem of attribution must be solved in a variety of contexts including rules concerning jurisdiction and jurisdictional immunities. It has lately become apparent that the problems of jurisdiction can be solved on a satisfactory basis by the use of the principle of substantial connection affirmed in the *Nottebohm* case.[1] Analogues of 'nationality for purposes of diplomatic protection' can be multiplied: in various contexts, 'substantial connection' is employed as a substitute for the concept of nationality, or 'nationality', when used, is defined in terms of substantial connection. The necessity for rules of attribution of a functional kind, not tied to an unworkable principle[2] of reference to municipal law and the autonomy of states in matters of 'nationality', is apparent when the issues of 'nationality' on the plane of international law are related to corporations, ships, aircraft, other national assets, and the assets of international organizations.

2. CORPORATIONS[3]

The attribution of legal persons (*personnes morales*) to a particular state for the purpose of applying a rule of domestic or international law is commonly based upon the concept of nationality. The borrowing of a concept developed in relation to individuals

---

[1] *Supra*, p. 407.

[2] *Supra*, pp. 373ff.

[3] On the issues of diplomatic protection and admissibility of claims see the literature cited *infra*, p. 459. Otherwise see Ginther, 15 *Öst. Z. für öff. R.* (1966), 27–59; Whiteman, viii. 17–22; Schwarzenberger, *International Law*, i (3rd edn., 1957), 388–412; Walker, 50 *AJ* (1956), 373–93; Vagts, 74 *Harv. LR* (1961),

is awkward in some respects but is now well established. A major point of distinction is the absence of legislative provisions in municipal law systems which create a national status for corporations: domestic nationality laws do not concern themselves with corporations. The consequences of this are twofold. First, the nationality must be derived either from the fact of incorporation, i.e. creation as a legal person, within the given system of domestic law, or from various links including the centre of administration (*siège social*) and the national basis of ownership and control. Secondly, the content of the nationality tends to depend on the context of the particular rule of law involved: nationality appears more as a functional attribution or tracing and less as a formal and general status of the kind relating to individuals.

A major issue concerning corporations is the right to exercise diplomatic protection in respect of the corporation and its shareholders. It is convenient to reserve this question for the discussion of admissibility of claims in Chapter 22.

Rules of municipal law may make use of the concept of nationality of legal persons even in the absence of special legislation creating such a status as such. Important areas of domestic law referring to the nationality of corporations are constitutional law, private international law (conflict of laws), the law relating to trading with the enemy, and taxation.

On the plane of international law and relations a great many treaty provisions define 'nationals' to include corporations (with functions of private law) for various purposes. Treaty provisions may or may not adopt the conflict of laws rule that the law of the place of creation determines whether an association has legal personality. For the purposes of the particular treaty unincorporated associations, including partnerships, may be assimilated to corporations. Public corporations may also be included.[4]

Treaties of commerce create standards of treatment in relation to 'nationals' and, or, 'companies' of the contracting parties. The Treaty of Commerce, Establishment and Navigation of 1959 between the United Kingdom and Iran defines 'companies' thus.[5]

The term 'companies'—
   (a) means all legal persons except physical persons;

1489–551; Note, ibid. 1429–51; Kronstein, 52 *Col. LR* (1952), 983–1002; Batiffol, *Droit international privé* (5th end., 1970), i. 233–62; Loussouarn and Bredin, *Droit du commerce international* (1969), 251–309; Goldman, 90 *JDI* (1963), 321–89; Caflisch, 24 *Ann. suisse* (1967), 119–60; Mann, 88 *LQR* (1972), 57–82 (also in Mann, *Studies in International Law* (1973), 524–52); Verzijl, *International Law in Historical Perspective*, v. (1972), 111–44; Bernhardt, *Encyclopedia*, III (1997), 495–501.

  [4] See the cases of *German Interests in Polish Upper Silesia* (1926) and *Peter Pázmány University* (1933), *infra*, p. 409.

  [5] Cmnd. 698, Art. 2, para. 4. See also the Treaty of Friendship, Commerce and Navigation, US and Italy, 1948, 79 UNTS 171, Art. II. See further Feliciano, 118 Hague *Recueil* (1966, II), 262–83; 56 *BY* (1985), 512–15, 58 *BY* (1987), 621–2.

(b) in relation to a High Contracting Party means all companies which derive their status as such from the law in force in any territory of that High Contracting Party to which the present Treaty applies;

(c) in relation to a country means all companies which derive their status as such from the law in force in that country.

Certain recent treaties concerned with the protection of investments employ a more complicated formulation.[6]

The Treaty establishing the European Economic Community provides in Article 58 that corporations under the law of a member state and having their 'siège statutaire', 'administration centrale', or 'principal établissement' within the Community are assimilated, for the purposes of the chapter on the right of establishment, to individuals who are 'ressortissant des États membres'.[7] For this purpose corporations include all legal persons whether of public or private law other than non-profit-making bodies.

Bilateral treaties concerned with double taxation contain rules of attribution which may invoke the concepts of nationality, residence, or fiscal domicile, while defining the crucial points of contact, which are commonly management and control.[8] Air transport agreements may require that airlines acquiring a foreign carrier permit satisfy a condition of substantial ownership and effective control by nationals of the other contracting party.[9] Important provisions ascribing a national character to corporations and other associations appear in peace treaties, agreements on reparation for war losses, treaties of cession, and agreements for compensation in case of nationalization and other events causing loss to foreign interests on state territory. In the *Peter Pázmány University*[10] case, the Permanent Court found that the University, as a legal person in Hungarian law, was a Hungarian national for the purpose of submitting a claim to restitution of property under Article 250 of the Treaty of Trianon, 1920. In general treaty provisions employ a variety of criteria including *siège social*,[11] the national source of actual control, ownership, and place of creation.

---

[6] See Mann, 52 *BY* (1981), 241 at 242.

[7] See also Conv. Establishing the European Free Trade Association, 1959, Art. 16, para. 6; European Conv. on Establishment of Companies, 1966, Art. 1.

[8] Ginther, 15 *Öst. Z. für öff. R.* (1966), 40–6; and see *Compagnie Financière de Suez et l'Union Parisienne* v. *United States*, 492 F. 2nd 798 (US Ct. of Claims, 20 Feb. 1974); 68 *AJ* (1974), 738; *Digest of US Practice* (1974), 532; ILR 61, 408.

[9] See *Aerolineas Peruanas, S.A., Foreign Permit Case*, ILR 31, 416, US Civil Aeronautics Board.

[10] PCIJ Ser. A/B, no. 61 (1933), at 228–32; Whiteman, viii. 21. See also *German Interests in Polish Upper Silesia*, PCIJ Ser. A, no. 7, pp. 73, 74–5 (1926); *Flexi-Van Leasing, Inc.* v. *Iran*, ILR 70, 497; *Ray Go Wagner Equipment Company* v. *Iran Express Terminal Corporation*, ibid. 71, 688.

[11] This concept of French law overlaps with residence and domicile. Normally the *siège social* is the place where the administrative organs operate and where general meetings are held. However, tribunals may insist that the *siège social* should not be nominal and thus relate the test to that of effective control. See Schwarzenberger, *International Law*, pp. 393–5; and *Bakalian and Hadjthomas* v. *Banque Ottomane*, 93 *JDI* (1966), 117.

3. SHIPS[12]

In the maintenance of a viable regime for common use of the high seas the law of the flag and the necessity for a ship to have a flag are paramount.[13] The opinion commonly expressed by jurists was strongly in favour of the unqualified freedom of each state to determine for itself the conditions under which national status could be conferred on vessels.[14] This view of state competence suffers from the organic faults considered in a wider setting in the previous chapter. The act of conferment of nationality (registration) is within the competence of states, but registration is in principle only evidence of nationality, and valid registration under the law of the flag state does not preclude issues of validity under international law. The *Nottebohm* principle applies equally here, and the Convention on the High Seas of 1958[15] provides in Article 5, paragraph 1:[16]

Each State shall fix the conditions for the grant of its nationality to ships, for the registration of ships in its territory, and for the right to fly its flag. Ships have the nationality of the State whose flag they are entitled to fly. There must exist a genuine link between the State and the ship; in particular, the State must effectively exercise its jurisdiction and control in administrative, technical and social matters over ships flying its flag.

The International Law Commission[17] had preferred a reference to 'a genuine link' without any further specification. The Commission observed: 'While leaving States a wide latitude in this respect, the Commission wished to make it clear that the grant of its flag to a ship cannot be a mere administrative formality, with no accompanying guarantee that the ship possess a real link with its new State'. Judge Jennings[18] has remarked that 'the assumption that the "genuine link" formula, invented for dealing

---

[12] See especially Whiteman, ix. 1–51; Meyers, *The Nationality of Ships* (1967); Jennings, 121 Hague *Recueil* (1967, II), 460–5; Singh, 107 Hague *Recueil* (1962, III), 38–64; Johnson, 8 *Indian Yrbk. of Int. Affairs* (1959), 3–15; Schwarzenberger, *International Law*, i (3rd edn.), 412–18; Pinto, 87 *JDI* (1960), 344–69; Watts, 33 *BY* (1957), 52–84; Goldie, 39 *BY* (1963), 220–83; de Visscher, *Les Effectivités du droit international public* (1967), 139–44; Laun in *Gedächtnisschrift Ludwig Marxer* (1963), 327–68; Fay, 77 *RGDIP* (1973), 1000–80; Verzijl, *International Law in Historical Perspective*, iv (1971), 196–200; v. 144–50. Osieke, 73 *AJ* (1979), 604–27; O'Connell, *The International Law of the Sea* (ed. Shearer), ii (1984), 750–61; Dupuy and Vignes, *Traité du nouveau droit de la mer* (1985), 354–9; McConnell, 16 *Journ. of Maritime Law and Commerce* (1985), 365–96; Nordquist and Wachenfeld, 31 *German Yrbk.* (1988), 138–64; Wolfrum, 28 *Virginia Journ.* (1988), 387–99; Oppenheim ii. 732–3; Bernhardt, *Encyclopedia*, IV (2000), 400–8.

[13] *Supra*, p. 228.

[14] See Gidel, i. 80; Rienow, *The Test of the Nationality of a Merchant Vessel* (1937), 218–19; Harv. Research, 29 *AJ* (1935), Spec. Suppl., pp. 518–19. Cf. the *Muscat Dhows*, *RIAA* xi. 83 (1905).

[15] *Supra*, p. 228.

[16] See further Whiteman, ix. 7–17; *Yrbk. ILC* (1956), ii. 278–9; UN Conference on the Law of the Sea, Off. Recs. i. 78, 83, 85, 91, 108, 111, 112; iv. 61ff.; the *I.M.C.O.* case, Pleadings (1960), 357–8 (Riphagen), 364–8 (Seyersted), 383 (Vallat); Permanent Statute of the Free Territory of Trieste, Art. 33, 42 *AJ* (1948), Suppl., p. 97; Jessup, 59 *Columbia LR* (1959), 234 at 256; id., Sep. Op., *Barcelona Traction* case (Second Phase), ICJ Reports (1970), at 184, 186–9.

[17] *Yrbk. ILC* (1956), ii. 278–9.

[18] 121 Hague *Recueil* (1967, II), 463.

with people, is capable of immediate application to ships and aircraft, smacks of a disappointing naiveté' and, further, that 'a provision which might seem to encourage governments to make subjective decisions whether or not to recognize the nationality of this aircraft or that vessel is clearly open to abuse and for that reason to grave criticism'.

The provision above has met with criticism from partisans of the exclusive competence of states to ascribe national character to vessels.[19] The United States Department of State had adopted a position which involves interpreting the provision in such a way that the requirement of a genuine link is not a condition for recognition of the nationality of the ship but an independent obligation to exercise jurisdiction and control effectively.[20]

The provisions of Article 5 of the High Seas Convention of 1958 are repeated in essence in Article 91 of the UN Convention on the Law of the Sea of 1982. However, the duties of the flag state are enumerated separately in Article 94. The general opinion is that the position remains the same, with the opponents of the 'genuine link' un-appeased. The UN Convention on Conditions for Registration of Ships[21] adopted by a diplomatic conference in 1986 seeks to impose precise modalities for the effective exercise of jurisdiction and control by the flag state. The Convention has not yet entered into force.

In relation to ships' crews, the International Law Commission has affirmed the right of the State of nationality of a ship's crew to exercise diplomatic protection on their behalf, while at the same time acknowledging that the State of nationality of the ship also has a right to seek redress on their behalf.[22]

In the decision on admissibility and merits in the *M/V Saiga (No. 2) Case*[23] the International Tribunal for the Law of the Sea rejected an objection to admissibility based upon the absence of a genuine link on the following grounds:

81. The Convention follows the approach of the 1958 Convention. Article 91 retains the part of the third sentence of Article 5, paragraph 1, of the 1958 Convention which provides that there must be a genuine link between the State and the ship. The other part of that sentence, stating that the flag State shall effectively exercise its jurisdiction and control in administrative, technical and social matters over ships flying its flag, is reflected in Article 94 of the Convention, dealing with the duties of the flag State.

---

[19] See McDougal, Burke, and Vlasic, 54 *AJ* (1960), 25–116; McDougal and Burke, *The Public Order of the Oceans* (1962), 1008–140; Boczek, *Flags of Convenience* (1962). The debate relates to the use of flags of convenience by American interests in competition with European shipping.

[20] Whiteman, ix. 27 at 29. For the contrary view: Recommendation 108, General Conference of the ILO, 1958; (144 votes to 0, 3 abstentions); Meyers, *Nationality of Ships*, p. 225.

[21] 26 *ILM* (1987), 1229. See Wefers Bettink, 18 *Neths. Yrbk.* (1987), 69–119.

[22] Draft articles adopted on a second reading in 2006: *Report of the International Law Commission, Fifty-eighth session* (2006), G.A. Off. Recs., *Sixty-first session*, Suppl. No.10 (A/61/10), 90-94 (draft Article 18). See also Dugard, *Fifth Report*, A/CN.4/538, 4 March 2004, 21–30.

[23] Judgment of 1 July 1999; ILR 120, 143 at 179–80. The Tribunal also held that the evidence was not sufficient to establish a genuine link.

82. Paragraphs 2 to 5 of Article 94 of the Convention outline the measures that a flag State is required to take to exercise effective jurisdiction as envisaged in paragraph 1. Paragraph 6 sets out the procedure to be followed where another State has 'clear grounds to believe that proper jurisdiction and control with respect to a ship have not been exercised'. That State is entitled to report the facts to the flag State which is then obliged to 'investigate the matter and, if appropriate, take any action necessary to remedy the situation'. There is nothing in Article 94 to permit a State which discovers evidence indicating the absence of proper jurisdiction and control by a flag State over a ship to refuse to recognise the right of the ship to fly the flag of the flag State.

83. The conclusion of the Tribunal is that the purpose of the provisions of the Convention on the need for a genuine link between a ship and its flag State is to secure more effective implementation of the duties of the flag State, and not to establish criteria by reference to which the validity of the registration of ships in a flag State may be challenged by other States.

84. This conclusion is not put into question by the United Nations Convention on Conditions for Registration of Ships of 7 February 1986 invoked by Guinea. This Convention (which is not in force) sets out as one of its principal objectives the strengthening of 'the genuine link between a State and ships flying its flag'. In any case, the Tribunal observes that Guinea has not cited any provision in that Convention which lends support to its contention that 'a basic condition for the registration of a ship is that also the owner or operator of the ship is under the jurisdiction of the flag State'.

In *The Juno Trader*[24] case the International Tribunal for the Law of the Sea found on the facts that there had been no change in the flag state and that accordingly there Tribunal had jurisdiction. However, in a Joint Separate Opinion Judges Mensah and Wolfrum rejected the view that a change in the ownership of a ship resulted in the automatic change of the flag of a ship, and explained the considerations involved thus:[25]

In this context we consider it important to emphasize the special importance of the nationality of a vessel, particularly in regard to the implementation and enforcement of the rules of international law pertaining to the rights and responsibilities of States in respect of the ship. According to article 91 of the Convention, it is for each State to establish the conditions for the granting of its nationality to ships and for the registration of ships. The term "nationality", when used in connection with ships, is merely shorthand for the jurisdictional connection between a ship and a State. The State of nationality of the ship is the flag State or the State whose flag the ship is entitled to fly; and the law of the flag State is the law that governs the ship. The jurisdictional connection between a State and a ship that is entitled to fly its flag results in a network of mutual rights and obligations, as indicated in part in article 94 of the Convention. For example, granting the right to a ship to fly its flag imposes on the flag State the obligation to effectively exercise its jurisdiction and control in administrative, technical and social matters. In turn, the ship is obliged to fully implement the relevant national laws of the State whose flag it is entitled to fly. All States which have established ships' registers provide for specific procedural and factual requirements to be met before a ship is entered on their registers or is granted the right to fly the flag of the particular State. Ships receive respective documents to prove that they are entitled to fly a particular flag. Similarly, the laws of these States establish clear procedures to be followed for ships to leave the register, including the conditions under which a ship may lose the right to remain on the register.

24 ILR 128, 267.
25 Ibid., p.303 at p.307.

Treaties may contain specialized rules of attribution.[26] In the *I.M.C.O.* case[27] the International Court was asked to give an advisory opinion on the proper constitution of the Maritime Safety Committee of the Inter-Governmental Maritime Consultative Organization. The relevant Convention provided, in Article 28(a), that 'The Maritime Safety Committee shall consist of fourteen Members elected by the Assembly from the Members, governments of those nations having an important interest in maritime safety, of which not less than eight shall be the largest ship-owning nations ...' Panama and Liberia had not been elected and they and other states contended that the proper test was registered tonnage and not beneficial ownership by nationals. The Court found that the reference in the Convention was solely to registered tonnage. This conclusion depended on the construction of the text and was assumed to be consistent with the general purpose of the Convention. The Court thus found it unnecessary to examine the argument that registration was qualified by the requirement of a genuine link. With little or no justification the United States Department of State regards this as evidence in support of its position relating to Article 5 of the High Seas Convention.[28]

The courts of the United States have refused to apply local law to the internal management of vessels in American ports flying Honduran or Liberian flags which had close contacts with the United States.[29] This refusal to go behind the law of the flag and the fact of registration was based in part upon the construction of the relevant Treaty of Friendship, Commerce and Consular Rights and in part upon the general principle governing jurisdiction over ships in port.[30]

4. AIRCRAFT[31]

The Convention for the Regulation of Aerial Navigation of 1919,[32] and later the Chicago Convention of 1944,[33] provided that the nationality of aircraft is governed by the state of registration. The former stipulated that registration could only take place in the state of which the owners were nationals, while the latter merely forbids dual

---

[26] See e.g. the Conv. on Fishing and Conservation of the Living Resources of the High Seas, 1958, Art. 14; Peace Treaty with Italy, 42 *AJ* (1948), Suppl.; p. 47, Art. 78(9)(c); Annex VI, Art. 33.

[27] ICJ Reports (1960), 150; ILR 30, 426. See Simmonds, 12 *ICLQ* (1963), 56–87; Colliard, *Ann. français* (1960), 338–61; Rosenne, 65 *RGDIP* (1961), 507–17; de Visscher, *Les Effectivités*, p. 143.

[28] Whiteman, ix. 27 at 29.

[29] *McCulloch* v. *Sociedad Nacional; McLeod* v. *Empresa Hondurena; National Maritime Union* v. *Empresa Hondurena*, 372 US 10 (1963); ILR 34, 51; Whiteman, ix. 30; *Incres* v. *International Maritime Workers union*, 372 US 24 (1963); ILR 34, 66.

[30] *Supra*, p. 318.

[31] See de Visscher, 48 Hague *Recueil* (1934, II), 294–301; id., *Les Effectivités* pp. 144–6; Honig, *The Legal Status of Aircraft* (1956); Nys, *Rev. française de droit aérien* (1964), 159–83; Mankiewicz, *Ann. français* (1952), 685 at 686–90; Whiteman, ix. 376–90, 429–41; Cooper, 17 *Journ. of Air Law and Com.* (1950), 292–316; Rousseau, iv. 611–12; Oppenheim, ii. 656–7; Milde, Bernhardt (ed.), *Encyclopedia*, I (1992), 86–7; Hailbronner, ibid., Vol. IV (2000), 605–7.

[32] Arts. 5–10.

[33] Arts. 17–21.

registration. Neither Convention applied in time of war, and the latter Convention does not apply to state aircraft, i.e. 'aircraft used in military, customs and police services'. The Tokyo Convention on Offences Committed on Board Aircraft[34] provides that the state of registration has jurisdiction over offences and acts committed on board. The more recent provisions may be thought to support a doctrine of freedom in conferring national status by registration, in contrast to Article 5 of the Convention on the High Seas.[35] However, in the absence of flags of convenience in air traffic, it may be that the issue was left on one side by the authors, the assumption being that registration in practice depended on the existence of substantial connections. In the absence of substantial connections the state of registry will not be in a position to ensure that the aircraft is operated in accordance with the Chicago Convention. However, the application of a genuine link test is by no means straightforward and, as in the case of naturalization of individuals, registration is itself a presumptively valid and genuine connection of some importance.[36] The problem is to isolate the role of registration: it may merely certify status under national law for the purpose of administering the particular convention.[37] Obviously the *Nottebohm* principle[38] ought to apply to aircraft as it does to ships. It must surely apply at the least to discover to which state non-civil aircraft belong, but it is probable that even where the Chicago Convention applies, issues of diplomatic protection are not precluded by registration. In bilateral treaties the United States has reserved the right to refuse a carrier permit to an airline designated by the other contracting party 'in the event substantial ownership and effective control of such airlines are not vested in nationals of the other contracting party'.[39]

In principle aircraft of joint operating agencies, for example, the Scandinavian Airlines System, must be registered in one of the states involved. However, in 1967 the Council of the International Civil Aviation Organization adopted a resolution requiring the constitution of a joint register in such cases for the purposes of Article 77 of the Chicago Convention and the designation of a state as recipient of representations from third states.[40] The Resolution applies both to joint operating agencies and intergovernmental agencies.

International agreement is called for on the legal status of different types of air-cushion craft, including hovercraft and hydrofoils.

---

[34] *Supra*, p. 320.

[35] See Makarov, *Annuaire de l'Inst.* 48 (1959), i. 359 ff.; ibid. 49 (1961), ii. 32ff. Cf *Affaire F. OABV, Ann. français* (1958), 282.

[36] See Jennings, 121 Hague *Recueil*, pp. 460–6.

[37] But parties to the Chicago Conv. may be precluded from contesting nationality based on registration: see Cheng, *The Law of International Air Transport* (1962), 128–31.

[38] *Supra*, p. 407.

[39] See *Aerolineas Peruanas, S.A., Foreign Permit Case*, ILR 31, 416.

[40] See Whiteman, ix. 383–90; Fitzgerald, 5 *Canad. Yrbk.* (1967), 193–216; ILA, *Report of the Fifty-Second Conference* (1966), 228–86; ILA, *Report of the Fifty-Third Conference* (1968), 147–56; Cheng, *Yrbk. of Air and Space Law* (1966), 5–31; Venkatramiah, 11 *Indian Journ.* (1971), 435–58.

5. SPACE OBJECTS[41]

The Space Treaty of 1967[42] does not employ the concept of nationality in relation to objects launched into outer space. Article VIII of the Treaty provides in part that the state of registration 'shall retain jurisdiction and control over such object, and over any personnel thereof, while in outer space or on a celestial body'. In the Convention on Registration of Objects Launched into Outer Space it is provided that the launching state shall maintain a register of space objects.[43] Each state of registry has a duty to furnish certain information to the Secretary-General of the United Nations.

6. PROPERTY IN GENERAL

Ownership in international law is normally seen either in terms of private rights under national law, which may become the subject of diplomatic protection and state responsibility, or in terms of territorial sovereignty.[44] However, rules of attribution exist which must create a counterpart of ownership on the international plane. This is the case for state ships, aircraft, space vehicles, and national treasures.[45] Many treaties confer 'property' or 'title' without referring this to the national law of the *situs* or to any other local law.[46] Transfers of materials may reserve 'title' to the transferor. Thus the United States agreed to lend a vessel to the Philippines for five years, title to remain in the United States and the transferee having the right to place the vessel under its flag.[47]

---

[41] See McDougal, Lasswell, and Vlasic, *Law and Public Order in Space* (1963), 513–87; Goedhuis, 109 Hague *Recueil* (1963, II), 301–8; Lachs, 113 Hague *Recueil* (1964, III), 55–61; id., *The Law of Outer Space* (1972), 68–78; Rousseau, iv. 640–3; Fawcett, *Outer Space* (1984), 27–8; Oppenheim, ii. (9th edn., 1992), 826–38; Cheng, Bernhardt (ed.), *Encyclopedia*, IV (2000), 557–65. See also the UK Outer Space Act 1986, ss. 1, 7, and 13(1).

[42] *Supra*, p. 255.

[43] Adopted by the UN General Assembly on 12 Nov. 1974; in force 15 Sept. 1976; for the text: 14 ILM (1975), 43; *Digest of US Practice* (1974), 401; ibid. (1976), 424.

[44] See generally Staker, 58 *BY* (1987), 151–252.

[45] See the Cambodian claim in the *Temple* case, ICJ Reports (1962), 6, for restitution of sculptures and other objects; and the Jordanian claim to the Temple Scroll, acquired by Israel, UNESCO, Executive Board meeting, Oct. 1969. See further Williams, 15 *Canad. Yrbk.* (1977), 146–72; UNGA Resol. on Restitution of Works of Art, 11 Nov. 1977. Note also the case of a sunken Soviet submarine (see Rubin, 69 *AJ* (1975), 855–8), and the Agreement between the UK and UAR concerning the Tutankhamen Exhibition (*Treaty Series* no. 19 (1972), Cmnd. 4898), Art. 1(4). On U.S. title to a Confederate warship: see 85 *AJ* (1991), 381–3.

[46] See the Soviet-Swedish Agreement on Construction of Embassy Buildings, 1958; 428 UNTS, no. 6184; and various agreements on disposition of defence equipment, hydraulic works on frontier waters, and proprietary rights in river waters. See also the contract between the International Atomic Energy Agency, the Government of the United States, and the Government of Pakistan for the transfer of enriched uranium and plutonium for a reactor, 1962; 425 UNTS, no. 6114.

[47] Agreement of 1961; 433 UNTS, no. 6232.

In the arbitration concerning *Monetary Gold* (1953)[48] Sauser-Hall, sole arbitrator, referred in his award to a concept of 'patrimoine nationale' which could extend to gold functioning as a monetary reserve, although the gold did not belong to the state concerned by its national law but to a private bank under foreign control. In general the notion of state immunity provides a paradigm of 'title' on the international plane.

The issue of title arises in more specialist contexts in which the concept of 'title' plays little or no active role, the outcome depending on the particular rules of law applicable. Problems of this kind concern the disposition of vessels taken in prize,[49] title to booty of war,[50] the taking of reparation in kind, the effect of territorial cession on public property in the territory concerned,[51] and claims by the victors of 1945 to German assets in neutral countries.[52] The recognition and enforcement by a municipal court of foreign legislation protecting the cultural heritage of the state concerned raises problems of jurisdiction but such legislation may be presumed to be in accordance with the public policy of the forum.[53] In the context the UNESCO Convention for the Protection of the World Cultural and National Heritage,[54] adopted in 1972, provides a guide to public policy.

7. ASSETS OF INTERNATIONAL ORGANIZATIONS[55]

If one approaches the problem of attribution by reference to the rules concerning states, then negatives are prominent: organizations cannot have territorial sovereignty[56] and have no competence to confer nationality on persons or assets. Nevertheless the functional competence of organizations may include significant powers of jurisdiction and a regime of jurisdictional immunities, and both jurisdiction and the immunities of assets from national jurisdictions[57] are analogues of ownership. It is undoubtedly the case that the resources of the International Monetary Fund and buffer stocks established under international commodity agreements are forms of property title to which is not derived from any system of municipal law.[58] In the case of ships used in

---

[48] ILR 20 (1953), 441 at 469ff.: *RIAA* xii. 13 at 43ff. See further 49 *AJ* (1955), 403; Lalive, 58 *RGDIP* (1954), 438; Fawcett, 123 Hague *Recueil* (1968, I), 248–51. Cf. *Monetary Gold Removed from Rome in 1943*, ICJ Reports (1954), 19. See also the *Standard Oil* case, *RIAA* ii. 777 at 795.

[49] Municipal legislation in some states confers nationality of the captor states on lawful prizes.

[50] Oppenheim, i. 401–2.

[51] See *German Interests in Polish Upper Silesia* (1926), PCIJ, Ser. A, no. 7, p. 41; *Peter Pázmány University* (1933), PCIJ, Ser. A/B, no. 61, p. 237; UN Trib. in Libya, *RIAA* xii. 363.

[52] See Mann, 24 *BY* (1957), 239–57; Simpson, 34 *BY* (1958), 374–84.

[53] Cf. *Nigerian Objets d'Art Export Case*, ILR 73, 226, Fed. Supr. Ct., FRG; *A.-G. of New Zealand* v. *Ortiz* [1982] QB 349, Staughton, J.; [1982] 2 WLR 10, CA; [1983] 2 WLR 809, HL.

[54] Text: 11 *ILM* (1972), 1358.

[55] See generally ch. 31 on international organizations.

[56] *Supra*, p. 167.

[57] See the Conv. on the Privileges and Immunities of the United Nations, 1946, s. 3; and Jenks, *International Immunities* (1961), 52–3.

[58] See further Fawcett, 123 Hague *Recueil* (1968, I), 237–40; id., 44 *BY* (1970), 173–4.

furtherance of the purposes of an organization, there is obviously a case for allowing the organization to fly its own flag and exercise some protection over the vessel. The question of competence is still open, and there are some serious obstacles. The law of the flag is an instrument for ensuring compliance with various rules; but an organization will normally lack the means of exercising the appropriate jurisdiction and there will be no applicable law.[59] Aircraft operated by the United Nations or other intergovernmental organizations must, it seems, use a state registration, provided the relevant treaty provisions (in the Chicago Convention) allow this.[60] The problem of accession to the Convention on the Liability of Operators of Nuclear Ships by organizations has been considered by a Standing Committee of the Diplomatic Conference on Maritime Law, which failed to reach agreement.[61]

---

[59] The first Law of the Sea Conference could not agree on the subject. The Conv. on the High Seas leaves the question open (Art. 7). See François, *Yrbk. ILC* (1956), ii. 102; ibid. (1963), ii. 178; Jennings, 121 Hague *Recueil* (1967, 11), 467–8; McDougal and Burke, *The Public Order of the Oceans*, pp. 773–7; Singh, 107 Hague *Recueil* (1962, III), 134–61; O'Connell, pp. 100, 608; Meyers, *Nationality of Ships*, pp. 323–51. Fishing vessels of the United Nations Korean Reconstruction Agency and one of the vessels of the United Nations Emergency Force in Egypt carried a UN flag without having any state registration. On other occasions vessels with a national registration have flown a UN flag.

[60] See Mankiewicz, *Ann. français* (1962), 691–717; Cheng, *The Law of International Air Transport*, pp. 131–2; Whiteman, ix. 383–90; Fitzgerald, 5 *Canad. Yrbk.* (1967), 193–216.

[61] Sørensen, pp. 259–60.

PART VIII

THE LAW OF RESPONSIBILITY

21

THE RESPONSIBILITY
OF STATES

1. THE RELATIONS OF THE SUBJECT

In international relations as in other social relations, the invasion of the legal interest of one subject of the law by another legal person creates responsibility[1] in various forms determined by the particular legal system. International responsibility is commonly considered in relation to states as the normal subjects of the law, but it is in essence a broader question inseparable from that of legal personality in all its forms. For the sake of convenience the question whether organizations and individuals have the capacity to make claims and to bear responsibility on the international plane has been treated separately.[2] However, while the treatment is conventional in singling out state responsibility, it is specialized in two respects. First, the question of the treatment of aliens and their property on state territory[3] is reserved for Chapter 24. This subject is an aspect of substantive law, and, logically, if it is to be included, then so also ought expositions of all the rights and duties of states. Nevertheless the treatment of aliens will be dealt with incidentally in connection with the general problems of responsibility. Secondly, the question of exhaustion of local remedies so often dealt with under our general rubric is segregated as being a part of a separate issue, that of the admissibility of claims. While certain aspects of admissibility require treatment in this chapter (section 14), the subject receives further consideration in Chapter 22.

The issues of responsibility of States may arise in the context of a (normally bilateral) negotiated diplomatic settlement. They may also arise in the context of resolutions of the Security Council or the General Assembly of the United Nations. Apart from such political contexts, issues of responsibility and, or, compensation are determined in a number of judicial settings, including the International Court of Justice, the European Court of Human Rights, the Inter-American Court of Human Rights, the International Tribunal for the Law of the Sea, the Iran–U.S. Claims Tribunal, and the courts of arbitration.

---

[1] See *infra*, p. 434.
[2] *Infra*, pp. 568ff.
[3] Including the problems concerning the international minimum standard, denial of justice, and expropriation.

2. THE BASIS AND NATURE OF STATE RESPONSIBILITY[4]

Today one can regard responsibility as a general principle of international law, a concomitant of substantive rules and of the supposition that acts and omissions may be categorized as illegal by reference to the rules establishing rights and duties. Shortly, the law of responsibility is concerned with the incidence and consequences of illegal acts, and particularly the payment of compensation for loss caused. However, this, and many other generalizations offered on the subject, must not be treated as dogma, or allowed to prejudice the discussion which follows. Thus the law may prescribe the payment of compensation for the consequences of legal or 'excusable' acts, and it is proper to consider this aspect in connection with responsibility in general.[5] A scientific treatment of the subject is hindered by the relatively recent generalization of the notion of liability. In the Middle Ages treaties laid down particular duties and specified the liabilities and procedures to be followed in case of breach. In recent times the inconvenience of private reprisals,[6] the development of rules restricting forcible self-help, and the work of the International Court have contributed towards a more normal conception of responsibility from the point of view of the rule of law. Of course the notions of reparation and restitution in the train of illegal acts had long been part

---

[4] See especially Jiménez de Aréchaga, in Sørensen, pp. 533–72; Sørensen, 101 Hague *Recueil* (1960, III), 217–26; Ago, First Report, *Yrbk. ILC* (1969), ii, 125–56; Second Report, *Yrbk. ILC* (1970), ii. 177–97; Third Report, ibid. (1971), ii. (Pt. 1), 199–274; Fourth Report, ibid. (1972), ii. 71–160; Fifth Report, ibid. (1976) ii. (Pt. 1), 3–54; Sixth Report, ibid. (1977) ii. (Pt. 1), 3–43; Seventh Report, ibid. (1978) ii. (Pt. 1), 31–60; Eighth Report, ibid. (1979) ii. (Pt. 1), 4–27; Reports of *ILC* to UN General Assembly, *Yrbk. ILC* (1973) ii. 165–98; ibid. (1974), ii. (Pt. 1), 269–90; ibid. (1975), ii. 51–106; ibid. (1976), ii. (Pt. 2), 69–122; Reuter, 103 Hague *Recueil* (1961, II), 583–97; Accioly, 96 Hague *Recueil* (1959, I), 353–70; de Visscher, *Bibliotheca Visseriana*, ii. (1924), 89–119; Anzilotti, *Cours de droit international*, (1929), i. 466ff.; Parry, 90 Hague *Recueil* (1956, II), 657–98; Quadri, 113 Hague *Recueil* (1964, III), 453–77; Queneudec, *La Responsabilité internationale de l'état pour les fautes personnelles de ses agents* (1966); Verzijl, *International Law in Historical Perspective*, vi. (1973), 616–774; Jiménez de Aréchaga, 159 Hague *Recueil* (1978, I), 267–87; Riphagen, in Macdonald and Johnston (eds.), *The Structure and Process of International Law* (1983), 581–625; Rousseau, v. 5–96, 209–50; Brownlie, *System of the Law of Nations: State Responsibility* (Pt. 1) (1983); Graefrath, 185 Hague *Recueil* (1984, II), 9–150; Dupuy, 188 Hague *Recueil* (1984, V), 9–134; *Neths. Yrbk.* (1985) (symposium); Spinedi and Simma (eds.), *United Nations Codification of State Responsibility* (1987). See also the collected works of Roberto Ago, *Scritti sulla responsabilità internazionale degli Stati*, i. (1979), ii. (1) and ii. (2) (1986); Thirlway, 66 *BY* (1995), 38–80; ILC Report, *Yrbk. ILC* (1996), ii. (Pt. 2), 57–73; ibid. (1998), ii. (Pt. 2), 60–87; Crawford, First Report, UN Doc. A/CN.4/490; Crawford, Second Report, A/CN.4/498; Crawford, Third Report, A/CN.4/507; Crawford, Fourth Report, A/CN.4/517; Crawford, *The International Law Commission's Articles on State Responsibility* (2002); *Report of the International Law Commission, Fifty-third session* (2001), G. A. Off. Recs, 56th Session, Suppl. No. 10 (A/56/10); Brownlie, *Documents*, 300–10. See further Fitzmaurice and Sarooshi (eds.), *Issues of State Responsibility before International Judicial Institutions* (2004); Ragazzi (ed.),*Essays in Memory of Oscar Schachter* (2005). Of continuing value are the eight reports produced by Arangio-Ruiz in the period 1988 to 1996.

[5] See *infra*, p. 464.

[6] Formerly sovereigns authorized private citizens to perform acts of reprisal (special reprisals) against the citizens of other states: Wheaton, *Elements* (1866), paras. 291, 292.

of the available stock of legal concepts in Europe, and the classical writers, including Grotius, often referred to reparation and restitution in connection with unjust war.[7]

The nature of state responsibility[8] is not based upon delict in the municipal sense, and 'international responsibility' relates both to breaches of treaty and to other breaches of a legal duty. There is no harm in using the term 'international tort' to describe the breach of duty which results in loss to another state,[9] but the term 'tort' could mislead the common lawyer. The compendious term 'international responsibility' is used by tribunals and is least confusing.

The relevant judicial pronouncements are as follows. In a report on the *Spanish Zone of Morocco Claims*[10] Judge Huber said: 'Responsibility is the necessary corollary of a right. All rights of an international character involve international responsibility. If the obligation in question is not met, responsibility entails the duty to make reparation'. In its Judgment in the *Chorzów Factory* (Jurisdiction)[11] proceedings, the Permanent Court stated that: 'It is a principle of international law that the breach of an engagement involves an obligation to make reparation in an adequate form. Reparation therefore is the indispensable complement of a failure to apply a convention and there is no necessity for this to be stated in the convention itself'.

In the Judgment on the *Chorzów Factory* (Indemnity)[12] the Court said:

...it is a principle of international law, and even a general conception of law, that any breach of an engagement involves an obligation to make reparation. In Judgment No. 8[13]...the Court has already said that reparation is the indispensable complement of a failure to apply a convention, and there is no necessity for this to be stated in the convention itself.

The *Corfu Channel* case involved a finding that Albania was liable for the consequences of a mine-laying in her territorial waters and the absence of a warning of the danger:[14] 'These grave omissions involve the international responsibility of Albania. The Court therefore reaches the conclusion that Albania is responsible under international law for the explosions which occurred...and for the damage and loss of human life which resulted from them, and that there is a duty upon Albania to pay compensation to the United Kingdom'.

---

⁷ See Gentili, *De Iure Belli Libri Tres*, Book, II, ch. iii; Grotius, *De Iure Belli ac Pacis*, Book III, ch. x, para. 4. Cf. the discussion of reparation in connection with the armistice conditions and peace treaties, 1918–21: Brownlie, *International Law and the Use of Force by States* (1963), 135–9. See also the Statute of the International Court, Art. 36(2), c, d.

⁸ The question of criminal responsibility of states may arise: see Pella, 51 *RGDIP* (1947), 1–27; Brownlie, *International Law and the Use of Force by States*, pp. 150–4; 44 *Annuaire de l'Inst.* (1952), i. 361–457.

⁹ See Schwarzenberger, *International Law*, i. 562, 563, 571, 581; the *Union Bridge Company* claim (1924), *RIAA* vi. 138 at 142; and Jenks, *The Prospects of International Adjudication* (1964), 514–33.

¹⁰ Translation; French text, *RIAA* ii. 615 at 641. See also *Coenca Bros. v. Germany, Ann. Digest* 4 (1927–8), no. 389.

¹¹ (1927), PCIJ, Ser. A, no. 9, p. 21. This is quoted in part in the Adv. Op. in the *Reparation* case, ICJ Reports (1949), 184.

¹² (1928), PCIJ, Ser. A, no. 17, p. 29. See also ibid. 27, 47; the *Peace Treaties* case, ICJ Reports (1950), 228; and *Phosphates in Morocco* (Prelim. Objections) (1938), PCIJ, Ser. A/B, no. 74, p. 28.

¹³ *Supra*, n. 11.

¹⁴ ICJ Reports (1949), 23. See *infra*, p. 427, on the main aspects of the case.

These pronouncements show that there is no acceptance of a contract and delict (tort) dichotomy. However, the emphasis on the duty to make reparation does present a broad concept akin to civil wrongs in municipal systems. The law of claims is of course *in personam* in its operation, and parties may waive their claims. However, the idea of reparation does not always work well, and tends to give too restrictive a view of the legal interests protected and the *locus standi* of plaintiffs.[15] The duty to pay compensation is a normal consequence of responsibility, but is not conterminous with it.

In general, broad formulae on state responsibility are unhelpful and, when they suggest municipal analogies, a source of confusion. Thus it is often said that responsibility only arises when the act or omission complained of is *imputable* to a state.[16] Imputability would seem to be a superfluous notion, since the major issue in a given situation is whether there has been a breach of duty: the content of 'imputability' will vary according to the particular duty, the nature of the breach, and so on.[17] Imputability implies a fiction where there is none, and conjures up the idea of vicarious liability where it cannot apply. Unhappily Oppenheim[18] draws a distinction between original and vicarious state responsibility. Original responsibility flows from acts committed by, or with authorization of, the government of a state; vicarious responsibility flows from unauthorized acts of the agents of the state, or nationals, and of aliens living within the territory of the state. It is to be admitted that the legal consequences of the two categories of acts may not be the same; but there is no fundamental difference between the two categories, and, in any case, the use of 'vicarious responsibility' here is surely erroneous.

3. BOUNDARIES OF RESPONSIBILITY

IN GENERAL

It is intended to consider available defences subsequently,[19] although of course the use of the category 'defence' may be rather arbitrary, involving assumptions about the incidence of the burden of proof on particular issues. When the general problem is approached, the impression received is that those general principles which may be extracted are too general to be of practical value, a quality which belongs to general principles offered in books on the English law of tort and crime. Thus in principle an act or omission which produces a result which is on its face a breach of a legal obligation gives rise to responsibility in international law, whether the obligation rests

---

[15] See further *infra*, pp. 441, 449.
[16] See e.g. Sørensen, 101 Hague *Recueil* (1960, III), 223.
[17] See Quadri, 113 Hague *Recueil*, pp. 457–9.
[18] i. 337–8, 341. See further Kelsen, *Principles of International Law* (2nd edn.), 119–200.
[19] *Infra*, pp. 465–7.

on treaty, custom, or some other basis.[20] However, many rules prescribe the conduct required without being very explicit about the 'mental state', or degree of advertence, required from the state organs involved. This is a common fault even in the case of the nominate torts of English law, and many of our criminal statutes use question-begging terms like 'knowingly'. Moreover, the issues in inter-state relations are often analogous to those arising from the activities of employees and enterprises in English law, where the legal person held liable is incapable of close control over its agents, and rules employing metaphors based on the intention (*dolus*)[21] or negligence (*culpa*)[22] of natural persons tend to be unhelpful. In some cases it is *relationship* rather than fault in the ordinary sense which is held to justify liability. Thus in international law objective tests are usually employed to determine responsibility, although of course it can happen that governments, as groups of morally responsible *natural* persons, are capable of proven *dolus* or *culpa*. Moreover, in certain types of case, *dolus* and *culpa* have a special role to play.[23]

4. OBJECTIVE RESPONSIBILITY

Technically, objective responsibility rests on the doctrine of the voluntary act: provided that agency and causal connection are established, there is a breach of duty by result alone. Defences, such as act of third party, are available, but the defendant has to exculpate himself.[24] In the conditions of international life, which involve relations between highly complex communities, acting through a variety of institutions and agencies, the public law analogy of the *ultra vires* act is more realistic than a seeking for subjective *culpa* in specific natural persons who may, or may not, 'represent' the legal person (the state) in terms of wrongdoing. Where, for example, an officer in charge of a cruiser on the high seas orders the boarding of a fishing vessel flying another flag, there being no legal justification for the operation, and the act being in excess of his authority, a tribunal will not regard pleas that the acts were done in good faith, or under a mistake of law, with any favour.[25] Moreover, in municipal systems of law, the precise mode of applying a *culpa* doctrine, especially in the matter of assigning the burden of proof, may result in a regime of objective responsibility.

It is believed that the practice of states and the jurisprudence of arbitral tribunals and the International Court have followed the theory of objective responsibility[26] as

[20] See *infra*, p. 612, on unilateral acts.
[21] See *infra*, p. 441.
[22] See *infra*, p. 440.
[23] See *infra*, p. 441.
[24] See Judge Azevedo, ICJ Reports (1949), 85–6.
[25] See the *Jessie* (1921), *RIAA* vi. 57; the *Wanderer* (1921), ibid. 68; the *Kate* (1921), ibid. 77; the *Favourite* (1921), ibid. 82.
[26] See Borchard, 1 *Z.a.ö.R.u.V.* (1929), 223 at 224–5; Schwarzenberger, *International Law*, i. (3rd edn.), 632–41; Guggenheim, ii. 52; Starke, 19 *BY* (1938), 115; Basdevant, 58 Hague *Recueil* (1936, IV), 670–5;

a general principle (which may be modified or excluded in certain cases). Objective tests of responsibility were employed by the General Claims Commission set up by a Convention between Mexico and the United States in 1923 in the well-known *Neer*[27] and *Roberts*[28] claims, and in the *Caire* claim,[29] Verzijl, President of the Franco-Mexican Claims Commission, applied:

the doctrine of the objective responsibility of the State, that is to say, a responsibility for those acts committed by its officials or its organs, and which they are bound to perform, despite the absence of *faute* on their part... The State also bears an international responsibility for all acts committed by its officials or its organs which are delictual according to international law, regardless of whether the official organ has acted within the limits of his competency or has exceeded those limits. ..However, in order to justify the admission of this objective responsibility of the State for acts committed by its officials or organs outside their competence, it is necessary that they should have acted, at least apparently, as authorised officials or organs, or that, in acting, they should have used powers or measures appropriate to their official character...

A considerable number of writers support this point of view, either explicitly,[30] or implicitly, by considering the questions of imputability, causation, and legal excuses without adverting to the question of *culpa* and *dolus*.[31] At the same time certain eminent opinions have supported the Grotian view that *culpa* or *dolus malus* provide the proper basis of state responsibility in all cases.[32] A small number of arbitral awards[33] give some support to the *culpa* doctrine: for example, in the *Home Missionary Society* case[34] the tribunal referred to a 'well-established principle of international law that no government can be held responsible for the act of rebellious bodies of men com-

---

Cheng, *General Principles of Law*, pp. 218–32 (very helpful); Schachter, 178 Hague *Recueil* (1982, V), 189–90; Rousseau, v. 14–27; Jiménez de Aréchaga, 159 Hague *Recueil* (1978, I), 269–71. See also the International Law Commission's Articles on Responsibility of States (2001), Art. 2, Commentary, paras. 1–4; and Gattini, *Europ. Journ.* 3 (1992), 253–84.

[27] (1926), *RIAA* iv. p. 60 at 61–2.

[28] (1926), *RIAA* iv. 77 at 80.

[29] (1929), *RIAA* v. 516 at 529–31.

[30] See *supra*, n. 27.

[31] See Sibert, *Traité* (1951), i. 309ff.; and García Amador, Special Rapporteur, *Yrbk. ILC* (1956), ii. 186; ibid. (1957), ii. 106. See also the International Law Commission's Articles on Responsibility of States (2001), Art. 2, Commentary, paras. 1–4.

[32] See Lauterpacht, 62 Hague *Recueil* (1937, IV), 359–64; id., *Private Law Sources and Analogies of International Law* (1927), 134–43; Eagleton, *Responsibility*, p. 209; Ago, 68 Hague *Recueil* (1939, II), 498. See also Accioly, 96 Hague *Recueil* (1959, I), 364–70, for an enumeration of the writers.

[33] Cases cited in this connection are: the *Casablanca* case (1909), Hague Court Reports, i. 110; *RIAA* xi. 119; *Cadenhead* (1914), 8 *AJ* (1914), 663; *Iloilo* claims (1925), *RIAA* vi. 158, 160; *Pugh* claim (1933), *RIAA* iii. 1439; *Award on the Wal-Wal Incident* (1935), *RIAA* iii. 1657 (but see Schwarzenberger, *International Law*, pp. 636–7). See also the *Davis* case (1903), *RIAA* ix. 460, 463; *Salas* case, ibid. x. 720.

[34] (1920), *RIAA* vi. 42 at 44. During a rebellion in the Protectorate of Sierra Leone the Home Missionary Society, an American religious body, suffered losses. The United States alleged that in the face of a crisis the British Government failed to take the proper steps for the maintenance of order and that the loss of life and damage was the result of this neglect and failure of duty. The claim was dismissed because (1) there was no failure of duty on the facts; (2) there had been an assumption of risk.

mitted in violation of its authority, where it is itself guilty of no breach of good faith, or of no negligence in suppressing insurrection'. However, many of the awards cited in this connection are concerned with the standard of conduct required by the law *in a particular context*, for example claims for losses caused by acts of rebellion, of private individuals, of the judiciary, and so on.[35] Thus in the *Chattin* claim[36] the General Claims Commission described the judicial proceedings in Mexico against Chattin as 'being highly insufficient' and referred, *inter alia*, to 'an unsufficiency of governmental action recognizable by every unbiased man'. Chattin had been convicted on a charge of embezzlement and sentenced by the Mexican court to two years imprisonment. The Commission referred to various defects in the conduct of the trial and remarked that 'the whole of the proceedings discloses a most astonishing lack of seriousness on the part of the Court'. Furthermore, both writers[37] and tribunals[38] may use the words *faute* or fault to mean a breach of legal duty, an unlawful act. *Culpa*, in the sense of culpable negligence, will be relevant when its presence is demanded by a particular rule of law. Objective responsibility would seem to come nearer to being a *general* principle, and provides a better basis for maintaining good standards in international relations and for effectively upholding the principle of reparation.

The proposition that the type of advertence required varies with the legal context provides an introduction to the Judgment of the International Court in the *Corfu Channel* case,[39] which is considered by Hersch Lauterpacht[40] to contain an affirmation of the *culpa* doctrine. In fact the Court was concerned with the particular question of *responsibility* for the creation of danger in the North Corfu Channel by the laying of mines, warning of which was not given. The basis of responsibility was Albania's knowledge of the laying of mines.[41] The Court considered 'whether it has been established by means of indirect evidence that Albania has knowledge of mine-laying in her territorial waters independently of any connivance on her part in this operation'. Later on it concluded that the laying of the minefield 'could not have been accomplished without the knowledge of the Albanian Government' and referred to 'every State's obligation not to allow knowingly its territory to be used for acts contrary to the rights of other States'.[42] Liability thus rested upon violation of a particular legal duty. The use of circumstantial evidence to establish Albania's knowledge does not alter the fact

---

[35] See *infra*, pp. 445ff.

[36] (1927), *RIAA* iv. 282. See also Huber, rapporteur, *Spanish Zone of Morocco* claims, *RIAA* ii. 644–6.

[37] See Accioly, 96 Hague *Recueil* (1959, I), 369–70.

[38] See the *Prats* case (1868), Moore, *Arbitrations*, iii. 2886 at 2894–5; *Russian Indemnity* case (1912), Hague Court Reports i. 532 at 543. See further Cheng, *General Principles of Law*, pp. 218–32.

[39] ICJ Reports (1949), 4. See further *infra*, p. 445.

[40] See Oppenheim, i. (8th edn. by Lauterpacht), 343, referring to ICJ Reports (1949), p. 18. And cf. Lauterpacht, *The Development of International Law by the International Court* (1958), 88. See also *Répertoire suisse* iii. 1695.

[41] See García Amador, 94 Hague *Recueil* (1958, II), 387; id., *Yrbk. ILC* (1960), ii. 62–3; Schwarzenberger, *International Law* (3rd edn.), i. 632–4; Cheng, *General Principles of Law*, pp. 231–2; Jiménez de Aréchaga, in Sørensen, p. 537; id., *Yrbk. ILC* (1963), ii. 236. Judge Badawi, dissenting, supported a doctrine of fault which was in fact based on the notion of the unlawful, voluntary, act: ICJ Reports (1949), 65–6.

[42] ICJ Reports (1949), 18, 22.

that knowledge was a condition of responsibility. The Court was not concerned with *culpa* or *dolus* as such, and it fell to Judge Krylov[43] and Judge *ad hoc* Eaer[44] to affirm the doctrine of *culpa*.

5. *CULPA*

The term *culpa* is used to describe types of blameworthiness based upon reasonable foreseeability, or foresight without desire of consequences (recklessness, *culpa lata*). Although *culpa* is not a general condition of liability, it may play an important role in certain contexts. Thus where the loss complained of results from acts of individuals not employed by the state, or from activities of licensees or trespassers on the territory of the state, the responsibility of the state will depend on an unlawful omission. In this type of case questions of knowledge may be relevant in establishing the omission or, more properly, responsibility for failure to act. This type of relevance is not necessarily related to the *culpa* principle.[45] However, tribunals may set standards of 'due diligence' and the like, in respect of the activities, or failures to act, of particular organs of state.[46] Thus the 'subjective element' constitutes the type of duty, the actual object of imputation. In effect, since looking for specific evidence of a lack of proper care on the part of state organs is often a fruitless task, the issue becomes one of causation.[47] In the *Lighthouses* arbitration[48] between France and Greece one of the claims arose from the eviction of a French firm from their offices in Salonika and the subsequent loss of their stores in a fire which destroyed the temporary premises. The Permanent Court of Arbitration said:

Even if one were inclined...to hold that Greece is in principle responsible for the consequences of that evacuation, one could not...admit a causal relationship between the damage caused by the fire, on the one part, and that following on the evacuation, on the other, so as to justify holding Greece liable for the disastrous effects of the fire...The damage was neither a foreseeable nor a normal consequence of the evacuation, nor attributable to any want of care on the part of Greece. All causal connection is lacking, and in those circumstances Claim No. 19 must be rejected.

In any case, as Judge Azevedo pointed out in his dissenting opinion in the *Corfu Channel* case,[49] the relations of objective responsibility and the *culpa* principle are

---

43 Ibid. 71–2, quoting Oppenheim (7th edn.), i. 311.
44 ICJ Reports (1949), 127–8, also quoting Oppenheim.
45 Cf. the *Corfu Channel* case, *supra*, p. 442. See also Lévy, 65 *RGDIP* (1961), 744–64.
46 See generally *infra*, pp. 445ff.
47 García Amador, *Yrbk. ILC* (1960), ii. 63.
48 *RIAA* xii. 217–18; ILR 23 (1956), 352–3.
49 ICJ Reports (1949), 85.

very close:[50] the effect, at least, of the Judgment was to place Albania under a duty to take reasonable care to discover activities of trespassers.

When a state engages in lawful activities, responsibility may be generated by *culpa* in the execution of the lawful measures.[51] The existence and extent of *culpa* may affect the measure of damages,[52] and, of course, due diligence, or liability for *faute* or *culpa*, may be stipulated for in treaty provisions.

6. INTENTION AND MOTIVE

The fact that an *ultra vires* act of an official is accompanied by malice on his part, i.e. an intention to cause harm, without regard to whether or not the law permits the act, does not affect the responsibility of his state.[53] Indeed, the principle of objective responsibility dictates the irrelevance of intention to harm, *dolus*, as a condition of liability: and yet general propositions of this sort should not lead to the conclusion that *dolus* cannot play a significant role in the law. Proof of *dolus* on the part of leading organs of the state will solve the problem of 'imputability' in the given case, and, in any case, the existence of a deliberate intent to injure may have an effect on remoteness of damage as well as helping to establish the breach of duty.[54]

Motive and intention are frequently a specific element in the definition of permitted conduct. Thus the rule is stated that expropriation of foreign property is unlawful if the object is that of political reprisal or retaliation.[55] Again, action ostensibly in collective defence against an aggressor will cease to be lawful if the state concerned in the action is proved to be intent on using the operation for purposes of annexation.[56] Similarly, where conduct on its face unlawful is sought to be justified on the grounds of necessity or self-defence,[57] the intention of the actor is important, since it may remove all basis for the defences.[58]

---

[50] See García Amador, *Yrbk. ILC* (1960), ii. 63.

[51] e.g. of sequestration of Italian property in Tunisia by the French Government after the defeat of Italy: *In re Rizzo*, ILR, 22 (1955), 317 at 322. The Conciliation Commission said: 'the act contrary to international law is not the measure of sequestration, but an alleged lack of diligence on the part of the French State—or, more precisely, of him who was acting on its behalf—in the execution of the said measure...'. See also the *Ousset* claim, ibid. 312 at 314; the *Philadelphia-Girard National Bank* case (1929), *RIAA* viii. 67, 69; and *Yrbk. ILC*, (1969), ii. 103 (paras. 6–8).

[52] See the cases of *Janes* (1926), *RIAA* iv. 82; *Baldwin* (1842), Moore, *Arbitrations*, iv. 3235; and *Rau* (1930), Whiteman, *Damages in International Law*, p. 26.

[53] e.g. *Baldwin* (1942), Moore, *Arbitrations*, iv. 3235; Meron, 33 *BY* (1957), 95–6.

[54] *Dix* case, *RIAA*, ix. 119, at 121; cf. *Monnot* case, ibid. 232 at 233.

[55] See *infra*, pp. 538–9.

[56] See Brownlie, *International Law and the Use by Force by States*, pp. 408–9.

[57] See *infra*, pp. 447–9.

[58] Of course, action in good faith is not necessarily justified by reason of the mistake as to necessity for action.

7. THE INDIVIDUALITY OF ISSUES: THE *CORFU CHANNEL* CASE

At this stage it is perhaps necessary to stress that over-simplification of the problems, and too much reliance on general propositions about objective responsibility, *culpa*, and intention, can result in lack of finesse in approaching particular issues. Legal issues, particularly in disputes between states, have an individuality which resists a facile application of general rules. Much depends on the assignment of the burden of proof, the operation of principles of the law of evidence, the existence of acquiescence and estoppels, the nature of the *compromis*, and the precise nature of the relevant substantive rules or treaty provisions. This note of caution can be justified by reference to the *Lotus*,[59] *Corfu Channel*,[60] and *Fisheries*[61] cases in the International Court.

The most interesting of these is perhaps the *Corfu Channel* case.[62] The approach adopted by the majority of the Court fails to correspond neatly with either the *culpa* doctrine or the test of objective responsibility. 'Intention' is a question-begging category and appears in the case only in specialist roles. Thus, in the case of the British passage 'designed to affirm a right which had been unjustly denied' by Albania, much turned on the nature of the passage.[63] Taking all the circumstances into account, the Court held that the passage of two cruisers and two destroyers, through a part of the North Corfu Channel constituting Albanian territorial waters, was an innocent passage. As to the laying of the mines which damaged the destroyers *Saumarez* and *Volage*, the Court looked for evidence of knowledge of this on the part of Albania. The case also illustrates the interaction of the principles of proof and responsibility. The Court said:[64]

...it cannot be concluded from the mere fact of the control exercised by a State over its territory and waters that that State necessarily knew, or ought to have known, of any unlawful act perpetrated therein, nor yet that it necessarily knew, or should have known, the authors. This fact, by itself and apart from other circumstances, neither involves *prima facie* responsibility nor shifts the burden of proof.

On the other hand, the fact of this exclusive territorial control exercised by a State within its frontiers has a bearing upon the methods of proof available to establish the knowledge of that State as to such events. By reason of this exclusive control, the other State, the victim of a breach of international law, is often unable to furnish direct proof of facts giving rise to responsibility. Such a State should be allowed a more liberal recourse to inferences of fact and circumstantial evidence...

---

[59] *Supra*, p. 302.
[60] ICJ Reports (1949), 4.
[61] *Infra*, pp. 176ff.
[62] See generally Brownlie, *International Law and the Use of Force by States*, pp. 283–9; Wilhelm, 15 *Ann. suisse* (1958), 116–30.
[63] ICJ Reports (1949), 30. The right was that of passage through an international strait: see ibid. 28–30.
[64] p. 18.

The Court must examine therefore whether it has been established by means of indirect evidence that Albania has knowledge of mine-laying in her territorial waters independently of any connivance on her part in this operation. The proof may be drawn from inferences of fact, provided they leave *no room* for reasonable doubt. The elements of fact on which these inferences can be based may differ from those which are relevant to the question of connivance.

The decision raises another issue. At the time of the British mission 'designed to affirm a right', there had been no finding that the North Corfu Channel was an 'international strait',[65] and the question of passage for warships through the territorial sea, whether or not forming part of such a strait, was controversial. No attempt at peaceful settlement had been made, and the naval mission was an affirmation of what were, at the time, only *putative* rights.[66] Against this it could be said that Albania, by her policy of exclusion, supported on a previous occasion by fire from coastal batteries, had also adopted an *ex parte* view of her right to exclude warships. However, it is possible that in such a case there is a presumption in favour of the right of the coastal state; and, in any case, the British action on 22 October remained nonetheless a forcible affirmation of *putative* rights. The better course would have been to regard the naval mission as illegal,[67] and to consider whether the laying of mines without warning was a legal means of dealing with trespassers even for a small state with no navy of its own. It is probable that the nature of the *compromis* prevented such an approach, which would have avoided the necessity of holding that the naval mission was involved in an innocent passage as well as the Court's unhappy assimilation of putative rights and legal rights, in a dispute which in part concerned the law applicable.

8. LIABILITY FOR LAWFUL ACTS ABUSE OF RIGHTS

It may happen that a rule provides for compensation for the consequences of acts which are not unlawful in the sense of being prohibited.[68] Thus, in the Convention on the High Seas of 1958, Article 22 provides for the boarding of foreign merchant ships by warships where there is reasonable ground for suspecting piracy and certain other activities. Paragraph 3 then provides: 'If the suspicions prove to be unfounded, and provided that the ship boarded has not committed any act justifying them, it shall be compensated for any loss or damage that may have been sustained'. One is reminded here of the doctrine of incomplete privilege.[69]

---

[65] See *supra*, p. 267.

[66] The status of the North Corfu Channel was very doubtful: see Brüel, *Festschrift für Rudolf Laun* (1953), 259 at 273, 276.

[67] See the Diss Op. of Judges Azevedo, ICJ Reports (1949), 109; and Krylov, ibid. 75. Self-help remains self-help whichever view of the law on the subject of the action is subsequently upheld.

[68] See Sørensen, 101 Hague *Recueil* (1960, III), 221–3; Quadri, 113 Hague *Recueil*, pp. 461–5.

[69] See *infra*, pp. 466–7. See also the Law of the Sea Convention, 1982, Art. 106.

Several systems of law know the doctrine of abuse of rights,[70] exemplified by Article 1912 of the Mexican Civil Code:[71] 'When damage is caused to another by the exercise of a right, there is an obligation to make it good if it is proved that the right was exercised only in order to cause the damage, without any advantage to the person entitled to the right'. This doctrine[72] has had limited support from the dicta of international tribunals.[73] In the case concerning *Certain German Interests in Polish Upper Silesia*[74] it was held that, after the peace treaty came into force and until the transfer of sovereignty over Upper Silesia, the right to dispose of state property in the territory remained with Germany. Alienation would constitute a breach of her obligations if there was 'a misuse'[75] of this right'. In the view of the Court German policy amounted to no more than the normal administration of public property. In the *Free Zones* case the Court held that French fiscal legislation applied in the free zones (which were in French territory), but that 'a reservation must be made as regards the case of abuse of a right, an abuse which, however, cannot be presumed by the Court'.[76] It is not unreasonable to regard the principle of abuse of rights as a general principle of law.[77] However, while it is easy to sympathize with exponents of the doctrine, the delimitation of its function is a matter of delicacy. After considering the work of the International Court, Lauterpacht observes:[78]

These are but modest beginnings of a doctrine which is full of potentialities and which places a considerable power, not devoid of a legislative character, in the hands of a judicial tribunal. There is no legal right, however well established, which could not, in some circumstances, be refused recognition on the ground that it has been abused. The doctrine of abuse of rights is therefore an instrument which… must be wielded with studied restraint.

---

[70] See Gutteridge, 5 *Camb. LJ* (1933), 22–45. See further the decision of the ILO Admin. Trib. in *McIntire* v. *F.A.O.* (1954), ILR 21 (1954), 356.

[71] Cf. Art. 226 of the German civil code.

[72] Generally, on abuse of rights in international law, see Oppenheim, i. 407–10; Lauterpacht, *The Function of Law in the International Community* (1933), 286–306; id., *Development*, pp. 162–5; Schwarzenberger, *International Law*, pp. 84–109; Cheng, *General Principles of Law*, pp. 121–36; Politis, 6 Hague *Recueil* (1925, I), 1–109; García Amador, 94 Hague *Recueil* (1958, II), 377–82; id., *Yrbk. ILC* (1960), ii. 58–60; Guggenheim, 74 Hague *Recueil* (1949, I), 249–54; Kiss, *L'Abus de droit en droit international* (1953); Fitzmaurice, 27 *BY* (1950), 12–14; 30 *BY* (1953), 53–4; 35 *BY* (1959), 210–16; Whiteman, v. 224–30; Ago, Second Report, UN Doc. A/CN.4/233, paras. 48, 49; Iluyomade, 16 *Harv. Int. LJ* (1975), 47–92; Taylor, 46 *BY* (1972–3), 323–52; Thirlway, 60 *BY* (1989), 25–9.

[73] Citations often involve *ex post facto* recruitment of arbitral awards, e.g. the *Portendick* claim (1843), Lapradelle and Politis, i. 512, and the collection of references to the principle of good faith. See also *Yrbk. ILC* (1953), ii. 219, para. 100.

[74] (1926), PCIJ, Ser. A, no. 7, p. 30.

[75] The Court said: 'Such misuse cannot be presumed, and it rests with the party who states that there has been such misuse to prove its statement'.

[76] (1930), PICJ, Ser. A, no. 24, p. 12. See also *Free Zones* case (1932), PCIJ, Ser. A/B, no. 46, p. 167. References in sep. and Diss. Op. are as follows: ICJ Reports (1948), 79, 80; ibid. (1955), 120. Cf. Judge Anzilotti, *Electricity Company of Sofia* case (1939), PCIJ, Ser. A/B, no. 77, p. 98. A constant exponent of the doctrine was Judge Alvarez: ICJ Reports (1949), 47; ibid. (1950), 15; ibid. (1951), 149ff.; ibid. (1952), 128–33.

[77] See Cheng and Lauterpacht, cited, n. 74, *supra*. See also Kiss, *L'Abus de droit*, pp. 193–6 (a general principle of international law).

[78] *Development*, p. 164. See also Schwarzenberger, 42 *Grot. Soc.* (1956) 147–79; Verzijl, *International Law in Historical Perspective* (1968), i. 316–20.

In some cases the doctrine explains the genesis of a rule of existing law, for example the principle that no state has a right to use or permit the use of its territory in such a manner as to cause injury by fumes to the territory of another.[79] Often it represents a plea for legislation or, which is nearly the same thing, the modification of rules to suit special circumstances. In general what is involved is the determination of the qualities of a particular category of permitted acts: is the power or privilege dependent on the presence of certain objectives? The presumption in the case of acts prima facie legal is that motive is irrelevant: but the law may provide otherwise. When the criteria of good faith, reasonableness, normal administration, and so on are provided by an existing legal rule, reference to 'abuse of rights' adds nothing. Similarly, in the case of international organizations, responsibility for excess of authority, *détournement de pouvoir*, exists independently of any general principle of abuse of rights. In conclusion it may be said that the doctrine is a useful agent in the progressive development of the law, but that, as a general principle, it does not exist in positive law. Indeed it is doubtful if it could be safely recognized as an ambulatory doctrine, since it would encourage doctrines as to the relativity of rights[80] and result, outside the judicial forum, in instability.

9. RESPONSIBILITY FOR THE ACTS OF STATE ORGANS, OFFICIALS, REVOLUTIONARIES, AND OTHERS

(a) General aspects

The subject of state responsibility suffers from too much categorization. The question of liability of the legal person, the state, is overlaid by categories of imputability,[81] direct and indirect responsibility, and of responsibility for acts of special groups, viz., state organs,[82] revolutionaries, and individuals. Strictly, every breach of duty on the part of states must arise by reason of the act or omission of one or more of the organs of state, and, since in many contexts the principle of objective responsibility applies, the emphasis is on causal connection and the 'conduct appropriate' to the given situation. 'Liability for the acts of State organs, etc.' is coextensive with the whole range of legal duties, and yet the categories are commonly employed solely in connection with special problems of the responsibility of states for harm to resident aliens.[83] The association of

---

[79] See the *Trail Smelter* arbitration (1941), *Ann. Digest* (1938–40), no. 104; *RIAA* iii. 1905. See also the *Corfu Channel* case, *supra*, p. 427.

[80] Cf. Bowett's views discussed *supra*, p. 142 n. 119.

[81] See *supra*, p. 436.

[82] And further, special treatment of the legislature, executive, judiciary, military forces, officials generally, and *ultra vires* acts of officials.

[83] See further ch. 24. This association in the literature of the subject is less justified today when other topics, e.g. the law concerning the use or threat of force, and the development of weapons, have at least an equal claim to special treatment.

propositions with a particular area of delict is unfortunate, since the nature of the harm determines the extent of liability for the acts and omissions of organs and individuals. Standards of conduct may be relatively strict in the case of foreign diplomatic and consular agents[84] present on state territory or harms caused by armed forces[85] or explosives[86] within the territory to the interests of a foreign state, but less strict elsewhere. The presence of *dolus* may affect the nature of causation in a given case.[87] Particular rules and fact situations are more important than general propositions about responsibility for the acts of the judiciary or other categories of official: the categories provide only very general guidance.[88] Thus there may be responsibility for *ultra vires* acts of officials[89] and yet no responsibility for the acts of an official, acting with apparent authority, proved to have acted under the orders of a foreign power. Many cases provide nothing more than examples of the standard of conduct required. The status of the individual actor is only a factor in establishing 'imputability', or causal connection between the corporate entity of the state and the harm done.

In some cases the categories of 'tortfeasor' provide no help at all. In the *Corfu Channel* case[90] Albania was held responsible for the consequences of mine-laying in her territorial waters by reason of the knowledge by the Albanian authorities of the presence of the mines. There was no finding as to the agency which did the mine-laying, and it was possible that a third state was involved. Similarly, a neutral state may be responsible for allowing armed expeditions to be fitted out within its jurisdiction which subsequently carry out belligerent operations against another state.[91] With these extensive reservations, attention may be directed to the problems associated with particular categories of organs and persons. It is to be noted that the subject-matter now to be examined is dealt with in the International Law Commission's Articles on Responsibility of States (2001), Articles 4 to 11.

(b) State organs[92]

(i) *Executive and administration*.[93] In the *Massey* claim[94] the United States recovered an award of 15,000 dollars by reason of the failure of the Mexican authorities to take adequate measures to punish the killer of Massey, a United States citizen working in

---

[84] See the *Chapman* claim (1930), *RIAA* iv. 632; 8 *Canad. Yrbk.* (1970), 355–6; Cole, 41 *BY* (1967), at 390–2.

[85] But see *infra*, pp. 454–5, on civil and international war.

[86] See the *Corfu Channel* case, *supra*, pp. 442–3.

[87] *Supra*, p. 441.

[88] Cf. the treatment in McNair, *Opinions*, ii. 207ff., Oppenheim, i. 357–69; and Schwarzenberger, *International Law* (3rd edn.), i. 613–31 (the most judicious treatment).

[89] *Infra*, p. 452–3.

[90] *Supra*, pp. 442–3.

[91] See the *Alabama* arbitration (1872), Moore, *Arbitrations*, i. 653.

[92] On the acts of heads of states, members of governments, and diplomatic envoys see Oppenheim, i. 358–9.

[93] See García Amador, 94 Hague *Recueil* (1958, II), 403; id., *Yrbk. ILC* (1956), ii. 187; ibid. (1957), ii. 107, 109; Accioly, 96 Hague *Recueil* (1959, I), 373, 392–4; McNair, *Opinions*, ii. 207–19; Schwarzenberger, *International Law* (3rd edn.), i. 615–18; Whiteman, vii. 807–19.

[94] (1927), *RIAA* iv. 155. The claim was brought on behalf of the widow individually and as guardian of two minor children of herself and Massey. See also the *Way* claim (1928), *RIAA* iv. 391.

Mexico. The opinion of Commissioner Nielsen stated:[95] 'I believe that it is undoubtedly a sound general principle that, whenever misconduct on the part of [persons in state service], whatever may be their particular status or rank under domestic law, results in the failure of a nation to perform its obligations under international law, the nation must bear the responsibility for the wrongful acts of its servants'. Unreasonable acts of violence by police officers and a failure to take the appropriate steps to punish the culprits will also give rise to responsibility.[96] Except for the operation of the local remedies rule,[97] the distinction between higher and lower officials has no significance for the placing of responsibility on the state.[98] In each case it will be for the relevant rule of law applied to the particular facts to establish whether responsibility flows from the act of the official as such or from the insufficiency of the measures taken by other organs to deal with the consequences of the act of the official. In the *Rainbow Warrior* incident (1985) the French Government admitted its responsibility for the destruction by agents of the Ministry of Defence of the vessel *Rainbow Warrior* in Auckland harbour. The mediation of the UN Secretary-General resulted in a complex settlement which involved the payment of seven million US dollars as compensation for the breach of New Zealand territorial sovereignty.[99] The Judgment of the International Court in the Merits phase of the *Nicaragua* case held the United States responsible for a pattern of hostile activities directed against Nicaragua and carried out by its agents.[100] The European Court of Human Rights has defined the principles applicable when a State, as a consequence of military action, exercises control of an area outside its national territory:[101]

52. As regards the question of imputability, the Court recalls in the first place that in its abovementioned Loizidou judgment (*preliminary objections*) (pp. 23–4, para. 62) it stressed that under its established case-law the concept of 'jurisdiction' under Article 1 of the Convention is not restricted to the national territory of the Contracting States. Accordingly, the responsibility of Contracting States can be involved by acts and omissions of their authorities which produce effects outside their own territory. Of particular significance to the present case the Court held, in conformity with the relevant principles of international law governing State responsibility, that the responsibility of a Contracting Party could also arise when as a consequence of military action—whether lawful or unlawful—it exercises effective control of an area outside its national territory. The obligation to secure, in such an area, the rights and freedoms set out in the Convention, derives from the fact of such control whether it be exercised directly, through its armed forces, or through a subordinate local administration. ...

---

[95] Ibid. at 159.

[96] *Roper* claim (1927), *RIAA* iv. 145; *Pugh* claim (1933), *RIAA* ii. 1439.

[97] On which see *infra*, p. 472.

[98] See the *Massey* claim and *Way* claim, *ubi supra*; Schwarzenberger, *International Law*, pp. 617–18. For another opinion: Borchard, *Diplomatic Protection of Citizens Abroad* (1928), 185–90.

[99] Ruling of the Secretary-General, 6 July 1986; *ILR* 74, 241; 26 *ILM* (1987), 1346.

[100] *Case Concerning Military and Paramilitary Activities in and Against Nicaragua*, ICJ Reports (1986), 14 at 146–9.

[101] *Loizidou* v. *Government of Turkey* (Merits), ILR 108, 443, 465. This passage was quoted by the Court in *Cyprus* v. *Turkey*, ILR 120, 10, 38 (para. 76).

In the *Case Concerning the Application of the Convention on the Prevention and Punishment of the Crime of Genocide* (*Bosnia and Herzegovina* v. *Serbia and Montenegro*), the International Court determined that the massacres at Srebrenica in July 1995 constituted the crime of genocide within the meaning of the Convention. The Court then dealt with the question whether the actions were attributable to the Respondent. The Judgment sets forth the precise form of the legal analysis:[102]

This question has in fact two aspects, which the Court must consider separately. First, it should be ascertained whether the acts committed at Srebrenica were perpetrated by organs of the Respondent, i.e., by persons or entities whose conduct is necessarily attributable to it, because they are in fact the instruments of its action. Next, if the preceding question is answered in the negative, it should be ascertained whether the acts in question were committed by persons who, while not organs of the Respondent, did nevertheless act on the instruments of, or under the direction or control of, the Respondent.

Having applied the rules of customary international law of state responsibility, the Court made the following determinations. In the first place, the Court decided that the persons alleged to have the status of state organs of Yugoslavia did not have such status at the material time (Judgment, paras. 385–9). The Court then moves to the argument of the Applicant that the agents of the Republika Srpska and its armed forces were in reality de facto organs of the Respondent. In this context the Court applied the criterion of control. In the words of the Judgment:

391. The first issue raised by this argument is whether it is possible in principle to attribute to a State conduct of persons – or groups of persons – who, while they do not have the legal status of State organs, in fact act under such strict control by the State that they must be treated as its organs of purposes of the necessary attribution leading to the State's responsibility for an internationally wrongful act. The Court has in fact already addressed this question, and given an answer to it in principle, in its Judgment of 27 June 1986 in the case concerning *Military and Paramilitary Activities in and against Nicaragua* (*Nicaragua v United States of America*) (*Merits, Judgment, I.C.J. Reports 1986*, pp. 62–64). In paragraph 109 of that Judgment the Court stated that it had to

'determine...whether or not the relationship of the *contras* to the United States Government was so much one of dependence on the one side and control on the other that it would be right to equate the *contras*, for legal purposes, with an organ of the United States Government, or as acting on behalf of that Government (p. 62).'

Then, examining the facts in the light of the information in its possession, the Court observed that "there is no clear evidence of the United States having actually exercised such a degree of control in all fields as to justify treating the *contras* as acting on its behalf" (para. 109), and went on to conclude that "the evidence available to the Court...is insufficient to demonstrate [the *contras'*] complete dependence on United States aid", so that the Court was "unable to determine that the *contra* force may be equated for legal purposes with the forces of the United States" (pp. 62–3, para. 110).

---

[102] Judgment dated 26 February 2007, para. 384.

The Court continues:

392. The passages quoted show that, according to the Court's jurisprudence, persons, groups of persons or entities may, for purposes of international responsibility, be equated with State organs even if that status does not follow from internal law, provided that in fact the persons, groups or entities act in "complete dependence" on the State, of which they are ultimately merely the instrument.

The Court determined that the persons involved in the massacres at Srebrenica did not have a relationship of 'complete dependence' on the federal authorities in Belgrade (Judgment, paras. 393–5). The Court then moved to the further alternative argument of the Applicant, namely, that the actions at Srebrenica were committed by persons who, although not having the status of organs of the Respondent, acted on its instructions or under its direction or control.

The Court next presented the bases of its approach as follows:

398. On this subject the applicable rule, which is one of customary law of international responsibility, is laid down in Article 8 of the ILC Articles on State Responsibility as follows:

Article 8

Conduct directed or controlled by a State

The conduct of a person or group of persons shall be considered an act of a State under international law if the person or group of persons is in fact acting on the instructions of, or under the direction or control of, that State in carrying out the conduct.

399. This provision must be understood in the light of the Court's jurisprudence on the subject, particularly that of the 1986 Judgment in the case concerning *Military and Paramilitary Activities in and against Nicaragua (Nicaragua v United States of America)* referred to (paragraph 391). In that Judgment the Court, as noted above, after having rejected the argument that the *contras* were to be equated with organs of the United States because they were "completely dependent" on it, added that the responsibility of the Respondent could still arise if it were proved that it had itself "directed or enforced the perpetration of the acts contrary to human rights and humanitarian law alleged by the applicant State" (*I.C.J. Reports 1986*, p., 64, para. 115); this led to the following significant conclusion:

"For this conduct to give rise to legal responsibility of the United States, it would in principle have to be proved that that State had effective control of the military or paramilitary operations in the course of which the alleged violations were committed." (*Ibid.*, p. 65).

400. The test thus formulated differs in two respects from the test – described above – to determine whether a person or entity may be equated with a State organ even if not having that status under internal law. First, in this context it is not necessary to show that the persons who performed the acts alleged to have violated international law were in general in a relationship of "complete dependence" on the respondent State; it has to be proved that they acted in accordance with the State's instructions or under its "effective control". It must however be shown that this "effective control" was exercised, or that the State's instructions were given, in respect of each operation in which the alleged violations occurred, not generally in respect of the overall actions taken by the persons or groups of persons having committed the violations.

The Court then applied these principles and concluded that there was no factual basis for finding the Respondent responsible on the basis of direction or control (Judgment, paras. 408–15).

(ii) *Armed forces.* The same principles apply to this category of officials, but it is probably the case that a higher standard of prudence in their discipline and control is required, for reasons which are sufficiently obvious.[103] Commissioner Nielsen, in his opinion on the *Kling* claim,[104] said: 'In cases of this kind it is mistaken action, error in judgment, or reckless conduct of soldiers for which a government in a given case has been held responsible. The international precedents reveal the application of principles as to the very strict accountability for mistaken action'. A recent example of responsibility arising from mistaken but culpable action by units of the armed forces is the Soviet action in shooting down a Korean commercial aircraft (1983).[105]

In the *Case Concerning Armed Activities on the Territory of the Congo* (*DRC* v. *Uganda*) the International Court addressed the question whether Uganda was responsible for the acts and omissions of her armed forces on the territory of the DRC. The Court formulated the legal position as follows:[106]

213. The Court turns now to the question as to whether acts and omissions of the UPDF and its officers and soldiers are attributable to Uganda. The conduct of the UPDF as a whole is clearly attributable to Uganda, being the conduct of a State organ. According to a well-established rule of international law, which is of customary character, "the conduct of any organ of a State must be regarded as an act of that State" (*Difference Relating to Immunity from Legal Process of a Special Rapporteur of the Commission on Human Rights, Advisory Opinion, I.C.J. Reports 1999 (I)*, p. 87, para. 62). The conduct of individual soldiers and officers of the UPDF is to be considered as the conduct of a State organ. In the Court's view, by virtue of the military status and function of Ugandan soldiers in the DRC, their conduct is attributable to Uganda. The contention that the persons concerned did not act in the capacity of persons exercising governmental authority in the particular circumstances, is therefore without merit.

214. It is furthermore irrelevant for the attribution of their conduct to Uganda whether the UPDF personnel acted contrary to the instructions given or exceeded their authority. According to a well-established rule of a customary nature, as reflected in Article 3 of the Fourth Hague Convention respecting the Laws and Customs of War on Land of 1907 as well as in Article 91 of Protocol 1 additional to the Geneva Conventions of 1949, a party to an armed conflict shall be responsible for all acts by persons forming part of its armed forces.

---

[103] See Huber in the *Spanish Zone of Morocco* claims (1925), *RIAA* ii. 617 at 645; Freeman, 88 Hague *Recueil* (1955, II), 285. Cf. the *Caire* case (1929), *RIAA* v. 516 at 528–9. See also the *Chevreau* case (1931), *RIAA* ii. 1115; the *Naulilaa* case (1928), ibid. 1013; *Eis Claim*, ILR 30, 116; *García and Garza* case. *RIAA* iv. 119; and the report of a League of Nations Commission of Inquiry, 1925, for which see Conwell-Evans, *The League Council in Action* (1929), 155–60; Garner, 20 *AJ* (1926), 337. See also Whiteman, viii. 825–30.

[104] (1930), *RIAA* iv. 575 at 579; Briggs, p. 686 at p. 689.

[105] See 22 *ILM* (1983), 1190–8, 1419; 54 *BY* (1983), 513.

[106] I.C.J. Reports (2005), 168 at p. 242.

(iii) *Federal units, provinces, and other internal divisions.*[107] A state cannot plead the principles of municipal law, including its constitution, in answer to an international claim.[108] Arbitral jurisprudence contains examples of the responsibility of federal states for acts of authorities of units of the federations.[109]

(iv) *The legislature.*[110] This organ is in normal circumstances a vital part of state organization and gives expression to official policies by its enactments. The problem specific to this category is to determine when the breach of duty entails responsibility. Commonly, in the case of injury to aliens, a claimant must establish damage consequent on the implementation of legislation or the omission to legislate.[111] However, it may happen that, particularly in the case of treaty obligations,[112] the acts and omissions of the legislature are without more creative of responsibility. If a treaty creates an obligation to incorporate certain rules in domestic law, failure to do so entails responsibility for breach of the treaty, Professor Schwarzenberger[113] observes:

It is a matter for argument whether the mere existence of such legislation or only action under it constitutes the breach of an international obligation. Sufficient relevant *dicta* of the World Court exist to permit the conclusion that the mere existence of such legislation may constitute a sufficiently proximate threat of illegality to establish a claimant's legal interest in proceedings for at least a declaratory judgment.[114]

(v) *The judicature.*[115] The activity of judicial organs relates substantially to the rubric 'Denial of justice', which will be considered subsequently in Chapter 24 on the treatment of aliens. However, it is important to bear in mind, what is perhaps obvious, that the doings of courts may affect the responsibility of the state of the forum in other ways. Thus in respect of the application of treaties McNair[116] states: '...a State has a right to

---

[107] See Accioly, 96 Hague *Recueil* (1959, I), 388–91; Schwarzenberger, *International Law*, i. (3rd edn.), 625–7; McNair, *Opinions*, i. 36–7.

[108] *Supra*, pp. 34–5.

[109] *Youmans* claim (1926), *RIAA* iv. 110; *Mallén* claim (1927), *RIAA* iv. 173; *Pellat* claim (1929), *RIAA* v. 534; *Metalclad Corporation* v. *United Mexican States*, ILR 119, 615; ICSID (Additional Facility); *S. D. Myers, Inc.* v. *Canada*, ILR 121, 72; Partial Award.

[110] See Sibert, 48 *RGDIP* (1941–5), 5–34; García Amador, 94 Hague *Recueil* (1958, II), 401–2; id., *Yrbk. ILC* (1956), ii. 182, 186; ibid. (1957), ii. 107, 108; Accioly, 96 Hague *Recueil* (1959, I), 374–5; McNair, *Opinions*, ii. 219–21; Schwarzenberger, *International Law* (3rd edn.), i. 614–15; Fitzmaurice, 92 Hague *Recueil* (1957, II), 89–90; Guggenheim, ii. 7–9; Jiménez de Aréchaga, in Sørensen, pp. 544–6.

[111] See the *Mariposa* claim (1933), *RIAA* vi. 338 at 340–1.

[112] Where, on a reasonable construction of the treaty, a breach creates a claim without special damage. In any case, representations may be made and steps to obtain redress, *quia timet*, may be taken. On the Panama Canal Tolls controversy between Great Britain and the United States, see McNair, *Law of Treaties* (1961), 547–50; Hackworth, vi. 59.

[113] *International Law*, p. 614.

[114] See ibid. 604–5.

[115] On the category 'judicial officer' see the *Way* claim (1928), *RIAA* iv. 391 at 400. Generally see Jiménez de Aréchaga, in Friedmann, Henkin, and Lissitzyn (eds.), *Transnational Law in a Changing Society* (1972), 171–87. See also *Loayza Tamayo* v. *Peru*, ILR 116, 338; Inter-American Court of HumanIghts; Advisory Opinion on the *Difference Relating to Immunity*, ICJ Reports (1999), 62, 86–88, paras 57–65; *Azinian* v. *United Mexican States*, ILR 121, 1 (ICSID (Additional Facility)).

[116] *Law of Treaties*, p. 346.

delegate to its judicial department the application and interpretation of treaties. If, however, the courts commit errors in that task or decline to give effect to the treaty or are unable to do so because the necessary change in, or addition to, the national law has not been made, their judgments involve the State in a breach of treaty'.

(vi) *Ultra vires acts of organs and officials.*[117] It has long been apparent in the sphere of domestic law that acts of public authorities which are *ultra vires* should not by that token create immunity from legal consequences. In international law there are other reasons for disregarding a plea of illegality under domestic law. Moreover, the lack of express authority cannot be decisive as to the responsibility of the state. Arbitral jurisprudence and the majority of writers support the rule that states may be responsible for *ultra vires* acts of their officials committed within their apparent authority or general scope of authority.[118] An act of arrest by a police officer, in fact carrying out a private policy of revenge, but seeming to act in the role of police officer to the average observer, would be within the category. The rule accords generally with a regime of objective responsibility.

In the *Union Bridge Company* case[119] a British official of the Cape Government Railways appropriated neutral (American) property during the Second Boer War, mistakenly believing it was not neutral: the tribunal considered that liability was not affected by the official's mistake or the lack of intention on the part of the British authorities to appropriate the material, stating that the conduct was within the general scope of duty of the official. In the *Caire* claim[120] a captain and a major in the Conventionist forces in control of Mexico had demanded money from M. Caire under threat of death, and had then ordered the shooting of their victim when the money was not forthcoming. In holding Mexico responsible for this act, Verzijl, President of the Commission, said:

The State also bears an international responsibility for all acts committed by its officials or its organs which are delictual according to international law, regardless of whether the official or organ has acted within the limits of his competency or has exceeded those limits...However, in order to justify the admission of this objective responsibility[121] of the State

---

[117] See Meron, 33 *BY* (1957), 85–114; García Amador, *Yrbk. ILC* (1957), ii. 107, 109–10; Accioly, 96 Hague *Recueil* (1959, I), 360–3; Guggenheim, ii. 5–7; Anzilotti, *Cours*, i. 470–4; Freeman, 88 Hague *Recueil*, 290–2; Quadri, 113 Hague *Recueil* (1964, III), 465–8; *Yrbk. ILC* (1975) ii. 61–70; International Law Commision's Articles on Responsibility, Art. 7, and Commentary.

[118] Meron, 33 *BY* (1957), 85–114; Jiménez de Aréchaga, in Sørensen, p. 548. See also the *Bases of Discussion* of the Conference for the Codification of International Law, 1930, for the views of governments and the proposals of the Preparatory Committee (see Meron, 33 *BY* (1957), 101–2). Basis no. 13 was adopted by the Third Committee of the Conference as Art. 8 (2): 'International responsibility is...incurred by a State if damage is sustained by a foreigner as a result of unauthorized acts of its officials performed under cover of their official character, if the acts contravene the international obligations of the State. International responsibility is, however, not incurred by a State if the official's lack of authority was so apparent that the foreigner should have been aware of it, and could, in consequence, have avoided the damage'.

[119] (1924), *RIAA* vi. 138; 19 *AJ* (1925), 215.

[120] (1929), *RIAA* v. 516 at 530; *Ann. Digest*, 5 (1929–30), no. 91. See also the *Case Concerning Armed Activities on the Territory of the Congo (DRC v. Uganda)*, ICJ Reports (2005),168 at p. 242 (para.214).

[121] See *supra*, pp. 437ff.

for acts committed by its officials or organs outside their competence, it is necessary that they should have acted, at least apparently, as authorized officials or organs, or that, in acting, they should have used powers or measures appropriate to their official character...

In the *Youmans* case[122] the Commission stated: 'Soldiers inflicting personal injuries or committing wanton destruction or looting always act in disobedience of some rules laid down by superior authority. There could be no liability whatever for such misdeeds if the view were taken that any acts committed by soldiers in contravention of instructions must always be considered as personal acts'. It is not always easy to distinguish personal acts and acts within the scope of (apparent) authority. In the case of higher organs and officials the presumption will be that there was an act within the scope of authority.[123] Where the standard of conduct required is very high, as in the case of military leaders and cabinet ministers in relation to control of armed forces, it may be quite inappropriate to use the dichotomy of official and personal acts: here, as elsewhere,[124] much depends on the type of activity and the related consequences *in the particular case*.[125]

Students of the English rules as to the liability of employers for the torts of employees may well suspect that the concepts of 'apparent authority' and 'general scope of authority' are means to an end and are not to be examined too closely. It is not difficult to find cases in which the acts of state agents were clearly *ultra vires* and yet responsibility has been affirmed. *Youmans*[126] was such a case, where troops sent to protect aliens besieged by rioters joined in the attack, in which the aliens were killed. In some cases the decisions for responsibility may be buttressed by circumstances indicating negligence by superior officers. So in the *Zafiro*[127] the United States was held responsible for looting by the civilian crew of a merchant vessel employed as a supply vessel by American naval forces, under the command of a merchant captain who in turn was under the orders of an American naval officer. The tribunal emphasized the failure to exercise proper control in the circumstances.[128] What really matters, however, is the amount of control *which ought to have been exercised* in the particular circumstances,

---

[122] (1926), *RIAA* iv. 110 at 116; 21 *AJ* (1927), 571 at 578; *Ann. Digest*, 3 (1925–6), no. 162.

[123] But see the *Bensley* case, Moore, *Arbitrations*, iii. 3018 (responsibility denied for the personal act of the governor of a Mexican state).

[124] See *supra*, p. 437.

[125] Cf. the finding of the International Military Tribunal for the Far East on the operations by the Japanese Kwantung Army at Nomonhan in 1939; Judgment (Far Eastern Comm. text), 331–3; Brownlie, *International Law and the Use of Force by States*, pp. 210–11. See also *Sandline International Inc., and Papua New Guinea*, ILR 117, 552; Interim Award.

[126] *Supra*, n. 120.

[127] (1925), *RIAA* vi. 160; 20 *AJ* (1926), 385; *Ann. Digest*, 3 (1925–6), no. 161. See also the *Metzger* case (1903), *RIAA* x. 417; the *Roberts* case, ibid. ix. 204; the *Crossman* case, ibid. 356.

[128] Viz., the absence of civil or military government in Manila during the Spanish–American war. The tribunal might seem to overemphasize the need for failure to control, but the case is different from those in which unauthorized acts of armed forces occur within the area of established sovereignty of the state to which the armed forces belong: cf. the *Caire* case, *supra*.

not the amount of actual control.[129] This principle is of particular importance in relation to administrative practices involving violations of human rights.

(c) Mob violence, insurrection, revolution, and civil war[130]

The general principles considered below apply to a variety of situations involving acts of violence either by persons not acting as agents of the lawful government of a state, or by persons acting on behalf of a rival or candidate government set up by insurgents. The latter may be described as a '*de facto* government'. In the case of localized riots and mob violence, substantial neglect to take reasonable precautionary and preventive action and inattention amounting to official indifference or connivance will create responsibility for damage to foreign public and private property in the area.[131] In the proceedings arising from the seizure of United States diplomatic and consular staff as hostages in Tehran, the International Court based responsibility for breaches of the law of diplomatic relations upon the failure of the Iranian authorities to control the militants (in the early phase) and also upon the adoption and approval of the acts of the militants (at the later stage).[132]

Lord McNair[133] extracts five principles from the reports of the legal advisers of the British Crown on the responsibility of lawful governments for the consequences of insurrection and rebellion. The first three principles are as follows:

(i) A State on whose territory an insurrection occurs is not responsible for loss or damage sustained by a foreigner unless it can be shown that the Government of that State was negligent in the use of, or in the failure to use, the forces at its disposal for the prevention or suppression of the insurrection;

(ii) this is a variable test, dependent on the circumstances of the insurrection;

---

[129] See *Case of Ireland against the United Kingdom*, Europ. Ct. of HR, 18 Jan. 1978, ILR 58, 190; Judgment, paras. 158–9; *Velasquez Rodriguez* case, Inter-Am. Ct. of HR, Judgment of 29 July 1988, ILR 95, 232; the *Gordon* case (1930), *RIAA* iv. 586; 25 *AJ* (1931), 380; *Ann. Digest*, 5 (1929–30), no. 103 (army doctors at target practice with privately acquired pistol); and the *Morton* case, ibid. 428 (murder in a *cantina* by a drunken officer off duty); and cf. the *Mallén* case (1927), ibid. 173; 21 *AJ* (1927), 803; the *Henriquez* case, ibid. x. 727.

[130] See Ago, *Yrbk. ILC* (1972), ii. 126–52; Report of the Commission, ibid. (1975), ii. 91–106; Accioly, 96 Hague *Recueil* (1959, I), 395–403; Schwarzenberger, *International Law* (3rd edn.), i. 627–30; Briggs, pp. 697–721; McNair, *Opinions*, ii. 238–73, 277; *British Digest*, vi. 175–99; Borchard, *Diplomatic Protection*, pp. 213–45; Harv. Research, 23 *AJ* (1929), Spec. Suppl., pp. 188–96; Oppenheim, i. 550–4; Silvanie, 33 *AJ* (1939), 78–103; Hackworth, v. 657–82; Eagleton, *Responsibility*, pp. 125–56; Whiteman, viii. 189–24, 830–7; de Visscher, *Les Effectivités du droit international public* (1967), 120–1; 8 *Canad. Yrbk.* (1970), 356–7; Jiménez de Aréchaga in Sørensen, pp. 561–4; Akehurst, 43 *BY* (1968–9), 49–70; *Répertoire suisse*, iii. 1738–43; Verzijl, *International Law in Historical Perspective*, vi. 694–705; Brownlie, *System of the Law of Nations* (Pt. 1), 167–79; Rousseau, v. 73–5, 81–8; International Law Commission, Articles on State Responsibility, Art. 10, and Commentary.

[131] *Ziat, Ben Kiran* claim, *RIAA* ii. 730; *Youmans* case, ibid. iv. 110; Whiteman, viii. 831 (claim against Libya); UK and Indonesia, Exchange of Notes, 1 Dec. 1966, *Treaty Series* no. 34 (1967), Cmnd. 3277; Cole, 41 *BY* (1965–6), 390–2; *Noyes* case (1933), *RIAA* vi. 308; *Pinson* case (1928), *RIAA* v. 327; *Sarropoulos* v. *Bulgaria* (1927), 7 Recueil des décisions des tribunaux arbitraux mixtes, p. 47 at p. 50; *Ann. Digest*, 4 (1927–8), no. 162; Hackworth, v. 657–65.

[132] *Case Concerning United States Diplomatic and Consular Staff in Tehran*, ICJ Reports (1980), 3 at 29–30, 33–6. *Short* v. *Islamic Republic of Iran*, ILR 82, 149. See also *Yeager* v. *Islamic Republic of Iran*, ibid., 179; *Rankin* v. *Islamic Republic of Iran*, ibid., 204.

[133] *Opinions*, ii. 245.

(iii) such a State is not responsible for the damage resulting from military operations directed by its lawful government unless the damage was wanton or unnecessary, which appears to be substantially the same as the position of belligerent States in an international war.

These principles are substantially similar to those presented by writers of various nationalities. The general rule of non-responsibility[134] rests on the premises that, even in a regime of objective responsibility, there must exist a normal capacity to act, and a major internal upheaval is tantamount to *force majeure*. This is straightforward enough, but uncertainty arises when the qualifications put upon the general rule are examined. At the outset it will be noted that the general rule and the qualifications are stated in respect of damage to aliens on the territory of the state: this is unfortunate, since the nature of the qualifications (the conditions of responsibility) may vary according to the object of harm, so that, for example, if a diplomatic or consular agent is involved, a higher standard of conduct will be required.[135] There is general agreement among writers that the rule of non-responsibility cannot apply where the government concerned has failed to show due diligence. However, the decisions of tribunals and the other sources offer no definition of 'due diligence'. Obviously no very dogmatic definition would be appropriate, since what is involved is a standard which will vary according to the circumstances. And yet, if 'due diligence' be taken to denote a fairly high standard of conduct the exception would overwhelm the rule. In a comment on the Harvard Research draft[136] it is stated that: 'Inasmuch as negligence on the part of the government in suppressing an insurrection against itself is improbable, the claimant should be deemed to have the burden of showing negligence; and claims commissions have so held...' The Special Rapporteur for the International Law Commission on state responsibility, García Amador,[137] concludes that the basic principle is that there is a presumption against responsibility, and proposes the following provision:[138] 'The State is responsible for injuries caused to an alien in consequence of riots, civil strife or other internal disturbances if the constituted authority was manifestly negligent in taking the measures which, in such circumstances, are normally taken to prevent or punish the acts in question'. There is some authority for the view that the granting of an amnesty to rebels constitutes a failure of duty and an acceptance of responsibility for their acts on the basis of a form of estoppel: but in many cases this inference will be unjustified.[139]

---

[134] See also Huber, *Spanish Zone of Morocco* claims (1924), *RIAA* ii. 615 at 642; and *RIAA*, ii. 730. Cf. the *Home Missionary Society* case (1920), *RIAA* vi. 42 at 44; *Pinson* claim (1928), *RIAA* v. 327 (also for a discussion of the terms 'insurrection' and 'revolution'); *Sambiaggio* claim (1903), *RIAA* x. 500 (and see the index); *Volkmar* case (1903), *RIAA* ix. 317; *Santa Clara Estates Company* case (1903), ibid. 455; *Standard-Vacuum Oil Company Claim*, ILR 30, 168; *Socony Vacuum Oil Company* claim, ILR 21 (1954), 55. Cf. also *Mossé* case, *RIAA* xiii. 486; *Treves* case, ibid. xiv. 262; *Levi* case, ibid. 272; *Fubini* case, ibid. 420. See also the *Gelbtrunk* claim, ibid. xv. 463.

[135] Moreover, it is sometimes said that resident aliens have consented to certain types of risk.

[136] p. 194.

[137] *Yrbk. ILC* (1957), ii. 121–3.

[138] See also ibid. 121, Art. 12, para. 1.

[139] See Accioly, 96 Hague *Recueil* (1959, I), 402–3.

The other two principles propounded by Lord McNair[140] are generally accepted:

(iv) such a State is not responsible for loss or damage caused by the insurgents to a foreigner after that foreigner's State has recognized the belligerency of the insurgents;

(v) such a State can usually defeat a claim in respect of loss or damage sustained by resident foreigners by showing that they have received the same treatment in the matter
of protection or compensation, if any, as its own nationals (the plea of *diligentia quam
in suis*).[141]

Victorious rebel movements are responsible for illegal acts or omissions by their forces
occurring during the course of the conflict.[142] They also become responsible for the
illegalities of the previous government.[143]

(d) The approval and adoption by a State of harmful acts[144]

Responsibility accrues, quite apart from the operation of other factors, if a State approves
or otherwise adopts the conduct of private persons or entities. The International Court
applied this principle to the actions of the militants in the *Case Concerning United
States Diplomatic and Consular Staff in Tehran*.[145]

10. AGENCY AND JOINT TORTFEASORS

The notion of agency may be applied to a number of legal relationships. Thus the concept extends or could extend to such diverse topics as diplomatic representation and
other aspects of the law governing acts of personal agents of states and organizations,
the distinction between acts of officials for which a state is responsible and their 'personal' acts, the continuity of governments, including the responsibility of states for
acts of previous revolutionary regimes, and the giving of diplomatic protection to non-
nationals. A vital question, which has a close relation to the responsibility of states,
is the extent to which a declaration of war by a state affects those states politically
depend-ent upon it.[146] The protecting state may by virtue of the legal relations between
it and the protected state *ipso facto* have control over the latter's foreign relations. In

---

[140] *Opinions*, ii. 452.

[141] See also García Amador, *Yrbk. ILC* (1957), ii. 122, para. 8.

[142] Ibid. 121 (Art. 12, para. 2), 128 (quoting *Bases of Discussion* of the Hague Codification Conference and
the Harvard Research); Rousseau, *Droit international public* (1953), 380; Schwarzenberger, *International
Law* (3rd edn.), i. 627–9; Hackworth, v. 681ff.; Borchard, *Diplomatic Protection*, p. 241; *Pinson* claim (1928),
RIAA v. 327; *Bolivar Railway Company* case (1903), *RIAA* ix. 445; International Law Commission's Draft
Articles on State Responsibility, Art. 10, and Commentary.

[143] *Supra*, p. 80 on continuity of governments.

[144] See Brownlie, *System of the Law of Nations: State Responsibility, Part I* (1983), 157–8; International
Law Commission, Articles on State Reponsibility, Art. 11, and Commentary.

[145] ICJ Reports (1980), 3 at 29–30, 33–6.

[146] See Oppenheim, i. 191, 193, 196 (n. 1), 206–7 (notes); McNair, *Opinions*, i. 39; *Katrantsios v. The
Bulgarian State*, *Ann. Digest*, 3 (1925–6), no. 27; *van Hoogstraten v. Low Lum Seng*, ibid. 9 (1938–40), no. 16.

other cases a state prima facie independent may be sufficiently under the control of another for agency to be established.

Two issues more directly affecting state responsibility demand attention. The first concerns both the transferred servant and the case of an official acting in different capacities. The *Chevreau* case[147] illustrates the latter situation. In that case part of the French claim against the United Kingdom related to loss flowing from the negligence of the British consul in Persia, acting at the material time as agent for the French consul, and the tribunal rejected this part of the claim. Formal capacity may create an estoppel, or at least a presumption of fact, in such cases, but on particular facts a control test may be necessary to do justice. The second problem concerns the dependent state.[148] In the case where the putative dependent state cannot be regarded as having any degree of international personality[149] because of the extent of outside control, then the incidence of responsibility is no longer in question. In other cases a state may by treaty or otherwise assume international responsibility for another government.[150] In dealing with the *Spanish Zone of Morocco* claims[151] Huber said:

...it would be extraordinary if, as a result of the establishment of the Protectorates, the responsibility incumbent upon Morocco in accordance with international law were to be diminished. If the responsibility has not been assumed by the protecting Power, it remains the burden of the protected State; in any case, it cannot have disappeared. Since the protected State is unable to act without an intermediary on the international level, and since every measure by which a third State sought to obtain respect for its rights from the Cherif, would inevitably have an equal effect upon the interests of the protecting Power, it is the latter who must bear the responsibility of the protected State, at least by way of vicarious liability...the responsibility of the protecting State...is based on the fact that it is that State alone which represents the protected State in international affairs...

However, in cases where the dependent state retains sufficient legal powers to maintain a separate personality and the right to conduct its own foreign relations, the incidence of responsibility will depend on the circumstances: here, if the suzerain,[152] or state in an analogous position, is responsible on the facts, the responsibility will not be vicarious or derivative.[153]

The principles relating to joint responsibility of states are as yet indistinct, and municipal analogies are unhelpful. A rule of joint and several liability in delict should

---

[147] (1931), *RIAA* ii. 1115 at 1141. See also *Prince Sliman Bey* v. *Minister for Foreign Affairs*, ILR 28, 79.

[148] See Schwarzenberger, *International Law* (3rd edn.), i. 624–5.

[149] See *supra*, p. 72.

[150] The basis of responsibility may then rest either on the actual extinction of the personality of the protected state or on estoppel. Cf. *Studer (United States)* v. *Great Britain* (1925), *RIAA* vi. 149; *AJ* (1925), 790. See also Guggenheim ii. 26–7. Cf. agreements for indemnification of the agent: *Zadeh* v. *United States*, ILR 22 (1955), 336; *Oakland Truck Sales Inc.* v. *United States*, ibid. 24 (1957), 952.

[151] (1925), *RIAA* ii. 615 at 648–9. See also *Trochel* v. *State of Tunisia*, ILR 20 (1953), 47.

[152] See *supra*, p. 114.

[153] See Schwarzenberger, *International Law*, i. 624–5, and the *Brown* claim (1923), *RIAA* vi. 120 at 130–1. Conceivably there could exist a joint liability.

certainly exist as a matter of principle, but practice is scarce.[154] Practice in the matter of reparation payments for illegal invasion and occupation rests on the assumption that Axis countries were liable on the basis of individual causal contribution to damage and loss, unaffected by the existence of co-belligerency.[155] However, if there is joint participation in specific actions, for example where state A supplies planes and other material to state B for unlawful dropping of guerrillas and state B operates the aircraft, what is to be the position? Must a plaintiff proceed by making a joint claim against both tortfeasors, or against the operator of the aircraft for all the damage, or may it go against states A and B separately for proportions of damage? In the *Case Concerning Certain Phosphate Lands in Nauru* (*Nauru* v. *Australia*) the International Court held that the possibility of the existence of a joint and several liability of three States responsible for the administration of the Trust Territory at the material time did not render inadmissible *in limine litis* a claim brought against only one of them.[156] The question of substance was reserved for the Merits phase. In fact, a negotiated settlement was reached[157] and, subsequently, the United Kingdom and New Zealand, the other States involved, agreed to pay contributions to Australia on an *ex gratia* basis.[158]

Article 47 of the International Law Commission's Articles on Responsibility (2001) provides as follows:

Plurality of responsible States

1. Where several States are responsible for the same internationally wrongful act, the responsibility of each State may be invoked in relation to that act.
2. Paragraph 1:
    (a) does not permit any injured State to recover, by way of compensation, more than the damage it has suffered;
    (b) is without prejudice to any right of recourse against the other responsible States.

In other words, each State is separately responsible and that responsibility is not reduced by the fact that one or more other States are also responsible for the same act (see the Commentary).

---

[154] See Brownlie, *System of the Law of Nations* (Pt. 1) 189–92. On the question of complicity see *Yrbk. ILC* (1978) ii. (Pt. 1), 52–60 (Ago, Seventh Report); ibid. (1978) ii. (Pt. 2), 98–105 (Report of the Commission); ibid. (1979) ii. (Pt. 1), 4–27 (Ago, Eighth Report); ibid. (1979) ii. (Pt. 2), 94–106 (Report of the Commission); Quigley, 57 *BY* (1986), 77–131; Case of *Nicaragua* v. *Honduras* (Merits), *Memorial of Nicaragua* (1989), Ch. 12.

[155] But cf. the *obiter dictum* of the US Court of Claims in *Anglo-Chinese Shipping Co. Ltd.* v. *United States*, ILR 22 (1955), 982 at 986. See also claims by the United Arab Republic in respect of the Suez attack in 1956, and claims against individual states involved in the joint occupation of Germany and Austria.

[156] ICJ Reports (1992), 240 at pp. 258–9, para. 48. See also President Jennings, ibid., p. 301.

[157] See 32 *ILM* 1471.

[158] See 65 *BY* (1994), 625–6 (U.K. agreement).

11. THE TYPES OF DAMAGE AND THE FORMS AND FUNCTIONS OF REPARATION[159]

IN GENERAL

These subjects must be treated with caution, since the problems involved lead back to substantial issues as to the nature of responsibility and are far from being a mere appendix to the law of state responsibility. Other aspects of the subject also justify circumspection. In the first place, while the science of responsibility in municipal law is helpful, in the sphere of international relations there are to be found important elements, including the rules as to satisfaction,[160] which would look strange in the law of tort and contract. Secondly, the terminology of the subject is in disorder, a fact which in part reflects differences of opinion on matters of substance. The usage adopted by the present writer is as follows. The term 'breach of duty' denotes an illegal act or omission, an 'injury' in the broad sense. 'Damage' denotes loss, *damnum*, whether this is a financial quantification of physical injury or damage, or of other consequences of a breach of duty. 'Reparation' will be used to refer to all measures which a plaintiff may expect to be taken by a defendant state: payment of compensation (or restitution), an apology, the punishment of the individuals responsible, the taking of steps to prevent a recurrence of the breach of duty, and any other forms of satisfaction. 'Compensation' will be used to describe reparation in the narrow sense of the payment of money as a 'valuation' of the wrong done. Confusion arises in the case where compensation is paid for a breach of duty which is actionable without proof of particular items of financial loss, for example the violation of diplomatic or consular immunities, trespass in the territorial sea, or illegal arrest of a vessel on the high seas. The award of compensation

---

[159] See generally García Amador, *Yrbk. ILC* (1956), ii. 209–14; ibid. (1958), ii. 67–70; ibid. (1961), ii. 2–45; and in 94 Hague *Recueil* (1958, II), 462–87; Schwarzenberger, *International Law* (3rd edn.), i. 53–81; Cheng, *General Principles of Law*, pp. 233–40; Briggs, pp. 742–7; Eagleton, 39 *Yale LJ* (1929), 52–75; Kozhevnikov (ed.), *International Law* (n.d.), 130–3. See further Whiteman, *Damages in International Law*, 3 vols. (1937–43); Reitzer, *La Réparation comme conséquence de l'acte illicite en droit international* (1938); Personnaz, *La Réparation du préjudice en droit international public* (1938); Ralston, *The Law and Procedure of International Tribunals* (1926), 241–69; id., Supplement (1936), 115–34; Jiménez de Aréchaga, in Sørensen, pp. 564–72; Przetacznik, 78 *RGDIP* (1974), 919–74; Verzijl, *International Law in Historical Perspective*, vi. 742–71; Subilia, *L'Allocation d'intérêts dans la jurisprudence internationale* (1972); Bollecker-Stern, *Le Préjudice dans la théorie de la responsabilité internationale* (1973); *Yrbk. ILC* (1980), ii. (Pt. 1), 107–29 (Riphagen); ibid. 1980), ii. 62–3 (Report of the Commission); ibid. (1981) ii. (Pt. 1), 79–101 (Riphagen, Second Report); ibid. (1981) ii. (Pt. 2), 142–5 (Report of the Commission); ibid. (1982) ii. (Pt. 1), 22–50 (Riphagen, Third Report); ibid. (1982), ii. (Pt. 2), 78–82 (Report of the Commission); ibid. (1983) ii. (Pt. 1), 3–24 (Riphagen, Fourth Report); ibid. (1983) ii. (Pt. 2), 40–3; ibid. (1984) ii. (Pt. 1), 1–4 (Riphagen, Fifth Report); ibid. (1984) ii. (Pt. 2), 99–104 (Report of the Commission); ibid. (1985) ii. (Pt. 1), 3–19 (Riphagen, Sixth Report); ibid. (1985), ii. (Pt. 2), 24–7 (Report of the Commission); ibid. (1986), ii. (Pt. 2), 35–9 (Report of the Commission); Rousseau, v. 209–50; Gray, *Judicial Remedies in International Law* (1987); International Law Commission, Articles on State Responsibility, Art. 34, and Commentary.

[160] See *infra*, p. 461.

for such illegal acts is sometimes described as 'moral' or 'political' reparation, terms connected with concepts of 'moral' and 'political' injury, and it is this terminology which creates confusion, since the 'injury' is a breach of *legal* duty in such cases and the only special feature is the absence of a neat method of quantifying loss, as there is, relatively speaking, in the case of claims relating to death, personal injuries, and damage to property.[161] It may happen that the particular rule of law makes loss to individuals or some other form of 'special damage' a condition of responsibility.

In the ordinary type of claim the object is similar to that of an action in the municipal sphere. In the *Chorzów Factory* (Indemnity) case[162] the Permanent Court declared that:

The essential principle contained in the actual notion of an illegal act—a principle which seems to be established by international practice and in particular by the decisions of arbitral tribunals—is that reparation must, as far as possible, wipe out all the consequences of the illegal act and re-establish the situation which would, in all probability, have existed if that act had not been committed. Restitution in kind, or, if this is not possible, payment of a sum corresponding to the value which a restitution in kind would bear; the award, if need be, of damages for loss sustained which would not be covered by restitution in kind or payment in place of it—such are the principles which should serve to determine the amount of compensation due for an act contrary to international law.

The normal type of claim has these objectives and primarily aims at the protection of the interests of the claimant state: it is thus to be distinguished from the type of case in which the individual state is seeking to establish its *locus standi* in order to protect legal interests not identifiable with that state alone or with any existing state.[163] Before attention is turned to the principal topics of restitution and compensation, two other forms of remedy associated with the normal type of claim, but having features of their own, must be considered, viz. the declaratory judgment and satisfaction.

DECLARATORY JUDGMENTS[164]

In some cases a declaration by a court as to the illegality of the act of the defendant state constitutes a measure of satisfaction (or reparation in the broad sense).[165] However, international tribunals may be empowered or may assume the power to give a declaratory judgment in cases where this is, or is considered by the parties to be,

---

[161] Even then, the 'compensation' awarded for a broken limb is an exaction for the legal wrong involved, and not all aspects of the injury, e.g. pain and suffering, can be 'quantified' in simple terms of compensation and equivalence.

[162] (1928), PCIJ, Ser. A, no. 17, p. 47.

[163] See *infra*, pp. 467–74.

[164] See Lauterpacht, *Development*, pp. 205–6, 250–2; García Amador, *Yrbk. ILC* (1961), ii. 14–16; Gross, 58 *AJ* (1964), 419–23; C. de Visscher, *Aspects récents du droit procédural de la Cour internationale de justice* (1966), 187–94; Shihata, *The Power of the International Court to determine its own Jurisdiction* (1965), 216–19; Borchard, 29 *AJ* (1935), 488–92; Ritter, *Ann. français* (1975), 278–93; Gray, *Judicial Remedies*, pp. 96–107; Brownlie, *Essays in Honour of Sir Robert Jennings* (1996), 559–64.

[165] See *infra*.

the appropriate and constructive method of dealing with a dispute and the object is not primarily to give 'satisfaction' for a wrong received.[166] While the International Court is unwilling to deal with hypothetical issues and questions formulated in the abstract, it has been willing to give declaratory judgments,[167] and in some cases, for example those concerning title to territory, it may in any case be appropriate to give a declaratory rather than an executory form to the judgment.[168] The applicant states in the *South West Africa* cases[169] were seeking a declaration that certain legislation affecting the territory was contrary to the obligations of South Africa under the Mandate. In the *Case Concerning United States Diplomatic and Consular Staff in Tehran*[170] the Judgment of the International Court included several declaratory prescriptions involving the termination of the unlawful detention of the persons concerned. In the *Nicaragua* case[171] the Judgment at the Merits phase contained an injunctive declaration 'that the United States is under a duty immediately to cease and refrain from all such acts as may constitute breaches of the foregoing legal obligations'.

SATISFACTION[172]

Satisfaction may be defined as any measure which the author of a breach of duty is bound to take under customary law or under an agreement by the parties to a dispute, apart from restitution or compensation. Satisfaction is an aspect of reparation in the broad sense. However, it is not easy to distinguish between pecuniary satisfaction and compensation in the case of breaches of duty not resulting in death, personal injuries, or damage to or loss of property. Claims of this sort are commonly expressed as a claim for an 'indemnity'. If there is a distinction, it would seem to be in the intention behind the demand. If it is predominantly that of seeking a token of regret and acknowledgment of wrongdoing then it is a matter of satisfaction. The objects of satisfaction are three, which are often cumulative: apologies or other acknowledgment of wrongdoing by means of a salute to the flag or payment of an indemnity; the punishment of the individuals concerned; and the taking of measures to prevent a recurrence

---

[166] See *Arabian-American Oil Co.* v. *Saudi Arabia*, ILR 27, 117 at 144–6.

[167] See *Certain German Interests in Polish Upper Silesia* (1926), PCIJ, Ser. A, no. 7, p. 18; and the *Interpretation of Judgments Nos. 7 and 8 (The Chorzów Factory)* (1927), ibid., no. 13, pp. 20, 21. And cf. the *Mavrommatis* case (1925), ibid., no. 5, p. 51, and see *infra*, p. 461 on the *Corfu Channel* case.

[168] See the *Eastern Greenland* case (1933), PCIJ, Ser. A/B, no. 53, pp. 23, 24, 75.

[169] ICJ Reports (1962), 319; ibid. (1966), 6; and see *infra*.

[170] ICJ Reports (1980), 3 at 44–5.

[171] *Case Concerning Military and Paramilitary Activities in and against Nicaragua*, ICJ Reports (1986), 14 at 146–9. See also the Joint Diss. Op. of four judges in the *Nuclear Tests Cases* (Australia v. France), ICJ Reports (1974), 253 at 312–19.

[172] See García Amador, *Yrbk. ILC* (1961), ii. 19–28; Schwarzenberger, *International Law* (3rd edn.), i. 658–9; Jiménez de Aréchaga, in Sørensen, p. 572; Whiteman, viii. 1211–14; International Law Commission's Articles on State Responsibility (2001), Art. 37 and Commentary. See further Bissonnette, *La Satisfaction comme mode de réparation en droit international* (1952); Rousseau, v, 218–20; Przetacznik, 78 *RGDIP* (1974), 919 at 944–74.

of the harm. In the *I'm Alone*[173] case the Canadian Government complained of the sinking on the high seas of a liquor-smuggling vessel of Canadian registration by a United States coastguard vessel, as a climax to a hot pursuit which commenced outside United States territorial waters but within the inspection zone provided for in the 'Liquor Treaty' between Great Britain and the United States. The Canadian claim was referred to Commissioners appointed under the Convention concerned, and in their final report the following appears:

We find as a fact that, from September, 1928, down to the date when she was sunk, the *I'm Alone*, although a British ship of Canadian registry, was *de facto* owned, controlled, and at the critical times, managed, and her movements directed and her cargo dealt with and disposed of, by a group of persons acting in concert who were entirely, or nearly so, citizens of the United States, and who employed her for the purposes mentioned[174]...The Commissioners consider that, in view of the facts, no compensation ought to be paid in respect of the loss of the ship or the cargo.

The act of sinking the ship, however, by officers of the United States Coast Guard, was, as we have already indicated, an unlawful act; and the Commissioners consider that the United States ought formally to acknowledge its illegality, and to apologize to His Majesty's Canadian Government therefor; and, further, that as a material amend in respect of the wrong the United States should pay the sum of $25,000 to His Majesty's Canadian Government; and they recommend accordingly.

A number of ancillary questions remain. It is sometimes suggested that an affront to the honour of a state or intention to harm are preconditions for a demand for satisfaction, but this is very doubtful. Such elements may enter into the assessment of compensation,[175] as also may the failure to undertake measures to prevent a recurrence of the harm or to punish those responsible. Measures demanded by way of apology should today take forms which are not humiliating and excessive.[176]

There is no evidence of a rule that satisfaction is alternative to and, on being given, exclusive of a right to compensation for the breach of duty.[177] In the *Corfu Channel* case[178] the Court declared that the mine-sweeping operation by the Royal Navy in Albania's territorial waters was a violation of her sovereignty, and then stated: 'This declaration is in accordance with the request made by Albania through her Counsel, and is in itself appropriate satisfaction'. In spite of the terminology, this is not an

---

[173] Whiteman, *Damages*, i. 155–7; *RIAA* iii. 1609. See Hyde, 29 *AJ* (1935), 296–301; Fitzmaurice, 17 *BY* (1936), 82–111. See also the *Borchgrave* case (Prelim. Objections) (1937), PCIJ, Ser. A/B, no. 72, no. 73, p. 5; and the *Panay* incident, *Documents on International Affairs* (*RIIA*, 1937), 757; Hackworth, v. 687–9.

[174] i.e. smuggling liquor.

[175] See *infra*, p. 465, on 'penal damages'.

[176] Cf. Stowell, *Intervention in International Law* (1921), 21–35, on measures of 'expiation' demanded in the past, and, on the *Tellini* incident, see Eagleton, 19 *AJ* (1925), 304. See now Art. 47(3) of the I.L.C. work (2001): 'Satisfaction shall not be out of proportion to the injury and may not take a form humiliating to the responsible State'.

[177] No mandatory rule, that is: parties to a dispute may agree otherwise.

[178] ICJ Reports (1949), 4 at 35. See also the *Carthage* and the *Manouba* (1913), Hague Court Reports, i. 329 at 335 and 341 at 349; *RIAA*, xi. 457 at 460, and 471 at 476; and *Rainbow Warrior* arbitration (*New Zealand* v. *France*), ILR 82, 499 at 574–7. And see Parry, 90 Hague *Recueil* (1956, II), 674–93.

instance of satisfaction in the usual meaning of the word: the declaration is that of a court and not a party, and is *alternative* to compensation. No pecuniary compensation had been asked for by Albania, and a declaration of this kind was therefore the only means of giving an effective decision on the matter.[179]

RESTITUTION IN KIND AND RESTITUTION IN INTEGRUM[180]

To achieve the object of reparation tribunals may give 'legal restitution', in the form of a declaration that an offending treaty, or act of the executive, legislature, or judicature, is invalid.[181] Such action can be classified either as a genuine application of the principle of *restitutio in integrum* or as an aspect of satisfaction. Restitution in kind, specific restitution, is exceptional, and the vast majority of claims conventions and *compromis* (agreements to submit to arbitration) provide for the adjudication of pecuniary claims only.[182] Writers[183] and, from time to time, governments and tribunals[184] assert a right to specific restitution, but, while it is safe to assume that this form of redress has a place in the law, it is difficult to state the conditions of its application with any certainty. In the disputes arising out of the Mexican oil expropriations of 1938 and the Iranian measures in respect of the oil industry in 1951, some of the states the corporations of which were affected[185] demanded restitution, but eventually agreed to compensation. In many situations it is clear that a remedy which accommodates the internal competence of governments,[186] while giving redress to those adversely affected, is to be preferred: restitution is too inflexible. At the same time it will not do to encourage the purchase of impunity by the payment of damages and specific

---

[179] Cf. Judge Azevedo, dissenting, ICJ Reports (1949), 113–14; *Aerial Incident* case (Prelim. Objections), ICJ Reports (1959), 127 at 129–31; and see Sørensen, 101 Hague *Recueil* (1960, III), 230.

[180] García Amador, *Yrbk. ILC* (1961), ii. 17–18; Baade, 54 *AJ* (1960), 814–30; Wortley, 55 *AJ* (1961), 680–3; Schwarzenberger, *International Law* (3rd edn.), i. 656–7; Jiménez de Aréchaga in Sørensen, pp. 565–7; Jiménez de Aréchaga, 159 Hague *Recueil* (1978, I) 285–6; Rousseau, 214–18; Gray, *Judicial Remedies*, pp. 95–6; Schachter, 178 Hague *Recueil* (1982, V), 190–1. See also Art. 35 of the I.L.C. work (2001), and the Commentary.

[181] Such action is unusual, but see the *Martini* case (1930), *RIAA* ii. 975 at 1002. See also McNair, *Opinions*, i. 78; and the *Barcelona Traction* case, ICJ Reports (1964), 6; (Second Phase), ICJ Reports (1970), 4; *South West Africa* cases (Second Phase), ICJ Reports (1966) 6 (with particular reference to the laws of apartheid).

[182] See also the General Act for the Pacific Settlement of International Disputes 1928, Art. 32. A revised General Act came into force on 20 Sept. 1950, 71 UNTS, p. 101.

[183] See especially Mann, 48 *BY* (1976–7), 1–65 at 2–5; Verzijl, *International Law in Historical Perspective*, vi. 742.

[184] See the *Walter Fletcher Smith* claim (1927), *RIAA* ii. 913 at 918; Whiteman, *Damages*, ii. 1409; *Central Rhodope Forests* (1933), *RIAA* iii. 1405 at 1432; *Ann. Digest*, 7 (1933–4), no. 39 at p. 99; Whiteman, ii. 1460 at 1483. In the latter two awards restitution was not considered appropriate for practical reasons. See further Whiteman, iii. 1581–2; and cf. the *Interhandel* case, ICJ Reports (1959), 6. See also *BP Exploration Company (Libya) Ltd.* v. *Government of Libyan Arab Republic*, ILR 53, 297 (1973) (*restitutio in integrum* not favoured); *Texaco* v. *Government of the Libyan Arab Republic*, ILR 53, 389 (1977) (*restitutio* affirmed as a principle); *LIAMCO* v. *Government of Libyan Arab Republic*, ILR 62, 140 (1977) (*restitutio* not favoured).

[185] In the first case, the UK and the Netherlands; in the second the UK.

[186] See *supra*, pp. 105–6, on sovereignty and jurisdiction; *infra*, pp. 546–8, on acquired rights and concessions.

restitution will be appropriate in certain cases. In exceptional cases customary law or treaty may create obligations to which is annexed a power to demand specific restitution. Thus in the *Chorzów Factory* case[187] the Permanent Court took the view that, the purpose of the Geneva Convention of 1922 being to maintain the economic status quo in Polish Upper Silesia, restitution was the 'natural redress' for violation of or failure to observe the treaty provisions. There is much that is uncertain, but it would seem that territorial disputes may be settled by specific restitution, although the declaratory form of judgments of the International Court masks the element of 'restitution'.[188] In imposing obligations on aggressor states to make reparation for the results of illegal occupation, the victims may be justified in requiring restitution of 'objects of artistic, historical or archaeological value belonging to the cultural heritage of the [retro]ceded territory'.[189]

12. COMPENSATION, DAMAGES (*DOMMAGES-INTÉRÊTS*)

The general aspects of reparation and satisfaction have been considered already, and it remains to refer to certain problems concerning assessment of pecuniary compensation.[190] International tribunals face the same problems as other tribunals in dealing with indirect damages and deal with the issues in much the same way.[191] It is important to appreciate, even if the tribunals are often obscure in this respect, the intrinsic connection between 'remoteness' and 'measure of damages', on the one hand, and, on the other, the rules of substance. The particular context of a breach of duty, i.e. the nature of the duty itself and the mode of breach, may determine the approach to the question of damages.[192] For the sake of argument, it may be that the rule of law is simply that if harm is caused by negligence in the course of some lawful activity then compensation

[187] (1927), PCIJ, Ser. A, no. 8, p. 28. See also ibid., no. 17, p. 47. *Italian Rep.* v. *Fed. Rep. of Germany*, ILR 29, 442 at 474–6; and *Amoco International Finance* v. *Iran*, 15 Iran–US, CTR 189 at 246–8 (Chamber Three, 14 July 1987). It is normal to release vessels mistakenly captured in prize in neutral waters (see Whiteman, *Damages*, ii. 1139), but there may be no obligation to replace foreign property requisitioned in wartime in kind (Hackworth, vi. 649). But cf. on the obligations of unlawful belligerents, Art. 78 of the Italian Peace Treaty, and the *Duc de Guise* claim, ILR 18 (1951), 423.

[188] See generally *supra*, p. 459, and in particular the *Eastern Greenland* case and the *Temple* case. In the latter the Court found, *inter alia* that Thailand was obliged to restore to Cambodia any sculpture, stelae, fragments of monuments, and pottery which might have been removed by the Thai authorities.

[189] See the Italian Peace Treaty, Arts. 12, 37, 78 and Annex XIV, para. 4, and cf. the *Franco-Ethiopian Railway Co.* claim (1956), ILR 24 (1957), 602. See further Pt. III of the Final Act of the Paris Conference on Reparations, para. A (text: ILR 20 (1953), 441).

[190] See the literature cited *supra*, p. 441; and further Salvioli, 28 Hague *Recueil* (1929, III), 235–86; Yntema, 24 *Columbia LR* (1924), 134–53; *Fisheries* case, Pleadings, I, p. 101.

[191] See Schwarzenberger, *International Law*, i. 664–81; Cheng, *General Principles of Law*, pp. 233–40.

[192] Cf. Jennings, 37 *BY* (1961), 156–82; Salvioli, 28 Hague *Recueil* (1929, III), 268; and the *Dix* case, *RIAA* ix. 119, 121. On causation see also Cheng, *General Principles of Law*, pp. 241–53.

is payable.[193] The scale of compensation will in such a case be less ambitious than that applicable to activity unlawful at birth, for example unprovoked attacks on the vessels of another state. There is some debate as to the possibility of penal damages in international law.[194] The problem concerns in part the granting of compensation for non-political loss, i.e. breach of legal duties as such, for example by unlawful intrusion into the territorial sea. Compensation in such cases is not correctly described as 'penal damages'.[195] However, it is true to say that tribunals are cautious in approaching cases of non-material loss,[196] and there is no simple solution to the problem of assessment. Thus in the *Janes* claim[197] the United States presented a claim based on a failure by Mexico to take adequate steps to apprehend the murderer of an American citizen. The award saw liability in terms of the damage caused to the individuals concerned rather than to the United States,[198] and gave compensation to the relatives of Janes for the 'indignity' caused by the non-punishment of the criminal. However, the United States was making no claim apart from that 'on behalf of' the dependants of Janes, and the Claims Commission was concerned to translate the Mexican breach of duty into damages. The problem was, as it were, one of quantification rather than ascription.

13. CIRCUMSTANCES PRECLUDING WRONGFULNESS[199]

Classifications of 'defences' or 'justifications' are conventional and not very logical. Separate treatment of quantities as 'defences' should denote the existence of a legal burden of proof on the proponents of defences, but this is not always the case.

---

[193] Cf. the rule that expropriation of alien property is lawful if compensation is paid: *infra*, pp. 509ff.

[194] See García Amador, *Yrbk. ILC* (1956), ii. 211–12; Schwarzenberger, *International Law*, i. 673–4; Jorgensen, 68 *BY* (1997), 247–66; Art. 36 of the I.L.C. work, Commentary, para. 4.

[195] Cf. *supra*, on the *I'm Alone* and *Corfu Channel* cases. See the *Lusitania* claims (1923), 18 *AJ* (1924) 361 at 368; and Cheng, *General Principles of Law*, pp. 235–8.

[196] See Parry, 90 Hague *Recueil* (1956, II), 669ff.

[197] (1925), *RIAA* iv. 82. See Brierly, 9 *BY* (1928), 42–9; Jennings, 121 Hague *Recueil* (1967, II) 496. Another problem is the effect of waiver of a right to restitution on damages: see Salvioli 28 Hague *Recueil* (1929, III), 238; Jennings, 37 *BY*, p. 172.

[198] See Art. I of the General Claims Conv. of 1923, set out in Briggs, p. 639.

[199] See Guggenheim, ii. 57–63; García Amador, *Yrbk. ILC* (1956), ii. 208–9; Whiteman, viii. 837–50; *Yrbk. ILC* (1978), ii. (Pt. 1), 61–227; ibid. (1979), ii. (Pt. 1), 27–66 (Ago, Eighth Report); ibid. (1979) ii. (Pt. 2), 106–36 (Report of the Commission); ibid. (1980), ii. (Pt. 1), 14–70 (Ago, Eighth Report, Add.); ibid. (1980), ii. (Pt. 2), 34–62 (Report of the Commission); ibid. (1981) ii. (Pt. 2), 142–3 (Report of the Commission); Rousseau, v. 89–96; Jagota, 16 *Neths. Yrbk.* (1985), 249–77; Elagab, *The Legality of Non-forcible Counter-Measures in International Law* (1988); Alland, in Spinedi and Simma (eds.), *United Nations Codification of State Responsibility*, pp. 143–95; Malanczuk, ibid. 197–286; Barboza, in *Essays in Honour of Manfred Lachs* (1984), 27–42; Salmon, ibid. 235–70; Thirlway, 66 *BY* (1995), 70–80; International Law Commission's Articles on State Responsibility (2001), Arts. 20 (Consent), 21 (Self-defence), 22 (Counter-measures), 23 (*Force majeure*), 24 (Distress), and 25 (Necessity), together with the Commentaries. See also the Reports prepared by Arangio-Ruiz: Third Report, *Yrbk. ILC* 1991, II (Pt. i), 1; Fourth Report, ibid., 1992, II (Pt. 1), 1.

Moreover, in international law the incidence of the burdens of proof is not dependent on a plaintiff-defendant relation as found in systems of municipal law.[200] Again, emphasis on objective responsibility and the specialized nature of many groups of rules narrows the scope of generally accepted defences. Extinctive prescription, and forms of consent (acquiescence or waiver), are usually considered as issues of admissibility of claims, but may be reserved as issues of merits in arbitral and judicial proceedings.[201]

Tribunals accept defences of assumption of risk of the particular harm[202] and contributory negligence.[203] These defences have operated in practice in cases concerning harm to aliens, and the conduct of the individuals concerned has been treated as assumption of risk and so on. The defences also apply, of course, where conduct of organs of the claimant state amounts to assumption of risk or contributory negligence. *Force majeure*[204] will apply to acts of war[205] and under certain conditions to harm caused by insurrection and civil war.[206] However, necessity as an omnibus category probably does not exist, and its availability as a defence is circumscribed by fairly strict conditions.[207] In particular contexts in the law of war, military necessity may be pleaded, and the right of angary allows requisition of ships belonging to aliens lying within the jurisdiction in time of war or other public danger.[208] The use of force in self-defence, collective self-defence, and defence of third states now involves a specific legal regime, though it related in the past to the ambulatory principle of self-preservation.[209] Armed reprisals are clearly excluded by the law of the United Nations Charter, but the propriety of economic reprisals and the plea of economic necessity is still a matter of controversy.[210] A useful principle is that of incomplete privilege according to which the defendant is privileged to commit what would otherwise be a trespass, but upon

---

[200] See Lauterpacht, *Development*, pp. 363–7.

[201] See *infra*, pp. 501–2.

[202] *Home Missionary Society* case (1920), *RIAA* vi. 42. Cf. *Yukon Lumber* case (1913), *RIAA* vi. 17 at 20. See also Whiteman, viii. 842–5; Brownlie, *Festschrift für F.A. Mann* (1977), 309–19.

[203] *Davis* case (1903), *RIAA* ix. 460; Salmon, in *Essays in Honour of Roberto Ago*, iii (1987), 371–99; Bederman, 30 *Virginia Journ.* (1989–90), 335–69.

[204] See UN Secretariat Study, ST/LEG/13, 27 June 1977 (390 pp.); Award of the Arbitral Tribunal in *New Zealand* v. *France* dated 30th April 1990, ILR 82, 499 at 551–5.

[205] *American Electric and Manufacturing Co.* case, *RIAA* ix. 145; *Russian Indemnity* case (1912), *RIAA* xi. 421 at 443; and the *Lighthouses* arbitration (1956), ILR, 23 (1956), 354; *RIAA* xii. 220 at 242. Cf. *Kelley* claim (1930), *RIAA* iv. 608; *Chevreau* case (1930) *RIAA* ii. 1113 at 1123. On special problems affecting contracts by state enterprises see Mann, 9 *ICLQ* (1960), 691–4; Domke, 53 *AJ* (1959), 788–806; and Riad, 108 Hague *Recueil* (1963, I), 646–52.

[206] *Spanish Zone of Morocco* claims (1924), *RIAA* ii. 615 at 642.

[207] Jiménez de Aréchaga in Sørensen, pp. 542–4; and see the Judgment of the International Court in the *Gabcikovo-Nagymaros Project* (Hungary/Slovakia), ICJ Reports (1997), 7 at 9–46. But cf. Cheng, *General Principles of Law*, pp. 73–4, 223–31.

[208] McNair, *Opinions*, iii. 398.

[209] See Chapter 33 below. On the use of force to enforce laws in a contiguous zone see *supra*, p. 192. Cf. Cheng, *General Principles of Law*, pp. 69–102.

[210] See Zoller, *Peacetime Unilateral Remedies* (1984); Elagab, *The Legality of Non-forcible Counter-Measures in International Law* (1988).

the terms that he shall compensate the plaintiff for any damage caused.[211] The right of angary is conditioned in this way. However, attractive as such a doctrine might be in municipal law, in international relations it would encourage too many breaches of the peace if widely adopted.

14. THE NATURE OF A LEGAL INTEREST: *LOCUS STANDI*[212]

The types of international claim considered so far in this chapter involve direct harm to the legal rights of the plaintiff state in a context of delict, but it can happen that individual states may ground a claim either in a broad concept of legal interest or in special conditions which give the individual state *locus standi* in respect of legal interests of other entities. In the *South West Africa* cases[213] Ethiopia and Liberia made applications to the International Court in which the Court was asked to affirm the status of South West Africa as a territory under mandate, and to declare that South Africa had violated various articles of the Mandate Agreement and Article 22 of the Covenant of the League of Nations in consequence of certain aspects of her administration of South West Africa and, in particular, of the practice of apartheid. To found the jurisdiction of the Court the applications relied on Article 7 of the Mandate and Article 37[214] of the Statute of the Court, and the Union of South Africa, in its objections to the jurisdiction, submitted that Ethiopia and Liberia had no *locus standi* in the proceedings. Article 7 of the Mandate provides, in part:

The Mandatory agrees that, if any dispute whatever should arise between the Mandatory and another Member of the League of Nations relating to the interpretation or the application of the provisions of the Mandate, such dispute, if it cannot be settled by negotiation, shall be submitted to the Permanent Court of International Justice...

Apart from the issue as to survival of jurisdiction of that Court by reason of Article 37 of the Statute of the present Court, South Africa argued that neither Ethiopia nor Liberia was 'another Member of the League of Nations' as required for *locus standi* by Article 7 of the Mandate. The Court rejected this argument as contrary to the meaning of the article.[215] Another objection to the jurisdiction rested on the proposition that the

---

[211] Described as such in American doctrine on the law of tort: Harper, James, and Gray, *The Law of Torts* (2nd edn., 1986), i. 71–6; *Vincent v. Lake Erie Transportation Company* (1910), 109 Minn. 456; Lawson and Markesinis, *Tortious Liability for Unintentional Harm in the Common Law and the Civil Law*, i. (1982), 21–2.

[212] See Mbaye, 209 Hague *Recueil* (1988, II), 227–341; Queneudec, 255 Hague *Recueil* (1995), 339–462.

[213] *South West Africa* cases (Prelim. Objections), ICJ Reports (1962), 319; ILR 37, 3. See Verzijl, 11 *Neths. Int. LR* (1963), 1–25; and the literature cited *infra*.

[214] This part of the argument based on Art. 37 is not relevant to the subject at present under discussion.

[215] ICJ Reports (1962), 335–42. Emphasis was placed on the importance of effective judicial protection of the 'sacred trust of civilization'.

dispute brought before the Court by the applicants was not a dispute as envisaged in Article 7, in particular because it did not affect any material interests of the applicant states or their nationals. As a matter of interpretation of Article 7 the Court rejected this argument also:[216]

For the manifest scope and purport of the provisions of this Article indicate that the Members of the League were understood to have a legal right or interest in the observance by the Mandatory of its obligations both toward the inhabitants of the Mandated Territory,[217] and toward the League of Nations and its Members.

Having rejected these and other South African preliminary objections, the Court held that it had jurisdiction to decide the merits of the dispute.[218] In his Separate Opinion Judge Jessup[219] argued at length that 'international law has long recognized that States may have legal interests in matters which do not affect their financial, economic, or other "material", or, say, "physical" or tangible interests', and referred to provisions for settlement of disputes in minorities treaties, the Genocide Convention, and the Constitution of the International Labour Organization, cases in which all states had a legal interest in the protection of general interests of mankind.

This highly interesting decision, by a narrow majority, can of course be confined to the specific issue of the interpretation of Article 7 of the Mandate Agreement. It is significant that the dissenting judges were much more cautious on the nature of a legal interest. Thus President Winiarski expressed himself as follows:[220]

The relevant words of Article 7 cannot be interpreted in such a way as to conflict with the general rule of procedure according to which the Applicant State must have the capacity to institute the proceedings, that is to say, a subjective right, a real and existing individual interest which is legally protected. 'No interest, no action': this old tag expresses in a simplified, but, on the whole, correct form the rule...of international law. We have seen it in the *Mavrommatis* case.[221] In the *Wimbledon* case[222] the Permanent Court of International Justice met the objection raised by Germany by saying...that 'each of the four Applicant Powers has a clear interest in the execution of the provisions relating to the Kiel Canal, since they all possess fleets and merchant vessels flying their respective flags'... [the Applicants] assert that they have a sufficient legal interest...: 'a legal interest in seeing to it through judicial process that the sacred trust of civilization created by the Mandate is not violated'. But such a legally protected interest has not been conferred on them by an international instrument...

---

[216] Ibid. 343.

[217] See further Judge Bustamante, Sep. Op., ibid. 355–6, 374, 378, 380; and Verzijl, 11 *Neths. Int. LR* (1963), at 25.

[218] By 8 votes to 7.

[219] ICJ Reports (1962), 424–33.

[220] Ibid. 455–7. See also the Joint Diss. Op. of Spender and Fitzmaurice, pp. 547–9; and the Diss. Op. of Morelli, pp. 569–71.

[221] (1925), PCIJ, Ser. A, no. 5.

[222] (1923), PCIJ, Ser. A, no. 1, p. 20.

Subsequently the view of the dissenting judges was to prevail. In the *South West Africa* cases (Second Phase),[223] contrary to the expectations of those appearing before the Court, the merits were not dealt with. There had been certain changes in the membership of the Court, and the minority of 1962 now appeared as a majority.[224] The view of the majority in 1966 was that the question of the legal interest of the applicants had not been finally settled in the first phase of the proceedings. A fine distinction was drawn between the right to invoke a jurisdictional clause and the question of legal interest, the latter being an issue of merits.[225] The Court disagreed with the view that the issue of legal interest was a question of admissibility disposed of in 1962. Even if the issue were treated as one of admissibility it would fall to be dealt with at the second phase.[226] In the event the Court treated the issue of legal interest as one of merits. In the view of the 'minority' of seven judges the consequence was to violate the principle of *res judicata* by reopening a question settled at the first phase.

On the matter of the legal interest of the applicants the Court took up the general position of the minority on the Court in 1962. It is important to record precisely what the Court in 1966 said on the issue of legal interest. The Court was concerned with the interpretation of a particular instrument, the Mandate for South West Africa, and refused to apply the teleological principle of interpretation of treaties.[227] As a matter of interpretation, individual states only had a legal interest in respect of certain provisions of the Mandate characterized by the Court as the 'special interests' provisions, for example those concerning freedom for missionaries who were nationals of members of the League of Nations to enter and reside in the territory for the purpose of prosecuting their calling.[228] The applicants were not invoking interests protected by such provisions but referred to various provisions classified by the Court as 'conduct' provisions in respect of which the only supervision provided for was through the political organs of the League of Nations.

Aside from the issue of interpretation of the relevant instrument, the Court made certain statements of general application. In considering the argument

---

[223] ICJ Reports (1966), 6; ILR 37, 243. For comment see Cheng, *Curr. Leg. Problems* (1967), 181–212; Katz, *The Relevance of International Adjudication* (1968), ch. 4; Higgins, 42 *Int. Affairs* (1966), 573–99; Falk, 21 *Int. Organization* (1967), 1–24; Jennings, 121 Hague *Recueil* (1967, II), 507–11; Nisot, 3 *Revue belge* (1967), 24–36; de Visscher, *Aspects récents du droit procédural de la Cour internationale de justice*, pp. 17–28; Gross, 120 Hague *Recueil* (1967, I), 375–84; Dugard, 83 *SALJ* (1966), 429–60; Fleming, 5 *Canad. Yrbk.* (1967), 241–52. See also on the concept of *actio popularis*, Seidl-Hohenveldern, *Comunicazioni e studi*, 14 (1975), 803–13; Schwelb, 2 *Israel Yrbk. of Human Rights* (1972), 46–56.

[224] The decision was by 7 votes, together with the casting vote of the President (Spender, Fitzmaurice, Winiarski, Spiropoulos, Morelli, Gros, and Van Wyk, the *ad hoc* judge for South Africa). The 'minority' of seven judges consisted of Wellington Koo, Koretsky, Tanaka, Jessup, Padilla Nervo, Forster, and Mbanefo, the *ad hoc* judge for Ethiopia and Liberia.

[225] ICJ Reports (1966), 36–8.

[226] pp. 42–3.

[227] pp. 35, 48.

[228] pp. 19–23, 31–2, 43–4.

that interpretation of the Mandate should proceed in the light of the necessity for effectiveness in the system of supervision, the Court said:[229]

Looked at in another way moreover, the argument amounts to a plea that the Court should allow the equivalent of an '*actio popularis*', or right resident in any member of a community to take legal action in vindication of a public interest. But, although a right of this kind may be known to certain municipal systems of law, it is not known to international law as it stands at present...

It is important to notice that the dissenting judges (the 1962 majority view) did not assert the existence of such a general principle. The difference of view consisted of two principal elements: (*a*) the minority of 1966 did not regard judicial supervision, as opposed to supervision by political organs, as very exceptional, and consequently were more prone to interpret the relevant provisions to the effect that individual states had an interest in observance of the instrument concerned; (*b*) the minority of 1966 were prepared to regard the common interest of the contracting parties in enforcement of a certain type of multilateral treaty as a normal feature of international law and relations and, in the process of interpretation, not to be ruled out as an eccentric possibility.[230]

The difference between the two sides of the Court is virtually one of presumption and style of interpretation in approaching the economic and social aspects of international relations. The Court in 1966 took an empirical view of legal interest as a general issue and refused to restrict the concept, as a matter of general principle, to provisions relating to a material or tangible object:[231]

Next, it may be said that a legal right or interest need not necessarily relate to anything material or 'tangible', and can be infringed even though no prejudice of a material kind has been suffered. In this connection, the provisions of certain treaties and other international instruments of a humanitarian character, and the terms of various arbitral and judicial decisions, are cited as indicating that, for instance, States may be entitled to uphold some general principle even though the particular contravention of it alleged has not affected their own material interests;—that again, States may have a legal interest in vindicating a principle of international law, even though they have, in the given case, suffered no material prejudice, or ask only for token damages. Without attempting to discuss how far, and in what particular circumstances, these things might be true, it suffices to point out that, in holding that the Applicants in the present case could only have had a legal right or interest in the 'special interests' provisions of the Mandate, the Court does not in any way do so merely because these relate to a material or tangible object. Nor, in holding that no legal right or interest exists for the Applicants, individually as States, in respect of the 'conduct' provisions, does the Court do so because any such right or interest would not have a material or tangible object. The Court simply holds that such rights or interests, in order to exist, must be clearly vested in those who claim them, by some text or instrument, or rule of law;—and

---

[229] p. 47.
[230] See Wellington Koo, ICJ Reports (1966), 225–9; Koretsky, pp. 242–8; Tanaka, pp. 251–4; Jessup, pp. 352–88; Padilla Nervo, pp. 461–4; Forster, pp. 478–82; Mbanefo, pp. 501–5.
[231] pp. 32–3. Cf. Winiarski, quoted *supra*.

that in the present case, none were ever vested in individual members of the League under any of the relevant instruments, or as a constituent part of the mandates system as a whole, or otherwise.

Very similar issues were raised by the *Northern Cameroons* case (Preliminary Objections),[232] arising from an application by the Cameroons of 30 May 1961 which requested the Court to declare that the United Kingdom, as administering authority for the Cameroons, failed to fulfil its obligations under the Trusteeship Agreement relating to that territory. On 21 April 1961 the General Assembly of the United Nations approved the results of a plebiscite in the Northern Cameroons and declared that British administration should terminate on 1 June 1961, when it would become a province of the Federation of Nigeria. The background of the application was the dissatisfaction on the part of the Cameroons Government with the manner in which preparations for the plebiscite were made and a belief that maladministration had resulted in a plebiscite which favoured union with Nigeria and not the Cameroons. The application was based on Article 19 of the Trusteeship Agreement (which was still in force when the application was made), a provision similar to Article 7 of the Mandate Agreement for South West Africa.[233] The Court held that there was a dispute in existence, thus disposing of the preliminary objections of the United Kingdom.[234] However, having established the *right* to exercise jurisdiction, the Court went on to decide against the *propriety* of exercising jurisdiction in this case. Since the Cameroons was not seeking reparation or a finding which would invalidate the union with Nigeria, the issue was 'remote from reality' in the Court's view. The Court said:[235]

The function of the Court is to state the law, but it may pronounce judgment only in connection with concrete cases where there exists at the time of the adjudication an actual controversy involving a conflict of legal interests between the parties. The Court's judgment must have some practical consequence in the sense that it can affect existing legal rights or obligations of the parties, thus removing uncertainty from their legal relations. No judgment on the merits in this case could satisfy these essentials of the judicial function.

A part of the judgment in the *Cameroons* case was devoted to the question whether in the case it would be proper to give a declaratory judgment. The Court thought not, since the treaty in question—the Trusteeship Agreement—was no longer in force and there was no opportunity for a future act of interpretation or application in accordance with the judgment.[236] It is not easy to justify this refusal in the light of the declaration in the *Corfu Channel* case[237] on the illegality of Operation Retail (in regard to which Albania did not ask for any reparation), and several dissenting judges thought that

---

[232] ICJ Reports (1963), 15; 58 *AJ*, p. 488; ILR 35, 353; and see Gross, 58 *AJ* (1964), 415–31; Johnson, 13 *ICLQ* (1964), 1143–92; Verzijl, 11 *Neths. Int. LR* (1964), 25–33.

[233] *Supra*, p. 467.

[234] ICJ Reports (1963), 27. On the definition of a 'dispute' see *infra* on admissibility.

[235] Ibid. pp. 33–4. See also the Sep. Op. of Fitzmaurice, pp. 97–100.

[236] Ibid. 37. See also Wellington Koo, Sep. Op., p. 41; Fitzmaurice, Sep. Op., p. 97.

[237] ICJ Reports (1949), 4 at 36. See further *supra*, p. 461. See also the *Right of Passage* case: ICJ Reports (1960) 6 and Gross, 58 *AJ* (1964), 427–8.

the *Corfu Channel* case should have been followed.[238] More difficult is the determination of the difference between the *Cameroons* and *South West Africa* cases in regard to the nature of a legal interest. In this respect the two adjudication clauses involved were identical, though, as adjudication clauses in different contexts, they might call for different interpretations.[239] In his dissenting opinion in the *South West Africa* cases (Second Phase)[240] Judge Jessup stated that, since the applicants were in effect asking for a declaratory judgment and not an award of damages for their individual benefit, after the decision in 1962 they were entitled to a declaratory judgment without any further showing of interest.[241] On this view the only distinction between the two cases is that the legal and political situation in the *Cameroons* case had precluded any pertinent pronouncement by the court. In the *Nuclear Tests* case (*Australia* v. *France*)[242] four judges were of the opinion that the purpose of the claim was to obtain a declaratory judgment. The majority of the judges thought otherwise and, in the light of a French undertaking not to continue tests, held that the dispute had disappeared.

In these cases much turns on the interpretations of the relevant adjudication clause, the definition of a dispute, and notions of judicial propriety. However, assuming that the hurdles of jurisdiction, admissibility,[243] and propriety are surmounted, there is no inherent limitation of the concept of legal interest to 'material' interests. In this respect generalization is to be avoided, and the law is still developing. Thus states acting in collective self-defence, or a war of sanction against an aggressor, would seem to have a claim for costs and losses, although the evidence is not as yet very abundant.[244] 'Protective' claims in respect of 'dependent' peoples may have special features; for example, a tribunal should be reluctant to reject a claim on account of prescription or laches of the protecting sovereign.[245] Such claims, and the type of legal interest which they represent, may be founded on the principle of self-determination[246] as a part of *jus cogens*[247] and on the General Assembly Declaration on the Granting of Independence to Colonial Countries and Peoples.[248]

---

[238] See ICJ Reports (1963), 150–1 (Badawi), 170, 180 (Bustamante), and 196 (Beb a Don). The suggested method of distinguishing the *Corfu Channel* case in the Sep. Op. of Fitzmaurice, ibid. 98 n. 2, is attractive but not conclusive. See also the Sep. Op. of Morelli, pp. 140–1.

[239] The majority judgment (see p. 35) in substance ignored this aspect of things. See, however, the Sep. Op. of Spender, ibid. 65–73, and the Diss. Op. of Bustamante, pp. 156ff.

[240] ICJ Reports (1966), 328.

[241] He quotes from the Sep. Op. of Fitzmaurice in the *Cameroons* case, pp. 99, 100.

[242] ICJ Reports (1974), 253; Joint Diss. Op. at pp. 312–21; and see Ritter, *Ann. français* (1975), 28–93.

[243] See *infra* ch. 22.

[244] See Brownlie, *International Law and the Use of Force by States*, p. 148. Cf. McNair, 17 *BY* (1936), 150 at 157, where he says of the General Treaty for the Renunciation of War (Kellogg–Briand Pact): 'it is a reasonable view, though I cannot assert it to be an established opinion, that a breach of the pact is a legal wrong not merely against the victim of the resort to armed force but also against the other signatories of the Pact'.

[245] See the *Cayuga Indians* case (1926), *RIAA*, vi. 173 at 189.

[246] *Infra*, pp. 579–82.

[247] *Infra*, pp. 510–12.

[248] *Infra*, p. 581.

15. CAUSES OF ACTION[249]

As a practical matter it is important to establish the precise subject of the particular legal dispute. In diplomatic correspondence it is helpful if the complainant state indicates with reasonable clarity what it is complaining about, and in particular, whether a legal demand is being advanced as opposed to a mere remonstrance or request for reparation or political action irrespective of the legal issues (as may happen). As a question of instituting proceedings before an international tribunal, the relevant special agreement or application employed to start proceedings must indicate the subject of the dispute and the parties.[250] In the case of proceedings by application the precise issue will be isolated by the tribunal in the light of the pleadings in general and the final submissions in particular.[251] There are no rigid forms of action in international law but the definition of the cause of action may have significance beyond the exercise, just noticed, by which a tribunal decides what it has to decide on the merits.

(a) Objections to jurisdiction *ratione temporis* or based upon the reserved domain of domestic jurisdiction require consideration of what is the subject of the dispute.[252]

(b) A tribunal may have to apply the principle of *res judicata* and thus decide whether in previous proceedings a particular issue was disposed of finally and without possibility of revision in proceedings affecting the same general subject-matter.[253]

(c) The operation of the rule of admissibility of claims requiring prior exhaustion of local remedies in certain cases may call for careful examination of the nature of the dispute as presented to the relevant municipal court and the dispute as presented on the international plane. It must be decided whether local remedies were available in respect of the particular harms complained of.[254] In the same connection a tribunal must consider whether the issue is exclusively one of national law.[255]

---

[249] See generally Brownlie, 50 *BY* (1979), 13–41; and also in *System of the Law of Nations* (Pt. 1), 53–88. The practical relevance of the topic is exemplified by the issues in the *Nicaragua* case, with particular reference to the effect of the multilateral treaty reservation forming part of the US Decl. accepting the jurisdiction of the Court: ICJ Reports (1986), 14 at 29–38; Judge Ago, Sep. Op., pp. 182–4; Judge Sette-Camara, Sep. Op., pp. 192–200; Judge Ni, Sep. Op., pp. 201–11; Judge Oda, Diss. Op., pp. 215–19; Judge Schwebel, Diss. Op., pp. 296–306; Judge Jennings, Diss. Op., pp. 529–36.

[250] See Art. 40 of the Statute of the International Court. See the comment by Mann, 46 *BY* (1972–3), 504–5, referring to the *Norwegian Loans* case, ICJ Reports (1957), 9.

[251] Cf. *Fisheries* case, ICJ Reports (1951), 126; *Interhandel* case, ibid. (1959), 19.

[252] *Right of Passage* case (Merits), ICJ Reports (1960), 32–6.

[253] See Rosenne, *The Law and Practice of the International Court* (1997), iii. 1655–61.

[254] See Read, Diss. Op., *Norwegian Loans* case, ICJ Reports (1957), 98–100; Lauterpacht, Sep. Op., ibid. 39.

[255] See Lauterpacht, Sep. Op., ibid. 36–8.

(*d*) In presenting the merits of a claim there may be some advantage in relating the evidence to more than one category of unlawful activity. Thus in the *Barcelona Traction* case[256] Belgium presented the general pattern of action by the Spanish courts and administrative authorities as amounting to a despoliation of the property of the Barcelona Traction Company. There was no expropriation or direct forced transfer as such, but the effect of wrongfully entertaining and enforcing bankruptcy proceedings, as alleged, and enabling a private Spanish group to purchase the assets of the Barcelona Traction group at a ridiculously low price, as alleged, was to bring about a despoliation, an unlawful deprivation of property. The facts relied upon were presented in terms of four legal categories: abuse of rights; usurpation of jurisdiction; denial of justice *lato sensu*; denial of justice *stricto sensu*. The claims for damage and reparation were not apportioned in relation to these heads separately but to each and all of them. In the *Nuclear Tests* cases[257] the applicant states had some difficulty in relating the deposit of radioactive fall-out to existing legal categories.[258]

The concept of causes of action also concerns two other issues. First, the requirement that the applicant state establish a legal interest may be described in terms of a need to show a cause of action.[259] Secondly, there is a relatively unexplored territory reminiscent of the problems in the common law of relating the form of action to the heads of damage. For example, in the English law of torts it is easier to obtain recovery for financial loss if this can be presented as a head of 'damage' related to a recognized head of 'liability', such as nuisance, or presented as the damages flowing from an acceptable type of loss, such as negligence causing physical harm. In international claims comparable issues have arisen. Thus, there is an interaction between the availability of local remedies and the type of harm which can be the subject of an international claim. Thus it may happen that a contract (governed by a system of private law) is broken by a diplomatic agent or government agency for which immunity from the local jurisdiction is claimed and in respect of which no remedy may exist in the national law of the state of origin. In such a case the state of the nationality of the other party to the contract will have a claim, arising from the breach of contract, on the international plane. Such transposed causes of action are difficult to characterize.[260]

---

[256] ICJ Reports (1970), 4 at 15–25, Final Submissions, preamble, and ss. I–V. See also Tanaka, Sep. Op., pp. 146, 153.

[257] *Australia* v. *France*, ICJ Reports (1974), 253; *New Zealand* v. *France*, ibid. 457.

[258] See, in particular the *Pleadings, Nuclear Tests* cases, 2 vols. (Australia v. France), I, p. 14; Handl, 69 *AJ* (1975), 50–76.

[259] See Jennings, 121 Hague *Recueil* (1967, II), 507–11.

[260] See Jessup, Sep. Op., *Barcelona Traction* case (Second Phase), ICJ Reports (1970), 168. Compare the items of loss in the *Janes* case, *supra*, p. 464; the *General Electric Company* claim, ILR 30, 140 at 142–3; and the *Singer* claim, ibid. 187 at 197.

22

THE ADMISSIBILITY OF
STATE CLAIMS

1. INTRODUCTION

A state presenting an international claim to another state, either in diplomatic exchanges or before an international tribunal, has to establish its qualifications for making the claim, and the continuing viability of the claim itself, before the merits of the claim come into question. In the case where the claim is presented before a tribunal the preliminary objections may be classified as follows.[1] Objections to the jurisdiction, if successful, stop all proceedings in the case, since they strike at the competence of the tribunal to give rulings as to the merits or admissibility of the claim. An objection to the substantive admissibility of a claim invites the tribunal to reject the claim on a ground distinct from the merits—for example, undue delay in presenting the claim. In normal cases the question of admissibility can only be approached when jurisdiction has been assumed, and issues as to admissibility, especially those concerning the nationality of the claimant and the exhaustion of local remedies, may be closely connected with the merits of the case. Even if a claim is not rejected on grounds of lack of jurisdiction or inadmissibility, a tribunal may decline to exercise its jurisdiction on grounds of judicial propriety:[2] this was the outcome of the *Cameroons* case.[3]

---

[1] See Fitzmaurice, 34 *BY* (1958), 12–14; id., Sep. Op. in the *Cameroons* case, ICJ Reports (1963), 100ff.; Rosenne, *The Law and Practice of the International Court* (1997), ii. 536–40, 837–46; Winiarski, Diss. Op. in the *South West Africa* cases, ICJ Reports (1962), 449; Morelli, Diss. Op., ibid. 573–4; Bustamante, Diss. Op. in the *Cameroons* case, ICJ Reports (1963), 180–1.

[2] See Fitzmaurice, 34 *BY* (1958), 21–2, 36–9; Sep. Op. in the *Cameroons* case, ICJ Reports (1963), 100–8. Fitzmaurice, ICJ Reports (1963), 103, describes questions of propriety as 'of a wholly antecedent or, as it were, "pre-preliminary" character'. See also Bustamante, ibid. 181–3; Beb a Don, pp. 189ff.

[3] See also Gross, 58 *AJ* (1964), 415 at 423–9. The Court (ICJ Reports (1963), 28) did not find it necessary to deal with the issue of admissibility.

2. DIPLOMATIC NEGOTIATIONS[4]

In the *Right of Passage* case (Preliminary Objections)[5] India made a preliminary objection as follows: 'Portugal, before filing her Application in the present case, did not comply with the rule of customary international law requiring her to undertake diplomatic negotiations and continue them to the point where it was no longer profitable to pursue them...' The Court said that, assuming the contention had substance, the condition related in the objection had been complied with 'to the extent permitted by the circumstances of the case'.[6] The recent jurisprudence of the Court establishes the clear principle that the existence of active negotiations between the parties is not an impediment to the Court's exercise of jurisdiction.[7] However, prior recourse to diplomatic negotiations may provide material evidence of the existence of a legal dispute, and an adjudication clause in a treaty may contain the condition.[8]

3. LEGAL DISPUTES

In the *South West Africa* cases (Preliminary Objections)[9] the third preliminary objection advanced by the Republic of South Africa ran as follows:[10] 'the conflict or disagreement alleged by [the Applicants] to exist between them and the Government of the Republic of South Africa, is...not a "dispute" as envisaged in Article 7 of the Mandate for South West Africa, more particularly in that no material interests of the Governments of Ethiopia and/or Liberia or of their nationals are involved therein or affected thereby'. The Court held that there was a dispute within the meaning of Article 7 of the Mandate.[11] Yet irrespective of the existence of a dispute within the meaning of the adjudication clause relevant to the proceedings, there was a prior question of admissibility—was there a legal dispute in existence in any case? Early in the Judgment[12] the Court dealt with this point, holding that there was a dispute in this sense and quoting the definition of a dispute in the *Mavrommatis* case[13] as 'a disagreement on a point of law

---

[4] See Bourquin, in *Hommage d'une génération de juristes au Président Basdevant* (1960), 43–55; Witenberg, 41 Hague *Recueil* (1932, III), 22–6; Soubeyrol, 68 *RGDIP* (1964), 319–49; Reuter, *Comunicazioni e studi*, 14 (1975), 711–33.

[5] ICJ Reports (1957), 125 at 130. Cf. ibid. 132–3.

[6] Ibid. 148–9.

[7] See the *Aegean Sea Continental Shelf* case, ICJ Reports (1978), 3 at 12; *Nicaragua v. United States* (Jurisdiction and Admissibility), ibid. (1984), 392 at 440; *Cameroon v. Nigeria* (Prelim. Objs.), ibid. (1998), 302–4.

[8] See the *Mavrommatis* case, PCIJ, Ser. A, no. 2, p. 13; the *South West Africa* cases, ICJ Reports (1962), 319, and the *Cameroons* case, ibid. (1963), 15. See also *Nicaragua v. Honduras*, ICJ Reports (1988), 69, 92–9.

[9] ICJ Reports (1962), 319; see *supra*, pp. 469–71.

[10] ICJ Reports (1962), 327.

[11] Ibid. 342–4. See also Judge Bustamante, Sep. Op., pp. 379–84; Judge Jessup, Sep. Op., pp. 422–33; Judge van Wyk, Diss. Op., pp. 658–62.

[12] Ibid. 328.

[13] PCIJ, Ser. A, no. 2, p. 11. See further Judge Morelli, Diss. Op., ICJ Reports (1962), 564–71. The same issue arose in the *Cameroons* case, ICJ Reports (1963), 15 at 20 (UK prelim. objections), 27. See also Judge Wellington Koo, Sep. Op., ibid. 43–4; Judge Fitzmaurice, Sep. Op., pp. 105, 108–11; Judge Morelli, Sep. Op.,

or fact, a conflict of legal views or of interests between two persons'. In the *Nuclear Tests* case (Australia v. France)[14] the application of the concept of a 'legal dispute' involved considerable differences of opinion within the International Court. In the Advisory Opinion relating to the applicability of the arbitration procedure provided for in the United Nations Headquarters Agreement (concerning the status of the PLO Observer Mission to the United Nations) the Court had to determine whether a dispute existed between the United Nations and the United States.[15] The ambit of the legal dispute subsisting between Nicaragua and Colombia caused a substantial difference of opinion within the Court in the *Territorial and Maritime Dispute*.[16] Several Judges considered that the issue of title to the principal islands should have been joined to the Merits.

4. ABSENCE OF A LEGAL INTEREST OF THE PLAINTIFF

The existence of a legal interest[17] on the part of a plaintiff is a question distinct from the existence of a *dispute* relating to a legal interest alleged to exist by the plaintiff state. At the same time the nature of the claim and the existence of a dispute are closely connected questions.[18] In the *Cameroons* case[19] the Court treated the issue as to the existence of a legal interest on the part of the applicants as a matter of judicial propriety.[20] Nevertheless, some members of the Court treated it as an issue of admissibility,[21] and Judge Wellington Koo[22] refers to the existence of a legal interest as 'the indispensable basis of a justiciable dispute'.

5. DIPLOMATIC PROTECTION: THE NATIONALITY OF CLAIMS

The problem of attribution of individuals to particular states and the relations of diplomatic protection and nationality have been explored previously.[23] A normal and important function of nationality is to establish the legal interest of a state when

---

pp. 131–41; Judge Bustamante, Diss. Op., pp. 164–7. See also the *Peace Treaties* case, ICJ Reports (1950), 74; *Case Concerning East Timor* (Portugal v. Australia), ibid. (1995), 90.

[14] ICJ Reports (1974), 253.

[15] ICJ Reports (1988), 12. See also the Sep. Ops. of Judges Oda, Schwebel, and Shahabuddeen.

[16] Judgment of 13 Dec. 2007.

[17] See generally *supra*, pp. 478ff. On the admissibility of claims for cumulative harm arising in part before statehood of the applicant, see Judge Fitzmaurice, ICJ Reports (1963), 129; White, *Camb. LJ* (1965), 9 at 11; and *Case Concerning Certain Phosphate Lands in Nauru*, ICJ Reports (1992), 240.

[18] Judge Morelli, Sep. Op., ICJ Reports (1963), 132.

[19] *Supra*, p. 471.

[20] See *supra*, p. 475.

[21] Judge Fitzmaurice, Sep. Op., ICJ Reports (1963), 101, 105; Judge Badawi, Diss. Op., pp. 150–3; Judge Bustamante, pp. 170–2, 181. Cf. Judge Morelli, Sep. Op., p. 132. Cf. the *South West Africa* cases, *supra*, pp. 466–70, and see President Winiarski, ICJ Reports (1962), 449–57.

[22] ICJ Reports (1963), 44–6 (Sep. Op.).

[23] *Supra*, ch. 19.

nationals, and legal persons with a sufficient connection with the state,[24] receive injury or loss at the hands of another state. The subject-matter of the claim is the individual and his property: the claim is that of the state.[25] Thus if the plaintiff state cannot establish the nationality of the claim, the claim is inadmissible because of the absence of any legal interest of the claimant.[26] However, the variety of problems involved necessitates separate and somewhat extended treatment of the principle of nationality of claims. At the outset certain important exceptions to the principle must be noticed.[27] A right to protection of non-nationals[28] may arise from treaty or an *ad hoc* arrangement establishing an agency. The other generally accepted exceptions are alien seamen on ships flying the flag of the protecting state[29] and members of the armed forces of a state. If the injured party was in the service of the claimant state the latter may be said to have suffered harm to a legal interest although the victim was an alien.[30]

THE OPERATION OF THE NATIONALITY RULE[31]

The rule is generally stated as follows:[32] 'from the time of the occurrence of the injury until the making of the award the claim must continuously and without interruption have belonged to a person or to a series of persons (*a*) having the nationality of the State by whom it is put forward, and (*b*) not having the nationality of the State against whom

[24] See *infra*, pp. 482–6.

[25] See *infra*, ch. 25, on the position of the individual in international law and the question of human rights.

[26] *Panevezys–Saldutiskis Railway* (1939), PCIJ, Ser. A/B, no. 76. But legal interest may exist on some other basis: Fitzmaurice, 27 *BY* (1950), 24–5.

[27] See Schwarzenberger, *International Law* (3rd edn., 1957), i. 592–6; Parry, 30 *BY* (1953), 257; id., *Nationality and Citizenship Laws of the Commonwealth*, i. 12; Oppenheim, i. 347. On the *Reparation* case, see *infra*, p. 684. On the position of aliens employed in diplomatic and consular services: Fitzmaurice, 27 *BY* (1950), 25 n. 1.

[28] That is, apart from the question of persons internationally attributable to a state, but outside internal nationality legislation.

[29] See Watts, 7 *ICLQ* (1958), 691–712. But see Schwarzenberger, *International Law*, pp. 593–4.

[30] Fitzmaurice, 27 *BY* (1950), 25. Cf. the *Reparation* case, *infra*, p. 648.

[31] Questions of nationality, including multiple and effective nationality, are discussed *supra*, ch. 19. On diplomatic protection and the operation of the nationality rule see generally, Sinclair, 27 *BY* (1950), 125–44; Borchard, 43 *Yale LJ* (1934), 359–92; id., *Bibliotheca Visseriana* (123), iii. 1–53; id., *Annuaire de l'Inst.* 36 (1931), i. 256ff.; ibid. 36 (1931), ii. 201ff.; ibid. 37 (1932), 235ff., 479ff.; ibid. 51 (1965), i. 5–225; ibid. ii. 157–253, 260–2; Parry, 90 Hague *Recueil* (1956, II), 699–712; García Amador, 94 Hague *Recueil* (1958, II), 426–39; id., *Yrbk. ILC* (1956), ii. 199–203; id., *Yrbk. ILC* (1958), ii. 61–7; Lillich, 13 *ICLQ* (1964), 899–924. See further: Lillich, *International Claims, Their Adjudication by National Commissions* (1962); id., *International Claims, Their Preparation and Presentation* (1962); id., *International Claims: Postwar British Practice* (1967); Weston, *International Claims: Postwar French Practice* (1971); Whiteman, viii. 1216–91; *Répertoire suisse*, ii. 607–55; Feller, *The Mexican Claims Commissions 1923–1934* (1935); Lillich and Weston, *International Claims: Their Settlement by Lump Sum Agreements*, 2 vols. (1975); id. *International Claims: Contemporary European Practice* (1982); Rousseau, v. 101–51; ILA, *New Delhi Conference Report* (2002), 228–98; ILA, Toronto Conference Report (2006), 353–405. On the work of the International Law Commission, see Dugard, First Report, A/CN.4/506, Add.1; and *Report of the International Law Commission* (2006), *Fifty-eighth session*, G.A. Off. Recs., *Sixty-first session*, Suppl. No. 10 (A/61/10), 13–100.

[32] Oppenheim, i. 512–3; Whiteman, viii. 1243–6; Lillich and Weston, *International Claims: Contemporary European Practice*, p. 2; *French National Compensation* case, ILR 74, 280.

it is put forward'. International agreements, and internal legislation putting these into effect, may avoid the principle or vary and refine the conditions of continuity.[33] The principle of continuity has been criticized because it permits incidental matters, e.g. change of nationality by operation of law including cession of territory, to affect reasonable claims, and also because, if the legal wrong is to the state of origin, then the wrong has matured at the time of injury and is unaffected by subsequent changes in the status of the individual. The essence of the rule is probably a desire to prevent the individual choosing a powerful protecting state by a shift of nationality.[34] This view does not support the application of the principle in cases of involuntary changes brought about by death or state succession[35] and there is a respectable body of opinion which would reject the principle altogether.[36] The principle appears to be well-entrenched in the practice of states, but it may be modified in cases of state succession.[37]

The first part of the rule of continuity does not give rise to too much difficulty: the relevant nationality must exist at the time of injury.[38] The second part of the rule is variously stated in terms of nationality continuing until the 'presentation of the award', or the filing of a claim before a tribunal, or the formal presentation of a diplomatic claim in the absence of submission to a tribunal. However, the majority of governments[39] and of writers[40] take the date of the award of judgment as the critical date. In any case much depends on the terms of the agreement creating the machinery for the settlement of claims.

SUCCESSION ON DEATH[41]

The nationality of an heir must be that of the state of which the decedent on whose behalf the claim would have been made was a national: in other words the principle

---

[33] See Lillich, 13 *ICLQ* (1964), 900–4; Sinclair, 27 *BY* (1950), 142. A common critical date is that of the coming into force of the treaty governing the settlement of claims. See also the *Orinoco Steamship Co.* case, *RIAA* ix. 180; and *Padavano* claim, ILR 26 (1958, II), 336. Cf. *Isaiah* v. *Bank Mellat*, ILR 72, 716 at 719; *Loewen* v. *U.S.A.*, ILR 128, 335 at 412–18.

[34] See Borchard, 43 *Yale LJ* (1934), 359–92 esp. at 377–80; and Briggs, pp. 733–5; *Loewen* v. *USA*, ILR 128, 335 at 412–18.

[35] See Borchard, 43 *Yale LJ* (1934), 388–9. The awkward results of the rule appear in the following cases of state succession. Tanganyika became independent in 1961 and Zanzibar in 1963. In 1964 the two states formed a union. Thus the populations concerned were the subjects of two changes of nationality.

[36] *Annuaire de l'Inst.* (1931), ii. 201–12; ibid. (1932), 479–529; Jennings, 121 Hague *Recueil*, pp. 474–7; O'Connell, ii. 1033–9; Fitzmaurice, Sep. Op., *Barcelona Traction* case (Second Phase), ICJ Reports (1970), 99–103. See also Rousseau, v. 118–23.

[37] See the Resol. of the Institute of Int. Law, *Annuaire*, 51 (1965), 260. See also Jessup, Sep. Op., *Barcelona Traction* case (Second Phase), ICJ Reports (1970), 202; and ch. 29, s. 5.

[38] Most writers state the rule in this way.

[39] *Bases of Discussion*, Hague Codification Conference, 1930, iii. 140–5.

[40] e.g. Hurst, 7 *BY* (1926), 180; Oppenheim, i. 512–13; Sørensen, pp. 576–7. See also Huber, *Spanish Zone of Morocco* claims, *RIAA* ii. 615 at 706; *Ann. Digest* 2 (1923–4), 189; *Eschauzier* claim (1931), *RIAA* v. 207 at 209; *Kren* claim, ILR 20 (1953), 233; and Schwarzenberger, *International Law* (3rd edn.), i. 597–8.

[41] See Diena, 15 *RDILC* (1934), 173–93; Blaser, *La Nationalité et la protection juridique internationale de l'individu* (1962), 39–44; Schwarzenberger, *International Law*, p. 599; Hurst, 7 *BY* (1926), 166–74; Hackworth, v. 788–94, 805, 849–51; Whiteman, viii. 1261–2; Lillich and Weston, *International Claims: Contemporary European Practice*, p. 5.

of continuous nationality is applied to the beneficial interest in the property.[42] Since the beneficial interest is crucial a claim will be denied if the residuary legatee does not have the requisite nationality although the executrix has.[43] It may happen that a claims commission will presume continuity of nationality in the heirs of the deceased creditor.[44]

ASSIGNMENT OF CLAIMS[45]

If during the critical period a claim is assigned to or by a non-national of the claimant state, the claim must be denied. However, assignment does not affect the claim if the principle of continuity is observed.

AGENTS AND PROCURATORS[46]

International jurisprudence would presumably adopt the principle of procuration or agency, but here, as elsewhere, it is the nationality of the real or beneficial owner which matters. If a person with a power of attorney successfully presents a claim to a domestic tribunal of the defendant state the claimant is bound by the acts of the attorney and is barred from presenting the claim to another tribunal.[47]

BENEFICIAL OWNERS[48]

The principle to be followed is set forth in the decision of the United States Foreign Claims Settlement Commission in the *American Security and Trust Company* claim:[49] 'It is clear that the national character of a claim must be tested by the nationality of the individual holding a beneficial interest therein rather than by the nationality of the nominal or record holder of the claim. Precedents for the foregoing well-settled proposition are so numerous that it is not deemed necessary to document it with a long list of authorities...'

---

[42] See the *Stevenson* claim (1903), *RIAA* ix. 385; *Flack* claim (1929), *RIAA* v. 61; *Eschauzier* claim (1931), ibid. 207; *Gleadell* (1929), ibid. 44; *Ann. Digest* 5 (1929–30), no. 17; *Kren* claim, ILR 20 (1953), 233; *Bogovic* claim, ibid. 21 (1954), 156. Cf. *Hanover Bank* claim, ibid. 26 (1958, II), 334.

[43] See *Gleadell, supra*. But see Diena, 15 *RDILC* (1934), 186.

[44] *Straub* claim, ILR 20 (1953), 228.

[45] Witenberg, 41 Hague *Recueil* (1932, III), 71–2; Hyde ii. 899–900; Hackworth, v. 846–8; *Perle* claim, ILR 21 (1954), 161; *First National City Bank of New York* claim, ibid. 26 (1958, II), 323; *Dubozy* claim, ibid. 345. See also *Batavian National Bank* claim, ibid. 346 (on assignment after filing of claim).

[46] See Moore, *Arbitrations*, 4681, 4683; Blaser, *La Nationalité*, pp. 45–6. Cf. ICJ Reports (1970), 93–9, 135–6, 211–19, 352–3.

[47] *Nartnick* claim, ILR 21 (1954), 149.

[48] See Oppenheim, i. 514; Lillich, 13 *ICLQ* (1964), 922–3; Whiteman, viii. 1261–3.

[49] (1957), ILR 26 (1958, II), 322. See also *Binder-Haas* claim, ILR 20 (1953), 236; *Knesevich* claim, ILR 21 (1954), 154; *First National City Bank of New York* claim, ILR 26 (1958, II), 323; *Methodist Church* claim, ibid. 279; *Hanover Bank* claim, ibid. 334; *Chase National Bank* claim, ibid. 483; Jessup, Sep. Op., *Barcelona Traction* case (Second Phase), ICJ Reports (1970), 218–19.

Thus in that case the claim was denied, as the beneficiaries were not nationals of the United States although the trustee presenting the claim was. Treaties, and internal legislation regulating the consequences of international settlements for lump sums, may allow trustees to claim irrespective of the nationality of the beneficiaries.[50]

INSURERS[51]

Insurers may claim on the basis of subrogation provided the principle of continuity of nationality is satisfied. Subrogation may be regarded as a form of assignment or a form of representation: in any case it could be supported as a general principle of law.[52] This at least represents the practice of the United States Foreign Claims Settlement Commission in the recent past. There are cogent arguments against allowing the nationality of the insurer to affect the nationality of the claim. In particular, because of the practice of reinsurance, the ultimate bearer of loss is not readily ascertainable.[53] However, if the insurer's interest is established and the principle of continuity is satisfied there would seem to be no very good reason for denial of a claim, although there is authority for the view that the insurer should bear the risks in the contemplation of the policy and should not qualify for protection.[54]

PARTNERSHIP CLAIMS[55]

In principle, as a firm is not a legal person in English law, partners who are British nationals would receive protection as individuals to the extent of their interest in the partnership. However, post-war British claims practice, reflected in settlement agreements and Orders in Council, has in general permitted claims by firms constituted under English law, as such, irrespective of the nationality of the partners.

[50] See UK Orders in Council relating to settlements with Yugoslavia and Czechoslovakia: [1952] 1 SI 1096–7 (no. 1414); [1952] 1 SI 1092–3 (no. 1413).

[51] See Oppenheim, i. 514; Ritter, 65 *RGDIP* (1961), 765–802; Blaser, *La Nationalité*, pp. 47–50; McNair, *Opinions*, ii. 290–2; Hackworth, v. 809–12; O'Connell, ii. 1050–2; Meron, 68 *AJ* (1974), 628–47.

[52] See the *Federal Insurance Company* claim, ILR 26 (1958, II), 316, in which the US Foreign Claims Settlement Commission said: 'By virtue of [a]...principle, recognized and applied alike by courts of law and equity...an insurer who indemnifies the person who has suffered loss through another's wrongdoing, thereby acquires, to the extent of such indemnification, the assured's rights against the wrong-doer...' See also the *Continental Insurance Company* claim, ibid. 318.
Cf. the third preliminary objection of Bulgaria in the *Aerial Incident* case (Prelim. Objections), ICJ Reports (1959), 127 at 133. The Court did not find it necessary to deal with this objection.

[53] Schwarzenberger, *International Law* (3rd edn.), i. 599–600.

[54] Guggenheim, i. 311, n. 2. This was the position taken by the British Government in 1929.

[55] Lillich, 13 *ICLQ* (1964), 907–8; *British Digest*, v. 481–502; Lillich and Weston, *International Claims: Contemporary European Practice*, pp. 3, 31–2, 148–50; Whiteman, viii. 1270 (quoting Jiménez de Aréchaga).

CORPORATIONS[56]

The 'nationality' of a corporation for purposes of public international law, and more especially with regard to exercise of diplomatic protection, is a quality not easily distinguished in the available sources from questions of municipal law and functional rules for the determination of 'enemy character' in connection with trading with the enemy, prize law, and so on.[57] Since a corporation is a legal person and rules as to diplomatic protection distinguish corporate and other entities, a preliminary question should arise as to which system of law is to be used to classify the entity as corporate or not, or, more precisely, whether the firm or association concerned has legal personality distinct from that of its members as individuals.[58] Reference to the country under whose law the entity was constituted is, on the plane of international law, neither a necessary nor a sufficient test and, in any case, internal law frequently does not provide rules as to the 'nationality' of associations whether with or without legal personality. In fact reference to 'nationality' or 'corporations' as a means of ascertaining the admissibility of international claims is clumsy. It is significant that agreements on settlement of claims frequently contain *ad hoc* definitions of nationality which deal, in part, with corporations.[59]

The evidence of state practice and jurisprudence is very difficult to evaluate: the right of protection is discretionary, and many treaties and judicial decisions are concerned with very narrow questions and do not provide a suitable basis for generalization. However, certain somewhat provisional conclusions may be offered. In the first place there is very little evidence in support of the view that a state may present a claim

---

[56] See generally Oppenheim, ii. 859–62; Schwarzenberger, *International Law* (3rd edn.), i. 387–412; Beckett, 17 *Grot. Soc.* (1931), 175–94; P. de Visscher, 102 Hague *Recueil* (1961, I), 427–62; Hackworth, iii. 420, v. 840; Watts, 33 *BY* (1957), 79–83; Parry, *Nationality and Citizenship Laws of the Commonwealth* (1957), i. 133–42; Rundstein, Guerrero, and Schücking, 22 *AJ* (1928), Spec. Suppl., pp. 157–214; Nial, 101 Hague *Recueil* (1960, III), 314–22; Bindschedler, 90 Hague *Recueil* (1956, II), 231–42; O'Connell, ii. 1039–43, 1047–8; *British Digest*, v. 503–35; de Hochepied, *La Protection diplomatique des societés et des actionnaires* (1965); Petrén, 109 Hague *Recueil* (1963, II), 503ff.; Ginther, 16 *Öst. Z. für öff. R.* (1966), 27–83; Khalid Al-Shawi, *The Role of the Corporate Entity in International Law* (1957); Harris, 18 *ICLQ* (1969), 275–317; Goldman, 90 *JDI* (1963), 321–89; Feliciano, 118 Hague *Recueil* (1966, II), 284–95; Caflisch, *La Protection des sociétés commerciales et des intérêts indirects en droit international public* (1969); *Répertoire suisse*, ii. 635–51; Diez de Velasco, 141 Hague *Recueil* (1974, I), 93–185; Whiteman, viii. 1269–70 (quoting Jiménez de Aréchaga); Rousseau, v. 128–31; Lillich and Weston, *International Claims: Contemporary European Practice*, pp. 3–4; Seidl-Hohenveldern, *Corporations in and under International Law* (1987), 7–12; International Law Commisson, Fourth Report on diplomatic protection by John Dugard, A/CN.4/530, 13 March 2003; Add.1, 6 June 2003.

[57] *Supra*, p. 406.

[58] In some systems associations other than corporations in the English style receive legal personality, and the recent tendency in English law is to give procedural capacity to unincorporated bodies.

[59] See Lillich, 13 *ICLQ* (1964), 908–11. On protection of investment clauses see 52 *BY* (1981), 498–9; 53 *BY* (1982), 491–3; 54 *BY* (1983), 523; 55 *BY* (1984), 572–3; 56 *BY* (1985), 512–3; 57 *BY* (1986), 605–6; 58 *BY* (1987), 621–2; 59 *BY* (1988), 560; 60 *BY* (1989), 681–2; 61 *BY* (1990), 813–14; 62 *BY* (1991), 655–7; 63 *BY* (1992), 778–9; 64 *BY* (1993), 690–1; 65 *BY* (1994), 666–7; 66 *BY* (1995), 691–3 (list of agreements at 693–4); 67 *BY* (1996), 813–14.

on behalf of a corporation on the sole basis of its incorporation under its law.[60] In general the evidence supports a doctrine that some substantial and effective connection between the legal entity and the claimant state is required,[61] but there is no certainty as to the criteria for determining such connection. Of course, there is probably no point in seeking rigid principles.

British and American practice requires the existence of a substantial beneficial interest owned by nationals in the corporation,[62] and Italy and Switzerland have relied on this criterion in making agreements, though not exclusively. In many instances the beneficial interest exists in connection with a corporation incorporated under the law of the claimant state, but the crucial question is whether, on the basis of the beneficial interest, protection may be exercised in respect of a corporation incorporated in another state, and even in the defendant state. The present writer would give an affirmative answer to this as an issue of principle, but the sources give no unequivocal answer.[63]

The other principles supported by a modicum of practice and jurisprudence must be considered. It will be seen that they are difficult to distinguish and are cognates of the concept of substantial connection. One of these principles depends on the *siège social* of the corporation, which seems to mean the place where its administrative organs function, the centre of control.[64] Tribunals have also relied on the 'domicile' of a corporation, defining it in terms similar to the usual explanation of *siège social*.[65] The control test, resting on the seat of economic control and influence, has appeared

---

[60] Parry, *Nationality and Citizenship Laws*, p. 139. For a different view: Beckett, 17 *Grot. Soc.* (1931), 185; Moore, *Digest*, vi. 641–2; Vallat, *International Law and the Practitioner* (1966), 25. (Parry remarks that the proposition is 'unsupported by any convincing precedent'.) See, however, the cases discussed by Schwarzenberger, *International Law* (3rd edn.), i. 397–402, and esp. the *Standard Oil Company case* (1926), *RIAA* ii. 779; 8 *BY* (1927), 156; 22 *AJ* (1928), 404. On the *Agency of Canadian Car and Foundry Company* case (1939) see Parry, *Nationality and Citizenship Laws*, pp. 139–40; Watts, 33 *BY* (1957), 80–1.

[61] See Schwarzenberger, *International Law*, pp. 389–90, 411–12; White, *Nationalisation of Foreign Property*, p. 67; de Visscher, 102 Hague *Recueil* (1961, I), 446–62; C. de Visscher, *Théories et réalités* (4th edn., 1970), 303–4; id., *Les Effectivités du droit international* (1967), 131–4; Caflisch, *La Protection des sociétés*. For the contrary view: Harris, 18 *ICLQ* (1969), 275–95, who favours a modification of the 'established rule'. See also *supra* in regard to individuals, and *UK Contemp. Practice* (1962), ii. 194.

[62] See Lillich, 13 *ICLQ* (1964), 908–11; White, *Nationalisation of Foreign Property*, pp. 62–5; Watts, 33 *BY* (1957), 80–3. See also the *Westhold Corporation* claim, ILR 20 (1953), 266; *Cisatlantic* claim, *ibid.* 21 (1954), 293. On the whole, the jurisprudence of arbitral tribunals is inconclusive: Schwarzenberger, *International Law*, pp. 406–10. See further the *I'm Alone* (1933–5), *RIAA* iii. 1609. *Contra: Interoceanic Railway of Mexico* claim (1931), *RIAA* v. 178 at 184. On the practice of the Iran–US Claims Tribunal (based upon an agreement) see *Alcan Aluminium Ltd. v. Ircable Corporation*, ILR 72, 725; *Sola Tiles, Inc. v. Islamic Rep. of Iran*, ILR 83, 460; *Sedco Inc. v. NIOC, ibid.*, 84, 483; *Starrett Housing v. Government of Islamic Rep. of Iran, ibid.*, 85, 349.

[63] See Parry, *Nationality and Citizenship Laws*, p. 140; Jones, 26 *BY* (1949), 227–31; and Watts, 33 *BY* (1957), 81–2. In particular see the *Delagoa Bay Railway* claim, Moore, *Arbitrations*, ii. 1865; *British Digest*, v. 559; and the *Standard Oil Company* case (1926), *RIAA* ii. 779; 8 *BY* (1927), 156.

[64] See de Visscher, 102 Hague *Recueil* (1961, I), 437–9; Schwarzenberger, *International Law*, pp. 393–5; Judge Jessup, Sep. Op., *Barcelona Traction* case (Second Phase), ICJ Reports (1970), 183. Cf. the *Canevaro* case (1912), Hague Court Reports, i. 284 at 287; and the *Wimbledon*, PCIJ, Ser. A, no. 1, p. 182 and C3, Suppl., p. 3.

[65] Schwarzenberger, *International Law*, pp. 395–7. See the *Madera Company* claim (1931), *RIAA* v. 156; 28 *AJ* (1934), 590.

in a number of treaties.[66] In a number of cases tribunals have applied two or more of the available criteria in conjunction. Thus in the *Flack* claim[67] the nationality of the company was held to depend on incorporation, domicile, and *siège social*, in each case in London.

In the draft articles on diplomatic protection adopted in 2006 the International Law Commission proposed the following draft on the nationality of a corporation (article 9):

For the purposes of the diplomatic protection of a corporation, the State of nationality means the State under whose law the corporation was incorporated. However, when the corporation is controlled by nationals of another State or States and has no substantial business activities in the State of incorporation, and the seat of management and the financial control of the corporation are both located in another State, that State shall be regarded as the State of nationality.

It may be pointed out that, if a doctrine of substantial connection is employed, some but not all of the difficulties of classification of an entity as a legal person are avoided. If the place of incorporation is not a sufficient criterion, one still has to choose a system which decides whether separate legal personality exists or not, for example in the case of a partnership. Tribunals seem to rely on municipal law in this respect, but in fact, by demanding the existence of *siège social*, control, domicile, and so on, they would seem to require a guarantee that the grant of personality is reasonable and not a device for limiting the proper sphere of protection of other governments.[68]

THE *BARCELONA TRACTION* CASE AND THE PROTECTION OF CORPORATIONS

The decision in the *Barcelona Traction* case (Second Phase) is considered fully below. For the present the case must be considered in relation to the diplomatic protection of corporations. The Barcelona Traction Company was incorporated under Canadian law and had its registered office in Canada. The International Court, in reaching the conclusion that Belgium had no capacity to espouse the claims of the, as alleged, Belgian shareholders in the company, considered the argument that such a claim was the only possibility of redress for the loss suffered since the company's national state lacked capacity to act on its behalf. This argument raised the question whether Canada was the national state of Barcelona Traction. The Court explained its view that Canada was the national state in these terms:[69]

In allocating corporate entities to States for purposes of diplomatic protection, international law is based, but only to a limited extent, on an analogy with the rules governing the

---

[66] de Visscher, 102 Hague *Recueil* (1961, I), 439–45 (criterion criticized); Schwarzenberger, *International Law*, pp. 402–6. See also Judge Jessup, *ubi supra*.

[67] (1929), *RIAA* v. 61.

[68] Cf. the *Canevaro* case, *ubi supra*; and *Ruden & Co.* (1870), Lapradelle and Politis, ii. 588.

[69] ICJ Reports (1970), 42. See also Judge Ammoun, Sep. Op., pp. 295–6, 300; and the very qualified expressions of Judge Fitzmaurice, p. 83.

nationality of individuals. The traditional rule attributes the right of diplomatic protection of a corporate entity to the State under the laws of which it is incorporated and in whose territory it has its registered office. These two criteria have been confirmed by long practice and by numerous international instruments. This notwithstanding, further or different links are at times said to be required in order that a right of diplomatic protection should exist. Indeed, it has been the practice of some States to give a company incorporated under their law diplomatic protection solely when it has its seat (*siège social*) or management or centre of control in their territory, or when a majority or a substantial proportion of the shares has been owned by nationals of the State concerned. Only then, it has been held, does there exist between the corporation and the State in question a genuine connection of the kind familiar from other branches of international law. However, in the particular field of the diplomatic protection of corporate entities, no absolute test of the 'genuine connection' has found general acceptance. Such tests as have been applied are of a relative nature, and sometimes links with one State have had to be weighed against those with another. In this connection reference has been made to the *Nottebohm* case. In fact the Parties made frequent reference to it in the course of the proceedings. However, given both the legal and factual aspects of protection in the present case the Court is of the opinion that there can be no analogy with the issues raised or the decision given in that case.

In the present case, it is not disputed that the company was incorporated in Canada and has its registered office in that country. The incorporation of the company under the law of Canada was an act of free choice. Not only did the founders of the company seek its incorporation under Canadian law but it has remained under that law for a period of over 50 years. It has maintained in Canada its registered office, its accounts and its share registers. Board meetings were held there for many years; it has been listed in the records of the Canadian tax authorities. Thus a close and permanent connection has been established, fortified by the passage of over half a century. This connection is in no way weakened by the fact that the company engaged from the very outset in commercial activities outside Canada, for that was its declared object. Barcelona Traction's links with Canada are thus manifold.

This passage is of considerable importance. The Court rejects the analogy of the *Nottebohm* case[70] and the 'genuine connection' principle applied in that case in the context of the naturalization of individuals. Nevertheless, the authority of this expression of opinion is reduced by three circumstances. First, since neither Belgium nor Spain contested the Canadian character of the Barcelona Traction Company the reference to the issue of 'genuine connection' was quite without point.[71] Secondly, the Court in fact takes the trouble to set out the 'manifold' links of the company with Canada. Thirdly, there is a considerable body of opinion both on the Court[72] and elsewhere[73] in favour of the application of the *Nottebohm* principle to the diplomatic protection of limited companies. It would seem that the process whereby an individual embarks on a voluntary naturalization and the incorporation of a company in the country of

---

[70] *Supra*, p. 407.

[71] See the judgment at pp. 42–3, and the joint decl. of Judges Petrén and Onyeama, ICJ Reports (1970), 52.

[72] See the joint decl. of Judges Petrén and Onyeama (previous note); and the sep. ops. of Judges Fitzmaurice, ibid. 79–83; Tanaka, p. 129 (but cf. pp. 140–1); Jessup, pp. 182–91, 195, 204–7; Padilla Nervo, p. 254; Gros, pp. 279–83. See also the Diss. Op. of Riphagen, Judge *ad hoc*, pp. 346–8, 351–2.

[73] See the material considered *supra*, pp. 419ff.

choice are significantly similar. Fears that the 'genuine' or 'effective' link principle will lead to instability and absence of diplomatic protection are by no means groundless. However, the *Nottebohm* principle is essentially the assertion that in referring to institutions of municipal law, international law has a reserve power to guard against giving effect to ephemeral, abusive, and simulated creations.[74] Moreover, there is probably a presumption of validity in favour of the nationality created by incorporation and, in the case of multi-national corporate bodies, no very exacting test of substantial connection should be applied.

SHAREHOLDERS[75]

There is considerable authority for the view that shareholders must rely upon the diplomatic protection available in favour of the corporation in which they have invested. The shareholders may receive diplomatic protection from the state of their nationality in certain situations, namely, when the act of the respondent state affects the shareholder's legal rights (for example, the right to receive dividends) as such, and also when the company has ceased to exist in law in the place of incorporation. Other exceptions may exist but they are controversial. The admissibility of claims on behalf of shareholders was at issue in the *Barcelona Traction* case (Second Phase).[76] An account of the law must focus on this decision, resting as it did upon a majority judgment the reasoning of which was supported by twelve judges.

The Barcelona Traction Company was incorporated in Canada in 1911 and had its head office in Toronto. The company was a holding company and formed a number of subsidiary companies for the purpose of developing the production and distribution of electric power in the Spanish province of Catalonia. Some of the subsidiaries were incorporated under Canadian law and had registered offices in Canada; the others were incorporated under Spanish law and had registered offices in Spain. The Belgian

---

[74] See Whiteman, viii. 1270–2, for some good examples.

[75] Whiteman, viii. 1269–91; Hyde, ii. 904–8; Hackworth, v. 827–45; *British Digest*, v. 535–71; C. de Visscher, 15 *RDILC* (1934), 624–51; Beckett, 17 *Grot. Soc.* (1931), 188–94; Jones, 26 *BY* (1949), 225–58; Bagge, 34 *BY* (1958), 169–75; P. de Visscher, 102 Hague *Recueil* (1961, I), 463–79; Feliciano, 118 Hague *Recueil* (1966, II), 295–310; Lillich, 13 *ICLQ* (1964), 911–21; id., *International Claims: Postwar British Practice*, pp. 40–52; Weston, *International Claims: Postwar French Practice*, pp. 167–71; Nial, 101 Hague *Recueil* (1960, III), 311–22; Kiss, in Université de Paris, Institut de droit comparé, *La Personnalité morale et ses limites* (1960), 179–210; Caflisch, *La Protection des sociétés*; de Hochepied, *La Protection diplomatique*; Sørensen, pp. 579–81; O'Connell, ii. 1043–9; Jiménez de Aréchaga, 4 *Phil. Int. LJ* (1965), 71–98; id., 159 Hague *Recueil* (1978, I), 288–91; Lillich and Weston, *International Claims: Contemporary European Practice*, pp. 4–5. Clay, 45 *Georgetown LJ* (1956), 1–19; Diez de Velasco, 141 Hague *Recueil* (1974, I), 93–185; Rousseau, v. 131–51; Stern, *J.D.I.* 116 (1990), 897–927; Lowe, *Liber Amicorum Judge Shigeru Oda* (2002), 269–84; International Law Commission, Fourth Report on diplomatic protection by John Dugard, A/CN.4/530, 13 March 2003; Add.1, 6 June 2003.

[76] ICJ Reports (1970), 3; 9 *ILM* (1970), 227; for comment see Briggs, 65 *AJ* 327–45; Lillich, ibid. 522–32; Metzger, ibid. 532–41; Caflisch, 31 *Z.a.ö.R.u.V.* (1971), 162–96; C. de Visscher, 6 *Revue belge* (1970), i–iv; id., 7 *Revue belge* (1971), 1–6; id., *Théories et réalités* (4th edn.), 303–5; Higgins, 11 *Virginia JIL* (1971), 327–43; various items, 23 *Revista española* (1971), nos. 2–3; Seidl-Hohenveldern, 22 *Öst. Z. für öff. R.* (1971–2), 255–309; Grisel, 17 *Ann. suisse* (1971), 31–48; Mann, 67 *AJ* (1973), 259–74.

contention was that by the outbreak of the Second World War the share capital of Barcelona Traction was in large part held by Belgian nationals, the principal shareholder being a Belgian company called Sidro.[77] During the Second World War large blocks of shares were transferred to American nominees and, for a time, were vested in a trustee. In the Belgian view the ownership of these remained Belgian. In the immediate post-war period the Spanish authorities refused to authorize foreign currency transfers to service sterling bonds issued by Barcelona Traction. As a consequence in 1948 three Spanish holders of recently acquired bonds brought bankruptcy proceedings against Barcelona Traction. Eventually Barcelona Traction and the subsidiary companies were declared bankrupt in Spain, and by 1952 the assets in Spain and the management of the subsidiaries had passed to Spanish interests as a result of a complicated series of proceedings in the Spanish courts.

As a result of the bankruptcy proceedings, Spain received diplomatic representations from several governments and from Canada in particular. Canada took little or no further action after 1952 and, after a failure to negotiate a settlement, Belgium submitted the dispute to the International Court of Justice,[78] claiming reparation for losses[79] caused to Belgian shareholders in Barcelona Traction as a consequence of various unlawful acts[80] by the Spanish courts and administrative authorities. In the Belgian view the bankruptcy proceedings were contrived with the object of transferring the control of the group of companies to Spanish interests and leading to the 'total despoliation' of the group.

The Court held that Belgium lacked a legal interest in the subject matter of the claim and hence did not proceed to the merits. Judge Jessup held that the Belgian ownership of the shares had not been established. Judge Gros held that the company lacked a genuine connection with the Belgian economy. Judge Tanaka decided in favour of Belgium on the issue of admissibility but held in favour of Spain on the merits. The other 12 judges of the Court[81] participated in the reasoning of the majority judgment, though Judge Fitzmaurice[82] had serious misgivings concerning 'an unsatisfactory state of the law that obliges the Court to refrain from pronouncing on the substantive merits of the Belgian claim, on the basis of what is really—at least in the actual circumstances of this case—somewhat of a technicality'.

[77] The principal shareholder in Sidro was another company, Sofina, in which, it was alleged, Belgian interests were preponderant.

[78] An earlier application in 1958 was discontinued, a step which Spain as respondent did not oppose. In 1964 the Court, on a new application of 1962, rejected two Spanish preliminary objections relating to jurisdiction and joined the other preliminary objections (relating to non-exhaustion of local remedies and lack of jus standi in respect of the shareholders) to the merits. The Spanish objection on the basis of lack of jus standi had two branches (a) absence of Belgian ownership of the shares in question; (b) the absence of a right of diplomatic protection in respect of shareholders by a state other than the national state of the company.

[79] A sum equivalent to 88% of the net value of the business at the time of the bankruptcy declaration in 1948, plus incidental damage and certain expenses. Apart from the interest element the total claimed was some 84 million dollars.

[80] On the issues of state responsibility raised by Belgium see supra, p. 473.

[81] Riphagen, ad hoc Judge for Belgium, dissented.

[82] ICJ Reports (1970), 64.

The Court[83] accepted the mechanism of the limited liability company (*société anonyme*) as a general feature of national legal systems which had become a fact of international economic life. The shareholder takes advantage, as he is entitled to do, of the device of incorporation. If the company is harmed, this indirectly causes prejudice to the shareholders; but in such a case what is affected is a simple interest and not the *rights* of the shareholders. The shareholders must look to the company and thence to the national state of the company for action. The Court was unimpressed by the argument that, in the absence of protection by Canada (which had ceased substantial diplomatic activity in 1952), the shareholders should have alternative protection. The Court simply pointed out that Canada had the power to exercise protection but such power was discretionary—it was a right, not an obligation.[84] Various issues as to the policy of the law are explored in the judgment and, among the considerations which found favour with the Court was the following:[85]

The Court considers that the adoption of the theory of diplomatic protection of shareholders as such, by opening the door to competing diplomatic claims, could create an atmosphere of confusion and insecurity in international economic relations. The danger would be all the greater inasmuch as the shares of companies whose activity is international are widely scattered and frequently change hands.

The Court recognized that the shareholder has an independent basis for protection if the act complained of is aimed at the direct rights of the shareholder as such, for example, the right to any dividend.[86] Apart from that case, the question remained whether there were special circumstances in which the corporate veil could be lifted in the interest of the shareholders. Treaties and decisions concerned with the treatment of enemy and allied property in the two world wars and the treatment of foreign property in cases of nationalization were forms of *lex specialis* and were not of general application. In the view of the Court[87] the only special circumstance was the case of the company having ceased to exist as a corporate entity capable in law of defending its rights in the relevant municipal courts.

The carefully argued separate opinions of Judges Tanaka,[88] Jessup,[89] and Gros[90] supported the diplomatic protection of shareholders as a principle.[91]

---

[83] See esp. pp. 34–8. See also the Sep. Ops. of Judges Morelli, pp. 231–42; Padilla Nervo, pp. 244–64; and Ammoun, pp. 296–333.

[84] pp. 41–5. See also at p. 37.

[85] pp. 48–50 at p. 49.

[86] p. 36.

[87] pp. 40–1.

[88] pp. 121ff., esp. pp. 130–5.

[89] pp. 168–201.

[90] pp. 268–79, on condition that the investments in question are 'connected with the national economy' of the protecting state.

[91] Also in support of the principle: Nial, 101 Hague *Recueil* (1960, III), 320–2; Wortley, *Expropriation in Public International Law* (1959), 11–12, 144; Judge Wellington Koo, *Barcelona Traction* case (Prelim. Objections), ICJ Reports (1964), 53–64; Verzijl, 12 *Neths. Int. LR* (1965), 34–40; Feliciano, 118 Hague *Recueil* (1966, II), 295–310; C. de Visscher, *Les Effectivités*, pp. 134–8; de Hochepied, *La Protection diplomatique;*

The Court rejected two propositions for which there had been some support in the sources of the law, and which thus deserve some consideration.

(i) Protection for shareholders may be justified when the corporation is 'completely paralysed' or 'practically defunct'.

The Court held that shareholders could only receive protection as such when the corporation had ceased to exist in law. This was not true of Barcelona Traction since, in spite of its economic paralysis in Spain and state of receivership in Canada, the Company still existed and was capable of legal action. The Court remarked that the description 'practically defunct' 'lacks all legal precision'.[92] On the other hand Judges Fitzmaurice,[93] Tanaka,[94] and Gros,[95] with the support of a fair amount of other opinion,[96] would assimilate the absence of effective personality with formal termination of corporate existence, on the basis that in the context of diplomatic protection the internal law criteria are to be applied with moderation.

(ii) Protection may be exercised where the corporation has the nationality of the very state responsible for the acts complained of.

The Court remarked that 'whatever the validity of this theory may be, it is certainly not applicable to the present case, since Spain is not the national State of Barcelona Traction'.[97] However, Judges Fitzmaurice,[98] Tanaka,[99] and Jessup[100] supported this form of protection, primarily on the basis that in such a case no claim on behalf of the company would be possible on the international plane since the company had local nationality. The separate opinions of Judges Morelli,[101] Padilla Nervo,[102] and Ammoun[103] rejected this form of protection and the authorities are much divided on the issue.[104] In truth the exception, if it exists, is anomalous 'since it ignores the

Jones, 26 BY (1949), 225–58 (with some caution); Proceedings, ASIL (1969), 30–53. See further the Ziat Ben Kiran claim, RIAA ii. 729; Ann. Digest, 2 (1923–4), no. 102. Against the principle: Jiménez de Aréchaga, 4 Phil. Int. LJ (1965), 71–98; id., in Sørensen, pp. 579–81; Bagge, 34 BY (1958), 171; Rousseau, v. 147–9. See also Arbitration between the United States and the Reparation Commission (1926), RIAA ii. 779; 8 BY (1927), 156.

[92] p. 41. See also Judges Jessup, pp. 193–4; Padilla Nervo, pp. 256–7; Ammoun, pp. 318–20; and Beckett, 17 Grot. Soc. (1931), 190–1.

[93] pp. 72–5.

[94] p. 134.

[95] p. 276. See also Riphagen, Judge ad hoc, pp. 344–5.

[96] P. de Visscher, 102 Hague Recueil (1961, I), 477; Bindschedler, 90 Hague Recueil (1956, II), 237–8. British practice is in accord: British Digest, v. 564; Hackworth, v. 840–3. See also Feliciano, 118 Hague Recueil (1966, II), 304.

[97] p. 48 and see, however, Judge Padilla Nervo, Sep. Op., ICJ Reports (1970), 257.

[98] pp. 72–4.

[99] p. 134.

[100] pp. 191–3.

[101] p. 240.

[102] pp. 257–9.

[103] p. 318.

[104] In favour of protection: Beckett, 17 Grot. Soc. (1932), 189–93; C. de Visscher, 61 RDILC (1934), 624, 651; P. de Visscher, 102 Hague Recueil (1960, I), 478–9; Petrén, 109 Hague Recueil (1963, II), 506, 510; Judge

traditional rule that a State is not guilty of a breach of international law for injuring one of its own nationals'.[105] It is arbitrary to allow the shareholders to emerge from the carapace of the corporation in this situation but not in others. If one accepts the general considerations of policy advanced by the Court then this alleged exception to the rule is disqualified.

In the draft articles on diplomatic protection adopted in 2006 the International Law Commission proposed the following provisions relating to shareholders:

Article 11

Protection of shareholders

A State of nationality of shareholders in a corporation shall not be entitled to exercise diplomatic protection in respect of such shareholders in the case of an injury to the corporation unless:

(a) The corporation has ceased to exist according to the law of the State of incorporation for a reason related to the injury; or

(b) The corporation had, at the date of injury, the nationality of the State alleged to be responsible for causing the injury, and incorporation in that State was required by it as a precondition for doing business there.

Article 12

Direct injury to shareholders

To the extent that an internationally wrongful act of a State causes direct injury to the rights of shareholders as such, as distinct from those of the corporation itself, the State of nationality of any such shareholders is entitled to exercise diplomatic protection in respect of its nationals.

INTERESTS IN SHIPS AND AIRCRAFT[106]

The question of the nationality of ships and aircraft arises in variety of contexts,[107] and many of the rules are of a functional kind.[108] In fact much that is written on the subject is not concerned with the problems of diplomatic protection, and it is not appropriate to fasten on general propositions about the nationality of ships, primarily relating to

---

Wellington Koo, Sep. Op., *Barcelona Traction* case (Prelim. Objections), ICJ Reports (1964), 58; Jones, 26 *BY* (1949), 257; Caflisch, *La Protection des sociétés*, pp. 153ff.; Kiss, *La Personnalité morale*. See also Vallat, *International Law and the Practitioner*, p. 28; Whiteman, viii. 1272–4. Opposing protection: Jiménez de Aréchaga, 4 *Phil. Int. LJ* (1965), 93–4; id., in Sørensen, p. 580; id., 159 Hague *Recueil* (1978, I), 290; Diez de Velasco, 141 Hague *Recueil* (1974, I), 163–6. See also O'Connell ii. 1043; *Kunhardt* case (1903), *RIAA* ix. 171; *Baasch and Römer* case (1903), *RIAA* x. 467.

[105] Judge Jessup, Sep. Op., p. 192.

[106] See especially Watts, 33 *BY* (1957), 52–84; and also Rienow, *The Test of the Nationality of a Merchant Vessel* (1937); Rousseau, iv. 284–94; Oppenheim, ii. 731–2; Meyers, *The Nationality of Ships* (1967); Bettink, *Neths. Yrbk.* 18 (1987) 69–119; Bernhardt, *Encyclopedia*, IV (2000), 400–8; Kamto, *Mélanges offerts à Laurent Lucchini et Jean-Pierre Quéneudec* (2003), 343–73.

[107] *Supra*, pp. 227–8, 315–18, 410–12.

[108] See *supra*, p. 406.

jurisdiction, as relevant to the issue of the admissibility of claims. In general the principle of real or genuine link[109] supported in the *Nottebohm* case[110] ought to apply here, and there is evidence for the view that *bona fide* national ownership, rather than registration or authority to fly the flag, provides the appropriate basis for protection of ships.[111] The determination of national ownership leads into the issues concerning beneficial interest, corporations, and shareholders considered previously. It would seem that the position is the same in the case of aircraft.

STATE INTERESTS IN CORPORATIONS[112]

Governments may themselves hold shares in corporations, and some novel issues may arise, for example concerning the need to exhaust local remedies,[113] when the corporation makes a claim which is adopted by the government under the law of which the corporation is constituted. In the *Anglo-Iranian Oil Company* case[114] the United Kingdom supported a claim in which it had a direct interest. A question arises as to the eligibility of corporations in which governments have interests to claim sovereign immunity.[115]

SUBROGATION

The term subrogation may describe the transfer of liabilities as a consequence of the principle of state succession (assuming that the principle could operate in this way).[116] The term more correctly describes the process of 'transfer' on the basis of agreement between the successor state and the claimant, or estoppel, in which case issues as to the existence and meaning of the agreement or estoppel concern the admissibility of the claim.[117]

THE RECOMMENDED PRACTICE (INTERNATIONAL LAW COMMISSION (2006))

In order to establish a more adequate connection between the institutions of diplomatic protection and the protection of the rights of individuals, in the draft articles

---

[109] See generally *supra*, pp. 407ff.

[110] ICJ Reports (1955), 4.

[111] Watts, 33 *BY* (1957), 73–83.

[112] See Johnson, 4 *ILQ* (1951), 159–77; McNair, *Opinions*, ii. 39.

[113] See *infra*, s. 6.

[114] ICJ Reports (1951), 89.

[115] McNair, *Opinions*, ii. 39, referring to a case in which the US District Court for the District of Columbia granted immunity to the Anglo-Iranian Oil Company Ltd., basing its decision on the 'public purpose' of the Company: 47 *AJ* (1953), 502.

[116] Cf. Schwarzenberger, *International Law* (3rd edn.), i. 175–9; and the *Lighthouses* arbitration (1956), PCA, *RIAA* xii. 188–9; ILR 23 (1956), 659 at 668. On state succession see ch. 29.

[117] See the *Mavrommatis* case (1924), PCIJ, Ser. A, no. 2, at p. 28; and *Blabon et al. v. United States*, ILR 28, 195.

adopted in the 2006 the International Law Commission proposed the following (Article 19):

Recommended practice

A State entitled to exercise diplomatic protection according to the present draft articles, should:

(a) Give due consideration to the possibility of exercising diplomatic protection, especially when a significant injury has occurred;

(b) Take into account, wherever feasible, the views of injured persons with regard to resort to diplomatic protection and the reparation to be sought; and

(c) Transfer to the injured person any compensation obtained for the injury from the responsible State subject to any reasonable deductions.

6. EXHAUSTION OF LOCAL REMEDIES[118]

An important rule of admissibility applies to cases of diplomatic protection as opposed to instances of direct injury to the state. A claim will not be admissible on the international plane unless the individual alien or corporation concerned has exhausted the legal remedies available to him in the state which is alleged to be the author of injury.[119] This is a rule which is justified by practical and political considerations and not by any logical necessity deriving from international law as a whole. The more persuasive practical considerations advanced are the greater suitability and convenience of national courts as forums for the claims of individuals and corporations, the need to avoid the multiplication of small claims on the level of diplomatic protection, the

---

[118] Or, 'épuisement des recours locaux', 'épuisement préalable des recours internes'. See generally Fawcett, 31 *BY* (1954), 452–8; Bagge, 34 *BY* (1958), 165–9; Amerasinghe, *State Responsibility for Injuries to Aliens* (1967), 169–269; id., 12 *ICLQ* (1963), 1285–325; id., 25 *Z.a.ö.R.u.V.* (1965), 445–77; id., 36 *Z.a.ö.R.u.V.* (1976), 727–59; García Amador, *Yrbk.* ILC (1958), ii. 55–61; Verzijl, *Annuaire de l'Inst.* 45 (1954), i. 5ff.; ibid. 46 (1956), 1ff.; Reuter, 103 Hague *Recueil* (1961, II), 613–19; Briggs, 50 *AJ* (1956), 921–7; Fitzmaurice, 37 *BY* (1961), 53–64; Law, *The Local Remedies Rule in International Law* (1961); Jenks, *The Prospects of International Adjudication* (1964), 527–37; Whiteman, viii. 769–807; de Visscher, 52 Hague *Recueil* (1935, II), 421–32; Sørensen, pp. 582–90; Mummery, 58 *AJ* (1964), 389–414; Schwebel and Wetter, 60 *AJ* (1966), 484–501; Head, 5 *Canad. Yrbk.* (1967), 142–58; Jennings, 121 Hague *Recueil* (1967, II), 480–6; Przetacznik, 21 *Öst. Z. für öff. R.* (1971), 103–12; P. de Visscher, 136 Hague *Recueil* (1972, II), 167–76; Chappez, *La Règle de l'épuisement des voies de recours internes* (1972); Cançado Trindade, 16 *Indian Journ.* (1976), 187–218; id., 12 *Revue belge* (1976), 499–527 id., ibid. (1978), 232–57; id., *The Application of the Rule of Exhaustion of Local Remedies in International Law* (1983); Rousseau, v. 152–69; Jiménez de Aréchaga, 159 Hague *Recueil* (1978, I), 291–7; Pocar, in *Essays in Honour of Roberto Ago* (1987), iii. 291–300; *Digest of US Practice* (1978), 1208–17; Perrin, in *Mélanges Bindschedler* (1980), 271–91. See also Ago, Sixth Report on State Responsibility, *Yrbk. ILC* (1977), II (Pt. 1), 3 at 20–43; Report of the Commission, ibid. (1977), ii (Pt. 2), 30–50; Amerasinghe, *Local Remedies in International Law* (1990); Oppenheim, i. 522–6; Thirlway, 66 *BY* (1995), 80–93; Warbrick, 37 *ICLQ* (1988), 1006–8; ILC, Dugard, Second Report on diplomatic protection, A/CN.4/514, 28 Feb. 2001; Third Report, A/ CN.4/523, 7 March 2002. See further the *Report of the International Law Commission, Fifty-eighth session* (2006), G.A. Off. Recs., *Sixty-first session*, Suppl. No. 10 (A/61/10), 70–86.

[119] The application of the rule may be avoided by agreement.

maner in which aliens by residence and business activity have associated themselves with the local jurisdiction,[120] and the utility of a procedure which may lead to classification of the facts and liquidation of the damages.[121] The role of the local remedies rule is seen more readily if three situations are distinguished.[122]

(1) When the act complained of is a breach of an international agreement or customary law, and is not a breach of local law, then the rule is inapplicable.

(2) When the act complained of is a breach of local law only, then it is only the subsequent conduct of the state of the forum which can create responsibility. If the authorities there interfere with the course of justice or certain standards are not observed, then a denial of justice has occurred and responsibility results from it.

(3) When the act complained of is a breach both of the local law and of an international agreement or customary law, the rule of the exhaustion of local remedies applies. In this type of case the function of the rule is procedural: it is a question of admissibility and not of substance.[123]

However, the distinction between the first and third situations does not depend entirely on the question whether there has been a breach of the local law. The incidence of the procedural rule is a difficult problem,[124] and probably any answer will be incomplete if the empirical nature of the rule and its dependence on criteria of reasonableness are ignored. The distinction which is commonly drawn is between cases of direct injury to a state, for example by inflicting damage on its warships[125] or the commission of acts directed against its ambassador, and cases of diplomatic protection, in which the interest of an individual (or other legal entity of private law) is affected and the legal interest of the state depends on the nationality of the individual concerned. It is only in the latter case that the exhaustion of local remedies is a condition of admissibility on the international plane. However, in drawing the distinction one is perhaps only stating the problem rather than providing the basis for a solution. Reliance on the existence or not of a breach of local law is not entirely satisfactory, since, in some cases normally regarded as examples of direct injury to a state, it is not clear that there is no breach of the local law of the defendant state. Meron[126] argues that the rule can-

---

[120] Cf. the problems of the real or genuine link in the context of nationality, *supra*, pp. 407ff.

[121] See McNair, *Opinions*, ii. 197–8, 312. See also Borchard, *Diplomatic Protection of Citizens Abroad* (1928), 817.

[122] See Fawcett, 31 *BY* (1954), 452–8.

[123] Fawcett, 31 *BY* (1954), 452–8; Judge Lauterpacht, Sep. Op., *Norwegian Loans* case, ICJ Reports (1957), 9 at 39–41. Fawcett is of opinion that the objection would not be admitted if the claim were not for judgment and damages but for a declaration only; on this point see also Simmonds, 10 *ICLQ* (1961), 537, 545; Amerasinghe, *State Responsibility*, p. 204. For a contrary view: Sørensen, p. 582. See also *Case of Ireland against the United Kingdom*, Europ. Ct. of HR; ILR 58, 190, Judgment, 18 Jan. 1978, para. 159; ibid., Judge Fitzmaurice, Sep. Op., paras. 8–11.

[124] On which see Meron, 35 *BY* (1959), 83–101.

[125] Cf. the *Corfu Channel* case (Merits), ICJ Reports (1949), 4; and see *Case Concerning the Air Services Agreement of 27 March 1946 (US v. France)*, ILR 54, 304 at 323–5; and *Digest of US Practice* (1978), 1208–17.

[126] 35 *BY* (1959), 84–5.

not apply in cases of direct injury by reason of the maxim *par in parem, non habet jurisdictionem,* but it could be said that the maxim loses much of its force if it rests on the difference between direct and indirect injury (in the persons of nationals) to states. In the latter case states in the first instance leave the determination of issues to the internal law after all.

CONDITIONS OF APPLICATION OF THE LOCAL REMEDIES RULE

The existence of the rule is undoubted and its application in practice is very common. Nevertheless, not a little confusion and complexity are presented by the conditions in which the rule is applied.

(a) What is the precise function of proceedings in the local courts?

The rule is often described rather loosely in terms of the possibility of 'obtaining redress' in the local courts. As an issue of admissibility the local proceedings are regarded retrospectively, but when proceedings are begun in the local courts various issues of law and fact may be at large. It will not always be clear whether there is a breach of international law, or local law, or of either. The alien claimant in the local courts may be able to seek a remedy for a breach of international law *as such*, or may employ a remedy of local law which involves no reference to matters of international law but gives substantial reparation for the harm complained of. Even in the case of direct injury to the interests of a foreign state, for example, damage to warships caused by agents of the state in which remedies are sought, it is not possible to *assume* that no remedy exists in municipal law.[127] The local proceedings may actually establish that an instance of state responsibility has occurred but it is surely incorrect to state[128] that resort to local remedies is 'required...in order to determine...whether or not [such] an act or omission is incompatible with international law'. The local proceedings may simply establish that a particular rule of local law stands in the way of redress and leave aside both the issue of compatibility of that rule with international law, and the whole question of whether the dispute has an international character.[129] Thus in general the exhaustion of local remedies will involve using such local procedures as are available to protect interests which correspond *as closely as may be and in practical terms* with the interests involved in a subsequent international claim.[130]

---

[127] Cf. Jennings, 121 Hague *Recueil* (1967, II), 482.

[128] See Briggs, 50 *AJ* (1956), at 925–6; also in Whiteman, viii. 786–7.

[129] See Lauterpacht, Sep. Op., ICJ Reports (1957), 38.

[130] See the *Finnish Ships Arbitration* (*infra*) and the *Interhandel* case (*infra*). Cf. Amerasinghe, *State Responsibility*, pp. 196–7. See further Bustamante y Rivero, ICJ Reports (1970), 57–63; Tanaka, ibid., 147–8.

(b) The local remedies rule only applies when effective remedies are available in the national system

In certain circumstances recourse to local remedies is excused. The remedies to be exhausted comprise all forms of recourse as of right, including administrative remedies of a legal nature 'but not extra-legal remedies or remedies as of grace'.[131] The best test appears to be that an effective remedy must be available 'as a matter of reasonable possibility'.[132] No effective remedy is available if a point of law which could have been taken on appeal has previously been decided by the highest court,[133] or if the only issue on appeal would be one of fact and the higher courts lack the power to review findings of fact.[134] However, the local law may be uncertain on such issues as the principles of sovereign immunity, the Act of State doctrine, or the interpretation of gold clauses, and the consequence is that an international tribunal should show caution in drawing conclusions on the availability of a local remedy.[135] It must be noted, however, that a fair number of writers[136] and arbitral awards[137] have been willing to presume ineffectiveness of remedies from the circumstances, for example on the basis of evidence that the courts were subservient to the executive.[138] A final and major point remains. A remedy is effective if it does justice to the claim in the local courts: 'a remedy cannot be *ineffective* merely because, if the claimant is in the wrong, it will not be *obtainable*'.[139]

(c) Should the local courts have jurisdiction in accordance with international law?

It may be that no effective remedy is available if the local courts do not have jurisdiction in relation to the matter in issue *in terms of local law*[140] (see (*b*) above). A different issue is whether the local remedies rule can apply when, according to international law, the local courts could not have jurisdiction over the matter in issue. Judge Fitzmaurice[141]

---

[131] Brierly, p. 281, citing the *Finnish Ships Arbitration* (1934), *RIAA* iii. 1479.

[132] See Lauterpacht, Sep. Op., *Norwegian Loans* case, ICJ Reports (1957), 39; Fitzmaurice, 37 *BY* (1961), 59–64; Tanaka, Sep. Op., *Barcelona Traction* case (Second Phase), ICJ Reports (1970), 144–5; Gros, Sep. Op., ibid. 284.

[133] *Panevezys* v. *Saldutiskis Railway* case, PCIJ, Series A/B, no. 76; *X* v. *Austria*, ILR 30, 268.

[134] *Finnish Ships Arbitration* (1934), *RIAA* iii. 1484 at 1535.

[135] Lauterpacht, Sep. Op., ICJ Reports (1957), 39–40; and see Cançado Trindade, *The Application of the Rule of Exhaustion of Local Remedies in International Law*, pp. 138–43.

[136] Sørensen, pp. 589–90; Oppenheim i. 525; Amerasinghe, *State Responsibility*, pp. 196–7, 242–4.

[137] e.g. *Forests in Central Rhodopia* (Merits), *Ann. Digest* (1933–4), no. 39; *RIAA* iii. 1405, 1420; 28 *AJ* (1934), 773, 789.

[138] See the *Brown* claim (1923), *RIAA* vi. 120; *Velasquez Rodriguez* case, Inter-Am. Ct. of HR, Judgment of 29 July 1988 (Annual Report of the Inter-American Ct. of Human Rights (1988), 35). See also Whiteman, viii. 784; Tanaka, Sep. Op., *Barcelona Traction* case (Second Phase), ICJ Reports (1970), 145–7.

[139] Fitzmaurice, 37 *BY* (1961), 60.

[140] See the Estonian argument and the Court's acceptance of the principle in the *Panevezys–Saldutiskis Railway* case, PCIJ, Ser. A/B, no. 76, p. 18; Whiteman, viii. 773.

[141] Sep. Op., *Barcelona Traction* case (Second Phase), ICJ Reports (1970), 103–10. See also Riphagen, Judge *ad hoc*, ibid. 355–6; Amerasinghe, *State Responsibility*, pp. 185–187; Jennings, 121 Hague *Recueil* (1967, II), 485–6.

has expressed the opinion that it could not, since no question of local remedies could arise in respect of proceedings which were a nullity in terms of international law, either as a consequence of excess of jurisdiction or on some other ground, such as lack of notification of proceedings.

(d) Issues arising from executive action

It is sometimes said to be the law that the rule does not apply when the issue arises from measures taken by 'the constitutional or legislative power or the highest executive organs'.[142] This view is too dogmatic since remedies may be available whatever the constitutional status of the agency taking the measure concerned. The test remains that of the reasonable possibility of an effective remedy.[143]

(e) In cases of diplomatic protection does the rule apply only if a sufficient link existed between the alien and the respondent state?

Some authorities hold the opinion that local remedies need not be exhausted unless, at the time of the original harm alleged, the alien has established some voluntary connection with the territory or jurisdiction of the respondent state.[144] This view receives no explicit support from the decided cases though it can be reconciled with the *Finnish Ships* and *Ambatielos* cases (see *infra*) by recourse to a broad definition of the link required and retrospective rationalization.[145] As a matter of principle the outcome depends upon one's view of the major basis in policy of the local remedies rule. If the major objective is to provide an alternative, relatively more convenient, recourse to that of proceeding on the international plane then no condition as to a link will apply. If the rule is related to assumption of risk by the alien and the existence of a proper basis for exercise of national jurisdiction, then the requirement of a voluntary link, such as residence, is good sense.

(f) The rule applies only in connection with state responsibility for an unlawful act and in the absence of direct injury to the claimant state

This is the assumption in the literature and jurisprudence of the subject and the Arbitral Tribunal for the Agreement on German External Debts has decided[146] that

---

[142] See Verzijl, *Annuaire de l'Inst.* 45 (1954), i. 112; Whiteman, viii. 785; *Annuaire de l'Inst.* 46 (1956), 266. See also the *U.S.* v. *Bulgaria*, ICJ Pleadings, quoted in Whiteman, viii. 783–4; and Lauterpacht, *International Law: Collected Papers*, i (1970), 397–8.

[143] See the judgment in the *Interhandel* case, ICJ Reports (1959), 27. See also Sørensen, p. 587.

[144] See Sørensen, p. 583; Meron, 35 *BY* (1959), 94–100; Amerasinghe, *State Responsibility*, pp. 182–7; O'Connell, ii. 950–2; *Aerial Incident* case (*Israel* v. *Bulgaria*), ICJ Pleadings (1959), 531–2; Whiteman, viii. 793; Jiménez de Aréchaga, 159 Hague *Recueil* (1978, I), 296; Schachter, 178 Hague *Recueil* (1982, V), 205. See also Reuter, 103 Hague *Recueil*, p. 615; *British Digest*, vi. 253; Jennings, 121 Hague *Recueil* (1967, II), 485–6. See further the I.L.C., Dugard, Third Report on diplomatic protection, A/CN.4/523, 7 March 2002, 26–35.

[145] Against the link requirement: Harvard draft, 1961; 55 *AJ* (1961), 577, Art. 19 (and see Whiteman, viii. 793–4); Am. Law Institute, Restatement, Second, *Foreign Relations Law*, paras. 206–10.

[146] *Swiss Confederation* v. *German Federal Republic (No. 1)* (1958), ILR 25 (1958, I), 33 at 42–50; and see Johnson, 34 *BY* (1958), 363–8.

the rule, as a consequence, cannot apply where the applicant state makes no claim for damages but merely requests a decision on the interpretation and application of a treaty. However, the general character of the claim will determine the issue, as a Chamber of the International Court held in the *Elettronnica Sicula* (*ELSI*) case.[147]

The operation of the local remedies rule will now be examined in the light of the leading cases.

FINNISH SHIPS ARBITRATION[148]

During the First World War, at a time when Finland was a part of Russia, the Russian Government requisitioned certain ships belonging to Finnish shipowners which were transferred to the British Government. The vessels were used in the service of the Allies, and at the end of the war the Finnish Government made claims against the British Government for compensation, on behalf of the owners, for the hire of some ships used, and the loss of others, in the Allied service. The claims were unfruitful, and, under the Indemnity Act 1920, the owners submitted the claims to the Admiralty Transport Arbitration Board. In 1926 the board dismissed the claims on the ground that the requisition complained of was by and on behalf of the Russian Government. There was no appeal from this finding of fact. Appeal was possible on points of law to the Court of Appeal and the House of Lords, but the owners did not appeal. Eventually the two governments agreed to submit to Bagge, the sole arbitrator, the question: 'Have the Finnish shipowners or have they not exhausted the means of recourse placed at their disposal by British law?' By reason of the failure to appeal the British Government argued that the remedies had not been exhausted. The Finnish Government contended that, in view of the finding of fact, the right of appeal was illusory and ineffective since an appeal was bound to fail. The arbitrator pointed out[149] that he was not concerned with the merits of the claim before the board. The test of effectiveness was applied on the assumption that all allegations of fact in the claim were true. On this basis, he found that the appealable points of law in the judgment of the board 'obviously would have been insufficient to reverse the decision of the Arbitration Board as to there not being a British requisition, and that, in consequence, there was no effective remedy against this decision'.[150] His answer to the question submitted to him was therefore that the local remedies had been exhausted.

---

[147] ICJ Reports (1989), pp. 42–3, paras. 49–52. See also the *Case Concerning the Air Services Agreement of 27 March 1946*, ILR 54, 303 at 322–5; and the *Heathrow Airport User Charges Arbitration*, ILR 102, 215 at 277–9.

[148] (1934), *RIAA* iii. 1479; *Ann. Digest*, 7 (1933–4), no. 91. See also Fachiri, 17 *BY* (1936), 19–36; Borchard, 28 *AJ* (1934), 729–33; Hostie, 43 *RGDIP* (1936), 327–57.

[149] *RIAA* iii. 1499, 1503–4.

[150] *RIAA* iii. 1535ff.

AMBATIELOS ARBITRATION[151]

In 1919 Mr Ambatielos, a Greek national, concluded a contract for the purchase of nine steamships, then under construction, with the United Kingdom Government. In due course Ambatielos sought remedies for loss resulting from late delivery of some of the vessels and cancellation of the contract of purchase in respect of two others. However, as the Board of Trade had instituted proceedings in the Court of Admiralty on mortgage deeds executed on some of the ships in 1920, the claim of Ambatielos was, by agreement between the parties, put forward as a defence to the proceedings. Mr Justice Hill gave judgment (January 1923) for the United Kingdom Government for possession and sale of certain vessels which had been delivered and for principal and interest due under the mortgage deeds. On appeal to the Court of Appeal Ambatielos asked for leave to call as a witness Major Laing, the British civil servant who had negotiated the contract for purchase of the ships. Leave was refused, and after judgment Ambatielos did not appeal to the House of Lords. In 1953 the International Court of Justice held[152] that the United Kingdom was bound to submit to arbitration the dispute as to the validity of the claim of Ambatielos under the Anglo-Greek Treaty of Commerce and Navigation of 1886. Under an agreement concluded in 1955 the claim was thus submitted to a Commission of Arbitration. The Greek claim consisted of the main claim A, for compensation for breach of the contract of sale, an alternative claim B based on unjust enrichment for return of a part payment of the price, and another alternative claim C in connection with the cancellation of the purchase of two of the vessels as from the date of judgment instead of the date on which the mortgage deeds were signed. The United Kingdom submitted, *inter alia*, that the procedural remedies in the English courts had not been exhausted.

One of the principal Greek arguments was that the rule was not applicable because the remedies open to Ambatielos were ineffective. The Commission applied the test propounded in the *Finnish Ships* arbitration, viz., that the truth of the facts on which the claimant bases the claim must be assumed in determining the applicability of the rule. On the application of the rule the Commission observed:

... 'local remedies' include not only reference to the courts and tribunals, but also the use of the procedural facilities which municipal law makes available to litigants before such courts and tribunals. It is the whole system of legal protection, as provided by municipal law, which must have been put to the test...

It is clear, however, that it cannot be strained too far:

In the view of the Commission the non-utilisation of certain means of procedure can be accepted as constituting a gap in the exhaustion of local remedies only if the use of these means of procedure were essential to establish the claimant's case before the municipal courts.

---

[151] (1956), Award, HMSO, 1956; *RIAA* xii. 83; ILR 23 (1956), 306; ibid. 24 (1957), 291. See also Pinto, 84 *JDI* (1957), 540–615; Amerasinghe, *State Responsibility*, pp. 1296ff. (dealing, *inter alia*, with the ops. of Alfaro and Spiropoulos).

[152] ICJ Reports (1953), 10; ILR 20 (1953), 547. See also the *Ambatielos* case (Prelim. Objection), ICJ Reports (1952), 28; ILR 19 (1952), no. 96.

The Commission found that the local remedies had not been exhausted. As regards claim A, Ambatielos had failed to exhaust local remedies by not calling Major Laing as witness in the High Court[153] and by not exhausting his rights of appeal. In the case of claim B, such remedies as were available for unjust enrichment in English law had not been tried. Nor had any claim of the kind presented in claim C been put forward in the English court: the claim before Mr Justice Hill had been for non-delivery and was the converse of the claim for non-cancellation of the purchase of two vessels on the date of the mortgage deeds.

THE *INTERHANDEL* CASE[154]

In 1942 the United States Government vested most of the shares of the General Aniline and Film Company (GAF) as enemy property under the provisions of the Trading with the Enemy Act 1917. The majority of GAF shares were owned by Interhandel, a Swiss firm, which, in the opinion of the United States Government, was under the control of IG Farben. The view of the Swiss Government was that, after remodelling in 1940, Interhandel had completely severed its ties with IG Farben, although in 1945 the Swiss Government had ordered a provisional blocking of Interhandel's assets. In 1946 the Washington Accord was signed between France, the United Kingdom, and the United States and, on the other side, Switzerland. This agreement provided, *inter alia*, for the liquidation of property in Switzerland owned or controlled by Germans in Germany, the unblocking of Swiss assets in the United States, and the submission of disputes as to the application of the Accord to arbitration. The dispute remained unsettled, and in 1948, on an appeal by Interhandel under the Accord procedure, the Swiss Authority of Review annulled the provisional blocking of assets. The Swiss Government claimed that the Allied powers were bound by this decision and claimed that the vested property should be restored or that there should be resort to the arbitration procedure provided for in the Accord. The United States Government contended that the Washington Accord and the ruling of the Swiss Authority of Review did not apply to property vested in the United States.

In 1958 proceedings on the preliminary objections of the United States began in the International Court as a consequence of a Swiss application which invoked the optional clause of the Statute. The Swiss application was made only after litigation by the corporation in the United States' courts between 1948 and 1957. The third preliminary objection of the United States, though framed as an objection to jurisdiction, was in effect directed against the admissibility of the application by reason of the non-exhaustion of local remedies. On the position in the United States' courts the International Court observed:[155]

The Court has indicated in what conditions the Swiss Government, basing itself on the idea that Interhandel's suit had been finally rejected in the United States courts, considered

---

[153] The Commission made the assumption that the testimony would have had the effect of establishing the claim.

[154] ICJ Reports (1959), 6. See also Meron, 35 *BY* (1959), 89–92; Simmonds, 10 *ICLQ* (1961), 495–547; Briggs, 53 *AJ* (1959), 547–63; C. de Visscher, 63 *RGDIP* (1959), 413–33.

[155] ICJ Reports (1959), 26–7.

itself entitled to institute proceedings by its Application of October 2nd, 1957. However, the decision given by the Supreme Court of the United States on October 14th, 1957... granted a writ of *certiorari* and readmitted Interhandel into the suit. The judgment of that Court on June 16th, 1958, reversed the judgment of the Court of Appeals dismissing Interhandel's suit and remanded the case to the District Court. It was thenceforth open to Interhandel to avail itself again of the remedies available to it under the Trading with the Enemy Act, and to seek the restitution of its shares by proceedings in the United States courts. Its suit is still pending in the United States courts. The Court must have regard to the situation thus created.

Switzerland had argued that the local remedies rule did not apply, since the failure of the United States to comply with the decision of the Swiss Authority of Review, based on the Washington Accord, constituted a direct breach of international law, causing immediate injury to the rights of the applicant state. The Court rejected the argument:[156] '...the Court would confine itself to observing that such arguments do not deprive the dispute which has been referred to it of the character of a dispute in which the Swiss Government appears as having adopted the cause of its national, Interhandel,[157] for the purpose of securing the restitution to that company of assets vested by the Government of the United States'. The objection based on the local remedies rule was therefore upheld[158] in regard to the principal submission of the applicant. In its alternative claim, the applicant asked the Court to declare its competence to decide whether the United States was under an obligation to submit the dispute to arbitration or conciliation. The Court[159] agreed with the United States contention that this claim involved the same interest as the principal claim and stated that 'the grounds on which the rule of the exhaustion of local remedies is based are the same, whether in the case of an international court, arbitral tribunal, or conciliation commission'. Thus the objection applied to the alternative claim also.

Dogmatic criticism of the decision in the *Interhandel* case is inappropriate, since much depended on matters of appreciation. Nevertheless two criticisms might be thought to have cogency. In the first place, particularly in respect of the alternative claim, it is very doubtful if the facts disclosed that the only interest of Switzerland was that of Interhandel and that no direct injury to the applicant was involved.[160] There was no remedy available to the latter in the United States courts for breach of treaty rights. Secondly, litigation lasting ten years and on which no term had been placed might not be regarded as 'adequate' or 'effective'.[161]

---

[156] Ibid. p. 28. See also p. 27.

[157] No preliminary objection similar to that in the *Nottebohm* case, *supra*, pp. 411ff., was advanced, although the facts seem to have warranted such an objection.

[158] By 9 votes to 6.

[159] p. 29.

[160] See the diss ops. of Judge *ad hoc* Carry, p. 32, and of Judges Winiarski, pp. 83–4, Armand-Ugon, pp. 87–9, and Lauterpacht, p. 120. See also Simmonds, 10 *ICLQ* (1961), 540–5.

[161] Judge Armand-Ugon, at p. 87, referring to the *Finnish Ships* arbitration.

THE INTERNATIONAL LAW COMMISSION: DRAFT ARTICLES ADOPTED IN 2006

The draft articles relating to local remedies are as follows:

Article 14

Exhaustion of local remedies

1. A State may not present an international claim in respect of an injury to a national or other person referred to in draft article 8 before the injured person has, subject to draft article 15, exhausted all local remedies.

2. 'Local remedies' means legal remedies which are open to an injured person before the judicial or administrative courts or bodies, whether ordinary or special, of the State alleged to be responsible for causing the injury.

3. Local remedies shall be exhausted where an international claim, or request for a declaratory judgment related to the claim, is brought preponderantly on the basis of an injury to a national or other person referred to in draft article 8.

Article 15

Exceptions to the local remedies rule

Local remedies do not need to be exhausted where:

(a) There are no reasonably available local remedies to provide effective redress, or the local remedies provide no reasonable possibility of such redress:

(b) There is undue delay in the remedial process which is attributable to the State alleged to be responsible;

(c) There was no relevant connection between the injured person and the State alleged to be responsible at the date of injury;

(d) The injured person is manifestly precluded from pursuing local remedies; or

(e) The State alleged to be responsible has waived the requirement that local remedies be exhausted.

In the context of draft article 14, the reference to persons referred to in draft article 8 is to a stateless person or refugee who is 'lawfully and habitually resident' in the state seeking to present an international claim.

7. EXTINCTIVE PRESCRIPTION[162]

The lapse of time in presentation may bar an international claim in spite of the fact that no rule of international law lays down a time limit. Special agreements may exclude categories of claim on a temporal basis, but otherwise the question is one

---

[162] Or, 'préscription libératoire'. See generally Simpson and Fox, *International Arbitration* (1959), 122–6; Borchard, *Diplomatic Protection*, pp. 825–32; King, 15 BY (1934), 82–97; Politis and C. de Visscher, *Annuaire*

for the discretion of the tribunal. The rule is widely accepted by writers and in arbitral jurisprudence.[163] In the *Gentini*[164] case Ralston, Umpire, observed: 'The principle of prescription finds its foundation in the highest equity—the avoidance of possible injustice to the defendant…' Commonly a state claim will be denied because of the difficulty the defendant has in establishing the facts, but where there is no clear disadvantage to the defendant tribunals will be reluctant to allow lapse of time *simpliciter* to bar claims in the conditions in which state relations are conducted. Broad considerations of justice predominate. Thus in the *Cayuga Indians Claim*[165] a protected minority were not held to be prejudiced by delay on the part of the territorial sovereign.

On some sets of facts prescription will be associated with questions of acquiescence and estoppel,[166] and a number of cases which are regarded as instances of prescription are in fact based on lapse of time as evidence of acquiescence or waiver.[167] The distinction between prescription and acquiescence is important: in the latter case lapse of time and considerations of equity are less germane than precise evidence of acts of the parties. In cases of state succession and subrogation it would be necessary to establish acquiescence binding on particular legal persons, whereas prescription is a 'universal' basis of inadmissibility.

8. WAIVER OF CLAIMS[168]

Abandonment of claims may occur by unilateral acts of waiver, acquiescence implied from conduct, and by agreement. In the *Case Concerning Certain Phosphate Lands in Nauru*[169] the International Court rejected, on the facts, the preliminary objec-

---

de l'Inst. 32 (1925), 1–24; García Amador, *Yrbk. ILC* (1958), ii. 61 (Art. 23), 67; *Ambatielos* case, ICJ Pleadings (1953), index; Ralston, *Law and Procedure of International Tribunals* (1926), 375–83, Suppl., pp. 185–7; Oppenheim, i. 526–7; Schwarzenberger, *International Law* (3rd edn.), i. 565–70; C. de Visscher, in *Hommage d'une génération de juristes au Président Basdevant* (1960), 525–33; Pinto, 87 Hague *Recueil* (1955), I), 438–48; Cheng, *General Principles of Law* (1953), 373–86; Hackworth, v. 713–18; Rousseau, v. 178–82; Perrin, in *Les Étrangers en Suisse* (University of Lausanne, 1982), 311–36; Hober, *Extinctive Prescription and Applicable Law in Interstate Arbitration* (2001); Bernhardt, *Encyclopedia*, III (1997), 1107–8.

[163] See King, 15 *BY* (1934), 82–97, and also the *Ambatielos* claim (1956), *RIAA* xii. 103; ILR 23 (1956), 306; and the *Lighthouses* arbitration (1956), *RIAA* xii. 186; ILR 23 (1956), 659.

[164] (1903), *RIAA* x. 552–5. See also the *Spader* claim (1903), *RIAA* ix. 223.

[165] (1926), *RIAA* vi. 173; 20 *AJ* (1926), 574; *Ann. Digest*, 3 (1925–6), no. 181. See also Oppenheim, i. 350 n. 2.

[166] See generally *infra*, pp. 643–5.

[167] See *Sarropoulos* v. *Bulgarian State* (1927), *Recueil des décisions des tribunaux arbitraux mixtes* vii. 47; *Ann. Digest*, 4 (1927–8), no. 173.

[168] See Witenberg, 41 Hague *Recueil* (1932, III), 31–33; García Amador, *Yrbk. ILC* (1958), ii. 57–8; Suy, *Les Actes juridiques unilatéraux en droit international public* (1962), 154–7; Rousseau, v. 182–6; *Haas* v. *Humphrey* (1957), ILR 24 (1957), 316; *Wollemborg* claim (1956), ibid. 654; *RIAA* xiv. 283; Bernhardt, *Encyclopedia*, IV (2000), 1327–31. On the Calvo clause see *infra*, pp. 548–9; International Law Commission's Articles on State Responsibility (2001), Art. 45 and Commentary.

[169] ICJ Reports (1992), 247–50, paras. 12–21. See also the *La Grand* case (Germany v. United States) (Merits), Judgment of 27 June 2001, paras. 53–7.

tion of Australia according to which the Nauruan Government had waived all claims relating to rehabilitation of the phosphate lands. In the same case the Court rejected a separate Australian preliminary objection based upon delay in submission of the claim. The Court nevertheless recognised that delay might, in particular circumstances, render a claim inadmissible.[170] As in cases of diplomatic protection the state is asserting its own competence, it follows that the state may compromise or release the claim, leaving the individual or corporation concerned without any remedy.[171] Conversely the waiver of a claim by the national in his private capacity does not bind his government.[172]

9. OTHER GROUNDS OF INADMISSIBILITY

Other grounds exist which deserve brief notice. An objection *ratione temporis* will raise a question of admissibility when it involves the submission that at the relevant time the applicant state, or claimant in other circumstances, had no *locus standi*, for example because there was a lack of legal personality.[173] It is obvious that failure to comply with the rules of court of the tribunal in making an application may provide a ground for an objection as to admissibility, although tribunals may be reluctant to give too much significance to matters of form.[174] Analogously to the local remedies rule, it may happen that a respondent can establish that adequate remedies have been or ought to be obtained in another tribunal, whether national or international.[175] Moreover, there will be a residue of instances in which questions of inadmissibility and 'substantive' issues are difficult to distinguish. This is the case with the doctrine of 'clean hands', according to which a claimant's involvement in activity illegal under either municipal or international law may bar the claim.[176]

---

[170] Ibid., 253–5, paras. 31–6. Certain aspects of the question were reserved to the Merits phase: ibid., 255, para. 36.

[171] Cf. *Public Trustee* v. *Chartered Bank of India, Australia and China*, ILR 23 (1956), 687 at 698–9, *Austrian Citizen's Compensation Case*, ILR 32, 153; *Inao Horimoto* v. *The State*, ibid. 161; *Togen Akiyama* v. *The State*, ibid. 233; *Jews Deported from Hungary Case*, ibid. 44, 301.

[172] The decision in the *Tattler* claim (1920), *RIAA* vi. 48, is in error. Cf. *First National City Bank of New York* claim (1957), ILR 26 (1958, II), 323 at 325.

[173] See the *Cameroons* case, ICJ Reports (1963), 46–7 (Judge Wellington Koo, Sep. Op.), 127–30 (Judge Fitzmaurice, Sep. Op.), 169 (Judge Bustamante, Diss. Op.). Both sides in the case treated the objection as a jurisdictional one.

[174] See Witenberg, 41 Hague *Recueil* (1932, III), 90–4; the *Cameroons* case, ICJ Reports (1963), 27–8, 42–3 (Judge Wellington Koo), 173–4 (Judge Bustamante). See also, on procedural inadmissibility, the latter at pp. 172–3.

[175] See the *Ottoz* claim ILR 18 (1951), no. 136; the *Nartnick* and *Mayer* claims, ILR 21 (1954), 149, 150 respectively; and see the defendant's arguments in *Luther* v. *Sagor* [1921] 1 KB 456; [1921] 3 KB 532. See also Rousseau, v. 186–7; Simpson and Fox, *International Arbitration*, pp. 231–5.

[176] See Witenberg, 41 Hague *Recueil* (1932, III), 63–70; Hackworth, v. 709–18; Rousseau, v. 170–7; Salmon, *Ann. français* (1964), 225–66; Miaja de la Muela, *Mélanges offerts à Juraj Andrassy* (1968), 189–213. See also Dugard, Sixth Report on diplomatic protection, A/CN.4/546, 11 August 2004.

10. COUNTER-CLAIMS[177]

Much that has been said above will apply, *mutatis mutandis*, to counter-claims. However, the overriding requirement, apart from questions of jurisdiction, is that the counter-claim should have a sufficient connection with the claim itself.[178]

11. FOREIGN ACTS OF STATE IN MUNICIPAL COURTS

One form of the Act of State doctrine is the principle (which is not a rule of public international law) that municipal courts will not pass on the validity of the acts of foreign governments performed in their capacities as sovereigns within their own territories. In this form the principle has been applied to foreign expropriation measures by courts in various states[179] and by the United States Supreme Court in the *Sabbatino* case.[180] The principle has obvious significance in the field of jurisdiction, and a variety of considerations of policy are thought to support it, including the need to leave the executive unencumbered in its conduct of international relations. There is, however, an aspect of the rule which justifies its mention in a chapter on the admissibility of state claims. The issue of admissibility is considered in the context of international tribunals, but, as is clear from study of the local remedies rule, admissibility is bound up with the maintenance of a sensible relationship between national and international courts. The Act of State doctrine, from this point of view, is a congener of the local remedies rule: certain issues are better left to procedures on the international plane.[181] But it is not a converse of that rule, as the incidents of its operation are very different and it does not, or should not, entail a general non-recognition of foreign public acts.[182]

What is called the *Sabbatino* principle, involving judicial self-limitation *vis-à-vis* the executive, has received criticism. However, the principle has been reaffirmed by

---

[177] See Simpson and Fox, *International Arbitration*, pp. 172–8; Rosenne, *Law and Practice*, pp. 434–6.

[178] See the *Asylum* case, ICJ Reports (1950), 266 at 280–1, 288; the *Orinoco Steamship Co.* case, *RIAA* ix. 180 at 201; Order of ICJ, *Case Concerning the Application of the Convention on the Prevention and Punishment of the Crime of Genocide*, 17 December 1997, ICJ Reports (1997), 243.

[179] On these decisions see Münch, 98 Hague *Recueil* (1959, III), 442–6. See also Note, 62 *Columbia LR* (1962), 1278–312; and the *Indonesian Corporation* case, 13 *Neths. Int. LR* (1966), 58.

[180] *Banco Nacional de Cuba* v. *Sabbatino*, 376 US 398 (1964); see Henkin, 64 *Columbia LR* (1964), 805–32; and Simmonds, 14 *ICLQ* (1965), 452–92. An attempt to limit the effect of the decision took the form of the Foreign Assistance Act of 1965, the so-called Second Hickenlooper Amendment. For comment: Note, 4 *NYU JIL* (1971), 260–74.

[181] Cf. the doctrine of sovereign immunity, *supra*, ch. 16, and cf. also *Bulgarian State* v. *Takvorian*, ILR 21 (1954), 265.

[182] See, in particular, Staker, 58 *BY* (1987), 237–50; Dicey and Morris, *The Conflict of Laws* (14th edn., 2006), 92–121.

the Supreme Court in *First National City Bank* v. *Banco Nacional de Cuba*.[183] The more recent developments indicate the difficulty in finding a satisfactory alternative.[184] In *Alfred Dunhill* v. *Republic of Cuba*[185] the Supreme Court employed the 'restrictive theory' of sovereign immunity as the basis for refusal to recognize repudiation of commercial obligations of a state instrumentality as an act of state.

---

[183] 406 US 759 (1972); 11 *ILM* 811, ILR 66, 102. See also American Law Institute, *Restatement of the Law, Third, Foreign Relations Law*, (1987) paras. 443–4.

[184] See Lowenfeld, 66 *AJ* (1972), 795–814.

[185] 425 US 682 (1976); 15 *ILM* 735; ILR 66, 212.

23

A SYSTEM OF MULTILATERAL PUBLIC ORDER: SOME INCIDENTS OF ILLEGALITY AND THE CONCEPT OF *JUS COGENS*[1]

1. THE VARYING CONTENT OF ILLEGALITY

The law of responsibility has a precarious existence in a decentralized system of international relations, lacking compulsory jurisdiction and automatically applicable enforcement procedures. Much of the law consists of rules of competence and functional co-operation,[2] and the normal instance is not a tribunal but diplomatic exchange and negotiated settlement. Thus acceptance of the delictual character of breaches of treaty and other rules and the appearance of sophisticated, municipal, principles of responsibility, linked to damages rather than the political 'indemnity' or 'satisfaction', are relatively recent. Rules develop in the customary law as liberties and prohibitions with no very precise definition of the content of illegality involved.

Beyond the incidence of responsibility for causing material harm, there exists a variety of situations in which the illegality is conditioned in special terms. Even in the normal sphere of international responsibility, acts of trespass, for example an intrusion into the territorial sea of another state not causing 'material harm', are regarded by some as an exceptional form of delict.[3] Some jurists are of the opinion that states may bear a criminal responsibility for certain categories of wrongdoing, including

---

[1] See generally Guggenheim, 74 Hague *Recueil* (1949, I), 195–268; Fitzmaurice, 92 Hague *Recueil* (1957, II), 117–28; Jennings, *Cambridge Essays in International Law* (1965), 64–87; Baade, 39 *Indiana LJ* (1964), 497–559; Cahier, 76 *RGDIP* (1972), 645–97; Mann, 48 *BY* (1976–7), 1–65; Verzijl, *International Law in Historical Perspective*, vi (1973), 50–104; P. de Visscher, 136 Hague *Recueil* (1972, II), 90–4; Dugard, *Recognition and the United Nations* (1987); Oppenheim i. 183–203.

[2] There is a strong analogy with principles of constitutional and administrative law.

[3] *Supra*, pp. 459–64. See esp. Parry, 90 Hague *Recueil* (1956, II), 674ff. Cf. the status of *ultra vires* jurisdictional acts unaccompanied by any immediate enforcement or material harm, e.g. unlawful extension of nationality law.

the launching of aggressive war; and, irrespective of the criminality of the act *qua* act of state, criminal responsibility of individuals participating may exist under international law.[4] In several instances the illegality is relative or conditional. Illegality may result only if no compensation is paid,[5] and may be excluded as a consequence of bilateral relations determined by estoppel or acquiescence.[6] The legality of reprisal is conditioned in part by a prior commission of a delict by the state against which the reprisal is directed.[7]

2. OBJECTIVE CONSEQUENCES OF ILLEGAL EVENTS

Illegal conduct may produce a legal regime contingent on the existence of the conduct rather than its illegality. Thus an 'armed conflict' or 'war', the inception of which may have been the result of a breach of the United Nations Charter, will nevertheless draw in its train most[8] of, if not all, the rules governing the conduct of war. Similarly, states have in some instances at least operated a principle of effectiveness.[9] Thus, where control of territory results from illegal annexation, it may be good policy to recognize grants of nationality by the wrongdoer, since nationality may be regarded as a status and nullification of grants may have harmful consequences.[10] In the law relating to acquisition of territorial sovereignty, including the delimitation of a territorial sea, and to rights of passage and other privileges, illegal activity may produce valid results by the operation of prescription, acquiescence, and estoppel.[11] Here the illegal conduct is merely a *causa sine qua non* and does not of itself produce legal consequences.

3. GENERAL WRONGS: ABUSE OF STATE COMPETENCE

The notion of *delicta juris gentium*, as opposed to torts as reparation obligations between tortfeasor and claimant, takes four forms: (1) that of high illegality or breach of *jus cogens*, as in the case of genocide (see section 5, *infra*); (2) reference to cases

---

[4] *Infra*, ch. 26.

[5] Cf. the law of expropriation, *infra*, pp. 531ff.; and see *supra*, pp. 448–9, on incomplete privilege.

[6] *Infra*, pp. 612ff. For examples of relativity in the law of belligerent occupation see Baxter, 27 *BY* (1950), 235ff. Cf. *Dralle* v. *Republic of Czechoslovakia*, ILR 17 (1950), no. 41 at p. 165. See also *Arbitral Award* case, ICJ Reports (1960), 192; ibid. 221–3, Diss. Op., Judge Urrutia Holguin.

[7] See Fitzmaurice, 92 Hague *Recueil* (1957, II), 119.

[8] For a possible qualification, see *infra*, n. 39 and ch. 24, n. 85.

[9] See generally Touscoz, *Le Principe d'effectivité dans l'ordre international* (1964); Lauterpacht, *The Development of International Law by the International Court* (1958), 227ff.

[10] See Brownlie, 39 *BY* (1963), 326–7, 344–5.

[11] *Supra*, pp. 146–53.

where international law recognizes a general competence to exercise jurisdiction to apprehend, and perhaps to punish, irrespective of the nationality of the wrongdoer, as in the case of piracy;[12] (3) acts which harm all states indiscriminately and which are difficult to trace to particular tortfeasors, as in the case of successive nuclear tests in the atmosphere;[13] (4) acts infringing principles of law creating rights the beneficiaries of which do not have legal personality or, more correctly, do not have presently effective means of protecting their rights, as, for example, non-self-governing peoples and the populations of mandate or trust territories.[14] These categories are, of course, related in their application to particular subject-matter: thus the principle of self-determination involves (1) and (4).

The abusive exercise of a state competence without material harm to some other state raises issues similar to those apparent in the *South West Africa* cases,[15] where the mandatory's abuse of competence was in issue and the question was whether states not harmed in their material interests were allowed to raise the issues. Thus a state may extend its nationality to part of the population of another state, deprive a part of its permanent population of nationality, legislate for a criminal jurisdiction of aliens well beyond the limits set by international law, refuse to accept responsibility for its territorial sea, or fail to exercise criminal jurisdiction when it alone has competence.[16] In these cases no justiciable issue arises until acts of administration and enforcement infringe the legal interest of another state.

In principle proceedings in municipal courts involving excess of jurisdiction are 'null and void *ab initio*, and without effect on the international plane.'[17]

4. *EX INJURIA NON ORITUR JUS*

The principle that no benefit can be received from an illegal act has been stated by jurists in the context of international law[18] and applied by tribunals. In the *Eastern Greenland*[19] case the Permanent Court took the view that Norway could not rely on her decree of 1931 affecting the disputed area, as Denmark had a prior title.[20] Municipal courts have often refused to give extra-territorial recognition to acts regarded as ille-

---

[12] Cf. the treaties concerning repression of slavery and prostitution: Oppenheim, i. 979–82; and Schwelb, 9 *ICLQ* (1960), 668. The approach here is in terms of a duty to apprehend and punish and it is not clear that the wrongdoing is to be classified as an 'international crime'.

[13] See *supra*, ch. 13.

[14] On the principles of self-determination, *infra*, pp. 579–82.

[15] *Supra*, pp. 467–72.

[16] Cf. the position of contributing states in relation to UN forces in the Congo.

[17] Judge Fitzmaurice, Sep. Op., *Barcelona Traction* case, ICJ Reports (1970), 103–6 at 106 (para. 72).

[18] See Verzijl, 15 *RDI* (La Pradelle) (1935), 284–339; Lauterpacht, 62 Hague *Recueil* (1937, IV), 287–96; Guggenheim, 74 Hague *Recueil* (1949, I), 195–268. See also Lauterpacht, *Recognition in International Law* (1947), 409ff., 421ff.

[19] *Supra*, pp. 126, 137. Other judicial applications of the principle are listed in Oppenheim, i. 142 no. 1.

[20] Cf. Judge Anzilotti, diss., PCIJ, Ser. A/B, no. 53 at pp. 94–5. See also *supra*, p. 120, on title.

gal under international law.[21] The principle itself leads to the wide field of problems as to the nullity of *ultra vires* acts, problems which cannot be properly approached by way of abstract generalizations.[22] Reference to the principle *ex injuria non oritur jus* does not provide a safe guide to the solution of specific problems. For example, acquiescence of a state may confirm the validity of an award of an arbitrator which was in principle open to challenge on the ground of excess of jurisdiction.[23]

5. *JUS COGENS*[24]

Jurists have from time to time attempted to classify rules, or rights and duties, on the international plane by use of terms like 'fundamental' or, in respect to rights, 'inalienable' or 'inherent'. Such classifications have not had much success, but have intermittently affected the interpretation of treaties by tribunals.[25] In the recent past both doctrine and judicial opinion have supported the view that certain overriding principles of international law exist, forming a body of *jus cogens*.[26]

The major distinguishing feature of such rules is their relative indelibility. They are rules of customary law which cannot be set aside by treaty or acquiescence but only by the formation of a subsequent customary rule of contrary effect. The least controversial

---

[21] See *In re Krüger*, ILR 18 (1951), no. 68; *Singapore Oil Stocks* case, ILR 23 (1956), 810; *Civil Air Transport Inc.* v. *Central Air Transport Corp.*, ILR 19 (1952), no. 20 at p. 97.

[22] See Jennings and Baade, *supra*, n. 1. On the *ultra vires* acts of organizations see *infra*, pp. 665ff. See also ch. 4, s. 7.

[23] See *Arbitral Award made by the King of Spain on 23 December 1906*, ICJ Reports (1960), 192.

[24] See generally Schwelb, 61 *AJ* (1967), 946–75; Verdross, 60 *AJ* (1966), 55–63; Scheuner, 27 *Z.a.ö.R.u.V.* (1967), 520–32; Barberis, ibid. 30 (1970), 19–45; Schwarzenberger, 43 *Texas LR* (1965), 455–78; C. de Visscher, 75 *RGDIP* (1971), 5–11; *Concept of Jus Cogens in International Law*, Conf. on Int. Law, Langonissi (Greece), 1966 (1967); Mosler, 25 *Ann. suisse* (1968), 9–40, Paul, 21 *Öst. Z. für öff. R.* (1971), 19–49; Ago, *Yrbk. ILC.* (1970), ii. 177, 184 (para. 23); ibid. (1971), ii (Pt. 1), 199, 210 (para 41); ibid. (1976), ii (Pt. 1), 3, 31–2 (paras. 98–9); Marek, in *Recueil d'études en hommage à Paul Guggenheim* (1968), 426–59; Riesenfeld, 60 *AJ* (1966), 511–15; Virally, *Ann. français* (1966), 5–29; Monaco, 125 Hague *Recueil* (1968, III), 202–12; Guggenheim, *Traité* (2nd edn.), i. 128–9; Morelli, 51 *Rivista di d.i.* (1968), 108–17; Schweitzer, 15 *Archiv des V.* (1971), 197–223; P. de Visscher, 136 Hague *Recueil* (1972, II), 102–11; Sztucki, *Jus Cogens and the Vienna Convention on the Law of Treaties* (1974); Mann, *Festschrift für Ulrich Scheuner* (1973), 399–418; Wolfke, 6 *Polish Yrbk.* (1974), 145–62; Rozakis, *The Concept of Jus Cogens in the Law of Treaties* (1976); Crawford, 48 *BY* (1976–7), 146–8; Nageswar Rao, 14 *Indian Journ.* (1974), 362–85; Tunkin, *Theory of International Law* (1974), 147–60; Akehurst, 47 *BY* (1974–5), 281–5; Sinclair, *The Vienna Convention on the Law of Treaties* (2nd edn., 1984), 203–37; Gómez Robledo, 172 Hague *Recueil* (1981, III), 9–127; Alexidze, ibid. 219–68; Gaja, ibid. 271–313; Jiménez de Aréchaga, 159 Hague *Recueil* (1978, I), 62–8; Daillier, and Pellet, *Droit international public* (2007), 202–8, 274–5; Meron, *Human Rights Law-Making in the United Nations* (1986), 173–202; Christenson, 28 *Virginia JIL* (1988), 585–648; Ragazzi, *The Concept of International Obligations Erga Omnes* (1997), 43–73; Bernhardt, *Encyclopedia*, III (1997), 65–9; Orakhelashvili, *Peremptory Norms in International Law* (2006).

[25] On sovereignty and the restrictive interpretation of treaties see Lauterpacht, *Recognition*, pp. 300–6.

[26] See Lauterpacht, 27 *BY* (1950), 397–8; id., *Yrbk. ILC* (1953), ii. 154–5, esp. para. 4; Fitzmaurice, 30 *BY* (1953), 30; id., 59 *BY* (1959), 224–5; id., 92 Hague *Recueil* (1957, II), 120, 122, 125. See also *In re Flesche, Ann. Digest*, 16 (1949), no. 87 at p. 269. For an early source: Anzilotti, *Opere*, i. 289 (3rd Ital. edn., 1927; also in *Cours de droit international* (1929), i. 340). See further *North Sea Continental Shelf* cases, ICJ Reports (1969), 97–8 (Padilla Nervo, Sep. Op.), 182 (Tanaka, Diss. Op.), 248 (Sørensen, Diss. Op.).

examples of the class are the prohibition of the use of force,[27] the law of genocide, the principle of racial non-discrimination,[28] crimes against humanity, and the rules prohibiting trade in slaves and piracy.[29] In the *Barcelona Traction* case (Second Phase),[30] the majority judgment of the International Court, supported by twelve judges, drew a distinction between obligations of a state arising *vis-à-vis* another state and obligations 'towards the international community as a whole'. The Court said:

Such obligations derive, for example, in contemporary international law, from the outlawing of acts of aggression, and of genocide, as also from the principles and rules concerning the basic rights of the human person, including protection from slavery and racial discrimination.

Other rules which have this special status include the principle of permanent sovereignty over natural resources[31] and the principle of self-determination.[32]

The European Court of Justice (Court of First Instance) has held that the norms of *jus cogens* constitute a basis for placing limits upon the principle that resolutions of the Security Council have binding effect. These two relevant decisions relate to the powers of the Council to override domestic law by adopting measures against individuals listed as associates of terrorist groups, and especially the freezing of funds.[33]

The concept of *jus cogens* was accepted by the International Law Commission[34] and incorporated in the final draft on the law of treaties in 1966, Article 50,[35] of which provided that: 'a treaty is void if it conflicts with a peremptory norm of general international law from which no derogation is permitted and which can be modified only by a subsequent norm of general international law having the same character'. The Commission's commentary makes it clear that by 'derogation' is meant the use of agreement (and presumably acquiescence as a form of agreement) to contract out of rules of general international law. Thus an agreement by a state to allow another state

[27] McNair, *Law of Treaties* (1961), 214–15; Dept. of State Memo., 74 *AJ* (1980), 418; judgment of the Court in the *Case Concerning Military and Paramilitary Activities in and against Nicaragua* (Merits), ICJ Reports (1986), 100–1 (para. 190); ILR 76, 434–5; 54 *BY* (1983), 379.

[28] See the 1966 edn. of this book, p. 417; Judge Tanaka, Diss. Op., *South West Africa* cases (Second Phase), ICJ Reports (1966), 298; Judge Ammoun, Sep. Op., *Barcelona Traction* case (Second Phase), ICJ Reports (1970), 304; Judge Ammoun, Sep. Op., *Namibia* opinion, ibid. (1971), 78–81. See further *infra*, p. 596. The principle of religious non-discrimination must have the same status as the principle of non-discrimination as to sex.

[29] This statement in the third edn. (p. 513) was quoted by the Inter-American Commission of Human Rights in the *Case of Roach and Pinkerton*, Decision of 27 Mar. 1987 (OAS General Secretariat), 33–6.

[30] ICJ Reports (1970), 3 at 32. See also *In re Koch*, ILR 30, 496 at 503; *Assessment of Aliens Case*, ILR 43, 3 at 8; *Tokyo Suikosha* case, 13 *Japanese Ann. of IL* (1969), 113 at 115; *East Timor Case*, I.C.J. Reports, 1995, 90 at 102.

[31] See the relevant UN Decl. *infra*, p. 539.

[32] Judge Ammoun, Sep. Op., *Barcelona Traction* case (Second Phase), ICJ Reports (1970), 304.

[33] *Yusuf v. Council and Commission*, Case No. T–306/01, Judgment 21/09/2005, paras. 277 and 280; *Kadi v. Council and Commission*, Case No. T–315-01, para. 226. See also Orakhelashvili, *Europ. Journ.*, 16 (2005), 59–88. See also the New Zealand Court of Appeal decision, *Zaoui v. Attorney-General (No.2)*, ILR 131.508, paras. 32–38. The Supreme Court left the issue aside.

[34] See *Yrbk. ILC* (1963), ii 187 at 198 (Art. 37), 211 (Art. 45), 216 (Art. 53). See also McNair, *Law of Treaties*, pp. 213–18; Lauterpacht, *Yrbk. ILC* (1953), ii. 154–5; and Fitzmaurice, ibid. (1958), ii. 27 (Art. 17), 40.

[35] See *Yrbk. ILC* (1966), ii. 247–9. See also pp. 261 (Art. 61), 266 (Art. 67).

to stop and search its ships on the high seas is valid, but an agreement with a neighbouring state to carry out a joint operation against a racial group straddling the frontier which would constitute genocide, if carried out, is void since the prohibition with
which the treaty conflicts is a rule of *jus cogens*. After some controversy, the Vienna
Conference on the Law of Treaties reached agreement on a provision (Art. 53)[36] similar to the draft article except that, for the purposes of the Vienna Convention on the
Law of Treaties, a peremptory norm of general international law is defined as 'a norm
accepted and recognized by the international community of States as a whole as a
norm from which no derogation is permitted and which can be modified only by a
subsequent norm of general international law having the same character'. Charles de
Visscher[37] has pointed out that the proponent of a rule of *jus cogens* in relation to this
article will have a considerable burden of proof.

Apart from the law of treaties the specific content of norms of this kind involves the
irrelevance of protest, recognition, and acquiescence: prescription cannot purge this
type of illegality. Moreover, it is arguable that *jus cogens* curtails various privileges, so
that, for example, an aggressor would not benefit from the rule that belligerents are not
responsible for damage caused to subjects of neutral states by military operations.[38]
Many problems remain: more authority exists for the category of *jus cogens* than exists
for its particular content,[39] and rules do not develop in customary law which readily correspond to the new categories. However, certain portions of *jus cogens* are the
subject of general agreement, including the rules relating to the use of force by states,
self-determination, and genocide. Yet even here many problems of application remain,
particularly in regard to the effect of self-determination on the transfer of territory.
If a state uses force to implement the principle of self-determination, is it possible to
assume that one aspect of *jus cogens* is more significant than another?[40] The particular
corollaries of the concept of *jus cogens* are still being explored.[41]

---

[36] See also Arts. 64 and 71.

[37] *Théories et réalités en droit international* (4th edn., 1970), 295–6. See also id, *RGDIP* (1971), 5–11.

[38] See McNair, *Opinions*, ii. 277; and Schwarzenberger, *International Law* (3rd edn., 1957), i. 646.
Authority also exists for the view that an aggressor does not acquire title to property acquired even if the
confiscation and requisition were within the Hague Regulations: references, Brownlie, *International Law
and the Use of Force by States* (1963), 406 n. 3. Scope for reliance on doctrines of reprisal and necessity will be
reduced. Can the principle of universal jurisdiction develop in relation to *jus cogens*? Cf. the *Eichmann* case,
supra, p. 305. Should the principle of self-determination, as an aspect of *jus cogens*, be used to widen concepts
of legal interest and *locus standi*? Cf. the *South West Africa* cases (Second Phase), ICJ Reports (1966), 6, on
which see *supra*, p. 471.

[39] See the trenchant comment by Schwarzenberger, who regards the principle as a source of instability in
treaty relations: 43 *Texas LR* (1965), 455–78; id., *Curr. Legal Problems* (1965), 191–214; also in *International
Law* (3rd edn.), i. 425–7; and *The Inductive Approach to International Law* (1965), 85–107. See further a reply
by Verdross, 60 *AJ* (1966), 55–63. For further sceptical opinion, see Rousseau, i. 149–51; Weil, 77 *AJ* (1983),
413–42; Virally, 183 Hague *Recueil* (1983, V), 175–8.

[40] See further *supra*, ch. 7, s. 24.

[41] See e.g. Gaja, 172 Hague *Recueil* (1981, III), 271–313 (issues of state responsibility); Schachter, Hague
Recueil (1982, V), 182–4 (rights of third states to take counter-measures); and the *Memorial* of Nicaragua in
Nicaragua v. *US* (Compensation Phase), ch. 8 (moral damage).

6. THE OBLIGATION OF PUTTING AN END TO AN ILLEGAL SITUATION

When competent organs of the United Nations make a binding determination that a situation is illegal, the states which are addressees of the resolution or resolutions concerned are under an obligation to bring that situation to an end.[42] Much depends on the precise manner in which such resolutions spell out the consequences. However, in the ordinary course the consequence of the illegality will involve a 'duty of non-recognition'. This duty may be observed irrespective of or in the absence of any directives from the United Nations if in the careful judgment of the individual state a situation has arisen the illegality of which is opposable to states in general.

In 1970 the Security Council adopted Resolution 276 in which that organ recognized the decision of the General Assembly to terminate the mandate of South West Africa and to assume direct responsibility for the territory until its independence. The same decision of the General Assembly declared that the presence of South African authority in South West Africa (otherwise Namibia) as well as all acts by that Government concerning Namibia were illegal and invalid. In Resolution 283 the Security Council called upon all states to take specific steps consequential upon the illegality of the South African presence, including the termination of diplomatic and consular representation as far as such relations extended to Namibia, the ending of dealings relating to the territory by state enterprises and the withdrawal of financial support from nationals and private corporations that would be used to facilitate trade or commerce with Namibia.

In Resolution 284 (1970) the Security Council asked the International Court for an advisory opinion in response to the question: 'What are the legal consequences for States of the continued presence of South Africa in Namibia, notwithstanding Security Council Resolution 276 (1970)'? In its Opinion[43] the Court considered a variety of issues including the legal status of the General Assembly Resolution by which the Mandate was terminated.[44] The Court held[45] that as a consequence of Security Council Resolution 276 (1970), which was mandatory within the terms of the United Nations Charter, member states were under an obligation to recognize the illegality and invalidity of South Africa's continued presence in Namibia. In the Opinion it

---

[42] See the *Namibia* Opinion, ICJ Reports (1971), 54; and the Decree No. 1 for the Protection of the Natural Resources of Namibia, U.N. Council for Namibia; approved by the UNGA on 13 Dec. 1974. See also *Loizidou* v. *Turkey* (Merits), Judgment of the Europ. Ct. of Human Rights, 18 December 1996, para. 45.

[43] ICJ Reports (1971), 16.

[44] *Supra*, p. 164.

[45] pp. 54–6 of the Opinion; supported by 11 votes to 4 (see p. 58). By 13 votes to 2 it was held that, the continued presence of South Africa in Namibia being illegal, South Africa was under an obligation to withdraw its administration immediately. Judges Fitzmaurice and Gros, dissenting, considered that the Mandate had not been validly terminated. Passages in Sep. and Diss. Op. dealing with the legal consequences of the presence of South Africa in Namibia are as follows: pp. 89–100 (Ammoun); 119–20 (Padilla Nervo); 133–7 (Petrén); 147–9 (Onyeama); 165–7 (Dillard); 217–19 (de Castro); 295–8 (Fitzmaurice). See Dugard, 88 *S. African LJ* (1971), 460–77.

was recognized that the precise determination of appropriate measures was a matter for the political organs. Thus the Court would 'confine itself to giving advice on those dealings with the Government of South Africa which, under the Charter of the United Nations and general international law, should be considered as inconsistent with the declaration of illegality and invalidity made in paragraph 2 of Resolution 276 (1970), because they may imply a recognition that South Africa's presence in Namibia is legal'. Matters touched upon in this connection included treaty relations in cases in which South Africa purported to act on behalf of or concerning Namibia, diplomatic relations, and economic dealings. The Opinion excepted acts such as registration of births, deaths, and marriages from the taint of invalidity. Finally, the Court expressed the view that the illegality of the situation was opposable to all states and not merely to members of the United Nations.

In legal terms the consequences of illegality, or 'the duty of non-recognition', are distinct from the application of economic and military sanctions, voluntary or mandatory, as a consequence of United Nations resolutions as, for example, in relation to Rhodesia consequent upon the unilateral declaration of independence by the Smith regime.[46] Politically speaking, the practical consequences of non-recognition are similar to non-military sanctions.[47] It may be true, as Judge Petrén suggests in his separate opinion, that the resolutions relating to Namibia impose certain duties which go beyond the effects of mere non-recognition in general international law.[48]

7. THE EMERGING SYSTEM OF MULTILATERAL PUBLIC ORDER[49]

The subject matter of the present chapter forms a pattern of conduct based upon the premiss that there are certain peremptory norms (*jus cogens*) and the acceptance of the corollary that there is a duty not to recognize a situation created by a breach of a peremptory norm.

After considerable debate the International Law Commission included Chapter III (of Part Two) in the Articles relating to the responsibility of states adopted on second reading in 2001. This represents a fairly cautious version of the subject matter presented in the present book since the first edition of 1966.

Chapter III (of Part Two) of the ILC work is as follows:

CHAPTER III. SERIOUS BREACHES OF OBLIGATIONS UNDER PEREMPTORY NORMS OF GENERAL INTERNATIONAL LAW

---

[46] See Resols. of 1965 and 1966: 60 *AJ* (1966), 921–6; 61 *AJ* (1967), 652–5, Resols. of 1968: 7 *ILM* (1968), 897, 1402. See also 9 *ILM* (1970), 636.

[47] See Judge Petrén, Sep. Op., ICJ Reports (1971), 127, 134–7.

[48] Ibid. 134–7. See also Judges Onyeama, Sep. Op., p. 148; Dillard, Sep. Op., p. 165; Fitzmaurice, Diss. Op., p. 297.

[49] See Hutchinson, *BY* 59 (1988), 151–215; and Koskenniemi, ibid., 72 (2001), 337–56.

Article 40. Application of this chapter

1. This chapter applies to the international responsibility which is entailed by a serious breach by a State of an obligation arising under a peremptory norm of general international law.

2. A breach of such an obligation is serious if it involves a gross or systematic failure by the responsible State to fulfil the obligation.

Article 41. Particular consequences of a serious breach of an obligation under this chapter

1. States shall co-operate to bring to an end through lawful means any serious breach within the meaning of Article 40.

2. No State shall recognise as lawful a situation created by a serious breach within the meaning of Article 40, nor render aid or assistance in maintaining that situation.

3. This Article is without prejudice to the other consequences referred to in this part and to such further consequences that a breach to which this chapter applies may entail under international law.

Certain related provisions appear in Part Three of the Articles as follows:

Article 48. Invocation of responsibility by a State other than an injured State

1. Any State other than an injured State is entitled to invoke the responsibility of another State in accordance with paragraph 2 if;
   (a) The obligation breached is owed to a group of States including that State, and is established for the protection of a collective interest of the group; or
   (b) The obligation breached is owed to the international community as a whole.

2. Any State entitled to invoke responsibility under Paragraph 1 may claim from the responsible State:
   (a) Cessation of the internationally wrongful act, and assurances and guarantees of non-repetition in accordance with Article 30; and
   (b) Performance of the obligation of reparation in accordance with the preceding articles, in the interest of the injured State or of the beneficiaries of the obligation breached.

3. The requirements for the invocation of responsibility by an injured State under Articles 43, 44 and 45 apply to an invocation of responsibility by a State entitled to do so under Paragraph 1.

Article 54. Measures taken by States other than an injured State

This chapter does not prejudice the right of any State, entitled under Article 48, paragraph 1, to invoke the responsibility of another State, to take lawful measures against that State to ensure cessation of the breach and reparation in the interest of the injured State or of the beneficiaries of the obligation breached.

These normative structures look very progressive on paper but, in certain political circumstances, the result may be to give the appearance of legitimacy to questionable policies based on objectives collateral to the enforcement of the law.

PART IX

THE PROTECTION OF INDIVIDUALS AND GROUPS

24

INJURY TO THE PERSONS
AND PROPERTY OF ALIENS
ON STATE TERRITORY

1. STATE AND INDIVIDUAL

The legal consequences of belonging to a political community with a territorial base have not changed a great deal since the feudal era, in spite of changes in the theory used to describe or explain the relation. Ties of allegiance, citizenship, and nationality have provided the basis for the legal community of the state, whether the state was regarded primarily as an organic unity expressed in terms of 'personal' sovereignty or as a territorial domain. Modern practice tends toward the latter view, but has not wholly abandoned the doctrine of Vattel. Vattel, in a much quoted passage,[1] stated that an injury to a citizen is an injury to the state. His principle is often described as a fiction, but it is surely inadequate so to characterize the legal relation between a 'corporate' legal person and its membership. In any case Vattel was not contending that any harm to an alien was an injury to his state: the relation simply provides a necessary basis for principles of responsibility and protection.[2] On the one hand, the state has a certain responsibility for the acts of its citizens or other persons under its control of which its agents know or ought to know and which cause harm to the legal interest of another state. On the other hand, the state has a legal interest represented by its citizens, and those harming its citizens may have to account to the state protecting the latter. This accountability may take the form of subjection to the extra-territorial application of the national criminal law to acts harming citizens.[3] More important than this, however, is the diplomatic protection exercised by a state, in respect of its nationals.[4] If nationals are subjected to injury or loss by an agency for which another state is responsible in law, then, whether the harm occurs in the territory of a state,

---

[1] *Le Droit des gens*, Bk.11, ch. 6, para. 71.

[2] But see Ammoun, Sep. Op., *Barcelona Traction* case (Second Phase), ICJ Reports (1970), 290–4 (and cf. the same opinion at p. 300, para. 10).

[3] Generally on jurisdiction: *supra*, ch. 15.

[4] The concept of nationality is examined in ch. 19. The means of establishing the existence of the legal interest based on nationality, and other issues of admissibility, are considered *supra*, pp. 476ff. Exceptionally,

or *res communis*, i.e. the high seas or outer space, or in *terra nullius*, the state of the persons harmed may present a claim on the international plane.

The last proposition begs many questions involving the conditions under which responsibility arises, and the principal object of the present chapter is to examine these conditions. The general principles of 'imputability', including responsibility for the unauthorized acts of officials, have been considered in Chapter 21.

2. ADMISSION, EXPULSION, AND LIABILITIES OF ALIENS

The problems of responsibility naturally arise most frequently when aliens and their assets are stationed on state territory, and, by way of preliminary, something must be said of the incidence of aliens within the state. In principle this is a matter of domestic jurisdiction: a state may choose not to admit aliens or may impose conditions on their admission.[5] Internal economic policies and aspects of foreign policy may result in restrictions on the economic activity of aliens. National policy may require prohibition or regulation of the purchase of immovables, ships, aircraft, and the like, and the practice of certain professions by aliens. Provisions for the admissions of aliens in treaties of friendship, commerce, and navigation are qualified by references to 'public order, morals, health or safety'.[6] The topic of expulsion of aliens has been included in the current programme of work of the International Law Commission.[7]

As might be expected, expulsion is also within the discretion of the state,[8] but tribunals and writers have at times asserted the existence of limitations on this

a state may have a legal interest in an individual on some basis other than nationality, e.g. if the individual enters the state service.

[5] This is the view of modern authorities, e.g. Oppenheim, ii. 897–8. For British practice see McNair, *Opinions*, ii. 105–8; and *Musgrove v. Chun Teeong Toy* [1891] AC 272. See generally on admission and exclusion of aliens: Goodwin-Gill, 47 *BY* (1974–5), 55–156; id., *International Law and the Movement of Persons between States* (1978); *Répertoire suisse*, ii. 698–973; *British Digest*, vi. 9–77; Hackworth, iii. 549–52, 690–705, 717ff.; Puente, 36 *AJ* (1942), 252–70; Bernhardt (ed.), *Encyclopedia*, I (1992), 107–9; Gaja, *Cursos Euromediterráneos Bancaja de Derecho Internacional*, Vol.III, 289–311. On the effect of the European Conv. on Human Rights on admission and expulsion see 23 ILR (1956), 393; 33 *BY* (1957), 317; and ILR 28, 208, 246. On the law of the EC see the *Movement of Workers* case, ILR 40, 280; Wyatt and Dashwood, *European Community Law* (3rd edn., 1993), 237–77. See also the European Conv. on Establishment, *Europ. Treaty Series* no. 19 and *Regina (Ullah) v. Special Adjudicator* [2004] 2 AC 323; ILR 131, 577.

[6] e.g. treaty between the United States and Italy, 1948; Briggs, p. 530.

[7] *Report of the International Law Commission, Fifty-ninth session*, 2007, G.A. Off. Recs., *Sixty-second session*, Suppl. No. 10 (A/62/10), 132–53. See also *Memorandum* by the Secretariat, *Expulsion of Aliens*, A/CN.4/565, 10 July 2006; Kamto, Prelim. Report, A/CN.4/554, Second Report, A/CN.4/573, Third Report, A/CN.4/581; Fourth Report, A/CN.4/594.

[8] See *British Digest*, vi. 83–241; Hackworth, iii. 690–705; McNair, *Opinions*, ii. 109–12; de Boeck, 18 Hague *Recueil* (1927, III), 443–650; *British Practice* (1964), 209–11; ibid. (1966), 111–15; ibid. (1967), 112–14; Whiteman, viii. 850–63; Bernhardt (ed.), *Encycl. of P.I.L.*, I (1992). Doehring, 109–12.

discretion.[9] In particular, the power of expulsion must be exercised in good faith and not for an ulterior motive. While the expelling state has a margin of appreciation in applying the concept of 'ordre public', this concept is to be measured against human rights standards. The latter are applicable also to the manner of expulsion.[10] In certain conditions expulsion may constitute genocide or may infringe the principle of non-discrimination (racial or religious) which is part of customary international law. Expulsion which causes specific loss to the national state receiving groups without adequate notice would ground a claim for indemnity as for incomplete privilege.[11] Finally, and most important of all, the expulsion of persons who by long residence have acquired prima facie the effective nationality[12] of the host state is not a matter of discretion, since the issue of nationality places the right to expel in question.

The liabilities of alien visitors under their own and under the local law lead to overlapping and conflicting claims of the state of origin and the host state in various areas of jurisdiction, including anti-trust regulation, legislation governing labour and welfare standards, monetary regulations, and taxation. The principles on which conflicts of jurisdiction may be approached have been considered in Chapter 15, and it is at present the intention to examine the limits of the competence of the host state in placing liabilities on aliens of a special kind, viz., duties to serve in the armed forces, militia, or police and to submit to requisitions in time of emergency.[13] The legal position is not in all respects clear. Thus there is authority and principle to support the rule that an alien cannot be required to serve in the regular armed forces of the host state.[14] However, American and recent Australian practice supports the view that the alien admitted with a view to permanent residence has an obligation to serve in local militia and police forces and also in forces to be used in external defence.[15] Where the alien has participated in the local political franchise the obligation may also arise.[16] The basis for obligations of this kind is the reciprocity between residence and local protection, on the one hand, and the responsibilities of a 'functional' citizenship.

---

[9] See generally Goodwin-Gill, *International Law and the Movement of Persons*, pp. 201–310; and in 47 *BY* (1974–5), 55–156; and also Oppenheim, ii. 940–1; Hackworth, iii. 690; *British Digest*, vi. 112ff.; Wooldridge and Sharma, 23 *ICLQ* (1974), 397–425. Cp. *Yeager* v. *Islamic Republic of Iran*, ILR 82, 179; *Rankin* v. *Islamic Republic of Iran*, ibid., 204; *Short* v. *Islamic Republic of Iran*, ibid, 148 at 159–61; and *LAFICO* v. *Republic of Burundi*, ILR 96, 279 at 309–20.

[10] The view is sometimes expressed that the expelling state must have complied with its own law: *British Digest*, vi. 151–2; Goodwin-Gill, *International Law and the Movement of Persons*, pp. 263–81; and 47 *BY* (1974–5), 122–35.

[11] Cf. *supra*, pp. 465–7.

[12] *Supra*, pp. 407ff.

[13] For British practice see *British Digest*, vi. 359–422; McNair, *Opinions*, ii. 113–37. See also Parry, 31 *BY* (1954), 437–52; id., *Nationality and Citizenship Laws of the Commonwealth* (1957), 120–1.

[14] Sørensen, pp. 489–90; Verdross, 37 Hague *Recueil* (1931, III), 379; Oppenheim, ii. 907; Guggenheim, i. 348; *Polites* v. *Commonwealth of Australia*, 70 CLR 60, 70, per Latham, CJ. The law of war and neutrality may reinforce the position when the host state is involved in civil or foreign war.

[15] See Greig, *Austral. Yrbk.* (1967), 249–56; *British Practice* (1966), 107; Whiteman, viii. 540–73.

[16] The analogue is the principle of allegiance or effective connection as a basis for criminal jurisdiction over aliens: *supra*, pp. 300–7.

In some cases the long residence and local connections may create a new, effective, nationality opposable to the state of origin.[17]

3. GENERAL PRINCIPLES

The exercise of diplomatic protection in respect to nationals visiting or resident in foreign countries has subsisted, with some changes of terminology and concept, since the Middle Ages. Practice with modern features appears in the late eighteenth century, when the grant of special reprisals, an indiscriminate right of private war, to citizens harmed by aliens disappeared. It is the nineteenth century which produced political and economic conditions in which the status of aliens abroad became a problem of wide dimensions. The history has been primarily but not entirely concerned with the conflict of interest between investor states and the economically exploited hosts to foreign capital. In the century after 1840 some sixty mixed claims commissions were set up to deal with disputes arising from injury to the interests of aliens.[18] Literature on protection of aliens from the point of view of investor states grew particularly after about 1890, and influential contributions were made by the Italian Anzilotti and the American jurists Moore, Borchard, and Eagleton.[19]

The area of law under discussion has always been one of acute controversy, and, in the period since 1945, concepts of economic independence and political and economic principles, favouring nationalization and the public sector in national economies have made considerable headway. The legal reasoning offered on precise issues stems from a small number of general principles and the nature of the relation between them. It is always admitted that presumptively the ordering of persons and assets is an aspect of the domestic jurisdiction of a state and an incident of its sovereign equality and independence in the territorial sphere. Customary law contains long-established exceptions to the territorial competence of states, the chief of which is the immunity from local jurisdiction of the premises and personnel of diplomatic missions.[20] Exceptions may of course be created by treaty, and in the past immunity for aliens has

---

[17] *Supra*, p. 418.

[18] Claims settlement conventions included conventions between Mexico and the United States of 1839, 1848, 1868, and 1923; the Venezuelan arbitrations of 1903 involving claims of ten states against Venezuela; and conventions between Great Britain and the United States of 1853, 1871, and 1908.

[19] See Anzilotti, 13 *RGDIP* (1906), 5–29, 285–309, also in *Opere*, ii. (1) (1956), 151–207; Moore, *Digest*, vi. ch. 21; Borchard, *The Diplomatic Protection of Citizens Abroad* (1915); and Eagleton, *The Responsibility of States in International Law* (1928). See further Dunn, *The Protection of Nationals* (1932), and Freeman, *The International Responsibility of States for Denial of Justice* (1938). The treatise by Borchard had particular influence. See also Brownlie, *System of the Law of Nations: State Responsibility* (Pt. 1) (1983), 1–9; Lillich (ed.), *International Law of State Responsibility for Injuries to Aliens* (1983); Rousseau, v. 36–88. See also Lillich, 161 Hague *Recueil* (1978, III), 329–442; id., *The Human Rights of Aliens in Contemporary International Law* (1984).

[20] See *supra*, ch. 17.

been coupled with the privilege of the sending state in maintaining a special system of courts for nationals on the territory of the receiving state. This arrangement, known as a regime of capitulations, applied in countries such as China, Iran, Turkey, and Egypt in the past. Apart from special cases supported by custom or treaty, the territorial competence of the state subsists, and the alien is admitted, in the discretion of the sovereign, as a visitor who as such has a duty to submit to the local law and jurisdiction. If the alien acquires domicile or permanent residence he is even more obviously obliged to accept local duties, including perhaps the duty to serve in the armed forces. However, residence abroad does not of itself deprive an individual of the protection of his own government. In the past writers have rested the right of protection on the right of self-preservation or a 'right of intercourse': the correct way of justifying diplomatic protection and the nationality of claims would seem to be the very existence of the relation of nationality and the general absence of an alternative and better means of grounding protection in existing law. Where the state authorities cause injury to the alien visitor, for example in the form of brutality by police officials, then the legal position is clear. The host state is responsible, but, as a condition for the presentation of the claim by the state of the alien, the latter is required to exhaust the remedies available (where this is so) in the local courts.[21] The reasons for this particular condition of admissibility are practical: small claims by individuals are handled better in municipal courts, governments dislike the multiplication of claims for diplomatic intervention, and it is reasonable, for the resident alien especially, to submit to the local system of justice.

Much more difficult are the cases where the alien is harmed by acts or omissions which are on their face merely a normal exercise of the competence of organs of administration and government of the host state. These situations include the malfunction of judicial organs dealing with acts which are breaches of the local law affecting the interests of the alien, so-called 'denial of justice',[22] and also general legislative measures, not directed at aliens as such, affecting the ownership or enjoyment of foreign-owned assets. There has always been a current of opinion to the effect that the alien, having submitted to the local law, can only expect treatment on a basis of equality with nationals of the host state. This view is pressed particularly in relation to the lack in most cases of any *major* interest of the state of the alien in respect to injuries to nationals. It is also said that the status of the alien is not the subject of a privilege as 'alien', but is simply that of an 'individual' within the territorial sovereignty and jurisdiction of the host state.[23] The issues raised by such arguments must now be considered.

[21] *Supra*, p. 492. Cf. *British Digest*, vi. 253, 345, 347.
[22] *Infra*, p. 529.
[23] See the opinions of Guha Roy, 55 *AJ* (1961), 863–91. See also Anand, 56 *AJ* (1962), 383 at 400–3; Sinha, 14 *ICLQ* (1965), 121 at 127–8; Casteñeda, 15 *Int. Organisation* (1961), 38–48; and the debate in the International Law Commission, *Yrbk. ILC* (1957), i. 154ff.

4. THE STANDARD OF NATIONAL TREATMENT[24]

There has always been considerable support for the view that the alien can only expect equality of treatment under the local law because he submits to local conditions with benefits and burdens and because to give the alien a special status would be contrary to the principles of territorial jurisdiction and equality. Before examining the validity of the principle of national treatment, it must be observed that it is agreed on all hands that certain sources of inequality are admissible. Thus it is not contended that the alien should have political rights in the host state as of right. Moreover, the alien must take the local law as he finds it in regard to regulation of the economy and restriction on employment of aliens in particular types of employment. Access to the courts may be maintained, but with modified rules in ancillary matters: thus an alien may not have access to legal aid and may have to give security for costs.[25] More general variations may of course be created by treaty. The various standards of treatment commonly employed in treaties are as follows: those of reciprocity, the open door, good neighbourliness, and of identical, national, most-favoured-nation, equitable, and preferential treatment.

The principle of national treatment has support from many jurists both in Europe and Latin America prior to 1940,[26] from a small number of arbitral awards,[27] and from seventeen of the states at the Hague Codification Conference in 1930.[28] At the latter 21 states opposed the principle, although some opponents had on occasion supported it in presenting claims to international tribunals.[29]

---

[24] See the works cited *supra*, n. 21, and, further: Strisower, *Annuaire de l'Inst.* (1927), i. 455–98; Verdross, 37 Hague *Recueil* (1931, III), 327–406; Harv. Research, 23 *AJ* (1929), Spec. Suppl., pp. 131–399; Jessup, 46 *Columbia LR* (1946), 903–28; and in *A Modern Law of Nations* (1948), 94–122; Roth, *The Minimum Standard of International Law Applied to Aliens* (1949); Sohn and Baxter, 55 *AJ* (1961), 545–84; García Amador, *Yrbk. ILC* (1956), ii. 201–3; *British Digest*, vi. 247–440, *passim*, e.g. p. 343 (but cf. pp. 291, 292); Whiteman, viii. 704–6; García Amador, Sohn, and Baxter, *Recent Codifications of the Law of State Responsibility for Injuries to Aliens* (1974).

[25] The *cautio judicatum solvi* of civil law systems.

[26] Including Strupp, De Louter, Sibert, Nys, Alvarez, and Yepes. See also the citations by Herz, 35 *AJ* (1941), 243 at 259, n. 66. The equality principle was advocated as early as 1868 by the Argentinian jurist Calvo.

[27] See the *Canevaro* case (1912), PCA, Hague Court Reports, i. 285; 6 *AJ* (1912), 746; *RIAA* xi. 397; *Cadenhead* case (1914), 8 *AJ* (1914), 663; and the *Standard Oil* case (1926), 8 *BY* (1927), 156; 22 *AJ* (1928), 404; *RIAA* ii. 781 at 794.

[28] See Roth, *Minimum Standard*, pp. 72–4. See also the report of Guerrero of 1916, 20 *AJ* (1926), Spec. Suppl., pp. 176ff.

[29] e.g. the United States in the *Norwegian Ships* arbitration (1922), *RIAA* i. 307. See also the Havana Conv. of 1928, Art. 5, 23 *AJ* (1929), Spec. Suppl., p. 234; draft Conv. proposed by the Paris Conference on the Treatment of Aliens, 1929, Art.17, Roth, *Minimum Standard*, p. 71; and the Montevideo Conv. of 1933, Art. 9, 28 *AJ* (1934), Suppl., p. 75.

5. THE INTERNATIONAL MINIMUM STANDARD

Since the beginning of the present century legal doctrine has opposed an 'international minimum standard', 'a moral standard for civilized states', to the principle of national treatment.[30] A majority of the states represented at the Hague Codification Conference supported the international standard, and this standard is probably affirmed in the Declaration of the United Nations General Assembly adopted in 1962 on Permanent Sovereignty over Natural Resources.[31] The standard has also enjoyed the support of many tribunals and claims commissions. Thus in the *Neer Claim*[32] the General Claims Commission set up by the United States and Mexico expressed the law as follows:

> ... the propriety of governmental acts should be put to the test of international standards ... the treatment of an alien, in order to constitute an international delinquency should amount to an outrage, to bad faith, to wilful neglect of duty, or to an insufficiency of governmental action so far short of international standards that every reasonable and impartial man would readily recognize its insufficiency.

6. THE TWO STANDARDS IN PERSPECTIVE

The controversy concerning the national and international standards has not remained within the bounds of logic, and this is not surprising, as the two viewpoints reflect conflicting economic and political interests. Thus those supporting the national treatment principle are not necessarily committed, as is sometimes suggested, to the view that municipal law has supremacy over international law. It is possible to contend that, as a matter of international law, the standard of treatment is to be defined in terms of equality under the local law. Protagonists of national treatment point to the role the law associated with the international standard has played in maintaining a privileged status for aliens, supporting alien control of large areas of the national economy, and providing a pretext for foreign armed intervention. The experience of the Latin American states and others dictates extreme caution in handling the international standard, but it is necessary to distinguish between, on the one

---

[30] Leading proponents include Anzilotti, Verdross, Borchard, Oppenheim, Guggenheim, de Visscher, Scelle, and Jessup. See the citations by Roth, *Minimum Standard*, p. 88; and Hertz, 35 *AJ* (1941), 260; and materials cited *supra*, nn. 29–32. See also American Law Institute, Restatement, Second, *For. Relations Law*, pp. 501–7; Whiteman, viii. 697–704; Schachter, 178 Hague *Recueil* (1982, V), 314–21.

[31] Examined *infra*, pp. 539–41.

[32] (1926), *RIAA* iv. 60. See also the *Roberts* claim (1926), *RIAA* iv. 41; the *Hopkins* claim (1926) *RIAA* iv. 411; and *British Claims in the Spanish Zone of Morocco* (1925), *RIAA* ii. 617 at 644. See also the cases on expropriation cited *infra*, pp. 531ff.

hand, the question as to the content of the standard and the mode of application and, on the other hand, the core principle, which is simply that the territorial sovereign cannot in all circumstances avoid responsibility by pleading that aliens and nationals had received equal treatment. Thus if a national law provides that all persons of a particular race resident within the state shall be sterilized[33] it will not satisfy the state of an alien within the category to point to the equal application of the law. Conversely, the rules of international law authorize at least a measure of discrimination, for example in matters of taxation and exchange control. In any case the host state owes a special duty to aliens acting as diplomatic or consular agents or in some other official capacity.[34]

A source of difficulty has been the tendency of writers and tribunals to give the international standard a too ambitious content, ignoring the odd standards observed in many areas under the administration of governments with a 'Western' pattern of civilization within the last century or so. Another cause of difficulty, connected with the first, has been the extension of delictual responsibility to the malfunction of administrative and judicial organs, as in the field of denial of justice. This aspect involves the imposition of the law of delict where the true analogy is the use of administrative law remedies to enforce a proper use of legal powers.[35] It will be suggested later that in regard to non-exercise or malfunction of legal powers the standard of national treatment rule has some significance, at least as creating a presumption of absence of *dolus* (intention).

The basic point would seem to be that there is no single standard. Circumstances, for example the outbreak of war, may create exceptions to the international treatment rule, even where this applies in principle. Where a reasonable care or due diligence standard is applicable, then *diligentia quam in suis*[36] might be employed, and would represent a more sophisticated version of the national treatment principle. *Diligentia quam in suis* would allow for the variations in wealth and educational standards between the various states of the world and yet would not be a mechanical national standard, tied to equality. Though the two are sometimes confused, it is not identical with national treatment. There is support for the view that *diligentia quam in suis* has long been accepted as the standard in relation to harm resulting from insurrection and civil war.[37] Finally, there are certain overriding rules of law including the proscription of genocide which are clearly international standards.[38]

---

[33] A form of genocide, on which see *infra*, Ch. 26.

[34] See chs. 16 and 17.

[35] See further *infra*, pp. 506–8, on denial of justice. See also *supra*, p. 501.

[36] i.e. national treatment but on the basis of the standard *ordinarily* observed by the particular state in its own affairs. References to such a standard: Judge Huber, *British Claims in Spanish Morocco* (1924), *RIAA* ii. 617 at 644; McNair, *Opinions*, ii. 198, 245, 247, 250, 254, 258–66.

[37] *Supra*, pp. 436–8, and McNair, *Opinions*, ii. 198, 245, 247, 250, 254, 258–66.

[38] See *Barcelona Traction* case (Second Phase), ICJ Reports (1970), 4 at 32; and see *infra*, ch. 25.

A recent development has been the appearance of attempts to synthesize the concept of human rights and the principles governing the treatment of aliens. Thus García Amador, Special Rapporteur of the International Law Commission on the subject of state responsibility, presented in his second report a draft chapter with the rubric 'violation of fundamental human rights'.[39] The first article provided:

1. The State is under a duty to ensure to aliens the enjoyment of the same civil rights, and to make available to them the same individual guarantees as are enjoyed by its own nationals. These rights and guarantees shall not however, in any case be less than the 'fundamental human rights' recognized and defined in contemporary international instruments.

2. In consequence, in case of violation of civil rights, or disregard of individual guarantees, with respect to aliens, international responsibility will be involved only if internationally recognized 'fundamental human rights' are affected.

In the article which follows, the expression 'fundamental human rights' is expanded by an enumeration, which is stated not to be exhaustive, of rights, e.g. inviolability of privacy, home, and correspondence, and respect for honour and reputation.

This particular synthesis of human rights and the standard of treatment for aliens involves codifying the 'international minimum standard', raising that standard, extending it to new subject matter, and relating internal affairs and local law to international responsibility to a degree which the majority of states would find intolerable. Moreover, the standard is unconscionably vague, and the draft provides that the rights and freedoms enumerated 'may be subjected to such limitations or restrictions as the law expressly prescribes for reasons of internal security, the economic well-being of the nation, public order, health and morality or to secure respect for the rights and freedoms of others'.[40] Moreover, as the Indian member of the Commission pointed out,[41] the draft of rights and freedoms involved the application to economic relations between states of the standard of rights which the non-Communist European states had hitherto prescribed for themselves in their domestic affairs: a standard of a particular economic and social system was held out as the universally just standard. The present writer considers that it is not possible to postulate an international minimum standard which in effect supports a particular philosophy of economic life at the expense of the host state.[42] It is certainly the case that since 1945 developments concerning human rights have come to provide a new content for the international standard

---

[39] *Yrbk. ILC* (1957), ii. 112. Generally on the individual in international law and human rights see *supra*, ch. 25. See also Jessup, *A Modern Law of Nations*, pp. 94–122 and in 46 *Columbia LR* (1946), 903–28; Parry, 90 Hague *Recueil* (1956, II), 653–725; Cavaré, in *Makarov Festgabe* (1958), 54–80.

[40] For criticisms of the draft see the discussion in *Yrbk. ILC* (1957), i. 154ff., and for the Special Rapporteur's answers, ibid. ii. 49.

[41] *Yrbk. ILC* (1957), i. 158 (Pal).

[42] See Fischer Williams, 9 *BY* (1928), 1 at 20, 25.

based upon those human rights principles which have become a part of customary international law. These principles include the principle of non-discrimination on grounds of race,[43] the prohibition of genocide,[44] and the prohibition of torture and of inhuman or degrading treatment or punishment. A careful synthesis of human rights standards and the modern 'treatment of aliens' standards is called for.[45] The concept of discrimination calls for more sophisticated treatment in order to identify unreasonable (or material) discrimination as distinct from the different treatment of non-comparable situations.[46]

7. RELEVANT FORMS OF DELICTUAL RESPONSIBILITY

The general principles of state responsibility were examined in the previous chapter, and they are applicable to cases where aliens are injured, whether this occurs within or without the territory of the defendant state. Thus one might expect to rely upon a rule that a state is liable for failure to show due diligence in matters of administration, for example by failing to take steps to apprehend the murderer of an alien. However, the position is far more complex. In the first place, as we have seen, there is no single standard but different standards relating to different situations.[47] Furthermore, reference to a particular standard presumes that the activity concerned is outside the reserved domain of domestic jurisdiction and is the subject of international duties. But in the cases of nationalization (or general expropriation), and termination by governments of concession agreements, this is the major issue. International law is not a system replete with nominate torts or delicts, but the rules are specialized in certain respects. Thus reference may be made to the source of harm, such as unauthorized acts of officials, insurrection, and so on,[48] or to the object and form of harm, as, for example, territorial sovereignty, diplomats and other official agents, or injury to nationals. The category of injury to nationals involves the problems considered in the preceding sections and also certain special topics, the principal of which are denial of justice and expropriation. These will now be considered, together with other related subjects.

---

[43] *Infra*, pp. 572–5.

[44] *Infra*, Ch. 26.

[45] This was pointed out in the first edition of this work of 1966, alongside criticism of Garcia Amador's formulation. See further McDougal, Lasswell, and Chen, 70 *AJ* (1976), 432–69; Lillich, 161 Hague *Recueil* (1978, III), 329–442; id., *The Human Rights of Aliens* (1984).

[46] See McDougal, Lasswell, and Chen, 70 *AJ* (1976), 450–1; Wex, 15 *Canad. Yrbk.* (1977), 198 at 222–6; Schachter, 178 Hague *Recueil* (1982, V), 314–21.

[47] *Supra*, pp. 437ff.

[48] Cf. *supra*, pp. 452ff.

8. DENIAL OF JUSTICE[49]

The term 'denial of justice' has been employed by claims tribunals so as to be coextensive with the general notion of state responsibility for harm to aliens,[50] but it is widely regarded as a particular category of deficiencies on the part of the organs of the host state, principally concerning the administration of justice. It has been pointed out that the term has been given such a variety of definitions that it has little value and the problems could be discussed quite adequately without it.[51] However, if the phrase has a presumptive meaning, the best guide to this is probably the Harvard Research draft,[52] which provides as follows:

Article 9. A State is responsible if an injury to an alien results from a denial of justice. Denial of justice exists when there is a denial, unwarranted delay or obstruction of access to courts, gross deficiency in the administration of judicial or remedial process, failure to provide those guarantees which are generally considered indispensable to the proper administration of justice, or a manifestly unjust judgment. An error of a national court which does not produce manifest injustice is not a denial of justice.

A helpful definition has been offered by the NAFTA Tribunal in *Azinian* v. *United Mexican States*[53] decided in 1999:

The possibility of holding a State internationally liable for judicial decisions does not, however, entitle a claimant to seek international review of the national court decisions as though the international jurisdiction seised has plenary appellate jurisdiction. This is not true generally, and it is not true for NAFTA ...

A denial of justice could be pleaded if the relevant courts refuse to entertain a suit, if they subject it to undue delay, or if they administer justice in a seriously inadequate way ...

There is a fourth type of denial of justice, namely the clear and malicious misapplication of the law. This type of wrong doubtless overlaps with the notion of "pretence of form" to

---

[49] See Freeman, *International Responsibility*; Eagleton, 22 *AJ* (1928), 538–59; Lissitzyn, 30 *AJ* (1936), 632–46; Spiegel, 32 *AJ* (1938), 63–81; Harvard draft, 23 *AJ* (1929), Spec. Suppl., pp. 173–87; Fitzmaurice, 13 *BY* (1932), 93–114; Puente, 43 *Michigan LR* (1944), 383–406; de Visscher, 52 Hague *Recueil* (1935, II), 369–440; Sørensen, pp. 550–7; Whiteman, viii. 706–20, 726–35, 863–85; García Amador, *Yrbk. ILC* (1957), ii. 110–12; Adede, 14 *Canad. Yrbk.* (1976), 73–95; Jiménez de Aréchaga, Hague Academy, vol. 159 (1978–I), 278–82; Vitanyi, 22 *Neths. Int. LR* (1975), 131–63; Bernhardt (ed.), *Encyclopedia*, I (1992), Verosta, 1007–10; Paulsson, *Denial of Justice* (2005). See also *supra*, pp. 519–23. See further *Amco Asia Corporation* v. *Republic of Indonesia*, ILR 89, 368 at 451–2, 502–3, 621–2; and *Azinian* v. *United Mexican States*, ILR 121, 1, 22–7; ICSID (Additional Facility).

[50] See the tribunal in the *Robert E. Brown* claim (1923), *RIAA* vi. 120.

[51] See Lissitzyn, 30 *AJ* (1936), 645, 646; Jessup, 46 *Columbia LR* (1946), 913; Briggs, pp. 679–80.

[52] 23 *AJ* (1929), Spec. Suppl., p. 173. Similar definitions and approval of this definition in Fitzmaurice, 13 *BY* (1932), 108; Dunn, *Protection of Nationals*, p. 148; Freeman, *International Responsibility*, p. 97; McNair, *Opinions*, ii. 295; Briggs, p. 679. See also Restatement, Second, *For. Relations Law*, pp. 502–3, 534–48; Tanaka, Sep. Op., *Barcelona Traction* (Second Phase), ICJ Reports (1970), at 144, 156; Padilla Nervo, Sep. Op., ibid. 252, 265.

[53] ILR 121, 1 at pp.23–4 (Paulsson, Civiletti and von Wobeser).

mask a violation of international law. In the present case, not only has such wrongdoing been pleaded, but the Arbitral Tribunal wishes to record that it views the evidence as sufficient to dispel any shadow over the bona fides of the Mexican judgments. Their findings cannot possibly be said to have been arbitrary, let alone malicious.

These findings were approved by another NAFTA Tribunal in *Mondev* v. *United States of America*[54] in the Award of 2002.

The rubric 'Denial of Justice' concerns the application to certain aspects of state administration of the international standard. Latin American opinion would limit the concept to a duty to allow foreigners easy access to the courts which would duly exercise jurisdiction, without any inquiry into the quality of the justice given.[55]

The most controverted issue is the extent to which erroneous decisions may constitute denial of justice. There is authority for the view that an error of law accompanied by a discriminatory intention is a breach of the international standard.[56] However, it is well established that the decision of a lower court open to challenge does not constitute a denial of justice and that the claimant must pursue remedies available higher in the judicial system.[57]

In the present context the international standard has been applied ambitiously by tribunals and writers and difficulties have arisen. First, the application of the standard may involve decisions upon very fine points of national law and the quality of national remedial machinery.[58] Thus, in regard to the work of the courts, a distinction is sought to be made between error and 'manifest injustice'.[59] Secondly, the application of the standard in this field seems to contradict the principle that the alien, within some limits at least, accepts the local law and jurisdiction. Thirdly, the concept of denial of justice embraces many instances where the harm to the alien is a breach of local law only and the 'denial' is a failure to reach a non-local standard of competence in dealing with the wrong in the territorial jurisdiction. Thus the concept of the foreign state wronged in the person of its nationals is extended to cases where the primary wrong is a breach of municipal law alone. We are concerned with what may be in part an eccentric application of the principles of responsibility in this context,[60] and it would be better if such claims were regarded as resting on an equitable basis only. The existence of the rule of admissibility that the alien should

---

[54] ILR 125, 99 at p.151 (Sir Ninian Stephen, Crawford and Schwebel).

[55] See the report of Guerrero quoted in Briggs, p. 678. See also Whiteman, viii. 727 (Inter-Am. Juridical C'ee Report, 1961).

[56] See Jiménez de Aréchaga, in Friedmann, Henkin, and Lissitzyn, *Essays in Honor of Philip C. Jessup* (1972), 171–87 at 179–85, referring to the submissions of both parties in the *Barcelona Traction* case, ICJ Reports (1970), 3; Whiteman, viii. 727–31; and see Adede, 14 *Canad. Yrbk.* (1976), 91. See further O'Connell, ii. 948.

[57] See *Loewen* v. *United States of America*, ILR 128,334 at pp.393–7 (paras. 141–57).

[58] Cf. the discussion in the article by Mann, 42 *BY* (1967), 26–9.

[59] See McNair, *Opinions*, ii. 305; and *British Digest*, vi. 287–95.

[60] Cf. Parry, 90 Hague *Recueil* (1956, II), 695–6; and the *Janes* case, discussed *supra*, p. 467. The application of principles of responsibility is eccentric in the context of international relations: of course there is no objection of legal principle to extension of responsibility to cases of maladministration.

first exhaust local remedies is a partial reflection of the special character of claims on behalf of aliens against the host state.[61]

9. EXPROPRIATION OF FOREIGN PROPERTY[62]

A state may place conditions on the entry of an alien on its territory and may restrict acquisition of certain kinds of property by aliens. Apart from such restrictions, an alien individual, or a corporation controlled by aliens, may acquire title to property within a state under the local law. The subject-matter may be shares in enterprises, single items such as estates or factories, or, on a monopoly basis, major areas of activities such as railways and mining. In a number of countries foreign ownership has extended to proportions of between fifty and one hundred per cent of all major industries, resources, and services such as insurance and banking. Even in *laissez-faire* economies, the taking of private property for certain public purposes and the establishment of state monopolies have long been familiar. After the Soviet revolution and the extension of the public sector in many economies, both socialist and non-socialist, the conflict of interest between foreign investors and their governments and the hosts to foreign capital, seeking to obtain control over their own economies, became more acute. The terminology of the subject is by no means settled, and in any case form should not take precedence over substance. The essence of the matter is the deprivation by state organs of a right of property either as such, or by permanent transfer of the power of management and control.[63] The deprivation may be followed

---

[61] *Supra*, p. 492. Cf. Guha Roy, 55 *AJ* (1961), 863 at 877. See further Ténékidès, 14 *RDILC* (1933), 514–35; de Visscher, 52 Hague *Recueil* (1935, II), 421–32.

[62] See Fachiri, 6 *BY* (1925), 159–71; id., 10 *BY* (1929), 32–55; Fischer Williams, 9 *BY* (1928), 1–30; Herz, 35 *AJ* (1941), 243–63; Friedman, *Expropriation in International Law* (1953); Bindschedler, 90 Hague *Recueil* (1956, II), 179–306; Foighel, *Nationalization and Compensation* (1964); Wortley, *Expropriation in Public International Law* (1959); White, *Nationalisation of Foreign Property* (1961); Domke, 55 *AJ* (1961), 585–616; McNair, 6 *Neths. Int. LR* (1959), 218–56; Rolin, ibid. 260–75; Verdross, ibid. 278–87; Fouilloux, *La Nationalisation et le droit international public* (1962); Petrén, 109 Hague *Recueil* (1963, II), 492–575; García Amador, *Yrbk. ILC* (1959), ii. 2–24; ILA, *Report of the Forty-Eighth Conference* (1958), 130–239; *Annuaire de l'Inst.* 43, i. 42–132; 44, ii. 251–323; 52, i. 402–527, 656–732; 52, ii. 400–63, 523–6, 560, 565; American Law Institute, Restatement, Third, *Foreign Relations Law of the United States* (1987), para. 712; Whiteman, viii. 1020–185; Delson, 57 *Columbia LR* (1957), 755–86; Ronning, *Law and Politics in Inter-American Diplomacy* (1963), 33–62; Bishop, 115 Hague *Recueil* (1965, II), 403–14; Sohn and Baxter, 55 *AJ* (1961), 545–84; Amerasinghe, *State Responsibility for Injuries to Aliens* (1967), 121–68; *Répertoire suisse*, ii. 661–98; Orrego Vicuña, 67 *AJ* (1973), 711–27; Francioni, 24 *ICLQ* (1975), 255–83; Jiménez de Aréchaga, 11 *NY Univ. Journ. of Int. Law and Politics* (1978), 179–95; Hossain (ed.), *Legal Aspects of the New International Economic Order* (1980); Akinsanya, *The Expropriation of Multinational Property in the Third World* (1980); Dolzer, 75 *AJ* (1981), 553–89; Schachter, 178 Hague *Recueil* (1982, V), 295–326; Higgins, 176 Hague *Recueil* (1982, III), 259–392; Rousseau, v. 46–66; Dolzer, 1 *ICSID Review* (1986), 41–65; Schachter, 78 *AJ* (1984), 121–30; id., 79 *AJ* (1985), 420–2; Asante, 37 *ICLQ* (1988), 588–628; Pellonpää and Fitzmaurice, 19 *Neths. Yrbk.* 1988, 53–178; Norton, 85 *AJ* (1991), 474–505; Bernhardt (ed.), *Encycl. of P.I.L.*, II (1995), Dolzer, 319–27; Waelde and Kolo, *ICLQ*, 50 (2001), 811–48.

[63] On the various procedures of taking see Sohn and Baxter, 55 *AJ* (1961), 553, 559; Domke, ibid. 588–90; Christie, 38 *BY* (1962), 307–38; Whiteman, viii. 1006–20; Weston, 16 *Virginia JIL* (1975–6), 103–75; Reisman and Sloane, 74 *BY* (2003), 115–50. See also the *ELSI* case, ICJ Reports (1989), 15, 67–71; *Sola Tiles Inc.* v.

by transfer to the territorial state or to third parties, as in systems of land distribution as a means of agrarian reform. The process is commonly described as expropriation. If compensation is not provided, or the taking is regarded as unlawful, then the taking is sometimes described as confiscation. Expropriation of one or more major national resources as part of a general programme of social and economic reform is now generally referred to as nationalization or socialization.

State measures, prima facie a lawful exercise of powers of government, may affect foreign interests considerably without amounting to expropriation. Thus foreign assets and their use may be subjected to taxation, trade restrictions involving licences and quotas,[64] or measures of devaluation.[65] While special facts may alter cases, in principle such measures are not unlawful and do not constitute expropriation. If the state gives a public enterprise special advantages, for example by direction that it charge nominal rates of freight, the resulting *de facto* or quasimonopoly is not an expropriation of the competitors driven out of business:[66] it might be otherwise if this were the primary or sole object of a monopoly regime. Taxation which has the precise object and effect of confiscation is unlawful.[67]

A constant difficulty is to establish the line between lawful regulatory measures and forms of indirect or creeping expropriation. In *Pope and Talbot* v. *Government of Canada*,[68] decided by an Arbitration Tribunal in 2001, Pope and Talbot constituted the Claimant/Investor for the purposes of NAFTA, and was concerned in the export of softwood lumber from Canada into the United States. The investor argued that the statutory regime of export control imposed by Canada involved a form of expropriation of the investment.

The analysis of the Tribunal in the Interim Award was as follows:[69]

99. Canada appears to claim that, because the measures under consideration are cast in the form of regulations, they constitute an exercise of 'police powers', which, if non-discriminatory, are supposedly beyond the reach of the NAFTA rules regarding expropriations. While the exercise of police powers must be analysed with special care, the Tribunal believes that Canada's formulation goes too far. Regulations can indeed be exercised in a way that would constitute creeping expropriation ...

Islamic Rep. of Iran, ILR 83, 460; *Otis Elevator Company* v. *Islamic Rep. of Iran*, ILR 84, 618; and *Starrett Housing Corporation* v. *Islamic Rep. of Iran*, ILR 85, 349 at 380–93 (Iran–U.S. Claims Trib.). On concession agreements see *infra*, pp. 522–6.

[64] Treaties may make such restrictions unlawful: e.g. under the GATT, the EFTA Treaty, 1960, and bilateral commercial treaties.

[65] Currency depreciation is lawful unless it is discriminatory: *Tabar claim*, ILR 20 (1953), 211; *Zuk claim*, ibid. 26 (1958, II), 284; *Furst claim*, ibid. 42, 153; *British Digest*, vi. 350; Wortley, *Expropriation*, pp. 107–9; 5 *Canad. Yrbk.* (1967), 268; Whiteman, viii. 982–8. Treaty obligations exist, *inter alia*, under IMF agreements: Mann, 26 *BY* (1949), 263–70. See also *Re Keim*, ILR 44, 102.

[66] See the *Oscar Chinn* case (1934), PCIJ, Ser. A/B, no. 63; World Court Reports, iii. 416. See further Christie, 38 *BY* (1962), 322, 334–6. This decision is also authority for the view that goodwill is not an item of property separate from an enterprise.

[67] See *British Practice* (1964), 202–6; Whiteman, viii. 980, 1016, 1044; *Tax on Mortgagors' Gains* case, ILR 44, 149 at 153–4.

[68] ILR 122, 293.

[69] Ibid., 335–7

Indeed, much creeping expropriation could be conducted by regulation, and a blanket exception for regulatory measures would create a gaping loophole in international protections against expropriation. For these reasons, the Tribunal rejects the argument of Canada that the Export Control Regime, as a regulatory measure, is beyond the coverage of Article 1110.

100. The next question is whether the Export Control Regime has caused an expropriation of the Investor's investment, creeping or otherwise. Using the ordinary meaning of those terms under international law, the answer must be negative. First of all, there is no allegation that the Investment has been nationalized or the Regime is confiscatory. The Investor's (and the Investment's) Operations Controller testified at the hearing that the Investor remains in control of the Investment, it directs the day-to-day operations of the Investment, and no officers or employees of the Investment have been detained by virtue of the Regime. Canada does not supervise the work of the officers or employees of the Investment, does not take any of the proceeds of the company sales (apart from taxation), does not interfere with management or shareholders' activities, does not prevent the Investment from paying dividends to its shareholders, does not interfere with the appointment of directors or management and does not take any other actions ousting the Investor from full ownership and control of the Investment.

101. The sole 'taking' that the Investor has identified is interference with the Investment's ability to carry on its business of exporting softwood lumber to the US. While this interference has, according to the Investor, resulted in reduced profits for the Investment, it continues to export substantial quantities of softwood lumber to the US and to earn substantial profits on those sales.

102. Even when accepting (for the purpose of this analysis) the allegations of the Investor concerning diminished profits, the Tribunal concludes that the degree of interference with the Investment's operations due to the Export Control Regime does not rise to an expropriation (creeping or otherwise) within the meaning of Article 1110. While it may sometimes be uncertain whether a particular interference with business activities amounts to an expropriation, the test is whether that interference is sufficiently restrictive to support a conclusion that the property has been 'taken' from the owner. Thus, the *Harvard Draft* defines the standard as requiring interference that would 'justify an inference that the owner ... will not be able to use, enjoy, or dispose of the property ...'. The *Restatement*, in addressing the question whether regulation may be considered expropriation, speaks of 'action that is confiscatory, or that prevents, unreasonably interferes with, or unduly delays, effective enjoyment of an alien's property'. Indeed, at the hearing, the Investor's Counsel conceded, correctly, that under international law, expropriation requires a 'substantial deprivation'. The Export Control Regime has not restricted the Investment in ways that meet these standards.

10. THE COMPENSATION RULE

The rule supported by all leading 'Western' governments and many jurists in Europe and North America is as follows: the expropriation of alien property is lawful if prompt, adequate, and effective compensation[70] is provided for. In principle, therefore,

---

[70] The formula appears in a Note from the US Secretary of State, Cordell Hull, to the Mexican Government dated 22 August 1938: Hackworth, iii. 658–9. The formula also appears in various modern commercial

expropriation, as an exercise of territorial competence, is lawful, but the compensation rule (in this version) makes the legality conditional. The justifications for the rule are based on the assumptions prevalent in a liberal regime of private property and in the principle that foreign owners are to be given the protection accorded to private rights of nationals, provided that this protection involves the provision of compensation for any taking. These assumptions are used to support the compensation principle as yet another aspect of the international minimum standard governing the treatment of aliens.[71] The emphasis is on respect for property rights as 'acquired rights'[72] and as an aspect of human rights.[73] Reference is also made to general principles of law, including those of unjust enrichment and abuse of rights. The principle of acquired rights is thought by many to be unfortunately vague, and the difficulty is to relate this principle to other principles of law: in short this and other general principles beg too many questions. Constitutional provisions,[74] legislation providing for compensation,[75] and municipal court decisions[76] provide a general guide but no more than that, since local versions of public policy are not necessarily significant for international law.

Whatever the nature of the justifications offered for the compensation rule, it has received considerable support from state practice and the jurisprudence of international tribunals. The United Kingdom, the United States, and France have supported the rule in relation to Mexican agrarian reform, post-war nationalization in Eastern Europe, the Iranian law of 1951 nationalizing the oil industry, the nationalization of the Suez Canal by Egypt, and so on.[77] Agreements involving provision for some sort of

---

treaties: e.g. the Anglo-Japanese Commercial Treaty of 1963, Art. 14; see Almond, 13 *ICLQ* (1964), 925 at 949. See also Whiteman, viii. 1085–9. It is also commonly stipulated that the taking should be 'in the public interest', but see *infra*, p. 545. On the criteria of adequacy, effectiveness, and promptness, see García Amador, *Yrbk. ILC* (1959), ii. 16–24; White, *Nationalisation*, pp. 235–43; Domke, 55 *AJ* (1961), 603–10; Sohn and Baxter, ibid. 553 (Art. 10/4), 559–60; ICJ Pleadings, *Anglo-Iranian Oil Co.* case (*United Kingdom v. Iran*), 100ff.; Jiménez de Aréchaga, *Yrbk. ILC* (1963), ii. 237–44; Cole, 41 *BY* (1965–6), 374–9; Whiteman, viii. 1143–85; Metzger, 50 *Virginia LR* (1964), 603–7.

[71] On which, *supra*, p. 525.

[72] The statements of the Permanent Court on the principle of respect for vested or acquired rights occur in the context of state succession; see *infra*, n. 81. See generally García Amador, *Yrbk. ILC* (1959), ii. 3–10; Foighel, *Nationalisation and Compensation*, pp. 124–8. See also the *Lighthouses* arbitration (1956), PCA, *RIAA* xii. 155, 236.

[73] Cf. the Additional Protocol to the European Conv. on Human Rights, Art. 1.

[74] See Shawcross, 102 Hague *Recueil* (1961, I), 339 at 347.

[75] See White, *Nationalisation*, pp. 184–93.

[76] Many of these depend on the public policy of the forum and conflict of laws rules. However, see the *S.S. Elise, Ann. Digest*, 15 (1948), no. 50 at p. 200; *Anglo-Iranian Oil Co.* v. *Idemitsu Kosan Kabushiki Kaisha*, ILR 20 (1953), 305; the *Rose Mary* [1953] 1 WLR 246; ILR 20 (1953), 316; *In re Rhein-Main-Donau A.G.*, ILR 21 (1954), 212. See further Gihl, *Liber Amicorum Algot Bagge* (1956), 56–66; and cf. *Czechoslovak Agrarian Reform* case, *Ann. Digest*, 4 (1927–8), no. 94.

[77] The pre-1914 practice involved the following cases: the Sicilian sulphur monopoly granted to a French company, thus harming British subjects (1836), 28 *BFSP*, 1163–242; 29 ibid., 175–204, 1225; 30 ibid., 111–20; the *Charlton* case (1841), 31 *BFSP*, 1025–32; the *Finlay* case (1846), 39 *BFSP*, 410; *British Digest*, vi. 341; the *King* case (1853), Moore, *Digest*, vi. 262; Whiteman, *Damages in International Law*, 3 vols. (1937–43), ii. 1387; the *Savage* case (1852), Moore, *Arbitrations*, ii. 1855; the *Delagoa Bay Railway*

compensation in the form of the 'lump sum settlement' are numerous, but jurists are in disagreement as to their evidential value: many agreements rest on a bargain and special circumstances, and it is difficult to see whether the compensation principle is assumed as the general norm or has been eroded by the frequency of compromise.[78] Although some awards were in substance diplomatic compromises,[79] a good number of international tribunals have supported the compensation rule and the principle of acquired rights.[80] *Dicta* in a number of decisions of the Permanent Court,[81] involving treaty interpretation and the effects of state succession on various categories of property, may be regarded as supporting the compensation principle, which is supported also by a majority of jurists in Western countries.[82]

case (1900), Martens, *N.R.G.* (2nd Ser.), vol. 30, 329; *British Digest*, v. 535; Whiteman, *Damages*, iii. 1694; La Fontaine, p. 398 (Portugal conceded the principle of compensation); *Portuguese Religious Properties case* (1920), *RIAA* i. 7; Hague Court Reports, ii. 1; the proposal for an insurance monopoly in Uruguay (1911), Hackworth, v. 588; the Italian life insurance monopoly (1912), ibid. On the work of the Brussels Conference, 1921, see McNair, *Opinions*, i. 9, and Wortley, *Expropriation*, p. 61. On the Cannes Conference of 1922 see H. of C., Sess. Papers XXIII, 1922 (but see Friedman, *Expropriation*, pp. 19, 101–3). More modern practice includes the following: US Notes to Mexico in 1938 and 1940, Hackworth, iii. 655, 658, 662; Briggs, pp. 556, 559; 33 *AJ* (1939), Suppl., pp. 181–207; UK Note to Mexico, 1938, Cmd. 5758; UK minute to Poland, *Treaty Series* no. 23 (1948), Cmd. 7403 (cf. Fawcett, 27 *BY* (1950), 372–3); UK Memorial, *Anglo-Iranian Oil Co.* case, ICJ Pleadings (1951), 100–9; US Note to Guatemala, 28 Aug. 1953, 29 *Dept. of St. Bull.* (1953), 357, 359; protests of France, UK, and US on Suez Canal Company nationalization, 1956; US views on Cuban and Ceylonese nationalizations, 56 *AJ* (1962), 166; 58 *AJ* (1964), 168; UK reaction to Indonesian measures, *British Practice* (1964), 194–200; to Tanzanian nationalization of banks, ibid., (1967), 118–20. Cf. also the Netherlands Note to Indonesia, 18 Dec, 1959, 54 *AJ* (1960), 484; Kiss, *Répertoire* (1962), iv. paras. 655–66.

[78] See White, *Nationalisation*, pp. 193–243; Friedman, *Expropriation*, pp. 86–101; Fawcett, 27 *BY* (1950), 372–3; Drucker, 10 *ICLQ* (1961), 238–54; Shawcross 102 Hague *Recueil* (1961, I), 348–50; Lillich, 16 *Syracuse LR* (1964–5), 735–6; id., *The Protection of Foreign Investment* (1965), 167–88; Lillich and Weston, *International Claims: Their Settlement by Lump Sum Agreements*, 2 vols. (1975); Whiteman, viii. 1107–29; Lillich and Weston, 82 *AJ* (1988), 69–80.

[79] See the *Delagoa Bay Railway* and *Expropriated Religious Properties* cases, *supra*, n. 74.

[80] *Norwegian Ships* arbitration (1921), PCA, *RIAA* i. 307, 338; Hague Court Reports, ii. 40; *French Claims against Peru* (1921), PCA, *RIAA* i. 215; Hague Court Reports, ii. 31; 16 *AJ* (1922), 480; *Landreau* claim (1921), *RIAA* i. 347, 365; *Spanish Zone of Morocco* claims (1925), *RIAA* ii. 615, 647; *Ann. Digest*, 2 (1923–4), no. 85; *Hopkins* claim (1927), *RIAA* iv. 41; 21 *AJ* (1927), 160; *Ann. Digest*, 3 (1925–6), no. 167; *Goldenberg* claim (1928), *RIAA* ii. 901, 909; 3 *RDI* (1929), 559; *Hungarian Optants* case (1927), *Rec. TAM* vii. 138; arbitral award between Portugal and Germany (1930), *RIAA* ii. 1035, 1039; *Ann. Digest*, 5 (1929–30), 150, 151; *Shufeldt* claim (1930), *RIAA* ii. 1079, 1095; 24 *AJ* (1930), 799; *Mariposa* claim (1933), *RIAA* vi. 338; *de Sabla* claim (1933), *RIAA* vi. 358, 366; *Ann. Digest*, 7 (1933–4), no.92 at p. 243; *Arabian-American Oil Co. v. Saudi Arabia* (1958), ILR 27, 117 at 144, 168, 205; *Amoco International Finance Corporation v. Iran*, ILR 83, 490 at 541–3.
See also the *El Triunfo* case (1901), *RIAA* xv. 467; *Upton* (1903), *RIAA* ix. 234; and *Selwyn* (1903), ibid. 380.

[81] See *German Interests in Polish Upper Silesia* (1926), PCIJ, Ser. A, no. 7. pp. 21, 22, 33, 42; *Chorzów Factory* case (Jurisdiction)(1927), Ser. A, no. 9, pp. 27, 31; and no. 13, p. 19; *Chorzów Factory* case (Indemnity)(1928), Ser. A, no. 17, pp. 46, 47; (cf. Fischer Williams, 9 *BY*, 8–10); *German Settlers in Poland* (1923), Ser. B, no. 6, pp. 23, 24, 38; *Peter Pázmány University* (1933), Ser. A/B, no.61, p. 243.

[82] See McNair, Rolin, Verdross, Wortley, White, and Petrén, cited *supra*, n. 61. See also García Amador's report, *Yrbk. ILC* (1959), ii. 2–24; Sørensen, 101 Hague *Recueil* (1960, III), 176ff.; Fitzmaurice, 92 Hague *Recueil* (1957, II), 128; Guggenheim i. 333–4; Briggs, p. 569; Shawcross, 102 Hague *Recueil* (1961, I), 339, 369; O'Connell, pp. 776–85.

Jurists supporting the compensation rule recognize the existence of exceptions, the most widely accepted of which are as follows:[83] under treaty provisions; as a legitimate exercise of police power, including measures of defence against external threats; confiscation as a penalty for crimes;[84] seizure by way of taxation or other fiscal measures; loss caused indirectly by health and planning legislation and the concomitant restrictions on the use of property; the destruction of property of neutrals as a consequence of military operations, and the taking of enemy property as part payment of reparation for the consequences of an illegal war.[85]

11. THE PRINCIPLE OF NATIONAL TREATMENT

A number of jurists[86] and a few tribunals[87] have subscribed to the view that an alien cannot complain provided he receives the same treatment as nationals: if nationals of the expropriating state receive no compensation the alien can expect none. Sir John Fischer Williams has pointed out that a general dogma as to the inviolability of private property can no more be erected into an international duty than other political and economic doctrines. Thus the exceptions to the compensation rule noticed above indicate the relativity of acquired rights even in states founded on private enterprise principles. For reasons offered earlier, it is not thought that the national treatment principle provides a reliable general formula. In relation to expropriation, as elsewhere, it plays a subsidiary role in the context of the positive legal principles.[88]

12. CONTROL OF MAJOR NATURAL RESOURCES

The classical model for expropriation has long been the taking of a single item of property, and the analogy has been the wrongful taking of property in private law. Cases in which expropriation is allowed to be lawful in the absence of compensation

---

[83] See Friedman, *Expropriation*, pp. 1–3; Wortley, *Expropriation*, pp. 40–57; Guggenheim, i. 333; Herz, 35 *AJ* (1941), 251–2; *Yrbk. ILC* (1959), ii. 11–12, paras. 43, 44; Sohn and Baxter, 55 *AJ* (1961), 553, 561–2, Art. 10(5); Fischer Williams, 9 *BY* (1928), 22–8; Petrén, 109 Hague *Recueil* (1963, II), 525–36.

[84] See *Allgemeine Gold-und Silberscheideanstalt* v. *Customs and Excise Commissioners* [1980] 2 WLR 555; 51 *BY* (1980), 305.

[85] See the *AKU* case ILR 23 (1956), 21; *Prince Salm-Salm* case, ibid. 24 (1957), 893. This view is controversial, however. See further *Assets of Hungarian Company in Germany* case, ILR 32, 565; *Re Dohnert, Muller, Schmidt & Co.*, ibid. 570.

[86] See Dunn, 28 *Col. LR* (1928), 166–80; Cavaglieri, 38 *RGDIP* (1931), 257–96; Brierly, p. 284; Fischer Williams, 9 *BY* (1928), 28–9. See further Herz, 35 *AJ* (1941), 259 n. 66.

[87] See the *Canevaro* case PCA (1912), Hague Court Reports, i. 285; 6 *AJ* (1912), 746; *RIAA* xi. 397; *Standard Oil Co. Tankers* (1926), *RIAA* ii. 781, 794; 8 *BY* (1927), 156; 22 *AJ* (1928), 404.

[88] See further *supra*, pp. 523, 526, *infra*, p. 544, and cf. Fischer Williams 9 *BY* (1928, 28–9; Friedman, *Expropriation*, pp. 133, 210.

are within the narrow concept of public utility prevalent in *laissez-faire* economic systems, i.e. exercise of police power, health measures, and the like. The fact is that a large proportion of the members of the community of states now regard the existence of a public sector as an important aspect of national independence and economic development. Many of the poorer states have accepted foreign investment at the expense of economic, and therefore political, independence. It is all very well to say that nationalization is possible—providing prompt and adequate compensation is paid. In reality this renders any major economic or social programme impossible, since few states can produce the capital value of a large proportion of their economies promptly. It is common for the poorer economies to be subjected to foreign ownership to a great extent,[89] and the analogy of private law ownership clashes sharply with the desire of states to govern their own economies. This impasse has led some eminent jurists to distinguish between general expropriation (nationalization, or socialization), on the one hand, and, on the other, small-scale expropriation. In the case of nationalization of a major industry or natural resource compensation would be on a basis of payments phased out over a period and calculated with reference to the general economic position in the state concerned. In other words, compensation of private interests is accommodated to the competence to nationalize.[90] The principle of nationalization unsubordinated to a full compensation rule may be supported by reference to principles of self-determination, independence, sovereignty, and equality.[91] Equitably based, the lump sum settlement (*indemnité globale forfaitaire*) short of the prompt, adequate, and effective standard has become common, and some authors regard the practice as evidence of an *opinio juris*.[92] The jurisprudence of the European Court of Human Rights, in relation to the guarantees in Protocol 1 of the European Convention on Human Rights,[93]

[89] See the percentages for the Polish economy in 1946, quoted in Friedman, *Expropriation*, p. 32.

[90] See the opinions of Lauterpacht, 62 Hague *Recueil* (1937, IV), 346; id., *International Law: Collected Papers*, i (1970), 387–90; Sørensen, pp. 485–9; Bishop, 115 Hague *Recueil* (1965, II), 409–10; Amerasinghe, *State Responsibility*, pp. 121–68; Oppenheim, i (8th ed., 1955), 352; La Pradelle, *Annuaire de l'Inst.* 43 (1950), i. 60–6; de Visscher, *Theory and Reality in Public International Law* (1957), 193–5; Rolin, *Annuaire de l'Inst.* 43 (1950), i. 97; id., 6 *Neths. Int. LR* (1959), 272; Friedman, *Expropriation*, pp. 206–11; Guggenheim, i. 334–5. See also Baade, 54 *AJ* (1960), 804, nn. 22, 23. Cf. the Mexican Note to the US of 3 Aug. 1938, Hackworth, iii. 657. For Asian and Latin American opinions see *Yrbk. ILC* (1957), i. 154ff. See further Petrén, 109 Hague *Recueil* (1963, II), 545ff.; Sohn and Baxter, 55 *AJ* (1961), 553 (Art. 10, para. 4), 559–60. See also Rosenberg, *Le Principe de Souveraineté des États sur leurs Ressources Naturelles* (1983).

[91] See the resolutions of the UN General Assembly considered below.

[92] See Rolin, *Annuaire de l'Inst.* 43 (1950), i. 97; id., 6 *Neths. Int. LR* (1959), 273. For doubts as to the *opinio juris*, see Sørensen, 101 Hague *Recueil* (1960, III), 180 and Bindschedler, 90 Hague *Recueil* (1956, II), 297. See further Fawcett, 27 *BY* (1950), 372–5; García Amador, *Yrbk. ILC* (1959), ii. 20–4. At the very least, the requirement of 'promptness' has been overshadowed by post-war practice: see on this the *Anglo-Iranian* case, ICJ Pleadings (1951), 106.

[93] 'Every natural or legal person is entitled to the peaceful enjoyment of his possessions. No one shall be deprived of his possessions except in the public interest and subject to the conditions provided for by law and by the general principles of international law.'

The preceding provisions shall not, however, in any way impair the right of a State to enforce such laws as it deems necessary to control the use of property in accordance with the general interest or to secure the payment of taxes or other contributions or penalties.' See also the American Conv. on Human Rights, Art. 21; and the African Charter on Human and Peoples' Rights, Art. 14.

has given no little emphasis to considerations of public interest both in relation to the occasion of interference with property and in relation to the measure of compensation. Thus in the *James* case the Court observed that:[94]

... the taking of property without payment of an amount reasonably related to its value would normally constitute a disproportionate interference which could not be considered justifiable under Article 1. Article 1 does not, however, guarantee a right to full compensation in all circumstances. Legitimate objectives of 'public interest', such as pursued in measures of economic reform or measures designed to achieve greater social justice, may call for less than reimbursement of the full market value.

13. EXPROPRIATION UNLAWFUL *PER SE*

The position achieved by the preceding discussion is as follows:

1. Expropriation for certain public purposes, e.g. exercise of police power and defence measures in wartime, is lawful even if no compensation is payable.

2. Expropriation of particular items of property is unlawful unless there is provision for the payment of effective compensation.

3. Nationalization, i.e. expropriation of a major industry or resource, is unlawful only if there is no provision for compensation payable on a basis compatible with the economic objectives of the nationalization, and the viability of the economy as a whole.

Thus expropriation under (2) and (3) is unlawful, if at all, only *sub modo*, i.e. if appropriate compensation is not provided for. The controversial difference between (2) and (3) is the basis on which compensation is assessed. However, whatever may be the relation of these two categories, there is evidence of a category of types of expropriation which are illegal apart from a failure to provide for compensation, in which cases lack of compensation is an additional element in, and not a condition of, the illegality. It has been suggested that this category includes interference with the assets of international organizations[95] and taking contrary to promises amounting to estoppels.[96] Certainly it includes seizures which are a part of crimes against humanity or genocide, involve breaches of international agreements,[97] are measures of unlawful retaliation

---

[94] Judgment of 21 Feb. 1986; ECHR Ser. A, no. 98, para. 54. See also *Sporrong and Lönnroth*, Ser. A, no. 52, paras. 56–75; *Lithgow*, Ser. A, no. 102, paras. 111–74; Higgins, 176 Hague *Recueil* (1982, III), 355–75; and Mendelson, 57 *BY* (1986), 33–76. Cf. the decision of the Iran–US Claims Tribunal in *INA Corporation* v. *Government of the Islamic Republic of Iran*, ILR 75, 595. See, most recently, ECHR Ser. A, no. 169, para. 47.

[95] See Delson, 57 *Columbia LR* (1957), 771.

[96] Friedmann, 50 *AJ* (1956), 505. On estoppel see *infra*, p. 645.

[97] Cf. *German Interests in Polish Upper Silesia* (Merits) (1926), PCIJ, Ser. A, no. 7; *Chorzów Factory* case (Indemnity) (1928), Ser. A, no. 17, pp. 46–7.

or reprisal against another state,[98] are discriminatory, being aimed at persons of particular racial groups or nationals of particular states,[99] or concern property owned by a foreign state and dedicated to official state purposes.[100]

The practical distinctions between expropriation unlawful *sub modo*, i.e. only if no provision is made for compensation, and expropriation unlawful *per se* would seem to be these: the former involves a duty to pay compensation only for direct losses, i.e. the value of the property, the latter involves liability for consequential loss (*lucrum cessans*);[101] the former confers a title which is recognized in foreign courts (and international tribunals), the latter produces no valid title.[102] The case-law of the Iran–US Claims Tribunal includes examination of the relevance of the distinction between lawful/unlawful expropriation in the remedial sphere.[103]

14. THE GENERAL ASSEMBLY RESOLUTION OF 1962 ON PERMANENT SOVEREIGNTY OVER NATURAL RESOURCES

The materials on which an assessment of the rules governing expropriation must be based include important projects canvassed within the United Nations. In 1955 the Third Committee of the General Assembly adopted a draft article, as a part of

---

[98] Netherlands Note to Indonesia, 18 Dec. 1959, 54 *AJ* (1960), 484; US Notes to Libya, 8 July 1973, *Digest of US Practice* (1973), 334–5; 20 June 1974, ibid. (1975), 490–1; US Court of Appeals, *Banco Nacional de Cuba* v. *Sabbatino* (1962), 56 *AJ*, p. 1085 at pp. 1101–4; *Banco Nacional de Cuba* v. *First National City Bank*, 270 F. Supp. 1004 (1967); ILR 42, 45; Seidl-Hohenveldern, in *Essays Presented to Kollewijn and Offerhaus* (1962), 470–9; Rolin, 6 *Neths. Int. LR* (1959), 274. An obvious difficulty is to determine when a reprisal is lawful: in principle it should be a reaction to a prior breach of legal duty and be proportionate.

[99] There is much authority for this: see White, *Nationalisation*, pp. 119–44; McNair, 6 *Neths. Int. LR* (1959), 247–9; Rolin, ibid. 269–70; Herz, 35 *AJ* (1941), 243, 249, 259; Sørensen, 101 Hague *Recueil* (1960, III), 178; US Court of Appeals, *Banco Nacional de Cuba* v. *Sabbatino* (1962), 56 *AJ* (1962), 1104–5; *In re Helbert Wagg & Co. Ltd.* [1956] 1 Ch. 323; ILR 22 (1955), 480; *Bank Indonesia* v. *Senembah Maatschappij*, ILR 30, 28.

The test of discrimination is the intention of the government: the fact that only aliens are affected may be incidental, and, if the taking is based on economic and social policies, it is not directed against particular groups simply because they own the property involved. See ICJ Pleadings, *Anglo-Iranian Oil Co.* case (1951), 97; *Anglo-Iranian Oil Co. Ltd.* v. *S.U.P.O.R.*, ILR 22 (1955), 23 at 39; Whiteman, viii. 1041–57. See also the *ELSI* case, ICJ Reports (1989), 15, 71–3.

[100] White, *Nationalisation*, pp. 151–3.

[101] See Sørensen, 101 Hague *Recueil* (1960, III), 178–9; Fatouros, *Government Guarantees to Foreign Investors* (1962), 307–9. Some writers require specific restitution in the latter case; see Baade, 54 *AJ* (1960), 807–30; 56 *AJ* (1962), 504–5; Wortley, 55 *AJ* (1961), 680–3. See also Sohn and Baxter, ibid. 556; Jennings, 37 *BY* (1961), 171–3; and the decision of the Iran–US Claims Tribunal in *Amoco International Finance* v. *Iran*, 15 Iran–US CTR 189 at 246–52.

[102] See Domke, 54 *AJ* (1960), 305–23; id., ibid. 55 (1961), 610–16; Baade, 54 *AJ* (1960), 801–35; id., ibid. 56 (1962), 504–7; Seidl-Hohenveldern, ibid. 507–10; ib., 49 *Michigan LR* (1951), 851–68. The writers are not agreed on these questions, and municipal courts often recognize measures lawful under the *lex situs*: *Luther* v. *Sagor* [1921] 3 KB 532; *In re Helbert Wagg & Co. Ltd.* [1956] 1 Ch. 323; ILR 22 (1955), 480; *Dutch Tobacco Firms in Indonesia*, ILR 28, 16. See Staker, 58 *BY* (1987), 151–252, for a detailed discussion.

[103] See (e.g.) *Amoco International Finance* v. *Iran*, supra.

the Human Rights Covenants, on the right of self-determination, the second paragraph of which stated: 'The peoples may, for their own ends, freely dispose of their natural wealth and resources without prejudice to any obligations arising out of international economic co-operation, based upon the principle of mutual benefit, and international law. In no case may a people be deprived of its own means of subsistence'. The concept of economic self-determination stemmed from a General Assembly resolution of 21 December 1952.[104] Much later, work in the UN Commission on Permanent Sovereignty over Natural Resources and the Economic and Social Council culminated in the adoption of Resolution 1803 (XVII) by the General Assembly on 14 December 1962.[105] The resolution was in the form of a Declaration on Permanent Sovereignty over Natural Resources. The *consideranda* to the resolution refer, *inter alia*, to 'the inalienable right of all States freely to dispose of their natural wealth and resources in accordance with their national interests', and to 'respect for the economic independence of States', and stipulate that the resolution has no bearing on the subject of succession of states and governments.

The substance of the Declaration is as follows:

1. The right of peoples and nations to permanent sovereignty over their natural wealth and resources must be exercised in the interest of their national development and of the well-being of the people of the State concerned;

2. The exploration, development and disposition of such resources, as well as the import of the foreign capital required for these purposes, should be in conformity with the rules and conditions which the peoples and nations freely consider to be necessary or desirable with regard to the authorization, restriction or prohibition of such activities;

3. In cases where authorization is granted, the capital imported and the earnings on that capital shall be governed by the terms thereof, by the national legislation in force, and by international law. The profits derived must be shared in the proportions freely agreed upon, in each case, between the investors and the recipient State, due care being taken to ensure that there is no impairment, for any reason, of that State's sovereignty over its natural wealth and resources;

4. Nationalization, expropriation or requisitioning shall be based on grounds or reasons of public utility, security or the national interest which are recognized as overriding purely individual or private interests, both domestic and foreign. In such cases the owner shall be paid appropriate compensation, in accordance with the rules in force in the State taking such measures in the exercise of its sovereignty and in accordance with international law. In any case where the question of compensation gives rise to a controversy, the national

---

[104] Resol. 626 (VII). See also Resols. 1314 (XIII), 12 Dec. 1958, and 1515 (XV), 15 Dec. 1960. See generally Hyde, 50 *AJ* (1956), 854–67; and UN Secretariat study, *The Status of Permanent Sovereignty over Natural Wealth and Resources* (1962). Resol. 626 (VII) was cited in *Anglo-Iranian Oil Co. Ltd.* v. *S.U.P.O.R.*, ILR 22 (1955), 23 at 40; and *Anglo-Iranian Oil Co.* v. *Idemitsu Kosan Kabushiki Kaisha*, ibid., 20 (1953), 305 at 313.

[105] Adopted by 87 votes to 2, 12 abstentions. See Gess, 13 *ICLQ* (1964), 398–449 (text of Resol., p. 400) and Fischer, *Ann. français* (1962), 516–28; *Texaco* v. *Libyan Government*, 17 *ILM* (1978), i; 104 *JDI* (1977), 350, Award on Merits, paras. 68, 80–1, 83–4, 87–8; *LIAMCO* Award, 20 *ILM* (1981), 1 at 78, 99–103, 131; *Aminoil* Award, 21 *ILM* (1982), 976 at 1021. See further Resol. 2158 (XXI) adopted on 25 Nov. 1966 by 104 votes to 0, 6 abstentions; 6 *ILM* (1967), 147; and the Vienna Conv. on Succession of States in respect of Treaties (1978), Art. 13.

jurisdiction of the State taking such measures shall be exhausted. However, upon agreement by sovereign States and other parties concerned, settlement of the dispute should be made through arbitration or international adjudication;

5. The free and beneficial exercise of the sovereignty of peoples and nations over their natural resources must be furthered by the mutual respect of States based on their sovereign equality;

6. International co-operation for the economic development of developing countries, whether in the form of public or private capital investments, exchange of goods and services, technical assistance, or exchange of scientific information, shall be such as to further their independent national development and shall be based upon respect for their sovereignty over their natural wealth and resources;

7. Violation of the rights of peoples and nations to sovereignty over their natural wealth and resources is contrary to the spirit and principles of the Charter of the United Nations and hinders the development of international co-operation and the maintenance of peace;

8. Foreign investment agreements freely entered into by, or between, sovereign States shall be observed in good faith; States and international organizations shall strictly and conscientiously respect the sovereignty of peoples and nations over their natural wealth and resources in accordance with the Charter and the principles set forth in the present resolution.

15. THE CHARTER OF ECONOMIC RIGHTS AND DUTIES OF STATES

Since 1972 the less developed states have pressed for the establishment of a 'new deal' in their relations with the industrialized nations. This pressure was reflected, in particular, in the United Nations General Assembly Resolution 3201 (S-VI) of 1 May 1974[106] containing a Declaration on the Establishment of a New International Economic Order. On 12 December 1974 the General Assembly adopted the Charter of Economic Rights and Duties of States (120 votes in favour; 6 against; 10 abstentions).[107]

---

[106] 13 *ILM* (1974), 715; 68 *AJ* (1974), 798. See also Resol. 3202 (S–VI), ibid. 720.

[107] Resol. 3281 (XXIX), 14 *ILM* (1975), 251; 69 *AJ* (1975), 484. For comment see Lillich, 69 *AJ* (1975), 359–65; Castañeda, *Ann. français* (1974), 31–56; Virally, ibid. 57–77; Brower and Tepe, 9 *Int. Lawyer* (1975), 295–318; Haight, ibid. 591–604; Feuer, 79 *RGDIP* (1975), 273–320; White, 24 *ICLQ* (1975), 542–52; id., 16 *Virginia JIL* (1975–6), 323–45; Mahiou, 12 *Revue belge* (1976), 421–50; Salem, 102 *JDI* (1975), 753–800; Rao, 16 *Indian Journ.* (1976), 351–70; Jiménez de Aréchaga, Hague *Recueil* (1978, I), 297–310; Brownlie, 162 Hague *Recueil* (1978, IV), 255–71; Bedjaoui, *Towards a New International Economic Order* (1979) Hossain (ed.), *Legal Aspects of the New International Economic Order*; Rosenberg, *Le Principe de souveraineté des états sur leurs ressources naturelles* (1983); Hossain and Chowdhury (eds.), *Permanent Sovereignty over Natural Resources in International Law* (1984); UNITAR, Final Report (Abi-Saab), UN Doc. A/39/504, 23 Oct. 1984; ILA, *Report of the 62nd Conference* (1986), 2–11, 409–87; Bulajib, *Principles of International Development Law* (1986); Makarczyk, *Principles of a New International Economic Order* (1988); Oppermann and Petersmann (eds.), *Reforming the International Economic Order* (1987). See also the Decl. of Lima, 26 Mar. 1975, Second General Conference of UNIDO; 14 *ILM* (1975), 826.

The states voting against the resolution were: Belgium, Denmark, German Federal Republic, Luxembourg, the United Kingdom, and the United States.

For present purposes the leading principles of the Charter are to be found in Article 2, as follows:

1. Every State has and shall freely exercise full permanent sovereignty including possession, use and disposal, over all its wealth, natural resources and economic activities.

2. Each State has the right:

... (c) to nationalize, expropriate or transfer ownership of foreign property, in which case appropriate compensation should be paid by the State adopting such measures, taking into account its relevant laws and regulations and all circumstances that the State considers pertinent. In any case where the question of compensation gives rise to a controversy, it shall be settled under the domestic law of the nationalizing State and by its tribunals, unless it is freely and mutually agreed by all States concerned that other peaceful means be sought on the basis of the sovereign equality of States and in accordance with the principle of free choice of means.

What effect do these formulations have on customary international law? Such resolutions are vehicles for the evolution of state practice and each must be weighed in evidential terms according to its merits. The Charter has a strong political and programmatic flavour and does not purport to be a declaration of pre-existing principles. The opinion has been expressed that Article 2 of the Charter is merely a *de lege ferenda* formulation.[108] This view is contradicted by evidence that Article 2(2) (c) is regarded by many states as an emergent principle, applicable *ex nunc*. In the first place, the language harks back to paragraph 4 of the 1962 Resolution (*supra*). Secondly, the attitude of states opposed to Article 2 indicates all too clearly that governments are aware of the need to 'contract out' of such formulations by reservations of position either by explanations of negative votes and abstention or by the making of specific reservations after adoption of a resolution by consensus (without formal vote).[109]

Assuming that the provisions of Article 2 are to be reckoned with, as evidence of new customary law, what are the consequences? The concept of permanent sovereignty over natural resources reinforces the existing principle that taking for public purposes is lawful. The compensation principle is not, as such, denied.[110] Recent comment has neglected to notice that, if the term 'compensation' has an objective content, then failure by the local courts to provide 'compensation' would be contrary to the principles of Article 2. It is also clear that liability for denial of justice may arise if

---

[108] *Texaco* v. *Libyan Government, supra*, Award on Merits, paras. 88–9. However, this approach is modified in paras. 90–1. In the *LIAMCO* case (Award of 12 Apr. 1977), the sole arbitrator, Dr Mahmassani, stressed the vagueness of Art. 2(2)(c): 20 *ILM* (1981), 1 at 76. See also the *Aminoil* Award (24 Mar. 1982), 21 *ILM* (1982), 976 at 1021–2 (para. 90), 1032 (para. 143); and the *SEDCO* case (Iran–US Claims Tribunal), *ILR* 84, 484 at 525–7.

[109] See 13 *ILM* (1975), 715 at 744, 749, 753, 759, 762.

[110] See Jiménez de Aréchaga, 11 *NY Univ. Journ. of Int. Law and Politics* (1978), 179 at 184; Schachter, 178 Hague *Recueil* (1982, V), 321–3.

certain standards are not observed.[111] Moreover, expropriation contrary to treaty,[112] or in breach of an independent principle of customary law, for example, the principle of non-discrimination on grounds of race or religion, will continue to be unlawful. It has been stated[113] that the reference to the domestic law of the nationalizing state is intended to give general recognition to the Calvo doctrine,[114] but in fact the reference to domestic law is exclusively in relation to 'compensation' and, as it has been suggested above, this is by no means a reference to domestic law willy-nilly.

In conclusion it is to be emphasized that, assuming that Article 2 of the Charter does bring about a change in the customary law, whatever this might be, the United States and its associates will not be bound since they have adopted the role of persistent objectors.[115]

16. CONCLUSIONS ON EXPROPRIATION

The Declaration of 1962 set out above, which constitutes evidence of the existing law,[116] places emphasis on the rights of the state host to or receiving foreign assets, and in a general way contradicts the simple thesis of acquired rights. However, its actual formulations tend to cover up the real differences of opinion on the law by reference to international law and the payment of 'appropriate compensation'. Question-begging though the provisions may be, it is significant that the right to compensation on whatever basis, is recognized in principle. In view of the real differences of opinion, any statement of conclusions can only be provisional. The present position, including the elements of confusion, can be expressed in a number of independent propositions.

1. A considerable number of states insist that expropriation can only take place on payment of adequate, effective compensation. In practice deferred payments are regarded as sufficient provided effective compensation takes place.[117] The requirement of promptness has become subordinated to the other conditions and also to economic realities relating to payment of large sums.

2. Neither the principle of acquired rights nor that of national treatment provide reliable guidance.

---

[111] Cf. Castañeda, *Ann. Français* (1974) at 51, 54; *Texaco* v. *Libyan Government, supra*, Award on Merits, paras. 90–1.

[112] For a different view: Jiménez de Aréchaga, 11 *NY Univ. Journ. of Int. Law and Politics* (1978) 179–80; and in 159 Hague *Recueil* (1978, I), 297.

[113] Lillich, 69 *AJ* (1975), 359 at 361.

[114] On which see *infra*, pp. 545–6.

[115] On the persistent objector: *supra*, p. 11. In the Second Committee of the General Assembly Art. 2(2)(c) of the Charter attracted negative votes or abstention from 22 delegations.

[116] See UK Note to the Government of Iraq, 4 Sept. 1967; *British Practice* (1967), p. 121.

[117] See Foighel, *Nationalization and Compensation*, pp. 255–7; ICJ Pleadings, *Anglo-Iranian Oil Co.* case, pp. 100ff.

3. The majority of states accept the principle of compensation, but not on the basis of the 'prompt, adequate, and effective' formula.[118]

4. Where major natural resources are concerned, cogent considerations of principle reinforced by the Declaration of 1962 and the Charter of Economic Rights and Duties of States, militate against the 'prompt, adequate, and effective' formula.[119]

5. Certain categories of expropriation are illegal *per se* and not merely in the absence of compensation.[120]

6. Reference to reprisal action, as a type of expropriation illegal *per se*, only leads to secondary questions as to the legality of the reprisal.

7. Reference to general principles that expropriation must be for purposes of public utility, or that it must not be 'arbitrary', only causes confusion.[121] The determination of public utility is primarily a matter for individual states, and categories of illegality (see proposition(5)) can only depend on particular rules of international law.

8. The 'orthodox' compensation rule is stated to have exceptions, principally on the basis of police power.[122] Here the concept of public utility in certain societies is employed to explain cases where no compensation is payable. The exceptions are an embarrassment since, as a matter of principle, this position is not very different from the view taken by some states with a different view of public utility, viz., that the compensation rule does not apply, at least in the 'prompt, adequate, and effective' form.

9. It is a fact that a very considerable number of hosts to foreign capital are willing to conclude treaties for the protection of investments which contain a provision for the payment of 'prompt, adequate, and effective' compensation in case of expropriation or, more frequently, 'just compensation'. While these are negotiated deals, the pattern of agreements surely constitutes evidence of an international standard based upon the principle of compensation.[123]

---

[118] See the references in the article by Gess, 13 *ICLQ* (1964), 427–9, to the General Assembly debate on the Decl. of 1962, which provides for 'appropriate compensation'. See further Jiménez de Aréchaga, Hague *Recueil* (1978, I), 21, 297–310.

[119] See Lauterpacht, 62 Hague *Recueil* (1937, IV), 346; and Sohn and Baxter, 55 *AJ* (1961), 553 (Art. 10(4)), 559–60.

[120] *Supra*, pp. 538–9.

[121] See White, *Nationalisation*, pp. 149–50, who states that the rule against non-discrimination suffices. But absence of discrimination is not by itself a sufficient guide to legality. For references to public utility see Herz, 35 *AJ* (1941), 252–3; *Yrbk. ILC* (1959), ii. 15–16; Sohn and Baxter, 55 *AJ* (1961), 553 (Art. 10); McNair, 6 *Neths. Int. LR* (1959), 218 at 243–7; and the Decl. of the UN General Assembly of 1962, *supra*, p. 515.

[122] *Supra*, p. 536.

[123] See ICC, *Bilateral Treaties* for *International Investment* (1983); 51 *BY* (1980), 467–8; 52 *BY* (1981), 495–7; 53 *BY* (1982), 488; 54 *BY* (1983), 517–18; 55 *BY* (1984), 570–1; 56 *BY* (1985), 509–10; 57 *BY* (1986), 602–4. See further Mann, 52 *BY* (1981), 241–54; Schachter, 178 Hague *Recueil* (1982, V) 299; Dolzer, 75 *AJ* (1981), 565.

17. LEGAL DEVICES ADOPTED BY INVESTORS AND HOSTS TO FOREIGN CAPITAL

There is a large literature on the means of protecting foreign investment, and suggestions are made for the creation of multilateral investment codes.[124] In practice legal protection (apart from general international law) is based upon bilateral investment and aid agreements, guarantees to investors by the governments of capital-exporting states, and agreements between the investor and the recipient state. Investor states attempt to keep issues out of the national courts of the latter by appropriate clauses on jurisdiction in case of dispute and on choice of applicable law.[125] On the proposal of the World Bank an International Centre for the Settlement of Investment Disputes has been set up.[126] The Centre has jurisdiction over 'any legal dispute arising directly out of an investment, between a Contracting State (or any constituent subdivision or agency of a State designated to the Centre by that State) and a national of another Contracting State, which the parties to the dispute consent to in writing to submit to the Centre'. Investor governments, however, are not committed to the view that concession agreements involving recipient states and foreign corporations are 'international agreements' and not contracts of private law.[127] The Convention Establishing the Multilateral Investment Guarantee Agency (MIGA)[128] concerns, *inter alia*, the issuing of guarantees to investors against non-commercial risks.

States receiving foreign investment have long sought means of assimilating the foreign investor and their own nationals, and in treaties they seek to establish a standard of equal treatment or reciprocity. In making concession contracts with aliens, it has been the practice of Latin American governments to insert a 'Calvo clause', under which the alien agrees not to seek the diplomatic protection of his own state and submits matters arising from the contract to the local jurisdiction.[129] The majority of jurists

---

[124] See Fatouros, *Government Guarantees to Foreign Investors*; Snyder, 10 *ICLQ* (1961), 469–94; Gros, *Mélanges Rolin* (1964), 125–33; ILA, *Report of the Fifty-Second Conference* (1966), 819–60; *Report of the Fifty-Third Conference* (1968); 667–707; Schwarzenberger, *Foreign Investments and International Law* (1969); 71 *Harv. LR* (1958), 1102–22; Lillich, *The Protection of Foreign Investment*; Rubin, *Foreign Development Lending: Legal Aspects* (1971); Shihata, 203 Hague *Recueil* (1987, III), 95–320; Salem, 113 *JDI* (1986), 579–626; Dicke (ed.), *Foreign Investment in the Present and the New International Economic Order* (1987).

[125] See Sereni, 96 Hague *Recueil* (1959, I), 133–232; Spofford, 113 Hague *Recueil* (1964, III), 121–234; Metzger, 50 *Virginia LR* (1964), 594–627.

[126] Conv. on the Settlement of Investment Disputes between States and Nationals of Other States; opened for signature 18 Mar. 1965; in force 14 Oct. 1966; 4 *ILM* (1965), 532. As of 30 June 1998 there were 129 contracting states.

[127] See *infra*, pp. 546–50.

[128] Entered into force on 12 Apr. 1988. Text: 24 *ILM* (1985), 1598. See further Shihata, 203 Hague *Recueil* (1987, III), 95–320; id., *MIGA and Foreign Investment* (1987).

[129] See Lipstein, 22 *BY* (1945), 130–45; Shea, *The Calvo Clause* (1955); García Amador, *Yrbk. ILC* (1958), ii. 58–9; O'Connell, ii. 1059–66; Sørensen, pp. 590–3; Whiteman, viii. 916–33; Freeman, 40 *AJ* (1946), 121–47; Summers, 19 *Virginia LR* (1932–3), 459–84; Feller, *The Mexican Claims Commissions 1922–1934* (1935), 185–200; Graham, 6 *Texas Int. Law Forum* (1970–1), 289–308; Rogers, 72 *AJ* (1978), 1–16; Jiménez de Aréchaga, 159 Hague *Recueil* (1978, III), 309–10; Dolzer, 75 *AJ* (1981), 570–3; García Amador, *Max Planck*

and governments have hitherto denied the validity of such clauses, but international tribunals have since 1926 given them a degree of acceptance.[130] In principle, a clause in a contract of private law cannot deprive a state of the right of diplomatic protection or an international tribunal of jurisdiction. However, a tribunal may interpret the agreement which confers jurisdiction in such a way as to incorporate the clause, particularly where the alien contractor is seeking to use diplomatic protection as a means of avoiding his obligations. In any case the operation of the local remedies rule often makes the clause superfluous,[131] since, subject to what is said below, breach of a private law contract is not an international wrong and the right of diplomatic protection will arise only if there is a denial of justice in the course of exhausting remedies in the local courts.[132] The clause is not superfluous if the agreement conferring jurisdiction upon an international tribunal excludes the operation of the local remedies rule but incorporates by reference the effect of the Calvo clause (or is so interpreted). The practical effect of the clause in arbitrations has been to prevent contractual disputes being the object of diplomatic protection or inter-state proceedings in the absence of a denial of justice.

18. BREACHES AND ANNULMENT OF STATE CONTRACTS

Governments make contracts of various kinds with aliens or legal persons of foreign nationality: loan agreements (including the issue of state bonds), contracts for supplies and services, contracts of employment, agreements for operation of industrial and other patent rights under licence, agreements for the construction and operation of transport or telephone systems, agreements conferring the sole right, or some defined right, to exploit natural resources on payment of royalties, and exploration and production sharing agreements. Agreements involving resource exploitation are sometimes described as 'concession agreements', but there is no firm reason for regarding 'concession agreements' as a term of art or, assuming they can form a defined category, as being significantly different from other state contracts.[133] The contracting

Encyclopaedia, viii. 62–4; Rousseau, v. 203–8; International Law Commission, Dugard, Third Report, Add. 1, A/CN.4/523/Add.1, 16 April 2002; Paulsson, The Denial of Justice in International Law (2005), 20–4, 28–32. The 'clause' (there is no single type) is named after the Argentinian jurist responsible for the device. See further Agreement of Cartagena, Decision of Commission, no. 24, Dec. 1970, Common Regime on Foreign Investments, 11 Virginia Journ. of IL (1971), 264.

[130] See the North American Dredging Co. claim (1926), RIAA iv. 26; (American-Mexican Claims Commission); and comment in Sørensen, p. 592.

[131] The Calvo clause would not be superfluous in a case like the North American Dredging Co. claim (last note) since the Conv. by which the adjudicating Commission was constituted contained a specific waiver of the local remedies rule.

[132] On which, supra, p. 529.

[133] Some authorities insist on treating concessions as a special category, e.g. O'Connell, ii. 976–97. For another view: Sohn and Baxter, 55 AJ (1961), 566–7. On the position of bonds see Hyde, ii. 1005. See also Mann, 54 AJ (1960), at 589–90.

government may act in breach of contract, legislate in such a way as to make the contract worthless (for example, by export or currency restrictions), use its powers under domestic law to annul the contract, or repudiate the contract by means illegal in terms of the domestic law. What, then, is the position in terms of international law?

In principle, the position is regulated by the general principles governing the treatment of aliens. Thus, the act of the contracting government will entail state responsibility if, by itself or in combination with other circumstances, it constitutes a denial of justice (in the strict sense) or an expropriation contrary to international law. The general view[134] is that a breach of contract (as opposed to its confiscatory annulment) does not create state responsibility on the international plane. On this view the situation in which the state exercises its executive or legislative authority to destroy the contractual rights as an asset comes within the ambit of expropriation.[135] It follows that such action will lead to state responsibility in the same conditions as expropriation. Thus, it is often stated that the annulment is illegal if it is arbitrary and, or, discriminatory.[136] These terms cover two situations. First, action directed against persons of a particular nationality[137] or race is discriminatory. Secondly, action which lacks a normal public purpose is 'arbitrary'. A government acting in good faith may enact exchange control legislation or impose trade restrictions which incidentally (and without discrimination) lead to the annulment or non-enforceability of contractual rights. It is difficult to treat such action as illegal on the international plane.[138]

There is a school of thought which supports the view that the breach of a state contract by the contracting government of itself creates international responsibility.[139]

[134] Mann, 54 *AJ* (1960), 572–91 (also, *Studies in International Law* (1973), 302–26); Jessup, *A Modern Law of Nations* p. 104; id., 46 *Columbia LR* (1946), 913; Dunn, *The Protection of Nationals*, pp. 165–7, 171; Amerasinghe, 58 *AJ* (1964), 881–913; id., *State Responsibility*, pp. 66–120; Bishop, 115 Hague *Recueil*, 399–400; Hyde, *International Law* (2nd edn., 1947), ii. 988–90; Fitzmaurice, 37 *BY* (1961), 64–5, Borchard, *Diplomatic Protection*, ch. 7; Briggs, pp. 664–5; Eagleton, *Responsibility*, pp. 157–68; Metzger, 50 *Virginia LR* (1964), 607–8; Lipstein, 22 *BY* (1945), 134–5; Feller, *Mexican Claims Commissions*, p. 174; Foighel, *Nationalization and Compensation*, pp. 178–93; Petrén, 109 Hague *Recueil*, 523–4; Wengler, 76 *RGDIP* (1972), 313–45; Rigaux, 67 *Revue critique de d.i. privé* (1978), 435–59; Jiménez de Aréchaga, 159 Hague *Recueil* (1978, I), 305–6; Schachter, 178 Hague *Recueil* (1982, V), 309–12; Lalive, 181 Hague *Recueil* (1983, III), 9–284; Bowett, 59 *BY* (1988), 49–74; Oppenheim, ii. 927–9.

The position of O'Connell, ii. 976–1010, is broadly the same but concession contracts and bond obligations are treated as legally distinct categories. See further Fatouros, *Government Guarantees to Foreign Investors*, pp. 232–301.

[135] See the *Shufeldt Claim* (1930), *RIAA* ii. 1083; Wortley, *Expropriation*, pp. 55–7; White, *Nationalisation*, pp. 162–79; Schwebel, *Essays in Honour of Roberto Ago* (1987), iii. 401–13. Cf. *Feierabend Claim*, ILR 42, 157; *Hexner Claim*, ibid. 169. See also *Valentine Petroleum Arbitration* (1967), ILR 44, 79 at 85–91; *Texaco v. Libyan Government*, ILR 53, 389; *BP Exploration Company v. Libya*, ILR 53, 297; *Revere v. O.P.I.C.*, ILR 56, 258; *LIAMCO v. Libya*, ILR 62, 140. Cp. *Mobil Oil Iran Inc. v. Iran*, ILR 86, 230 at 274–6; *LETCO v. Government of the Republic of Liberia*, ILR 89, 313 at 337–8; *Amco Asia Corporation v. Republic of Indonesia* (Merits), ILR 89, 405 at 466–8.

[136] See e.g. Mann, 54 *AJ* (1960), 574–5; Sohn and Baxter, 55 *AJ* (1961), 566–70; Whiteman, viii. 933, 942.

[137] On this issue see *supra*, p. 538.

[138] Some authorities would regard this on the same basis as expropriation lawful *sub modo*; see White, *Nationalisation*, pp. 162–3, 178. Cf. also O'Connell, ii. 986–9; García Amador, *Yrbk. ILC* (1959), ii. 14–15, 24–36; Hyde, 105 Hague *Recueil* (1962, I), 322–3; the *LIAMCO* Award, *supra*, Pt. 3, V(6).

[139] See Harv. Research, 1929, Art. 8, 23 *AJ* (1929), Spec. Suppl., pp. 167–8 (but the comment considerably modifies the text); Carlston, 52 *AJ* (1958), 760–79; ILA, *Report of the Forty-Eighth Conference* (1958), 161.

Jennings[140] has argued persuasively (though with some deliberate caution) that there are no basic objections to the existence of an international law of contract. He points out that in the field of nationality, for example, rights created in municipal law may be evaluated according to international law standards. Again, the cases of contractual situations giving rise to denial of justice to be found in arbitral jurisprudence are treated as cases of contract when the issues of remedy and reparation are dealt with. Jennings also refers to the Calvo clause,[141] which, in so far as it has validity on the international plane, is not a mere question of domestic jurisdiction. Exponents of the international law character of state contracts also use arguments based upon the doctrine of acquired rights[142] and the principle of *pacta sunt servanda*, and refer to certain decisions of international tribunals.[143]

Apart from the merits of these arguments, it has to be recognized that there is little solid evidence that the position they tend to support corresponds to the existing law. The practice of the leading capital-exporting states, the United States[144] and the United Kingdom,[145] clearly requires some element, beyond the mere breach of contract, which would constitute a confiscatory taking or denial of justice *stricto sensu*. On analysis most of the arbitral decisions cited in support of the view that breach of contract by the contracting state is an international wrong are found not to be in point, either because the tribunal was not applying international law or because the decision rested on some element apart from the breach of contract.[146] There is no evidence that the principles of acquired rights and *pacta sunt servanda* have the particular consequences contended for. Exponents of acquired rights doctrine

See also Am. Law Inst., Restatement, Third, *Foreign Relations Law*, para. 712. O'Connell, ii. 993–4, comes close to this position in respect of concession contracts. See further *Annuaire de l'Inst.* (1952), ii. 318, and Schwebel, *Essays in Honour of Roberto Ago* (1987), iii. 401–13.

[140] 37 *BY* (1961), 156–82.

[141] *Supra.*

[142] See Jennings, 37 *BY* (1961), pp. 173–5, 177; O'Connell, ii. 984–5; Hyde, 105 Hague *Recueil* (1962, I) 315–18. The award in *Saudi Arabia v. Arabian-American Oil Co.* (*supra*, p. 535), referred to acquired rights as a 'fundamental principle'. See also McNair, 33 *BY* (1957), 1 at 16–18.

[143] e.g. the *Delagoa Bay Railway* case (*supra*, n. 77); *El Triunfo* claim (*supra*, n. 80); *Landreau* claim (ibid.); *Shufeldt* claim (ibid.); *Rudloff* case, *RIAA* ix. 244; and *Saudi Arabia v. Arabian-American Oil Co.* (*supra*, n. 80). See also the *Sapphire–N.I.O.C.* arbitration, ILR 35, 136; see Lalive, 13 *ICLQ* (1964), 987–1021; and *Texaco v. Libyan Government*, ILR 53, 389; 17 ILM (1978), 1; see Lalive, ibid. 319–49; Rigaux, 67 *Revue critique de d.i. privé* (1978), 435–59.

[144] Moore, *Digest*, vi. 705; Hackworth, v. 611; Whiteman, viii. 906–7. For a different view of the US position see Wetter, 29 *Univ. of Chicago LR* (1962), 275 at 305–22; Sohn and Baxter, 55 *AJ* (1961), 573.

[145] Pre-1900 items; McNair, *Opinions*, ii. 201–4; *British Digest*, vi. 358. See further *Anglo-Iranian Oil Co.* case, Pleadings, UK Memorial, pp. 83–6, 96–8; *Ambatielos* case, Pleadings, pp. 389, 475; *British Practice* (1966), 108–11. The position of France, the UK, and US on the nationalization of the Suez Canal Company by Egypt in 1956 rested on the special character of the Company as an 'international agency' and on the allegation of breaches of the Conv. of Constantinople: see 6 *ICLQ* (1957), 314; Whiteman, iii. 1084–130. However, compensation was paid to stockholders for the nationalization: E. Lauterpacht (ed.), *The Suez Canal Settlement* (1960).

[146] See Mann, 54 *AJ* (1960), 575–80; Amerasinghe, *State Responsibility*, pp. 77–84. The award in *Saudi Arabia v. Arabian-American Oil Co.* (*ut supra*, pp. 144–6) had a declaratory character as the principle of acquired rights had been recognized by both parties.

commonly give it a modified form which leaves room for exercise of local legislative competence. Moreover, if one is to apply general principles of municipal law then it becomes apparent the government contracts have a special status and in some systems lack enforceability.[147] It is a striking fact that in English law when the executive receives money paid over by a foreign government in settlement of contract claims (on an *ex gratia* or some other basis), the executive is under no legal duty to pay over the sums received to the private claimants. The arguments based upon acquired rights could be applied to a number of reliance situations created by the host state by the grant of public rights such as citizenship or permission to reside or to work. The distinction drawn by partisans of responsibility in contract situations between loan agreements, concessions, and other contracts is unsatisfactory. Why do they prefer their reasoning only in certain contract or reliance situations?

There is a further issue which requires consideration. In the proceedings arising from the Iranian cancellation of the 1933 Concession Agreement between the Iranian Government and the Anglo-Iranian Oil Company, the United Kingdom contended that violation of an explicit undertaking in a concession by the government party not to annul was illegal quite apart from the law relating to expropriation on payment of adequate compensation.[148] This view almost certainly does not represent the positive law but it is not without merit.[149] An undertaking not to annul by legislative action is a voluntary acceptance of risk comparable to the undertaking given by an alien in the form of a Calvo clause.

The rules of public international law accept the normal operation of rules of private international law and when a claim for breach of a contract between an alien and a government arises, the issue will be decided in accordance with the applicable system of municipal law designated by the rules of private international law. Further questions are raised if the parties to a state contract expressly choose an applicable law other than a particular system of local law, either 'general principles of law' or public international law.[150] A choice by the parties of public international law is assumed by some writers to place the contract on the international plane, but this cannot be correct since a state contract is not a treaty and cannot involve state responsibility as an international obligation.[151] In practice choice of law clauses in state contracts often

[147] Note also that decisions of English courts have upheld legislative abrogation of gold clauses: *R.* v. *International Trustee* [1937] AC 500. See also *Kahler* v. *Midland Bank* [1950] AC 24 and Mann, *The Legal Aspect of Money* (4th edn., 1971), 167–75, 290ff.

[148] UK Memorial, *Anglo-Iranian Oil Co.* case, Pleadings, pp. 86–93. See comment by Mann, 54 *AJ* (1960), 587; and cf. *Digest of US Practice* (1975), 489–90.

[149] A few writers give it support: White, *Nationalisation*, pp. 163, 175–9; O'Connell, ii. 993–4. See also *Radio Corporation of America* case, *RIAA* iii. 1621.

[150] See McNair, 33 *BY* (1957), 1–19; Sereni, 96 Hague *Recueil* (1959, I), 133–232; Mann, 35 *BY* (1959), 34–7; id., 42 *BY* (1967), 1–37; O'Connell, ii. 977–84, 990–1; Weil, 128 Hague *Recueil* (1969, III), 120–88; id., *Mélanges Reuter* (1981), 549–82; Greenwood, 53 *BY* (1982), 27–81; *Annuaire de l'Inst.* 57, i. 192–265; ibid. 58, ii. 192 (Resol.); Mann *et al.*, *Revue belge* (1975), 562–94; the *Abu Dhabi* arbitration, ILR 18 (1951), no. 37.

[151] *Annuaire de l'Inst.* 57, i. 246–7 (Report of van Hecke); Schachter, 178 Hague *Recueil* (1982, V), 301–9. For a different view: *Texaco Award*, ILR 53, 389, paras. 26, 46–8, 71, *per* Dupuy, sole arbitrator. See also Von Mehren and Kourides, 75 *AJ* (1981), 476–552.

specify the local law 'and such principles and rules of public international law as may be relevant', and in face of such clauses arbitrators have a certain discretion in selecting the precise role of public international law.[152] The tribunal in the case of *Aminoil* v. *Kuwait*[153] decided that by implication the choice of law was that of Kuwait, that public international law was a part of the law of Kuwait, and that in any event considerable significance was to be accorded to the 'legitimate expectations of the parties'.

Specialized standards are prescribed in the North American Free Trade Agreement. Thus Article 1105 provides that: 'Each Party shall accord to investments of investors of another Party treatment in accordance with international law, including fair and equitable treatment and full protection and security'.[154]

19. STABILIZATION CLAUSES[155]

The term 'stabilization clause' relates to any clause contained in an agreement between a government and a foreign legal entity by which the government party undertakes neither to annul the agreement nor to modify its terms, either by legislation or by administrative measures. The legal significance of such clauses is inevitably controversial, since the clause involves a tension between the legislative sovereignty and public interest of the state party and the long-term viability of the contractual relationship. If the position is taken that state contracts are, in categorical terms, valid on the plane of public international law (see the discussion *supra*), then it follows that a breach of such a clause is unlawful and to be compensated as a form of expropriation.[156] Another view is that stabilization clauses as such are invalid in terms of public international law as a consequence of the principle of permanent sovereignty over natural resources.[157]

In general the problem calls for careful classification. If a state party to a contract effects an annulment this may, depending on the circumstances, constitute an

---

[152] See *B.P. Exploration Company* v. *Libya*, ILR 53, 297; *Texaco* v. *Libya*, ibid. 389; *LIAMCO* v. *Libya*, ILR 62, 140; *AGIP* v. *Congo*, ILR 67, 318; *Benvenuti and Bonfant* v. *Congo*, ibid. 345.

[153] ILR 66, 518. For comment: Mann, 54 *BY* (1983), 213–21; Redfern, 55 *BY* (1984), 65–110.

[154] See *S.D. Myers, Inc.* v. *Canada*, ILR 121, 72, NAFTA Arbitration Tribunal; *Page and Talbot, Inc.* v. *Canada*, ILR 122 (the same); *Mondev* v. *United States of America*, 125, 99 at pp. 139–63. See also Brower and others, *ASIL Proceedings* (2002), 9–22.

[155] See generally: Weil, 128 Hague *Recueil* (1969, III), 229–34; id., *Mélanges offerts à Charles Rousseau* (1974), 301–28; Jiménez de Aréchaga, 159 Hague *Recueil* (1978, I), 307–9; Schachter, 178 Hague *Recueil* (1982, V), 313–14; Higgins, 176 Hague *Recueil* (1982, III), 298–314; Greenwood, 53 *BY* (1982), 60–4; Lalive, 181 Hague *Recueil* (1983, III), 56–61, 147–62; Redfern, 55 *BY* (1984), 98–105; Paasivirta, 60 *BY* (1989), 315–50.

[156] See the view of the sole arbitrator in *Texaco* v. *Libya*, ILR 53, 389 at 494–5. In the *LIAMCO* case, ILR 62, 140 at 196–7, the sole arbitrator held that breach of a stabilization clause was lawful but gave rise to a right to receive an equitable indemnity. The issue was not considered in the *B.P.* Award. See also *Revere* v. *OPIC*, ILR 56, 258 at p. 278–94; Weil, *Mélanges oerts à Charles Rousseau*, pp. 301–28.

[157] See Jiménez de Aréchaga, 159 Hague *Recueil* (1978, I), 297–8, 307–9. See also Rosenberg, *Le Principe de souveraineté*, pp. 297–332.

expropriation: and the legality of the annulment will then depend on the general principles relating to expropriation (see *supra*). The legal position will not, on this view, depend upon the existence of a stabilization clause. If there is a provision for arbitration, then the issue will be governed either by the express choice of law (if there is one) or by the choice of law derived by a process of interpretation. If the choice of law involves elements of public international law, the arbitral tribunal will then approach the stabilization clause in the light of all the relevant circumstances, includ- ing the history of the relationship, the conduct of the parties, and the reasonable expectations of the parties.[158] It is to be noted that the tribunal in the *Aminoil* case adopted the view that stabilization clauses were not prohibited by international law, but gave a cautious interpretation to the particular undertaking in question. Thus, such a clause could operate but only in respect of 'nationalisation during a limited period of time'. In the instant case, the clause could not be presumed to exclude nationalization for a period of 60 years.[159]

---

[158] See the majority Award in the *Aminoil* case, ILR 66, 518, paras. 90–101. In his Sep. Op., Sir Gerald Fitzmaurice stated that the stabilization clauses rendered the expropriation (in effect) unlawful (see the Opinion, paras. 19–20). See further Mann, 54 *BY* (1983), 213–21; Redfern, 55 *BY* (1984), 98–105.

[159] Award, paras. 90–101, and paras. 94–5, in particular.

25

THE PROTECTION OF
INDIVIDUALS AND GROUPS:
HUMAN RIGHTS AND
SELF-DETERMINATION

1. INTRODUCTION: THE APPLICABLE LAW

The events of the Second World War and concern to prevent a recurrence of catastrophes associated with the policies of the Axis Powers led to increased concern for the legal and social protection of human rights and fundamental freedoms. A notable pioneer in the field was Hersch Lauterpacht, who stressed the need for an International Bill of the Rights of Man.[1] The provisions of the United Nations Charter also provided a basis for the development of the law. The more important results of the drive to protect human rights will be recorded in due course, but at the outset some comment may be made on the forms assumed by the campaign. Inevitably it has carried to the international forum the ideologies and concepts of freedom of the various leading states, and ideological differences have influenced the debates.

Human rights is a broad area of concern and the potential subject matter ranges from the questions of torture and fair trial to the so-called third generation of rights, which includes the right to economic development and the right to health.

---

[1] See Lauterpacht, *International Law and Human Rights*; id. *An International Bill of the Rights of Man* (1945). See further Robertson and Merrills, *Human Rights in the World* (4th edn., 1996); Brownlie and Goodwin-Gill (eds.), *Human Rights* (5th edn., 2006); UN, *Human Rights: A Compilation of International Instruments*, i (1994); ii (1997); Higgins, 48 BY (1976–7), 281–320; Humphrey, in Bos (ed.), *The Present State of International Law* (1973), 75–105; McDougal, Lasswell, and Chen, *Human Rights and World Public Order* (1980); Henkin (ed.), *The International Bill of Rights: The Covenant on Civil and Political Rights* (1981); Meron (ed.), *Human Rights in International Law*, 2 vols. (1984); id., *Human Rights Law-Making in the United Nations* (1986); Buergenthal, *International Human Rights* (1988); McGoldrick, *The Human Rights Committee* (1991); Oppenheim, ii. 983–1030; Alston, *The United Nations and Human Rights* (1992); Clapham, *Human Rights in the Private Sphere* (1993); Craven, *The International Covenant on Economic, Social and Cultural Rights* (1995); Loucaides, *Essays on the Developing Law of Human Rights* (1995); Provost, *International Human Rights and Humanitarian Law* (2002); Baderin, *International Human Rights and Islamic Law* (2003).

Many lawyers in academic life refer to an entity described as 'International Human Rights Law' which is assumed to be a separate body of norms. While this is a convenient category of reference, it is also a source of confusion. Human rights problems occur in specific legal contexts. The issues may arise in domestic law, or within the framework of a standard-setting convention, or within general international law. But there must be reference to the specific and relevant applicable law. There is thus the law of a particular State, *or* the principles of the European Convention on Human Rights, *or* the relevant principles of general international law. In the real world of practice and procedure, there is no such entity as 'International Human Rights Law'.

2. THE HISTORICAL PERSPECTIVE

The appearance of human rights in the sphere of international law and organizations is often traced to the era of the League Covenant of 1919, and the Minorities Treaties and League of Nations mandated areas which were associated with the Covenant. There can be no question that the Minorities Treaties, in particular, constituted an important stage in the recognition of human rights standards and provided 'an instrument of supervision in the interest alike of the individual and of international peace'.[2]

The emphasis upon the League Covenant and the Minorities Treaties of 1919–1920 is in fact misplaced. Neither the Mandates system nor the Minorities regimes were representative in character. The League Covenant did not contain a general minorities clause. Amongst the proposals which were discarded was the following Japanese amendment:

The equality of nations being a basic principle of the League of Nations, the High Contracting Parties agree to accord as soon as possible to all aliens nationals of states members of the League equal and just treatment in every respect making no distinction either in law or fact on account of their race or nationality.[3]

The Minorities Treaties at least presented a model, even if the model was applied selectively. The idea of universal human rights awaited the wartime planning in the United States relating to post-war organization, and a draft bill of rights was prepared as early as December 1942.[4]

Although its work may appear specialized, the International Labour Organization (ILO), created in 1919, has in fact for four generations done an immense quantity of work towards giving practical expression to a number of very important human rights and towards establishing standards of treatment. Its agenda has included forced labour,

---

[2] *Oppenheim's International Law*, ed. H. Lauterpacht, i, (8th edn., 1955), 715–16.

[3] David Hunter Miller, *The Drafting of the League Covenant* (New York, 1928), ii. 229 at 323–5. See also McKean, *Equality and Discrimination under International Law* (Oxford, 1983), 14–26.

[4] Russell and Muther, *A History of the United Nations Charter* (Washington, DC, The Brookings Institution, 1958), 323–9, 777–89.

freedom of association, discrimination in employment, equal pay, social security, and the right to work.[5] The ILO's Constitution has a tripartite character, and there is separate representation of employers and workers, as well as governments, in the Governing Body and in the General Conference. In addition, there are provisions for union and employer organizations to make representations and complaints. This constitutional procedure was augmented in 1949 when the ILO Governing Body established a fact-finding and conciliation commission on freedom of association.[6]

The procedure for enforcement of ILO conventions is important. The Constitution requires member States to make separate annual reports upon the measures taken by them to give effect to conventions adopted by it, and these reports are examined closely by a committee of experts, which may raise questions with the governments concerned. A member State may file a complaint with the International Labour Office if it is dissatisfied with another member's observance of a convention by which it is bound. The complaint may be referred to a commission of inquiry, and any government concerned in the complaint may refer the findings of the commission to the International Court of Justice. In February 1962 the first commission of inquiry reported, having been appointed upon a complaint by Ghana against Portugal alleging the existence of forced labour in Portuguese African territories contrary to the Convention Concerning the Abolition of Forced Labour of 1957.[7] It is clear that such inquiries have a judicial aspect, and the composition of the commission just referred to reinforces this view.[8] Moreover, the breadth of subject-matter open to inquiry in this manner indicates a considerable erosion of domestic jurisdiction.

3. HUMAN RIGHTS AND THE CHARTER OF THE UNITED NATIONS

The United Nations Charter provides the base line of human rights. The issue of human rights is directly addressed and the Charter, for the first time, employs the terminology of human rights.

---

[5] See Jenks, *The International Protection of Trade Union Freedom* (1957); id., *Human Rights and International Labour Standards* (1960); id., *Social Justice in the Law of Nations* (1970); *The I.L.O. and Human Rights* (Report of the Director-General (Pt. I) to the International Labour Conference, Fifty-second Session, 1968); Brownlie and Goodwin-Gill, *Human Rights*, 497–591; McNair, *The Expansion of International Law* (1962), 29–52; International Labour Office, *The Impact of International Labour Conventions and Recommendations* (1976); Wolf in Meron (ed.), *Human Rights in International Law*, ii. 273–305; Bernhardt, *Encyclopedia* II (1995), 1150–56.

[6] See Nørgaard, *Position of the Individual*, at 139–58.

[7] 45 ILO Official Bull., no. 2, Supp. no. II (1962); ILR 35, 285. Both governments accepted the findings. For a further inquiry into a Portuguese complaint against Liberia: 46 ILO Official Bull., no. 2, Supp. No. II (1963); ILR 36, 351. See also Vignes, *Ann. Français* (1963), 438–59; Osieke, 47 *BY* (1974–5), 315–40; Valticos, *Essays in Honour of Roberto Ago*, ii (1987), 505–21. Other inquiries (involving freedom of association) related to Poland (1982) and the German Federal Republic (1985).

[8] See *South West Africa* cases, ICJ Reports (1962), 427–8 (Sep. Op. of Judge Jessup).

In the preamble the members 'reaffirm faith in fundamental human rights, in the equal rights of men and women...'. Article I defines the purpose of the United Nations to include co-operation 'in promoting and encouraging respect for human rights and for fundamental freedoms for all without distinction as to race, sex, language, or religion'. Of key importance is Article 55, which states that 'the United Nations shall promote: (a) higher standards of living, full employment, and conditions of economic and social progress and development.... (c) universal respect for, and observance of, human rights and fundamental freedoms for all...'. Article 56 provides: 'All Members pledge themselves to take joint and separate action in co-operation with the Organization for the achievement of the purposes set forth in Article 55'.[9]

As treaty provisions applicable both to the Organization and its members these prescriptions are of paramount importance. Article 55 is perhaps oblique—the United Nations 'shall promote'. However, Article 56 is stronger and involves the members; and the political and judicial organs of the United Nations have interpreted the provisions as a whole to constitute legal obligations.[10] Two possible sources of weakness require notice. First, the legal obligation is general in provenance, and work has gone forward to supplement the Charter by the adoption of covenants giving more specific content to the rights protected, and providing more sophisticated enforcement procedures. Thus, while it may be doubtful whether states can be called to account for every alleged infringement of the rather general Charter provisions, there can be little doubt that responsibility exists under the Charter for any substantial infringement of the provisions, especially when a class of persons, or a pattern of activity, is involved.

The second source of weakness is the absence of precise definition. If the intention of the draftsman is respected, it will be clear that the concept of human rights has a core of reasonable certainty. Moreover, in 1948, the General Assembly adopted a Universal Declaration of Human Rights[11] which is comprehensive and has to some extent affected the content of national law. The Declaration has been expressly invoked by domestic courts.[12]

The political organs of the United Nations have been prepared to exercise a general power of investigation and supervision in this field,[13] but there is a lack of specific machinery for dealing with complaints. The existing agencies have difficulty in

---

[9] Other references to human rights exist in Arts. 62, 68, and 76. Art. 76 refers to the encouragement of respect for human rights in stating the basic objectives of the trusteeship system. Where attempts were made by private individuals in the United States to invoke the provisions of Arts. 55 and 56, relief was denied on the basis that the Charter, while binding on the United States as a treaty, was not self-executing. See *Rice* v. *Sioux City Memorial Park Cemetery, Inc.*, 245 Iowa 147, 60 NW 2d 110 (1953), ILR 20 (1953), 244; *Fujii* v. *State of California*, 28 Cal. 2d 718, 242 P. 2d 617 (1952), ILR 19 (1952), 312; *Comacho* v. *Rogers*, 199 F. Suppl. 155 (1961); ILR 32, 368. See further *Re Drummond Wren* (1945), 3 DLR 674, *Ann. Digest*, 12 (1943–5), no. 50; *Re Noble and Wolfe* (1948), 4 DLR 123; (1949), 4 DLR 475; (1951), I DLR 321; *Ann. Digest*, 16 (1949), no. 100; *Oyama* v. *State of California* (1948), 332 US 633; *Ann. Digest*, 16 (1949), no. 79.

[10] See the Adv. Op. on Namibia: ICJ Reports (1971), at 56–7. See further Schwelb, 66 *AJ* (1972), 337–51.

[11] Whiteman, v. 237; Brownlie, *Documents*, 192; id., *Basic Documents on Human Rights* (5th edn. (2006), 23). See Oppenheim, ii. 744–6; Waldock, 106 Hague *Recueil* (1962, II), 198–9.

[12] See below.

[13] In practice, Art. 2(7) of the Charter has not been very restrictive.

dealing with particular cases; discussion normally centres on political implications rather than settlement of actual cases. Nevertheless publicity, fact-finding machinery, and other 'measures' under Article 14 of the Charter can achieve useful objectives. Article 14 provides:

Subject to the provisions of Article 12, the General Assembly may recommend measures for the peaceful adjustment of any situation, regardless of origin, which it deems likely to impair the general welfare or friendly relations among nations, including situations resulting from a violation of the provisions of the present Charter setting forth the Purposes and Principles of the United Nations.

For long the nearest approach to permanent machinery for supervision of the problem of protection is the Commission on Human Rights set up by the Economic and Social Council in 1946. The Commission, however, with the approval of the Economic and Social Council, early on decided that it had no power to take any action in regard to any complaints concerning human rights. The Commission receives thousands of private communications, which are in substance complaints, and the governments concerned are invited to reply, after being given an indication of the nature of the complaint.[14] The principal functions of the Commission have included the preparation of the texts of the Universal Declaration, the Convention on the Political Rights of Women, and draft covenants supplementing the Universal Declaration.[15] Since 1967 (under the 1235 Procedure) the Commission has established investigatory procedures in respect of country-specific complaints of gross violations.[16]

In 2006 growing unease with the way in which the Commission functioned led to its replacement by the Human Rights Council, consisting of 47 Member States.[17] In Resolution 60/251, adopted on 15 March 2006, the General Assembly made the following principal dispositions:

1. *Decides* to establish the Human Rights Council, based in Geneva, in replacement of the Commission on Human Rights, as a subsidiary organ of the General Assembly; the Assembly shall review the status of the Council within five years;

2. *Decides* that the Council shall be responsible for promoting universal respect for the protection of all human rights and fundamental freedoms for all, without distinction of any kind and in a fair and equal manner;

---

[14] The complainant's identity is not divulged. See generally Nørgaard, *Position of the Individual*, 104–7. See also Art. 64 of the Charter for the power of the Economic and Social Council to obtain reports from members on progress in the field of human rights.

[15] See further Humphrey, *René Cassin: Amicorum Discipulorumque Liber I* (1969), 108; id., 62 AJ (1968), 869–88; ILA, *Report of the Fifty-Fifth Conference* (1972), 571–8; Marie, *La Commission des Droits de l'Homme de l'ONU* (1975).

[16] See Alston (ed.), *The United Nations and Human Rights* (1992), 126–210 (an excellent account). See, for example, Draft Report of the Commission to the Economic and Social Council, Fifty-Ninth Session of the Commission, E/CN.4/2003/L.11 (and Addenda).

[17] See U.N. Doc A/RES/60/251, 3 April 2006; U.N. General Assembly, G.A./10449, Dept. of Public Information, 15 March 2005; U.K. Foreign and Commonwealth Office, Written Answer, 26 June 2006, 77 BY (2006), 726; Ghanea, *ICLQ*, 55 (2006), 695–705; *A.J.*, 100 (2006), 697–9. There were four votes against the resolution: the United States, Israel, Marshall Islands and Palau.

3. *Decides also* that the Council should address situations of violations of human rights, including gross and systematic violations, and make recommendations thereon. It should also promote the effective coordination and the mainstreaming of human rights within the United Nations system;

4. *Decides further* that the work of the Council shall be guided by the principles of universality, impartiality, objectivity and non-selectivity, constructive international dialogue and cooperation, with a view to enhancing the promotion and protection of all human rights, civil, political, economic, social and cultural rights, including the right to development;...

The Council has a duty to submit an annual report to the General Assembly and is mandated to assume and review all the responsibilities of the Commission on Human Rights with the purpose, *inter alia*, of maintaining a complaint procedure.

4. ACTION AUTHORISED BY THE SECURITY COUNCIL TO PREVENT OR AMELIORATE HUMANITARIAN CRISES

The General Assembly of the United Nations lacks enforcement powers under the Charter, although it can recommend the application of sanctions. Nonetheless it has not infrequently expressed concern about human rights issues, including the human rights aspects of the Peace Treaties with Bulgaria, Hungary, and Romania (1948), the situation in Rhodesia (1962), the situation in the Portugese colonies (1965), the treatment of the Palestinian population of the Occupied Territories (1968), and the treatment of Kurdish Refugees in Iraq (1991).

The Security Council was unable to act effectively, prior to the end of the Cold War, because of the veto, but did use its powers of investigation under Chapter VI from time to time, as in relation to the situation arising in South Africa (1960). In the period after 1990 the Council began to use its powers in respect of peacekeeping (and on the basis of Chapter VII of the Charter), to ensure the provision of humanitarian assistance, as in the case of Somalia in 1992.[18] Extensive operations were undertaken in Bosnia in 1993 with the stated purpose of delivering humanitarian assistance. The mandate also included the creation of safe areas and the power to use force to protect UN-established safe areas. These various operations were based upon powers delegated to member States by the Security Council. In 1994 the Council authorized certain member States, on a short-term basis, to establish a safe haven in Rwanda for the protection of displaced persons, refugees, and civilians at risk.

---

[18] See Sarooshi, *The United Nations and the Development of Collective Security* (1999), 210–29; Gray, *International Law and the Use of Force* (2000), 153–99; Chesterman, *Just War or Just Peace?* (2001), 127–218; Ramcharan, *The Security Council and the Protection of Human Rights* (2002).

5. STANDARD-SETTING: MULTILATERAL NON-BINDING INSTRUMENTS

It is true to say that the more or less generalized references to human rights in the Charter left much to be done and the United Nations organs embarked upon an extended programme of codification which eventually resulted in the two International Covenants and other multilateral standard-setting conventions. The importance of such multilateral treaties goes without saying, but in historical sequence it was a non-binding instrument which surfaced before the International Covenants, the Universal Declaration of Human Rights adopted by the General Assembly of the United Nations on 10 December 1948. Another non-binding instrument, the Helsinki Final Act (1 August 1975), was also to have considerable significance in practice.

The two instruments have particular interest for lawyers because they demonstrate that the normative impact of an instrument does not necessarily depend upon its formal legal status.

(i) THE UNIVERSAL DECLARATION OF HUMAN RIGHTS, 1948[19]

In 1948, the General Assembly adopted a Universal Declaration of Human Rights which is comprehensive and has to some extent affected the content of national law, being expressly invoked by tribunals.[20] The Declaration is not a legal instrument, and some of its provisions, for example the reference to a right of asylum, could hardly be said to represent legal rules. On the other hand, some of its provisions either constitute general principles of law or represent elementary considerations of humanity.[21] Perhaps its greatest significance is that it provides an authoritative guide, produced by the General Assembly, to the interpretation of the provisions in the Charter.[22] No doubt there is an area of ambiguity, but the indirect legal effect of the Declaration is not to be underestimated, and it is frequently regarded as a part of the 'law of the United Nations'.[23] The Declaration has been invoked by the European Court of Human Rights, as an aid to

---

[19] Whiteman, v. 237; Brownlie and Goodwin-Gill, *Human Rights* (5th edn., 2006), 23. See Oppenheim, ii. 744–6; Waldock, 106 Hague *Recueil* (1962, II), 198–9.

[20] e.g. *In re Flesche, Ann. Digest* (1949), at 269; *The State (Duggan)* v. *Tapley, ILR* 18 (1951), at 342; *Robinson* v. *Sec-Gen. of the U.N., ILR* 19 (1952), at 496 (UN Admn. Trib.); *Extradition of Greek Nationals* case, ILR 22 (1955), at 524; *Beth-El Mission* v. *Minister of Social Welfare,* ILR 47, 205; *Artzet* v. *Secretary-General of the Council of Europe (No. 1),* ILR 51, 438 at 444; *Waddington* v. *Miah,* ILR 57, 175 at 177; *Iranian Naturalization* case, ILR 60, 204 AT 207; *M.* v. *United Nations and Belgium,* ILR 69, 139 AT 142–3; *Police* v. *Labat,* ILR 70, 191 at 203; *Basic Right to Marry* case, ILR 72, 295 at 298. See further Skubiszewski, 2 *Polish Yrbk.,* 99–105 and Hannum, *26 Ga. J. Int. & Comp. L.* (1995–6), 287–397.

[21] Cf. *Corfu Channel* case (Merits), ICJ Reports (1949).

[22] See Waldock, 106 Hague *Recueil* (1962, II), 199. But see Oppenheim, ii. 745.

[23] See Schwelb, 66 *AJ* (1972), at 673–5; and Waldock, *ICLQ,* Suppl. Public. No. II (1965), at 14. See also Security Council Resol. 310 (1972); comment by Schwelb, 22 *ICLQ* (1973), 161–3.

interpretation of the European Convention of Human Rights,[24] and by the International Court in relation to the detention of hostages 'in conditions of hardship'.[25]

The Declaration is a good example of an informal prescription given legal significance by the actions of authoritative decision-makers, and thus it has been used as a standard reference in the Helsinki Declaration, the second of the 'non-binding' instruments which have been of considerable importance in practice.

(II) THE HELSINKI FINAL ACT, 1975[26]

On 1 August 1975 there was adopted the Final Act of the Conference on Security and Co-operation in Europe in Helsinki. This contains a declaration of principles under the heading 'Questions Relating to Security in Europe'. The Final Act was signed by the representatives of 35 States, including the United States and the USSR.

The document was obviously not in treaty form, and therefore not legally binding as such. The United States, along with other signatories, affirmed that the instrument was not legally binding.[27] At the same time the document constitutes evidence of the acceptance by the participating States of certain principles as principles of customary or general international law, including the standards of human rights.

The significance of the Helsinki Final Act was recognized by the International Court in its Judgment on the merits in *Nicaragua* v. *United States*. In the words of the Court:

Also significant is United States acceptance of the principle of the prohibition of the use of force which is contained in the declaration on principles governing the mutual relations of States participating in the Conference on Security and Co-operation in Europe (Helsinki, 1 August 1975), whereby the participating States undertake to 'refrain in their mutual relations, *as well as in their international relations in general*', from the threat or use of force. Acceptance of a text in these terms confirms the existence of an *opinio juris* of the participating States prohibiting the use of force in international relations.[28]

(III) THE PARIS CHARTER, 1990[29]

In this Declaration the participating States in the Conference on Security and Cooperation in Europe (34 in all) reaffirmed their commitment to the principles of the Helsinki Final Act.

---

[24] *Golder* case, ILR 57, 201 at 216–17.
[25] *Case Concerning United States Diplomatic and Consular Staff in Tehran*, ICJ Reports (1980), 3 at 42 (para. 91).
[26] Brownlie and Goodwin-Gill (2006), 817.
[27] United States Department of State, *Digest of United States Practice in International Law*, 1975, USGPO, Washington, DC, 325–7.
[28] *ICJ Reports 1986*, 100, para. 189, emphasis added; and see also 133, para. 264.
[29] Brownlie and Goodwin-Gill, *Human Rights* (5th edn., 2006), 866.

(IV) ILO DECLARATION ON FUNDAMENTAL PRINCIPLES AND RIGHTS AT WORK 1998[30]

The key provisions of the Declaration are as follows:

The International Labour Conference
1. Recalls:
   (a) that in freely joining the ILO, all Members have endorsed the principles and rights set out in its Constitution and in the Declaration of Philadelphia, and have undertaken to work towards attaining the overall objectives of the Organization to the best of their resources and fully in line with their specific circumstances;
   (b) that these principles and rights have been expressed and developed in the form of specific rights and obligations in Conventions recognized as fundamental both inside and outside the Organization.

2. Declares that all Members, even if they have not ratified the Conventions in question, have an obligation arising from the very fact of membership in the Organization to respect, to promote and to realize, in good faith and in accordance with the Constitution, the principles concerning the fundamental rights which are the subject of those Conventions, namely:
   (a) freedom of association and the effective recognition of the right to collective bargaining;
   (b) the elimination of all forms of forced or compulsory labour;
   (c) the effective abolition of child labour; and
   (d) the elimination of discrimination in respect of employment and occupation.

3. Recognizes the obligation on the Organization to assist its Members, in response to their established and expressed needs, in order to attain these objectives by making full use of its constitutional, operational and budgetary resources, including, by the mobilization of external resources and support, as well as by encouraging other international organizations with which the ILO has established relations, pursuant to Article 12 of its Constitution, to support these efforts:
   (a) by offering technical cooperation and advisory services to promote the ratification and implementation of the fundamental Conventions;
   (b) by assisting those Members not yet in a position to ratify some or all of these Conventions in their efforts to respect, to promote and to realize the principles concerning fundamental rights which are the subject of these Conventions; and
   (c) by helping the Members in their efforts to create a climate for economic and social development.

These provisions recognize that ILO Members generally have an obligation to respect 'in good faith and in accordance with the Constitution, the principles concerning the fundamental rights' which are the subject of the ILO Conventions, even in the absence of ratification.

---

[30] Brownlie and Goodwin-Gill, *Human Rights* (5th edn., 2006), 570. For comment see Alston, *Europ. Journ.*, Vol.15 (2004), 457–521 and Alston, *Europ. Journ.*, 16 (2005), 467–80; Langille, ibid., 409–37; Maupain, 439–65.

6. STANDARD-SETTING: BINDING MULTILATERAL CONVENTIONS

There can be no doubt that the main corpus of human rights standards consists of an accumulated code of multilateral standard-setting conventions. These fall into four general categories. First of all, the two comprehensive International Covenants on Economic, Social and Cultural Rights and on Civil and Political Rights adopted in 1966. Secondly, the comprehensive regional conventions: the European Convention on Human Rights of 1950, the American Convention on Human Rights of 1969, and the African Charter on Human and Peoples' Rights of 1981. Thirdly, the conventions dealing with specific wrongs, such as genocide, torture, or racial discrimination. Fourthly, the conventions related to the protection of particular categories of people: women, children, refugees, and migrant workers.

The classical and still general method of enforcement is by means of the duty of performance of treaty undertakings imposed on the States Parties. It is the domestic legal systems of the States Parties to the given convention which are the vehicles of implementation. Thus the International Covenant on Civil and Political Rights contains express provisions setting forth the duty to ensure that domestic law provides sufficient means of maintenance of the treaty standards. It is also a characteristic of such treaties that the means of implementation of the treaty provisions are a matter of domestic jurisdiction. In this context it is helpful to recall the remonstrance of Sir Robert Jennings that it is a mistake to think of domestic jurisdiction in '"either/or" terms'.[31]

It is also normal to impose monitoring mechanisms in the form of a duty to submit reports and to create an optional competence to consider communications from individuals who claim to be victims of a violation by a State Party of any of the rights set forth in the relevant standard-setting convention. This is the system adopted in respect of the International Covenant on Civil and Political Rights and its Optional Protocol.

7. CUSTOMARY OR GENERAL INTERNATIONAL LAW

The vast majority of States and authoritative writers would now recognize that the fundamental principles of human rights form part of customary or general international law, although they would not necessarily agree on the identity of the fundamental principles. In 1970 the International Court, delivering judgment in the *Barcelona*

---

[31] 'General Course on Principles of International Law', *Recueil des cours*, Vol. 121 (1967–II), 502.

Traction case, referred to obligations *erga omnes* in contemporary international law, and these were stated to include 'the principles and rules concerning the basic rights of the human person, including protection from slavery and racial discrimination'.[32] The Final Act of the Helsinki Conference of 1975[33] included a 'Declaration of Principles Guiding Relations between Participating States'. This Declaration includes a section on human rights and the following paragraph appears in that section:

In the field of human rights and fundamental freedoms, the participating States will act in conformity with the purposes and principles of the Charter of the United Nations and with the Universal Declaration of Human Rights. They will also fulfil their obligations as set forth in the international declarations and agreements in this field, including *inter alia* the International Covenants on Human Rights, by which they may be bound.

It is evident that the participating States recognize that human rights standards form part of general international law: thus the *Digest of United States Practice in International Law*[34] sets forth the Declaration referred to in the previous paragraph under the heading: 'Rights and Duties of States'.

The significance of the role of the 'customary international law of human rights' is recognized in the most recent edition of the *Restatement of the Law: The Third*. Under the rubric just quoted the following proposition appears:

A State violates international law if, as a matter of State policy, it practices, encourages, or condones
  (1) genocide
  (2) slavery or slave trade,
  (3) the murder or causing the disappearance of individuals,
  (4) torture or other cruel, inhuman or degrading treatment or punishment,
  (5) prolonged arbitrary detention,
  (6) systematic racial discrimination, or
  (7) a consistent pattern of gross violations of internationally recognised human rights.[35]

The literature of human rights tends to neglect the role of customary law. There are, however, illustrious exceptions among whom are Professors Schachter[36] and Meron.[37]

In the case concerning *Legal Consequences of the Construction of a Wall in the Occupied Palestinian Territory*, the International Court of Justice in its Advisory Opinion found that the construction of the wall by Israel, the occupying power, in the Occupied Palestinian Territory, and the associated regime, 'are contrary to international law'. In approaching the issues raised by the request from the General

---

[32] ICJ Reports (1970), 3 at 32.

[33] Brownlie and Goodwin-Gill (5th edn., 2006), 817.

[34] United States Department of State, *Digest of United States Practice in International Law* (1975), 7.

[35] American Law Institute, *Restatement of the Law, the Third, the Foreign Relations Law of the United States*, 1987, Vol. 2, 161, para. 702.

[36] Schachter, *Recueil des cours*, Vol. 178 (1982–V), 333–8.

[37] Meron, *Human Rights and Humanitarian Norms as Customary International Law* (Oxford, 1989).

Assembly for an advisory opinion, the Court first determined the sources of the applicable law. In its view:[38]

The Court will now determine the rules and principles of international law which are relevant in assessing the legality of the measures taken by Israel. Such rules and principles can be found in the United Nations Charter and certain other treaties, in customary international law and in the relevant resolutions adopted pursuant to the Charter by the General Assembly and the Security Council. However, doubts have been expressed by Israel as to the applicability in the Occupied Palestinian Territory of certain rules of international humanitarian law and human rights instruments. The Court will now consider these various questions.

In resolving certain questions raised by Israel, the Court had recourse to various aspects of customary international law concerning the substance of international humanitarian law.[39] Considerations of general international law were also relied upon in determining that the United Nations Covenants of 1966 apply both to individuals present within a State's territory and to individuals outside that territory but subject to that State's jurisdiction.[40]

8. THE GENERAL PRINCIPLES OF HUMANITARIAN LAW

In the *Nicaragua* case the International Court at the Merits phase applied 'general principles of humanitarian law', based upon Article 3 common to the four Geneva Conventions, to the armed conflict inside Nicaragua in so far as the acts of the United States were concerned. In the words of the Judgment:

The Court however sees no need to take a position on that matter since in its view the conduct of the United States may be judged according to the fundamental general principles of humanitarian law; in its view, the Geneva Conventions are in some respects a development, and in other respects no more than the expression, of such principles. It is significant in this respect that, according to the terms of the Conventions, the denunciation of one of them

> shall in no way impair the obligations which the Parties to the conflict shall remain bound to fulfil by virtue of the principles of the law of nations, as they result from the usages established among civilized peoples, from the law of humanity and the dictates of the public conscience (Convention I, Art. 63; Convention II, Art. 62; Convention III, Art. 142; Convention IV, Art. 158).

Article 3 which is common to all four Geneva Conventions of 12 August 1949 defines certain rules to be applied in the armed conflicts of a non-international character. There is no doubt

---

[38] ICJ Reports (2004), 136 at 171, para. 86.
[39] Ibid., 172–7, paras. 89–101.
[40] Ibid., 177–81, paras. 102–13.

that, in the event of international armed conflicts, these rules also constitute a minimum yardstick, in addition to the more elaborate rules which are also to apply to international conflicts; and they are rules which, in the Court's opinion, reflect what the Court in 1949 called 'elementary considerations of humanity' (*Corfu Channel, Merits, I.C.J. Reports 1949*, p. 22; paragraph 215 above). The Court may therefore find them applicable to the present dispute, and is thus not required to decide what role the United States multilateral treaty reservation might otherwise play in regard to the treaties in question.[41]

In the result the phrase 'general principles of humanitarian law' appears in six passages of the Judgment.[42] It is of some interest that this locution was produced by the Court of its own accord, Nicaragua having, for its own reasons, avoided the introduction of the issue as to whether or not an armed conflict existed.

9. THE SUBSTANTIVE RIGHTS: THE INTERNATIONAL COVENANTS, 1966

The adoption of the Universal Declaration of Human Rights was widely regarded as a first step toward the preparation of a Covenant, which would be in the form of a treaty. The Declaration, of course, was contained in a resolution of the General Assembly and was not intended to be binding. After extensive work in the Commission on Human Rights and the Third Committee of the General Assembly, the latter in 1966 adopted two Covenants and a Protocol: the International Covenant on Economic, Social, and Cultural Rights (151 parties to date); the International Covenant on Civil and Political Rights (154 parties to date); and an Optional Protocol[43] to the latter (105 parties to date), relating to the processing of communications from individuals. In 1990 a Second Protocol was adopted, aiming at the abolition of the death penalty (56 parties to date).[44]

The Covenants, which came into force in 1976, have legal force as treaties for the Parties to them and constitute a detailed codification of human rights. The Covenant on Economic, Social and Cultural Rights contains various articles in which the Parties 'recognize' such rights as the right to work, the right of everyone to social security and to an adequate standard of living for himself and his family.[45] The type of obligation is

---

[41] ICJ Reports (1986), 113–14, para. 218.

[42] Ibid., 113–14, para. 218; 114, para. 220; 129, para. 255; 130, para. 256 (twice); 148, *dispositif*, para. 9.

[43] For the text, Brownlie and Goodwin-Gill, *Human Rights* (5th edn., 2006), 348, 358, 375. For comment: Schwelb, 62 *AJ* (1968), 827–68; id., in Eide and Schou (eds.), *International Protection of Human Rights*, 103–29; Capotorti, ibid. 131–48; Schwelb, in *René Cassin: Amicorum Discipulorumque Liber I*, 301–24; Robertson, 43 *BY* (1968–9), 21–48; Vierdag, 9 *Neths. Yrbk.* (1978), 69–105; Henkin (ed.), *The International Bill of Rights*; Meron, *Human Rights Law-Making in the United Nations*, 83–127; Jhabvala, 15 *Israel Yrbk. on HR* (1985), 184–203.

[44] Brownlie and Goodwin-Gill, 379.

[45] On the basis of Arts. 11 and 12 of the Covenant the Committee on Economic, Social and Cultural Rights has held that there is a human right to water: see General Comment No. 15: 29th Session, 11–29 November 2002.

programmatic and promotional, except in the case of the provisions relating to trade unions (Art. 8). Each Party 'undertakes to take steps…to the maximum of its available resources, with a view to achieving progressively the full realization of the rights recognised in the present Covenant by all appropriate means, including particularly the adoption of legislative measures'. The rights recognized are to be exercised under a guarantee of non-discrimination, but there is a qualification in the case of the economic rights 'recognized' in that 'developing countries…may determine to what extent they would guarantee' such rights to non-nationals. The machinery for supervision consists of an obligation to submit reports on measures adopted, for transmission to the Economic and Social Council of the United Nations. Since 1986 an expert Committee on Economic, Social and Cultural Rights has assisted in supervising compliance with obligations under this Covenant.[46]

The International Covenant on Civil and Political Rights is more specific in its delineation of rights, stronger in statement of the obligation to respect the rights specified, and better provided with means of review and supervision. The provisions clearly owe much to the European Convention on Human Rights and the experience based upon it. Article 2, paragraph I, contains a firm general stipulation: 'Each State Party to the pres-ent Covenant undertakes to respect and to ensure to all individuals within its territory and subject to its jurisdiction the rights recognized in the present Covenant, without distinction of any kind, such as race, colour, sex, language, religion, political or other opinion, national or social origin, property, birth, or other status'.[47] The rights are defined with as much precision as can reasonably be expected and relate to the classical issues of liberty and security of the person, equality before the law, fair trial, and the like. There is an obligation to submit reports on measures adopted to give effect to the rights recognized by the Covenant to a Human Rights Committee.[48] There is also a complaints procedure under which parties to the Covenant may complain of non-compliance, subject to a bilateral attempt at adjustment and prior exhaustion of domestic remedies, provided that such complaints are only admissible if both the States concerned have recognized the competence of the Committee to receive complaints (the procedure under Art. 41). The Committee may make use of *ad hoc* Conciliation Commissions in resolving issues raised in this manner. In addition the Optional Protocol to this Covenant provides for applications to the Human Rights Committee created by the Covenant from individuals subject to its jurisdiction who claim to be victims of violations of the provisions of the Covenant, and who have exhausted all available domestic remedies.[49] The State charged with a violation is under an obligation to submit to the Committee 'written explanations or statements

---

[46] Alston, in Alston (ed.), *The United Nations and Human Rights* (1992), 473–508.

[47] However, the firmness of the stipulation is placed in question by para. 2, which makes it apparent that States may become parties on the basis of a *promise* to bring their legislation into line with the obligations of the Covenant: see Robertson, 43, *BY* (1968–9), at 25.

[48] See Jhabvala, 6 *Human Rights Qtly.* (1984), 81–106; Robertson, in Henkin, *The International Bill of Rights*, 332–51.

[49] See de Zayas, Möller, Opsahl, 28 *German Yrbk.* (1985), 9–64; Ghandi, 57 *BY* (1986), 201–51.

clarifying the matter and the remedy, if any, that may have been taken by that state'. Subsequently, the Committee 'shall forward its views to the State Party concerned and to the individual'. Thus no public determination of the issue on a judicial or quasi-judicial basis results, in contrast to the possibilities provided in the European Convention to be considered later. However, the 'views' of the Committee in substance involve decisions of issues of law and fact and a selection of these decisions is published periodically.

10. THIRD GENERATION RIGHTS

Originating in the Algiers Declaration of 1978[50] a doctrine of the Rights of Peoples has appeared in the literature.[51] A fairly typical prospectus of these rights would include the right to food, the right to a decent environment, the right to development, and the right to peace. They are commonly referred to as 'third generation' human rights (as opposed to the first two generations, consisting of civil and political rights and, subsequently, economic, social, and cultural rights), and it is commonly suggested, or assumed, that they are not part of existing law, but are 'emerging'.

The subject requires careful handling, not least because some of its proponents are unable, or unwilling, to place it in a proper relation with the structure of general international law. In one version of the doctrine at least, it appears to involve a refusal of legitimacy to recognized governments and to be an ally of a principle of intervention on very broad grounds of oppression.[52] The best approach appears to be to assume that the class of rights is heterogeneous, in terms both of historical provenance and legal implications. Thus the right to development already has a prominent position in both literature and diplomacy,[53] and is the subject of a Declaration on the Right to Development adopted by the UN General Assembly on 4 December 1986.[54] Similarly

[50] Text in Cassese and Jouvé (eds.), *Pour un droit des peuples* (1978), 27.

[51] See generally Falk, *Human Rights and State Sovereignty* (1981); Marks, 33 *Rutgers LR* (1980–81), 435–52; Alston, 29 *Neths. Int. LR* (1982), 307–22; id., 78 *AJ* (1984), 607–21; Rich, 23 *Virginia JIL* (1983), 287–328; Crawford (ed.), *The Rights of Peoples* (1988). See also Higgins, *Problems and Process* (1994), 102–4.

[52] In fact the decision of the International Court in the case of *Nicaragua* v. *United States* (Merits phase), ICJ Reports (1986), 14 (at 132–5) is strongly inimical to such a principle (see 133 (para. 263), in particular).

[53] See Schachter, 15 *Columbia Journ. Trans. Law* (1976), 1–16; Dupuy (ed.), *The Right to Development at the International Level* (1980); Gros Espiell, 16 *Texas Int. LJ* (1981), 189–205; Metdagh, 28 *Neths. Int. LR* (1981), 30–53; Rich, 23 *Virginia JIL* (1983), 287–328; id., in Crawford (ed.), *The Rights of Peoples*, 39–54; Mbaye, in *Essays in Honour of Manfred Lachs* (1984), 163–77; Flory, Mahiou, Henry (eds.), *La Formation des normes en droit international du développement* (1984); Bedjaoui, *Essays in Honour of Roberto Ago* (1987), ii. 15–44; Pellet, *Le Droit international de développement* (2nd edn., 1987); Snyder and Slinn (eds.), *International Law of Development* (1987); De Waart, Peters, Denters (eds.), *International Law and Development* (1988). See also the Award in the *Guinea-Guinea (Bissau)* case, 14 February 1985, 25 ILM (1986), 251, paras. 121–2, ILA, *Report of the 62nd Conference* (1986), 2 (Resol. para. 6).

[54] Resol. 41/128. Recorded vote: 146 in favour; 1 against (US); 8 abstentions. Art. 1 provides as follows: '1. The right to development is an inalienable human right by virtue of which every human person and all peoples are entitled to participate in, contribute to and enjoy economic, social, cultural and political

the right to an adequate standard of living (otherwise, the Right to Food) has received substantial recognition as a legal standard.[55] The 'rights of peoples' also forms a part of the African Charter on Human and Peoples' Rights (adopted in 1981).[56] Certainly, some of the literature of the Rights of Peoples is in many ways eccentric, ignoring the principles of non-intervention and playing down the principle of self-determination, which has a claim to be the only genuine example of the genre.[57]

11. REGIONAL MACHINERY FOR THE PROTECTION OF HUMAN RIGHTS

Machinery for the protection of human rights may be created on a regional basis. The European Convention for the Protection of Human Rights and Fundamental Freedoms[58] is a comprehensive bill of rights on the Western liberal model, born of the Council of Europe. The contracting parties undertake to secure to 'everyone within their jurisdiction' the rights and freedoms defined in section I of the Convention. The precise definition therein has enabled some of the parties to incorporate the rights in their national law as self-executing provisions. In order to make the draft acceptable to Governments certain qualifications on its field of application had to be incorporated. Article 17 provides: 'Nothing in this Convention may be interpreted as implying for any State, group or person any right to engage in any activity or perform any act aimed at the destruction of any of the rights and freedoms set forth herein...'. Article 15 permits measures derogating from the obligations under the Convention 'in time of war

development, in which all human rights and fundamental freedoms can be fully realised. 2. The human right to development also implies the full realisation of the right of peoples to self-determination, which includes, subject to relevant provisions of both International Covenants on Human Rights, the exercise of their inalienable right to full sovereignty over all their natural wealth and resources.' See Kiwanuka, 35 *Neths. Int. LR* (1988), 257–72; Brownlie, *The Human Right to Development*, Commonwealth Secretariat (1989).

[55] See Art. II of the International Covenant on Economic, Social and Cultural Rights, and UNGA Resol. 3348 (XXIX) of 17 December 1974. See also: Alston and Tomasevski (eds.), *The Right to Food* (1984); Eide, Goonatilake, Gussor, Omawale (eds.), *Food as a Human Right* (1984); Brownlie, *The Human Right to Food*, Commonwealth Secretariat (1987).

[56] *Supra.*

[57] *Infra.*

[58] Signed on 4 November 1950; entered into force on 3 September 1953. Text of Conv. and 11 protocols: Brownlie and Goodwin-Gill (2006), 609. See further the European Social Charter, signed on 18 October 1961, entered into force on 26 February 1965. Text: Brownlie and Goodwin-Gill (2006), 645. See generally Fawcett, *The Application of the European Convention on Human Rights* (2nd edn., 1987); Eissen, *Ann. Francais* (1959), 618–58; Higgins, 48 *BY* (1976–7), 281–320; id., Meron (ed.), *Human Rights in International Law*, ii. 495–536; Waldock, *Human Rights LJ* (1980), 1–12; id., *Mélanges offerts à Paul Reuter* (1981), 535–47; Harris, *The European Social Charter* (1984); Van Dijk, Van Hoof, Van Rijn, and Zwaak, *Theory and Practice of the European Convention on Human Rights* (4th edn., 2006); Pettiti, Decaux, and Imbert, *La Convention Européenne des Droits de l'Homme: Commentaire Article par Article* (1995) ; Harris, O'Boyle, and Warbrick, *Law of the European Convention on Human Rights* (1995); Jacobs and White, *The European Convention on Human Rights* (1996). All members of the Council of Europe are parties, 41 States in all. The Conv. may apply to overseas territories: Art. 63.

or other public emergency threatening the life of the nation'. However, no derogation shall be made under this provision from Articles 2 (right to life) (except in respect of deaths resulting from lawful acts of war), 3 (torture and inhuman punishment), 4(1) (slavery or servitude), and 7 (no retrospective punishment).

The principal organ (in the original scheme of things) was the European Commission of Human Rights, to which every complaint went. Any Party might refer an alleged breach of the Convention by another Party to the Commission (Art. 24): see, for example, the four Applications submitted by Cyprus in respect of the conduct of Turkey in Northern Cyprus.[59] In addition, Parties might by declaration recognize the competence of the Commission to receive petitions from any person claiming to be a victim of a violation of the Convention.

The human rights protected by the treaty were originally implemented by three organs, the European Commission of Human Rights, the European Court of Human Rights, and the Committee of Ministers of the Council of Europe. The original institutional structure operated from 1953 until 1998. In November 1998 it was replaced by a new system in accordance with the provisions of Protocol II. Under the new system the European Court of Human Rights deals with individual applications and inter-State cases and the Commission is abolished. The final judgments of the Court are binding. The various functions of the system are allotted to committees, Chambers of the Court, and the Grand Chamber of the Court.

The Commission in the old system did not have the powers of a court, but in its hand-ling of petitions it may be said to have been acting judicially, and the procedure for hearing petitions is of interest. Any High Contracting Party might refer to the Commission any alleged breach of the Convention (Art. 24).[60] However, in addition, individual complainants were given *locus standi* before the Commission. This right of individual petition (Art. 25) was described by the Legal Committee of the Consultative Assembly of the Council of Europe as 'a right of individuals to seek a remedy directly', but in the treaty it had been made a 'right' only at the option of governments. The government concerned must have recognized the competence of the Commission (now the Court) to receive petitions from individuals by express declaration. With this limitation, the Commission might receive petitions addressed to the Secretary-General of the Council of Europe from any person, non-governmental organization, or group of individuals claiming to be the victim of a violation by one of the parties of the rights protected by the Convention. The Commission (now the Court) shall accept petitions after all domestic remedies have been exhausted 'according to the generally recognized rules of international law' (Art. 26). These words were added in order to refer to the juris-prudence according to which improper delay by national tribunals is deemed to be an exhaustion of local remedies. A considerable proportion of applications are rejected as 'manifestly ill-founded' (Art. 35(3)). The main duty of

[59] See the Commission's decision of 26 May 1975, 18 *Yrkb. of the Europ. Conv.* (1975), 82; Commission's decision of 10 July 1978, ibid., vol. 21, 100; ILR 62, 4.

[60] Thus a State may support the rights of nationals of other States: see e.g. *Denmark, Norway, Sweden and Netherlands* v. *Greece* (1967); *Ireland* v. *United Kingdom* (1971).

the Commission (now the Court) is to investigate alleged breaches of the Convention, for which purpose the States concerned are to provide the necessary facilities, and to secure, if possible, an amicable settlement. The final judgment of the Court shall be transmitted to the Committee of Ministers, which 'shall supervise its execution' (Art. 45(2)). The Committee of Ministers will no longer have the power to decide 'whether there has been a violation of the Convention', as it did in relation to certain classes of cases coming from the Commission by virtue of the former Article 32. This is a major improvement.

The work of the Commission and the Court has provided valuable material on the elaboration of the provisions on civil liberties and the concept of exhaustion of local remedies. However, the procedure used is less than expeditious, and the amount of direct protection conferred is somewhat limited. At the same time the working of the machinery has exposed anomalies in national systems of law, and the Convention has influenced decisions of national courts[61] and the policy of the national legislatures involved.[62]

The Inter-American system for the protection of human rights[63] is complex, mainly because it consists of two overlapping mechanisms with different diplomatic starting points. In the first place the Inter-American Commission on Human Rights was first created in 1960 as an organ of the Organization of American States with the function of promoting respect for human rights. As amended by the Protocol of Buenos Aires, the OAS Charter contains a substantial list of economic, social, and cultural standards, and the Commission, as reordered in accordance with the American Convention on Human Rights[64] of 1969, has an extensive competence in these matters in relation to OAS members. On the basis of this Convention an additional system for the promotion of human rights was created. The Inter-American Commission of Human Rights was re-established and retains its broad powers within the context of the OAS (Arts. 41, 42, and 43). At the same time the Commission has responsibilities arising from the provisions of the American Convention. Thus it has jurisdiction *ipso facto* to hear complaints against the parties from individual petitioners (Art. 44). In addition, the

---

[61] See Golsong, 33 *BY* (1957), 317–21; id., 38 *BY* (1962), 445–56; Buergenthal, *ICLQ*, Suppl. Public. no. 11 (1965), 79–106; Petzold, 46 *BY* (1972–3), 401–4; 47 *BY* (1974–5), 356–61; Khol, 18 *Am. Journ. Comp. Law* (1970), 237; *S. v. Free State of Bavaria*, ILR 45, 316; *Association Protestante v. Radiodiffusion-Télévision Belge*, ILR 47, 198.

[62] The *De Becker* case (see Robertson, *Human Rights in Europe* (1963), 63) resulted in a change in Belgian legislation. The work of the Commission has, e.g. focused on the West German and Austrian practice of permitting long terms of detention pending trial. See Scheuner, in Eide and Schou (eds.), *International Protection of Human Rights*, 193–215.

[63] See Schreiber, *The Inter-American Commission on Human Rights* (1970); Vasak, *La Commission interaméricaine des droits de l'homme* (1968); Gros Espiell, 145 Hague *Recueil* (1975), II, 1–55; Buergenthal, 69 *AJ* (1975), 828–36; id., 76 *AJ* (1982), 231–45; id., in Meron (ed.), *Human Rights in International Law*, ii. 439–93; Shelton, 26 *German Yrbk.* (1983), 238–68; *Pertaining to Human Rights in the Inter-American System* (1985); Medina Quiroga, *The Battle of Human Rights* (1988); Davidson, *The Inter-American Court of Human Rights* (1992).

[64] Text: Brownlie and Goodwin-Gill (2006), 933. See also the Protocol of San Salvador, 14 November 1988; 28 *ILM* (1989), 156.

Commission may deal with inter-State disputes provided that both parties have made a declaration recognizing its competence in this respect (Art. 45).

In accordance with the American Convention (Arts. 52 to 69) an Inter-American Court of Human Rights has been constituted and began to function in 1979. The Court has an adjudicatory jurisdiction according to which the Commission and, if they expressly accept this form of jurisdiction, the States Parties may submit cases concerning the interpretation and application of the Convention (Arts. 61 to 63).[65] Article 64 creates an advisory jurisdiction according to which OAS member States (and the organs listed in Chapter X of the Charter of the OAS) may consult the Court regarding 'interpretation of this Convention or of other treaties concerning the protection of human rights in the American States'.[66]

In general the American Convention draws upon the European Convention, the American Declaration of the Rights and Duties of Man (1948),[67] and the International Covenant on Civil and Political Rights, and the result is a very extensive set of provisions. Only OAS members have the right to become parties and to date 25 of the members have become parties.[68]

In practice the Inter-American Commission has exercized its OAS competence in respect of petitions (concerning the execution of juveniles) on behalf of individuals, against the United States, which is not a party to the American Convention, but was held to be bound by the American Declaration of the Rights and Duties of Man.[69]

On 17 June 1981 the Eighteenth Assembly of the Heads of State and Government of the Organization of African Unity adopted the African Charter on Human and Peoples' Rights.[70] While the Charter has much in common with its European and American predecessors, it also has features of its own. Not only are the rights of 'every individual' specified, but also the duties (Chapter II). Several provisions define the rights of 'peoples', for example, to 'freely dispose of their wealth and resources' (Arts. 19 to 24). There are no derogation clauses comparable to Article 15 of the European Convention (war or other public emergency). In the sphere of institutional safeguards, there is an absence of a judicial or quasi-judicial organ. The relevant organ is the African Commission on Human and Peoples' Rights, the mandate of which is in very general terms but which includes the interpretation of the Charter at the request of a State Party (Art. 45). The emphasis is on conciliation. The Commission may investigate complaints by States of violations of the Charter (Arts. 47 to 54) and endeavour to reach an amicable solution

---

[65] 17 States have accepted the jurisdiction to date.

[66] See Adv. Op. dated 13 November 1985; ILR 75, 31. See also Adv. Op. dated 14 July 1989, ILR 96, 416.

[67] Text: Brownlie and Goodwin-Gill (2006), 925.

[68] Out of 32 members.

[69] See Case no. 3/87, *Roach and Pinkerton*, Decision of 27 Mar. 1987, paras. 44–8.

[70] Text: 21 *ILM* (1982), 58. The Charter entered into force on 21 October 1986, and has received not fewer than 51 ratifications. For comment see Gittleman, 22 *Virginia JIL* (1981–2), 667–714; Kunig, 25 *German Yrbk.* (1982), 138–68; Umozurike, 77 *AJ* (1983), 902–12; Bello, 194 Hague *Recueil* (1985, V), 13–268; D'Sa, 10 *Austral Yrbk.* (1987), 101–30; Weston, Lukes, Hnatt, 20 *Vanderbilt Journ. of Transnational Law* (1987), 608–14; Murray, *The African Commission on Human and Peoples' Rights in International Law* (2000); Nmehielle, *The African Human Rights System* (2001).

(Arts. 52 and 53). The Commission may also, subject to certain conditions, consider complaints ('communications') from individuals (Arts. 55 and 56). Only where a complaint reveals 'a series of serious or massive violations' of rights is the Commission bound to involve the OAU Assembly, which 'may then request the Commission to undertake an in-depth study of these cases, and make a factual report, accompanied by its findings and recommendations' (Art. 58). Each State Party has a duty to report on legislative implementation every two years (Art. 62).

12. THE STANDARD OF NON-DISCRIMINATION

The Charter of the United Nations, which entered into force in 1945, contains a significant number of references to 'human rights and fundamental freedoms for all without distinction as to race, sex, language or religion'.[71] These somewhat general and to some extent promotional provisions have provided the background to the appearance of a substantial body of multilateral conventions and practice by the organs of the United Nations. By 1965, at the latest, it was possible to conclude that in terms of the Charter the principle of respect for and protection of human rights had become recognized as a legal standard.[72] In 1970 the majority of the International Court, consisting of 12 judges, delivering judgment in the *Barcelona Traction* case (Second Phase)[73] referred to obligations *erga omnes*[74] in contemporary international law which included 'the principles and rules concerning the basic rights of the human person, including protection from slavery and racial discrimination'.

There is indeed considerable support for the view that there is in international law today a legal principle of non-discrimination which applies in matters of race.[75] This principle is based, in part, upon the United Nations Charter, especially Articles 55 and 56, the practice of organs of the United Nations, in particular resolutions of the General Assembly condemning apartheid, the Universal Declaration of Human Rights, the International Covenants on Human Rights, and the European Convention on Human

---

[71] See Arts. 1(3), 13(1), 55, 56, 62(2) and 76.

[72] Judge Tanaka, Diss. Op., *South West Africa* cases (Second Phase), ICJ Reports (1966), at 300; *Namibia* Opinion, ibid. (1971), 57, para. 131.

[73] ICJ Reports (1970), 3 at 32.

[74] i.e. binding on all States and also having the status of peremptory norms (*jus cogens*), on which see *supra*, 514–17.

[75] See the Diss. Ops. of Judge Tanaka, ICJ Reports (1966), at 286–301; and Padilla Nervo, ibid. 455–6, 464, 467–9. Cf. the Sep. Op. of Judge van Wyk, ibid. 154–5, 158–72. See further Whiteman, v. 244–6; and viii. 376–83; Huston, 53 *Iowa LR* (1967), 272–90; Vierdag, *The Concept of Discrimination in International Law with Special Reference to Human Rights* (1973); Partsch, 14 *Texas Int. LJ* (1979), 191–250; Ramcharan, in Henkin (ed.), *The International Bill of Rights* (1981), 246–69; McKean, *Equality and Discrimination under International Law* (1983); Greenberg, in Meron (ed.), *Human Rights in International Law*, i. 307–43; Meron, *Human Rights Law-Making in the United Nations*, 7–52; Bernhardt, *Encyclopedia*, I (1992), 1079–83; and see the decision in the *European Roma* case [2005] 2 AC 1; ILR 131, 652, paras. 32–47, 72–105, and 109–14.

Rights.[76] There is also a legal principle of non-discrimination in matters of sex, based upon the same set of multilateral instruments,[77] together with the Convention on the Elimination of All Forms of Discrimination against Women adopted by the UN General Assembly in 1979.[78]

There is a growing body of legal materials on the criteria by which illegal discrimination may be distinguished from reasonable measures of differentiation, i.e. legal discrimination.[79] The principle of equality before the law allows for factual differences such as sex or age and is not based on a mechanical conception of equality. The distinction must have an objective justification;[80] the means employed to establish a different treatment must be proportionate to the justification for differentiation;[81] and there is a burden of proof on the Party seeking to set up an exception to the equality principle.[82] The provisions of Article I of the International Convention on the Elimination of All Forms of Racial Discrimination, 1966 (170 parties to date),[83] are of particular interest:

1. In this Convention, the term 'racial discrimination' shall mean any distinction, exclusion, restriction or preference based on race, colour, descent, or national or ethnic origin which has the purpose or effect of nullifying or impairing the recognition, enjoyment or exercise, on an equal footing, of human rights and fundamental freedoms in the polit-ical, economic, social, cultural or any other field of public life.

2. This Convention shall not apply to distinctions, exclusions, restrictions or preferences made by a State Party to this Convention between citizens and non-citizens.

3. Nothing in this Convention may be interpreted as affecting in any way the legal provisions of States Parties concerning nationality, citizenship or naturalization, provided that such provisions do not discriminate against any particular nationality.

---

[76] See Art. 14, on which see Eissen, *Mélanges offerts á Polys Modinos*, 122–45; Guggenheim, *René Cassin: Amicorum Discipulorumque Liber I*, 95–100.

[77] On sexual equality see Daw, 12 *Malaya LR* (1970), 308–36; McDougal, Lasswell, and Chen, 69 *AJ* (1975), 497–533; McKean, *Equality and Discrimination under International Law*, 166–93; *United Nations Action in the Field of Human Rights* (UN, New York, 1983), 81–124; Meron, *Human Rights Law-Making in the United Nations*, 53–82. On the definition of discrimination in this context see *Chollet (née Bauduin) v. Commission*, Europ. Ct. of Justice, *Recueil*, 18 (1972), 363; *Zanoni v. E.S.R.O.*, ILR 51, 430; *Artzt v. Secretary-General*, ibid. 438; *Leguin v. Secretary-General*, ibid. 451.

[78] Text: Brownlie and Goodwin-Gill (2006) 388. In force between 180 states.

[79] See *Minority Schools in Albania* (1935), PCIJ, Ser. A/B, no. 64. *Association Protestante v. Radiodiffusion-Télévision Belge*, ILR 47, 198; *Beth-El Mission v. Minister of Social Welfare*, ILR 47, 205.

[80] See Judge Tanaka, ICJ Reports (1966), at 302–16; *Belgian Linguistics* case (Merits), ECHR Judgment of 23 July 1968, ILR 45, 136, 163–6, 173–4, 180–1, 199–201, 216–17; *National Union of Belgian Police* case, ECHR, Ser. A, vol. 19, 19–92; *Swedish Engine Drivers' Union* case, ibid., vol. 20, 1617; *Schmidt and Dahlström* case, ibid., vol. 21, 16–18; *Case of Engel and Others*, ibid., vol. 22, 29–31; *Marckx* case, ibid., vol. 87, 12–16; *Abdulaziz* case, ibid., vol. 94, 35–41; *James and Others*, ibid., vol. 98, 44–6; *Lithgow and Others*, ibid., vol. 102, 66–70; *Gillow* case, ibid., vol. 109, 25–6; *Mathieu-Mohin and Clerfayt* case, ibid., vol. 113, 26; *Monnell and Morris* case, ibid., vol. 115, 26–7; *Bouamar* case, ibid., vol. 129, 25–6.

[81] *Belgian Linguistics* case, last note; *Société X, W et Z v. République Federale d'Allemagne*, Europ. Comm. of HR, *Collection of Decisions*, vol. 35, 1.

[82] Judge Tanaka, Diss. Op., ICJ Reports (1966), at 309.

[83] Brownlie and Goodwin-Gill, *Human Rights*, 336. See further *Gerhardy v. Brown* (1985), 57 ALR 472, and Crawford (ed.), *The Rights of Peoples*, 6–11.

4. Special measures taken for the sole purpose of securing adequate advancement of certain racial or ethnic groups or individuals requiring such protection as may be necessary in order to ensure such groups or individuals equal enjoyment or exercise of human rights and fundamental freedoms shall not be deemed racial discrimination, provided, however, that such measures do not, as a consequence, lead to the maintenance of separate rights for different racial groups and that they shall not be continued after the objectives for which they were taken have been achieved.[84]

The picture is completed by the Declaration on the Elimination of All Forms of Intolerance and Discrimination Based on Religion or Belief, adopted by the UN General Assembly on 25 November 1981 (by consensus).[85] The Declaration (Art. 8) is intended to be complementary to the Universal Declaration of Human Rights and the International Covenants.

The issue of non-discrimination in relation to treatment of aliens has been considered elsewhere. It is noteworthy that there is some authority for propositions which employ non-discrimination (on the basis of nationality) as a principle limiting the normal liberties of States in particular contexts, including expropriation,[86] currency devaluation,[87] taxation,[88] and the export trade.[89] It would be reasonable to suppose that arbitrary discrimination in the exercise of the power to expel aliens would be unlawful. There are two issues in such cases. First, whether the particular liberty is subject to limitation of this type: if the particular standard of non-discrimination is *jus cogens* (as in racial discrimination), the answer will be affirmative. Secondly, whether standards have developed for determining the distinction between lawful differentiation and unlawful, arbitrary, discrimination.

In a very significant determination in 2001 the European Court of Human Rights held that discriminatory treatment as such could be categorised as degrading treatment within the terms of Article 3 of the European Convention. In the words of the Court:[90]

302. The applicant Government alleged that, as a matter of practice, Greek Cypriots living in the Karpas area of northern Cyprus were subjected to inhuman and degrading treatment, in particular discriminatory treatment amounting to inhuman and degrading treatment.

303. They submitted that the Court should, like the Commission, find that Article 3 had been violated. The applicant Government fully endorsed the Commission's reasoning in this respect.

304. The Commission did not accept the respondent Government's argument that it was prevented from examining whether the totality of the measures impugned by the applicant Government, including those in respect of which it found no breach of the Convention,

---

[84] Cf. Judge Tanaka, Diss. Op., ICJ Reports (1966), at 306–10, in which he takes the view that any distinction on a racial basis is contrary to the principle of non-discrimination.

[85] Resol. 36/55. Text: 21 *ILM* (1982), 205. For comment: Sullivan, 82 *AJ* (1988), 487–520.

[86] *Supra*, 538.

[87] *Supra*, 532.

[88] *Supra*, 532.

[89] See Fawcett, 123 Hague *Recueil* (1968, I), 267–74, with particular reference to GATT.

[90] *Cyprus* v. *Turkey*, Judgment of 10 May 2001; ILR 120, 10 at 91–3, paras. 302–11.

provided proof of the pursuit of a policy of racial discrimination amounting to a breach of Article 3 of the Convention. The Commission had particular regard in this connection to its report under former Article 31 in the *East African Asians* v. *United Kingdom* case adopted on 14 December 1973 (Decisions and Reports 78–A, p. 62). Having regard to the fact that it found the Convention to be violated in several respects, the Commission noted that all the established interferences concerned exclusively Greek Cypriots living in northern Cyprus and were imposed on them for the very reason that they belonged to this class of persons. In the Commission's conclusion, the treatment complained of was clearly discriminatory against them on the basis of their 'ethnic origin, race and religion'. Regardless of recent improvements in their situation, the hardships to which the enclaved Greek Cypriots were subjected during the period under consideration still affected their daily lives and attained a level of severity which constituted an affront to their human dignity.

[...]

306. The Court further recalls that the Commission, in its decision in the above-mentioned *East African Asians case*, observed, with respect to an allegation of racial discrimination, that a special importance should be attached to discrimination, based on race and that publicly to single out a group of persons for differential treatment on the basis of race might, in certain circumstances, constitute a special affront to human dignity. In the Commission's opinion, differential treatment of a group of persons on the basis of race might therefore be capable of constituting degrading treatment when differential treatment on some other ground would raise no such question (*loc. cit.*, p. 62, para. 207).

[...]

310. In the Court's opinion, and with reference to the period under consideration, the discriminatory treatment attained a level of severity which amounted to degrading treatment.

311. The Court concludes that there has been a violation of Article 3 of the Convention in that the Greek Cypriots living in the Karpas area of northern Cyprus have been subjected to discrimination amounting to degrading treatment.

13. LEGAL CONCEPTS RELATING TO THE PROTECTION OF INDIVIDUALS BY JUDICIAL SUPERVISION

The work of the European Commission and the European Court of Human Rights over a long period has produced a set of legal concepts within the framework of the European Convention for the Protection of Human Rights. These concepts are also to be found in the determinations of judicial bodies applying the provisions of other regional conventions. At the outset it must be emphasized that these concepts, in part, rest upon the political premises that the State involved as Respondent is itself democratic and that there must be a fair balance between the general interest and the interests of the individual. In what follows there is a brief exposition of some of the pertinent legal concepts.

(A) THE MARGIN OF APPRECIATION[91]

This takes the form of a legal discretion which recognizes that the Respondent State can be presumed to be best qualified to appreciate the necessities of a particular situation affecting its jurisdiction. This margin takes the form of a presumption and its application will depend on the subject matter.

In the *James and Others* case[92] the Court rejected the complaint against the leasehold reform legislation of the United Kingdom and observed:[93]

Because of their direct knowledge of their society and its needs, the national authorities are in principle better placed than the international judge to appreciate what is 'in the public interest'. Under the system of protection established by the Convention, it is thus for the national authorities to make the initial assessment both of the existence of a problem of public concern warranting measures of deprivation of property and of the remedial action to be taken. Here, as in other fields to which the safeguards of the Convention extend, the national authorities accordingly enjoy a certain margin of appreciation.

Furthermore, the notion of 'public interest' is necessarily extensive. In particular, as the Commission noted, the decision to enact laws expropriating property will commonly involve consideration of political, economic and social issues on which opinions within a democratic society may reasonably differ widely. The Court, finding it natural that the margin of appreciation available to the legislature in implementing social and economic policies should be a wide one, will respect the legislature's judgment as to what is 'in the public interest' unless that judgment be manifestly without reasonable foundation. In other words, although the Court cannot substitute its own assessment for that of the national authorities, it is bound to review the contested measures under Article 1 of Protocol No. 1 and, in so doing, to make an inquiry into the facts with reference to which the national authorities acted.

(B) RESTRICTIONS UPON FREEDOMS 'NECESSARY IN A DEMOCRATIC SOCIETY'[94]

In the European Convention on Human Rights several key provisions are expressed to be subject to restrictions which are 'necessary in a democratic society'. In the case of *Silver and Others* v. *United Kingdom*, the Court explained the general principles as follows:[95]

97. On a number of occasions, the Court has stated its understanding of the phrase 'necessary in a democratic society', the nature of its functions in the examination of issues turning

---

[91] See Merrills, *The Development of International Law by the European Court of Human Rights* (1988), 136–57.

[92] ECHR, Judgment of 21 February 1986, Series A, no. 98.

[93] Para. 46.

[94] See Merrills, op. cit., 113–34; and Marks, 66 BY (1995), 209–38.

[95] ECHR, Judgment of 25 March 1983, Series A, No. 61; ILR 72, 334, 369, para. 97.

on that phrase and the manner in which it will perform those functions. It suffices here to summarise certain principles:

(a) the adjective 'necessary' is not synonymous with 'indispensable', neither has it the flexibility of such expressions as 'admissible', 'ordinary', 'useful', 'reasonable' or 'desirable' (see the *Handyside* judgment of 7 December 1976, Series A no. 24, p. 22, para. 48);

(b) the Contracting States enjoy a certain but not unlimited margin of appreciation in the matter of the imposition of restrictions, but it is for the Court to give the final ruling on whether they are compatible with the Convention (ibid., p. 23, para. 49);

(c) the phrase 'necessary in a democratic society' means that, to be compatible with the Convention, the interference must, *inter alia*, correspond to a 'pressing social need' and to be 'proportionate to the legitimate aim pursued' (ibid., pp. 22–3, paras. 48–9);

(d) those paragraphs of Articles of the Convention which provide for an exception to a right guaranteed are to be narrowly interpreted (see the above-mentioned *Klass and others* judgment, Series A no. 28, p. 21, para. 42).

The issue arises regularly in the more critical cases concerning the right to respect for private and family life;[96] freedom of thought, conscience, and religion; freedom of expression;[97] and freedom of assembly.[98]

(c) PROPORTIONALITY: THE BALANCE BETWEEN THE GENERAL INTEREST AND THE INTERESTS OF THE INDIVIDUAL

The provisions of the Convention seek to maintain a balance between the general interest (a pressing social need) and the rights and interests of the individual. This balance is referred to by the Court as the principle of proportionality. Thus a legitimate aim, for example, the licensing of restaurants serving alcohol in the public interest, may be furthered by a means which is disproportionate (revocation of the licence).[99] In the *Dudgeon* case,[100] which concerned legislation in Northern Ireland concerning homosexuality, the Court explained the principles thus:

53. Finally, in Article 8 as in several other Articles of the Convention, the notion of 'necessity' is linked to that of a 'democratic society'. According to the Court's case-law, a restriction on a Convention right cannot be regarded as 'necessary in a democratic society'—two hallmarks of which are tolerance and broadmindedness—unless, amongst other things,

---

[96] *Klass and Others*, Judgment of 6 September 1978; ECHR, Series A, No. 28, ILR 58, 423; paras. 46–60; *Silver and Others*, Judgment of 25 March 1983, ECHR, Series A, No. 61; ILR 72, 334, 369, para. 97.

[97] *Handyside*, Judgment of 7 December 1976; ECHR, Series A, No. 24, paras. 49–59; *Sunday Times*, Judgment of 26 April 1979; ECHR Series A, No. 30, paras. 58–68; *Lingens*, Judgment of 8 July 1986; ECHR, Series A, No. 103, paras. 42–7; *Müller and Others*, Judgment of 24 May 1988; ECHR, Series A, No. 133, paras. 31–33.

[98] *United Communist Party of Turkey Case*, Judgment of 30 January 1998; para. 42.

[99] *Tre Traktörer Aktiebolag* case, ECHR, Judgment of 7 July 1989, Series A, No. 159.

[100] ECHR, Judgment of 22 October 1981; Series A, No. 45; ILR 67, 395, paras. 53, 59–61.

it is proportionate to the legitimate aim pursued (see the above-mentioned *Handyside* judgment, p. 23, para. 49, and the above-mentioned *Young, James and Webster* judgment, p. 25, para. 63)...

Notwithstanding the margin of appreciation left to the national authorities, it is for the Court to make the final evaluation as to whether the reasons it has found to be relevant were sufficient in the circumstances, in particular whether the interference complained of was proportionate to the social need claimed for it (see paragraph 53 above).

To sum up, the restriction imposed on Mr Dudgeon under Northern Ireland law, by reason of its breadth and absolute character, is, quite apart from the severity of the possible penalties provided for, disproportionate to the aims sought to be achieved.

This factor of proportionality has played a major role in the jurisprudence.[101] Whilst the factor is on its face a logical principle, it inevitably entails significant choices of policy. In the case of *Fogarty* v. *United Kingdom*[102] the Court held that, as an aspect of the issue of proportionality, it was appropriate to interpret the Convention as far as possible in harmony with other rules of international law, including those relating to the grant of State immunity.

(D) THE ABSENCE OF AN OFFICIAL INVESTIGATION CONSTITUTING EVIDENCE OF A VIOLATION

In a long series of decisions the European Court has responded to the extraordinary circumstances prevailing in certain regions of Turkey. In order to deal effectively with cases involving ill-treatment,[103] disappearances,[104] the destruction of a village,[105] the death of the Applicant's sister,[106] and shooting by unidentified persons,[107] the Court has relied upon the evidence of a lack of effective investigation, or of any investigation, by the authorities, as evidence of violations of Article 2 (the right to life), Article 3 (prohibition of torture), Article 5 (the right to liberty and security of person), and Article 8 (the right to home and family life). In addition, such lack of an effective investigation was held to constitute a violation of Article 13 (the right to an effective

---

[101] See also *Rasmussen*, Judgment of 28 November 1984, ECHR, Series A, No. 87, para. 38; *Lithgow and Others*, ECHR, Judgment of 8 July 1986, Series A, No. 102, para. 374; *Gillow*, ECHR, Judgment of 24 November 1986, Series A, No. 109, paras. 55–8; *Mathieu-Mohin and Clerfayt*, ECHR, Judgment of 26 March 1987, Series A, No. 116, para. 67; *Mellacher*, ECHR, Judgment of 19 December 1989, Series A, No. 169, paras. 51–3; *Pine Valley Developments Ltd.*, ECHR, Judgment of 29 November 1991, Series A, No. 222; *Open Door and Dublin Well Woman*, ECHR, Judgment of 29 October 1992, Series A, No. 246, para. 72; *Steel*, ECHR, Judgment of 23 September 1998; *Fayed*, ECHR, Judgment of 21 September 1994, Series A, No. 294B, para. 75.

[102] ECHR, Judgment of 21 November 2001 (Grand Chamber), paras. 35–6.

[103] *Aksoy*, ECHR, Judgment of 18 December 1996, paras. 98–100; *Timurtas*, ECHR, Judgment of 29 October 1998, paras. 305–10.

[104] *Kurt*, ECHR, Judgment of 25 May 1998; *Cakici*, ECHR, Judgment of 8 July 1999, paras. 81–87.

[105] *Mentes*, Judgment of 28 November 1997.

[106] *Ergi*, ECHR, Judgment of 28 July 1998, paras. 78–86.

[107] *Kaya*, ECHR, Judgment of 19 February 1998, paras. 84–92; *Ergi*, ECHR, Judgment of 28 July 1998, paras. 79–86.

remedy).[108] Similar principles have been applied by the Inter-American Human Rights.[109]

(E) THE CONDITION THAT LOCAL REMEDIES BE EXHAUSTED[110]

The Convention, in Article 35(1), provides that 'the Court may only deal with the matter after all domestic remedies have been exhausted, according to the generally recognised rules of international law and within a period of six months from the date when the final decision was taken'. This condition of competence reflects the role of the Court, which is supervisory and not appellate. The Court, and formerly the Commission, have developed certain useful clarifications of the condition of prior exhaustion of domestic remedies. In the first place, the Court will usually not require such recourse if the violation originates in an administrative practice of the organs of the Respondent State.[111] This principle applies to both inter-State cases and individual applications.

14. THE PRINCIPLE OF SELF-DETERMINATION[112]

It is not necessarily the case that there is a divorce between the legal and human rights of groups, on the one hand, and individuals, on the other. Guarantees and standards governing treatment of individuals tend, by their emphasis on equality, to protect groups as well: this is obviously so in regard to racial discrimination. Many

---

[108] *Aksoy*, ECHR, Judgment of 18 December 1996, paras. 98–100; *Kaya*, ECHR, Judgment of 19 February 1998, paras. 106–8; *Cakici*, paras. 108–14; *Yasa*, paras. 109–15.

[109] See *Paniagua Morales et al.*, Int. Human Rights Reports, Vol. 6, 1067; Vol. 10, 698. See also the Inter-American Commission, *Extrajudicial Executions and Forced Disappearances v. Peru*, ibid., Vol. 10, 829.

[110] See Merrills, op. cit., 190–4; Jacobs and White, *The European Convention on Human Rights* (2nd edn., 1996), 354–8.

[111] See *Ireland* v. *United Kingdom*, ILR 58, 190; Judgment, paras. 156–9.

[112] See Rousseau, ii. 17–35; Scelle, *Spiropoulos Festschrift* (1957), 385–91; Tunkin, *Theory of International Law* (1974), 60–9; Lachs, 1 *Indian Journ.* (1960–1), 429–42; Whiteman, vi. 38–87; id., xiii. 701–68; Emerson, 65 AJ (1971), 459–75; Bastid, in *Mélanges offerts á Juraj Andrassy* (1968), 13–30; Verzijl, *International Law in Historical Perspective*, i. (1968), 321–36; Kaur, 10 *Indian Journ.* (1970), 479–502; Fawcett, 132 Hague *Recueil* (1971, 1), 387–91; Umozurike, *Self-Determination in International Law* (1972); Rigo Sureda, *The Evolution of the Right of Self-Determination: A Study of United Nations Practice* (1973); Calogeropoulos-Stratis, *Le Droit des peuples á disposer d'eux-mêmes* (1973); Crawford, 48 BY (1976–77), 149–73; Brossard, 15 *Canad. Yrbk* (1977), 84–145; Sinha, 14 *Indian Journ.* (1974), 332–61; Jiménez de Aréchaga, Hague *Recueil* (1978: 1), 99–111; Crawford, *The Creation of States in International Law* (2nd edn., 2006) 107–48; id. (ed.), *The Rights of Peoples* (index); Cristescu, *The Right to Self-Determination* (New York, 1981), 147–70; Cassese, in Henkin, *The International Bill of Rights in International Law*, i. 193–6; Thürer, Bernhardt, *Encyclopedia*, Vol.4 (2000), 364–74; Shaw, *Title to Territory in Africa* (1986), 59–144; Wilson, *International Law and the Use of Force by National Liberation Movements* (1988), 55–88; Cassese, *Self-determination* (1993); Brownlie, 255 Hague *Recueil* (1995), 55–61; Franck, *Fairness in International Law and Insitutions* (1995), 140–69; Laing, *California Western Int. LJ* (1991–2), 209–308; Higgins, *Problems and Process* (1994), 111–28; Crawford, 69 BY (1998), 85–117; Quane, *I.C.L.Q.* 47 (1998), 537–72.

instruments of the type recorded earlier stipulate for rights 'without distinction as to race, sex, language, or religion'.[113] However, in certain contexts, such as the trusteeship system in the United Nations Charter, the rights of a certain population are protected.

The rights of important groups as such become particularly prominent in connection with the principle, or right, of self-determination,[114] viz., the right of cohesive national groups ('peoples') to choose for themselves a form of political organization and their relation to other groups. The choice may be independence as a State, association with other groups in a federal State, or autonomy or assimilation in a unitary (non-federal) State. Until recently the majority of Western jurists assumed or asserted that the principle had no legal content, being an ill-defined concept of policy and morality.[115]

Since 1945 developments in the United Nations have changed the position, and West-ern jurists generally admit that self-determination is a legal principle.[116] The generality and political aspect of the principle do not deprive it of legal content: it may be recalled that in the *South West Africa* cases (Preliminary Objections)[117] the International Court regarded the terms of Article 2 of the Mandate Agreement concerned as disclosing a legal obligation, in spite of the political nature of the duty 'to promote to the utmost the material and moral well-being and the social progress of the inhabitants of the territory'.

Although reference is often made to the declarations in the Atlantic Charter of 14 August 1941,[118] the key development was the appearance of references to 'the principle of equal rights and self-determination of peoples' in Article 1, paragraph 2, and Article 55 of the United Nations Charter.[119] Many jurists and governments were prepared to interpret these references as merely of hortatory effect, but the practice of United Nations organs has established the principle as a part of the law of the United Nations. In Resolution 637A (VII) of 16 December 1952[120] the General Assembly recommended,

---

[113] Cf. UN Charter, Art. 1(3); European Conv. for the Protection of Human Rights, Art. 14. Many applications to the European Commission of Human Rights from Belgian sources have concerned the rights of communities in relation to the language question in Belgium.

[114] French equivalents are: *droit des peuples à disposer d'eux-mêmes, droit ou principe de libre disposition, d'auto-disposition, de libre détermination.*

[115] Prior to 1945 reference in the legal sources are rare. See, however, the report of the Committee of Jurists on the Aaland Islands question in 1920: see Padelford and Andersson, 33 *AJ* (1939), 465 at 474. Cf. Hyde, i. 363, 389; Hackworth, i. 422. The principle is referred to in Soviet treaties concluded in the period 1920–2.

[116] See Scelle, *Spiropoulos Festschrift*; Quincy Wright, 98 Hague *Recueil* (1959, III), 193; Wengler, 10 *Rev. hell. de.d.i.* (1958), 26–39.

[117] ICJ Reports (1962), 319. Cf. the division of opinion in the *South West Africa* cases (Second Phase), ibid. (1966), 6.

[118] Text: 35 *AJ* (1941), Suppl., 191. Adherence by the USSR and other states in a Decl. of 1 Jan 1942: 36 *AJ* (1942), Suppl., 191.

[119] See also chs. XI (Decl. Regarding Non-self-governing Territories) and XII (International trusteeship system).

[120] The Commission on Human Rights and the Third Committee have been concerned with the subject, and it appears in the Covenants on Civil and Political Rights and Economic, Social, and Cultural

inter alia, that 'the States Members of the United Nations shall uphold the principle of self-determination of all peoples and nations'. Most important is the Declaration on the Granting of Independence to Colonial Countries and Peoples adopted by the General Assembly in 1960[121] and referred to in a series of resolutions concerning specific territories since then.[122] The Declaration regards the principle of self-determination as a part of the obligations stemming from the Charter, and is not a 'recommendation', but is in the form of an authoritative interpretation of the Charter.[123] The principle has been incorporated in a number of international instruments.[124] The United States[125] and many other governments support the principle, which appears in the Declaration of Principles of International Law concerning Friendly Relations adopted without vote by the United Nations General Assembly in 1970.[126] The Advisory Opinion of the International Court relating to the *Western Sahara*[127] confirms 'the validity of the principle of self-determination' in the context of international law. In the case concerning the *Legal Consequences of the Construction of a Wall in the Occupied Palestinian Territory* the International Court recognised the principle of self-determination as one of the rules and principles relevant to the legality of the measure taken by Israel. In the words of the Court:[128]

88. The Court also notes that the principle of self-determination of peoples has been enshrined in the United Nations Charter and reaffirmed by the General Assembly in resolution 2625 (XXV) cited above, pursuant to which "Every State has the duty to refrain from any forcible action which deprives peoples referred to [in that resolution]...of their right to self-determination." Article 1 common to the International Covenant on Economic, Social and Cultural Rights and the International Covenant on Civil and Political Rights reaffirms the right of all peoples to self-determination, and lays upon the States parties the obligation to promote the realisation of that right and to respect it, in conformity with the provisions of the United Nations Charter.

Rights, *supra*, 572. The principle was invoked during discussion by the General Assembly, *inter alia*, of the Algerian, Tunisian and Cyprus cases: Sohn, *Cases on United Nations Law*, 420ff., 812.; and Higgins, *Development*, 90–106.

[121] Resol. 1514 (XV); Brownlie, *Documents*, 228; Whiteman, xiii, 701–68. See also Resol. 1314 (XIII).

[122] The GA established a Special Committee to implement the Decl. See the resols. on implementation of the Decl. in *UK Contemp. Practice* (1962, II), 280–2, 287; ibid. (1963, II), 216–20; *British Practice* (1964), 173, 237.

[123] See Waldock, 106 Hague *Recueil* (1962, II), 33; Annual Report of the Secretary-General (1961), 2. Cf. Judge Moreno Quintana, ICJ Reports (1960), 95–6.

[124] The Pacific Charter, 8 Sept. 1954, *Dept. of St. Bull.* 31 (1954), 393; Communique of the Bandung Conference, 24 Apr. 1955; *Ann. francais* (1955), 723; Decl. of the Belgrade Conference of Non-aligned Countries, 6 Sept. 1961 (25 states); Decl. of the Cairo Conference of Non-aligned Countries, Oct. 1964 (47 states), 4 *Indian Journ.* (1964), 599. See also UNGA Resol. 1815 (XVII): *UK Contemp. Practice* (1962, II), 290; and Resol. 1966 (XVIII), ibid. (1963, II), 225.

[125] See 61 *AJ* (1967), 595; statement in UNGA, 12 Oct. 1966.

[126] Resol. 2625 (XXV), Annex. Text: 65 *AJ* (1971), 243; Brownlie, *Documents*, 27.

[127] ICJ Reports (1975) 12 at 31–3. See also the *Namibia* Opinion, ibid. (1971), 16 at 31; *Georg K. v. Ministry of the Interior*, ILR 71, 284; and *Case Concerning East Timor*, ICJ Reports (1995), 102.

[128] ICJ Reports (2004), 136 at 171–2.

The Court would recall that in 1971 it emphasised that current developments in 'international law in regard to non-self-governing territories, as enshrined in the Charter of the United Nations, made the principle of self-determination applicable to all [such territories]'. The Court went on to state that 'These developments leave little doubt that the ultimate objective of the sacred trust' referred to in Article 22, paragraph 1, of the Covenant of the League of Nations 'was the self-determination . . . of the peoples concerned' (*Legal Consequences for States of the Continued Presence of South Africa in Namibia (South West Africa) notwithstanding Security Council Resolution 276 (1970), Advisory Opinion, I.C.J. Reports 1971*, p.31, paras 52–53). The Court has referred to this principle on a number of occasions in its jurisprudence (*ibid*: see also *Western Sahara, Advisory Opinion, I.C.J. Reports 1975*, p.,68, para 162). The Court indeed made it clear that the right of peoples to self-determination is today a right *erga omnes* (see *East Timor (Portugal v Australia), Judgment, I.C.J. Reports 1995*, 102, para 29).

The present position is that self-determination is a legal principle, and that United Nations organs do not permit Article 2, paragraph 7, to impede discussion and decision when the principle is in issue.[129] Its precise ramifications in other contexts are not yet worked out, and it is difficult to do justice to the problems in a small compass. The subject has three aspects. First, the principle informs and complements other general principles of international law,[130] viz., of State sovereignty, the equality of states, and the equality of peoples within a State. Thus self-determination is employed in conjunction with the principle of non-intervention in relation to the use of force and otherwise.[131] Secondly, the concept of self-determination has been applied in the different context of economic self-determination.[132] Lastly, the principle appears to have corollaries which may include the following: (1) if force be used to seize territory and the object is the implementation of the principle, then title may accrue by general acquiescence and recognition more readily than in other cases of unlawful seizure of territory; (2) the principle may compensate for a partial lack of certain *desiderata* in the fields of statehood and recognition; (3) intervention against a liberation movement may be unlawful and assistance to the movement may be lawful; (4) territory inhabited by peoples not organized as a State cannot be regarded as *terra nullius* susceptible to appropriation by individual States in case of abandonment by the existing sovereign.

---

[129] On domestic jurisdiction: *supra*, 292ff. On the practice of UN organs in the present connection see Higgins, *Development*, 90–106.

[130] On the relation of self-determination to *jus cogens* see *supra*, 510.

[131] Cf. the Punta del Este Decl. 56 AJ (1962), 601, 607; and the UNGA Resol. on the Hungarian situation in 1956 (see Higgins, *Development*, 184–5, 211).

[132] See the Decl. on Permanent Sovereignty over Natural Resources, *supra*, 539, and Art. 1 common to the Covenants produced by the Third Committee of the General Assembly, *supra*, 565.

15. OTHER ORGANS CREATED TO ENHANCE COMPLIANCE WITH HUMAN RIGHTS STANDARDS

It is impossible in a general work to provide a detailed picture of the multiform and numerous institutions involved in the protection of human rights. However, even in a small compass, attention must be drawn to certain other organs. Several of the multilateral standard-setting treaties on special questions provide for monitoring of compliance by investigating committees. In temporal sequence the first such organ was the Committee on the Elimination of Racial Discrimination which supervises the implementation of the International Convention on the Elimination of All Forms of Racial Discrimination.[133] The Committee held its first session in 1970.

The second organ of this type is the Committee on the Elimination of Discrimination against Women. This began its work in 1981 and its task is to supervise the implementation of the Convention on the Elimination of All Forms of Discrimination against Women.[134]

The third organ is the Committee against Torture set up in accordance with Article 17 of the Convention against Torture and other Cruel, Inhuman or Degrading Treatment or Punishment, which entered into force on 26 June 1987.[135] The Convention has at least 123 Parties. In 2002 an Optional Protocol was adopted to establish a system of regular visits to prisons and other places of detention. Finally, the General Assembly adopted the Convention on the Rights of the Child on 20 November 1989, Article 43 of which provides for the establishment of a committee 'for the purpose of examining the progress made by the States Parties in achieving the obligations undertaken in the present Convention...'.[136] The Committee began to function in 1991.

In 1993 the General Assembly created the office of the UN High Commissioner for Human Rights.[137] A perusal of the substantial and complex provisions of the General Assembly resolution establishing the mandate of the High Commissioner will indicate that each High Commissioner must select his or her priorities. As Professor Merrills has pointed out, the principal task of the High Commissioner is to provide leadership in the human rights field.[138]

---

[133] Brownlie and Goodwin-Gill, *Human Rights* (2006), 336. See further Partsch, in Alston (ed.), *The United Nations and Human Rights* (1992), 339–68; Oppenheim, ii. 1009–10.

[134] Brownlie and Goodwin-Gill, op. cit., 388. See further Jacobson, in Alston (ed.), *The United Nations and Human Rights* (1992), 444–72; Byrnes, *Yale J.I.L.* 14 (1989), 1–67.

[135] Brownlie and Goodwin-Gill, op. cit., 405. See further Byrnes, in Alston (ed.), *The United Nations and Human Rights* (1992), 509–46.

[136] Brownlie and Goodwin-Gill, op. cit., 429.

[137] Resol. 48/141; *ILM* 33 (1994), 303; Brownlie and Goodwin-Gill, op. cit., 191. See further Clapham, *Europ. Journ.* 5 (1994), 556–68.

[138] Merrills, *Human Rights in the World* (4th edn., 1996), 112–14.

16. AN EVALUATION

The above account of human rights represents a legal treatment of the subject and is, it should be emphasized, an analysis from the perspective of public international law. This approach is appropriate for several reasons, including the fact that human rights as legal standards were invented by international lawyers, together with the normative development of significant human rights standards as part of customary or general international law.

An evaluation of the existing human rights system must begin by placing emphasis on three elements. In the first place, the 'system', such as it is, depends for its efficacy upon the domestic legal systems of States. The decisions and recommendations of the supervisory and monitoring bodies can only be implemented by means of the legislatures and administrations of the States Parties to the various standard-setting conventions. Secondly, the application of human rights forms part of a larger problem, the belief in, and the maintenance of, the Rule of Law, including the existence of an independent judiciary, within domestic legal systems.

The third element is particularly related to the second. Adherence to human rights instruments, like the European Convention, presupposes that the States adhering will apply the standards, and that implementation will not be a problem. In practice, such a system fails when it has to face the worst case scenarios, and the recalcitrant Respondent State. Practitioners within the Strasbourg system (and Governments) are well aware of the failure of Turkey to implement decisions of the European Court of Human Rights, including the *Case of Loizidou* v. *Government of Turkey*, and the Judgments in the series of Applications brought by the Republic of Cyprus against Turkey. These cases concern the rights of large groups, and long-lasting situations.

The question of the efficacy of the system of human rights leads to a wider problem. On occasion the Security Council may decide to take coercive action under Chapter VII of the United Nations Charter, precisely to deal with the worst cases. This, then, appears to be the solution. But, in practice, such action has been taken on a very selective basis and has been shadowed by *ad hoc* geopolitical reasons unconnected with human rights. This element of discrimination can best be illustrated by instances of failure to act, and, in particular, the failure of the Security Council to take any action in face of the gross and persistent measures of discrimination and breaches of humanitarian law on the part of Israel against the Palestinian people and their institutions.[139] The issue of selectivity can lead to claims of human rights violations being used as a powerful political weapon.

Probably the most egregious example of this is provided by the case of Iraq. The Iraq–Iran War raged for eight years (1980–8). Iran was not the aggressor. During the conflict leading Western powers gave assistance to the Iraqi Government in the form

---

[139] See the Resolution adopted on 15 April 2003 by the U.N. Commission on Human Rights by 50 votes to 1. The United States voted against and Australia and Costa Rica abstained.

of matrices for chemical weapons (which were used against Iran) and satellite intelligence. The Security Council took no action under Chapter VII of the Charter. In contrast, in the period from 1991 up to the United States attack on Iraq in March 2003, the same States took a strong line on the bad rights record of the Iraqi regime and the attack was justified in public statements in part by reference to the human rights factor. Here is revealed a purely cyclical version of human rights, contingent upon collateral political considerations.

Such problems of consistency and efficacy affect all systems of law, and not only public international law and human rights. The appalling realities of power politics must be balanced against the fifty years of successful formulation of legal standards of human rights and the development of mechanisms of supervision and monitoring. Such formulation, at the very least, puts the question of enforcement on the agenda.

26

INTERNATIONAL CRIMINAL JUSTICE

1. INTRODUCTION

The concept of international criminal justice is both simple and complex. It is simple in the sense that certain types of wrongdoing are generally recognized as international crimes, which may be prosecuted both before national courts and, in so far as they have competence, international criminal courts. The concept is also complex in the sense that the relation between the role of national courts and international criminal courts is problematical. The subject is further complicated by the tendency of the Security Council to limit recourse to national courts in certain selected situations, as in the 'former Yugoslavia', Rwanda, and Sierra Leone. The International Criminal Tribunal for the Former Yugoslavia and the International Criminal Tribunal for Rwanda were both created by the Security Council, in 1993 and 1994 respectively, under Chapter VII, the enforcement chapter, of the United Nations Charter.

2. CRIMES UNDER INTERNATIONAL LAW[1]

It is necessary to begin by identifying those offences recognized as crimes under international law for which individuals can be held responsible. An historical sequence is called for because, as in the *Pinochet* case[2] in the English courts, it is possible that the date on which an offence became a part of general or customary international law may be legally relevant.

(A) THE NUREMBERG CHARTER AND THE RESOLUTIONS OF THE GENERAL ASSEMBLY OF THE UNITED NATIONS

The International Military Tribunals at Nuremberg and Tokyo functioned on the basis of Charters which required the punishment of individuals for war crimes, crimes

---

[1] See generally Cassese, *International Criminal Law* (2003).
[2] [1999] 2 WLR 827; ILR 119, 135.

against humanity and crimes against peace. In Resolution 95(I) adopted unanimously on 11 December 1946, the General Assembly affirmed 'the principles of international law recognised by the Charter of the Nuremberg Tribunal and the Judgment of the Tribunal'.

On 21 November 1947 the General Assembly established the International Law Commission and on the same day another resolution was adopted in which that Commission was directed to:

(a) Formulate the principles of international law recognized in the Charter of the Nuremberg Tribunal and in the judgment of the Tribunal, and

(b) Prepare a draft code of offences against the peace and security of mankind, indicating clearly the place to be accorded to the principles mentioned in sub-paragraph (a) above.

In response the International Law Commission formulated the following 'crimes under international law':[3]

Principle VI. The crimes hereinafter set out are punishable as crimes under international law:
  a. Crimes against peace:
    (i) Planning, preparation, initiation or waging of a war of aggression or a war in violation of international treaties, agreements or assurances;
    (ii) Participation in a common plan or conspiracy for the accomplishment of any of the acts mentioned under (i).

  b. War crimes:
    Violations of the laws or customs of war which include, but are not limited to, murder, ill-treatment or deportation to slave-labour or for any other purpose of civilian population of or in occupied territory, murder or ill-treatment of prisoners of war or persons on the seas, killing of hostages, plunder of public or private property, wanton destruction of cities, towns, or villages, or devastation not justified by military necessity.

  c. Crimes against humanity:
    Murder, extermination, enslavement, deportation and other inhuman acts done against any civilian population, or persecutions on political, racial or religious grounds, when such acts are done or such persecutions are carried on in execution of or in connexion with any crime against peace or any war crime.

Principle VII. Complicity in the commission of a crime against peace, a war crime, or a crime against humanity as set forth in Principle VI is a crime under international law.

When the work of the International Law Commission was examined by the Sixth (Legal) Committee of the General Assembly, eighteen states considered that the Nuremberg Charter and the principles derived from it had become a part of international law.[4]

---

[3] *Yearbook*, ILC, 1950, ii, 374–8.
[4] See Brownlie, *International Law and the Use of Force by States* (1963), 191–4.

(B) THE DRAFT CODE OF CRIMES AGAINST THE PEACE AND SECURITY OF MANKIND

In 1996 the International Law Commission adopted twenty draft articles constituting a Code of Crimes against the Peace and Security of Mankind.[5] The Commission recommended that the General Assembly select 'the most appropriate form which would ensure the widest possible acceptance of the draft Code'. The Code is related to the responsibility of individuals for the relevant crimes. Inevitably, the draft articles have become more or less redundant in face of the successful negotiation of the Statute of the International Criminal Court: see below.

(C) INTERNATIONAL CRIMES: THE POSITION IN GENERAL INTERNATIONAL LAW

There is, at this stage in the historical development of the concept of international crimes, sufficient material to provide a reliable assessment of those offences which are recognized as a part of general or customary international law. In this context the provisions of the Statute of the International Criminal Court constitute good evidence of the offences forming part of general international law. The provisions defining international crimes are as follows:

(i) *Crimes within the jurisdiction of the Court (Art. 5)*

1. The jurisdiction of the Court shall be limited to the most serious crimes of concern to the international community as a whole. The Court has jurisdiction in accordance with this Statute with respect to the following crimes:
   (a) The crime of genocide;
   (b) Crimes against humanity;
   (c) War crimes;
   (d) The crime of aggression.

2. The Court shall exercise jurisdiction over the crime of aggression once a provision is adopted in accordance with Articles 121 and 123 defining the crime and setting out the conditions under which the Court shall exercise jurisdiction with respect to this crime. Such a provision shall be consistent with the relevant provisions of the Charter of the United Nations.

Genocide (Art. 6)

For the purpose of this Statute, 'genocide' means any of the following acts committed with intent to destroy, in whole or in part, a national, ethnical, racial or religious group, as such:

(a) Killing members of the group:

(b) Causing serious bodily or mental harm to members of the group;

---

[5] *Yrbk.*, ILC, 1996, II (pt. ii), 15–56. See Allain and Jones, *Europ. Journ.* 8 (1997), 100–17.

(c) Deliberately inflicting on the group conditions of life calculated to bring about its physical destruction in whole or in part;

(d) Imposing measures intended to prevent births within the group;

(e) Forcibly transferring children of the group to another group.

In the Nuremberg Charter the category of 'crimes against humanity' encompassed genocidal acts but genocide did not emerge as a special category until the adoption of the Convention on the Prevention and Punishment of Genocide in 1948. Article 6 of the ICC Statute is based upon Article II of the Genocide Convention.

Crimes against humanity (Art. 7)

1. For the purpose of this Statute, 'crime against humanity' means any of the following acts when committed as part of a widespread or systematic attack directed against any civilian population, with knowledge of the attack:
   (a) Murder
   (b) Extermination;
   (c) Enslavement;
   (d) Deportation or forcible transfer of population;
   (e) Imprisonment or other severe deprivation of physical liberty in violation of fundamental rules of international law;
   (f) Torture;
   (g) Rape, sexual slavery, enforced prostitution, forced pregnancy, enforced sterilisation, or any other form of sexual violence of comparable gravity;
   (h) Persecution against any identifiable group or collectivity on political, racial, national, ethnic, cultural, religious, gender as defined in paragraph 3, or other grounds that are universally recognised as impermissible under international law, in connection with any act referred to in this paragraph or any crime within the jurisdiction of the Court;
   (i) Enforced disappearance of persons;
   (j) The crime of apartheid;
   (k) Other inhumane acts of a similar character intentionally causing great suffering, or serious injury to body or to mental or physical health.

Paragraph 2 of Article 7 provides a series of definitions of terms used in paragraph 1. Crimes against humanity were included in the Charter of the Nuremberg IMT (Article 6(c)), but they were to some extent related to the war. This association was removed in the Principles formulated in 1950 by the International Law Commission (see above). In the *Pinochet* case Lord Browne-Wilkinson held that 'ever since 1945 torture on a large scale has featured as one of the crimes against humanity...'.[6] The definition in the ICC Statute is not qualified in a similar way, and does not involve a pattern.

---

[6] [1999] 2 WLR 827, 841; ILR 119, 135, 149.

War crimes (Art. 8)[7]

1. The Court shall have jurisdiction in respect of war crimes in particular when committed as a part of a plan or policy or as a part of a large-scale commission of such crimes.

2. For the purpose of this Statute, 'war crimes' means:

(a) Grave breaches of the Geneva Conventions of 12 August 1949, namely, any of the following acts against persons or property protected under the provisions of the relevant Geneva Convention:

(i) Wilful killing;

(ii) Torture or inhuman treatment, including biological experiments;

(iii) Wilfully causing great suffering, or serious injury to body or health;

(iv) Extensive destruction and appropriation of property, not justified by military necessity and carried out unlawfully and wantonly;

(v) Compelling a prisoner of war or other protected person to serve in the forces of a hostile Power;

(vi) Wilfully depriving a prisoner of war or other protected person of the rights of fair and regular trial;

(vii) Unlawful deportation or transfer or unlawful confinement;

(viii) Taking of hostages.

(b) Other serious violations of the laws and customs applicable in international armed conflict, within the established framework of international law, namely, any of the following acts (in part only):

(i) Intentionally directing attacks against the civilian population as such or against individual civilians not taking direct part in hostilities;

(ii) Intentionally directing attacks against civilian objects, that is, objects which are not military objectives;...

Article 8 also deals with the standards applicable 'in the case of an armed conflict not of an international character', based upon Article 3 common to the four Geneva Conventions of 12 August 1949: see Article 8(2)(c), (d), (e), and (f) of the Statute of the ICC.

(ii) *The Crime of Aggression*

The Statute of the International Criminal Court also includes the crime of aggression, as Article 5 (above) indicates. The content of the crime is subject to the outcome of further negotiations.[8] The Nuremberg Charter of 1945 defined 'crimes against peace' as follows:

namely planning, preparation, initiation or waging of a war of aggression, or a war in violation of international treaties, agreements or assurances, or participation in a Common Plan or Conspiracy for the accomplishment of any of the foregoing.

---

[7] On the relation between war crimes and crimes against humanity see Bing Bing Jia, *Essays in Honour of Ian Brownlie* (1999), 243–71. On the status of the Geneva Conventions as customary international law see the Eritrea-Ethiopia Claims Commission, Decisions of 1 July 2003, *Ethiopia's Claim 4* (Prisoners of War) and *Eritrea's Claim 17* (Prisoners of War).

[8] See the Preparatory Commission for the International Criminal Court, Proceedings of the Preparatory Commission at its fifth session (12–30 June 2000), PCNICC/2000 L.3/Rev. 1, 6 July 2000, 8.

The definition of aggression adopted by consensus in the General Assembly in 1974 placed emphasis (in Article 1) upon violations of the Charter of the United Nations (see *infra*). The Draft Code of Crimes against the Peace and Security of Mankind adopted by the International Law Commission in 1996 defines the crime of aggression as follows in Article 16:

An individual who, as leader or organiser, actively participates in or orders the planning, preparation, initiation or waging of aggression committed by a State, shall be responsible for a crime of aggression.[9]

(iii) *Torture in time of Peace*

It is reasonable to categorize torture in time of peace as an international crime, and Judge Cassese has adopted this approach.[10] Such an approach has several advantages. First, it confirms the status of torture as an offence which exists independently both of the existence of war or armed conflict, and of crimes against humanity. In the latter context the association with crimes against humanity had the consequence that it was sometimes assumed that torture was only an international crime if it involved a pattern of activity. Recent decisions in various jurisdictions have confirmed the status of torture as a crime under general international law without requiring a pattern of activity. A particularly important decision in this respect is that of the ICTY in *Furundzija*,[11] where the Court referred to the Declaration adopted by the General Assembly in 1975[12] and the United Nations Convention Against Torture adopted in 1984.[13]

In spite of these developments the categorisation issue still appears in the provisions of the Statute of the ICTY, the Rwanda Tribunal, and the Rome Statute of the ICC, in which torture is listed as a form of crimes against humanity.

(D) TEMPORALITY

In practice it may be necessary for a court to determine what the scope of an international crime was at the time of the offence, and also whether an offence included in an indictment or request for extradition was recognized as a crime at a particular date. In the House of Lords appeal in the *Pinochet* case six of the seven judges decided that extra territorial torture became a crime in the United Kingdom only in 1988 when the crime was incorporated into local legislation.[14] Lord Millett, in a substantial speech, held as follows:[15]

In my opinion, the systematic use of torture on a large scale and as an instrument of state policy had joined piracy, war crimes and crimes against peace as an international crime of

---

[9] *Yrbk*. ILC. 1996, II (pt. ii), 42–3.
[10] *International Law* (2001), 254–6.
[11] Judgment of the Trial Chamber of 10 December 1998; ILR 121, 254–65.
[12] Resol. 3452 (XXX), 9 Dec. 1975; *Digest of U.S. Practice* (1975), 217. Adopted by consensus.
[13] *ILM* 23 (1984), 1027. States Parties: 123.
[14] [1999] 2 WLR 827; ILR 119, 135.
[15] [1999] 2 WLR 904–13, at 912.

universal jurisdiction well before 1984. I consider that it had done so by 1973. For my own part, therefore, I would hold that the courts of this country already possessed extraterritorial jurisdiction in respect of torture and conspiracy to torture on the scale of the charges in the present case and did not require the authority of statute to exercise it.

In the Statute of the Criminal Tribunal for the Former Yugoslavia the scope of the subject-matter jurisdiction is linked directly with the requirement that the crimes concerned formed part of customary international law at the material time.

3. ENFORCEMENT BY NATIONAL COURTS

Provided certain standards of legality are observed, national courts are at liberty to exercize jurisdiction in respect of international crimes. It is increasingly recognized that the principle of universal jurisdiction is an attribute of the existence of crimes under international law.[16] On occasion courts have punished aliens guilty of harming deported nationals on the basis of the principle of passive nationality.[17] At the end of the Second World War nineteen States adhered to the London Agreement on the prosecution of war criminals and charges were brought before the national courts of China, France, Poland, and other States.[18]

An aspect of the role of national courts is the choice as to the content of the indictment. Thus, it would seem perfectly logical to characterize unlawful killing of civilians as murder under the law of Norway, the law of war being relevant to any issues of exculpation.[19] The indictment of *Eichmann* in the Israeli courts included the count of murder. The nature of the offences committed during the war in Nazi-occupied territory justified the application of universal jurisdiction on an inter-temporal basis. In the words of the Supreme Court of Israel:[20]

We have thus far stated our reasons for dismissing the first two contentions of counsel for the appellant in reliance upon the rules that determine the relationship between Israel municipal law and international law. Our principal object was to make it clear—and this is by way of a negative approach—that under international law no *prohibition* whatsoever falls upon the enactment of the Law of 1950 either because it created *ex post facto* offences or because such offences are of an extra-territorial character. Nevertheless, like the District Court, we too do not content ourselves with this solution but have undertaken the task of showing that it is impossible to justify these contentions even from a positive approach—that in enacting the said Law the Knesset only sought to set out the principles of

---

[16] See *In re Gerbsch*, ILR 16, 399.

[17] See *In re Rohrig*, ILR 17, 393.

[18] See the *History of the United Nations War Crimes Commission* (HMSO, London, 1948).

[19] See *In re Hans*, ILR 14, 305.

[20] *A.G. of the Government of Israel* v. *Adolf Eichmann*, ILR 36, 5, 287, para. 10.

international law and embody its aims. The two propositions on which we propose to rely will therefore be as follows:

(1) The crimes created by the Law and of which the appellant was convicted must be deemed today as having always borne the stamp of international crimes, banned by the law of nations and entailing individual criminal responsibility.

(2) It is the peculiarity universal character of these crimes that vests in every State the authority to try and punish anyone who participated in their commission.

The role played by national courts and military tribunals has been episodic and far from consistent.[21] The reluctance of governments to prosecute their own nationals inevitably provides a part of the policy basis for the establishment of international criminal courts.

However, the role of national courts has been given emphasis in the Statute of the International Criminal Court, where it is stated in the preamble that the Court 'shall be complementary to national criminal jurisdictions'. The International Criminal Tribunal for the Former Yugoslavia does not deprive national courts of their jurisdiction over the relevant international crimes but does have a significant super-visory role.

4. TEMPORAL JURISDICTION

The temporal limits of the jurisdiction of international criminal courts are set by their constituent instruments. Thus the temporal jurisdiction of the ICTY is established in Article 8 of the Statute to begin on 1 January 1991.[22] The Statute of the International Criminal Court provides, in Article II, that the Court 'has jurisdiction only with respect to crimes committed after the entry into force of this Statute', and, in Article 24, that no person 'shall be criminally responsible under this Statute for conduct prior to the entry into force of this Statute'.

The question of jurisdiction *ratione temporis* was raised by Yugoslavia in the *Genocide* case before the International Court of Justice. The Court rejected the argument:[23]

... it remains for the Court to specify the scope of that jurisdiction *ratione temporis*. In its sixth and seventh preliminary objections, Yugoslavia, basing its contention on the principle of the non-retroactivity of legal acts, has indeed asserted as a subsidi-ary argument that, even though the Court might have jurisdiction on the basis of the Convention, it could only deal with events subsequent to the different dates on which the Convention might have become applicable as between the Parties. In this regard, the Court will confine itself to the observation that the Genocide Convention—and

---

[21] See Schabas, *Journ. of Int. Crim. Justice*, 1 (2003), 39–63.
[22] On the factors lying behind this choice of date see Shraga and Zacklin, *Europ. Journ.* 5 (1994), 362–3.
[23] ICJ Reports (1996), 617, para. 34.

in particular Article IX—does not contain any clause the object or effect of which is to limit in such manner the scope of its jurisdiction *ratione temporis*, and nor did the Parties themselves make any reservation to that end, either to the Convention or on the occasion of the signature of the Dayton-Paris Agreement. The Court thus finds that it has jurisdiction in this case to give effect to the Genocide Convention with regard to the relevant facts which have occurred since the beginning of the conflict which took place in Bosnia and Herzegovina.

In the remainder of this passage there is a certain suggestion that temporal limitations do not attach to genocide *per se*.[24]

5. THE APPLICABILITY OF STATUTORY LIMITATIONS TO INTERNATIONAL CRIMES

A source of problems is the application of municipal rules on limitation to war crimes and other crimes against international law.[25] In principle the *erga omnes* character of crimes against international law excludes the application of principles of limitation. In 1968 the General Assembly adopted the Convention on the Non-Applicability of Statutory Limitations to War Crimes and Crimes against Humanity.[26] A distinct but analogous issue is whether particular legislation is retroactive as opposed to being retrospective.[27]

6. MULTILATERAL TREATY REGIMES

Certain threats to international public order have been addressed by means of multilateral standard-setting conventions. A significant example is the Montreal Convention of 1971 for the Suppression of Unlawful Acts against the Safety of Civil Aviation.[28] The Convention provides that each Contracting Party has a duty to arrest and try an offender present in its territory (Article 6). It is further provided that if the Contracting State with custody of the offender does not extradite him, then it is obliged to try the offender, whether or not the offence was committed in its territory (Article 7). In relation to the destruction by an act of terrorism of the Pan-Am flight 103 over Lockerbie in Scotland, causing 270 deaths, Libya declared its readiness to prosecute the suspects in Libya. In face of the unwillingness of the United Kingdom and the United States

---

[24] See below.
[25] See the *Barbie* case in the French courts: see ILR 78, 125, 136 (Ct. of Cassation (Criminal Chamber)).
[26] In force 11 November 1970; *ILM* 8 (1969), 8. See generally Weiss, 53 *BY* (1982), 163–95.
[27] See *In re Finta*, ILR 82, 424; Canada: High Ct.; *Regina* v. *Finta*, ILR 98, 520; Ontario Court of Appeal.
[28] Text: *ILM* 10 (1971), 1151.

to countenance this course, the Libyan Government began proceedings against both States in the International Court concerning the interpretation and application of the Convention.[29]

Another important standard-setting Convention of the same type is the Convention against Torture adopted by the General Assembly on 10 December 1984.[30]

7. NORMS HAVING THE CHARACTER OF OBLIGATIONS *ERGA OMNES*

In its Judgment in the *Genocide* case (*Bosnia and Herzegovina* v. *Yugoslavia*) the International Court adopted the view that territorial restrictions do not apply to rights and obligations which are *erga omnes*. In the words of the Court:[31]

...as to the territorial problems linked to the application of the Convention, the Court would point out that the only provision relevant to this, Article VI, merely provides for persons accused of one of the acts prohibited by the Convention to 'be tried by a competent tribunal of the State in the territory of which the act was committed...'. It would also recall its understanding of the object and purpose of the Convention, as set out in its Opinion of 28 May 1951, cited above:

The origins of the Convention show that it was the intention of the United Nations to condemn and punish genocide as 'a crime under international law' involving a denial of the right of existence of entire human groups, a denial which shocks the conscience of mankind and results in great losses to humanity, and which is contrary to moral law and to the spirit and aims of the United Nations (Resolution 96(I) of the General Assembly, December 11th 1946). The first consequence arising from this conception is that the principles underlying the Convention are principles which are recognised by civilised nations as binding on States, even without any conventional obligation. A second consequence is the universal character both of the condemnation of genocide and of the co-operation required 'in order to liberate mankind from such an odious scourge' (Preamble to the Convention).' (*I.C.J. Reports 1951*, p. 23).

It follows that the rights and obligations enshrined by the Convention are rights and obligations *erga omnes*. The Court notes that the obligation each State thus has to prevent and to punish the crime of genocide is not territorially limited by the Convention.

---

[29] See *Case Concerning Questions of Interpretation and Application of the 1971 Montreal Convention Arising from the Aerial Incident at Lockerbie* (Libyan Arab Jamahiriya v. United Kingdom) (Preliminary Objections), I.C.J. Reports, 1998, 9; the same case against the United States, ibid., 115.

[30] Text: *ILM* 23 (1984), 1027. States Parties: 123.

[31] ICJ Reports (1996), 615–16.

There is a suggestion of similar thinking by the Court in relation to the finding on temporal jurisdiction. The Court stated that 'this finding is, moreover, in accordance with the object and purpose of the Convention as defined by the Court in 1951 ... '[32]

In a related context, the presiding Judge in the *Pinochet* appeal, Lord Browne-Wilkinson, linked the '*jus cogens* nature of the international crime of torture' with the justification of resort to universal jurisdiction on the part of States.[33] The Judgment of the Trial Chamber of the ICTY in *Furundzija* emphasized the character of the prohibition of torture and the consequent obligations for States as obligations *erga omnes*, and also having the status of *jus cogens*.[34]

A further question is whether in general international law the *erga omnes* quality of international crimes has the consequence that States receiving suspects on their territory have a duty to prosecute.[35]

8. CRIMINAL TRIBUNALS ESTABLISHED BY THE SECURITY COUNCIL ACTING UNDER CHAPTER VII OF THE CHARTER OF THE UNITED NATIONS

(A) THE INTERNATIONAL CRIMINAL TRIBUNAL FOR THE FORMER YUGOSLAVIA (ICTY)[36]

At a certain point in the development of the armed conflict in Yugoslavia, beginning in 1991, the Security Council decided to create a tribunal to deal with those responsible for breaches of international humanitarian law (violations of the Geneva Conventions, crimes against humanity and genocide).[37] On the basis of a Report of the Secretary-General, which included a draft Statute, the Security Council approved the Statute of the International Tribunal without change.[38] The Court began to function in 1995. It consists of three Trial chambers and an Appeals chamber. Its seat is in The Hague. Its early tasks included the preparation of a code of criminal procedure and various regulatory matters, including regulations governing the treatment of detainees.

---

[32] ICJ Reports (1996), 617, para. 34.

[33] [1999] 2 WLR 827, 841; ILR 119, 135, 149.

[34] Judgment of 10 December 1998; ILR 121, 260–2.

[35] See Goodwin-Gill, *Essays in Honour of Ian Brownlie* (1999), 199–223.

[36] See Meron, *AJ* 88 (1994), 78–87; O'Brien, *AJ* 87 (1993), 639–59; Shraga and Zacklin, *Europ. Journ.* 5 (1994), 360–80; Cassese, *Encycl. of P.I.L.* (ed. Bernhardt), IV, 1608–16; Kolb, *BY* 71 (2000), 259–315.

[37] See S. C. Resol. 808 (1993), adopted on 22 February 1993.

[38] See Resol. 827 (1993), adopted on 25 May 1993. For the text of the Report see *ILM* 32 (1993), 1203.

Article 8 of the Statute defines the limits of territorial and temporal jurisdiction as follows:

The territorial jurisdiction of the International Tribunal shall extend to the territory of the former Socialist Federal Republic of Yugoslavia, including its land surface, airspace and territorial waters. The temporal jurisdiction of the International Tribunal shall extend to a period beginning on 1 January 1991.

The subject-matter jurisdiction of the Tribunal extends to grave breaches of the Geneva Conventions of 1949, violations of the laws and customs of war, genocide and crimes against humanity. The background is elucidated by Shraga and Zacklin as follows:[39]

The establishment of the Tribunal under Chapter VII of the United Nations Charter delimited not only its territorial and temporal jurisdiction, but also circumscribed the scope of its subject-matter jurisdiction and imposed strict criteria on the choice of the applicable law. The fact that the Security Council is not a legislative body mandated that the subsidiary organ it created would not be endowed with competence the parent body did not have. Likewise it could not be seen as creating a new international law binding upon the parties to the conflict.

The Tribunal was, accordingly, empowered to apply only those provisions of international humanitarian law which are beyond any doubt part of customary international law, irrespective of their codification in any international instrument, and regardless of whether the State or States in question had adhered to them and duly incorporated their provisions into their national legislation. The list of international humanitarian law violations that are of an undoubtedly customary international law nature, was further limited to those which have customarily entailed the criminal liability of the individual, and includes, according to Articles 2 to 5 of the Statute: grave breaches of the Geneva Conventions, violations of the laws or customs of war, the crime of genocide and crimes against humanity.

As a consequence, the case law of the Tribunal touches upon the requirement that the violations concerned must involve individual criminal responsibility under customary law. This issue appears constantly in the case law. In the *Tadic* case[40] the context included grave breaches of the Geneva Conventions of 1949, and crimes against humanity, whilst in *Furundzija* the context consisted of torture[41] and also rape and serious sexual assaults.[42]

The issue of 'individual criminal responsibility' is dealt with comprehensively in Article 7 of the Statute:

1. A person who planned, instigated, ordered, committed or otherwise aided and abetted in the planning, preparation or execution of a crime referred to in Articles 2 to 5 of the present Statute, shall be individually responsible for the crime.

2. The official position of any accused person, whether as Head of State or Government or as a responsible Government official, shall not relieve such person of criminal responsibility nor mitigate punishment.

---

[39] *Europ. Journ.* 5 (1994), 363.
[40] Trial Chamber II, 7 May 1997; ILR 112, 1, 201–23.
[41] Trial Chamber II, 10 December 1998; ILR 121, 213, 254–65.
[42] Ibid., 266–73.

3. The fact that any of the acts referred to in Articles 2 to 5 of the present Statute was committed by a subordinate does not relieve his superior of criminal responsibility if he knew or had reason to know that the subordinate was about to commit such acts or had done so and the superior failed to take the necessary and reasonable measures to prevent such acts or to punish the perpetrators thereof.

4. The fact that an accused person acted pursuant to an order of a Government or of a superior shall not relieve him of criminal responsibility, but may be considered in mitigation of punishment if the International Tribunal determines that justice so requires.

These provisions reflect generally accepted principles governing individual responsibility, but with the qualification that the denial of immunity is controversial: see below. In this context it is to be recalled that the ICTY forms part of a radical and coercive regime imposed by the Security Council acting on the basis of Chapter 7 of the United Nations Charter.

In spite of this background the Statute retains a role for national courts and thus provides for concurrent jurisdiction as follows in Article 9 of the Statute:[43]

1. The International Tribunal and national courts shall have concurrent jurisdiction to persecute persons for serious violations of international humanitarian law committed in the territory of the former Yugoslavia since 1 January 1991.

2. The International Tribunal shall have primacy over national courts. At any stage of the procedure, the International Tribunal may formally request national courts to defer to the competence of the International Tribunal in accordance with the present Statute and the Rules of Procedure and Evidence of the International Tribunal.

The modalities of intervention and deferral are elaborated in the Rules of Procedure and Evidence of the Tribunal.

In respect of enforcement powers, there are serious difficulties. The Tribunal has the power to issue warrants for arrest and subpoenas, but does not have the necessary enforcement powers. The Tribunal is thus reliant upon States for the execution of its orders.[44] In practice use has been made of IFOR to enforce arrest warrants in Bosnia and Herzegovina, and of UNTAES in the Eastern Slavonian region of Croatia.[45]

(B) THE INTERNATIONAL CRIMINAL TRIBUNAL FOR RWANDA (ICTR)

This Tribunal was established by virtue of Security Council Resolution 955 (1994), adopted on 8 November 1994, and the Annex contains the Statute of the Tribunal.[46] Its competence is described in Article 1 as follows:

The International Tribunal for Rwanda shall have the power to prosecute persons responsible for serious violations of international humanitarian law committed in the territory of

---

[43] See further Shraga and Zacklin, op. cit., 371–2.

[44] See Cassese, Bernhardt (ed.), *Encycl. of P.I.L.*, IV, 1613.

[45] See Lamb, *BY*, 70 (1999), 165–244.

[46] *ILM* 33 (1994), 1600. See also the *Yearbook of the United Nations*, Vol. 50 (1996), 1194–1201. See also Kolb, *BY* 71 (2000), 259–315.

neighbouring States, between 1 January 1994 and 31 December 1994, in accordance with the provisions of the present Statute.

The elements of subject-matter jurisdiction and personal jurisdiction are similar to those of the ICTY examined above.

9. THE INTERNATIONAL CRIMINAL COURT (ICC)[47]

In 1994 the International Law Commission adopted a Draft Statute for an International Criminal Court, which was recommended to the General Assembly.[48] Most delegations in the General Assembly expressed support for the establishment of an international criminal court. Part of the background to the evolution of opinion was the belief that such a court would be more appropriate than the *ad hoc* 'regional' criminal tribunals being created by the Security Council. After much work in the Preparatory Commission and elsewhere, in 1998 a Diplomatic Conference was convened in Rome on the establishment of an International Criminal Court. After a series of significant compromises had been achieved, the Statute of the Court was signed on 17 July 1998.[49] In accordance with the provisions of Article 126, the Statute entered into force when sixty states had ratified, accepted, or approved it, or acceded to it. It is a momentous development and has provoked some political opposition, chiefly, but by no means exclusively, from the United States.

Part 4 of the Statute is concerned with the composition of the Court. It consists of eighteen judges, serving for nine years, after the first election (groups of six selected by lot to serve for three, six, and nine years). The judges are not (with some minor exceptions) eligible for re-election.

The subject-matter jurisdiction (Article 5) extends to the crime of genocide; crimes against humanity; war crimes; and the crime of aggression: see above. The definition of the crime of aggression is still the subject of negotiation. The key provisions on jurisdiction otherwise are as follows:

ARTICLE 12

PRECONDITIONS TO THE EXERCISE OF JURISDICTION

1. A State which becomes a Party to this Statute thereby accepts the jurisdiction of the Court with respect to the crimes referred to in article 5.

---

[47] See Cassese, Gaeta and Jones (eds.), *The Rome Statute of the International Criminal Court: A Commentary*, 3 Vols. (2002); Arsanjani and Reisman, *AJ*, 99 (2005), 385–403; and Akhavan, ibid., 403–21.

[48] See the Report of the ILC on the work of its 46th Session; *Yrbk* ILC 1994, II (pt. ii), 26–74.

[49] See Cassese, Gaeta and Jones, *Materials* vol.; and United Nations Diplomatic Conference of Plenipotentiaries, 15 June–17 July 1998: *Off. Recs.*, 3 vols.

2. In the case of Article 13, paragraph (a) or (c), the Court may exercise its jurisdiction if one or more of the following States are Parties to this Statute or have accepted the jurisdiction of the Court in accordance with paragraph 3:

   (a) The State on the territory of which the conduct in question occurred or, if the crime was committed on board a vessel or aircraft, the State of registration of that vessel or aircraft;

   (b) The State of which the person accused of the crime is a national.

3. If the acceptance of a State which is not a Party to this Statute is required under paragraph 2, that State may, by declaration lodged with the Registrar, accept the exercise of jurisdiction by the Court with respect to the crime in question. The accepting State shall cooperate with the Court without any delay or exception in accordance with Part 9.

ARTICLE 13

EXERCISE OF JURISDICTION

The Court may exercise its jurisdiction with respect to a crime referred to in Article 5 in accordance with the provisions of this Statute if:

   (a) A situation in which one or more of such crimes appears to have been committed is referred to the Prosecutor by a State Party in accordance with Article 14;

   (b) A situation in which one or more of such crimes appears to have been committed is referred to the Prosecutor by the Security Council acting under Chapter VII of the Charter of the United Nations; or

   (c) The Prosecutor has initiated an investigation in respect of such a crime in accordance with Article 15.

The jurisdiction of the ICC depends upon the consent of the States Parties. In this respect it is similar to the crimes, such as terrorism directed against aircraft, governed by multilateral standard-setting treaties. The ICC also leaves considerable powers and responsibilities in the hands of States. Thus the principle of complementarity gives States Parties the first opportunity to investigate and prosecute persons responsible for the relevant crimes: see the Statute, Articles 17 and 18.

In accordance with Article 13 of the Statute, jurisdiction arises on the basis of three trigger mechanisms: reference to the Prosecutor by a State Party; reference to the Prosecutor by the Security Council; and the initiation of an investigation by the Prosecutor *proprio motu*. Three States have referred situations to the Office of the Prosecutor: the Central African Republic, the Congo, and Uganda. On 31 March 2005 the Security Council referred the situation in Darfur. In 2008 the hearing schedule contained three cases.

A source of difficulty concerns the impact of the Statute on third States.[50] It is, of course, perfectly normal for States to exercise criminal jurisdiction in respect of the nationals of other States, if certain conditions are satisfied. However, concerns have

---

[50] See Danilenko, in Cassese, Gaeta and Jones, op. cit., 1871–97; and Mégret, *Europ. Journ.*, 12 (2001), 247–68.

been expressed about referrals to the ICC of cases in which American nationals are charged with crimes resulting from forcible interventions abroad or lawful peacekeeping operations.[51] As Professor Wedgwood states the problem:[52]

Another issue that was inadequately analysed in Rome—and of central importance in evolving American attitudes towards the Court—is the question of taking jurisdiction over nationals of states that have not ratified the treaty. The issue of universal jurisdiction was not discussed at all in plenary sessions, and was compromised in a way that left all sides unhappy. One argument in favour of allowing the prosecution of the nationals of non-treaty parties is that states often prosecute foreign nationals for matters that occur within their state territories (the principle of territoriality), or affect their citizens as victims (the principle of passive personality), or merely affect state interests (the principle of protective jurisdiction). The consent of the foreign national's state is not required....

...All states claiming territorial integrity and political independence within the Westphalian system are bound to respect the domestic governance of other countries, including their legitimate exercise of public authority over criminal behaviour, limited by the jurisdictional rules of international law. But, one might argue, states are not obliged to participate in an international body. The genius behind the Rome Statute was to build a stable regime founded on state consent, rather than the peremptory authority of the Security Council. It may, then, seem in tension to prosecute third party nationals under that regime.

The regime of arrest and surrender for trial depends upon the co-operation of custodial States in accordance with the Statute and involves certain complexities regarding the mechanism for distributing national and international prosecutions.[53]

10. IMMUNITY FROM JURISDICTION[54]

A problem which has faced the International Court, and various national courts, since the last edition of this book is the relationship between the immunity of Heads of State and government ministers from criminal jurisdiction in respect of conduct during their periods of office and the concept of international crimes having the character of jus cogens. In its Judgment in the *Arrest Warrant* case (Democratic Republic of Congo v. Belgium), the International Court, dealing with the status of an incumbent Minister for Foreign Affairs drew the following conclusions:[55]

53. In customary international law, the immunities accorded to Ministers for Foreign Affairs are not granted for their personal benefit, but to ensure the effective performance of

---

[51] See Wedgwood, *Europ. Journ.* 10 (1999), 93–107; Scheffer, *AJ* 93 (1999), 12–21; Monroe Leigh, *AJ* 95 (2001), 124–31. The United States has concluded at least 25 agreements with other States to prevent the prosecution of its nationals.

[52] Ibid., 99.

[53] See generally Young, *BY* 71 (2000), 317–56.

[54] See Watts, Hague Academy, *Recueil des cours*, Vol. 247 (1994, III), 19–130; *Annuaire de l'Institut*, Vol. 69 (2000–2001), 441–709; Fox, *The Law of State Immunity* (2002), 421–48.

[55] *ILM* 41 (2002), 536, 549–50. See Cassese, *Europ. Journ.*, 13 (2002), 853–75; Spinedi, ibid., 895–9.

their functions on behalf of their respective States. In order to determine the extent of these immunities, the Court must therefore first consider the nature of the functions exercised by a Minister for Foreign Affairs. He or she is in charge of his or her Government's diplomatic activities and generally acts as its representative in international negotiations and inter-governmental meetings. Ambassadors and other diplomatic agents carry out their duties under his or her authority. His or her acts may bind the State represented, and there is a presumption that a Minister for Foreign Affairs, simply by virtue of that office, has full powers to act on behalf of the State (see, e.g. Art. 7, para 2(a), of the 1969 Vienna Convention on the Law of Treaties). In the performance of these functions, he or she is frequently required to travel internationally, and thus must be in a position freely to do so whenever the need should arise. He or she must also be in constant communication with the Government, and with its diplomatic missions around the world, and be capable at any time of communicating with representatives of other States. The Court further observes that a Minister for Foreign Affairs, responsible for the conduct of his or her State's relations with all other States, occupies a position such that, like the Head of State or the Head of Government, he or she is recognized under international law as representative of the State solely by virtue of his or her office. He or she does not have to present letters of credence: to the contrary, it is generally the Minister who determines the authority to be conferred upon diplomatic agents and countersigns their letter of credence. Finally, it is to the Minister for Foreign Affairs that chargés d' affaires are accredited.

54. The Court accordingly concludes that the functions of a Minister for Foreign Affairs are such that, throughout the duration of his or her office, he or she when abroad enjoys full immunity from criminal jurisdiction and inviolability. That immunity and that inviolability protect the individual concerned against any act of authority of another State which would hinder him or her in the performance of his or her duties.

The decision involved upholding such immunity even in respect of alleged crimes under international law, namely, war crimes and crimes against humanity. The European Court of Human Rights has also maintained the application of the principle of immunity in cases based upon the European Convention.[56]

However, certain senior municipal courts have challenged the validity of the principle of immunity in cases involving charges of international crimes. In the Pinochet case[57] the House of Lords, in the second appeal, dealt with charges of torture brought against a former Head of State of Chile by the Spanish Government. Several Law Lords in the second appeal stated that the standard of whether torture was lawful or not was set by international law, not by domestic law, and thus torture cannot constitute acts committed in performance of the official function of a Head of State. This logic was applied to the position of a former Head of State, who could only claim the benefit of immunity ratione materiae. However, the same logic should surely apply to the position of a serving Head of State and immunity ratione personae.

---

[56] Al-Adsani v. United Kingdom (21 Nov. 2001); Fogarty v. United Kingdom (21 Nov. 2001); and McElhinney v. United Kingdom (21 Nov. 2001). See Orakhelashvili, German Yrbk. Vol.45 (2002), 227–67; Leiden Journ., Vol.15 (2002), 703–14.

[57] [1999] 2 WLR 827.

11. SOME REFLECTIONS ON THE RULE OF LAW

The subject of international criminal justice is benighted by strong elements of paradox. On the face of things the Rule of Law has been strengthened by a proliferation of international criminal tribunals, including the International Criminal Court, whose Judges were elected by the General Assembly in 2003. But the picture includes negative elements. In some situations the creation of a Tribunal has appeared to be a substitute for more effective preventive action by the international community, as in the case of the genocide in Rwanda. Moreover, in the case of the ICTY the creation of the Tribunal was associated with a specialized political campaign to destabilize the multi-ethnic State of Yugoslavia, with the ultimate aim of bringing about 'regime change' in Serbia. The Tribunal formed part of a coercive order created by the Security Council, and some observers have raised questions about the independence of the prosecution process from external influences. In the case of the Rwanda Tribunal the trial process is very slow and thousands of prisoners await trial.

In any event a variety of institutional forms of criminal justice are now appearing.[58] A recent example is the Sierra Leone Special Court.[59] This is based on the consent of the State concerned and has jurisdiction exclusively over international crimes. The Special Court has concurrent jurisdiction with, and primacy over, the domestic courts of Sierra Leone. The overall problem remains. Political considerations, power, and patronage will continue to determine who is to be tried for international crimes and who not.

---

[58] See Mundis, *AJ* 95 (2001), 934–52.
[59] See Resol. 1315 (2000), *ILM* 40 (2001), 247; and Mundis, op. cit., 935–42. See also the draft Agreement between the United Nations and the Royal Government of Cambodia concerning the Prosecution under Cambodian Law of Crimes Committed during the Period of Democratic Kampuchea: Annex to U.N. General Assembly Resol. 57/228, 13 May 2003.

PART X

INTERNATIONAL TRANSACTIONS

27

THE LAW OF TREATIES

1. INTRODUCTION[1]

A great many international disputes are concerned with the validity and interpretation of international agreements, and the practical content of state relations is embodied in agreements. The great international organizations, including the United Nations, have their legal basis in multilateral agreements. Since it began its work the International Law Commission has concerned itself with the law of treaties, and in 1966 it adopted a set of 75 draft articles.[2]

These draft articles formed the basis for the Vienna Conference which in two sessions (1968 and 1969) completed work on the Vienna Convention on the Law of Treaties, consisting of 85 articles and an Annex. The Convention[3] entered into force on 27 January 1980 and not less than 105 states have become parties.[4]

---

[1] The principal items are: the Vienna Conv. on the Law of Treaties (see n. 3); the commentary of the International Law Commission on the Final Draft Articles, *Yrbk. ILC* (1966), ii. 172 at 187–274; Whiteman, xiv. 1–510; Rousseau, i. 61–305; Guggenheim, i. 113–273; McNair, *Law of Treaties* (1961); Harvard Research, 29 *AJ* (1935), Suppl.; O'Connell, i. 195–280; Sørensen, pp. 175–246; Jennings, 121 Hague *Recueil* (1967, II), 527–81; *Répertoire suisse*, i. 5–209; Elias, *The Modern Law of Treaties* (1974); Reuter, *Introduction au droit des traités* (2nd edn., 1985); id., *Introduction to the Law of Treaties* (1989). See further: Rousseau, *Principes généraux du droit international public*, i (1944); Basdevant, 15 Hague *Recueil* (1926, V), 539–642; Detter, *Essays on the Law of Treaties* (1967); Gotlieb, *Canadian Treaty-Making* (1968); various authors, 27 *Z.a.ö.R.u.V.* (1967), 408–561; ibid. 29 (1969), 1–70, 536–42, 654–710; Verzijl, *International Law in Historical Perspective*, vi (1973), 112–612; Sinclair, *The Vienna Convention on the Law of Treaties*, 2nd ed. (1984); Thirlway, 62 *BY* (1991), 2–75; id., 63 *BY* (1992), 1–96; Oppenheim, ii. 1197–1333; Rosenne, *Developments in the Law of Treaties, 1945–1986* (1989); Aust, *Modern Treaty Law and Practice* (2000).

[2] The principal items are as follows: International Law Commission, Reports by Brierly, *Yrbk.* (1950), ii; (1951), ii; (1952), ii; Reports by Lauterpacht, *Yrbk.* (1953), ii; (1954), ii; Reports by Fitzmaurice, *Yrbk.* (1956), ii; (1957), ii; (1958), ii; (1960), ii; Reports by Waldock, *Yrbk.* (1962), ii; (1963), ii; (1964), ii; (1965), ii; (1966), ii; Draft articles adopted by the Commission, I, Conclusion, Entry into Force and Registration of Treaties, *Yrbk.* (1962), ii. 159; 57 *AJ* (1963), 190; *Yrbk.* (1965), ii. 159; 60 *AJ* (1966), 164; Draft Articles, II, Invalidity and Termination of Treaties, *Yrbk.* (1963), ii. 189; 58 *AJ* (1964), 241; Draft Articles, III, Application, Effects, Modification and Interpretation of Treaties, *Yrbk.* (1964), ii; 59 *AJ* (1965), 203, 434; Final Report and Draft, *Yrbk.* (1966), ii. 172; 61 *AJ* (1967), 263.

[3] Text: 63 *AJ* (1969), 875; 8 *ILM* (1969), 679; Brownlie, *Documents*, p. 270. For the preparatory materials see: items in n. 2; *United Nations Conference on the Law of Treaties, First Session, Official Records*, A/CONF. 39/11; *Second Session*, A/CONF.39/11; Add. 1; Rosenne, *The Law of Treaties* (1970). For comment see Reuter, *La Convention de Vienne sur le droit des traités* (1970); Elias, *The Modern Law of Treaties* (1974); Sinclair, *The Vienna Convention on the Law of Treaties*; (2nd edn., 1984); Kearney and Dalton, 64 *AJ* (1970), 495–561; Jennings, 121 Hague *Recueil* (1967, II), 527–81; Deleau, *Ann. français* (1969), 7–23; Nahlik, ibid. 24–53; Frankowska, 3 *Polish Yrbk.* (1970), 227–55.

[4] Art. 84.

The Convention is not as a whole declaratory of general international law: it does not express itself so to be (see the preamble). Various provisions clearly involve progressive development of the law; and the preamble affirms that questions not regulated by its provisions will continue to be governed by the rules of customary international law. Nonetheless, a good number of articles are essentially declaratory of existing law and certainly those provisions which are not constitute presumptive evidence of emergent rules of general international law.[5] The provisions of the Convention are normally regarded as a primary source: as, for example, in the oral proceedings before the International Court in the *Namibia* case. In its Advisory Opinion in that case the Court observed:[6] 'The rules laid down by the Vienna Convention ... concerning termination of a treaty relationship on account of breach (adopted without a dissenting vote) may in many respects be considered as a codification of existing customary law on the subject'.

The Convention was adopted by a very substantial majority at the Conference[7] and constitutes a comprehensive code of the main areas of the law of treaties. However, it does not deal with (*a*) treaties between states and organizations, or between two or more organizations;[8] (*b*) questions of state succession;[9] (*c*) the effect of war on treaties.[10] The Convention is not retroactive in effect.[11]

A provisional draft of the International Law Commission[12] defined a 'treaty' as:

any international agreement in written form, whether embodied in a single instrument or in two or more related instruments and whatever its particular designation (treaty, convention, protocol, covenant, charter, statute, act, declaration, concordat, exchange of notes, agreed minute, memorandum of agreement, *modus vivendi* or any other appellation), concluded between two or more States or other subjects of international law and governed by international law.

The reference to 'other subjects' of the law was designed to provide for treaties concluded by international organizations, the Holy See, and other international entities such as insurgents.[13]

---

[5] Cf. *North Sea Continental Shelf Cases, supra,* p. 12.

[6] ICJ Reports (1971), 16 at 47. See also *Appeal relating to Jurisdiction of ICAO Council*, ICJ Reports (1972), 46 at 67; *Fisheries Jurisdiction Case*, ICJ Reports (1973), 3 at 18; *Case Concerning Sovereignty over Pulao Ligitan and Pulao Sipidan*, Judgment of 17 December 2002, para. 37; *Case Concerning the Land and Maritime Boundary Between Cameroon and Nigeria*, Judgment of 10 October 2002, para. 263; *Iran–United States, Case No. A/18*; ILR 75, 176 at 187–8; *Lithgow*, ibid. 439 at 483–4; *Restrictions on the Death Penalty* (Adv. Op. of Inter-American Ct. of HR, 8 Sept. 1983), ILR 70, 449 at 465–71; *Asian Agricultural Products Ltd.* v. *Republic of Sri Lanka*, ILR 106, 416, 437–46; *Ethyl Corporation* v. *Government of Canada*, ILR 122, 250, 278–80; *Pope and Talbot* v. *Government of Canada*, ILR 22, 293 (Interim Award, 316, paras. 64–9).

[7] 79 votes in favour; 1 against; 19 abstentions.

[8] *Infra,* p. 679.

[9] *Infra,* p. 649.

[10] See *infra,* p. 620.

[11] See McDade, 35 *ICLQ* (1986), 499–511.

[12] *Yrbk. ILC* (1962), ii. 161.

[13] See ch. 3 on legal personality.

In the Vienna Convention, as in the Final Draft of the Commission, the provisions are confined to treaties between states (Art. 1).[14] Article 3 provides that the fact that the Convention is thus limited shall not affect the legal force of agreements between states and other subjects of international law or between such other subjects of international law or between such other subjects. Article 2(1)(a) defines a treaty as 'an international agreement concluded between States in written form and governed by international law, whether embodied in a single instrument or in two or more related instruments[15] and whatever its particular designation'. The distinction between a transaction which is a definitive legal commitment between two states, and one which involves something less than that is difficult to draw but the form of the instrument, for example, a joint communiqué, is not decisive.[16] Article 2 stipulates that the agreements to which the Convention extends be 'governed by international law' and thus excludes the various commercial arrangements, such as purchase and lease, made between governments and operating only under one or more national laws.[17] The capacity of particular international organizations to make treaties depends on the constitution of the organization concerned.[18]

2. CONCLUSION OF TREATIES[19]

(a) Form[20]

The manner in which treaties are negotiated and brought into force is governed by the intention and consent of the parties. There are no substantive requirements of form, and thus, for example, an agreement may be recorded in an exchange of letters or the minutes of a conference.[21] In practice form is governed partly by usage, and thus form will vary according to whether the agreement is expressed to be between states, heads of states, governments (increasingly used), or particular ministers or departments.

---

[14] On the concept of a treaty see Widdows, 50 *BY* (1979), 117–49; Virally, in *Festschrift für Rudolf Bindschedler* (1980), 159–72; Thirlway, 62 *BY* (1991), 4–15; Malgosia Fitzmaurice, 73 *BY* (2002), 141–85.

[15] The conclusion of treaties in simplified form is increasingly common. Many treaties are made by an exchange of notes, the adoption of an agreed minute and so on. See: *Yrbk. ILC* (1966), ii. 188 (Commentary); Hamzeh, 43 *BY* (1968–9), 1779–89; Smets, *La Conclusion des accords en forme simplifée* (1969); Gotlieb, *Canadian Treaty-Making* (1968).

[16] See the *Aegean Sea Continental Shelf Case*, ICJ Reports (1978), 3 at 38–44; and the *Nicaragua* case (Merits), ibid. (1986), 14 at 130–2.

[17] See Mann, 33 *BY* (1957), 20–51; id., 35 *BY* (1959), 34–57; and cf. the *Diverted Cargoes* case, *RIAA* xii. 53 at 70. See also *British Practice* (1967), 147.

[18] On the capacity of members of federal states: *supra*, pp. 58–9, 74.

[19] The effect on the validity of treaties of non-compliance with internal law is considered in s. 5. On participation in multilateral treaties, see *infra*, p. 667.

[20] See generally Aust, 35 *ICLQ* (1986), 787–812. On 'gentleman's agreements' see E. Lauterpacht, *Festschrift für F. A. Mann* (1977), 381–98; Eisemann, *JDI* (1979), 326–48; Virally, *Annuaire de l'Inst.* 60 (1983), i. 166–374; ibid. 60, ii. 284 (Resol.); Thirlway, 63 *BY* (1991), 18–22.

[21] See *Case Concerning Maritime Delimitation and Territorial Questions (Qatar v. Bahrain)*, ICJ Reports, 1994, 112 at 120–2.

The Vienna Convention applies only to agreements 'in written form' but Article 3 stipulates that this limitation is without prejudice to the legal force of agreements 'not in written form'. Obviously substantial parts of the Convention are not relevant to oral agreements: the fact remains that important parts of the law, for example, relating to invalidity and termination, will apply to oral agreements.[22]

(b) Full powers and signature[23]

The era of absolute monarchs and slow communications produced a practice in which a sovereign's agent would be given a Full Power to negotiate and to bind his principal. In modern practice, subject to a different intention of the parties, a Full Power involves an authority to negotiate and to sign and seal a treaty. In the case of agreements between governments Full Powers, in the sense of the formal documents evidencing these and their reciprocal examinations by the negotiators, are often dispensed with.[24]

The successful outcome of negotiation is the adoption and authentication of the agreed text. Signature has, as one of its functions, that of authentication, but a text may be authenticated in other ways, for example by incorporating the text in the final act of a conference or by initialling. Apart from authentication, the legal effects of signature are as follows. Where the signature is subject to ratification, acceptance, or approval (see *infra*), signature does not establish consent to be bound. However, signature qualifies the signatory state to proceed to ratification, acceptance, or approval and creates an obligation of good faith to refrain from acts calculated to frustrate the objects of the treaty.[25] Where the treaty is not subject to ratification, acceptance, or approval, signature creates the same obligation of good faith and establishes consent to be bound. Signature does not create an obligation to ratify.[26] In recent times signature has not featured in the adoption of all important multilateral treaties: thus the text may be adopted or approved by the General Assembly of the United Nations by a resolution and submitted to member states for accession.[27]

(c) Ratification[28]

Ratification involves two distinct procedural acts: the first is the act of the appropriate organ of the state, which is the Crown in the United Kingdom, and may be called

---

[22] See Whiteman, xiv. 29–31; *Yrbk. ILC* (1966) ii. 190, Art. 3, commentary, para. 3.

[23] See Mervyn Jones, *Full Powers and Ratification* (1946); ILC draft, Art. 1(i)(d)(e), 4–7, 10–11; *Yrbk. ILC* (1962), ii. 164ff; Waldock, ibid. 38ff.; *Yrbk. ILC* (1966), ii. 189, 193–7; Whiteman, xiv. 35–45; Vienna Conv., Arts. 7–11.

[24] Other exceptions exist in modern practice. Thus heads of state, heads of government, and Foreign Ministers are not required to furnish evidence of their authority.

[25] See Vienna Conv. Art. 18; *Upper Silesia* case, PCIJ, Ser. A, no. 7, p. 30; McNair, *Law of Treaties*, pp. 199–205; Fauchille, *Traité*, i. pt. iii (1926), 320.

[26] *Yrbk. ILC* (1962), ii. 171. But see Lauterpacht, ibid. (1953), ii. 108–12; and Fitzmaurice, ibid. (1956), ii. 112–13, 121–2.

[27] See the Conv. on the Privileges and Immunities of the United Nations, *infra*, pp. 652–3.

[28] See Whiteman, xiv. 45–92; Mervyn Jones, *Full Powers*; Delhousse, *La Ratification des traités* (1935); Sette-Camara, *The Ratification of International Treaties* (1949); Fitzmaurice, 15 *BY* (1934), 113–37; id., 33 *BY* (1957), 255–69; Blix, 30 *BY* (1953), 352–80; Frankowska, 73 *RGDIP* (1969), 62–88.

ratification in the constitutional sense; the second is the international procedure which brings a treaty into force by a formal exchange or deposit of the instruments of ratification. Ratification in the latter sense is an important act involving consent to be bound. However, everything depends on the intention of the parties, where this is ascertainable, and modern practice contains many examples of less formal agreements not requiring ratification and intended to be binding by signature.[29] A problem which has provoked controversy concerns the small number of treaties which contain no express provision on the subject of ratification. The International Law Commission[30] at first considered that treaties in principle require ratification[31] and specified exceptional cases where the presumption was otherwise, for example if the treaty provides that it shall come into force upon signature. However, the Commission changed its view, partly by reason of the difficulty of applying the presumption to treaties in simplified form. Article 14 of the Vienna Convention regulates the matter by reference to the intention of the parties.

(d) Accession, acceptance, and approval[32]

'Accession', 'adherence', or 'adhesion' occurs when a state which did not sign a treaty, already signed by other states, formally accepts its provisions. Accession may occur before or after the treaty has entered into force. The conditions under which accession may occur and the procedure involved depend on the provisions of the treaty. Accession may appear in a primary role as the only means of becoming a party to an instrument, as in the case of a convention approved by the General Assembly of the United Nations and proposed for accession by member states.[33] Recent practice has introduced the terms 'acceptance' and 'approval' to describe the substance of accession. Terminology is not fixed, however, and where a treaty is expressed to be open to signature 'subject to acceptance', this is equivalent to 'subject to ratification'.

(e) Expression of consent to be bound

Signature, ratification, accession, acceptance, and approval are not the only means by which consent to be bound may be expressed. Any other means may be used if so agreed, for example an exchange of instruments constituting a treaty.[34]

---

[29] See the *Case Concerning the Land and Maritime Boundary Between Cameroon and Nigeria*, Judgment of 10 October 2002, para. 264.

[30] ILC draft, Arts. 1(1)(d), 12; *Yrbk. ILC* (1962), ii. 171; Waldock, ibid. 48–53. See the Final Draft, Arts. 2(1)(b), 10, 11 and 13; *Yrbk. ILC* (1966), ii. 197–8; and the Vienna Conv., Arts. 2(1)(b), 11, 14, 16.

[31] See McNair, *Law of Treaties*, p. 133; Detter, *Essays*, 15–17. Some members of the Commission were of opinion that no specific rule on the question existed. See also *British Practice* (1964), i. 81–2 and the *Ambatielos* case, ICJ Reports (1952), 43.

[32] ILC draft, Arts. 1(1)(d), 13–16. See the Final Draft, Arts. 2(1)(b), 11, 12, and 13; *Yrbk. ILC* (1966), ii. 197–201; Vienna Conv. Arts. 2(1)(b), 11, 14–16.

[33] As in the case of the Conv. on the Privileges and Immunities of the United Nations. See McNair, *Law of Treaties*, pp. 153–5.

[34] Vienna Conv., Arts. 11 and 13.

3. RESERVATIONS[35]

In the Vienna Convention, a reservation is defined as 'a unilateral statement, however phrased or named, made by a State, when signing, ratifying, accepting, approving or acceding to a treaty, whereby it purports to exclude or to modify the legal effect of certain provisions of the treaty in their application to that State'. This definition begs the question of validity, which is determined on a contractual and not a unilateral basis. The formerly accepted rule for all kinds of treaty was that reservations were valid only if the treaty concerned permitted reservations and if all other parties accepted the reservation. On this basis a reservation constituted a counter-offer which required a new acceptance, failing which the state making the counter-offer would not become a party to the treaty. This view rests on a contractual conception of the absolute integrity of the treaty as adopted.[36]

In the period of the League of Nations (1920–46) the practice in regard to multi-lateral conventions showed a lack of consistency. The League Secretariat, and the later the Secretary-General of the United Nations, in his capacity as depositary of conventions concluded under the auspices of the League, followed the principle of absolute integrity. In contrast the members of the Pan-American Union, later the Organization of American States, adopted a flexible system which permitted a reserving state to become a party *vis-à-vis* non-objecting states. This system, dating from 1932, promotes universality at the expense of depth of obligation. Thus a state making sweeping reservations could become a party though bound only in regard to two or three non-objecting states and, even then, with large reservations.

Following the adoption of the Convention on the Prevention and Punishment of the Crime of Genocide by the General Assembly of the United Nations in 1948, a

---

[35] ILC draft, Arts. 1(1)(f), 18–22; *Yrbk. ILC* (1962), ii. 175–82; Waldock, ibid. 60–8; Final Draft, Arts. 2(1) (d), 16–20; *Yrbk. ILC* (1966), ii. 189–90, 202–9; Vienna Conv., Arts. 19–23; Lauterpacht, *Yrbk. ILC* (1953), ii. 123–36; Fitzmaurice, 2 *ICLQ* (1953), 1–27; id., 33 *BY* (1957), 272–93; Holloway, *Les Réserves dans les traités internationaux* (1958); id., *Modern Trends* (1967), 473–542; McNair, *Law of Treaties*, ch. 4; Bishop, 103 Hague *Recueil* (1961), ii. 249–341; Anderson, 13 *ICLQ* (1964), 450–81; Whiteman, xiv. 137–93; Detter, *Essays*, pp. 47–70; Jennings, 121 Hague *Recueil* (1967, II), 534–41; Cassese, *Recueil d'études en hommage á Guggenheim* (1968), 266–304; Tomuschat, 27 *Z.a.ö.R.u.V.* (1967), 463–82; Kappeler, *Les Réserves dans les traités internationaux* (1958); Mendelson, 45 *BY* (1971), 137–71; Ruda, 146 Hague *Recueil* (1975, III), 95–218; Gaja, *Ital. Yrbk.* (1975), 52–68; id., *Essays in Honour of Roberto Ago*, i (1987), 307–30; 49 *BY* (1978), 378–80; Bowett, 48 *BY* (1976–7), 67–92; McRae, 49 *BY* (1978), 155–73; Imbert, *Les Réserves aux traités multilatéraux* (1979); Sinclair, *The Vienna Convention*, pp. 51–82; Gamble, 74 *AJ* (1980), 372–94; Horn, T.M.C. Asser Instituut, Swedish Institute, *Studies in International Law*, Vol. 5 (1988); Cameron and Horn, 33 *German Yrbk.* (1990), 62–129; Clark, 85 *AJ* (1991), 281–321; Redgwell, 64 *BY* (1993), 245–82; Sucharipa-Behrmann, 1 *Austrian Review of Int. and Europ. Law* (1996), 67–88; Greig, *Austral. Yrbk.*, 16 (1995), 21–172. See further Pellet, Second Report on Reservations to Treaties, UN Doc. A/CN. 4/477; Third Report, A/CN. 4/491; Add.1–6; Fourth Report, A/CN.4/499; Fifth Report, A/CN.4/508, Add.1–4; Sixth Report, A/CN.4/518, Add.1–3; Seventh Report, A/CN.4/526, Add.1–3; Eighth Report, A/CN.4/526, Add.1; Ninth Report, A/CN.4/544; Tenth Report, A/CN.4/558, Add.1–2; Eleventh Report, A/CN.4/574; Twelfth Report, A/CN.4/584. See also *Report of the International Law Commission, Fifty-ninth session*, G.A. Off. Recs., *Sixty-second session*, Suppl. No. 10 (A/62/10), 46–66.

[36] See *Reservations to Genocide Convention*, ICJ Reports (1951), 15 at 21, 24.

divergence of opinion arose on the admissibility of reservations to the Convention, which contained no provision on the subject. The International Court was asked for an advisory opinion, and in giving its opinion[37] stressed the divergence of practice and the special characteristics of the Convention, including the intention of the parties and the General Assembly that it should be universal in scope. The principal finding of the Court was that 'a State which has made ... a reservation which has been objected to by one or more of the parties to the Convention but not by others, can be regarded as being a party to the Convention if the reservation is compatible with the object and purpose of the Convention ...'. In 1951 the International Law Commission rejected the 'compatibility' criterion as too subjective and preferred a rule of unanimous consent. However, in 1952 the General Assembly requested the Secretary-General of the United Nations to conform his practice to the opinion of the Court in respect of the Genocide Convention; and, in respect of *future*[38] conventions concluded under the auspices of the United Nations of which he was depositary, to act as depositary without passing upon the legal effect of documents containing reservations and leaving it to each state to draw legal consequences when reservations were communicated to them. In its practice the Secretariat adopted the 'flexible' system for future conventions, and in 1959 the General Assembly reaffirmed its previous directive and extended it to cover *all* conventions concluded under the auspices of the United Nations, unless they contain contrary provisions. In 1962 the International Law Commission decided in favour of the 'compatibility' doctrine.[39] The Commission pointed out that the increase in the number of potential participants in multilateral treaties made the unanimity principle less practicable.

The Final Draft of the Commission was followed in most respects by the Vienna Convention. Article 19 of the Convention indicates the general liberty to formulate a reservation when signing, ratifying, accepting, approving or acceding to a treaty and then states three exceptions. The first two exceptions are reservations expressly prohibited and reservations not falling within provisions in a treaty permitting specified reservations and no others. The third class of impermissible reservations is cases falling outside the first mentioned classes in which the reservation is 'incompatible with the object and purpose of the treaty'.

Article 20 provides as follows for acceptance of and objection to reservations other than those expressly authorized by a treaty:[40]

2. When it appears from the limited number of the negotiating States and the object and purpose of a treaty that the application of the treaty in its entirety between all the parties

---

[37] Last note.

[38] Concluded after 12 Jan. 1952, when the resolution was adopted.

[39] Draft Art. 18(1)(d) and 20(2). The Commission rejected a 'collegiate' system which would require acceptance of the reservation by a given proportion of the other parties for the reserving state to become a party: cf. Anderson, 13 *ICLQ* (1964), 450–81. See also *British Practice* (1964), i. 83–4.

[40] Special provisions concerning the making of reservations may present difficult problems of interpretation: see the *Anglo-French Continental Shelf Arbitration*, ILR 54, 6 at 41–57 (paras. 34–74); and Bowett, 48 *BY* (1976–7), 67–92.

is an essential condition of the consent of each one to be bound by the treaty, a reservation requires acceptance by all the parties.

3. When a treaty is a constituent instrument of an international organization and unless it otherwise provides, a reservation requires the acceptance of the competent organ of that organization.

4. In cases not falling under the preceding paragraphs and unless the treaty otherwise provides:

> (a) acceptance by another contracting State of a reservation constitutes the reserving State a party to the treaty in relation to that other State if or when the treaty is in force for those States;
>
> (b) an objection by another contracting State to a reservation does not preclude the entry into force of the treaty as between the objecting and reserving States unless a contrary intention is definitely expressed by the objecting State;[41]
>
> (c) an act expressing a State's consent to be bound by the treaty and containing a reservation is effective as soon as at least one other contracting State has accepted the reservation.

5. For the purposes of paragraphs 2 and 4 and unless the treaty otherwise provides, a re-servation is considered to have been accepted by a State if it shall have raised no objection to the reservation by the end of a period of twelve months after it was notified of the reservation or by the date on which it expressed its consent to be bound by the treaty, whichever is later.

The 'compatibility' test is the least objectionable solution but is by no means an ideal regime,[42] and many problems remain. The application of the criterion of compatibility with object and purpose is a matter of appreciation, but this is left to individual states. How is the test to apply to provisions for dispute settlement, or to specific issues in the Territorial Sea Convention of 1958,[43] such as the right of innocent passage? In practical terms the 'compatibility' test approximates to the Latin-American system and thus may not sufficiently maintain the balance between the integrity and the effectiveness of multilateral conventions in terms of a firm level of obligation.

The reason for the approximation to the Latin-American system[44] is that each state decides for itself whether reservations are incompatible and some states might adopt a liberal policy of accepting far-reaching reservations. The particular difficulty which international tribunals face in practice is the determination of the precise legal consequences of a decision that a particular reservation is incompatible. In the

---

[41] This provision reverses the presumption against entry into force contained in the proposals of the International Law Commission: see Zemanek, in *Essays in Honour of Manfred Lachs* (1984), 323–36.

[42] See Waldock, *Yrbk. ILC* (1962), ii. 65–6; *ILC*, 1966 Report, ibid. (1966), ii. 205–6; Sinclair, 19 *ICLQ* (1970), 53–60.

[43] *Supra*, pp. 173ff.

[44] For the Standards on Reservations adopted in 1973 by the OAS see *Digest of US Practice* (1973), 179–81. For the history: Ruda, 146 Hague *Recueil* (1975, II), 115–33.

Belilos[45] and *Loizidou*[46] cases the European Court of Human Rights treated the objectionable reservation as severable. The issue of severability in relation to human rights treaties is the subject of controversy.

In respect of the International Government on Civil and Political Rights, 1966, the United Nations Human Rights Committee has addressed the issue of reservations in this way:[47]

6. The absence of a prohibition on reservations does not mean that any reservation is permitted. The matter of reservations under the Covenant and the First Optional Protocol is governed by international law. Article 19(3) of the Vienna Convention on the Law of Treaties provides relevant guidance. It stipulates that where a reservation is not prohibited by the treaty or falls within the specified permitted categories, a State may make a reservation provided it is not incompatible with the object and purpose of the treaty. Even though, unlike some other human rights treaties, the Covenant does not incorporate a specific reference to the object and purpose test, that test governs the matter of interpretation and acceptability of reservations.

7. In an instrument which articulates very many civil and political rights, each of the many articles, and indeed their interplay, secures the objectives of the Covenant. The object and purpose of the Covenant is to create legally binding standards for human rights by defining certain civil and political rights and placing them in a framework of obligations which are legally binding for those States which ratify; and to provide an efficacious supervisory machinery for the obligations undertaken.

8. Reservations that offend peremptory norms would not be compatible with the object and purpose of the Covenant. Although treaties that are mere exchanges of obligations between States allow them to reserve *inter se* application of rules of general international law, it is otherwise in human rights treaties, which are for the benefit of persons within their jurisdiction. Accordingly, provisions in the Covenant that represent customary international law (and *a fortiori* when they have the character of peremptory norms) may not be the subject of reservations. Accordingly, a State may not reserve the right to engage in slavery, to torture, to subject persons to cruel, inhuman or degrading treatment or punishment, to arbitrarily deprive persons of their lives, to arbitrarily arrest and detain persons, to deny freedom of thought, conscience and religion, to presume a person guilty unless he proves his innocence, to execute pregnant women or children, to permit the advocacy of national, racial or religious hatred, to deny to persons of marriageable age the right to marry, or to deny to minorities the right to enjoy their own culture, profess their own religion, or use their own language. And while reservations to particular clauses of Article 14 may be acceptable, a general reservation to the right to a fair trial would not be.

---

[45] *European Court of Human Rights*, Series A, No. 132. See further Cameron and Horn, 33 *German Yrbk.* (1990), 69–129; Marks, 39 *ICLQ* (1990), 300–27; Chinkin and Others, *Human Rights as General Norms and a State's Right to Opt Out* (1997).

[46] Ibid., Series A, No. 310 (*Loizidou* v. *Turkey* (Preliminary Objections)).

[47] General Comment No. 24, 11 Nov. 1994; ILR 107, 65. The response of the U.K. Government was critical: see 66 *BY* (1995), 655–61. See also Hampson, Working Paper, E/CN.4/Sub.2/1999/28, 28 June 1999; Simma, *Liber Amicorum Professor Ignaz Seidl-Hohenveldern* (1998), 659–82; and Helfer, *Columbia LR*, 102 (2002), 1832–911.

4. ENTRY INTO FORCE, DEPOSIT, AND REGISTRATION[48]

The provisions of the treaty determine the manner in which and the date on which the treaty enters force. Where the treaty does not specify a date, there is a presumption that the treaty is intended to come into force as soon as all the negotiating states have consented to be bound by the treaty.[49]

After a treaty is concluded, the written instruments, which provide formal evidence of consent to be bound by ratification, accession, and so on, and also reservations and other declarations, are placed in the custody of a depositary, who may be one or more states, or an international organization. The depositary has functions of considerable importance relating to matters of form, including provision of information as to the time at which the treaty enters into force.[50] The United Nations Secretariat plays a significant role as depositary of multilateral treaties.

Article 102 of the Charter of the United Nations[51] provides as follows:

1. Every treaty and every international agreement entered into by any Member of the United Nations after the present Charter comes into force shall as soon as possible be registered with the Secretariat and published by it.

2. No party to any such treaty or international agreement which has not been registered in accordance with the provisions of paragraph 1 of this Article may invoke that treaty or agreement before any organ of the United Nations.

This provision is intended to discourage secret diplomacy and to promote the availability of texts of agreements. The *United Nations Treaty Series* includes agreements by non-members which are 'filed and recorded' with the Secretariat as well as those 'registered' by members. The Secretariat accepts agreements for registration without conferring any status on them, or the parties thereto, which they would not have otherwise. However, this is not the case where the regulations governing the article provides for *ex officio* registration. This involves initiatives by the Secretariat and extends to agreements to which the United Nations is a party, trusteeship agreements,

---

[48] ILC drafts, Arts. 23–5; *Yrbk. ILC* (1962), ii. 182–3; Waldock, ibid. 68–73; Final Draft, Arts. 21, 22, and 75; *Yrbk. ILC* (1966), ii. 209–10, 273–4; Vienna Conv., Arts. 24, 25, 80. On registration see Whiteman, xiv. 113–26; McNair, *Law of Treaties*, ch. 10; Brandon, 29 BY (1952), 186–204; id., 47 AJ (1953), 49–69; Boudet, 64 RGDIP (1960), 596–604; Broches and Boskey, 4 *Neths. Int. LR* (1957), 189–92, 277–300; Higgins, *The Development of International Law through the Political Organs of the United Nations* (1963), 328–36; Detter, *Essays*, pp. 28–46.

[49] Vienna Conv., Art. 24(2).

[50] Vienna Conv., Arts. 76, 77; Rosenne, 61 AJ (1967), 923–45; ibid. 64 (1970), 838–52; Whiteman, xiv. 68–92.

[51] A similar but not identical provision appeared in Art. 18 of the Covenant of the League of Nations: McNair, *Law of Treaties*, pp. 180–5.

and multilateral agreements of which the United Nations is a depositary. It is not yet clear in every respect how wide the phrase 'every international engagement' is, but it seems to have a very wide scope. Technical intergovernmental agreements, declarations accepting the optional clause in the Statute of the International Court, agreements between organizations and states, agreements between organizations, and unilateral engagements of an international character[52] are included.[53] Paragraph 2 is a sanction for the obligation in paragraph 1, and registration is not a condition precedent for the validity of instruments to which the article applies, although these may not be relied upon in proceedings before United Nations organs.[54] In relation to the similar provision in the Covenant of the League the view has been expressed that an agreement may be invoked, though not registered, if other appropriate means of publicity have been employed.[55]

5. INVALIDITY OF TREATIES[56]

(a) Provisions of internal law[57]

The extent to which constitutional limitations on the treaty-making power can be invoked on the international plane is a matter of controversy, and no single view can claim to be definitive. Three main views have received support from writers. According to the first, constitutional limitations determine validity on the international plane.[58] Criticism of this view emphasizes the insecurity in treaty-making that it would entail. The second view varies from the first in that only 'notorious' constitutional limitations are effective on the international plane. The third view is that a state is bound irrespective of internal limitations by consent given by an agent properly authorized according to international law. Some advocates of this view qualify the rule in cases where the other state is aware of the failure to comply

---

[52] McNair, *Law of Treaties*, p. 186, and see *infra*, p. 640.

[53] If an agreement is between international legal persons it is registrable even if it be governed by a particular municipal law; but cf. Higgins, *Development*, p. 329. It is not clear whether special agreements (*compromis*) referring disputes to the International Court are required to be registered.

[54] If the instrument is a part of the *jus cogens* (*supra*, p. 510), should non-registration have this effect?

[55] *South West Africa* cases (Prelim. Objections), ICJ Reports (1962), 319 at 359–60 (Sep. Op. of Judge Bustamante) and 420–2 (Sep. Op. of Judge Jessup). But cf. Joint Diss. Op. of Judges Spender and Fitzmaurice, ibid. 503.

[56] See also *infra*, p. 629, on conflict with prior treaties. See generally: Elias, 134 Hague *Recueil* (1971, III), 335–416.

[57] See *Yrbk. ILC* (1963), ii. 190–3; Waldock, ibid. 41–6; *ILC*, Final Report, *Yrbk. ILC* (1966), ii. 240–2; McNair, *Law of Treaties*, ch. 3; Blix, *Treaty-Making Power* (1960); Lauterpacht, *Yrbk. ILC* (1953), ii. 141–6; P. de Visscher, *De la conclusion des traités internationaux* (1943), 219–87; id., 136 Hague *Recueil* (1972, II), 94–8; Geck, 27 *Z.a.ö.R.u.V.* (1967), 429–50; *Digest of US Practice* (1974), 195–8; Meron, 49 *BY* (1978), 175–99.

[58] This was the position of the International Law Commission in 1951; *Yrbk.* (1951), ii. 73.

with internal law or where the irregularity is manifest. This position, which involves a presumption of competence and excepts manifest irregularity, was approved by the International Law Commission, in its draft Article 43, in 1966. The Commission stated that 'the decisions of international tribunals and State practice, if they are not conclusive, appear to support' this type of solution.[59]

At the Vienna Conference the draft provision was strengthened and the result appears in the Convention, Article 46:[60]

1. A State may not invoke the fact that its consent to be bound by a treaty has been expressed in violation of a provision of its internal law regarding competence to conclude treaties as invalidating its consent unless that violation was manifest and concerned a rule of its internal law of fundamental importance.

2. A violation is manifest if it would be objectively evident to any State conducting itself in the matter in accordance with normal practice and in good faith.

(b) Representative's lack of authority[61]

The Vienna Convention provides that if the authority of a representative to express the consent of his state to be bound by a particular treaty has been made subject to a specific restriction, his omission to observe the restriction may not be invoked as a ground of invalidity unless the restriction was previously notified to the other negotiating states.

(c) Corruption of a state representative

The International Law Commission decided that corruption of representatives was not adequately dealt with as a case of fraud[62] and an appropriate provision appears in the Vienna Convention, Article 50.

(d) Error[63]

The Vienna Convention, Article 48,[64] contains two principal provisions which probably reproduce the existing law and are as follows:

1. A State may invoke an error in a treaty as invalidating its consent to be bound by the treaty if the error relates to a fact or situation which was assumed by that State to exist at the time when the treaty was concluded and formed an essential basis of its consent to be bound by the treaty.

---

[59] *Yrbk. ILC* (1966), ii. 240–2.

[60] See the *Case Concerning the Land and Maritime Boundary Between Cameroon and Nigeria*, Judgment of 10 October 2002, para. 265.

[61] ILC draft, Art. 32; *Yrbk. ILC* (1963), ii. 193; Waldock, ibid. 46–7; Final Draft, Art. 44; *Yrbk. ILC* (1966), ii. 242; Vienna Conv., Art. 47.

[62] *Yrbk. ILC* (1966), ii. 245.

[63] See Lauterpacht, *Yrbk. ILC* (1953), ii. 153; Fitzmaurice, 2 *ILCQ* (1953), 25, 35–7; Waldock, *Yrbk. ILC* (1963), ii. 48–50; Oraison, *L'Erreur dans les traités* (1972); Thirlway, 63 *BY* (1992), 22–8.

[64] See also *Yrbk. ILC* (1966), ii. 243–4.

2. Paragraph 1 shall not apply if the State in question contributed by its own conduct to the error or if the circumstances were such as to put that State on notice of a possible error.[65]

(e) Fraud[66]

There are few helpful precedents on the effect of fraud. The Vienna Convention provides[67] that a state which has been induced to enter into a treaty by the fraud of another negotiating state may invoke the fraud as invalidating its consent to be bound by the treaty. Fraudulent misrepresentation of a material fact inducing an essential error is dealt with by the provision relating to error.

(f) Coercion of state representatives[68]

The Vienna Convention, Article 51, provides that 'the expression of a State's consent to be bound by a treaty which has been procured by the coercion of its representative through acts or threats directed against him shall be without legal effect'. The concept of coercion extends to blackmailing threats and threats against the representative's family.

(g) Coercion of a state[69]

The International Law Commission in its draft of 1963 considered that Article 2, paragraph 4, of the Charter of the United Nations, together with other developments, justified the conclusion that a treaty procured by the threat or use of force in violation of the Charter of the United Nations shall be void. Article 52 of the Vienna Convention so provides.[70] An amendment with the object of defining force to include any 'economic or political pressure' was withdrawn. A Declaration condemning such pressure appears in the Final Act of the Conference.

(h) Conflict with a peremptory norm of general international law (*jus cogens*)

See Chapter 23, section 5.

---

[65] See the *Temple* case, ICJ Reports (1962), 26. See also the Sep. Op. of Judge Fitzmaurice, ibid. p. 57.

[66] See Lauterpacht, ibid. (1953), ii. 152; Fitzmaurice, ibid. (1958), ii. 25, 37; Waldock, ibid. (1963), ii. 47–8; Oraison, 75 *RGDIP* (1971), 617–73.

[67] Art. 49. See also the Final Draft, *Yrbk. ILC* (1966). ii. 244–5.

[68] Fitzmaurice, ICJ Reports (1958), ii. 26, 38; Waldock, ibid. (1963), ii. 50; Final Draft, Art. 48; *Yrbk. ILC* (1966), ii. 245–6.

[69] ILC draft, Art. 36; *Yrbk. ILC* (1963), ii. 197; Waldock, ibid. 51–2; Lauterpacht, ICJ Reports (1953), ii. 147–52; McNair, *Law of Treaties*, pp. 206–11; Brownlie, *International Law and the Use of Force by States* (1963), 404–6; Fitzmaurice, *Yrbk ILC* (1957), ii. 32, 56–7; ibid. (1958), ii. 26, 38–9; Bothe, 27 *Z.a.ö.R.u.V.* (1967), 507–19; Jennings, 121 Hague *Recueil*, pp. 561–3; Ténékidès, *Ann. français* (1974), 79–102; De Jong, 15 *Neths. Yrbk.* (1984), 209–47. See also *Fisheries Jurisdiction* case (*United Kingdom* v. *Iceland*), ICJ Reports, (1973) 3 at 14; Briggs, 68 *AJ* (1974), 51 at 62–3; Thirlway, 63 *BY* (1992), 28–31.

[70] See also the Final Draft, Art. 49; *Yrbk. ILC* (1966), ii. 246–7; Whiteman, xiv. 268–70; Kearney and Dalton, 64 *AJ* (1970), 532–5.

6. WITHDRAWAL, TERMINATION AND SUSPENSION OF TREATIES[71]

(a) *Pacta sunt servanda*

The Vienna Convention prescribes a certain presumption as to the validity and con-tinuance in force of a treaty,[72] and such a presumption may be based upon *pacta sunt servanda* as a general principle of international law: a treaty in force is binding upon the parties and must be performed by them in good faith.[73]

(b) State succession[74]

Treaties may be affected when one state succeeds wholly or in part to the legal personality and territory of another. The conditions under which the treaties of the latter survive depend on many factors, including the precise form and origin of the 'succession' and the type of treaty concerned. Changes of this kind may of course terminate treaties apart from categories of state succession (section (*h*), *infra*).

(c) War and armed conflict[75]

Hostile relations do not automatically terminate treaties between the parties to a conflict. Many treaties, including the Charter of the United Nations, are intended to be no less binding in case of war, and multipartite law-making agreements such as the Geneva Conventions of 1949 survive war or armed conflict.[76] However, in state practice many types of treaty are regarded as at least suspended in time of war, and war conditions may lead to termination of treaties on grounds of impossibility or fundamental change of circumstances. In many respects the law on the subject is uncertain. Thus, it is not yet clear to what extent the illegality of the use or threat of force has had effects on the right (where it may be said to exist) to regard a treaty as suspended or

---

[71] See generally *Annuaire de l'Institut*, 49, i (1961); 52, i. ii (1967); Fitzmaurice, *Yrbk. ILC* (1957), ii. 16–70; McNair, *Law of Treaties*, chs. 30–35; Tobin, *Termination of Multipartite Treaties* (1933); Detter, *Essays*, pp. 83–99; Whiteman, xiv. 410–510; Capotorti, 134 Hague *Recueil* (1971, III), 419–587; Haraszti, *Some Fundamental Problems of the Law of Treaties* (1973), 229–425; Jiménez de Aréchaga, 159 Hague *Recueil* (1978, I), 59–85; Thirlway, 63 *BY* (1992), 63–96; Oppenheim, ii. 1296–1311.

[72] Art. 42. See also ILC draft, Art. 30; *Yrbk. ILC* (1963), ii. 189; Final Draft, Art. 39; ibid. (1966), ii. 236–7.

[73] See the Vienna Conv. Art. 26; the ILC Final Draft, Art. 23; *Yrbk. ILC* (1966), ii. 210–11; and McNair, *Law of Treaties*, ch. 30.

[74] See ch. 29, pp. 633–7. In its work on the law of treaties the International Law Commission put this question aside: Final Draft, Art. 69; *Yrbk*. (1966), ii. 267; and see the Vienna Conv., Art. 73.

[75] See McNair, *Law of Treaties*, ch. 43; Briggs, pp. 934–46; Scelle, 77 *JDI* (1950), 26–84; La Pradelle, 2 *ILQ* (1948–9), 555–76; Edwards, 44 *Grot. Soc.* (1958), 91–105; Whiteman, xiv. 490–510; Broms, *Annuaire de l'Inst.* 59 (1981), i. 201–84; ibid. ii. 175–244 (debate); Broms, ibid. 61 (1985), i. 1–27; ibid. 61, ii. 199–255 (debate); 278 (Resol.). The question was put aside by the International Law Commission: Final Draft, Art. 69; *Yrbk*. (1966), ii. 267; and see the Vienna Conv., Art. 73.

[76] See *Masinimport* v. *Scottish Mechanical Light Industries*, ILR 74, 559 at 564 (Scotland, Court of Session).

terminated.[77] The International Law Commission decided to include the topic 'effects of armed conflicts on treaties' on its agenda in 2004 and in the course of 2006 and 2007 the first three reports of the Special Rapporteur (the present writer) had been examined.[78]

(d) Operation of the provisions of a treaty

A treaty may of course specify the conditions of its termination, and a bilateral treaty may provide for denunciation by the parties.[79] Where a treaty contains no provisions regarding its termination the existence of a right of denunciation depends on the intention of the parties, which can be inferred from the terms of the treaty and its subject-matter, but, according to the Vienna Convention, the presumption is that the treaty is not subject to denunciation or withdrawal.[80] At least in certain circumstances denunciation is conditional upon a reasonable period of notice. Some important law-making treaties, including the Conventions on the Law of the Sea of 1958, contain no denunciation clause. Treaties of peace are presumably not open to unilateral denunciation.

(e) Termination by agreement

Termination or withdrawal may take place by consent of all the parties.[81] Such consent may be implied. In particular, a treaty may be considered as terminated if all the parties conclude a later treaty which is intended to supplant the earlier treaty or if the later treaty is incompatible with its provisions.[82] The topic of 'desuetude', which is probably not a term of art, is essentially concerned with discontinuance of use of a treaty and its implied termination by consent.[83] However, it could extend to the

---

[77] ILC draft Pt. II, commentary; *Yrbk. ILC* (1963), ii. 189, para. 14.

[78] See the Report of the Commission for 2006 (G.A. Off. Recs., Sixty-first session, Suppl. No. 10 (A/61/10)), 382–93; and the Report of the Commission for 2007, G.A. Off Recs., Sixty-second session, Suppl. No. 10 (A/62/10)), 154–77. See also Bannelier, *Mélanges Salmon* (2007), 125–59.

[79] Vienna Conv., Art. 54; ILC Final Draft, Art. 51; *Yrbk. ILC* (1966), ii. 249.

[80] Vienna Conv., Art. 56; ILC draft, Art. 39; *Yrbk. ILC* draft, Art. 39; *Yrbk. ILC* (1963), ii. 200–1; Waldock, ibid, 64–70; Fitzmaurice, ibid. (1957), ii. 22; McNair, *Law of Treaties*, pp. 502–5, 511–13; ILC, Final Draft, Art. 53; *Yrbk.* (1966), ii. 250–1; Jiménez de Aréchaga, 159 Hague *Recueil* (1978, I), 70–1; Widdows, 53 *BY* (1982), 83–114; Sinclair, *The Vienna Convention*, pp. 186–8; Plender, 57 *BY* (1986), 143–53. See also the Adv. op. on the Interpretation of the Agreement of 25 Mar. 1951 between the WHO and Egypt, ICJ Reports (1980), 73 at 94–6; 128–9 (Mosler, Sep. Op.); 159–62 (Ago, Sep. Op.); 176–7 (El-Erian, Sep. Op.); 184–9 (Sette-Camara); and the *Nicaragua* case (Jurisdiction), ICJ Reports (1984), 392 at 419–20 (para. 63).

[81] Vienna Conv., Art. 54; ILC draft Art. 40, *Yrbk.* (1963), ii. 203–4; ILC Final Draft, Art. 54, *Yrbk.* (1966), ii. 251–2. See also Kontou, *The Termination and Revision of Treaties in the Light of New Customary International Law* (1994).

[82] Vienna Conv., Art. 59; ILC draft, Art. 41, *Yrbk.* (1963), ii. 203–4; ILC Final Draft, Art. 56; *Yrbk.* (1966), ii. 252–3; Plender, 57 *BY* (1986), 153–7. See also the Sep. Op. of Judge Anzilotti, *Electricity Company of Sofia* case, *PCIJ*, Ser. A/B, no. 77, p. 92. See also *infra*, p. 600.

[83] See ILC Final Draft, Art. 39, Commentary, para. 5; *Yrbk.* (1966), ii. 237; Fitzmaurice, *Yrbk. ILC* (1957), ii. 28, 47–8, 52; McNair, *Law of Treaties*, pp. 516–18; Yuille, *Shortridge Arbitration*, Lapradelle and Politis, ii. 105; *Nuclear Tests* case (Australia v. France), ICJ Reports (1974) 253 at 337–8 (Joint Diss. Op.), 381 (De Castro, Diss.) 404, 415–16 (Barwick, Diss.); 55 *BY* (1984), 517 (UK); Sinclair, *The Vienna Convention*,

distinct situation of a unilateral renunciation of rights under a treaty. Moreover, irrespective of the agreement of the parties, an ancient treaty may become meaningless and incapable of practical application.[84]

(f) Material breach[85]

It is widely recognized that material breach by one party entitles the other party or parties to a treaty to invoke the breach as the ground of termination or suspension. This option by the wronged party is accepted as a sanction for securing the observance of treaties. However, considerable uncertainty has surrounded the precise circumstances in which such right of unilateral abrogation may be exercised, particularly in respect of multilateral treaties. Article 60 of the Vienna Convention[86] deals with the matter with as much precision as can be reasonably expected:

1. A material breach of a bilateral treaty by one of the parties entitles the other to invoke the breach as a ground for terminating the treaty or suspending its operation in whole or in part.
  2. A material breach of a multilateral treaty by one of the parties entitles:

(a) the other parties by unanimous agreement to suspend the operation of the treaty in whole or in part or to terminate it either:

(i) in the relations between themselves and the defaulting State, or

(ii) as between all the parties.

(b) a party specially affected by the breach to invoke it as a ground for suspending the operation of the treaty in whole or in part in the relations between itself and the defaulting State;

(c) any party other than the defaulting State to invoke the breach as a ground for suspending the operation of the treaty in whole or in part with respect to itself if the treaty is of such a character that a material breach of its provisions by one party radically changes the position of every party with respect to the further performance of its obligations under the treaty.

3. A material breach of a treaty, for the purposes of this article, consists in:[87]

(a) a repudiation of the treaty not sanctioned by the present Convention; or

(b) the violation of a provision essential to the accomplishment of the object or purpose of the treaty.

---

pp. 163–4; Plender, 57 *BY* (1986), 138–45; Kontou, op. cit. *supra*, 24–31; Thirlway, 63 *BY* (1992), 94–6. See also *Widjatmiko* v. *NV Geobroeders Zomer*, ILR 70, 439.

[84] See Parry, in Sørensen, p. 235.

[85] McNair, *Law of Treaties*, pp. 553–71; Sinha, *Unilateral Denunciation of Treaty Because of Prior Violations of Obligations by Other Party* (1966); Detter, *Essays*, pp. 89–93; Fitzmaurice, *Yrbk. ILC* (1957), ii. 31, 54–5; *Tacna–Arica Arbitration, RIAA.* ii. 929, 943–4; *Ann. Digest* (1925–6), no. 269; Whiteman, xiv. 468–78; Simma, *Öst. Z. für öff. R.* 20 (1970), 5–83; Briggs, 68 *AJ* (1974), 51–68; Jiménez de Aréchaga, 159 Hague *Recueil* (1978, I), 79–85; Sinclair, *The Vienna Convention* (2nd edn., 1984), pp. 188–90; Plender, 57 *BY* (1986), 157–66.

[86] See also ILC draft, Art. 42, *Yrbk. ILC* (1963), ii. 204; Waldock, ibid. 72–7; Final Draft, Art. 57; ibid. (1966), ii. 253–5.

[87] This definition was applied by the International Court in the *Namibia* Opinion, ICJ Reports (1971), 46–7, in respect of South African violations of the Mandate for South West Africa (Namibia) and the consequent termination of the Mandate by the UN General Assembly.

4. The foregoing paragraphs are without prejudice to any provision in the treaty applicable in the event of a breach.

5. Paragraphs 1 to 3 do not apply to provisions relating to the protection of the human person contained in treaties of a humanitarian character, in particular to provisions prohibiting any form of reprisals against persons protected by such treaties.

A State may by its own conduct prejudice its right to terminate a treaty on the ground of material breach.[88]

(g) Supervening impossibility of performance[89]

The Vienna Convention provides[90] that a party 'may invoke the impossibility of performing a treaty as a ground for terminating it if the impossibility results from the permanent disappearance or destruction of an object indispensable for the execution of the treaty'. Situations envisaged include the submergence of an island, the drying up of a river, or destruction of a railway, by an earthquake or other disaster. The effect of impossibility is not automatic, and a party must invoke the ground for termination. Impossibility of performance may not be invoked by a party to the relevant treaty when it results from that party's own breach of an obligation flowing from the treaty.[91]

(h) Fundamental change of circumstances[92]

The principles have been expressed in Article 62 of the Vienna Convention as follows:

1. A fundamental change of circumstances which has occurred with regard to those existing at the time of the conclusion of a treaty, and which was not foreseen by the parties, may not be invoked as a ground for terminating or withdrawing from the treaty unless:

(a) the existence of those circumstances constituted an essential basis of the consent of the parties to be bound by the treaty; and

(b) the effect of the change is radically to transform the extent of obligations still to be performed under the treaty.

---

[88] See the *Gabčikovo-Nagymaros Project* (Hungary/Slovakia), Judgment, paras. 105–10.

[89] See generally McNair, *Law of Treaties*, pp. 685–8; Fitzmaurice, *Yrbk. ILC* (1957), ii. 50–1; Sinclair, *The Vienna Convention*, pp. 190–2.

[90] Art. 61(1); ILC draft, Art. 43, *Yrbk. ILC* (1963), ii. 206; Waldock, ibid. 77–9; Final Draft, Art. 58, ibid. (1966), ii. 255–6. Another example of impossibility arises from the total extinction of one of the parties to a bilateral treaty, apart from any rule of state succession which might allow devolution: see Waldock, ibid. (1963), ii. 77–9. and ibid., commentary at pp. 206–7.

[91] See the *Gabiikovo-Nagymaros Project* (Hungary/Slovakia), Judgment, paras. 102–3.

[92] ILC draft, Art. 44, *Yrbk. ILC* (1963), ii. 207; Waldock, ibid. 79–85; Final Draft, Art. 59, ibid. (1966), ii. 256–60; Fitzmaurice, ibid. (1957), ii. 56–65; McNair, *Law of Treaties*, pp. 681–91; Rousseau, *Principles généraux*, i. 580–615; Chesney Hill, *The Doctrine of 'Rebus sic Stantibus'* (1934); Harvard Research, 29 *AJ* (1935), Suppl., pp. 1096–126; van Bogaert, 70 *RGDIP* (1966), 49–74; Whiteman, xiv. 478–90; Lissitzyn, 61 *AJ* (1967), 895–922; Poch de Caviedes, 118 Hague *Recueil* (1966), ii. 109–204; Schwelb, 29 *Z.a.ö.R.u.V.* (1969), 39–70; Note, 76 *Yale LJ* (1967), 1669–87; Pastor Ridruejo, 25 *Ann. suisse* (1968), 81–98; Verzijl, *Festschrift für Walter Schätzel*, pp. 515–29; Rousseau, i. 224–30; Haraszti, *Some Fundamental Problems of the Law of Treaties* (1973), 327–420; id.; 146 Hague *Recueil* (1975, III), 1–94; Toth, *Juridical Review* (Edinburgh) (1974), 56–82, 147–78, 263–81; Jasudowicz, 8 *Polish Yrbk.* (1976), 155–81; *Répertoire suisse*, i. 178–86; Jiménez de Aréchaga, 159 Hague *Recueil* (1978, I), 71–9; Sinclair, *The Vienna Convention*, pp. 192–6; Cahier, in *Essays in Honour of Roberto Ago*, i. (1987), 163–86; Thirlway, 63 *BY* (1992), 75–82.

2. A fundamental change of circumstances may not be invoked as a ground for terminating or withdrawing from a treaty:

(a) if the treaty establishes a boundary; or

(b) if the fundamental change is the result of a breach by the party invoking it either of an obligation under the treaty or of any other international obligation owed to any other party to the treaty.

3. If, under the foregoing paragraphs, a party may invoke a fundamental change of circumstances as a ground for terminating or withdrawing from a treaty it may also invoke the change as a ground for suspending the operation of the treaty.

An example of a fundamental change would be the case where a party to a military and political alliance, involving exchange of military and intelligence information, has a change of government incompatible with the basis of alliance. The majority of modern writers accept the doctrine of *rebus sic stantibus* which is reflected in this provision. The doctrine involves the implication of a term that the obligations of an agreement would end if there has been a change of circumstances. As in municipal systems, so in international law it is recognized that changes frustrating the object of an agreement and apart from actual impossibility may justify its termination. Some jurists dislike the doctrine, regarding it as a primary source of insecurity of obligations, more especially in the absence of a system of compulsory jurisdiction. The Permanent Court in the *Free Zones* case[93] assumed that the principle existed while reserving its position on its extent and the precise mode of its application. State practice and decisions of municipal courts[94] support the principle, for which three juridical bases have been proposed. According to one theory the principle rests on a supposed implied term of the treaty, a basis which involves a fiction and, where it does not, leaves the matter as one of interpretation. A second view is to import a 'clausula' *rebus sic stantibus* into a treaty by operation of law, the clause operating automatically. The third view, which represents the modern law, is that the principle is an objective rule of law, applying when certain events exist, yet not terminating the treaty automatically, since one of the parties must invoke it. The International Law Commission and the Convention exclude treaties fixing boundaries from the operation of the principle in order to avoid an obvious source of threats to the peace.

In the *Fisheries Jurisdiction* case (*United Kingdom v. Iceland*)[95] the International Court accepted Article 62 of the Vienna Convention as a statement of the customary

---

[93] (1932), *PCIJ*, Ser. A/B, no. 46, pp. 156–8; *Ann. Digest* (1931–2), 362 at 364. The Court observed that the facts did not justify the applications of the doctrine, which had been invoked by France.

[94] e.g. *Bremen v. Prussia, Ann. Digest* 3 (1925–6), no. 266; *In re Lepeschkin*, ibid. 2 (1923–4), no. 189; *Sransky v. Zivnostenska Bank*, ILR 22 (1955), 424–7.

[95] ICJ Reports (1973), 3 at 20–1. See also ibid, 49 (*Fed. Rep. of Germany v. Iceland*); and Briggs, 68 *AJ* (1974), 51–68.

law but decided that the dangers to Icelandic interests resulting from new fishing techniques 'cannot constitute a fundamental change with respect to the lapse or subsistence' of the jurisdictional clause in a bilateral agreement. In the *Hungary/ Slovakia* case the Court rejected the Hungarian argument in these terms:[96]

Hungary further argued that it was entitled to invoke a number of events which, cumulatively, would have constituted a fundamental change of circumstances. In this respect it specified profound changes of a political nature, the Project's diminishing economic viability, the progress of environmental knowledge and the development of new norms and prescriptions of international environmental law ...

The Court recalls that, in the *Fisheries Jurisdiction* case (*I.C.J. Reports 1973*, p. 63, para. 36), it stated that,

Article 62 of the Vienna Convention on the Law of Treaties, ... may in many respects be considered as a codification of existing customary law on the subject of the termination of a treaty relationship on account of change of circumstances.

The prevailing political situation was certainly relevant for the conclusion of the 1977 Treaty. But the Court will recall that the Treaty provided for a joint investment programme for the production of energy, the control of floods and the improvement of navigation on the Danube. In the Court's view, the prevalent political conditions were thus not so closely linked to the object and purpose of the Treaty that they constituted an essential basis of the consent of the parties and, in changing, radically altered the extent of the obligations still to be performed. The same holds good for the economic system in force at the time of the conclusion of the 1977 Treaty. Besides, even though the estimated profitability of the Project might have appeared less in 1992 than in 1977, it does not appear from the record before the Court that it was bound to diminish to such an extent that the treaty obligations of the parties would have been radically transformed as a result.

The Court does not consider that new developments in the state of environmental knowledge and of environmental law can be said to have been completely unforeseen. What is more, the formulation of Articles 15, 19 and 20, designed to accommodate change, made it possible for the parties to take account of such developments and to apply them when implementing those treaty provisions.

The changed circumstances advanced by Hungary are, in the Court's view, not of such a nature, either individually or collectively, that their effect would radically transform the extent of the obligations still to be performed in order to accomplish the Project. A fundamental change of circumstances must have been unforeseen; the existence of the circumstances at the time of the Treaty's conclusion must have constituted an essential basis of the consent of the parties to be bound by the Treaty. The negative and conditional wording of Article 62 of the Vienna Convention on the Law of Treaties is a clear indication moreover that the stability of treaty relations requires that the plea of fundamental change of circumstances be applied only in exceptional cases.

---

[96] ICJ Reports (1997), 7 at 64–5, para. 104.

(i) New peremptory norm

A treaty becomes void if it conflicts with a peremptory norm of general international law (*jus cogens*) established after the treaty comes into force.[97] This does not have retroactive effects on the validity of a treaty.

7. INVALIDITY, TERMINATION, AND SUSPENSION: GENERAL RULES[98]

The application of the regime of the Vienna Convention concerning the invalidity, termination, and suspension of the operation of treaties is governed by certain general provisions. The validity and continuance in force of a treaty and of consent to be bound is presumed (Art. 42).[99] Certain grounds of invalidity must be invoked by a party[100] and so the treaties concerned are not void but *voidable*. These grounds are: incompetence under internal law, restrictions on authority of representative, error, fraud, and corruption of a representative. The same is true of certain grounds of termination, namely, material breach, impossibility, and fundamental change of circumstances. On the other hand a treaty is *void* in case of coercion of a state (invalidity), and conflict with an existing or emergent peremptory norm (*jus cogens*) (invalidity or termination). Consent to be bound by a treaty procured by coercion of the representative of a state 'shall be without any legal effect' (Art. 51, invalidity). The rules governing separability of treaty provisions (Art. 44), that is, the severance of particular clauses affected by grounds for invalidating or terminating a treaty, do not apply to the cases of coercion of a representative, coercion of a state, or conflict with an *existing* peremptory norm (*jus cogens*). Provisions in conflict with a *new* peremptory norm may be severable, however.[101]

8. APPLICATION AND EFFECTS OF TREATIES[102]

(a) Justification for non-performance or suspension of performance

The grounds for termination have been considered in section 6, and the requirements of essential validity in section 5. However, the content of those categories does not exhaust the matters relevant to justification for non-performance of

---

[97] Vienna Conv., Art. 64; ILC draft, Art. 45; *Yrbk. ILC* (1963), ii. 211; Waldock, ibid. 77, 79 (para. 8); Final Draft, Art. 61; ibid. (1966), ii. 261; Fitzmaurice, ibid. (1957), ii. 29–30, 51. See also *supra*, p. 584. Generally on *jus cogens* see ch. 23, s. 5.

[98] See further the Vienna Conv., Arts. 69–72 and 75; and Cahier, 76 *RGDIP* (1972), 672–89.

[99] See also Art. 26 and *supra*.

[100] On the procedure see Arts. 65–8. See further Briggs, 61 *AJ* (1967), 976–89; Thirlway, 63 *BY* (1992), 85–94.

[101] See *Yrbk. ILC* (1966), ii. 238–9. 261. For comment on this distinction see Sinclair, 19 *ILCQ* (1970), 67–8.

[102] Vienna Conv., Arts. 28–30, 34–9; ILC draft, Arts. 55–64; 59 *AJ* (1965), 210ff.; Final Draft, Arts. 24–6, 30–4.

obligations, an issue which can arise irrespective of validity or termination of the *source* of obligation, the treaty itself. The topic of justification belongs to the rubric of state responsibility (Chapter 21, section 13). Clearly a state may plead necessity, or *force majeure*, for example, the effects of natural catastrophe or foreign invasion.[103] In the same connection legitimate military self-defence in case of armed conflict and civil strife provides a more particular justification.[104] Non-performance by way of legitimate reprisals raises highly controversial issues of the scope of reprisals in the modern law.[105] The Vienna Convention does not prejudice any question of state responsibility (Art. 73).

(b) Obligations and rights for third states[106]

The maxim *pacta tertiis nec nocent nec prosunt* expresses the fundamental principle that a treaty applies only between the parties to it. The final draft of the International Law Commission and the Vienna Convention refer to this as the 'general rule', and it is a corollary of the principle of consent and of the sovereignty and independence of states. Article 34 of the Convention provides that 'a treaty does not create either obligations or rights for a third State without its consent'.

The existence and extent of exceptions to the general rule have been matters of acute controversy. The Commission was unanimous in the view that a treaty cannot by its own force create obligations for non-parties. The Commission did not accept the view that treaties creating 'objective regimes', as, for example, the demilitarization of a territory by treaty or a legal regime for a major waterway, had a specific place in the existing law.[107] Article 35 of the Vienna Convention provides that 'an obligation arises for a third State from a provision of a treaty if the parties to the treaty intend the provision to be the means of establishing the obligation and the third State expressly accepts that obligation in writing'.

However, two apparent exceptions to the principle in respect of obligations exist. Thus a rule in a treaty may become binding on non-parties if it becomes a part of international custom.[108] The Hague Convention concerning rules of land warfare and, perhaps, certain treaties governing international waterways fall within this category. Further, a treaty may provide for lawful sanctions for violations of the law which are

---

[103] See UN Secretariat Study, ST/LEG/13, 27 June 1977.

[104] See Fitzmaurice, *Yrbk. ILC* (1959), ii. 44–5, 64–6.

[105] Fitzmaurice, ibid. 45–6, 66–70; McNair, *Law of Treaties*, p. 573; Schwarzenberger, *International Law*, i. 537. Cf. Art. 2(3) of the UN Charter.

[106] Vienna Conv. Arts. 34–8; ILC draft, Arts. 58–62; 59 *AJ* (1965), 217–27; Final Draft, Arts. 30–4; *Yrbk. ILC* (1960), ii. 69–107; Jiménez de Aréchaga, 50 *AJ* (1956), 338–57; McNair, *Law of Treaties*, pp. 309–21; Lauterpacht, *The Development of International Law of the International Court* (1958), 306–13; Guggenheim (2nd edn.), i. 197–204; Lachs, 92 Hague *Recueil* (1957, II), 313–19; Detter, *Essays*, 100–18; Whiteman, xiv. 331–53; Jennings, 20 *ICLQ* (1971), 433–50; Rousseau, i. 182–93; Cahier, 143 Hague *Recueil* (1974, III), 589–736; Rozakis, 35 *Z.a.ö.R.u.V.* (1975), 1–40; *Répertoire suisse*, i. 139–48; Napoletano, *Ital. Yrbk.* (1977), 75–91; Sinclair, *The Vienna Convention* (2nd edn., 1984), pp. 98–106; Thirlway, 60 *BY* (1989), 63–71; Chinkin, *Third Parties in International Law* (1993), 25–114; Oppenheim, ii. 1260–6.

[107] See McNair, *Law of Treaties*, p. 310, and see further *supra*, pp. 276, 377.

[108] Vienna Conv., Art. 38; ILC Final Draft, Art. 34; *Yrbk. ILC* (1966), ii. 230.

to be imposed on an aggressor state.[109] The Vienna Convention contains a reservation in regard to any obligation in relation to a treaty which arises for an aggressor state 'in consequence of measures taken in conformity with the Charter of the United Nations with reference to the aggression' (Art. 75). The precise status of Article 2, paragraph 6, of the United Nations Charter is a matter of some interest. Kelsen,[110] among others, holds the view that the provision creates duties, and liabilities to sanctions under the enforcement provisions of the Charter, for non-members. Assuming that this was the intention of the draftsmen, the provision can only be reconciled with general principles by reference to the status of the principles in Article 2 as general or customary international law.

More controversial is the conferment of rights on third parties, the *stipulation pour autrui*. Not infrequently treaties make provisions in favour of specified third states or for other states generally, as in the case, it would seem, of treaties concerning certain of the major international waterways, including, on one view, the Panama Canal.[111] The problem is to discover when, if at all, the right conferred becomes perfect and enforceable by the third state. The rule is that the third state only benefits in this sense if it expressly or implicitly assents to the creation of the right, a proposition accepted by the leading authorities.[112] Another view, supported by some members of the International Law Commission, was that the right which it was intended to create in favour of the third state was not conditional upon any specific act of acceptance by the latter.[113] Some authority for this view exists in the Judgment in the *Free Zones* case.[114] In that case the rights contended for by Switzerland, viz., the benefit of a free customs zone in French territory under multipartite treaties to which France was a party, but Switzerland was not, rested in fact on agreements of 1815 and 1816 to which Switzerland was a party.[115] However, the statement by the Court appears to accept[116] the principle that the creation of rights for third states is a matter only of the intention of the grantor states.

In its Final Report the Commission took the view that the two opposing views, referred to above, did not differ substantially in their practical effects. Article 36 of the Vienna Convention creates a presumption as to the existence of the assent of the third state:

1. A right arises for a third State from a provision of a treaty if the parties to the treaty intend the provision to accord that right either to the third State, or to a group of States

---

[109] *Yrbk. ILC* (1966), ii. 227, Art. 31, commentary, para. 3; ibid., Art. 70, p. 268.

[110] *The Law of the United Nations* (1951), 106–10. *Contra*, Bindschedler, 108 Hague *Recueil* (1963, I), 403–7. Cf. McNair, *Law of Treaties*, pp. 216–18.

[111] *Supra*, pp. 264–5.

[112] Rousseau and McNair *ut supra* n. 97. See the Final Draft, 1966, Art. 32.

[113] See Lauterpacht, Fitzmaurice, Jiménez de Aréchaga, *ut supra*, n. 105.

[114] (1932), PCIJ, Ser. A/B, no. 46, pp. 147–8. See also the Committee of Jurists on the Aaland Islands question; 29 *AJ* (1935), Suppl., Pt. III, pp. 927–8; and *Jews Deported from Hungary* case, ILR 44, 301 at 314–15. The point was not really in issue in the *River Oder Commission* case, PCIJ, Ser. A, no. 23, 19–22.

[115] See McNair, *Law of Treaties*, pp. 311–12.

[116] See the comment by Cahier, 143 Hague *Recueil* (1974, III), 629–30, who refers to the ambiguity in the reference by the Ct. to acceptance of the right 'as such' by the third state.

to which it belongs, or to all States, and the third State assents thereto. Its assent shall be presumed so long as the contrary is not indicated, unless the treaty otherwise provides.

2. A State exercising a right in accordance with paragraph 1 shall comply with the conditions for its exercise provided for in the treaty or established in conformity with the treaty.

The third state may, of course, disclaim any already inhering right expressly or tacitly through failure to exercise the right. The right of a third state may not be revoked or modified by the parties if it is established that it was intended that this could only occur with the consent of the third state: Article 37(2).

(c) Treaties having incompatible provisions[117]

The relation of treaties between the same parties and with overlapping provisions is primarily a matter of interpretation, aided by presumptions. Thus it is to be presumed that a later treaty prevails over an earlier treaty concerning the same subject-matter. A treaty may provide expressly that it is to prevail over subsequent incompatible treaties, as in the case of Article 103 of the Charter of the United Nations. Further, it is clear that a particular treaty may override others if it represents a norm of *jus cogens*.[118]

9. AMENDMENT AND MODIFICATION OF TREATIES[119]

The amendment[120] of treaties depends on the consent of the parties, and the issue is primarily one of politics. However, the lawyer may concern himself with procedures for amendment, as a facet of the large problem of peaceful change in international relations. Many treaties, including the Charter of the United Nations (Arts. 108 and 109), provide for the procedure of amendment. In their rules and constituent instruments, international organizations create amendment procedures which in some cases show considerable sophistication. In the League Covenant (Art. 19) and, less explicitly, in the Charter of the United Nations (Art. 14) provision for peaceful change was made as a part of a scheme to avoid threats to the peace.

---

[117] Vienna Conv., Arts. 30, 59; ILC draft, Art. 63; 59 *AJ* (1965), 227–40; Final Draft, Arts. 26, 56; *Yrbk. ILC* (1966), ii. 214–17, 252–3; Lauterpacht, ibid. (1953), ii. 156; ibid. (1954), ii. 133; Fitzmaurice, ibid. (1958), ii. 27, 41–5; Waldock, ibid. (1963), ii. 53–61; McNair, *Law of Treaties*, pp. 215–24; Rousseau, *Principes généraux*, i. 765–814; Jenks, 30 *BY* (1953), 401–53; Cahier, 76 *RGDIP* (1972), 670–2; Sciso, 38 *Öst. Z. für öff. R.* (1987), 161–79.

[118] *Supra*, p. 510.

[119] Vienna Conv., Arts. 39–41; ILC draft, Arts. 65–8; 59 *AJ* (1965), 434–45; Final Draft, Arts. 35–8; *Yrbk. ILC* (1966), ii. 231–6; *Annuaire de l'Inst.* 49 (1961), i. 229–91; 52 (1967), i. 5–401; Handbook of Final Clauses, ST/LEG/6, pp. 130–52; Hoyt, *The Unanimity Rule in the Revision of Treaties* (1959); Blix, 5 *ICLQ* (1956), 447–65, 581–96; Whiteman, xiv. 436–42; Detter, *Essays*, pp. 71–82; Sinclair, *The Vienna Convention*, pp. 106–9.

[120] There is no distinction of quality between 'amendment' of particular provisions and 'revision' of the treaty as a whole.

Apart from amendment, a treaty may undergo 'modification' when some of the parties conclude an '*inter se* agreement' altering the application of the treaty between themselves alone.[121]

Modification may also result from the conclusion of a subsequent treaty or the emergence of a new peremptory norm of general international law.[122] The Final Draft of the International Law Commission[123] provided that 'a treaty may be modified by subsequent practice in the application of the treaty establishing the agreement of the parties to modify its provisions'. This article was rejected at the Vienna Conference on the ground that such a rule would create instability.[124] This result is unsatisfactory. In the first place Article 39 of the Convention provides that a treaty may be amended by agreement without requiring any formality for the expression of agreement. Secondly, a consistent practice may provide cogent evidence of *common* consent to a change. Thirdly, modification of this type occurs in practice: witness the inclusion in practice of fishing zones as a form of contiguous zone for the purposes of the Territorial Sea Convention.[125] The process of interpretation through subsequent practice (section 10(*f*)) is legally distinct from modification, although the distinction is often rather fine.

10. INTERPRETATION OF TREATIES[126]

(a) Competence to interpret

Obviously the parties have competence to interpret a treaty, but this is subject to the operation of other rules of the law. The treaty itself may confer competence on an *ad hoc* tribunal or the International Court. The Charter of the United Nations is interpreted by its organs, which may seek advisory opinions from the Court of the Organization.[127]

---

[121] Vienna Conv., Art. 41.

[122] See pp. 510–12.

[123] Art. 38, *Yrbk. ILC* (1966), ii. 236.

[124] *Official Records, First Session*, pp. 207–15. See also Kearney and Dalton, 64 *AJ* (1970), 525.

[125] See also US and France, *Air Transport Services Agreement Arbitration*, 1963, ILR, 38, 182; *RIAA* xvi. 5; Award, P.IV, s. 5.

[126] Rousseau, *Droit international public*, i. 241–305; Guggenheim (2nd edn.), i. 245–68; Whiteman, xiv. 353–410; McNair, *Law of Treaties*, chs. 20–29; Fitzmaurice, 28 *BY* (1951), 1–28; id., 33 *BY* (1957), 203–38; Lauterpacht, *Development*, esp. pp. 116–41; id., 26 *BY* (1949), 48–85; *Annuaire de l'Inst.* 43 (1950), i. 366–460; 44 (1952), ii. 359–401; 46 (1956), 317–49; de Visscher, *Problémes d'interprétation judiciaire en droit international public* (1963); Sinclair, 12 *ICLQ* (1963), 508–51; Degan, *L'Interprétation des accords en droit international* (1963); Berlia, 114 Hague *Recueil* (1965, I), 287–332; Jacobs, 18 *ICLQ* (1969), 318–46; Rosenne, 5 *Columbia Journ. Trans. Law* (1966), 205–30; Yasseen, 151 Hague *Recueil* (1976, III), 1–114; Haraszti, *Some Fundamental Problems of the Law of Treaties*, pp. 13–228; Sinclair, *The Vienna Convention* (2nd edn., 1984), pp. 114–58; Thirlway, 62 *BY* (1991), 16–75; and 77 *BY* (2007), 1–82; Oppenheim, ii. 1266–84.

[127] See further, *infra*, p. 694.

(b) The status of 'rules of interpretation'

Jurists are in general cautious about formulating a code of 'rules of interpretation', since the 'rules' may become unwieldy instruments instead of the flexible aids which are required.[128] Many of the 'rules' and 'principles' offered are general, question-begging, and contradictory. As with statutory interpretation, a choice of a 'rule', for example of 'effectiveness' or 'restrictive interpretation', may in a given case involve a preliminary choice of meaning rather than a guide to interpretation. The International Law Commission in its work confined itself to isolating 'the comparatively few general principles which appear to constitute general rules for the interpretation of treaties'.

(c) The text and the intentions of the parties

The Commission and the Institute of International Law[129] have taken the view that what matters is the intention of the parties *as expressed in the text*, which is the best guide to the more recent common intention of the parties. The alternative approach regards the intentions of the parties as an independent basis of interpretation. The jurisprudence of the International Court supports the textual approach,[130] and it is adopted in substance in the relevant provisions of the Vienna Convention:[131]

ARTICLE 31

General rule of interpretation

1. A treaty shall be interpreted in good faith in accordance with the ordinary meaning to be given to the terms of the treaty in their context and in the light of its object and purpose.

2. The context for the purpose of the interpretation of a treaty shall comprise, in addition to the text, including its preamble and annexes:

(a) any agreement relating to the treaty which was made between all the parties in connection with the conclusion of the treaty;

(b) any instrument which was made by one or more parties in connection with the conclusion of the treaty and accepted by the other parties as an instrument related to the treaty.

3. There shall be taken into account, together with the context:

(a) any subsequent agreement between the parties regarding the interpretation of the treaty or the application of its provisions;

(b) any subsequent practice in the application of the treaty which establishes the agreement of the parties regarding its interpretation;

---

[128] For the case in favour of having rules: Beckett, *Annuaire de l'Inst.* 43 (1950), i. 435–40.

[129] *Ut supra*, p. 607. The first rapporteur of the Institute, Lauterpacht, preferred more direct investigation of intention.

[130] See Fitzmaurice, 28 *BY* (1951), 1–28; id. 33 *BY* (1957), 203–38.

[131] On interpretation of treaties authenticated in two or more languages see Art. 33; Hardy, 37 *BY* (1961), 72–155; *James Buchanan and Co. Ltd. v. Babco (U.K.) Ltd.* [1977] AC 141; ILR 74, 574; *Young Loan Arbitration*, ILR 59, 495; Ago (Sep. Op.), *Nicaragua* case (Jurisdiction), ICJ Reports (1984), 522–3; Jennings (Sep. Op.), ibid. 537–9; Schwebel (Diss. Op.), ibid. 575–6.

(c) any relevant rules of international law applicable in the relations between the parties.

4. A special meaning shall be given to a term if it is established that the parties so intended.

ARTICLE 32
Supplementary means of interpretation

Recourse may be had to supplementary means of interpretation, including the preparatory work of the treaty and the circumstances of its conclusion, in order to confirm the meaning resulting from the application of Article 31, or to determine the meaning when the interpretation according to Article 31:

(a) leaves the meaning ambiguous or obscure; or

(b) leads to a result which is manifestly absurd or unreasonable.

This economical code of principles follows exactly the Final Draft of the International Law Commission.[132] At the Vienna Conference the United States proposed an amendment with the object of removing the apparent hierarchy of sources by combining the two Articles, and thus giving more scope to preparatory work and the circumstances in which the treaty was concluded. This proposal received little support. In its Commentary[133] the Commission emphasized that the application of the means of interpretation in the first article would be a single combined operation: hence the heading 'General rule' in the singular. The various elements present in any given case would interact. The Commission pointed out that the two articles should operate in conjunction, and would not have the effect of drawing a rigid line between 'supplementary' and other means of interpretation. At the same time the distinction itself was justified since the elements of interpretation in the first article all relate to the agreement between the parties 'at the time when or after it received authentic expression in the text'. Preparatory work did not have the same authentic character 'however valuable it may sometimes be in throwing light on the expression of agreement in the text'.

(d) Textual approach: natural and ordinary meaning[134]

The first principle stated in Article 31 of the Vienna Convention is that 'a treaty shall be interpreted in good faith in accordance with the ordinary meaning to be given to the terms of treaty . . . '.[135] In the Advisory Opinion on the *Polish Postal Service in Danzig*[136] the Permanent Court observed that the postal service which Poland was entitled to establish in Danzig under treaty was not confined to operation inside the postal

---

[132] Arts. 27, 28.

[133] *Yrbk. ILC* (1966), ii. 219–20.

[134] There seems to be no real difference between the principle of actuality (or textuality) and the principle of natural and ordinary meaning in the scheme of Fitzmaurice.

[135] See the *Admissions* case, ICJ Reports (1950), 8.

[136] (1925), PCIJ, Ser. B, no. 11 at p. 37. See also the *Eastern Greenland* case (1933), PCIJ, Ser. A/B, no. 53 at p. 49; US-Italy Arbitration, *Interpretation of Air Transport Services Agreement, RIAA*, xvi. 75 at 91.

building, as 'postal service' must be interpreted 'in its ordinary sense so as to include the normal functions of a postal service'. A corollary of the principle of ordinary meaning is the principle of integration: the meaning must emerge in the context of the treaty as a whole[137] and in the light of its objects and purposes.[138] Another corollary is the principle of contemporaneity: the language of the treaty must be interpreted in the light of the rules of general international law in force at the time of its conclusion,[139] and also in the light of the contemporaneous meaning of terms.[140] In the *Bankovic*[141] case the European Court of Human Rights referred to the relevant rules of international law and state practice when determining that the 'jurisdiction' of States, for the purposes of Article 1 of the European Convention, did not extend to military missions involving Contracting States acting extraterritorially. The applicants were relatives and injured survivors of a NATO air attack on a television station in Belgrade, during the military operations of 1999. The doctrine of ordinary meaning involves only a presumption: a meaning other than the ordinary meaning may be established, but the proponent of the special meaning has a burden of proof.[142] The fact remains that in complex cases the tribunal will be prepared to make a careful inquiry into the precise object and purpose of a treaty.[143]

(e) Context to be used

The context of a treaty for purposes of interpretation comprises, in addition to the treaty, including its preamble[144] and annexes, any agreement or instrument related to the treaty and drawn up in connection with its conclusion.[145]

(f) Subsequent practice

The parties may make an agreement regarding interpretation of the treaty. It follows also that reference may be made to 'subsequent practice in the application of the treaty which clearly establishes the understanding of all the parties regarding its

---

[137] See the Vienna Conv., Art. 31(1); *Competence of the I.L.O. to Regulate Agricultural Labour* (1922), PCIJ., Ser. B, nos. 2 and 3, p. 23; *Free Zones* case (1932), Ser. A/B, no. 46, p. 140; US-France Arbitration, *Case Concerning the Air Services Agreement of 27 March 1946*, RIAA xviii. 417 at 435; ILR 54, 304 at 328–9.

[138] See the Vienna Conv., Art. 31(1); *U.S. Nationals in Morocco*, ICJ Reports (1952), 183–4, 197–8; *Case Concerning Sovereignty over Pulao Ligitan and Pulao Sipadan*, Judgment of 17 December 2002, paras. 37, 49–52.

[139] See the *Grisbadarna* case, *RIAA* xi. 159–60. Generally on inter-temporal law *supra*, p. 126.

[140] *U.S. Nationals in Morocco, supra*, p. 132. See also Fitzmaurice, 33 *BY* 225–7.

[141] ILR 123, 94, 108–13.

[142] For critical comment on the concept of natural or plain meaning see Lauterpacht, *Development*, pp. 52–60.

[143] See the *Case Concerning the Gabcikovo-Nagymaros Project*, ICJ Reports (1997), 7 at 35–46, paras. 39–59; and see also the Award of the Arbitral Tribunal in *Fraport* v. *Philippines*, dated 16 August 2007, paras. 334–56.

[144] See Fitzmaurice, 33 *BY* 227–8.

[145] See the Vienna Conv., Art. 31(2); and *Young Loan Arbitration*, ILR 59, 495 at 534–40 (Decision), 556–8 (Diss. Op.).

interpretation'.[146] Subsequent practice by individual parties also has some probative value.

(g) Practice of organizations[147]

In a series of important advisory opinions the International Court has made considerable use of the subsequent practice of organizations in deciding highly controversial issues of interpretation.[148] Two points arise. The first is that constitutionally members who were outvoted in the organs concerned may not be bound by the practice.[149] Secondly, the practice of political organs involves elements of politics and opportunism, and what should be referred to, subject to the constitutional issue, is the reasoning *behind* the practice, which can reveal its legal relevance, if any.[150]

(h) Preparatory work

When the textual approach, on the principles referred to already, either leaves the meaning ambiguous or obscure, or leads to a manifestly absurd or unreasonable result, recourse may be had to further means of interpretation, including the preparatory work of the treaty and the circumstances of its conclusion.[151] Moreover, such recourse may be had to verify or confirm a meaning that emerges as a result of the textual approach.[152] In general the International Court, and the Permanent Court before it, have refused to resort to preparatory work if the text is sufficiently clear in itself.[153] On a number of occasions the Court has used preparatory work to confirm a conclusion reached by other means.[154] Preparatory work is an aid to be employed with discretion, since its use may detract from the textual approach, and, particularly in the case of multilateral agreements, the records of conference proceedings, treaty drafts, and so on may be confused or inconclusive. The International Law Commission has taken the

---

[146] See the Vienna Conv., Art. 31(3)(b); *Yrbk ILC* (1966), ii. 221, para. 15; *Air Transport Services Agreement Arbitration* (1963), ILR 38, 182 at 245–8, 256–8; *Air Transport Services Agreement Arbitration* (1965), *RIAA* xvi. 75 at 99–101; *Young Loan Arbitration*, ILR 59, 495 at 541–3 (Decision), 573–4 (Diss. Op.). See also Fitzmaurice, 28 *BY* 20–1; 33 *BY* 223–5, where subsequent practice is commended for its 'superior *reliability*' as an indication of meaning.

[147] See Engel, 16 *ICLQ* (1967), 865–910; Judge Spender, *Expenses* case, ICJ Reports (1962), 187ff.; Judge Fitzmaurice, ibid. 201–3.

[148] *Competence of the General Assembly*, ICJ Reports (1950), 9; *IMCO* case, ibid. (1960), 167ff.; and the *Expenses* case ibid. (1962), 157ff.

[149] See further *infra*, pp. 691ff.

[150] See the Sep. Op. of Judge Spender in the *Expenses* case, pp. 187ff. The ILC did not deal with the problem in the present draft: 59 *AJ* (1965), 456 (para. 14).

[151] See the Vienna Conv., Art. 32, *supra*; *Yrbk. ILC* (1966), ii. 222–3, paras. 18–20; Jennings, 121 Hague *Recueil*, pp. 550–2; *Young Loan Arbitration*, ILR 59, 495 at 543–8 (Decision), 562–7 (Diss. Op.); *Fothergill* v. *Monarch Airlines Ltd.* [1981] AC 251; ILR 74, 627; *Commonwealth of Australia* v. *State of Tasmania* (1983) 46 ALR 625; ILR 68, 266.

[152] See further Lauterpacht, *Development*, pp. 116–41; 48 *Harv. LR* (1935), 549–91; McNair, *Law of Treaties*, ch. 23.

[153] *Admissions* case, ICJ Reports (1948), 63; *Competence of the General Assembly*, ibid. (1950), 8. See Fitzmaurice, 28 *BY* 10–3; 33 *BY* 215–20.

[154] e.g. *Convention of 1919 concerning the Work of Women at Night* (1932), PCIJ, Ser. A/B, no. 50, p. 380. See also *Bankovic* v. *Belgium and Others*, ILR 123, 94, 110–11 (paras. 63–5); Europ. Ct. of Human Rights.

view that states acceding to a treaty and not taking part in its drafting cannot claim for themselves the inadmissibility of the preparatory work, which could have been examined before accession.[155]

(i) Restrictive interpretation[156]

In a number of cases the Permanent Court committed itself to the principle that provisions implying a limitation of state sovereignty should receive restrictive interpretation.[157] As a general principle of interpretation this is question-begging and should not be allowed to overshadow the textual approach: in recent years tribunals have given less scope to the principle.[158] However, in cases which give rise to issues concerning regulation of rights and territorial privileges the principle may operate:[159] in these instances it is not an 'aid to interpretation' but an independent principle. The principle did not find a place in the provisions of the Vienna Convention.

(j) Effective interpretation[160]

The principle of effective interpretation is often invoked, and suffers from the same organic defects as the principle of restrictive interpretation. The International Law Commission did not give a separate formulation of the principle, considering that, as a matter of the existing law, it was reflected sufficiently in the doctrines of interpretation in good faith in accordance with the ordinary meaning of the text (paragraph (d) above).[161] The International Court has generally subordinated the principle to the textual approach.[162] In the *Peace Treaties* case[163] the Court made this clear and avoided revision of the treaties by refusing to remedy a fault in the machinery for settlement of disputes not curable by reference to the texts themselves.

(k) The teleological approach[164]

The International Law Commission and the Vienna Convention gave a cautious qualification to the textual approach by permitting recourse to further means of interpretation when the latter 'leads to a result which is manifestly absurd or unreasonable

---

[155] Differing thus from the *River Oder Commission* case (1929), PCIJ, Ser. A, no. 23. See further Sinclair, 12 *ICLQ* (1963), at 512–17; *Arbitral Comm. on Property, etc., in Germany,* ILR 29, 442 at 460–8.

[156] See Lauterpacht, 26 *BY* (1949), 48–85; id., *Development,* pp. 300–6; McNair, *Law of Treaties,* pp. 765–6.

[157] e.g. *River Oder Commission* case, *ut supra,* p. 261.

[158] See, however, *De Pascale Case, RIAA* xvi. 227; *De Leon Case,* ibid. 239. Cf. *Droutzkoy Case,* ibid. 273 at 292.

[159] *Supra,* pp. 369ff.

[160] See *Annuaire de l'Inst.* 43 (1950), i. 402–23; McNair, *Law of Treaties,* ch. 21.

[161] *Yrbk. ILC* (1966), ii. 219, para. 6.

[162] Fitzmaurice, 28 *BY* 19–20; 33 *BY,* 211, 220–3.

[163] ICJ Reports (1950), 229. See also the *South West Africa* cases (Prelim. Objections), ibid. (1962), 511–13 (Diss. Op. of Judges Spender and Fitzmaurice); *South West Africa* cases (Second Phase), ibid. (1966), 36, 47–8.

[164] See Fitzmaurice, 28 *BY* 7–8, 13–14; 33 *BY* 207–9; Waldock, *Mélanges offerts à Paul Reuter* (1981), 535–47.

in the light of the objects and purposes of the treaty'.[165] Somewhat distinct from this procedure is the more radical teleological approach according to which a court determines what the objects and purposes are and then resolves any ambiguity of meaning by importing the substance 'necessary' to give effect to the purposes of the treaty. This may involve a judicial implementation of purposes in a fashion not contemplated in fact by the parties. At the same time the textual approach in practice often leaves the decision-maker with a choice of possible meanings and in exercising that choice it is impossible to keep considerations of policy out of account. Many issues of interpretation are by no means narrow technical inquiries.

In advisory opinions concerning powers of organs of the United Nations, the International Court has adopted a principle of institutional effectiveness and has freely implied the existence of powers which in its view were consistent with the purposes of the Charter.[166] This tendency reached its apogee in the opinion given in the *Expenses* case, and the problems raised by this decision are considered elsewhere.[167] The work of the European Court of Human Rights has involved a tendency to an effective and 'evolutionary' approach in applying the European Convention on Human Rights.[168]

The teleological approach has many pitfalls. However, in a small specialized organization, with supranational elements and efficient procedures for amendment of constituent treaties and rules and regulations, the teleological approach, with its aspect of judicial legislation, may be thought to have a constructive role to play. Yet the practice of the Court of the European Communities has not shown any special attraction to this approach, and it would seem that the delicate treaty structure with its supranational element dictates a generally textual and relatively conservative approach to texts.

11. CLASSIFICATION OF TREATIES

A number of distinguished writers have developed or supported classifications of treaties. Lord McNair long ago pointed to the variety of functions which the treaty performs and the need to free ourselves from the traditional notion that the treaty is governed by a single undifferentiated set of rules.[169] As he suggests, some treaties, dispositive of territory and rights in relation to territory, are like conveyances in private

---

[165] ILC, Final Draft, Art. 28; Vienna Conv., Art. 32.

[166] The cases are cited *infra*, pp. 686–8. See further the *International Status of South West Africa*, ICJ Reports (1950), 128, the *South West Africa* cases, ibid. (1962), 319, and the *Namibia* Opinion, ibid. (1971), 16 at 47–50. See also the opinions of Fitzmaurice, in the *Expenses* case, ICJ Reports (1962), 198ff. See further Gordon, 59 *AJ* (1965), 794–833. Cf., however, the Joint Dissent of Fitzmaurice and Spender in the *South West Africa* cases, ICJ Reports (1962), at 511–22; and the view of the Court in the *South West Africa* cases (Second Phase), ICJ Reports (1966), 36, 47–8.

[167] *Infra*, pp. 694ff.

[168] See Waldock, *Mélanges offerts à Paul Reuter*.

[169] 11 *BY* (1930), 100–18; also in *The Law of Treaties*, pp. 739–54. See also Rousseau, *Principes généraux*, i. 132–41, 677, 728–64; Vitta, *Ann. français* (1960), 225–38. On the special role of multilateral treaties see Lachs, 92 Hague *Recueil* (1957, II), 233–341.

law. Treaties involving bargains between a few states are like contracts; whereas the multilateral treaty creating either a set of rules, such as the Hague Conventions on the Law of War, or an institution, such as the Copyright Union, is 'law-making'. Moreover, the treaty constituting an institution is akin to a charter of incorporation. It is certainly fruitful to contemplate the unique features of parts of the large terrain to which the law of treaties applies and to expect the development of specialized rules. Thus it is the case that the effect of war between parties varies according to the type of treaty involved. However, Lord McNair and others have tended to support the position that the genus of treaty (the contents of the genus may themselves be a matter of dispute) produces fairly *general* effects on the applicable rules. Thus the law-making character of a treaty is said (1) to rule out recourse to preparatory work as an aid to interpretation; (2) to avoid recognition by one party of other parties as states or governments; and (3) to render the doctrine of *rebus sic stantibus* inapplicable.[170] More especially, Lord McNair,[171] Sir Gerald Fitzmaurice,[172] and Sir Humphrey Waldock,[173] among others, have regarded certain treaties as creating an 'objective regime' creating rights and duties for third states. Examples given include the treaty regimes for international waterways,[174] regimes for demilitarization,[175] and treaties creating organizations.[176] Significantly the International Law Commission deliberately avoided any classification of treaties along broad lines and rejected the concept of the 'objective regime' in relation to the effects of treaties on non-parties.[177] The Commission has accepted specialized rules in a few instances,[178] but has been, correctly it would seem, empirical in its approach. In formulating the general rules of interpretation the Commission did not consider it necessary to make a distinction between 'law-making' and other treaties.[179] The drafts of the Commission and the Vienna Convention treat the law of treaties as essentially a unity.[180] The evidence is that jurists are today less willing to accept the more doctrinal versions of the distinction between treaty-contract (*vertrag*) and treaty-law (*vereinbarung*),[181] the latter category representing multilateral treaties making rules for future conduct and framing a generally agreed legislative policy. The contrast intended is thus between the bilateral political bargain and the 'legislative act' produced by a broad international conference. But in fact the distinction is less

---

[170] See McNair, *Law of Treaties*.

[171] *Law of Treaties*, ch. 14.

[172] *Yrbk. ILC* (1960), ii. 96ff. (with considerable caution).

[173] 106 Hague *Recueil* (1962, II), 78–81 (with some caution).

[174] *Supra*, pp. 260–4.

[175] See the Committee of Jurists on the Aaland Islands question, 29 *AJ* (1935), Suppl., Pt. III, pp. 927–8.

[176] Cf. the *Reparation* case, *infra*, p. 676.

[177] *Supra*, s. 8(b); *infra*, s. 12. See also, in the context of aids to interpretation, 59 *AJ* (1965), 449–50 (commentary on the draft).

[178] See the Vienna Conv., Art. 62(2), *supra*, p. 623. Cf. the provisions on reservations, *supra*, pp. 612–15.

[179] *Yrbk. ILC* (1966), ii. 219, para. 6. But note the view of Berlia, 114 Hague *Recueil*, 287 at 331.

[180] See Dehaussy, *Recueil d'études en hommage à Guggenheim*, pp. 305–26; and Reuter, *Introduction au droit des traités*, pp. 37–9.

[181] For the history see Lauterpacht, *Private Law Sources and Analogies of International Law* (1927), para. 70.

clear: for example, it is known that political issues and cautious bargaining lie behind law-making efforts like the Geneva Conventions on the Law of the Sea. Further, the distinction obscures the real differences between treaty-making and legislation in a municipal system.[182]

12. PARTICIPATION IN GENERAL MULTILATERAL TREATIES

In an early draft (Article 1(1)(c)) the International Law Commission defines a 'general multilateral treaty' as 'a multilateral treaty which concerns general norms of international law and deals with matters of general interest to States as a whole'. Such a treaty has been described as 'the nearest thing we yet have to a general statute in international law'.[183] United Nations practice in convening a conference to draw up a treaty is to leave the question of composition to a political organ, the General Assembly, and a number of Communist states[184] were excluded as a result. In the Commission it was proposed that states should have a right to become parties to this type of treaty. This solution was adopted in a provisional draft in the insubstantial form that the right existed except where the treaty or the rules of an international organization provide otherwise.[185] The Final Draft of the Commission contained no provision on the subject and amendments intended to give 'all States a right to participate in multilateral treaties' were defeated at the Vienna Conference.[186]

---

[182] Waldock, 106 Hague *Recueil* (1962, ii), 74–6.

[183] ibid., 81. See also Lachs, 92 Hague *Recueil* (1957, II), 233–41.

[184] For a long time Mongolia; also China, East Germany, North Vietnam, and North Korea. These states were not represented at the Law of the Sea Conference in 1958.

[185] ILC draft, Art. 8; *Yrbk. ILC* (1962), ii. 167–9; Waldock, ibid. 53–8.

[186] *Yrbk. ILC* (1966), ii. 200; UN Secretariat Working Paper, A/CN. 4/245, 23 Apr. 1971, pp. 131–4. See also Lukashuk, 135 Hague *Recueil* (1972, I), 231–328.

28

OTHER TRANSACTIONS INCLUDING AGENCY AND REPRESENTATION

1. INFORMAL AGREEMENTS

The law of treaties does not contain mandatory requirements of form, and the rapporteurs on the subject of the International Law Commission have admitted the validity of unwritten agreements.[1] In the *Railway Traffic Between Lithuania and Poland* case[2] the Permanent Court accepted the view that participation by two states, parties to a dispute, in the adoption of a resolution by the Council of the League of Nations constituted a binding 'engagement'. Again, in the *Eastern Greenland* case[3] the Court placed reliance in part on an oral statement by the Norwegian Minister of Foreign Affairs, Mr Ihlen, to the Danish Minister accredited to Norway, relating to Norwegian accept-ance of the Danish claim to the whole of Greenland. Though apparently unilateral, the Court regarded this statement, and a Danish disclaimer of interests in Spitzbergen, as interdependent.

2. QUASI-LEGISLATIVE ACTS

The nature of a mandate agreement was in issue in the *South West Africa* cases (Preliminary Objections).[4] The applicant states founded jurisdiction on its nature as 'a treaty or convention in force' providing for reference of disputes to the Permanent Court and kept alive in this respect by Article 37 of the Statute of the present Court.[5]

---

[1] See the Sep. Op. of Judge Jessup, *South West Africa* cases (Prelim. Objections), ICJ Reports (1962), 402–5.

[2] (1931), PCIJ, Ser. A/B, no. 42, pp. 115, 116. See also McNair, *Law of Treaties* (1961), 14.

[3] (1933), PCIJ, Ser. A/B, no. 53 at pp. 71–3. See also McNair, *Law of Treaties*, pp. 9–10; Hambro, *Festschrift für Jean Spiropoulos* (1957), 227–36; Aust, 35 *ICLQ* (1986), 807–11.

[4] ICJ Reports (1962), 319. Cf. *South West Africa* cases (Second Phase), ICJ Reports (1966), 6; *Namibia* Opinion, ibid. (1971), 16.

[5] See *infra*, p. 714.

In its preliminary objections South Africa, the mandatory state, contended, *inter alia*, that the Mandate was not *ab initio* a 'treaty or convention', since its original authority was a resolution of the Council of the League of Nations. The Court held that the Mandate was an agreement in spite of the confirmation by the Council of the League.[6] However, in a Joint Dissenting Opinion, Judges Spender and Fitzmaurice took a different view, concluding that the Mandate was 'a quasi-legislative act of the League Council'.[7] As the Court itself pointed out, the Mandate Agreement had special features. These may be described as 'quasi-legislative': but it does not follow that it is not a 'treaty or convention', for certain purposes at least. Similar problems arise in the case of trusteeship agreements under Chapter 12 of the United Nations Charter.[8] The Permanent Court assimilated mandates to treaties for purposes of interpretation.[9] However, in the context of interpretation such quasi-legislative acts cannot be approached in quite the same way as bilateral treaties.[10]

3. UNILATERAL ACTS

(a) In general

Acts and conduct of governments may not be directed towards the formation of agreements and yet are capable of creating legal effects in a great many ways. The formation of customary rules and the law of recognition are two of the more prominent categories concerned with the 'unilateral' acts of states. Some authors have been prepared to bring unilateral acts, including protest, promise, renunciation, and recognition, within a general concept of 'legal acts', either contractual or unilateral, based upon the manifestation of will by a legal person.[11] The writer is of opinion that this approach may provide a useful framework for discussion of problems and yet may

---

[6] At pp. 330–1 of the Judgment.

[7] Ibid. 482–90. See also the Diss. Op. of Judge Basdevant, p. 461. Cf. Sep. Op. of Judge Morelli, *Northern Cameroons* case, ICJ Reports (1963), 142; and *Namibia* Opinion, ibid. (1971), 266–8, Judge Fitzmaurice, Diss. Op., 338–9, Judge Gros, Diss. Op.

[8] See Detter, *Law Making by International Organizations* (1965), 187–201.

[9] *Mavrommatis Palestine Concessions* case, PCIJ, Ser. A, No. 2.

[10] See Hardy, 37 *BY* (1961), 76–8.

[11] See especially Suy, *Les Actes juridiques unilatéraux en droit international public* (1962), at 22. See further Dehaussy, 92 *JDI* (1965), 41–66; Cahier, *Recueil d'études de droit international en hommage à Paul Guggenheim* (1968), 237–65; Rousseau, i. 416–32; Verzijl, *International Law in Historical Perspective*, vi (1973), 105–11; Jacqué, *Mélanges offerts à Paul Reuter* (1981), 327–45; Martin, *L'Estoppel en droit international public* (1979); Paul de Visscher, *Essays in Honour of Manfred Lachs* (1984), 459–65; Oppenheim, ii. 1187–96; Skubiszewski, in Bedjaoui (ed.), *International Law: Achievements and Prospects* (1991), 221–39; Bernhardt, *Encyclopedia*, IV (2000), 1018–23; Reisman and Arsanjani, *ICSID Review*, 19 (2004), 328–43; Rodríguez-Cedeño, First Report on Unilateral Acts of States, UN Doc. A/CN.4/486; Second Report, UN Doc. A/CN.4/500; Third Report, UN Doc. A/CN.4/505; Fourth Report, UN Doc. A/CN.4/519; Fifth Report, UN Doc. A/CN.4/525; Sixth Report, UN Doc. A/CN.4/534; Seventh Report, U.N. Doc.A/CN.4/542; Eighth Report, U.N. Doc.A/CN.4/557; Ninth Report, U.N. Doc.A/CN.4/569; ibid., Add.1 (6 April 2006); and Suy, *Mélanges Salmon* (2007), 631–42.

obscure the variety of legal relations involved. Moreover, analysis in terms of categories of 'promise', 'protest', and the like is superficial, and tends to confuse conditioning facts and legal consequences. In terms of result, a great deal will depend on the context in which a 'promise' or 'protest' occurs, including the surrounding circumstances and especially the effect of relevant rules of law.[12]

(b) Unilateral declarations

A state may evidence a clear intention to accept obligations *vis-à-vis* certain other states by a public declaration which is not an offer or otherwise dependent on reciprocal undertakings from the states concerned.[13] Apparently the terms of such a declaration will determine the conditions under which it can be revoked.[14] In 1957 the Egyptian Government made a Declaration on the Suez Canal and the Arrangements for its Operation[15] in which certain obligations were accepted. The Declaration was communicated to the Secretary-General of the United Nations together with a letter which explained that the Declaration was to be considered as an 'international instrument' and registered as such by the Secretariat. Such a declaration may implicitly or otherwise require acceptance by other states as a condition of validity.[16]

In the *Nuclear Tests* case (Australia v. France)[17] the International Court held that France was legally bound by publicly given undertakings, made on behalf of the French Government, to cease the conduct of atmospheric nuclear tests. The criteria of obligation were: the intention of the state making the declaration that it should be bound according to its terms; and that the undertaking be given publicly. There was no requirement of a *quid pro quo* or of any subsequent acceptance or response. With one exception[18] the judges expressing views in separate or dissenting opinions made no reference to this matter. As a result of the French undertaking, so interpreted, the dispute, it was held, had disappeared and 'the claim advanced by Australia no longer has any object'. While the principle applied by the Court—that a unilateral declaration may have certain legal effects—is not new, when the declaration is not directed to a specific state or states but is expressed *erga omnes*, as here, the detection of an intention to be legally bound, and of the structure of such intention, involves very careful

---

[12] See the treatment by Venturini, 112 Hague *Recueil* (1964, II), 367–467. See also Reuter, 103 Hague *Recueil* (1961, II), 547–82.

[13] See McNair, *Law of Treaties*, p. 11; Brierly, *Yrbk. ILC* (1950), ii. 227; Lauterpacht, ibid. (1953), ii. 101ff.; Judge Jessup, Sep. Op., *South West Africa* cases (Prelim. Objections), ICJ Reports (1962), 402–4, 417–18; Fitzmaurice, 33 *BY* (1957), 229–30; *Répertoire suisse*, i. 213 (and see iii. 1326); Lachs, 169 Hague *Recueil* (1980, iv), 198.

[14] Cf. Fitzmaurice, *Yrbk. ILC* (1960), ii. 79 (Art. 12), 81 (Art. 22), 91, 105.

[15] *Supra*, p. 264.

[16] Cf. the Austrian Decl. of 1955, contained in a Statute on Austria's permanent neutrality; on which see Kunz, 50 *AJ* (1956), 418–25.

[17] ICJ Reports (1974), 253 at 267–71. See also *Nuclear Tests* case (*New Zealand* v. *France*), ibid. 457 at 472–5. For comment see: Carbone, 1 *Ital. Yrbk.* (1975), 166–72; Rubin, 71 *AJ* (1977), 1–30; Paul de Visscher, *Essays in Honour of Manfred Lachs*, pp. 459–65; Thirlway, 60 *BY* (1989), 8–17.

[18] Judge de Castro, Diss. Op., ICJ Reports (1974), 372 at 373–4, accepting the principle, but deciding on the facts that the French statements lay within 'the political domain'.

appreciation of the facts. In the *North Sea Continental Shelf* cases[19] the International Court stated that unilateral assumption of the obligations of a convention by conduct was 'not lightly to be presumed', and that 'a very consistent course of conduct' was required in such a situation. In any event the principle recognized in the *Nuclear Tests* cases was applied by the International Court in the *Nicaragua* case (Merits)[20] and also by a Chamber of the Court in the *Case Concerning the Frontier Dispute* (Burkina Faso v. Mali).[21]

(c) Reliance on voidable transactions

A specific instance of waiver, reinforced by estoppel (see *infra*), is provided for in Article 45 of the Vienna Convention on the Law of Treaties:[22]

A State may no longer invoke a ground for invalidating, terminating, withdrawing from or suspending the operation of a treaty under Articles 46 to 50[23] or Articles 60 and 62,[24] if, after becoming aware of the facts:

(a) it shall have expressly agreed that the treaty is valid or remains in force or continues in operation, as the case may be; or

(b) it must by reason of its conduct be considered as having acquiesced in the validity of the treaty or in its maintenance in force or in operation, as the case may be.

(d) Evidence of inconsistent rights

Unilateral declarations involve, in principle at least, concessions which are intentional, public, coherent, and conclusive of the issues. However, acts of acquiescence and official statements may have probative value as admissions of rights inconsistent with the claims of the declarant in a situation of competing interests, such acts individually not being conclusive of the issues. Thus in the *Eastern Greenland* case[25] the Court attached significance to the fact that Norway had become a party to several treaties which referred to Danish sovereignty over Greenland as a whole, Norway having contended that Danish sovereignty had not been extended over the whole of Greenland. The legal significance of this type of admission depends on the aspect of inconsistency between the admission and the position later taken on the disposition of legal rights in a sphere in which the claims are in conflict.

---

[19] ICJ Reports (1969), 4 at 25 (paras. 27–8).

[20] *Case Concerning Military and Paramilitary Activities in and against Nicaragua (Nicaragua v. United States)*; ICJ Reports (1986), 14 at 132 (para. 261). See also ibid. 384–5 (para. 248) (Schwebel, Diss. Op.).

[21] ICJ Reports (1986), 554 at 573–4 (paras. 39–40). See also the decision of the Court of Arbitration in the *Gulf of St. Lawrence* case (*Canada–France*), 17 July 1986; 90 *RGDIP* (1986), 713 at 756.

[22] See the Final Draft, 1966, Art. 42; *Yrbk. ILC* (1966), ii. 239, commentary.

[23] *Supra*, p. 617.

[24] *Supra*, pp. 622–4.

[25] (1933), PCIJ, Ser. A/B, no. 53, pp. 70–1. See also the *Minquiers* case, ICJ Reports (1953), 47 at 66–7, 71–2.

(e) Estoppel and status

On the basis of stability in matters of status, rather than principles of good faith and consistency, nationality[26] and diplomatic protection[27] may rest on estoppel. Official conferment of status may be upheld although in the first instance acquisition of the status rested on error of fact or law. This form of estoppel does not depend on reliance having been placed upon the representation by another state.[28]

(f) Opposable situations

Acceptance of the existence of rights inconsistent with those contended for provides evidence for the competitor when the dispute is resolved subsequently (para. (d), supra). This acceptance may be circumstantial and indirect. However, when the competitor's claim or encroachment is palpable, and a dispute is already known to exist, the other side may damage its case seriously by its recognition or acquiescence. The counterpart to the latter is the protest of a state disputing the claim or, at the least, reserving its rights. Acquiescence,[29] recognition, or implied consent may have the result of conceding lawfully held rights to a usurper, subject to the operation of rules of *jus cogens* preventing this.[30] A similar yet somewhat distinct role appears when a state is claiming rights on a basis which is plausible to some extent, and yet rests either on an ambiguous state of fact, or on a contention that the law has changed or provides an exception in its favour. Here acquiescence by the 'loser' involves an acceptance of the legal basis of the opponent's claim, and perhaps such acquiescence can be more readily proved than in the case of the state faced by an undoubted usurper.[31]

4. ESTOPPEL

There is a tendency among writers to refer to any representation or conduct having legal significance as creating an estoppel, precluding the author from denying the 'truth' of the representation, express or implied. By analogy with principles of municipal law, and by reference to decisions of international tribunals, Professor Bowett[32] has stated the essentials of estoppel to be: (1) a statement of fact which is clear and

[26] *Supra*, pp. 399–400.

[27] On the relation of this and nationality, *supra*, pp. 402–3. See further *British Digest*, v. 89, 369–70, 374, 379–80, 461, 467–73.

[28] Cf. the definition of Bowett, *infra*.

[29] On acquiescence and protest generally see MacGibbon, 30 *BY* (1953), 293–319; 31 *BY* (1954), 143–86. On prescription and acquiescence in regard to acquisition of territory *supra*, pp. 150ff. See also Bowett, 33 *BY* (1957), 197–201; Cahier, in *Recueil d'études en hommage à Paul Guggenheim* (1968), 237–65; Barale, *Ann. français* (1965), 389–427; Bentz, 67 *RGDIP* (1963), 44–91.

[30] On *jus cogens*, *supra*, pp. 510–12.

[31] See the *Fisheries* case, ICJ Reports (1951), at 138–9, and *supra*, pp. 176ff., in relation to the Norwegian system of straight baselines for delimiting the territorial sea.

[32] *BY* (1957), 176 at 202. This author takes some pains to isolate estoppel from other things. See further Dominicé, in *Recueil d'études en hommage à Paul Guggenheim*, pp. 327–65 at pp. 364–5; Martin, *L'Estoppel*

unambiguous; (2) this statement must be voluntary, unconditional, and authorized; and (3) there must be reliance in good faith upon the statement either to the detriment of the party so relying on the statement or to the advantage of the party making the statement. A considerable weight of authority[33] supports the view that estoppel is a general principle of international law, resting on principles of good faith and consistency. It is now reasonably clear that the essence of estoppel is the element of conduct which causes the other party, in reliance on such conduct, detrimentally to change its position or to suffer some prejudice.[34] Without dissenting from this as a general and preliminary proposition, it is necessary to point out that estoppel in municipal law is regarded with great caution, and that the 'principle' has no particular coherence in international law, its incidence and effects not being uniform.[35] Thus before a tribunal the principle may operate to resolve ambiguities and as a principle of equity and justice:[36] here it becomes a part of the evidence and judicial reasoning. Elsewhere, its content is taken up by the principles noted in the last section, which are interrelated and yet are specialized to some degree.[37]

Examples of judicial application of the broader version of the principle are the *Arbitral Award by the King of Spain*[38] and the *Temple* case.[39] In the former case Nicaragua challenged the validity of the award on several grounds: the Court held the award valid and stated that it was no longer open to Nicaragua, who, by express declaration and by conduct, had recognized the award as valid, to challenge its validity. In the *Temple* case Thailand sought to avoid a frontier agreement on the ground of error. In this case also the Court held that Thailand was precluded by her conduct from asserting that she did not accept the treaty. These cases support a particular type of estoppel (see section 3, para. (*c*), *supra*), but the rule concerned could operate independently of any general doctrine of estoppel. In the Jurisdiction Phase of the *Nicaragua* case the International Court held that the 'constant acquiescence' of Nicaragua in the various public statements (for example, in the *Yearbook* of the Court)

en droit international public (1979); Thirlway, 60 *BY* (1989), 29–49; Bernhardt (ed.), *Encyclopedia*, II (1995), 116–19.

[33] See Judges Alfaro and Fitzmaurice in the *Temple* case, ICJ Reports (1962), 39–51, 61–5; Bowett, 33 *BY* (1957), at 202; MacGibbon, 7 *ICLQ* (1958), 468–513; Lauterpacht, *The Development of International Law by the International Court* (1958), 168–72; Report of the International Law Commission on the Law of Treaties, *Yrbk. ILC* (1963), ii. 212–13; Waldock, ibid. 39–40; Report of ILC, *Yrbk. ILC* (1966), ii. 239.

[34] See the *North Sea Cases*, ICJ Reports (1969), 26, para. 30; *Gulf of Maine* case, ibid. (1984), 309, para. 145. See also *Application to Intervene by Nicaragua*, ibid. (1990), p. 118, para. 63.

[35] See the Diss. Op. of Judge Spender, *Temple* case, ICJ Reports (1962), 143.

[36] Cf. Cheng, *General Principles of Law* (1953), 141–58; Schwarzenberger, 87 Hague *Recueil* (1955, I), 312ff.; Lauterpacht, *Development*, pp. 168–72; Bowett, 33 *BY* (1957), 195.

[37] See the comments of Venturini, 112 Hague *Recueil* (1964, II), 370–4. Bowett uses the principle of reliance to isolate 'simple' or 'true' estoppel from the other principles. However, in some contexts, such as renunciation, reliance is not active in determining legal consequences. Nor does his distinction as to statements of fact have much viability. See further Vallée, 77 *RGDIP* (1973), 949–99.

[38] ICJ Reports (1960), 192 at 213. See Johnson, 10 *ICLQ* (1961), 328–37.

[39] ICJ Reports (1962), 6 at 32. See Johnson, 11 *ICLQ* (1962), 1183–204; and, on the relation of estoppel and acquisition of territory, *supra*, p. 153. See further the *Argentine–Chile Frontier* case, Award of 1966, ILR 38, 10 at 76–9.

to the effect that Nicaragua was bound by its 1929 Declaration 'constitute a valid mode of manifestation of its intent to recognize the compulsory jurisdiction of the Court under Article 36, paragraph 2, of the statute...'.[40] In the *Case Concerning Territorial and Maritime Dispute between Nicaragua and Honduras in the Caribbean Sea*, the Court insisted that 'The evidence of a tacit legal agreement must be compelling'.[41]

5. AGENCY AND REPRESENTATION

(a) States and organizations as agents

States and organizations of states act as agents for various purposes, including the making of treaties.[42]

(b) State organs

The state organs include the head of state, head of government, heads of executive departments, and diplomatic representatives.[43] However, the legal boundaries of the state are not to be defined in simple terms, a view supported by the experience of municipal law. Specific authority may be given to individuals constituting delegations to conferences or special missions to foreign governments.[44] The existence of authority in a particular instance may be a matter regulated in part by international law. Thus, in treaty-making and in the making of unilateral declarations a Foreign Minister is presumed to have authority to bind the state he represents.[45] Moreover, the quality of 'the state' varies on a functional basis: thus 'sovereign immunity' from other state jurisdictions extends to the agents of the state, including its armed forces and warships, and state property in general.[46]

---

[40] ICJ Reports (1984), 392 at 411–13 (paras. 43–7); and see also pp. 413–15 (paras. 48–51) on issues of estoppel. See further Ruda (Sep. Op.), pp. 458–60; Mosler (Sep. Op.), pp. 463–5; Oda (Sep. Op.), pp. 483–9; Ago (Sep. Op.), pp. 527–31; Schwebel (Diss. Op.), pp. 595–600.

[41] Judgment dated 8 October 2007, para. 253.

[42] See ch. 30, s. 2.

[43] See *British Digest*, vii; Sørensen, 101 Hague *Recueil* (1960, III), 58–68; *Yrbk. ILC* (1962), ii. 164–6.

[44] On *ad hoc* diplomacy see ch. 17.

[45] Cf. *Eastern Greenland* case (1933), PCIJ, Ser. A/B, no. 53, p. 71; McNair, *Law of Treaties*, pp. 73–5; and Vienna Conv. on the Law of Treaties, 1969, Art. 7(2)(a). See also *Case Concerning the Land and Maritime Boundary Between Cameroon and Nigeria*, Judgment of 10 October 2002, paras. 265–6.

[46] Or, at least, property used for public purposes. On sovereign immunity see ch. 16. On the immunity of armed forces see ch. 18, s. 1(*e*).

PART XI

TRANSMISSION OF RIGHTS AND DUTIES

29

STATE SUCCESSION[1]

1. STATE SUCCESSION AS A CATEGORY

State succession arises when there is a definitive replacement of one state by another in respect of sovereignty over a given territory in conformity with international law. The political events concerned include total dismemberment of an existing state, secession, decolonization of a part of a state, merger of existing states, and partial cession or annexation of state territory. In general the process involved is that of a permanent displacement of sovereign power and thus temporary changes resulting from belligerent occupation or grants of exclusive possession of territory by treaty are excluded. Distinct also is the case where one state acts as the delegate or agent of another for legal purposes.

When the sovereignty of one state replaces that of another state then a number of legal problems arise. Is the successor state bound by all or any of the treaties of the predecessor? Do the inhabitants of the territory concerned automatically become nationals of the successor? Is the successor state affected by international claims involving the predecessor, by the predecessor's national debt and its other obligations under the system of municipal law now supplanted? It is of great importance to note that the phrase 'state succession' is employed to *describe* an area, or a source of problems: the term does not connote any principle or presumption that a transmission or succession

---

[1] The principal items of literature are as follows: O'Connell, *State Succession in Municipal Law and International Law*, 2 vols. (1967); id., 130 Hague *Recueil* (1970, II), 95–206; Zemanek, 116 Hague *Recueil* (1965, III), 187–300; Castrén, 78 Hague *Recueil* (1951, I), 379–506; Whiteman, ii, ch. 4; Schwarzenberger, *International Law* (3rd edn., 1957), 164–79; Jennings, 121 Hague *Recueil* (1967, II), 437–51; *Yrbk. ILC* (1962), ii. 101, 131; (1963), ii. 95, 260; (1968), ii. 1, 87, 94, 213; (1969), ii. 23, 45, 69; (1970), ii. 25, 61, 102, 136, 170; (1971), ii (Pt. 1), 143, 157; (1971), ii (Pt. 2), 111; (1972), ii. 1, 60, 61, 223; (1973), ii. 3, 198; (1974), ii (Pt. 1), 1, 89, 91, 162; (1975), ii. 106; (1976), ii (Pt. 1), 55; (1976), ii (Pt. 2), 122; (1977), ii (Pt. 1), 45; (1977), ii (Pt. 2), 51; (1978), ii (Pt. 1), 229, 244; (1978), ii (Pt. 2), 106; (1979), ii (Pt. 1), 67; (1979), ii (Pt. 2), 10; (1980), ii (Pt. 1), 1; (1980), ii (Pt. 2), 7; (1981), ii (Pt. 1), 3; (1981), ii (Pt. 2), 9–113; Rousseau, iii. 329–511; Verzijl., *International Law in Historical Perspective*, vii (1974); Bardonnet, *La Succession d'états à Madagascar* (1970); *Répertoire suisse*, iii. 1297–1403; Bedjaoui, 130 Hague *Recueil* (1970, II), 455–586; Crawford, 51 BY (1980), 2–47; Makonnen, *International Law and the New States of Africa* (1983); id., 200 Hague *Recueil* (1986, V), 93–234; Daillier, and Pellet, 538–56; Oppenheim, i. 208–44; Torres Bernardez, in Bedjaoui (ed.), *International Law: Achievements and Prospects* (1991), 381–404; Hafner and Kornfeind, 1 *Austrian Review of Int. and Comp. Law* (1996), 1–49; Craven, *Europ. Journ.*, vol. 9 (1998), 142–62; Bernhardt (ed.) *Encyclopedia*, IV (2000), 641–56.

of legal rights and duties occurs. The phrase 'state succession' is well established in spite of its misleading suggestion of the municipal law analogy of continuity of legal personality in an individuals general property, passing as an inheritance, this involving a complete or 'universal succession'.

State succession is an area of great uncertainty and controversy. This is due partly to the fact that much of the state practice is equivocal and could be explained on the basis of special agreement and various rules distinct from the category of state succession. Indeed, it is perfectly possible to take the view that not many settled legal rules have emerged as yet.[2]

2. THE PRE-EMPTION OF PROBLEMS BY TREATY, ACQUIESCENCE, AND ESTOPPEL

A number of major issues have been dealt with in the past by multilateral peace treaties which actually constituted new states and regulated succession problems as a part of the territorial rearrangement. Thus the Treaty of St Germain of 1919 provided for the responsibility of the successor states of the Austro-Hungarian Monarchy for the public debts of the predecessor.[3] Provisions of the Italian Peace Treaty of 1947, and the United Nations Resolution on 'Economic and Financial Provisions Relating to Libya', determined various questions concerning the relations of Italy and its former colony of Libya.[4] On other occasions the conduct of states may produce informal novation by means of unilateral declarations and forms of acquiescence or estoppel. In 1958 when the United Arab Republic was created by the Union of Egypt with Syria, the Minister of Foreign Affairs of the Union made a statement, as follows, in a Note to the Secretary-General of the United Nations: '... all international treaties and agreements concluded by Egypt or Syria with other countries will remain valid within the regional limits prescribed on their conclusion and in accordance with the principles of international law'. Such a declaration of itself could not bind third states parties to treaties with the former states of Egypt and Syria. However, third states appear to have acquiesced in the position adopted by the United Arab Republic and the United States expressly took cognizance of the assurance given.[5] New states may become parties to

---

[2] Cf. *Yangtze (London) Ltd.* v. *Barlas Bros. (Karachi) Ltd.*, ILR 34, 27 at 32–3, SC of Pakistan; *Pales Ltd.* v. *Ministry of Transport*, ILR 22 (1955), 113 at 122, SC of Israel (as Ct. of Civil Appeals); Guggenheim, i. 461.

[3] Art. 203 of the Treaty. See also Tripartite Claims Comm., Admin. Decision no. 1, *RIAA* vi. 203; and the *Ottoman Debt Arbitration* (1925), *RIAA* i. 529.

[4] UN Tribunal in Libya, decisions of 18 Feb. 1952 and 31 Jan. 1953, *RIAA* xii. 356; ILR 24 (1957), 103 and (1958, I), 2.

[5] Whiteman, ii. 959–62, 1014. See also Waldock, *Yrbk. ILC* (1971), ii (Pt. 1), 145–53; *Yrbk. ILC* (1972), ii. 272–7; ibid. (1974), ii (Pt. 1), 236–41. See also *D.C.* v. *Public Prosecutor*, ILR 73, 38 (Netherlands Supr. Ct.); *R.* v. *Director of Public Prosecutions, ex parte Schwartz*, ibid. 44 (Jamaica, Full Ct. of the Supr. Ct.); *M.* v. *Federal Department of Justice and Police*, ILR 75, 107 (Switzerland, Fed. Trib.).

treaties by notices of succession the validity of which is accepted by other states, by international organizations and, if necessary, by the International Court.[6]

On a considerable number of occasions the inheritance or devolution of treaty rights and obligations has been the subject of agreements between the predecessor and successor states.[7] The United Kingdom made such agreements with Burma, Ceylon, the Federation of Malaya, Ghana, Cyprus, the Federation of Nigeria, Sierra Leone, Jamaica, Trinidad and Tobago, The Gambia, and Malta. Such agreements promote certainty and stability of relations. They also create certain problems. First, the agreement may appear to be a part of the bargain exacted by the outgoing colonial power at independence and the new state may seek legal means of disputing its validity and application.[8] Secondly, third states cannot be legally bound by inheritance agreements unless by express declaration or conduct they agree to be bound.[9]

3. TERRITORIAL SOVEREIGNTY AND DOMESTIC JURISDICTION

After a change of sovereignty various issues may be raised in the context of municipal law, viz., the destiny of the property of the ceding or former state, the continuity of the legal system, the status of private property rights, including rights deriving from contracts and concessions concluded under the former law, and nationality problems. Hyde[10] and other writers have maintained that the municipal law of the predecessor remains in force until the new sovereign takes steps to change it. O'Connell[11] and other authorities[12] support a principle of vested or acquired rights. This principle is to the effect that a change of sovereignty has no effect on the acquired rights of foreign nationals. The principle has received support from tribunals[13] but it is a source of confusion since it is question-begging and is used as the basis for a variety of propositions. For some, it means simply that private rights are not affected by the change of sovereignty as such. For others it appears to mean that the successor state faces restrictions on its powers in relation to private rights of aliens additional to the ordinary rules of international law governing treatment of aliens apart from a case of succession.

---

[6] Cp. *Application of the Convention on the Prevention and Punishment of Genocide* (Bosnia and Herzegovina v. Yugoslavia), ICJ Reports, 1996, 595, 612, paras. 17–23.

[7] See generally E. Lauterpacht, 7 *ICLQ* (1958), 524–30; O'Connell, *State Succession*, ii. 352–73.

[8] See on unequal treaties, *supra*, p. 591; and *infra*, p. 488, on issues concerning *jus cogens*.

[9] See the UK–Venezuela Agreement, 1966, Art.VIII, *British Practice* (1966), 72; Waldock, Second Report, *Yrbk. ILC* (1969), ii. 54–62; *Yrbk. ILC* (1972), ii. 236–41; ibid. (1974), ii (Pt. 1), 183–7.

[10] Hyde, i. 397ff.

[11] *International Law* (2nd edn., 1970), i. 377–81, 388–9; *State Succession* (2nd edn.), chs. 6 and 10; 130 Hague *Recueil* (1970, II), 134–46.

[12] Oppenheim, i. (8th edn., 1955), 160 n. 3. See also Waldock, *Yrbk. ILC* (1969), i. 74–5; Tsuruoka, ibid. 87–8. Zemanek, 116 Hague *Recueil* (1965, III), 279, points out that only when one assumes that the chain of continuity is broken does it become necessary to have recourse to a special rule on vested rights.

[13] *Lighthouses* case, *RIAA* xii. 155 at 236; *Forests of Central Rhodopia* case, *RIAA* ii. 1389 at 1431–6.

Moreover, writers often fail to relate the concept of acquired rights to the other principles affecting a change of sovereignty. The new sovereign receives the same sort of sovereignty as the transferor has had, and this involves normal powers of legislation and jurisdiction deriving from sovereign equality and the reserved domain of domestic jurisdiction. Survival of the old law depends on the consent of the new sovereign.[14] Indeed some proponents of acquired rights formulate the principle in a qualified form. Thus O'Connell[15] states that 'the principle of respect for acquired rights in international law is no more than a principle that change of sovereignty should not touch the interests of individuals more than is necessary', and goes on to say that the successor state which alters or cancels acquired rights must comply with the minimum standards of international law. In the case of decolonization, the continuation of the pre-independence economic structure, which commonly involves extensive foreign ownership of major resources, would produce a situation in which political independence and formal sovereignty were not matched by a normal competence to regulate the national economy. The declaration of the United Nations General Assembly on 'Permanent Sovereignty over Natural Resources'[16] contains a proviso thus:

Considering that nothing in paragraph 4 below in any way prejudices the position of any Member State on any aspect of the question of the rights and obligations of successor States and Governments in respect of property acquired before the accession to complete sover-eignty of countries formerly under colonial rule.

(a) State property[17]

It is generally conceded that succession to the public property of the annexed or ceding state is a principle of customary international law and the jurisprudence of the Permanent Court of International Justice supports this position.[18] Another approach would be to say that the 'principle' is really a presumption that acquisition of state

---

[14] Briggs, p. 237; Guggenheim, i (1953), 136; Kaeckenbeeck, 17 *BY* (1936), 1 at 13ff.; Rosenne, 27 *BY* (1950), 267 esp. at 273, 281–2; Zemanek, 116 Hague *Recueil* (1965, III), 281; Bedjaoui, *Yrbk. ILC* (1968), ii. 115; and ibid. (1969), ii. 69. See the debate: *Yrbk. ILC* (1969), i. 53ff., and Bedjaoui, 130 Hague *Recueil* (1970, II), 531–61. Various writers have pointed out that the often-quoted passage in the case of *German Settlers in Poland* (1923) (PCIJ Ser. B, no. 6, p. 36), that, in the instance of German territory transferred to Poland after the First World War, German law had continued to operate in the territory in question, is a factual statement that German law was continued in force after the cession. See further *L. and JJ.* v. *Polish State Railways*, ILR 24 (1957), 77, Polish Supr. Ct.

[15] *State Succession* at p. 266. O'Connell (at p. 107) points out that the principle of continuity of law is only a presumption. See also 130 Hague *Recueil* (1970, II), 141.

[16] *Supra*, p. 539.

[17] See *Yrbk. ILC* (1970), ii. 131; ibid. (1971), ii (Pt. 1), 157; ibid. (1973), ii. 3; ibid. (1974), ii (Pt. 1), 91; ibid. (1975), ii. 110; ibid. (1976), ii (Pt. 1), 55; ibid. (1976), ii (Pt. 2), 122; ibid. (1981), ii (Pt. 2), 24–47; *Union of Burma* v. *Kotaro Toda*, ILR 53, 149; Resol., Institut de Droit International, Vancouver, 2001; *Annuaire de l'Inst.*, vol. 69 (2000–2001), 713.

[18] *Peter Pázmány University* case (1933), PCIJ, Ser. A/B, no. 61 at p. 237. See also *Haile Selassie* v. *Cable and Wireless, Ltd.* (no. 2), [1939] Ch. 182, 195. On the definition of state property see Schwarzenberger, *International Law*, i. (3rd edn.), 167–9; UN Tribunal for Libya, *supra*; and Guggenheim, i. (1953), 468–9. See also Bedjaoui, *Yrbk. ILC* (1968), ii. 106–8, and ibid. (1970), ii. 131, 144–51.

property is inherent in the grant of territorial sovereignty and is a normal consequence of the acquisition of sovereignty in situations apart from a grant or cession. The position is in general confirmed by the provisions of the Vienna Convention on Succession of States in respect of State Property, Archives and Debts, adopted in 1983,[19] although the Convention propounds a rather different legal regime for the case where the successor is a 'newly independent state'.

(b) Public law claims and public debts[20]

It follows from what has already been said that the successor state has a right to take up fiscal claims belonging to the former state, including the right to collect taxes due.

Much more a matter of controversy is the fate of the public debts of the replaced state. It may be that there is no rule of succession established,[21] but some writers[22] have concluded that in cases of annexation or dismemberment, as opposed to cession, where the ceding state remains in existence, the successor is obliged to assume the public debts of the extinct state. Zemanek[23] confines succession to the situation where before independence an autonomous political dependency has through the agency of the metro-politan power contracted a 'localized debt' which is automatically attributed to the new state after separation. In practice municipal courts will enforce obligations of the predecessor state against the successor only when the latter has recognized them.[24] The Vienna Convention on Succession of States in respect of State Property, Archives and Debts, adopted in 1983 (see above) provides for the passing of the state debt to the successor state (as a general principle) with a reduction according to an equitable proportion in the cases of transfer of part of a state, secession, or dissolution of a state (Arts. 36–37, 39–41). However, when the successor state is a 'newly independent State', no state debt shall pass, except by agreement (and then only if certain other conditions are satisfied) (Art. 38). According to Article 2(1)(e) a 'newly independent State'

---

[19] Text: 22 *ILM* (1983), 298, 306. The Conv. has not been universally acceptable, and was adopted by 54 votes in favour, 11 against, with 11 abstentions. For comment, see Streinz, 26 *German Yrbk.* (1983), 198–237; Monnier, *Ann. Français* (1984), 221–9. See further Arbitration Commission, Conference on Yugoslavia, *Opinion No. 1*, ILR 92, 162; id., *Opinion No. 9*, ibid., 203.

[20] In addition to the literature referred to *supra*, p. 649, see ILA, *Report of the Fifty-Third Conference* (1968), 598 at 598, 603; Lauterpacht, *International Law: Collected Papers*, iii (1977), 121–37; Bedjaoui, *Yrbk. ILC* (1971), ii (Pt. 1), 185; ibid. (1977), ii (Pt. 1), 45; ibid. (1977), ii (Pt. 2), 59; ibid. (1978), ii (Pt. 1), 229; ibid. (1978), ii (Pt. 2), 113; ibid. (1979), ii (Pt. 2), 40; ibid. (1981), ii (Pt. 2), 72–113. As to state archives see ibid. (1979), ii (Pt. 1), 67; ibid. (1979), ii (Pt. 2), 77; ibid. (1980), ii (Pt. 1), 1; ibid. (1980), ii (Pt. 2), 11; ibid. (1981), ii (Pt. 2), 47–71.

[21] See the *Ottoman Debt Arbitration* (1925) *RIAA* i. 531 at 573; Brierly, p. 159; Rousseau, iii. 426–70; Hackworth, i. 539; Castrén, 68 Hague *Recueil* (1951, I), 458–84 at 465; Guggenheim, i. (1953), 469; *Franco-Ethiopian Railway Company Claim*, ILR 24 (1957), 602 at 629.

[22] Feilchenfeld, *Public Debts and State Succession* (1931); Sack, 80 *U. of Penn. LR* (1931), 608; Briggs, p. 234; Oppenheim, i. 214–15; Sørensen, p. 293. See further O'Connell, *State Succession*, i. 369ff.; and the *Lighthouses Arbitration*, ILR 23 (1956), at 659.

[23] 116 Hague *Recueil* (1965, III), 255–70. See also Guggenheim, i. (1953), 472; Bedjaoui, *Yrbk. ILC* (1968), ii. 109–10; and *Pittacos v. État Belge*, ILR 45, 24 at 31–2.

[24] See e.g. *West Rand Central Gold Mining Company* v. *The King* [1905] 2 KB 391; *Shimshon Palestine Portland Cement Company Ltd.* v. *A.-G.*, ILR 17 (1950), 72, Israel SC (sitting as Ct. of Civil Appeals); *Dalmia Dadri Cement Company Ltd* v. *Commissioner of Income Tax*, ILR 26 (1958, II), 79, India, SC.

means a successor state the territory of which had been 'a dependent territory for the international relations of which the predecessor State was responsible'. This distinction between 'newly independent States' and other successor states is problematical.

(c) State contracts and concessions

As in the case of all rights acquired under the municipal law of the predecessor state, rights deriving from state contracts and concessions are susceptible to change by the new sovereign. Limitations on such interference derive only from any relevant international standards concerning aliens or human rights in general.[25] However, a number of writers[26] state the principle that the acquired rights of a concessionaire must be respected by a successor state.[27] There is a certain anomaly in the selection of concessions as beneficiaries of the principle, which could be related to other matters, including contracts of employment and pension rights. It will be appreciated that judicial pronouncements to the effect that the mere change of sovereignty does not cancel concession rights[28] do not give support to the acquired rights doctrine in the form that *after* the change of sovereignty the new sovereign must maintain the property rights of aliens acquired before the change of sovereignty.

In the *Lighthouses Arbitration*[29] between France and Greece before the Permanent Court of Arbitration certain claims were concerned with an alleged Greek responsibility for breaches of concessions occurring prior to extension of Greek sovereignty over the autonomous state of Crete. These claims raise issues of succession in the context of state responsibility which are examined below. However, the Tribunal also approached the matter on the basis of recognition and adoption by Greece of the violation of the concession contract occurring before and even after the change of sovereignty over the island in question. The Tribunal said:[30]

... the Tribunal can only come to the conclusion that Greece, having adopted the illegal conduct of Crete in its recent past as autonomous State, is bound, as successor State, to take upon its charge the financial consequences of the breach of the concession contract. Otherwise, the avowed violation of a contract committed by one of the two States ... with the assent of the other, would, in the event of their merger, have the thoroughly unjust consequence of cancelling a definite financial responsibility and of sacrificing the undoubted rights of a private firm holding a concession to a so-called principle of non-transmission of debts in cases of territorial succession, which in reality does not exist as a general and absolute principle.

---

[25] See chs. 24 and 25; Castrén, *Yrbk. ILC* (1969), i. 63, para. 45; Ruda, ibid. 82, para. 39; Ago, ibid. 88, para. 22; Guggenheim, i (1953), 474; Schwarzenberger, *International Law*, p. 173, commenting on the case of *Certain German Interests in Polish Upper Silesia* (1926), PCIJ Ser. A, no. 7, pp. 21, 22; ILA, *Report of the Fifty-Fifth Conference* (1972), 654 at 660.

[26] e.g.: Rousseau, iii. 393–425; O'Connell, *State Succession*, i. 304ff. esp. at 345 (but see also p. 266 and *supra*, p. 649); Guggenheim, i (1953), 476–7.

[27] See *supra*, pp. 651–2, on the principle. See also Bedjaoui, *Yrbk. ILC* (1968), ii. 115–17; *Répertoire suisse*, iii. 1394–403.

[28] *Sopron-Köszeg Railway* case (1929), *RIAA* ii. 961, 967.

[29] ILR 23 (1956), 79; *RIAA* xii. 155. Of some interest, though depending on treaty provisions, is the *Mavrommatis Jerusalem Concessions* case (1925), PCIJ, Ser. A, no. 5, pp. 21, 27.

[30] ILR 23 (1956), at 92; *RIAA* xii, at p. 198.

In this case the Greek Government with good reason commenced by recognising its own responsibility.

The short point remains that territorial change of *itself* neither cancels nor confers a special status on private rights. Where the private rights involve a substantial foreign control of the economy, then some modern exponents of the principle of vested or acquired rights are moved to formulate certain large qualifications concerning 'odious concessions' or 'concessions contrary to the public policy of the successor state',[31] for example, a major concession granted on the eve of independence and involving vital resources. Qualified to this degree, the principle would seem to lose its viability.

4. THE INTERACTION OF RULES OF LAW

A common fault of writers is to classify issues primarily as 'succession' and consequently to consider particular issues in isolation from the matrix of rules governing the subject-matter, which might involve, for example, the law of treaties or nationality. It has been pointed out earlier in this chapter that principles of acquiescence and estoppel are often dominant, and in the previous section the issues of succession to state property and private law rights were related to general principles of international law governing transfers of sovereignty. The need to consider problems precipitated by a change of sovereignty in relation to the particular body of legal principles is illustrated very well by the law relating to nationality and the law of treaties.

5. PARTICULAR LEGAL ISSUES

(a) Nationality[32]

The problem involved is that of the nationality of inhabitants of territory which is the subject of a change of sovereignty. If assumptions as to matters of principle may be made at the outset, the writer's opinion is that no help is to be derived from the categories of the law of state succession.[33]

---

[31] Zemanek, 116 Hague *Recueil* (1965, III), at 282–9 (and note p. 288). See also Sørensen, p. 292; and 44 *Annuaire de l'Inst.* (1952), ii. 472.

[32] See the International Law Commission, *Report on the Work of its Fifty-first session (3 May–23 July 1999)*, G.A. Off. Recs., Fifty-fourth Session, Suppl. No. 10 (A/54/10), 12–90. See also Memorandum by the Secretariat, *Nationality in relation to the succession of states*, UN Doc. A/CN.4/497, 8 March 1999. The Draft Articles adopted by the Commission were brought to the attention of Governments by G.A. resol. 55/153, dated 30 Jan. 2001.

[33] Cf. Weis, *Nationality and Statelessness in International Law* (2nd edn., 1979), 136, 144. At pp. 144–5 he observes: 'Most of the principles referred to in connection with universal succession apply, *mutatis mutandis*, to the effects of partial succession on nationality. This is, however, subject to two qualifications: (a) questions of nationality will, in cases of partial succession, more frequently be regulated by treaty; and (b) since the predecessor State continues to exist, two nationalities, the nationality of the predecessor and that of the successor State are involved. There thus arises not only the question of acquisition of the new nationality, but also that of the loss of the old nationality'. These qualifications hardly raise serious issues of principle.

In the submission of the present writer, the evidence is overwhelmingly in support of the view that the population follows the change of sovereignty in matters of nationality. At the end of the First World War the Versailles and associated treaties contained a number of provisions, more or less uniform in content, relating to changes of sovereignty which exhibited all the variations of state succession.[34] Thus the Minorities Treaty signed at Versailles provided as follows:

Article 4 (cp. Art. 3). Poland admits and declares to be Polish nationals *ipso facto* and without the requirements of any formality persons of German, Austrian, Hungarian or Russian nationality who were born in the said territory of parents habitually resident there, even if at the date of the coming into force of the present Treaty they are not themselves habitually resident there.

Nevertheless, within two years after coming into force of the present Treaty, these persons may make a declaration before the competent Polish authorities in the country in which they are resident stating that they abandon Polish nationality, and they will then cease to be considered as Polish nationals. In this connexion a declaration by a husband will cover his wife and a declaration by parents will cover their children under 18 years of age.

Article 6. All persons born in Polish territory who are not born nationals of another State shall *ipso facto* become Polish nationals.

The Treaties of St Germain, Trianon, and Paris[35] have similar provisions, except that the Treaties of St Germain and Trianon refer to persons born of parents 'habitually resident or possessing rights of citizenship [*pertinenza—heimatrecht*] as the case may be there'. It is thought that the precedent value of such provisions is considerable in view of their uniformity and the international character of the deliberations preceding the signature of these treaties. The objection that they give a right of option does not go very far, since the option is a later and additional procedure. Only if and when the option is made does the nationality of the successor state terminate: there is no statelessness before then. The Treaty of Peace with Italy of 1947 provided in Article 19 that Italian citizens domiciled, in the sense of habitual residence, in territory transferred shall become citizens of the transferee; and a right of option is given.

State practice evidenced by the provisions of internal law is to the same effect. The law of the United Kingdom has been expressed as follows by Lord McNair:[36]

The normal effect of the annexation of territory by the British Crown, whatever may be the source or cause of the annexation, for instance, a treaty of cession, or subjugation by war, is that the nationals of the State whose territory is annexed, if resident thereon, become British subjects; in practice, however, it is becoming increasingly common to give such nationals an option, either by the treaty of cession or by an Act of Parliament, to leave the territory and retain their nationality.

---

[34] See *Laws Concerning Nationality* (1954), 586ff. See also the Treaty of Neuilly-sur-Seine, Arts. 51 and 52, ibid. 587; and the Treaty of Lausanne, Arts. 30–6, ibid.

[35] Art. 4. The Treaty of Paris concerned Romania. See also *Markt* v. *Prefect of Trent, Ann. Digest*, 10 (1941–2), no. 76. See also Caggiano, 2 *Ital. Yrbk.* (1976), 248 at 264–71.

[36] *Opinions*, ii. 24. See also Parry, *Nationality and Citizenship Laws of the Commonwealth* (1957), 274–5. Cf. the British Nationality Act 1948, 11 (repealed by the British Nationality Act 1981).

The practice of the United States is to confer nationality on nationals of the predecessor state resident in the territory,[37] although on occasion persons who were 'citizens' of the territory annexed acquired citizenship.[38] In view of the state practice it is hardly surprising to find works of authority stating that persons attached to territory change their nationality when sovereignty changes hands.[39] Somewhat surprising is the caution of Dr Weis in his conclusion on these issues. In his view:[40]

To sum up, it may be said that there is no rule of international law under which the nationals of the predecessor State acquire the nationality of the successor State. International law cannot have such a direct effect, and the practice of States does not bear out the contention that this is inevitably the result of the change of sovereignty. As a rule, however, States have conferred their nationality on the former nationals of the predecessor State, and in this regard one may say that there is, in the absence of statutory provisions of municipal law, a *presumption* of international law that municipal law has this effect.

Variations of practice, and areas of doubt, certainly exist, but by their nature they are hardly inimical to the general rule. Some difficulties merely concern modalities of the general rule itself.[41] Thus the position of nationals of the predecessor state who at the time of the transfer are resident outside the territory the sovereignty of which changes is unsettled. The rule probably is that, unless they have or acquire a domicile in the transferred territory, they do not acquire the nationality of the successor state.[42] This, it seems, is the British doctrine.[43]

The general principle is that of a substantial connection with the territory concerned by citizenship or residence or family relation to a qualified person. This principle is

---

[37] Moore, *Digest*, iii. 311ff.; Hackworth, iii. 116ff.

[38] Annexations of Hawaii and Texas: see Hackworth, iii. 119; and Moore, *Digest*, 314.

[39] See Oppenheim, i. (8th edn., 1955) 551, 571, 656–7; Rousseau, iii. 343; Hyde, ii. 1090; Briggs, p. 503. See further the opinion of the US Attorney-General quoted by Briggs, p. 503, and the Harvard draft, Art. 18, 23 *AJ* (1929), Spec. Suppl., p. 61. The ninth edition of Oppenheim denies any automatic change: Oppenheim, i. 218–19.

[40] *Nationality*, pp. 143–4. Under the rubric 'Partial succession' he concludes (pp. 147–8), '... one may speak of a positive rule of international law on nationality to the effect that, under international law and provided the territorial transfer is based on a valid title, the predecessor State is under an obligation *vis-à-vis* the successor State to withdraw its nationality from the inhabitants of the transferred territory if they acquire the nationality of the successor State. In the absence of explicit provisions of municipal law there exists a presumption of international law that the municipal law of the predecessor State has this effect'. A formula involving a presumption as to the effect of municipal law is infelicitous. Other authors are of similarly cautious opinions: see Graupner, 32 *Grot. Soc.* (1946), 87 at 92; Mervyn Jones, *British Nationality Law* (1956), 20–6; Parry, 28 *BY* (1951), 426–7. See also Whiteman, viii. 104–12.

[41] By analogy, the validity of the baseline principle in the law of the territorial sea was not thought to be affected by the absence (at least before 1958) of clear evidence as to its application to all permutations arising in coastal formations and relations.

[42] See Weis, *Nationality*, pp. 140–4, 149–53; O'Connell, *The Law of State Succession* (1956), 253; Mervyn Jones, *British Nationality Law*, pp. 23–4; *Slouzak Minority in Teschen (Nationality)* case, *Ann. Digest*, 11 (1919–41), no. 93; *Ministry of Home Affairs* v. *Kemali*, ILR 40, 191; *North Transylvania Nationality* case, ibid. 43, 191. Cf. *In re Andries*, ILR 17 (1950), no. 26 (dual nationality arising).

[43] McNair, *Opinions*, ii. 21–6; Weis, *Nationality*, p. 140. Parry, *Nationality and Citizenship Laws*, pp. 163–4, 275, is of the opinion that the rule was uncertain. See also *Murray* v. *Parkes* [1942] 2 KB 123.

perhaps merely a special aspect of the general principle of the effective link.[44] However, it could be argued that for the individuals concerned, at the moment of transfer, the connection with the successor state is fortuitous. Whatever the merits of this, the link, in cases of territorial transfer, has special characteristics. Territory, both socially and legally, is not to be regarded as an empty plot: territory (with obvious geographical exceptions) connotes population, ethnic groupings, loyalty patterns, national aspirations, a part of humanity, or, if one is tolerant of the metaphor, an organism. To regard a population, in the normal case, as related to particular areas of territory, is not to revert to forms of feudalism but to recognize a human and political reality, which underlies modern territorial settlements. Modern thinking on human rights and the principle of self-determination has the same basis, and the latter has tended to create demands for changes in territorial sovereignty. If these assumptions are justifiable, it may be worthwhile to draw on the ideas inherent in the concepts of mandated and trust territories, and the principles of Chapter 11 of the United Nations Charter.[45] Sovereignty denotes responsibility, and a change of sovereignty does not give the new sovereign the right to dispose of the population concerned at the discretion of the government. The population goes with the territory: on the one hand, it would be illegal, and a derogation from the grant, for the transferor to try to retain the population as its own nationals, and, on the other hand, it would be illegal for the successor to take any steps which involved attempts to avoid responsibility for conditions on the territory, for example by treating the population as *de facto* stateless or by failing to maintain order in the area. The position is that the population has a 'territorial' or local status, and this is unaffected whether there is a universal or partial successor and whether there is a cession, i.e. a 'transfer' of sovereignty, or a relinquishment by one state followed by a disposition by international authority.[46] In certain cases other considerations arise. Where there is a question of the continuity of states difficulties will arise which do not depend on nationality law, and in principle the result will be as in other cases of state succession.[47] When a new status is created by international

---

[44] *Supra*, pp. 407ff. See also the Secretariat survey of 14 May 1954, *Yrbk. ILC* (1954), ii. 61, para. 39: 'The opinion is widely held that, in case of change of sovereignty over a territory by annexation, or its voluntary cession by one State to another, the annexing State is obliged to grant its nationality to the inhabitants of the territory concerned who were citizens of the ceding State, at least if they have, at the time of annexation, their permanent residence in the ceded territory. In most instances these questions are settled by treaty...' And cf. the United Nations Conv. on the Reduction of Statelessness, 1961, Art. 10.

[45] See further the *South West Africa* cases, ICJ Reports (1962), 319 at 354–7; 374, 378, 380 (Judge Bustamante, Sep. Op.), 422, 429–32 (Judge Jessup, Sep. Op.), 479–82, 541ff. (Judges Spender and Fitzmaurice, Joint Diss. Op.).

[46] It may happen that title is renounced without the territory becoming a *res nullius*. Relinquishment is thus distinct from abandonment, and is usually accompanied by recognition of title in another state, or recognition of a power of disposition to be exercised by another state or group of states. See e.g. the Treaty of St Germain, 10 Sept. 1919, Arts. 36, 43, 46, 47, 53, 54, 59, 89–91.

[47] See *Costa* v. *Military Service Commission of Genoa, Ann. Digest*, 9 (1938–40), no. 13, *United States, ex rel. Reichel* v. *Carusi*, ibid. 13 (1946), no. 49; *Re Tancredi*, ILR 17 (1950), no. 50; Austrian Supr. Ct. ILR 26 (1958, II), 40 at 42; German Fed. Rep., Supr. Admin. Ct., ibid. 21 (1954), 175; Fed. Const. Ct., ibid., 22 (1955), 30 (cf. Weis, *Nationality*, pp. 150–2); Fed. Supr. Ct., in *In re Feiner*, ibid. 23 (1956), 367, and in the *Austro-German Extradition* case, ibid. 364. In the last two cases the Court observed: 'Nor are there any binding rules

quasi-legislative acts, as in case of the creation of a mandate regime or trust territory, there may be no automatic change.[48] Lastly, though it cannot be dealt with here, the question of the legality of population transfer (apart from voluntary exercise of rights of option) arises.

(b) Diplomatic claims and the principle of continuous nationality

The operation of the nationality rule has been examined in Chapter 22. In principle the requirement of continuity of nationality between the time of injury and the presentation of the claim (or, in cases of resort to judicial settlement, the making of the award) is not satisfied if the individual concerned suffers a change of nationality as a result of a change of territorial sovereignty. At least one of the arguments used to support the continuity principle, namely that it prevents the injured citizen choosing his own protector by a shift of nationality, has no application to a change of nationality in the present connection. The rule of continuous nationality would adversely affect the whole citizen population of Tanzania after the voluntary union of Tanganyika and Zanzibar. In some cases of transfer the predecessor and successor states may act jointly in espousing claims on behalf of persons of their nationality successively, but this solution is inapplicable in case of mergers and dismemberment of states. It is surely the case that the correct solution in principle is a rule of substitution or subrogation, putting the successor in charge of claims belonging to the predecessor. This would be consonant with the conception of an effective change of sovereignty.

In the *Panevezys–Saldutiskis Railway* case[49] the Permanent Court was concerned with an Estonian claim and a Lithuanian counter-claim relating to the property of a company established under the law of the Russian Empire and operating in the territory which in 1918 constituted the new states of Estonia and Lithuania. In 1923 the company became an Estonian company with registered offices in Estonia. Estonia subsequently claimed compensation for the assets of the company remaining in Lithuania of which Lithuania had taken possession in 1919 and the Court upheld the Lithuanian preliminary objection based upon non-exhaustion of local remedies. The only Judgment[50] delivered which concerned the principle of continuity of nationality expressly in the context of state succession was the Dissenting Opinion of Jonkheer

---

of international law governing the question of acquisition and loss of nationality in the event of State succession'. However, decisions permitting Germans nationality arising from the Anschluss to subsist after the re-establishment of Austria in 1945 seem to rest on the rule that extra-territorial residence avoids the result of the change of sovereignty. Cf. *Austrian Nationality* case, ILR 20 (1953), 250; *Loss of Nationality (Germany)* case, ILR 45, 353. On 17 May 1956 the German Federal Republic enacted a law under which those who were German nationals by virtue of the Anschluss ceased to be such on 26 Apr. 1945. However, such persons were entitled to regain German nationality by declaration, with retroactive effect, to the date of loss, that they had had 'perman-ent residence' since 26 Apr. 1945 'within the territory of the German Reich as constituted on 31 December 1937 (Germany)': *Laws Concerning Nationality*, Suppl. (1959), 122.

[48] See *Westphal et Uxor v. Conducting Officer of Southern Rhodesia*, Ann. Digest, 15 (1948), no. 54; Parry, *Nationality and Citizenship Laws*, p. 668.

[49] (1939), PCIJ, Ser. A/B, no. 76; World Court Reports, iv. 341.

[50] But one may argue that the majority Judgment (p. 16) deals with the point when it holds that the principle of continuity applied. However, the issue was whether there was proof of the Estonian nationality of

van Eysinga.[51] He referred to the 'inequitable results' of a rule requiring continuity and concluded that it had not been established that the rule could not resist the normal operation of the law of state succession.

(c) Transmissibility of state responsibility

The preponderance of authority is in favour of a general rule that liability for an international delict is extinguished when the wrongdoing state ceases to exist either by annexation or voluntary cession.[52] It seems that such liability is 'personal' and there is no good reason for succession to responsibility. This reasoning clearly cannot have general application and is less cogent in relation to voluntary merger or voluntary dissolution.[53] Nor does it apply when a successor state accepts the existence of succession, thus creating an estoppel in various particular respects.[54] In the *Lighthouses Arbitration*[55] it was held in connection with one claim that Greece had by her conduct adopted an illegal act by the predecessor state and recognized her responsibility. Recently certain writers[56] have challenged the application of a rule of non-transmission of responsibility to claims in respect of wrongful deprivation of private property: apparently this position is a logical extension of the view that rights under concessions survive changes of sovereignty.

The substantial problem would appear to be the doubtful status of the local remedies rule when, for example, a taking of property has occurred under the law of the previous sovereign. If the new state refuses to accept continuity of the municipal law, then a possible but not a necessary consequence is that no 'local remedies' are available and in any case international responsibility does not pass to the successor. If continuity of the legal system is accepted, does it follow that the successor by providing 'local remedies' is estopped from contesting succession to responsibility after such remedies have been exhausted?

the company concerned *at the time of injury* in 1919, i.e. when state succession had already occurred: see the Sep. Op. of de Visscher and Rostworowski, at pp. 27–8.

[51] At pp. 32–5. See also O'Connell, *State Succession*, i. 537–41, Jennings, 121 Hague *Recueil* (1967, II), 476; and Monnier, *Ann. français* (1962), 68–72.

[52] Oppenheim, i. 218; Hurst, 5 *BY* (1924), 163; Guggenheim, i. (1953), 474; Rousseau, iii. 505–11; Briggs, p. 233; Daillier, and Pellet, *Droit international public*, p. 555; *Brown Claim* (1923), *RIAA* vi. 120; *Hawaiian Claims* (1925), *RIAA* vi. 157; Monnier, *Ann. français* (1962), 65–90; Czaplinski, 28 *Canad. Yrbk.* (1990), 339–59. But see Dumberry, *German Yrbk.*, 49 (2006), 413–47; and *Minister of Defence* v. *Mwandinghi*, ILR 91, 341, Namibia S.C.

[53] Cf. the *Lighthouses Arbitration*, above; and Brierly, pp. 160–1. However, the decision rests on the element of adoption of the wrongful act by Greece and thus is not in principle inconsistent with the other authorities. The PCA nevertheless is sceptical as to the existence of any general rule and refers to 'the vagaries of international practice and the chaotic state of authoritative writings': ILR 23 (1956), at 91–2; *RIAA* xii, at p. 198. See further Verzijl, *International Law in Historical Perspective*, vii. 219–28; *Minister of Defence, Namibia* v. *Mwandinghi*, ILR 91, 341.

[54] *Infra*, pp. 666–7.

[55] *Supra*, p. 654.

[56] See, in particular, O'Connell, *State Succession*, i. 482–6; and Jennings, 121 Hague *Recueil* (1967, II), 449–50.

(d) Claims to territory and the benefit of local customs[57]

In both the *Right of Passage* case (Merits)[58] and the *Temple* case (Merits)[59] the successor states in relation to local customs and boundary treaties, respectively, relied on
the materiality of evidence of the position before transfer of sovereignty by the United
Kingdom and France, respectively. The basis for this in both cases was recognition.
In the *Island of Palmas*[60] and *Clipperton Island*[61] cases the United States and Mexico,
respectively, were claiming as successors to Spain.

(e) The law of treaties: in general[62]

It seems to be generally accepted that in cases of 'partial succession', i.e. annexation
or cession, where the 'losing' state is not extinguished, no succession to treaties can
occur. Of course, existing treaties of the acquiring state will apply prima facie to the
territories concerned. The rest of the area of problems is approached on the basis, first,
that the law of treaties is the prime reference and thus the fact of succession must be
fitted into that context, and, secondly, that the case where a continuing identity of legal
personality is established is reserved for separate treatment.[63]

When a new state emerges it is not bound by the treaties of the predecessor sovereign by virtue of a principle of state succession. In many instances the termination of
a treaty affecting a state involved in territorial changes will be achieved by the normal
operation of provisions for denunciation or the doctrine of fundamental change of
circumstances.[64] However, as a matter of general principle a new state, *ex hypothesi* a
non-party, cannot be bound by a treaty, and in addition other parties to a treaty are not
bound to accept a new party, as it were, by operation of law.[65]

The rule of non-transmissibility (forming part of general international law) applies
both to secession of 'newly independent states' (that is, to cases of decolonization) and
to other appearances of new states by the union or dissolution of states. The distinctions drawn by the International Law Commission in this respect in its drafts and,
subsequently, in the provisions of the Vienna Convention on Succession of States in

[57] See Bedjaoui, *Yrbk. ILC* (1968), ii. 112–14. On boundary treaties, see *infra*, p. 635.

[58] ICJ Reports (1960), 6; on which see *supra*, p. 10.

[59] Ibid. (1962), 6.

[60] *Supra*, p. 136.

[61] *Supra*, p. 141.

[62] In addition to the literature referred to *supra*, p. 621, see *Yrbk. ILC* (1950), ii. 206–18; the ILA, *Report
of the Fifty-Third Conference* (1968), 596; and *Report of the Fifty-Fourth Conference* (1970); ILA, *The Effect of
Independence on Treaties* (1965); Mochi Onory, *La Succession d'états aux traités* (1968); Udokang, *Succession
of New States to International Treaties* (1972); O'Connell, in: ILA, *The Present State of International Law*
(1973), 331–8; Caggiano, *Ital. Yrbk.* (1975), 69–83; Mériboute, *La Codification de la succession d'états aux
traités* (1984).

[63] *Infra*, p. 666.

[64] *Supra*, p. 623.

[65] Oppenheim, i. 211–12; McNair, *Law of Treaties* (1961), 592, 600–1, 629, 655; Brierly, p. 153; Sørensen,
pp. 294–5, 298–9; Jennings, 121 Hague *Recueil* (1967, II), 442–6; Guggenheim, i. 463; *Yrbk. ILC* (1970), ii.
31–7; ibid. (1972), ii. 227, 250–4; ibid. (1974), ii (Pt. 1), 7–9, 168–9, 211–14. See further ILA, *Report of the
Fifty-Third Conference* (1968), pp. xiii, 589ff.; *Yrbk. ILC* (1950), ii. 214–18 (the Israeli practice), in particular
para. 23; 69 *AJ* (1975), 863–4 (US practice).

respect of Treaties,[66] adopted in 1978, are not reflected by the practice of states.[67] This is not to deny that considerations of principle and policy may call for a different outcome in the case of a union of states (see the Vienna Convention, Arts. 31, 32, and 33). However, the distinction between a secession and the dissolution of federations and unions is unacceptable, both as a proposition of law and as a matter of principle.

To the general rule of non-transmissibility (the 'clean slate' doctrine) certain important exceptions are often stated to exist. These may now be considered.

(i) *Treaties evidencing rules of general international law.* Certain multilateral conventions contain rules which are generally accepted as declaratory of general international law, as, for example, the Convention on the High Seas and parts of the Convention on the Continental Shelf.[68] A successor state is bound by such rules in the same way as other states.

(ii) *'Objective regimes' and localized treaties in general.* A number of writers, including O'Connell[69] and McNair,[70] have taken the view that there is a category of dispositive or localized treaties concerning the incidents of enjoyment of a particular piece of territory in the matter of demilitarized zones, rights of transit, navigation, port facilities, and fishing rights. This category of treaties in their view is transmissible. The subject-matter overlaps considerably with the topic of international servitudes considered elsewhere.[71] The present writer, in company with others,[72] considers that there is insufficient evidence in either principle or practice for the existence of this exception to the general rule. First, much of the practice is equivocal and may rest on acquiescence. Secondly, the category is very difficult to define[73] and it is not clear why the treaties apparently included should be treated in a special way. Supporters of the alleged exception lean on materials which are commonly cited as evidence of an independent concept of state servitudes.[74] However, the Vienna Convention on Succession of States in Respect of Treaties of 1978 provides that a succession of states shall not affect obligations, or rights, 'relating to the use of territory', and 'established by a treaty

---

[66] Text: 17 *ILM* (1978), 1488. The Swiss Federal Tribunal has recognized the ILC Final Draft as 'authoritative': *M. v. Federal Department of Justice and Police*, ILR 75, 107. See further Sinclair, *Essays in Honour of Erik Castrén* (1979), 149–83. See also Arbitration Commission, Conference on Yugoslavia, *Opinion No. 1*, ILR 92, 162; *Opinion No. 9*, 203.

[67] Reports to UNGA; *Yrbk. ILC* (1972), ii. 250, 286; ibid. (1974), ii (Pt. 1), 211, 252. The evidence set forth in the Reports does not satisfy the criteria of a rule of customary law. See also *R. v. Commissioner of Correctional Services, ex parte Fitz Henry*, ILR 72, 63 (Jamaica, Full Ct. of the Supr. Ct.).

[68] See chs. 10 and 11.

[69] *State Succession*, ii. 12–23, 231ff.

[70] *Law of Treaties*, pp. 655–64. See also Zemanek, 116 Hague *Recueil* (1965, III), 239–44; Rousseau, iii. 491–4; Oppenheim, i. 213; Sørensen, pp. 297–8; Guggenheim, i. (1953), 465. See further: *Répertoire suisse*, iii. 1333–4, 1339–40, 1358–92.

[71] *Supra*, p. 376.

[72] See e.g. Castrén, 78 Hague *Recueil* (1951, I), 448–9. Sceptical are Brierly, p. 154; and Jennings, 121 Hague *Recueil* (1967, II), 442.

[73] See the miscellany in McNair, *Law of Treaties*.

[74] See *Free Zones* case (1932), PCIJ, Ser. A/B, no. 46; World Court Reports, ii. 448, and the *Wimbledon* (1923), PCIJ, Ser. A, no. 1; World Court Reports, i. 163.

for the benefit of any territory of a foreign state and considered as attaching to the territories in question' (Art. 12). In the *Case Concerning the Gabcikovo-Nagymaros Project* (Hungary/Slovakia) the International Court had to determine whether the relevant Treaty of 1977 between Hungary and Czechoslovakia had survived the dissolution of Czechoslovakia and the appearance of the Czech Republic and the Slovak Republic. The Court held that Article 12 'reflects a rule of customary international law' and, further, that the content of the 1977 Treaty indicated that it must be regarded as establishing a territorial regime within the meaning of Article 12.[75]

(iii) *Boundary treaties*. Many jurists who are unable to accept the existence of the category of localized treaties as an exception to the 'clean slate' rule nevertheless regard boundary treaties as a special case depending on clear considerations of stability in territorial matters. It would seem that the question depends on normal principles governing territorial transfers: certainly the change of sovereignty does not as such affect boundaries.[76] This principle is contained in the Vienna Convention of 1978 (Art. 11) and a Chamber of the International Court has referred to the obligation to respect preexisting boundaries in the event of a State succession.[77]

(iv) *Certain other categories*. The majority of writers are of the view that no other exceptions exist. However, a number of authorities consider that in the case of general multilateral or 'law-making' treaties there is a transmission. The view of O'Connell[78] is that in such cases the successor state is obliged by operation of law. However, the actual practice does not support this thesis but rather indicates that the successor has an *option* to participate in such a treaty in its own right irrespective of the provisions of the final clauses of the treaty on conditions of participation.[79] It is probable that the regular acquiescence of states parties to such conventions and of depositaries in such informal participation indicates an *opinio juris*. However, there is some difficulty in producing a neat definition of general multilateral treaties for this purpose. The type includes the Conventions on the Privileges and Immunities of the United Nations, White Slave Traffic, Narcotic Drugs, Obscene Publications, Slavery, the Law of the Sea, Customs Facilities for Touring, various Customs conventions, Refugees, ILO Conventions, the Geneva Conventions of 1949 on the conduct of war, and the Warsaw Conventions for the Unification of Certain Rules relating to International

---

[75] ICJ Reports, 1997, 7, 69–72, paras. 116–23.

[76] On the principle of *uti possidetis* see *supra*, p. 129. See also O'Connell, *State Succession*, ii. 273; Waldock, *Yrbk. ILC* (1968), ii. 92–3; Bedjaoui, ibid. 112–14; Waldock, *Yrbk. ILC* (1972), ii. 44–59; ibid. 298–308; ibid. (1974), ii (Pt. 1), 196–208.

[77] *Case Concerning the Frontier Dispute (Burkina Faso-Mali)*, ICJ Reports (1986), 554 at 566 (para. 24). See also Kaikobad, 54 *BY* (1983), 119–41; 56 *BY* (1985), 49–109; Award of the Tribunal in the *Guinea-Guinea (Bissau) Maritime Delimitation* case (1985), ILR 77, 636 at page 657 (para 40).

[78] *State Succession*, i. 212–29.

[79] See Waldock, *Yrbk. ILC* (1968), i. 130–1, paras. 47–8, and pp. 145–6, paras. 14–16; Castañeda, ibid. 137, paras. 37–41; Waldock, *Yrbk. ILC* (1970), ii. 37–60; *Yrbk. ILC* (1972), ii. 254–72; ibid. (1974), ii (Pt. 1), 214–36; and Indonesian Note in UN Legis. Series ST/LEG/SER B/14, *Materials on Succession of States* (1967), 37. See further the Secretariat studies in *Yrbk. ILC* (1968), ii. 1; (1969), ii. 23; (1970), ii. 61.

Carriage by Air.[80] Common characteristics are the generality of participation allowed for in the conventions themselves, and the primary object of providing a comprehensive code of rules or standards for the particular subject-matter.[81] The Vienna Convention of 1978 adopts a fairly restrictive view of participation in multilateral treaties but allows an informal regime of participation for 'newly independent States' on the basis of 'a notification of succession' (see Arts. 10, 17 to 23, and 31).

In practice problems of succession are dealt with by devolution agreements,[82] by original accession to conventions by new states and by unilateral declarations. In 1961 the Government of Tanganyika made a declaration to the Acting Secretary-General of the United Nations in the following terms:[83]

As regards bilateral treaties validly concluded by the United Kingdom on behalf of the territory of Tanganyika, or validly applied or extended by the former to the territory of the latter, the Government of Tanganyika is willing to continue to apply within its territory on a basis of reciprocity, the terms of all such treaties for a period of two years from the date of independence...unless abrogated or modified earlier by mutual consent. At the expiry of that period, the Government of Tanganyika will regard such of these treaties which could not by the application of rules of customary international law be regarded as otherwise surviving, as having terminated.... The Government of Tanganyika is conscious that the above declaration applicable to bilateral treaties cannot with equal facility be applied to multilateral treaties. As regards these, therefore, the Government of Tanganyika proposes to review each of them individually and to indicate to the depositary in each case what steps it wishes to take in relation to each such instrument—whether by way of confirmation of termination, con-firmation of succession or accession. During such an interim period of review, any party to a multilateral treaty which has prior to independence been applied or extended to Tanganyika may, on the basis of reciprocity, rely against Tanganyika on the terms of such treaty.

This approach has been adopted, though with variations, by a considerable number of states in a similar situation.[84] In a general way such declarations combine a vague or general recognition[85] that certain unspecified treaties do survive as a result of the application of rules of customary law with an offer of a grace period in which treaties remain in force on an interim basis without prejudice to the declarant's legal position and with a requirement of reciprocity.[86] These arrangements are consistent with

---

[80] UN Secretariat Memo. A/CN4/150, *Yrbk. ILC* (1962), ii. 106, ch. 11.

[81] See Jennings, 121 Hague *Recueil* (1967, II), 444.

[82] *Supra*, p. 650.

[83] *Materials on Succession of States*, p. 177. See also Seaton and Maliti, *Tanzania Treaty Practice* (1973); Waldock, *Yrbk. ILC* (1969), ii. 62–8; *Yrbk. ILC* (1972) ii. 241–6; ibid. (1974), ii (Pt. 1), 187–93.

[84] Including Uganda, Kenya, Barbados, Guyana, Swaziland, Nauru, Mauritius, Botswana, Lesotho, Zambia, Burundi, Rwanda and Malawi. See also UN Legis. Series, *Materials on Succession of States*, p. 233 (Malagasy Note); and Waldock, Second Report, *Yrbk. ILC* (1969), ii. 62–8; 52 *BY* (1981), 384–5 (Kiribati); 52 *BY* (1981), 443–4 (Suriname).

[85] See the Zambian declaration.

[86] But see *Molefi* v. *Principal Legal Adviser*, ILR 39, 415, Lesotho High Ct., 1969; [1971] AC 182, PC, in which the Privy Council treated a declaration of this type as an accession to the 1951 Conv. Relating to the Status of Refugees.

the existence of an option to participate in multilateral treaties but are not positive evidence in support of such an option. The practice based on such declarations supports the view that what eventually occurs is either termination or novation as the case may be in respect of the particular treaty.

The actual practice concerning the optional continuance of treaties in force is, it will be appreciated, not confined to multilateral conventions.[87] The question arises whether the practice in relation to general multilateral conventions is to be interpreted on the basis that the new state has the option to participate as of right. The answer is, probably, yes, but this can only be a tentative view and the practice in the case of continuance (apart from a new accession) of treaties of all types may be explicable simply as a novation of the original treaty by the new state and the other pre-existing contracting party or parties.[88]

(f) Constitutions of international organizations[89]

The prevailing doctrine is to the effect that in so far as new states may succeed to treaty obligations of their predecessors under principles of general international law, such principles have no application to membership in international organizations. The position is determined by the provisions of the constitution of the particular organization. In the case of the United Nations all newly independent states are required to apply for membership in the United Nations. However, the member states by general tacit agreement or acquiescence may treat particular cases in a special way. When an original member of the United Nations, India, was partitioned in 1947 the General Assembly treated the surviving India as the successor to pre-1947 India and admitted Pakistan as a new member of the United Nations. The union of Egypt and Syria in 1958 as the United Arab Republic and the dissolution of the union in 1961 resulted in informal consequential changes in membership of the Organization rather than formal admission, in the first instance of the United Republic, and in the second instance of the restored Egypt (still the United Arab Republic) and Syria.

(g) The law of treaties: succession to signature, ratification and reservations

Within the existing possibilities of inheritance of treaties, there is considerable practice to the effect that a new state can inherit the legal consequences of a ratification by a predecessor of a treaty which is not yet in force, but it is doubtful if a new state can inherit the consequences of signature of a treaty which is subject to ratification.[90] A further issue, as yet unsettled, is whether a state 'inheriting' or continuing the treaties

---

[87] See the unilateral declarations noted above; Zemanek, 116 Hague *Recueil* (1965, III), 243; ILA, *The Effect of Independence on Treaties* (1965), 99–100, 109, 144ff.; *Materials on Succession of States*, pp. 37, 42, 218.

[88] See the UK view on a bilateral treaty with France as affecting Laos: *Materials on Succession of States*, pp. 188–9; *Yrbk. ILC* (1969), ii. 60.

[89] O'Connell, *State Succession*, ii. 183–211; Zemanek, 116 Hague *Recueil* (1965, III), 254–54; Schachter, 25 *BY* (1948), 101–9; Whiteman, ii. 1016–27; UN Doc. A/CN4/149 and Add. 1, *Yrbk. ILC* (1962), ii. 101; ibid. 106 at paras. 144–9; *Yrbk. ILC* (1968), ii. 1; (1969), ii. 23; Green, in Schwarzenberger (ed.), *Law, Justice and Equity* (1967), 152–67.

[90] See *Yrbk. ILC* (1962), ii. 124, paras. 143, 151.

of a predecessor inherits the latter's reservations or is entitled to make reservations and objections of its own.[91] The Vienna Convention on Succession of States in respect of Treaties of 1978 contains a number of provisions creating privileges in matters of this kind in favour of 'newly independent States' (Arts. 18 to 20).

(h) *Jus cogens*: succession in relation to the principle of self-determination

Several members of the International Law Commission have pointed out[92] that rules concerning succession must conform with any existing principles of *jus cogens*.[93] Points about *jus cogens* are made with particular reference to the principle of self-determination[94] and the possible continuance of political and economic domination after formal independence has been attained. The legal status of devolution treaties and economic concessions standing over from the pre-independence regime may be challenged on this basis in particular circumstances.[95]

6. RELEVANCE OF THE POLITICAL FORM OF TERRITORIAL CHANGE

There is clearly some relation between the nature of the territorial change and the transmissibility of rights and duties. Thus it is generally agreed that a cession of a part of territory will not affect the treaties of the parties to the transfer. Similarly, there are reasons of principle for approaching the issue of state responsibility differently in the cases of merger or voluntary dissolution of states. However, apart from the results of empirical inquiry in the context of such legal categories as treaties or state responsibility, there seems to be little or no value in establishing, as major *legal* categories, concepts of cession, dismemberment, merger, decolonization, and the like.[96] It may be that decolonization attracts special principles but there is no *general* significance in the distinction between decolonization, dismemberment, secession, and annexation. Too ready a reliance on such distinctions produces harmful results. In the first place, particular factual situations are presented as though they are legal categories. Secondly, distinctions are made in the legal rules adduced which may seem anomalous or invidious. Thus O'Connell[97] employs the category of 'annexation' and accepts the

---

[91] See Gaja, i. *Italian Yrbk.* (1975), 52–68; Waldock, *Yrbk. ILC* (1970), ii. 46–52.

[92] *Yrbk. ILC* (1968), i. 102, para. 35 (Bedjaoui); p. 125, paras. 22, 23 (Ustor); p. 125, paras. 26–8 (Castañeda); p. 132, para. 69 (Tabibi); p. 138, para. 57 (Bartoš); p. 144, para. 63 (El-Erian).

[93] *Supra*, p. 510.

[94] *Supra*, p. 579.

[95] See Bedjaoui, *Yrbk. ILC* (1968), ii. 115–17; and (1969), i. 53–6; Bartoš, ibid. 56–7.

[96] But see Bedjaoui, *Yrbk. ILC* (1968), ii. 100–1. Other members of the Int. Law Comm. adopted a similar point of view: *Yrbk. ILC* (1969), i. 53ff.

[97] *State Succession*, ii, chs. 2 and 8. O'Connell and Jennings (121 Hague *Recueil* at pp. 447–8) regard 'evolution towards independence' within the British Commonwealth as creating a continuity in personality

view that annexation terminates 'personal' treaties. He adopts a different approach to survival of treaties in the case of 'grants of independence' without explaining adequately why there should be such a different outcome.

This much having been said, the factual and political events producing a change of sovereignty may nevertheless have legal relevance in particular circumstances. Thus if the successor either repudiates or acknowledges political continuity with the predecessor then this may produce some effects of preclusion or estoppel in respect of legal matters. Thus Poland refused to accept that there was continuity after she regained her independence in 1918.[98] There will be a presumption against continuity in cases where the political and legal machinery of change has involved relinquishment of sovereignty followed by reallocation in the form of a multilateral territorial settlement, as in the case of the peace treaties in Europe in 1919–20.[99] Similarly, there will be a presumption against continuity in the case of a forcible secession or its equivalent, as in the case of the appearance of Israel.[100] In those instances in which there is no 'transfer' of sovereignty then it is inappropriate to argue from the principle of a *grant* of sovereignty. Of course, the reference to either acknowledged or repudiated political (and thus legal) continuity with a predecessor state raises problems for third states which are not bound to accept the political determination of the putative successor.[101] The recognition of continuity by third states must be an important element since assessment of political continuity is very much a matter of choice and appreciation.[102] This is also the case where complicated political change produces a double succession within a short space of time as in the case of India and Pakistan, and Senegal and Mali. Normally, of course, these matters will be regulated by treaty: thus, for example, Turkey as a new political entity was held to be identical with the Ottoman Empire in provisions of the Treaty of Lausanne.[103]

7. THE DISINTEGRATION OF FEDERAL STATES

The substance of the previous section has been particularly relevant in the context of the disintegration, or partial disintegration, of the Soviet Union and the Socialist Federal Republic of Yugoslavia, both being federations. The political processes

---

with the pre-independence colonial government. This view is not reflected in the relevant legal position except in the rather different case where a protectorate is held to have had international personality before the subordinate status was removed: see Zemanek, 116 Hague *Recueil* (1965, III), 195–202; UN Legis. Series, *Materials on Succession of States* (1967), 184. Cf. also Rosenne, 27 *BY* (1950), 267.

[98] *Yrbk. ILC* (1963), ii. 129, paras. 305ff.; p. 131, paras. 326ff.

[99] *Supra*, p. 130 and cf. *RIAA* i. 429 at 441–4. Special provision was made in the treaties for the maintenance of public debts.

[100] UN Legis. Series, *Materials on Succession of States* (1967), 38; *Shimshon Palestine Portland Cement Factory Ltd. v. A.-G.*, ILR 17 (1950), 72.

[101] Whiteman, ii. 758–9; *Répertoire suisse*, iii. 1337–57.

[102] *Supra*, p. 80. See *D.C. v. Public Prosecutor*, ILR 73, 38 (Netherlands Supr. Ct.).

[103] See also the *Ottoman Debt Arbitration*, *RIAA* i. 529 at 571–4, 590–4, 599.

involved were casual and included elements of civil strife. In the case of the Russian Federation, the principal surviving component of the Soviet Union, the States of the European Community declared that this was the continuation of the former Soviet Union. Russia was also accepted by the members of the Security Council as the continuing State of the former Soviet Union.

In the wake of the disintegration of Yugoslavia, the two surviving units, Serbia and Montenegro, then denominated as the Federal Republic of Yugoslavia, declared that it was the sole successor of the former Yugoslavia. This position was unacceptable to the European Community and its member States.[104] Apparently as a consequence of this difference, Yugoslavia has been prevented from exercising its rights as a member of the United Nations, but without this affecting its rights and duties arising from its status as a party to the Statute of the International Court of Justice. It is difficult to give legal articulation to these episodes in State practice.

8. DOCTRINE OF REVERSION[105]

It is possible that a continuity by virtue of general recognition by third states (see the last section) arises in the form of a reversion. Thus the successor state may be regarded as recovering a political and legal identity displaced by an intervening period of dismemberment or colonization.[106] Such cases will be rare and the logical consequences of a doctrine of reversion may create a threat to the security of legal relations: thus it would follow that the successor would not be bound by territorial grants or recognition of territorial changes by the previous holder. The suggestion has been made that, quite apart from recognition by third states, in a case of post-colonial reversion, the principle of self-determination may create a presumption in favour of the successor state.[107] This raises large issues of the relation between principles of *jus cogens*, of which self-determination[108] is an example in the view of some authorities, and the law relating to state succession.[109]

---

[104] See *Opinion No. 9*, Conference on Yugoslavia, Arbitration Commission, ILR 92, 203. See also the other Opinions of this body: Opinon No. 11, ILR 96, 718; Opinion No. 12, ibid., 723; Opinion No. 13, ibid., 726; Opinion No. 14, ibid., 729. See also *Federal Republic and National Bank of Yugoslavia* v. *Republics of Croatia, Slovenia, Macedonia and Bosnia-Herzegovina*, ILR 128, 627, France, Court of Cassation.

[105] See Alexandrowicz, 45 *International Affairs* (1969), 465–80; Jain, 9 *Indian Journ.* (1969), 525–7.

[106] Cf. the history of Poland and India.

[107] See the Diss. Op. of Judge Moreno Quintana in the *Right of Passage* case, ICJ Reports (1960), 6 at 93–6, esp. at 95. Cf. Bedjaoui, *Yrbk. ILC* (1968), i. 128, para. 10. In the *Red Sea Islands Arbitration* (Phase One), the Yemeni argument based on reversion was rejected on the facts: see the Award, ILR 114, 2, 115–17. However, it is not clear whether the Court of Arbitration appreciated the precise historical sequence of events.

[108] *Supra*, p. 579.

[109] See *supra*, s. 5(*h*).

30

OTHER CASES OF TRANSMISSION OF RIGHTS AND DUTIES

1. SUCCESSION BETWEEN INTERNATIONAL ORGANIZATIONS[1]

It happens from time to time that an international organization is dissolved and its functions are in substance assumed by a new organization with similar objects and composition. When the League of Nations was dissolved in 1946, practical arrangements had been made for the transfer of its property and certain of its functions to the United Nations. There was no automatic transfer and the element of continuity depended on the consent of the United Nations.[2] In the case of functions under treaties, transfer of functions to the United Nations required the consent of the parties to the treaties. Instruments containing acceptances of the jurisdiction of the Permanent Court of International Justice (which was dissolved in 1946) were deemed to be acceptances of the jurisdiction of the new Court by specific provisions in the new Statute.[3]

There is no rule of automatic succession between organizations and the primary criterion must be the intention of the member states at the material times. In the Advisory Opinion on the *International Status of South West Africa*[4] the International Court was concerned to discover the legal consequences of the dissolution of the League of Nations the organs of which had supervised the execution of the Mandate for South

---

[1] Fitzmaurice, 29 *BY* (1952), 8–10; Oppenheim, i (8th edn., 1955), 168–9; Kiss, *Ann. français* (1961), 463–91; Chiu, 14 *ICLQ* (1965), 83–120; Hahn, *Duke LJ* (1962), 379–422, 522–57; also in 13 *Öst. Z. für öff. R.* (1963–4), 167–239; Bernhardt (ed.), *Encyclopedia* II (1995), 1340–43; Judge Fitzmaurice, Diss. Op., *Namibia* Opinion, ICJ Reports (1971), 227–63; Schwarzenberger, *International Constitutional Law* (1976), 99–114; Ranjeva, *La Succession des organisations internationales en Afrique* (1978); Jacqué, *Ann. français* (1981), 747–67; Myers, *Succession between International Organizations* (1993); Thirlway, 67 *BY* (1996), 9–12; Schermers and Blokker, *International Institutional Law* (3rd edn., 1997), 1015–19; Sands and Klein, *Bowett's Law of International Institutions*, 5th edn. (2001), 526–31.

[2] See Whiteman, xiii. 263–300.

[3] See *infra*, p. 714.

[4] ICJ Reports (1950), 128. See also *South West Africa* cases (Prelim. Objections); ibid. (1962), 319; and the *Namibia* Opinion, ibid. (1971), 16. See generally Cheng, 20 *Current Leg. Problems* (1967), 181–212.

West Africa and South Africa's refusal to conclude a Trusteeship Agreement. On a number of grounds not relating to any principle of succession between organizations, the Court found that the Mandate continued to exist. It also found that the appropriate organs of the United Nations were to exercise the supervisory functions of the League of Nations in spite of the fact that such functions 'were neither expressly transferred to the United Nations nor expressly assumed by the organization'.[5] The reasoning of the court is not easy to characterize. The principal basis of this finding was 'the necessity for supervision' which continued to exist despite the disappearance of the supervisory organ under the Mandates system—the Council of the League of Nations. Judge Fitzmaurice has expressed the view that the Advisory Opinion is authority for the proposition that an 'automatic devolution' of functions from one organization to another *may* occur and that in certain conditions there is a presumption that such a devolution occurs.[6] If the Court was purporting to construe the provisions of the United Nations Charter and relying upon a teleological or purposive approach to interpretation, then Judge Fitzmaurice was in error.[7] However, the principle of necessity may seem to go beyond mere treaty interpretation and, if that be so, then *in effect* the Court was discovering a case of 'automatic' succession.[8]

Judge Fitzmaurice has his own view of the matter.[9] He considers that 'there are only three ways in which the United Nations could, upon the dissolution of the League, have become invested with the latter's powers in respect of mandates as such: namely, (a) if specific arrangement to that effect had been made, (b) if such a succession must be implied in some way, or (c) if the mandatory concerned—in this case South Africa— could be shown to have consented to what would in effect have been a *novation* of the reporting obligation, in the sense of agreeing to accept the supervision of, and to be accountable to, a new and different entity, the United Nations, or some particular organ of it'. With respect, this formulation must be correct. The essential difference between Judge Fitzmaurice and the Court as a whole probably consists in the manner of application of these principles to the evidence of what actually happened upon the dissolution of the League.

2. CASES OF AGENCY

States may act on behalf of other states for various purposes, provided that authority to do so exists and is not exceeded. States may appoint other states as agents for various purposes, including the making of treaties. This agency may arise from the

---

[5] ICJ Reports (1950), 136.

[6] 29 *BY* (1952), 8. See also Oppenheim, i. (8th edn., 1955), 168–9; Lauterpacht, *The Development of International Law by the International Court* (1958), 277–81.

[7] See Schwarzenberger, *International Law* (3rd edn., 1957), i. 178; Bowett, *International Institutions*, p. 382; Chiu, 14 *ICLQ* (1965), 105–6. See also Cheng 20 *Curr. Leg. Problems* (1967), 187–91.

[8] The formulations of the Ct. in the *Namibia* Opinion, ICJ Reports (1971), at 28–45, do not take the matter any further.

[9] ICJ Reports (1971), 227. See also the joint dissent of Judges Spender and Fitzmaurice, *South West Africa* cases, ICJ Reports (1962), at 516ff.

existence of a relation of federation or dependence or protection[10] or otherwise.[11] By agreement an organization may become an agent for member states, and others, in regard to matters outside its normal competence and a state may act as agent for an organization.[12]

3. ASSIGNMENT

In considering the effects of a devolution agreement[13] the International Law Commission has pointed out that it was 'extremely doubtful' whether such a purported assignment by itself could change the position of any of the interested states. The Vienna Convention on the Law of Treaties contains no provisions regarding assignment of rights or obligations. As the Commission has pointed out: 'The reason is that the institution of "assignment" found in some national systems of law by which under certain conditions contract rights may be transferred without the consent of the other party to the contract does not appear to be an institution recognized in international law'.[14]

---

[10] Cf. *supra*, pp. 72–4.

[11] See the ILC Report on the Law of Treaties, 59 *AJ* (1965), 203 at 209, referring to the Belgo-Luxembourg Economic Union, under which treaties may be concluded by one state on behalf of the Union. See also the Utilities Claims Settlement Agreement between the Government of the United States as Unified Command, on its own behalf and on behalf of Certain Other Governments, and the Government of the Republic of Korea, 1958, *Treaty Series*, no. 57 (1959), Cmnd. 796.

[12] *Infra*, p. 688.

[13] On which see *supra*, p. 650.

[14] *Yrbk. ILC* (1969), ii. 56, para. 10. For a different view: Mann, 30 *BY* (1953), 475–8 (also in Mann, *Studies* (1973), 360–5); and see also Starke, 13 *Indian Journ.* (1973), 519–29.

PART XII

INTERNATIONAL ORGANIZATIONS AND TRIBUNALS

PART XII

INTERNATIONAL
ORGANIZATIONS AND
TRIBUNALS

31

INTERNATIONAL ORGANIZATIONS

1. INTRODUCTION

In the nineteenth century states advanced from the bilateral treaty and reliance on diplomatic contact to other forms of co-operation. The Congress of Vienna heralded an era of international conferences and multilateral treaties, and later there appeared administrative unions such the European Danube Commission, and the International Telegraph Union. After 1920 the League of Nations and the United Nations provided the more developed notion of universal peace-keeping institutions, and there appeared an ever-increasing number of specialized institutions concerned with technical, economic, and social co-operation. Permanent organizations with executive and administrative organs paralleled but did not completely replace the system of *ad hoc* diplomacy involving, *inter alia*, conferences.[1] The general study of international organization and the multiplicity of institutions and agencies is a department of the political and social sciences, and in the present chapter the object is to indicate only the legal problems arising from the function of organizations of states.[2]

---

[1] Cf. the United Nations Conferences on the Law of the Sea and other subjects. On *ad hoc* diplomacy: ch. 17, s. 11.

[2] See esp. Sands and Klein, *Bowett's Law of International Institutions* 5th edn. (2001); Colliard, *Institutions des relations internationales* (8th edn., 1985); Morgenstern, 48 BY (1976–7), 241–57, id., *Legal Problems of International Organizations* (1986); Rousseau, ii. 449–691; Schwarzenberger, *International Constitutional Law* (1976); Kirgis, *International Organizations in Their Legal Setting* (1977); Daillier, Pellet, *Droit international public* (7th edn., 2002), 571–642; Dupuy (ed.), *A Handbook of International Organizations* (1988); Thirlway, 67 BY (1996), 1–73; White, *The Law of International Organisations* (1996); Amerasinghe, *Principles of the Institutional Law of International Organizations* (1996); id., *Austrian Journ.*, 47 (1995), 123–45; Schermers and Blokker, *International Institutional Law*, 3rd edn. (1997); Bernhardt (ed.), *Encycl. of PIL*, II (1995), Bindschedler and others, 1289–1346; Diez de Velasco Vallejo, *Les organisations internationales* (2006); Sarooshi, *International Organizations and Their Exercise of Sovereign Powers* (2005).

2. LEGAL PERSONALITY[3]

The international community has no legal and administrative process comparable to that of incorporation in municipal law, but it is significant that the latter may recognize unincorporated associations as legal persons.[4] Where there is no constitutional system for, as it were, recognizing and registering associations as legal persons, the primary test is functional. Indeed, it would be fatuous to work from an abstract model in face of the existence of some 170 organizations of states. In the *Reparation* case[5] the International Court was asked for an advisory opinion on the capacity of the United Nations, as an organization, to bring an international claim in respect of injury to its personnel, on the lines of diplomatic protection, and in respect of injury to the United Nations caused by the injury to its agents. The Charter did not contain any explicit provision on the legal personality of the Organization,[6] but the Court drew on the implications of the Charter as a whole:[7]

The subjects of law in any legal system are not necessarily identical in their nature or in the extent of their rights, and their nature depends upon the needs of the community. Throughout its history, the development of international law has been influenced by the requirements of international life, and the progressive increase in the collective activities of States has already given rise to instances of action upon the international plane by certain entities which are not States. This development culminated in the establishment in June 1945 of an international organization whose purposes and principles are specified in the Charter of the United Nations. But to achieve these ends the attribution of international personality is indispensable.

The Charter has not been content to make the Organization created by it merely a centre 'for harmonizing the actions of nations in the attainment of these common ends' (Article I, para. 4). It has equipped that centre with organs, and has given it special tasks. It has defined the position of the Members in relation to the Organization by requiring them to give it every assistance in any action undertaken by it (Article 2, para. 5), and to accept and carry out the decisions of the Security Council; by authorizing the General Assembly to make recommendations to the Members; by giving the Organization legal capacity and privileges and immunities in the territory of each of its Members; and by providing for the conclusion of agreements between the Organization and its Members. Practice—in

---

[3] Generally see *supra*, Ch. 3.

[4] Cf. *Knight and Searle v. Dove* [1964] 2 QB 631.

[5] ICJ Reports (1949), 174.

[6] Art. 104 relates solely to legal capacity of the Organization in the municipal law of member states, on which see Bridge, 18 *ICLQ* (1969), 689.

[7] ICJ Reports (1949), 178–9. See also the Advisory Opinion concerning *Interpretation of the Agreement of 25 March 1951 between the WHO and Egypt*, ICJ Reports (1980), 73 at 89–90 (para. 37); *Westland Helicopters v. A.O.I.*, ILR 80, 596, ICC Court of Arbitration; *A.O.I. v. Westland Helicopters*, ibid., 622, Swiss proceedings; Advocate-General's Opinion, *Maclaine Watson & Co. Ltd. v. Council of the EC and Commission of the EC*, 1 June 1989, ILR 96, 201 (EC Ct. of Justice); *LAFICO v. Republic of Burundi*, ibid., 279 (Arbitral Tribunal), 4 March 1991; Advisory Opinion concerning *Legality of the Use by a State of Nuclear Weapons in Armed Conflict*, ICJ Reports (1996) 66 at 78–81, paras. 24–26.

particular the conclusion of conventions to which the Organization is a party—has confirmed this character of the Organization, which occupies a position in certain respects in detachment from its Members, and which is under a duty to remind them, if need be, of certain obligations. It must be added that the Organization is a political body, charged with political tasks of an important character, and covering a wide field namely, the maintenance of international peace and security, the development of friendly relations among nations, and the achievement of international co-operation in the solution of problems of an economic, social, cultural or humanitarian character (Article I); and in dealing with its Members it employs political means. The 'Convention on the Privileges and Immunities of the United Nations' of 1946 creates rights and duties between each of the signatories and the Organization (see, in particular, Section 35). It is difficult to see how such a convention could operate except upon the international plane and as between parties possessing international personality.

In the opinion of the Court, the Organization was intended to exercise and enjoy, and is in fact exercising and enjoying, functions and rights which can only be explained on the basis of the possession of a large measure of international personality and the capacity to operate upon an international plane. It is at present the supreme type of international organization, and it could not carry out the intentions of its founders if it was devoid of international personality. It must be acknowledged that its Members, by entrusting certain functions to it, with the attendant duties and responsibilities, have clothed it with the competence required to enable those functions to be effectively discharged.

Accordingly, the Court has come to the conclusion that the Organization is an international person. That is not the same thing as saying that it is a State, which it certainly is not, or that its legal personality and rights and duties are the same as those of a State. Still less is it the same thing as saying that it is 'a super-State', whatever that expression may mean. It does not even imply that all its rights and duties must be upon the international plane, any more than all the rights and duties of a State must be upon that plane. What it does mean is that it is a subject of international law and capable of possessing international rights and duties, and that it has capacity to maintain its rights by bringing international claims.

The criteria of legal personality in organizations may be summarized as follows:

1. a permanent association of states, with lawful objects, equipped with organs;

2. a distinction, in terms of legal powers and purposes, between the organization and its member states;

3. the existence of legal powers exercisable on the international plane and not solely within the national systems of one or more states.[8]

[8] See further Jenks, 22 BY (1945), 267–75; Ginther, Die völkerrechtliche Verantwortlichkeit internationaler Organisationen gegenüber Drittstaaten (1969); Skubiszewski, 12 Ann. français (1966), 544 at 556–60; Quadri, 113 Hague Recueil (1964, III), 423–33; Seyersted, 34 Acta Scandinavica (1964), 46–61; id., 4 Indian Journ. (1964), 1–74, 233–68; Pescatore, 103 Hague Recueil (1961, II), 27–52, 67–74; Dupuy, 100 Hague Recueil (1960, II), 467–88, 529–61; Fawcett, 34 BY (1957), 313–14; Broches, 98 Hague Recueil (1959, III), 323–9; Weissberg, The International Status of the United Nations (1961); Bishop, 115 Hague Recueil (1965, II), 261–8; Osakwe, 65 AJ (1971), 502–21; Dupuy (ed.), Handbook, pp. 43–55.

These criteria relate to delicate issues of law and fact and are not always easy to apply. However, many important institutions undoubtedly have legal personality, including the specialized agencies of the United Nations (such as the International Labour Organ-ization), the European Union, the Organization of American States, the African Union, and the Organization of the Islamic Conference and, as will appear subsequently, the really difficult questions concern the particular capacities of the organization as a legal person and its relations to members, third states, and other organizations. Before these questions are considered it may give more point to the criteria summarized above if certain distinctions are drawn. Thus an organization may exist but lack the organs and objects necessary for legal personality: the British Commonwealth is an association of this kind. Similarly, a multilateral convention may be institutionalized to some extent, making provision for regular conferences, and yet not involve any separate personality.[9] Joint agencies of states,[10] for example an arbitral tribunal or river commission, may have restricted capacities and limited independence, with the executive and jurisdictional powers, and legal personality is only a matter of degree. This is also the case with the agencies and subsidiary organs of organizations, such as the United Nations Conference on Trade and Development, the High Commissioner for Refugees, and the Technical Assistance Board in relation to the United Nations.[11] If an organization has considerable independence and power to intervene in the affairs of member states, the latter may come to have a status akin to that of membership in a federal union. It may be noted also that, while an organization with legal personality is normally established by treaty, this is by no means necessary and the source could equally be the resolution of a conference of states or a uniform practice.[12] The constitutional basis of the United Nations Conference on Trade and Development (UNCTAD) and of the United Nations Industrial Development Organization (UNIDO) must be found in resolutions of the General Assembly.[13]

Finally, some other relations of the subject-matter may be mentioned. An institution may lack the features of an 'organization' and yet have legal personality on the international plane. Thus the 'contracting parties' of the General Agreement on Trade and Tariffs have some legal personality, partly by reason of the exercise by them of a quasi-judicial function in the complaint procedures between contracting parties. Moreover, a formal presentation may concentrate too much on 'international legal personality', ignoring the powers of organizations, and institutions like the GATT, to

---

[9] Cf. conflicting decisions of Italian courts on the status of the North Atlantic Treaty Organization: *Branno* v. *Ministry of War*, ILR 22 (1955), 756; *Mazzanti* v. *H.A.F.S.E.*, ibid., 758.

[10] See further *supra*, 61. Cf. the Commonwealth Secretariat Act 1966. See also Dale, 31 *ICLQ* (1982), 451–73.

[11] See Reuter, *Hommage au Président Basdevant* (1960), 415–40; Dale, 23 *ICLQ* (1974), 576–609; Morgenstern, *Legal Problems of International Organizations*, pp. 23–6.

[12] On the formation of the World Tourism Organization, see Gilmour, 18 *Neths. Int. LR* (1971) 275–98. Cf. *Zoernsch* v. *Waldock* [1964] 1 WLR 675, on the constitution of an organ of an organization.

[13] See Gutteridge, *The United Nations in a Changing World*, (1969), 75–85.

make local law contracts such as leases of buildings. In practice the latter competence may flow from the international legal personality.

3. PERFORMANCE OF ACTS IN THE LAW

The analogue for the successful exercise of legal functions in international relations is the state, in spite of the obvious dangers of assuming automatic and extensive parallels. The most viable type of organization will have a number of legal powers similar to those normally associated with statehood. The enumeration of acts in the law which organizations may perform will establish the dynamics of the subject and provide a necessary background to the subjects of implied powers and interpretation of basic instruments developed later. At the same time the individuality of each organization must be emphasized: in the first instance the evidence of legal capacity is to be found in the constituent treaty of the particular organization.

(a) The treaty-making power[14]

The existence of legal personality does not of itself support a power to make treaties, and everything depends on the terms of the constituent instrument of the organization. The constituent instrument does not normally confer a general treaty-making power, but this may be established by interpretation of the instrument as a whole and resort to the doctrine of implied powers (*infra*). The United Nations Charter contains provisions expressly authorizing certain agreements, such as the trusteeship agreements (Chapter 12) and relationship agreements with the specialized agencies (Arts. 57 and 63). However, the United Nations, together with other organizations, has concluded headquarters agreements with states and agreements on co-operation with other organizations, although the constituent instrument contains no express authority for these types of agreement. In practice organizations readily assume a treaty-making power. The Vienna Convention on the Law of Treaties between States and International Organizations or between International Organizations was adopted

---

[14] See Broches, 98 Hague *Recueil* (1959, III), 329ff.; Pescatore, 103 Hague *Recueil* (1961, II), 55–67; Dupuy, 100 Hague *Recueil* (1960, II), 489ff.; Detter, 38 *BY* (1962), 421–44; Karunatilleke, 75 *RGDIP* (1971), 12–91; Hungdah Chiu, *The Capacity of International Organizations to Conclude Treaties, and the Special Legal Aspects of the Treaties So Concluded* (1966); Whiteman, xiii. 28–31; Zemanek (ed.), *Agreements of International Organ-izations and the Vienna Convention on the Law of Treaties* (1971); *Yrbk. ILC* (1974), ii (pt. 2), 3 (biblio); Bernhardt (ed.), *Encycl. of P.I.L.*, II (1995), Zemanek, 1343–6. The specific provisions of drafts of the International Law Commission on the law of treaties applied to the treaties of states only, but the Commission has recognized that in principle it considers the international agreements to which organizations are parties to fall within the scope of the law of treaties: *Yrbk. ILC* (1963), ii. 177–8 (paras. 113–15). See ILC, Final Draft on the Law of Treaties, 1966, Art. 3; *Yrbk. ILC* (1966), ii. 190; and the Vienna Conv. on the Law of Treaties, 1969, Art. 3. See also Report on the ILC 1980, Draft Articles on treaties concluded between states and International Organizations or between International Organizations; *Yrbk ILC* (1980), (Pt. 2), 64–103; ibid (1982), (Pt. 2), 9–77 (on the basis of the work of Reuter as rapporteur); and *Annuaire de l'Inst.* (1973), 55, 214–415.

on 21 March 1986.[15] Its content is very similar to the Vienna Convention on the Law of Treaties of 1969. Organizations participating in the Conference which adopted the Convention have the competence to sign the Convention and to execute acts of formal confirmation (equivalent to ratification by states).[16] The Convention is also open for accession 'by any organization which has the capacity to conclude treaties'.[17]

(b) Privileges and immunities[18]

In order to function effectively, international organizations require a certain minimum of freedom and legal security for their assets, headquarters, and other establishments and for their personnel and representatives of member states accredited to the organizations. By analogy with the privileges and immunities accorded to diplomats, the requisite privileges and immunities in respect of the territorial jurisdiction of host states are recognized in the customary law. However, there is as yet no general agreement on the precise content of the customary law concerning the immunities of international organizations. The minimum principle appears to be that officials of international organizations are immune from legal process in respect of all acts performed in their official capacity.[19] In any case, the international immunities are highly specialized and inevitably vary a great deal. As experience with United Nations peace-keeping forces shows, the relationship with the host state will depend a great deal on the specific function involved and all the circumstances.[20] The decisions of national courts do not as yet produce a coherent body of principles. Some decisions rely upon the analogy of diplomatic immunities, while others take a more rigorously functional view.[21] Naturally the immunity given to judges of the International Court

---

[15] Text: 25 *ILM* (1986), 543. For comment: Gaja, 58 *BY* (1987), 253–69.

[16] Arts. 82, 83.

[17] Art. 84. But see Art. 85 on entry into force.

[18] Jenks, *International Immunities* (1961); Lalive, 84 Hague *Recueil* (1953, III), 291–385; Weissberg, pp. 141–69; Brandon, 28 *BY* (1951), 90–113; Schröer, 75 *RGDIP* (1971), 712–41; Whiteman, xiii. 32–188; Secretariat Study, *Yrbk. ILC* (1967), ii. 154–324; El-Erian, ibid. 133–53; ibid. (1968) ii. 119–62; ibid. (1969), ii. 1–21; ibid. (1970), ii. 1–24; ibid. (1971), ii (Pt. 1), 1–142; *Privileges and Immunities of International Organizations* (Resol. (69) 29 of the Committee of Ministers) Council of Europe, 1970; Michaels, *International Privileges and Immunities* (1971); *Digest of US Practice* (1978), 90–124; ibid. (1979), 189–216; ibid. (1980), 63–75; ibid. (1981–88, I), 337–404; Dominicé, 187 Hague *Recueil* (1984, IV), 149–238; Glenn, Kearney, Padilla, 22 *Virginia JIL* (1981–2), 247–90; Duffar, *Contribution à l'étude des privilèges et immunités des organisations internationales* (1982); Dominicé, *Festschrift Seidl-Hohenveldern* (1998), 85–96; Singer, *Virginia Journ.*, 36 (1995), 53–165; Thirlway, 67 *BY* (1996), 36–9; Bernhardt (ed.), *Encycl. of P.I.L.*, II (1995), Szasz, 1325–33; Sands and Klein, *Bowett's Law of International Institutions*, 5th edn. (2001), 486–512; Gaillard and Pingel-Lenuzza *ICLQ* 51 (2002), 1–16; Robert, *Mélanges Salmon* (2007), 1432–60.

[19] See Jenks, *International Immunities*, pp. 114–21; Rousseau, ii. 601–3; Schermers, *International Institutional Law*, 291–3 (paras. 484–7); Dupuy (ed.), *Handbook*, p. 192.

[20] See esp. Bowett, *United Nations Forces* (1964), pp. 428–67. On the transfer of the seat of an organization (or its Regional Office) from the territory of a host state see the Advisory Opinion concerning the *Interpretation of the Agreement of 25 March 1950 between the WHO and Egypt*, ICJ Reports (1980), at 92–6 (paras. 43–50).

[21] See e.g. *Porru v. F.A.O.*, ILR 71, 240; *Re Pisani Balestra di Mottola*, ibid. 565; *M. v. Cantonal Appeals Commission of Berne*, ILR 75, 85; *X. v. Department of Justice and Police of Canton of Geneva*, ibid. 90; *Stahel v. Bastid*, ibid. 76; *Weidner v. I.T.S.O.*, ILR 63, 191; *Broadbent v. O.A.S.*, ibid. 337; *M. v. United Nations*

and other holders of judicial offices is of special importance and is equated to diplomatic privileges.[22] As in the case of diplomatic immunities, international immunities are subject to waiver. In the opinion of the English courts even the inviolability of official archives may be lost as a consequence of the communication of documents forming part thereof by member states of the organization (or their representatives) to third parties.[23]

Article 105 of the United Nations Charter provides that 'the Organization shall enjoy in the territory of each of its members such privileges and immunities as are necessary for the fulfilment of its purposes', and, further, that 'representatives of the Members of the United Nations and officials of the Organization shall similarly enjoy such privileges and immunities as are necessary for the independent exercise of their functions in connection with the Organization'. If the constituent treaty contains only general stipulations, then further arrangements are necessary. In the case of the United Nations the principal instrument involved is the General Convention on the Privileges and Immunities of the United Nations.[24] In 1999 a difference arose between the United Nations and the Government of Malaysia relating to the immunity from legal process of the Special Rapporteur of the Commission on Human Rights on the Independence of Judges and Lawers. In response to a request from the Economic and Social Council, the International Court rendered an Advisory Opinion upholding the immunity of the Special Rapporteur.[25] The United Nations and the United States concluded a Headquarters Agreement in 1947.[26] In 1987 a dispute arose between the host state and the United Nations as a result of pressure from Congress to close the PLO Observer Mission in New York.[27] For constitutional and other reasons states implement treaty obligations of this kind by municipal legislation, and in the United Kingdom the applicable legislation is the International Organizations Acts 1968[28] and 1981.

---

and Belgium, ILR 69, 139; *I.A.E.A. Representative Immunity* case, ILR 70, 413; *International Patents Institute Employee* case, ibid. 418; *Clarsfield* v. *Office Franco-Allemand pour la Jeunesse*, ILR 72, 191; *Tuck* v. *P.A.H.O.*, ibid. 196; *ESOC Official Immunity* case, ILR 73, 683; *Bari Institute* v. *Jasbez*, ILR 77, 602; *Girod de l'Ain*, ILR 82, 85; *African Reinsurance Corporation* v. *Abate Fantaye*, ILR 86, 655; *FAO* v. *INDPAI*, ILR 87, 1; *Cristiani* v. *Italian Latin-American Institute*, ibid., 20; *Mininni* v. *Bari Institute*, ibid., 28; *Sindicato UIL* v. *Bari Institute*, ibid., 37; *ECOWAS* v. *B.C.C.I.*, ILR 113, 472; *League of Arab States* v. *I*, ILR 127, 94.

[22] See Art. 19 of the Statute of the International Court; and 93 *JDI* (1966), 176.

[23] *Shearson Lehman Bros. Inc.* v. *Maclaine Watson & Co. Ltd. (No. 2)* [1988] 1 All ER 116, HL.

[24] Approved by the General Assembly on 13 Feb. 1946. Text: 1 UNTS 15. See *M.* v. *Organization des Nations Unies et État Belge*, ILR 45, 446. There is a separate Conv. on the Privileges and Immunities of the Specialized Agencies, approved on 21 Nov. 1947. Text: 33 UNTS 261.

[25] ICJ Reports (1999), 62.

[26] 11 UNTS 18. See *US* v. *Melekh*, 190 F. Supp. 67; 193 F. Supp. 586; ILR 32, 308; *U.S. ex rel. Casanova* v. *Fitzpatrick*, 214 F. Supp. 425; ILR 34, p. 154; *People* v. *Coumatos*, 224 NYS 2d 507; ILR 35, 222. On the OPEC Fund Headquarters Agreement with Austria see *Firma Baumeister Ing. Richard L.* v. *O.*, *United Nations Juridical Yearbook*, 2004, 394.

[27] See the Advisory Opinion of the International Court in the *PLO Observer Mission* case, ICJ Reports (1988), 12.

[28] See also the Diplomatic and Other Privileges Act 1971. See further *Zoernsch* v. *Waldock* [1964] 1 WLR 675.

The question of privileges and immunities is governed by the Vienna Convention on the Representation of States in their Relations with International Organizations of a Universal Character,[29] adopted in 1975 in face of opposition from the major 'host states'. It is to apply to permanent missions constituting representation of the sending state to the organization concerned, and also delegations sent to an organ or a conference convened by the organization. The provisions have been criticized by a number of governments on the basis that the interest of the host state receives insufficient protection. The privileges and immunities are modelled on the provisions of the Vienna Convention on Diplomatic Relations.[30] The United States, for example, does not accept that the provisions of the present Convention represent the existing international law on the subject.[31]

It should be noted that some Governments and municipal courts have adopted the view that immunity exists by virtue of customary international law.[32] On occasion the immunity has been recognized by the courts of non-member States.[33] At least certain aspects of the immunity have the status of general principles of law.[34]

(c) Capacity to espouse international claims

In the Advisory Opinion in the *Reparation* case, quoted in part earlier, the International Court held unanimously that the United Nations was a legal person with capacity to bring claims against both member and non-member[35] states for direct injuries to the Organization. The power to espouse claims for direct injuries was regarded, it seems, as a concomitant of legal personality, since the Court leaned on the general ambience of purposes and functions as it did when examining the preliminary issue of personality. However, the Court[36] expressed its conclusion in terms of implied powers and effectiveness, of which more later. A similar reasoning may apply to other organizations. The capacity to espouse claims thus depends (1) on the existence of legal personality and (2) on the interpretation of the constituent instrument in the light of the purposes and functions of the particular organization.[37] In contrast, the existence of immunities is not conditioned by separate legal personality on the part of the agency concerned.

---

[29] Text: 69 *AJ* (1975), 730; *Digest of US Practice* (1975), 40. The Conv. requires 35 ratifications or accessions before it comes into force. Thirty-two States have become parties. For comment: Fennessy, 70 *AJ* (1976), 62. For the Report of the International Law Commission, see *Yrbk. ILC* (1971), ii (Pt. 1), 278.

[30] See ch. 17.

[31] See *Digest of US Practice* (1973), 25–9, referring to Art. 36 of the ILC draft articles (n. 28, *supra*).

[32] See *Iran–US Claims Tribunal* v. *AS*, ILR 94, 321 (Neths. S.C.) and *Eckhardt* v. *Eurocontrol (No. 2)*, ibid., 331 (Neths. District Ct. of Maastricht).

[33] See, in relation to the League of Arab States: *ZM* v. *Permanent Delegation of the League of Arab States to the United Nations*, ILR 116, 643 (Labour Court of Geneva).

[34] See the authorative view of Szasz, Bernhardt (ed.), *Encycl. of PIL*, II (1995), 1325–33.

[35] ICJ Reports (1949), 184–5, 187.

[36] At p. 180.

[37] Sørensen, 101 Hague *Recueil* (1960, III), 139, relates the capacity directly to legal personality.

(d) Functional protection of agents and persons entitled through them[38]

The Court in the *Reparation* case used similar reasoning[39] to justify its opinion that the United Nations could espouse claims for injury to its agents on the basis of a functional protection. This view provoked several dissenting opinions,[40] and certainly this capacity cannot readily be invoked for other organizations, especially when their functions do not include peace-keeping.[41] In 1997 the Fifth Committee of the General Assembly decided that the costs resulting from an Israeli bombardment (in 1996) of the headquarters of the U.N. Interim Force in Lebanon (1,773,618 dollars) should be borne by Israel.[42] A problem which remains to be solved is the determination of priorities between the state's right of diplomatic protection and the organization's right of functional protection.[43]

(e) *Locus standi* before international tribunals

When an organization has legal personality it ought in principle to have *locus standi* before international jurisdictions. Everything depends on the statute governing the tribunal or the *compromis* concerned. Whilst certain organizations have access to the International Court through its advisory jurisdiction, the Statute still confines *locus standi* to states (Art. 34).[44]

(f) Responsibility[45]

Organizations may have extensive functions involving the conclusion of treaties, the administration of territory, the use of armed forces, and the provision of technical assistance. If an organization has a legal personality distinct from that of the member states, and functions which in the hands of states may create responsibility, then it is

---

[38] See El-Erian, *Yrbk. ILC* (1963), ii. 159 at 181–3; Eagleton, 76 Hague *Recueil* (1950, I), 369–72; Hardy, 37 *BY* (1961), 516–26; *Yrbk. ILC* (1967), ii. 218–19.

[39] ICJ Reports (1949), 181–4. Cf. *Jurado* v. *I.L.O.* (No. 1), ILR 40, 296.

[40] See Hackworth, p. 196, Badawi, p. 205, and Krylov, p. 217. Winiarski, p. 189, in general shared the views of Hackworth.

[41] Pescatore, 103 Hague *Recueil* (1961, II), 219–21, denies the capacity for the European Communities.

[42] Report of Fifth C'ee (Part II), Doc. A/5/725/Add.1, 11 June 1997.

[43] ICJ Reports (1949), 185–6; Bowett, *United Nations Forces*, pp. 151, 242–8; 448.

[44] See, on the whole question, Jenks, *The Prospects of International Adjudication* (1964), 185–224 (see also in 32 *Grot. Soc.* (1946), 1–41).

[45] García Amador, *Yrbk. ILC* (1956), ii. 173 at 189–90; Seyersted, 37 *BY* (1961), 420–3; 431, 473–5; Fitzgerald, 3 *Canad. Yrbk.* (1965), 265–80; Arsanjani, *Yale Journ. of World Public Order*, Vol. 7 (1981), 131–76; Bernhardt (ed.), *Encycl. of P.I.L.*, II (1995), Ginther, 1336–40; Sands and Klein, op. cit., 512–26; *Yrbk. ILC* (1967), ii. 219–20; ibid., (1975), ii. 87–91. See also the Western European Union Conv. of 1958; 7 *ICLQ* (1958), 568; Cmnd. 389; the UNGA Decl. on Outer Space, fifth principle, *supra*, p. 267; and Art. 6 of the Outer Space Treaty, *supra*, p. 267. See further the Report of Professor Higgins, *Annuaire de l'Inst.* Vol. 66, I (1995), 249–469; and the Resolution adopted in 1996, ibid., Vol. 66, II (1996), p. 445. The topic is on the agenda of the International Law Commission: see Gaja, First Report, A/CN.4/532, 26 March 2003; Second Report, A/CN.4/541; Third Report, A/CN.4/553; Fourth Report, A/CN.4/564, Add.1–2; Fifth Report, A/CN.4/583. See also the *Report of the International Law Commission, Fifty-eighth session* (2006), G.A. Off. Recs., *Sixty-first session*, Suppl. No. 10 (A/61/10), 246–92; and Report of the Commission, *Fifty-ninth session* (2007), G.A. Off.Recs., *Sixty-second session*, Suppl. No. 10 (A/62/10), 178–220. See also ILA, *Berlin Conference Report* (2004), 164–241.

in principle reasonable to impute responsibility to the organization. In a very general way this follows from the reasoning of the Court in the *Reparation* case. However, regard must be had to each set of circumstances. In relation to the use of forces under the authority of the United Nations in peace-keeping operations, the general principle is that the issue of financial responsibility is determined by the relevant agreements between governments contributing forces and the United Nations,[46] and between the latter and the host state. There is no evidence of a presumption in law that the United Nations bears either an exclusive or a primary responsibility for the tortious acts of such forces, and the law remains undeveloped. In practice the United Nations has accepted responsibility for the acts of its agents.[47] However, in the case of more specialized organizations with a small number of members, it may be necessary to fall back on the collective responsibility of the member states. There is a strong presumption against a delegation of responsibility by a state to an organization arising simply from membership therein. Evidence must be sought of the intention of the states establishing the particular organ-ization. In certain cases the organization may be conceived of as creating risks and incurring liabilities in the course of its activities and as a vehicle for the distribution of costs and risks.[48] In adopting draft articles on the responsibility of international organizations for wrongful acts (on a first reading), the International Law Commission has accepted the view that member States cannot generally be regarded as responsible for the internationally wrongful acts of the organization.[49] At the same time it would be contrary to good sense if a State could avoid responsibility by creating an interna-tional organization.[50]

In the litigation pursued in the English courts as a consequence of the inability of the International Tin Council to meet its liabilities, the issues of public international law (for example, the question of the residual responsibility of the member states) were not faced head on and the decisions turned to an extent on the construction of the International Tin Council (Immunities and Privileges) Order in relation to matters essentially of English law.[51] However, in his Judgment in the Court of Appeal in the 'direct actions' by creditors against the member states Kerr, LJ, concluded 'In sum, I cannot find any basis for concluding that it has been shown that there is any rule of international law, binding upon the member states of the I.T.C., whereby they can be held liable, let alone jointly and severally, in any national court to the creditors of the

---

[46] See *Nissan* v. *A.G.* [1970] AC 179; LR 44, 359; for comment see 43 *BY* (1968–9), 217–26.

[47] See *Yrbk. of the United Nations* (1965), 138; Whiteman, xiii. 28; *M.* v. *Organization des Nations Unies et État Belge*, ILR 45, 446; *Yrbk. ILC* (1967), ii. 216–20.

[48] See: The European Launcher Development Organization; European Space Research Organization. See further the Conv. on Liability for Damage Caused by Space Objects, 1972, Art. XXII.

[49] See the Report of the Commission (2006), draft article 29, 286–91.

[50] See the European Court of Human Rights, *Waite and Kennedy* v. *Germany*, ILR 118, 121 at 135, para. 67. See further Brownlie, *Essays in Memory of Oscar Schachter* (2005), 355–62; Sienho Yee, ibid., 435–54.

[51] *International Tin Council Appeals* [1988] 3 All ER 257, CA.

I.T.C. for the debts of the I.T.C. resulting from contracts concluded by the I.T.C. in its own name'.[52] The House of Lords agreed with this view.[53]

(g) Administration of territory

See Chapter 8, section 2.

(h) Right of mission[54]

The constituent instrument of an organization may expressly or by implication permit the sending of official representatives to states and other organizations. Though there is a similarity to the sending of diplomatic missions in state relations the analogy cannot be pressed very far.

(i) Recognition of states

See *supra*, Chapter 5, section 9.

4. INTERPRETATION OF THE CONSTITUENT INSTRUMENT: INHERENT AND IMPLIED POWERS[55]

The constitutional structure of an international organization involves a nice distribution of powers between the organization and the reserved domain of domestic juris-diction of member states, and also between the various organs of the organization itself. Considerable problems of interpretation may arise in two contexts. First, the issue may be faced before any action is taken. If a competent organ holds that action contemplated would be *ultra vires*, then procedures for amendment may be followed: in Article 235 of the European Economic Community Treaty the Council of the Community is given power to make appropriate provision. Secondly, the challenge to constitutionality may occur during the process of decision-making, or even after action has been taken, as was the case in the disputes within the United Nations over expenditure on the peace-keeping force placed in Egypt in 1956 and the United Nations operation in the Congo. Basically the problems are those of treaty interpretation, complicated by the fact that political organs may determine the conditions in

---

[52] Ibid., 307. Ralph Gibson, LJ, expressed a similar view (pp. 341–56). See also Nourse, LJ, pp. 326–34, who proposed a residual liability of the member states for debts not discharged by the ITC itself (p. 334).

[53] [1989] 3 WLR 969; ILR 81, 670: see Lord Templeman (at pp. 983–4) and Lord Oliver of Aylmerton (at pp. 1010–12). See also Higgins, *Liber Amicorum Ibrahim F. I. Shihata*, 443–8; and Marston, *ICLQ* 40 (1991), 403–24.

[54] See further Pescatore, 103 Hague *Recueil* (1961, II), 187–97; Seyersted, 34 *Acta Scandinavica* (1964), 21–4.

[55] See Bindschedler, 108 Hague *Recueil* (1963, I), 312–418; Vallat, 97 Hague *Recueil* (1959, II), 203–91; Hexner, 53 *AJ* (1959), 341–70; Lauterpacht, *The Development of International Law by the International Court* (1958), 267–81; Rosenne, *Comunicazioni e studi*, 12 (1966), 21–29; Amerasinghe, 65 *BY* (1994), 175–209; Bernhardt (ed.), *Encyclopedia*, II (1995), Zuleeg, 1312–14; Thirlway, 67 *BY* (1996), 20–8.

which an issue is adjudicated upon and the consequence of any judicial opinion on interpretation.

The International Court has applied the doctrine of implied powers in interpreting the United Nations Charter. In the *Reparation* case the Court observed in its Advisory Opinion[56] that 'the rights and duties of an entity such as the Organization must depend upon its purpose and functions as specified or implied in its constituent documents and developed in practice'. In practice the reference to implied powers may be linked to a principle of institutional effectiveness. Thus in the same Opinion[57] the Court stated: 'Under international law, the Organization must be deemed to have those powers which, though not expressly provided in the Charter, are conferred upon it by necessary implication as being essential to the performance of its duties'. The Court has also held that a capacity to establish a tribunal to do justice between the Organization and staff members 'arises by necessary intendment out of the Charter', there being no express provision in this regard.[58] Judicial interpretation may lead to expansion of the competence of an organization if resort be had to the teleological principle according to which action in accordance with the stated purposes of an organization is *intra vires* or at least is presumed to be.[59] The view has also been expressed that, when the issue of interpretation relates to the constitution of an organization, a flexible and effective approach is justifiable.[60] Obviously the judicial power of appreciation is wide, and the principles enunciated in this fashion may be used as a cloak for extensive legislation. The process of interpretation cannot be subordinated to arbitrary devices. Thus in his Dissenting Opinion in the *Reparation* case[61] Judge Hackworth observed: 'Powers not expressed cannot freely be implied. Implied powers flow from a grant of expressed powers, and are limited to those that are "necessary" to the exercise of powers expressly granted'. Moreover, where a particular issue calls for a measure of appreciation, a great deal must depend on the context and the interplay of various relevant principles. In the context of the United Nations Charter, the principles of implied powers and effectiveness may beg the very question at issue, and, in any case, such principles must be related to Article 2(1) of the Charter, which states that 'the

---

56   ICJ Reports (1949), 174 at 180.

57   At p. 182. See also the *International Status of South West Africa* case, ICJ Reports (1950), 128 at 136–8; the *Voting Procedure* case, ibid. (1955), 67; the *Petitioners* case, ibid. (1956), 23; and *South West Africa* cases (Prelim. Objections), ibid. (1962), 319 at 328–9, 331ff. On the *Namibia* Opinion of 1971 see *supra*, p. 517.

58   *Effects of Awards of Compensation made by the U.N. Administrative Tribunal*, ICJ Reports (1954), 47 at 56–7.

59   See the *Expenses* case, ICJ Reports (1962), 151 at 167–8, and *infra*, pp. 701ff. See also the Sep. Op. of Judge Fitzmaurice, ICJ Reports (1962), 204–5; id., 28 *BY* (1951), 7–8, 13–14; id., 33 *BY* (1957), 207–9. See further the *Namibia* Opinion, ICJ Reports (1971), 16 at 47–9, and esp. 52. See also ibid. 132 (Judge Petrén, Sep. Op.); 150, 163–4 (Judge Dillard, Sep. Op.); 184–9 (Judge de Castro, Sep. Op.); 223–4, 279–95 (Judge Fitzmaurice, Diss. Op.); 338–41 (Judge Gros, Diss. Op.).

60   Vallat, 97 Hague *Recueil* (1959, II), 249–50.

61   ICJ Reports (1949), at 198. See also the Diss. Op. of Judges Winiarski and Moreno Quintana in the *Expenses* case, ICJ Reports (1962), at 230, 245, respectively; the Joint Diss. Op. of Judges Spender and Fitzmaurice in the *South West Africa* cases (Prelim. Objections), ibid. 511ff.; and Judge Fitzmaurice, Diss. Op., *Namibia* case, ICJ Reports (1971), 281–2.

Organization is based on the principle of the sovereign equality of all its Members', and also to Article 2(7), which refers to the domestic jurisdiction of states. Particular care should be taken to avoid an automatic implication, from the very fact of legal personality, of particular powers, such as the power to make treaties with third states[62] or the power to delegate powers.[63]

5. RELATIONS WITH MEMBER STATES

(a) Decision-making

Decisions by international conferences and organizations can in principle only bind those states accepting them. Indeed, in the League of Nations decisions could only be taken on a basis of unanimity. Today the principle of majority decision is commonly adopted, and voting rules may vary considerably between various organizations and organs of the same organization.[64] In some bodies, such as the International Monetary Fund, weighted voting has been introduced, and in the United Nations Security Council the five permanent members have a voting privilege known as the 'veto'. The trend away from the principle of unanimity and other aspects of the existing voting systems create considerable problems of controlling the powers of organizations. The constitutional issues arising from disputes over interpretation of the basic instrument and decisions alleged to be *ultra vires* will be noticed later on.[65]

(b) Domestic jurisdiction[66]

The type of international co-operation undertaken through an organization and its constituent treaty will normally leave the reserved domain of domestic jurisdiction untouched. Action in pursuit of particular objects rests on the basis of agreement in the constituent instrument, and any administrative or executive measures or recommendations by organs of the organization relate to governments and, whilst perhaps creating obligations to take certain steps within the national jurisdiction, do not of themselves affect state organs within that sphere. Since the constitution of an organization usually defines its objects and powers with some care, an express reservation of domestic jurisdiction will not always be necessary. When the powers of the organization are extensive, as in the case of the United Nations, an express

---

[62] See Pescatore, 103 Hague *Recueil* (1961, II), 62; but see *Commission* v. *Council* [1971] CMLR 335; and see Akehurst, 46 *BY* (1972–3), 439 at 440.

[63] See Reuter, *Hommage à Président Basdevant*, p. 415 at pp. 426, 431–7; and *Meroni & Cie et al.* v. *The High Authority*, ILR 25 (1958, I), 369.

[64] See *Bowett's Law of International Institutions*, 5th edn. by Sands and Klein, 2001, pp. 261–96; Skubiszewski, 18 *Int. Organization* (1964), 700–805; Jenks, *Cambridge Essays*, pp. 48–63.

[65] *Infra*, pp. 665ff. These problems recur in relation to amendment of constitutional texts and apportionment of expenses of organizations. On the latter see Bowett, *The Law of International Institutions*, pp. 414–21.

[66] See generally *supra*, pp. 292–4; see also *infra*, on the relation of organizations to municipal law.

reservation occurs (Article 2(7) of the Charter). However, the Charter does not allow the reservation to affect the application of enforcement measures against states under Chapter 7.[67]

(c) Agency

By agreement between the states and the organization concerned, the latter may become an agent for member states, and others, in regard to matters outside its ordinary competence. Conversely, a state may become an agent of an organization for a particular purpose, for example, as an administering authority of a trust territory under Article 81 of the United Nations Charter.

(d) The law applicable[68]

An organization obviously enters into a variety of legal relations both on the international plane and with persons of private law within particular systems of municipal law. In principle the relations of the organization with other persons of international law will be governed by international law, including general principles of law, with the norms of the constituent treaty predominating when relations with member states of the organizations are concerned. When an issue arises from relations with persons of private law, the question may be regulated by a choice of law provision in a treaty which refers to a system of municipal law or to 'general principles of law'. Otherwise, everything will depend on the forum before which the issue is brought and the rules of conflict of laws applicable.

6. THE FUNCTIONAL CONCEPT OF MEMBERSHIP[69]

Whilst organizations are normally composed of states, a number of organizations have operated in effect a functional concept of membership compatible with their special purposes. Thus the Universal Postal Union is a union of postal administrations, the International Monetary Fund a union of currency areas, and the World Meteorological Organization a union of states and territories having their own meteorological service. In this type of membership regime dependent territories have a functional equality with sovereign states. However, in some organizations[70]

---

[67] On the relation of Art. 2(7) to action taken outside ch. 7, see Bowett, *United Nations Forces*, pp. 196–200, 282–3.

[68] On the related questions of the control of acts of organizations and the power of interpretation of constituent instruments see *infra*, pp. 698ff. On choice of law see Fawcett, 36 *BY* (1960), 321 at 336–40; Jenks, *The Proper Law of International Organizations* (1962); Seyersted, 122 Hague *Recueil* (1967, III), 434–624; Valticos, *Annuaire de l'Inst.* (1977), i. 1–191.

[69] See Fawcett, 36 *BY* (1960), 321 at 340–1; id., *The British Commonwealth in International Law* (1963), 229–31; Osieke, 51 *BY* (1980), 189–229.

[70] The ITU, WHO, IMCO, UNESCO, and FAO.

dependent territories are given 'associate' membership although in practice they may have an equality with other members. In accordance with resolutions of the General Assembly of the United Nations, prior to the achievement of statehood by Namibia, the UN Council for Namibia was accorded full membership in certain organizations (FAO and ILO) and associate membership in another (WHO), apparently in its capacity 'as the legal Administering Authority for Namibia'.[71]

7. RELATIONS WITH STATES NOT MEMBERS

The general rule is that only parties to a treaty are bound by the obligations contained in it, and this rule applies in principle to the constituent instruments of organizations of states. An exception to the rule appears in the Charter of the United Nations, Article 2(6) of which provides: 'The Organization shall ensure that States which are not Members of the United Nations act in accordance with the Principles so far as may be necessary for the maintenance of international peace and security'.

The exception[72] rests on the special character of the United Nations as an organization concerned primarily with the maintenance of peace and security in the world and including in its membership the great powers as well as the vast majority of states. Whilst third states are not in principle bound by the basic treaty of an international organization, the possession of legal personality by an organization may give rise to certain obligations on the part of non-member states under general international law. Thus an organization may possess a capacity to bring claims against both members and non-members.[73]

In the *Reparation for Injuries*[74] case the International Court, with little elaboration, regarded a power to bring claims against non-members of the United Nations as a sort of corollary of the power to do so in respect of member states. The Court produced a statement which represents an assertion of political and constitutional fact rather than a reasoned conclusion:

On this point, the Court's opinion[75] is that fifty States, representing the vast majority of the members of the international community, had the power, in conformity with international law, to bring into being an entity possessing objective international personality, and not

---

[71] See Herman, 12 *Canad Yrbk.* (1975), 306–22; Osieke, 51 *BY* (1980), 189–229.

[72] For the view that the provision does not bind non-members: Bindschedler, 108 Hague *Recueil* (1965, I), 404–6. For the more usual view, accecpted in the text: Kelsen, *The Law of the United Nations* (1951), 85–6, 106–10. The view, surely incorrect, is sometimes expressed that regional organizations can take enforcement action against non-members without the authorization of the Security Council (Art. 53(1)). On the selective blockade of Cuba in 1962, *inter alia* directed against the USSR, an extraregional power, see Campbell, 16 *Stanford LR* (1963–4), 160–76; Wright, 57 *AJ* (1963), 546–65; Giraud, 67 *RGDIP* (1963), 501–44; Nizard, 66 *RGDIP* (1962), 486–545. See also Akehurst, 42 *BY* (1967), 175–227.

[73] *Supra*, p. 682.

[74] ICJ Reports (1949), p. 174 at 184–5. See also the *Namibia* Opinion, ibid. (1971), 16 at 56.

[75] The only opposing view was that of Judge Krylov, at pp. 218–19.

merely personality recognized by them alone, together with capacity to bring international claims.

It is sometimes appropriate and necessary for courts, both national and international, to state propositions of this type. The difficulty which remains arises from the fact that the statement, being related to the setting up of the United Nations, a special case, provides no useful guide for other cases.

It has been suggested that a rule is forming according to which an organization as a legal person can expect the same immunities and privileges as a state,[76] but the general equation of the legal personality of organizations with that of states would be incautious. Certainly, third states may and do enter into agreements with organizations which are valid on the international plane.[77] It is also probable that a principle operates to the effect that constitutional limitations within the structure of the organization cannot be pleaded by the organization, or third states, as a justification for avoiding their mutual obligations.[78] Non-member states may also enter into relations with an organization by means of special missions and vice versa. However, the existence of a legal personality in an organization does not connote a whole range of legal capacities, and the constituent instrument remains the prime determinant of specific powers in the matter of relations with third states. This is particularly obvious when it is necessary to inquire to what extent, if at all, the agreements concluded by an organization bind the members of the organization also.

8. RELATION TO MUNICIPAL LAW[79]

An organization will necessarily enter into relations within particular systems of municipal law, both in the state in which the headquarters is sited and in the course of its activities there and elsewhere. The extent to which the particular system recognizes its legal personality will depend on the local law as modified by the obligations of any relevant agreement. Thus the Treaty of Rome provides (Art. 211) that the European Community shall be accorded legal capacity in each member state to the greatest extent accorded to corporate entities ('les personnes morales'). The effect of such provisions is of course dependent on the constitutional doctrine of each state on the incorporation of the agreements into internal law.[80] In the case of the International Civil Aviation Organization the Constitution makes no provision as to the precise

[76] Sørensen, 101 Hague *Recueil* (1960, III), 139.

[77] On the agreements between the International Bank and Switzerland, a non-member, see Broches, 98 Hague *Recueil* (1959, III), 374–84.

[78] See the *Expenses* case, ICJ Reports (1962), 151 at 168; the Sep. Op. of Judge Fitzmaurice, ibid., 199–200; and Seyersted, 34 *Acta Scandinavica* (1964), 32–40.

[79] See O'Connell, 67 *RGDIP* (1963), 26–9, 34; Skubiszewski, 2 *Polish Yrbk.*, pp. 80–108; Schreuer, 27 *ICLQ* (1978), 1–17. On the effect on validity of treaties of constitutional limitations within the legal systems of the parties, see *supra*, p. 589 and Broches, 98 Hague *Recueil* (1959, III), 387–408.

[80] *Supra*, pp. 44–5.

content of its legal personality, and as a consequence the status of the organization varies according to the uncoordinated municipal laws of the member states. To refuse all legal protection on state territory to personnel and assets of an organization may entail international responsibility quite apart from treaty obligations. Private law disputes relating to property or operations of the organization will be settled according to the principles of conflict of laws, apart from the effect of the jurisdictional immunity of the organization as defined by the relevant agreement, or, perhaps, arising from general international law.

In the case of the English courts a foreign entity will only be recognized as having legal personality if it has been accorded legal personality under the law of a foreign state recognized by the United Kingdom. An international organization will be accorded legal personality (and the capacity to sue) if it has been accorded the legal capacity of a corporation under the law of one or more of the member states or of the law of the state where it has its seat, if that state is not a member state.[81]

9. LAW-MAKING BY ORGANIZATIONS[82]

The varied roles played by organizations may be distinguished as follows:

(a) Forums for state practice

Statements on legal questions by governments through their representatives in organs and committees of organs provide evidence of customary law. So it is also with the voting on resolutions concerned with legal matters, for example the resolution of the General Assembly affirming the principles of the Nuremberg Charter.[83]

(b) Prescriptive resolutions

A resolution not in itself binding[84] may prescribe principles of international law and be, or purport to be, merely declaratory. However, the mere formulation of principles

---

[81] *Arab Monetary Fund* v. *Hashim (No. 3)*, [1991] 2 AC 114 at pp. 161 *per* Lord Templeman; *Westland Helicopters Ltd.* v. *A.O.I.* [1995] 2 WLR 126 at pp. 140–1 (Colman, J). See also Staker, 62 *BY* (1991), 433–7; 66 *BY* (1995), 491–6; and Marston, *ICLQ* 40 (1991), 403–24.

[82] Skubiszewski, 41 *BY* (1965–6), 198–274; id., *Recueil d'études en hommage à Guggenheim* (1968), 508–20; Waldock, 106 Hague *Recueil* (1962, II), 26–35, 96–193; Hahn, 108 Hague *Recueil* (1963, I), 226–34; Virally, *Ann. français* (1956) 66–96; Johnson, 32 *BY* (1955–6), 97–122; Sørensen, 101 Hague *Recueil* (1960, III), 91–108; Sloan, 25 *BY* (1948), 1–33; id., 58 *BY* (1987), 39–150; McMahon, 41 *BY* (1965–6), 1–102; Yemin, *Legislative Powers in the United Nations and Specialized Agencies* (1969); Buergenthal, *Law-Making in the International Civil Aviation Organization* (1969); Cheng, 5 *Indian Journ.* (1965), 23–48; Vignes, in Macdonald and Johnston (eds.), *The Structure and Process of International Law* (1983), 809–53; Skubiszewski, *Annuaire de l'Inst.* 69 (1985), 29–358; ibid. 69 (1987), ii. 65–126, 274–89 (Resol.).

[83] See further *supra*, p. 589.

[84] Thus resolutions of the UN General Assembly are recommendations creating prima facie no legal obligation. See, however, Judge Lauterpacht, Sep. Op. *South West Africa* case (Voting Procedure), ICJ Reports (1955), 67 at 118–19, 122; Skubiszewski, *ASIL Proc.* (1964), 153–62; and *Digest of US Practice* (1975), 85.

may elucidate and develop the customary law.[85] When a resolution of the General Assembly touches on subjects dealt with in the United Nations Charter, it may be regarded as an authoritative interpretation of the Charter: obvious examples are the Universal Declaration of Human Rights[86] and the Declaration on the Granting of Independence to Colonial Countries and Peoples[87] contained in resolutions of the General Assembly. Resolutions on new legal problems provide a means of corralling and defining the quickly growing practice of states, while remaining hortatory in form.[88]

(c) Channels for expert opinion

Organizations often establish bodies of legal experts in connection with projects for the codification or progressive development of the law, the most important being the International Law Commission of the United Nations General Assembly,[89] and, like governments, organizations have a staff of legal advisers from whom proceed expert and highly influential opinions.[90]

(d) Decisions of organs with judicial functions

Clearly decisions of judicial organs, such as the Court of Justice of the European Communities, may contribute to the development of the law of treaties, principles of interpretation, and general international law.[91] The specialized function of such bodies may of course limit their contribution to the latter.

(e) The practice of political organs

Political organs, and particularly the General Assembly and Security Council of the United Nations, make numerous recommendations and decisions relating to specific issues, which involve the application of general international law, or, where there is no identity of the two, the provisions of the Charter or some other constituent instrument. Such practice provides evidence of the state of the law and also of the meaning of texts, and has considerable legal significance.[92] However, as with the practice of states, the nature of the particular decision and the extent to which legal matters were considered must be examined before much legal weight is given to the decision. Futhermore, to give legal significance to an omission of an organ to condemn[93] is problematical, since this omission turns often on the political attitude of the majority

---

85 See *supra*, p. 14.

86 *Supra*, p. 559.

87 *Supra*, p. 579.

88 See the decl. of principles governing activities in outer space: *supra*, p. 255.

89 On which see *supra*, p. 31.

90 On the legal opinions of the UN Secretariat: Schachter, 25 *BY* (1948), 91–125.

91 See McMahon, 37 *BY* (1961), 320–50.

92 See Higgins, *The Development of Intenational Law through the Political Organs of the United Nations* (1963); id., 64 *AJ* (1970), 1–18; id., *Proc. ASIL* (1970), 37–48; and Schachter, 58 *AJ* (1964), 960–5. On the interpretation of the UN Charter by the organs see further *infra*, pp. 694–8.

93 See the statements by Higgins in 37 *BY* (1961), 269 at 319. Cf. Schachter, 59 *AJ* (1965), 168.

in the organ concerned. Moreover, many jurists regard the decisions of political organs in terms of the arithmetic of voting, the decisions being taken to represent the views of *n* states in the majority and their cogency being roughly on a scale *n* majority divided by *n* minority states. Obviously states cannot by their control of numbers of international organizations raise in some sense the value of their state practice by reference to the 'practice of organizations'.[94]

In certain instances a consistent and uniform interpretation by members of an organ placed upon a persistent practice, for example, in matters of voting, adopted *by that organ* will be opposable to *all* members provided that there is substantial evidence of general acceptance by members of the organization. On this basis in its Advisory Opinion in the *Namibia* case[95] the International Court rejected the South African argument that the key Security Council resolution was invalid since two permanent members had abstained. The consistent practice of the members of the Security Council had been to interpret such abstention as not constituting a bar to the adoption of resolutions in spite of the provisions of Article 27, paragraph 3, of the Charter which refer to the 'concurring votes' of the permanent members.

(f) External practice of organizations

Organizations may make agreements with member and non-member states and with other organizations, and may present international claims and make official pronouncements on issues affecting them. Subject to what has been said above about the need for care in evaluating acts of political organs, the practice of organizations provides evidence of the law.

(g) Internal law-making

Organizations have considerable autonomy in making rules on internal matters such as procedure and the relations of the organization and its staff. Resolutions of organs of the United Nations on questions of procedure create internal law for members. However, questions of internal powers, for example concerning budgetary control, have a delicate relation to issues as to external *ultra vires*, if budgetary approval were given to sums allocated for operations under resolutions alleged to be *ultra vires* the Charter as a whole.[96] The United Nations has developed a code of staff regulations and rules governing the conditions of service of its officials, and the General Assembly has established a United Nations Administrative Tribunal to adjudicate upon applications alleging non-observance of employment contracts of staff members of the Secretariat.[97]

---

[94] Cf. Sørensen, 101 Hague *Recueil* (1960, III), 100–1, 105–6. For views on the reliability of subsequent practice of organs in interpretation of the Charter see the Sep. Op. of Judges Spender and Fitzmaurice in the *Expenses* case, ICJ Reports (1962), at 187ff., 210ff., respectively, and Gross, 17 *Int. Organization* (1963), 1 at 14ff.

[95] ICJ Reports (1971), 16 at 22.

[96] See the *Expenses* case, *infra*, pp. 666–7.

[97] See Amerasinghe, *The Law of the International Civil Service*, 2 vols. (1988); id., *Documents on International Administrative Tribunals* (1989); *Effect on Awards of Compensation made by the UN Administrative Tribunal*, ICJ Reports (1954), 47.

10 CONTROL OF ACTS OF ORGANIZATIONS

(a) Responsibility under general international law

As we shall gather later, there is no compulsory system for review of the acts of organizations by bodies external to them. In this situation the controls, such as they are, are provided by general international law. The correlative of legal personality and a capacity to present international claims is responsibility.[98] Moreover, when creating institutions states cannot always hide behind the organization when its activities cause damage to the interests of states or other organizations. General international law provides criteria according to which an organization may be held to be unlawful in conception and objects, and, apart from this, particular acts in the law may be void if they are contrary to a principle of the *jus cogens*.[99]

(b) Internal political and judicial control

The question of control in practice turns on the powers of the executive and deliberative organs and the constitutional limitations under which these political organs are placed.[100] The divisions of competence between organs and the limits to the powers of the organization as a whole may be carefully drawn, and, as in the Charter of the United Nations, the obligations set out in the relevant instrument may be expressed to apply to the organization itself, and the organs.[101] Interpretation of the constituent treaty by organs is the general rule. In the United Nations Charter, reference to the International Court depends on the readiness of political organs to request an advisory opinion, and any opinion given is not necessarily acted upon subsequently. Similarly, with bodies like the International Monetary Fund, which is concerned with politically sensitive issues, judicial powers are conferred on the executive board or other executive organ and there is no provision for direct judicial control by a separate judicial organ.[102] In the *Namibia* Opinion[103] the International Court remarked that 'undoubtedly, the Court does not possess powers of judicial review or appeal in respect of the decisions taken by the United Nations organs concerned'. However, in the same Advisory Opinion the Court did consider the validity of acts of organs 'in the exercise of its judicial function and since objections have been advanced…'

Organs may produce an impressive and consistent case-law on points of interpretation. However, political organs may support constitutional developments which

---

[98] *Supra*, p. 655. See generally Klein, *La Responsabilité des Organisations internationales* (1998); Wellens, *Remedies against International Organisations* (2002); Dominicé, *Melanges Virally* (1991), 225–38.

[99] On this see *supra*, pp. 510–12.

[100] See generally Bindschedler, 108 Hague *Recueil* (1963, I), 312–418; and Hahn, ibid. 195–297.

[101] See the Charter, Arts. 2, 24(2), and 55.

[102] On the IMF see Fawcett, 36 *BY* (1960), 321–42. On the European Free Trade Association see Darwin, ibid. 354–9. On the International Bank, see Broches, 98 Hague *Recueil* (1959, III), 312–13. On the ILO, see Osieke, 48 *BY* (1967–7), 259–80.

[103] ICJ Reports (1971), 16 at 45. See further the *Tadic* case, Decision of 2 October 1995, 35 ILM (1996), 32; *Lockerbie* case (Preliminary Objections), Judgment of 27 February 1998, 37 ILM (1998), 587.

are distinctly controversial and regarded as *ultra vires* the organs by a minority of member states. The most obvious examples are the machinery created by the Uniting for Peace Resolution of the General Assembly of the United Nations in 1950 and the use of that machinery for the creation of a United Nations Emergency Force in 1956 to serve in Egypt. A minority of states contended that only the Security Council had the power to take enforcement action, and on this basis they refused to contribute to the expenses incurred in carrying out the operation in Egypt. A similar situation arose when the Security Council gave a mandate to the Secretary-General to organize forces for operations in the Congo (ONUC). There is no automatic recourse which can settle disputes on points of interpretation by members; individual states have no right to request opinions and minority opinion can be over-ridden. States in a minority may withdraw from the organization, acquiesce in what they regard as illegal operations, resist military forces acting under putative authority of the organization, or withhold financial contribution. The latter course was adopted in the cases of UNEF and ONUC, and eventually the General Assembly requested an advisory opinion from the Court.[104] Even at this juncture political control was prominent. The request was formulated in a manner calculated to narrow the issue somewhat artificially to the interpretation of 'expenses of the Organization within the meaning of Article 17, paragraph 2, of the Charter of the United Nations'. Moreover, the Court's opinion was sought retrospectively, long after the actions were authorized and enormous expenditure incurred.[105] As a general matter, the problems arising from the *ultra vires* acts of international organizations are far from being resolved, and in any case are not susceptible to resolution by means of simplified formulations.[106]

(c) External political control

Organizations usually lack external restraints, but exceptionally one organization may be made subordinate to another in one or more respects. Thus 'regional arrangements and agencies' are regulated in a general way by Chapter VIII of the United Nations Charter, and more particularly by Article 53(1), which provides that no enforcement action shall be taken by such arrangements or agencies 'without the authorization of the Security Council'.[107]

---

[104] On the *Expenses* case see further *infra*, p. 697. See also Fitzmaurice, Sep. Op., ICJ Reports (1962), 203–4; Winiarski, Diss. Op., at p. 232; and Bustamante, Diss. Op., at pp. 304–5. Similar issues arose when the General Assembly terminated the Mandate for South West Africa: see the *Namibia* Opinion, ICJ Reports (1971), 16. See also Waldock, 106 Hague *Recueil* (1962, II), 35–6; and cf. Fawcett, 33 *BY* (1957), 311–16.

[105] See Judge Basdevant, ICJ Reports (1962), p. 237.

[106] See generally E. Lauterpacht, *Cambridge Essays* (1965), 88–121; Cahier, 76 *RGDIP* (1972), 645, 659; Osieke, 48 *BY* (1967–7), 259–80; id., 28 *ICLQ* (1979), 1–26; id., 77 *AJ* (1983), 239–56; Furukawa, *Mélanges offerts à Paul Reuter* (1981), 293–314; Bernhardt, *Essays in Honour of Krzysztof Skubiszewski* (1996), 599–609.

[107] Cf. *supra* pp. 687–88.

(d) Direct judicial control[108]

Organizations are commonly given immunity on a functional basis from municipal law,[109] but policy may favour a different regime. Thus the International Bank is subject to suit in a member state by private legal persons but not by member states.[110] Direct judicial control of the acts of organizations by a specially created organ is rare, but it appears in a developed form in the European Court of Justice.[111] This Court has considerable powers of review in respect of acts of organs of the European Union on grounds of incompetence, violation of the relevant treaty or rules for its application, procedural irregularity, and *détournement de pouvoir*.[112] The European Community Treaty provides for a reference to a judicial organ of the question of compatibility with the basic treaty of an agreement at the stage of negotiation.[113]

(e) External rights of appeal

Some organizations, such as the Food and Agricultural Organization, rely on their own organs to decide disputes, but provide a right of appeal to an appropriate international court or arbitral tribunal.[114] Certain constituent treaties provide for recourse to arbitration.[115]

(f) Interpretation by advisory opinions *(and see para.* (b) *above)*

The General Assembly and Security Council of the United Nations, and the specialized agencies, have the power to request the International Court for advisory opinions.[116] Such requests must relate to the mandate of the organ or agency concerned.[117] This procedure has been described as involving 'indirect' judicial control of organizations, but this is misleading. The opinions are only 'advisory' it is true, but they are influential and may relate to matters of high controversy. Moreover, the opinions come from a body less closely integrated with the institution controlled than the judicial organ of the European Union, and thus the control is more 'external' in some measure.[118] The

---

[108] See generally on judicial control the proceedings of the Institute of International Law: *Annuaire de l'Inst.* 44, (1952), i. 224ff.; 45 (1954), i. 265ff.; 47 (1957), i. 5ff.; 47 (1957), ii. 274ff. Text of resol.: ibid. 476, 488; 52 *AJ* (1958), 105.

[109] *Supra*, p. 680.

[110] See Broches, 98 Hague *Receuil* (1959, III), 309.

[111] See McMahon, 37 *BY* (1961), 320–50.

[112] See Fawcett, 33 *BY* (1957), 311–16. Very simply, the term means the arbitrary exercise of a discretionary power.

[113] Art. 228 of the EC Treaty.

[114] See the FAO Constitution, Art. 17. On the interpretation of Art. 84 of the Chicago International Civil Aviation Convention see the *Appeal Relating to the Jurisdiction of the ICAO Council (India* v. *Pakistan)*, ICJ Reports (1972), 46.

[115] See the ITU Constitution, Art. 28(2); UPU Constitution, 1964, Art. 32; UPU General Regulations, Art. 126.

[116] *Infra*, p. 721.

[117] *Legality of the Use by a State of Nuclear Weapons in Armed Conflict* (Advisory Opinion), ICJ Reports (1996) 66.

[118] It is noteworthy that the specialized agencies have been reluctant to request advisory opinions: cf. Fawcett, 36 *BY* (1960), 321 at 327.

'direct' control of the Court of the European Union exists in a highly specialized political and legal context.

The supranational European institutions are not subject to 'external' judicial interpretation whilst the Charter of the United Nations is. Moreover, the International Court has been unwilling to refuse to give opinions on the ground that the issue was political.[119] In the *Expenses* case[120] the Court faced an issue on which members of the United Nations were completely divided, the constitutional basis for the use of armed forces in UNEF and ONUC.[121] The issue took the form of a request for an interpretation of Article 17(2) of the Charter, but in substance the obligations of members were in issue and not merely the budgetary competence of the General Assembly in making resolutions authorizing expenditure for the operations concerned. The Court pursued a policy of 'institutional effectiveness' and stated that 'when the Organization takes action which warrants the assertion that it was appropriate for the fulfilment of one of the stated purposes of the United Nations, the presumption is that such action is not *ultra vires* the Organization'.[122] The majority opinion held that the operations were in pursuance of the stated purposes and that member states were bound by the resolutions of the General Assembly authorizing the expenditure involved, which were 'expenses of the Organization' under Article 17(2). The reasoning of the Court has been subjected to cogent criticism by Gross.[123] The main points of criticism are as follows. The General Assembly can only make recommendations, yet the Court's view permits non-obligatory recommendations to result in binding financial obligations. This gives the General Assembly a supranational budgetary power denied to more closely integrated communities. Moreover, the presumption against *ultra vires* runs contrary to the principle of the sovereign equality of members and points to creation of 'a super state'.[124] As a matter of treaty interpretation, the Court's approach to Article 17(2) was open to grave doubt. Further, reference by the Court to the subsequent practice of organs as an aid to interpretation involved the use of evidence which did not unequivocally bear on the issues before the Court.[125] Many lawyers may warm to any decision which gives more power to the Organization, but the Organization is not an abstraction, and political alliances, however transient, may give direction to decisions of political organs. To speak of

---

[119] Fawcett, 36 *BY* (1960), 321 at p. 730.

[120] ICJ Reports (1962), 151; ILR 34, 281. For comment see Gross, 16 *Int. Organization* (1963), 1–35; Jennings, 11 *ICLQ* (1962), 1169–83; Simmonds, 13 *ICLQ* (1964), 854–98; Verzijl, 10 *Neths. Int. LR* (1963), 1–32; Bindschedler, 108 Hague *Recueil* (1963, I); 353–64; E Lauterpacht, *Cambridge Essays*, pp. 106ff.

[121] See generally Bowett, *United Nations Forces.*

[122] ICJ Reports (1962), 168. See also Judge Fitzmaurice, at pp. 204, 208; Morelli, at p. 223; Bustamante, Diss. Op. at p. 298. Another opinion concerning the issue of *ultra vires* is the *IMCO* case, ICJ Reports (1960), 150.

[123] 16 *Int. Organization* (1963), 1–35.

[124] Cf. ICJ Reports (1949), 179. See also ICJ Pleadings (*Expenses* case), 134, 403, 425; Winiarski, Diss. Op., ICJ Reports (1962), at 230, 232; Moreno Quintana, Diss. Op., at p. 248; Bustamante, Diss. Op. at pp. 302, 304–5.

[125] See Judge Spender, ICJ Reports (1962), 187ff.; Judge Fitzmaurice, pp. 210ff.; Winiarski, Diss. Op., at pp. 230–2.

'institutional effectiveness' or 'implied powers' is to beg a great many questions.[126] The issue in the case was both legal and political, and the choice before the Court involved large assumptions about the structure of the Charter. This type of judicial control does not settle the problem of reconciling major divisions between member states: indeed, the present opinion may have exacerbated a crisis which might have had a disastrous outcome but was settled by negotiation.[127]

The general issues presented by the *Expenses* case also attended the termination of the Mandate for South West Africa by a General Assembly resolution, consequential action by the Security Council and a request by the latter to the Court for an advisory opinion on the legal consequence for states of the presence of South Africa in South West Africa (Namibia) in defiance of the resolutions.[128] The view of the South African and French Governments presented to the Court was that the relevant resolutions of the General Assembly and Security Council were *ultra vires*. On this question the Court observed:[129]

Undoubtedly, the Court does not possess powers of judicial review or appeal in respect of the decisions taken by the United Nations organs concerned. The question of the validity or conformity with the Charter of General Assembly Resolution 2145 (XXI) or of related Security Council resolutions does not form the subject of the request for advisory opinion. However, in the exercise of its judicial function and since objections have been advanced the Court, in the course of its reasoning, will consider these objections before determining any legal consequences arising from those resolutions.

Nevertheless a significant minority[130] of judges preferred the principle that any relevant issue of law was a matter for the Court and accepted the corollary that the legal qualities of the basic resolutions could be relevant to the legal consequences of South African rejection of the resolutions. In short, if a political organ refers a matter to the principal judicial organ of the United Nations, the latter is entitled and, indeed, bound to act as such.[131]

---

[126] See Moreno Quintana, Diss. Op., at p. 245; 'Each organ has its due function. The implied powers which may derive from the Charter so that the Organization may achieve all its purposes are not to be invoked when explicit powers provide expressly for the eventualities under consideration'. See also Koretsky, Diss. Op., at pp. 272–4; and the views of Judges Hackworth, Spender, and Fitzmaurice cited *supra*, n. 55.

[127] The United States invoked Art. 19 of the Charter in consequence of the Opinion and for a whole session no voting took place in the General Assembly. See 4 *ILM* (1965), 1000.

[128] ICJ Reports (1971), 16. See further *supra*, p. 490.

[129] At p. 45 of the Opinion. See also pp. 71 (Judge Ammoun, Sep. Op.); 105 (Padilla Nervo, Sep. Op.); 180–2 (de Castro, Sep. Op.).

[130] See pp. 130–1 (Judge Petrén, Sep. Op.); 141–5 (Judge Onyeama, Sep. Op.); 151–2 (Judge Dillard, Sep. Op.); 301–4 (Judge Fitzmaurice, Diss. Op.); 331–2 (Judge Gros, Diss. Op.).

[131] See also the Advisory Opinion in the *Expenses* case, ICJ Reports (1962), 151 at 157. The issue was not raised in such a sharp form in the *Expenses* case in which the terms of the request for an opinion directly raised the issue whether expenditures had been validly authorized: see the *Namibia* case, p. 181 (Judge de Castro, Sep. Op.).

(g) Administrative tribunals

A number of organizations possess their own administrative tribunals to hear disputes concerning staff contracts.[132]

---

[132] The UN Administrative Tribunal and the ILO Tribunal serve a number of other organizations. See further Akehurst, *The Law Governing Employment in International Organizations* (1967). On the machinery for review of decisions of the UN Administrative Tribunal see Advisory Opinions on *Application for Review of Judgment No. 158*, ICJ Reports (1973), 166; *Application for Review of Judgment No. 273*, ibid. (1982), 325; *Application for Review of Judgment No. 333*, ibid. (1987), 18. Note, in particular, ibid. 107–9 (paras. 4–7) (Ago, Diss. Op.).

32

THE JUDICIAL SETTLEMENT OF INTERNATIONAL DISPUTES

1. PEACEFUL SETTLEMENT IN GENERAL

The settlement of disputes between states by judicial action is only one facet of the enormous problem of the maintenance of international peace and security. In the period of the United Nations Charter the use of force by individual states as a means of settling disputes is impermissible. Peaceful settlement is the only available means.[1] However, there is no obligation in general international law *to settle* disputes, and procedures for settlement by formal and legal procedures rest on the consent of the parties. The context of judicial settlement in international relations is thus very different to that of the function of municipal courts, and this type of settlement is relatively exceptional in state relations. The object of this chapter is to consider the technical problems involved in legal process between states. The large field of settlement by political means, including action by organs of international organizations, must be left on one side.[2] Yet it must not be thought that there is a complete divorce between the two approaches to settlement. Political organs, like the General Assembly and Security Council of the United Nations, may and often do concern themselves with evidence and legal argument, although the basis for action remains primarily political.[3] The General Assembly, in particular, has provided a useful forum for settling disputes although its work in this respect tends to be forgotten. So also governments conducting negotiations with a view to settling disputes commonly take legal advice, and confidential legal advice from specialist advisers to the executive may be weighty and reasonably objective.

---

[1] See the UN Charter, Arts. 2(3), 2(4), and 33.

[2] See chs. 6 and 7 of the UN Charter; Goodrich, Hambro, and Simons, *Charter of the United Nations* (3rd edn., 1969); Vallat, *Cambridge Essays* (1965), 155–77; Simma (ed.), *The Charter of the United Nations* (2 vols. 2nd edn., 2002); Conforti, *The Law and Practice of the United Nations* (1996).

[3] See Higgins, *The Development of International Law through the Political Organs of the United Nations* (1963); id., 64 *AJ* (1970), 1–18; Schachter, 58 *AJ* (1964), 960–5.

2. ARBITRATION[4]

In both national and international legal history, the mature judicial process develops out of relatively informal administrative and political procedures. International practice has long included negotiation, good offices, and mediation as informal methods of settling disputes.[5] Treaties establishing machinery for peaceful settlement frequently provide for these methods and also for conciliation. Conciliation is distinct from mediation and grew out of the commissions of inquiry provided for in the Hague Conventions for the Pacific Settlement of International Disputes of 1899 and 1907 and the commissions which figured in the series of arbitration treaties concluded by the United States in 1913 and 1914 (the Bryan treaties). Conciliation has a semi-judicial aspect, since the commission of persons empowered has to elucidate the facts, may hear the parties, and must make proposals for a settlement which, normally, do not bind the parties.

Before conciliation appeared as an established technique, the process of arbitration had long been a part of the scene, having the same political provenance. However, the practice of arbitration evolved as a sophisticated procedure similar to judicial settlement. Modern arbitration begins with the Jay Treaty of 1794 between the United States and Great Britain, which provided for adjudication of various legal issues by mixed commissions. The popularity of arbitration increased considerably after the successful *Alabama Claims* arbitration of 1872 between the United States and Great Britain.[6] In this early stage of experience arbitral tribunals were often invited by the parties to resort to 'principles of justice and equity' and to propose extra-legal compromises. However, by the end of the century, arbitration was primarily if not exclusively associated with a process of decision according to law and supported by appropriate procedural standards. In recent times the distinction between arbitration and judicial settlement has become formal. The contrasts are principally these: the agency of decision in arbitration would be designated 'arbitral tribunal',

---

[4] See generally Sohn, 108 Hague *Recueil* (1963, I), 9–113; id., 150 Hague *Recueil* (1976, II), 195–294; id., 23 *Virginia JIL* (1982–3), 171–89; Stuyt, *Survey of International Arbitrations, 1794–1970* (1972); ILA, *Report of the Fifty-Second Conference* (1966), 287–356; Whiteman, xii. 1020–152; Mosler and Bernhardt (eds.), *Judicial Settlement of International Disputes* (1974), 417–552; Verzijl, *International Law in Historical Perspective*, viii (1976), 161–323; Caflisch, *Ann, français* (1979), 10–45; Rousseau, v. 304–93; Gray and Kingsbury, 63 *BY* (1992), 97–134; Collier and Lowe, *The Settlement of Disputes in International Law* (1999). See also *Case Concerning the Arbitral Award of 31 July 1989*, ICJ Reports (1991), 53 at 68–9; Conference on Yugoslavia, Arbitration Commission, 4 July 1992, ILR 92, 194 at 197.

[5] On these, and on conciliation, see Hackworth, vi. 1–57; Rousseau, v. 257–71, 286–95; Merrills, *International Dispute Settlement* (3rd edn., 1998), 1–87; *Handbook on the Peaceful Settlement of Disputes between States*, (United Nations, New York 1992). On conciliation see further *Annuaire de l'Inst.* (1959), i. 5–130; Cot, *La conciliation internationale* (1968); David Davies Memorial Institute, *International Disputes: The Legal Aspects* (1972); Bowett, 180 Hague *Recueil* (1983, II), 185–90. See also the *Jan Mayen Continental Shelf Conciliation* (1981), ILR 62, 108. On commissions of inquiry: see Bar-Yaacov, *The Handling of International Disputes by Means of Inquiry* (1974); Bensalah, *L'Enquête internationale dans le règlement des conflits* (1976); Rousseau, v. 272–85; *Re Letelier and Moffitt*, ILR 88, 727 (Chile–U.S. International Commission).

[6] Award: Moore, *Arbitrations*, i. 653. Great Britain was required to pay 15,500,000 dollars.

'umpire';[7] the tribunal consists of an odd number, usually with national representatives (but this element may be present in standing courts); the arbitral tribunal is usually created to deal with a particular dispute or class of disputes; and there is more flexibility than there is in a system of compulsory jurisdiction with a standing court.[8]

3. PERMANENT COURT OF ARBITRATION[9]

Between 1900 and 1920 the Permanent Court of Arbitration was the major organization for arbitration. It was set up under the Hague Convention for the Pacific Settlement of International Disputes of 1899[10] and consists not of a court but of machinery for the calling into being of tribunals. There is the Permanent Administrative Council and the International Bureau, which acts as a secretariat or registry for the tribunals set up. The basis of the 'Court' is a panel of arbitrators to which parties may nominate a maximum of four persons. When parties to the Convention agree to submit a dispute to the Permanent Court of Arbitration, each appoints two arbitrators from the panel, and the four arbitrators select an umpire. Thus a tribunal is constituted only to hear a particular case. The Permanent Court of Arbitration has had a useful but hardly spectacular existence. Between 1900 and 1932 20 cases were heard, but no cases have been dealt with since then.[11]

4. CODES OF ARBITRAL PROCEDURE

Apart from provisions relating to the Permanent Court of Arbitration, the Hague Conventions of 1899 and 1907 contain a code of arbitral procedure which applies to tribunals created under the Permanent Court machinery or by other means unless the parties have agreed on special rules of procedure. In 1953 the International Law Commission adopted a draft Convention on Arbitral Procedure,[12] which did

---

[7] There is no fixed terminology, and judicial functions are carried out by agencies labelled 'mixed claims commission', or even 'conciliation commission' (as in the case of the Conciliation Commissions set up to hear claims arising under Art. 83 of the peace treaty with Italy, 1947).

[8] See the circular of the Secretary-General of the PCA of 3 Mar. 1960, 54 *AJ* (1960), 933.

[9] See the official publication: *Permanent Court of Arbitration: Basic Documents* (n.d.), Peace Palace, The Hague. The volume includes the Permanent Court of Arbitration Optional Rules for Arbitrating Disputes between Two Parties of Which Only One is a State (1992): see 32 *ILM* (1993), 572.

[10] Most states supporting the 'Court' became parties to the Conv. of 1899. The Conv. of 1907, which received few ratifications, was not radically different. See generally Hudson, *Permanent Court of International Justice 1920–1942* (1943), 6–36; Guyomar, *Ann. français* (1962), 377–90; François, 87 Hague *Recueil* (1955, I), 461–551; id., 9 *Neths. Int. LR* (1962), 264–72; Rousseau, v. 369–74.

[11] In recent years attempts have been made to revive interest in the PCA and several important arbitrations have had the benefit of P.C.A. facilities, e.g. *Larsen v. The Hawaiian Kingdom*, ILR 199, 566.

[12] See *Yrbk. ILC* (1953), ii. 201, 208; and A/CN.4/92, *Commentary on the Draft Convention on Arbitral Procedure* (1955).

not find favour with governments and was reformulated as a set of Model Rules on Arbitral Procedure.[13] The Model Rules were identified as a statement of customary international law by the Tribunal in the *Sharjah/Dubai Boundary Case*.[14] The object of the draft Convention was to provide for cases where the validity of awards is challenged on various grounds,[15] and also to safeguard the effectiveness of the obligation to arbitrate arising from agreement. A key issue in any agreement to arbitrate is the appointment of the arbitrators,[16] and especially the neutral member of a tribunal or commission. Treaties normally contain carefully drawn provisions on the appointment of the neutral member, but the relevant provisions in the peace treaties with Bulgaria, Hungary, and Romania of 1947 failed because failure by one side to appoint its own member of the tribunal rendered them inoperative.[17] This problem was considered by the International Law Commission at its fourth, fifth, and tenth sessions, and the material part of the provision finally adopted is as follows:[18]

2. If the tribunal is not constituted within three months from the date of the request made for the submission of the dispute to arbitration, or from the date of the decision on arbitrability, the President of the International Court of Justice shall, at the request of either party, appoint the arbitrators not yet designated. If the President is prevented from acting or is a national of one of the parties, the appointments shall be made by the Vice-President. If the Vice-President is prevented from acting or is a national of one of the parties, the appointments shall be made by the oldest member of the Court who is not a national of either party.

Critics of this provision regard it as in conflict with the principle of the autonomy of the parties in international arbitration and as creating a procedure halfway between arbitration and normal legal procedure.

5. JUDICIAL SETTLEMENT

It is not intended to draw a sharp line between arbitration and judicial settlement: the latter category can properly be applied to the work of any international tribunal settling disputes between states in accordance with rules of international law.

---

[13] *Yrbk. ILC* (1958), ii. 81. The Model rules were adopted by the UNGA in Resol. 1262 (XIII), 14 Nov. 1958. They are optional.

[14] See the Award, ILR 91, 543 (at 575).

[15] e.g. that the tribunal exceeded the powers conferred in the agreement to arbitrate. Cf. *Case Concerning the Arbitral Award by the King of Spain*, ICJ Reports (1960), 192.

[16] See Sohn, 108 Hague *Recueil* (1963, I), 60–81; Johnson, 30 *BY* (1953), 152–77.

[17] In a request for an adv. op. the General Assembly submitted the following question to the Court: 'If one party fails to appoint a representative to a Treaty Commission under the Treaties of Peace ... where that party is obligated to appoint a representative to the Treaty Commission, is the Secretary-General of the United Nations authorized to appoint the third member of the Commission upon the request of the other party to a dispute according to the provisions of the respective Treaties?' The court replied in the negative: *Interpretation of Peace Treaties* (Second Phase), ICJ Reports (1950), 221. The Court remarked (p. 229): 'It is the duty of the Court to interpret the Treaties, not to revise them'.

[18] *Yrbk. ILC* (1958), ii. 83; Art. 3. See also the European Conv. for the Peaceful Settlement of Disputes, 1957, 320 UNTS, 243, Art. 21.

Moreover, the more institutionalized types of jurisdiction developed historically from arbitral experience. Apart from the International Court of Justice, judicial settlement has included the activity of many *ad hoc* arbitral tribunals[19] and mixed commissions, and of specialized tribunals of a semi-permanent character,[20] including the United Nations Tribunal in Libya,[21] the United Nations Tribunal in Eritrea, the Supreme Restitution Court of the German Federal Republic,[22] the Arbitral Commission on Property, Rights, and Interests in Germany,[23] the Arbitral Tribunal and Mixed Commission for the Agreement on German External Debts,[24] the Property Commissions set up as a consequence of Article 15(a) of the Peace Treaty with Japan,[25] the Austrian–German Arbitral Tribunal,[26] the Iran–United States Claims Tribunal,[27] and the International Centre for Settlement of Investment Disputes between states and nationals of other states.[28] Two circumstances are paramount: (1) the existence of a dispute; and (2) decision by a tribunal which, in virtue of its source of authority, composition, immunity from local jurisdiction, and powers of jurisdiction, is international rather than national. The definition of

---

[19] See, in particular, the *Rann of Kutch Arbitration* (1968), ILR 50, 2; *Beagle Channel Arbitration* (1977), ILR 52, 93 (Award of 18 Feb. 1977); *Delimitation of the Continental Shelf* (UK and France), Decisions of 30 June 1977 and 14 Mar. 1978, ILR 54, 6 and 139; *Case Concerning the Air Services Agreement of 27 March 1946* (*US v. France*), ILR 54, 304; *Young Loan Arbitration*, ILR 59, 494; *Guinea/Guinea-Bissau Maritime Boundary Arbitration* (1985), 25 ILM (1986), 251; *Red Sea Islands Arbitration* (First Phase) (Award of 9 October 1998), ILR 114, 1; (Second Phase) (Award of 17 December 1999), ILR 119, 417; *Barbados and Republic of Trinidad and Tobago Maritime Boundary Arbitration* (Award of 11 April 2006).

[20] See generally *Ann. français*, 'Chroniques'; and International Law Reports (ed. Lauterpacht); Mosler and Bernhardt (eds.), *Judicial Settlement of International Disputes*, pp. 83–190, 285–416; Charney, Hague *Recueil*, 271 (1998), 104–382.

[21] See *Italy v. Libya*, ILR 22 (1955), 103.

[22] Conv. on the Settlement of Matters Arising out of the War and the Occupation of 1952, amended by the Paris Protocol, 1954, 49 *AJ* (1955), Suppl., pp. 69, 83. Cf. *Casman v. Herter*, 117 F. Supp. 285; ILR 28, 592; Application no. 235/56, *Year-book of the European Conv. on Human Rights* (1958–9), 256 at 288.

[23] Conv. on the Settlement of Matters Arising out of the War and the Occupation, 49 *AJ* (1955), Suppl., pp. 69, 113.

[24] Agreement on German External Debts, 27 Feb. 1953, 333 UNTS 3; Cmnd. 8781. See the *Young Loan Arbitration*, ILR 59, 494.

[25] Agreement of 1952; 138 UNTS 183. See ILR 29 and 30; and Summers and Fraleigh, 56 *AJ* (1962), 407–32.

[26] Austrian–German Property Treaty, 15 June 1957. See Seidl-Hohenveldern, *The Austrian–German Arbitral Tribunal* (1972).

[27] Claims Settlement Agreement (Declaration of the Government of Algeria), 19 Jan. 1981; 20 *ILM* (1981), 230. See the *Iran–US Claims Tribunal Reports*; Lillich (ed.), *The Iran–United States Claims Tribunal, 1981–1983* (1984); Mapp, *The Iran–United States Claims Tribunal: The First Ten Years 1981–1991* (1993); Aldrich, *The Jurisprudence of the Iran–United States Claims Tribunal* (1996); Brower and Brueschke, *The Iran–United States Claims Tribunal* (1998).

[28] Text of Conv. establishing the centre: 60 *AJ* (1966), 892 UK Arbitration (International Investment Disputes) Act 1966, Sched. See Lauterpacht, *Recueil d'etudes en hommage à Paul Guggenheim* (1968), 642–64; Delaume, 93 *JDI* (1966), 26–49; Broches, *Liber Amicorum for Martin Domke*, pp. 12–22; id., 136 Hague *Recueil* (1972, II), 331–410; Roulet, 22 *Ann. suisse* (1965), 121–54; Lalive, 51 *BY* (1980), 123–61.

a 'dispute' and the nature of a legal interest have been considered elsewhere.[29] The international character of the tribunal is a question of both its organization and its jurisdiction. A municipal tribunal may apply international law and when it does so is no longer *merely* an organ of the national system of law: but it is not acting independently of the national system, it is not settling issues between legal persons on the international plane, and its jurisdiction does not rest on agreement on the international plane.[30] *For the present purpose*, therefore, the municipal tribunal would not be an international tribunal. While the advisory jurisdiction of the International Court will be considered, what follows is concerned primarily with the problems of contentious jurisdiction in ordinary international claims. Again, commissions of inquiry set up by the International Labour Organization to investigate breaches of ILO conventions,[31] and decisions to permit waiver in the GATT system, have a judicial aspect.[32] In the 1994 Agreement Establishing the World Trade Organization, significant changes were made in the GATT dispute settlement procedure. Provision for settlement of disputes by arbitration appears in the constituent instruments of international organ-izations, such as the Universal Postal Union,[33] in commodity agreements, such as the International Coffee Agreement of 1968,[34] and in bilateral air transport agreements.[35]

The UN Convention on the Law of the Sea of 1982 established an International Tribunal for the Law of the Sea (ITLOS), which consists of 21 judges.[36] The Convention has created a permissive jurisdictional regime. Thus States may choose between the Tribunal, the International Court, and various types of arbitration. The only form of compulsory jurisdiction relates to deep seabed mining disputes arising under Part XI of the Convention. The Tribunal dealt with its first case in 1997.[37]

---

[29] *Supra*, pp. 467–72, 476–7.

[30] Cf. the Foreign Claims Settlement Commission in the United States and the Foreign Compensation Commission in the United Kingdom. See Lillich, *International Claims: Their Adjudication by National Commissions* (1962); id., 13 *ICLQ* (1964), 899–924; id., *International Claims: Postwar British Practice* (1967); the *Flegenheimer* claim, ILR 30, 532; Freidberg, 10 *Virginia JIL* (1970), 282–99; Weston, ibid. 223–81; Weston, *International Claims: Postwar French Practice* (1971); Lillich and Weston, *International Claims: Contemporary European Practice* (1982).

[31] *Supra*, pp. 554–5.

[32] General Agreement on Tariffs and Trade, Cmnd. 8048, Art. 23.

[33] Constitution, 1964, Art. 126. See also the Int. Telecommunications Conv., 1965, Art. 28(2), Annex 3.

[34] Art. 44; and see the arbitration reported in 8 *ILM* (1969), 564. See also the subsequent Agreements of 1976 and 1983.

[35] See Award, 1963, US–France; *RIAA* xvi. 5; 3 *ILM* (1964), 668; Adv. Op., 1965, *US–Italy*; *RIAA* xvi. 75; 4 *ILM* (1965), 974; Decision, 1978, *US–France*; RIAA xviii 417; ILR 54, 304.

[36] See Ranjeva, in Dupuy and Vignes (eds.), *Traité du Nouveau Droit de la Mer* (1985), 1105–67; Adede, *The System for Settlement of Disputes under the United Nations Convention on the Law of the Sea* (1987); Merrills, *International Dispute Settlement* (3rd edn., 1998), 185–93; Collier and Lowe, *The Settlement of Disputes in International Law* (1999), 84–90; Rosenne, 89 *AJ* (1995), 806–14; Guillaume, 44 *ICLQ* (1995), 854–5; Oda, ibid., 863–72.

[37] *M/V Saiga*, ILR 110, 736 (4 December 1997); *M/V Saiga (No. 2)* (Request for Interim Measures), ILR 117, 111 (11 March 1998); *M/V Saiga (No. 2)* (Admissibility and Merits), ILR 120, 143 (1 July 1999).

6. THE PERMANENT COURT OF INTERNATIONAL JUSTICE AND THE INTERNATIONAL COURT OF JUSTICE[38]

The 'World Court' is the label commonly applied to the Permanent Court of International Justice and the International Court of Justice, the latter appearing as a new creation in 1945 but being substantially a continuation of the earlier body. The Permanent Court began to function in 1922, but as a new standing tribunal it grew out of previous experience. Arbitral practice contributed to the development in two ways. Its positive influence shows in the similarity in certain respects between the Court and arbitral practice, viz., the institution of national judges,[39] the power to decide *ex aequo et bono*,[40] the use of special agreements to establish jurisdiction, and the application of some basic principles, for example, that in the absence of agreement to the contrary, an international tribunal has the right to decide questions of its own jurisdiction.[41] The negative influence was the more decisive, since criticism of the Permanent Court of Arbitration, to the effect that it was not a standing court and could not develop a jurisprudence, led to proposals for and a good measure of agreement on a draft Convention Relative to the Creation of a permanent Court of Arbitral Justice at the Second Hague Peace Conference in 1907. The Convention failed of adoption because of disagreement on the number of judges on the Court, some representatives requiring as many judges as there were states members of the Court.[42]

In 1920 the Council of the League of Nations appointed an advisory committee of jurists to prepare a draft Statute for a Permanent Court of International Justice.[43] The draft Statute sprang from three sources: the draft Convention of 1907, a proposal

---

[38] Generally see Rosenne, *The Law and Practice of the International Court 1920–1996* (1997); Guyomar, *Commentaire du règlement de la Cour internationale de justice* (2nd edn., 1983); Fitzmaurice, 29 *BY* (1952), 40–62; 34 *BY* (1958), 8–161; Hudson, *Permanent Court*; Gross, 65 *AJ* (1971), 253–326; Elias, *The International Court of Justice and Some Contemporary Problems* (1983); Jennings, *Essays in Honour of Roberto Ago* (1987), iii. 139–51; Oda, 244 Hague *Recueil* (1993-vii), 9–190; Schwebel, *Justice in International Law* (1994), 1–168; Guillaume, 44 *ICLQ* (1995), 848–54; Lowe and Fitzmaurice (eds.), *Essays in Honour of Sir Robert Jennings* (1996); Muller, Raic and Thuránsky (eds.), *The International Court of Justice* (1997); Bowett and Others, *The International Court of Justice: Process, Practice and Procedure* (1997); Collier and Lowe, *The Settlement of Disputes in International Law* (1999), 124–85; Jennings, 68 *BY* (1997), 1–63; Watts, *Max Planck Yrbk. of United Nations Law*, 5 (2001), 21–39; Brown, *A Common Law of International Adjudication* (2007).

[39] See *infra*, p. 710.

[40] See *infra*, p. 720.

[41] *Nottebohm* case (Prelim. Objection), ICJ Reports (1953), 111 at 119. See further *supra*, p. 19, for references to arbitral decisions in the practice of the Court.

[42] As 46 states were invited to the conference, there would be a tribunal of 46 judges, in three groups sitting at various periods: see Scott, 2 *AJ* (1908), 772–810; Hudson, *Permanent Court*, pp. 80–4. For the proposal for an International Prize Court in 1907 see Hudson, *Permanent Court*, pp. 71–9. On the not very successful Central American Court of Justice, which functioned from 1908 to 1918, see Hudson, *Permanent Court*, pp. 42–70; id., 26 *AJ* (1932), 759–86; Mosler and Bernhardt (eds.), *Judicial Settlement of International Disputes*, pp. 315–22.

[43] See Art. 14 of the League Covenant.

of neutral states for compulsory jurisdiction, and the Root–Phillimore plan for the election of judges, of which more subsequently. The draft Statute provided for compulsory jurisdiction, but in the Council and the Assembly of the League the great powers and their supporters were able to prevail in their opposition to this. In the Assembly, however, a weak compromise was agreed on in the form of the 'optional clause'.[44] As amended, the Statute came into force in 1921. A defect in the Statute was that it contained no provision for its own amendment and all changes required unanimous approval from the parties, a slow procedure. After the Second World War the Permanent Court could have been revived, but the committee seized of the problem at the San Francisco conference decided to create a new court, two important considerations being the dislike of bodies related to the League of Nations felt by the United States and Soviet Union, and the problem of amending the Statute if the old Court were to be related to the United Nations Organization.[45]

The new court has a much closer relation with the United Nations than the old had with the League. The Charter provides (Art. 92) that the International Court of Justice is 'the principal judicial organ of the United Nations', and all members of the latter are *ipso facto* parties to the Statute of the Court (Art. 93).[46] In substance if not in form, the new Court is a continuation of the old: the Statute is virtually the same; jurisdiction under instruments referring to the old Court has been transferred to the new;[47] and there is continuity in the jurisprudence of the Court. The new Statute contains provisions on its amendment (Arts. 69 and 70).

7. ORGANIZATION OF THE COURT[48]

The problem which merits particular notice is the appointment of judges,[49] the key point in the creation of a standing international tribunal in which states may have confidence. The Statute of the Court goes far towards maintaining the independence of judges once appointed. No member of the court may exercise any political or administrative function, or engage in any other occupation of a professional nature (Art. 16, para. 1), or act as agent or counsel in any case, or participate in the decision of a case with which he has previously been connected in some other capacity (Art. 17). Dismissal can only occur on the basis of the unanimous opinion of the

---

[44] *Infra*, p. 716.

[45] See Hudson, 51 *AJ* (1957), 569–73.

[46] On the relation to the United Nations see further *infra*.

[47] See *infra*, p. 714.

[48] In the remainder of the chapter, references to 'the Court' denote the functioning of the two Courts except where the context determines otherwise.

[49] See generally Lauterpacht, *The Function of Law in the International Community* (1933), 156–7, 202–41; Rosenne, *Law and Practice*, iii. 1097–1164; Guerrero, *Annuaire de l'Inst.* 44 (1952), ii. 439–52; Huber *et al.*, ibid. 45 (1954), i. 407–554, and ii. 60–106; Hambro, *Festgabe für Makarov* (1958), 141; Gross (ed.), *The Future of the International Court of Justice* (1976), in particular, pp. 377–441 (Rosenne).

other members of the Court (Art. 18, para. 1). Members engaged on business of the Court have diplomatic privileges and immunities (Art. 19).[50] Salaries are fixed by the General Assembly and may not be decreased during the term of office and are free of all taxation (Art. 32).

However, the conditions governing the appointment of judges and the machinery of nomination and election are political in character. The membership of the Court cannot be equal to that of the United Nations, since it must have viability as a tribunal,[51] and yet its composition must be broad enough to give states sufficient confidence to resort to the Court. Before 1929 there was a Court of 11. The present Court has fifteen judges with partial or 'regular' elections of five judges every three years.[52] Article 2 of the Statute provides that 'the Court shall be composed of a body of independent judges, elected regardless of their nationality from among persons of high moral character, who possess the qualifications required in their respective countries for appointment to the highest judicial offices, or are jurisconsults of recognized competence in international law'. This formula takes in professors, professional lawyers, and civil service appointees: in practice many judges of the Court have been former advisers to national Foreign Ministries.[53] In other provisions of the Statute the question of nationality acquires significance. It is provided that no two members may be nationals of the same state (Art. 3, para. 1), and Article 9 requires electors to bear in mind 'that in the body as a whole the representation of the main forms of civilization and of the principal legal systems of the world should be assured'. The principle stated is unimpeachable, but it is difficult to translate into practice, and in any case the system of election ensures that the composition of the Court reflects voting strength and political alliances in the Security Council and General Assembly. The permanent members of the Security Council normally have judges on the Court. The judges are elected as individuals and do not represent their states of origin.

Nomination of candidates for election to the court (Statute, Arts. 4–7) is by the national groups of the Permanent Court of Arbitration:[54] members of the United Nations not so represented may create national groups for the purpose. Groups may and often do nominate persons of other nationalities.[55] The system of nomination is to ensure that independent persons are nominated. However, the national groups are themselves nominated by governments, and nominations are sent through Foreign

---

[50] See *Armand Ugon* v. *Banco Italiano del Uruguay*, 93 JDI (1966), 176.

[51] It has been suggested that the maximum allowing for viability and successful collective functioning is 17. Proposals to increase the number of judges were made in the United Nations in 1956–7: Schwelb, 64 AJ (1970), 880 at 882.

[52] Members may be re-elected. In the general election in 1946 the allocation of 3-, 6-, and 9-year terms was settled by lot. The quorum is 9.

[53] See the *ICJ Yearbook* for biographical notes on the judges. See also Fitzmaurice, *Livre du Centenaire, 1873–1973* (Institut de droit international) (1973), 286–90.

[54] Cf. *supra*, p. 703.

[55] Art. 6 provides: 'Before making these nominations, each national group is recommended to consult its highest court of justice, its legal faculties and schools of law, and its national academies and national sections of international academies devoted to the study of law.' See Baxter, 55 AJ (1961), 445.

Ministries. In spite of criticism the system of indirect nomination, as opposed to direct nomination by governments, was maintained in the new Statute of 1945.

The system of election is based on the Root–Phillimore plan of 1920 and involves independent, simultaneous, voting by the Security Council and the General Assembly. States which are parties to the Statute of the Court but not members of the United Nations are permitted[56] to take part in the procedures of nomination and election: for elections the General Assembly is thus specially augmented. Candidates must obtain an absolute majority in both organs to be elected (Art. 10 of the Statute). In practice the Security Council and General Assembly do not vote independently, and more or less discreet consultation occurs.[57] In post-war elections political calculations have been prominent, and the attitude of judges in particular cases has on occasion affected the voting when candidates have been presented for re-election.[58] The political basis for elections has been the object of adverse comment, particularly with regard to the post-1945 system of partial elections every three years, but it is difficult to see a way out: the political basis for elections would seem to be a condition of the Court's existence.

A further concession to the political conditions of the Court's existence is to be found in Article 31 of the Statute. This provides that a party to a case before the Court has a right, in effect, to representation on the Court by a national judge, and, if there is no judge of its nationality, a judge *ad hoc* may be appointed (who may be of some other nationality). The judge *ad hoc* is appointed by the party concerned and commonly supports its view of the case when on the bench. The institution is reminiscent of the national commissioners in *ad hoc* arbitral bodies and is justified if at all by expediency alone.

8. JURISDICTION OF THE COURT IN CONTENTIOUS CASES[59]

The court has jurisdiction in contentious cases between states,[60] on the basis of the consent of the parties. The Court has often referred to the fact that the jurisdiction of the Court to hear and decide a case on the merits depends on the will of the parties.[61]

---

[56] Resol. 264 (III), 8 Oct. 1948.

[57] For procedures to deal with deadlock, see Arts. 11 and 12 of the Statute. Informal consultation is used to obviate resort to a joint conference. See further Sørensen, pp. 700–1.

[58] For comment on particular elections: Hudson, 46 *AJ* (1952), 38–9; Simpson, 37 *BY* (1961), 527–35; Hogan, 59 *AJ* (1965), 908–12.

[59] See esp. Shihata, *The Power of the International Court to Determine its Own Jurisdiction* (1965); Fitzmaurice, 34 *BY* (1958), 8–138; Rosenne, *Law and Practice* ii. 517–984; Abi-Saab, *Les Exceptions préliminaires dans la procédure de la Cour internationale* (1967); Guyomar, *Commentaire du règlement de la Cour internationale de justice,* pp. 496–518; Thirlway, 69 *BY* (1998), 1–83; 70 *BY* (1999), 3–63; 71 *BY* (2000), 73–90; 72 *BY* (2001), 37–211; 74 *BY* (2003), 7–114. On the use of the terms 'competence' and 'jurisdiction': Fitzmaurice, 29 *BY* (1952), 40–2; 34 *BY* (1958), 8–9.

[60] Art. 34, para. 1, of the Statute provides: 'Only states may be parties in cases before the Court.'

[61] See e.g. the *Anglo-Iranian Oil Co.* case, ICJ Reports (1952), at 102–3; and the *Monetary Gold* case, ibid. (1954), at 32. See further Fitzmaurice, 34 *BY* (1958), 66–97.

This principle, reflected in Article 36 of the Statute, rests on international practice in the settlement of disputes and is a corollary of the sovereign equality of states.[62] As it has been pointed out elsewhere,[63] the competence of a tribunal to deal with the merits of a claim may be challenged on a number of grounds. Objections to the jurisdiction strike at the competence of the tribunal to give rulings as to the merits or admissibility of the claim. An objection to the admissibility of a claim, for example on the grounds that local remedies have not been exhausted, involves a challenge to the validity of a claim distinct from issues as to jurisdiction or merits. Normally the question of admissibility can only be approached when jurisdiction has been assumed, and issues of admissibility, especially those concerning the nationality of the claimant and the exhaustion of local remedies, may be closely connected with the merits of the case. It is possible for cases to go through three phases, involving distinct proceedings concerned successively with preliminary objections to jurisdiction, preliminary objections to admissibility, and the ultimate merits of the case. In practice, the Court may join certain types of preliminary objection to the merits provided that 'the objection does not possess, in the circumstances of the case, an exclusively preliminary character' (Art. 79(7) of the Rules of Court, 1978). For example, objections to jurisdiction by reference to the concept of domestic jurisdiction, or the existence of a dispute before the date of acceptance of jurisdiction in an instrument excluding past disputes, involve issues which could not be pronounced upon without prejudging the merits.[64] Finally, the court may decline to exercise a jurisdiction which it has, or which may be found to exist in the given case, on grounds of judicial propriety.[65]

As a further preliminary, consideration must be given to the effects of becoming a party to the Statute of the Court.[66] States do not submit to the jurisdiction of the

[62] *Supra*, pp. 289ff. In their Joint Diss. Op. in the *South West Africa* cases (Prelim. Objections), ICJ Reports (1962), 319 at 473–4, Judges Spender and Fitzmaurice stated that the Court has a duty to be satisfied beyound a reasonable doubt that jurisdiction does exist.

[63] *Supra*, ch. 22.

[64] *Right of Passage* case (Prelim. Objections), ICJ Reports (1957), 125 at 149–52. See also Rosenne, *Law and Practice*, pp. 464–6; Fitzmaurice, 34 *BY* (1958), 23–5; Lauterpacht, *The Development of International Law by the International Court* (1958), 113–15; Shihata, *Power of the International Court*, pp. 113–16; the *Barcelona Traction* case (Prelim. Objections), ICJ Reports (1964), 6 at 41–7; Morelli, Diss. Op., ibid. 97–115; ibid. (Second Phase), ICJ Reports (1970), 51; Bustamante y Rivero, Sep. Op., p. 57; Fitzmaurice, Sep. Op., pp. 110–13; Tanaka, Sep. Op., p. 115; Gros, Sep. Op., p. 268 n., Ammoun, Sep. Op., pp. 286–7; Riphagen, Diss. Op., pp. 356–7. In the *Interhandel* case (Prelim. Objections), ICJ Reports (1959), at 27–9, the Court refused to join an objection of non-exhaustion of local remedies to the merits: for comment see Jenks, *The Prospects of International Adjudication* (1964), 532–4; Shihata, *Power of the International Court*, pp. 279–82. See further on the relation of issues of admissibility and merits and also on the status of decisions on preliminary objections, the *South West Africa* cases (Second Phase), ICJ Reports (1966), 6 (see Cheng, 20 *Curr. Leg. Problems* (1967), 181 at 199–205); and the *Nuclear Tests* case (*Australia* v. *France*), ICJ Reports (1974), 253.

[65] See the *Cameroons* case, ICJ Reports (1963), 15; *supra*, p. 453.

[66] Art. 93(1) of the United Nations Charter provides that all members of the Organization are *ipso facto* parties to the Statute of the Court, and Art. 35(1) of the Statute states that the Court shall be open to parties to it. Art. 93(2) of the Charter provides that a state which is not a member of the United Nations may become a party to the Statute of the Court 'on conditions to be determined in each case by the General Assembly upon the recommendation of the Security Council.' Switzerland, Liechtenstein, San Marino, and Nauru have become parties under this provision.

Court as a result of signing the Statute, and some further expression of consent is required. On the other hand, states not parties to the Statute are not unconditionally barred from the Court.[67] Signature of the Statute, though it may not ground jurisdiction in the ordinary way, does have some important consequences. In the first place, without more, parties to the Statute are bound to accept the jurisdiction of the Court to determine its own competence (the *compétence de la compétence*): Article 36(6) of the Statute provides that 'In the event of a dispute as to whether the court has jurisdiction, the matter shall be settled by the decision of the Court.'[68] Secondly, the Statute in Article 41 supports a jurisdiction to indicate 'interim measures of protection' (or, 'provisional measures') to preserve the respective rights of the parties. Unless there are circumstances which make it apparent that there is no consent to the jurisdiction, the Court will assume the power to indicate such measures, without prejudice to the question of the jurisdiction of the Court to deal with the merits of the case.[69] In the *La Grand Case* (Germany v. United States of America)[70] the Court established that such interim measures are binding in character. Lastly, under Article 62 of its Statute the Court has power to permit third-party intervention in cases in which a state has an interest of a legal nature which may be affected by the decision in the case.[71]

9. HEADS OF JURISDICTION

(a) Matters specially provided for in the Charter of the United Nations

Article 36(1) of the Statute includes within the jurisdiction 'all matters specially provided for in the Charter of the United Nations'. These words were inserted during the drafting of the present Statute in the expectation that the Charter would contain

---

[67] Art. 35(2) of the Statute stipulates as follows: 'The conditions under which the Court shall be open to other states shall, subject to the special provisions contained in treaties in force, be laid down by the Security Council, but in no case shall such conditions place the parties in a position of inequality before the court.' In the *Corfu Channel* case (Prelim. Objections), ICJ Reports (1947–8), 53, Art. 35(2) was not regarded as exclusive in effect: see Rosenne, *Law and Practice*, pp. 278–84.

[68] See the *Nottebohm* case (Prelim. Objection), ICJ Reports (1953), 119–20, where the Court regarded this power as grounded in international law apart from any explicit provision in the Statute. See further Shihata, *Power of the International Court*; Fitzmaurice, 34 *BY* (1958), 25–31; Berlia, 88 Hague *Recueil* (1955, II), 109–54. On the power of the Court to determine the jurisdiction of another international tribunal see the *Ambatielos* case (Merits: Obligation to Arbitrate), ICJ Reports (1953), 10, and Fitzmaurice, 34 *BY* (1958), 31–66.

[69] *Anglo-Iranian Oil* case, ICJ Reports (1951), 89 at 92–3; *Nicaragua* case, Order of 10 May 1984; ICJ Re-ports (1984), 169 at 179–80. See further Shihata, *Power of the International Court*, pp. 179–80; Fitzmaurice, 34 *BY* (1958), 107–19; Lauterpacht, *Development*, pp. 110–13; the Joint Dissent of Winiarski and Badawi, ICJ Reports (1951), 96–8; and the Sep. Op. of Lauterpacht, *Interhandel* case, ICJ Reports (1951), 117.

[70] ILR 118, 37 (Order of 3 March 1999); Judgment on the Merits, 27 June 2001, paras. 98–109. See Thirlway, 72 *BY* (2001), 111–26; and Jennings, *The Law and Practice of International Tribunals* (2002), I, 13–54.

[71] On intervention under Arts. 62 and 63 of the Statute in general: Rosenne, *Law and Practice* iii. 1481–1555; Fitzmaurice, 34 *BY* (1958), 124–9; Elias, *Festschrift für Hermann Mosler* (1983), 159–72; Oda, *ibid*. 629–48; Chinkin, 80 *AJ* (1986), 495–531; id., *Third Parties in International Law* (1993), 147–217.

some provision for compulsory jurisdiction. Apart from a controversial construction of Article 36(3) of the Charter, no such provision was made. In the *Corfu Channel* case (Preliminary Objections)[72] the United Kingdom argued that Article 36(1) of the Statute could be referred to Article 36(1) and (3) of the Charter, which provide for reference of legal disputes to the Court on the recommendation of the Security Council; and, further, that a recommendation involved a decision which was binding in accordance with Article 25 of the Charter. The Court did not find it necessary to deal with the point, but in a joint separate opinion seven judges rejected the argument, *inter alia* on the ground that in its normal meaning the term 'recommendation' was non-compulsory.[73]

(b) Consent *ad hoc*: jurisdiction by special agreement and unilateral application

The consent of the parties may be given *ad hoc* to the exercise of jurisdiction over a dispute the existence of which is recognized by both parties. Normally, as in the *Minquiers and Ecrehos*[74] case between France and the United Kingdom, the consent will take the form of a special agreement (*compromis*). However, the special agreement is not an essential requirement of form, and the Court has taken the view that consent *ad hoc* may arise where the plaintiff state has accepted the jurisdiction by a unilateral application followed by a separate act of consent by the other party, either by a communication to the Court or by taking part in the initiation of proceedings.[75] In other words, the voluntary jurisdiction is not to be restricted by requirements of form, and Article 36(1) of the Statute states simply that 'the jurisdiction of the Court comprises all cases which the parties refer to it'.

(c) Consent *ante hoc*: treaties and conventions[76]

Article 36(1) of the Statute refers also to 'all matters specially provided for ... in treaties and conventions in force'.[77] A great many multilateral and bilateral treaties contain clauses granting jurisdiction in advance over classes of disputes arising from their

[72] ICJ Reports (1947–8), 15.

[73] Ibid. 31–2. Jurists generally agree with the Joint Sep. Op.: see Fitzmaurice, 29 *BY* (1952), 31–2, 44; Oppenheim, 7th ed. (1948), ii. 115. For a different approach: Rosenne, *Law and Practice*, ii. 692–5; Gross, 120 Hague *Recueil* (1967, I), 351–5.

[74] ICJ Reports (1953), 47. In this case a special agreement was employed, although the parties had both accepted jurisdiction under the optional clause (Statute, Art. 36(2)).

[75] *Corfu Channel* case (Prelim. Objections), ICJ Reports (1948), 27–8. See futher Hudson, *Permanent Court*, pp. 435–8; Fitzmaurice, 29 *BY* (1952), 43–4; id., 34 *BY* (1958), 79–80; Rosenne, *Law and Practice*, ii. 695–725.

[76] See Rosenne, *Law and Practice*, i. 332–5; *Ambatielos* case (Prelim. Objections), ICJ Reports (1952), 28 at 39; Briggs, in *Recueil d'études en hommage à Guggenheim*, pp. 628–41; Charney, 81 *AJ* (1987), 855–87.

[77] i.e., in force on the date of the institution of proceedings. Nor can a unilateral suspension of a treaty *per se* render jurisdictional clauses inoperative: *Appeal relating to the Jurisdiction of the ICAO council*, ICJ Reports (1972), 46 at 53–4.

subject-matter.[78] Although the jurisdiction is by the consent of the parties, like all types of jurisdiction in the present context, it can be described as 'compulsory' in the sense that agreement, in binding form, is given in advance of the appearance of particular disputes. However, the label 'compulsory jurisdiction' is often used to describe simply jurisdiction arising under Article 36(2) of the Statute.[79] In the *Nicaragua* case (Jurisdiction Phase)[80] the court (14 votes to 2) decided that jurisdiction existed by virtue of the Treaty of Friendship, Commerce and Navigation between the United States and Nicaragua of 1956.

(d) Transferred jurisdiction: Articles 36(5) and 37 of the Statute[81]

The Statute of the Permanent Court provided for jurisdiction on the basis of compromissory clauses in treaties or conventions, and when the Statute was redrafted in 1945 it was desired to save such clauses. Article 37 of the new Statute thus provides:

Whenever a treaty or convention in force provides for reference of a matter to a tribunal to have been instituted by the League of Nations, or to the Permanent Court of International Justice, the matter shall, as between the parties to the present Statute, be referred to the International Court of Justice.

Two limitations are prominent here: the treaty or convention must be 'in force' between the litigating states, and all the parties to the dispute must be parties to the new Statute. Article 37 has operated to support jurisdiction in the *Ambatielos* case (Preliminary Objection),[82] the *South West Africa* cases (Preliminary Objections),[83] and the *Barcelona Traction* case (Preliminary Objections).[84] The application of Article 37 to particular situations leads to a variety of difficult questions which are, however, incidental to the operation of Article 37 itself. An issue bearing directly on the effect of the article was highlighted by the *Aerial Incident* case (Preliminary Objections).[85] There the issue was the survival of a Bulgarian declaration of acceptance of jurisdiction under the optional clause (Statute, Art. 36(2)), made in 1921. Article 36(5) of the Statute of the present Court, drafted in 1945, provides:

Declarations made under Article 36 of the Statute of the Permanent Court of International Justice and which are still in force shall be deemed, as between the parties to the present

---

[78] On the drafting of compromissory clauses: Guggenheim, *Annuaire de l'Inst.* 45 (1954), i. 310–43; ibid. 46 (1956), 178–264.

[79] See the *Ambatielos* case, ICJ Reports (1952), at 39.

[80] ICJ Reports (1984), 392 at 426–9, See also Ruda (Sep. Op.), pp. 452–4; Schwebel (Diss. Op.), pp. 628–37.

[81] See Rosenne, *Law and Practice*, ii. 677–91; Fitzmaurice, 34 *BY* (1958), 137–8.

[82] ICJ Reports (1952), 28.

[83] Ibid. (1962), 319 at 334–5. Cf. the Joint Diss. Op. of Spender and Fitzmaurice, ibid., at pp. 469, 494–503, 505–6, 512–13; the Sep. Op. of Bustamante, pp. 367, 376–7; Sep. Op. of Jessup, pp. 415–16; the Sep. Op. of Mbanefo, pp. 437–8; the Diss. Op. of Van Wyk, pp. 613–15. See also the *Status of South West Africa* case, ICJ Reports (1950), 128 at 138.

[84] ICJ Reports (1964), 6.

[85] Ibid. (1959), 127. See Gross, 57 *AJ* (1963), 753–66.

Statute, to be acceptances of the compulsory jurisdiction of the International Court of Justice for the period which they still have to run and in accordance with their terms.

The Government of Israel, as plaintiff, argued that the effect of the declaration of 1921 was revived when Bulgaria again became a party to the Statute on joining the United Nations in 1955, as a consequence of Article 36(5). The majority of the Court interpreted the latter to apply only to states which were signatories of the 1945 Statute, prior to the dissolution of the Permanent Court, and not to a state in the position of Bulgaria, not a signatory, and becoming a party to the Statute many years later as an automatic consequence of admission to the United Nations.[86] The Court emphasized that a different construction would run counter to the principle that the jurisdiction of the Court is founded on the consent of states.[87] In a carefully reasoned joint dissenting opinion,[88] Judges Lauterpacht, Wellington Koo, and Spender interpreted Article 36(5) in a different way, taking the view that declarations, in regard to that provision, and treaties and conventions, in regard to Article 37, did not lose validity on the dissolution of the Permanent Court on 18 April 1946.[89] As a consequence of a formalistic approach to points of interpretation, the joint dissent reduces the consensual basis of the Court's jurisdiction in this context to a shadow. The problem left over was this: if the view in the joint dissent, that Articles 36(5) and 37 were to be treated alike, was correct, then the majority interpretation of 36(5) could be used to reduce the effect of Article 37. In the *South West Africa* cases (Preliminary Objections) the issue was not faced: the Court was influenced by the need to exercise effective supervision over a territory with a special status, and, in any case, the parties were all signatories of the Statute at San Francisco. But in the *Barcelona Traction* case the principal second preliminary objection of Spain raised the issue: Spain was not a party to the Statute before the dissolution of the Permanent Court in 1946. The court held that Article 37 could not be approached in this way and that the date on which the respondent became a party to the Statute was irrelevant.[90] The decision in the *Aerial Incident* case[91] was distinguished on the following grounds: (1) a different category of instrument was involved in Article 37; (2) the phrase 'in force' in Article 37 bore on the instrument containing the jurisdictional clause and not the clause; (3) the *Aerial Incident* case was *sui generis* and could have gone in favour of Bulgaria on other grounds. As a further reason for not following the *Aerial Incident* decision, the Court pointed out that a decision concerning Article 37 must affect a considerable number of treaties and general multilateral conventions.[92]

---

[86] See also the Sep. Op. of Badawi, p. 148. In the Sep. Op. of Armand-Ugon. p. 152, the view is taken that Art. 36(5) only applies to declarations of acceptance for a fixed term and not to declarations, such as that of Bulgaria in 1921, without a time limit.

[87] At p. 142 of the Judgment.

[88] p. 156.

[89] pp. 163, 166, 171, 180–2. See also Jessup, ICJ Reports (1962), 415.

[90] ICJ Reports (1964), 26–39. See also the *Nuclear Tests* case (*Australia* v. *France*), ibid. (1974), 332–3 (Joint Diss. Op.), 375–80 (De Castro, Diss. Op.).

[91] ICJ Reports (1959), 127. See also the *Temple* case (Prelim. Objections), ICJ Reports (1961), 17, distinguished in the present decision at p. 30.

[92] ICJ Reports (1964), 29–30.

On the plane of formal logic the distinctions offered are not in all respects impressive, and the Court would seem to have tempered consistency with expediency.[93]

In the *Nicaragua* case (Jurisdiction Phase),[94] the International Court held that the Nicaraguan Declaration of 1929 constituted a valid acceptance of the Court's jurisdiction by virtue of Nicaragua's ratification of the United Nations Charter (and automatic acceptance of the Court's Statute) in 1945, in spite of the fact that prior to this acceptance of Article 36, paragraph 5, of the Statute, the Declaration of 1929 had not acquired 'binding force'.

(e) Consent *ante hoc*: declarations under the optional clause[95]

Article 36(2) of the Statute, commonly referred to as the optional clause, provides as follows:

The States parties to the present Statute may at any time declare that they recognise as compulsory *ipso facto* and without special agreement, in relation to any other state accepting the same obligation, the jurisdiction of the Court in all legal disputes concerning:

(a) the interpretation of a treaty;

(b) any question of international law;

(c) the existence of any fact which, if established, would constitute a breach of an international obligation;

(d) the nature or extent of the reparation to be made for the breach of an international obligation.

Acceptance of jurisdiction is by means of unilateral declarations deposited with the Secretary-General of the United Nations, the declarant state being bound to accept jurisdiction *vis-à-vis* any other declarant so far as the acceptances coincide. In the *Nicaragua* case (Jurisdiction Phase),[96] the Court held that the conduct of Nicaragua constituted 'a valid mode of manifestation of its intent to recognise the compulsory jurisdiction of the Court under Article 36, paragraph 2, of the Statute'. On the principle of reciprocity, the lowest common factor in the two declarations is the basis for jurisdiction, and thus a respondent state can take advantage of a reservation or condition

---

[93] Spender and Wellington Koo did not discern any decisive distinction (pp. 47, 51–3). Spiropoulos considered that the *Aerial Incident* Judgment was decisive in the present case (p. 48). In his Sep. Op. Tanaka concluded that the present decision 'substantially overruled' the *Aerial Incident* decision (pp. 65–77): only by expressly overruling the previous decision could the Court have reconciled considerations of consistency with those of policy. In Diss. Ops. Morelli and Armand-Ugon (Judge *ad hoc*) held that Art. 37 ceased to operate after the dissolution of the Permanent Court (pp. 86–97, 134–59, respectively).

[94] ICJ Reports (1984), 392 at 397–411. For criticism of this reasoning see Mosler (Sep. Op.), pp. 461–3; Oda (Sep. Op.), pp. 473–89; Ago (Sep. Op.), pp. 517–27; Jennings (Sep. Op.), pp. 533–45; Schwebel (Diss. Op.), pp. 562–600.

[95] See Waldock, 32 *BY* (1955–6), 244–87; Briggs, 93 Hague *Recueil* (1958, I), 229–363; Rosenne, *Law and Practice*, ii. 727–836; Fischer Williams, 11 *BY* (1930), 63–84; Fitzmaurice, 34 *BY* (1958), 74–9; Crawford, 50 *BY* (1979), 63–86; Merrills, ibid. 87–116; Thirlway, 15 *Neths. Yrbk.* (1984), 97–138; Merrills, 64 *BY* (1993), 197–244. Merrills, *Liber Amicorum Judge Shigeru Oda*, Vol.1 (2002), 435–50; Orrego Vicuña, ibid., 463–79.

[96] ICJ Reports (1984), 392 at 411–13 (paras. 43–7). For criticism of this view see Ruda (Sep. Op.), pp. 458–60; Mosler (Sep. Op.), pp. 463–5; Oda (Sep. Op.), pp. 483–9; Ago (Sep. Op.), pp. 527–31; Schwebel (Diss. Op.), pp. 595–600.

in the declaration of the applicant state.[97] The independent declarations are binding in the senses that they can only be withdrawn in accordance with principles analogous to the law of treaties,[98] and operate contractually with a suspensive condition, viz., the filing of an application by a state with a coincident declaration.[99] This type of jurisdiction involves acceptance of jurisdiction in advance for categories of disputes which are usually mere contingencies. The commitment *ante hoc*, in relation to any other state fulfilling the conditions of the Statute, is usually described as a compulsory jurisdiction, although, as in the case of jurisdiction by treaty or convention, the basis is ultimately consensual. The basis of the optional clause lay in a compromise, first achieved in 1920, and maintained in the new Statute in 1945, between a system of true compulsory jurisdiction based on unilateral applications by plaintiffs, and jurisdiction based on treaties concluded independently. The expectation was that a general system of compulsory jurisdiction would be generated as declarations multiplied. The conception was sound enough, but the conditions in which the system has functioned have reduced its effectiveness. In 1934 there were forty-two declarations in force, the number reducing to thirty-two by 1955 but increasing since then.[100] The point is of course that since 1955 the figures represent a low proportion of the total of independent states (some 185 are parties to the Statute of the Court). The negative factors are principally the lack of confidence in international adjudication on the part of governments, the practice, accepted by the Court, of making declarations subject to various reservations and conditions, frequently arbitrary in extent and ambiguous in form, and the tactical advantages of staying out of the system.

Before the nature of certain of the conditions and reservations is examined, some general points must be made about the drafting of Article 36(2). In the first place, the paragraph refers to 'all legal disputes', whereas paragraph (1) refers to 'all cases' and 'all matters', an indication that the latter is not restricted to 'disputes'. However, both paragraphs involve the distinction between legal and political issues, and the distinction is less easy to maintain if no 'dispute' exists.[101] In spite of the reference to legal disputes in Article 36(2), some declarations state the limitation as a reservation. More important in practice is the condition of reciprocity in Article 36(2), expressed in the words 'in relation to any other state accepting the same obligation'.[102] This condition is a

---

[97] See the *Electricity Company of Sofia and Bulgaria* case (1939). Ser. A/B, no. 77, pp. 80–2; *Anglo-Iranian Oil Company* case, ICJ Reports (1952), 93 at 103; *Case of Certain Norwegian Loans*, ibid. (1957), 9 at 23–4; *Aegean Sea Continental Shelf* case, ibid. (1978), 3 at 37.

[98] See the *Nicaragua* case (Jurisdiction), ICJ Reports (1984), 392 at 415–21 (paras. 52–66). See also ibid., Mosler (Sep. Op.), pp. 466–7; Jennings (Sep. Op.), p. 547; Schwebel (Diss. Op.), pp. 620–8.

[99] The declarations are valid without ratification, but may be made subject to ratification. They are registered as 'international agreements' under Art. 102 of the Charter. On their interpretation: ICJ Reports (1952), 103. On the question whether two optional clause declarations are a form of treaty *inter se*: *Nuclear Tests* case (*Australia* v. *France*, ICJ Reports (1974), 352–6 (Joint Diss. Op.)).

[100] There are currently 65 acceptances.

[101] On the definition of a dispute: *supra*, pp. 476–7. On the important question of justiciability and the distinction between legal and political disputes *see* Lauterpacht, *Function*; Sohn, 108 Hague *Recueil* (1963, I), 41ff.; 76–81; Brownlie, 42 *BY* (1967), 123–43.

[102] This does not mean, as it could be taken to mean, that the declarations must be identical. Generally, on reciprocity, see Briggs, 93 Hague *Recueil* (1958, I), 237–68; Thirlway, 15 *Neths. Yrbk.* (1984), 97–138.

part of the Statute itself and applies to declarations expressed to be made 'unconditionally'. It follows that reservations as to reciprocity in acceptances are superfluous. Article 36(3), rather confusingly, refers to a condition of reciprocity which is optional and not a part of the Statute: declarations may contain a suspensive condition referring to acceptance of compulsory jurisdiction by other states. An important point is that reciprocity applies when a case is submitted to the Court and not before: thus in the *Right of Passage* case (Preliminary Objections)[103] India was unsuccessful in her contention that reciprocity applied so as to allow the respondent to take advantage of a reservation in the declaration of the applicant, Portugal, of a right to exclude any given category or categories of disputes, on notification to the Secretary-General. Portugal had filed her application only three days after depositing her declaration. In the *Nicaragua* case (Jurisdiction Phase) the Court held that the concept of reciprocity did not apply to the formal conditions upon which a state accepted the jurisdiction of the Court, such as the conditions for termination of the undertaking. Moreover, 'it appears clearly that reciprocity cannot be invoked in order to excuse departure from the terms of a state's own declaration ...'.[104]

Particular conditions and reservations met with require brief examination.[105]

(i) *Matters of domestic jurisdiction.* A plea that the issue concerned is a matter of domestic jurisdiction may appear as a preliminary objection or as a plea on the merits: strictly speaking the plea is available, apart from any reservation on the subject, in accordance with the general principles of international law.[106] One form of this reservation has created controversy. In 1946 the United States deposited a declaration with a reservation of 'disputes with regard to matters which are essentially within the domestic jurisdiction of the United States of America as determined by the United States of America', and seven other states have used this 'automatic' or 'peremptory' reservation.[107] In principle this form of reservation is incompatible with the Statute of the Court, since it contradicts the power of the Court to determine its own jurisdiction and is not a genuine acceptance of jurisdiction *ante hoc*.[108]

---

[103] ICJ Reports (1957), 125 at 143–4, 147–8.

[104] ICJ Reports (1984), 392 at 419–21 (and, in particular, para. 62). See also Mosler (Sep. Op.), pp. 465–8; Oda (Sep. Op.), pp. 510–12; Jennings (Sep. Op.), pp. 546–53; Schwebel (Diss. Op.), pp. 616–18, 625–8.

[105] For other reservations see Briggs, 93 Hague *Recueil* (1958, I), 296–308. Reservations as to reciprocity and legal disputes have been noted already.

[106] On the general question of domestic jurisdiction before international tribunals: *supra*, pp. 296–8. Many declarations, including the current UK declaration, contain no reservation concerning domestic jurisdiction.

[107] See generally Briggs, 93 Hague *Recueil* (1958, I), 328–63; Shihata, *Power of the International Court*, pp. 271–97; Gross, 56 *AJ* (1962), 357–82; Henkin, 65 *AJ* (1971). The other declarations with this reservation were those of France (1947), Mexico (1947), Liberia (1952), South Africa (1955), India (1956), Pakistan (1957), the Sudan (1958), Malawi (1966), Philippines (1972).

[108] The Court has avoided the issue when it has been raised, as in the *Case of Certain Norwegian Loans*, ICJ Reports (1957), 9; and the *Interhandel* case, ibid. (1959), 6. However, a number of judges have held the reservation to be illegal: see ICJ Reports (1957), 42ff. (Lauterpacht), 68–70 (Guerrero);

(ii) *Time-limits and reservations ratione temporis.*[109] Declarations may be expressed to be for a term of years, but some are expressed to be terminable after, say, six months' notice and some immediately on notice to the Secretary-General. While a power of termination immediately on notice weakens the system of compulsory jurisdiction, it would seem to be compatible with the Statute of the Court.[110] Indeed, the court has held that, in the absence of such a reservation, by analogy with the law of treaties notice of termination of a declaration may be given (provided a reasonable period of notice is allowed).[111] Once the Court is seized of a case on the basis of declarations in force at the date of an application, the subsequent expiry of a declaration of one of the parties does not affect the Court's jurisdiction in that case.[112]

(iii) *Reservation of past disputes.* Reservation of past disputes as a type of reservation *ratione temporis* is common, and the reservation may be taken further, as in the 'Belgian formula', which refers to all disputes arising after a certain date 'with regard to situations or facts subsequent to the said date'. Disputes often have a long history, and this formula is ambitious. In its jurisprudence the Court has taken the view that the limitation takes in only situations or facts which are the source, the real cause, of the dispute.[113]

(f) Consent *post hoc: forum prorogatum*[114]

Lauterpacht writes[115] that 'exercise of jurisdiction by virtue of the principle of *forum prorogatum* takes place whenever, after the initiation of proceedings by joint

---

ibid. (1959), 55–9 (Spender), 76–8 (Klaestad), 92–4 (Armand-Ugon), 97ff. (Lauterpacht). See also *Annuaire de l'Inst.* (1959), ii. 359 (Resol. 2); Guerrero, *Festschrift für Jean Spiropoulos* (1957), 207–12; Jennings, 7 *ICLQ* (1958), 355–63; Goldie, 9 *UCLA Law Rev.* (1961–2), 277–359; and Simmonds, 10 *ICLQ* (1961), 522–32. Juristic opinion is against the validity of the reservation: Oppenheim, 7th edn. (1948), ii. 62–3; Hudson, 41 *AJ* (1947), 9–14; Waldock, 31 *BY* (1954), 131–7; Briggs, 93 Hague *Recueil* (1958, I), 363; id., 53 *AJ* (1959), 301–18; Jennings, 7 *ICLQ* (1958), 355–63. Note, however, the careful analysis of Crawford, 50 *BY* (1979), 87–116.

[109] Generally on competence *ratione temporis*: Briggs, 93 Hague *Recueil* (1958, I), 269–95; Rosenne, *Law and Practice*, ii. 782–802.

[110] See the view of the Court on an analogous reservation in the *Right of Passage* case (Prelim. Objections), ICJ Reports (1957), 125 at 143–4. See further Briggs, 93 Hague *Recueil* (1958, I), 273–7.

[111] See the *Nicaragua* case (Jurisdiction Phase), ICJ Reports (1984), 392 at 418–20. See also ibid., Mosler (Sep. Op.), pp. 466–7; Jennings (Sep. Op.), p. 550, Schwebel (Diss. Op.), pp. 620–8.

[112] *Nottebohm* case (Prelim. Objection), ICJ Reports (1953), 111 at 122–3. See also Fitzmaurice, 34 *BY* (1958), 14–19.

[113] See the *Phosphates in Morocco* case, PCIJ, Ser. A/B, no. 74, pp. 23–4; *Electricity Company of Sofia and Bulgaria* case, ibid., no. 77, p. 82; *Right of Passage* case (Merits), ICJ Reports (1960), at 33–6. See further Briggs, 279–95.

[114] See Rosenne, *Law and Practice*, ii. 695–725; Shihata, *Power of the International Court*, pp. 128–35; Waldock, 2 *ILQ* (1948), 377–91; Lauterpacht, *Development*, pp. 103–7; Fitzmaurice, 34 *BY* (1958), 80–6; Stillmunkes, 68 *RGDIP* (1964), 665–86; Winiarski, *Festschrift für Jean Spiropoulos* (1957), 445–52; Thirlway, 69 *BY* (1998), 27–30; Sienho Yee, *Towards an International Law of Co-Progressiveness* (2004), 85–100.

[115] *Development*, p. 103.

or unilateral application, jurisdiction is exercised with regard either to the entire dispute or to some aspects of it as the result of an agreement, express or implied...'. The principle operates because the Statute and rules of court as interpreted contain no mandatory rules as to specification of the formal basis on which the applicant founds jurisdiction, nor as to the form in which consent is to be expressed. Consent may take the form of an agreement on the basis of successive acts of the parties, and the institution of proceedings by unilateral application is not confined to cases of compulsory jurisdiction. Thus, in the *Corfu Channel* case (Preliminary Objection),[116] after the United Kingdom had made a unilateral application, Albania accepted the jurisdiction in an official commun-ication to the Court. Informal agreement, agreement inferred from conduct, or a formal agreement, in each case *after* the initiation of proceedings, may result in prorogated jurisdiction. However, the Court will not accept jurisdiction unless there is a real, and not merely apparent, consent.[117] Resort to technical constructions in order to promote jurisdiction in particular cases may in the long run discourage appearances before the Court, and the judicial practice has not developed *forum prorogatum* as a true principle of estoppel. 'Automatic and compulsory' jurisdiction, in so far as it occurs at all, is confined to (1) instances in the practice of the Court where preliminary objections in fact independent of the merits are joined to the merits without the consent of both parties;[118] (2) the operation of Articles 36(5) and 37 prior to the dissolution of the Permanent Court and, on one view, subsequently;[119] (3) the competence to decide on matters of jurisdiction and similar powers based on the Statute.[120]

(g) Jurisdiction to decide *ex aequo et bono*[121]

Article 38(2) of the Statute gives the Court power to decide a case *ex aequo et bono* if the parties agree to this. This provision qualifies Article 38(1), which refers to the function of the Court as being to decide 'in accordance with international law' such disputes as are submitted to it.[122] The exercise of this power, which has not yet occurred, may not be easy to reconcile with the judicial character of the tribunal.

---

[116] ICJ Reports (1947–8), at 27. But the institution of proceedings was based on a special agreement.

[117] See the *Ambatielos* case, ICJ Reports (1952), 28 at 39; and the *Anglo-Iranian Oil Company* case, ibid. 93 at 114.

[118] See the Diss. Op. of Armand-Ugon in the *Barcelona Traction* case (Prelim. Objections), ICJ Reports (1964), 6 at 164. See also the Diss. Op. of Morelli, ibid. 97ff., on the entertainment of 'preliminary objections' inadmissible as such. On the effect of the *non ultra petita* rule on jurisdiction see Rosenne, *Law and Practice*, pp. 594–6; and Fitzmaurice, 34 *BY* (1958), 98–107.

[119] *Supra*, p. 714.

[120] *Supra*, p. 716.

[121] See Lauterpacht, *Development*, pp. 213–23; Fitzmaurice, 34 *BY* (1958), 132–7; Rosenne, *Law and Practice*, pp. 587–94.

[122] It seems also to qualify Art. 36(2), which refers to 'all legal disputes'. But under Art. 36(2) (and possibly 36(1)) the existence of a 'legal dispute' is a precondition for jurisdiction, on whatever basis the dispute is decided.

10. THE ADVISORY JURISDICTION OF THE COURT[123]

Article 65(1) of the Statute provides as follows: 'The Court may give an advisory opinion on any legal question at the request of whatever body may be authorized by or in accordance with the Charter of the United Nations to make such a request.' The Charter in Article 96 empowers the General Assembly and Security Council so to request, and provides that on the authorization of the General Assembly a similar power may be given to other organs and to specialized agencies.[124] The uses of the advisory jurisdiction are to assist the political organs in settling disputes and to provide authoritative guidance on points of law arising from the function of organs and specialized agencies. Thus some requests for opinions relate to specific disputes or situations, like those emanating from the League Council under the old Statute,[125] and the various opinions relating to South West Africa (Namibia);[126] and such requests involve use of political organs as an indirect means of seizing the Court of precise disputes. Other requests, as in the cases concerning the *Competence of the Assembly*[127] and *Reservations to the Genocide Convention*,[128] have involved fairly general and abstract questions. The origin of many requests in actual disputes, and the very nature of the judicial function, have given a contentious aspect to advisory proceedings. Thus Article 68 of the Statute provides that the Court shall be guided by the provisions applicable in contentious cases 'to the extent to which it recognizes them to be applicable'.[129] In the *Eastern*

---

[123] Hudson, *Permanent Court*, pp. 483–524; id., 42 *AJ* (1948), 15–19, 630–2; Rosenne, *Law and Practice*, ii. 985–1061; id., 39 *BY* (1963), 1–53; Lauterpacht, *Development*, pp. 107–10, 248–50, 352–8; Fitzmaurice, 29 *BY* (1952), 45–55; id., 34 *BY* (1958), 138–49; Greig, 15 *ICLQ* (1966), 325–68; Gross, 120 Hague *Recueil* (1967, I), 319–440; Keith, *The Extent of the Advisory Jurisdiction of the International Court of Justice* (1971); Pratap, *The Advisory Jurisdiction of the International Court* (1972); Pomerance, *The Advisory Function of the International Court in the League and U.N. Eras* (1973); Waldock, *Aspects of the Advisory Jurisdiction of the International Court of Justice* (1976); Reisman, 68 *AJ* (1974), 648–71; Rousseau, v. 420–7; Guyomar, *Commentaire du règlement*, pp. 641–92; Thirlway, 71 *BY* (2000), 91–144; Higgins, *Essays in Honour of Sir Robert Jennings* (1996), 567–81; Brower and Bekker, *Liber Amicorum Judge Shigeru Oda*, Vol.1 (2002), 351–68.

[124] Authorizations have been given to the Economic and Social Council, the Trusteeship Council, the Interim Committee of the General Assembly, the Committee on Applications for Review of the Judgments of the United Nations Adminstrative Tribunal, the various specialized agencies (with the exception of the Universal Postal Union), and the International Atomic Energy Agency. Agreements to which the United Nations or a specialized agency is a party may contain obligations to request and to accept advisory opinions: see Rosenne, *Law and Practice*, ii. 682–6.

[125] e.g. the case of *Nationality Decrees in Tunis and Morocco*, PCIJ, Ser. B, no. 4 (1923). The disputants here had not been able to agree on arbitration.

[126] Arising out of South Africa's refusal to recognize the international status of South West Africa as a territory under mandate.

[127] ICJ Reports (1950), 4. The issue was whether under Art. 4 of the Charter the General Assembly had a power to admit to membership unilaterally.

[128] ICJ Reports (1951), 15. Here the issue was the conditions under which reservations to multilateral conventions could be made.

[129] Art. 83 of the Rules of Court provides for appointment of judges *ad hoc* if the request concerns 'a legal question actually pending between two or more States'.

Carelia case[130] the Council of the League of Nations asked for an opinion on a dispute between Finland and the Soviet Union, the latter objecting to the exercise of jurisdiction, and the Court refused jurisdiction on the ground that the requesting organ was not competent to request an opinion in the circumstances: no state can be compelled to submit disputes to a tribunal without its consent, and the Soviet Union was not bound by the League Covenant. In the *Namibia*[131] and *Western Sahara*[132] cases the *Eastern Carelia* case was distinguished on the basis that the situations involved did not constitute a dispute: and in each case the political organ making the request for an opinion was concerned in the exercise of *its own* functions under the Charter of the United Nations, and not the settlement of a particular dispute.[133]

While there is no separate proceeding to deal with preliminary objections, as there is in contentious proceedings, and perhaps should be in advisory procedure, objections to the jurisdiction arise frequently and relate both to jurisdiction as such and to propriety. Objections to jurisdiction might involve the incapacity of the requesting body either *in limine*[134] or in relation to the subject-matter of the request, as where a plea of domestic jurisdiction is made.[135] In a recent case the Court held that the question put was not a question which related to matters 'within the scope of the activities' of the requesting organization (the World Health Organization).[136]

In practice objections have often challenged the power of the Court to deal with political questions. Article 65 of the Statute refers to 'any legal question', and the Court has taken the view that, however controversial and far reaching in their implications, issues of treaty interpretation, arising in the context of the United Nations Charter, are legal questions.[137] As the Court is unwilling to decline jurisdiction by adverting to the political implications of opinions, the issue then becomes one of propriety.[138]

---

[130] PCIJ, Ser. B, no. 5 (1923). The rule still holds, although in the *Peace Treaties* case, ICJ Reports (1950), 65, the Court distinguished the *Eastern Carelia* case, *inter alia* by emphasizing its duty to comply with the request of another organ of the United Nations. See Lauterpacht, *Development*, pp. 352–8; Shihata, *Power of the International Court*, pp. 121–3. See further Gross, 120 Hague *Recueil* (1967, I), 359–70.

[131] ICJ Reports (1971), 16 at 23–4.

[132] ICJ Reports (1975), 12 at 24–6.

[133] See further Waldock, *Aspects of the Advisory Jurisdiction*, 3–10.

[134] As in the *Eastern Carelia* case (*supra*) and the *Peace Treaties* case, ICJ Reports (1950), 65.

[135] See the *Peace Treaties* case, ibid. 70.

[136] Advisory Opinion on *Legality of the Use by a State of Nuclear Weapons in an Armed Conflict*, ICJ Reports (1996), 66. Judges Shahabuddeen, Weeramantry, and Koroma dissented.

[137] See the *Admissions* case, ICJ Reports (1948), 61; *Competence of the General Assembly*, ibid. (1950), 6–7; the *Expenses* case, ibid. (1962), 155. At the San Francisco conference it was decided not to grant a power to settle disputes on interpretation of the Charter: 13 UNCIO, 668–9, 709–10. See also *Genocide* case, ICJ Reports (1951), 20.

[138] Objections to the advisory jurisdiction do not always stress the distinction between propriety and jurisdiction. See further on the distinction between legal and political questions, ICJ Reports (1948), 69ff. (Sep. Op. of Judge Alvarez), 75ff. (Sep. Op. of Judge Azevedo), 94–5 (Judge Zoričić, Diss. Op.), 107–9 (Judge Krylov, Diss. Op.); ICJ Reports (1962), 249–52 (Moreno Quintana), 253–4 (Koretsky). A connected question raised in the *Expenses* case concerned the extent to which the requesting organ could limit the issues to be examined.

In the *Admissions*[139] and the *Expenses*[140] cases the Court concerned itself with issues of interpretation which had considerable political ramifications, and, significantly, the organs concerned were unable to act on these two opinions. In refusing to decline requests by virtue of its discretion in the matter of advisory jurisdiction, the Court has reiterated the view that as it is an organ of the United Nations a request for an advisory opinion should not, in principle, be refused.[141] Furthermore, the principle of the *Eastern Carelia* case, that the matter concerned a dispute between two states and jurisdiction could not be exercised without their consent, can be advanced as an issue both of jurisdiction and of propriety.[142]

11. AN EVALUATION OF THE COURT[143]

In the period 1922–46 the Permanent Court dealt with 33 contentious cases and 28 requests for advisory opinions; while from 1946 to 2007 the new Court has dealt with approximately 107 contentious cases[144] and 24 requests for advisory opinions. The tempo of resort to the Court has fluctuated since 1945, and acceptance of compulsory jurisdiction under the optional clause has been slow to develop. The following factors explain the reluctance of states to resort to the Court: the political fact that hauling another state before the Court is often regarded as an unfriendly act; the greater suitability of other tribunals and other methods of review for both regional and technical matters; the general conditions of international relations; and a preference for the flexibility of arbitration in comparison with a compulsory jurisdiction. Given the conditions of its existence, the Court has made a reasonable contribution to the maintenance of civilized methods of settling disputes, but it has not been at all

---

[139] *Conditions of Admission to Membership of the United Nations*, ICJ Reports (1947–8), 57. See also *Competence of the General Assembly*, ibid. (1950), 4; and Rosenne, 39 *BY* (1963), 39–42.

[140] ICJ Reports (1962), 151.

[141] See the *Peace Treaties* case (First Phase), ICJ Reports (1950), 71–2; *Reservations* case, ibid. (1951), 19; *Administrative Tribunal of the ILO*, ibid. (1956), 86; the *Expenses* case, ibid. (1962), 155. Cf. Fitzmaurice, 29 *BY* (1952), 53.

[142] See the *Peace Treaties* case, ICJ Reports (1950), 70–1. See further Gross, 121 Hague *Recueil* (1967, II), 355–70.

[143] See generally Mosler and Bernhardt (eds.), *Judicial Settlement of Disputes*; Gross (ed.), *The Future of the International Court of Justice*, 2 vols.; Dugard, 16 *Virginia JIL* (1976), 463–504; P. de Visscher, 136 Hague *Recueil* (1972, II), 178–202. Fitzmaurice, in *Livre du Centenaire* (Institut de Droit International) pp. 275–97; Rosenne, 20 *Israel LR* (1985), 182–205; Jennings, *International Courts and International Politics* (1986); Jiménez de Aréchaga, 58 *BY* (1987), 1–38; Lachs, 169 Hague *Recueil* (1980, IV), 226–31; id., 10 *Syracuse Journal of Int. Law and Commerce* (1983), 239–78; Damrosch (ed.), *The International Court of Justice at a Crossroads* (1987); Lowe and Fitzmaurice (eds.), *Fifty Years of the International Court of Justice: Essays in Honour of Sir Robert Jennings* (1996); Muller, Raic, Thuránsky (eds.), *The International Court of Justice* (1997); Jennings, 68 *BY* (1997), 1–63; Higgins, *ICLQ*, 50 (2001), 121–32.

[144] This figure does not include unilateral applications in which the applicant did not allege that the Court had jurisdiction but requested the Court to communicate the application to the other party: e.g. *Case Concerning the Aerial Incident of September 4th, 1954*, ICJ Reports (1958), 158.

prominent in the business of keeping the peace; indeed, the provisions of the United Nations Charter do not place emphasis on the role of the Court. In certain respects, however, the Court has been influential, viz., in the development of international law as a whole as a result of its jurisprudence and in the giving of advisory opinions on the interpretation of the United Nations Charter[145] and other aspects of the law of international organizations.[146] Assessment of its jurisprudence ought not to be based on facile generalizations, and characterization of a particular decision as conservative or radical must depend on the view taken of the relevant pieces of law. British writers have been critical of decisions like those in the *Fisheries*,[147] *Reservations*,[148] and *Nottebohm*[149] cases as being too radical, and, whether this be so or not, it is certain that the Court has developed the law as often as it has applied it. When, in its advisory opinions,[150] the Court has pronounced on the interpretation of the United Nations Charter, it has trenched boldly on political issues (which did not cease to be such because they were also legal issues) of the first magnitude.

The life of the Court in the last twenty years or so has been characterized by a variety of elements. In the first place, since 1980 the number of contentious cases taken to the Court has significantly increased, and this in spite of a number of disputes being referred to *ad hoc* courts of arbitration. Many of the new cases have been based upon special agreements (*Libya–Tunisia*;[151] *Gulf of Maine* case (*Canada–US*)[152] *Libya–Malta*;[153] *Burkina Faso–Mali*;[154] *United States–Italy*;[155] *El Salvador–Honduras*,[156] *Libya–Chad*;[157] *Hungary–Slovakia*; *Botswana–Namibia*; *Indonesia–Malaysia*; and *Malaysia–Singapore*). In this context, the new chamber procedure created by the Rules of Court adopted in 1978 has been utilized on four occasions (*Gulf of Maine* case; *Burkina Faso–Mali*; *El Salvador–Honduras*;[158] and the *Case Concerning Elettronica Sicula S.p.A. (ELSI)*).[159] However, the practice of resort to chambers involved various drawbacks and the market for this procedure has dwindled. There have also been

---

[145] *Reparation for Injuries* case, ICJ Reports (1949), 174; *Admissions* case, ibid. (1947–8), 57; *Competence of the General Assembly*, ibid. (1950), 4; *Voting Procedure* (South West Africa), ibid. (1955), 67; the *Expenses* case, ibid. (1962), 151; *Namibia* Opinion, ibid. (1971), 16.

[146] *Supra*, ch. 31.

[147] *Supra*, pp. 176ff.

[148] *Supra*, p. 613.

[149] *Supra*, p. 417ff.

[150] *Supra*, p. 721.

[151] ICJ Reports (1982), 18; and see also ibid. (1985), 192.

[152] Ibid. (1984), 246.

[153] Ibid. (1985), 13.

[154] Ibid. (1986), 554.

[155] Ibid. (1987), 3 (constitution of a Chamber of five judges).

[156] Ibid. (1987), 10 (constitution of a Chamber of five judges).

[157] Ibid. (1994), 6.

[158] See Zoller, 86 *RGDIP* (1982), 305–24; Schwebel, 81 *AJ* (1987), 831–54; Oda, 82 *AJ* (1988), 556–62.

[159] ICJ Reports (1989) 15.

cases begun by unilateral application[160] and a number of proceedings resulting from applications for permission to intervene in existing proceedings.[161] In recent years the Court has had a consistently full calendar of contentious cases.

[160] Cases begun by application in the recent past include *Nicaragua* v. *Honduras*; *Nicaragua* v. *Costa Rica* (discontinued); *Denmark* v. *Norway* (Maritime Delimitation between Greenland and Jan Mayen Island); *Iran* v. *United States* (Aerial Incident) (discontinued); *Libya* v. *United Kingdom* (Lockerbie); *Libya* v. *United States* (Lockerbie); *Iran* v. *United States* (Oil Platforms); *Spain* v. *Canada* (Fisheries); *Cameroon* v. *Nigeria* (Land and Maritime Boundary); *Pakistan* v. *India* (Aerial Incident); *Congo* v. *Uganda* (Armed Activities); *Congo* v. *Rwanda* (Armed Activities); *Nicaragua* v. *Colombia* (Territorial and Maritime Dispute).

[161] Fiji Application, ICJ Reports (1974), 530; Malta Application, ibid. (1981), 3; Italian Application, ibid. (1984), 3; El Salvador Declaration, ibid. (1984), 215; Nicaraguan Application, ibid. (1990), 92.

PART XIII

THE USE OR THREAT OF FORCE BY STATES

PART XIII

THE USE OR THREAT OF FORCE BY STATES

33

THE USE OR THREAT OF FORCE BY STATES

1. INTRODUCTION

The long history of just war in various cultural traditions must be sought elsewhere.[1] However, the current legal regime, which is based upon the United Nations Charter, can only be understood adequately in relation to certain antecedents, and these must be examined.

In the practice of States in nineteenth-century Europe, war was often represented as a last resort, that is, as a form of dispute settlement. However, the prevailing view was that resort to war was an attribute of statehood and it was accepted that conquest produced title. Thus, the conquest of Alsace-Lorraine by the German Empire was not the object of a policy of non-recognition either by France or by third States. Certain other aspects of nineteenth-century practice are worth recalling. In the first place, there was a somewhat nebulous doctrine of intervention, which was used, to a certain extent, in conjunction with coercive measures short of a formal 'State of war', such as reprisals or pacific blockade. This evasion was useful both diplomatically and to avoid internal constitutional constraints on resort to war.

The nineteenth-century practice is relevant to an understanding of the approach adopted by the League of Nations Covenant drawn up in 1919, the provisions of which essentially reflected nineteenth-century thinking. There were innovations, of course, and these took the form of procedural constraints on resort to war. But, provided the procedures foreseen in Articles 11 to 17 were exhausted, resort to war was permissible. This appeared to be the intention of the draftsmen in spite of the provisions of Article 10, according to which there was an obligation by members to respect and preserve as against external aggression the territorial integrity and existing independence of all members of the League.[2]

Independently of the League Covenant, certain groups of States were concerned to establish the illegality of conquest. A recommendation of the International Conference

---

[1] See generally Brownlie, *International Law and the Use of Force by States* (1963), 3–50. On the European theories see Russell, *The Just War in the Middle Ages* (1975); Sereni, *The Italian Conception of International Law* (1943).

[2] See Brownlie, *International Law and the Use of Force by States* (1963), 55–65.

of American States at Washington in 1890 contained the principle that cessions of territory made under threats of war or in the presence of an armed force should be void.[3]

The Sixth Assembly of the League adopted a resolution on 25 September 1925 which stated that a 'war of aggression' constituted 'an international crime', in accordance with a proposal of the Spanish delegation which had been studied in the First Commission. The report of the First Commission had noted that unhappily the principle that a war of aggression was an international crime had not yet entered positive law. At the Eighth Assembly a Polish proposal for a resolution prohibiting wars of aggression was adopted unanimously on 24 September 1927. Sokal, of Poland, stated that the proposal did not constitute a juridical instrument properly so called but had 'moral and educational' significance.

2. THE GENERAL TREATY FOR THE RENUNCIATION OF WAR (1928)

The more important development was the conclusion in 1928 of a legally binding multi-lateral treaty, the General Treaty for the Renunciation of War. The provisions were as follows:

Article I. The High Contracting Parties solemnly declare in the names of their respective peoples that they condemn recourse to war for the solution of international controversies, and renounce it as an instrument of national policy in their relations with one another.

Article II. The High Contracting Parties agree that the settlement or solution of all disputes or conflicts of whatever nature or of whatever origin they may be, which may arise among them, shall never be sought except by pacific means.

This instrument has been ratified or adhered to by 63 States and is still in force. It contains no provision for renunciation or lapse. The treaty was of almost universal obligation since only four States in international society as it existed before the Second World War were not bound by its provisions.[4]

The General Treaty, often referred to as the Kellogg-Briand Pact, constituted the background to the formation of customary law in the period prior to the appearance of the United Nations Charter, and it is in this context that the Kellogg-Briand Pact comes into prominence as the foundation of the State practice in the period 1928 to 1945, including the prosecution case in the International Military Tribunals in Nuremberg and Tokyo. The Kellogg-Briand Pact, as interpreted by the parties, prefigures the legal regime of the Charter. There is, in fact, a degree of continuity between the practice of the period from 1928 to 1945 and the legal regime of the Charter.[5]

---

[3] Moore, *Digest* (1906), i, 292.
[4] See Brownlie, op. cit., 74–111.
[5] Brownlie, op. cit., 66–111, 216–50.

The principal parties to the Kellogg-Briand Pact made reservations, which were accepted by the other parties, relating to self-defence.[6] The regime which emerged includes the following elements:

First: the obligation not to have recourse to war for the solution of international controversies.

Secondly: the obligation to settle disputes exclusively by peaceful means.

Thirdly: the reservation of the right of self-defence and also of collective self-defence.

Fourthly: the reservation of the obligations of the League Covenant.

Thus, the Kellogg-Briand Pact, seen in its context and in relation to the practice of the parties, constituted a realistic and comprehensive legal regime.

In the period following the conclusion of the Pact, it played a considerable role in the practice of States. Thus, the United States invoked the Pact in relation to hostilities between China and the Soviet Union in 1929, again in 1931 in relation to the conflict between China and Japan, and also in the context of the Leticia dispute between Peru and Ecuador in 1933. The Pact continued to play a role until 1939, when, for example, the Pact was cited in the condemnation by the League Assembly of Soviet action against Finland.[7] The practice of the parties was not in all respects consistent, however, and the Italian conquest of Ethiopia was accorded recognition by a number of States, this recognition being rescinded in 1941. This was the legal regime which was the actual precursor of the United Nations Charter.

3. THE LEGAL REGIME OF THE UNITED NATIONS CHARTER[8]

The essentials of the legal regime just outlined reappear in the United Nations Charter brought into force on 24 October 1945. Article 2 thereof formulates certain principles which bind both the Organisation and its Members. The key provisions for present purposes are as follows:

3. All Members shall settle their international disputes by peaceful means in such a manner that international peace and security, and justice, are not endangered.

---

[6] Ibid., 235–47.

[7] Ibid., 75–111; and Hackworth, *Digest, VI*, 46, 51–2.

[8] Russell and Muther, *A History of the United Nations Charter* (1958); Simma, *The Charter of the United Nations: A Commentary*, 2 vols. (2nd edn., 2002); Pellet, *La Charte des Nations Unies* (1985); Brownlie, op. cit. See also Gardam, *Necessity, Proportionality and the Use of Force by States* (2004); Stürchler, *The Threat of Force in International Law* (2007); and the Chatham House Principles on Use of Force in Self-defence, *ICLQ*, 55 (2006), 963–72.

4. All Members shall refrain in their international relations from the threat or use of force against the territorial integrity or political independence of any State, or in any other manner inconsistent with the Purposes of the United Nations.

Article 2(4) has been described as 'the corner-stone of the Charter system'.[9]

Article 51 reserves the right of individual or collective self-defence 'if an armed attack occurs against a Member of the United Nations', and this is described as 'the inherent right'. At the Merits phase of the *Nicaragua* case it was recognized that this formulation refers to pre-existing customary law. In the words of the Court:

As regards the suggestion that the areas covered by the two sources of law are identical, the Court observes that the United Nations Charter, the convention to which most of the United States argument is directed, by no means covers the whole area of the regulation of the use of force in international relations. On one essential point, this treaty itself refers to pre-existing customary international law; this reference to customary law is contained in the actual text of Article 51, which mentions the 'inherent right' (in the French text the 'droit naturel') of individual or collective self-defence, which 'nothing in the present Charter shall impair' and which applies in the event of an armed attack. The Court therefore finds that Article 51 of the Charter is only meaningful on the basis that there is a 'natural' or 'inherent' right of self-defence, and it is hard to see how this can be other than of a customary nature, even if its present content has been confirmed and influenced by the Charter.[10]

It is reasonable to assume that the Court was referring in principle to the customary law existing in 1945, together with any subsequent developments.

The Charter regime presents some questions of interpretation. The first question concerns the formulation 'against the territorial integrity or political independence of any State'. Some writers have relied on this language to produce substantial qualifications of the prohibition of the use of force, and the United Kingdom employed this type of argument to defend the mine-sweeping operation to collect evidence within Albanian waters in the *Corfu Channel* case.[11] However, the preparatory work of the Charter is sufficiently clear and this phrasing was introduced precisely to provide guarantees to small States and was not intended to have a restrictive effect.[12] A further and particularly difficult issue of interpretation relates to the phrase 'armed attack' in Article 51. The present writer takes the view that 'armed attack' has a reasonably clear meaning, which necessarily rules out anticipatory self-defence, but this position calls for clarification. Since the phrase 'armed attack' strongly suggests a trespass it is very doubtful if it applies to the case of aid to revolutionary groups and forms of subversion which do not involve offensive operations by the forces of a State. Sporadic operations by armed bands would also seem to fall outside the concept of 'armed attack'. However, it is conceivable that a co-ordinated and general campaign by powerful bands of

---

[9] Brierly, *The Law of Nations* (6th edn., by Waldock, 1963), 414.
[10] ICJ Reports (1986), 94, para. 176.
[11] ICJ Reports (1949), 4.
[12] Brownlie, op. cit., 265–8.

irregulars, with obvious or easily proven complicity of the government of a State from which they operate, would constitute an 'armed attack', more especially if the object were the forcible settlement of a dispute or the acquisition of territory.[13]

The definition of armed attack had obvious importance in the *Nicaragua case*[14] where the complaint of Nicaragua and the counter-case assertions of the United States involved alleged support to the operations of irregular forces.

4. THE LEGALITY OF ANTICIPATORY OR PRE-EMPTIVE ACTION BY WAY OF SELF-DEFENCE AND THE PROVISIONS OF THE CHARTER

Article 51 of the Charter provides:

Nothing in the present Charter shall impair the inherent right of individual or collective self-defence if an armed attack occurs against a Member of the United Nations, until the Security Council has taken measures necessary to maintain international peace and security. Measures taken by members in the exercise of this right of self-defence shall be immediately reported to the Security Council and shall not in any way affect the authority and responsibility of the Security Council under the present Charter to take at any time such action as it deems necessary in order to maintain or restore international peace and security.

There is a long-standing controversy as to whether the Charter provisions definitively exclude the possibility of anticipatory self-defence. Much of the literature advocating the legality of such action relies upon two related propositions. The first proposition is that Article 51 of the Charter reserves a right of self-defence which exists in customary law: this view is reasonable in itself. The reference to customary law is important because on its face the text of Article 51 is incompatible with anticipatory action. Thus the partisans of anticipatory self-defence find it necessary to invoke customary law in order to seek to legitimate such action.

The second proposition is that the customary law concerned was formed in the nineteenth century and, in particular, as a result of the correspondence exchanged by the United States and Britain in the period from 1838 to 1842.[15] The cause of the exchange was the seizure and destruction (in 1837) in American territory by British armed forces of a vessel (the *Caroline*) used by persons assisting an armed rebellion in

---

[13] See Brownlie, op. cit., 278–9, 361.

[14] ICJ Reports (1986), 14.

[15] For the documents see Jennings, at 32 *AJ* (1938), 82–99. The problems presented by the activities of insurgent groups on the territory of a neighbouring State formed a major element in the *Case Concerning Armed Activities on the Territory of the Congo* (DRC v. Uganda), ICJ Reports, 2005. See further Okowa, 77 *BY* (2006), 203–55.

Canada. In protesting the incident the U.S. Secretary of State Daniel Webster required the British Government to show the existence of:

> ...necessity of self-defence, instant, overwhelming, leaving no choice of means, and no moment for deliberation. It will be for it to show, also, that the local authorities in Canada, even supposing the necessity of the moment authorised them to enter the territories of the United States at all, did nothing unreasonable or excessive; since the act justified by the necessity of self-defence, must be limited by that necessity, and kept clearly within it.

Lord Ashburton (for the British Government) in his response on 28 July 1842 did not dispute Webster's statement of principle. The formula used by Webster has proved valuable as a careful formulation of anticipatory self-defence but the correspondence made no difference to the legal doctrine, such as it was, of the time. Self-defence was then regarded either as synonymous with self-preservation or as a particular instance of it. Webster's Note was an attempt to describe its limits in relation to the particular facts of the incident.

The statesmen of the period used self-preservation, self-defence, necessity, and necessity of self-defence as more or less interchangeable terms, and the diplomatic correspondence was not intended to restrict the right of self-preservation which was in fact reaffirmed. Many works on international law both before and after the *Caroline* case regarded self-defence as an instance of self-preservation and subsequently discussed the *Caroline* under that rubric.

The reference to the period 1838 to 1842 as the critical date for the customary law said to lie behind the United Nations Charter, drafted in 1945, is anachronistic and indefensible. It is surely more appropriate to know the state of customary law in 1945 rather than 1842, and it is far from clear that in 1945 the customary law was so flexible. Since 1945 the practice of States generally has been opposed to anticipatory self-defence. The Israeli attack on an Iraqi nuclear reactor in 1981 was strongly condemned as a 'clear violation of the Charter of the United Nations' in Security Council Resolution 487 (1981) (adopted unanimously). The Bush doctrine, published in 2002, claims a right of 'pre-emptive action' against States who are seen as potential adversaries. This doctrine is applicable in the absence of any proof of an attack or even an imminent attack.[16] This doctrine lacks a legal basis, but it does have an historical parallel, the attack on Serbia by Austria-Hungary in 1914. When the United States Expeditionary Force began military operations against Iraq in March 2003, the letter to the Security Council of 20 March relied upon Security Council resolutions as the putative legal basis of the action, rather than the principles of general international law.[17]

---

[16] See the document: *The National Security Strategy of the United States of America*, White House, Washington, September 2002, 15; see Gray, *Chinese Journ. of I.L.*, 2 (2002), 437–47; and Farer, *AJ* 96 (2002), 359–64.

[17] See U.N.Doc.S/2003/351. See further the United Kingdom letter of the same date, which also places reliance exclusively upon Security Council resolutions: U.N.Doc.S/2003/350; and the similar Australian letter of the same date: U.N.Doc.S/2003/352. See also *ICLQ* 52 (2003), 811–14.

5. THE RIGHT OF COLLECTIVE SELF-DEFENCE (ARTICLE 51 OF THE CHARTER)

The right of collective defence was accepted in general international law prior to the appearance of the United Nations Charter but is now given express recognition in the provisions of Article 51 of the Charter.[18] It may be recalled that, in response to the Iraqi attack on Kuwait, Security Council Resolution 661 (1990) made express reference in the preamble to the 'inherent right of individual or collective self-defence, in response to the armed attack by Iraq against Kuwait'. In the *Nicaragua* case (Merits), the International Court indicated two conditions for the lawful exercise of collective self-defence. The first such condition is that the victim State should declare its status as victim and request assistance.[19] The second condition is that the wrongful act complained of must constitute an 'armed attack'.[20]

6. THE DEFINITION OF AGGRESSION

In 1974 the General Assembly adopted a resolution on the definition of aggression which provided as follows in the first three articles:[21]

Article 1

Aggression is the use of armed force by a state against the sovereignty, territorial integrity or political independence of another state or in any other manner inconsistent with the Charter of the United Nations, as set out in this definition.

Article 2

The first use of armed force by a state in contravention of the Charter shall constitute *prima facie* evidence of an act of aggression although the Security Council may in conformity with the Charter conclude that a determination that an act of aggression has been committed would not be justified in the light of other relevant circumstances including the fact that the acts concerned or their consequences are not of sufficient gravity.

Article 3

Any of the following acts, regardless of a declaration of war, shall, subject to and in accordance with the provisions of Article 2, qualify as an act of aggression:

  (a) The invasion or attack by the armed forces of a state of the territory of another state, or any military occupation, however temporary, resulting from such invasion

---

[18] See generally: Bowett, *Self-Defence in International Law* (1958), 200–48; Dinstein, *War, Aggression and Self-Defence* (3rd edn., 2001), 222–45; Gray, *International Law and the Use of Force* (2000), 120–43; Simma (ed.), *The Charter of the United Nations* (2nd edn., 2002), i, 802–3.

[19] ICJ Reports (1986), 14, 103–5.

[20] Ibid., 102–4, 110, 127.

[21] Rovine, *Digest of United States Practice in International Law 1974*, Dept of State, 696–8.

or attack, or any annexation by the use of force of the territory of another state or part thereof;

(b) Bombardment by the armed forces of a state against the territory of another state or the use of any weapons by a state against the territory of another state;

(c) The blockade of the ports or coasts of a state by the armed forces of another state;

(d) An attack by the armed forces of a state on the land, sea or air forces, marine and air fleets of another state;

(e) The use of armed forces of one state, which are within the territory of another state with the agreement of the receiving state, in contravention of the conditions provided for in the agreement or any extension of their presence in such territory beyond the termination of the agreement;

(f) The action of a state in allowing its territory, which it has placed at the disposal of another state, to be used by that other state for perpetrating an act of aggression against a third state;

(g) The sending by or on behalf of a state of armed bands, groups, irregulars or mercenaries, which carry out acts of armed force against another state of such gravity as to amount to the acts listed above, or its substantial involvement therein.

The final paragraph of this definition calls for some commentary. Such activity is characterized not as 'indirect aggression' but as an 'act of aggression'.

Moreover, the phrase 'or its substantial involvement therein' strongly indicates that the formulation extends to the provision of logistical support.[22]

The remaining Articles are as follows:

Article 4

The acts enumerated above are not exhaustive and the Security Council may determine that other acts constitute aggression under the provisions of the Charter.

Article 5

No consideration of whatever nature, whether political, economic, military or otherwise, may serve as a justification for aggression.

A war of aggression is a crime against international peace. Aggression gives rise to international responsibility.

No territorial acquisition or special advantage resulting from aggression are or shall be recognised as lawful.

Article 6

Nothing in this definition shall be construed as in any way enlarging or diminishing the scope of the Charter including its provisions concerning cases in which the use of force is lawful.

---

[22] The drafting history of para. (g) is examined in the Dissenting Opinion of Judge Schwebel in the *Nicaragua* case: ICJ Reports (1986), 341–6, paras. 162–71.

Article 7

Nothing in this definition, and in particular Article 3, could in any way prejudice the right to self-determination, freedom and independence, as derived from the Charter, of peoples forcibly deprived of that right and referred to in the Declaration on Principles of International Law concerning Friendly Relations and Cooperation among States in accordance with the Charter of the United Nations, particularly peoples under colonial and racist regimes or other forms of alien domination; nor the right of these peoples to struggle to that end and to seek and receive support, in accordance with the principles of the Charter and in conformity with the above-mentioned Declaration.

Article 8

In their interpretation and application the above provisions are interrelated and each provision should be construed in the context of the other provisions.

The definition was adopted by consensus and, as a consequence, contains a number of general provisos and loose ends. None the less, it constitutes a useful epitome of the law and is a form of State practice. The provisions on complicity in relation to the activities of armed bands and irregulars are of obvious relevance today. As Article 6 makes clear, the definition is without prejudice to the provisions of the United Nations Charter.

7. REGIONAL ARRANGEMENTS: CHAPTER VIII OF THE UNITED NATIONS CHARTER

Chapter VIII of the United Nations Charter, under the heading 'Regional Arrangements' provides (in part) as follows:

Article 52

1. Nothing in the present Charter precludes the existence of regional arrangements or agencies for dealing with such matters relating to the maintenance of international peace and security as are appropriate for regional action, provided that such arrangements or agencies and their activities are consistent with the Purposes and Principles of the United Nations.'

Article 53

1. The Security Council shall, where appropriate, utilise such regional arrangements or agencies for enforcement action under its authority. But no enforcement action shall be taken under regional arrangements or by regional agencies without the authorisation of the Security Council, with the exception of measures against any enemy State, as defined in paragraph 2 of this Article, provided for pursuant to Article 107 or in regional arrangements directed against renewal of aggressive policy on the part of any such State, until such time as the Organisation may, on request of the Governments concerned, be charged with the responsibility for preventing further aggression by such a State.

The Charter thus gives a certain constitutional role to regional arrangements.[23] The supposition behind both Articles is that these organizations will have a role which is complementary to that of the Security Council, both in respect of peaceful settlement of disputes and in respect of enforcement action under the authority of the Security Council. Such organizations currently include the Organization of American States, the Arab League, the African Union, the Organization for Security and Cooperation in Europe (OSCE), and the Organization of Eastern Caribbean States (OECS). In practice the Security Council has been pragmatic in accepting the status of organizations as regional arrangements for the purpose of using its powers to authorize enforcement action.

The important distinction is between the concept of a collective self-defence organization, which hinges on a member being the victim of an armed attack, and the looser concept of a 'threat to the peace of the region'. In the Cuban missile crisis the United States justified the blockade of Cuba on the basis of the provisions in the Inter-American Treaty of Reciprocal Assistance which related to the regional peace-keeping function, no doubt because the emplacement of Soviet missiles in Cuba did not constitute an 'armed attack'.[24]

8. THE UNITED NATIONS AS A SYSTEM OF PUBLIC ORDER

The analysis of the legal regime of the United Nations Charter presented thus far stands in need of completion. The design of the United Nations constitutes a comprehensive public order system. In spite of the weakness involved in multilateral decision-making, the assumption is that the Organization has a monopoly of the use of force, and a primary responsibility for enforcement action to deal with breaches of the peace, threats to the peace or acts of aggression. Individual Member States have the exceptional right of individual or collective self-defence. In the case of regional organizations the power of enforcement action is in certain conditions delegated by the Security Council to the organizations concerned.

Enforcement action may involve the use of force on behalf of the community against a State. However, the practice has evolved of authorizing peacekeeping operations which are contingent upon the consent of the State whose territory is the site of the operations. In recent history the roles of peacekeeping and enforcement action have on occasion become confused, with unfortunate results.[25]

---

[23] Simma, *Charter of the United Nations* (2nd edn., 2002), i, 807–95; Gray, *International Law and the Use of Force* (2000), 204–6, 233–6; Dinstein, *War, Aggression and Self-defence* (3rd edn., 2001), 268–73.

[24] See Akehurst, 42 *BY* (1967), 175–227.

[25] See Gray, *International Law and the Use of Force* (2000), 150–75.

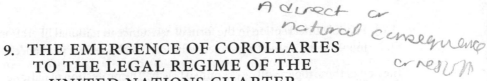

A direct or natural consequence or result

9. THE EMERGENCE OF COROLLARIES TO THE LEGAL REGIME OF THE UNITED NATIONS CHARTER

At this point, it is useful to look briefly at the crystallization of corollaries to the legal regime as it has developed. The corollaries include the following legal principles:

First: The principle of non-recognition of territorial acquisitions obtained by use or threat of force.[26]

Second: The principle that any treaty the conclusion of which was procured by the threat or use of force in violation of the Charter of the United Nations shall be void.[27]

These two principles are the most significant of the corollaries. There can be no doubt that the conclusion of the Kellogg-Briand Pact gave an impetus to the development of corollaries, particularly in the form of the Stimson doctrine of non-recognition formulated in 1932 in relation to the invasion of Manchuria by Japan.[28] The appearance of such corollaries is both significant in itself and provides evidence of the maturity and internal consistency of the legal regime.

The emergence of corollaries can be seen in the Vienna Convention on the Law of Treaties (1969), Article 52, dealing with the invalidity of treaties procured by coercion, and in the draft articles on State Responsibility produced by the International Law Commission in 2001.

10. SOURCES OF CONTROVERSY SINCE 1945

It is now time to return to the examination of the general structure of the legal regime. In the period since the adoption of the United Nations Charter in 1945 there were four significant sources of controversy in the rather tidy legal regime presented thus far in this Chapter.

These sources of controversy were as follows:

(a) The alleged right of forcible intervention to protect nationals:

(b) Hegemonial intervention on the basis of regional arrangements in the absence of explicit Security Council authorisation.

(c) Forcible intervention in a State on the basis of consent of the territorial sovereign; and

---

[26] See Brownlie, op. cit., 410–23; Whiteman, *Digest*, Vol. 2 (1963), 1145–61.

[27] Brownlie, op. cit., 404–5; Whiteman, *Digest*, Vol. 5 (1965), 871–2; McNair, *Law of Treaties* (1961), 209–11, 234–6.

[28] Brownlie, op. cit., 411–12.

(d) Forcible intervention in the form of assistance to national liberation movements conducting armed conflicts to achieve independence.

The first of these topics will be examined briefly. The protection of nationals was one of several justifications invoked by the United States in relation to the use of force against Panama in 1989.[29] In her examination of the practice Dr Christine Gray observes that few States accept a legal right to protect nationals abroad.[30] Some writers regard the right to protect nationals by the use of force as an aspect of the customary law right of self-defence.[31]

The second of the sources of controversy involved resort to hegemonial intervention on the basis of regional arrangements in the absence of the explicit authorization of the Security Council in accordance with Articles 52 to 54 of the Charter. Three episodes may be recalled, starting with the action taken by the OAS in the Cuban Missile crisis. On 22 October 1962 President Kennedy announced that the OAS would be asked to invoke Articles 6 and 8 of the Rio Treaty of 1947.

Article 6 provides as follows:

If the inviolability or the integrity of the territory or the sovereignty or political independence of any American State should be affected by an aggression which is not an armed attack or by an extra-continental or intra-continental conflict, or by any other fact or situation that might endanger the peace of America, the Organ of Consultation shall meet immediately in order to agree on the measures which must be taken in case of aggression to assist the victim of the aggression or, in any case, the measures which should be taken for the common defence and for the maintenance of the peace and security of the Continent.

Thus, the action taken was not related to Article 3 of the Rio Treaty which is predicated upon the existence of an armed attack and the provisions of Article 51 of the Charter. The point to be observed is that the *casus foederis* of regional arrangements extends to mere threats to the peace of the region, and is not limited to the concept of self-defence.

In the second place there was the crisis in the Dominican Republic in 1965 and the dispatch of an Inter-American Peace Force. In this case the jurisdiction of the Security Council was recognized in principle at least. Lastly, there was the Soviet-led Warsaw Pact invasion of Czechoslovakia in 1968. In this instance the parties to the Warsaw Pact treated it as a regional arrangement, in spite of the fact that the language of the Pact was contingent upon the existence of an armed attack. No armed attack on Czechoslovakia had in fact taken place, prior to the action of the Warsaw Pact States. The problem presented by this type of action by regional arrangements is that it gives

[29] See Wedgwood, *Columbia Journal of Trans. Law*, Vol. 29, 609; Chesterman in *Essays in Honour of Ian Brownlie* (1999), 57–94.

[30] *International Law and the Use of Force* (2000), 108.

[31] See Bowett, *Self-defence in International Law* (1958), 87–105; Waldock, Hague Academy, *Recueil des Cours*, Vol. 81, 451, 466–7; Dinstein, *War, Aggression and Self-defence* (3rd edn., 2001), 203–7. See also Bowett in Cassese (ed.). *The Current Legal Regulation of the Use of Force* (1986), 39–55; and Franck, *Recourse to Force* (2002), 76–96.

rise to a second-hand and low-level legitimacy without the more objective constraints of the provisions of Article 51.

The third source of controversy is the incidence of intervention based upon the consent of the territorial sovereign.[32] The title of such intervention is clear: the consent of States. The problem is, of course, the fact that in many cases the status of the consenting government is problematical. The worst case scenario is the situation in which competing *de facto* governments sponsor foreign intervention.

The fourth source of controversy in the period from 1945 to 1990 was the existence of recognized national liberation movements and the legality of external assistance to such movements.[33] In 1974 the General Assembly of the United Nations admitted as Observers those liberation movements which were recognized by regional organizations at that time. Such recognition was accorded to the Angolan, Mozambican, Palestinian, and Rhodesian movements.

The member States of the United Nations, or at least the majority, recognized the legality of wars of liberation in certain conditions and, as a consequence, the legality of external assistance to such armed conflicts. The relevant documents are the Declaration on Principles of International Law Concerning Friendly Relations and Cooperation among States in accordance with the Charter of the United Nations[34] and Article 8 of the Definition of Aggression adopted by the General Assembly in 1974.[35]

11. THE AUTHORISATION OF THE USE OF FORCE BY INDIVIDUAL STATES AS DELEGATED ENFORCEMENT ACTION UNDER THE CHARTER OF THE UNITED NATIONS

It is necessary to move on to review certain other sources of controversy in the period since 1990. The first particular source of problems in this period is the authorization by the Security Council of the use of force by individual States, or a group of States, by way of delegated enforcement action.[36] The action in Korea in 1950 was a precursor to this phenomenon. A major case of delegation followed the invasion of Kuwait by Iraq in 1991. In Resolution 678 the Security Council authorized the use of force against

---

[32] See Brownlie, op. cit., 317–27.

[33] See Abi-Saab, Hague Academy, *Recueil des Cours*, Vol. 165, 371–2; Abi-Saab, *Recueil des Cours*, Vol. 207, 410–16; Cassese, *Self-determination of Peoples* (1995), 150–5; Gray, *International Law and the Use of Force* (2000), 45–50; Shaw, *International Law* (5th edn., 2003), 220–3.

[34] Annex to General Assembly Resol. 2625 (XXV), adopted by consensus, 24 October 1970; Brownlie, *Basic Documents*, 27.

[35] General Assembly Resol. 3314 (XXIX), 14 December 1974. For the text see above.

[36] Blokker, Europ. Journ., Vol. 11, 541–68; Dinstein, *War, Aggression and Self-defence* (3rd edn., 2001), 256–73; Sarooshi, *The United Nations and the Development of Collective Security* (1999); Gray, *International Law and the Use of Force* (2000), 165–99; Sicilianos, 106 *REDIP* (2002), 5–50.

Iraq by a group of States assisting Kuwait and acting by way of collective self-defence in accordance with Article 51 of the Charter.[37]

Such action has an independent legal basis in Article 51 of the Charter, and is particularly justifiable in the absence of stand-by United Nations forces. However, the grant of delegated powers by the Security Council may, and sometimes does, lead to the conferment of a pseudo-legitimacy upon military operations which have political objectives unrelated to genuine peace keeping or enforcement action.

12. THE USE OF FORCE TO PREVENT OR CURTAIL HUMANITARIAN CATASTROPHES (HUMANITARIAN INTERVENTION)

Historically speaking, there have been two models for humanitarian intervention.[38] The late nineteenth-century model has been described as follows:[39]

By the end of the nineteenth century the majority of publicists admitted that a right of humanitarian intervention (*l'intervention d'humanité*) existed. A state which had abused its sovereignty by brutal and excessively cruel treatment of those within its power, whether nationals or not, was regarded as having made itself liable to action by any state which was prepared to intervene. The action was thus in the nature of a police measure, and no change of sovereignty could result.

The doctrine was inherently vague and its protagonists gave it a variety of forms. Some writers restricted it to action to free a nation oppressed by another; some considered its object to be to put an end to crimes and slaughter; some referred to 'tyranny', others to extreme cruelty; some to religious persecution, and, lastly, some confused the issue by considering as lawful intervention in case of feeble government or 'misrule' leading to anarchy.

Much of the time it appeared as a cloak for episodes of imperialism, including the invasion of Cuba by the United States in 1898, and the doctrine of humanitarian intervention did not survive the post-1919 era.

The second model is connected with the NATO bombing of targets throughout Yugoslavia for a period of 78 days, commencing on 24 March 1999. There is a preliminary and major difficulty in classifying the action. This is because the authenticity

---

[37] In fact authorization by the Security Council is not necessary in cases of self-defence: see Kaikobad, 63 *BY* (1992), 299–366.

[38] On humanitarian intervention see generally Gray, *International Law and the Use of Force* (2000), 26–42; Brownlie, *International Law and the Use of Force by States* (1963), 338–42; Brownlie, in Lillich (ed.), *Humanitarian Intervention and the United Nations* (1973), 139–48; Franck, Hague Academy, *Recueil des Cours*, Vol. 240 (1993–III), 256–7; Higgins, Hague Academy, Vol. 236 (1991–V), 313–16; Verwey, in Cassese (ed.), *The Current Legal Regulation of the Use of Force* (1986), 57–78; Murphy, *Humanitarian Intervention: the United Nations in an Evolving World Order* (1996); Simma, *Europ. Journ.*, 10 (1999), 1–22; Chesterman, *Just War or Just Peace?* (2001); Simma, *The Charter of the United Nations* (2nd edn., 2002), i, 130–32; Holzgrefe and Keohane (eds.), *Humanitarian Intervention* (2003); 71 *Nordic Journ.* (2002), 523–43; Hilpold, *Europ. Journ.*, 12 (2001), 437–67; Goodman, *AJ*, 100 (2006), 107–41.

[39] Brownlie, *Use of Force*, 338.

of the subsequent claims that the action had humanitarian motives is substantially undermined by the fact that, beginning in October 1998, the threats of force were linked directly to a collateral political agenda, that is, the acceptance by Yugoslavia of various *political* 'demands' concerning the status of Kosovo, these 'demands' being presented under threat of a massive bombing campaign. This background has been ignored by many commentators.

The official position of the United Kingdom was set forth in a statement by the Permanent Representative to the United Nations, Sir Jeremy Greenstock, on 24 March 1999. The key passages are as follows:

Mr President,

In defiance of the international community, President Milosevic has refused to accept the interim political settlement negotiated at Rambouillet; to observe the limits on security force levels agreed on 25 October; and to end the excessive and disproportionate use of force in Kosovo.

Because of his failure to meet these demands, we face a humanitarian catastrophe. NATO has been forced to take military action because all other means of preventing a humanitarian catastrophe has been frustrated by Serb behaviour.

* * *

Mr President,

The action being taken is legal. It is justified as an exceptional measure to prevent an overwhelming humanitarian catastrophe. Under present circumstances in Kosovo there is convincing evidence that such a catastrophe is imminent. Renewed acts of repression by the authorities of the Federal Republic of Yugoslavia would cause further loss of civilian life and would lead to displacement of the civilian population on a large scale and in hostile conditions.

Every means short of force has been tried to avert this situation. In these circumstances, and as an exceptional measure on grounds of overwhelming humanitarian necessity, military intervention is legally justifiable. The force now proposed is directed exclusively to averting a humanitarian catastrophe, and is the minimum judged necessary for that purpose.

This statement makes the clear assertion that the action is legal but no specific international law source is invoked and, in particular, no reference is made to the United Nations Charter.

In May 1999 Yugoslavia sued 10 Member States of NATO before the International Court of Justice in respect of the bombing campaign and its consequences, including civilian deaths, injuries, and privations, the effect on navigation on the Danube of the destruction of bridges, and damage to the environment. The first procedural development involved a request by Yugoslavia for interim measures of protection.[40]

The position in 1999, when the operations took place, was that there was little or no authority and little or no state practice to support the right of individual States to

---

[40] ICJ Reports (1999); Orders dated 2 June 1999.

use force on humanitarian grounds in international law.[41] The legal situation may be
different in cases where the Security Council or a regional organization takes such
action in accordance with the provisions of the Charter. State practice has been overwhelmingly hostile to the concept of intervention on such a selective and subjective
basis. The weak legal position was recognized by the United Kingdom Government
when it informed the Select Committee on Foreign Affairs of the House of Commons
of its aim of establishing in the United Nations 'new principles governing humanitarian intervention'.[42]

Any discussion of this question must take account of the Ministerial Declaration
produced by the meeting of Foreign Ministers of the Group of 77 held in New York
on 24 September 1999, three months after the NATO action against Yugoslavia had
ended. The key passage for present purposes appears in paragraph 69:

> The Ministers stressed the need to maintain clear distinctions between humanitarian
> assistance and other activities of the United Nations. They rejected the so-called right of
> humanitarian intervention, which has no basis in the UN Charter or international law.

This represents the opinion of 132 States. This total includes 23 Asian States, 51 African
States, 22 Latin American States, and 13 Arab States.

Those international lawyers who espouse the right of humanitarian intervention,
few in number, tend to ignore the practice of States, including the opinion of the 132
States quoted above. Instead of the practice of States generally, reliance is placed upon
a number of ambiguous episodes, which, it is optimistically asserted, either presage or
constitute a change in the customary law.[43]

The material relied upon includes two highly problematical developments, the first
of which is the Air Exclusion Zone in northern Iraq, created in 1991. This involved
the use or threat of force with the object of excluding the exercise of Iraqi power in
order to protect the Kurds of northern Iraq. This Air Exclusion Zone is, in the view
of the British Government, justified by 'the customary international law principle
of humanitarian intervention'.[44] However, no sources were provided to support this
view, and the legal status of the air patrols is problematical to say the least. The Air
Exclusion Zone in southern Iraq, created in 1992, is equally controversial and was,
like its predecessor, based upon a Security Council resolution.[45] The third episode
invoked in this connection is the ECOWAS—authorized operations in Liberia in
1990. The operations (by ECOMOG) were in reality a regional peacekeeping exercise
which, at a certain stage, received the support of the Security Council and the OAU.[46]
Contemporary observers did not recognize the episode as a form of humanitarian

---

[41] See Brownlie and Apperley, *ICLQ*, 49 (2000), 878–910.

[42] House of Commons, Foreign Affairs Committee, Fourth Report, Kosovo, Vol. I, liii, para. 144,
pp. cxi–cxii (para. 23).

[43] See Greenwood, *ICLQ*, Vol. 49 (2000), 926–34. See also Franck, *Recourse to Force* (2002), 135–73.

[44] See the quotations, *ICLQ*, Vol. 49 (2000), 882–3.

[45] See ibid., 906–7.

[46] See ibid., 907–8.

intervention. The practical basis of the action was the need to restore order in a state without an effective Government. The 'practice', such as it is, involves a small number of adherent States, and the contempor-ary debates in the Security Council reveal marked divisions of opinion.[47] Finally, the partisans of humanitarian intervention either ignore the conditions for the formation of new principles of customary law or, on occasion, propose that the requirement of *opinio juris* be relaxed.[48]

13. FORCIBLE MEASURES TO OCCLUDE SOURCES OF TERRORISM[49]

The atrocities in New York and Washington in September 2001, appalling as they were, involved a phenomenon already familiar to other States, including the United Kingdom (both in Northern Ireland and in England), and Nicaragua (during the operations of the *Contras* with external assistance).[50] There is no category of the 'law of terrorism' and the problems must be characterized in accordance with the applicable sectors of public international law: jurisdiction, international criminal justice, State responsibility, and so forth. The present focus is upon the use of force, in the absence of the consent of the territorial sovereign, by individual States, in order to occlude or remove sources of terrorism.

In principle, the normal criteria apply. If the terrorist attack involves the responsibility of a State, it may, depending on the circumstances, constitute an armed attack and therefore justify action by way of self-defence. In 1998 the embassies of the United States in Kenya and Tanzania were the targets of terrorist attacks, which killed nearly 300 people, including 12 Americans. The United States, using cruise missiles, attacked 'terrorist facilities', namely, para-military training camps in Afghanistan and a target in the Sudan (described as a 'chemical weapons facility').

The United States reported the operations to the Security Council as follows:[51]

These attacks were carried out only after repeated efforts to convince the Government of Sudan and the Taliban regime in Afghanistan to shut these terrorist activities down and to cease their cooperation with the Bin Laden organisation. That organisation has issued a series of blatant warnings that 'strikes will continue from everywhere' against American targets, and we have convincing evidence that further such attacks were in preparation from these same terrorist facilities. The United States, therefore, had no choice but to use armed force to prevent these attacks from continuing.

---

[47] Note the Security Council debate on 24 and 26 March 1999: see Chesterman, *Just War or Just Peace?* (2001), 211–13.

[48] See Franck, *Recourse to Force* (2002), 191.

[49] See Byers, ICLQ, 51 (2002), 401–14, Paust, *Cornell I.L.J.*, 35 (2002), 533–57; BY 72 (2001), 679–92.

[50] ICJ Reports (1986), 66–9, 129–30: referring to the Manual on *Psychological Operations in Guerrilla Warfare*, published and disseminated by the United States.

[51] Letter dated 20 August 1998. See generally Murphy, 93 AJ (1999), 161–7.

In doing so, the United States has acted pursuant to the right of self-defence confirmed by Article 51 of the Charter of the United Nations. The targets struck, and the timing and method of attack used, were carefully designed to minimise risks of collateral damage to civilians and to comply with international law, including the rules of necessity and proportionality.

In spite of the invocation of the Charter, such operations are problematical at several levels, including the rule of law problems arising from unilateral fact-finding (as in the case of the Sudanese target, which was in fact a pharmaceutical factory).

The first Security Council resolution adopted after the events of 11 September 2001 refers expressly to 'the inherent right of individual or collective self-defence in accordance with the Charter'.[52] In response to the attacks by individuals of different nationalities (none of Afghan nationality) the United States adopted the view that the *de facto* government of Afghanistan was complicit and used military force in order to remove the government and to seek to extirpate the organization responsible for the attacks in New York and Washington, and its Afghan supporters. On one view of the evidence, the American operations were partly a response to an armed attack, respons-ibility for which attached to the Afghan *de facto* government, and partly action by way of anticipatory self-defence to occlude sources of terrorism for the future.

Almost insoluble issues of policy emerge. It is difficult to bring forcible regime change within the concept of self-defence or the principle of self-determination. Would the process of occlusion justify a regime of occupation unlimited in time?

14. REFLECTIONS ON POLICY

In 1999 10 member States of NATO mounted a bombing campaign against Yugoslavia without the authorization of the Security Council and in the absence of any other justification founded in the provisions of the United Nations Charter. At least some of the States involved pleaded the urgent need for humanitarian intervention. The ultimate question in such crises, as in the crisis relating to Iraq in 2003, is not whether the use of force may be justified beyond the cases provided for in the Charter, but who makes the determination that such action is necessary. The security system based upon the primary role of the Security Council is not an abstract scheme but reflects the international consensus that individual States, or a group of States, cannot resort to force (for purposes other than self-defence) except with the express authorization of the United Nations.

---

[52] See Resol. 1368 (2001), 12 September 2001; and also Resol. 1373 (2001), 28 September 2001.

15. DETERMINATIONS OF THE USE OR THREAT OF FORCE BY STATES: THE LEGAL CONTEXTS

In conclusion it is necessary to remind the reader of the various legal contexts in which determinations of the use or threat of force occur. The principal contexts are as follows:

(a) The incidence of State responsibility for illegal acts or omissions and the resulting duty to provide reparation.

(b) The criminal responsibility of individuals for acts of aggression: such responsibility was imposed by the International Criminal Tribunals at Nuremberg and Tokyo after the Second World War.

(c) There is also the (as yet unresolved) issue of the criminal responsibility of States for acts of aggression.

(d) The application of the United Nations Charter by the political organs and, in particular, the exercise by the Security Council of its competence under Chapter VII of the Charter relating to 'any threat to the peace, breach of the peace, or act of aggression'.

(e) The application of the provisions of multilateral conventions concerned with collective self-defence and/or regional peace-keeping.

(f) The application of the provisions of bilateral treaties of mutual assistance or friendship, commerce, and navigation.[53] Such treaties may provide a jurisdictional clause relating to the International Court in cases in which the Respondent State has not otherwise accepted the jurisdiction of the Court.

---

[53] See the *Oil Platforms* case (Iran v. United States) (Preliminary Objection), ICJ Reports (1996), 803; and the *Nicaragua* case (Nicaragua v. United States), ICJ Reports (1986), 14, 115–17, 135–42.

INDEX

[all references are to page number]